The Judgements
Concerning the Permissible and the Prohibited

By

Imam al-Hādi ila al-Haqq Yahya b. al-Hussein

Translation and Annotations by

The Imam Rassi Society

Contents

Translator's Introduction **1**

Brief biography of Imam al-Hādi Yahya b. al-Hussein 5

The *Ahkām*: its significance and context 7

Al-Hādi's approach to the Fundamentals of Jurisprudence (*Ušūl al-fiqh*) 12

A. The Qur'an and its sciences 12

B. Sunnah and hadith 15

C. The use of analogy 16

D. The statements, judgements and consensus of the imams of Ahl al-Bayt 18

Al-Hādi and disagreement 22

Al-Hādi and the *Musnad Imam Zayd* 24

A. An overview 25

B. Analysis of the responses to the discrepancies 27

C. An alternative response to the discrepancies 28

Key features of this translation 33

Acknowledgements **36**

Author's Introduction **38**

The Book of Ritual Purity **50**

Concerning the one who intends to relieve oneself, what is recommended and what one should be wary of 50

Description of purification 51

Concerning that which invalidates the ritual ablution and what necessitates its renewal 52

Concerning what is narrated from the Prophet regarding purification for the prayer using a *mudd* of water and the purification wash using a *šā'* 53

Concerning various issues regarding the ritual ablution 54

Concerning that which is impermissible to purify from the remains of beasts and what is ritually impure from them 55

Concerning the purification wash from the state of major ritual impurity 56

Concerning what obligates the purification wash 57

Concerning the one in the state of major ritual impurity with smallpox and wounds 57

Concerning the breaking of a limb and what one is to do 58

Concerning what the one in the state of major ritual impurity should do if such person intends to eat or sleep 58

Concerning the state of major ritual impurity with an ailment that prevents washing 58

Concerning the state of major ritual impurity with menstruation 59

Concerning the purification wash for women 59

Concerning the man who had intercourse with his wife and wanted to repeat it before performing ritual ablution 59

Concerning the one in the state of major ritual impurity who immerses himself in water 59

Concerning what is discouraged and not discouraged when performing the ritual ablution with the water of ponds and wells 60

Concerning incontinence of urine and discharge from wounds 60

Concerning an ailment in which one's clothes are soiled by blood, vomit and the like 61
Concerning the dust purification and when it is obligatory 61
Concerning the boundaries of the dust purification and its explanation 62
Concerning the one in the state of major ritual impurity who cannot find water or pure earth 63
Concerning the traveller who entered the state of major ritual impurity but fears that if he were to perform the purification wash with the water he has, he would perish from thirst 63
Concerning the presence of water and when it is found 64
Concerning menstruation as well as its minimum and maximum 64
Concerning what is impermissible for the menstruating woman to do 65
Concerning what is encouraged for the menstruating woman to do 65
Concerning what the pregnant woman does if she sees blood 65
Concerning postpartum bleeding (*an-nifās*), an explanation of what is obligatory regarding it and how long a woman waits with it 66
Concerning vaginal bleeding, its explanation and what one does about it 66
Concerning the man who wants to have intercourse with his menstruating wife once the blood discontinues 68
Concerning wiping over the leather socks, sandal straps, feet, headscarf, turban or cap 68
The Book of the Ritual Prayer 70
The beginning of the chapters regarding the prayer and the explanation of its obligation in the Book 70
The call to prayer and its mention in the Qur'an 70
Concerning payment for the muezzin 71
Concerning the call to prayer before the dawn 71
Concerning the call to prayer without the ritual ablution and speech during the call to prayer 72
Concerning the call to prayer by a blind man, son of a fornicator or slave 72
Concerning the designation of the prayers and their numbers in the Book 73
Concerning the time limits of the prayers 73
Concerning the opening supplication of the prayer as well as its permissible and prohibited 74
Concerning entering the prayer and its actions 76
Concerning what one says in the first sitting in the first two units of a prayer consisting of three or four units 77
Concerning what one does in the last two units of a prayer consisting of three or four units 77
Concerning a response to the proof against glorifying Allah in the last two units of the prayer 77
Concerning an explanation of the prayer lines with the prayer leader 82
Concerning a woman leading others in the prayer 82
Concerning the narrated statement of the Prophet: ((Every prayer in which one does not recite the *Fātiha* of the Book, is aborted)) 83
Concerning the recitation of *Bismillah ar-Rahmān ar-Rahīm* audibly 83
Concerning those discouraged actions in the prayer 84
Concerning what one does behind the imam, what one recites in the prayer behind him and what one does not recite 84
Concerning the *qunūt* and which prayers it is in 85
Concerning what is said in the *qunūt* 85

Concerning the clothes of the one praying and which clothing is sufficient for men and women 86
Concerning the one who laughs in the prayer 87
Concerning who can and cannot lead the prayer 87
Concerning what one must do if he were to enter upon the congregational prayer and not find space in the prayer line 88
Concerning the prayer leader who recites a prostration verse in the prayer 89
Concerning forgetfulness in the prayer 89
Concerning what a man does when he catches the prayer leader in a part of the prayer 90
Concerning when the prayer leader declares Allah's greatness and what interrupts the prayer 91
Concerning the one who unknowingly prays without facing the *qibla* and concerning repeating the prayer in its time and outside of its time as well as what one does not repeat 93
Concerning the prayer of an infirmed person and how he prays as well as the unconscious person in the prayer 93
Concerning praying on a ship, praying naked or praying on the water where one cannot find land 94
Concerning the Friday congregational prayer and its virtues 94
Concerning shortening the prayer and when it is shortened 96
Concerning the joining of two prayers during travel 99
Concerning what one can pray on or towards as well as concerning the final salutations, the place and clothing in the prayer 99
Concerning praying in leather socks and sandals 101
Concerning counting one's prayers with pebbles or lines and concerning a man who uses the earth for support or counts the numbers of verses in the prayer 101
Concerning assisting the imam during the prayer and concerning the prayer of the traveller with the resident and the resident with the traveller 102
Concerning the eclipse prayer: solar and lunar 103
Concerning the rain prayer 103
Concerning the Eid prayers and what is done in them 104
Concerning what the imam does during the Pilgrimage, how he prays, how many prayers he prays, where he delivers the sermon and what he says during the sermon 105
Concerning the joining of the Eid with the Friday prayer 105
Concerning whether it is permissible for one who performed the dust purification due to not finding water to lead those who performed the ritual ablution in prayer 106
Concerning the prayer of the nude with the clothed and the prayer of the seated with the standing 107
Concerning the urging to pray the voluntary night prayers 107
Concerning the prayer of the imam for the Eid and the Friday congregational prayer during travel and the declaration of Allah's greatness for the two Eids 108
Concerning when two men intend to make the other one the prayer leader while he does not know 108
The Book of Funeral Rites (*Al-Janā'iz*) 110
The beginning of the chapters regarding funeral rites 110
Concerning turning the corpse toward the *qibla* 110
Concerning the reward of bathing the dead and hastening to bury 111
Concerning the bathing and shrouding of Allah's Messenger 111
Concerning the one who dies while travelling with a non-marriageable person and concerning the man and his

wife who travels and one of them dies 112

Concerning a woman who dies during travel and there is no non-marriageable person with her or no one else to bathe her 112

Concerning what one does with a martyr 112

Concerning the prayer over the stillborn, the one burned by fire, the drowning victim and the one who was stoned 113

Concerning the prayer over a child of fornication and the uncircumcised 114

Concerning carrying the funeral bier and its burial 114

Concerning embalming with scented musk and how many times one shrouds the corpse in garments 115

Concerning the declaration of Allah's greatness at the funeral prayer, the number of times one does it and what one says in every declaration 116

Concerning the *dhimmi* woman who dies while there is a Muslim in her womb and concerning giving condolences to the *dhimmi* 118

Concerning the tombs and sepulchres 118

Concerning the bed for the body in the grave and the plastering of a grave and its decoration 119

Concerning burying a group in one grave out of necessity 119

Concerning the one who cannot find shrouding and concerning the funeral of men, women, children and slaves 120

Concerning an explanation of washing the dead and its manner 121

Concerning the times for the prayer over the dead 122

Concerning where the prayer leader is to stand during the prayer over the dead 122

Concerning what is to be done to the graves 122

Concerning a woman who dies while a living baby is in her womb 122

The Book of the Purification Dues 124

The beginning of the chapters regarding the purification dues 124

Concerning the purification dues on gold 125

Concerning the purification dues on silver 125

Concerning the purification dues on camels 125

Concerning the purification dues on cows 126

Concerning the purification dues on sheep 126

Concerning the explanation of the Prophet's statement: ((One is to not part what is joined or join what is parted for fear of the purification dues)) 127

Concerning the minimum amount of livestock and what Allah's Messenger pardoned, as well as the explanation of what livestock the dues collector is to count 128

Concerning the designation of what Allah's Messenger pardoned, the meaning of what he pardons and when such pardon occurs 129

Concerning the designation of lands 129

Concerning what is accepted from the *dhimmi* in Muslim lands and their renting of such 130

Concerning what is taken from the commerce of the *dhimmi* 130

Concerning the purification dues on what is extracted from the earth 131

Concerning the purification dues taken from grapes 132

Concerning taking unmeasured wealth as dues 132

Concerning the dues on melons, cucumbers and other fruits that yield without stopping and cannot be enumerated ... 132
Concerning the dues on jujube, berries, pistachios, hazelnuts, acorns and other things extracted from the earth 133
Concerning the dues on linen and hemp ... 133
Concerning the dues on henna, cotton and reeds as well as what one is to do with them and when one is to take the dues from them ... 133
Concerning the categories, when they are joined and when the measurement for each category has not reached five *wasq*s ... 134
Concerning the purification dues on categories of fruit whose yield has not reached two hundred dirham ... 134
Concerning joining gold and silver as well as the method according to us ... 134
Concerning the manner in which the purification dues are taken ... 135
Concerning when the purification dues are taken from everything that obligates it ... 135
Concerning the purification dues on ornaments ... 136
Concerning the mining of gold and silver as well as what is obligatory on it ... 136
Concerning what is obligatory on ambergris, pearls and musk as well as what is obtained as booty on land and sea ... 136
Concerning the purification dues on honey ... 136
Concerning what is obligatory of treasure ... 137
Concerning the purification dues on the orphan's wealth and on the debt that one man owes another ... 137
Concerning an oppressive ruler taking the purification dues on wealth and what is to be taken ... 137
Concerning taking the dues from owners ... 138
Concerning those for whom the dues are obligated and prohibited and concerning the designation of those categories that Allah mentions ... 139
Concerning the purification dues taken from one land to another and concerning the land tax as well as what is obligatory regarding it ... 141
Concerning an explanation of the one who takes the dues, who does not take the dues and how much one in need can take ... 142
Concerning the amount that one in need is to take from the dues ... 142
Concerning the one who earns wealth and had wealth for which the dues are obligated before it and concerning the dues on lost wealth, stolen wealth or usurped wealth ... 142
Concerning that which the idolaters usurp from the Muslims' wealth ... 143
Concerning the man who has a profit but owes a debt or he has wealth that he owes the like of it as purification dues but owes the like of it as a debt ... 143
Concerning the man who exchanges his money in a business transaction and buys supplies with it but then their value decreases or increases ... 144
Concerning the purification dues on wealth from camels jointly owned by two men ... 144
Concerning the purification dues on wealth from cows jointly owned by two men ... 144
Concerning the purification dues on wealth from sheep jointly owned by two men ... 145
Concerning what two owners are to do when one has more than the other and the manner in which the purification dues are taken ... 145
Concerning what one takes from camels of obligatory age ... 146
Concerning the delaying of the purification dues on cattle for two or three years ... 146

Concerning delaying the purification dues on gold.....146
Concerning delaying the purification dues on silver.....147
Concerning combining gold with silver.....147
Concerning the ruling regarding the people of the purification dues when the collector is delayed in collecting it from them and then later approaches them for it but they had already paid it to the poor and needy.....147
Concerning what is collected from the Banu Taghlib, the Christians of the Peninsula.....148
Concerning the fast-breaking dues (*zakat al-fitr*).....149
Concerning the designation of the fast-breaking dues, its limit and those people for whom it is obligatory.....149
Concerning when the fast-breaking dues are collected and until when it is permissible for one to delay it.....150
Concerning the one who cannot find foodstuffs to distribute for the fast-breaking dues: Is it permissible to distribute money?.....150
Concerning what the owner of the dues must do concerning the fast-breaking and preparation.....150
Concerning what one does with the wealth of one who is absent and not present during the time of the fast-breaking and concerning what is distributed from each dependent.....151
Concerning the one who has produce such as dates and other things that obligate the dues as well as when it is not possible to leave it until the time of drying for fear of spoilage.....151
Concerning an explanation of distributed dues and its meaning as well as its exposition from the Book, the Sunnah and language.....151
Concerning various issues regarding the purification dues.....152
The Book of Fasting.....156
Concerning the obligation of fasting and its legalisation in the Book as well as an explanation of what Allah commands regarding it.....156
Concerning what has come regarding the virtue of fasting the month of Ramadan.....159
Concerning the type of speech from which the faster and the one not fasting should refrain.....160
Concerning how a man should be careful from his family while fasting.....160
Concerning that which is encouraged for the faster.....160
Concerning fasting on the day of doubt.....161
Concerning the time to break the fast.....162
Concerning the fasting on 'Āshūra, daily (*ad-dahr*), on the white days and on the Day of 'Arafat.....162
Concerning the faster cupping and applying kohl.....163
Concerning the faster who has intercourse with his wife, eats or drinks out of forgetfulness during Ramadan.....163
Concerning the faster who has intercourse with his wife deliberately as well as kisses or looks at her and ejaculates during Ramadan.....164
Concerning fasting while travelling.....164
Concerning the man who fasts during some of Ramadan but then travels during some of it and concerning the distance that one is permitted to break the fast.....164
Concerning the faster who wakes up in the state of major ritual impurity during Ramadan.....165
Concerning the menstruating woman making it up.....165
Concerning the one who intends a voluntary fast but breaks the fast.....166
Concerning the one who breaks the fast while falsely assuming that the sun had set and concerning making up during Ramadan and its manner.....166
Concerning religious seclusion and the fast of the Prophet.....167

Concerning the time for the pre-dawn meal 168
Concerning the one who breaks the fast a day or more intentionally during Ramadan 168
Concerning the faster who applies eye-drops, injections and salve to the urethra or the ears 168
Concerning the one who kisses or touches and then ejaculates 169
Concerning vomit from the faster and what breaks the fast by entering one's throat 170
Concerning the one who vows a fast on himself for Allah 170
Concerning the menstruating woman who is purified in the middle of the day and had eaten in the beginning as well as the traveller who returns to his family at the end of the day after having eaten in the beginning 171
Concerning the one who is permitted to refrain from fasting during Ramadan 171
Concerning the one who breaks the fast for Ramadan and then does not make it up until the coming month 172
Concerning the fast for unlawful pronouncements 172
Concerning when the fast becomes religiously obligatory upon the male and female child 174
Concerning the witnessing of the new moon 174
Concerning the supplication one makes when witnessing the new moon 174
Concerning various issues regarding the fast and religious seclusion 175
Concerning the one who swears by the religious seclusion 177
Concerning fasting for unintentional manslaughter 178
The Book of the Hajj pilgrimage 180
The beginning of the chapters related to the Hajj pilgrimage 180
Concerning the entry points Allah's Messenger designated 181
Concerning entering the Hajj pilgrimage 181
Concerning the *talbiya* 182
Concerning what is encouraged for the pilgrim whenever he wants to mount an animal after assuming the pilgrim garb in the desert 182
Concerning that which is obligatory for the pilgrim to avoid 183
Concerning what is encouraged for the pilgrim to do when landing at the landing place 183
Concerning what is permissible for the pilgrim to kill 184
Concerning the pilgrim justifying the wearing of clothes due to some misfortune and extreme cold 184
Concerning the pilgrim's entrance to the Sanctified Site (*al-Haram*) 184
Concerning what the pilgrim says when viewing the Ka'ba 184
Concerning the two-unit prayer after the circumambulation behind the *maqām* and the entrance to Zamzam ... 185
Concerning the departure to Ŝafa and Marwa and the actions that are to take place between them 186
Concerning beginning the Hajj pilgrimage on the Day of *Tarwiya* in Mecca 186
Concerning the one who enters Mecca intending a solitary pilgrimage (*mufrida*) or performing the 'Umra pilgrimage 187
Concerning what the one who combines the pilgrimages (*al-qārin*) says and does as well as the manner in which they assume the pilgrim garb 187
Concerning the declaration of Allah's greatness on the Days of *Tashrīq* 188
Concerning the stopping points on 'Arafat and what one is to do there 188
Concerning what one does in Muzdalifa 189

Concerning what one does at the Sacred Site 189
Concerning pressing forward in multitudes (*al-Ifāḍa*) from the Sacred Site 189
Concerning the stoning of the *jamrats* and the actions regarding that 191
Concerning the first departure for Mina and the actions regarding that 192
Concerning the second departure for Mina and the actions regarding that 193
Concerning the assumption of the pilgrim garb for 'Umra and Hajj pilgrimages together if one intends to join them 193
Concerning what the one performing the separate joint pilgrimages (*al-mutamattu'*) does in his pilgrim state and leaving such state of 'Umra 194
Concerning what the restricted person (*al-muhaṣṣir*) does 195
When the restricted one and others reach the Hajj pilgrimage 195
Concerning what is permissible for the restricted person who is able to free himself in enough time to catch the Hajj pilgrimage 196
Concerning what is permissible for the pilgrim to do out of necessity 196
Concerning the one who approaches his entry point ill, unconscious and unable to do anything 197
Concerning what the pilgrim is to do—what is obligatory and impermissible 198
Concerning the she-camel, cow or ewe for sacrifice and the sufficient amount 199
Concerning what a woman does if she were to approach an entry point or Mecca while in the state of menstruation 200
Concerning a woman who enters 'Umra while in the state of menstruation and does not purify until departing for the Hajj pilgrimage 200
Concerning the garb of a woman in the state of pilgrim sanctity 200
Concerning the child who reaches puberty, the slave that is freed and the *dhimmi* who embraces Islam during the days of Hajj 201
Concerning the time in which the pilgrim garb is assumed 201
Concerning mistakes in the wording of the *talbiya* with a different intention in the state of pilgrim sanctity 202
Concerning the 'Umra pilgrimage and its months as well as the month in which one is to assume and relinquish the state of pilgrim sanctity for it 202
Concerning the performer of 'Umra and the time in which he separates the 'Umra and Hajj pilgrimages 203
Concerning the time that it is permissible and impermissible for the one who avoided the 'Umra pilgrimage to make it up 203
Concerning the expiation due for the pilgrim who wears clothing during the times of prohibition 203
Concerning the shade of the pilgrim 204
Concerning the difference between the combined, solitary and separate joint pilgrimages 204
Concerning cupping for the pilgrim 205
Concerning the pilgrim who kisses or hugs and then ejaculates 205
Concerning the Hajj pilgrimage on behalf of the dead and the one who avoids the Hajj while not having the ability 206
Concerning the pilgrim who has intercourse and shaves after stoning the *jamrat* of al-'Aqaba as well as the one who joins the pilgrimages and has intercourse before trimming the hair 207
Concerning the pebbles one uses for the *jamrats*, the place from which they take them and the time one stones the *jamrats* as well as stoning the *jamrats* while riding and stoning with multiple pebbles at once 207

Concerning the stoning of the *jamrats* without the ritual ablution and stoning before sunrise 208

Concerning what is permissible and impermissible to slaughter as well as the shaving and trimming 208

Concerning the one who enters for the separate joint pilgrimages but cannot find a sacrificial animal as well as the one who vows to walk to the House of Allah 209

Concerning the times for the circumambulation, the shortening in the journey from Mecca to 'Arafat and the break in the circumambulation.... 210

Concerning a woman dyeing while in the state of pilgrim sanctity....211

Concerning the expiation for the one who performs the combined and solitary pilgrimages 211

The penalty for killing game 211

Concerning the slaughtered animals that are permissible and impermissible for the pilgrim to eat....214

Concerning the taming of wild livestock and domesticated livestock becoming wild 214

Concerning the pilgrim buying game animals in the Sanctified Site 214

Concerning the one who performed the circumambulation in the state of major ritual impurity or outside of the state of ritual purity.... 214

Concerning the one who forgot the brisk walking between Ŝafa and Marwa....215

Concerning the one who forgot to stone the *jamrats* 215

Concerning the she-camel that gives birth, its milk and the time to sacrifice it in homelands 215

Concerning the pilgrim who delays the sacrifice until the days of sacrifice pass 216

Concerning the one who fears ruin for his sacrifice as well as substituting another for it 216

Concerning the one who vowed to sacrifice his son or anyone else in Mecca or Mina....216

Concerning the man who says that he will use all his possessions in the way of Allah or that he will sacrifice everything he owns to the House of Allah or that he vows such or that he appoints everything to Allah 217

Concerning the one who vows to sacrifice for his brother, father, sons, non-marriageable relatives, any other relatives, slaves or anyone else from his wealth.... 217

Concerning the penalty for a slave or child who kills a game animal as well as the obligatory expiation due on them.... 217

Concerning the one who sends his sacrificial animal with people and they promised to mark it with a garland on a day but then did not act upon it after days pass.... 218

Concerning a woman and slave who assumes the state of pilgrim sanctity without their guardian's permission 218

The Book of Marriage.... 220

The beginning of the chapters regarding marriage and the explanation regarding what Allah has made permissible in marriage.... 220

Concerning those from whom Allah prohibits marriage and the explanation of its judgement in the Qur'an.....221

Concerning the invalidity of marriage without a guardian and two witnesses....223

Concerning the explanation of guardians 224

Concerning giving virgins in marriage and concerning the dowry and concerning two guardians giving in marriage to two men.... 225

Concerning the *muta'* marriage and concerning the deputation of giving in marriage as well as the giving away in marriage by the appointee 226

Concerning the slave who marries without his master's permission and concerning the man who openly presents a dowry contrary to the agreement between them 229

Concerning a woman whose husband dies without him having had intercourse with her and determined her dowry and concerning a man who marries a slave woman over a free woman and concerning a man who sleeps with a woman and then marries her 229

Concerning sexual impotence (*al-iynayn*) and concerning two *dhimmis* when one of them embraces Islam and concerning a man who owns two sisters as slaves as well as the withdrawal from a free woman 230

Concerning stipulation in marriage and a man who marries a man's widow and daughter 232

Concerning the one who has four wives and divorces one of them and the time that it is permissible for him to remarry and concerning what is permissible for a man to do with his wife while she is menstruating 232

Concerning the wife of a missing person and concerning the meaning of the Glorified's statement {The male fornicator marries not save the female fornicator} as well as a man who marries the daughter of a woman and her mother without having had intercourse with either 233

Concerning a prohibition not prohibiting a permission and whether it is permissible for a man to look at a woman he intends to marry and concerning when it is permissible for the divorced woman who has not had intercourse to remarry 235

Concerning the exegesis of Allah's statement {or those without desire amongst men} and concerning the woman who marries during her waiting period and the explanation of suitability 236

Concerning the one who fornicates with a virgin and the meaning of the statement of Allah's Messenger ((A man does not propose against the proposal of his brother or bargain against the bargain of his brother)) 237

Concerning beating the hand drum (*ad-duff*) during a wedding 238

Concerning a man who marries a woman on the judgement of one without intellect as well as a man who gives away his relative in marriage below the dowry of one like her 238

Concerning a man who makes the manumission of his slavewoman her dowry and the statement regarding the waiving of a girl 238

Concerning a woman who gifts her dowry to her husband as compensation 239

Concerning one who marries a wife for something in particular and then it is destroyed before the marriage commences 240

Concerning the girl who is given in marriage by her brother or uncle while she is pre-pubescent but then reaches puberty and chooses for herself 240

Concerning the one who is not permitted to be a guardian even if the person is a non-marriageable relative 241

Concerning a man who marries a virgin or non-virgin and how long he stays with each as well as concerning a wife who gives her days to another wife 241

Concerning a woman who owns her husband fully or partly 242

Concerning the woman who is given in a suitable marriage by her guardian but her mother dislikes her marriage 242

Concerning the man who marries a woman and stipulates that she financially maintains him and gives him her dowry as well as the woman who stipulates that she be given the right of intercourse and divorce 243

Concerning whether a woman can take responsibility for the marriage contract of another woman or not 243

Concerning the one who marries with women as witnesses 243

Concerning the son's wife and the father's wife and concerning the woman who claims that a man married her while he objects to that and concerning a man who marries a woman and his son marries her daughter 243

Concerning a man and his son who marry two women and one of them mistakenly has intercourse with the other's wife 244

Concerning two men—one who contracts a marriage to a woman and the other who contracts a marriage with her daughter—and one is mistakenly given in marriage to the wife of the other 245

Concerning the prohibition from marrying *dhimmis* as well as the explanation of that from the Book, Sunnah and intellect 245

Concerning the woman who is with a husband while her son from another dies as well as concerning a woman who breastfeeds her husband within two lunar years 250

Concerning that which makes it permissible for a woman to remarry her first husband and the designation of defects for which a woman can be returned if she deceives him 251

Concerning the one who apostatises from Islam 251

Concerning the one in the domain of war (*al-harbi*) who embraces Islam and emigrates while having a pre-pubescent wife in the domain of war 252

Concerning the idolater who embraces Islam while having ten wives: among them are some he married with a joint contract and among them are some he married separately and concerning the one in the domain of war who departed to the domain of Islam in safety 252

Concerning the apostasy of the pre-pubescent child and concerning one who embraces Islam and then apostatises before his wife embraces Islam 253

Concerning the *dhimmi* or his wife who embraces Islam and then divorces during her waiting period as well as a female *dhimmi* who embraces Islam while she has a pre-pubescent husband 253

Concerning the one who owns a non-marriageable relative and one who owns a marriageable relative 254

Concerning the slave girl of two men who gives birth to the child of one of them 254

Concerning the purification of a slave woman at the time of buying and selling as well as concerning the man who marries a slave woman and then buys her 255

Concerning marriage to slaves and their divorce 255

Concerning the women one is permitted to marry 256

Concerning an absentee who was announced as dead and his inheritance is distributed but then he returns 257

Concerning the marriage of an indentured labourer and his purchase of his wife 257

Concerning what obligates the dowry 257

Concerning one who gives a manservant, maidservant or more in marriage as a dowry 258

Concerning a man who marries a woman for a slave woman as dowry specifically and then has intercourse with the latter before she is given to her 258

Concerning deputation (*al-wikāla*) in marriage 258

Concerning an old man who had intercourse and died because of his wife 259

Concerning the one who contracts a marriage with a woman and then her sister is deceptively given to him as well as what is binding upon her regarding her husband 259

Concerning the child of a free woman from a slave 259

Concerning a slave woman who escaped, claimed that she was free, was married to a free man, had children and then was caught 259

Concerning a woman who is deceived by a slave and she marries him assuming that he is a free man 260

Concerning marriage to a eunuch 260

Concerning *shighār* 261

Concerning two men who have intercourse with a slave woman during the same period of purity and she gives birth without knowing the identity of the father 261

Concerning the narration of the Prophet regarding the reward for having intercourse with one's wife 261

Concerning the prohibition of women's anuses from their husbands 262

Concerning a man who marries a woman and another woman says "I am the mother of them both" in that she breastfed him and his wife 262

Concerning the wife of one imprisoned in the domain of war 263

Concerning equity between wives...263
Concerning the choice of a boy between his mother and paternal uncle...263
Concerning that which is obligatory on the husband and wife regarding service and maintenance in matters of their home...263
Concerning what a man should do when approaching his wife...264
Concerning a man who has intercourse with his wife with someone else in the room...264
The Book of Divorce...266
The beginning chapters regarding divorce as well as an explanation of what Allah commands regarding it and the proof for it...266
Concerning the sunnah divorce and it being a divorce of the waiting period...266
Concerning that from which a woman in her waiting period should refrain and concerning the one whose menstruation is delayed...269
Concerning the one who divorces before having intercourse and concerning the waiting period of the woman who initiated divorce and the *umm walad*...270
Concerning the waiting period of the *dhimmi* and the female apostate...271
Concerning the declarations of freedom (*al-bariyya*), release (*al-khaliyya*), separation (*al-bāyin*), settlement (*al-batta*), prohibition (*al-harām*) and "Your rope is upon your own withers"...271
Concerning the statement "Your affair is in your hands" and concerning choice and divorce before marriage..271
Concerning unlawful pronouncements...273
Concerning the oath of abstention (*al-ilā`u*) and the statement regarding it...276
Concerning divorce of slaves and concerning divorce of the severely inflicted, child, compelled, person with pleurisy and intoxicated...278
Concerning that which one writes to divorce his wife what he does not say...279
Concerning one who has four wives and divorced one of them without it being known which one he divorced and without the clear intention as to which one it was...279
Concerning when a woman with two children in her womb can marry after being divorced...280
Concerning the financial maintenance of a woman whose husband has died and when it is counted—when she comes to know of his death or from the day he died?...280
Concerning the one who divorces three times simultaneously and one who divorces contrary to the sunnah divorce...281
Concerning involuntary divorce...291
Concerning one who says to his wife: "Observe your waiting period!"...291
Concerning a man who says to his wife "You are not my wife" or "You are released" or "You are free"...292
Concerning the stating of exceptions in divorce...292
Concerning continuation between divorces...292
Concerning a man who calls out to one of his wives by name and another wife answers and then he divorces her...292
Concerning one who divorces with part of the pronouncement...293
Concerning one who swears by divorce and unknowingly breaks the oath...293
Concerning one who swears by divorce of different wives or all of them collectively...293
Concerning an unlawful pronouncement of a slave woman...293
Concerning one who declares an unlawful pronouncement on two, three or four wives...294

Concerning one who declares an unlawful pronouncement on his wives twice, thrice or four times ... 294

Concerning one who swears an oath of abstention and then divorces his wife during this abstention ... 294

Concerning one who divorced a pre-pubescent girl and she menstruates before the completion of three months in which she observed her waiting period ... 295

Concerning the divorce of male slaves and the waiting period of female slaves ... 295

Concerning one who swears by divorce that he would do such and such but then dies before he is able to do it ... 296

Concerning the one who deserves the child and concerning the compulsion of the guardian to financially maintain the pre-pubescent child ... 297

Concerning the one who says to his wife "You are divorced to this month" or "...this year" ... 298

Concerning mutual cursing (*al-li'ān*) ... 298

Concerning the one who says to his wife: "You are divorced if Allah wills" ... 299

Concerning a man who divorces a slave woman with three divorces and then buys her afterwards ... 300

Concerning a woman whose husband dies in absentia and when she observes the waiting period ... 300

Concerning the waiting period of the *umm walad* regarding manumission and death ... 301

Concerning the post-divorce compensation which is binding on the slave ... 301

Concerning the waiting period for the woman with vaginal bleeding ... 301

Concerning the *khula'* divorce and when it is permissible for a man to declare a *khula'* divorce ... 302

Concerning the woman who was *khula'* divorced ... 302

The Book of Suckling ... 304

The beginning of the chapters regarding suckling ... 304

Concerning what is prohibited from suckling—more or less ... 304

Concerning milk relations after weaning ... 305

Concerning the 'milk of the man' (*laban al-fahl*) ... 306

Concerning the suckling of the People of the Book ... 306

Concerning a boy and girl being given the milk of two different children from the same nurse mother with two years or more between ... 306

Concerning a woman who gives her husband her breastmilk to drink without him knowing ... 307

The Book of Financial Maintenance (*an-Nafaqāt*) ... 308

Concerning the financial maintenance of a pregnant woman whose husband has died ... 308

Concerning a slave who marries a free woman that has children from him and who financially maintains the children ... 308

Concerning the financial maintenance of a divorcee who is impermissible until after remarriage ... 308

Concerning a man who is unable to financially maintain his wife ... 309

Concerning a disbeliever who embraces Islam—either he or his wife—and whether he is obligated to financially maintain her ... 310

Concerning the financial maintenance of a slave's wife ... 311

Concerning the judgement that financial maintenance of the one in straitened circumstances is upon the abled heir ... 311

Concerning the Muslim who has a poor relative who is a disbeliever ... 312

Concerning that which is binding upon the abled regarding a relative in straitened circumstances ... 312

The Book of Sales (*al-Buyū'*) **314**

The beginning of the chapters regarding sales 314

Concerning profit, merchandise and strictness regarding usury 316

Concerning that which is weighed or measured when one sells to another 318

Concerning that which is discouraged in sales 319

Concerning uncertainty and protecting one's family from it 320

Concerning the choice of a transaction 323

Concerning the sale of a slave who is freed at the master's death as well as the *umm walad* and concerning the one who buys something but then notices that it has a defect 324

Concerning the sale of a copy of the Qur'an, recitation and instruction 326

Concerning increase in a delayed sale and concerning a sale of unknown weight and measure as well as concerning an oath during a sale 326

Concerning selling a slave's services, the merchandise of the idolaters and selling a slave without his master's permission 327

Concerning the purchase of fresh clovers, herbs, cucumber and melon 328

Concerning one who buys a commodity and returns it with extra 329

Concerning one who buys a slave woman and comes to know that she is his *umm walad* 329

Concerning one who hires out a slave or riding beast and then another hires them out for more than what was hired out to him 329

Concerning what is discouraged of uncertain sales 330

Concerning resale for profit (*al-murābaha*) 330

Concerning a commodity resold for profit by two partners and the manner in which it is resold for profit 330

Concerning a commodity taken by a man to show it and then if the one who is shown it likes it, he buys it 330

Concerning the sale of price-marked clothing (*ar-ruqūm*) 330

Concerning the sale of that of which one does not take possession 330

Concerning the option of one who buys something and takes possession of it but does not look at or inspect it 331

Concerning the partner's sale from his partners or others that was not shared by them 331

Concerning one who wanted to buy a commodity, postponed its payment and then bought it from its owner for less than its price 331

Concerning one who bought something and then it was damaged before he could take possession of it 332

Concerning the option when there was a stipulation of three days, more or less 332

Concerning working for a third or fourth of something 332

Concerning that which is damaged by the manufacturer 332

Concerning one who acts contrary to another's command regarding his wealth 333

Concerning the meaning of the Prophet's statement: ((No city-dweller should sell for a Bedouin)) 333

Concerning the Messenger's prohibition of intercepting cattle drivers (*al-jalūba*) 334

Concerning something in which some differ in designation from others 334

Concerning difference in two types and what is permissible in terms of sales 334

Concerning the sale of an animal for another 334

Concerning additional money with two animals 334

Concerning the sale of meat for an animal 335

Concerning the purchase of one meat with other types of meat 335
Concerning the purchase of dates with their receptacles 335
Concerning a slave being permitted to buy and sell in business 335
Concerning one who sells himself or commands another to sell him 336
Concerning that which is impermissible regarding buying and selling as well as that which is permissible to buy and sell for the other 336
Concerning exchange as well as substituting silver for silver, gold for gold, gold for silver and silver for gold. 339
The Book of Prepayment (*as-Salam*) 342
The beginning of the chapters regarding prepayment 342
Concerning the one who prepays for a damaged good and concerning when the one who was prepaid considers that for which he prepaid to be ruined 346
Concerning prepayment for that whose value varies in itself and whose measure differs in itself, such as pomegranates, citrons, quince, pears, melons, cucumbers, bananas as well as eggs such as ostrich eggs and chicken eggs, the Indian nut (*rānij*) and the like 347
Concerning prepayment for meat, heads and roasted meat (*ash-shiwā*) 348
The proof for the soundness of prepayment related from the Prophet 348
Concerning that which is impermissible in prepayment in regard to time and days 350
Concerning that which is permissible in prepayment in regard to time and days 350
Concerning prepayment for clothes, outer garments, furnishings and other things from that category 352
Concerning one who prepays for an item to an appointed time and then the one he prepaid asks to take some of the item as food and return the rest in money 353
Concerning the one who engages in a valid prepayment transaction to an appointed time but the one who is prepaid or the one who prepays says "Hurry for me..." or "Allow me to hurry..." or "Delay for me and I'll give you more" or the one who prepays says "I will delay for you if you give me more" 353
Concerning the surrender of some wealth by the one who prepays and the one who is prepaid from one another 353
Concerning a man who prepays two categories for one category 354
Concerning the one who prepays another with a debt or deposit (*al-wadī'a*) 354
Concerning the man who partners with another in a prepayment agreeing on the rate and amount 355
Concerning when the one who prepaid and the one who was prepaid disagree in claims 355
Concerning a guarantee and taking a security deposit (*rahn*) in the prepayment transaction 356
Concerning the one who borrowed something 356
The Book of Pre-Emption (*ash-Shufa'*) 358
The beginning of the chapters regarding pre-emption: Concerning pre-emption 358
Concerning what is obligatory regarding pre-emption 358
Concerning distinguishing the pre-emptors: the first and then the foremost 358
Concerning the choice of pre-emptor as well as what is permissible and impermissible 358
Concerning the one who buys a garden or house and then part of it is damaged or added to and then the pre-emptor seeks its pre-emption 359
Concerning the one who sells and then cancels it and what is incumbent on the pre-emptor 360
Concerning a man who sells a house or estate for a price and the pre-emptor increases it and then reverts it to another price without knowing the original price until after the transaction 360

Concerning an estate or house that is bought for a price and sold for more than that before its pre-emption is sought 361

Concerning the man who buys land but then stipulates that he has the option of three days or the seller stipulates that on him or the two of them stipulate that the both of them have the option of three days 362

Concerning a transaction in which a pre-emptor takes for a price but then another pre-emptor who is more entitled comes to claim pre-emption 362

Concerning one who buys a house with a house or land with land or a gifted item from that and the seeking of an equivalent for a particular item and the statement regarding a gift or charity 362

Concerning the obligation of seeking pre-emption between seller and buyer 363

Concerning pre-emption 364

Also concerning pre-emption 366

The Book of Partnership 368

Concerning partnership: A co-partnership (*al-mufāwaḍa*) 368

Concerning a partnership that is other than a co-partnership 369

Concerning two men who form a partnership but have no wealth to buy and sell with their reputations 370

Concerning two carpenters, two tailors, two farmers, two cuppers, two weavers and other manufacturers who share in what they manufacture 370

The Book of Speculative Partnership (*al-Muḍāraba*) 372

Concerning a speculative partnership 372

Concerning speculative partnership 375

Concerning that for which the speculator is not responsible 376

The Book of Security Deposits (*ar-Rahn*) 378

Concerning security deposits: the depositor and the depositee 378

Concerning security deposits 379

Also concerning security deposits 379

Concerning disagreements between the depositor and depositee 380

The Book of Suretyship (*al-Kafāla*), Guaranty (*aḍ-Ḍamān*), Debt Transfer (*al-Hawāla*) and Deputation (*al-Wakāla*) 382

Concerning suretyship and guaranty 382

Concerning deputation 382

The Book of Misappropriation (*al-Ghaṣb*) and Confessions (*al-Iqrār*) 384

Concerning the misappropriation of living property 384

Concerning one who misappropriates livestock and then slaughters it 384

Concerning one who misappropriates dates, date pits, any type of fruit or eggs 384

Concerning one who misappropriates a small or large date palm or tree 384

Concerning one who misappropriates an enslaved minor, lamb or baby animal 385

Concerning one who misappropriates a garment, cotton, wool or hair 385

Concerning the misappropriated item 385

Concerning one who buys something and uses it but then its right is demanded afterwards 385

Concerning one who takes an animal or any other unmeasurable and unweighable commodity without the owner's permission and then it is ruined 386

Concerning one who confesses a right that necessitates the prescribed punishment 386
Concerning the confession of the slave 386
Concerning that for which a person is permitted to confess 387
The Book of Insolvency (*at-Taflīs*) 388
Concerning one who becomes insolvent while having a creditor's commodity 388
Concerning one who buys a slave girl from another man and she gives birth while with him and then he becomes insolvent 389
Concerning one who becomes insolvent while having a slave for which he had not paid and was given wealth as a gift 389
Concerning one who buys barren land but then harvests date palms on it or constructs on it but then becomes insolvent 390
Concerning one who sells something and takes possession of some of its price but then the buyer becomes insolvent while he owes the remainder of the price 390
Concerning one who leaves a security deposit that is more or less than its value and then he becomes insolvent 390
Concerning a man who buys a house, demolishes it, builds another one and then becomes insolvent 391
Concerning debt 391
Concerning imprisonment for debt 392
The Book of Settlements (*aš-Šulh*) 394
Concerning the making of settlements between Muslims 394
Concerning settlements of gold for silver and silver for gold in repayment 394
The Book of Oaths, Vows and Expiations 396
Concerning the judgement of expiations for oaths and concerning one who swears invalidly while knowing that 396
Concerning repetition of an oath regarding one thing 398
Concerning what is to happen for the one who swears the oath 398
Concerning which slaves are valid to be used as expiations 398
Concerning a man who swears an oath and then makes an exception after ending his statement 399
Concerning one who swears by other than Allah 399
Concerning one who must observe expiation but cannot find needy Muslims and whether it is permissible to feed or clothe the needy *dhimmi* 400
Concerning one who was forced to swear a false oath and concerning one who confesses that a child is his but then denies it 400
Concerning one who swore an oath to a particular time 400
Concerning one who swore an oath while he was a minor and then breaks the oath while still a minor or after maturing and concerning the breaking of an oath by a slave 401
Concerning one who swore an oath that he would not buy something, sell something or marry 401
Concerning one who is obligated to expiate a number of times when he can only find ten needy people 402
Concerning that for which none can swear 403
The Book of Claims 404
Concerning oaths and evidence as well as for whom they are obligated 404
Concerning a woman who claims family ties against a man 404

The Book of Sharecropping (*al-Muzāra'a*) 406
Concerning sharecropping and what is related 406
Concerning the yard of wells and streams as well as their surroundings 406
Concerning one who constructs a building on an estate without or with the landowner's permission 406
Concerning two partners in regard to the lower level and upper level 406
Concerning roads, streets and alleyways that come from every direction when their people dispute regarding their capacity and narrowness 407
Concerning two partners who share land and one of them digs a well on the other's land 407
The Book of Gifts, Charity, Life Grants (*al-'Umra*), *Ruqba*, Loaned Items (*al-Ā'riya*) and Entrusted Items (*al-Wadī'a*) 410
Concerning what is permissible and impermissible regarding gifts 410
Concerning gifts for the slave 410
Concerning gifts and charity when they are known, recognised and determined 411
Concerning donating a house, land or wealth as charity to a man and he does not take possession of it 411
Concerning one who gifts something seeking an equivalent and concerning an indentured labourer being bought as a slave with what remains 411
Concerning reclamation of charity 412
Concerning life grants and *ruqba* 412
Concerning a guarantee of loaned items and concerning a man who dies while owing the dowry to his wife 412
Concerning entrusted items and what Allah commands regarding it 413
The Book of Lost and Found Items 414
Concerning lost and found items 414
Concerning male and female foundlings when they are found 414
The Book of Prescribed Punishments (*al-Hudūd*) 416
Concerning the prescribed punishment for fornication in the Book 416
Concerning when the prescribed punishment is obligated upon the married and unmarried by witness 422
Concerning when the prescribed punishment is obligated upon the one who confesses to fornication 423
Concerning the establishment of the prescribed punishment on the slave by his master 425
Concerning what takes place with a man and woman of consummative marriage 425
Concerning some witnesses who retract 426
Concerning the retraction of one witness regarding the marriage state of the punished 427
Concerning one who hires, is loaned or given a slave woman as a deposit and then he has intercourse with her and says "I thought that she was permissible for me" 427
Concerning a man who was accused of fornication but was later discovered to have been insane after the prescribed punishment was applied 427
Concerning a woman who was accused of fornication but was later discovered to have had a closed-up vagina (*ratqā*) or to have been a virgin after the prescribed punishment was applied 428
Concerning men and women accused of fornication who were husband and wife but not in a consummative marriage 428
Concerning a witness who was discovered to be a *dhimmi*, blind or insane 428
Concerning the *umm walad*, female indentured labourer and female slave who is freed upon her master's death when they fornicate 428

Concerning *ta'zīr* and whether it is permissible 429
Concerning one who fornicated with an unmarriageable relative 429
Concerning a woman who claimed that a man forced her 429
Concerning one who married invalidly and whether he would be considered in a consummative marriage or not as well as concerning the minor and insane person who fornicates.................... 430
Concerning a man who fornicated with three or four women 430
Concerning an infirmed person against whom a testimony is established for fornication as well as the slave who testifies against himself for fornication 430
Concerning the prescribed punishment for the *dhimmi* 430
Concerning the prescribed punishment for the one who fornicates with a woman in her anus 431
Concerning the prescribed punishment for homosexual acts....................431
Concerning the prescribed punishment for slander 431
Concerning the explanation of slander and when the prescribed punishment is obligatory....................432
Concerning the son who slanders the father and the father who slanders the son 432
Concerning one who slanders a group....................433
Concerning a Muslim who slanders a *dhimmi* or slave 433
Concerning a man who says to another "O one who fornicates with his mother!" or "O sinner!" or "O openly disobedient one!".................... 433
Concerning one who is flogged for slander and then slanders again before his flogging is complete 434
Concerning the *dhimmi* who slanders a Muslim 434
Concerning the *dhimmi* who is slandered by a Muslim but then embraces Islam afterwards as well as a slave who is slandered by a free person but then is manumitted or slanders a free person....................434
Concerning the man and woman confirmed each other's statements....................435
Concerning the man and child who slanders....................435
Concerning the one who slandered the son of an *umm walad* from her master or slanders her 436
Concerning the testimony of women....................436
Concerning the *dhimmi* who fornicates with a Muslim woman and concerning when she is forced against her will.................... 437
Concerning the one who attempts magic and the cuckold (*duyūth*)....................438
Concerning the prescribed punishment for heretics and apostates 438
Concerning the prescribed punishment for women who have intercourse with women....................438
Concerning the prescribed punishment for the thief and what Allah obligates upon him in the Qur'an 439
Concerning the thief who is amputated but then repeats 439
Concerning the one who confesses to theft....................440
Concerning the testimony of two witnesses of theft against the thief 440
Concerning the one who climbs the wall of a house or opens its door and takes an item from it....................441
Concerning a group of thieves among whom some enter, some transport the stolen item and some keeping watch 441
Concerning one for whom amputation is not obligatory when bringing it out to one for whom amputation is obligatory.................... 442
Concerning the number of times the one who confesses to theft is to confess before being amputated....................442

Concerning one who stole something from a protected place but then returned it before he was brought to the imam 442

Concerning the slave who steals his master's property..... 443

Concerning one who steals intoxicants from the *dhimmi* 443

Concerning one who steals a slave child or free child 444

Concerning one who steals an animal..... 444

Concerning one who steals agriculture or dates..... 444

Concerning one who confesses that the stolen item is with him..... 445

Concerning the prescribed punishment for the grave robber (*an-nabāsh*) 445

Concerning snatching (*al-khulsa*)..... 445

Concerning one who violates a trust or pilfers in buying and selling..... 445

Concerning one whose left hand is mistakenly amputated 446

Concerning those who make war 446

Concerning intoxicants and its prohibition from the Book of Allah 448

Concerning the prescribed punishment for intoxicants..... 449

Concerning what the imam should do with the prescribed punishments 450

Concerning various points related to the prescribed punishments..... 450

Concerning the one who slanders his wife who is a pre-pubescent girl..... 451

Concerning the man who slanders his wife with a slave, Jew, Christian or Magian..... 451

Concerning the man who slanders his wife and then dies before performing the mutual cursing with her or she dies 451

Concerning the slave who slanders a free woman or slave woman when she is married to him and concerning a free man who slanders his wife who is a slave..... 452

Concerning one who said to the son of a woman who engaged in a mutual cursing "You are not the son of so-n-so" meaning the one who engaged in the mutual cursing with his mother and concerning one who slandered his wife by a specific man 452

Concerning one who said to his wife "I found you to not be a virgin"..... 452

Concerning the proofs of the one who claims that there is no prescribed punishment for intoxication and the refutation of the one who claims that the Commander of Believers revoked the prescribed punishment for such 452

The Book of Indemnity, Injuries and Offences 458

Beginning of the judgement regarding indemnity in the Book and what Allah decrees against the one who intentionally kills a soul 458

Concerning what Allah mentions about retaliatory compensation (*al-qišāš*) 460

Concerning indemnities and injuries..... 463

Concerning how the indemnity is to be taken..... 464

Concerning the delineation of the indemnity and its designation from wealth..... 464

Concerning injuries for which there is no retaliation 464

Concerning the indemnity for the one upon whom it is obligatory..... 465

Concerning the numbers of indemnity for the people..... 465

Concerning the free person who kills a slave and a man who kills a woman out of rebellion and causing corruption in the land 465

Concerning the kinds of manslaughter 466
Concerning a one-eyed person who gouged a healthy eye....466
Concerning the nail and tooth that are blackened....466
Concerning the two ovaries....467
Concerning the blind eye, lame hand or leg and mute tongue 467
Concerning the injuries by a child and slave and concerning a herniated bladder 467
Concerning a man and child who share in intentional manslaughter or injuries together 467
Concerning the injuries by men and women as well as concerning the injuries of the foetus of a free woman, slave woman, livestock, slaves and children 467
Concerning the injuries by an *umm walad*, a slave freed upon his master's death and an indentured labourer...468
Concerning the free person who injured a slave and the injuries by slaves....469
Concerning that for which the clan (*al-'aqila*) does not pay the bloodwite 469
Concerning a slave who strikes the stomach of his master's wife and she gives birth to a living foetus or stillborn 469
Concerning the one who castrated a slave....470
Concerning a man who kills a woman intentionally....470
Concerning a *dhimmi* who kills a Muslim 470
Concerning a Muslim who kills a *dhimmi* 471
Concerning the one who removes something from his borders and it injures a person and concerning a riding beast that injures its leg 471
Concerning a man who kills his son and a son who kills his father 472
Concerning the indemnity that one who killed unintentionally is to not inherit....472
Concerning the killer who is pardoned by some of the guardians when he intentionally killed....472
Concerning one who confessed to manslaughter—whether intentional or unintentional 473
Concerning a group who kills a person unintentionally or intentionally 473
Concerning the pardon of an enslaved killer....473
Concerning taking indemnities for an injury....473
Concerning swearing an oath....473
Concerning a pregnant woman who is killed....474
Concerning a murder victim who was found among a people who were declared innocent by the victim's guardians but then they claimed that it was someone else.... 475
Concerning one who plucks out all a person's teeth 475
Concerning a man who commits a number of injuries 475
Concerning that which the clan is to be fined 475
Concerning the doctor, circumciser and healer who ruined what they were supposed to treat....475
Concerning a leaning wall that collapses on a person and concerning one who dies as a result of retaliation.....476
Concerning a man who was killed but has small children and concerning a woman who was forced by a sinner against her will and she killed him 476
Concerning swearing oaths and a rabid dog....477
Concerning various issues regarding indemnities 477
Concerning one who inherits from indemnity 478

Concerning one who bit a person's hand and removed a chunk of hand from his mouth along with his own tooth or teeth ... 478

Concerning one who brands his slave with fire ... 478

Concerning one who did an action that causes damage without the intention of the doer ... 479

Concerning two ships that collide with each in the sea ... 479

The Book of Inheritance Shares ... 480

The beginning of the chapters regarding inheritance shares ... 480

Concerning the inheritance shares from the sunnah and what is agreed upon ... 480

Concerning those men who have inheritance shares allotted to them and concerning one who inherits from his paternal relatives and others ... 481

Concerning those women who have inheritance shares allotted to them and how much is inherited from them481

The designation of those men and women who do not inherit ... 481

The designation of family inheritance shares and what has come regarding urging the study of inheritance ... 482

Concerning the inheritance shares of the two parents ... 482

Concerning the one whom the mother exempts and the one who exempts her from the third ... 482

Concerning the inheritance of the offspring and with whom s/he inherits and does not inherit as well as which of the offspring exempts the paternal relatives and does not exempt them ... 483

Concerning paternal/maternal brothers and sisters as well as who exempts and who is exempted and the grandfather ... 484

Concerning an explanation of the inheritance of brothers and sisters from the father and with whom they inherit as well as concerning the one who exempts them from inheritance ... 485

Concerning an explanation of the inheritance of the mother's offspring as well as the amount they can exempt from the inheritance and the amount of their inheritance ... 486

Concerning all the brothers and sisters as well as the brothers' offspring and an explanation of their inheritances ... 487

Concerning the sharing among the paternal/maternal brothers and maternal brothers regarding the third as well as who among them does not share ... 488

Concerning the inheritance of paternal uncles ... 490

Concerning the inheritance of paternal cousins ... 490

Concerning the inheritance of nieces and nephews ... 491

Regarding the inheritance of the indirect heirs (*al-kalāla*) ... 492

Concerning the *munāsakha* ... 493

Concerning the *'awl* regarding inheritance shares ... 493

Concerning redistribution (*ar-radd*) ... 494

Concerning the inheritance shares of the grandfather ... 494

Concerning the inheritances of the drown victim, burn victim, demolish victim and missing altogether as well as the inheritance shares for similar ... 495

Concerning the accounting of inheritance shares and its summation ... 496

Concerning the inheritance of the hermaphrodite ... 498

Concerning the one who dies and leaves behind a pregnant woman and heirs and then they rush to distribute it before knowing that she is pregnant ... 499

Concerning the inheritance of a missing person ... 500

Concerning bequests 500
Concerning confessions and denials 500
Concerning the maternal relatives 501
Concerning the inheritances of the Magians 502
Concerning the inheritance of the son of a couple that performed a mutual curse 502
Concerning the inheritance of the People of the Book 503
Concerning the inheritance between Muslims and *dhimmis* 503
Concerning the inheritance of the apostate 503
Concerning the inheritances of the free and the slaves 503
Concerning clientage and manumitted slaves as well as an explanation of the inheritance of the freed slave and those who inherit from him 504
Concerning clientage and manumitted slaves in family relations (*as-ŝulb*) 505
Concerning an explanation of one who manumits one who was manumitted by a woman 505
Concerning the hermaphrodite in clientage 506
Concerning the maternal relatives in clientage and its explanation 508
Concerning a missing person and concerning pregnant woman in clientage 509
Concerning clientage regarding the drown victim, burn victim, demolish victim as well as similar deaths for which one does not know who died before his companion 509
Concerning the apostasy of the manumitter and manumitted 510
Concerning the clientage of the People of the Book and the Magians 510
Concerning clientage in claims and denials 511
Concerning a Magian's clientage for a Magian 512
Concerning clientage 512
The Book of Hunting Game (*as-Ŝayid*) 514
Beginning of the chapters regarding hunting game and its explanation in the Book 514
Concerning hunting game with the dogs of the Magians, Jews and Christians 515
Concerning hunting at night 515
Concerning the caught fish of the Magians and idolaters 516
Concerning the one who shoots an arrow at a game animal or sends one's dog on it then it is hidden from sight and one later finds it 516
Concerning fish that died and were not caught game 516
Concerning the game caught by an untrained dog as well as that game that is shared between a trained and untrained dog 517
Concerning the use of a bow and arrow to shoot a game animal and the statement regarding an arrow with no feathers or head (*al-mi'rāḍ*) 517
Concerning hunting with clay pellets (*al-julāhiq*) 517
Concerning a game animal that is thrown to the ground or falls into water 517
Concerning properly sacrificing the game animal 517
The Book of Sacrificed Meats (*adh-Dhabā`ih*) 520
The beginning of the chapters regarding sacrificed meats and its explanation in the Book 520
Concerning a woman's sacrifice as well as that of a child, person in the state of major ritual impurity and a

menstruating woman ... 522
Concerning sacrifice with a sharp stake, nail, stone or bone ... 523
Concerning the sacrifice performed by the mute, runaway slave and uncircumcised ... 523
Concerning the sacrifice of a foetus and what has been narrated that its sacrifice is the sacrifice of its mother .. 523
Concerning that which is permissible and impermissible in respect to sacrifice ... 524
Concerning one who steals a lamb and sacrifices it ... 525
Concerning the *aqīqa* ... 525
The Book of Foods, Drinks and Clothing ... 528
The beginning of the chapters regarding foods and the explanation of what is prohibited regarding them in the Book and Sunnah ... 528
Concerning washing the hands before eating ... 529
Concerning the virtue of the table spread (*mā`ida*) of Muhammad's Progeny as well as the virtue of the one who eats with them ... 529
Concerning flies, beetles, mice and similar that fall in the food ... 529
Concerning eating lizard ... 530
Concerning that which is discouraged to eat ... 530
Concerning the blessing (*baraka*) of that from which Allah's Messenger ate and drank ... 531
Concerning one who is compelled to eat carcass and the amount he is to eat as well as whether he can take it as provisions ... 531
Concerning eating clay and vinegar ... 531
Concerning accepting an invitation and what is encouraged regarding festive gatherings (*al-walīma*) ... 532
Concerning eating with the left hand ... 532
Concerning the intestines of the disbeliever ... 532
Concerning drinks ... 533
Concerning the intoxicants and intoxication ... 533
Concerning drinking out of gold and silver containers ... 534
Concerning the one who drinks and wants to give some to his companions ... 535
Concerning what has been narrated regarding the prohibition of drinking from golden and silver containers 535
Concerning the chapters related to clothing ... 535
Concerning concealing oneself in water and bathhouses ... 535
Concerning one who wears fox skin, tiger skin and other predatory animals ... 536
Concerning a woman who weaves her hair with another's hair and concerning changing grey hair ... 536
Concerning that which one should avoid wearing ... 536
Concerning allowing the sarong to drag ... 537
Concerning beautifying oneself with nice clothing ... 537
Concerning clothing as well as which clothing and other things are prohibited to wear ... 539
The Book of Bequests ... 540
Concerning what the living can do on the dead's behalf, such as Hajj, manumission, charity and other acts of righteousness ... 540
Concerning the bequest of the sick, pregnant and those engaged in fighting ... 542

Concerning the bequest to the heir 543
Concerning the bequest 544
Concerning the deceased's gesturing with his head in the bequest 544
Concerning the act of bequeathing 544
Concerning the man who bequeaths some of his wealth to another man 545
Concerning the bequest of the child, idiot, insane and weakling 545
The Book of the Contract of Indentureship, Slaves Freed by Their Master's Death, Manumission, the *Umm Walad* and the Like 548
Concerning the contract of indentureship and its mention in the Book 548
Concerning the one under the contract of indentureship 548
Concerning the contract of indentureship 549
Concerning the slave freed upon his master's death and manumission in health and illness 549
Concerning manumission 550
Concerning a slave that is owned by two people and one of them manumitted his share 550
Concerning a slave that is manumitted and joins the disbelievers as an apostate but then is acquired as war booty by the Muslims 551
Concerning a slave who is sold while owing a debt 551
Concerning claim of liability (*'uhda*) for a runaway slave 552
Concerning the indentured labourer and manumitted slave left behind by their master without any other property except them 552
Concerning one who makes an exception in manumission 552
Concerning the *umm walad* of a *dhimmi* or his slave woman who embraces Islam 553
Concerning one who manumits a part of his slave 553
Concerning the one who manumits his slave to an appointed time 554
Concerning a man who says to his slave that does not belong to him: "You are free from my ownership" 555
Concerning manumission by announcement 555
The Book of the Magistrate, Magistrates and Testimonies 556
Concerning that which is obligatory for the magistrate to do 556
Concerning magistrates and the one who claims hearing loss 558
Concerning magistrates and a stream of water divided among estates 558
Concerning judgements between the people of the marketplaces and setting up 558
Concerning those characteristics that a magistrate must have 559
Concerning granting the magistrate provisions for his office of judgement 559
Concerning judgements with oaths accompanied by a witness 559
Concerning the testimony of newly pubescent youths against each other in cases of head wounds and bodily injuries 560
Concerning those from whom testimonies are not accepted and those for whom testimonies are permitted 560
Concerning some testimonies 560
Concerning bribery in court cases, the prostitute's hire, the pay to a fortune-teller (*al-kāhin*), the contracting of a mercenary and the price of a dog 561
Concerning dispersing witnesses 561

Concerning the testimony of a child when he gets older and the disbeliever when he embraces Islam 561
The Book of Expeditions (*as-Siyar*) **562**
Introductory statement regarding expeditions 562
Concerning the description of the imam and the statement regarding that...562
Concerning the imamate which is established by an imam..562
Concerning two men from the Prophet's Progeny who share in these qualities...564
Concerning the removal of the imam from the imamate...564
Concerning what is permissible for the imam to do regarding his subjects as well as when it is permissible to depart from his command and refrain from him 565
Concerning that which is narrated from the Prophet: ((Whoever dies without knowing the imam will die the death of the pre-Islamic era)) 566
Concerning what Allah obligates upon the imam: anger in His affair, establishment of His proof and diligent effort in His obedience 566
Concerning what is narrated regarding the Mahdi 567
Concerning seeking assistance from enemies against the oppression of the disobedient..........................568
Concerning one who refuses to pledge allegiance to a just imam or is discouraged from him...................570
Concerning that which is obligatory for the just imam regarding the subjects and what is obligatory for them regarding him 570
Concerning the one who breaks the oath of allegiance to a rightful ruler..572
Concerning acting as a scribe for an oppressor and causing fear to the tyrants 572
Concerning what is obligatory upon the believers who cannot change the oppressor's actions that they see 573
Concerning what the imam should do before fighting the enemy...573
Concerning what the imam of truth does when he marches towards jihad against the enemies and meets the disobedient 573
Concerning the distribution of war booty among the army..575
Concerning the distribution of the fifth of the war booty 577
Concerning those women, children, slaves and *dhimmi*s who are present in war and the distribution of war booty 579
Concerning the captives who should not be killed 579
Concerning fighting the people of the *qibla* in their towns 580
Concerning attacking by night (*al-bayāt*)..581
Concerning spoils and its explanation..581
Concerning how the imam should admonish his forces when dispatching them or his soldiers when addressing them... 581
Concerning one who carries out a military expedition for hire..582
Concerning that which is in the possession of the oppressors and their helpers 582
Concerning the judgement of rebels regarding their *jizya* and herds 582
Concerning mercantile wealth of rebel soldiers...582
Concerning the wealth of women and children who were among the soldiers of wrongdoers and transgressors 583
Concerning the imam who says to a man: "If you kill so-n-so, you can have his plunder" 583
Concerning that which the imam can appoint for the killer 584

Concerning the wealth of dominions and other places that were conquered 584
Concerning what is required regarding fulfilling the trust of the imam 584
Concerning partiality towards a group who is advancing 584
Concerning waiting for the rightful imam 585
Concerning whether there is a fifth paid from plunder 585
Concerning commanding the good and forbidding the evil and concerning one who takes control of the Muslims' affairs 585
Concerning the virtue of a just imam 587
Concerning the code of conduct regarding the rebels 588
Concerning spies and concerning the code of conduct of warfare in the domain of war 588
Concerning the imposition of taxes upon conquered lands and then it was left and not divided, as what was done with dominions and other parts of the Levant, Egypt, and so on 589
Concerning the people of Islam granting safety to the people of idolatry 590
Concerning a Muslim captive who is granted safety in the domain of war by someone 591
Concerning a Muslim who enters one of the villages of the idolaters after being granted their safety and then they are suddenly attacked and captured while he is among them: Is he permitted to buy them? 591
Concerning a man from the domain of war and the *dhimmi* who embraces Islam at the hand of a Muslim man 591
Concerning a slave who embraced Islam in the domain of war 591
Concerning the one in the domain of war who embraces Islam and then emigrates to the domain of Islam while having children in the domain of war and then the Muslims take over that domain: What is to happen to his children? 591
Concerning the people from the domain of war who embrace Islam while there are Muslim slaves in their possession whom they took as booty from the Muslims prior to their embracing Islam 592
Concerning an indentured labourer and *umm walad* who are captured by idolaters and then the latter embrace Islam while owning both 592
Concerning a Muslim slave who is captured by the people of the domain of war and then apostatises from Islam in the domain of war but some of them embraces Islam and departs with him to the domain of Islam 593
Concerning one from the domain of war who accepts the *dhimmi* status and agrees to pay the *jizya* while he owns Muslim slaves from the slaves of the Muslims 593
The Book of Asceticism (*az-Zuhd*), Etiquette and Other Matters Related to Ennobling Character 594
Concerning disagreements among Muhammad's Progeny 594
Concerning the virtue of visiting the Prophet's grave 594
Concerning the urging towards obedience to Allah, the Mighty and Majestic 595
Concerning seeking forgiveness 595
Concerning seeking permission 596
Concerning weeping out of fear of Allah and concerning visiting one's brothers in Allah 596
Concerning the will of the Commander of Believers, 'Ali b. Abi Ṭālib 596
Concerning inciting animals to fight 597
Concerning the acts of the people of Lot which Allah's Messenger prohibited 597
Concerning memorising the Qur'an and the virtue of reciting the Qur'an 598
Concerning righteousness towards parents and maintaining family ties 599

Concerning the right of a Muslim on another Muslim and the right of a neighbour....600
Concerning reliance upon Allah....601
Concerning those who love one another for the sake of Allah....601
Concerning men who resemble women and women who resemble men....601
Concerning seeking the best choice (*al-istikhāra*)....602
Concerning the virtue of worship during the pre-dawn....603
Concerning good character and the virtues of prayers upon the Prophet and the virtues of the Friday congregational prayer....603
Concerning humility, patience and gratitude....604
Concerning generosity, deeds for Allah and stinginess....605
Concerning kindness....605
Concerning aiding the oppressors....606
Concerning commanding the good and forbidding the evil as well as supplicating to Allah....607
Concerning observing trusts, fulfilling covenants and being truthful in speech....608
Concerning backbiting and arrogance....608
Concerning major sins and their explanation....609
Concerning charity....609
Concerning constantly doing favours....609
Concerning apologies and the urging its acceptance....610
Concerning one who is compelled or forgets....610
Concerning the sanctity of Medina....610
Concerning the virtue of Medina....611
Concerning shyness....611
Concerning anger....611
Concerning the fortune-teller, physiognomist, astrologer and soothsayer....611
Concerning discouraged speech....612
Concerning a Muslim staying away from his Muslim brother....612
Concerning identifying the needy....612
Concerning seeking protection and invocations (*ar-ruqya*) for illness....613
Concerning dreams....613
Concerning greetings....614
Concerning images....614
Concerning owning a dog....614
Concerning calamity one should fear....614
Concerning playing chess....615
Concerning names that are discouraged....615
Concerning what was narrated from the Prophet regarding cupping and concerning clipping the moustache....615
Concerning what is encouraged of speech and actions related to travel....616
Concerning isolation (*al-wahda*)....616

Translator's Introduction

In the Name of Allah, the Most Merciful, the Most Gracious…

All praise is due to Allah, the Exalted and Majestic; the One who has no partners or associates; the One who provides the light of guidance to His slaves so that they may attain spiritual perfection and illumination by means of it. May Allah send His choicest blessings upon His slave and seal of the Messengers, Muhammad b. 'Abdullah. May Allah bless his pure Progeny, righteous Companions, and those who follow them in excellence until the Day of Judgement. As to what follows…

One of the most complex, nuanced and often misunderstood aspects of Islam is its jurisprudence. Indeed, as of the writing of this introduction, one of the biggest fears confronting 'Western' countries is the application of the dreaded 'Shari'ah law' in their environs. Media pundits and conservative right advocacy groups alike tend to fan the flames of this fear by presenting it is an antiquated and violent throwback to the medieval times. It is rather unfortunate that the whole of Islamic law—with its various branches that include laws regarding prayer, fasting, financial transactions, contractual obligations and the like—is discarded and overshadowed by imaginary visions of chopping blocks bloodied by the severed hands of thieves. Although the prescribed punishments are an aspect of the system of Islamic law, it is only a small part of an integrated whole. However, it is only this part that is emphasised by those seeking to forward the anti-Islamic agenda and purposely obfuscate the noble *Shari'ah*.

Regardless, the Islamic *Shari'ah* stands as one of the most enduring institutions to date, as all other contenders have either been severely crippled or rendered ineffectual in the wake of the onslaught of postmodernism. This, I believe, is the fear of its opponents. Despite the attempts to completely annihilate Islamic law and relegate it to the landfill of history as it has done with Western Christendom, Eastern emperor-worship and Soviet-bloc communism, Islam's jurisprudential relevance remains ever so vibrant in the hearts of its billion plus adherents. Indeed, this is even more evident in the realm of world economics as in the dark shadow of the 21st century economic crisis, even non-Muslims were looking to Islamic economic structures as alternatives. This just goes to demonstrate the perpetually relevant nature of Islamic law as well as its innate ability to draw upon the collective humanist potential. By 'humanist,' we do not mean the misnomered bastard child of the European Enlightenment and Social Darwinism—both of which ironically deprive the human of humanity by confining him/her to animalistic origins and bestial social tendencies. By 'humanist,' we mean the quality of the being ennobled by a noble Creator to reach the highest peak of nobility by realising his/her humanity. This has been, is and will always be the intended goal of Islamic law.

According to Qur'anic cosmology, the human being is the one whom Allah has favoured above all other Earthly creatures. Allah says: **{Verily, We hath ennobled the children of Adam and hath carried them upon land and sea. We hath provided them with the best of foods and hath greatly favoured them over much of what We've created} (Q. 17:70)**. Such nobility is based upon whether the human being adheres to that which is the basis of his/her nobility and favour—the God-given intellect. Despite differences in psychological and cultural make-up, the human intellect is universal.

Also, the human is gregarious and communal by nature. That withstanding, the human intellect alone is not sufficient in governing the affairs of the community. Another essential element is required to maintain the homeostasis of the community. Left to its own devices, reason could very well justify its own interests over those of the collective—even at the detriment of the collective. Allah says: **{…and ever-present with the souls is greed} (Q. 4:128)**.

Although human logic can support the virtue of those internal qualities that affect the collective such as honesty and justice, selflessness as well as other virtuous qualities that affect the individual spirit seem to be those for which the human being cannot attain based on reason alone. Rather, these qualities, which are held as universally virtuous, are taught to humankind from a source other than humankind because, as we mentioned, there is nothing individually logical about their virtue. Allah says that He **{...taught humankind what he knew not. Nay! Indeed, humankind is wont to transgress, considering himself to be wholly independent. Yet, unto Allah shall be the return}** **(Q. 96:5-8)**. That is to say that humankind was instructed in that which they do not have the capacity to teach themselves inherently; such is not organic in human make up. Without such teaching, we are bound to sin and arrogantly assume that we are self-sufficient and above all criticism.

This Divine guidance, as it were, serves to instruct humankind out of a sense of collective social-responsibility as well as engender a sense of individual spirituality. Indeed, without the intellect coupled with Divine guidance, the existence of the human being is relegated to that of a dumb beast. The Qur'an alludes to this when it says: **{...whilst those who disbelieve engage in enjoyment and eat as the cattle eat. And the Hellfire is for them a final destination}** **(Q. 47:12)**. The Glorified also says: **{They are like cattle. Nay! They are more astray. They are heedless!}** **(Q. 7:169)**.

Allah's guidance to humankind came through the tongue and actions of His Prophets and Messengers, upon them be peace. In addition to being charged with providing human beings with Allah's pure and noble conveyances, the Prophets and Messengers were also to establish systems of justice. The logic of such is that individual ethics and morality cannot exist within a vacuum outside of the communal collective. Otherwise, the overarching influence of society can eventually corrupt the individual. Regarding this role of the Prophets and Messengers, Allah declares: **{Verily, We sent Our Messengers with clear proofs and revealed with them the Book and the Scale (*al-mizān*) that humankind can establish justice}** **(Q. 57:25)**. This **{Scale}** symbolically refers to the establishment of systems dispensing justice.

Although justice is a universal concept, it logically follows that the application of such justice would depend on the idiosyncrasies of the relevant community in which it exists. It is this that is termed '*Shari'ah*' in the Qur'an. Allah says: **{Unto each of thee, We hath appointed for thee a law (*shir'atan*) and methodology}** **(Q. 5:48)**. This is the only instance in the Qur'an where the word *Shari'ah*, or at least its derivative, appears. The word literally denotes a path or street, and it idiomatically denotes a code of law specific to a community.

Earlier communities had their own *Shari'ah* as is evidence in the Qur'an. Allah says regarding previous iterations of the sacred law: **{Verily, We revealed the Torah as a source of guidance and light by which the Prophets who submitted judged the Jews, as did the rabbis and the priests by such of Allah's Book as they were bidden to preserve and were witnesses. So fear not humankind, but fear Me. And barter not My revelations for paltry gain. And whosoever judges not by that which Allah hath revealed—they are the disbelievers. And We decreed for them therein: A soul for a soul, an eye for an eye, a nose for a nose, an ear for an ear, a tooth for a tooth and injuries as retaliatory compensation. But whosoever forgives it as charity—it shall be for him an expiation. And whosoever judges not by that which Allah hath revealed—they are the wrongdoers. And We placed upon their footsteps Jesus, the son of Mary, confirming that which was with them of the Torah. And We gave unto him the Gospel; in it was guidance and light, confirming that which was with him of the Torah, guidance and an exhortation for the God-conscious. Let the people of the Gospel judge according to what Allah hath revealed therein. And whosoever judges not by that which Allah hath revealed—they are the disobedient}** **(Q. 5:44-47)**.

The duty of dispensing justice as well as the subsequent delineation of a *Shari'ah* was not exclusive to the Prophets of old. Allah says to the Prophet Muhammad, peace and blessings be upon him and his progeny: {**Say: "I am not an innovator amongst the Messengers…"**} (**Q. 46:9**). That is to say that Allah's last Messenger, peace and blessings be upon him and his progeny, was not unique from the previous Prophets and Messengers in his duties and functions. Neither was the one who came without a *Shari'ah.*

Indeed, it was the *Shari'ah* of the {**Seal of the Prophets**} (**Q. 33:40**) that was to supersede all previous codes of sacred law. Allah says: {**And We revealed unto thee the Book in truth, confirming that which is with them from the scripture as a guardian over it. Therefore, judge between them by that which Allah hath revealed and follow not their whims regarding what has come unto thee of the truth**} (**Q. 5:48**). In this holy verse, Allah's Messenger, peace be upon him and his progeny, is commanded to judge the previously-mentioned religious communities using the judgements of the Qur'an.

Such concept regarding the supersession of the *Shari'ah* of Islam is furthermore exemplified in the verse of the Qur'an: {**And when Allah took a covenant through the Prophets "If there, after I hath given thee the Book and wisdom, comes unto thee a Messenger confirming that which is with thee, ye must believe in him and help him." He said: "Doth ye confess and accept based on this?" They said: "We confess!" He said: "So, bear witness, and I am with thee as a Witness."**} (**Q. 3:81**).

During the presence of Allah's Messenger, peace and blessings be upon him and his progeny, he functioned as the sole source of Islamic legislation. Through his statements, actions and silences, the Muslim *Ummah* was able to ascertain the Divine Will and implement the *Shari'ah* without much ambiguity. However, with the passing of the Prophet, there existed a perpetual need for an interpretive function that would carry out the Divine precepts lest the community fall back into its pre-Islamic ignorance. Regarding this, Allah says: {**Muhammad is but a messenger. Verily, the Messengers before him passed away. If he were to die or is slain, will ye turn back on thy heels? And whosoever turns back on his heels shall never harm Allah in the slightest**} (**Q 3:144**).

This interpretive function is not something that could be left to any and every one. This position was such that required the utmost sensitivity insomuch that the slightest error or mistake could completely undo all that which the Lawmaker established. The person who fulfilled this role was one whose knowledge and authority could not be questioned or placed under scrutiny. Neither could such person be accused of missteps and errors because this would entail a faulty transmission of a perfect message. On the contrary, the person who fulfils this role must be one who consistently demonstrates mastery and proficiency in executing the law in word and spirit. Regarding this type of person, Allah says: {**Is the one who guides to the truth worthier to be followed or the one who cannot guide unless he is guided? What aileth thee? How doth thou judge?**} (**Q. 10:35**).

This rhetorical question posed by the Creator does not leave room for the affairs of the *Ummah* to be left to one who is inferior or less virtuous. Rather, Allah demands that the function of guidance and leadership be given to one who is most knowledgeable, capable and virtuous.

In addition to this function being exclusive to the one who exhibits these characteristics, the record of religious history and scripture testifies to this role being fulfilled by members of the immediate families of the Messengers and Prophets, upon them be peace. The Exalted says: {**...or do they envy people for what Allah has given them from His bounty? Verily, We have given the family of Abraham the Book and wisdom. We have given them great dominion!**} (**Q. 4:54**).

Also, Allah quotes Moses, upon him be peace, as saying: {**"And make for me a vizier from my family—Aaron, my brother. Increase my strength through him, and allow him to share in my affair so that we may glorify Thee much and remember Thee abundantly. Verily, Thou**

are upon us Ever-Seeing!" He [i.e. Allah] **said: "Thou hast been granted what thou ask, O Moses!"} (Q. 20:29-36).**

In these cases and others, the Qur'an highlights those instances in which the family members of the Prophets assisted them in establishing the precepts of the *Shari'ah.* The descendants are said to fulfil this function by serving as imams, or leaders, of their respective communities. The Qur'an highlights this by mentioning the conversation between Allah and the Prophet Abraham, upon him be peace: **{"Verily, We shall make thee an imam for the people!" He** [i.e. Abraham] **asked: "And from my descendants?" He** [i.e. Allah] **replied: "Our covenant reaches not the wrongdoers!"} (Q. 2:124).**

Allah fulfilled this covenant by appointing the imamate for Abraham's descendants. He says: **{And We bestowed unto him Isaac and Jacob as an addition, and We made all of them to be righteous. And We made them imams, guiding by Our command. We inspired them to do acts of goodness, establish the prayer and render the purification dues} (Q. 21:72).**

Thus, we see that the Abrahamic covenant did not restrict his descendants to simply act as exemplars; rather, they were to lead the community in establishing the *Shari'ah.* We also see from the above-mentioned Qur'anic references that this covenant is firmly established for those who are righteous and not wicked. So, Prophetic descent alone is insufficient if it is not coupled with a sense of social responsibility and personal piety.

Furthermore, Abraham, upon him be peace, prayed: **{"Lord, make this city secure and keep me and my sons away from worshipping idols. Lord, they have led many amongst humankind astray. Whosoever follows me is of me. Whosoever disobeys me—verily, Thou art Oft-Forgiving, Most Compassionate! Our Lord, I have settled some of my descendants in an uncultivated valley near Thy Sacred House, O Lord, so that they may establish prayer. So make the hearts of the people incline towards them and provide for them from the fruits so that they may be grateful..."} (Q. 14:35-37).**

Consequently, Prophet Abraham, upon him be peace, blessed the holy city of Mecca by his supplication as well as the presence of his descendants. The Patriarch prayed that his offspring be kept away from idolatry in all its forms, for those who engage in such would not be considered the scions of Abraham, upon him be peace, and therefore not included among the inheritors of his covenant.

Chief among these Abrahamic descendants was Prophet Muhammad, peace and blessings be upon him and his progeny. He fulfilled all of the criteria of Abraham's prayer since he guided by Allah's command, did acts of righteousness, established the prayer, imposed the purification dues and had never engaged in idol worship. As confirmation, Allah says: **{The people who have more right to Abraham are those that follow him, this Prophet, and those who believe…} (Q. 3:68).**

By extension, those descendants of Prophet Muhammad, peace and blessings be upon him and his progeny, who meet the same criteria are those who are to be imams based upon the requests and supplications of Abraham, upon him be peace. They are those who similarly refrained from idolatry during their lifetimes, as well as established the precepts of Allah upon their subjects. They are those for whom Abraham, upon him be peace, prayed in the aforementioned supplication: **{"…So make the hearts of the people incline towards them…"} (Q. 14:35-37).**

This supplication corresponds to the request from the Prophet Muhammad, peace and blessings be upon him and his progeny, when he asked: **{Say: "I ask thee for no reward but only affection toward the kin."} (Q. 42:23)**. This **{affection}** towards the family members of the Prophet, peace and blessings be upon him and his progeny, was a command from Allah and subsequently an answer to Abraham's supplication. One of these descendants who was an answer to the supplication was the Imam of Yemen known as Imam al-Hādi ila al-Haqq Yahya b. al-Hussein, upon him be peace.

Brief biography of Imam al-Hādi Yahya b. al-Hussein

He was Imam al-Hādi ila al-Haqq is Abul-Hussein Yahya bin al-Hussein b. al-Qāsim b. Ibrāhīm b. Ismā'īl b. Ibrāhīm b. al-Hasan b. al-Hasan b. 'Ali b. Abi Ṭālib, upon them be peace. As we can readily notice from his lineage, he was a Hasani *sayyid*.

As for his maternal lineage, he was also a descendant of the Prophet, peace and blessings be upon him and his progeny. His mother was Umm al-Hasan bt. al-Hasan b. Muhammad b. Suleiman b. Dāwūd b. al-Hasan b. al-Hasan b. Fātima bt. Prophet Muhammad, peace and blessings be upon him and his progeny. He was a Hasani sayyid on both sides of his lineage.

Al-Hādi was born in Medina in the year 245 AH/860 CE. His mother was pregnant with him during the lifetime of his illustrious grandfather, Imam al-Qāsim b. Ibrāhīm Rassi, upon him be peace. After she delivered the child, Imam Rassi recited the call to prayer in his grandson's ears and supplicated for him.

His biographers relate that Imam Rassi then asked his son, al-Hussein, as to what he intended to name the child. When al-Hussein responded by saying "Yahya," the imam is recorded to have then said: "By Allah, he will be the Master (*Sāhib*) of Yemen!" This prophecy came into fruition when Imam al-Hādi emigrated to Yemen and became its imam. Imam Rassi, upon him be peace, would not live long enough to see his grandson fulfil this prophecy because he only lived one year after the birth of Imam al-Hādi, upon him be peace.

Al-Hādi followed a rigorous system of education and upbringing, drawing from the wellsprings of the Prophet's Descendants. Even in the ***Ahkām***, he references statements and narrated traditions on the authorities of his grandfather, father and uncles. The son of al-Hādi, Imam Murtaḍa Muhammad, related that his father achieved mastery of some of the highest levels of sacred sciences at the age of seventeen.

The depth of his knowledge did not go unnoticed by his contemporaries as well as those after them. Another great imam from the Prophetic Household who ruled a part of Persia during the lifetime of al-Hādi, Imam Nāsir al-Utrūsh, upon him be peace, said of him: "He, by Allah, is one of the imams of divine guidance!" When the news of al-Hādi's death reached him, he wept bitterly and said: "Today, a pillar of Islam has fallen!" It is also related that the former Mu'tazilite, al-Hākim al-Jishumi, said of al-Hādi: "In him were all the preconditions for the imamate and the example of bravery!"

Al-Hādi was called to Yemen in 280 AH by a group of Yemenis to quell dissension and settle disputes. He initially set out to one of the eastern provinces, the village of the Bani Hishaysh to the east of modern day Sana'a. However, after settling there briefly, he was opposed by a group of disobedient rebels and not supported. Disappointed, he returned to the Hejaz. Soon after, he received a missive from the people of Yemen openly declaring their loyalty to him if he were to return. This was said to have taken place in Dhul-Qa'da in the year 283 AH. He accepted their invitation and was seen off by some of the prominent Prophetic Descendants, one of whom was his paternal uncle, Muhammad b. al-Qāsim. His uncle offered his support of the imam before the latter set off to Yemen.

Al-Hādi headed to Sa'da, Yemen on the 7th of Safar in the year 284 AH. He was able to bring the warring tribes together and unify them as brothers. He established justice there and ruled northern Yemen and parts of the Hejaz as imam. He even had the Friday sermons recited in his name in Mecca for seven years.

Al-Hādi's presence and subsequent significance in Yemen was chronicled by traditionalists and historians alike. The Sunni commentator on ***Ŝahīh al-Bukhāri***, Ibn Hajar al-Asqalāni, alluded to al-Hādi in his ***Fat hal-Bāri***. Commenting on the hadith ((This matter will remain in the Quraysh even if there only remain two of them)), he states the following:

> So the matter remains in the Quraysh from country to country in summation. The greatest of them—that is, the people of the Yemen—is called the imam. No one among them can assume the role of imam except the most knowledgeable and most just. [...] As for the one in Sa'da and other parts of Yemen, there is no doubt that he is from the Quraysh because he is from the descendants of al-Hussein b. 'Ali.

Ibn Hajar affirms that the rule in Yemen was achieved by one from the Prophet's Progeny. Although he mistakenly mentioned that the imam was a descendant of al-Hussein b. 'Ali instead of al-Hasan b. 'Ali, he nonetheless saw the Imamate of Yemen as a fulfilment of the Prophetic utterance since one of al-Hādi's descendants was the imam of that time.

A more explicit example is that of the reference to al-Hādi in the book ***Riyāḍ al-Mustāba*** by historian and traditionalist, Sheikh Yahya b. Abi Bakr al-'Amrāni. He stated:

> Then, from the time of al-Mu'tamid, al-Mu'tadid, al-Muqtadir to al-Musta'sim, the last of the Abbasid kings, the Ahl al-Bayt moved to countries where they were not able to before, such as Gilan and Daylām and the neighbouring countries of the Persians. Another example is parts of Yemen, such as Sana'a, Sa'da and its destinations. About twenty imams, the first of them and most memorable is Imam al-Hādi Yahya b. al-Hussein b. al-Qāsim b. Ibrāhīm b. Ismā'īl b. Ibrāhīm b. al-Hasan al-Muthanna. He was born in Medina, originated in the Hejaz, and was taught there and in Iraq. The manifestation of his rule in Yemen was in the year 280 AH. He came to Yemen while the prevailing doctrine there was that of the Qarmatians and the Esotericists. So he fought them hard in more than eighty battles, in none of which was he defeated. He had extensive knowledge and excessive courage.

The two groups mentioned by Sheikh Yahya—the Qarmatians and Esotericists—refer to two extremist sects of the Ismā'īli Shi'ites who formed the primary source of antagonism for Imam al-Hādi in Yemen. A member of one of these groups poisoned the imam; leading to the latter's death at the age of 53.

Scholar of lineage, Najm ad-Dīn 'Ali b. Abil-Ghanā`im al-'Umari (d. 441 AH) said in his ***Al-Majdi fī Ansāb at-Ťālibiyīn***:

> Al-Hādi, the great warrior of the religion and the pious imam of the Zaydis, was a compiler and poet who appeared in Yemen. He died in the year 298 AH. He died undertaking jihad himself. He used to wear a woollen robe and practice asceticism, may Allah have mercy on him.

The famous Ẑāhirite scholar, Allama 'Ali b. Hazm (d. 456), better known as Ibn Hazm, said in his ***Jamharat Ansāb al-'Arab***:

> And among them are some who settled in Sa'da, a place in Yemen. They include Ja'far who was nicknamed 'ar-Rashīd,' al-Hasan al-Muntakhab, al-Qāsim al-Mukhtār, Muhammad al-Mahdi—all of whom were the sons of Ahmed an-Nāsir b. Yahya al-Hādi b. al-Hussein b. al-Qāsim Rassi b. Ibrāhīm Tabataba`i. This Yahya, who was nicknamed 'al-Hādi,' had a position in the judgements of jurisprudence. I've seen it, and it is not that far from the positions of the Collective (*al-Jamā'a*).

Historian, Ahmed b. Muhammad al-Qurtubi (d. 600 AH) said in his ***Ta'rīf bil-Ansāb***:

> The arrival of al-Hādi Yahya b. al-Hussein to Sa'da was the sixth of Safar in the year 284. There was great strife between the tribes of Khawlān and Rabi'a, so he reconciled the two. All of them agreed to such. Khawlān were the owners of the land so they marched with him to Yemen until he became its ruler. They carried out his command as well as his organisation of the state. And they continued doing so during the lifetimes of Yahya b. al-Hussein al-Hādi as well as that of his sons Muhammad b. Yahya and an-Nāsir b. Yahya.

Historian and traditionalist, Allama Muhammad b. Ahmed ad-Dhahabi (d. 748 AH) said in his ***Tārikh al-Islām*** under the entry 'Yahya b. al-Hussein b. al-Qāsim b. Tabataba`i al-Alawi':

> He conquered Yemen and was called to Sanā` and its surrounding areas. Coinage was minted in his name. He then left Sanā after it was conquered by the Qarmatians. He went to Sa'da and was called 'al-Hādi Abul-Hussein' as well as the ruler of Najrān and the surrounding areas. The sermons were preached with him being addressed as the Commander of Believers (*amīr al-mu`minīn*). He was of righteous conduct (*hasan as-sīra*). He died in the year 298 and was succeeded by his son, Muhammad, who was nicknamed al-Murtaḍa.

Historian, Ahmed b. 'Ali (d. 828 AH), better known as Ibn 'Anba, said in his ***'Umdat at-Ťālib***:

> As for Yahya al-Hādi b. al-Hussein b. Rassi, his patronym was Abul-Hussein. He was one of the Zaydi imams, a venerable warrior, a scrupulous man and a poet. He appeared in Yemen and was nicknamed "al-Hādi ila al-Haqq." He died undertaking jihad himself and used to wear a woollen robe. He composed great works on jurisprudence, which was close to that of Abu Hanīfa.

Not all historians were as objective regarding the presence of al-Hādi in Yemen. Twelfth-century historian, 'Umar b. 'Ali b. Samra al-Ja'di related in his ***Tabaqāt Fuqahā al-Yemen***:

> And in such and such year, two great controversies took place in Yemen: one of them was the controversy of 'Ali b. al-Faḍl and his calling people to disbelief, and the other was the controversy of Sharīf Yahya b. al-Hussein Rassi and his calling people to Shi'ism.

Here he likened the presence of al-Hādi in Yemen to that of the heretic, 'Ali b. al-Faḍl. The most amazing thing about this comparison is that the chief opponent of al-Hādi was 'Ali b. al-Faḍl, who headed the Qarmatians! Nevertheless, it is evident that the role of Imam al-Hādi and his descendants in the history of Yemen cannot be neglected.

Before and during his reign as imam in Yemen, al-Hādi's primary concern was the beliefs and practices of his subjects. He authored a number of letters and treatises to provincial governors and scholars all clarifying issues regarding doctrine and praxis. Due to the influence of the aforementioned heretical sects as well as that of the various Sunnite factions, Yemen became a hotbed of sectarianism. It is this backdrop that forms the context of al-Hādi's magnum opus, ***Kitāb al-Ahkām fil-Halāl wal-Harām***.

The *Ahkām*: its significance and context

There is no other book that can be said to have established the jurisprudence of Ahl al-Bayt in Yemen which has had the amount of influence and authority than the ***Ahkām*** of al-Hādi. Indeed, this book occupies a unique place in jurisprudence in Yemen. This statement is in agreement with that of the imams and scholars from the past to the present.

One of the most famous commentators of the ***Ahkām***, Abul-'Abbās 'Ali b. Bilāl, wrote in the introduction of his ***Sharh al-Ahkām***:

> For when I saw the scholars of the opposition and the increase of their victory on behalf of their predecessors among their scholars as well as the strengthening of their doctrines

by their explanations of their narrations and books and their evidence against their opponents, I noticed that they multiplied their learners and spread their mention by their perseverance in teaching their books. I did not find the same to be the case among the Ahl al-Bayt of Allah's Messenger, peace and blessings be upon him and his progeny—those whom Allah commanded to be followed by His mention. Nor was there a desire for the sciences and teachings of their elders, which were neglected. There was no desire to instruct it to their youth, along with what they have classified and derived regarding the dilemmas of various issues and the foundational statements of our masters and imams, may Allah's blessings be upon them, about what I said. Insomuch that the populace assumed there was an indifference on the part of the scholars when they did not look into it, and they thought that they were not knowledgeable of or familiar with such while among them. This was something due to their neglect of it and perseverance in it.

> Desire and familiarity with the truth called me to compose a commentary on one of the books of our imams, ***Kitāb al-Ahkām fil-Halāl wal-Harām***. Al-Hādi, upon him be peace, was unique in classifying and extracting it as a request of him for the benefit of his offspring, partisans and those who came after him. Therefore, he composed these chapters and issues to branch out on them and to come out in each part of his book on its subcategories. When he presented and resolved it, Allah took him unto Himself while being pleased with his work, and He rewarded him for his effort.

Sayyid Imam al-Mutawakkil 'ala Allah Ahmed b. Suleiman (d. 566 AH), an imam of Ahl al-Bayt who ruled Yemen in the 12th century, similarly stated in the introduction of his ***Ušūl al-Ahkām***:

> Verily, when I came upon many of the primary places of the Ahl al-Bayt as well as those of the other tribes, I found that the jurists of the Generality authored books on Islamic Law, reports, narrated traditions and other issues. We also found that they authored books on the narrated traditions from the Prophet, peace and blessings be upon him and his progeny, by day and by night. They compiled those traditions that they use as proofs; however, I did not find the same case with our pure imams or their devoted scholars. They were prevented from that due to their constant engaging in jihad as well as their being dispersed throughout the lands. It is also due to their fear of the people of stubborn opposition as well as oppression of those disbelievers and disobedient who oppressed them. They narrated many traditions in their books, as well as their sciences, reports and poems; however, the best book of Islamic Law they authored was the book ***Al-Ahkām*** of al-Hādi ila al-Haqq, upon him be peace.

Sayyid Allama Majiddin al-Mu'ayyadi (d. 1428 AH) stated in his ***Lawāmi' al-Anwār***:

> Yes. I will now speak, with Allah's help, about the predominance of the two books of the two trusted guides of the Ummah and masters of the imams—the ***Majmu'*** of the great imam, imam of the saved sect and guiding relatives, Abul-Hussein, Zayd b. 'Ali b. al-Hussein b. 'Ali as well as the ***Ahkām*** of the imam of imams and guide of the Ummah Abul-Hussein Yahya b. al-Hussein b. al-Qāsim b. Ibrāhīm, upon them be the best of greetings and peace.
>
> I say—and may Allah bring us to the correct and it is upon Him that we rely and from Him that we seek help from every issue which is the extent of our knowledge and the limit of our ability—that the two books, the ***Majmu'*** and ***Ahkām***, are more authoritative and authentic than other them. This is because we transcribed the both of them upon the backs of our imams and their partisans, and the both of them were accepted by the later scholars from their predecessors insomuch that their successive mass transmission cannot be denied by the most expert and experienced scholars in all regions.

> That which the imam of Yemen narrated from the great imam, the guardian who is son of the guardian, Zayd b. 'Ali, or from the latter's grandfather, the Luminary of the Messenger's Progeny [i.e. al-Qāsim b. Ibrāhīm] is considered the most correct, foremost and reliable.

The late Sayyid Majiddīn al-Mu'ayyadi, may Allah have mercy on him, mentioned the dual relationship between the ***Ahkām*** and ***Musnad Imam Zayd,*** upon him be peace. We will dwell upon the relationship between these two books later, Insha'Allah. However, it suffices to say that the authority of the ***Ahkām*** was and is seen to be predominant as evident from the statements of the above imams.

As for the context of the ***Ahkām***, much of it can be derived from the text itself, as Imam al-Hādi justified his writing of the text in his introduction. He said:

> We know that those who oppose the Messenger's Family, upon them be peace, have embellished ignorance. They have presumptuously claimed knowledge and perfection. Regarding it, they have spoken from their whims. They have left the emulation of the people of knowledge whom Allah commands them to emulate—namely, the People of their Prophet's Household. They [i.e. the People of the House] are the ones who are to be imitated and asked. That is from the statement of Allah, Glorified be He: **{Ask the People of the Reminder if ye know not} (Q. 21:7)**. The **{People of the Reminder}** are the Progeny of Muhammad. Allah revealed the Book upon them. They guide by means of it towards the correct. Therefore, rejecting the Progeny of the Messenger, peace and blessings be upon him and his progeny, is injustice and rebellion.
>
> To Allah, they remain in opposition and defiantly disobedient. They speak by their caprices about that which was revealed concerning the permissible and prohibited. They act insolently against the Possessor of Majesty and Nobility and in that, they oppose Muhammad's Progeny, upon them be peace. Their statements contravene the Book, Sunnah and intellect. Blessed be Allah, Possessor of Majesty! They are not contented with that until they decry the one unlike them as a disbeliever! They all claim ignorance for such a one and allege that the truth is in their hands while the other is far from what is true and correct. They also allege that such person is misguided and follows caprice and deviation. By such, they repulse Allah's slaves away from Him and manifest resistance. They throw back the curtain of truth from the fixed place Allah chose it to be. Yet, He has appointed it to be known and built the pillar of the religion by it. As He—Glorified and Majestic be He—says: **{And thy Lord creates what He wills and chooses for them that which is best} (Q. 28:68)** and **{Allah is most knowing of where to place His Message} (Q. 6:124)**. Then, He says: **{Then, We have caused to inherit the Book those whom We have chosen amongst Our slaves} (Q. 35:32)**.
>
> Therefore, we saw that composing a thorough book was paramount. In it is the foundation of the permissible and prohibited narrated from the Messenger, upon him be peace. Thereby, one can act upon it and rely upon that which we mentioned. In so doing, one does not incline towards the ignorance and deviance of the people of blindness who remain in the place of rebelliousness and disaster.

He alluded to the travesty of the Muslim *Ummah*, in that the majority of the Muslims have left the pure source of Islamic knowledge as exemplified by the Prophet's Progeny. This claim is very significant because the religious landscape of Yemen was very varied prior to and after the arrival of al-Hādi. Yemen was host to various factions of Muslims, which included the aforementioned Isma'ili sects as well as the various madhhabs of the Generality. The apparent abandonment of the various Sunni sects regarding the exclusive authority of the Ahl al-Bayt is well known and needs no explanation. However, it is with great interest that al-Hādi similarly faulted the Ismā'īli Shi'ite sects for their leaving the guidance of the Ahl al-Bayt. This would seem as contradictory due to the latter claiming adherence to the imams of Ahl al-Bayt. Nevertheless, much like his grandfather before him, al-Hādi did not hold his tongue when countering the claims of those 'Rafidites' who he believed misrepresented the doctrine of the Prophet's Progeny. Throughout his ***Ahkām***, he relates traditions on the authorities of the prominent imams of the Ahl al-Bayt in order to counter the aberrant doctrines of those he deemed 'Rafidites.'

For example, when dwelling on the divisive issue of whether the pronouncement of three divorces in one sitting constitutes a valid divorce, he argued that although the practice is an innovation, it nevertheless is a valid divorce. He cited a series of Qur'anic verses to justify his claim as well as presented some analogous reasoning. In addition to that, he also referenced various imams from the Prophet's Progeny who held to his view at variance to the Rafidite Shia. This list of imams included but was not limited to Imams Zayd b. 'Ali, Muhammad al-Bāqir and Ja'far as-Ŝādiq, upon them be peace; the reference to the latter two imams was even more significant due to the fact that the Imami Shi'ites consider them to be infallible imams.

Therefore, according to al-Hādi's contention, those factions of Ismā'īli Shi'ites prevalent throughout Yemen represented an inauthentic 'Shi'ism' rife with erroneous doctrines and practices falsely attributed to the Prophetic Household. Furthermore, he even decried an unnamed false claimant to the imamate by contrasting the virtues of those he considered 'true' imams of Ahl al-Bayt and the actions of this false claimant. He says regarding this pseudo-imam:

> According to Allah, he is considered amongst those who slumber, as well as one who is listless and weak. They are also amongst the seekers of leisure and comfort. He presents himself before them, and the idea enters their hearts that he is the leader and that he comes out against the oppressors as a warrior. They falsely assume that, and he presents himself to them as such so that he may milk from them their money and consume their wealth.
>
> Verily, he confuses them in their affairs by pretending that it is the right way. By his pretending, he diverts them from their Lord. By means of their confusion, they are prevented from their obligations and injunctions made binding upon them by their Creator. He is persistent in consuming their wealth because he has confused them. They remain ignorant due to his pretending to be a leader and making believe to be one who will rebel against the oppressors. By Allah! He knows the intimate details of the affair, and that it is not as the ignorant falsely assume! It is decreed that he is amongst those who stray and deviate from His path in rebellion.
>
> According to his Lord, he destroys himself by his deeds and that of others, as well as by deviating from the truth and the truthful—bringing together all matters of sin. By such, the oppressors could institute a claim, and the rulers of open disobedience could establish a pillar of support. The ignorant would falsely assume his claim to be the truth and truthful due to his pretending. Filth would be on their hands. He would consume ill-gotten property without right. He would commit grievous offenses with calamitous results and turn many away from Allah. He would be disengaged from the statements of the believers and scatter the opinions of the Muslims. They would not be able to interpret the truth out of confusion. He would interpret with his own interpretations, and they would plunge heedlessly into dangers. Every one of his actions would be disputed secretly due to the fear of manifesting it in the open. He would attempt to deceive Allah and those who believe, but he would only be deceiving himself.

So, the ***Ahkām*** acts as a manifesto of sorts, clearly delineating the jurisprudence of the Prophet's Progeny in the face of those who were seen as either intentionally neglecting it or apparently perverting it.

As for the timing of the ***Ahkām***, Muhammad Yahya 'Izzān said in his preface to the 1997 edition of the jurisprudential text, ***At-Tahrīr***:

> And he [i.e. al-Hādi], peace be upon him, began to write the book ***Al-Ahkām*** in Medina. When he reached the Sales section, it was agreed that he would leave for Yemen. He became preoccupied with warfare there. Therefore, after the Sales section, he would dictate it to his scribe whenever there was a break in the war campaign. He had intended to write more, but fate prevented him from that, peace be upon him.

Al-Hādi began his monumental work while in the illuminated city of his grandfather, the Prophet, peace and blessings be upon him and his progeny. This is of great significance due to the fact that Medina served as an intellectual hub of Islamic activity. After all, it is the city where the Prophet and his followers fled when being pursued by the Meccan idolaters. Allah's Messenger, peace and blessings be upon him and his progeny, spent the later part of his years in Medina and thus firmly established the blessed city as a centre for Islamic praxis. Unlike the other frontier provinces of intellectual importance—such as Kufa, Baghdad and Basra—Medina is where the Prophetic precedent was witnessed and enacted. Additionally, it is the city where a large number of the Prophet's Descendants resided and taught. That withstanding, al-Hādi's presence there during the initial authoring of the ***Ahkām*** served as source material for his judgements.

Indeed, Yemen was fertile ground for the doctrine of the ***Ahkām*** to take root. It was a place whose major tribes, one of which is the powerful Hamdhāni tribe, boasted support for the Alawi cause. During the lifetime of the Prophet, peace and blessings be upon him and his progeny, 'Ali was dispatched to Yemen in order to preach the message of Islam to her tribes. Many of the tribes readily accepted the message and became loyal supporters of the fledgling faith due to the efforts of 'Ali, upon him be peace.

Even with the various winds of dynasties that blew across Yemen, there still remained a loyal core who held to the Alawi cause. Perhaps, this is the reason why much of Yemen held sway to the various Ismā'īli sects due to the Rafidites' supposed adherence to the Ahl al-Bayt. It is also the reason why the different warring tribes sought out the Prophetic Descendants to settle their disputes as is indicated in the biography of Imam al-Hādi, upon him be peace. Therefore, it was more likely that the ***Ahkām*** would be well received by the Yemenite tribes. That is not to say that the whole of Yemen would fall under the banner of the ***Ahkām***, as it would be under the imamates of subsequent imams centuries later that Yemen would do so. However, much of central and northern Yemen, as well as Najrān in present-day Saudi Arabia, came under the jurisdiction of Imam al-Hādi, upon him be peace.

As for the audience of the ***Ahkām***, the text's tone seems to indicate that it was a book whose intended addressees were the common Muslims. The language used in the text does not overtly employ the use of scholarly jargon that would differentiate it from the lay. Rather, its tone is wholly accessible to all.

The text is similarly not bogged down with too many textual proofs and evidences from the primary sources of the religion. That is not to say that al-Hādi avoids citing evidences for his positions; rather, the book's main purpose—to lay out the basics of Islamic practice—is not lost to an overabundance of Qur'anic verses and narrated traditions. The onus of textual citations and references to the Qur'an and narrated traditions would fall on the later imams and scholars who authored works such as ***Shifā al-Awām***, ***Ušūl al-Ahkām*** and ***Sharh at-Tajrīd***—all of which served to justify al-Hādi's positions using the primary textual sources.

Al-Hādi's approach to the Fundamentals of Jurisprudence (*Uṣūl al-fiqh*)

Imam al-Hādi, upon him be peace, was not without a methodology in his approach to the jurisprudence of the ***Ahkām***. These established fundamentals of jurisprudence, although not explicitly articulated in the ***Ahkām***, nevertheless permeated throughout the text. We will now look at some examples of how he exemplified some of the more well-known principles of the fundamentals of jurisprudence.

A. The Qur'an and its sciences

There is no disagreement that the Qur'an serves as the primary source of jurisprudence in Islam. Even after a glance at the Holy Book, one could easily identify those verses of a legislative nature—whether explicit or implicit. Sayyid Imam Ahmed b. Yahya b. al-Murtaḍa (d. 840 AH), also known as Imam Ibn al-Murtaḍa, said in his ***Al-Bahr az-Zakhkhār*** that five hundred verses of the Qur'an have been utilised as having legal function. However, it is from these verses that a myriad of laws are derived. That would necessitate that there exist various sciences from which these laws are derived. We will take a brief look at some examples of six of these sciences al-Hādi utilised in order to derive laws and legal rulings.

The principal of these sciences is an in-depth knowledge of the Arabic language because the Almighty says regarding the Qur'an **{...in a clear Arabic tongue...} (Q. 26:195)**. Therefore, a prerequisite knowledge of the language is required to derive rulings from the Qur'an. Al-Hādi, upon him be peace, demonstrated mastery in this field with some of his evidences for judgements. For example, when expounding upon the verse that mentions the punishment of the highway robber [i.e. **{Q. 5:33}**], he draws from the interchangeability of conjunctions known by Arabic linguists. He says:

> The meaning of **{they are to be put to death or (*aw*) crucified}** is: "...and crucified." It [i.e. the Arabic word for 'or'] is used as a conjunction of inclusion that does not carry the meaning of choice. This is what the Arabs do in their speech. Regarding that, Allah says: **{...and We sent unto him one hundred thousand or (*aw*) more...} (Q. 37:147)**. By that, the Glorified means "...and more..." It is used as a conjunction of inclusion here just as it is used in the verse **{...or crucified...}**. If it were a conjunction of alternative in the phrase **{...or more...}**, it would imply uncertainty. And Allah—the Blessed and Exalted—is free of such, and the Glorified is highly exalted from such! Rather, He is the most knowing, and there is nothing hidden from Him—whether it be in secret or in the open. It is as He says **{He knows the treachery of the eyes and whatsoever the breasts conceal} (Q. 40:19)** and **{He knows the secret and what is more hidden} (Q. 20:7)**.

Another of these Qur'anic disciplines is the science related to the 'reason for revelation' (*asbāb an-nuzūl*). Such science relies upon the narrations that mention the purported circumstances surrounding the revelation of a Qur'anic verse or series of verses. As for its role in jurisprudence, it serves to demonstrate the historic context of the verse as well as the subsequent application of such verse to a jurisprudential ruling. An example of this is the narration that mentions the revelation of the verses regarding unlawful pronouncements. Al-Hādi, upon him be peace, said:

> Regarding that is what Allah—the Blessed and Exalted—says when He revealed to His Prophet regarding the unlawful pronouncement of Aws b. as-Sāmit al-Anŝāri to his wife Khawla bt. Tha'laba. He was looking at her while she was praying and was aroused by her. He then commanded her to come to him, and she refused. After she completed her prayer, he was angry with her and said: "You are to me as the back (*žahr*) of my mother!" This was the method of divorce in the pre-Islamic era of ignorance and an unlawful pronouncement. He regretted doing so, and she also regretted. She approached Allah's Messenger, peace and blessings be upon him and his progeny, and mentioned that to him. She said: "Look. Is there repentance for him?" He replied: ((I do not see that

> there is repentance for him in returning to you)). She raised her hands to Allah and said; "O Allah! Verily Aws divorced me while I am old in age, weak in my body, frail in my bones and the desire of men has left me!" Allah had mercy on her and revealed the expiation. Allah's Messenger, peace and blessings be upon him and his progeny, summoned him and said: ((Free a slave)). He replied: "I do not have one." The Prophet, peace and blessings be upon him and his progeny, then said: ((Fast two consecutive months)). He replied: "O Messenger of Allah, if I do not eat three times a day, I could not withstand it!" He, peace and blessings be upon him and his progeny, then said: ((Feed sixty needy people)). He replied: "I do not have anything to give in charity unless Allah and His Messenger gives it to me." Allah's Messenger, peace and blessings be upon him and his progeny, helped him with an *araq* of dates. An *araq* is a large bucket. In it was thirty *šā'* of dates for charity. He said: "O Messenger of Allah, by the One who sent you as a Prophet in truth, there is no family more in need than us!" The Prophet, peace and blessings be upon him and his progeny, then said: ((Go ahead and eat—you and your family. Have sexual intercourse with your wife)). Then, Allah revealed what He revealed regarding these two Anŝāris: **{Those who make an unlawful pronouncement to their wives and then goes back on what they said, they are to free a slave before they touch one another. That is for thee to take exhortation. And Allah is aware of what ye do. Whosoever cannot find one, then he fasts for two months continuously before they touch one another. Then whosoever cannot, he is to feed sixty needy people}** **(Q. 58:4)**.

A third of these Qur'anic sciences is the knowledge of abrogation (*naskh*). This science entails that the scholar be aware of certain judgements mentioned in the Qur'an and the manner in which they were later repealed and substituted in favour of other judgements. The importance of such in relations to jurisprudence is reflected in the question as to whether one continues to act upon a Qur'anic judgement or not. Al-Hādi exemplified this principle in various places in his ***Ahkām***; one of which is when referring to contracting a debt and establishing trusts. He said:

> As for the statement of the Mighty and Majestic **{And if one of thee entrusts another, let he who is entrusted return his trust} (verse 283)**, this verse is abrogated by the statement of Allah **{O ye who believe! When ye contract a debt for a fixed term, write it down. Let a scribe record it in writing amongst thee equitably} (verse 282)**.

By such, he demonstrates that the action of pledging verbal trusts between two was later abrogated by the practice of appointing a scribe to write it down. Such abrogation was seen as being necessary as many of the early Muslims who could not read or write started to encounter later Muslims who were functionally literate and could therefore transcribe the conditions of a transaction and/or debt.

A fourth of the Qur'anic sciences utilised by Imam al-Hādi is that of identifying that which needs to be explicated (*al-mujmal*) as well as that which explicates (*al-mubayyan*). According to this science, there are verses that state a general action to be done without mentioning their manner, and there are verses that specify the way in which it is to be enacted. An example of the first type is mentioned by al-Hādi in respect to certain actions that we are obligated to do without being informed of their manner. He says:

> He detailed and explained its rudimentary actions upon the tongue of Gabriel, upon him be peace. This includes the prayer, the number of its obligations and bowings, as well as the purification dues, an explanation of what Allah desires to be taken and the minimum and maximum of wealth that necessitates it. He establishes the basis of the command with His statement **{Establish the prayer and render the purification dues} (Q. 73:20)**. The believers would not know what he has obligated them of their wealth nor when they are obligated to pay the purification dues from what is in their possession

unless Allah differentiates and explains it after stating its basis and obligation in the Book. He explained the details to His Prophet, peace and blessings be upon him and his progeny, upon the tongue of Gabriel, upon him be peace. Gabriel then commanded the Messenger, peace and blessings be upon him and his progeny, and the Messenger commanded his *Ummah* to do so just as Allah commanded him. He made the noon prayer four units, the late noon prayer four units, the sunset prayer three units, the night prayer four units and the dawn prayer two units. However, the numbers of units and details did not come in the Book.

In other words, although we are clearly commanded to pray and render the purification dues, their details are not mentioned in the Qur'an. There are scant references to some of the postures of the prayer, for example, but its complete performance is not elaborated upon. Instead, the manner was demonstrated by Allah's Messenger, peace and blessings be upon him and his progeny.

As for the second type—that which explains the details of a general command or action—an example of this is when Imam al-Hādi enumerates the shares of the inheritance laws from the Qur'an. Such laws are not in need of explication as they very clearly convey the details by which inheritance shares are to be distributed.

A fifth category of the Qur'anic sciences utilised in the ***Ahkām*** is differentiating the absolute (*al-muṫlaq*) from the restricted (*al-muqayyad*). The role of this distinction in jurisprudence is so that the jurist can properly apply the Qur'anic judgement in general without restrictions or establish restrictions and limits for the general judgement. An example of this in the ***Ahkām*** is when al-Hādi discusses the manner of performing the dust purification. He distinguishes the entire face—which the verse implies a general body part without specifying boundaries—from the arms, for which the verse states a specific limit to the limb to be washed. He says:

> The boundary of the dust purification is to the elbows. It is impermissible for one to perform the dust purification to the wrists. The boundary of the one who performs the dust purification is like the boundary of the washing for the one who found water. As Allah—Glorified be He—says: **{O ye who believe, when ye stand for the prayer, wash thy faces and thy hands to the elbows, wipe thy heads and** [wash] **thy feet to the ankles} (Q. 5:6)**.

A sixth science of the Qur'an utilised by Imam al-Hādi is that which differentiates the general (*al-u'mūm*) from the specific (*al-khuṡūṡ*). The importance of this science is that the jurist is able to designate those duties and prohibitions that are for the general body of Muslims and that which is for a specific class or category among them. One example that demonstrates this is the distinction between the marriage of the Prophet and that of the other believers. The believing men are allowed to marry up to four wives based on the verse: **{And wed those whom seem goodly to thee of women—two, three and four} (Q. 4:3)**. However, the Prophet was specified in being able to marry only nine. Imam al-Hādi says:

> Allah allowed him to marry those who are named the daughters of paternal uncles and aunts, daughters of maternal uncles and aunts as well as those female slaves whom the right hand possesses for the Messenger of the Lord of creation and all the Muslims. Then, He allowed him to marry the believing woman who gave herself to His Prophet, peace and blessings be upon him and his progeny. He warned other than him and made them specific for him instead of the believers. That is stated in His clear Book: **{...specifically for thee in the stead of the believers}**. The Blessed and Exalted permitted him to marry nine and joined them. However, He did not permit the Muslims to join more than four of any women—be they female slaves or far cut-off [i.e. not related].

B. Sunnah and hadith

The secondary source of jurisprudence is the collection of narrated traditions ascribed to the Prophet, peace and blessings be upon him and his progeny. It would be beyond the scope of this introduction to prove the validity of the Prophetic Sunnah. However, it suffices that the earliest community of Muslims were keen to take note of the Prophet's statements and actions insomuch that they even recorded his most seemingly mundane actions such as which sandal he put on first.

According to Imam al-Hādi, the Prophetic Sunnah was not subordinate to the primary source of the Qur'an but rather an equally valid source of legislation. In his ***Tafsīr Ma'na as-Sunnah***, he argues that the Prophetic Sunnah is not something from the Prophet himself but rather from Allah. Therefore, it commands as much attention and adherence as the Book of Allah. He says:

> Allah's Messenger, peace be upon him, would not have invented anything without Allah, glory be to Him. It is as he, peace and blessings be upon him and his progeny, said when he says: **{"I follow naught save what is revealed to me."} (Q. 7:203)**. Also, he said, peace be upon him: **{"...and I am not amongst those who pretend."} (Q. 38:86)**. And we say that Allah, Glory be to Him, did not entrust His Prophet to invent any portion of his matter, nor legislate it, nor impose it, nor prove it since Allah has charged him with an excess of His command and obliged him in respect to his action. Rather, the saying about that is clear, and the clear truth is certainty that Allah, Exalted be He above all His affairs, is the ultimate source of his obligations in the Clear Book, and he revealed it to the Seal of the Prophets.
>
> Therefore, He made in His Book the foundations of whatever he obligated from the religion, and he explained it to everyone, so the foundations of the religion were in the entire Book. And the details of it as well as the branches came to the Prophet, peace be upon him, from Allah, the Possessor of Majesty and Honour upon the tongue of the honourable Angel, Gabriel, the trustworthy spirit. Insomuch that he [i.e. Gabriel] descended with the laws of religion and the branches of the foundations of the Qur'an that was made clear to Muhammad, may Allah's prayers and peace be upon him and his progeny, just as he, peace be upon him, descended with the foundations. His descent was with the branches, just as his descent was with the combined general principles. And Gabriel, the trustworthy spirit, conveyed to Muhammad, the Seal of the Prophets, the branches of the laws of religion from Allah, the, Lord of creation, just as He conveyed to him the principles of the Clear Qur'an.

Therefore, according to the imam, the Sunnah served as another principle source of Islamic legislation. Laws cannot exist within a vacuum; every theory needs a methodology. Therefore, it would only make sense that the Source of the methodology be the same as that of the theory. Otherwise, a theory without a clear methodology can be misapplied, which could result in invalidating the theory itself.

Al-Hādi, upon him be peace, utilised various narrated traditions in his ***Ahkām***. This method involved both affirmation and negation of these traditions. Affirmation refers to those narrations that support his point of view, and negation refers to those narrations he deemed inauthentic because they contradict his point of view. In this, he is not unlike any other jurist.

Regarding those affirmative narrated traditions, al-Hādi quoted well-known narrations that appear in various other corpus of hadith. He generally uses the phrase "It is narrated that..." before quoting a hadith without relaying the chain of narrators. Another common phrase repeated more than one hundred seventy times throughout his book when quoting most of these traditions is "It has reached us... (*balaghanā*)." This phrase, when used by al-Hādi, denotes a narrated tradition that has been related to him through a source considered reliable to him though the chain of narrators may not be mentioned.

Both Prophetic hadith as well as traditions from Imam 'Ali and others adhere to this same formula. When the imam says "It has reached us…" he most likely assumes that the addressee relies upon his criteria in accessing the narration's authenticity. Similarly, Imam al-Hādi uses the phrase "It has been narrated to us…" about fifteen times to convey the same idea.

That is not to say that the imam does not relate traditions with chains of narrators. He relates some of the chains of narrators on the authority of his grandfather, Sayyid Imam al-Qāsim b. Ibrāhīm, who sometimes named the narrators from whom he related the hadith.

As for the negation of narrated traditions, Imam al-Hādi ascribed fabrication to those narrated traditions he deemed inauthentic. He did not indicate any clear methodology in declaring the narrations as inauthentic. For example, he did not do so due to weakening or criticising a narrator or sub-narrator, as was the practice of other scholars of hadith. However, there is one instance in which Imam al-Hādi falsified the 'hadith' ((One or two sucklings do not make prohibited)) due to its contradicting the Qur'an. Mostly though, he simply stated that those reports were not authentically attributed to Allah's Messenger or Imam 'Ali, upon them be peace, without stating the reason he considered them so.

C. The use of analogy

As for the use of analogy, the term refers to the process used by jurists in the absence of a clear textual reference. In his ***Al-Bahr az-Zakhkhār***, Imam Ibn Murtaḍa defines 'analogy (*qiyās*)' as 'applying one thing to another by striking a comparison.' Because it is a jurisprudential principle that is not agreed upon by all jurists, we saw fit to briefly examine its criticisms and justifications.

There are some criticisms of analogy and analogous reasoning. Some of its critics posit the view that analogy, as a non-textual method of derivation, negates the all-encompassing nature of the primary source texts. Other critics claim that the practice is invalid because although the primary sources may be used, they say that those sources are used in a way outside of their original intent. For example, Twelver Shia philosopher and jurist, Murtaḍa al-Mutahhari (d. 1399 AH) argued that the weakness of analogy in jurisprudence is that the whole process is based on guesswork and conjectural similarities. That is to say that analogous reasoning allows one to freely apply the principles of an explicit judgement to a situation whose resemblance to the initial judgement cannot be firmly established. Thus, as they say, one would be comparing apples to oranges without explicit proof that such comparison is valid. Such would entail reliance on assumption, and a legal principle and practice—they say—cannot be based on assumption.

We say in reply that the practice of analogy actually employs the use of the primary source texts and does not negate them. Its usage affirms the all-encompassing and timeless nature of the Qur'an and narrated traditions because it expands the meanings of the texts to include those things that are seemingly not covered by the primary source texts. The key to understanding this relationship is to determine whether the explicit text from the primary sources forms a clear principle in itself or whether it serves as an example of an unstated overarching principle. If it is the former, the reach of analogy would be severely restricted due to the explicit text being limited in scope. However, if one argues that the explicit text is but an example of a principle, the principle can then be derived from the example and equally applied to similar cases insomuch that the principle is the same though the variables are different. It is this second understanding that Sayyid Imam al-Qāsim b. Muhammad (d. 1029 AH), upon him be peace, alludes to in his ***Al-I'tiṣām*** when he says:

> As for analogy, that which proves the obligation to act upon it is the statement of the Exalted: **{And on whatsoever ye may differ, the judgement is to Allah} (Q. 42:10)**. That is, one is to refer to what has come from Allah in His decisive Book and upon the tongue of Allah's Messenger, peace and blessings be upon him and his progeny. It is also based on the statement of the Exalted: **{Then if ye dispute on a thing, refer to Allah and the Messenger} (Q. 4:59)**. That is, one is to refer to the Book of Allah and the Sunnah of His

> Messenger, peace and blessings be upon him and his progeny. Referring to the fundamental of the Book and Sunnah is the reality of analogy when one cannot find any explicit reference.

Thus, we see from the imam's quote that proper analogy uses the text of the Qur'an and Sunnah to derive judgements and arrive at a legislative principle. Imam al-Hādi himself defends the use of analogy in his treatise ***Kitāb al-Qiyās*** in which he said:

> The meaning that is firmly established as its intended meaning as well as a proof for light and guidance is that when a scholar who is well-versed in his knowledge and firm in his understanding encounters a matter, he employs the use of analogy based on the Book of Allah and the Sunnah of Allah's Messenger, peace and blessings be upon him and his progeny. And the meaning of our saying 'he employs the use of analogy' is: he reflects, he envisions, he thinks and he distinguishes, and he extracts it from the Book of Allah, the Sunnah of His Prophet and his intellect so that he, at the descent of the calamity, dives in the seas of the Book and Sunnah until he extracts by his inference the knowledge of his need from the Book of his Lord and the Sunnah that He revealed to His Prophet.

Therefore, correct analogy utilises the primary source texts to derive a ruling even when the relevance of its application may not be clear. Rather than imply that the primary source texts are insufficient, the use of analogy presents the Qur'an and Sunnah as perpetually relevant in the face of obscure matters as well as ever-changing times and circumstances. Its non-use would imply negligence and insufficiency on the part of the Lawgiver and revealed text. Also, as Imam al-Hādi says, one is to be a penetrating scholar deeply steeped in the various sciences of the Qur'an and Sunnah in order to effectively derive rulings through analogy as to avoid the mistakes of the uninitiated.

As for the criticism that a judgement cannot be based on assumption and conjecture, Imam Ibn Murtaḍa responded in his ***Al-Bahr*** that there are various examples of judgements based on assumption and uncertainty. He cited as examples the process of determining the *qibla* as well as identifying the prayer times during overcast. In these cases, one cannot do such with certainty, so one must rely on assumption and conjecture.

We will now look at an example of Imam al-Hādi's use of analogy in the ***Ahkām***. In it, he discusses the penalty for killing a game animal while one is in the state of pilgrim sanctity for the Hajj. He says:

> The penalty for killing is a ewe. If one cannot find a ewe, he must feed ten needy people if he wants or fast for ten days. This is because the equivalent of a ewe is fasting, as Allah stipulates for the performer of separate joint pilgrimages to fast three days during the Hajj pilgrimage and seven days when he returns [Ref. **Q. 2:196**]. Just as we find that Allah has established a ten-day fast to take the place of the minimum penalty—which is a ewe according to us—we say that the equivalent of every ewe is a ten-day fast.
>
> We also say that the equivalent of a ewe is feeding ten needy people because we established that feeding ten needy people takes the place of the ten-day fast. Similar is established by the Ever-Living and Self-Sustaining when He says regarding the unlawful pronouncement (*až-žihār*): {**Whosoever cannot find one, then he fasts for two months continuously before they touch one another. Then whosoever cannot, he is to feed sixty needy people**} (**Q. 58:4**). It is then established that feeding a needy person takes the place of fasting a day. Therefore, it is sound according to us that a ewe is equivalent to fasting for ten days or feeding ten needy people.

In this example, Imam al-Hādi equates the penalty of a ewe with fasting for ten days or feeding ten needy people. There is no explicit reference in the Qur'an or Prophetic statements that the number of needy people to feed must be ten or that one must fast ten days for such infringement. We are simply told that the expiation of one who does such **{is to feed the needy or the equivalent thereof is fasting}** (**Q. 5:95**) without specifying the number. We are also told in the Qur'an **2:196** that the fast and feeding can take place for those who do not have a sacrificial animal when performing the separate joint pilgrimages. Thus, the imam's judgement is based on the analogous relationship between all these variables mentioned in the Qur'anic verses.

D. The statements, judgements and consensus of the imams of Ahl al-Bayt

Now that we've dealt with those elements of Islamic jurisprudence which have credence amongst the majority of scholars and schools, we will now cover that element which differentiates the school of Ahl al-Bayt from others—the authority of the imams of the Prophet's Descendants. In addition to the textual sources that form the foundation of Islamic jurisprudence about which all agree—the Qur'an and Sunnah—there are also the narrated statements and consensus of those imams held to be authoritative by their followers. This fundamental, although held to not be authoritative to others, nevertheless forms an essential part of what is termed 'Zaydi' jurisprudence. Due to this, we saw fit to elaborate on the basis of this very important jurisprudential fundamental and respond to its opponents, with the help of Allah.

Before that, we would like to first define the parameters of what we mean by the collective statements of the imams of Ahl al-Bayt as well as their consensus. The first parameter we mean to define is to whom the term 'imams of Ahl al-Bayt' refer. By such term, we refer to the descendants of al-Hasan b. 'Ali and al-Hussein b. 'Ali, upon both of them be peace. The term is a direct reference to a portion of the Qur'anic verse known as the Verse of Purification (*Ayat at-Taṫhīr*) in which the immediate family of the Prophet is addressed. The verse is as follows: **{Verily, Allah only desires to prevent from thee filth, O Ahl al-Bayt, and purify thee with a thorough purification}** (**Q. 33:33**). The verse itself does not name these family members that are referenced; however, narrated traditions highlight their identities. For the sake of brevity, we will cite one such tradition. Sunni traditionalist, at-Tirmidhi, related on the authority of Umm Salama:

> The verse **{Verily, Allah only desires to prevent from thee filth, O *Ahl al-Bayt*, and purify thee with a thorough purification}** (**Q. 33:33**) was revealed in my house while I was sitting at the door of my house. In the house was Allah's Messenger, 'Ali, Fāṭima, al-Hasan and al-Hussein. He covered them with a cloak and said: ((O Allah, these are my Ahl al-Bayt! Prevent from them filth and purify them with a thorough purification!)) I asked: "O Messenger of Allah, am I not among the Ahl al-Bayt?" He replied: ((You are upon good. You are among the wives of Allah's Messenger)).

Such tradition is explicit and denotes that Ahl al-Bayt referred exclusively to the Prophet, 'Ali, Fāṭima, al-Hasan and al-Hussein, upon them be peace. This is evident from various perspectives. First, he had not gathered anyone else under the cloak although he had wives and other relatives present. Second, he did not say "These are amongst (*min*) my Ahl al-Bayt" as to include them among a larger group; rather, he exclusivised them by saying ((These are my Ahl al-Bayt!)). Third, he excluded one of his wives, Umm Salama, who sought to be included.

This is further substantiated by the narrations on the authority of Anas b. Mālik in which the Prophet, peace and blessings be upon him and his progeny, referred to 'Ali, Fāṭima, al-Hasan and al-Hussein as Ahl al-Bayt on other occasions. In it, he relates that Allah's Messenger, peace and blessings be upon him and his progeny, used to pass the door of Fāṭima for sixth months when departing for the dawn prayer. He would say: ((The prayer, O Ahl al-Bayt! **{Verily, Allah only desires to prevent from thee filth, O *Ahl al-Bayt*, and purify thee with a thorough purification}** (**Q. 33:33**))).

One may ask how the term 'Ahl al-Bayt' can only be applied to the descendants of al-Hasan and al-Hussein, upon them be peace, but not include the other offspring of 'Ali, upon him be peace.

After all, they say, 'Ali had more children from other wives after Fāṭima. Why would not these offspring be considered Ahl al-Bayt as well? The reply is that the term refers exclusively to the Prophet's Descendants through Fāṭima because in other narrations, the Prophet used the term 'my descendants' which would restrict the meaning to only those through the line of Fāṭima, upon her be peace, and not through any other of 'Ali's wives after her. This is coupled by the fact that the Prophet, peace and blessings be upon him and his progeny, referred to them as ((…my Ahl al-Bayt…)) in traditions further emphasising his connection to them. This would entail that any other connection outside of the Fatimid line is not connected to the Prophet and is therefore not from among his Ahl al-Bayt.

Now that it is established who the term 'Ahl al-Bayt' refers to, it must now be demonstrated how this blessed verse is used to prove the exclusive authority of the Ahl al-Bayt in matters of religion. Sayyid Imam al-Manṣūr Billah 'Abdullah b. Hamza (d. 652 AH), upon him be peace, said in his ***Sharh ar-Risālat an-Nāṣiha bi Adillat al-Wāḍiha*** regarding the proof of the verse:

> As for the statement regarding the proof of this verse, Allah informs us that He desires to prevent filth from them and purify them thoroughly. It is one of the following: Either He desires to purify them from literal impurities such as urine, defecation, carcass and blood; or He desires to purify them from the filth of disobedience and the impurity of sin; or He does not desire to purify them from either one. It is invalid that He does not desire to purify them from either of the two types of impurities because the Exalted has already informed us that He desires to do such, and His desire is amongst His actions that is to occur. The contrary statement in this regard would be impossible. It is also invalid that He desires to purify them from literal impurities and actual filth because they would be the same as others; their judgement and the judgement of the Muslim community would be exactly the same. The only remaining view is that He desires to purify them from committing obscenities and avoiding obligations, and this cannot take place except by means of absolute infallibility from their deeds. By the evidence of such, their consensus is established a proof.

Hence, the interpretation that the Ahl al-Bayt is protected from sin and error by the word of the Qur'an forms one of the textual proofs used to justify the adoption of their collective opinion as a proof.

However, one of the pressing questions is around whether such protection affords the Ahl al-Bayt individual authority or collective authority. The Qur'anic verse mentions a general protection without specifying whether such is indicative of the individual members or their consensual agreement. This is usually addressed by emphasising that the Prophet's statements designate the infallibility of each individual member of the Companions of the Cloak [i.e. 'Ali, Fāṭima, al-Hasan and al-Hussein]. However, this is not the case regarding their descendants. Various statements of Allah's Messenger, peace and blessings be upon him and his progeny, seemingly convey the protection of the Companions of the Cloak from sin and error. Some examples include but are not limited to the following: (('Ali is with the truth and the truth is with 'Ali)), ((Al-Hasan and al-Hussein are the masters of the youths of Paradise)), ((Fāṭima is the mistress of the women of creation)) and ((Fāṭima is a part of me. Whoever angers her [i.e. Fāṭima] angers me)). Such statements are emphatic in their denotation. However, since no similar statements exist for any other individual member of the Ahl al-Bayt, it is understood to mean that their collective opinion and judgements are deemed as infallible.

As for the statements of the Prophet, peace and blessings be upon him and his progeny, which apparently support the doctrine of the proof for their collective opinion, there are several. One of the clearest is the hadith known as the Hadith of Two Weighty Things (*ath-Thaqalayn*). The wording of the mass-transmitted report whose authenticity is agreed upon is ((Verily, I leave you that by which if you hold on to it, you will never go astray after me: the Book of Allah and my Descendants, my Ahl al-Bayt. Verily, the Subtle and Aware informed me that they will never separate until they meet me at the Basin)). Such hadith emphasises the role of the Ahl al-Bayt as a source of divine guidance next to the Qur'an. It also illustrates that the two would not separate from each other, which demonstrates their continuous connection and association even after the lifetimes of the Companions of the Cloak, upon them be peace.

Similar is also conveyed, such as the following: ((My Ahl al-Bayt are like the ark of Noah. Whoever embarks upon them will be saved and whoever does not will be drowned)) and ((My Ahl al-Bayt are a means of safety to the People of the earth just as the stars are a means of safety to the people of the heavens)). With such explicit statements, the authority of the Ahl al-Bayt in terms of religion is further substantiated.

Given the import on all of the above, Imam al-Hādi, upon him be peace, relied on the individual statements of Imam 'Ali and the consensus of the Prophet's Descendants as definitive proofs, as well as the individual judgements of al-Hādi's grandfather, Imam al-Qāsim Rassi, and that of the other prominent imams of Ahl al-Bayt. As for the judgements of the Commander of Believers, 'Ali b. Abi Ṭālib, upon him be peace, as well as the proof of the consensus of Ahl al-Bayt, they are considered proofs in and of themselves because of the aforementioned proofs regarding the infallibility of Ahl al-Bayt in general and 'Ali in particular. His views are also held to be authoritative because of the assumption that any of his actions and judgements were that which he heard and saw from the Prophet, peace and blessings be upon him and his progeny. For example, when discussing the preference for reciting the glorification (*tasbīh*) rather than the recitation of *Surat al-Fātiha* (Q. 1) in the last two units of the prayer, Imam al-Hādi cited that it was the practice from Imam 'Ali and said:

> However, we choose to do what was narrated from the Commander of Believers, may Allah be merciful to him. This is because we know that he did not do anything unless Allah's Messenger, peace and blessings be upon him and his progeny, did it. Allah's Messenger, peace and blessings be upon him and his progeny, did not do anything unless he was commanded by Allah to do so. He chose it for him to do in the religion.

Such admission recognises the glorification in the last two units as the Prophetic precedent despite the absence of any reports that attribute such practice to Allah's Messenger, peace and blessings be upon him and his progeny. However, since this practice was attributed to 'Ali, al-Hādi nevertheless ascribes it to the Prophet by extension.

As for the consensus of the Prophet's Descendants, Imam al-Hādi referred to it as a proof and a fundamental basis for his judgements. For example, he says regarding the number of declarations in the funeral prayer: "The consensus of the Progeny of Allah's Messenger, peace and blessings be upon him and his progeny, holds to the view that the declaration of Allah's greatness in the funeral prayer takes place five times."

The imam cited the consensus of the Ahl al-Bayt in several forms. In addition to explicitly stating it, he also utilised phrases and expressions to imply their collective agreement. For example, he uses the phrase "...according to us..." more than one hundred times throughout the ***Ahkām*** as to suggest the mutual agreement of the Ahl al-Bayt. He also repeats the phrase "We say..." throughout the text to convey the same meaning. Another interesting convention he uses is the phrase "Others say..." in order to differentiate the opinions of the Ahl al-Bayt from those of others. The literal translation of the Arabic is "Those other than us say..." This clearly sets the positions of the imams of Ahl al-Bayt apart from that of other than them. According to al-Hādi, therefore, most of his judgements reflected the collective consensus of the Ahl al-Bayt, upon them be peace. It also implies that any contrary opinion, even if it were related from 'Ali or any other imam, is considered unacceptable, invalid and falsely attributed to them. We will dwell on this in the next two sections, God willing.

Imam al-Hādi's assertion must be qualified as he thoroughly familiarised himself with the various views of those imams and scholars of Ahl al-Bayt. As we mentioned earlier, his residence in Medina afforded him the opportunity to collect and take from the opinions of the prominent Descendants based there. His travels also took him to places such as modern-day Iraq and Iran in order to gather and corroborate the statements and judgements of the Ahl al-Bayt in those regions as well.

Perhaps, the most accessible source of the collective consensus of the Ahl al-Bayt was that which was reported from his grandfather, Imam al-Qāsim b. Ibrāhīm Rassi, upon him be peace. The rulings of Imam Rassi permeate the ***Ahkām*** and form the bulk of what will be known as Hadawi jurisprudence. It has been authentically attributed to Imam al-Qāsim b. Ibrāhīm that he said: "I have met the elders of the Prophet's progeny among the descendants of al-Hasan and al-Hussein, and there were no disagreements that occurred between them." This statement of his has been reported and authenticated by Sayyid Imam Humaydān b. Yahya in his ***Majmu'***, Sayyid Imam al-Qāsim b. Muhammad in his ***Al-Irshād***, as well as Amīr 'Ali b. 'Abdullah al-Hasani (d. 1190 AH) in his ***Buluugh al-Arab***.

We will dwell more on the import of this statement in the next section; however, it suffices that this admission of Imam Rassi, upon him be peace, establishes the principle that his views represented that of the collective consensus of Ahl al-Bayt. Otherwise, he would be forced to acknowledge that his views were contrary to those of their consensus. It is more likely that he made this statement to further justify his views as being those of the collective agreement of the Prophet's Descendants.

It is evident that Imam al-Hādi, upon him be peace, considered the views of his grandfather to represent the views of the collective Ahl al-Bayt. As we mentioned, he cites the judgements of Imam Rassi as definitive proofs in his ***Ahkām***. However, in ***Al-Muntakhab***—a text that chronologically appears after the ***Ahkām***, in which the compiler, Muhammad b. Suleiman al-Kufi, records his questions and al-Hādi's answers regarding multiple jurisprudential issues—the citations of the individual judgements of Imam al-Qāsim Rassi are substituted with the statement "...the statement of the scholars of the progeny of Allah's Messenger..."

As an example, Imam al-Hādi relates in the ***Ahkām*** that Imam Rassi stated regarding prostrating in the prayer due to reciting a verse of prostration: "We do not hold to the view that one prostrates in the obligatory prayers any additional prostration due to the recitation of a prostration verse." However, in ***Al-Muntakhab***, al-Hādi attributes such view to the collective Ahl al-Bayt when he says:

> As for my statement and the statement of the scholars of the Messenger's Progeny, we hold to the view that one does not prostrate due to reciting a verse of prostration in the obligatory prayer because it is an addition to the prayer. There is no addition to the prayer just as there is no subtraction from it.

In ***Al-Muntakhab***, the imam did not mention it as being the view of Imam Rassi, as he did in ***Al-Ahkām***; rather, he said that it was the view of the scholars of Ahl al-Bayt. It is for this reason we say that it is clear that al-Hādi considered the judgements of his grandfather to be synonymous with that of the collective scholars of the Prophet's Descendants.

Of course, such view raises the question as to where this places those independent judgements (*ijtihād*) of imams from the Ahl al-Bayt, which are not corroborated by the collective consensus. That is to say, according to al-Hādi, do the independent rulings of an imam constitute a proof in the fundamentals of jurisprudence? We say in reply that Imam al-Hādi was not opposed to employing independent judgements whenever there was no consensus on an issue. In several instances, he makes the statement "The best of what I heard..." which implies a choice out of various valid views. This would suggest that there exists a number of independent judgements on a particular issue. In another instance, he makes it clear that he utilised his own judgement and not a narrated statement from any authoritative reference.

When discussing the recitations to take place in the eclipse prayer, he states some Qur'anic verses and afterwards states: "This which we have mentioned regarding the recitation in the eclipse prayer is not mentioned on the authority of anyone; rather, I hold it to be the best and the choicest." Therefore, he considered independent judgements as valid as long as they did not contradict the fundamental sciences of religion.

The allowance of scholarly independent judgements will undoubtedly lead to a myriad of opinions and would therefore open the door to conflicting opinions among the scholars of Ahl al-Bayt. This brings us to the question: What happens when there is disagreement among the Ahl al-Bayt?

Al-Hādi and disagreement

One of the criticisms of the aforementioned jurisprudential principle is that the descendants of the Prophet, peace and blessings be upon him and his progeny, have spread and scattered throughout the earth and that they have adopted various schools of thought historically. They say that you have Hasani and Husseini sayyids that belong to the wide spectrum of Islamic ideologies and praxis. There are Prophetic Descendants that are Maliki, Shafi'i, Hanafi, Hanbali, Ismā'īli, Ja'fari, Zaydi, etc. Therefore, they ask, how can one accurately assess their collective consensus? Furthermore, there have even been scholarly disagreements among those scholars of the Ahl al-Bayt within the same school. Contradictory statements exist among the imams of Ahl al-Bayt regarding many jurisprudential issues. It would therefore seem implausible that collective agreement could exist among them when there has been so much collective disagreement.

In his ***Ahkām***, Imam al-Hādi set forth his thesis in a section dedicated specifically to the issue of disagreement among the Ahl al-Bayt. In it, he says:

> There is no disagreement from the Progeny of Muhammad, peace and blessings be upon him and his progeny, except in the case of negligence. So, whoever of them neglects the knowledge of his forefathers and does not follow the knowledge of his father's family from his father until it ends with 'Ali b. Abi Ṭālib, may Allah bless him, and the Prophet, peace and blessings be upon him and his progeny, and shares with the Generality in their sayings and follow their interpretations—such would necessitate disagreement. This is the case especially if such one has no insight and discernment and does not refer what has been reported to him back to the Book nor refer the allegorical to the decisive.
>
> As for those of them who quote from their forefathers—father from father—until they end up to the foundation while neither considering what others have said nor drawing attention to the opinion of others with a distinct understanding based on what came to him from the Book and agreed-upon Sunnah and the intellect which Allah appointed as a proof regarding it and refers all his affairs to the Book referring the allegorical to the decisive, it will never be a source of misguidance, nor will it contradict the truth in the first place.

Thus, the imam affirmed that there is no difference of opinion among the Ahl al-Bayt. Any disagreement, he says, is attributed to abandoning the doctrine of their forefathers.

In addition to this, a more detailed explanation is narrated from him in his ***Kitāb al-Qiyās***. When asked about the possibility of disagreements that occur among the Prophetic Descendants, he replied by saying:

> Verily, disagreement from the progeny of Allah's Messenger—O one who questions about their reports—never occurred and will never occur except in two situations. As for the first of them, it is due to being forgetful of something after something and due to an error in what was narrated and transmitted. And this is a small and minor matter because the forgetful among them can turn from his forgetfulness and refer back to the established statement that is mentioned to him after encounter and debate.

> As for the second of them, it is the graver of the two as well as the most dangerous and difficult. It is that some of them are influenced, learn and take knowledge from other than their forefathers. Such person was not enlightened by the light of their wisdom nor was he illuminated by their light when confronted by the darkness of other doctrines. When matters were ambiguous, he did not rely on their jurisprudence. Rather, he turned from them to others. He took what he had from his knowledge from their opponents, insomuch that his knowledge became the knowledge of others and his doctrine became the doctrine of others. He considered their statements, may Allah bless them, as being insignificant since he knew that which he cited from others and understood without him being ignited by them. Therefore, he equated his matter with other than theirs. His knowledge became like the knowledge of those who taught him, and his statement became like the statement of those whose statements he observed. The light of his illumination became like the light of knowledge in his possession. Therefore, he and the one from whom he took such became equal in opposing the Ahl al-Bayt of Allah's Messenger, peace and blessings be upon him and his progeny. Even if he were from their lineage, his knowledge is not the same as their knowledge, and neither is his opinion regarding judgements in which there is disagreement like their opinion. The proof against the one who opposed the original fundamentals of the Prophet's Progeny is like the proof against other slaves of Allah who went against the original fundamentals and abandoned them.

So, Imam al-Hādi was very clear in his view that there is no disagreement among the imams of Ahl al-Bayt, upon them be peace. He also made it clear that if any disagreement were to occur between them, it would be due to intentional or unintentional neglect of the doctrine passed down from their forefathers or errors in transmission of their views. Such view of al-Hādi leaves no room for contradictions or variant opposing opinions and rulings from the Prophet's progeny.

What must be qualified is that by disagreement, we do not mean the difference between declaring something obligatory or praiseworthy. Such difference in designation is not known as disagreement. By disagreement, we mean the difference between declaring something permissible and prohibited. Such disagreement on the part of Ahl al-Bayt is seen as being impermissible and impossible. Indeed, such disagreement would have theological implications, as it would entail that a source of divine guidance contradicts itself. That withstanding, all of the proofs regarding the Ahl al-Bayt being a source of guidance next to the Qur'an would be rendered ineffectual if they contradicted each other in judgements and opinions.

This discrepancy was recognised by our earliest imams, and this is the reason that they adamantly denied the possibility of disagreement among them. In sermon 147 in the ***Nahj al-Balāgha***, Imam 'Ali, upon him be peace, is recorded to have said regarding the Ahl al-Bayt: "They do not act contrary to the religion, nor do they differ from one another." Sayyid Imam Ahmed b. 'Isa b. Zayd b. 'Ali, upon them be peace, is recorded to have said in ***Al-Jāmi' al-Kāfi wa al-U'lūm*** when asked about whether the Ahl al-Bayt disagree: "If it is regarding those judgements of Allah, they never disagree."

Sayyid Imam 'Abdullah b. Hamza, upon him be peace, said in his ***Ash-Shāfi'***:

> Don't you know that the differences between the Descendants is like the differences between the Prophets...How can the Descendants differ from their forefathers when the Prophet testified to their integrity saying: ((They will never separate until they meet me at the Basin))?

The son of Imam al-Hādi, Sayyid Imam al-Murtaḍa Muhammad b. Yahya (d. 316 AH), upon them be peace, similarly said in his reply to the people of Tabaristān:

> The imams differ only in what is not permissible and impermissible as well as in explanation and speech. Each imam in his time has calamities that descend upon him and

> must judge them by that which Allah grants him to deduce from the Book of Allah and the Sunnah of His Prophet, peace and blessings be upon him and his progeny, as well as from the argument of reason by which he is to infer from the Book which may be obscure. He is to extract from it the truth and correct, and if this issue came upon the first, he would have extracted it as the latter extracts it. The imams have been entrusted with the people; Allah, the Mighty and Majestic, has commanded them to have a good conduct among them and give them advice. Perhaps, in the imam's era, one of the subjects' causes will be judged as correct, for which the Book testifies to, and then that same calamity will occur in another age of the imams who will not be able to enforce the ruling in it, as it was possible for the first. In such case, he will be excused by Allah.

Sayyid Imam al-Qāsim b. 'Ali al-Ayāni (d. 393 AH), upon him be peace, said in his ***Kitāb at-Tafrī'***:

> That which attributes disagreement to the imams is impossible. Such cannot be attributed to them except out of ignorance of that which is between truth and falsehood. Rather, they only differ regarding the outward aspects of their lives and interpretations. They are in agreement with justice and do not depart from it.

Evidently, the imams of Ahl al-Bayt saw the concept of disagreement in matters related to the permissible and prohibited as being impossible and untenable.

If we return to al-Hādi's statement regarding the possible reasons for their being contrary statements from the imams, we see that he attributes such to negligence as well as mistaken transmissions. Even in the ***Ahkām***, he relates those traditions inaccurately narrated from the imams, specifically Imam 'Ali, upon him be peace. For example, he mentioned that it was narrated from 'Ali that he prohibited the caught fish of the Magians; however, he declared that such report was inauthentically attributed to 'Ali, upon him be peace. In this way, al-Hādi enacted his methodology of falsifying those reports from the imams, which imply disagreement in judgements.

This brings us to the discussion as to the relationship between the judgements of al-Hādi mentioned in the ***Ahkām*** and those narrations relayed in the earliest book of reports attributed to Imam 'Ali as related by Imam Zayd b. 'Ali known as ***Musnad Imam Zayd***.

Al-Hādi and the *Musnad Imam Zayd*

If the dear reader can recall, we cited the statement of Sayyid Majiddīn al-Mu'ayyadi in his ***Lawāmi' al-Anwār*** in which he said that the two most authentic books were the ***Ahkām*** and the ***Musnad*** of Imam Zayd b. 'Ali, upon them be peace. It is important to note that the relationship between these two texts reflects both confirmation and contradiction.

As a preface to this discussion, it is necessary to first highlight the significance of the ***Musnad Imam Zayd***. The ***Musnad Imam Zayd***, also known as the ***Majmu' al-Fiqh***, was said to have been compiled by a student of Imam Zayd named Abu Khālid 'Amr b. Khālid al-Wāsiṭi (d. 150 AH). Although, most traditionalists of the Generality held him to be an unreliable narrator of hadith, he was nonetheless relied upon by the imams of Ahl al-Bayt. There seems to not have been any criticism of him in the books of the Ahl al-Bayt, and Imam al-Hādi even related from him in the ***Ahkām***. That being the case, his attribution of the ***Musnad Imam Zayd*** to Imam Zayd b. 'Ali goes relatively unchallenged outside of Sunni circles though 13th century Sunni traditionalist and biographer, Hāfiẓ Jamaludīn al-Mizzi, acknowledged in ***Tahdhīb al-Kamāl*** that Abu Khālid narrated from Imam Zayd and composed a compilation (*naskha*) from him.

This compilation, the ***Musnad Imam Zayd***, contains various reports on the authority of Imam Zayd from his father from his grandfather from 'Ali from the Prophet, peace and blessings be upon him and his progeny. Therefore, such short chain of narrators demonstrates the chronological primacy of this text. It is held as being the first book of hadith related to jurisprudence since it pre-empted the earliest book of

Sunni jurisprudential narrated traditions, the ***Muwatta*** of Imam Mālik, by several decades. The book is also said to contain the recorded judgements of Imam 'Ali and Imam Zayd, upon them be peace.

A. An overview

As we said earlier, we find that there tends to be a sense of agreement and disagreement between Imam al-Hādi and the ***Musnad Imam Zayd***. We will first look at the relationship of agreement between the texts. The instances of agreement can be divided into those which agree implicitly and those which agree explicitly. An example of a report in the ***Ahkām*** that can be found directly in the ***Musnad*** is the wording of the testimony of faith that is declared during the prayer. In the ***Musnad Imam Zayd***, it says:

> Zayd b. 'Ali, upon them be peace, used to say in the testimony of faith after the first two units: "*Bismillâhi wa Billahi wa alhamdulillahi wal-asmā`ul-husna kulluhā lillahi. Ashhadu an lā ilāha ila Allāhu wahdahu lā sharīka lahu wa ashhadu anna Muhammadan abduhu wa rasūluhu.* (Tr. "In the Name of Allah and in Allah! All Praise is due to Allah! The most beautiful Names belong to Allah! I testify that there is no god but Allah, the One in which there is no partner! I testify that Muhammad is His Messenger and Slave.")."

Imam al-Hādi, upon him be peace, cites this wording in his ***Ahkām*** and says that his father and grandfather related this from Imam Zayd, upon him be peace. The imam was also quoted in the ***Muntakhab*** as ascribing the same wording of the testimony of faith to Zayd b. 'Ali, upon them be peace.

As for an example of the implicit conformity between what is related in the ***Musnad Imam Zayd*** and the ***Ahkām***, Imam al-Hādi relates in the section dealing with the declaration of Allah's greatness that Imam 'Ali recited it from the end of the dawn prayer on the day of 'Arafat to the last day of *Tashrīq*. However, he did not attribute such report to Imam Zayd, upon him be peace. Yet, the following is reported in the ***Musnad***:

> Zayd b. 'Ali related to me [i.e. Abu Khālid] from his father—his grandfather—'Ali, upon them be peace, that the Prophet, peace and blessings be upon him and his progeny, said to him: ((O 'Ali, declare Allah's greatness at the end of the dawn prayer on the day of 'Arafat until the late noon prayer on the last day of *Tashrīq*)).

In this case, there is harmony between the two texts although Imam al-Hādi had not referenced Imam Zayd, upon him be peace.

Although in most cases there is agreement, what is of more interest to us is the contradictory relationship that exists between the two texts. Similar to the instances of implicit and explicit agreements, there are examples of implicit and explicit contradictions. By the term 'implicit' contradiction, we mean those contradictions in which Imam al-Hādi passes a judgement contrary to what is narrated in the ***Musnad*** without referencing the report itself or attributing it with falsehood. By the term 'explicit,' we mean a contradiction in which a report from the ***Musnad*** is clearly attributed with falsehood.

As for an example of an implicit disagreement between the judgements in the ***Ahkām*** and the narrations in the ***Musnad***, there is a judgement regarding the recitation of the supplication, known as the *qunūt*, in the prayer. In the ***Ahkām***, Imam al-Hādi, upon him be peace, declares:

> According to us, the *qunūt* is after the bowing; we do not hold to the view that it is before it. According to us, there is nothing after the *qunūt* except the declaration of Allah's greatness and the descending to prostrate.

In this, he simply states the judgement without referencing that contradictory reports exist to justify the opposite. Yet, in the ***Musnad Imam Zayd***, the following is reported:

> Zayd b. 'Ali related to me from his father—his grandfather—'Ali, upon them be peace, used to recite the *qunūt* in the dawn prayer before the bowing and in the witr prayer after the bowing. Then, in Kufa, he recited the *qunūt* in the witr prayer before the bowing.
>
> Zayd b. 'Ali, upon them be peace, used to recite the *qunūt* in the dawn and witr prayers before the bowing.

In this example, Imam al-Hādi, upon him be peace, passed a judgement contrary to what was narrated from Imam Zayd on the authority of his forefathers to 'Ali, upon them be peace, without referencing the report.

There are several instances within the ***Ahkām*** in which Imam al-Hādi, upon him be peace, explicitly attributes falsehood to reports that appear in the ***Musnad Imam Zayd***. An example of this is the question as to whether one can sell an *umm walad*. The following is narrated in the ***Musnad***:

> Zayd b. 'Ali related to me from his father—his grandfather—'Ali, upon them be peace, that he permitted the sale of *ummahāt al-awlād* (plural of '*umm walad*'). He used to say: "If her master dies while she has a child from him, she would be free from his share because the child owns a share from her. If she does not have a child, she is sold."

Therefore, according to the ***Musnad***, Imam 'Ali, upon him be peace, permitted the *umm walad* to be sold. However, Imam al-Hādi, upon him be peace, related in his ***Ahkām***:

> As for what the riffraff (*hamaj*) narrate in which the Commander of Believers, upon him be peace, permitted the sale of them [i.e. *umm walad*], it is not truthfully from him nor would anyone who knew him attribute that to him. Regarding that, my father related to me that his father was asked about the sale of the *umm walad* and he said: "This is impermissible, nor can one pass such judgement on them. As for what the people of ignorance narrated from the Commander of the Believers, upon him be peace, one does not accept that from them, and it is not truthfully attributed to him."

Thus, we see that not only does al-Hādi not permit the selling of the *umm walad*, but he also attributes fabrication to the report in which Imam 'Ali was reported to say otherwise. Also, he denigrates those who narrated such report as 'riffraff (*hamaj*)!' This Arabic word denotes one who is foolish, stupid and dishonourable. The same judgement regarding the report is repeated in the ***Muntakhab*** where he was asked about the permissibility of selling an *umm walad*. He replied by saying: "Others hold to that view and narrate it from 'Ali b. Abi Ṫālib, upon him be peace. But it is not authentically attributed to him according to us. Rather, it is a lie and falsehood attributed to him."

There is another instance of contradiction between the two texts that deserves attention. In the ***Ahkām***, Imam al-Hādi passed the judgement that the purification dues are to be paid from the wealth of orphans. He justified his judgement by citing a report in which Imam 'Ali, upon him be peace, was reported to have taken the purification dues from the wealth of the children of Abu Rāfi'. However, a contrary report is narrated in the ***Musnad Imam Zayd***. The report is as follows:

> I [i.e. Abu Khālid] asked Zayd b. 'Ali, upon them be peace, about the wealth of the orphan and whether the purification dues are collected from it. He replied: "No." I said: "Verily, the progeny of the sons of Abi Rāfi' narrate from 'Ali that he used to take the purification dues from their wealth." He replied: "We, the Ahl al-Bayt, object to that."

In this report, not only did Imam Zayd reject the judgement, but he also stated that the collective Ahl al-Bayt objected to the report. On one hand, we have Imam al-Hādi who narrates Imam 'Ali's judgement through the Ahl al-Bayt and on the other hand, we have Imam Zayd who objects to such on the authority of the Ahl al-Bayt.

Another interesting relationship that exists between the two texts that neither reflects agreement nor disagreement is that of the existence of reports from Imam Zayd in the ***Ahkām*** that do not appear in the ***Musnad***. An example of this can be seen in the following report in the ***Ahkām***:

> It has reached us on the authority of Zayd b. 'Ali from his fathers that 'Ali b. Abi Ṭālib, upon him be peace, said: "Allah's Messenger, peace and blessings be upon him and his progeny, ascended the pulpit and said: ((O people! Verily, Gabriel came to me, stood before me and said: *O Muhammad! Whoever reaches the month of Ramadan and does not seek forgiveness and dies will enter the Hellfire; Allah will curse him. Say: 'Ameen.'* And I said: 'Ameen.' Then he said: *Whoever encounters a just imam and does not seek forgiveness for him, Allah will curse him. Say: 'Ameen.* And I said: 'Ameen.' Then he said: *Whoever encounters his parents and does not seek forgiveness for them, Allah will curse him. Say: 'Ameen.'* And I said: 'Ameen'))."

This report, although related from Imam Zayd in the ***Ahkām***, has not been related in the ***Musnad Imam Zayd*** either in its entirety or abbreviated form.

B. Analysis of the responses to the discrepancies

The discrepancies that exist between these two texts have generally garnered more attention from the opponents of the Hadawi madhhab than from the proponents. For example, in his works, Imam Muhammad b. 'Ali ash-Shawkāni (d. 1255), a former Hadawi who became amongst its harshest critics, highlighted the differences between what is narrated in the ***Musnad*** and the judgements of al-Hādi. Similarly, Amir Muhammad b. Ismā`īl as-Sana'ani (d. 1182) dedicated a lot of ink towards refuting the Hadawi madhhab by juxtaposing the reports and judgements in the ***Musnad*** against Imam al-Hādi's rulings.

The proponents of al-Hādi have traditionally responded to these discrepancies by either ignoring them or seeking to reconcile between them by the use of *ta`wīl*, or a variant interpretation. None of them have ever breached the possibility of ascribing weakness or fabrication to the conflicting narrations in the ***Musnad***. There has almost been a hallowed sanctity given to the ***Musnad Imam Zayd*** insomuch that even the staunchest Hadawi would never deny its complete authenticity despite the statements of al-Hādi himself. We will now critically examine these traditional responses to the discrepancies.

The first response attempts to ignore the contradictions between the ***Musnad*** and the ***Ahkām*** by relegating the differences to independent scholarly effort (*ijtihād*). That is to say that any discrepancy between the two is seen as being a result of the exercise of free and uninhibited thought. They say: "Imam Zayd said this, and Imam al-Hādi said that. Neither one is infallible, so one is free to take whichever opinion one likes." Consequently, one imam of Ahl al-Bayt is presented as differing from another in judgements due to the freedom Islam affords to difference of opinion and disagreement.

We say that this response is wholly unsatisfactory because it seeks to gloss over the fact that these differing judgements are based on conflicting narrations between the two. All are assumed to be attributed to the Ahl al-Bayt; but, if they disagree in matters related to the permissible and prohibited, it creates the theological quagmire we referenced earlier. It also contradicts the cited statements that the Ahl al-Bayt do not disagree. In the examples of contradictions, we mentioned in the previous section, there are clear statements and narrated reports in one book, which are at odds with what is narrated in the other book. With such clear and glaring inconsistencies, one is either forced to accept one or the other; however, one cannot accept both.

Even if one says that al-Hādi's falsifying a report in the ***Musnad*** is a result of his own scholarly *ijtihād*, we reply by saying that such response does not negate the root of the problem. This is because the root of the problem, as we said, is not in the difference in judgements but rather in the difference in the attribution of such judgements to Imam 'Ali and the Ahl al-Bayt. Imam al-Hādi, upon him be peace, falsified the report because it was at variance with what was related to him; it was not the result of his own personal *ijtihād*.

The second traditional response to the contradictions between the judgements of Imam al-Hādi and the ***Musnad*** employs the use of *ta`wīl* in order to reconcile the two. This method involves interpreting one text to conform to the other. In this way, one is able to seemingly maintain the authenticity of both without sacrificing the integrity of either.

We say that this response is also untenable for two reasons. The first reason is that although *ta`wīl* is an attempt to reconcile two contradictory narrations, it can only effectively be utilised when there is ambiguity in the text to allow for such a variant interpretation. That is to say that when the text allows for *ta`wīl* due to its vagueness, one is free to use it. However, when such vagueness is not apparent from the text, one cannot use *ta`wīl*. For example, in the case of the kinds of manslaughter, Imam al-Hādi relates in the ***Ahkām*** that there are only two types: intentional and unintentional. Also, he categorically denies the existence of a third type. He quotes from his grandfather, Imam al-Qāsim Rassi, upon him be peace: "It is narrated that 'Ali, upon him be peace, said that 'almost intentional' is that which was committed by a staff and projected with a large stone. But this is not authentically attributed to him according to us."

However, in the ***Musnad Imam Zayd***, the following is related from Abu Khālid:

> Zayd b. 'Ali related to me from his father—his grandfather—'Ali, upon them be peace, said: "Intentional killing is with a sword and iron, almost intentional killing is with a stone and staff, and unintentional killing is when the killer does not intend to kill another but does so mistakenly."

Thus, it is evident that one text posits that there are only two types of manslaughter without a third, and the other text states that there are three types. Furthermore, the text that says that there are three attributes the statement to the Commander of Believers, 'Ali b. Abi Ṭālib, upon him be peace, and the other text attributes falsehood to such report. This leaves no room for a variant interpretation; there are either two types of manslaughter or three. There is no ambiguity between these two extremes, as both are very clear in their denotation. We therefore say that although the *ta`wīl* approach may be able to explain away some inconsistencies, the gap between the two extremes are so vast in many other cases that variant interpretation just becomes an exercise in futility.

The second reason why the *ta`wīl* method proves to be unsatisfactory in attempting to reconcile these texts is that such pursuit completely ignores those instances in which others understood there to be irreconcilable differences between the two views. That is to say that if we attempt to present the view that there is no disharmony between what is narrated from Imam Zayd and the judgements of Imam al-Hādi, we would have to disregard the statements of those imams and scholars who have acknowledged the disagreement between the rulings of the two imams.

For example, regarding the aforementioned issue of whether the purification dues are paid on an orphan's wealth, two different views are attributed to the two imams. In his ***Sharh at-Tajrīd***, Imam al-Mu`ayyad Billah, upon him be peace, related that Imam al-Hādi held to the view that the purification dues are extracted from the orphan's wealth. He similarly related a contrary view from Imam Zayd, upon him be peace. Their contrary views were highlighted without attempting to reconcile them as the same view. It should also be noted that this issue is regarding a religious obligation, and two differing views regarding a religious obligation is not a light matter.

C. An alternative response to the discrepancies

Given all of the above, it should be quite evident to the reader that Imam al-Hādi, upon him be peace, was completely unaware of the ***Musnad Imam Zayd***. Such assertion, of course, creates a series of uncomfortable questions that must be addressed. First, if it is affirmed that Imam al-Hādi was ignorant of the ***Musnad Imam Zayd*** as a text and it was said to have been compiled about a hundred years prior to Imam al-Hādi, one is forced to ask: Where did the text come from? Second, if it is affirmed that Imam al-Hādi circulated among the scholars and authorities of the Ahl al-Bayt of his time, why had he not heard about this compilation or referred to it in his judgements? Third, how was he able to confidently claim the consensus of Ahl al-Bayt regarding those issues for which contrary was related in the ***Musnad***? Fourth, why and how does Imam al-Hādi explicitly declare the reports found in the ***Musnad*** as not authentically attributed to Imam 'Ali, upon him be peace? Fifth, why and how does Imam al-Hādi narrate some reports from Imam Zayd b. 'Ali, upon him be peace, in his ***Ahkām*** that can be found in the ***Musnad***, yet attribute falsehood to other reports that can be found in the same book? Sixth, why and how does he similarly relate reports from the compiler of the ***Musnad***, Abu Khālid al-Wāsiti, yet attribute falsehood to other reports found in the latter's book? Seventh, why and how does Imam al-Hādi relate traditions from Imam Zayd, upon him be peace, that do not appear in the ***Musnad***? Eighth, why and how does Imam al-Hādi pass judgements contrary to the explicit reports found in the ***Musnad***? Ninth, why and how does Imam al-Hādi ascribe foolishness and stupidity to the one who related a report that appears in the ***Musnad Imam Zayd*** by referring to such person as *hamaj*? Tenth, why is it that the ***Musnad*** had not reached Yemen from Iraq until centuries after al-Hādi?

It is the translator's humble opinion that the conclusion of all of the aforementioned questions makes it plausible that some of the ***Musnad Imam Zayd*** have been subjected to forgery and interpolation. Although such view may not be considered 'orthodox' in Zaydi circles, it is nonetheless the most satisfactory way that one can address the discrepancies that exist between the texts.

This should not be considered far-fetched, as the imams of Ahl al-Bayt often alluded to the fact that words and statements have been falsely attributed to them by both enemies and partisans alike. Sayyid Imam al-Qāsim b. 'Ali al-Ayāni, upon him be peace, related that when it was perceived that there was a disagreement between Imams 'Abdullah b. al-Hasan and Ja'far b. Muhammad, upon them be peace, the latter said: "By Allah and by this edifice to which I direct myself to! I have been lied upon; our doctrine (*al-madhhab*) is the same!"

Not only does Imam Ja'far b. Muhammad, upon him be peace, acknowledge that lies were attributed to him, but he also affirms that there are no disagreements in the doctrine of Ahl al-Bayt.

A similar statement was made by the son of Imam al-Qāsim b 'Ali, Sayyid Imam al-Hussein b. al-Qāsim al-Ayāni (d. 404 AH), upon him be peace, said in his ***Mukhtasar al-Ahkām***:

> Not everything that has been narrated from Allah's Messenger, peace and blessings be upon him and his progeny, is truthfully attributed to him due to the small number of reliable people and long period of time. Insomuch that during my own lifetime, I have heard false narrations attributed to me, which I never said or did! Perhaps, even Allah's allies (*awliyā*) may hear such and attribute truthfulness to it while living around the same time. How much more so is the case with the Prophet, peace and blessings be upon him and his progeny, who lived a longer period of time ago?

Therefore, we suggest that even the ***Musnad Imam Zayd*** may have had forged traditions and reports inserted between her two covers not unlike other texts. Additionally, we say that such may have taken place at the hands of the Kufans in Iraq, as there are certain peculiarities that point to Iraq. Various 'signposts' support this assertion which we would like to briefly touch upon.

I. The nullification of the ritual ablution due to laughter in the prayer

First, in his ***Ahkām***, Imam al-Hādi, upon him be peace, makes reference to whether laughter during the prayer invalidates the ritual ablution or not. He states regarding this issue: "Regarding what the Iraqis say—that is, laughter interrupts the prayer and invalidates the ritual ablution—we do not say what they say nor do we ascribe to their view."

He clearly states that it is the view of 'the Iraqis' that laughter during the prayer invalidates the ritual ablution. This is a reference to the Hanafis, as they are generally regarded as the 'Kufans' in particular, and 'the scholars of Iraq' in general since the Hanafi base of scholarship was in Iraq. Also, it is well known that Imam Abu Hanīfa held to the view that laughter invalidates the ritual ablution.

Consequently, in the ***Musnad***, Imam Zayd, upon him be peace, is recorded to have said that laughter during the prayer invalidates the ritual ablution. The report is as follows:

> Zayd b. 'Ali, upon him be peace, said: "One can resume the prayer after the performance of these three actions [i.e. nosebleeds, vomit and flatulence]. However, there are three actions for which one cannot resume the prayer: urination, defecation and laughing. They nullify the ritual ablution and the prayer."

It is plausible that this ruling was interpolated and falsely attributed to Imam Zayd, upon him be peace, in Kufa. This is because in another place in the ***Musnad***, the following report appears from Abu Khālid:

> I asked Imam Zayd b. 'Ali, upon them be peace, about that which nullifies the ritual ablution. He replied: "Urination, defecation, flatulence, nosebleeds, vomiting, pus, pus with blood and sleep in a reclining position."

In this latter report, no mention is made of laughing during the prayer; although it mentions urination and defecation as in the previous report. One may argue that the reason it does not mention laughter in the prayer is because all of the other actions mentioned as nullifiers of the ablution occur outside of the prayer. However, we respond by saying that the questioner asked about nullifiers of the ablution in general without specifying whether they take place outside the prayer or during it. It would have therefore been appropriate for Imam Zayd to have mentioned laughter during the prayer; but, he did not.

II. The *Tarāwīh* prayer

The *Tarāwīh* prayer is a voluntary congregational prayer prayed in the mosques during the month of Ramadan. This prayer has universal acceptance among the scholars and jurists of the Generality, although some of their jurists hold to the view that praying this prayer alone in one's home is preferable. A contrary view is said to be held by the imams of Ahl al-Bayt insomuch that they apparently considered the practice an innovation.

It is narrated in ***Al-Jāmi' al-Kāfi*** that Sayyid Imam al-Hasan b. Yahya b. al-Hussein b. Zayd b. 'Ali (d. 260 AH), upon them be peace, said:

> The consensus of the Progeny of Allah's Messenger, peace and blessings be upon him and his progeny, is that the *Tarāwīh* prayer is not from the *Sunnah* of Allah's Messenger, peace and blessings be upon him and his progeny, nor that of the Commander of Believers [i.e. 'Ali b. Abi Ťālib]. Rather, 'Ali b. Abi Ťālib used to prohibit that. According to them, it is better to pray it individually. Similar is the case with the other *sunnah* prayers, except the obligatory prayers which are better to pray in congregation.

According to this reference, it is the consensus of the imams of Ahl al-Bayt, upon them be peace, that the *Tarāwīh* prayer is an innovation that was not practiced by the Prophet, peace and blessings be upon him and his progeny, nor Imam 'Ali, upon him be peace. Furthermore, it is stated that Imam 'Ali, upon him be peace, used to forbid the practice. Let the reader also take note that this statement was recorded from the great grandson of Imam Zayd b. 'Ali, upon them be peace, who was held as an authority in Kufa. So, if the *Tarāwīh* prayer was something advocated by his ancestors, he would know.

A similar statement is made in the same book on the authority of al-Qūmisi:

> I asked al-Qāsim bin Ibrāhīm, upon him be peace, about standing in voluntary congregational prayer during Ramadan, and he said: "It is unknown." He narrated on the authority of 'Ali, upon him be peace, that he used to prohibit that.
>
> 'Abdullah b. al-Hasan, upon him be peace, used to pray with his family in his house during the nights of Ramadan like one would pray *Tarāwīh* in the mosques.

Although there is no reference to the *Tarāwīh* prayer in the ***Ahkām***, Imam al-Hādi was asked about it in one of his treatises known as ***Jawāb Masā'il Abil-Qāsim ar-Rāzi***. In it, he vociferously forbade it as an innovation that has no support among the Prophetic Descendants, upon them be peace.

Regardless, the following is narrated in the ***Musnad***:

> Zayd b. 'Ali narrated on the authority of his father—his grandfather—'Ali, upon him be peace, that he commanded that the one who stands in prayer with the people during Ramadan and pray twenty units should give the final salutations after every two units. He should take a break (*yarāwah*) after four units so one is free to relieve oneself and repeat the ritual ablution. He should pray the *witr* prayer at the last part of the night before leaving.

This is a quite apparent reference to the *Tarāwīh* prayer. Many scholars and commentators have tried to reconcile this report with the explicit prohibition of the practice in other sources. Even I, in my zeal to resolve the apparent contradiction, employed the use of *ta'wīl* to maintain the integrity of the report yet condemn the prayer in my article "The *Tarāwīh* Prayer: Praiseworthy *Sunnah* or Blameworthy Innovation?" At that time, I was unwilling to entertain the possibility that the report was fabricated and falsely attributed to Imam 'Ali, upon him be peace, despite evidence to the contrary. However, all such attempts at reconciliation prove to be unsatisfactory for the reasons we will mention.

As for the report's explicit support for the *Tarāwīh* prayer, the dear reader should note the following about the contents of the report. One, the report begins by saying that Imam 'Ali, upon him be peace, 'commanded' the actions that are mentioned subsequently regarding the prayer. This command in the Arabic language can either denote an actual imperative, recommendation or permission as is known in the sciences of the fundamentals of jurisprudence. Two, it mentions that one should 'stand in prayer with the people.' This cannot be interpreted to refer to other than the congregational prayer because the same phrase is used to denote the congregational prayer in other narrated traditions. Three, the phrase 'with the people' is not restricted to one's family because the word 'family' was not used. Four, the report explicitly mentions Ramadan and no other occasion for which this specific prayer is to be performed. Five, the report mentions that twenty units are to be prayed in this particular prayer. Six, the Arabic word for 'take a break' (*yarāwah*) is the word from which the name *Tarāwīh* is derived. All of that withstanding, those who hold to the textual integrity of the ***Musnad Imam Zayd*** as well as maintain that the text is accurately and authentically attributed to Imams 'Ali and Zayd, upon them be peace, have no grounds to condemn or dissuade anyone from praying the *Tarāwīh* prayer in congregation. Such discouragement would run counter to an explicit report in the ***Musnad***.

Our assertion that the report in the ***Musnad*** is an explicit endorsement of *Tarāwīh* is shared by some imams of the Ahl al-Bayt, upon them be peace. For example, Sayyid Imam Yahya b. Hamza (d. 749 AH), upon him be peace, said in his ***Al-Intiṣār 'ala 'Ulamā al-Amṣār***: "This view which we have chosen regarding it [i.e. the *Tarāwīh* prayer] being a sunnah during the nights of Ramadan has been narrated from Zayd b. 'Ali, 'Abdullah b. al-Hasan and 'Abdullah b. Musa b. Ja'far."

As is evident, Imam Yahya b. Hamza, upon him be peace, even recognised and acknowledged that Imam Zayd related a narration in support of the *Tarāwīh* prayer. This leaves no room for doubt and uncertainty regarding the explicitness of the report in the ***Musnad Imam Zayd*** and its endorsement for the *Tarāwīh* prayer, as we know it.

We have reason to believe that this report in the ***Musnad*** is an example of a Kufan forgery. First, as we mentioned, the *Tarāwīh* prayer was regarded by the earliest imams of Ahl al-Bayt as an innovation. In addition to that which we related from ***Al-Jāmi' al-Kāfi'***, there are also very explicit statements from prominent imams from the Prophetic Household that declare the practice as an innovation. It should be noted that, according to the same reference, the consensus of the Ahl al-Bayt was said to be reached regarding its invalidity. It should also be noted that despite Imam Yahya b. Hamza's reference to the practice being endorsed by Imam 'Abdullah b. al-Hasan, the reference from ***Al-Jāmi' al-Kāfi*** records him as praying in his home as opposed to praying *Tarāwīh* in the mosque. Second, according to the reference from the same book, Imam al-Hasan b. Yahya b. al-Hussein b. Zayd b. 'Ali, upon them be peace, expressly denied the *Tarāwīh* prayer's attribution to Imam 'Ali, upon him be peace. This is significant because the aforementioned imam was the great grandson of Imam Zayd, upon him be peace. If he knew of his great grandfather's attribution of the practice to 'Ali, it is unlikely that he would negate the import of the report which narrates such practice. Instead, he affirms that such was not the Sunnah of the Prophet nor that of Imam 'Ali, upon them be peace. Third, the same imam reports that 'Ali, upon him be peace, used to prohibit such practice; however, the report in the ***Musnad*** says that he 'commanded' it. Such stark contrast between the two reports indicates that the reporter of one was completely unaware of the other or that one disregarded the other. Fourth, the manner in which the *Tarāwīh* prayer is said to be prayed in the ***Musnad*** as well as the number of units matches that which was narrated from Kufan authority, Imam Abu Hanīfa, as well as the other jurists of the Generality.

III. Reference to Abu Hanīfa in the *Musnad*

There is a sole reference to Abu Hanīfa in the ***Musnad*** that deserves our attention. Of course, he is regarded as the 'founder' of the Hanafi madhhab as he occupied the position of a prominent scholar of Kufa. Although the primary sources of his madhhab are from his two students known as Qaḍi Abu Yusuf and Imam Muhammad ash-Shaybāni, the madhhab was named after him and similarly attributed to Kufa, Iraq. As for the reference to him in the ***Musnad***, it is as follows:

> Abu Khālid said: "When Imam Zayd b. 'Ali, upon them be peace, arrived in Kufa, he hid himself in the house of 'Abdullah b. az-Zubayr [al-Asadi]. When [the news of such] came to Abu Hanīfa, he spoke to Mu'awiya b. Ishaq as-Salmi, Naṣr b. Khuzayma al-'Abbasi and Sa'id b. Khuthaym, and they all visited Imam Zayd b. 'Ali, upon him be peace. They said [i.e. to Zayd b. 'Ali]: 'Here is one of the scholars of Kufa [i.e. referring to Abu Hanīfa].' Zayd b. 'Ali, upon him be peace, asked him: 'What is the key to prayer? How does one initiate it? What is the opening of prayer? What is that which makes certain things prohibited in it (*tahrīmuha*) and what is that which makes those things permissible again (*tahlīluha*)?'
>
> Abu Hanīfa replied: 'The key to prayer is ritual purity. That which makes certain things prohibited in it is the declaration of *Allāhu Akbar*, and that which makes those things permissible again is the final salutations (*at-taslīm*). The initiation of the prayer is the declaration of *Allāhu Akbar* because the Prophet, peace and blessings be upon him and his progeny, used to initiate the prayer by declaring *Allāhu Akbar* and would raise his hands. The opening of the prayer is: *Glory and Praise be to You, O Allah! And blessed be Your Name! You are the Almighty and Exalted! And there is no God other than You!* This is because it is narrated that the Prophet, peace and blessings be upon him and his progeny, used to recite this opening in the prayer.' Zayd, upon him be peace, was amazed by this from him."

We say that this passage in the ***Musnad*** alludes to a possible Kufan insertion. There are some striking features in it that support this assertion. It is well known that Imam Abu Hanīfa an-Nu'mān b. Thābit was a student of Imam Zayd, upon him be peace. Moreover, it is also known that he held Imam Zayd, upon him be peace, in high regard. Therefore, it would make sense that a student would want to seek out his teacher.

However, what is noticeable is the prominence given to Abu Hanīfa in this passage. In it, Imam Zayd, upon him be peace, asks him a series a questions to which he answers all of them satisfactorily to the point that Imam Zayd is 'amazed' at his responses. Indeed, the majority of the report contains the words of Abu Hanīfa, not Imam Zayd. Furthermore, Imam Zayd, upon him be peace, had other well-known students. Yet, Abu Hanīfa is given precedence over all other students in the ***Musnad*** insomuch that similar is not said or related about any other student; this report is unique in this sense. We say that the reason for this is that it is a possible Kufan interpolation.

It should therefore not be surprising to the reader that because of the precedence given to Abu Hanīfa in particular and his Kufan school in general in parts of the ***Musnad***, the book was translated into Urdu by Deobandi scholar and mufti, Maulana Muhammad Ashraf of Pakistan.

In conclusion, we say that the ***Musnad Imam Zayd***, although a great book in terms of its significance, has nonetheless suffered from interpolation. We cannot accurately say when or how it happened; however, it should suffice the reader to know that our assertion is shared by Imams al-Qāsim Rassi and al-Hādi, upon them be peace. In their works, principal of which is the ***Ahkām*** of al-Hādi, some traditions and reports found in the ***Musnad*** are attributed with falsehood and fabrication. It should therefore not be considered 'improper' or 'unorthodox' for us to say the same thing that the imams said.

Key features of this translation

Much like our previous translation projects, we have endeavoured to accurately represent the thoughts and views of the author to the best of our ability. We have translated the text of the ***Ahkām*** as literally as possible without employing the use of too many idiomatic expressions. However, in those cases in which the idiomatic expression serves to make the meaning clear, we have utilised such.

The arrangement and organisation of the book was not something that Imam al-Hādi, upon him be peace, initiated. It must be duly noted that the sections and sub-headings throughout the book were not present in the original text. Rather, all of such was a feature added by one of the sub-narrators in order to make the book easier to follow and more accessible to the reader. This sub-narrator, Abul-Hasan 'Ali b. al-Hasan b. Ahmed b. Abi Harīsa (d. 325), said in his introduction to the ***Ahkām*** that he found the book to be scattered with one chapter here and another one there without there being a single copy. When he was asked about such, he replied that due to Imam al-Hādi, upon him be peace, constantly engaged in warfare, the imam was unable to compile his work in a collection. Abu Harīsa said that he then worked to compile the chapters into one book out of fear that the imam would die before he was able to do so. We therefore owe a debt of gratitude to this companion of Imam al-Hādi who saw fit to construct the book and enumerate its chapters and sub-headings into a comprehensible book!

We have retained the popular Anglicised spellings and renderings of those names of people, places and things for the ease and familiarity of the English reader. For example, instead of rendering the name of the Prophet as 'Isa, upon him be peace, for which he is more well known to Arabic-speakers, we rendered his name as 'Jesus' because of the familiarity of that rendering by the English-speaking audience. Similar is the case with some transliterations. For example, the properly transliterated *Ramažān* is instead rendered as 'Ramadan' due to this spelling being better known to English speakers.

We have opted for our own translation of the Qur'an as opposed to utilising a published Qur'anic translation. The Qur'anic text is differentiated from other text by the use of brackets ({ }) as well as bold text. The reader may notice the difference in wording and style between the Qur'anic references and the non-Qur'anic references. This is because we wanted to attempt to accurately represent the difference between the Speech of the Creator and speech of the created.

We have differentiated the Prophetic hadiths by inserting the translation of the Prophet's statements in double parenthesis [(( ))]. An example is the statement of the Prophet, peace and blessings be upon him and his progeny: ((There is no marriage except with a guardian and two witnesses)). We did this to draw a distinction between his statements and those of anyone else.

We have also sought to emphasise the text's comprehensiveness by including a wealth of annotations. These explanatory annotations serve to aid the reader in understanding the depth of al-Hādi's knowledge by drawing upon companion texts that support his views. However, we did not want to weigh the annotation section down by including textual evidence for every single jurisprudential issue and judgement. Instead, some of our future translation projects will include those texts which imams and scholars authored that cite textual justifications for al-Hādi's *madhhab*, if Allah wills.

Also, in the annotations, we wanted to provide some sources and references for the narrated traditions which were cited by al-Hādi, upon him be peace. The list of texts from the hadith corpus is by no means exhaustive. Rather, they only represent a portion of those books of hadith, which relate the same tradition literally or similarly. Some of the hadith texts of the Generality, Zaydi and Twelver Shi'ite schools were referenced in the annotated footnotes.

It should similarly be noted that when citing the hadith or narration, the main text of the ***Ahkām*** may attribute such narration to one narrator or Companion; however, the references of the hadith in other sources, which were listed in the annotations, may be related from a different Companion or narrator. But, the text of the hadith and report remains the same or similar.

Another key feature in the annotations is the inclusion of references that mention a possible alternate judgement or ruling from al-Hādi in other texts. Texts, such as the ***Muntakhab***, may narrate a contrary ruling from al-Hādi that seemingly counters his judgement mentioned in the ***Ahkām***. However, we address these instances in the annotations by consulting the book known as ***Al-Qawl al-Awwal wa ath-Thāni lil-Imam al-Hādi ila al-Haqq Yahya b. al-Hussein*** that was compiled by 'Abdul-Karīm Muhammad 'Abdullah al-Waḍḍāf in 1428 AH. This text was extremely helpful in pointing out these differences as well as explaining the possible reasons and attempting to reconcile them.

Some of the references we consulted include ***At-Tāj al-Mudhhab Li Ahkām al-Madhhab*** authored by Chief Justice Ahmed b. Qāsim al-A'nasi (d. 1390 AH). This text is an extensive commentary on the standard of Zaydi jurisprudence, ***Al-Azhār*** and continues to be referenced until this day. One of the other texts referenced is ***Al-Bahr az-Zakhkhār al-Jāmi' Li Madhāhib 'Ulamā al-Amšār***, which is a comprehensive encyclopaedia of comparative jurisprudence which serves as a reference for all the various issues of Islamic law. Its author, Imam Mahdi Ahmed b. Yahya b. al-Murtaḍa (d. 840 AH), was also known as Ibn al-Murtaḍa.

At the appendices of the book, we have placed a short biography of all the personalities mentioned in the book, as well as indicated personality with the (§) symbol after their names the first time the name appears. We have also placed a dictionary of jurisprudential terminology at the end of the book.

We pray that the dear reader is able to gather benefit from the translation of this important text. We also pray that that any mistakes or misrepresentations of the original text are not misconstrued as the fault of the original author but rather the sole responsibility of the translator. By such, we hope that our humble effort is not overshadowed by the existence of any such errors and that the reader is nonetheless blessed by the sincerity of our original intent.

Imam Rassi Society
Shawwal 17, 1445 AH

Acknowledgements

We would first like to acknowledge and thank the efforts of our members who have sacrificed and toiled for the completion of this book. We pray that Allah blesses their families as well for their sacrifice in allowing us to maximise our utilisation of them. We would like to specifically acknowledge our member, **Ibn Zabāra**, who selflessly worked towards editing portions of the translation and offering suggestions.

We would similarly like to thank our brother, **Muhammad Al-Shareef** for his invaluable contributions towards translation assistance as well as for consulting the scholars regarding the meanings of the more obscure passages and concepts.

We pray for and acknowledge the work and efforts of the late **Dr Murtaḍa al-Muhatwary**, may Allah have mercy on him, whose published manuscript of the ***Ahkām*** we consulted for the majority of our translation. We also greatly benefited from his annotations, references and preface. May Allah bless his family as well as those involved in the publishing of the manuscript!

We similarly ask Allah to bless and have mercy on those scholars and imams from whom we have received the ***Ahkām*** from its author.

Translation of *Al-Ahkām fi al-Halāl wal-Harām*:

In the Name of Allah, the Most Gracious, the Most Merciful…

Author's Introduction

All praises are due to Allah, the One who is not seen by eyes, encompassed by thoughts or described by describers![1] His Grace cannot be fully recompensed by those who perform abundant deeds! He is the One praised in good and bad days, as well as in comfort and discomfort. He has no limits one can reach, nor does He have a likeness. You cannot strike a parable for Him. He is the Possessor of strength, power and the impossible. He draws close while we move away. His knowledge and conveyance is not fenced in by anything. He brought things into being as they are. There is nothing to prevent Him—Glorified be He—from bringing anything into being.

There is no concealed secret hidden from Him! Rather, He knows everything that will be just as He knows what has been. It is not concealed from Him that which you intend, incline towards or that which is in the hearts. The subtleties of those things unknown are not removed from Him. By His command, He causes the trees to grow. By His Power, He carries the raindrops. By His Strength, He causes the seas to flow. By His Will, He causes the torrents of rain to fall.

I bear witness that, truly, there is no god but Allah! This statement indicates slavery to Allah, the Glorified, and a sincere statement of truth from the slaves.

I bear witness that Muhammad was His Slave and Messenger to His creation. He is the one He entrusted with His Revelation. He is the one He sent His Message to convey, and he faithfully conveyed what he was commanded to. He strove hard for his Lord and sincerely advised his *Ummah*. He was a slave to his God until he attained certainty. He strove hard, advised, accounted himself and enslaved himself until he established the call to Reality and manifested the words of truth. He declared the Oneness of Allah publically and worshipped Him day and night. Then, Allah took him unto Himself while He was satisfied with his deeds. He accepted his efforts and praised his affair. Upon him be the best prayers of those who supplicate! Similarly, may prayers be upon the Purified People of His House!

Then, we say—after praising and extolling Allah as well as sending prayers and peace upon Muhammad and his Progeny—as to what follows...

We have looked into our affairs, as well as that of our descendants, brothers and followers who come after us. This includes those who incline towards the Family of the Messenger, peace and blessings be upon him and his progeny, and connect to them by their love, hold firmly to their religion, embrace their guardianship and declare that which Allah makes obligatory regarding their virtues. And when we looked into that, we knew we would eventually die. And to Allah we will arrive, and from the place of delusional arrogance we will leave. And to the place of passage we will return. And to discussions and accounting we will return. **{Whosoever comes with a good deed shall find ten like unto it, but whosoever comes with a bad deed shall find its like, and they are not oppressed} (Q. 6:160)**.

We know that those who oppose the Messenger's Family, upon them be peace, have embellished ignorance. They have presumptuously claimed knowledge and perfection. Regarding it, they have spoken from their whims. They have left the emulation of the people of knowledge whom Allah commands them to emulate—namely, the People of their Prophet's Household. They [i.e. the People

[1]Sayyid Abul-Abbās Ahmed b. Ibrāhīm al-Hasani narrated with a complete chain of narrators to Zayd b. 'Ali—his aunt, Zaynab bt. 'Ali that Fātima az-Zahrā, upon her be peace, said in her famous sermon: "All praise is due to Allah…the One who is prevented from the sight of vision, from the tongue of the describers and from being encompassed by imaginations!"

of the House] are the ones who are to be imitated and asked. That is from the statement of Allah, Glorified be He: **{Ask the People of the Reminder if ye know not} (Q. 21:7)**. The **{People of the Reminder}** are the Progeny of Muhammad.[2] Allah revealed the Book upon them. They guide by means of it towards the correct. Therefore, rejecting the Progeny of the Messenger, peace and blessings be upon him and his progeny, is injustice and rebellion.

To Allah, they remain in opposition and defiantly disobedient. They speak by their caprices about that which was revealed concerning the permissible and prohibited. They act insolently against the Possessor of Majesty and Nobility and in that, they oppose Muhammad's Progeny, upon them be peace. Their statements contravene the Book, Sunnah and intellect. Blessed be Allah, Possessor of Majesty! They are not contented with that until they decry the one unlike them as a disbeliever! They all claim ignorance for such a one and allege that the truth is in their hands while the other is far from what is true and correct. They also allege that such person is misguided and follows caprice and deviation. By such, they repulse Allah's slaves away from Him and manifest resistance. They throw back the curtain of truth from the fixed place Allah chose it to be. Yet, He has appointed it to be known and built the pillar of the religion by it. As He—Glorified and Majestic be He—says: **{And thy Lord creates what He wills and chooses for them that which is best} (Q. 28:68)** and **{Allah is most knowing of where to place His Message} (Q. 6:124)**. Then, He says: **{Then, We have caused to inherit the Book those whom We have chosen amongst Our slaves} (Q. 35:32)**.

Therefore, we saw that composing a thorough book was paramount. In it is the foundation of the permissible and prohibited narrated from the Messenger, upon him be peace. Thereby, one can act upon it and rely upon that which we mentioned. In so doing, one does not incline towards the ignorance and deviance of the people of blindness who remain in the place of rebelliousness and disaster.

The foremost thing that we should mention, describe, prove and elaborate on is the Divine Oneness of our Lord. The statement of truth is that He created us. We said that the foremost thing to the one who seeks refuge from destruction and seeks to enter the door of salvation is that he knows that Allah is One. He has no equal, similarity or likeness. He is different from anything that one can imagine or think of. Therefore, one should negate from Him any capricious statement, any ascription of likeness to His creation, as well as any of their defects and shortcomings of their hands, feet, faces, lips, tongues, ears, parts and eyes until one extracts such from their hearts. Such is sound to the intellect and belief. He is unlike anything that we mentioned of the creation.[3]

---

[2] Imam Rassi, upon him be peace, echoes this sentiment in his work ***Al-Imām al-Muftarāḍ aṭ-Ṭā'a.*** He said:

> Allah makes following the scholars an obligation saying: **{Ask the People of the Reminder if ye know not}**. Allah calls His Messenger "a Reminder" in His saying: **{Fear Allah, O those of understanding who have believed! Allah has sent down to thee a Reminder, a Messenger} (Q. 65:10-11).** The Chosen, Pure, and Knowledgeable People of His House are the ones whom Allah commands to ask.

[3] There are intellectual and textual proofs of Allah not resembling His creation. As for an intellectual proof, since creation is comprised of created attributes (ex. colour, distance, and hardness), it is impossible for the Creator to have the same attributes because if the Creator bought the created attributes into being from nothing, He was and, therefore, is independent of such attributes.

As for the textual proofs, Allah says: **{He is unlike anything.} (Q. 42:11).** It is narrated that Allah's Messenger, peace and blessings be upon him and his progeny, was asked about the greatest of sins, and he said: ((Attributing to Allah an equal while He created you)). The Commander of Believers, 'Ali b. Abi Ṭālib said: "Whoever attributes to Him conditions does not believe in His Divine Oneness, nor does the one who ascribes likeness to Him grasp His reality."

That withstanding, one knows that everything Allah mentions about Himself has a meaning and interpretation that is well known to the scholars of Revelation—those who command towards justice and those who call to Him. We have elaborated on all of this in ***Kitāb at-Tawhīd***, a book we composed for the one who desires to attain gnosis of Allah.[4]

When one knows that as sound and negates from Allah any likeness of His creation—the large and small of it—it is obligatory for one to know that Allah, Glorified and Majestic, is Just in His actions and all affairs. He is innocent of all of the statements of the ignorant. He is Holy and set apart from the oppression of oppressors. He is remote from decreeing the corruption of the corrupt. He is Highly Exalted from being satisfied with the disobedience of the disobedient. He is innocent of the slaves' actions.[5] He does not cause corruption in His slaves. He does not extract goodness and righteousness from them. How can such be possible for One All-Wise? How can it be an attribute for One All-Merciful? Highly Exalted and Holy is Allah that this can be the case!

How can He decree disobedience yet prohibit it, dispraise the disobedient, command obedience and reward the obedient? If that were the case, why does one strive and not call creation towards disobedience? On the contrary, they all promote obedience and faith, as well as truthful speech and right actions. If it were that He decreed disobedience and disbelief upon the disbelievers as well as God-consciousness and belief upon the believers, it would be for each slave to obey that which the Glorified commanded for them. They would act by His Decree and move according to His Will. One would find no one of disobedience; rather, all of them would be obedient to Allah and be people of belief. Then, one knows that Allah does not decree immorality and the objectionable. He does not will anything but obedience. Concerning that, the possessor of Majesty says: **{Allah orders not immorality. Dost thou say about Allah what ye know not?} (Q. 6:48)** and **{Verily, Allah commands justice, goodness, and giving towards kin and forbids immorality, evil, and oppression. He admonishes thee that thou may remember} (Q. 16:90)**.[6]

It is obligatory for one to know that all the promises and threats of the Majestic One are undoubtedly true. There is no confusion regarding the accounting of deeds as well as the Gathering *(al-Hashr)*. Similarly, the punishment that Allah promises the disbelievers and the reward He promises for the believers are true.[7]

---

[4] We know of no extant copies of a text by this name; however, as evident from the existing writings of Imam al-Hādi, he delves into the topic of Divine Oneness and theology quite extensively. One can easily refer to his ***Kitāb al-Bāligh al-Mudarrik***, ***Al-Murtashid fī at-Tawhīd*** and ***Usūl ad-Dīn*** just to name a few.

[5] There are intellectual and textual proofs that the slaves' actions are from them and not Allah. As for an intellectual proof, the nature of a command and prohibition necessitates that the one who commands be independent of the one commanded. Otherwise, it would be superfluous for there to be a command or prohibition.

As for the textual proofs, Allah says: **{...and thou create falsehood.} (Q. 29:17)**. It is narrated that Allah's Messenger, peace and blessings be upon him and his progeny, said: ((Whenever you perform an action, Allah gives you your full due for it. Whoever finds good should praise Allah. Whoever finds contrary to that, the blame is on none but himself)). Imam 'Ali b. Musa narrates that the Commander of the Believers, 'Ali b. Abi Ṭālib said: "As for that which is not from Allah, it is oppression to His slaves."

[6] Sayyid Abul-Abbās al-Hasani narrated with a complete chain of narrators to Imam Ja'far as-Sādiq, upon him be peace, who said regarding the aforementioned verse: "Every act of mercy, kindness and pleasure is from Allah and attributed to Allah. Every act of obscenity and objection is from the Devil."

[7] The truthfulness of the divine promise and divine threat is proven intellectually and textually. As for the intellectual proof, their truthfulness hinges on the truthfulness of the Prophets and Messengers who promised Paradise for the righteous and Hell for the wicked. If their promises and threats are proven false, everything they came with would be subject to belying.

As for the textual proofs, Allah says: **{And who is truer in speech than Allah?} (Q. 4:87)**. It is narrated that the Prophet, peace and blessings be upon him and his progeny, said addressing Allah: ((You are the Truth, and Your promise is true! Your meeting is true, and Your speech is true. Your paradise is true, and Your Hellfire is true. And Your Prophets are true, and Muhammad is true...)). The Commander of Believers, 'Ali b. Abi Ṭālib said: "Allah sent Prophets by means of distinguishing them with His Revelation. ...He invited them [i.e. the people] with a truthful tongue to the right path."

Whoever enters Paradise and Hell amongst the righteous and wicked, will never exit therefrom. The ignorant say that some will exit the place of torment and enter the place of the God-conscious and believers.[8] To that, the Lord of creation says: **{...therein to abide forever} (Q. 4:57)**. The Powerful and Majestic also says: **{They desire to exit the Fire but they shall not exit therefrom. For them is a lasting punishment!} (Q. 5:22)**. In all of that, He declares that anyone who enters the Fire will remain there and not exit. We seek refuge in Allah from such ignorance and blindness! We ask for aid and guidance for He is the Guardian of everything we are blinded from and the One who repels all evils.

When one knows and believes that, one's gnosis of his Creator will be sound. Such person—by Allah's permission—will be a knower of Allah. Such person will be amongst the monotheists as well as one who can speak about Allah with truth and certainty.

Afterwards, it is obligatory for one to know that everything that the Messenger, upon him be peace, came with—that which he legislated as prohibited or permissible, the Sunnah and its urging, the religious injunctions upon the *Ummah*—is an obligation from the Possessor of Majesty and Nobility. This is based upon the Word of Allah, Glorified be He: **{Whatsoever the Messenger gives thee, take it. Whatever he prohibits thee from, leave it} (Q. 59:7)** and **{Obey Allah and obey the Messenger} (Q. 64:12).**

One must know that he did not obligate anything major or minor except that Allah was satisfied with it. He, peace and blessings be upon him and his progeny, sincerely called Allah's slaves towards Him and struggled to rectify affairs in his land. Then Allah took him unto Himself while being satisfied with him. He [i.e. Allah] accepted that from him.

One must know that he did not leave the Muslims blind in any affair; rather, he made clear to them everything and demonstrated to them that which will bring salvation. He elaborated everything that they needed with luminous proofs, decisive signs, sufficient guidance and truthful speech. **{...that those who perish would have perished upon evidence and those who live would have lived upon evidence. Verily, Allah is All-Hearing, All-Knowing} (Q. 8:42)**. When one understands that, it will remain in one's innermost heart.

It is obligatory for one to know, understand, believe in and be cognisant of the Guardianship of the Commander of Believers and Imam of the God-conscious, 'Ali b. Abi Ṭālib[§]—may Allah have mercy on him. It is an injunction from Allah, the Lord of creation, upon all Muslims. One will not be saved from the punishment of the Most-Merciful nor will the name 'belief' be applied to one unless he/she believes that with utmost certainty. This is because Allah says: **{Verily, thy only Guardian is Allah, His Messenger, and those who believe—those who establish the prayer and render the dues whilst bowing} (Q. 5:55)**. That was the Commander of Believers—may Allah have mercy on him—to the exclusion of the other Muslims. This refers to when he gave charity during his prayer seeking closeness to his Lord through his dues.[9]

---

[8] It is the belief of the Generality that the disobedient Muslim who goes to Hell will eventually be taken out and placed in Paradise because of the Intercession of the Prophet, peace and blessings be upon him and his progeny. They interpret some of the Qur'anic verses to justify this belief as well as narrate traditions to support it. However, such interpretations are wanting due to the explicitness of the verses that affirm the eternal indwelling of the disobedient in the Hellfire. Similarly, those narrated reports that seemingly implies this doctrine are not beyond scrutiny.

[9] This verse known as "the Verse of Guardianship" is overwhelmingly reported to be revealed about 'Ali b. Abi Ṭālib. Jalāludīn as-Suyūti relates multiple chains of transmission in his book ***Durr al-Manthūr***. It is also related in ***Al-Jami' Bayna as-Sihāh as-Sitta*** by Razīn al-'Abdari, ***Asbāb an-Nuzūl*** of al-Wāhidi, ***Tafsīr at-Tha'labi***, ***Tafsīr at-Tabari***, ***Tafsīr al-Jalālayn*** and others

Concerning him, the Most-Merciful says in His revealed Qur'an: {**The forerunners** [in faith] **are the forerunners. They are the ones brought nigh** [to Allah] **in Gardens of Paradise**} (**Q. 56:10-12**). He was the forerunner to his Lord to the exclusion of others.[10]

Concerning him, the Blessed and Exalted says: {**Is the one who guides to the truth worthier to be followed or the one who cannot guide unless he is guided? What aileth thee? How doth thou judge?**} (**Q. 10:35**).[11] He was the guide to the Truth to the exclusion of others, as well as the caller to the straight path and wayfarer upon the path of the Pure Messenger. He was a forerunner to Allah. He was the guide through the ambiguous laws of Allah.

He was the most deserving of the Imamate. Because he preceded them, he was most worthy to guide them. Since he was most worthy to guide them, he was the most God-conscious of them. Since he was the most God-conscious of them, he was the best of them. Since he was the best of them in all good, he was the most deserving to be their guardian. The beautiful remembrances that have come concerning him in the Clear Revelation are many and not few.

Concerning him, Allah revealed to His Messenger at the pond (*ghadīr*) of Khumm: {**O Messenger, convey what has been revealed unto thee from thy Lord. If thou dost not do so, thou hast not delivered His message. Allah shall protect thee from the people**} (**Q. 5:67**). He, peace and blessings be upon him and his progeny, stopped and did not proceed one step until he carried out that which he determined to regarding 'Ali, upon him be peace. Then, he went under a tree with widespread branches, gathered all of the people and said: ((O people! Do I not have more right over you than you have over yourselves?)). They said: "Indeed, O Messenger of Allah!" Then he said: ((O Allah, bear witness! O Allah, bear witness! Then, whomsoever I was his Guardian, 'Ali is his Guardian! O Allah, help those that help him and oppose those that oppose him! Abandon those that abandon him and assist those that assist him!))[12]

He, peace and blessings be upon him and his progeny, said concerning him: (('Ali is to me as Aaron was to Moses except that there will be no prophet after me)).[13] In that is a proof that whatever was obligatory concerning Aaron with Moses was obligatory concerning him [i.e. 'Ali] except Prophecy. Aaron, upon him be peace, was most deserving of the position of Moses. He was his partner in every affair and was the foremost to him to the exclusion of other people. Regarding that, Moses, upon him be peace, requested the Possessor of Majesty and Nobility: {**"And make for me a vizier from my family—Aaron, my brother. Increase my strength**

---

[10] Al-Hākim al-Jishumi related in his ***Tanbīh al-Ghāfilīn*** regarding this verse:

> It is said that it refers to those who prayed to the two *qiblas* [i.e. Jerusalem and Mecca] and preceded in Islam. It is said that it refers to the earliest in obedience. It is said that it refers to the earliest in Emigration. It is said that it refers to the earliest in answering the call of the Messenger. All of such applies to and is present in the Commander of Believers as has been mentioned.

[11] It is also narrated in ***Tanbīh al-Ghāfilīn*** regarding this verse:

> The Guide to the Truth is Allah's Messenger and 'Ali after him. The proof for that is the statement of the Exalted: {**But thou art simply a warner, and to every people [there is] a guide**} (**Q. 13:7**). It is narrated that the guide is the Commander of Believers, 'Ali, upon him be peace.

Imams ath-Tha'labi, Ibn Abi Hātim, at-Tabarāni, Ibn Mardawayh, Ibn Asākir and al-Hākim narrated that the verse {**and to every people [there is] a guide**} (**Q. 13:7**) refers to 'Ali. Al-Hākim even authenticated the report based upon the criteria of al-Bukhāri and Muslim.

[12] This hadith known as *Hadith al-Ghadīr* is narrated in many books of hadith and has reached the status of 'mass-transmitted' (*mutawātir*), the highest level of authenticity. Sunni traditionalist, Jalāludīn as-Suyūti includes it in his compilation of mass-transmitted traditions, ***Al-Ahādīth al-Mutawātira***. Traditionalist and historian, Muhammad b. Ahmed adh-Dhahabi stated in his ***Sīra 'Alām an-Nubalā*** (5:415): "The hadith is firmly established (*thābit*) without a doubt." He also said in the same book (8:334): "Its text is mass-transmitted."

[13] This hadith known as *Hadith al-Manzila* is narrated in many books of hadith and has similarly reached the status of 'mass transmitted.' In addition to being narrated with numerous chains in the most authoritative texts of the Generality and others, it has been authenticated by classical and modern scholars alike. Imam al-Hākim declared the hadith authentic and mass-transmitted in his ***Al-Mustadrak***.

through him, and allow him to share in my affair so that we may glorify Thee much and remember Thee abundantly. Verily, Thou are upon us, Ever-Seeing!" He [i.e. Allah] **said: "Thou hast been granted what thou ask, O Moses!"} (Q. 20:29-36)**. Allah gave Moses a partner in his affair: Aaron.

Whoever objects to the fact that 'Ali was the most deserving of the position of the Messenger, peace and blessings be upon him and his progeny, rejects the Book of Allah, Possessor of Majesty and Nobility, and invalidates the statements of the Lord of creation. Such a one also counters what is clearly stated in the Decisive Book and removes Aaron from the affairs of Moses. Such a one also belies the statement of Allah's Messenger, peace and blessings be upon him and his progeny, and invalidates what he legislated regarding the Commander of Believers. It necessitates that the one who belies these two principles in Allah's religion, is declared wicked (*fājir*) and to all Muslims, a disbeliever.

My father related to me that his father was asked whether the Imamate of 'Ali b. Abi Ťālib, may Allah be merciful to him, was a religious injunction from Allah. He replied:

> This is what we and the scholars of the Messenger's Progeny say, upon him and them be peace. They all say the same thing, and there is no disagreement amongst them concerning that. It is due to his precedence in belief in Allah and his knowledge regarding Allah's rulings. He was the most knowledgeable of Allah's slaves and the most God-conscious. It is as Allah, the Glorified, says: **{The only ones amongst His slaves that fear Allah are the scholars** (or **"the most knowledgeable"). Verily, Allah is All Powerful, Most Forgiving} (Q. 35:28)**.
>
> The most fearing of them are the most guided and the most guided of them are the most God-conscious. It is as Allah, the Glorified, says: **{Is the one who guides to the truth worthier to be followed or the one who cannot guide unless he is guided? What aileth thee? How doth thou judge?} (Q. 10:35)**. The Blessed and Exalted also says: **{The forerunners** [in faith] **are the forerunners. They are the ones brought nigh** [to Allah] **in Gardens of Paradise} (Q. 56:10-12).**
>
> He preceded the believers to his Lord. He was the first among them in this.
> He achieved more nearness than them, and out of them, he was the noblest.
> He was the noblest slave to Allah and most deserving of imamate in religion.
> This is clear, so all praises due to Allah for everything sought as an ambition!
>
> 'Ali b. Abi Ťālib! May Allah shower His mercy upon him!
> None is ignorant of him except the ignorant steeped in oppression!
> None objects to the truth concerning him except out of contention!

My father related to me that his father was asked about the one who made war against the Commander of Believers. He was also asked regarding the one who differed from him in war but did not fight with him or against him. He replied:

> Whoever made war against him, made war against Allah and His Messenger.[14]
> Whoever refrained from him without permission is astray and religiously lesser.

My father related to me that his father was asked about one who heaps curses on the Commander of Believers or scornfully reviles him and his family while being ignorant of the unique virtues that have come from Allah regarding him, upon him be peace. He said:

> The imam judges based on one's view or the abuse of the abuser.
> Otherwise, such person can only be considered a disbeliever and evildoer.

---

[14] It is related in the ***Ŝaḥīḥ*** of Ibn Hibbān and ***Al-Mustadrak*** that the Prophet, peace and blessings be upon him and his progeny, looked at 'Ali, Fātima, al-Hasan, and al-Hussein and said: ((I am at war with whomever you are at war with and I am at peace with whoever you are at peace with)).

If he understood the Guardianship of *Amīr al-Mu'minīn* and its belief,
And he declared it in all matters, whether they be done publicly or discreet,
He must believe in and declare the Imamates of al-Hasan and al-Hussein.
They are the honoured grandsons of the Messenger, the ones he proclaimed;
The ones the Messenger indicated whom Allah made love obligatory for.
Their descendants who follow their example, we are also obligated to adore.

He said to His Messenger, peace and blessings be upon him and his progeny: **{Say: "I ask thee for no reward but only affection toward the kin."}** (Q. 42:23)[15] and **{O ye who believe, fear Allah and be with the truthful}** (Q. 9:119).[16]

He says regarding the two of them, as well as their grandfather, father, and mother: **{Verily, the righteous shall drink of a cup mixed with camphor—a spring where the slaves of Allah doth drink whilst it flows in abundance. They observe vows and fear a Day in which the evil is widespread}** (Q. 76:5-7).[17]

Regarding what the Messenger, upon him be peace, said about them both: ((Every child is connected to their father except the two children of Fãtima.§ I am the father of them both and their paternal relations)).[18]

Then, both are his sons and offspring by Allah's injunction and decree.
Concerning that, Allah, the Blessed says about Abraham, upon him be peace:

{...as well as from his descendants: David, Solomon, Job, Joseph, Moses, and Aaron. In this way, We reward those who do good. Also, Zachariah, John, Jesus, and Elijah—all of them were among the righteous!} **(Q. 6:85-86).**

He mentions that Jesus was from amongst the descendants of Abraham,
As well as of Moses and Aaron. Allah only makes him born through Miriam.
Allah makes the meaning of kinship and birth the same—son and daughter.
Jesus and Moses were made to flow from the same stream of Abraham's water.

He, peace and blessings be upon him and his progeny, said: ((Al-Hasan§ and al-Hussein§ are the masters of the youth of Paradise)).[19] He, peace and blessings be upon him and his progeny, also said: ((Verily, I leave you that by which if you hold on to it, you will never go astray after me: the Book of Allah and my Descendants, my Ahl al-Bayt. Verily, the Subtle and Aware will never separate them until they meet me at the Basin)).[20]

---

[15] There is disagreement as to whether this verse refers to the Prophet's clan generally or his descendants specifically. The books of hadith, exegesis and history relate that when the Messenger, peace and blessings be upon him and his progeny, was asked the identity of the {**kin**} in this verse, he replied with (('Ali, Fatima and their two sons)) or similar.

[16] It is also narrated in ***Tanbīh al-Ghāfilīn*** regarding this verse:

> The exegetes differ regarding about whom this verse is revealed. It is said that it means to be with 'Ali b. Abi Ťālib and his companions; al-Kalbi narrated this on the authority of Ibn Abbās. It is said that this means to be with the Progeny of Muhammad; this is narrated on the authority of Abu Ja'far Muhammad b. 'Ali. It is said that this means to be with Muhammad and his Companions. It is said that it means to be with the *Muhājirūn* and *Ansār*; this is narrated from Ibn Jurayj. There is no doubt that 'Ali is included amongst them.

[17] It is narrated in ***Tanbīh al-Ghāfilīn***: "It is said that it was revealed regarding 'Ali, Fatima, al-Hasan, al-Hussein and a slave woman named Fiźźa on the authority of Ibn Abbās and Mujāhid."

[18] Similarly narrated in ***Al-Mu'jam al-Kabīr, Musnad Abu Ya'la, Tārikh al-Baghdādi, Al-Mustadrak***. Imam al-Hākim said: "This hadith has an authentic chain of narrators although they [i.e. al-Bukhāri and Muslim] did not relate it."

[19] Similarly narrated in ***Musnad Imam Zayd, Amāli Abu Ťālib, Musnad Ahmed, Sunan at-Tirmidhi, Ŝahīh Ibn Hibbān, Al-Mustadrak***, ***Bihār al-Anwār*** and ***Sunan Ibn Māja***. Imam as-Suyūti said in his ***Al-Jāmi' as-Saghīr*** regarding this *hadith*: "It is mass-transmitted."

[20] Similarly narrated in ***Musnad Imam Zayd, Amāli Abu Ťālib, Ŝahīh Muslim, Sunan at-Tirmidhi, Al-Mustadrak, Manāqib*** of al-Kufi, ***Musnad Ahmed, Mušannaf Ibn Abi Shayba, Dhakhā'ir al-U'qba, Jāmi' al-Ušūl, Majmu' az-Zawā'id, Al-Mu'jam al-Kabīr, Al-Mu'jam al-Awsat, Sunan al-Bayhaqi, Sunan ad-Dārimi, As-Sawā'iqa al-Muhriqa, Ušūl al-Kāfi, Bihār al-Anwār.***

He, peace and blessings be upon him and his progeny, also said: ((My Ahl al-Bayt are like the ark of Noah. Whoever embarks upon them will be saved and whoever does not will be drowned))[21] and ((One does not love us, O Ahl al-Bayt, except that his feet will be firmly established until Allah saves him on the Day of Judgement)).[22]

Regarding them, he said, peace and blessings be upon him and his progeny: ((The stars are a means of safety to the people of the heavens. When the star goes from the sky, it is a promise to the people of the heavens. My Ahl al-Bayt are a means of safety to the people of the earth. When my Ahl al-Bayt go from the earth, it is a promise to the people of the earth)).[23]

They are the righteous among his Family, peace and blessings be upon him and his progeny. What beautiful remembrance has come regarding them in the Book of the Possessor of Majesty and Nobility! What the Messenger, peace and blessings be upon him and his progeny, has said regarding them! It would take too long to mention such in a book. A little should suffice over a lot, as it is enough for the people of faith to not engage with much.

When one has reached full knowledge of both of their Guardianships [i.e. that of Imams al-Hasan and al-Hussein], virtues and Imamates, it is obligatory to know that the one among their descendants who has more right to the affair, is he who calls creation to obedience.

One must also know that the right of command, prohibition, judgement and imamate after them belongs to their descendants and none other. Otherwise, it is impermissible. The imam after them among their descendants must follow their path and be like them. He must follow their steps as well as be God-conscious, pure, ardent concerning struggle in Allah's affair and indifferent towards the ephemeral things of this world. He must understand those necessary things and be familiar with the interpretations of those opposed to him. He must be courageous and valiant, generous and liberal. He must be merciful and compassionate towards his subjects, as well as forbearing and pardoning. He must give to them of himself and partner with them in his affair without being easily influenced by them. He must not judge them by anything other than Allah's judgements. He must be well known as a warrior. He must call towards his Lord and raise high His banner. He must struggle hard in his call and make it widespread in the land, and not shrink from solidarity with the slaves.

He must be a source of fear to the oppressors and a source of security for the believers. The defiantly disobedient should not feel safe and secure with him; rather, he should seek them out and they should seek him out. He should manifest them, and they should manifest him. He should be hostile against them, and they should be hostile against him. Thereby, they would establish their treachery against him and seek to destroy him, rebel against him and muster the tribes to fight him. But they should fear that he would exile them, and he must be a source of fright for them. He must not renege his call towards Allah's affair or change due to fear. He must not shrink from his struggle against them out of trembling. He must rally all of his forces and not fall short of that.

If the aforementioned is the case for a descendant of the two Grandsons—al-Hasan and al-Hussein, he is the imam religiously obligatory to obey, and it is an obligation upon the Muslims to help him. Whoever falls short of that and does not connect himself to Allah, does not make his sword known, does not expose the oppressors and they him, does not manifest his affair, does not raise his banner so that the perfect evidence of his Lord is visible for all to see, and does not demonstrate a good example—it is not

---

[21] Similarly narrated in ***Manāqib*** of al-Kufi, ***Amāli Abi Ťālib***, ***Fadā`il Sahāba*** of Ahmed b. Hanbal, ***Al-Mu'jam al-Awsaṭ***, ***Al-Mu'jam al-Kabīr***, ***Al-Mustadrak***, ***Bihār al-Anwār***

[22] Similarly narrated in the ***Amāli*** of Sheikh as-Ŝadūq and Sheikh at-Ťūsi in his ***Amāli***.

[23] Similarly narrated in ***Manāqib*** of al-Kufi, ***Amāli Abi Ťālib***, ***Al-Mustadrak***, ***Tārikh Dimashq***

obligatory for the Muslims to obey such a one, emigrate to him or be patient with him.

Whoever amongst the Muslim *Ummah* does that after it has been made clear to them that he is their guardian, and he has aspired towards his Lord, made his sword known and uncovered the manifestations of the oppressors, his call to Allah is religiously obligatory. Whoever falls short of that would have Allah's proof against him, which is firm, established, decisive and manifest. His proof is decisive **{...that those who perish would have perished upon evidence and those who live would have lived upon evidence. Verily, Allah is All-Hearing, All-Knowing}** (**Q. 8:42**).

There are examples from both their descendants among the Muslim *Ummah*, who were pure, patient with Allah and good-doers. One example is Zayd b. 'Ali,[§] may Allah be satisfied with him. He was a God-conscious imam who established the proof of the Lord of creation. Another example is his son, Yahya,[§] who imitated his actions.

Other examples include the likes of Muhammad b. 'Abdullah[§] and his brother, Ibrāhīm,[§] who were guides to Allah, resolute in the affairs of Allah and blameless before Allah. They both were illuminated—step by step, patient, self-accountable and thus, similar to their fathers and uncles. They fought against open opponents. Nothing prevented the both of them from establishing the affair of their Creator or striving for their Lord's pleasure. May the prayers and blessings of Allah be upon the souls of these elders!

They were patient with Allah and self-accountable. They did not lose assurance or courage but they, as Allah mentions about their ancestors who passed: **{...never lost assurance with what afflicted them in the way of Allah, nor did they weaken or settle. And Allah loves the patient!}** (**Q. 3:146**).

Another example is al-Hussein b. 'Ali al-Fakhi,[§] the martyr who was purified by Allah—Glorified be He. He was blameless and sacrificed his soul for Allah with a small band of believers. They commanded the good and forbade the evil. They fought and fought until they met Allah and He was satisfied with them and accepted their deeds. May Allah shower His Mercy and Blessings on them!

Then, there was Yahya b. 'Abdullah b. al-Hasan,[§] the one who established the proof of Allah. He was self-accounting and patient with Allah amidst intensity and anger. Then there was Muhammad b. Ibrāhīm b. Ismā'īl,[§] the one who established the proof of Allah. He called towards the Truth, prevented open disobedience and promoted the Oneness of Allah. He was patient in all his affairs and judged all matters with the truth.

Another example was al-Qāsim b. Ibrāhīm,[§] the noble scholar. He unsheathed his sword, was blameless and sacrificed his soul. He made manifest the oppressors and called towards the Manifest Truth. May the prayers, blessings and mercy of Allah be upon them all!

Whoever is like that among the descendants of al-Hasan and al-Hussein, is the imam of all Muslims and it is prohibited to disobey him. It is not religiously permitted for them to abandon him, rather it is religiously obligatory to obey and aid him. Allah will punish the one who abandons him, and He will firmly establish the one who helps him. He will be an Ally to the one who is an ally to him and be an Enemy to the one who is an enemy to him.

However, whoever fools himself and seeks to establish it in his family and descendants for the sake of amusement—they become oppressors and pretenders. He fulfils their needs, and they fulfil his needs. He becomes on intimate terms with them, and they become on intimate terms with him. He trusts them, and they trust him. They refrain from him, and he refrains from them. He sheathes his sword, withdraws his banner and hides himself from them. He misrepresents to the ignorant, as well as to the people of heedlessness and deviancy. He may falsely claim the

Imamate, but by their whims, he intends to establish it.[24]

According to Allah, he is considered amongst those who slumber, as well as one who is listless and weak. They are also amongst the seekers of leisure and comfort. He presents himself before them, and the idea enters their hearts that he is the leader and that he comes out against the oppressors as a warrior. They falsely assume that, and he presents himself to them as such so that he may milk from them their money and consume their wealth.

Verily, he confuses them in their affairs by pretending that it is the right way. By his pretending, he diverts them from their Lord. By means of their confusion, they are prevented from their obligations and injunctions made binding upon them by their Creator. He is persistent in consuming their wealth because he has confused them. They remain ignorant due to his pretending to be a leader and making believe to be one who will rebel against the oppressors. By Allah! He knows the intimate details of the affair, and that it is not as the ignorant falsely assume! It is decreed that he is amongst those who stray and deviate from His path in rebellion.

According to his Lord, he destroys himself by his deeds and that of others, as well as by deviating from the truth and the truthful—bringing together all matters of sin. By such, the oppressors could institute a claim, and the rulers of open disobedience could establish a pillar of support. The ignorant would falsely assume his claim to be the truth and truthful due to his pretending. Filth would be on their hands. He would consume ill-gotten property without right. He would commit grievous offenses with calamitous results and turn many away from Allah. He would be disengaged from the statements of the believers and scatter the opinions of the Muslims. They would not be able to interpret the truth out of confusion. He would interpret with his own interpretations, and they would plunge heedlessly into dangers. Every one of his actions would be disputed secretly due to the fear of manifesting it in the open. He would attempt to deceive Allah and those who believe, but he would only be deceiving himself.

As Allah, the Exalted, says: **{They attempt to deceive Allah and those who believe but they only deceive themselves and know not. In their hearts is a sickness, and Allah increases it in sickness. For them shall be a painful punishment} (Q. 2:9-10)**.

It is as if he had not heard Allah say: **{Whether thou conceal thy speech or make it known, He is most knowing of what is in the breasts} (Q. 67:13)**. He plots against Allah and the believers, but Allah plots against him and He is the Best of Plotters!

He brings affliction upon himself due to the misappropriation of dinar and dirham and the continuation of considering his blessings as trivial. He wears silk and brocade and reclines on blankets and pillows of sable, satins and silks. He is not overly concerned about Allah's affairs, nor does he rectify the affairs of Allah's slaves. Where can all of that be except by means of the Imamate?!

By his life! He is far distant from it indeed. He is nowhere near it. He is only kidding himself. He has duped others by means of embellishing his outer form, as well as by his speech and lies. Allah will punish him. **{Whosoever doeth that shall meet a penalty. Punishment shall be multiplied for him on the Day of Judgement, and he shall eternally abide therein utterly humiliated} (Q. 25:68-69)**.

By my life! If that were the case, he is far distant from that which he claims, and he falsely assumes the role that Allah has not given him. He [i.e. Allah] has not required this path for him.

---

[24] Imam al-Hādi seems to be alluding to a false claimant among the Ismailis or a sect of theirs. After mentioning examples of true imams and their characteristics, he mentions the antithesis of the imams. Contrary to the aforementioned imams, the pseudo-imam is said to be a cowardly and money-hungry opportunist. It is possible that he is referring to false claimants in general—as they were many before the time of al-Hādi as well as during his time. It is also possible that he is referring to someone in particular. Refer to the **Translator's Introduction** regarding Imam al-Hādi's chief opponents, an extremist Ismā'īli sect known as the Qarmatians.

How can it be that we mentioned some of what was mentioned of him regarding his claims out of extremism and peril? It is from the direct quotations of his partisans and the statements of his own followers.

Concerning him, they are satisfied to be liars and outside of the Truth. They declare that he claims the attributes of the Overpowering One (*al-Jabbār*) and that he participates in the secret sciences. They say he has knowledge of what is in the depths of the oceans and that he has the power to transform what he wants and establish what he wants. He permits unlawful sexual activity as well as the open display of indecency and acting on corrupt desires and lusts—all of which are acts of disobedience to Allah and prohibited in the verses of the Qur'an.

He promotes the avoidance of the prayers, the withholding of the purification dues (*az-zakāt*) and the rejection of the Ramadan fast. By such, he annuls everything that is spoken of in the Criterion [i.e. the Qur'an]. He advocates for the abandonment of the purification wash for those in the state of major ritual impurity. He promotes the committing of every indecency and other things that are mentioned of him.

He magnifies his affairs by means of extremism and the objectionable. That is because they say, "I know your imam. I act upon what I desire without fear of punishment or reprisal." Those are their statements according to the whole Muslim *Ummah*.

Their statements of blasphemy are well known, as well as their false ascriptions to Allah and words of disbelief of the Most Merciful. By their claims, they attribute corporeality to their Creator, making Him in the form of a man. According to them, He eats, drinks, enters, exits, buys and sells. They make Him to comprise of Moses, Jesus and 'Ali. They claim that he is in the form of the children of Adam. Similarly, they narrate from the devils that He takes the form of slaves.[25] Blessed be Allah from being attributed to that! The Lord of creation is too Holy to be ascribed to that by the ignorant and astray! Whoever says that, may he be met with woe, calamity and punishment! The heavens almost collapse at such statements, the earth almost cleaves asunder, and the mountains almost crumble!

When the rightly-guided comes to know that and becomes aware of their description we mentioned, as well as their leader and that which Allah makes clear about their government, it is religiously obligatory to believe in the virtue of fighting and of commanding the good and prohibiting the bad. One should know that it is the greatest of the obligations stipulated by Allah. Therefore, he should come out and fight against the oppressors, and he should intend thereby to expose the openly disobedient. He should do so by his hand, his tongue, his heart and by any other means that he is able to with his group.[26]

---

[25] Here the imam seems to reference some of the deviant beliefs of a group of extremist Shi'ites present during his era as well as that of his grandfather, Imam al-Qāsim Rassi, upon him be peace. One of these beliefs included the corporeality of Allah something repugnant to all who hold to the transcendence of the Almighty. Imam Rassi, upon him be peace, said in his ***Kitāb al-Mustarshid***:

> The people of prayer agree with us that our God will not be perceived by the sight except a sect of Rafidites and the interpolators who agree with them. They say that the Prophet, peace and blessings be upon him and his progeny, saw his Lord as a fair-skinned white man with a loss of hair. They also narrate a story that he saw Him in the form of an adolescent boy.

[26] In ***Sharh al-Ahkām***, Abul-Hasan 'Ali b. Bilāl related the following:

> It has been related to us that the Commander of Believers, upon him be peace, said: "The greatest jihad is the one with the heart, hand and tongue. Then, it is that with the tongue and heart. Then, it is that with the heart, and that is the weakest. Whoever does not cause his heart to command the good and prohibit to the bad—such person will sink into degeneracy."

Then, after that, it is religiously obligatory to purify oneself for the prayers—keeping in mind the rules of purification. They should pray them with their established rules and within the times that Allah has appointed for them. One is religiously obligated to observe what Allah commanded regarding the purification dues as is legislated by the Messenger, upon him be peace. He is the one who establishes the religious injunction regarding the values of cattle. One is religiously obligated to fast the month of Ramadan as is stipulated by the All-Merciful. One is religiously obligated to make the pilgrimage to the Oft-Frequented House. One is to observe all the religious injunctions stipulated by Allah regarding the Greater Pilgrimage. One is to act upon everything commanded by Allah and His Messenger, and one is to avoid everything prohibited by Allah and His Messenger.

One is to speak the truth even if it is against oneself. One is to establish testimony as it is, observe their trusts and avoid treachery. One is to show righteousness towards parents and maintain family ties with relations. If one does that and is true to that, such person is truly a believer and one who has made oneself a slave to Allah—Glorified be He—following His commands. If that is the case, the name of 'belief' can apply to such person and it is binding that Allah reward him/her with good. Such person will be amongst those who have no fear nor will they grieve.[27]

After that, it is religiously obligatory to consider what has been stipulated from His commands concerning the permissible and prohibited, as well as all its reasons. Verily, Allah is too majestic from being flippant in what He says, and He is not satisfied for His slaves and protected friends to be ignorant and deficient. Indeed, He desires to increase them in all good and excellence.

Therefore, it is religiously obligatory for one to seek that which one should seek from the knowledge of the People of the Prophet's Household, peace and blessings be upon him and his progeny, and follow the best of it.[28] It is that which is the closest to the Book. For Allah—Glorified be He—says: **{Glad tidings be to the slaves who listen to speech and follow the best of it. They are those who Allah has guided and those of understanding} (Q. 39:17-18)**.

With the will and success of Allah, we will compose that which will be of benefit in this world and the next. We will say in it that which has been firmly established, as well as what would illuminate the hearts of the one seeking substantiation. We do so by the power of Allah, for He is the only One we seek help from in our affair. We rely upon Him in our matters. Allah is sufficient and enough as the Protector of our affairs. We rely upon Him, and He is the Lord of the Throne!

> It has been related to us that the Commander of Believers, may the Lord of creation bless him, said: "I heard Allah's Messenger, peace and blessings be upon him and his progeny, say: ((Whoever among you sees something objectionable, let him change it with his tongue. If he is unable to with his tongue, let him hate it with his heart. If he does that, he would be considered to having changed it. That is because if a man were to kill another in the east and the news of such were to reach the west while the people are content with his action, they would be considered his partners in such. But if one were to hate it with his heart while unable to change it with his tongue, he would be considered as to having changed it)).

[27] It is here where Imam al-Hādi lays out the basic format of this book. He begins with the outward religious injunctions in terms of worship and transactions. After which, he delves into those matters related to character and asceticism in the last chapter of the book.

[28] Regarding the obligation of seeking knowledge, Sheikh 'Ali b. Bilāl related in his ***Sharh al-Ahkām*** that Sayyid Abul-Abbās al-Hasani related with his chain of narrators to Anas b. Mālik that Allah's Messenger, peace and blessings be upon him and his progeny, said: ((Seek knowledge even in China. Verily, the seeking of knowledge is incumbent upon every Muslim)). He also related with a complete chain of narrators to 'Ali, upon him be peace:

> Seek out knowledge before it is raised. As for me, I do not say to you that it would be like this (he then motioned his hand to the sky). Rather, it is the person of knowledge in the tribe. He will die and knowledge will disappear with him. The people will take the ignorant as leaders. They will ask and be given edicts, whereby they will go astray and lead others astray. They will speak by their own opinions and abandon traditions. When that happens, this *Ummah* will be destroyed.

The Book of Ritual Purity

In the Name of Allah, the Most Gracious, the Most Merciful...

Concerning the one who intends to relieve oneself, what is recommended and what one should be wary of

The following is encouraged for one who intends to relieve oneself—relieving oneself is done in a covered place, one should not uncover one's nakedness until sitting, one should seek refuge in Allah from the evil of the accursed devil of filthiness,[1] and one should not sit facing the *qibla* nor should one turn one's back to it. The *qibla* should be to one's left or right.[2]

When one has relieved oneself and risen to purify oneself, one should praise Allah for the harm that He has removed from him. Similar is narrated from the Commander of Believers, may Allah have mercy on him. It is narrated that when he would exit the latrine, he would say: "All praise is due to Allah, the One who has brought health to my body! All praise is due to Allah, the One who has removed harm from me!"[3]

One should not cleanse ones private parts with the right hand because it has reached us on the authority of Allah's Messenger, peace and blessings be upon him and his progeny, that he prohibited his Companions from relieving themselves while facing the *qibla* or turning their backs towards it and from cleansing their private parts with their right hands.[4]

He has prevented and discouraged them from defecating while facing and turning their backs to the *qibla* out of the great esteem and respect that Allah gives to it. When He appointed it a rendezvous point and a destination for Allah's injunctions as well as a place with blessings and the traces of His Pure Prophets; this is so that He obligates it as a place of great esteem to all creation.

Regarding his prohibiting cleansing the private parts with the right hand, the Prophet, peace and blessings be upon him and his progeny, only did so based on consideration for the believers. It was done for them as a benefit due to their eating [i.e. with the right hand] and doing other things during times when water was scarce and used for the purification of other limbs. Because of that, he prohibited them from cleansing the private parts with the right hand in order to prevent harm and injury.

Before the prayer and after eating, the Muslims should not be heedless of using tooth-sticks in their mouths during purification. However, this is not obligatory upon them; it is merely encouraged for them. It has reached us on the authority of Zayd b. 'Ali from his fathers from 'Ali b. Abi Ṭālib, may Allah be satisfied with him, that Allah's Messenger, peace and blessings be upon him and his progeny, said: ((Had I not feared the burden on my community, I would have made using the tooth-stick obligatory with purification. Whoever can tolerate the tooth-stick during the purification should not abandon it)).[5]

---

[1] In the book ***Al-Muntakhab***, Imam al-Hādi was asked about the wording of this. He replied: "One should say: *Bismillâhi. Allumma Inni a'ûdhu bika min ar-rijs al-khabîth al-makhabbith ash-shaytânir-rajîm.* (Tr. "In the Name of Allah. O Allah, I seek refuge in You from the impurity, filth, and nastiness of the filthy and rejected Satan!")." This supplication is similarly narrated in ***Musnad Imam Zayd*** and ***Amāli Ahmed b. 'Isa*** with identical wording except that it includes the word "*an-najas*" after the word "*ar-rijs.*"

[2] The wording used by the imam seeming implies that facing the *qibla* while relieving oneself is considered discouraged (*makruh*) rather than prohibited. However, in ***Al-Muntakhab***, the implication is that the imam held it to be prohibited. Later imams noted this and narrated that al-Hādi held to two different positions [Ref. ***Sharh at-Tajrīd***, ***Al-Intiṣār***, ***Al-Bahr***]. We reconcile this by saying that according to the ***Ahkām***, the imam considered it prohibited rather than discouraged due to the subsequent wording that the Prophet "prohibited his Companions from relieving themselves…" as well as his statement "He has prevented and discouraged them from defecating…"

[3] The same wording is narrated in the ***Musnad Imam Zayd***, as well as the ***Amāli Ahmed b. 'Isa*** with a complete chain of narrators to Imam Zayd—his ancestors—'Ali, upon them be peace.

[4] Similarly narrated in ***Sharh at-Tajrīd***, ***Ŝahīh Muslim***, ***Sunan an-Nisā'i***, ***Sunan Abu Dāwūd***, ***Sunan at-Tirmidhi***

[5] Similarly narrated in ***Musnad Imam Zayd***, ***Ŝahīh al-Bukhāri***, ***Muwatta***, ***at-Tirmidhi***, ***Bihār al-Anwār***, ***Uṣūl al-Kāfi***

Description of purification

The first thing that the one making ablution should do is wash both hands. Then, such person washes the privates from the top of the anus. When one cleans it thoroughly and removes all of the impurities from it, one cleanses downwards until reaching the bottom of the anus. Then, one washes the hands and cleanses them from any traces of impurities from the privates.

Then, one rinses the mouth and nose three times, scooping with one handful of water each time. One disperses enough water that the nose and mouth are fully clean. Then, one washes the face—bottom and top—with water. It is not sufficient to wipe it with a wet palm; one must carry the water from the hands and wash the face with it. This includes the cheeks, forehead and temples, as well as penetrating the beard. Then, with the left palm, one washes the right arm up until and including the elbow, three times. After that, one washes the left arm in the same manner that one washed the right arm. Then, he wipes the whole head from the front to the back. One passes the hands over the head through the hairs and rubs the wet fingers in the ears as well as the outside, top and bottom.

It is encouraged for one to engage in the verbal remembrance of Allah's Name when beginning the purification, as well as the middle and the end. One says what has been related from the Commander of Believers—upon him be the prayers of the Lord of creation!

It has reached us on his authority that he used to say when approaching the place of purification: "In the Name of Allah, with Allah, and upon the path of Allah's Messenger, peace and blessings be upon him and his progeny." Then, he would wash his private parts and say: "O Allah, by Your Mercy, protect my private parts from disobedience to You!" Then he would rinse his mouth and say: "O Allah, my declaration is my proof on the Day of meeting You!" Then, he would rinse his nose and say: "O Allah, do not prevent me from the scents of Paradise!" Then he would wash his face and say: "O Allah, whiten my face on the day that faces are whitened and blackened!" Then he would wash his right hand and say: "O Allah, give me my book in my right hand and forgive my sin!" and wash his left hand and say: "O Allah, do not give me my book in my left hand and pass over all of my deeds!" He then would wipe his head and say: "O Allah, cover me with Your Mercy and complete for me Your Favour!" He would then pass his hand over his nape and say: "O Allah, quench my thirst on the Day of Accounting!" Then he would wash his feet to the ankles and say: "O Allah, establish my feet on the straight path on the Day feet will fail! O Possessor of Majesty and Nobility!"[6] He would rub the water between his toes and begin the washing with his right.

---

[6] 'Ali's supplication is also related with slightly different wording in the ***Amāli Ahmed b. 'Isa*** with a complete chain to Muhammad b. Hanifiya:

> I entered upon my father, 'Ali b. Abi Ťālib, upon him be peace, and to his right was a container of water. He called for it and poured it over his right hand and washed it. Then, he cleansed his privates and said: "O Allah, protect my private parts and cover my nakedness and do not allow my enemies to gloat over me!" Then, he washed his mouth and nose and said: "O Allah, my declaration is my proof and do not prevent me from the scents of Paradise!" Then he washed his face and said: "O Allah, whiten my face on the day that faces are blackened and do not blacken my face on the day that faces are whitened!" Then, he poured water on his right hand and said: "O Allah, give me my book in my right hand and not the left!" Then, he poured water on his left hand and said: "O Allah, do not give me my book in my left hand and do not make it chained to my neck!" Then, he wiped his head and said: "O Allah, cover us with Your mercy for verily we fear Your punishment! O Allah, do not join our forelocks to our feet!" He then wiped the nape of his neck and said: "O Allah, save us from the severances of the Fire and its extreme thirst!" Then he washed his feet and said: "O Allah, establish my feet on the straight path on the Day that feet will fail!" Then he returned to the standing position and said: "O Allah, just as we have purified ourselves with water, purify us from our sins!" Then he indicated with his hands like this with water dripping from his fingertips and said: "O my dear son, do as I have done for there is no drop of water from your fingertips except that Allah will create an Angel to seek forgiveness for you till the Day of Judgement! And it will be a reward will be an Angel glorifying Allah for you on the Day of Judgement! O my dear son, it is from this action of mine that sins fall just as the leaves of a tree fall on a windy day!"

If one were to say other than that, it would be sufficient; any remembrance of Allah is sufficient. If one were to forget to supplicate, it does not invalidate the ablution nor does one invalidate one's ritual purity. This is because the religion is enough, and one's declaration of Allah's Oneness suffices. When one's ritual ablution is complete, one has achieved the opening to the prayer—ritual purity.

Regarding the completion of the ritual ablution, it has reached us that Allah's Messenger, peace and blessings be upon him and his progeny, said: ((A believer does not perform the ritual ablution in an excellent way and then prays except that Allah forgives him for his sins between that prayer and the next)).[7]

This hadith correlates with the Book of Allah where the Glorified says: **{Establish the prayer at the two ends of the day and at the approach of the night. Verily, good deeds efface bad deeds. That is a reminder for those who remember} (Q. 11:114)**. Allah—Glorified be He—declares that good deeds destroy bad deeds. The prayer is the utmost of the slaves' good deeds and after that is Allah's urging towards jihad. This only applies to the obedient and right-acting believers.

However, regarding the one who persists in acts of disobedience and remains heedless of and avoids obedience, Allah will not accept any of their acts of worship, let alone their voluntary acts. Concerning that, the Lord of creation says: **{Verily, Allah only accepts from the God-conscious} (Q. 5:27)**. Whoever is not included amongst the God-conscious, Allah will not accept their deeds. Neither will He accept from the persistent sinners; rather, they are odious to Allah. There is no doubt that they will be amongst those who are eternally punished in the Hereafter.

Concerning the completion of ablution, it has also reached us that Allah's Messenger, peace and blessings be upon him and his progeny, said:

> ((Shall I not inform you of what causes Allah to efface transgressions and raise ranks? It is the completion of the ritual ablution, the taking of many steps to the mosques and the waiting for the prayer after the prayer. That is the fortress for you)).[8]

Regarding the one who says that rinsing the nose and mouth is *sunnah* and not obligatory[9], one cannot claim that because Allah orders the washing of the face. These two things are included in the face and therefore, included in the command. That withstanding, it is obligatory to rinse them just as it is obligatory to wash the face. There is no doubt that they are a part of the face; they carry the filth on one's face. If one is ordered to wash every limb and remove filth from them, such person would take care to remove all filth and clean it. How can it be that Allah orders one to wash the face, yet not order one to wash the part of the face that carries dirt and filth?

Concerning that, my father related to me that his father, al-Qāsim b. Ibrāhīm—may Allah have mercy on them—was asked about one who forgets to rinse the nose and mouth. He said: "It is not sufficient unless one rinses the nose and mouth because the mouth and the nostrils are a part of the face. Allah says: **{...and wash thy faces...} (Q. 5:6)**, and they are part of the face."

Concerning that which invalidates the ritual ablution and what necessitates its renewal

The ritual ablution is invalidated and requires renewal due to worms exiting the anus, flatulence, defecation, urination, as well as prostatic fluid and penile discharge that occurs without passion. The purification wash is not obligatory in that case; semen discharge that occurs due to sexual passion obligates one to perform the purification wash. Vomit; blood that flows or drips due to something like cupping, nosebleeds, and the like; discharge from wounds, lesions and the like; and sleep that removes

---

7 Similarly narrated in ***Musnad Imam Zayd*, *Ŝahīh Muslim, Sunan an-Nisā`i, Sunan al-Kubra*** of an-Nisā`i, ***Muwaṫṫa, Jāmi' al-Ušūl***

8 Similarly narrated in ***Amāli Abi Ťālib, Mušannaf Ibn Abi Shayba, Musnad Ahmed, Sunan Ibn Mājah, Bihār al-Anwār***

9 Although the vast majority of jurists consider the rinsing of the nose and mouth to be a recommended Sunnah and not an obligation, there is disagreement regarding its judgement. Some jurists held to the view that both rinsing the nose and the mouth were obligatory, and others said that rinsing the nose was obligatory and rinsing the mouth was encouraged. [Ref. ***Al-Bidāyat al-Mujtahid***].

the intellect—if any of that were to occur, one must renew one's ritual ablution and purity.

If one were in the prayer, one would have to repeat it from the beginning. Whoever does not renew his ritual ablution, the prayer would not be valid. This is because the key to the prayer is purity, the opening declaration of Allah's greatness (*al-takbīr*) renders its permissible prohibited and the final salutations (*at-taslīm*) render its prohibited permissible.

My father related to me that his father, al-Qāsim b. Ibrāhīm—may Allah be satisfied with him—was asked about an elderly man, an ill person or an infirmed person who has worms coming out of the anus after ritual ablution. "Does such person have to renew it?" He replied: "Such a person has to perform the ritual ablution unless it is something that occurs continuously without interruption." This is because such cannot come out except that it is an excuse.

Whoever prays without ritual purity, the prayer is not accepted. Similarly, charity is not accepted out of malevolence. It has reached us on the authority of Zayd b. 'Ali from his fathers that 'Ali b. Abi Ťālib, may Allah be satisfied with him, said:

> Allah's Messenger, peace and blessings be upon him and his progeny, said: ((The prayer is not accepted except by ritual purification. The prayer is not accepted except by recitation of the Qur'an. The prayer is not complete except by the purification dues. Charity is not accepted out of malevolence)).[10]

My father related to me that his father said:

> Abu Bakr b. Abi Uways§ related to us on the authority of Hussein b. 'Abdullah b. Ḋumayra§ from his father§ from his grandfather§ from 'Ali b. Abi Ťālib, may Allah be satisfied with him: "Whoever has a nosebleed during the prayer should depart, perform the ritual ablution and repeat the prayer."[11]

Concerning what is narrated from the Prophet regarding purification for the prayer using a *mudd* of water and the purification wash using a *šā'*

This hadith was narrated, and Allah knows best regarding its authenticity.[12] If that is the case, Allah's Messenger, peace and blessings be upon him and his progeny, used to purify himself teaching the minimum amount for purification. In that which Allah's Messenger, peace and blessings be upon him and his progeny, ate, drank and purified himself with there is a blessing that did not exist with anyone other than him.

According to us, there is no limit to that. It is not an intentional command nor is it measurement understood to be compared to. It is only that it was the amount that was used on all the limbs, and he washed what Allah commanded him to using the minimum amount of water. It is sufficient for the ones who purify themselves and make ablution with it. Similarly, the sufficient amount for the one who performs the purification wash for major ritual impurity is that one washes all the limbs, hair, skin, front and back with water until it is all cleansed.

---

[10] Similarly narrated in ***Musnad Imam Zayd, Amāli Abi Ťālib, Šahīh Muslim, Šahīh Ibn Hibbān, Sunan at-Tirmidhi, Bihār al-Anwār***

[11] Similarly narrated in ***Sharh at-Tajrīd, Bihār al-Anwār***. It is also related on the authorities of A'isha, Ibn 'Umar and Abu Sa'īd al-Khudri in ***Mušannaf Ibn Abi Shayba, Sunan al-Bayhaqi*** and ***Sunan ad-Dārqutni*** respectively. Although the hadith was declared 'weak' due to the presence of rejected sub-narrators, the import of the hadith agrees with the agreed-upon authentic report in which the Prophet commanded a woman with a continuous flow of blood to repeat the ablution before each prayer. Analogously, such action demonstrates the judgement that flowing blood nullifies the ritual ablution.

[12] It is narrated in ***Al-Muntakhab*** that Imam al-Hādi said:

> Others say that the amount is a *mudd* for the ritual ablution and a *sā'* for the purification wash. They have narrated that from the Prophet, peace and blessings be upon him and his progeny; but it is not authentic. As for me, my statement and that of the scholars of the Messenger's Progeny is that there is no limit or minimum amount of water one can use for purification.

The one performing the ritual ablution washes the parts of the body that such person is commanded to wash. This is sufficient, and it fulfils the religious injunction—whether it is a lot or a little. This is because Allah never mentioned whether it should be a lot of water or a little; He simply commanded one to purify oneself thoroughly. Therefore, the one who purifies oneself is rendered purified, and that is sufficient.

Concerning various issues regarding the ritual ablution

The man or woman who sleeps until the intellect is removed—whether in the state of standing, sitting, bowing or prostrating—invalidates the ritual ablution and has to renew it. One would have to renew the prayer that it occurred in if it was an obligatory prayer. If it occurred in a supererogatory prayer, one has the choice to renew the ritual ablution and prayer or not. There is no prayer for the one who is asleep in it.

My father related to me that his father was asked about a person in the state of minor ritual purity who fell asleep sitting with his head nodding, sitting cross-legged, leaning against something, prostrating or standing. He replied:

> Sleep does not invalidate the ritual ablution or the prayer except if one's intellect is removed in any of the aforementioned states. Whoever loses intellect—such one must renew the ritual ablution and prayer due to the loss of intellect.

I prefer that the one who makes the ritual ablution while preoccupied with the affairs of this world prolong the ritual ablution until one forgets about one's wealth, buying, selling, and conversation, as long as one does not delay the prayer beyond its time. If one can renew the ritual ablution, one should because if one is preoccupied with anything other than the prayer, one has not established it. Allah—the Blessed and Exalted—says: **{O ye who believe! When thou stand for the prayer, wash thy faces and hands until the elbows...} (Q. 5:6)**. The verse obligates the ritual ablution for the prayer when establishing it. However, the one who is preoccupied with other than it, has not established it.

Whoever tells a lie, one's lie obligates the renewal of one's ritual ablution. Similar is the case for one who is obscene, transgresses or is lewd in speech and action.[13]

If a man kisses, hugs, touches or embraces his wife, the ritual ablution is not invalidated unless something comes out of him. My father related to me that his father was asked about a person in the state of minor ritual purity who kissed his wife. He replied: "His ritual ablution would not be invalidated unless something came out of him."

If a man performed the ritual ablution but forgot to wash his right arm and prayed, he has to go back and wash his right arm. After that, he must wash his left arm. Then, he must wipe his head and ears and wash his feet to the ankles. This is because he washed what he washed from incorrectness. When there is incorrectness in a religious injunction, one has to renew it.

Regarding a man who performed the ritual ablution, does he return to the face or not? If that is where he left off, he washes his face and the arms after the face. Then he wipes the head and washes the feet—as Allah has commanded—including the ankles. The washing of them enters into the command to wash until the water is on them. The shinbone is the extent to what one washes. Similarly, whoever avoids the heels or inside of the feet did not wash what they were commanded to wash. After that, one enters the prayer and its religious injunction.

---

[13] This would include every intentional major sin, such as gossiping, backbiting and injuring a Muslim—whether physically or verbally. [Ref. ***At-Tāj***].

It has reached us that Allah's Messenger, peace and blessings be upon him and his progeny, said ((Woe to the heels from the Fire!))[14] and ((Woe to the inside of the feet from the Fire!)).[15] By that, he, peace and blessings be upon him and his progeny, intended to urge that they should be washed. The heels are made obligatory by stressing the avoidance of it or part of it.

Similarly, one is obligated to rub water between the toes until one attains certainty that they are completely clean and water has run between them. Otherwise, one would have to repeat and rub water between the toes. Then, one can begin the prayer with the certainty of one's ritual purity. Regarding that, it has reached us that Allah's Messenger, peace and blessings be upon him and his progeny, said: ((Permeate the toes with water before you are permeated with the Fire!)).[16]

Regarding a man who performed the ritual ablution and completed the prayer, but then the doubt occurs to him, "Did I wash my face first or my arms?"—if he prayed and it had not occurred to him before or during the prayer but only after, his prayer and ritual purity would be considered sound. He does not have to return to the prayer. If he is certain that he preceded with that which should have been postponed or postponed that which should have been preceded, he has to renew his ritual ablution and repeat the prayer.

Concerning that which is impermissible to purify from the remains of beasts and what is ritually impure from them

The pure is rendered ritually impure when it comes into contact with a dog, pig, as well as the remains of that from which the idolater drinks or sticks their hands into. Regarding the horse, mule, donkey and other livestock, if one can clearly determine that their remains altered the smell, taste or colour [of the water], one cannot perform the ritual ablution with it. If one cannot clearly determine that their remains altered the smell, taste and colour, there is no problem performing the ritual ablution with it.

There is no problem with a man who purifies himself with the leftover water of his menstruating wife, as long as a drop does not fall into it or she does not place her hand in it before washing it.

Regarding a man who purifies himself from major ritual impurity in a large washbasin, this leftover water is fine; there is no problem for one to purify oneself with it. There should not be bodily ritual impurities in it, nor should he enter his hands into it before washing them. If one sees any traces of bodily ritual impurities or enters his hands into it before purifying them, one cannot make the ritual ablution with it—neither him nor anyone else.

Regarding two or three drops of urine or intoxicants in a container of water, one cannot make ritual ablution with it because it is considered ritually impure. Rather, one empties the container of the impure drops and cleans the container from the ritual impurities.

One is not allowed to drink from it either. If one is unable to clearly determine the colour and taste of the water in the container because it is not clear, Allah has prohibited one from drinking even a small amount of it just as He has prohibited one from drinking a large amount. If it is clear to him that it is not pure and contains that which Allah has prohibited one to drink, it is impermissible for him to drink or purify himself with any of it. Rather, he should remove it and stay away from it.

These containers are not like wells, ponds or pools whose water is not placed into containers to drink or purify oneself with. A container is used to contain water for the one performing ritual ablution—whether one, two or three—in order to purify oneself with and/or drink from. There is a clear difference between that which is placed in a container and that which is not.

---

[14] Similarly narrated in ***Sharh at-Tajrīd, Amāli Abi Ṭālib, Sunan Ibn Mājah, Sharh Ma'ani al-Athār, Mušannaf Ibn Abi Shayba***

[15] The hadith appears as ((Woe to the heels and insides of the feet!)) in the following texts: ***Sunan at-Tirmidhi, Al-Mustadrak, Musnad Ahmed, Sunan ad-Dārqutni, Sunan al-Bayhaqi, Jāmi' al-Ušūl*** and ***Majmu' az-Zawā'id.***

[16] Similarly narrated in ***Sharh at-Tajrīd, Sunan ad-Dārqutni***

Regarding the urine of donkeys, horses, mules and other animals prohibited to eat—if a drop were to fall in a container, one cannot purify oneself with the water in that container. One is not allowed to drink from it or use it.

Regarding the urine of camels and sheep—if one were to come into contact with it or it fell in the water that one is using for purification, there is no problem purifying oneself with it, as long as it does not alter its taste, colour or smell.

Concerning the purification wash from the state of major ritual impurity

Among the obligations for the one in the state of major ritual impurity is to wash the right hand. One is to pour out enough water until it is thoroughly cleansed. Then, one washes the left hand. One scoops the water with the right hand until one thoroughly cleans it [i.e. the left hand]. Then, one washes one's private parts until it is clean. Afterwards, one strikes the earth with the hands and cleanses the private parts with the dust. One strikes the earth again and washes it with the dust that remains. Then, one performs the ritual ablution for the prayer.

One then pours water on the head three times, or if one has a small tin of water, one pours it on the head until it is clean and rubs the water into the scalp. Afterwards, one pours the water onto the right side of one's body and then the left—rubbing each side with the hand until it is clean. Then, one completes the rest of the ritual ablution for the prayer because one cannot complete the ritual ablution until the body is purified from ritual impurities.

My father related to me from his father that Allah's Messenger, peace and blessings be upon him and his progeny, used to wash from the state of major ritual impurity and then perform the ritual ablution. He washed his hands and then, private parts. He poured water on his left with his right hand and then washed his hand. He rinsed his mouth and nose and then washed his face. He washed his forearms three times. He then wiped his head, poured water onto his head and washed the rest of his body—rubbing his body with his hands. Then, he started with the place that he left off and washed his feet. Finally, he repeated the ritual ablution for the prayer.[17]

> Whoever is in the state of major ritual impurity and performs the purification wash without urinating first—such person is not purified in my opinion because semen still remained in the urethra and was not excreted until after the purification wash. Is it not true that if he were to excrete semen after the purification wash—even if he had not urinated—he would have to repeat the purification wash?

---

[17] Sheikh 'Ali b. Bilāl related in his ***Sharh al-Ahkām*** that Abul-Abbās al-Hasani related with his chain of narrators to Zayd b. 'Ali—his ancestors—'Ali, upon him be peace:

> During the government of 'Umar, a group from Kufa came before him. He [i.e. 'Umar] said: "Who are you people?" They said: "We are a group of Iraqis." He said: "[Did you come] with permission or without permission?" They said: "No. With permission." He said: "If that weren't the case, then I would kill you because that is the punishment for a breach." They said: "We came to ask you about something." He said: "Go ahead." They said: "We want to ask you about the purification wash from major ritual impurity and the matters related to it." He replied: "Woe unto you! Are you bewitched? You asked me about things which I had not asked Allah's Messenger, peace and blessings be upon him and his progeny, about! Are you not present, O Abul-Hasan?" I said: "Indeed." He said: "Then answer with that which Allah's Messenger, peace and blessings be upon him and his progeny, replied. You are better at remembering that than I." I then said: "I asked him, upon him be peace, about the purification wash from major ritual impurity, and he said: ((You wash your hands before placing them in your container. Then, you wipe your private parts with your hand until it is clean. Then you rub the earth with your hands. Afterwards, you wash it with water. Rinse your nose and mouth three times. You then wash your face and arms three times. Wipe your head and then wash your feet. Pour water over your head three times. Then, pour water over your body. Then rub your whole body with both hands))."

A similar report exists in the ***Amāli Ahmed b. 'Isa*** with a shorter chain of narrators on the authority of Zayd b. 'Ali—his ancestors—'Ali, upon them be peace.

If one were to urinate and then something comes out along with it after the purification wash, one does not have to repeat it. However, this is only the case with prostatic discharge and not semen. My father related to me that his father said regarding the man who was in the state of major ritual impurity but excreted semen after the purification wash:

> If it was a liquid excreted due to pleasure, one would have to repeat the purification wash. If it was prostatic discharge or anything else, the ritual ablution would be sufficient instead of the purification wash.

The one in the state of major ritual impurity washes each limb separately. One is to wash each limb after the other, even if the first limb dries before the second one. This comes from what Allah has commanded regarding the washing of all the body. The same is the case with both men and women.

Concerning what obligates the purification wash

The purification wash is obligatory upon all people who have a wet dream. It is also obligatory in the awakened state when the two circumcised parts meet. My father related to me that his father was asked about a man who had intercourse with his wife but had not ejaculated. "Do they have to perform the purification wash?" He replied:

> There is disagreement in that which is narrated from the Prophet, upon him be peace. There is also disagreement in that which is narrated from 'Ali—may Allah have mercy on him—as well as what is narrated from the Emigrants (*al-Muhājirūn*) and the Anŝār. There are many narrations; however, out of precaution, one should perform the purification wash. It has been said that what obligates the prescribed punishment obligates the purification wash.[18]

If a man dreams that he is having intercourse but awakens and had not ejaculated, he does not have to perform the purification wash. However, if one is awakened until the point that the two circumcised parts meet, one is obligated to perform the purification wash. It is the same for men and women.

If a man dreams that he is having intercourse but wakes up and discovers that the wetness on himself is prostatic discharge and he is absolutely certain that he had not ejaculated, he is not obligated to perform the purification wash.

If he found semen on his clothes, he is obligated to perform the purification wash because he found something on his clothes that necessitated the purification wash. It may be possible that one may forget what one sees in one's dream. However, it is not possible that one ejaculates in one's clothes except that he had a wet dream.

Concerning the one in the state of major ritual impurity with smallpox and wounds

If one afflicted by smallpox does not fear that the purification wash would not cause injury to the pox, one uses water. If one fears that the smallpox would worsen, one uses the dust purification (*tayammum*).[19] This is sufficient according to the Praiseworthy One because Allah—Glorified be He—says: **{And make not thine own hands contribute to destruction} (Q. 2:195)** and **{...and slay not thyself. Verily, Allah hath been merciful unto thee}** (Q. 4:29) and **{Allah desires ease for thee, and He desires not hardship for thee...}** (Q. 2:185).

---

[18] It is narrated in the ***Amāli Ahmed b. 'Isa*** with a complete chain of narrators to Abul-Jārūd who said:

> I heard Abu Ja'far say that the Quraysh and the Ansār met. The Ansār came forward and said "Water is from water." The Quraysh said: "When the two circumcised parts meet, the purification wash is obligatory." They raised the issue to 'Ali, upon him be peace. 'Ali said: "O Ansār, is the prescribed punishment obligatory?" They said: "Yes!" He then asked: "Is the bridal dowry obligatory?" They said: "Yes." He then said: "What is with you that the prescribed punishment and bridal dowry are obligatory but not the water? Therefore, do so." And they did so.

[19] Ibn Rushd similarly narrated that the view that the dust purification can be used for major ritual impurity was the view of Imam 'Ali, upon him be peace. [Ref. ***Al-Bidāyat al-Mujtahid***]

Similarly, if one has sores or lesions and fears water, one washes everything other than the lesion. It is sufficient for one to wash all of the body parts except the afflicted limb. My father related to me that his father was asked about someone with smallpox who was in the state of major ritual impurity but unable to perform the purification wash and ritual ablution. He said: "Whoever fears injury and harm due to smallpox, sickness or wounds, performs the dust purification. That would be sufficient for him."

Concerning the breaking of a limb and what one is to do

If one breaks a limb, wears a splint and fears that by loosening the splint, water would make the injury worse, it would be invalid to loosen the splint. It would be sufficient for him to avoid washing that limb altogether. The prayer would be obligatory for such person, even if they had avoided washing the broken limb.

Regarding the statement of the one who says that one is to wipe over the broken limb, it is invalid according to us. This is because Allah obligates the washing of limbs, yet one would avoid it due to the fear that the loosening [of the splint] and the presence of water would cause greater harm. Therefore, it is sufficient for one that Allah's judgement allows for one to avoid washing that limb altogether due to the accident.

Therefore, one does not have to wipe over the splint because the splint differs from the limb that Allah commands to be washed.[20] One is not obligated in the Book or Sunnah to wash a bandaged splint during the ritual ablution just as one is commanded to wash the hands and feet. However, if one is secure from harm in loosening it, it would be invalid to avoid it. It is obligatory to wash it as Allah commands.

By that, one is to take into account the safety of one's religion and consideration for one's self. One should consider what one does and strive towards the truth in what one acts upon. Whether one acts in the open without concealing anything or secretly, it is as Allah says: **{He knows the deceptions of the eyes and whatsoever the heart conceals} (Q. 40:19)**.

Concerning what the one in the state of major ritual impurity should do if such person intends to eat or sleep

Such person should wash the private parts and hands, as well as rinse the mouth before one eats or sleeps. If one were to do other than that, it would not be religiously prohibited. Such person would just be acting contrary to tradition.

My father related to me that his father said regarding the one in the state of major ritual impurity who wanted to eat or sleep: "There is no problem with that. It's preferable to us that he washes his hands and then washes the private parts if he wants to eat or sleep."

Concerning the state of major ritual impurity with an ailment that prevents washing

If a man enters the state of major ritual impurity and then falls into a fire and burns his body before he is able to perform the purification wash, he is to perform the dust purification with high dry earth if he fears further harm from water. Such person does not wash and must perform the dust purification for each prayer. Also, such person does not have to perform the purification wash due to the state of major ritual impurity.

---

[20] A contrary statement is related from Imam al-Hādi in ***Al-Muntakhab*** in which he purportedly states that one is to wipe over the splint. All four Sunni schools are in agreement with this judgement as well as the Twelver Shia jurists. These contrary statements from al-Hādi deserve much attention because although the text ***Al-Muntakhab*** came chronologically after the ***Ahkām***, there are no statements from the imams or scholars that al-Hādi abrogated or repealed his earlier statement. Consequently, both statements (i.e. the impermissibility of wiping over the splint and the permissibility) are narrated from al-Hādi in subsequent texts, and later imams found themselves on either side of the issue.

Concerning the state of major ritual impurity with menstruation

If a woman in the state of major ritual impurity menstruates before she is able to perform the purification wash, she performs the purification wash for her state of major ritual impurity once her blood starts to slacken. However, if her menstrual discharge is copious, it is sufficient for her to perform one purification wash for both at the end of her cycle.

My father related to me that his father said regarding the woman who menstruated before she was able to wash from the state of major ritual impurity:

> It is preferable to us that she performs the purification wash from the state of major ritual impurity if her menstrual blood is not overwhelming. However, if her blood does not slacken or dry, she performs one purification wash for both.

Concerning the purification wash for women

It is religiously obligatory for a woman to undo her hair when she performs the purification wash for menstruation. She does not have to loosen it when she performs the purification wash for any other major ritual impurity. However, she must collect it in her two palms, pour water on it, shake it and squeeze it three times until she knows that the water has penetrated to her roots and passed around the sides. The same is the case with men.

My father related to me that his father was asked if a woman is to undo her hair when she performs the purification wash for major ritual impurity. He said:

> She does not undo her hair as long as water is able to penetrate all of it. However, she must collect it in her two palms, pour water on it, shake it and squeeze it until she knows that the water has penetrated to her roots. Likewise is narrated on the authority of Umm Salama,[§] the wife of the Prophet, peace and blessings be upon him and his progeny, that he commanded her to do so. She had lots of thick hair but he did not command her to undo it. However, when she purified herself from menstruation, she was obligated to undo her hair.[21]

Concerning the man who had intercourse with his wife and wanted to repeat it before performing ritual ablution

If a man had intercourse with his wife but wanted to repeat it before performing ritual ablution, there is no restriction in that. It is permissible for him to repeat it with his wife many times—even without performing the purification wash and ritual ablution in between. Even if he had four wives, it would be permissible for him to have intercourse with each of them without renewing the ritual ablution between intercourses.

My father related to me that his father was asked about a man who had intercourse with his wife but wanted to repeat it before renewing the ritual ablution between them. He said: "There is no problem if he repeats it without performing the ritual ablution. The last of that is similar to the first."

Concerning the one in the state of major ritual impurity who immerses himself in water

If the person in the state of major ritual impurity immerses himself in water while having bodily ritual impurities, such person should rub it off their bodies until it is cleansed. If water was brought to him, that would be sufficient.

---

[21] Similarly narrated in ***Ŝaḥīḥ Muslim, Sunan at-Tirmidhi, Abu Dāwūd, Sunan Ibn Mājah, Sunan an-Nisā'i, Al-Mu'jam al-Kabīr, Al-Mu'jam al-Awsaṭ, Jāmi' al-Uŝūl, Sunan al-Bayhaqi, Sunan ad-Dārqutni, Sunan ad-Dārimi***

If he immersed himself but had not cleansed his body from the filth, even if the water penetrated all of the hair—inside and outside—such person would not be considered clean or ritually pure. Similar is the case for one who immersed oneself in the ocean many times due to there being abundant water—the slave would not have cleansed that which he was commanded to. This would not apply to a small amount of water if one were to perform the purification wash with it.

My father related to me that his father was asked about a person in the state of major ritual impurity who immersed himself in water until he was completely submerged. Would such person be ritually purified? He replied:

> Yes. It would be sufficient unless such person did not cleanse what one is commanded to cleanse—front and back. Perhaps, such person would not be completely clean from one immersion. That withstanding, if such person were to cleanse all of their limbs, such person would be clean and ritually purified.

Concerning what is discouraged and not discouraged when performing the ritual ablution with the water of ponds and wells

The water of ponds and wells is not rendered ritually impure except by that which alters its water. It is rendered ritually impure if there is alteration of its colour, smell or taste. If there is a change in its smell, taste or colour, it is not valid to use it to purify oneself. That withstanding, there is nothing that can invalidate their water's ritual purity if it were to fall in it—whether it be carcass or any other ritually impure thing.

My father related to me that his father was asked if wells, ponds or springs were rendered ritually impure if a ritually impure thing were to fall in it. He replied:

> It is not rendered ritually impure as long as the ritually impure thing does not overwhelm it. It is not rendered ritually impure by carcass or any other thing like it as long as the ritually impure thing does not overwhelm the water's colour, smell and taste.

Similar is the case with anything that falls in the water—whether it be small or large—in a container, pit, hollow or earthenware jar. If something like rosewater, oxymel, broth, intoxicants, sugar or similar alters the water's colour, taste and smell and prevents it from being considered the 'pure water' that Allah created for use in ritual purification—one is not allowed to perform the ritual ablution with it because it is not considered water. If one cannot find other than it [i.e. pure water], one is to use high, pure earth for dust purification. Because one is not able to find the water that Allah commanded one to use for purification, it is binding for such person to perform the dust purification for any major ritual impurity and for the prayer.

My father related to me that his father said:

> If something alters the taste, smell and colour of water, one cannot perform the ritual ablution with it, nor can one purify oneself with it. If it is altered by vinegar, milk or cheese, and it overwhelms it insomuch that it can no longer be called 'pure water', one cannot perform the ritual ablution with it.
>
> Allah only makes ritual purity by means of pure water, as He says: **{Water hath been sent down to thee from the heavens, that thou may purify thyself} (Q. 8:11)**. The Mighty and Powerful also says: **{We have sent down pure water from the heavens} (Q. 25:48)**, and the Glorified says: **{If thou find not water, perform the dust purification with high, pure earth} (Q. 4:43)**. If one found water that has been altered, one has not found water.

Concerning incontinence of urine and discharge from wounds

If a person has incontinence of urine or constant flow from a wound and they are unable to stop it, such person—whether male or female—is to pray and not pay heed to what is coming out of them.

This is the case if there is no possibility to stop the flow.

It is preferable that the person who has incontinence of urine inserts cotton in the place of the affliction. It is also preferable that the person with constant flow from the wound wraps and bandages the afflicted limb. Whatever comes after such efforts have been made is excused and the person prays. One is not to pay heed to that which flows afterwards.

My father related to me that his father said that the one who is unable to stop the flow of urine simply performs the ritual ablution for the prayer and prays. There is no harm if such person does that because they are incapable of stopping the flow.

Concerning an ailment in which one's clothes are soiled by blood, vomit and the like

Such person should wash their clothes from what soiled it, as long as there remains time for the prayer. However, there is no harm if such person were to leave it. We prefer that such person not leave it more than a day and night of five prayers if he does not have another article of clothing. If he has another article of clothing, he prays in it. When the prayer is finished, he washes the soiled clothes and wears the washed one for each prayer.

If that is not possible due to difficulty or some other reason, it is sufficient to wash it once a day, every two days or every three days. It would be impermissible for such person to avoid washing it altogether unless there exist a valid reason that prevents one from doing so. This is because he should not leave it on his clothes altogether; such would be indecent and filthy.

My father related to me that his father said regarding a man who is covered in ulcers, leprosy or scabies and it leaked on his clothing:

> If the person who had such ailment was unable to stop the flow by washing and cleaning, he does not have to perform the ritual ablution because of it. Even if he had to perform the purification wash, a dispensation is also given to such person as is mentioned in the narrated traditions.

Concerning the dust purification and when it is obligatory

Dust purification is religiously obligatory upon the one who cannot find pure water.[22] Pure water refers to that which we have previously mentioned. The dust purification would be religiously obligatory upon one whether the person was a resident or a traveller.

Dust purification is impermissible except at the end of the prayer time. If it were night time and one would not be able to locate water before sunrise and before the time of the prayers elapses, such person performs the dust purification. Similarly, if it were day time and the person would not be able to find water before sunset and before the time of the prayers elapses, such person performs the dust purification.

It is impermissible to pray two prayers with one dust purification unless it is an obligatory prayer and a supererogatory prayer. In that case, it would be permissible. For example, if one were to pray the late noon prayer (*al-'asr*) before sunset after performing the dust purification but is unable to find water before the sunset prayer (*al-maghrib*), it would be impermissible for him to pray the sunset prayer with that same dust purification. This is because it is obligatory for him to seek out water. He is to exercise much effort to locate water. If the person is unable to locate water at the end of its prayer time, one performs another dust purification. This is because it is a means that Allah makes one desirous of performing it, mindful of His Grace and hopeful for rain or other than that.

[22] This inability to find water is further elaborated on in texts such as ***At-Tāj al-Mudhhab,*** which expands this concept. For example, if one were able to locate water but was physically unable to retrieve it or feared harm or ruin of oneself/another or contact with a ritual impurity from doing such, such person would be obligated to perform the dust purification. One would also be obligated to perform the dust purification if such person feared the elapse of a prayer for which one cannot make up, such as the funeral prayer and Eid prayers.

My father related to me that his father was asked "When does one perform the dust purification?" He replied: "One performs the dust purification at the end of the prayer time when there is no possibility to locate any pure water."

My father related to me that his father was asked "How many prayers can one perform with the dust purification?" He replied: "Only perform one prayer. Such person performs the dust purification at the end of each prayer time."

My father related to me that his father said:

> A questioner asked about a man who is unable to find water and is incapable of performing the dust purification with high, clean earth. What does he do? What is religiously obligatory for such person?
>
> He must pray because he cannot perform the dust purification except with high, clean earth. This is because it is high, pure earth with which Allah commands one to perform the dust purification. Allah does not mention purification except by means of water and high, pure earth. Allah has instructed the people in everything other than these two things yet He commands the believers that it [purification] be by only these two things.
>
> Whoever is in the state of major ritual impurity and cannot find pure water or high, pure earth, the obligation of purity that Allah commanded him with is removed from him. However, he must still pray even if he is not pure.

The 'time' refers to that time in which the one performing the dust purification must perform it. It is the time in which if one were to find water after the end of the prayer time. One is not obligated to perform the ritual ablution with that water or repeat the prayer since it was found after the prayer time elapsed.

It is impermissible for one to perform the dust purification if there is still time to locate water before the prayer time elapses. If one finds water, it is obligatory for such person to perform the ritual ablution and repeat the prayer within that time. This is because one located water within the time that one is obligated to pray.

Concerning the boundaries of the dust purification and its explanation

The boundary of the dust purification is to the elbows. It is impermissible for one to perform the dust purification to the wrists. The boundary of the one who performs the dust purification is like the boundary of the washing for the one who found water. As Allah—Glorified be He—says: **{O ye who believe, when ye stand for the prayer, wash thy faces and thy hands to the elbows, wipe thy heads and** [wash] **thy feet to the ankles} (Q. 5:6)**.

He—Glorified be He—obligates the washing of the entire face from the hairline to the boundary of the ears to the cheekbones to the chin. He also obligates the washing of the hands to the elbows. The meaning of **{...to the elbows}** is: 'until the elbows.' The intended meaning is 'Wash your faces and your hands until the elbows'—with 'until' taking the place of 'to.' Similarly, when He says **{...to the ankles}**, the intended meaning is 'until the ankles.' These prepositions are called descriptive prepositions, and one can be used in place of another. For example, the poet says: "They drank the water of the ocean then mount / Before (*ladā*) the green chasm with breezy sound." The phrase 'before the green chasm' only means 'upon the green chasm'—with 'upon' taking the place of 'before.'

A proof of that is the statement of Allah—Glorified be He—when He quotes Pharaoh as saying: **{"I shall crucify thee in the trunks of palm trees..."} (Q. 20:71)**. The preposition 'in' only means 'on'—with 'on' taking the place of 'in.'

It is religiously obligatory for the one performing the dust purification to use high, pure earth that does not contain anything impure or filthy. One is to strike the high, pure earth with both hands fully spread twice. One strike is for the face and the other strike is for the forearms. Then, after the first strike, one wipes the entire face. With the second strike, one wipes the right forearm with the left hand—from the fingernails to the elbows. Then, one turns the left palm to the inside of the right forearm and wipes it. One does the same thing to the left arm that one did with the right—using the high, pure earth on one's hand.

My father related to me that his father said:

> Abu Bakr b. Abi Uways§ related to us on the authority of al-Hussein b. 'Abdullah b. Ḋumayra from his father from his grandfather that 'Ali b. Abi Ťālib, may Allah be satisfied with him, said regarding the dust purification: "The face and the arms until the elbows."

My father related to me that his father said regarding the dust purification: "The boundary for the dust purification with high, pure earth is up until the elbows, similar to the boundaries for the ritual ablution." He then mentioned on the authority of 'Ali b. Abi Ťālib, may Allah be satisfied with him, that he used to command that.[23]

Concerning the one in the state of major ritual impurity who cannot find water or pure earth

Any person in the state of major ritual impurity who cannot find water or pure earth must pray without performing the dust purification. The same is the case whether one is in the state of major ritual impurity or not. One cannot perform the dust purification with anything other than high, pure earth as Allah commands. He makes it the means of purification for one who cannot find water.

High, pure earth is dust and nothing else [such as pebbles and stones, which are considered invalid to use for dust purification. Ref. ***At-Tāj***]. The one who cannot find dust is like the one who cannot find water. It is obligatory for such person to observe the prayer that Allah has made an injunction, even if the person is not pure. If one is unable to find water or high, pure earth to purify oneself with, it is still a religious injunction for such person to pray because avoidance is only for the one who is incapable to do it and cannot find a means with a valid excuse. The same is the case for any of the religious obligations.

Concerning the traveller who entered the state of major ritual impurity but fears that if he were to perform the purification wash with the water he has, he would perish from thirst

Whoever is travelling and fears that he would perish from thirst if he were to perform the ritual ablution with the water he has—it is impermissible for such person to purify oneself with that water. It is religiously obligatory for him to perform the dust purification because Allah does not burden any of His slaves with hardships; rather, He facilitates their affairs with ease. In so doing, He gives them more, and prohibits them from killing themselves and causing their own destruction by means of their hands.

Regarding that, Allah says: **{And make not thine own hands contribute to destruction} (Q. 2:195)** and **{...and slay not thyself. Verily, Allah hath been merciful unto thee} (Q. 4:29)** and **{Allah desires ease for thee, and He desires not hardship for thee...} (Q. 2:185)**. Therefore, it is religiously obligatory for one who fears destruction if one were to purify oneself with the water one has, to not purify oneself with that water because purifying oneself with that water would be religiously prohibited. Self-preservation is obligatory, and it is impermissible to do anything contrary to that.

My father related to me that his father was asked about a traveller who had water but feared that if he were to purify himself with it, he would perish from thirst. He replied:

> It is not religiously permissible for him to perform the ritual ablution with that water if that is the case. This is because Allah forbids one to injure oneself and prohibits destruction. As He says: **{...and slay not thyself. Verily, Allah hath been merciful unto thee. Whosoever does that out of enmity and injustice—We shall drive him into the Fire! That is for Allah easy} (Q. 4:29-30)**.

[23] Sheikh 'Ali b. Bilāl related in his ***Sharh al-Ahkām*** that Sayyid Abul-Abbās al-Hasani related with his chain of narrators to 'Ali b. Abi Ťālib, upon him be peace: "The dust purification is the face and hands to the elbows three times similar to the ritual ablution."

> He is to perform the dust purification as Allah commands. He wipes his face and arms with it, and keeps the water for himself. The same is the case if one feared an oppressive ruler, bandits or predatory animals if one were to search for water. In that case, one performs the dust purification with high, pure earth. In all of that, it is religiously prohibited to subject oneself to injury or destruction.

The intended meaning of his statement, may Allah be satisfied with him, '...if one feared an oppressive ruler, bandits or predatory animals if one were to search for water...' is a man who has water, knows where water is, but fears that if he were to retrieve this water, he would be assaulted by the oppressive ruler, bandit or predatory animal. He is to drink the water that is with him and perform the dust purification instead of seeking out the water that may lead to destruction.

Concerning the presence of water and when it is found

Whoever knows where water is, knows that he can reach it before the prayer times elapse and does not fear for himself any ruin—it is religiously obligatory for him to seek out this water. Similar is the case if he were to buy it for a price and it was a suitable price for the water. If the person did not fear loss of wealth or lack of financial maintenance (*an-nafaqa*), it would be religiously obligatory to buy that water. Otherwise, the fear of the loss of wealth and lack of financial maintenance would be included in that which leads to destruction.

One should make effort to seek out water. Whoever enters the state of major ritual impurity in the night or the day while there is water at some distance, and he knows that he can reach it before sunrise if it is night or before sunset if it is day, it is religiously obligatory for him to demand it unless there is something that prevents him from doing so.

My father related to me that his father said:

> If a traveller was only able to find water that was sold for an expensive price and he could afford it, he must buy it. This is because its availability in price means that it was found, as Allah says: **{If thou find not water, perform the dust purification with high, pure earth} (Q. 4:43)**. In the language, 'find' can mean availability by price. The exception is if the water's price is unjust or leads to undue destruction. Then, one would not be obliged to purchase such water. Such person should perform the dust purification with high, pure earth.

If the person in the state of major ritual impurity performs the dust purification but later finds water within the prayer time, he must perform the purification wash and repeat the prayers he made. If one was unable to find water until after a day, night, two days or two nights, one is to perform the purification wash. However, such one does not have to make up any of the prayers prayed with the dust purification; he has already observed his injunction and acted on what he was commanded.

Concerning menstruation as well as its minimum and maximum

The minimum amount of time for the menstruation is three nights, and the maximum amount of time is ten nights. Any time less than three nights is not considered menstruation.

It is religiously obligatory that she avoid the prayer during its [i.e. menstruation's] time until she cleanses and purifies herself. After she performs the purification wash, she can pray and fast. Any time outside of the time of menstruation is not considered menstruation; it is simply a form of illness. Nevertheless, it is impermissible for her to avoid the prayer during this time.

The menstruation can be four, five, six, seven, eight, nine, or ten days to the extent that women know for themselves. Their menstruation is by their own experiences. However, if her blood extends beyond ten days, it is considered vaginal bleeding. One is to do what the woman with vaginal bleeding does. She stops praying at the time of her menstrual discharge, which she knows for herself. She performs the purification wash after she is purified from it, which she knows for herself. She then can pray and fast. Her husband can approach her during this time. The avoidance of the prayer occurs only during the ten days. Menstruation only lasts up to ten days; nothing beyond that is considered menstruation but rather vaginal bleeding.

Concerning what is impermissible for the menstruating woman to do

It is impermissible for a menstruating woman to enter a mosque, touch a copy of the Qur'an and recite the Qur'an. It is likewise prohibited for her to pray because there is no prayer except by recitation of the Qur'an, and the menstruating woman cannot recite the Qur'an. It is also prohibited for her husband to approach her in the place of cultivation.

My father related to me that his father was asked: "Is it permissible for the person in the state of major ritual impurity and the menstruating woman to recite the Qur'an or not?" He replied: "The both of them can glorify Allah and engage in His remembrance, but they cannot recite the Qur'an."

Concerning what is encouraged for the menstruating woman to do

It is encouraged for the menstruating woman to—at the time of each prayer—clean herself, perform the ritual ablution, go to a pure place, sit there, face the *qibla* and engage in the glorification of Allah, declare that there is no God but Allah, seek forgiveness from Allah and depart.

It is encouraged that she places kohl on her eyes, comb her hair and beautify herself in her house. She is not to neglect herself, leave her hair dishevelled or debase herself. She is to adhere to excellence in her affairs.

Concerning what the pregnant woman does if she sees blood

If a pregnant woman sees blood, she should make effort to wash it from herself. If she fears that there is something to that, it is merely an accidental occurrence and not menstruation. Even if it occurred during the time that she normally experiences menstruation, it cannot be menstruation because menstruation cannot occur when a woman is pregnant. Consequently, Allah makes it that way. It is such that the womb cannot be the place for both menstruation and a baby. If it carries a baby, then menstruation departs. Thusly, Allah makes the departure of menstruation the sign that a woman is pregnant.

Regarding that, Allah—Glorified be He—says: **{...those who no longer anticipate menstruation from thy women—if thou are in doubt, their waiting period is three months, as well as those who have not menstruated} (Q. 65:4)**. He has made three months the waiting period for those who no longer anticipate menstruation, as well as for those pre-pubescent girls who have not menstruated. Therefore, when women still have menstruation and calculate it with their husbands, it is obligatory for her to refrain just as she would if she were pregnant until the matter is made clear to her and it is freed from her womb.

Because of that, we say that it is religiously obligatory for the woman in that situation to be wary of those things that wariness makes obligatory. An example would be a medication that one fears for the foetus and other than that which may cause harm to her. And due to that is what is said regarding the woman when her husband divorces her then she menstruates and finally, her menstruation discontinues. She will be considered amongst those menstruating women who cannot anticipate it because of her advanced age.

She is to anticipate her own menses to the time of its discontinuance, which is when she reaches sixty years. When she reaches sixty years, her waiting period is three months. Afterwards, she is permissible to marry. Using the analogy, it is religiously obligatory for one who is married but intends to marry his wife's sister, to divorce the wife and wait for her menstrual cycle and waiting period to end before he marries her sister. This is the case for one who does not anticipate her cycle and does not see blood at the end of her menstruation. The other alternative to that is for him to wait until she reaches the age of no longer anticipating menstruation and wait for three months. It is only after that time that he can divorce her sister. Anything other than that is impermissible because she does not anticipate it.

If that is the case, the only waiting period for her is her menstrual cycle. This is the limit. It is only an illness for her. It is not religiously obligatory for her waiting period to be other than the time of her menses, which Allah made for her. Her menses will always be her waiting period, which she inherited and passed down. When that is the case, it is impermissible for him to marry her sister.

My father related to me that his father was asked about the pregnant woman who sees blood and would this be considered menstruation. He replied: "No, it is not menstruation. However, it is some type of occurrence that happens to her just as an occurrence happens to other than her."

Concerning postpartum bleeding (*an-nifās*), an explanation of what is obligatory regarding it and how long a woman waits with it

A woman is to wait up to forty days for her postpartum bleeding unless she notices that she is pure before then. If that is the case, she purifies herself and cleans herself from blood. If she does not see that she is pure before the forty days, forty days is the limit of her postpartum bleeding. After which, she purifies herself, and it is not longer than that. If she sees blood after that time, she does what she would do in the case of vaginal bleeding.

Likewise, has been related to us that Allah's Messenger, peace and blessings be upon him and his progeny, said: ((The period of postpartum bleeding is forty days unless one notices purity before that)).[24] It has also been related to us that 'Ali b. Abi Ṭālib, may Allah be merciful to him, said:

> The time for the postpartum bleeding is forty days. When the forty days have elapsed, she performs the purification wash and prays. It is similar to vaginal bleeding. She can fast and pray. Her husband can approach her, also.[25]

The woman with postpartum bleeding purifies herself from it just as she would purify herself from menstruation because postpartum bleeding and menstruation are the same in meaning. Both involve the issuance of blood. The Arabs call menstruation *nifāsa.*

Regarding that, it is narrated that Allah's Messenger, peace and blessings be upon him and his progeny, was with one of his wives and she leaped up. He asked: ((What's wrong? Are you bleeding (*nafasti*)?))[26] By that he meant, 'Are you menstruating?' In pure Arabic, the Arabs call menses *nifāsa.*

Allah—Blessed and Exalted—obligates the purification wash for menstruation. Likewise, it is obligatory for postpartum bleeding because it is the root and meaning of menstruation. The only difference between the two words is in the wording and name.

Concerning vaginal bleeding, its explanation and what one does about it

According to us, vaginal bleeding does not have a specific time outside of what the woman knows for herself during the days of menstruation. If she experiences vaginal bleeding and knows the days of menstruation, she calculates it from that. If it is the time of her menstruation, she does not pray, fast, recite Qur'an or have intercourse with her husband. When the times of her menstruation has passed, she can pray, fast, recite and have intercourse with her husband if he likes.

It is religiously obligatory that she establish the days of her irregular menstruation. At the end of the days of her irregular menstruation, she purifies herself and performs the purification wash as she

---

[24] Similarly narrated in ***Sharh at-Tajrīd*, *Sunan Ibn Mājah, Sunan ad-Dārqutni*, *Sunan al-Bayhaqi***

[25] Similarly narrated in ***Amāli Ahmed b. 'Isa***. A condensed version appears in ***Bihār al-Anwār***.

[26] Similarly narrated in ***Sharh at-Tajrīd, Amāli Ahmed b. 'Isa, Ŝahīh al-Bukhāri, Ŝahīh Muslim, Sunan an-Nisā`i, Sunan al-Bayhaqi, Sunan Ibn Mājah, Musnad Ahmed, Sunan ad-Dārimi, Jāmi' al-Ušūl, Al-Mu'jam al-Kabīr, Al-Mu'jam al-Awsat***

would for her normal menstruation. Then, she inserts cotton, stops her flow as a man with incontinence would do and prays her prayer. She is to delay her noon prayer until the beginning of the late noon prayer time. She inserts cotton, stops her flow, performs the ritual ablution and prays the noon and late noon prayers together. Likewise, she does the same for the sunset and night prayers.

Similar is narrated from Allah's Messenger, peace and blessings be upon him and his progeny, that he used to order his wives to do so.[27] Its limit was in the prayer times. He ordered them to join the noon and late noon prayers at the end of its first time [i.e. the end of the sunset prayer's time] as well as the sunset and night prayers at the beginning of its last time [i.e. the beginning of the night prayer's time]. Verily, Allah's Messenger, peace and blessings be upon him and his progeny, only ordered them and others to do this out of mercy due to their tribulations. However, if a woman is able to insert cotton, perform the ritual ablution and hold it for every prayer time, this is best—only if she is able to do so. If not, Allah does not burden a soul except with what it can bear.

If the woman who has vaginal bleeding did not menstruate before this vaginal bleeding and the blood continues, she establishes it for a longer time than the menstruation time of other woman, including her sisters and aunts. We do not establish a set time for her in this situation or an exact number of days unless she exceeds ten days. Nothing beyond ten days is considered menstruation.

My father related to me that his father, al-Qāsim b. Ibrāhīm—may Allah be satisfied with him—was asked: "What does a woman with vaginal bleeding do? Can her husband approach her?" He replied:

> She establishes the days of her menstruation. Then she performs the purification wash afterwards and performs the ritual ablution for each prayer. Her husband can have intercourse with her, if he likes; however, she is to cleanse herself from blood when he intends to have intercourse with her. Any blood that exceeds its normal time is considered similar to the blood of a wound, injury or discharge.
>
> According to us, any time beyond the normal menstruation time is known by the woman and what she can sense for herself. However, if she had never menstruated before but experienced postpartum or vaginal bleeding, she calculates its maximum time to that of her female relations. According to us, there is no set time as others say. We do not specify a set time as long as it does not exceed ten days.
>
> This is based on what Allah's Messenger, peace and blessings be upon him and his progeny, ordered Fātima bt. Abu Hubaysh[§] to do. He ordered her to establish the days of her menstruation, and he did not set a specific time for her.[28] Analogy is not possible in that except that it would be rushing foolhardily into one's own opinion.

Yellowness and cloudiness during the days of menstruation indicate menses; its judgement is that of blood. Outside of the days of menstruation, it is vaginal bleeding. When yellowness and cloudiness appears or it comes from the water a woman cleanses her private parts with, it is all the same. It is considered menses during the time of menstruation. She is to avoid the prayer, as well as refrain from entering the mosques, reciting the Qur'an, praying, fasting and having intercourse with her husband.

My father related to me that his father was asked about yellowness and cloudiness. He replied:

> If it were to take place during the days of menstruation, it is considered menses, and its ruling is the same as that of blood. If it were to take place outside of the days of menstruation, it is not the menses. Rather, it is as vaginal bleeding.

---

[27] Similarly narrated in ***Sharh at-Tajrīd, Sunan Abu Dāwūd, Sunan ad-Dārimi***

[28] Similarly narrated in ***Sharh at-Tajrīd, Sunan Ibn Mājah, Musnad Ahmed***

Concerning the man who wants to have intercourse with his menstruating wife once the blood discontinues

A man does not have intercourse with his wife until she performs the purification wash with water, even if she cleansed herself and no longer sees blood. She is to cleanse herself from all of its traces, as Allah says: **{...and approach them not until they hath purified themselves} (Q. 2:222)**.

The meaning of **{purified themselves}** is 'performed the purification wash and cleaned themselves,' and it does not mean when her blood has discontinued.

Haven't you considered that the term 'purification' does not apply to anything except one who purifies? One can only be considered purified if such person underwent purification. One is purified by the purification wash and cleansing. That is why we said that the meaning of **{purified themselves}** is: performed the purification wash and cleaned themselves from impurities and any blood.

My father related to me that his father was asked, "If a menstruating woman completed her cycle and cleansed herself, can her husband have intercourse with her before she performs the purification wash?" He replied:

> Her husband cannot have intercourse with her until she performs the purification wash. Concerning that, Allah says: **{...and approach them not until they hath purified themselves} (Q. 2:222)**. It is interpreted to mean '...until they have performed the purification wash.'

Concerning wiping over the leather socks, sandal straps, feet, headscarf, turban or cap

The consensus of the Progeny of Allah's Messenger, peace and blessings be upon him and his progeny, is that it is impermissible to wipe over any of those things. If one were to wipe over these things, there would be no ritual ablution for that person; there is no prayer except with ritual ablution.[29]

Regarding what the Rafidites say about wiping over the feet—this is invalid, impossible and baseless.[30] Verily, the prohibition of wiping over the leather socks, feet or sandals, is stated by Allah, Glorified be He: **{O ye who believe! When thou stand for the prayer, wash thy faces and hands until the elbows, wipe thy heads and** [wash] **thy feet to the ankles} (Q. 5:6)**. The phrase **{thy feet to the ankles}** is in the accusative case and is connected to the washing of the face.

My father related to me that his father said:

> I have never seen anyone from the Progeny of the Messenger, peace and blessings be upon him and them, doubt that the recitation of Allah's Messenger, peace and blessings be upon him and his progeny; 'Ali b. Abi Ṭālib, may Allah be merciful to him; their progeny; and the Emigrants was **{...and** [wash] **thy feet}** with the phrase in the accusative case. The conjunctive **{and}** connects it back to the washing of the face.

---

[29] The vast majority of Sunni jurists adhere to the permissibility of wiping over the leather socks. Their opinions are divided between its absolute and conditional permissibility. Those who hold to its absolute permissibility say that one is free to wipe over them as a resident and during travel; whereas those who hold to its conditional permissibility say that they should only be wiped over in the case of travel since travel entails a degree of difficulty. They also disagreed regarding the extent to which the leather socks are to be wiped, the time that they are to be wiped, the state of the one who wipes as well as the condition that the leather socks must be in before they can be wiped. Coupled with this is the related issue of whether it is permissible to wipe over the non-leather socks. All such disagreements are based on conflicting narrated traditions and analogy. [Ref. ***Bidāyat al-Mujtahid***]. It is narrated in ***Al-Jāmi' al-Kāfi*** on the authority of Qūmisi that Imam al-Qāsim Rassi, upon him be peace, declared that the consensus of the Prophet's Progeny is to avoid wiping over the leather socks.

[30] The Twelver Shia and the Ismā'ilis hold to the legitimacy of wiping over the feet. They argue that such practice is based upon a reading of the Qur'an as well as was advocated by the Imams of *Ahl al-Bayt*. [Ref. ***Bihār al-Anwār***]. However, it is narrated in ***Al-Jāmi' al-Kāfi***:

> Imam al-Hasan b. Yahya said: "The consensus of the Prophet's Progeny is for washing the feet as well as for the prohibition from wiping over the leather socks. It [i.e. the consensus] also prohibits wiping over the feet, headscarf, turban and cap. If any of that were to occur, the ritual purity of both men and women would be invalidated according to them."

One is prohibited from wiping over the feet in the verse. The verse only obligates the washing of the feet due to impurities, dirt and filth. Wiping over the top of them is not washing them, and not washing them is not cleaning them. Allah is obeyed by washing and cleaning them as well as the removal of filth from them. Wiping over the tops of the feet while neglecting the sides and bottoms, does not clean them.

It is obligatory that they be washed. It is narrated from the Messenger, peace and blessings be upon him and his progeny, that he said: ((Woe to the heels and inside of the feet from the Fire!)). This proves that he, peace and blessings be upon him and his progeny, made it obligatory for the one performing the ritual ablution to wash all of the feet—their insides and outsides.

If the word **{feet}** was pronounced as the object of the preposition, then wiping would have been obligatory. Yet, how could the wiping be obligatory when Allah's Messenger, peace and blessings be upon him and his progeny, said: ((Woe to the heels and inside of the feet from the Fire!))? It is because he, peace and blessings be upon him and his progeny, intended that the feet be washed. For certain, Allah commanded that they be washed.

Regarding that, it is narrated that he [i.e. the Prophet] said: ((Permeate the toes with water before you are permeated with the Fire!)). That proves that they are to be permeated and cleaned. Washing their insides and outsides is religiously obligatory upon every Muslim who seeks purity.

Why on earth would I wipe over my feet or wipe over my leather socks? Why on earth would I wipe over my leather socks or wipe over my saddle? Severing the feet is more preferable to me than wiping over the leather socks or feet, as well as avoiding washing them. Consequently, it is a religious injunction to wash them as we have mentioned. Our evidence is, as we stated firstly, from the statement of Allah, as well as that of Allah's Messenger, peace and blessings be upon him and his progeny.

The proof against the one who advocates for wiping the feet and recites the verse with **{thy feet}** as an object of the preposition, is Allah's statement **{to the ankles}**. When it says **{to the ankles}**, we know for a certainty that it can only mean washing. Also, it is in the accusative case and the conjunctive connects it to the washing of the face. That is because it does not say 'wipe until the ankles.' It cannot say **{to the ankles}** unless washing is meant.

The Book of the Ritual Prayer

In the Name of Allah, the Most Gracious, the Most Merciful...

The beginning of the chapters regarding the prayer and the explanation of its obligation in the Book

Allah, the Majestic, says regarding its bestowal: {**They were commanded naught save to worship Allah sincerely. For Him is the religion of uprightness. They establish the prayer and render the purification dues; that is the right religion**} (**Q. 98:5**). He—Glorified be He—says: {**...then, establish the prayer, for the prayer is decreed upon the believers at established times**} (**Q. 4:103**).

He said to His Prophet, peace and blessings be upon him and his progeny: {**Command thy family to pray and be ye steadfast therein. We ask thee not for provision; We provide for thee. The end is for the God-conscious**} (**Q. 20:130**). The intended meaning of {**thy family**} is 'your people.'

He—Glorified be He—says: {**Confuse not truth with falsehood. Conceal not the truth whilst thou know. Establish the prayer, render the purification dues and bow with those who bow**} (**Q. 2:42**) and {**Safeguard the prayer, especially the middle prayer. Stand before Allah as devout ones**} (**Q. 2:238**).

The call to prayer and its mention in the Qur'an

Allah—the Blessed and Exalted—says: {**And when thou are called to the prayer, they take it as jest and play. That is because they are people who use not their intellect**} (**Q. 5:58**). He—Glorified be He—also says: {**O ye who believe, when the call to prayer is made on the day of congregation, rush towards the remembrance of Allah and leave trade. It is better for thee if ye only but knew**} (**Q. 62:19**).

The wording of the call to prayer and that of the pre-prayer call are doubled. Regarding the call to prayer, one says:

> *Allāhu Akbar. Allāhu Akbar. Ash-hadu 'an lā ilāha illa Allāh. Ash-hadu 'an lā ilāha illa Allah. Ash-hadu anna Muhammadan rasūlullāh. Ash-hadu anna Muhammadan rasūlullāh. Hayya 'ala as-salāt. Hayya 'ala as-salāt. Hayya 'ala al-falāh. Hayya 'ala al-falāh. Hayya 'ala khayrul amal. Hayya 'ala khayrul amal. Allāhu Akbar. Allāhu Akbar. Lā ilāha illa Allāh.* (Tr. "Allah is the Greatest. Allah is the Greatest. I testify that there is no god but Allah. I testify that there is no god but Allah. I testify that Muhammad is the Messenger of Allah. I testify that Muhammad is the Messenger of Allah. Come to the prayer. Come to the prayer. Come to prosperity. Come to prosperity. Come to the best of deeds. Come to the best of deeds. Allah is the Greatest. Allah is the Greatest. There is no god but Allah.")

According to us, the pre-prayer call is similarly doubled.[1] However, after saying *Hayya 'ala khayrul amal,* one is to say: *Qad qāmat as-salāt* (Tr. "The prayer has been established."). *Qad qāmat as-salāt. Allāhu Akbar. Allāhu Akbar. Lā ilāha illa Allāh.*

The phrase *Hayya 'ala khayrul amal* is authentic to us. It existed during the time of Allah's Messenger, peace and blessings be upon him and his progeny.[2] The muezzin used to recite that, and it was not abandoned until the time of 'Umar b. al-Khattāb.[§] He ordered that it be abandoned and said:

---

[1] In ***Al-Jāmi' al-Kāfi***, it is narrated on the authority of al-Qūmisi the Imam al-Qāsim, upon him be peace, said: "The consensus of the Prophet's Progeny, peace and blessings be upon him and his progeny, is that the call to prayer and pre-prayer call are both doubled."

[2] In the book ***Al-Adhān bi Hayya 'ala Khayrul Amal***, Sharīf Muhammad b. 'Ali al-Alawi narrated multiple reports with various chains of narration that the following recited *Hayya 'ala Khayrul amal* in the call to prayer: The Prophet, 'Ali b. Abi Ṭālib, al-Hasan, al-Hussein, Sahl b. Hunayf, 'Abdullah b. 'Umar, Muhammad b. al-Hanifiyya, 'Ali b. al-Hussein Zayn al-'Abidīn and Muhammad b. 'Ali al-Bāqir. The book ***Al-Jāmi' al-Kāfi*** also narrates that Imam al-Hasan b. Yahya declares that the practice is established by the consensus of the Prophet's Progeny.

"I fear that the people would rely on it." He ordered that the phrase *As-salāt khayral min an-nawm* (Tr. "Prayer is better than sleep") take its place.[3]

The original call to prayer was taught to Allah's Messenger, peace and blessings be upon him and his progeny, during the Night of the Ascension. Allah sent an angel to teach it to him.[4] Regarding the statement of the ignorant who say that it came in a dream of one of the Anŝār who informed the Prophet about it and he ordered that it be taught to Bilāl[§]—this is impossible.[5] The intellect cannot accept this because the call to prayer is from the foundations of the religion. A man cannot teach any foundation of the religion to Allah's Messenger, peace and blessings be upon him and his progeny.

My father related to me that his father said regarding the call to prayer and pre-prayer call: "There is disagreement concerning that; however, the most authentic that we heard is that the wording of both is repeated."

It is encouraged that the one who hears the muezzin repeat what he says. When he reaches the phrase *Hayya 'ala as-salāt*, say: "Glorified and praised be You, O Allah! Blessed be Your Name! Majestic be Your praise! Exalted be Your greatness! There is no god other than You!" When he says *Hayya 'ala al-falāh*, say: "O Allah, make us among those who succeed (*al-muflihīn*) and who are safe on the Day of Judgement! When he says *Hayya 'ala khayrul amal*, say: "O Allah! Make us among those who observe what they are obligated to observe! Make us among those who have certainty regarding their limits and those who are firm upon them! Verily, You are the hearer of supplications!"

When the pre-prayer call is made and he says *Qad qāmat as-salāt*, say: "O Allah! Guide us to the most correct deeds and establish us upon that in which You are satisfied! Send blessings upon Muhammad, our Prophet as well as upon the People of His Pure and Chosen Household—those who are truthful, righteous and those who have had impurity removed from them and have been purified with a thorough purification!"

Concerning payment for the muezzin

There is no problem if the muezzin takes payment for calling to prayer as long as he does not make it a condition for doing so and would not call to prayer if he were not paid. There is also no problem with chanting the call to prayer as long as it is complete and clear in its wording.

My father related to me that his father said regarding chanting the call to prayer: "There is no problem with chanting the call to prayer as long as it is complete and clear. There is also no problem with one taking payment for the call to prayer as long as it is not stipulated as a condition."

Concerning the call to prayer before the dawn

It is impermissible for the call to prayer to take place before the dawn. The call to prayer is only during the times of the five obligatory prayers for which the people are summoned to be present. Regarding the time outside of the prayers and before their times have entered, one does not call to the prayer during those times because it may confuse the people.

It was narrated that Bilāl gave the call to prayer one night. The Prophet, peace and blessings be upon him and his progeny, summoned him and said: ((What is with you that you make the night prayer at

---

[3] Similarly narrated in ***Sharh at-Tajrīd, Sunan at-Tirmidhi, Mušannaf Ibn Abi Shayba, Sunan Abu Dāwūd, Al-Muwatta***. Although it is generally held that this additional phrasing is considered licit according to all Sunni schools of law, there is also evidence to suggest that Imam ash-Shāfi' discouraged it. It is nevertheless considered prohibited by all Shi'ite sects and the Ibādhis [Ref. ***Al-Bahr az-Zakhkhār, Al-Bidāyat al-Mujtahid***].

[4] It is narrated in ***Amāli Ahmed b. 'Isa, Al-Jāmi' al-Kāfi, Sahīfa 'Ali b. Musa ar-Rida, Ash-Shifā*** of Amīr al-Hussein, ***Majmu' az-Zawā'id*** and ***Al-Mu'jam al-Awsat*** that the call to prayer was taught to the Prophet during the Night of Ascension.

[5] The traditionalists of the Generality report that when the Muslims were trying to decide on a method to signal the prayer, 'Abdullah b. Zayd al-Ansāri saw a man in his dream who taught him the wording of the call to prayer. Some also report that 'Umar b. al-Khattāb dreamt the call to prayer. Imam al-Qāsim b. Muhammad refuted this claim and belief in his ***Al-I'tisām***.

the time of the day prayer and the day prayer in the time of the night prayer? Return, then call out that the slave should sleep)).[6] Bilāl ascended and said "Would that Bilāl bereave his mother and blood drip from his forehead!" Bilāl then called out that the people can sleep, and he repeated the call to prayer after the dawn arrived.

It has reached us on the authority of Zayd b. 'Ali, may Allah be merciful to him: "Whoever gives the call to prayer before the approach of dawn has made permissible what Allah has prohibited and has prohibited what Allah has permitted."[7]

It has reached us that 'Ali b. Abi Ťālib, may Allah be satisfied with him, said: "Whoever gives the call to prayer before the approach of dawn has to repeat it. Whoever gives the call to prayer before its prayer time has to repeat it."[8]

Concerning the call to prayer without the ritual ablution and speech during the call to prayer

There is no problem for the muezzin to do so without having performed the ritual ablution. However, one cannot perform the pre-prayer call unless he performed the ritual ablution and has attained ritual purity because there is nothing after the pre-prayer call except the prayer. We do not like that one summon to it while he is not in the state to perform it.

The muezzin is not to speak in the call to prayer or in the pre-prayer call unless it is out of necessity. My father related to me that his father said: "The muezzin is not to speak in the call to prayer or in the pre-prayer call unless it is out of necessity or there is an urgent need."

Concerning the call to prayer by a blind man, son of a fornicator or slave

There is no problem for any of these people to call to the prayer as long as they are people of religion, knowledge and certainty. There is also no problem if any of them lead the prayer and the people pray behind them. There is no problem if one man gives the call to prayer and another one gives the pre-prayer call if they choose.

My father related to me that his father said:

> There is no problem for a blind man to give the call to prayer because Ibn Umm Maktūm§ used to call to prayer for the Prophet, peace and blessings be upon him and his progeny, and he was blind. There is no problem for a blind man, son of a fornicator or slave to give the call to prayer or lead others in the prayer as long as they are people of purity and scrupulousness.

My father related to me that his father said: "There is no problem if the one who gives the pre-prayer call is not the same as the one who gives the call to prayer if they so choose."

It is not for women to call to the prayer or give the pre-prayer call because the call to prayer and pre-prayer call are a summoning to the prayer. One cannot summon to the prayer unless they are made leaders of the men and women who will pray behind them. Women cannot lead men in the prayer.

---

[6] Similarly narrated in ***Sharh at-Tajrīd, Sunan Abu Dāwūd, Sunan ad-Dārqutni, Sunan al-Bayhaqi***

[7] Similarly narrated in ***Musnad Imam Zayd***

[8] Similarly narrated in ***Amāli Ahmed b. 'Isa, Al-Jāmi' al-Kāfi***

Also, the summoning to the prayer cannot be except with the raising of the voice. Women are commanded to be concealed, and it is obligatory for them to conceal their voices, just as it is obligatory for them to conceal their faces and beauty.[9]

Concerning the designation of the prayers and their numbers in the Book

Allah—Glorified be He—says: **{Establish the prayer at the descent of the sun to the darkness of the night and the recitation at the dawn. Verily, the recitation at dawn is ever witnessed} (Q. 17:78)**. His statement **{descent of the sun}** refers to the noon prayers. The word **{descent}** means 'decline from the meridian.'

His statement **{to the darkness of the night}** refers to the sunset prayer. The **{darkness of the night}** refers to its entering, and its entering refers to its manifestation. Its manifestation refers to the stars of the night being made visible. One can only see the stars when it is dark. One cannot see stars during the day. It is for this reason the Allah says when mentioning His Prophet Abraham, upon him be peace: **{When the night covered him, he saw a star...} (Q. 6:76)**. He mentions that the sign and manifestation of night is the appearance of a star. There is no **{darkness of the night}** unless there is the appearance of a star. The prayer is impermissible nor can one break the fast until this time.

His statement **{and the recitation at the dawn. Verily, the recitation at dawn is ever witnessed}** proves the obligation of the dawn prayer. It is impermissible to pray the dawn prayer until the dawn has broken and the light of twilight can be seen. When one is able to witness the light of dawn, then the prayer becomes obligatory as decreed by the Lord of creation.

Then, He says: **{By the Afternoon (*al-'Asr*)! Surely, humankind is at a loss!}**. He mentions the late noon prayer by name. This proves its mention specifically. Its injunction is further designated by what Allah's Messenger, peace and blessings be upon him and his progeny, has clarified.

Then, He says: **{O ye who wraps himself! Arise in the night, except for a little—half of it or subtract from or add to it a little—recite the Qur'an with a measured recitation} (Q. 73:1-4)**. He then says: **{Verily thy Lord knows that thou stand almost two-thirds of the night or half or one-third of it with a group of those with thee. Allah measures the day and the night knowing that thou are not able to do it, and He hast turned to thee. Therefore, recite whatsoever is easy from the Qur'an} (Q. 73:20)**. He commands them to recite what is easy for them in the Qur'an in their standings and prayer. This is proven by what is made binding upon them of the recitation in these times.

Their standing for the prayer in the night was made clear by the Messenger, upon him be peace. It is the night prayer that Allah specifically named in the verse: **{...and after the night prayer} (Q. 24:58)**. The night prayer is that which the people call the night prayer. These are the five prayers that Allah has made binding upon the believers. These are the times that Allah has appointed for them, and He has made evident their number and names.

Concerning the time limits of the prayers

The beginning of the noon prayer time is at the descent of the sun from the meridian. When the sun starts to

---

[9] This statement from al-Hādi seems to imply that he considered the woman's face to be a part of her nakedness (*'awra*) for which she is obligatory to cover. However, in the section dealing with marriage, he permits a man to look at a woman's face for whom he intends to marry. This would seem like a contradiction; however, this is due to a confusion of what is considered nakedness and what is not. The permissibility of a woman uncovering her face is not seen as being absolute. Also, it is evident that al-Hādi did not consider her face as her nakedness because she is to uncover her face for the prayer and Hajj pilgrimage and one cannot display any part of one's nakedness for the prayer or hajj pilgrimage by consensus. Rather, it is more precise to say that al-Hādi obligated a woman to cover her face without it being considered her nakedness. Imam al-Mu'ayyad Billah said in his ***Sharh at-Tajrīd***: "We do not hold to that. We simply permit one to look at her face for the reason of marriage, testimony or other necessities when such looking does not lead to the forbidden. A person must be aware of those matters for which he is not safe from falling into sin."

decline from the meridian and its descent is clear, it is the beginning time for the noon prayer. The beginning of the late noon prayer time is when the shadow of everything becomes the same length as that thing. The beginning of the sunset prayers time is when the night enters. The entering of the night is made evident by the appearance of a star that one cannot see except in the darkness of the night.

Concerning that, Allah says about His forbearing Prophet, Abraham: {**When the night covered him, he saw a star...**} (**Q. 6:76**). The beginning of the night prayer's time is the disappearance of the twilight. The twilight's appearance is red, not white. This is because the whiteness is not hidden except after a portion of the night. The redness is measured at a seventh of the night. It is the beginning of the night prayers. The beginning of the dawn prayer is the approach of dawn, which is visible by its light. These are the established times for the prayers of those who establish the prayers in the mosques.

The times between these established times are when one can pray. Whoever fears its elapse, the time between the sun's decline and its yellowing is that of the noon and late noon prayers. This is also true for the one who is ill, in fear, preoccupied with the affairs of Allah, as well as a menstruating woman who has become pure from the yellowness we mentioned. Similarly, if a menstruating woman were to become pure at the last part of the day and she is able to purify herself and pray at least five units, it is obligatory for her to pray the noon and late noon prayers together—even if the sun sets while she is praying the last of her late noon prayer. Likewise is the case with the person who is unconscious due to illness; if he were to regain consciousness in the time that one could pray at least five units, it is obligatory for him to pray the noon and late noon prayers together. One has the full extent of the day if one is afflicted by any of what we mentioned above.

Similarly, one has the full extent of the night if one is compelled. The full extent of the sunset and night prayers are proven by Allah's statement to His Prophet, peace and blessings be upon him and his progeny: {**O ye who wraps himself! Arise in the night, except for a little—half of it or subtract from or add to it a little—and recite the Qur'an with a measured recitation**} (**Q. 73:1-4**). That shows that the extent of the times for the sunset and night prayers is a religious injunction from Allah—the Mighty and Majestic. My proof that it is a religious injunction from Allah is His statement: {**Allah measures the day and the night knowing that thou are not able to do it, and He hast turned to thee. Therefore, recite whatsoever is easy from the Qur'an. He knew that there shall be amongst thee those who are ill and others who travel through the earth seeking of Allah's provision, as well as others who fight in Allah's way. Therefore, recite what is easy from it, and establish the prayer and render the purification dues**} (**Q. 73:20**).

His statement {**establish the prayer and render the purification dues**} proves that the prayer is just as a religious injunction as rendering the purification dues because they are joined. Supererogatory prayers cannot be joined with obligatory purification dues. Likewise, we find that Allah mentions both the prayer and the purification dues together in the Qur'an. He would not mention the prayer with the purification dues unless the prayers are an established injunction just as the purification dues are an established injunction. This proves that the prayer is a religious injunction.

If it were supererogatory, Allah would have mentioned it as thus, just as He mentioned other things as supererogatory. He decreed it as such for His Prophet, peace and blessings be upon him and his progeny, when Allah—Glorified be He—said: {**...and a part of the night, establish a night vigil prayer (*tahajjud*) as supererogatory for thee. Perhaps thy Lord shall resurrect thee to a praiseworthy station**} (**Q. 17:79**). He—Blessed be He—has decreed that matters are obligatory, supererogatory or permissible. He has differentiated them, and their boundaries are clear.

Concerning the opening supplication of the prayer as well as its permissible and prohibited

It has reached us on the authority of Allah's Messenger, peace and blessings be upon him and his progeny:

((The key to the prayer is ritual purity. The opening declaration of *Allāhu Akbar* (*at-takbīr*) makes prohibited, and the final salutations (*at-taslīm*) makes permissible. The prayer is not valid if one does not recite the *Fātiha* and the Qur'an with it)).[10]

The best of what we heard concerning the opening supplication and what we hold to is that the one praying faces the *qibla* and says: "I seek refuge in Allah—the All-Hearing, the All-Knowing—from Satan, the rejected." Then, he says: "**{I have turned my face towards the One who has formed the heavens and earth** [as an upright Muslim]. **I am not amongst those who associate partners (Q. 6:79). Verily, my prayer, my sacrifice, my life, and my death are for Allah, the Lord of creation. He has no partners. With this I am commanded} (Q. 6:162-163) {And I am from amongst those who submit} (Q. 10:90)**." Then one says: "**{All praise is due to Allah who has not taken a son. There is no partner who shares in [His] dominion. He has no protector out of weakness} (Q. 17:111)**" Afterwards, one recites the opening declaration of Allah's greatness by saying: *Allāhu Akbar*. Then one begins the prayer with: *Bismillah ar-Rahmān ar-Rahīm*. Then they recite the *Fātiha* and an additional *surah*. This is the best of what we heard concerning the opening supplication.

My grandfather, al-Qāsim b. Ibrāhīm—may Allah be satisfied with him—derived this from the Qur'an. Allah—Glorified be He—commanded His Prophet, peace and blessings be upon him and his progeny: **{Be not loud in thy prayer, nor be silent in it. Rather, adopt a way in between} (Q. 17:110)**. He said that one should not be loud in the recitation for the noon and late noon prayers, and one should not be silent in recitation for the sunset, evening and dawn prayers. Rather, one is to **{adopt a way in between}**; that is, one is to do both of them in that.

Then, it says that He commands the one who intends to begin the prayer: **{Say: "All praise is due to Allah who has not taken a son. There is no partner who shares in [His] dominion. He has no protector out of weakness"} (Q. 17:111)**. Afterwards, He commands him to declare Allah's greatness in the opening supplication of the prayer. He says: **{And declare Allah's greatness} (Q. 17:111)**. This means that the one praying is to say: *Allāhu Akbar.* Then, the one praying begins the recitation with the *Fātiha* and that which is easy from the Qur'an. Therefore, according to us, this is the most authentic opening supplication. It is the best and the one that most resembles the Divine Revelation.

It is the seeking of refuge from Satan, the opening and then, the saying: "**{All praise is due to Allah who has not taken a son. There is no partner who shares in [His] dominion. He has no protector out of weakness} (Q. 17:111)**." After that, one declares Allah's greatness saying *Allāhu Akbar* after the entire opening supplication.

We do not hold to the view that the opening supplication is after the declaration of Allah's greatness because Allah commands that the opening supplication take place before the declaration of Allah's greatness. He says: **{Say: "All praise is due to Allah who has not taken a son. There is no partner who shares in [His] dominion. He has no protector out of weakness."}** Then, He says: **{And declare Allah's greatness} (Q. 17:111)**. Therefore, He commands that the declaration of Allah's greatness take place after the opening supplication. It is for that reason we say that there is nothing after the opening supplication except the recitation of Qur'an.[11]

My father related to me that his father said: "The opening supplication is before the declaration of Allah's greatness, and the declaration of Allah's greatness is after the opening supplication. The verse says **{And declare Allah's greatness} (Q. 17:111)**."

---

[10] Similarly narrated in ***Musnad Imam Zayd, Amāli Abi Ťālib, Sharh at-Tajrīd, Sunan at-Tirmidhi, Sunan Abu Dāwūd, Sunan Ibn Māja***

[11] There is a difference of opinion regarding whether the opening supplication is before the declaration of Allah's greatness or after it. There are narrations that support both views. For example, in ***Musnad Imam Zayd***, it is related that 'Ali recited the opening supplication after the declaration of Allah's greatness. This view was echoed by Muhammad b. Manšūr who narrated this opinion from the Prophet, 'Ali and other imams of *Ahl al-Bayt*. However, whenever we have two opposing views narrated from the same authorities, we choose the view that is in more conformity with the Qur'an, as was stated by Imam al-Hādi, upon him be peace. And Allah knows best!

We do not hold to the view that the one praying raises his hands while declaring Allah's greatness—whether it is in the beginning, during the bowing or during the prostration. Regarding that, it is narrated on the authority of Allah's Messenger, peace and blessings be upon him and his progeny: ((Why is it that the people raise their hands like the tails of unruly horses? If they do not cease, Allah will do something to them and He will do it)).[12]

My father related to me that his father said:

> Do not raise the hands in the declaration of Allah's greatness. The limbs should be settled. This is because the prayer is simply submissive humility to Allah and lowliness. Being settled is closest to lowliness and submissive humility. It more so resembles submission to Allah—Glorified be He.

Concerning entering the prayer and its actions

One stands in the prayer and begins with the opening supplication. Then, he declares Allah's greatness. It is obligatory for him to recite the *Fātiha* as well any other *surah* that one can read from the Qur'an. Afterwards, one declares Allah's greatness and bows. In the bowing state, one says: *Subhāna Allahi al-Ažīm wa bihamdihi* (Tr. "Glorified be Allah, the Great, and praised be He") three times. Then, one returns to the upright position from the bowing and says: *Sami'a Allahu līman hamida* (Tr. "Allah hears those who praise Him.") Then one remains tranquil and starts to prostrate. One declares Allah's greatness and prostrates by laying one's forehead and nose on the ground completely with one's knees away from one's chest, elbows away from one's trunk, hands situated between the shoulders and ears, and feet in an erected position with the bottom of the toes on the ground. Then, one says: *Subhāna Allahi al-A'la wa bihamdihi* (Tr. "Glorified be Allah, the Exalted, and praised be He") three times.[13] He returns to the upright sitting position with the right foot erected and the left laying down and declares Allah's greatness. One sits with ones hands firmly placed on the knees in a settled position. Then one prostrates a second time repeating the glorification one did in the first prostration. Afterwards, one returns to the standing position while declaring Allah's greatness. One does in the second unit what he did in the first. One recites the *Fātiha* and what is easy or preferred from the Qur'an. It is as Allah—Blessed and Exalted be He—says: **{Therefore, recite whatsoever is easy from the Qur'an} (Q. 73:20)**.

It is said that it is sufficient for the one praying to recite any three verses of the Qur'an along with the *Fātiha*. The recitation of three verses is analogous to reciting all of *Al-Kawthar* (Q. 108) which comprises of three verses. It is preferable to us that one recites a complete *surah* of the Qur'an along with the *Fātiha*.

---

[12] Similarly narrated in ***Sharh at-Tajrīd, Ŝahīh Muslim, Sunan an-Nisā'i, Musnad Ahmed, Sunan Abu Dāwūd, Mušannaf Ibn Abi Shayba, Sunan al-Bayhaqi, Al-Mu'jam al-Kabīr, Bihār al-Anwār***. The second clause ((…If they do not cease…)) appears only in ***Sharh at-Tajrīd***. All other references include the clause ((…Be settled in the prayer)). Imam al-Hādi repeats the aforementioned hadith with the second clause ((…Be settled in the prayer)) in ***Al-Muntakhab***.

[13] In the books of the Generality as well as ***Musnad Imam Zayd*** and others, the glorifications in the bowings and prostrations substitute the Name of Allah with 'Lord' (*Rabb*), insomuch that the worshipper says: *Subhāna Rabbi al-Ažīm wa bihamdihi* and *Subhāna Rabbi al-A'la wa bihamdihi* respectively. When asked the justification for using the Divine Name instead of 'Lord', ***Al-Muntakhab*** records al-Hādi as saying:

> In their language, the Arabs permit the use of terms 'lord of the house' or 'lord of the village' to mean 'head of the house' or 'emir of the village.' When we know that, we take the statement of the Commander of Believers regarding the glorification in the bowings and prostrations. It is that which was narrated on the authority of 'Ali b. Rajā—al-Hasan b. al-Hussein al-Arabi—'Ali b. al-Qāsim al-Kindi—Muhammad b. Ubaydullah b. 'Ali b. Abi Rāfi'—his father—his grandfather that 'Ali used to say *Subhāna Allahi al-Ažīm wa bihamdihi* in his bowings and *Subhāna Allahi al-A'la wa bihamdihi* in his prostrations. This Name cannot be shared with any of creation because He says: **{Knowest thou any with His Name?} (Q. 19:65)**; that is, 'Can anyone be called Allah other than Allah?' Therefore, we prefer this [i.e. the glorification with the Name] because there is no atheism or idolatry in such statement.

Then one declares Allah's greatness and bows until the back is straight with space under his armpits. He places his palms on his knees with slight space between his fingers while they [i.e. his knees] face the *qibla*. One does not bend them [i.e. the knees] to the sides. One keeps his head straight without bowing it low or raising it high. Placing it between these two ways is best. One glorifies Allah in this position with the same glorification one did in the first bowing. Then one raises the head from the bowing and says: *Sami'a Allahu līman hamida.* Then one remains tranquil until the back and limbs return to their places. Then, one declares Allah's greatness and begins to prostrate. One does in the second prostration the same thing that one did in the first.

Concerning what one says in the first sitting in the first two units of a prayer consisting of three or four units

The best of what we heard and hold to is that when the praying person sits for the testimony of faith (*at-tashahhud*) after the first two units of the noon, afternoon, sunset and night prayers, he says:

> *Bismillâhi wa Billahi wa alhamdulillahi wal-asmā`ul-husna kulluhā lillahi. Ashhadu an lā ilāha ila Allāhu wahdahu lā sharīka lahu wa ashhadu anna Muhammadan abduhu wa rasūluhu.* (Tr. "In the Name of Allah and in Allah! All Praise is due to Allah! The most beautiful Names belong to Allah! I testify that there is no god but Allah, the One in which there is no partner! I testify that Muhammad is His Messenger and Slave.").

Then, one returns to the standing position.

Concerning what one does in the last two units of a prayer consisting of three or four units

According to us, the most authentic is what is narrated on the authority of the Commander of Believers—may Allah be merciful to him—from the Prophet, peace and blessings be upon him and his progeny, that he used to glorify Allah in the last two units. He would say: *Subhāna Allāhi. Alhamdulillāhi. Lā ilahāha ila Allāh. Allāhu Akbar.* (Tr. "Glorified be Allah. All Praise is due to Allah. There is no god but Allah. Allah is the Greatest."). He repeated this three times. Afterwards, he would bow.

That is what we saw from the elders of the Messenger's Progeny, peace and blessings be upon him and his progeny. We heard this from them, and we do not restrict one to recite *Al-Hamd* [i.e. the *Fātiha*] in them. However, we choose to do what was narrated from the Commander of Believers, may Allah be merciful to him. This is because we know that he did not do anything unless Allah's Messenger, peace and blessings be upon him and his progeny, did it. Allah's Messenger, peace and blessings be upon him and his progeny, did not do anything unless he was commanded by Allah to do so. He chose it for him to do in the religion.

My father related to me that his father, al-Qāsim b. Ibrāhīm, upon him be peace, said:

> One is to glorify Allah in the last two units. That is what we saw from the elders of the Progeny of Allah's Messenger, peace and blessings be upon him and his progeny. Likewise, it is narrated to us from the Commander of Believers, may Allah be merciful to him, that he used to glorify Allah in three times in the units and say: *Subhāna Allāhi. Alhamdulillāhi. Lā ilahāha ila Allāh. Allāhu Akbar.*

Concerning a response to the proof against glorifying Allah in the last two units of the prayer

One may say that it is impermissible to glorify Allah in the last two units of the noon, afternoon and night prayers as well as the third unit of the sunset prayer. He says that it is religiously obligatory for one to recite *Al-Hamd*.[14] What is your proof for that? What demonstrates that it is to be as such?

He replies: "It is because Allah says: **{Therefore, recite whatsoever is easy from the Qur'an} (Q. 73:20)**." Say to him: Does one not recite what is easy from the Qur'an in the prayer during the first two units? We know that whoever recites in the first two units of each prayer has recited what is easy in the Qur'an, unless there is a verse—may Allah be merciful to you—that explicitly obligates recitation in every unit. Similar would be the case if there is proof that Allah made it a religious injunction upon the slaves. If you cannot find a proof for your statement or cite an established narration, then you have no evidence against one who recites in the first two units and glorifies Allah in the last two units. This is because one does recite what is easy, as Allah—the Exalted and Great—commands.

If he says "My proof for that is also what is narrated from the Prophet, peace and blessings be upon him and his progeny ((Every prayer in which one does not recite the *Fātiha* of the Book, is aborted)),[15]" say to him the following: You have proven that which is contrary to what you intend to prove. Don't you notice that you're saying that if so-n-so intended to pray four units for the noon prayer and four units for the late noon prayer, but instead prayed three units for the late noon prayer or two units for the noon prayer, that person did not pray the late noon prayers? Nor is it valid for you to say that someone prayed the noon prayer because he prayed three units for the late noon prayer and it consists of four. Similar is the case for the noon prayer; you cannot be a resident and pray two. It should be clear to you regarding these two situations that they are to be prayed in full with four units and not less. The soundness of the first of it is established by the soundness of the last of it, and the soundness of the last of it is established by the soundness of the first of it.

If that is the case, this proves the correctness of what we said. It establishes that whoever recites in the first part of the prayer or in some of it, has acted on what was commanded in the injunction to recite what is easy. Also, they have acted upon the command [in the *hadith*] and their prayers are not aborted because they did recite in it, even if they recited in some of it.

Have you not considered that that Arabs say "So-n-so launched an arrow..." or "...two arrows at the army" but yet mean that he launched it at some of the army? This is permissible for one to say. Similarly, the Arabs say: "Yesterday, we remained at the rest house." By that, he simply meant that he remained at a part of it. They also say: "So-n-so threw a stone..." or "...two stones at the house of so-n-so." However, the intended meaning is that the person threw a stone at part of the house or a portion of it.

Even if there is a connection between all of something or a part of it, part of it could be intended. Therefore, this can be applied to the statement of the Prophet, peace and blessings be upon him and his progeny: ((Every prayer in which one does not recite the *Fātiha* of the Book is aborted)). Therefore, you have no proof from the Book of Allah or the agreed-upon narrations of Allah's Messenger, peace and blessings be upon him and his progeny.

If he had said "Every unit in which one does not recite the *Fātiha* of the Book, is aborted," then you would have a clear proof against us, and it would invalidate our position. It is established that whoever recites in the first two units and engages in glorification in the last two has acted upon the statement of Allah—the Mighty and Majestic: **{Therefore, recite whatsoever is easy from the Qur'an} (Q. 73:20)** by clear proof and evidence.

Then, one says to one who says that: "Are we not in agreement with you and everyone else that the last two units of a four-unit prayer and the third unit of the sunset prayer are not said audibly?" You

---

[14] The jurists have disagreed over the obligation of reciting the *Fātiha* in the last two units of a four-unit prayer and the last unit of a three-unit prayer. Some jurists such as Mālik and ash-Shāfi' held to its desirability or obligation, but others such as Abu Hanīfa held to the view that the Fātiha was not necessary in the last two units of the prayers. [Ref. ***Al-Bidāyat al-Mujtahid***]

[15] Similarly narrated in ***Musnad Imam Zayd, Sharh at-Tajrīd, Ŝahīh Muslim, Sunan at-Tirmidhi, Sunan an-Nisā'i, Musnad Ahmed, Sunan Ibn Mājah, Sunan al-Bayhaqi, Muwatta, Sunan ad-Dārqutni, Al-Mu'jam al-Awsat, Bihār al-Anwār***. Some references include the wording: ((Every prayer in which one does not recite the Mother of the Book…))

will not find anyone who would not say: "Yes. We and others are in agreement with you that this is the case." If that is the case, it is said: "Is there anything in the Qur'an greater than *Al-Hamd*?" It is the Mother of the Book and in it are the Names of Allah, the Lord of lords. In it is the declaration of His Oneness as well as the sanctification of His Names.

Regarding what Allah has designated and magnified of it, it is narrated that the Prophet, peace and blessings be upon him and his progeny, said:

> ((By the One who sent me with the truth as a Prophet, there is nothing in the Torah, Noble Gospels, Psalms or Great Criterion [i.e. the rest of the Qur'an] that is like it! It is the seven oft-repeated verses and the great recitation (or "Qur'an") that I was given)).[16]

Also, from that, it is narrated:

> ((It is not recited over a sick person except that he is made well. It is not recited for a grieved person except that it is sufficient and succour. One does not use it as an intercessor to Allah except that He grants one's desires)).[17]

If that is the case, why do you recite it silently and not audibly in the night prayers? When you recite it and another verse with it, why not recite it audibly in the last two units since it is the greatest thing that we recite? Yet, you recite it. Regarding that are narrations that you and we narrate.

One may say: "We do not recite it silently; we only follow those narrations in which loud recitation is avoided in the last two units. We recite it and other than it audibly in the first two units." The reply is: Both we and you narrate that. However, that [i.e. the recitation of the *Fātiha* in the last two units] is not narrated as such. This matter is not one of agreement between you and us. Rather, we differ with you by what we narrate and act upon. You cannot find a proof for yourself that counters what we've said nor can you negate it. By that, you promote the opposite of what you attempt to obligate in what you are silent in and abandon its audible recitation. How can you attribute to your Prophet, peace and blessings be upon him and his progeny, that which you discourage from yourself?

A proof is established for us as evidence and witness by Allah's statement to His Prophet, upon him be peace: **{Be not loud in thy prayer, nor be silent in it. Rather, adopt a way in between}** (**Q. 17:110**). We recite audibly in some of the prayers and silently in others.

It is said that the intended meaning of **{Be not loud in thy prayer, nor be silent in it. Rather, adopt a way in between}** refers to the prayer times and the prayer itself. By such, Allah separates the morning and noon prayers. The **{way in between}** refers to the time between these two periods. If you do not hold to the view that there is a division in the prayer units that Allah has joined, Allah commanded His Prophet, peace and blessings be upon him and his progeny, to recite audibly in the night prayers and silently in the day prayers based upon the verse **{adopt a way in between}**. One may also apply the meaning that He—Glorified be He—prohibited His Messenger, peace and blessings be upon him and his progeny, from reciting too loud insomuch that those listening discouraged it and too silently insomuch that those listening could not hear it at all. Rather, he was commanded to adopt a middle way between these two extremes and recite at a volume between both. In this case, the **{way in between}** refers to the middle path between these two situations.

---

[16] Similarly narrated in ***Ṣahīh Ibn Khuzayma, Musnad Ahmed, Sunan at-Tirmidhi***

[17] I was unable to locate this hadith; however, its meaning is sound and has been corroborated by other authenticated traditions. Regarding the Qur'an as a source of healing, it has been narrated on the authority of Abu Sa'īd that ***Surah Fātiha*** (**Q. 1**) was recited over a man who was stung by a scorpion or bitten by a snake, and he was thereafter healed. As for the Qur'an being a means of removing grief, it is narrated that the Prophet, peace and blessings be upon him and his progeny, used to recite in his supplication: "I ask You…to make the Qur'an the spring of my heart, light of my breast, banisher of my sadness and reliever of my distress!" Regarding the Qur'an being a means of intercession, it is narrated on the authority of Abu Hurayra that Allah's Messenger, peace and blessings be upon him and his progeny, said that ***Surah al-Mulk*** (**Q. 67**) intercedes for its reciter until he is forgiven.

If it is as you mentioned—that he was commanded to recite audibly in the first two units and silently in the last two—then it should be that he recites audibly in the first two units of the noon and late noon prayers just as he recites audibly in the first two units of the sunset and night prayers. This is because the verse does not differentiate the night from the day. Where is the difference exemplified? Since you do not have a proof in abandoning the loud recitation in the two-day prayers, it is necessary to refer back to what we said and our proof that we mentioned. Otherwise, you would take an invalid position that is impossible to prove and establish.

Both you and we agree and establish the fact that the Messenger, peace and blessings be upon him and his progeny, could not be heard reciting in the last two units and that whatever he said was silent. Based on this statement in which there is consensus amongst the Muslims, we teach that he did not recite the Qur'an in the last two units. If he did recite anything from the Book of the Most Merciful, he did so audibly and made it manifest and clear because all of it is light, guidance, a light-giving explanation and a healing. There is nothing contemptible in it that it should be concealed. Allah only makes it as a source of benefit for all people, and He commands His Prophet to manifest it to all creation and recite it to the ears of all listeners. He commands His slaves to listen attentively and silently. In it are explanations for those who hear it and confirmation for the one who speaks by its verses. The Qur'an is too great to have some of its recitation concealed from anyone who may listen to its verses. Therefore, when Allah's Messenger, peace and blessings be upon him and his progeny, was silent in the last two units, this teaches us that he engaged in the remembrance of Allah in them and that which is different to what he did in the first two units before. He—Glorified be He—mentions recitation of the Qur'an in the first two units, so it should be done audibly. He mentions the glorification of Allah in the last two units, so it should be done silently.

Thus, he, peace and blessings be upon him and his progeny, differentiates between the glorification and the recitation of Qur'an. In so doing, he demonstrates the esteem held for that which Allah has magnified by the revelation of the Criterion. It is that which He has made as a proof and guidance for all people. Therefore, the silence in the last two units is a proof that one is to engage in the verbal remembrance of Allah and not the recitation of the Qur'an. He used to engage in glorification means that he used to glorify Allah.

Do you not notice that the whole prayer is built upon the wording in it? There are six types of speech in the standings and the sittings, and no other type of speech is permissible in it. One is not allowed to say anything other than these. The first of these is the call to prayer, as is stated by Allah, Glorified be He: **{O ye who believe, when the call to prayer is made on the day of congregation, rush towards the remembrance of Allah and leave trade. It is better for thee if ye only but knew}** (Q. 62:19). The second of these is the opening supplication one says in the prayer which is derived from the verse: **{Say: "All praise is due to Allah who has not taken a son. There is no partner who shares in [His] dominion. He has no protector out of weakness"}** (Q. 17:111). The third of these is the declaration of Allah's greatness, which prohibits the permissible. This is derived from what Allah commands His Prophet to do after the opening supplication **{"...He has no protector out of weakness"}** with the statement **{And declare Allah's greatness}** (Q. 17:111). The fourth of these is the recitation in it, and that is derived from the statement of the Mighty and Majestic: **{Therefore, recite whatsoever is easy from the Qur'an}** (Q. 73:20). The fifth of these is the glorification, and that is derived from the statement of the Glorified: **{Glorify the Name of thy Lord, the Exalted, the One who created and then proportioned, the One who measured and then guided...}** (Q. 87:1-3). The sixth of these is the final salutations that makes permissible, and this is derived from Allah's statement, Glorified be He: **{When the prayer is completed, disperse within the earth and seek from the bounty of Allah. Remember Allah often that ye may succeed}** (Q. 62:10). The phrase **{is completed}** indicates an act or worship that has been concluded. The final salutations make permissible the speech and deeds that were previously deemed prohibited.

The call to prayer is known, and the opening supplication is evident and understood. The opening declaration of Allah's greatness is made clear by evidence, and the recitation in the night prayers are audible by clear evidence. The glorifications in the bowings and prostrations of the prayers are silent, and the final salutations are audible without being silent or concealed. The Muslim *Ummah* is in agreement with this, and all this is well known and mutually understood. When we recognise all of that as well as that which one is to say in the prayer, we find that the only thing that is said silently is the glorification and opening supplication.

One may say that there are no restrictions in the opening supplication, and one can recite it audibly. However, we find that only the call to prayer, opening declaration of Allah's greatness, recitation of Qur'an and the final salutations are recited audibly. We never found that the opening supplication was ever recited except that it was said silently. It is a Prophetic practice from the past, stemming from the Messenger, peace and blessings be upon him and his progeny. Then, we find that the Messenger, peace and blessings be upon him and his progeny, was always silent in the last two units of the prayer and taught this to us.

We narrate that the glorification of Allah is true from two perspectives: first, it is related from reliable sources among the Messenger's Progeny; and second, we have made it clear to the intellect. This is because he was silent in the last two units, and the only thing said silently in the prayer is the glorification of Allah, as is evident in the bowings and prostrations. We find that the glorifications are always said silently in the bowings and prostrations. We also find that he, peace and blessings be upon him and his progeny, was always silent in some of the units of the prayer. This teaches us that he said the same thing in the last two units as he said in the prostrations and bowings. This is because the glorifications were similarly said silently in both.

This is alluded to in the statement of the Glorified: **{Establish the prayer for My remembrance} (Q. 20:14).** The intended meaning is "Establish the prayer by My remembrance." The best remembrance after recitation of the Qur'an is the glorification of the One, the Most Merciful.

It is narrated on the authority of 'Ali b. Abi Ťālib—may Allah be merciful to him—that he used to glorify Allah in the last two units.[18] It consisted of the wording: *Subhāna Allāhi. Alhamdulillāhi. Lā ilahāha ila Allāh. Allāhu Akbar.* He used to say it three times. All of that is authentic according to us. It is narrated from our ancestors and authenticated by us that the glorification of Allah is in the last two units of the prayer. This is based upon what we proved, and this should be sufficient to the one with knowledge and discernment.

My father related to me that his father was asked what one says in the last two units of every four-unit prayer. He said:

> One glorifies Allah in it by saying: *Subhāna Allāhi. Alhamdulillāhi. Lā ilahāha ila Allāh. Allāhu Akbar.* It is related to us on the authority of 'Ali b. Abi Ťālib—may Allah be merciful to him—that he used to glorify Allah in them.

The Commander of Believers would not have done that unless he learned it from the Seal of the Messengers.

When one sits in the last unit of a three- or four-unit prayer, one says:

> *Bismillâhi wa Billahi wa alhamdulillahi wal-asmā`ul-husna kulluhā lillahi. Ashhadu an lā ilāha ila Allāhu wahdahu lā sharīka lahu wa ashhadu anna Muhammadan abduhu wa rasūluhu. Allāhumma salli 'ala Muhammad wa āli Muhammad. Wa bārik 'ala Muhammad wa āli Muhammad. Ka mā salayta wa bārakta 'ala Ibrāhīm wa 'ala āli Ibrāhīm. Innaka Hamīdun Majīd.* (Tr. "In the Name of Allah and in Allah! All Praise is due to Allah! The most beautiful Names belong to Allah! I testify that there is no god but Allah, the One in which there is no partner! I testify that Muhammad is His Messenger and Slave. O Allah, pray upon Muhammad and the Progeny of Muhammad, and bless Muhammad and the

[18] Similarly narrated in ***Musnad Imam Zayd, Sharh at-Tajrīd, Mušannaf Ibn Abi Shayba***.

Progeny of Muhammad just as You have prayed and blessed Abraham and the Progeny of Abraham. Verily, You are the Praiseworthy and Glorious.")

Then, one recites the final salutations. If one desires, one can supplicate to Allah afterwards. Similar was related to me on the authority of my father from his father. Both of them narrated this from Zayd b. 'Ali—may Allah be merciful to him—on the authority of his fathers from 'Ali b. Abi Ťālib—may Allah be merciful to him.[19]

Concerning an explanation of the prayer lines with the prayer leader

If a man is praying with a prayer leader, he stands to the right of the prayer leader. If there are two men, they form a line, place him [i.e. the prayer leader] forward and pray with him. If there is a congregation, they form a line, two lines or more depending on the number of people present and the space they have. They stand shoulder to shoulder without allowing any space between them in a straight line without differing. This is based upon what has reached us from Allah's Messenger, peace and blessings be upon him and his progeny. He said: ((Straighten your lines and do not differ lest Allah causes your hearts to differ)).[20]

It is impermissible for a man to pray with women if there is no other man with him. If there is a man with them, there is no problem for him to pray with him and them. The man is to stand to the right of the prayer leader and the women form a line behind them. If there is a man and a woman, the man stands to the right of the prayer leader and the woman stands behind them.

If there is a hermaphrodite with the man and woman and the hermaphrodite urinates from a penis, he is to be considered a man. He and the other man are to pray behind the prayer leader, and the woman prays behind them. If the hermaphrodite were to urinate from an opening, he is to be considered a woman. The man would pray to the right of the prayer leader, and the woman and hermaphrodite would pray behind them. If the hermaphrodite were to urinate from two openings, he is to be considered a full hermaphrodite. The man would pray to the right of the prayer leader, the hermaphrodite would pray behind them and the woman would pray behind the hermaphrodite.

If the prayer leader were to invalidate his ritual purity, he is to depart the prayer and each person in the aforementioned congregation continues the prayer by him or herself. The man to the right is not to be placed forward to lead; rather, he is to complete the prayer by himself. This is because if he were placed forward to lead, a man would be left to pray alone with a woman and hermaphrodite.

It is impermissible for a man to pray with a woman if there is not another man with her, unless the woman is a part of his family. There is no problem for a man to pray a supererogatory prayer at home in congregation with his wife and family.

If there are two men, two full hermaphrodites and two women with the prayer leader, the two men stand behind the prayer leader, the two hermaphrodites stand behind the men and the two women stand behind the hermaphrodites. If the prayer leader's ritual ablution is invalidated, one of the two men is placed forward to lead and the other man stands to his right. He completes the prayer and does not have to repeat the unit in which the former prayer leader's ritual ablution was invalidated.

Concerning a woman leading others in the prayer

Women can lead each other in the prayer. They should appoint the purest, most righteous and one who is best at reciting the Book of their Lord to lead them in the prayer. The one who is appointed as the prayer leader should stand in the centre and the others should stand at both sides—to her left and right. She should not be placed forward to lead. If there are two women, one is to stand to the right of the

[19] Similarly narrated in ***Sharh at-Tajrīd*** and ***Amāli Ahmed b. 'Isa***. It is also related in ***Bihār al-Anwār***.

[20] Similarly narrated in ***Musnad Imam Zayd, Musnad Ahmed, Sunan Abu Dāwūd, Al-Mustadrak, Al-Mu'jam al-Kabīr, Bihār al-Anwār***

other. If there are three women, the leader is to stand in the centre and one woman stands to her right and the other woman stands to her left. Similarly, a servant girl or blind woman can be appointed as prayer leader as long as they are people of righteousness, uprightness and God-consciousness.

That is based upon what has reached us from Allah's Messenger, peace and blessings be upon him and his progeny. He entered upon Umm Salama and there were women praying near her. He, peace and blessings be upon him and his progeny, said to her: ((Will you not lead them in the prayer?)) She replied: "O Messenger of Allah, is that valid?" He replied: ((Yes. However, you are not to lead them from the front or behind. They are to stand to your right and left)).[21]

Concerning the narrated statement of the Prophet: ((Every prayer in which one does not recite the *Fātiha* of the Book, is aborted))

It has reached us on the authority of Allah's Messenger, peace and blessings be upon him and his progeny: ((Every prayer in which one does not recite the *Fātiha* of the Book, is aborted)). It has similarly reached us on the authority of the Commander of Believers, 'Ali b. Abi Ťālib, may Allah be merciful to him: "Every prayer without recitation of the Qur'an, is aborted."[22]

'Aborted' means something deficient and incomplete. Anything incomplete is invalid. Allah's Messenger, peace and blessings be upon him and his progeny, simply means by that any prayer of four and three units. If one were to recite it in one or two units of the prayer, it would not be considered aborted. It would be sound because Allah's Messenger, peace and blessings be upon him and his progeny, only invalidated it if one did not recite the Qur'an in any part of the prayer. This is the consensus of the Progeny of Allah's Messenger, peace and blessings be upon him and his progeny. All of them agree that if one were to forget the recitation of the Qur'an in one of two units, he is to perform two prostrations of forgetfulness. His prayer would be sound and complete if he were to recite in some of the units.

Concerning the recitation of *Bismillah ar-Rahmān ar-Rahīm* audibly

According to us, there is no prayer for the one who does not recite *Bismillah ar-Rahmān ar-Rahīm* audibly [i.e. in an audible prayer].[23] My proof for this is that one cannot neglect any verse of the Qur'an. If it is a verse of the Qur'an, it is obligatory for one to recite when reciting *Al-Hamd*. It is an established verse in every *surah* of the Qur'an. Allah—the Blessed and Exalted—repeats it and makes it the opening verse. The repetition of something demonstrates the greatness that Allah affords to it. This is because it contains two of His Great Names, and it mentions the One who is Majestic and Noble.

Since that is the case, it is impermissible to neglect it. One cannot conceal it because it is a part of all the *surahs*[24] and is situated at the beginning of each. When one conceals it in *Al-Hamd*, it is considered deficient and altered. Why recite all of it audibly if you recite a part of it silently? It is the first part of the *surah* and subsequently, the first thing that should be made manifest and recited audibly because it is its key.

In addition to what we mentioned and elaborated on regarding the greatness of *Bismillah ar-Rahmān ar-Rahīm* and its praiseworthiness and the mention of the Names of the One Majestic, if it were not a part of the Qur'an, it would be impermissible to recite it in the prayer—whether it be silently or audibly. This is because if it was the case, it would be an interpolation and addition in the prayer, and speech is not allowed in it.

---

[21] Similarly narrated in ***Musnad Imam Zayd, Sharh at-Tajrīd, Mušannaf Ibn Abi Shayba***

[22] Similarly narrated in ***Sharh at-Tajrīd*** and ***Sunan at-Tirmidhi***

[23] It is narrated in ***Al-Jāmi' al-Kāfi*** that Imams al-Hasan b. Yahya and Muhammad b. Manšūr related that the consensus of the Prophet's Progeny holds to the view that *Bismillah ar-Rahmān ar-Rahīm* is to be recited audibly in the two *surahs* that are recited in the prayer.

[24] That is, it is at the beginning of all the *surahs* except *Surah at-Tawba* (**Q. 9**).

My father related to me on the authority of al-Qāsim b. Ibrāhīm, upon him be peace, from Abu Bakr b. Abi Uways from al-Hussein b. 'Abdullah b. Ḍumayra from his father from his grandfather that 'Ali b. Abi Ṭālib, may Allah be merciful to him, said: "Whoever does not recite *Bismillah ar-Rahmān ar-Rahīm* audibly, his prayer is aborted."[25]

It has reached us on the authority of Allah's Messenger, peace and blessings be upon him and his progeny: ((Every prayer in which *Bismillah ar-Rahmān ar-Rahīm* is not recited audibly is a verse that was stolen by Satan)).[26]

Concerning those discouraged actions in the prayer

It is discouraged for the one praying to blow in his prayer, as well as point, wipe the traces of prostration from the forehead, play with the beard, crack the fingers, raise one of the legs while standing, blow the nose or rotate to the left or right. Regarding that, it has reached us on the authority of Allah's Messenger, peace and blessings be upon him and his progeny, that he saw a man playing with his beard in the prayer. He said: ((If he was tranquil in the heart, he would be tranquil in the limbs)).[27]

I have never seen any of the scholars of the Messenger's Progeny, peace and blessings be upon him and his progeny, say *Amīn* after the recitation of *Al-Hamd* in the prayer, nor have I heard that from them. We do not hold to the view that it is said in the prayer because it is not a part of the Qur'an. Anything that is not a part of the Qur'an is impermissible to say in the prayer. My father related to me that his father was asked about saying *Amīn* in the prayer. He replied: "I discourage that it should be said because it is not a part of the Qur'an."

Concerning what one does behind the prayer leader, what one recites in the prayer behind him and what one does not recite

One does not recite behind the prayer leader in the audible prayers; however, one does recite behind him in the inaudible prayers because Allah—Glorified be He—commands that one pay heed and listen silently. The one who recites does not listen silently, and whoever does not listen silently does not pay heed. That is based upon the statement of Allah—Glorified be He: **{When the Qur'an is recited, pay heed to it and listen silently that thou may receive mercy} (Q. 7:204)**. The Blessed and Exalted commands that one pays heed and listen silently to the recitation of the prayer leader. That is why we say that it is impermissible for one to recite behind the prayer leader when he recites audibly.

Regarding the prayers that are not recited audibly, one must recite *Al-Hamd* and what is easy from the Qur'an behind the prayer leader because silent listening is only obligatory when one is able to hear. When the prayer leader does not recite audibly, listening silently becomes invalid and one is obligated to recite in the prayer.

My father related to me from his father, al-Qāsim b. Ibrāhīm, upon him be peace, that he used to advocate for recitation behind the prayer leader in those prayers that are recited silently. He also discouraged recitation behind a prayer leader who recited audibly. He used to say: "Allah—Glorified be He—commands that that one listen silently and pay heed when it is recited. One recites when one cannot hear and does not listen silently."

---

[25] Similarly narrated in ***Sharh at-Tajrīd*** and ***Amāli Ahmed b. 'Isa***

[26] Ibid.

[27] Similarly narrated in ***Musnad Imam Zayd*** and ***Sharh at-Tajrīd***

Concerning the *qunūt* and which prayers it is in

We do not advocate for the *qunūt* except in the morning and *witr* prayers.[28] According to us, the *qunūt* is encouraged, and we prefer that it not be abandoned. According to us, the *qunūt* is after the bowing; we do not hold to the view that it is before it.[29] According to us, there is nothing after the *qunūt* except the declaration of Allah's greatness and the descending to prostrate.

The *qunūt* is a *sunnah*, and whoever abandons it has not invalidated anything of his religion.[30] We prefer that one not be heedless of it and abandon it. However, we do not say that it is an obligation like the other known obligations of the prayer. My father related to me that his father was asked about the *qunūt* and said: "It is not an obligation. It is a good *sunnah* that one is encouraged to perform."

Concerning what is said in the *qunūt*

It is preferred that one recite verses from the Qur'an in it [i.e. the *qunūt*]. This comprises of supplications, praises and remembrances of Allah, the One the Praiseworthy. An example is the statement of Allah, the Majestic and Powerful: **{Allah burdens not a soul except with what it can bear. To it belongs what it hast earned and upon it is what it hast earned. Our Lord, take us not to task for that which we hath forgotten or erred. Our Lord, burden us not with that which Thou hast burdened those before us. Our Lord, burden us not with that which we cannot bear. Pardon us, forgive us and show us mercy. Thou are our Master, so grant us victory over the disbelieving folk} (Q. 2:286).** Allah—Glorified be He—also says: **{Our Lord, grant us the good of this world and the good of the hereafter, and prevent us from the punishment of the Fire} (Q. 2:201).**

If you want to supplicate after the final salutations of the *witr* prayer, you can recite the *qunūt* that the Prophet, peace and blessings be upon him and his progeny, taught his son, al-Hasan b. 'Ali, may Allah have mercy on him. It is related on the authority of 'Ali b. Abi Ṭālib, may Allah be satisfied with him:

> Verily, Gabriel—may Allah bless him—taught the following supplication to the Prophet, peace and blessings be upon him and his progeny, and the Prophet, peace and blessings be upon him and his progeny, taught it to his son al-Hasan: ((O Allah, guide me among those whom You have guided. Align Yourself to me in friendship with those whom You have align Yourself with. Pardon me with those whom You have pardoned. Bless me with what You have granted. Save me from the evil that You have decreed. Verily You judge and there is none to judge against You. Whoever aligns himself to You will not be abased. Whoever has opposed You will not be honoured. You are Blessed and Exalted!)).[31]

---

[28] It is narrated in ***Al-Jāmi' al-Kāfi*** that Imams al-Hasan b. Yahya and Muhammad b. Manšūr related that the consensus of the Prophet's Progeny is that the *qunūt* is recited. It is also narrated that they said: "The *qunūt* in the dawn and witr prayers is a past Sunnah according to us. It is the consensus of the Ahl al-Bayt of the Prophet, peace and blessings be upon him and his progeny, that the *qunūt* is recited in the dawn prayer." This is confirmed by Imam al-Hādi in ***Al-Muntakhab*** when he stated: "As for the statement of the scholars of the Prophet's Progeny and myself, the *qunūt* is only in the dawn and witr prayers."

[29] There are conflicting narrations regarding whether the *qunūt* is before or after the bowing. In the ***Amāli Ahmed b. 'Isa***, there are some reports that say that 'Ali recited the *qunūt* before the bowing and there are others that say that he recited it after the bowing. In the ***Musnad Imam Zayd***, it says that 'Ali used to recite the *qunūt* in the dawn prayer before the bowing and in the *witr* prayer after the bowing; however, he recited it in the *witr* prayer before the bowing after moving to Kufa. Despite these reports, Imam al-Hādi is reported to have said in ***Al-Muntakhab***:

> Others say that it is before the bowing; however, that has not been related to us except on the authority of 'Uthmān and those who say what he says. As for the statement of the scholars of the Messenger's Progeny and myself, the *qunūt* for the dawn prayer and the *witr* prayer is after the bowing.

[30] According to ***Al-Muntakhab***, al-Hādi was asked whether the one who forgets the qunūt is to repeat the prayer and he replied in the negative. Then he was asked whether the one who forgets such is to perform the two prostrations of forgetfulness due to its abandonment to which he replied in the affirmative.

[31] Similarly narrated in ***Musnad Imam Zayd, Sharh at-Tajrīd, Amāli Abi Ṭālib, Sunan at-Tirmidhi, Sunan Abu Dāwūd, Sunan Ibn Mājah, Sunan an-Nisā'i, Al-Mustadrak, Sunan ad-Dārimi, Musnad Ahmed, Al-Mu'jam al-Kabīr, Mušannaf Ibn Abi Shayba, Sunan al-Bayhaqi, Ṣahīh Ibn Khuzayma, Bihār al-Anwār***

> Then, Allah's Messenger, peace and blessings be upon him and his progeny, added to that: ((O Allah, I ask You for guidance, God-consciousness, righteousness and independence. I seek refuge in You from the victory of debt and the victory of enemies!)).[32]

This *qunūt* was after the final salutations of the *witr* prayer. We do not prefer that this take place before the final salutations because it is not from the Qur'an. One cannot make a *qunūt* in the prayer except with that which is in the Book of Allah, the Majestic and Powerful.

It is also said that those two supplications from Allah's Messenger, peace and blessings be upon him and his progeny, took place before speech was prohibited in the prayer.[33]

Another supplication that is preferred is that of the Commander of Believers, 'Ali b. Abi Ťālib, may Allah be satisfied with him. He used to supplicate after the final salutations of the *witr* prayer similarly saying:

> O Allah, it is to You that the sights are raised, hands are stretched forth, hearts are turned and tongues supplicate. It is to You that actions are carried out. O Allah, open the truth between us and our people. Verily, You are the best of Openers! We complain to You that our Prophet has been slandered, our enemies have increased and our numbers have decreased. Affliction has become manifest, and times have become hard. O Allah, grant us a speedy victory, and cause the authority of truth to be made manifest. O God of creation! *Amīn*.[34]

The Commander of Believers, 'Ali b. Abi Ťālib used to supplicate with this *qunūt* and curse certain men by name.[35] They included Mu'awiya b. Abi Sufyān,[§] 'Amr b. al-'Ās,[§] Abul-A'war as-Sulami[§] and Abu Musa al-Asha'ri.[§]

Every supplication other than the Qur'an is impermissible; we hold to the view that there is no supplication in the obligatory prayers or other prayers except from the Qur'an.

Concerning the clothes of the one praying and which clothing is sufficient for men and women

It is sufficient for the man who prays to do so in a one-piece long shirt as long as it covers him. The garment is tied with two ends around the nape. Similarly, it is narrated that when Allah's Messenger, peace and blessings be upon him and his progeny, prayed the last prayer with the people during his fatal illness, he was wearing a Khaybari cloak with its two ends tied around the nape.[36]

One does not pray wearing one article of clothing unless it is thick [enough so that one cannot see the colour of one's body underneath the garment. Ref. ***At-Tāj***]. The one praying should not be able to be described. It must be long, flow down over the knees and come near to the border of the ankles for the ritual ablution. The one praying must wear a garment that is fastened and must loosen its sides until the tops of the shoulders are covered. If the one praying is in a special garment for the Pilgrimage, he does not fasten the two ends around the nape and cover the chest; rather, he is to wrap the garment with one of the ends over the shoulders.

It is valid for a woman to pray in one garment that covers her head and body if she does not have a headscarf with which to cover her head. She must wrap the sides of the garment over her forearms and

[32] Similarly narrated in ***Amāli Ahmed b. 'Isa***. The first part of the supplication appears in texts such as ***Ŝahīh Muslim, Sunan at-Tirmidhi, Sunan Ibn Mājah, Musnad Ahmed, Mušannaf Ibn Abi Shayba, Kanz al-'Ummāl, Al-Mu'jam al-Kabīr, Al-Mu'jam al-Awsaṫ***. The second part appears in texts such as ***Sunan an-Nisā'i, Al-Mustadrak, Musnad Ahmed, Mušannaf Ibn Abi Shayba, Kanz al-'Ummāl, Al-Mu'jam al-Kabīr***.

[33] That is to say that the *qunūt* taught to Imam al-Hasan and the addition were recited during the ritual prayers prior to speech being prohibited in the prayers. This view reconciles those narrations in which the *qunūt* of al-Hasan was said to have been recited in the prayer and the ruling that speech was prohibited.

[34] Similarly narrated in ***Musnad Imam Zayd, Waqa'at Siffīn, Amāli Abi Ťālib, Amāli Ahmed b. 'Isa, Bihār al-Anwār***

[35] Similarly narrated in ***Tārikh at-Tabari, Manāqib*** of al-Kufi, ***Waqa'at Siffīn, Bihār al-Anwār.*** It is also narrated in ***Tārikh Dimashq*** that 'Ali used to curse Mu'awiya and his partisans in his *qunūt* for forty days.

[36] Similarly narrated in ***Sunan at-Tirmidhi, Musnad Ahmed, Majmu' az-Zawā'id, Al-Mu'jam al-Awsaṫ, Musnad al-Bazzār***

other limbs. She must take care that the garment covers her back, belly, shoulders, head, chest and shins. If all she has is one long shirt, she must stick her head into one of the pockets and take care as to not uncover any part of her body out of scrupulousness so that her prayer is valid. She must guard herself in the garment so that no part of her chest is shown during her bowing and prostration.

It is permissible for a man to pray in pants and a long sheet over his shoulders. If he does not have a sheet but has a turban, he can wrap it around his shoulders and have the ends hanging on the sides or in front of him. Similarly, if he wears a sarong, he should raise the top of it to the navel. Then, he lowers what he can of his garments—whether a sheet, turban or other articles of clothing—on his shoulders. He takes the ends and folds it over his chest and breast.

Concerning the one who laughs in the prayer

Whoever laughs in the prayer insomuch that laughter fills his mouth or any other type of laughter that interrupts the recitation or distracts one from the prayer—it is religiously obligatory for the person to rise and repeat the prayer.

Regarding what the Iraqis say— that is, laughter interrupts the prayer and invalidates the ritual ablution— we do not say what they say nor do we ascribe to their view.[37] This is because laughter only interrupts the prayer insomuch that it distracts from the prayer and interrupts the one reciting. It [i.e. laughter] is a sound that issues forth, even if it is a soft sound. Whereas the ritual ablution is interrupted by loud sounds, not low sounds, or continuous and serious speech. Speech does not interrupt the ritual ablution, but it is discouraged by the Most Merciful, as well as the one who speaks successively during it. Nothing invalidates the ritual ablution except that which we elaborated on in the section dealing with the ritual ablution.

Concerning who can and cannot lead the prayer

It is permissible to pray behind the people of religion, scrupulousness, virtue, truth, faith and similar. Even if the person is blind, a slave or a child of fornication, they can lead the prayer as long as they know the rules of the prayer and have memorised what is needed from the Qur'an. Similar is the case with the Bedouin, as long as he knows the rules of the prayer and has memorised what he is supposed to recite from the Qur'an.

If someone is a Muslim of scrupulousness and virtue and is known as such, there is no problem to pray behind such person. It is only discouraged to pray behind a Bedouin if he is ignorant of those things of which he should not be ignorant.

According to us, it is impermissible to pray behind one who is reckless in his religion among the defiantly disobedient.[38] This includes one who intakes intoxicants, betrays trusts, commits major sins, is an oppressor, consumes the prohibited, is a tyrant, bears false testimonies, disobeys their parents, accepts bribes or is known for lying and false testimonies. This is because Allah—Glorified be He—says: **{It is those who forge lies who believe not in the signs of Allah} (Q. 16:105)**.

---

[37] It is the view of Abu Hanīfa that laughter in the prayer invalidates the ritual ablution and prayer. It is said to be based on a *mursal* tradition—that is, a tradition in which the Companion is missing in the chain of narrators. However, many jurists rejected it because of its grade and because of the fact that it makes an action during the prayer invalidate the ritual purity which does not invalidate ritual purity outside of the prayer. [Ref. ***Al-Bidāyat al-Mujtahid***]

[38] It is related in ***Al-Jāmi' al-Kāfi*** that Imam al-Hasan b. Yahya said:

> It is the consensus of the Prophet's Progeny, peace and blessings be upon him and his progeny, that one does not place forward anyone to lead the prayer unless there is agreement regarding such person's reliability and that one does not pray behind open sinners for the Friday congregational prayer or the congregational prayers.

Imam al-Mu`ayyad Billah similarly related in ***Sharh at-Tajrīd*** that there is consensus of Ahl al-Bayt regarding the prohibition of praying behind an open sinner. He then added: "I do not know of any disagreement among them regarding it."

It is not permitted for the one who commits acts of disobedience for which Allah punishes because the prayer of the follower is dependent upon the prayer of their prayer leader. Their sittings depend upon his sitting, their standings depend upon his standing, and their final salutations depend upon his final salutations. Whatever invalidates his prayer invalidates their prayers.

The prayers of the defiantly disobedient are not accepted by the Lord of creation because Allah—Glorified be He—says: **{Verily, Allah accepts only from the God-conscious}** (Q. 5:27). If the prayer leader's prayer is not accepted, it is invalid. If the prayer leader's prayer is invalid, the prayers of those who follow him are invalid. Is it not true that if [the prayer leader] were to forget something and the followers did not forget anything, he and they would have to prostrate twice for forgetfulness even though they had not forgotten anything? Similarly, if he were to pray with them without ritual purity, the prayer would be invalid. The prayers of those behind him would similarly be invalid.

Regarding that, it is narrated that the Prophet, peace and blessings be upon him and his progeny, said: ((When you venture out and purify yourselves for the prayer, place the best of you forward to lead)).[39] Also regarding that, it is narrated that when the Bani Majammam came to him, he asked: ((Who led you in the prayer?)) They replied: "So-n-so." He said: ((Do not appoint as your prayer leader one who is reckless in his religion)).[40]

My father related to me that his father, al-Qāsim b. Ibrāhīm, was asked about the blind man, slave and son of fornication leading the prayer. He replied: "It is permissible for all of them to lead the prayer as long as they are not known to have committed any major sins and there is no doubt about them."

If one is unjustly forced to be present at a prayer behind someone who is impermissible to follow and such person would not be safe from harm if he were to leave the congregation, he is to use dissimulation and stand with them as if he is praying behind the prayer leader. It should not be that one is made to lead the Muslims unless there is satisfaction in his religion.

Concerning what one must do if he were to enter upon the congregational prayer and not find space in the prayer line

If one were to enter the congregation while they are praying with the prayer leader and not find space in the prayer line, he should pull one of the men in the prayer line back and stand next to him. Then, he prays the prayer with their prayer leader. This is because an individual should not pray alone when there is a congregation in prayer lines unless there is a valid reason.[41]

One should not prevent his Muslim brother from pulling him back in order to pray with him. Praying next to one another is better than praying in one's original place.

The best place for men in the prayer line is the first line close to the prayer leader. The worst place for women in the prayer line is the front line close to the men. Out of scrupulousness, the women should avert their gazes from the men during their bowings and prostrations. The women should preoccupy their gazes by looking towards the ground. That is purer for their prayers and in closer proximity to their Lord.

---

[39] Similarly narrated in ***Sunan ad-Dārqutni, Tārikh Baghdād, Al-Mustadrak, Bihār al-Anwār***

[40] Similarly narrated in ***Sharh at-Tajrīd*** and ***Amāli Abi Ṭālib***

[41] The valid reasons for praying alone and avoiding the prayer in congregation are the following: if the prayer leader is an open sinner or a minor; if the prayer leader is a resident and you are a traveller; if the prayer prays sitting and you pray standing; if the prayer leader has performed the dust purification and you have performed the ritual ablution; if the prayer leader is praying a prayer (such as the noon prayer) and you are praying another prayer (such as the late noon prayer); if the prayer leader and you disagree regarding the prayer times, the direction of the *qibla* or ritual purity. In all such cases, one is permitted to pray alone outside the congregation [Ref ***Al-Azhār***].

Concerning the prayer leader who recites a prostration verse in the prayer

It is discouraged for the prayer leader to recite a prostration verse in the obligatory prayers because that would entail an extra prostration. One should not add to it [i.e. the prayer] just as one should not decrease from it. It is religiously obligatory that one observe in it that which Allah has mandated, and He has not mandated any additions or subtractions. This is the closest to guidance and what is best.[42]

As for the supererogatory prayers, the one who performs them has a choice; he is not restricted in what he does. The better of the two matters is that one not adds to it anything that is not established in it. One could observe it [i.e. the prostrations for recitation of the prostration verses] in the supererogatory prayers but not the obligatory prayers.

Others differ with us in that and narrate reports concerning that. We do not recognise these narrations, nor do we do in our prayer what they do. That is because—according to us—it is not authentically attributed to the Messenger, peace and blessings be upon him and his progeny, nor is it established by the proof of the intellect.[43]

My father related to me that his father said: "We do not hold to the view that one prostrates in the obligatory prayers any additional prostration due to the recitation of a prostration verse."

Concerning forgetfulness in the prayer

Two prostrations of forgetfulness are obligatory upon one who stands in the place of sitting, sits in the place of standing, bows in the place of prostration, prostrates in the place of bowing, glorifies Allah in the place of recitation or recites in the place of glorification. It is also said that they are for the one who performs the final salutations outside of its place.

It is related that the Prophet, peace and blessings be upon him and his progeny, prayed the dawn prayer with the people. He prayed only one unit and departed. Then, a man named Dhul Shimālayn[§] asked: "O Messenger of Allah, did you forget or was it removed from the prayer?" He replied: ((What is that, O Dhul Shimālayn?)) He informed him that this was so, and he walked a circuit around the prayer lines. He asked: ((Is this right? He claimed that I only prayed one unit)). They replied: "Yes, O Messenger of Allah. You only prayed one unit." Allah's Messenger, peace and blessings be upon him and his progeny, prayed another unit, prostrated twice for forgetfulness and then performed the final salutations.

I do not know of the authenticity of this hadith of the Prophet, peace and blessings be upon him and his progeny, regarding prayer after the final salutations. I do not hold it to be authentically attributed to the Allah's Messenger, peace and blessings be upon him and his progeny.[44] Rather, I say that whoever forgets and performs the final salutations outside of its place and then remembers before speaking or

---

[42] It is encouraged for one to prostrate when reciting or hearing one of the following Qur'anic verses—7:206, 13:15, 16:50, 17:109, 19:58, 22:18, 22:77, 25:60, 27:26, 32:15, 38:24, 41:37, 53:62, 84:21 and 96:19. One is to not recite *Allahu Akbar*, the testimony of faith nor the final salutations. One is to be in the state of ritual purity and must face the *qibla*. If any of these verses are recited by the imam or one praying an obligatory prayer alone, one is to not prostrate. This would invalidate the prayer as it would entail an intentional addition to the prayer [Ref. ***Tāj al-Mudhhab***].

[43] It is narrated in ***Musnad Imam Zayd*** on the authority of 'Ali that the Prophet recited a verse of prostration in the Friday dawn prayer and prostrated for it. This same hadith is narrated in the 'Sound Six' (*Sihāh Sitta*) books of the Generality without mentioning that he prostrated for it. In ***Al-Muntakhab***, it is interesting to note that when Imam al-Hādi was asked about prostrating after reciting a verse of prostration in the Friday dawn prayer, he replied that one is to not do so. It is as if he completely disavows the narrated tradition.

[44] The said hadith has been narrated with many conflicting details. First, there is a disagreement as to the identity of the speaker. Some narrate that it was Dhul-Shimālayn, others narrate it with the name Dhul-Yadayn; still others substitute it with the names of Abu Hurayra and Ťalha b. Ubaydullah. Some tried to reconcile the difference between Dhul-Shimālayn and Dhul-Yadayn by stating that they were the same person; however, one was martyred in the Battle of Badr while the other entered Islam much later. A second contradictory detail is whether the Prophet purportedly recited the final salutations after two units or three; there are reports that mention either. A third contradictory detail is whether it took place before the prohibition of speech in the prayer or after. A fourth contradictory detail is whether it was the dawn prayer, late noon prayer or night prayer—all of which are reported.

turning his face from the place where his prayer was discontinued, he is to complete it and begin it from where it was discontinued. He should observe what is mandated upon him of its rules.

Regarding the two prostrations of forgetfulness, they do not complete the prayer nor do they subtract from it. They are only performed to counter the promptings of Satan. They do not take place except after the final salutations and the completion of the prayer in which there was forgetfulness.[45]

As for it taking place before the final salutations, this is impermissible according to us because such would entail an addition to the prayer. The final salutations make every prohibited action that took place before it permissible; it is a part of it and from it.

My father related to me that his father was asked whether the two prostrations of forgetfulness take place before or after the final salutations. He replied:

> The two prostrations of forgetfulness take place after the final salutations because if they were to take place before it, this would entail an addition in the prayer. The two prostrations only take the place of forgetfulness and the promptings of Satan, as Allah's Messenger, peace and blessings be upon him and his progeny, said. It is related authentically that the Prophet, peace and blessings be upon him and his progeny, used to prostrate twice after the final salutations.[46]

Concerning what a man does when he catches the prayer leader in a part of the prayer

If one catches the prayer leader bowing, such person is to declare Allah's greatness and bow with him. Then, he prays the rest of the prayer with the prayer leader. When the prayer leader performs the final salutations, that person is to stand and complete the remainder of the prayer. He is to omit that unit that he caught with the prayer leader when the latter was bowing—even if he had not recited in it.

If he catches [the prayer leader] prostrating, he is to prostrate with him. When the prayer leader stands, the man is to declare Allah's greatness and intend to perform the prayer from the beginning. He performs the rest of the prayer with the prayer leader—sitting when he sits and standing when he stands. When [the prayer leader] performs the final salutations, he stands and completes the remainder of the prayer. He does not count that unit in which he prostrated with the prayer leader because he missed the bowing. If he had caught the bowing, he would have caught that unit. This is because Allah, the Glorified, says in His Book: **{O ye who believe, bow and prostrate} (Q. 22:77).** He causes the prayer to consist of bowings as well as prostrations. Therefore, whoever catches the bowings has caught the unit, and whoever misses the bowing cannot be recompensed by the prostrations.

Others say that when one reaches the prayer leader while he is prostrating, one is to declare Allah's greatness for his prayer. Then, he is to prostrate and stand with the prayer leader with the first declaration of Allah's greatness being sufficient for him after his standing. We do not hold to that view nor do we hold to the view that one declares Allah's greatness except after the prayer leader and he stands. This is because his declaration of Allah's greatness enters him into the prayer, and we do not hold to the view that one can enter upon it in the state of sitting or prostration. We do not hold to the view that anything comes after the declaration of Allah's greatness except the recitation if the prayer leader recites silently and listening if the prayer leader recites audibly.

If one catches an individual praying while the latter is bowing in the second unit of a two-unit prayer, he is to declare Allah's greatness, bow and he should count this unit as the beginning of his prayer.

---

[45] It is narrated in the ***Musnad Imam Zayd*** from his ancestors that 'Ali said: "The prostrations of forgetfulness are after the final salutations, before speech and valid for additions and deficiencies." The same is narrated from 'Ali on the authority of Ja'far as-Sādiq in the ***Amāli Ahmed b. 'Isa.*** Imam Ahmed b. 'Isa also related:

> I used to perform the prostration of forgetfulness before the final salutations, and that was my view. However, when I saw that the consensus on the authority of the Commander of Believers was that he used to prostrate after the final salutations, I began prostrating after the final salutations for both additions and deficiencies.

[46] Similarly narrated in ***Sharh at-Tajrīd, Sunan Ibn Mājah, Sunan Abu Dāwūd, Sunan al-Bayhaqi, Ŝahīh al-Bukhāri, Sunan at-Tirmidhi***

Then, he prostrates with the prayer leader. When the prayer leader sits the second time in the last unit, he is to sit with him. If this was the first unit, he is to stand when the prayer leader stands, and when the prayer leader completes the prayer, he is to sit with him until the prayer leader declares the final salutations. When the prayer leader completes his prayer, the follower's prayer is also completed. There is no problem with what the prayer leader has established if it was not established by the follower in that case.

That withstanding, if a man were to catch the prayer leader during his sunset prayer while the latter is in the second unit, he declares Allah's greatness and enters the prayer with him. When the prayer leader bows and prostrates, the man bows and prostrates. When the prayer leader sits for his second unit, the man sits with him even if this is the man's first unit of prayer. Then, the prayer leader stands for the third unit and the man stands with him. When the prayer leader sits and performs the testimony of faith (*at-tashahhud*), the man performs his testimony of faith for the second unit of his prayer and continues sitting until the prayer leader declares the final salutations. When the prayer leader declares the final salutations, the man stands up to pray his third unit. He then sits, performs his third testimony of faith and declares the final salutations.

He is to sit in every unit is sitting position when the prayer leader does so; this is permissible. It is impermissible for the follower to differ from the prayer leader in anything he does. He cannot sit when he stands, stands when he sits, bows when he prostrates or prostrates when he bows. Rather, he does what he does and acts upon in the prayer what he acts upon. Similar is the case with a woman who catches the prayer; she must do everything the man does.

If two men or more enter the mosque and find that the people have already completed the prayer, they have a choice whether to make one a prayer leader and pray in congregation or pray alone individually. Allah mandates that it is one's choice.

My father related to me that his father was asked about a group who enters the mosque after the congregation has completed the prayer. Should they form another congregation or pray alone individually? He replied: "There is no problem if they were to pray together in congregation even if there was already a congregation before them."

Praying in congregation is better than praying individually just as Friday is better than other days. Similar is narrated by us and has reached us on the authority of the Commander of Believers, 'Ali b. Abi Ťālib, may Allah have mercy on him:

> Allah's Messenger, peace and blessings be upon him and his progeny, said: ((My *Ummah* will remain as long as there does not appear from it usury, the open manifestation of bribes, the severing of family ties, the avoidance of prayers in congregation and the abandoning of this house to lead the prayer elsewhere. If one were to leave this house to lead the prayer, do not consider it)).[47]

Similar is the case with any major sin that Allah threatens with the Fire.

Concerning when the prayer leader declares Allah's greatness and what interrupts the prayer

When the muezzin recites the pre-prayer call and says *Hayya 'ala as-salāt. Hayya 'ala as-salāt.* The prayer leader stands, as well as those who want to pray with him. They stand in their rows and straighten their prayer lines while the prayer leader stands in front of them. When he says *Qad qāmat as-salāt*, the prayer leader declares Allah's greatness and does not wait.

[47] Similarly narrated in ***Musnad Imam Zayd*** and ***Amāli Abi Ťālib***

Similar has reached us on the authority of 'Ali b. Abi Ťālib, may Allah have mercy on him, who said: "When the muezzin said, *Qad qāmat as-salāt*, Allah's Messenger, peace and blessings be upon him and his progeny, used to declare Allah's greatness without waiting."[48]

I do not hold to the view that anything interrupts the prayer of a Muslim, but the Muslim should prevent it the best that he can. He should not pray without a barrier if it is possible. It is narrated that Allah's Messenger, peace and blessings be upon him and his progeny, used to place a spear in front of him and then pray. It has also reached us that the Commander of Believers, 'Ali b. Abi Ťālib, may Allah have mercy on him, said:

> Allah's Messenger, peace and blessings be upon him and his progeny, used to lead us in the prayer and placed a spear in front of him. Then, a dog, donkey and woman passed in front of him. When he departed, he said: ((Verily, I saw what you saw; however, nothing interrupts the prayer of a Muslim. They should prevent it if they can)).[49]

There is no problem with one who prays in an open field if he cannot find a barrier to place in front of him. It is said that one may place a line in front of him, and there is no problem in that. However, one does not do that if they can find a barrier to place in front of them.

There is no problem with praying in camel stalls or sheep pens as long as there are no ritual impurities or traces of pus and discharge. It has been related that Allah's Messenger, peace and blessings be upon him and his progeny, discouraged praying in camel stalls and sheep pens; however, it is not authentic according to us.[50]

It has been related to me from my father that his father was asked about prayer in camel stalls or sheep pens. He said:

> There is no problem with that. It has been narrated on the authority of Ibn al-Mughaffal[§] and others that the Prophet, peace and blessings be upon him and his progeny, prohibited prayer in camel stalls or sheep pens. However, this is not authentic according to us.[51]

The people agree that the urine or dung of a camel do not render the clothes ritually impure if it were soiled by them. Therefore, how can it be discouraged to pray in camel stalls as long as there are no traces of ritual impurities, such as flowing blood? How could the earth be rendered ritually impure by their dung and urine while those things do not render the clothes ritually impure? They claim that the sun purifies that which falls on the earth but do not say that it purifies that which falls on the clothes? So how can it be permissible to pray in clothing with cattle urine but impermissible to do so in a camel pen with puddles and heaps?

By the life of their fathers! Such statement is invalidated by analogy. What they say swerves from the path of truth and correctness, and the rule of intellect negates it from the truth. It is therefore impermissible to mention it in connection with the Messenger and ascribe such to him. This is due to disagreement and its being far from truth and correctness.

---

[48] Similarly narrated in ***Musnad Imam Zayd, Amāli Ahmed b. 'Isa, Sharh at-Tajrīd, Al-Jāmi' al-Kāfi.*** Similar is narrated in ***Musnad al-Bazzār*** and ***Sunan al-Bayhaqi.***

[49] Similarly narrated in ***Musnad Imam Zayd, Sharh at-Tajrīd, Al-Jāmi' al-Kāfi, Amāli Ahmed b. 'Isa, Sunan Abu Dāwūd, Ŝahīh al-Bukhāri, Ŝahīh Muslim, Sunan an-Nisā'i, Bihār al-Anwār***

[50] As for the report, it is narrated in ***Al-Jāmi' as-Saghīr*** of as-Suyūti: "The Prophet, peace and blessings be upon him and his progeny, said: ((Pray in sheep pens, but do not pray in camel pastures)). This was narrated by at-Tirmidhi on the authority of Abu Hurayra. Ibn Mājah narrated it on the authority of 'Abdullah b. al-Mughaffal." It is also narrated in ***Musnad Imam Zayd*** that when the Prophet was asked whether it was permissible to pray in camel stalls, he replied in the negative.

[51] Imam al-Qāsim's reply is narrated in more detail in ***Al-Jāmi' al-Kāfi***. In it, he says:

> There is no problem praying in camel stalls or sheep pens. That which is narrated in which the Prophet discouraged prayer in camel stalls and that it was created from the devils is not authentically attributed to him. The amazing thing is that this narration contradicts the Book of Allah. Allah says: { **...eight pairs—twain of sheep and twain of goats. Say: "Hath He forbidden two males or two females or whatsoever is contained in the wombs of the female? Inform me if ye art indeed truthful"} (Q. 6:143).**

Concerning the one who unknowingly prays without facing the *qibla* and concerning repeating the prayer in its time and outside of its time as well as what one does not repeat

Anyone who prays without facing the *qibla* ignorantly but then comes to know of it afterwards while there is still time for the prayer should repeat it. According to me, it is invalid for one to not repeat it if it is in its time. If it is outside of its time, it is not obligatory to repeat it. This is because he prays while believing that he is facing the *qibla* and then does not know of his error in the prayer until after its time. The prayer is that in which its time remains.

If one were to pray after purifying with ritually impure water ignorantly but then later comes to know of it during the prayer time, it is religiously obligatory for him to repeat the ritual ablution with pure water and repeat the prayer. Similarly, one who prays after performing the dust purification and then finds water after the prayer while still in its time has to perform the ritual ablution with water and repeat the prayer he performed. This is similar to the occurrence of an unintentional error where one is obligated to repeat it while there is time. If the time elapsed, it is not obligatory to repeat it.

As for the prayer that one can perform outside of its time, it is a prayer that one forgot to pray—even if it is outside of its time. He is to repeat it when reminded. Similar is the case with one who prays after performing ritual ablution with ritually impure water while knowing that it is impure. He is to repeat the prayer even after its time elapsed and repent to his Lord for what he did. Similar is the case with one who forgot that he was in the state of major ritual impurity and then performed the ritual ablution and prayer. Afterwards, he was reminded after the prayer times elapsed that he was in the state of major ritual impurity. He is to perform the purification wash and repeat the prayer that he prayed. Similar is the case with one who performed the ritual ablution, forgot to wash his face and then was reminded after its time elapsed that he forgot to wash his face. He is to repeat the ritual ablution and prayer. As for the one who does not repeat the prayer among the slaves, such person will have no deficiency or invalidation.

Concerning the prayer of an infirmed person and how he prays as well as the unconscious person in the prayer

The infirmed person prays in any way he can. If he can stand, he stands. If he can sit, he sits. If one prays seated, he sits cross-legged and then declares Allah's greatness, recites and places his hands on his two knees for the bowing. He then sits while straightening his legs and goes into prostration while bending his legs. He then sits upon his left leg with the right foot upright and then repeats the prostration. Afterwards, he sits cross-legged, recites and does the same for the rest of the prayer as he did in that unit.[52]

If one is not able to prostrate, one gestures nodding with his head. His prostration should be lower than his bowing. If he is not able to sit and face the *qibla*, he is to gesture and nod. He does what he is able in the prayer. This is because Allah only places upon one that which one can bear out of His Mercy for the one in hardship. This is based upon the statement of the Glorified and Exalted: **{Allah burdens not a soul except with what it can bear} (Q. 2:286)**. He—Blessed and Exalted be He—also says: **{Allah desires for thee ease, and He desires not hardship for thee} (Q. 2:185)**.

---

[52] In ***Al-Muntakhab***, al-Hādi was asked: "Is it permissible for a man who is praying seated to declare the opening declaration of *Allāhu Akbar* while sitting and then recite some of the *surahs* standing and then bow afer completing the *surah*?" To which, he replied:

> That is not preferable to us, though others say that it is permissible. As for us, we do not hold to that view. Rather, we hold to the view that if a man begins the prayer standing, he is to complete the prayer standing. And if he begins the prayer sitting, he is to complete the prayer sitting in the supererogatory prayers. As for the obligatory prayers, no one is to pray sitting except the one with a valid excuse.

Others say that such person is to bring his face close to something to prostrate on. He then is to lay his face on something during the prostration. According to us, this is nothing because the prostration is either by normal ability or a nodding gesture.

Regarding the unconscious person, if he were to regain consciousness at the end of the day, he performs the prayers for that day. If he were to regain consciousness at the end of the night, he performs the prayers for that night. If he is unconscious for a full day, two days or three days and then regains consciousness, he is to only pray from the time that he regained consciousness. If he were to regain consciousness during the day, he prays the prayers of that day; and if he were to regain consciousness during the night, he prays the prayers of that night.

It has been related to me from my father that his father was asked how an infirmed person prostrates. "Does he gesture or prostrate on a cushion if he is not able to prostrate on the ground?" He replied: "If he can prostrate on the ground, he prostrates on it. If he is unable to do that, he nods with his head. The nodding gestures for his prostration should be lower than the nodding gestures of his bowing."

Concerning praying on a ship, praying naked or praying on the water where one cannot find land

Anyone on a ship prays in any way he can if he can find a way to do so and can endure it whether the vessel is in motion or has stopped in its journey. This is the case even if the ship has shifted from facing the *qibla* and has turned from it completely in the water.

Regarding the naked person, he is to sit cross-legged and place any grass he can over his nakedness. He is to then use nodding gestures like those of the infirmed person. He is to stay on the ground while he gestures so as to not uncover his nakedness in the prayer. If he cannot find any grass, he is to cover his nakedness with his left hand. He then does what we previously mentioned.

If there is a naked congregation with him and they made him the imam, they are all to sit while covering their nakedness with their hands. They form one prayer line just as a group of praying women with a woman as their prayer leader. The naked one leading the prayer sits in the centre and not in front of them. They pray to his right and left in a single prayer line.

Regarding the one who is standing in water, he uses nodding gestures. If he is able to sit in it, he sits and uses nodding gestures. If he is not able to sit, he prays standing in it. If there is a congregation, they are to appoint one of them as a prayer leader. If they are naked in water and cannot cover their nakedness, they only place him forward if the water is opaque. Otherwise, he is to stand in the centre of them, as the naked person leading the prayer. If the water that covers them is opaque, they place him forward and pray behind him. He is to use nodding gestures for the bowing and prostrations.

Concerning the Friday congregational prayer and its virtues

It has reached us that Allah's Messenger, peace and blessings be upon him and his progeny, said: ((Increase in your prayers upon me on Friday. Verily, [the reward for] deeds are doubled on it)).[53]

It is encouraged for the one praying the sunset prayer on the night before Friday to recite *Ađ-Ďuha* (Q. 93) and *Al-Qadr* (Q. 97). It is also encouraged for the one praying the night prayer then to recite *Al-Jumu'a* (Q. 62) and *Al-Munāfiqūn* (Q. 63). In the dawn prayer, one is encouraged to recite *Al-A'la* (Q. 87) and *Al-Ghāshia* (Q. 88).

When the sun first passes the horizon, the imam is to go to the mosque as well as the Muslims with him. When the imam ascends the pulpit, everyone in the mosque is to be silent. When the muezzin says at the end of the call to prayer *Allāhu Akbar Allāhu Akbar*, the imam is to stand. When the

[53] Similarly narrated in ***Musnad Imam Zayd, Amāli Ahmed b. 'Isa, Amāli Abi Ťālib, Sunan Ibn Mājah, Sunan Abu Dāwūd, Sunan an-Nisā'i, Uṡūl al-Kāfi, Bihār al-Anwār***

muezzin says at the end of the call to prayer *Lā ilāha ila Allah*, the imam speaks. The prayers of all the people stop at this point; it is religiously obligatory for them to listen silently and pay heed.

After he delivers the first sermon, he sits briefly. Then, he stands and delivers the second sermon. In it, he engages in the verbal remembrance of Allah and prays upon the Prophet, peace and blessings be upon him and his progeny, as well as his Ahl al-Bayt. He supplicates for the Muslim men and Muslim women, the believing men and believing women. When he is finished, he descends, and the muezzin declares the pre-prayer call. When he says *Hayya 'ala as-salāt*, the imam stands in his prayer place and the Muslims stand behind him. When the muezzin says *Qad qāmati as-salāt*, the imam declares Allah's greatness and recites *Al-Hamd* (Q. 1) and *Al-Jumu'a* (Q. 62) audibly. Then, he recites in the second unit *Al-Hamd* (Q. 1) and *Al-Munāfiqūn* (Q. 63), or he recites *Al-A'la* (Q. 87) and *Al-Ghāshia* (Q. 88). Anything that he does is sufficient in that regard.

When he declares the final salutations, he rises from his place going to the right or left and then performs voluntary prayers. It is preferable to perform voluntary prayers; otherwise, he is to disperse amongst the earth along with the Muslims.[54]

It is encouraged that the one going to the Friday congregational prayer bathe before going. It is also encouraged that the imam goes towards it on foot and barefooted time after time, if he is able to. This is because that is narrated that the Commander of Believers 'Ali b. Abi Ťālib, may Allah have mercy upon him, used to do this time after time.[55] One should not stroll to the Friday congregational prayer nor rush to it before the descent of the sun from its horizon in the sky.

According to us, the Friday congregational prayer is the **{middle prayer}** that is mentioned by Allah, the Exalted and Most High. On the other days, it refers to the noon prayer. Similar has reached us from the Commander of Believers 'Ali b. Abi Ťālib, may Allah have mercy upon and pleasure with him. My father related to me that his father said:

> Abu Bakr b. Abi Uways has related to me on the authority of al-Hussein b. 'Abdullah b. Ḋumayra from his father from his grandfather that 'Ali b. Abi Ťālib, may Allah have mercy on him, said: "The **{middle prayer}** is the Friday congregational prayer. On the other days, it refers to the noon prayer."[56]

The Muslims should display beauty on Friday. They should wear the best clothes, adorn their attire, wear their best scents and eat the best food. Similarly, they should relieve themselves of their work and entertain their servants, for it is a great and blessed day. Allah chose it for this *Ummah* and gave it virtue over the other days. He has made it a festival for the people of Islam and has obligated them to distinguish it from other days. This is because Allah, the Mighty and Majestic, has distinguished it from the other days in its blessings as well as its virtue among them.

---

[54] Although not mentioned in this text, we saw fit to mention some questions posed to al-Hādi regarding the Friday congregational prayer. The intent is to establish some principles that can be applied. In ***Al-Muntakhab***, it says:

> I asked: "What do you say regarding a man who missed the Friday sermon? How many units does he pray?" He replied: "He is to pray four." "If he were to reach while the imam was on the pulpit and he had already completed the sermon but the man had not heard any part of it before the imam descends and leads the people in prayer. Is the man to join with the people?" "He is to pray four units—two with the imam and then complete the last two after the imam recites the final salutations." "What if he reaches while the imam is on the pulpit and he says at the end of the sermon **{Verily, Allah commands justice, goodness…} (Q. 16:90)**?" "If he were to reach while the imam is on the pulpit delivering the last of his sermon, he is to pray two units with the imam and recite the final salutations when he does." "Does he pray the complete prayer if he missed one unit with the imam after the latter recited the final salutations?" "He is to pray three units along with the one he caught with the imam."

[55] Similarly narrated in ***Musnad Imam Zayd, Amāli Ahmed b. 'Isa, Bihār al-Anwār***

[56] Similarly narrated in ***Sharh at-Tajrīd, Amāli Ahmed b. 'Isa, Uṡūl al-Kāfi, Bihār al-Anwār***

Concerning shortening the prayer and when it is shortened

When a traveller decides to travel a *barīd*, which is twelve miles [or nineteen kilometres], he begins to shorten after departing from his home and when he is invisible from the people of his house. When the traveller intends to settle in a place for ten days, he prays the full prayer. If he does not intend to remain ten days, stays in his city and says to himself each day "I will leave today or tomorrow," he continues to shorten until a month's time. If he stays for more than a month, he prays the full prayer—even if he were to remain one day after the month.

Shortening refers to that which occurs with the four unit prayers. It does not refer to the three units outside of the four units because shortening is halving a prayer. Halving is when the traveller prays half the prayer that a resident would pray, and one cannot halve a three-unit prayer. One cannot observe Allah's injunction in that regards. Similar is the case with the dawn prayer. One cannot halve it because it is two units, and there is no prayer other than a prayer that is two units in number—whether an obligatory or a supererogatory prayer.

Concerning that, there is consensus amongst the Messenger's Progeny, peace and blessings be upon him and his progeny, that the supererogatory prayer—whether day or night—is prayed in twos and not other than twos. Given all of that, one cannot shorten the dawn prayer.

Regarding the one who says that the prayer cannot be shortened except in the case of fear,[57] we do not acknowledge that nor does one act upon that. Rather, shortening is an injunction from Allah upon every traveller—whether they travel by land or sea and whether in the state of righteousness or disobedience. This is because when Allah first made the prayer an injunction upon the believers, it was prayed in two units. Then, He added to it two more units at the end. He made it four units for the resident and kept the original injunction of two units for the traveller. It became obligatory for the traveller to shorten due to travel, and it became obligatory for the resident to pray it in full due to residency.[58] Therefore, one praying a full prayer during travel is like one praying the shortened prayer during residency. One has not acted upon the injunction that Allah appointed upon him. Similarly, one who cuts it short during residency has not observed that which Allah has made for him in his residency.

My father related to me that his father said:

> The best of what we heard concerning the shortening is the statement of the majority of the Progeny of Allah's Messenger, peace and blessings be upon him and his progeny. They said that it is a *barīd*; a *barīd* is four *farsakh*s. Similarly, the people of Mecca shorten in their departure in the Hajj pilgrimage to 'Arafat.
>
> The traveller prays the full prayer when he goes to a place and decides to stay for ten days. If he had not decided to remain there that long, he shortens for a month. He then prays it in full after that month.

Then ask the one who says that one does not shorten the prayer except in the case of fear or war: What is the fear prayer according to you? How do you perform it in your opinion? One has no excuse in presenting it as it is, and they must describe it the way that Allah has described it.

Then, he will say: The fear prayer is the division of the Muslims into two groups. One half of the Muslims pray with the prayer leader, and the other half stands face-to-face with the enemy to defend their praying brothers. They keep them safe from the enemy until they complete one unit with imam. Then the prayer leader stands with the first group, lengthens the recitation, and completes one unit of prayer with them. Afterwards, they pray the last unit by themselves without a prayer leader and pronounce the final salutation. Then the first group departs and stands in the place of their brothers

---

[57] There is an opinion narrated from A'isha that the prayers can only be shortened in the state of fear. She cited the verse as her justification. **{...there is no sin upon thee to shorten the prayer if ye fear that those who disbelieve would attack thee. Verily, the disbelievers are to thee a manifest enemy}** (**Q. 4:101**). [Ref. ***Al-Bidāyat al-Mujtahid***]

[58] Similarly narrated in ***Musnad Imam Zayd, Sharh at-Tajrīd, Ŝahīh Ibn Khuzayma. Muwatta***

face to face with the enemy while the second group begins their prayer. They stand behind the prayer leader pray the last unit with him. He then performs the testimony of faith and the final salutation while the second group continues to pray their last unit on their own. They then depart to fight their enemy. It is to be that all of them pray a unit with the prayer leader and another one.

Then, he would say that the prayer according to him is in the state of fear as he said. If the fear prayer is divided into two groups of Muslims and shortened with the prayer leader as you described, the prayer is simply shortened into two shortenings and halved twice—first, when the four units are halved into two and second, when the two halves are divided among the ones praying with the prayer leader in two divisions. They pray one part with their prayer leader and then the other group comes and prays the other part with him. This clarifies what the two divisions are.

This is not mentioned to us by Allah in the Qur'an. No one says that it is because Allah only mentions one shortening; He does not mention a second shortening. If he says that Allah indeed mentions two shortenings, ask about the shortening that is mentioned twice. God willing, he will not find any evidence in that regard and it would be better to leave the debate due to his apparent ignorance. It will be clear that such person was just arrogant and just wants to debate. However, if he comprehends, returns to the right and connects himself to the light of truth, he knows that there is only one shortening of the prayer. He also knows that the Muslims shorten the prayer in their travel and divide them among themselves with a prayer leader in fear of their enemy or in fear for themselves in general. Each one takes a portion of it and prays a part with the prayer leader.

If the travel prayer were four units like that of a resident without fear of an enemy, then they would pray two divisions due to the state of fear. The Muslims would then divide it into two parts of two units. The prayer leader would pray half of it with them, and they will face off the enemy for the other half while their brethren pray with the imam. Each half would comprise of two units based on the claim of the one who says that the travel prayer is not shortened and consists of four units like the prayer of the resident. Then, they would complete the last half of the prayer by themselves and then face off the enemy. The remaining group would then pray with the prayer leader as the others did and thereby take a portion of the prayer leader's prayer. Then all of them would have prayed two portions of two units. But there is no scholar who advocates this or anyone else with an intellect among the ignorant.

If it is established that the fear prayer is two units and that the two units are divided into two parts, then it is established that the travel prayer is two units. They are a religious injunction from Allah upon all. It is impermissible to increase it or decrease it. Allah says: **{…there is no sin upon thee to shorten the prayer if ye fear that those who disbelieve would attack thee. Verily, the disbelievers are to thee a manifest enemy} (Q. 4:101)**. It is its shortening to two units with the prayer leader that Allah has made an injunction. All praise is due to Allah! This should be clear to the one who comprehends and knows the interpretation of the Word of the Most Merciful.

Have you not heard what our Lord has said to His Messenger? **{And when thou art amongst them and establish for them their prayer, let only a party of them stand with thee and let them take their arms. Then when they have prostrated, let them fall to the rear and let another party come that hath not prayed. Let them pray with thee, and let them take their precaution and their arms. Those who disbelieve long for thee to neglect thy arms and thy baggage that they may attack thee once for all} (Q. 4:102)**. In the beginning of the verse, when it says **{when they have prostrated}**, this means: when they have completed one unit and prostrated twice. Then, they complete the second unit by themselves and depart to face their enemy. Afterwards, the party that has not prayed prays the second unit with you. Everyone has divided the prayer into two parts and prayed one part with the prayer leader and the other by themselves. This is the meaning of shortening.

My father has related to me that his father used to say that shortening the prayer during travel is a religious obligation upon the traveller. He also used to say:

> We say that the traveller shortens the prayer whether in obedience or disobedience because it was originally two units for the resident and the traveller. Our statement and derivation are based upon what we have understood from the Clear Book of Allah. We do not derive that from their narrations. All praise is due to Allah! We do not accept that which they have narrated. We say what Allah has said about that specifically and hold to what we have understood from Allah by means of what He has made clear to His Messenger.
>
> **{When ye strike the earth…}** The phrase 'to strike it' means: to travel upon it. **{…there is no sin upon thee to shorten the prayer if ye fear that those who disbelieve would attack thee. Verily, the disbelievers are to thee a manifest enemy} (Q. 4:101)**. The verse itself makes it clear that it is shortened during travel. It also proves that two units are religiously obligatory. In both of them [i.e. travel during war and peace] there is the 'striking of the earth.' The shortening mentioned in this verse only refers to halving it with the prayer leader and the congregation with him.
>
> Have you not heard how Allah addresses His Messenger with the words: **{And when thou art amongst them and establish for them their prayer, let only a party of them stand with thee and let them take their arms. Then when they have prostrated…} (Q. 4:102)**? This means: when they have completed one unit and prostrated, let the second party that has not prayed pray the second unit with you after that. Then, each group of the two would have shortened the prayer and completed that which they did not with the Messenger, upon him be peace. This is the fear prayer that Allah has mentioned. When they pray in the state of fear, they shorten their prayer. If they were to not shorten it and were in the state of safety, they pray the complete prayer with the prayer leader—two units and two units. Regarding that, Allah says: **{…but when ye are in security, remember Allah as He hath taught thee, which ye knew not} (Q. 2:239)**. He is saying: Complete the full prayer with your Messenger when you are in the state of security and do not shorten it. Praying the full prayer with the prayer leader is what they were commanded to do.
>
> They used to pray the noon and late noon prayers in two units each as you observe in travel. They were increased to four units in residence. It did not matter whether they were disobedient or righteous or whether the travel was good or evil. The prayer is not increased during the journey nor is it decreased during residency. Whoever increases in what Allah has mandated upon him of the prayer during a journey—such person must repeat his prayer. Such would be similar to a person who increased in the prayer while a resident; his prayer would be invalidated and he would have to repeat it.
>
> The same judgement of shortening that we mentioned applies to the prayer leader and two units during travel. He must pray the complete prayer. Similarly, it was a religious injunction to both the traveller and resident originally. Then, there can be no shortening except as we previously mentioned regarding it. It is impermissible for one to say "The prayer is shortened" except in the manner which we have mentioned regarding shortening. Shortening cannot be approached except in the way that we have explained. One can only say that the prayer has been increased but not that it is shortened except in the manner that we have mentioned. It would be a contradiction in what we were commanded to do. The two units that we were commanded to do during travel and residence was a religious injunction from Allah. Then, He increased it in the prayer of the resident and kept it as two for the traveller. All of that was a religious injunction from Allah. Whoever increases or decreases from that has to repeat the prayer.

Concerning the joining of two prayers during travel

Whoever is in his house during the time that the sun passes its zenith and he intends to travel, he can join the prayers by praying the noon prayer and then the late noon prayer immediately after it. If he wants to pray the voluntary prayers between them, he can do so. If the sun declines while he is travelling, he can delay the noon prayer and continue his journey until the shadow of an object is its size or half its size if he wants. Then, he dismounts and prays the noon and late noon prayers together. Similar has reached us from Allah's Messenger, peace and blessings be upon him and his progeny.[59]

Likewise is done for the sunset and night prayers. One can join them even if one is in his house when the stars of night become visible, but he does not wait until the light of day. If one is on a journey when the red of dawn is visible, one dismounts at the sun's setting or before its setting and join the two prayers.

My father related to me that his father said that the one who joins the prayer can intend to do so before sunset or after it. My father also related to me that his father said that there is no problem in joining the two prayers during travel. He also said:

> We did not accompany the elders of Muhammad's Progeny, upon him be peace, except that we saw that they joined the prayers during travel when the sun descended between noon and afternoon. Similarly, the sunset and night prayers were joined when it was dark; this is general. All of them mentioned that Allah's Messenger, peace and blessings be upon him and his progeny, joined the prayers in the state of residency without sickness or rain.[60] They used to join the prayers when there was rain even when there was no illness or a journey.

Concerning what one can pray on or towards as well as concerning the final salutations, the place and clothing in the prayer

A man can pray in anything except silk.[61] It is discouraged to pray in hide if he does not have anything else with it. It is also discouraged for a man to pray in a garment completely saturated with dye. One does not pray in a garment unless it is ritually pure and cleansed from impurities.

I discourage praying in unknown skins (*khazz*) because I do not know what it is, what animal it is from and the trustworthiness of the manufacturers. I fear that they may have assembled it using the living and the dead as well as the recently killed and the tanned.

I do not prefer that one prostrate on anything other than that which grows from the earth. It is said that whatsoever is permissible to pray in is impermissible to prostrate on. Precaution regarding that is preferable. According to me, the best thing is that one places the forehead on the low part of the earth or any of the herbage from it, such as the papyrus plant, as well as what grows in it like old cotton (*al-kursuf*), linen (*al-kattān*) and other herbs.

My father related to me that his father was asked about coarse wool, felt and similar. He replied:

> It is preferable to me that the one praying place his forehead on the dust or the lowest part of the earth. It is necessary that one prostrate on that which grows from the earth, like herbage and the like. The exception is if one fears injury from extreme heat or cold. Then, one should be God-conscious by what he is wary of and prostrate on what he likes.

---

[59] Similarly narrated in ***Sharh at-Tajrīd, Musnad Ahmed, Sunan Abu Dāwūd, Sunan al-Bayhaqi, Sunan ad-Dārqutni***

[60] Similarly narrated in ***Muwatta, Ŝahīh Muslim, Sunan at-Tirmidhi, Sunan Abu Dāwūd, Musnad Ahmed, Ŝahīh Ibn Hibbān, Sunan an-Nisā'i, Sharh at-Tajrīd***

[61] Although not mentioned here, the imam holds to the view that a man praying in silk blends in which the non-silk material exceeds the amount of silk would be considered permissible. Please refer to the section on clothing. However, in ***Al-Muntakhab***, the imam was asked about a man wearing and praying in silk blends in which silk comprises of half the garment and he permitted such. We reconcile these two views by saying that the imam's ruling in the ***Ahkām*** is based on the independent judgement of Imam Rassi and is more precautionary. However, the imam's later ruling in ***Al-Muntakhab*** reflects more of his own independent judgement.

Regarding prostrating on cotton garments as well as linen, it is valid for people to use. My grandfather, al-Qāsim b. Ibrāhīm, held to this view when he said 'prostrate on what he likes.'

It is not preferable to me that one prostrate on a piece of one's turban. It has been related from the Prophet, peace and blessings be upon him and his progeny, that he prohibited that.[62] If the one prostrating fears extreme heat or cold, fold its side under and prostrate on the piece that was folded under.

My father related to me that his father was asked about prostrating on a piece of one's turban. He replied:

> It is not preferable to me that one prostrates on a piece of one's turban unless one fears injury due to extreme heat or cold. It is encouraged that one places the forehead on the earth and has dust on the face. This is out of debasement to and magnification of Allah.
>
> He is to similarly place his nose on the earth when prostrating. However, if he does not do that with his nose, it would not be any deficiency in his prayer. There is no problem if he uses his garments on the earth due to extreme heat or cold. That has been narrated from Allah's Messenger, peace and blessings be upon him and his progeny.

When the one praying has ended his prayer and intends to pronounce the final salutations, he is to pronounce the final salutations to the right and the final salutations to the left intending the two Angels that Allah mentions are to his right and left. This is the case even if one is praying alone. This is based on what Allah says: **{When the two Receivers receive on the right and left, he utters not a word except that with him is an observer prepared} Q. 50:17-18**). If he is a prayer leader, he is to intend by his salutations the two Angels as well as the believers to the right and left.

As for others who say that the final salutations are only recited once to the right or that one intends the imam when one recites the final salutations—we do not know of that, hold to that view, advocate for that nor see that as factual.

My father related to me that his father was asked about the manner of the final salutations and he replied:

> One is to recite two final salutations—one to the right and one to the left. This is to be done whether there is an imam or not. If one is alone one intends by that the two Angels. If one is in a congregation, one intends the Angels as well as the people praying with him to the right and left. He is to say: *As salāmu alaykum wa rahtmatullah. As salāmu alaykum wa rahtmatullah.*

One does not pray in the houses of latrines based upon what one may come into contact with there. This includes the washings of the major ritually impure and that which is soiled from the impurities of the body. It is those impurities, filth, contaminants, dirt and urine that people are commanded to purify themselves from. If there are places in which there are none of these aforementioned things nor are there any places soiled based upon one's knowledge and not ignorance, there is no problem for the Muslims to pray there or to take a seat there.

As for the graveyards, we do not hold to the view that one can pray there—whether it be dilapidated or furnished. We discourage that—as well as our ancestors—because it is not devoid of the righteous and obedient person buried there nor is it devoid of the disobedient and wicked. Those among the past righteous there and those of obedience to the Glorified are people who are too dignified to be prayed over. Also included among them are those who did not fear Allah, and they diverted from the truth. It is therefore upon Him—the Glorified—to act in accordance to that. Therefore, it is impermissible to pray near him just as it is impermissible to ask for mercy for him. This is because he is a great impurity and an ignoble creation to Allah. Consequently, it is discouraged to pray among the graveyards of the Muslims and around the [dead] believers.

We also hold to the view that one cannot pray in the middle of the road of travellers so as to block the way. This is because the prayer there is a source of harm for the passer-by. It is impermissible for a

[62] Similarly narrated in ***Mušannaf Ibn Abi Shayba, Sunan al-Bayhaqi, Musnad Ahmed***

Muslim to harm the people of Islam. It is something that Allah and His Messenger prohibited. Regarding that, Allah says: **{A mother should not be harmed because of her child, nor should he to whom the child is born be harmed because of his child}** (Q. 2:233) and **{Hold not to them in harm that ye transgress}** (Q. 2:231) and **{…or a debt without harm…}** (Q. 4:12). Regarding that, Allah's Messenger, peace and blessings be upon him and his progeny, said: ((There is no harming or reciprocating harm in Islam)).[63]

My father related to me that his father was asked about the prayer in the middle of the road, in the bathhouses and in the graves. He said:

> As for the outdoor, clean bathhouses where there are no impurities—there is no prohibition with praying there. It is only discouraged to pray in the indoor bathhouses due to impurities. As for the graves—prayer is discouraged there out of respect for its people if they were believers and out of avoidance of the ritual impurity and contamination of its people if they were disbelievers. As for the prayer in the middle of the road—it is only prohibited due to the harm that it may cause to the passer-by. Harming someone is not from the character of the believers. Allah's Messenger, peace and blessings be upon him and his progeny, said: ((There is no harming or reciprocating harm in Islam)).

Concerning praying in leather socks and sandals

There is no problem in praying in leather socks and sandals even if one does not know whether the leather was a result of a disbeliever slaughtering the animal—as long as one did not see any ritual impurities. But if the slaughterer was a disbeliever, Jew, Magian, one who does not know the Most Merciful or one who does not adhere to any religion, it is impermissible to pray in any skins from the animal they slaughtered. We do not hold to the view that that it is religiously permissible for the Muslims to eat from it or take any benefit from it. Similarly, if a drop of its blood were to stain one's clothing or if it were stained by many intoxicants, pus and its urine—it is impermissible to pray in or on that garment.

It is religiously impermissible for one to pray in a synagogue or church due to the ritual impurity of those in both places. They render both ritually impure by their treading upon them as well as by their sweat, bodies and disbelief. This is because it is impermissible for them to enter mosques in which one prays based upon Allah's statement: **{Verily, the idolaters are impure. So, they are not to approach the Holy Mosque after this year}** (Q. 9:28). Allah prevents them from entering the mosques in order to cause one to know of their ritual impurity and contamination. If it is apparent that Allah prevents them from the places of the Muslims' prayers, it is therefore impermissible to pray in the places of the idolaters. This is because they render ritually impure any place where they are. Every place where they enter is rendered ritually impure due to their being there. It is for that reason that we say that it is impermissible to pray in their places.

It is impermissible for a Muslim to make an image on the wall a *qibla* and pray towards it. The exception is if he places something over to cover it or removes it off the wall in front of him.

Concerning counting one's prayers with pebbles or lines and concerning a man who uses the earth for support or counts the numbers of verses in the prayer

There is no problem for a man to draw a line on the earth to enumerate the number of units he performs. Nor is there a problem for him to use stones to count them or the number of verses as long as he does that to remember as a method of thorough examination in his religion and if he fears doubt and forgetfulness in the prayer.[64]

---

[63] Similarly narrated in ***Sharh at-Tajrīd, Musnad Ahmed, Sunan Ibn Mājah, Al-Mustadrak, Sunan al-Bayhaqi, Al-Mu'jam al-Awsat, Muwatta, Usūl al-Kāfi, Bihār al-Anwār***

[64] In ***Al-Muntakhab***, when al-Hādi was asked the reason that such actions do not invalidate the prayer, he responded by saying:

There is no problem for a man to use the earth or a wall for support if he needs something to hoist himself in the prayer due to injury or old age. Similar is narrated from Allah's Messenger, peace and blessings be upon him and his progeny, that he used to lean on a pole in front of him while hoisting himself for the prayer.[65] Today, that pole is in the *qibla* of his mosque in Medina.

Concerning assisting the imam during the prayer and concerning the prayer of the traveller with the resident and the resident with the traveller

If the imam is confused and doubts something in his recitation of Qur'an insomuch that his doubt is extended for a period of time and he cannot seem to remember the recitation, there is no problem for some of the believers to assist him in remembering. This is narrated from the Commander of Believers, may Allah have mercy on and contentment with him.

My father related to me that his father was asked about an imam who was confused in his recitation and stopped. Can one behind him assist him in remembering? He replied:

> If his confusion lasted a period of time, there is no problem for someone behind him to assist him in remembering. There will be no fault on the one assisting him. It has been narrated from the Commander of Believers, 'Ali b. Abi Ṭālib—may Allah have mercy on him—that he used to permit that.[66]

The traveller should not enter upon the prayer of the resident,[67] but there is no problem for the resident to enter upon the prayer of the traveller. We only say that because, according to us, there cannot be final salutations from the follower before that of the imam. He can only pronounce the final salutations after the prayer leader. There is no problem for the prayer leader to pronounce the final salutations and then the follower completes the rest of the prayer after the prayer leader's final salutations.

Have you not considered that the one who catches the noon and late noon prayers with the prayer leader must wait until the prayer leader performs the final salutations before he can complete the last two units in the rest of the prayer? Isn't it impermissible for a resident to pray two units for the noon prayer by himself and then join a congregational prayer to pray his two remaining units and pronounce the final salutations after the two units while the congregation continues their prayer? Since that is impermissible for him to do, we similarly say that the traveller cannot pray behind a resident and then end his prayer with the final salutations before the prayer leader ends his prayer with the final salutations.

I simply said that any action outside of the actions of the prayer discontinues and invalidates it. As for these actions, they are amongst those actions that preserve the prayer and establish their number, bowings and prostrations. Therefore, it is amongst those actions that correct the prayer, not invalidate it. Its preservation and assistance in its establishment when there is a need is not problematic for the one who fears the effects of doubt and the whisperings of Satan as well as from the tribulations associated with such. It would therefore be obligatory for such person to do everything that will help him to remember what has elapsed due to the whisperings of Satan. He would therefore establish what he intended of the prayer out of obedience to the Most Merciful.

[65] Similarly narrated in ***Sharh at-Tajrīd, Sunan Abu Dāwūd, Al-Mustadrak, Sunan al-Bayhaqi***

[66] Similarly narrated in ***Sharh at-Tajrīd, Sunan al-Bayhaqi***

[67] A contrary view is said to have been narrated from Imam al-Hādi in ***Al-Muntakhab***. Imam Yahya related in his ***Al-Intiṣār*** as well as Imam Ibn Murtaḍa in ***Al-Bahr*** that al-Hādi held to two different views regarding the permissibility of the prayer of the traveller behind the resident: the view from the ***Ahkām*** that it is impermissible and the view from ***Al-Muntakhab*** that it is permissible. However, upon close scrutiny of this claim, it is evident that the two imams erred. This is because in all extant copies of ***Al-Muntakhab***, al-Hādi is reported to have said that it is impermissible for the traveller to pray behind the resident. It is possible that the aforementioned imams utilised a manuscript of the text, which had an error. Even if we were to assume that the manuscripts in our possession are flawed and those in the aforementioned imams' possession were correct, it would still be possible to reconcile the two seemingly different views by saying that al-Hādi's judgement regarding the impermissibility of the traveller praying behind the resident refers to the four-unit prayers which are shortened. And his judgement regarding its permissibility refers to the two- and three-unit prayers which are not shortened. This reconciliation was also articulated by Imam Abu Ṭālib in his ***At-Tahrīr***. [Ref. ***Al-Qawl al-Awwal wa ath-Thāni lil-Imam al-Hādi***]

My father related to me that his father was asked whether the traveller could enter the prayer of the resident and whether the resident can enter the prayer of the traveller. He replied:

> We do not hold to the view that the traveller can pray behind the residents because his religious obligation is different to theirs and his judgement is different to theirs. If the resident enters upon the prayer of travellers, he is to complete his prayer after the travellers pronounce the final salutations.

Concerning the eclipse prayer: solar and lunar

The best of what we heard concerning the eclipse prayer is that it consists of ten bowings with four prostrations. The explanation of that is that the prayer leader stands and the people select him due to his scrupulousness. He then declares Allah's greatness and recites *Al-Hamd* (Q. 1) as well as *Al-Ikhlāŝ* (Q. 112) and *Al-Falaq* (Q. 113) seven times. After which, he bows and then raises his head and recites *Al-Hamd* (Q. 1) as well as *Al-Ikhlāŝ* (Q. 112) and *Al-Falaq* (Q. 113) seven times. After which, he bows and then raises his head and repeats what he recited before. He is to do this five times—reciting what we mentioned in each unit. After doing this for five bowings, he is to prostrate with two prostrations.

Afterwards, he stands, recites and bows. Then, he recites and bows continuously until he has completed the last five bowings. He is to recite what he recited in the first set of bowings. Then, he is to prostrate with two prostrations, recite the testimony of faith, pronounce the final salutations and then remain in his place. He is to increase in seeking forgiveness, supplications, reciting *Lā ilaha ila Allah* and declaring Allah's greatness.

One is to listen out of scrupulousness; he is to not yell it loudly. He is to supplicate for those present, including himself and the Muslims. He is to ask Allah to complete the desired of every blessing, avert from him the detested of every wrath and then he departs.

This which we have mentioned regarding the recitation in the eclipse prayer is not mentioned on the authority of anyone; rather, I hold it to be the best and the choicest. As for the number of bowings, it has been narrated. My father related to me that his father was asked about the eclipse prayer and he replied:

> There is difference in opinion regarding that but all of them are possible. It has been narrated that the Prophet, peace and blessings be upon him and his progeny, used to pray six units with four prostrations.[68] Other than that has also been mentioned. However, this is not authentically attributed to him according to us.[69]
>
> It has also been narrated that 'Ali b. Abi Ťālib, upon him be peace, used to pray the eclipse prayer with ten bowings and four prostrations. According to us, this narration is authentic.[70] He certainly would not have done that unless he took it from Allah's Messenger, peace and blessings be upon him and his progeny.[71]

Concerning the rain prayer

The most preferable and choicest prayer for seeking rain is that the Muslims who are suffering from drought in the city depart to a public square in their city. Then, they gather and place a prayer leader in front of them. They are to pray four units with him pronouncing the final salutations after every two units. They recite in every unit *Al-Hamd* (Q. 1) and *An-Nasr* (Q. 110) along with three verses from *Al-Furqān* (Q. 25) **{And He is the one who sends wind as glad tidings before His mercy, and We**

---

[68] Similarly narrated in ***Ŝahīh Muslim, Musnad Ahmed, Ŝahīh Ibn Khuzayma***

[69] There are reports that mention four bowings and four prostrations in ***Ŝahīh al-Bukhāri, Ŝahīh Muslim, Sunan an-Nisā'i, Musnad Ahmed***. There are also reports that mention that it consists of eight bowings and four prostrations in ***Musnad Ahmed, Ŝahīh Muslim, Sunan an-Nisā'i, Sunan al-Bayhaqi***

[70] Similarly narrated in ***Majmu' Imam Zayd, Sharh at-Tajrīd, Sunan al-Bayhaqi***

[71] The same is narrated from the Prophet in ***Musnad Ahmed, Sunan Abu Dāwūd, Sunan at-Tirmidhi, Al-Mu'jam al-Awsaṫ, Al-Mustadrak***

send down from the heavens pure water that We may bring life thereby to a dead land and provide as drink to those of many livestock and man We created. And We hath verily distributed it amongst them that they may remember. Yet, most men are naught but ungrateful} **(Q. 25:48-50)** and the last part of *Al-Hashr* (Q. 59) from the verse **{Not equal are the companions of the Fire and the companions of Paradise. The companions of Paradise are the triumphant...}** **(Q. 59:20)** until the end of the *surah*.

When one has prayed the four units and recited what we mentioned of the verses, one is to seek Allah's forgiveness and seek it for the Muslims. They are to persist in supplications and the asking for mercy and forgiveness. They are to renew their repentance with Allah and ask Him to accept their repentance. They are to seek forgiveness for any past misdeeds and the prayer leader is to say:

> O Allah! It is only to You that we call and aim. It is You that we seek from, and it is by Your Mercy that we present ourselves to You. You are our God, Master, Creator and our Merciful Benefactor. Do not frustrate our calls to You! Do not cut off our hopes in You! Verily, You are the Most Merciful of the Merciful!

Then he flips part of his cloak that was on his right onto his left and the part of his cloak that was on his left onto his right. He then departs and the people depart with him to their homes. On the way, they recite from the Qur'an. They recite *Yā Sīn* (Q. 36) until the end of it and then say seven times: "There is no strength or power except by Allah, the Exalted and the Great! Upon Him do we place our trust. He is the Lord of the Great Throne!" They then recite the last verse of *Al-Baqara* (Q. 2).

Concerning the Eid prayers and what is done in them

It is obligatory upon the imam—when it is the day of breaking the fast—to depart to the public square of his city or to the side. He is to then pray two units with the people. He recites *Al-Hamd* (Q. 1) and another *surah* of the Qur'an in the first unit. He then declares Allah's greatness seven times saying in every declaration: *Allahu Akbar kabīra. Al-hamdulillahi kathīra. Subhana Allah bukra wa aṣīla.* (Tr. "Allah is the Greatest over all. Abundant praise is due to Allah. Glorified be Allah in the morning and late noon.")

He bows and then stands and prostrates twice. He returns to the standing position and recites *Al-Hamd* (Q. 1) and another *surah*. He then declares Allah's greatness five times like the declaration he made in the beginning. He then bows, lifts his head and prostrates twice. After which, he recites the testimony of faith and pronounces the final salutations. At the end of the prayer, he declares Allah's greatness thrice and then rises.

He ascends to his riding beast or a pulpit and addresses the people with a sermon. He declares Allah's greatness nine times before he addresses the people and after he completes it, he declares Allah's greatness seven times. He instructs the people in what they need to know concerning the fast-breaking dues (*fitr*) and teaches then that it is the Sunnah of their Prophet. He emphasises to them that it is binding and religiously obligatory upon them. He commands them to observe it by distributing it to the free poor among them, as well as to the slaves—young and old. He reminds them how much it should be and its obligatory amount upon the men among them. It is a *ṣā'* of dates, corn, barley, yoghurt or wheat.

The people can distribute to their poor any staple that they eat and have earned. Similar is the case with lentils, chickpeas, cottage cheese or green beans if the people of that place eat it and use it as a means of earning. They are not held responsible for what they cannot find or extract from other than what they earn because Allah says: **{Allah burdens not a soul except with what it can bear}** **(Q. 2:286)** and **{...except with what He hath given it}** **(65:7)**.

Allah's Messenger, peace and blessings be upon him and his progeny, has said regarding the charge of slaves: ((Fear Allah regarding the one whom your right hands own. Feed them with what you eat and clothe them with what you wear)).[72] He, peace and blessings be upon him and his progeny, commanded that the slaves be fed with what their masters eat. Similarly, we say that it is religiously obligatory for one to use as one's dues that which one earns for oneself.

When the imam has completed the sermon, he is to sit briefly and then deliver a second sermon. In it, he is to praise Allah, the Exalted Lord. Then, he declares Allah's greatness seven times and dismounts. Afterwards, he departs, as do the Muslims with him.

In the case of the prayer of the Eid of the Sacrifice, the prayer is before the sermon just as the Eid of the Fast-Breaking. There is no call to prayer or pre-prayer call just as the Eid of the Fast-Breaking. One declares Allah's greatness in the two units of the Eid of the Sacrifice in the same manner that one declares Allah's greatness in the Eid of the Fast-Breaking—seven [in the first unit] and then five times [in the second unit]. Then he ascends the riding beast or pulpit and declares Allah's greatness nine times. Afterwards, he begins the sermon and addresses the people. He inserts in his speech the declaration of Allah's greatness by saying:

> *Allahu Akbar*! *Allahu Akbar*! *Lā ilaha ila Allah*! *Allahu Akbar kabīra*! *Al-hamdulillahi kathīra 'ala ma a'tānā wa awlānā wa ahala lanā min bahayma al-'anām*! (Tr. "Allah is the Greatest! Allah is the Greatest! There is no god but Allah! Allah is the Greatest over all! Abundant praise is due to Allah for what He has given us, appointed for us and made permissible for us from cattle!")

Then he returns to the place where he ended the sermon and continues speaking. He pauses to declare Allah's greatness and then returns to his speech until he has declared Allah's greatness three times in his sermon. When the imam has completed the sermon, he is to sit briefly and then stand to deliver a second sermon. He declares Allah's greatness seven times and then descends.

Concerning what the imam does during the Pilgrimage, how he prays, how many prayers he prays, where he delivers the sermon and what he says during the sermon

The imam must address the people in Mecca before the *tarwiya* that day. He must explain to them their rites and teach them on the day of their Pilgrimage. He must explain to them the defects of their sacrifices that are discouraged and command them to observe all of the rites—their manner, method and the state of pilgrim sanctity.

Then he is to address them on the Day of 'Arafat [i.e. the ninth of Dhul-Hijja]. He is to command and prohibit them. He is to make them to observe what is religiously obligatory for them to observe. He is to make it audible for one to hear and keep his speech short. He is to insert the *talbiya* in his sermon saying:

> *Labayk Allāhumma labayk. labayk lā sharīka laka labayk. Inna al-hamda wan- ni'mata laka wal-mulk. Lā sharīka lak.* (Tr. "I am at Your service, O Allah. I am at Your service. You have no partners. I am at Your service. Verily, the praise and blessings belong to You, as well as the dominion. You have no partners.")

Then, he is to return to his topic in the sermon, pause to recite the *talbiya* and then return to the sermon. Afterwards, he pauses to recite the *talbiya* and return to the sermon. He recites the *talbiya* three, five or seven times—depending upon the length of the sermon.

Concerning the joining of the Eid with the Friday prayer

When the Eid falls on a Friday—one can be present for the Friday congregational prayer if one desires, or one could forfeit it due to one's presence at the Eid prayer and sermon if one desires. Similar has reached us from Allah's Messenger that when the two Eids were joined during his time,

---

[72] Similarly narrated in ***Majmu' Imam Zayd, Amāli Abi Ťālib, Ŝahīh Muslim, Musnad Ahmed, Al-Mu'jam al-Kabīr, Bihār al-Anwār***

he prayed the Eid prayer with the people and addressed them saying: ((One can come to the Friday congregational prayer if one wants or one does not have to come if one wants)).[73]

Whoever bathes for the Eid prayer when it is joined with the Friday congregational prayer and intends thereby the Eid and congregational prayer—that bath would be sufficient for the bath on Friday. The purification wash on Fridays is not religiously obligatory. Allah's Messenger, peace and blessings be upon him and his progeny, only ordered it upon his Companions because they used to be covered in dust and sweat while working. Then the time for the Friday congregational prayer would come and they would be present for the prayer while in that state. They would be crowded together and the smell of the dust and sweat would emanate among them. Some of them would abuse others due to this. Therefore, Allah's Messenger, peace and blessings be upon him and his progeny, commanded them to bathe on Friday and they did it. Consequently, that odour disappeared and they used the water to remove from them what caused them to smell.[74]

The Friday congregational prayer is obligatory upon all Muslims except the child, woman, slave and ill person [as well as the traveller and prisoner. Ref. ***At-Tāj***]. Whoever among them is able to attend, such person can attend. This is good, but it is not religiously obligatory for such person.

The covering of the women is the best for rectifying affairs, and their remaining in their houses renders the greatest reward. My father related to me from his father all the way to the Prophet, peace and blessings be upon him and his progeny: ((Women are weak (*'iyyun*) and deficient; therefore, approach their weakness by means of silence and their deficiency by means of the houses)).[75]

Concerning whether it is permissible for one who performed the dust purification due to not finding water to lead those who performed the ritual ablution in prayer

It is impermissible for one who has performed the dust purification to lead in prayer those who have performed the water purification. Similar has been related to us from Allah's Messenger, peace and blessings be upon him and his progeny: ((The one who has performed the dust purification does not lead in prayer the one who performed the ritual ablution with water)).

It has also reached us that the Commander of Believers, 'Ali b. Abi Ťālib—may Allah be merciful to him—said: "The one with dust purification cannot lead in prayer those with the ritual ablution."[76]

---

[73] Similarly narrated in ***Majmu' Imam Zayd, Musnad Ahmed, Sunan Abu Dāwūd, Sunan an-Nisā'i, Sunan Ibn Māja***

[74] Similarly narrated in ***Majmu' Imam Zayd, Sharh at-Tajrīd, Amāli Abi Ťālib, Ŝahīh al-Bukhāri, Al-Muwatta, Sunan an-Nisā'i***

[75] Similarly narrated in ***Sharh at-Tajrīd, Amāli al-Murshid Billah, Bihār al-Anwār***. Commenting on this hadith in the footnotes, Dr Murtaḍa al-Muhatwary (d. 2015 CE) said:

> The said narration does not agree with the Qur'an and the intellect according to the principles of the *madhhab*. As for the Qur'an, Allah says: {**And the believing men and believing women are guardians one to another. They command the good and forbid the evil. They establish the prayer and render the purification dues, and they obey Allah and His Messenger. And Allah shall have mercy upon them. Verily, Allah is Almighty and Most-Wise**} (**Q. 9:71**). If they [i.e. the women] were weak and deficient in the absolute sense, they would not be held responsible for commanding the good and forbidding the evil like men.
>
> As for the intellect, they are similar to men without any differences except in femininity, and men have deficiencies also. Women are obligated to cover their bodies because of their enchantment and temptation insomuch that men are commanded to lower their gazes. Women are also commanded to do so.
>
> As for the Sunnah, they were present with the Prophet in the mosque, in wars and all situations. Regarding the Mother of Believers, Khadīja; as well as her daughter, [Fātima] az-Zahrā; az-Zahrā's daughter, Zaynab; as well as the daughters of al-Hussein, they are examples of strong and powerful women despite modesty as well as played their part in their service to Islam and Muslims. And Allah knows best!

Other scholars reply by saying that the narration is not at all incongruent with the principles of the *madhhab* because the imams who narrated this hadith, such as al-Hādi, al-Murshid Billah and al-Mu`ayyad Billah, all similarly held the Qur'an and intellect as the barometer to judge its authenticity, yet they had not criticised it nor subjected it to scrutiny based on its text.

[76] Similarly narrated in ***Majmu' Imam Zayd, Sharh at-Tajrīd, Sunan ad-Dārqutni, Sunan al-Bayhaqi***

Concerning the prayer of the nude with the clothed and the prayer of the seated with the standing

The nude person does not lead the clothed person in prayer, nor does the seated person lead the standing person in prayer. That is because Allah has placed more virtue in the covering of nakedness and more virtue in praying standing over sitting.

It has been narrated that Allah's Messenger, peace and blessings be upon him and his progeny, said to his Companions when he was sick and led them in the prayer while he was sitting: ((The prayer of the one seated is half that of the one standing)).[77]

Concerning the urging to pray the voluntary night prayers

It is encouraged for the one who can and has the strength and health to not neglect praying eight units in the last part of the night. One is to pray them in twos and recite what is easy from the Qur'an in every unit. In this is great virtue and the best of this world and the hereafter. Regarding that, it has reached us that Allah's Messenger, peace and blessings be upon him and his progeny, said: ((Whoever prays eight units in the night—other than the *witr* prayer—and he continues doing so until he meets Allah—Allah will open for him twelve doors of Paradise)).[78]

It has also reached us that Allah's Messenger, peace and blessings be upon him and his progeny, said: ((Two units of prayer in the last half of the night is better than the world and whatever is in it. Had it not been a difficulty upon my *Ummah*, I would have made the both of them binding upon them)).[79]

It is encouraged for one who has the strength to do so even if he is upon the back of a riding beast.[80] He is to gesture and his prostrations should be lower than his bowings. If he can, he turns his face towards the *qibla*. If he was on his riding beast, he turns his riding beast towards it.

As for the religiously obligatory prayers, the earth is the earth [i.e. one is to pray on the ground] unless there is a great hardship in doing so or there is fear to the body. If that is the case, Allah does not burden a soul except with what it can bear. As the Blessed and Exalted says: **{Allah desires ease for thee, and He desires not hardship for thee...}** (Q. 2:185) and **{Allah burdens not a soul except with what it can bear}** (Q. 2:286). The Blessed and Exalted means by the phrase **{what it can bear}**: its capacity and what it can do. It has reached us from Allah's Messenger, peace and blessings be upon him and his progeny, that he used to pray the voluntary prayers on the back of his riding beast in the direction that it faced.[81]

---

[77] Similarly narrated in ***Sharh at-Tajrīd, Amāli Abi Ťālib, Al-Muwaťťa, Sunan at-Tirmidhi, Musnad Ahmed, Sunan ad-Dārimi, Sunan an-Nisā'i, Sunan Ibn Mājah, Mušannaf Ibn Abi Shayba, Kanz al-'Ummāl, Majmu' az-Zawā'id, Al-Mu'jam al-Kabīr, Al-Mu'jam al-Awsaṫ***

[78] Similarly narrated in ***Musnad Imam Zayd, Amāli Ahmed b. 'Isa, Al-Jāmi' al-Kāfi, Amāli Abi Ťālib***. In the ***Majmu'***, it says ((…eight doors of Paradise)); however, the other texts mention ((…twelve doors…)). It is also narrated that the Prophet prayed eight voluntary units in texts such as ***Musnad Ahmed, Sunan an-Nisā'i, Ŝahīh Ibn Khuzayma***

[79] Similarly narrated in ***Musnad Imam Zayd*** with the wording ((…the last third of the night…)). Also narrated in ***Amāli Ahmed b. 'Isa*** with the wording: ((…last part of the night…))

[80] According to ***Al-Muntakhab***, al-Hādi stated that the minimum number of supererogatory prayers that one should perform is the two-unit prayer before the dawn prayer, two units after the noon prayer, two units after the sunset prayer and three units of witr. However, he says, one is not obligated to observe these prayers and must do that which is according to one's ability.

[81] Similarly narrated in ***Musnad Imam Zayd, Sharh at-Tajrīd, Ŝahīh al-Bukhāri, Ŝahīh Muslim, Sunan Abu Dāwūd, Ŝahīh Ibn Khuzayma***

Concerning the prayer of the imam for the Eid and the Friday congregational prayer during travel and the declaration of Allah's greatness for the two Eids

When the imam is on a journey as well as those with him and the Friday congregational prayer or one of the Eids occur in the villages of the Muslims, he should join in, pray and address the Muslims. He prays two units for the Friday prayer.

Likewise, I say that it is religiously obligatory for the people of the village and springs if there is a congregation and a mosque in the village. The Friday congregation prayer is religiously obligatory upon them, and they are to choose an imam for themselves to deliver the sermon and pray with them.

I hold to the view that it is only religiously obligatory upon them if the imam that they supplicate for and mention in their sermons is a just and rightful imam for whom the imamate is permissible. This is because Allah has commanded that all people rush towards the Friday congregation prayer and did not make an exception. He says: **{O ye who believe, when the call to prayer is made on the day of congregation, rush towards the remembrance of Allah and leave trade. It is better for thee if ye only but knew} (Q. 62:19)**.[82]

As for the declaration of Allah's greatness for the Eid of Breaking the Fast, it takes place when the imam departs to deliver the sermon. As for the declaration of Allah's greatness for the Eid of the Sacrifice, it is from the dawn prayer on the Day of 'Arafat to the late noon prayer in the last days of *Tashrīq*. It is the day of the great sacrifice. Likewise has reached us from the Commander of Believers, 'Ali b. Abi Ṭālib—may Allah be merciful to him—that he used to do that.[83]

My father related to me that his father was asked about the declaration of Allah's greatness, and he said: "It is from the dawn prayer on the Day of 'Arafat to the late noon prayer in the last days of sacrifice."

The declaration of Allah's greatness is at the end of every obligatory and supererogatory prayer. It is that one says: *Allāhu Akbar. Allāhu Akbar. Lā ilāha ila Allāh. Wa Allāhu Akbar kabīra. Wa alhamdulillāhi kathīra wa subhāna Allahi bukratan wa aṡīla.*

Concerning when two men intend to make the other one the prayer leader while he does not know

If each of the two men choose the other to lead the prayer while the one he chose is ignorant of that and the two of them pray, their prayers would be sound. Even if each of the two of them did not intend to lead the other in the prayer, their prayers would be sound. We only say that because we do not find that either of them prayed by himself without designating the other to lead. That withstanding, we say that their prayers would be sound. When each of them designated the other as the leader while

[82] This statement of al-Hādi emphasises the established principle that the Friday congregational prayer is invalid without the manifestation of a just imam of the Muslims. He further elucidates this point in his replies to a series of questions posed to him as recorded in the ***Muntakhab***:

> I asked: "Is it permissible for a man to pray two units of the Friday congregational prayer with the people if he is not under the jurisdiction of the imam?" He [i.e. al-Hādi] replied: "If the man is in a land far from the imam but still calls and urges to him, he would be permitted to pray [i.e. the Friday congregational prayer] with the people." "What if he is unable to supplicate for the imam in the sermon, but only able to supplicate for the people of uprightness and truth?" "If he does so intending thereby the imam, it [i.e. the prayer] would be permissible." "What if a man who was appointed by the imam to pray was addressing the people with a sermon on the pulpit and then the news came to him that the imam had died while the former was on the pulpit? Should he pray the two units with the people?" "Yes. This is because when he began the prayer, the time had already entered while he was under his [i.e. the imam's] jurisdiction." "What if a man intends to pray the Friday congregational prayer with the people before the manifestation of the imam while he advocates for the just imam? Is he to pray the two-unit prayer with the people?" "The two-unit Friday congregational prayer is not obligatory without the establishment of a just and rightful imam."

This judgement is further emphasised by the statement of Imam al-Mu`ayyad Billah, who states in his ***Sharh at-Tajrīd*** that the judgement regarding the invalidity of the Friday congregational prayer without a just imam is 'the madhhab of Ahl al-Bayt.' This indicates their consensus.

[83] Similarly narrated in ***Musnad Imam Zayd, Sharh at-Tajrīd, Amāli Abi Ṭālib, Muṡannaf Ibn Abi Shayba, Sunan al-Bayhaqi***

believing in the prayer of the other, he made him the imam within himself. He intended by such the belief in the sittings, bowings, prostrations and standings of the other.

If the both of them did not believe that the other was the leader of the prayer, their prayers would be invalid because the both of them did not pray for themselves individually nor did one of them lead the other. The intention for each of them is that the follower relies on his brother even if the brother was not aware of that. That withstanding, we say that their prayers would not be sound.

This is the case even if the following were to occur: A man had prayed the noon prayer and entered upon the prayer leader praying with the congregation to pray a voluntary prayer with them. Then, the prayer leader's ritual purity was invalidated by an impure occurrence. The man who had already prayed was placed forward to lead in the prayer leader's place due to his piety. However, it was not known that despite leading them in the prayer, he was praying a voluntary prayer. Their prayer would be invalid because they unknowingly made a person praying his voluntary prayers their prayer leader while they were praying their obligatory prayers.

One does not make one a leader of the obligatory prayers unless that person is praying that obligatory prayer. As for the one who is praying other than that, he is to not be made the prayer leader. It is therefore religiously obligatory upon them that they place someone else forward to lead if they come to know of that. They must repeat the prayer and not count it.

The Book of Funeral Rites (*Al-Janā`iz*)

In the Name of Allah, the Most Gracious, the Most Merciful...

The beginning of the chapters regarding funeral rites

The one to whom death approaches should appoint an executor of his will and bear witness to his appointment. The beginning of his appointment should include the wording of what Allah decrees as a testimony of truth:

> In the Name of Allah, the Most Gracious, the Most Merciful. This is what I appoint to so-n-so, the son of so-n-so to bequeath. It is that I bear witness that there is no god but Allah, the One with whom are no partners. And I bear witness that Muhammad is His slave and messenger, peace and blessings be upon him and his progeny. He was sent with guidance and the religion of Truth so that he could warn those that were alive and prove true the word against the disbelievers.
>
> O Allah, I bear witness to You, and sufficient for me is You as a Witness! I also bear witness to the Bearers of Your Throne, the people of Your heavens and Your earth, as well as that which You created, formed and measured that You are Allah. There is no god but You. You are One and have no partners. I also bear witness that Muhammad is Your slave and messenger. I also bear witness that the Hour is coming and there is no doubt in it and that Allah will resurrect the dead from the tombs. I am saying it along with the one who says thus and make it sufficient against the one who rejects its acceptance. There is no power and strength except by means of Allah, the Exalted and the Great!
>
> O Allah, to the one who testified to what was testified to him, write his testimony along with my testimony. As for the one who rejected any of it, write my testimony in the place of his testimony. Make it for me a sound contract on the Day of meeting You. Verily, You do not act contrary to what You promised.

This resembles the bequest of the Commander of Believers, 'Ali b. Abi Ṫālib, upon him be peace.[1]

Then, one faces his lying cushion in the direction of the *qibla* and says:

> O Allah! Bless me in death and after death. I am not among the idolaters. Facilitate for me the extraction of my soul and make easy for me my difficulty. My affair is by means of Allah's Name, by Allah and upon the path of Allah's Messenger, peace and blessings be upon him and his progeny, as an upright Muslim.

Then, one can bequeath anything else one wills. One is not permitted to bequeath a third of another's wealth except with the permission of his heir. Afterwards, he testifies to the bequest and gives it to a reliable person to distribute it after his death.

Concerning turning the corpse toward the *qibla*

The best place to turn the corpse is towards the *qibla.* According to me, it is best for him to urge the dead to recite *Lā ilaha ila Allah* at the time of death and bathe him on his back. He should also face him towards the *qibla* and turn both of his feet towards the *qibla* so that his face faces it completely.

It is religiously impermissible for one to wail or yell over him. It is also religiously impermissible to slap or scratch one's cheeks and rip one's pockets. It has reached us from Allah's Messenger, peace and blessings be upon him and his progeny, that he used to strongly prohibit that. He, peace and

[1] Similarly narrated in ***Amāli Ahmed B. Isa***

blessings be upon him and his progeny, said: ((Eyes may tear and hearts may rend, but we do not say that which angers the Lord)).[2]

It has also reached us from Allah's Messenger, peace and blessings be upon him and his progeny:

> ((There are two sounds that are evil and accursed in this world and the next: the sound of affliction when one rips the pockets and scratches the face with the chime of Satan and also the sound of blessings when one plays the flutes of Satan)).[3]

Concerning the reward of bathing the dead and hastening to bury

It has reached us from Allah's Messenger, peace and blessings be upon him and his progeny, that he used to say:

> ((The Muslim male does not bathe his Muslim brother without soiling him, looking at his private parts or mentioning evil about him and then prays over him except that his sins are rendered void as the latter is placed in his tomb)).[4]

The one who died in the beginning of the day should not be housed in any place except his tomb. It is preferable to us that the one who died at the beginning of the night not be delayed until the morning before being placed in the tomb unless it has drowned, was mutilated, or contracted leprosy. It is preferable to us that they be delayed. It has reached us from Allah's Messenger, peace and blessings be upon him and his progeny, that he did similar.[5]

Concerning the bathing and shrouding of Allah's Messenger

It has reached us from the Commander of Believers, 'Ali b. Abi Ṫālib, upon him be peace:

> When I went to bathe Allah's Messenger, peace and blessings be upon him and his progeny, I heard someone call out from the side of the house, "Do not remove the shirt!" We bathed Allah's Messenger, peace and blessings be upon him and his progeny, with his shirt on. Verily, I saw myself as bathing him, and a hand other than mine would turn him; I was being assisted in turning him. Verily, I wanted to turn him completely over yet someone called out to me that I should not turn him over.[6]

It has also reached us from him that he said: "I shrouded Allah's Messenger, peace and blessings be upon him and his progeny, in three garments: two Yemeni garments—a worn garment and a shirt that he used to beautify himself with."[7]

It is encouraged for the one who bathed the dead to perform the purification wash. Similar has reached us from 'Ali, upon him be peace. My father related to me that his father was asked whether the one who bathed the dead should perform the purification wash. He replied: "Yes. The one who bathed the dead should perform the purification wash. This is a statement from 'Ali, upon him be peace, as well as other than him from among the Companions and Followers."[8]

---

[2] Similarly narrated in ***Amāli Ahmed b. 'Isa, Ŝahīh al-Bukhāri, Ŝahīh Muslim, Sunan at-Tirmidhi, Sunan Abu Dāwūd, Sunan al-Bayhaqi, Sunan Ibn Mājah, Musnad Ahmed, Mušannaf Ibn Abi Shayba, Al-Mu'jam al-Kabīr, Al-Mu'jam al-Awsaṫ, Ušūl al-Kāfi, Bihār al-Anwār***

[3] Similarly narrated in ***Sunan al-Bayhaqi*** and ***Majmu' az-Zawā'id.*** Ibn Hajar said in the latter book: "Al-Bazzār narrated it and his narrators are reliable."

[4] Similarly narrated in ***Musnad Imam Zayd, Amāli Abi Ṫālib, Sunan Ibn Mājah, Sunan al-Bayhaqi, Al-Mustadrak***

[5] Sheikh 'Ali b. Bilāl related in his Sharh al-Ahkām that Allah's Messenger, peace and blessings be upon him and his progeny, said: ((It is from the ennobling of the deceased to hasten its burial)). Similar is narrated in ***Sharh at-Tajrīd*** and ***Al-Mu'jam al-Kabīr***

[6] Similarly narrated in ***Musnad Imam Zayd*** and ***Amāli Ahmed b. 'Isa***

[7] Similarly narrated in ***Musnad Imam Zayd, Sunan Abu Dāwūd, Sunan Ibn Mājah, Sunan al-Bayhaqi***

[8] Sheikh 'Ali b. Bilāl reported in his ***Sharh at-Ahkām*** that it was related to him from Sayyid Abul-Abbās al-Hasani narrated with a complete chain of narrators to 'Ali: "Whoever bathes the dead should perform the purification wash similar to that for major ritual impurity." He narrated similar with another chain of narrators to Zayd b. 'Ali—his father—his grandfather—'Ali, upon them be peace. It is also narrated in ***Musnad Imam Zayd, Sharh at-Tajrīd, Sunan Ibn Mājah*** and ***Sunan al-Bayhaqi.***

Concerning the one who dies while travelling with a non-marriageable person and concerning the man and his wife who travels and one of them dies

If a man were to die among women or a woman were to die among men, and there is a non-marriageable person with either of them—such person is to clothe them in a sarong and pour out water on them and wash their bodies with their hands. However, one is to not rub over the private parts; one simply pours water over them. Similar is the case if a man were to die during travel and his wife accompanied him or a woman were to die and her husband accompanied her.

There is no problem with a man bathing his wife and a woman bathing her husband. The both of them should be cautious about looking at the private parts. Verily, 'Ali, upon him be peace, bathed Fāṭima, the daughter of Allah's Messenger, Allah's blessings be upon him and her.[9]

My father related to me that his father was asked about a man whose daughter died during travel and there are no women present. He replied: "He should bathe her and refrain from looking at her private parts."

My father also related to me that his father was asked if a man could bathe his wife and if a woman could bathe her husband. He replied: "There is no problem with that because 'Ali, upon him be peace, bathed Fatima, the daughter of Allah's Messenger, may Allah's blessings be upon him and the choicest of their progeny."

Concerning a woman who dies during travel and there is no non-marriageable person with her or no one else to bathe her

If a woman died and she was accompanied by an unrelated man and there were no non-marriageable people with her, one is to simply pour water over her body without uncovering her arms, feet or hair. If a man died amongst unrelated women, they are to simply pour water over him.[10]

Concerning what one does with a martyr

If a martyr died in the battlefield, one is to bury him in the clothes he died in. This excludes leather socks, belt or pelt. One is to remove them or their pants unless they were soiled with his blood. In that case, he is to be buried in them.

He is to not be bathed if he died in the battlefield. If he was around the battlefield in which he was struck and there was a little life left in him, one is to do to him what one would do with any other dead body—bathe him, shroud him, pray over him and bury him. Similarly, one is to pray over the martyr because he is most deserving of prayer and purification. They are the people of forgiveness and blessings.

My father related to me that his father was asked if the martyr is bathed. He replied: "If the martyr died in the battlefield, he is not bathed. If he was moved and there was still a little life in him and then he died, one does with him what one would do to any other dead body."

My father related to me that his father was asked if the martyr is prayed over or not. He replied:

> The martyr is prayed over because the Prophet, peace and blessings be upon him and his

---

[9] Similarly narrated in ***Sharh at-Tajrīd, Sunan al-Bayhaqi, Bihār al-Anwār***

[10] In the ***Muntakhab***, it is reported that when al-Hādi was asked about bathing an unrelated woman whose relatives are not accessible, he replied:

> Others, such as Sufyān and others, say that one is to perform the dust purification on her. However, we do not acknowledge their statement regarding that. Rather, we hold to the view that she is to be bathed with water above her clothes and her clothes on her are to be cleansed along with her. If it is possible to perform such without looking at her in order to shroud her, one must do it. Otherwise, they should try to do the bathing by pouring water over the clothes until the water reaches her body. And that which is under her clothes that she has washed in cleanliness is to be purified, inserted into her shrouds and buried.

progeny, prayed over his uncle al-Hamza,§ may Allah be satisfied with him.[11] He declared Allah's greatness over him seventy times. Some people lifted him and others placed him down. Al-Hamza was placed down and he declared Allah's greatness over him and upon the others who were martyred with him on the day of Uhud.

Whoever does not observe the prayer over the martyr is a deviant innovator. Who is more deserving of the prayer and mercy than the martyr?

Concerning the prayer over the stillborn, the one burned by fire, the drowning victim and the one who was stoned

If a baby dies after childbirth, one prays over it and does with it what one would do over any other dead body. Its inheritance is distributed and it is named. If it died before childbirth, one should not do any of the above. The sign of its life is its yell. If four women bear witness to that or if two upright believing women do so, its judgement would be considered that of a stillborn.

If someone died from being burned with fire and water would afflict the body, one is not to touch the skin if one fears that it would be damaged. As for the one who died by drowning, one is to bathe it just as one would bathe another dead body. One is to also pray over them, shroud them and do with them what one does with other dead Muslims. As for the one who was stoned and it is known that such person was religious, there is no disagreement from the Muslim *Ummah* that such person is to be bathed, shrouded and prayed over.

As for the one who was stoned openly and forgiveness and repentance was heard from such person—one is to seek forgiveness for him when one prays at his funeral. One can pray over such person out of fear (*al-mudārāt*) if one needs to. However, if one does not need to due to fear, one does not pray over him and one is to refrain from seeking forgiveness for a person who died upon sin and had not repented to his Lord.

My father related to me that his father was asked whether one is to pray over a stoned person. He replied:

> As for the one to whom repentance was established, there is no disagreement that one is to pray over and shroud such individual as well as do with them what one would do with other dead Muslims. Similar is narrated from Allah's Messenger, peace and blessings be upon him and his progeny. He commanded that to be done with Mā'iz b. Mālik al-Aslami§ when he was stoned.[12]
>
> The same is also narrated from the Commander of Believers, 'Ali b. Abi Ṫālib, upon him be peace, when a woman from Hamadhān was stoned. He commanded that she be shrouded, washed and prayed over.
>
> As for the one who was stoned openly, there are some who say that he is to be prayed over and there are some who say that he should not be prayed over because the prayer is the seeking of mercy and forgiveness. Whoever persists in a major sin that obligates the Hellfire—one is to not pray over such person because he is condemned if he did not repent. He is to be condemned just as what was narrated from al-Hussein b. 'Ali, upon him be peace, and his supplications against Sa'īd b. al-A'š§ when he died. Also, Allah says in response to the opponents of such view: **{...and pray not over any of them who died, and stand not over their tomb} (Q. 9:84)**.

My father related to me that his father was asked about bathing the one who drowned. He replied: "The drowned victim is to be bathed like any other." My father also related to me that his father was

---

[11] Similarly narrated in ***Sharh at-Tajrīd, Amāli Ahmed b. 'Isa, Sunan at-Tirmidhi, At-Tabaqāt al-Kubra, Sunan al-Bayhaqi, Tārikh Dimashq, Tārikh Baghdād, Uṡūl al-Kāfi, Bihār al-Anwār***

[12] It is narrated that he prayed over Ghāmidiya who committed fornication in ***Ŝahīh Muslim, Mušannaf Ibn Abi Shayba, Sunan al-Bayhaqi***

asked whether one is to pray over the stillborn that died. He replied: "It is not to be prayed over unless it was alive from the womb. Then, one prays over it."

Concerning the prayer over a child of fornication and the uncircumcised

One is to pray over the child of fornication just as one would pray over anyone else. One is to seek forgiveness for such child if he was known for piety because he is not harmed by the sin of his parents if he was a believer.

As for the uncircumcised person—if he avoided circumcision due to making light of the Sunnah of Allah's Messenger, peace and blessings be upon him and his progeny, and out of neglect for what Allah has obligated upon him—he is to not be prayed over. If he avoided such due to fear for himself or a valid excuse of his Lord, he is to be prayed over just as anyone else.

Regarding that, it has reached us from Allah's Messenger, peace and blessings be upon him and his progeny, that a man from the People of the Book entered Islam. He was a young man who was uncircumcised. [The Prophet], peace and blessings be upon him and his progeny, told him to get circumcised, and the young man replied: "I fear for myself." He then said: ((If you fear for yourself, it is sufficient)). Then, the young man slaughtered an animal for him, and the latter ate from it. When the young man died, he prayed over him.[13]

My father related to me from his father that he was asked about the prayer over the child of fornication. He replied: "One is to pray over the child of fornication just as one would pray over anyone else because he is not blamed for the sins of his parents."

Concerning carrying the funeral bier and its burial

One is to begin on the right of the bed and carry it. Then, one is to make their way to the back on the right while carrying it. Afterwards, one makes one's way around and carries it from the left. Then, one moves towards the back of the left side. One should walk behind the funeral bier and not in front of it because one is to follow and not be followed.

My father related to me from his father that he was asked about carrying the funeral bier and which side one should begin on. He replied: "One should begin on the right and then make one's way around it on every side as long as it does not cause any difficulty on him."

My father related to me from his father that he was asked about walking in front of the funeral bier. He replied:

> It is narrated that the Commander of Believers, 'Ali b. Abi Ťālib, upon him be peace, used to walk behind it.[14] He used to say: "Verily, I only follow, and I am not followed." It is most preferred to the Progeny of Allah's Messenger, peace and blessings be upon him and his progeny, unless one carries it from the front.

It is discouraged for women to follow the funeral bier. They should stay away and must be isolated from men. They must not raise their voices in wailing or display their faces. When it is buried, they should depart to their houses. It is not preferable for them to visit the graves.

---

[13] Similarly narrated in ***Musnad Imam Zayd, Amāli Ahmed b. 'Isa, Sharh at-Tajrīd***

[14] Sheikh 'Ali b. Bilāl reported in his ***Sharh al-Ahkām*** that Sayyid Abul-Abbās related with a complete chain of narrators to Abu Umāma:

> Abu Sa'īd said to 'Ali, upon him be peace: "O Abul-Hasan, inform me on how one is to walk behind a funeral bier?" He, upon him be peace, replied: "O Abu Sa'īd, I was asked similar by another person. By Allah, walking behind the funeral bier is as superior to walking in front of it just as the obligatory prayers are superior to the voluntary prayers." He then said that he heard that from Allah's Messenger, peace and blessings be upon him and his progeny.

Similarly narrated in ***Sharh at-Tajrīd, Sunan at-Tirmidhi, Sunan Abu Dāwūd, Sunan al-Bayhaqi***

My father related to me from his father that he was asked about women accompanying the funeral bier and if it is permissible for a woman to visit the graves. He replied:

> It has been reported that the Prophet, peace and blessings be upon him and his progeny, discouraged that.[15] Then it was repealed so that there was no longer a problem with a woman to follow the funeral bier. This is the case as long as they stay away from men and are prevented from intermixing with them. They must also be adequately covered in their clothes. I discourage women to visit the graves.

I do not deem it permissible for people to do what they have been doing. They yell at the funeral procession due to the death of the person, and they wail for him in the markets and streets. Rather, they can seek the permission from the guardians of the deceased to usher him in with a messenger. It has been reported that the Prophet, peace and blessings be upon him and his progeny, discouraged that [i.e. wailing].

My father related to me from his father that he was asked about ushering in the funeral procession. He replied:

> It is preferable that one not yell. It has been reported that Allah's Messenger, peace and blessings be upon him and his progeny, prohibited wailing. He said: ((It is from the acts of the pre-Islamic era)).[16] There is no problem in ushering it in. It is good if one seeks permission from his companions, brothers and relatives.

Concerning embalming with scented musk and how many times one shrouds the corpse in garments

There is no problem if one embalms the corpse with scented musk. Some people have discouraged it, but we do not discourage it based upon what has been reported in the traditions. Allah's Messenger, peace and blessings be upon him and his progeny, was embalmed with it, as well as the Commander of Believers, 'Ali b. Abi Ťālib, upon him be peace.[17]

As for the shrouding, it is based on what his companions are capable of and what is possible. If one shrouds with seven garments, this is good. If one shrouds with five garments, this is good. If one shrouds with three garments, this is good. It has been narrated that Allah's Messenger, peace and blessings be upon him and his progeny, was shrouded in three garments.[18]

If there is nothing other than one garment, it is sufficient. Allah's Messenger, peace and blessings be upon him and his progeny, shrouded his uncle, al-Hamza b. 'Abdul-Muttalib, may Allah be satisfied with him, in a Khaybari cloak. When he used it to cover his head, his feet were exposed. When he used it to cover his feet, his head was exposed. He placed some herbage over his uncle's feet to cover them.[19]

If one shrouds with three pieces, one clothes it in a sarong and wraps it with two shrouding cloths. If one shrouds in five pieces, one includes a shirt, turban and three pieces of shrouding cloths.[20] If one shrouds in seven pieces, one includes a shirt, sarong, turban and four pieces of shrouding cloths. The same applies to a woman except that one substitutes a head covering for the turban.

---

[15] Similarly narrated in ***Sunan Ibn Mājah*** and ***Sunan al-Bayhaqi***

[16] Similarly narrated in ***Sunan at-Tirmidhi, Sunan Ibn Mājah, Sunan al-Bayhaqi***

[17] Similarly narrated in ***Musnad Imam Zayd, Sharh at-Tajrīd, Sunan al-Bayhaqi, Mušannaf Ibn Abi Shayba, Al-Mustadrak***

[18] Similarly narrated in ***Musnad Imam Zayd, Mušannaf Ibn Abi Shayba, Musnad Ahmed, Sunan Abu Dāwūd, Sunan Ibn Mājah, Al-Mu'jam al-Kabīr, Sunan al-Bayhaqi, Ušūl al-Kāfi, Bihār al-Anwār***

[19] Similarly narrated in ***Sharh at-Tajrīd, Mušannaf Ibn Abi Shayba, Sunan al-Bayhaqi***

[20] Imam Abu Ťālib in his ***At-Tahrīr***, Imam al-Mu`ayyad Billah in his ***Sharh at-Tajrīd***, Imam Ibn Murtaḍa in his ***Al-Bahr*** and Imam Yahya b. Hamza in his ***Al-Intišār*** note that al-Hādi has two different statements regarding the five pieces of shrouding. In ***Al-Muntakhab***, he is quoted as saying that the five pieces of shrouding are to consist of a shirt, sarong and three pieces of shrouding cloths—with the sarong taking the place of the turban. It is possible that he changed his judgement based on the different circumstances that existed between Medina and Yemen. It is generally held that al-Hādi began the ***Ahkām*** while in Medina until he got to the Book of Sales. Then, he continued after arriving to Yemen and was later asked the questions that are included in ***Al-Muntakhab***. [Ref. ***Al-Qawl al-Awwal***]

My father related to me from his father that the latter was asked about embalming with scented musk. He replied:

> I saw the Progeny of Muhammad, upon him be peace, and some of them discouraged it while others did not see a problem in it. It is reported that the Prophet, peace and blessings be upon him and his progeny, was embalmed with scented musk. It is also reported from 'Ali, upon him be peace, that he ordered that he be embalmed with scented musk.[21] It was preferred from the embalming of the Prophet, peace and blessings be upon him and his progeny.

My father related to me from his father that the latter was asked how many times should a man, woman and child be shrouded. He replied:

> A man is to be shrouded in one garment if nothing else can be found and three garments if it can be found. Allah's Messenger, peace and blessings be upon him and his progeny, was shrouded in three garments. And Allah's Messenger, peace and blessings be upon him and his progeny, shrouded his uncle, al-Hamza b. 'Abdul-Muṫṫalib, may Allah be satisfied with him, in a Khaybari cloak while it was folded.
>
> If possible, the woman should be shrouded in seven garments—either a single dress, two dresses or three. Then her head is to be covered with a scarf.[22]

He was then asked about the dead woman's hair and whether it should be combed or braided. He replied: "It is collected together but it is not tied by other than it."

Concerning the declaration of Allah's greatness at the funeral prayer, the number of times one does it and what one says in every declaration

The consensus of the Progeny of Allah's Messenger, peace and blessings be upon him and his progeny, holds to the view that the declaration of Allah's greatness in the funeral prayer takes place five times. It is narrated from the Prophet, peace and blessings be upon him and his progeny, that he used to declare Allah's greatness five times.[23]

The one praying is not restricted in what he says in the prayer, nor is he limited in what he can supplicate for in his declarations of Allah's greatness.[24] After that, one prays for the Prophets and Messengers, supplicates for the deceased and seeks forgiveness for him.

It is encouraged that one says in the first unit after declaring Allah's greatness: "There is no God but Allah, the One with whom are no partners. To Him belongs dominion and to Him belongs the praise. He gives life and He gives death. And He is powerful over all things."

Then, one recites *Al-Hamd* (Q. 1). After that, one declares Allah's greatness and afterwards says:

> O Allah, bless Muhammad, Your Slave and Messenger, the best of Your creation. Bless the

---

[21] Similarly narrated in ***Musnad Imam Zayd, Mušannaf Ibn Abi Shayba, Al-Mustadrak***

[22] Although not mentioned in this text, al-Hādi was asked about the specific description of the garments in which the deceased is to be shrouded in ***Al-Muntakhab***. The dialogue is as follows:

> I asked: "Is it permissible for a woman to be shrouded in dyed garments?" He replied: "Yes. Haven't you considered that it is permissible for her in the prayer? That which is permissible for her to pray in is similarly permissible for her to be shrouded in." "Similarly, can a man be shrouded in dyed garments?" "He can be washed and shrouded with it even if it is not white. However, white is preferable to us."

[23] Similarly narrated in ***Musnad Ahmed, Sunan ad-Dārqutni, Sunan an-Nisā'i, Al-Mu'jam al-Kabīr, Al-Mu'jam al-Awsaṫ, Uṡūl al-Kāfi, Bihār al-Anwār.*** The majority of the Sunni narrations relate that the Prophet declared Allah's greatness four times. However, five times also appears in the aforementioned narrations, and both four and five are related in ***Ŝahīh Muslim, Sunan at-Tirmidhi, Sunan Ibn Mājah*** and ***Sunan Abu Dāwūd*** on the authority of 'Abdur-Rahmān b. Abi Layla. As for the five declarations of the funeral prayer being the collective consensus of the Ahl al-Bayt, the same is narrated in the ***Amāli Ahmed b. 'Isa*** and ***Al-Jāmi' al-Kāfi***.

[24] It is also related in Al-***Muntakhab*** that when al-Hādi was asked about what the one praying the funeral prayer should say, he replied by saying: "As for my statement and the statement of the scholars of the Prophet's Progeny, upon them be peace, all that one recites or supplicates for the dead is permissible. One is not restricted in that."

People of his Family, the Pure, Noble and Truthful—the ones from whom Allah has removed filth and purified thoroughly—just as You have blessed Abraham and the Progeny of Abraham. Verily, You are the Praiseworthy and Glorious!

Then, one recites **{Say: He is Allah, the One...}** **(Q. 112)** and afterwards declares Allah's greatness. Then, one says:

> O Allah, bless Your Near Angels. O Allah, honour their builds and magnify their affairs. O Allah, bless Your Prophets that were sent. O Allah, make excellent their rewards and ennoble their recompense. Raise their station with You. O Allah, make Muhammad the intercessor for his community and make us amongst those who receive his intercession by Your Mercy. O Allah, make us among his group and cause us to enter his intercession. Make us amongst those who take refuge in his garden.

Then, one recites **{Say: "I seek refuge in the Lord of the Dawn..."}** **(Q. 113)** and afterwards declares Allah's greatness. Then one says:

> Glorified be the One who is glorified by the heavens and earths. Glorified be our Lord, the Highly Exalted. Glorified and Exalted be He! O Allah, verily this is Your slave and the son or Your two slaves. He has arrived to You, and we have verily come with him seeking intercession for him. We ask for forgiveness on his behalf. So, forgive him of his sins, and pardon him of his transgressions. Cause him to meet his Prophet, Muhammad, peace and blessings be upon him and his progeny. Expand his grave, make easy his affair. Make him to taste Your Mercy and Pardon, O the Most Generous of generous!
>
> O Allah, provide for us a good preparation similar to this day and do not cause us to experience hardship after it. Render our deeds and days good, and cause us to experience good on the Day we meet You.

Then, one is to declare Allah's greatness and afterwards recite the final salutations to the right and left.

This supplication is only recited for the believer who was righteous and God-conscious. As for the openly disobedient, wrongdoing sinner—it is impermissible to recite it for such person. We do not love them; rather, we declare Allah free of them. We ask that He dishonour them and prepare punishment for them.

My father related to me from his father that the latter was asked about the number of declarations of Allah's greatness in the funeral prayer. He was also asked regarding the supplication that one make in each declaration and whether one raises the hands for every declaration or not. He replied:

> As for the declaration of Allah's greatness—according to the Progeny of Allah's Messenger, peace and blessings be upon him and his progeny—it is to be declared five times. It has been narrated from the Prophet, peace and blessings be upon him and his progeny, that he declared Allah's greatness over the body of the Negus[§] five times and raised his hands in the first declaration.[25] After that, he settled his limbs as he did in the regular prayer.

---

[25] Similarly narrated in ***Al-Mu'jam al-Kabīr*** and ***Al-Mu'jam al-Awsaṭ***. It is believed that there is a conflict between the ***Ahkām*** and ***Al-Muntakhab*** regarding whether the hands are to be raised in the funeral prayer or not. Imam Yahya b. Hamza states in his ***Al-Intiṣār*** that two views are related from Rassi and al-Hādi regarding this issue: the recommendation of raising the hands in the first declaration of the funeral prayer as implied in ***Ahkām*** and the discouragement of raising them as explicitly stated in ***Al-Muntakhab***. We say that since the ***Ahkām*** does not directly state that Imam Rassi advocated for the hands to be raised and since al-Hādi stated that they are to not be raised at all, the most authoritative view is that the hands are to not be raised at the onset of the funeral prayer similar to the other prayers. As for Imam Rassi's narration that the Prophet raised his hands at the onset of the funeral prayer of the Negus, it is possible that this took place before the practice of raising of the hands in the prayer was abrogated. [Ref/ ***Al-Qawl al-Awwal***]

He recited the *Fātiha* (Q. 1) and the prayers upon the Prophet, peace and blessings be upon him and his progeny, after the first declaration. After the second declaration, he supplicates for the Messengers and Muslims. Then in the rest of it, he supplicates for the dead and whoever is present. One does not abandon the supplication if the deceased was amongst the righteous.

Whoever misses something from the declarations of Allah's greatness over the funeral bier completes it after the departure of the people and before the lifting of the body. Whoever fears that the time would elapse before one is able to pray over the dead, makes dust purification and then prays.

My father related to me that his father said regarding a man outside of the state of ritual purity who fears that the time would elapse before he is able to pray over the dead: "If he fears that the time for the prayer would elapse, he makes dust purification and then prays over it."

Concerning the *dhimmi* woman who dies while there is a Muslim in her womb and concerning giving condolences to the *dhimmi*

There is no problem in giving them condolences as long as one does not supplicate for them, praise their dead or say a good word about them.[26] One should not bear witness to their funeral procession because Allah has prohibited prayer on them as well as standing over the graves of their brothers and the hypocrites. He said to His Prophet, peace and blessings be upon him and his progeny: **{...and pray not over any of them who died, and stand not over their tomb} (Q. 9:84)**.

As for the *dhimmi* woman with a Muslim baby in her womb—if she were to die, she is to be buried in the graveyard of her coreligionists with it. One is to not consider what is in her womb because it was not disconnected from her and had not exited her womb. Therefore, its judgements are the judgements of other than her.

Even if a disbeliever were to bear witness to the truth once before his soul departs, his judgement concerning shrouding, burial, prayers and wash is the same as that of other Muslims. This is because, by means of his bearing witness, he has departed from the status of an idolater and become—by the permission of Allah—one of the believers.

My father related to me that his father was asked about the Jewess and Christian who dies with a Muslim child in her womb. He replied: "One is to bury them both in the graveyard of her coreligionists as long as it has not separated from her womb."

My father related to me that his father was asked about the disbeliever who bore witness to the truth only once when death approached him. "Is he buried and where is he buried?" He replied: "His status regarding the prayer and shrouding is the same as that of other Muslims."

Concerning the tombs and sepulchres

It is religiously obligatory that the *Ummah* of Muhammad, peace and blessings be upon him and his progeny, bury their dead in a hole beside the grave unless the graves are located in preventative places that one cannot access for burial. If one is not able to do so, then one can utilise a sepulchre after all excuses and efforts have been exhausted. This is similar to what the people of Mecca and others did.

Regarding that, it has reached us that when Allah's Messenger, peace and blessings be upon him and his progeny, passed away, a voice said: "Where will the Prophet, peace and blessings be upon him and his progeny, be buried?" 'Ali, upon him be peace, responded: "If you want, I can relate a hadith to

---

[26] If both the deceased and grieving family member were openly disobedient Muslims or disbelievers, one is permitted to say: "To Allah we belong and to Allah we will return!" as a condolence. Conversely, if the deceased was an outwardly righteous Muslim, one can say as condolences: "May Allah increase the reward of your family member!" or "May Allah forgive your family member!" As for the proper time for giving condolences, it is after the burial since this is the time where grief and sadness are the strongest. [Ref ***Al-Azhār***]

you." They said: "Relate the hadith to us." He said: "I heard Allah's Messenger, peace and blessings be upon him and his progeny, say: ((Allah cursed the Jews and the Christians for taking the graves of their Prophets as places of prostration. A Prophet never passed away except that he was buried in the same place where he passed away))."[27] As soon as that came from his mouth, they went towards his bed and dug a hole where the bed was. When they finished, they asked: "Should we bury him or construct a sepulchre?" 'Ali, upon him be peace, said: "I heard Allah's Messenger, peace and blessings be upon him and his progeny, say: ((Burial is for us, and sepulchres are for other than us))."[28] Then, they buried Allah's Messenger, peace and blessings be upon him and his progeny.

My father related to me that his father was asked about tombs and sepulchres. He replied:

> The Prophet, peace and blessings be upon him and his progeny, was buried. Burial is most preferred by us because the Prophet, peace and blessings be upon him and his progeny, said: ((Burial is for us, and sepulchres are for other than us)). That refers to the Pre-Islamic peoples from the Quraysh and the Arab idolaters that followed them.

Concerning the bed for the body in the grave and the plastering of a grave and its decoration

It is not preferable to me that one place anything over the body in the grave nor should anything other than the shrouding be placed in it. As for decorating the grave—it is not preferable to us because when one has died, beautification has gone from them. Since beautification has gone from their souls, it is a beautification that is further than that of their house and grave.

As for the erecting stones as markers around it or over it so that it is recognised from other than it—there is no problem with that. Similarly, there is no problem with plastering it with clay so that it can remain as a landmark for the dependents.

My father related to me from his father that the latter was asked if one could place a garment or felt over the dead. He replied: "One is to not place anything over the body in its grave after shrouding it except herbage from the earth in the burial."

My father related to me from his father that the latter was asked about plastering the graves with clay or bricks, as well as demanding payment for doing that. He replied: "As for demanding payment for it—it is discouraged. It is similarly discouraged to use bricks on it. However, there is no problem with plastering it with clay."

Concerning burying a group in one grave out of necessity

When the body is placed on the edge of his tomb, the head should be drawn out and turned towards the *qibla*. One should lay his head upon something in his tomb—either dust or an elevated place due to the burial. One is to not lay the head upon anything other than what is in the tomb due to burial.

If the people are compelled to bury a group in one grave, they are to place between each body dust, stones or clay. My father related to me from his father that the latter was asked about the body and from where should it be placed in the grave. He replied: "One is to take the body and enter it into the grave from the shoulders and chest. Then, one faces it towards the *qibla* and brings the legs inside."

---

[27] Similarly narrated in ***Musnad Imam Zayd, Sharh at-Tajrīd, Amāli Ahmed b. 'Isa.*** The same hadith is related on the authorities of 'Umar, A'isha, Zayd b. Thābit and Abu Hurayra in the following collections with slight variations: ***Ŝahīh al-Bukhāri, Ŝahīh Muslim, Sunan an-Nisā`i, Sunan Abu Dāwūd, Musnad Ahmed, Mušannaf Ibn Abi Shayba, Majmu' az-Zawā`id, Al-Mu'jam al-Kabīr***.

[28] Similarly narrated in ***Musnad Imam Zayd, Sharh at-Tajrīd*** and ***Amāli Ahmed b. 'Isa.*** The same hadith is related on the authority of Ibn Abbās and Jarīr b. 'Abdullah in the following collections: ***Sunan at-Tirmidhi, Sunan an-Nisā`i, Sunan Abu Dāwūd, Sunan Ibn Mājah, Sunan al-Bayhaqi, Musnad Ahmed, Al-Mu'jam al-Kabīr.***

My father related to me from his father that he was asked about two or three men who were buried in one grave and how one is supposed to bury them. He replied:

> One is to not bury them in the same grave unless one does so out of necessity. If they are buried out of necessity, one is to place between each body dust or earth. Allah's Messenger, peace and blessings be upon him and his progeny, once ordered the burial of people in twos and threes in one grave. This was because his Companions were many and there were many casualties among them.[29]

It has reached us that Allah's Messenger, peace and blessings be upon him and his progeny, said: ((Whoever pours three handfuls of dust on the grave of his brother—Allah will remove from him his evil deeds)).[30]

It has reached us that the Commander of Believers, 'Ali b. Abi Ťālib, upon him be peace, used to supplicate when pouring dust on the dead:

> O Allah! Verily, we believe in You and we confirm the truth of Your Messengers. We are certain of Your resurrection. This is what Allah and His Messenger has promised. Allah and His Messenger have spoken the truth.

He then said: "Whoever does that—there will be counted for him a good deed for every grain of dust."[31]

Concerning the one who cannot find shrouding and concerning the funeral of men, women, children and slaves

If one cannot find shrouding for the dead due to expediency or any other reason, one can use herbage from the earth if possible. If it is not possible to use herbage, then one uses what one can because Allah—the Blessed and Exalted—says: **{Allah burdens not a soul except with what it can bear} (Q. 2:286)**.

If there is a group funeral prayer that consists of freemen, one places the funeral bier of the free man in front of the prayer leader. The funeral biers of the free man's male children are placed in front of his funeral bier so that they can follow the free man's funeral bier. The slave's funeral bier follows that of the free man's children. The free woman's funeral bier follows that of the slave's.[32] The funeral bier of the slave woman follows that of the free woman's. Then the prayer leader declares Allah's greatness over all of them collectively just as he would declare it over one of them. He does so five times and intends by such the prayer over all of them collectively.

My father related to me from his father that the latter was asked about the dead for whom no shrouding could be found. He replied: "One shrouds them in what one is able of the herbs of the earth. If one cannot find that, bury them in what one is able to bury them in."

My father related to me from his father that the latter was asked about the funeral of men, women, children and slaves together. He replied: "The men are to be placed forward, then the free male children. After that is the male slaves, then the freewomen and the remainder insomuch that they all face the *qibla*."

---

[29] Similarly narrated in ***Sharh at-Tajrīd, Sunan at-Tirmidhi, Sunan Abu Dāwūd, Sunan an-Nisā'i***

[30] Similarly narrated in ***Sharh at-Tajrīd*** and ***Amāli Ahmed b. 'Isa***

[31] Sheikh 'Ali b. Bilāl reported this in his ***Sharh al-Ahkām*** from Sayyid Abul-Abbās al-Hasani with the latter's chain of narrators to 'Ali, upon him be peace. The only difference is that in the said text, it says: "We confirm the truth of Your Messenger…" in the singular. It is also narrated in ***Amāli Ahmed b. 'Isa*** with the same chain of narrators as the ***Sharh al-Ahkām***; however, its wording is the same as what appears in the ***Ahkām***.

[32] In ***Al-Muntakhab***, the imam is reported to have said that slave's bier is to follow that of the freewoman. These two contrary statements attributed to al-Hādi are reported in ***Al-Bahr***, ***At-Tahrīr*** and ***Sharh at-Tajrīd***. However, we say that al-Hādi's statement in the ***Ahkām***—that is, the freewoman's bier is to follow that of the male slave—is considered more authoritative due to the fact that this judgement was taken directly from his grandfather, Imam Rassi. According to ***Majmu' al-Murtaḍa***, Imam al-Murtaḍa b. al-Hādi stated that any narrated divergence between Rassi and al-Hādi should be disregarded because al-Hādi would never pass a judgement contrary to that of his grandfather. Also, refer back to the **Translator's Introduction** regarding Imam al-Hādi's methodology.

Concerning an explanation of washing the dead and its manner

The first thing that one begins with is the laying of the body to be washed. Then, one is to extend the neck so that it faces the *qibla.* Afterwards, the private parts must be covered and the clothes are removed. The tummy is then pressed three times unless it is the body of a pregnant woman. In that case, her tummy is not pressed. The washer wraps a rag around the hand and cleans the two openings while pouring water onto the hand. The two openings are to be completely washed. One should avoid looking at the private parts. One should not bathe the dead unless such person is the foremost of its people and the purest of its religion.

Then, one performs the ritual ablution on it, as one would do for the prayer. One washes the hands, as well as the mouth, teeth, lips and nose. One cleans what one is able. Afterwards, one is to wash the face completely. Next, one washes the right forearm to the elbow and then the left arm to the elbow. Then, one wipes the head and then washes the feet to the ankles—beginning with the right and then left.

After that, one washes the head and then the whole body—turning the body on the right and then left. One begins with the right side before the left. One is to be careful in thoroughly washing the inside and outside. Then, one washes the whole body using the herb known as *huruḍ*[33] in that wash. One is to rub the *huruḍ* over all of it. After that, one washes it with the herb known as *sidr.*[34] One is to begin with the head and wash it as well as the beard. If it is the body of a woman, one is to not comb her hair. One washes the whole body with *sidr*—the sides, the back and front. Then, one washes the *sidr* from it. Afterwards, one washes the body a third time using water with camphor and cleans the whole body completely. This includes the head, face, arms, feet, tummy and back.

If an impure occurrence takes place after that, one is to redo the complete wash five times. If an impure occurrence takes place after that, one is to redo the complete wash seven times. As for the impure occurrence that takes place after that washing—it would be prudent to use linen at the place to prevent soiling the shroud. Whatever hair falls from the body—one is to wash it and return it to the shroud.

My father related to me from his father that the latter was asked about washing the dead and what is sufficient of it. He replied:

> The bathing of the dead is like the bathing of the one in the state of major ritual impurity. It is discouraged to heat the water for the body unless it is necessary due to overwhelming cold or that the dead body will become too dirty. Then, one can heat the water.

My father related to me from his father that the latter was asked whether the one in major ritual impurity or a menstruating woman could bathe the dead. He replied: "It is not preferable that both of them do that unless one cannot find anyone else to do it. However, if either were to do it, it is sufficient as long as they are clean."

If there is a need for either of the two of them to bathe the dead, the one in the state of major ritual impurity should use the excess water to perform the purification wash if there is any. If there is no excess water and one cannot assess the amount of water, he should perform the dust purification. As for the menstruating woman—she should wash her hands in any case before bathing the dead.

My father related to me from his father that the latter was asked about anything that may fall from the dead body, such as nails or hair. He replied: "If anything were to fall from the dead body, it is encouraged for one to return it to the shroud. One is to not clip the nails."

---

[33] This term refers to the trees or plants from which people derive potash. It is also known as kali or glasswort. [Ref. **Lane's Arabic English Lexicon**]

[34] This refers to a genus of lote-tree known as the 'Christ thorn jujube' or *spina Christi.* It renders a fruit known as *nabeca.* [Ref. **Lane's Arabic English Lexicon**]

Concerning the times for the prayer over the dead

The best times to pray over the dead are the times for the obligatory prayers. All of the day and night times are the times for one to pray over the dead except the three times that the prayers are prohibited. They are the following: during the time of sunrise until it has completely risen and become white, during the time of its zenith until it starts to descend and during the time of its setting until its colour changes and it has completely set.

My father related to me from his father that the latter was asked about the times that one is to bury and pray over the dead. He replied:

> It is encouraged for it to not take place during times of necessity for the people of the funeral. It is also not encouraged for the burial to take place during the prayer times. There is no problem to bury it and pray over it after the dawn prayer or after the late noon prayer. However, if the funeral bier is present and the prayer has begun, one can choose whichever one wants as long as there is no hardship on the people and one does not fear that the obligatory prayer time will elapse.

Concerning where the prayer leader is to stand during the prayer over the dead

In the funeral prayer, the prayer leader is to stand at the navel of the man and at the chest and shoulders of the woman. My father related to me from his father that the latter was asked about where the prayer leader is to stand. He replied:

> At the funeral prayer of a man, the prayer leader is to stand between their chests and private parts. In the case of women, the prayer leader is to stand between their chests and faces.

Concerning what is to be done to the graves

Flattening the graves is more preferred than constructing domes.[35] However, if one were to construct a dome, there is no problem with it. There is also no problem with inscribing one's name on a stone erected at the head. Stone is more preferable than wooden boards, but there is no problem with the latter.

Concerning a woman who dies while a living baby is in her womb

If a pregnant woman dies and one is certain that she is dead and her baby is alive moving in her womb, it is to be removed from her gently. Then, her belly is to be stitched up well. Afterwards, one does with her as one would do with any other dead body, including the bathing, shrouding and burial.

---

[35] It is narrated in ***Al-Jāmi' al-Kāfi*** that Imams al-Hasan b. Yahya and Muhammad b. Manšūr said that it is the consensus of the Prophet's Progeny that the graves should be flattened and the dead drawn in.

The Book of the Purification Dues

In the Name of Allah, the Most Gracious, the Most Merciful...

The beginning of the chapters regarding the purification dues

It has reached us from the Commander of Believers, 'Ali b. Abi Ťālib, may Allah's mercy and pleasure be upon him: "Allah's Messenger, peace and blessings be upon him and his progeny, said: ((The prayer is not complete except by means of the purification dues, and charity is not accepted out of malevolence))."[1]

It has also reached us that he, peace and blessings be upon him and his progeny, said: ((Whoever refrains from the purification dues and consumes usury has made war against me in this world and the hereafter)).[2]

Also, it has reached us that the Commander of Believers, may Allah's mercy and pleasure be upon him, called his son, al-Hasan, as death approached the former and said: "I adjure you to render the purification dues in its proper place. Verily, the prayer is not accepted from one who refrains from rendering the purification dues."[3]

It has reached us that Allah's Messenger, peace and blessings be upon him and his progeny, said: ((The purification dues are the arch of Islam)).[4]

The purification dues are a religious obligation from Allah upon every person just as the prayer is a religious obligation. One's faith is not complete except by means of its observance. Regarding that, Allah says: **{Establish the prayer and render the purification dues and bow with those who bow} (Q. 2:43)**. He—Majestic and Mighty—also says: **{They were commanded naught save to worship Allah sincerely. For Him is the religion of uprightness. They establish the prayer and render the purification dues; that is the right religion} (Q. 98:5)**.

He also says: **{Woe be unto the idolaters! [They are] those who render not the purification dues...} (Q. 41:6-7)**. He names them **{idolaters}** due to their refraining from rendering the purification dues as well as for rejecting the dues that Allah commanded them to pay from their wealth.

Then, the Blessed and Exalted commanded His Prophet, peace and blessings be upon him and his progeny, to take charity from their wealth. He says: **{Take from their wealth dues, wherewith thou may purify them and sanctify them. And pray for them; verily, thy prayer is source of tranquillity for them. Allah is All-Hearing, All-Knowing} (Q. 9:103)**. Therefore, Allah has obligated the Prophet, peace and blessings be upon him and his progeny, and the believers to take it as a tariff and payment.

Then, He says: **{Whatsoever the Messenger gives thee, take it. Whatsoever he prohibits thee from, leave it. And be wary of Allah. Verily, Allah is severe in punishment} (Q. 59:7)**. Therefore, he obligates the Muslim *Ummah* to accept and do what Allah's Messenger, peace and blessings be upon him and his progeny, has commanded them. Then, he, peace and blessings be upon him and his progeny, explained what Allah has obligated upon the Muslim *Ummah* regarding the purification dues as a religious injunction. He made clear how much is to be taken, when it is to be taken and from how much is to be taken. He pardoned the minimum amount until it reaches the limit that he, peace and

---

[1] Similarly narrated in ***Musnad Imam Zayd, Amāli Abi Ťālib, Amāli al-Murshid Billah, Ŝahīh Muslim, Sunan at-Tirmidhi, Sunan an-Nisā'i, Sunan Abu Dāwūd, Sunan Ibn Mājah, Musnad Ahmed, Ŝahīh Ibn Hibbān, Sunan al-Bayhaqi, Kanz al-'Ummāl, Majmu' az-Zawā'id, Al-Mu'jam al-Kabīr, Al-Mu'jam al-Awsat, Bihār al-Anwār***

[2] Similarly narrated in ***Musnad Imam Zayd*** and ***Amāli Ahmed b. 'Isa***

[3] Similarly narrated in ***Amāli Ahmed b. 'Isa, Majmu' az-Zawā'id, Al-Mu'jam al-Kabīr, Bihār al-Anwār***

[4] Similarly narrated in ***Amāli Ahmed b. 'Isa, Al-Mu'jam al-Awsat, Al-Mu'jam al-Kabīr, Majmu' az-Zawā'id, Bihār al-Anwār***

blessings be upon him and his progeny, prescribed. Also, he pardoned the minimum amount of livestock (*al-awqāš*), which is that in between two obligatory amounts of animals.[5]

Concerning the purification dues on gold

It is not religiously obligatory for the purification dues to be paid on gold until the weight reaches twenty mithqal.[6] Once the weight reaches twenty mithqal, 2.5% of it is due. This amounts to half a dinar. Then whatever exceeds twenty mithqal—whether a little or a lot—only 2.5% of it is due based upon the first amount. For forty mithqal of gold, only a mithqal is due. This is 2.5%, and it applies to whatever exceeds that.

Concerning the purification dues on silver

It is not religiously obligatory for the purification dues to be paid on silver until the amount reaches two hundred dirham.[7] At that point, 2.5% is due—which amounts to five dirham. If one adds two dirhams to that two hundred dirham or more or less, one is to sum up all of that and pay 2.5% on it. This is the case whether it is a lot added to it or a little; it is calculated based on this amount.

If it reaches the amount of four hundred dirhams, ten dirhams is due. If it reaches eight hundred, twenty dirhams is due. If it reaches one thousand, twenty-five dirhams is due. Whatever exceeds that is similarly calculated—whether a little or a lot.

My father related to me that his father said:

> There are no purification dues paid for less than two hundred dirhams. But, once it reaches this amount, five dirhams is due. There are no purification dues paid for less than twenty mithqal of gold. But, once it reaches this amount, 2.5% of it is due—which amounts to half a dinar. Whatever exceeds that is similarly calculated as thus. Likewise is narrated on the authority of 'Ali, may Allah have mercy on him.[8]

Concerning the purification dues on camels

There are no purification dues on less than five camels. When the number reaches five and they are freely grazing and pastured, one lamb is due. If there are ten, two lambs are due. Then, there is no other due until the number reaches fifteen. Afterwards, three lambs are due. Then, there is no other due until the number reaches twenty. After that, four lambs are due. Then, there is no other due until the number reaches twenty-five. Then, one owes a *bint makhād*[9] until the number reaches thirty-five. For anything more than that, a *bint labūn*[10] is due until the number reaches forty-five. When that number is increased by one, one owes a *hiqqa*[11] until the number reaches sixty. When there are sixty-one camels, one owes a *jadha'* until the number reaches seventy-five. When there are seventy-six camels, one owes two *bint labūn*s until the number reaches ninety. When there are ninety-one, one owes two *hiqqa*s until the number reaches one

---

[5]After defining the word *awqāš*, ***Lane's Arabic English Lexicon*** says: "…for instance when camels amount in number to five, one sheep or goat is to be given for them; and nothing is to be given as such as exceed that number until they amount to ten: thus what is in between the five and ten is termed *waqqaš*"

[6] Twenty mithqal of gold equals roughly 70 to 73 grams.

[7] Two hundred mithqal of silver equals roughly 520 grams.

[8] Similarly narrated in ***Musnad Imam Zayd, Sharh at-Tajrīd***

[9] According to ***Al-Muntakhab***, when Imam al-Hādi was asked the meaning of the name *bint makhād*, he replied: "Because its mother has produced milk (*tatamakhad*) with a baby in its womb and she follows her."

[10] According to ***Al-Muntakhab***, when Imam al-Hādi was asked the meaning of the name *bint labūn*, he replied: "Because its mother had given birth while she was providing milk to her. Then she became a *bint labūn*"

[11] According to ***Al-Muntakhab***, when Imam al-Hādi was asked the meaning of the name *hiqqa*, he replied: "Because she is suitable (*astahaqat*) to be mounted by the stallion. That is why she is called a *hiqqa*."

hundred twenty camels. For every fifty camels after that, one owes a *hiqqa*.[12]

My father related to me that his father said:

> There are no purification dues on less than five camels. When the number reaches five, one lamb is due. If there are ten, two lambs are due. When there are fifteen, three lambs are due. When there are twenty, four lambs are due. When there are twenty-five, one *bint makhāḍ* is due. If one cannot find a *bint makhāḍ*, then a male *bint labūn* is due until the number reaches thirty-five. For one more than that, a *bint labūn* is due until the number reaches forty-five. When that number is increased by one, one owes a *hiqqa* until the number reaches sixty. When that number is increased by one, one owes a *jadha'* until the number reaches seventy-five. When that number is increased by one, one owes two *bint labūn*s until the number reaches ninety. When that number is increased by one, one owes two *hiqqa*s until the number reaches one hundred twenty camels. For every fifty camels after that, one owes a *hiqqa*.

Concerning the purification dues on cows

There are no purification dues on less than thirty cows. When the number reaches thirty cows, a male or female calf is due. The calf refers to a male or female yearling. Then, only the yearling is due until the number of cows reaches forty. When the number reaches forty, a full-grown cow is due. Nothing else is due until the number reaches sixty—after which, two calves are due. Then, nothing else is due until the number reaches seventy. When that happens, a calf and a full-grown cow are due. Nothing else is due after that until the number reaches eighty—after which, two full-grown cows are due. Nothing else is due until the number reaches ninety—after which, three calves are due. Nothing else is due until the number reaches one hundred—after which, a full-grown cow and two calves are due. Nothing else is due until the number reaches one hundred ten—after which, two full-grown cows and a calf are due. Nothing else is due until the number reaches one hundred twenty—after which, three full-grown cows are due. Nothing else is due until the number reaches one hundred thirty—after which, a full-grown cow and three calves are due. Nothing else is due until the number reaches one hundred forty—after which, two full-grown cows and two calves are due. Nothing else is due until the number reaches one hundred fifty—after which, three full-grown cows and one calf is due. Whatever number of cows exceeds that, one is to account a full-grown cow for every additional forty and a male or female calf for every additional thirty.

My father related to me that his father said: "There are no purification dues on less than thirty cows. For every thirty cows, one owes a male or female calf. For every forty cows, one owes a full-grown cow."

Concerning the purification dues on sheep

There are no purification dues on less than forty sheep. When there are forty sheep, one lamb is due. Then, there is nothing else due until the number reaches one hundred twenty sheep. When that number is increased by one, two lambs are due until the number reaches two hundred. When the two hundred sheep are increased by one, three lambs are due until the number reaches three hundred. Then, there is a lamb owed for every one hundred sheep.

---

[12] Imam Abu Ťālib relates in his ***At-Tahrīr***, as well as Imam Yahya b. Hamza in his ***Al-Intišār*** and al-Mu`ayyad Billah in his ***Sharh at-Tajrīd*** that two different rulings are narrated from al-Hādi. One judgement—which is here in the ***Ahkām***—is that once the number of camels reaches one hundred twenty, a *hiqqa* is due for every fifty camels after that. The implication of the statement from the ***Ahkām*** is that one would not owe anything else after one hundred twenty camels until the number reaches fifty. The other judgement—which is in ***Al-Muntakhab***—is that the obligatory dues would start over from the beginning insomuch that after the number of camels exceeds one hundred twenty, one would owe a lamb after the excess reaches five camels and so forth. We say that one statement does not necessarily preclude the other. In ***Sharh at-Tajrīd***, Imam Abul-Abbās al-Hasani is narrated to have reconciled these two seemingly contradictory statements by saying that one would begin anew after the number of camels reaches one hundred twenty, as stated in ***Al-Muntakhab***; however, one would owe a hiqqa when the number reaches fifty instead of forty-five, as stated in the ***Ahkām***. [Ref. ***Al-Qawl al-Awwal***]

It has reached us that the Commander of Believers, 'Ali b. Abi Ṭālib, upon him be peace, said:

> Allah's Messenger, peace and blessings be upon him and his progeny, stood before us one day and said: ((Regarding sheep—for forty sheep, one lamb is due. This is until the number reaches one hundred twenty. When there is one additional sheep added to that number, two lambs are due until the number reaches two hundred. When one more is added to that, three lambs are due; this is until the number reaches three hundred. When there is an additional one hundred sheep added to that number, one lamb is due. One is to not part what is joined or join what is parted for fear of the purification dues. Nor should the dues collector take the most outstanding of the sheep, the decrepit or that which has a blemish)).[13]

By that, Allah's Messenger, peace and blessings be upon him and his progeny, meant that the dues collector is to not take the choicest lamb or the one in the prime of its youth. Nor is he to take one with any defect.

Concerning the explanation of the Prophet's statement: ((One is to not part what is joined or join what is parted for fear of the purification dues))[14]

The meaning of 'what is parted' that is to not be joined is: whatever the owner divided even though it was joined as one flock. The meaning of 'what is joined' that is to not be parted is: whatever the owner joined even though the flock was divided.[15]

The meaning of his joining is that which one man owns is to not be separated even if he has three sheep in three different flocks. In that case, it is religiously obligatory for the dues collector to join all of them, calculate them and take the purification dues from him. He is to not look at the physical separation of the flock but rather join the possessions of the owner.

The meaning of the parting that is to not be joined is demonstrated by the following. If there is one flock of two hundred and one sheep that belong to six different people—one owns thirty-eight, another owns thirty-nine, another owns thirty-seven, another owns thirty-six, another owns thirty-five and another owns fifteen—it is not religiously obligatory for the dues collector to take the purification dues from any of them because not one owner has forty sheep. This is the judgement of the Seal of Prophets, peace and blessings be upon him and his progeny.[16]

The dues collector is to not incline towards the one from whom he collects the dues. Nor is he to accept a gift out of fear of consumption. If he were to accept anything, that would belong to the public treasury of the Muslims. This would not be religiously permissible for him unless it was granted to him by the imam of the Muslims. If he grants it to him—even a portion—this would be permissible for him. Otherwise, it would be religiously impermissible for him.

Similar is the case for all the imam's workers who accept gifts from the levies of the Muslims. This is because they only gave him gifts due to his position in the government. The government is simply a

---

[13] Similarly narrated in ***Sharh at-Tajrīd***

[14] Similarly narrated in ***Musnad Imam Zayd, Amāli Ahmed b. 'Isa, Sharh at-Tajrīd, Sunan ad-Dārqutni, Sunan al-Bayhaqi, Ŝahīh al-Bukhāri, Sunan Ibn Mājah, Musnad Ahmed, Mušannaf Ibn Abi Shayba***

[15] It is narrated in ***Al-Muntakhab*** that Imam al-Hādi said regarding this tradition: "This report has been authentically transmitted from [the Prophet]; however, the ignorant among the Generality do not know the intended meaning of Allah's Messenger." Ibn Rushd said in his ***Al-Bidāyat al-Mujtahid*** regarding this tradition and the reasons of dispute among the scholars: "Each faction interpreted this tradition according to their own assumptions."

[16] In Al-***Muntakhab***, al-Hādi was presented with various scenarios related to the application of the aforementioned hadith.

> I asked: "If a man died and left behind one hundred sheep as well as three sons and his wealth was not divided until the passing of a lunar year, what is the dues collector supposed to do?" He replied; "He is to take a sheep from each." "How can that be since the wealth was parted?" "The wealth after being joined is not that which was divided. Have you not considered that each one of them had not known what specific portion of the sheep belonged to them?" "Similarly, what if it remained in their possession for ten years without having been divided and then it decreased until it became forty when the lunar year passed over it?" "The reply is the same. The purification dues would be obligatory on that which was not distributed even if each one of them knew which of the sheep belonged to each."

trust of Allah and His Messenger, peace and blessings be upon him and his progeny, as well as that of the imam to keep due diligence over. Therefore, whatever is pilfered from the wealth of the government—it is impermissible and religiously prohibited to take it because they do not give him anything except by the reason of his belonging to the government. For that reason, we say that every benefit that belongs to the government is the wealth of Allah. It is therefore impermissible and religiously prohibited to take the wealth of Allah unless permitted by the leader, the one who considers Allah's affairs and rectifies them in the earth.

It is impermissible for the imam to permit that for any of his workers or anyone else unless it is out of consideration of the Muslims and rectification for the land of the Lord of creation. It is neither permissible for the workers to consume more of Allah's wealth in what they drink, wear, ride, use or reside in until after the imam permits it.

The dues collector should—when approaching the watering place that the livestock constantly uses—divide the sheep of every man into two parts and then choose from the two parts. Then, he is to take the dues from the part which left by the owner of the sheep. After then, he is to leave the rest for the owner. Similar is to be done for cows and camels.

My father related to me that his father was asked about the purification dues on the sheep. He replied:

> There are no purification dues on sheep for less than forty. When the number reaches forty, a sheep is due until the number reaches one hundred twenty. When that number increases by one, two sheep are due. Then, there is nothing else due until the number reaches two hundred. When that number increases by one, three sheep are due until the number reaches three hundred. When that number of sheep increases, a sheep is due for every one hundred sheep.
>
> One is to not separate what has been joined nor join what has been separated out of fear for the purification dues. One is to not take a male goat, a decrepit, a defective animal, the choicest or the one in the prime of its youth as purification dues. One is to take that which is in the middle.

Concerning the minimum amount of livestock and what Allah's Messenger pardoned, as well as the explanation of what livestock the dues collector is to count

The minimum amount of livestock that Allah's Messenger, peace and blessings be upon him and his progeny, pardoned refers to those camels, cows and sheep that fall between two ages and the number that is between the two ages.

For example, it is that amount that falls between what obligates a *bint al-makhāḍ* and what obligates and *bint labūn*. Those ten camels are pardoned by Allah's Messenger, peace and blessings be upon him and his progeny, because after twenty-five, a *bint makhāḍ* is due. Then, there is nothing else due until the number reaches thirty-five. After that is increased, one owes a *bint labūn* because he, peace and blessings be upon him and his progeny, did not appoint any purification dues for that which falls between these two amounts. Likewise is the case for everything.

Similarly, the minimum amount of cows is that which falls between thirty and forty cows as well as that which is between the yearling and the full-grown cow. There is nothing appointed after a yearling as an obligation when the number reaches thirty until the number reaches forty; then, a full-grown cow is due.

Similar is the case for the minimum amount of sheep. There is nothing appointed for any number of sheep under forty. Then, when there is forty, a lamb is due. After that, there are no purification dues for anything that exceeds the minimum amount of forty until the number reaches one hundred twenty. When that number is increased, two lambs are due until the number reaches two hundred. That which is between these two amounts and two limits is the minimum amount that is pardoned by Allah's Messenger, peace and blessings be upon him and his progeny.

The dues collector counts from the livestock and calculates from that which grazes freely in a pasture as well as from the young camels, cows and sheep that eat. My father related to me that his father said: "The dues collector counts from the old and young. He is to take from the young that which he is able to and not take the decrepit or the choicest."

Concerning the designation of what Allah's Messenger pardoned, the meaning of what he pardons and when such pardon occurs

Allah's Messenger, peace and blessings be upon him and his progeny, pardoned camels that are used for labour—those that are stall-fed and bear burdens—even if the number reaches five. Also, forty sheep are pardoned if they are stall-fed in the town, are milking and do not pasture. If they pasture outside of the town and graze, the purification dues are obligatory upon them. Similar is the case with cows if they do not pasture. Allah's Messenger, peace and blessings be upon him and his progeny, similarly pardoned the domestic animals, those used for service, clothing as well as the horse.[17]

He, peace and blessings be upon him and his progeny, simply pardoned those things when the owner does not use it for business and trade seeking profit. As for the one who bought all of that and other things such as carpet, jars of copper, clay pots, lead, iron, equipment, pottery, stones, wood or other things to use for business or seek a profit therefrom and gets money for it—the purification dues are obligatory on all that. One is to render the purification dues on that by its value if the value reaches the amount that obligates the purification dues.[18] As for pearl and sapphire, it is also due on that after the amount for the fifth dues (*khumus*) has been extracted.

Concerning the designation of lands

The lands refer to those places forcibly conquered by the Muslims, and they share and divide it amongst themselves; it has become their property. In that case, they only will be obligated to pay the tithe. It is the land of Khaybar that Allah's Messenger, peace and blessings be upon him and his progeny, conquered. He divided it and took some of it as property. He obligated his Companions to pay a tithe on it. He worked on half of it and left those who were there from before to work on the other half and render the other half to pay in taxes. Whatever is taken from it is between all the Muslims to take to the public treasury.

The land the Muslims conquered is the land that is taxed and situated as before, such as rural Kufa and other places like Egypt, the Levant, Khorasan and the like. Everything taken from those lands is to be taken to the Muslim public treasury.

The land in which there is a treaty with its people—there is nothing that is to be taken from them unless there was an amount stipulated in the treaty. An example is the people of Najrān and others. This money is to also be taken to the Muslim public treasury.

The land that the people abandoned without being killed or expelled by expedition with either cavalry or camelry, such as Fadak, is to be the property for the imam of the Muslims; he can use it for whatever he wants. All of what we designated regarding this wealth is religiously permissible for the Progeny of Allah's Messenger, peace and blessings be upon him and his progeny. They are most

---

[17] Similarly narrated in ***Musnad Imam Zayd, Sharh at-Tajrīd, Amāli Ahmed b. 'Isa, Bihār al-Anwār***

[18] In ***Al-Muntakhab***, al-Hādi is recorded to have further clarified the difference between those pieces of equipment used for trade and those used for manufacturing. The conversation is as follows:

> I asked: "If a man were to have a lunar year pass over his wealth while it is twenty mithqal and he has shop equipment—such as perfumery equipment, cobbler equipment or similar—is he obligated to include its value with his wealth and extract the entire purification dues from them?" He replied: "No. He is only obligated to render it from that equipment which he sells and not the equipment that he makes use of in his business. Similar is the case with the equipment of a manufacturer: it is not obligated for him to render the dues from its value because it is that from which he earns the wealth the dues are extracted from."

preferred than other than them because those other than them can gain from the tithes but they [i.e. the Prophet's Descendants] cannot. It is permissible for the imam of the Muslims to acquire this wealth with them as well as eat, drink, ride and marry from it. He can also benefit from it as he benefits the Muslims by means of it.

The lands in which its people entered Islam—there is a tithe due on it. This refers to lands such as the lands of Yemen and the Hejaz. It is obligatory for the people to—when the fruit has ripened—pay the fifth dues on it in addition to the purification dues. Whatever is taken from it is charity that is to be distributed to those designated by Allah from His statement: **{Verily, the dues are for the poor and needy and workers and those to whose hearts are to be reconciled and those to be freed and the indebted and those in the way of Allah and the traveller. It is a religious injunction from Allah. Allah is All-Knowing, All-Wise} (Q. 9:60)**.

As for the land to which a Muslim man gave life—it will belong to him and his inheritors after him; a tithe is taken from it. Similar has reached us from Allah's Messenger, peace and blessings be upon him and his progeny, in which he said: ((Whoever gives life to a land—it belongs to him)).[19] The intent of 'it will belong to him' is that no one before him previously owned it and that no one other than him farmed on it; there are no signs on it nor has anyone else claimed it.[20]

If someone set up barriers on a piece of land and established banners to indicate his ownership but had not lived on it and yielded crops on it, thereby neglecting it for three years, and someone else came and gave life to it—that which is yielded will belong to the one who gave life to it.

Concerning what is accepted from the *dhimmi* in Muslim lands and their renting of such

There are many different things said about that. The most preferred and that which I hold to is that the *dhimmi* are not to be allowed to do so; that is, they are to be prevented from farming on the lands of the Muslims because that would be unfair seizure of the Muslims' wealth. It would be injurious to them because the *dhimmi* is not obligated to render the purification dues on that which they extract from the farmland. The purification dues are only obligatory upon the Muslims. If the *dhimmi* does not farm on the farmland of the Muslims, the latter would be able to benefit their poor and rectify their situation.

Similarly, I do not hold to the view that they can sell the Muslims' land lest the tithes that the Muslims owe on it be invalidated. As for what had previously belonged to them from the past, they are not prevented from selling it because it is something that had not belonged to the Muslims before nor do they benefit from it now.

Concerning what is taken from the commerce of the *dhimmi*

Half a tithe is to be taken from the money of the traders among the *dhimmi*. It is the wealth that they bring with them and trade with the Muslims within the lands of Islam. That is to only be taken from the one who comes from a large country to another country, like the *dhimmi* of the Levant who come with their commerce to the Hejaz, Iraq, Yemen or any place other than the people of the Levant when they trade from a far country to that of the Muslims.

---

[19] Similarly narrated in ***Sharh at-Tajrīd, Ŝaḥīḥ al-Bukhāri, Muwaṭṭa, Musnad Ahmed, Sunan ad-Dārimi, Mušannaf Ibn Abi Shayba, Sunan al-Bayhaqi, Sunan at-Tirmidhi, Sunan Abi Dāwūd, Ŝaḥīḥ Ibn Hibbān, Majmu' az-Zawā'id, Al-Mu'jam al-Kabīr, Al-Mu'jam al-Awsat, Bihār al-Anwār***

[20] Imams Abu Ṫālib, Yahya b. Hamza and Ibn Murtaḍa relate that Imam al-Hādi held to to different opinions between the ***Ahkām*** and ***Al-Muntakhab*** regarding ownership of unclaimed land. They say that according to the ***Ahkām***, land will belong to the one who gives life to it; whereas in ***Al-Muntakhab***, he says that it will belong to the imam of the Muslims. We say that there is no disagreement between the two because the land in the ***Ahkām*** refers to land without an owner, but the land referred to in ***Al-Muntakhab*** refers to land conquered by the Muslims. This is confirmed by another statement in ***Al-Muntakhab*** in which the imam echoed his statement from the ***Ahkām***: "The land to which a Muslim gives life shall belong to him and his heirs after him; a tithe is taken from it."

As for the one who was in any of the nearby villages—one is to not take anything from them in those villages where they have settled. One is only to take from the one who moved his commerce from the country in which he lives to a far country. As for the commerce in a country—none of it is to be taken. If they left to another country, one is to take from them just as one would take from other than them.

Concerning the purification dues on what is extracted from the earth

According to me, the purification dues are obligatory upon everything extracted from the earth as well as everything that is taken from it—whether weighable or not. This is because Allah says to His Prophet, peace and blessings be upon him and his progeny: {**Take from their wealth dues, wherewith thou may purify them and sanctify them. And pray for them; verily, thy prayer is source of tranquillity for them. Allah is All-Hearing, All-Knowing**} (**Q. 9:103**).

The term {**wealth**} refers to everything people gain and are enriched by as well as that which they rely upon for their livelihood.[21] It is that which is weighable or not. This is because much of what we find is disregarded by other than us, and one earns from wealth everything that a man and woman owns. This is the case insomuch that perhaps one would not be able to measure the abundance and plenitude that is greater than that which one can measure. For that reason, we are obligated to render the dues from all that.

Allah has obligated such upon all wealth in order to elucidate that. According to the one with intellect and comprehension as well as the one who adheres to His Book, the Glorified teaches it by means of His statement: {**Take from their wealth dues, wherewith thou may purify them and sanctify them**}. These important things are not lacking to the one who owns wealth or does not own wealth. If they have wealth, Allah obligates it from the wealth.

Linguistically, it cannot be called 'wealth' if it is nothing in it for any human being. You will never—God willing—find in the language or among the linguists except that it is designated as 'wealth.' It is not known by any other name or designation. We will explain—God willing—what is obligatory on those possessions of wealth that can be measured and cannot be measured.

Therefore, the fundamental of what obligates a lot or little is that which is watered by flowing water in the earth, that which is watered by the heavens and those trees that grow without need of irrigation—there is a tithe due on all of the produce that occurs or date palms.

As for that which is watered by camels, cows and other animals that carry water—there is to be half a tithe paid on it when its yield has reached the amount of five *wasq*s. A *wasq* equals sixty *šā'*s from the *šā'* of the Prophet, peace and blessings be upon him and his progeny. That is what was the amount determined by Allah's Messenger, peace and blessings be upon him and his progeny. Equally, he determined the amount of five *wasq*s. There are no dues obligated for any measured amount less than five *wasq*s.

My father related to me that his father said:

> The purification dues are obligated on every herb that is extracted from the earth. This is the preferred statement based on the statement of Allah: {**Take from their wealth dues, wherewith thou may purify them and sanctify them**} (**Q. 9:103**).

My father related to me that his father said: "The purification dues are not obligated on any measured amount less than five *wasq*s. A *wasq* equals sixty *šā'*s. One is to take the suitable amount from that which exceeds five *wasq*s."

---

[21] According to the ***Lane's Lexicon***, the Arabic word for wealth (*māl*) denotes: "Whatever one possess; property; wealth…whatever men possess of dirham, or deenars or gold or silver or wheat or barley, or bread, or beasts, or garments or pieces of cloth, or weapons, or other things."

He was asked about the weight of a *šā*, and he replied:

> It is nothing but a measurement because Allah's Messenger, peace and blessings be upon him and his progeny, said: ((A *wasq* is sixty *šā's*)).[22] This proves that it is a measurement, and it is not sound that it is a weight.

Concerning the purification dues taken from grapes

As for those things from grapes which dries—one takes a tithe from it or half a tithe from it when it has become completely dry [depending on its method of watering]. As the Glorified says: **{...and give its due the day of its harvest} (Q. 6:141)**. As for that which has not dried—one is to consider a possible amount and estimate.[23]

Anything that comes from any vine or vines in the possession of one man is to be joined. After five *wasq*s of grapes have dried, one is to take from it half a tithe or a tithe. The method is that one dispatches a competent person to divide the portions into ten without dealing excessively generous or stingy while the owner is present. Then one says to him: "Choose five portions from these ten portions." Each portion is recognisable and known due to some type of indicator. When the owner chooses from the vines five portions out of ten, the divider with the dues-collector takes a portion from the remaining five portions; that is the tithe that is to be taken from the vines. This is the case when the dues are a tithe.

If there is half a tithe from what is obligatory, the dues collector divides that portion between him and the owner of the vines. Then, he can display it for selling. If the owner of the vines wants to buy it after having investigated it for its sale, he has more right to pay for it and buy it. Otherwise, it is sold to another person.

My father related to me that his father was asked about the lands in which are many grapes that have not dried. Is it obligatory for them to pay a tithe for its juice or its value? He replied: "One is to render the purification dues based upon that which one can estimate. Then, one is to take from it based upon the measure of its amount."

Concerning taking unmeasured wealth as dues

As for pomegranates, apples, peaches, quinces, apricots, carobs, figs, plums, sugarcane, bananas, pears and other fruits extracted from the earth that cannot be measured—the method is that one dispatches one who is competent to classify them. If there is no doubt from the one dispatched and the owner of wealth that each classification of those fruits has reached the amount of two hundred dirhams, one is to take either a tithe or half a tithe, depending on the method of its watering. Then one takes the purification dues from each of the yield and not gold or silver for it. If the amount of each classified yield has reached less than two hundred dirhams, the owner does not take anything of that which is less. This is the best method regarding those things that cannot be measured.

Concerning the dues on melons, cucumbers and other fruits that yield without stopping and cannot be enumerated

The best method regarding the dues on the aforementioned items that are not extracted altogether and cannot be held from its beginning until its end due to some of it being harvested after others is that one

---

[22] Similarly narrated in ***Musnad Imam Zayd, Sharh at-Tajrīd, Mušannaf Ibn Abi Shayba, Sunan ad-Dārqutni***

[23] It has been mentioned in ***At-Tahrīr*** and ***Sharh at-Tajrīd*** that two different rulings were passed by al-Hādi regarding grapes that have not been dried. In contrast to what is stated in the ***Ahkām***, he is quoted to have said in ***Al-Muntakhab*** that the purification dues from non-dried grapes are to be treated as unmeasured wealth. That is, its monetary value is to be classified by a competent person and if its monetary value is assessed to be greater than two hundred dirhams, one is to take a tithe or half a tithe of the yield from it. Imam al-Mu`ayyad said in his ***Sharh at-Tajrīd*** that the ruling in the ***Ahkām*** is the most reliable and strongest opinion due to its conformity with what has been narrated from the Prophet regarding the estimation of the grapes. The intent, he says, for the ruling in ***Al-Muntakhab*** is when one cannot find the *nišāb*.

entrusts a person who has knowledge about what is extracted. Such person calculates or corroborates with the owner if he is certain that he is trustworthy. He then leaves it with him if he knows that he would observe what is obligatory upon him and is cautious of himself in respect to Allah regarding it.

If there is no blame on him, he [i.e. the owner] is to swear that he is truthful until he investigates the purchase of the yield considering what yield he attained. If it was two hundred dirhams, one is to take a tithe or half a tithe from it. If the yield is more than two hundred, one is to calculate based on that. If it is less than two hundred, one does not take dues from it.

Concerning the dues on jujube, berries, pistachios, hazelnuts, acorns and other things extracted from the earth

For every owned thing extracted from the earth that one can measure by a *mikyāl* [a unit of dry measurement for grains]—one is to pay a tithe on it. Or one pays half a tithe if the aforementioned things are irrigated as well as on those aforementioned things which cannot be measured. One is to take the dues as we first mentioned regarding those things that cannot be measured.

Concerning the dues on linen and hemp

There is half a tithe due on everything watered by buckets, camels, cows and other artificial means. The full tithe is due on the produce if the watering source is from natural flowing water, water from the heavens or rivers and springs. One is to not take anything from these things until it becomes obligatory to pay dues on it. The obligation of the purification dues is when the minimum reaches the amount that obligates the dues on wealth, and that amount is two hundred dirhams. When it reaches that amount, one is to take a tithe or half a tithe.

Concerning the dues on henna, cotton and reeds as well as what one is to do with them and when one is to take the dues from them

Regarding these three things, one is to consider each of them individually. If its portion equals two hundred dirham, one is to take half a tithe or a complete tithe on that which is cut or picked depending on whether its source of water is natural or not. Thusly, if its portion does not reach the amount of two hundred dirhams, one does not extract anything from it from one year to another. If one were to extract from it an amount that is two hundred dirhams after a complete year, one takes from each of that which is cut or picked for that year. It is a simple affair.

One does not observe it if each category does not reach the amount of two hundred dirhams in a year. One does not take anything from it—whether cut or picked as well as once or many times a year. It is also not observed if the portions do not reach two hundred dirhams in a year.

We have only employed the method that what was and is must reach two hundred dirhams in a year because it is the established standard forever. One does not extract the entire yield together in a year.

We already dealt with the principle that one is to take the dues from the value of the yield of fruits and other things each year. We have made the year the extent of time for the aforementioned cotton, henna and reeds. The value of these yields is known by means of it just as the value of fruits is known by it when one has divided it in a year. Therefore, we hold to the view that the year is the best time to use for measure.

When the yield does not reach the amount of two hundred dirhams unless at the head of the year, the matter is simple. If it does not reach the amount of two hundred dirhams each year, there is nothing due on such person. The exception is that if there was an increase in its production and the yield were to increase and grow abundantly. If that is the case, he owes as we have previously explained and elaborated on.

We simply say that if the amount of yield had not reached two hundred dirhams—whether cut or picked—in a year, there is nothing due on its owners and keepers. This is the measure that is for fruits and the like per year that is already known by the owners of these crops.

When we find that these crops' yield has fallen short of two hundred dirhams in a year, one does not take the purification dues from it. We say that there is nothing due on that yield in less than a year if it had not reached two hundred dirhams just as the purification dues are not obligatory on the yield that falls short of two hundred dirhams in a complete year.

Two hundred dirham is the extent for that which cannot be measured just as five *wasq*s is the extent for that which can be measured. That, according to us and in our view, is the most just and closest to the truth, God willing. There is no strength, assistance and power for us except by Allah!

Concerning the categories, when they are joined and when the measurement for each category has not reached five *wasqs*

When each category of those things that can be measured has not reached the amount of five *wasq*s, there are no purification dues on it. You do not mix wheat with barley or dates with raisins. There are no purification dues from a measureable category that is combined with another measureable category.

The explanation of that is that if it is five *wasq*s but a fourth of wheat or four *wasq*s of barley, one is to not combine one with the other. There are no purification dues to be paid from either one. Similarly, for every type of yield, one is to not combine one category with another.

Concerning the purification dues on categories of fruit whose yield has not reached two hundred dirham

Similarly, if each category of immeasurable fruit and other things does not reach the value of two hundred dirhams, there are no purification dues to be paid on them. One is to not combine one with the other.

An explanation of that can be seen from the following: A man has pomegranates that value at one hundred and eighty dirhams. He also has peaches that value at one hundred and ninety dirhams. He is not obligated to pay the purification dues on them because each category has not reached the value of two hundred dirhams. One category is not combined with the other. Based upon this, the method regarding those things that grow from the earth and are watered is that one is not combined with the other at the time in which the purification dues are paid; rather, one takes it from the wealth.

Concerning joining gold and silver as well as the method according to us

If a man had fifteen mithqal of gold and a hundred and fifty dirhams, he is to join the dirham with the dinar and calculate their joint value. Then, he reckons the value in dinar and extracts a half dinar from twenty mithqal. Anything in addition to that is calculated accordingly. And if he had fifty dirham and ten dinar, he is to join the dinar—based on the value of the dirham[24]—to the fifty dirham. He is then to extract the purification dues to the value of two hundred and fifty dirhams. Anything in addition to that is calculated accordingly.

---

[24] Although it wasn't mentioned in this text, there was apparently a discrepancy in calculating the value of the dirham by the time ***Al-Muntakhab*** was composed. The influx of minted coinage from other regions created a confusion regarding the worth of the dirham. This prompted the compiler of al-Muntakhab to ask al-Hādi about it. He responded by saying: "This dirham in the possession of the people in Iraq and its outskirts is the dirham which applies. It is the dirham which weighs forty-two barley grains." He also clarified that it was this dirham that existed during the era of the Prophet. Regarding the history of the dirham and dinar, please refer to the end of the last section of the **Book of Sales**.

And if he had one hundred dirhams and six dinars, he is to join the dirham with the dinar and calculate their joint value in dirham until it reaches two hundred. Afterwards, one extracts the purification dues from it.

The explanation of that is that the six dinar are calculated accordingly. He expends the twenty dinar to one hundred and twenty dirhams. This one hundred and twenty is joined to the one hundred. This would be two hundred and twenty, and he is to extract 2.5 % as purification dues. Therefore, if a man has eighteen mithqal and fifty dirhams, it would be obligatory for him to convert that fifty dirham to the value of dinar and join it to the eighteen mithqal. Twenty dirham converted to dinar equals to two dinars and a half. All of that equals twenty mithqal and a half. The purification dues would be 2.5% of that. It would be half a dinar and a quarter Iraqi *qīrāṭ*. The value of a dinar is twenty *qīrāṭ*.[25]

Similar is the case with gold and silver. One is to join one with the other and calculate the value of the purification dues on them collectively. One is to not join one category of things to other categories except in the case of gold and silver.

Concerning the manner in which the purification dues are taken

One is to take the purification dues of wheat from wheat, barley from barley, raisins from raisins, dates from dates and everything else which grows from the ground in which the dues are obligatory. One takes the purification dues from that same thing. One does not take the purification dues of one thing from another. Similarly, one takes the dues of a light-footed animal from a light-footed animal and a cloven-footed animal from a cloven-footed animal.

However, there is no problem taking the dues of gold from silver or the dues of silver from gold based upon the value of one of them. We can only combine their joint values in the case of gold and silver because we hold to the view that the joining of one to the other in the dues relates to the meaning of one currency in the purification dues only. As for other than that, it is not the case. In the case of commerce, gold only has the value of gold, and silver only has the value of silver.

Concerning when the purification dues are taken from everything that obligates it

One is to take the purification dues from that which grows from the earth at the time of its harvest. This is based on Allah's statement: **{...and give its due the day of its harvest} (Q. 6:141)**.

As for gold, silver, camels, cows and sheep—after a lunar year passes over those, which he owns, the purification dues are to be paid on it. The purification dues are not obligatory upon any of those things until after a lunar year passes over it.

---

[25] According to ***Al-Muntakhab***, al-Hādi was similarly asked about the worth of a mithqal. The conversation took place as follows:

> He said: "This mithqal which is in the people's possession is twenty Iraqi *qīrāṭ* and twenty-four Hejazi and Basran *qīrāṭ*." I asked: "How can there be a disagreement in that—twenty *qīrāṭ* on one hand and twenty-four *qīrāṭ* on the other?" "There is no disagreement in that; all of that means the same." "How is that?" "This is because the Iraqi *qīrāṭ* is three barley grains; therefore, the mithqal is twenty *qīrāṭ*. The total number of mithqal would be sixty barley grains. As for the Hejazi and Basran *qīrāṭ*, it is the weight of two and a half barley grains. It is for that reason that the mithqal would also be twenty-four *qīrāṭ*. As for the mithqal in itself, it is that which Allah mentioned to Muhammad, peace and blessings be upon him and his progeny, which is the dinar. He says in His Book: **{And amongst the People of the Book are some of whom if ye were to entrust him to a treasure, he would return it unto thee. And there are some who if ye were to entrust him with a dinar, he would not return it unto thee save that ye remain standing over him...} (Q. 3:75)**. This is the dinar that Allah caused Muhammad, peace and blessings be upon him and his progeny, to know upon the tongue of Gabriel. He informed him that the minimum that one is obligated to render for the purification dues is twenty dinars. When it reaches twenty mithqal, half a mithqal is due."

Concerning the purification dues on ornaments

As for every ornament belonging to women as well as that which is on saddles, swords, copies of the Qur'an or other than that, such as belts and reins and the other ornaments of the people of Islam—there is to be a 2.5% dues paid on them similar to the aforementioned half a mithqal paid on each twenty mithqal. Five dirham is to be paid on each two hundred dirhams.

If each category of ornaments reaches the amount that does not obligate the purification dues, one is to combine one of them with the other until it reaches the amount that obligates the purification dues. Afterwards, one extracts the purification dues from the total—which is 2.5% of the sum total.

Concerning the mining of gold and silver as well as what is obligatory on it

Everything that is taken from mining—whether one mithqal or one thousand mithqal—is considered booty (*ghanīma*). It is a gift from Allah and was found as booty. Regarding booty, Allah's judgement on that is that the fifth dues are to be paid on it. That is based on the statement of the Blessed and Exalted: **{And know that whatsoever ye take as booty, verily a fifth thereof is for Allah, and for the Messenger and for the kin and orphans and the needy and the wayfarer} (Q. 8:41)**. It is therefore religiously obligatory for the owner at the time of finding it. If he knows the imam will use it to rectify affairs, he is to pay it to him. It is impermissible to not pay it to him and keep it.

If he does not know his [i.e. the imam's] location, he is to distribute it. It is for those to whom Allah designated it. The most entitled to it among the people is the Progeny of Allah's Messenger, peace and blessings be upon him and his progeny; this includes their orphans, needy and travellers. This is because others can receive charity, but they [i.e. the Prophet's Family] cannot receive or take anything from it.

When the fifth dues are extracted from mining, there are no dues on the rest of it until a lunar year has passed over it. Then, it becomes obligatory to take 2.5% from its wealth after the passing of a lunar year if it amounts to twenty mithqal or two hundred dirhams and beyond that.

Concerning what is obligatory on ambergris, pearls and musk as well as what is obtained as booty on land and sea

All of the aforementioned that are obtained as booty from land and sea[26]—whether little or a lot—are similar to that which is mined—fifth dues are due on it. One is to pay it when you pay the fifth dues on that which is mined.

Concerning the purification dues on honey

The best view regarding the purification dues on honey is that one takes a tithe from it every year when its value reaches two hundred dirham.[27] Regarding that is what has reached us on the authority

---

[26] The term 'booty' is considered general and therefore encompasses anything that one obtains and/or catches. Although not mentioned in the present text, al-Hādi's rulings regarding the fifth dues on game from the sea appear in ***Al-Muntakhab***.

> I asked: "What if a fisherman caught a fish (*huwt*) whose value equals a *dāniq* [i.e. a sixth of a dirham]?" He replied: "He is to pay the fifth dues." "What if he caught a big fish, ate some of it and sold some of it for two hundred dirhams and a lunar year passes over it after having extracted the fifth dues?" "He is to render the purification dues from it since a year passes over it." "How much?" "He is to render 2.5% because the first situation had passed and the amount of wealth that he acquired equals that which necessitates the purification dues." "If the fisherman intended to eat it along with his family and not sell any portion of it, would he still owe the fifth dues?" "Yes, because all of such would be considered booty." "If he were not a fisherman but rather a farmer and desired to get water for his crops by opening a river stream but then a fish comes out of the sea on to land and the man takes it after the water dries up, would he owe anything?" "Yes, because it was that which was extracted from the sea." "Similarly, everything extracted from any body of water would be considered booty?" "Yes."

of Abu Sayāra al-Muta'i.§ He said to the Prophet, peace and blessings be upon him and his progeny: "O Messenger of Allah, I have bees." Allah's Messenger, peace and blessings be upon him and his progeny, replied: ((Then, render the tithe from each hive)).[28]

My father related to me that his father was asked about honey and whether the purification dues are paid on it. The latter replied:

> It has been narrated from the Prophet, peace and blessings be upon him and his progeny, that he took a tithe from it. It was narrated on the authority of Abu Sayāra that he mentioned to the Prophet, peace and blessings be upon him and his progeny, that he had bees. The latter commanded him to render the tithes from it. According to me, it is no different from any other wealth and provisions that Allah has caused His slave to own.

Concerning what is obligatory of treasure

It is the booty that Allah provided for such. Included in it is that which is obtained by mining, which one takes a fifth dues from. One is to pay it when you pay the fifth dues on that which is mined to those whom Allah designated the fifth dues.

Concerning the purification dues on the orphan's wealth and on the debt that one man owes another

One is to pay the purification dues on the wealth of an orphan [or any minor under whom one has charge. Ref. ***At-Tāj***]. Regarding that, it is narrated that the Commander of Believers, 'Ali b. Abi Ṭālib—may Allah's mercy be upon him—used to pay the purification dues from the wealth of the sons of Abi Rāfi'.[29]

It is encouraged for the appointee to look after it for them so that he may reclaim some of the profit for the purification dues unless the purification dues would completely deplete it. Whoever has a debt, it is similarly obligatory to pay the purification dues on it a year after it was retained. However, it should not be depleted to the point below that which obligates the purification dues.

Concerning an oppressive ruler taking the purification dues on wealth and what is to be taken

I do not hold to the view that what an oppressive ruler takes from a person waives his obligation; rather, I hold to the view that it is obligatory for such person to extract the dues from the remainder and distribute it to those for whom Allah commands. One does not count that which an oppressive ruler takes as from him.

My father related to me that his father was asked whether that which an oppressive ruler takes is waived from being counted. He replied: "It is not waived and the proprietor must count it."

An oppressive ruler is one for whom it is impermissible to pay any portion of the purification dues. Whoever pays any portion of it to him willingly without being compelled to do so and while he is able to avoid paying him—such person is ruined in respect to Allah and has not observed that which Allah has

---

[27] A contrary view is narrated in the ***Kanz al-'Ummāl, Amāli Ahmed b. 'Isa*** and ***Sunan al-Bayhaqi***. The chain of narrators in the last two references includes Ja'far b. Muhammad on the authority of his ancestors. According to the narration, Imam 'Ali is reported to have said: "There are no purification dues on honey." However, we reconcile the narrations by saying that the statement recorded from the imam was abbreviated. The complete narration is "There are no purification dues on that honey one consumes or is in one's home." Muhammad b. Manṣūr narrated this in ***Al-Jāmi' al-Kāfi*** and ***Amāli Ahmed b. 'Isa***. Thus, it is clear that the honey which is sold in commerce and not consumed by the owner is that from which the purification dues are rendered.

[28] Similarly narrated in ***Sharh at-Tajrīd, Sunan Abu Dāwūd, Majmu' az-Zawā'id, Al-Mu'jam al-Kabīr, Al-Mu'jam al-Awsat***. Other sources simply say that the Prophet took a tithe from honey; these sources include the following: ***Al-Jāmi al-Kāfi, Amāli Ahmed b. 'Isa, Sunan Ibn Mājah, Sunan al-Bayhaqi, Bihār al-Anwār***

[29] Similarly narrated in ***Sharh at-Tajrīd, Muṣannaf Ibn Abi Shayba, Sunan al-Bayhaqi, Sunan ad-Dārqutni, Kanz al-'Ummāl***.

commanded him regarding paying it and its judgement regarding the eight categories who are to receive it. It is therefore the responsibility of such person to distribute it among the deserving people himself.

If he is forced and compelled to pay it or it is taken forcefully from his possession, his wealth takes priority. This is because of the oppression that has come upon him regarding the wealth that Allah has appointed for His slaves. The dues that an oppressor takes is therefore not counted against the owner.

Concerning taking the dues from owners

It is for the imam to force his subjects to pay the purification dues to him from everything that necessitates the purification dues. This is because Allah says: **{Take from their wealth dues, wherewith thou may purify them and sanctify them. And pray for them. Verily, thy prayer is a source of tranquillity for them. Allah is All-Hearing, All-Knowing}** (Q. 9:103). He commands it to be taken, and none can be commanded to take anything except out of obedience or force. Whoever rejects obedience—it is necessary to take it by force.

Others say that if people are entrusted with gold and silver, they can render the purification dues however they want. If they want, they can pay it to the imam. If they want, they can distribute it themselves. This is, according to me, invalid. There is no authentic narration that has been narrated to support this, nor is there a reported tradition that relates this. This is because it contradicts the Book of Allah. And that which contradicts the Book is not the truth, and that which does not counter it is correct.

I believe that the one who said this only did so to conceal the blessings and wealth from the people of oppression due to fear and to prevent their wealth from the oppressors. The interpretation of their statement is as thus. According to me, the purification dues on this wealth are otherwise invalid. The purification dues on this misappropriated wealth would not be a religious injunction of Allah upon them to render it to those Allah designates. Nor would it be religiously obligatory for them to pay any portion of it.

If it is a religious injunction for them to pay the purification dues, it is religiously obligatory that they pay it to the ruler of the Muslims whom Allah commands to take it from them. Allah emphasises to him and them that it should be taken from their hands in order to distribute it to wherever he is commanded and to observe it in respect to those who have it. They are commanded to be submissive to him in that.

Regarding Allah's command for him to take it from them is His statement: **{Take from their wealth dues, wherewith thou may purify them and sanctify them. And pray for them. Verily, thy prayer is a source of tranquillity for them. Allah is All-Hearing, All-Knowing}** (Q. 9:103). These are the dinar and dirham. However, it is not devoid of either being wealth or other than wealth. If it is wealth, it is upon the imam to take from it that which is obligatory. It is not for any of creation to say that it is not wealth; rather, they are the choicest of wealth. Allah would not make the purification dues on this wealth obligatory upon them and not obligate them to pay any of it to the people of charity among the poor and needy—in secret or public—by giving it to them or their imam. Then say to the one that says that they are entitled to it and are to pay it without the imam: "What is your proof for that?" Can we find any proof for that in the Clear Book or the agreed-upon traditions of the Messenger of the Lord of creation in which there is no disagreement? Is there a proof for that in rule of the intellect and the understanding of one with intellect?

Is that like what we can find for you among the verses of the Decisive Book wherein Allah says **{Take from their wealth dues}** (Q. 9:103)? Is that like what we can find for you narrated on the authority of the Messenger, peace and blessings be upon him and his progeny, regarding what he took from al-'Abbās who was one of the closest of his relatives? Both we and you narrate that Allah's Messenger, peace and blessings be upon him and his progeny, hurried to take the purification dues from al-'Abbās before the time that the dues became obligatory.[30] Is it like what we can find for you in the proof of the intellect when we previously mentioned that it is not devoid of either being wealth or other than wealth? If it is wealth, what is due on it is that which is due on wealth.

The imam is most entitled to take it, as he is commanded to take it. If there were no wealth, there would be nothing for the imam from which to take the purification dues. It would not be obligatory for the owners to pay the dues to anyone else—whether in secret or public. There is no other way to pay it. It would not be for the fair-minded person to reiterate any statement regarding that.'

Concerning those for whom the dues are obligated and prohibited and concerning the designation of those categories that Allah mentions

The dues are obligatory for those slaves whom Allah designates in His statement: **{Verily, the dues are for the poor and needy and workers and those to whose hearts are to be reconciled and those to be freed and the indebted and those in the way of Allah and the traveller. It is a religious injunction from Allah. Allah is All-Knowing, All-Wise} (Q. 9:60).**

It is between eight categories. Whenever one category is waived among them, its portion is allotted to those who are in most need. It is the option of the imam of the Muslims to distribute it to one of the categories designated by Allah. He distributes it without injustice; no one among the people in these categories is to be treated unfairly in that regard.

As for the **{poor}**, they are those who do not own anything except a house, a servant and a garment to cover their trunks; these are considered **{the poor}**. The **{needy}** whom we prefer to take the dues are the people of poverty and insufficiency who are compelled to take it. The **{workers}** are the collectors who exact the full amount from the hands of its owners and take it.

The ones **{whose hearts are to be reconciled}** are the people of this world who are inclined to it. They would not follow the truthful unless it is paid to them. The Muslims would not be safe from them otherwise and their hearts would not be reconciled to them due to the fear of their opposition. They would be cautious of them, and the latter would refrain from helping them against their enemies. This is similar to what Allah's Messenger, peace and blessings be upon him and his progeny, used to do. It is religiously obligatory upon the imam to reconcile them by means of that. He should attempt to influence them by some of what they desire.

As for **{those to be freed}**—they are those who are contracted to serve as slaves for a determined period of time. It is religiously obligatory for the imam to appropriate for them the amount needed to fulfil their terms and time specificity.

As for **{the indebted}**—they are those who have debts that were not accrued out of extravagance, foolishness or disobedience. It is religiously obligatory for the imam to cover the cost of their debts. After that, he is to give to them that which will help establish them, provide a livelihood for them, sustain them and be sufficient for them.

As for **{those in the way of Allah}**—it is that he provides a portion to strengthen those warriors and support them in preparation against the oppressors. Those things that strengthen include horses, weaponry and necessary equipment for them. That is based upon what Allah commands regarding them: **{And prepare for them whatsoever ye are able of strength and of steeds of war that ye may terrify the enemies of Allah and thy enemies...} (Q. 8:60).**

As for the **{traveller}**—it refers to a weak traveller travelling to and fro on the path. He is to be provided for with that which would strengthen him and suffice for him—whether a little of a lot. The imam is to pay for him from that which he possesses to cover his wages and expenditure. If such

[30] Similarly narrated in ***Sharh at-Tajrīd, Mušannaf Ibn Abi Shayba, Al-Mu'jam al-Kabīr***

person is naked, he is to provide clothing. All of such occurs until the traveller ends his journey and returns to his homeland.

As for those who do not have a right to the dues—they are the progeny of Allah's Messenger, peace and blessings be upon him and his progeny. They are those whom Allah has exempted from taking it and purified them from its consumption and the filth of it due to the hands of the Muslims. In exchange of that, he gives them the fifth dues from the booty of the idolaters—wealth and lands. This also includes that which was obtained from the rebellious who took it from its rightful owners. This is based on the statement of Allah: **{And know that whatsoever ye take as booty, verily a fifth thereof is for Allah, and for the Messenger and for the kin and orphans and the needy and the wayfarer} (Q. 8:41)**. This is for them a substitute for the aforementioned dues that is impermissible for them.

If a man from the progeny of Allah's Messenger takes, consumes and spends from the purification dues while ignorant of its impermissibility, he is to pay back that which he used and give it to those whom Allah designated. If he were to do such while cognisant of its impermissibility, he is to return it and sincerely repent to his Lord. If he took it from them out of need and compulsion and no one else could be found to give it to and if there was fear that he would perish otherwise, it is religiously obligatory that he pay back what he took after that without exception.

If such person were to find a portion of purification dues and carcass, he should still not consume any of the purification dues because of its impermissibility for him. He should reject the notion of paying back what he consumed. He should consider consuming some of the carcass out of necessity unless he fears for his life or fears sicknesses and untoward accidents if he were to eat it. Then he should not avoid it if he fears for his life because Allah says in His Book: **{Allah desires ease for thee, and He desires not hardship for thee...} (Q. 2:185)** and **{...and slay not thyself. Verily, Allah hath been merciful unto thee} (Q. 4:29)** and **{And make not thine own hands contribute to destruction} (Q. 2:195)**.

If one does not fear for his life, one is to not take any portion of the purification dues believing it to be out of necessity. The exception is if it is understood to be a loan and one would pay back what he took. As for the idea that it would be religiously permissible for him to consume it out of necessity—it is not the case. The exception is the aforementioned condition that he pays it back.

We said this because Allah deems it permissible for him to eat enough carcass out of necessity in order to preserve his life. However, He does not deem it permissible in His Book that any of the progeny of Allah's Messenger, peace and blessings be upon him and his progeny, consumes any portion of the dues that are religiously prohibited from them. The exception is if it is considered a loan with the notion of paying back what he consumed. If a man other than them who belonged to one of the aforementioned categories were compelled to take from the purification dues, he would not be obligated to pay it back because he belonged to one of the categories mentioned by Allah, such as the needy and the traveller.

Allah only obligates the progeny of Allah's Messenger, peace and blessings be upon him and his progeny, to pay it back because it is not a condition on other than them, and their state is not like that of others. Rather, their state concerning it is the state of one who does not take from it. It is therefore binding that they pay it back to its owners and distribute it among its people.

My father related to me that his father was asked about charity for the Bani Hāshim. He replied:

> The charity is not religiously permissible for them because Allah ennobled His Prophet, peace and blessings be upon him and his progeny, by means of the fifth dues that He made for them. This is due to the emphasis on him and them, peace and blessings be upon him and his progeny.

Concerning the purification dues taken from one land to another and concerning the land tax as well as what is obligatory regarding it

One should not extract a people's purification dues from their city to another city while there is one among them who needs it. The exception is if the imam observes that others are people of Islam who are in more need. Then, he should act upon his opinion because he looks into the affairs of the Muslims and is most responsible for the believing slaves of Allah.

My father related to me that his father was asked about the purification dues extracted from one land and taken to another. He replied: "The order of the purification dues is to the imams. Only the imam can distribute the amount to those categories. He must be familiar with the affairs of the Muslims."

Everything that is in one's possession from those conquered lands that land taxes are paid on—it is binding upon him to extract the lease of the land; it is the land tax. It is binding upon him due to what Allah has made binding concerning those herbs from which are extracted a tithe or half a tithe observing its purification.

The purification dues are different to the land taxes, and the land taxes are different to the purification dues. This is because the land does not belong to him; it belongs to Allah, His Messenger and the Muslims. It is only leased to him based upon the leased taxes on it from them. Leasing property does not remove from the Muslim the obligation of the purification dues on that which grows there. Rather, it is upon him to observe that on the day of its harvest just as Allah has commanded.

Verily, the likeness of taxable land in the possession of the farmer is like that which one person leases to another by means of the payment for the crops. It is upon him to render the paid land tax to the owner, as well as the lease let as a condition. If one taxes the yield of Allah, which grows and is extracted on the day of its harvest—it is a tithe or half a tithe depending on the method of how the land was watered.

My father related to me that his father was asked about conquered land and the taxes on it. "Does one pay the tithe on it along with the land tax or not?" He replied:

> One pays the tithe on it because there is no interrelation between it and the tax or rent. Rent is a different monetary obligation, and the conquered land tax is a different monetary obligation. The tithe is a purification due and charity in Muslim property.

It is obligatory for the imam to take from them the lease of the lands of Allah. It is this that is called 'taxes' that is paid on the land that was conquered. This is because it is a lease, even if it is called 'taxes.' That in which is a compensation is a monetary obligation that should be placed in Allah's wealth. It is an obligatory transaction imposed on all Muslims—young and old, Hashemite and Bedouin, Persian and non-Arab. One takes the dues from them, which Allah has obligated after being extracted from this earth once the amount of the same type has reached five *wasq*s. The full tithe is due on the produce if the watering source is from natural flowing water, water from the heavens or rivers and springs even if it was irrigated from the roots without intervention. Half a tithe is due on everything watered by buckets, camels, cows and other artificial means.

One is to distribute the tithe or half a tithe to those people of charity whom Allah designated. That which one takes from these lands differs in judgement even if it is just one. Whatever one takes from lands conquered by force, its condition and judgement is the same. The judgement of what one takes from the dues of the Muslims, which Allah extracts, is the same judgement as other types of dues. One is to distribute it to those nine categories that Allah designates in His statement: **{Verily, the dues are for the poor and needy and workers and those to whose hearts are to be reconciled and those to be freed and the indebted and those in the way of Allah and the traveller} (Q. 9:60)**.

If the imam decides to distribute it all to one category in order to rectify the affairs of the Muslims, it is permissible for him to do so. This mandate would be to him, and consideration of the Muslims is obligatory upon him.

Concerning an explanation of the one who takes the dues, who does not take the dues and how much one in need can take

The one who has in his possession any of the aforementioned categories of food, money, livestock or land that obligate the dues—such person does not take from the dues. This is the case even if that land is dispensable. The one who takes from the dues is the one whose yield does not obligate the dues. That is, if the amount is less than five *wasq*s, such person takes from the dues. But if his yield comes to five *wasq*s and he fears that his yield would be completely depleted or he is certain that it would not be enough for his family, he does not take anything from the dues even if he fears for his life and his family is in need. This is because he has in his possession that which obligates the dues. He should not fear for himself nor should the wealth of the Muslims bring him certainty because with today is tomorrow. Perhaps Allah will remove his fear and alleviate tomorrow his provisions that were restricted today.

Allah—Glorified be He—says: **{For, verily, with hardship is ease. Verily, with hardship is ease}** **(Q. 94:5-6)**. The Glorified also says: **{And there is not a beast in the earth but that the sustenance thereof depends upon Allah. He knows its dwelling and repository. All is in a manifest decree}** **(Q. 11:6)**. With that, this man may have what he needs for today from his yield which reaches the limit of its time period but someone else among the poor Muslims may not have anything to fulfil his need. The latter would be in more of a need to seek that which is taken from the dues.

Concerning the amount that one in need is to take from the dues

It is impermissible for the poor or one in need to take the amount that obligates the dues from the dues. Rather, he is to take less than that or that which is less or more than the amount of his need and that of his family. If he is single, he is to take fifty dirham or its value from the other things. If he has a family, he is to take nineteen mithqal of gold currency. If he takes silver, he is to take one hundred ninety dirhams. If he takes a dry measure of grain, he is to take five *wasq*s minus a third. If he takes camels, he is to take four of them. If he takes cows, he is to take nineteen of them. If he takes sheep, he is to take thirty-nine ewes. If he takes fruit from trees, such as pomegranates, apples or other fruits, one is to take the amount of one hundred ninety-five dirhams.

If there is no just imam to whom one renders the purification dues, one is to distribute it among its people to whom it is an obligation to pay. Their wealth is paid to those who remember Allah and who are designated as brothers. The owner of the dues is to begin with the one whom he is not obligated to maintain among his relatives, kin and neighbours. Then, one is to spread it among any deserving Muslim to whom he can render the dues; this includes the people of scrupulousness among the Muslims. As for the one who inclines towards opposition in the religion, such person is the furthest from the believers in deserving it.

Concerning the one who earns wealth and had wealth for which the dues are obligated before it and concerning the dues on lost wealth, stolen wealth or usurped wealth

Whoever had thirty-five mithqal while less than a lunar year passes over it and then he earns more wealth, he is to pay the dues from the last and the first once the lunar year has passed. Similarly, if he buys a slave, horse or goods with it for the purpose of business while anticipating profit and then his wealth increases and he buys another horse with it, he is to pay the dues for all of the aforementioned to the amount of its value on the first day after the lunar year has passed. He is to not consider an approximate amount at the end. The dues are only obligated from the wealth in his possession that was newly earned that lunar year.

As for the one who lost or misplaced his wealth and two years pass before he finds it, he is to extract from it the obligated amount for each year once it is found. For the first year, 2.5% of twenty-five is extracted. It is twelve and a half Iraqi *qīrāṭ*; the amount of a dinar is twenty *qīrāṭ*. For the second year, one extracts twelve *qīrāṭ* and a half *habb*[31] and a sixteenth of a *habb*.

Similarly, when stolen wealth is recovered, he extracts the dues from the stolen wealth for the two years. Similar is the case for any wealth that a Muslim misappropriates in the lands of Islam because even though it was in the possession of the usurper for two years, no amount was extracted from his hand. The imam of the Muslims is mandated to seize and remove it from the hand of the usurper by the mandate of the Lord of creation.

Concerning that which the idolaters usurp from the Muslims' wealth

If the idolaters usurp the wealth of some Muslims—whether livestock or anything else—and it remains in their possession for a year or two before the Muslims reclaim it, each owner is most entitled to it and it is not shared among the Muslims. When it is taken, there is no purification dues paid from it because he did not own any quantity while it was in the hands of the usurping idolaters.

We simply say that it is not counted and that it is not like other wealth. If the divider comes before its owner can claim his portion or his possessions are recognised, it is not religiously obligatory for it to be taken from the one that this happened to unless its value was extracted. Then, he is more entitled to it after its yield was extracted. This is the difference between what was usurped by idolaters and that which was taken by Muslims. Afterwards, the recapture of the Muslims is to be returned to their owners from the idolaters. There is also a difference between that which was usurped in the lands of Islam by the people of rebellion and that which is judged as being returned by the people of belief.

Concerning the man who has a profit but owes a debt or he has wealth that he owes the like of it as purification dues but owes the like of it as a debt

Whoever owes two *wasq*s of food and extracted five *wasq*s from his land, he is to pay a fifth of the *wasq*s as the purification dues. He is not to consider as his yield that which obligates his debt. This is because if he were to extract what he owes from that, there would not remain anything that would obligate the purification dues. Rather, he is to pay the purification dues first and then the debt after rendering that which Allah has obligated in His land. Similarly, if his yield is ten *wasq*s and he owes ten *wasq*s, he extracts the purification dues from the total and then pays the debt. Similarly, if he owes twenty dinars and has twenty dinars in his possession, he is obligated to pay the purification dues on what he has even if he owes the same amount as a debt.

We do not acknowledge the opinion of those cheapskates who say otherwise because these dinars are not devoid of ownership even if the amount of his debt is the same or he does not have in his possession the amount that they claim as his debt. Therefore, if he does have in his possession that which permits charity, as well as that which is used for marriage, food and drink, it similarly necessitates that he renders the purification dues from it. If he is not able to use it for charity, marriage, food and drink, he is not obligated to render the purification dues from it. Therefore, I do not know what could be clearer to the one with sound intellect, analogical reasoning and understanding that he can eat from it and marry with it! Similar is the case with one who owes two hundred dirhams and has two hundred dirhams in his possession. After a lunar year passes over it, he is religiously obligated to render the purification dues from it; he is to not consider the debt he owes.

[31] A unit of weight that approximates to the weight of a barley seed. [Ref. **Lane's Arabic English Lexicon**]

Concerning the man who exchanges his money in a business transaction and buys supplies with it but then their value decreases or increases

If a man exchanged money that necessitates the purification dues regarding commercial supplies—whether they be dry goods, raw material (*qazz*), food or animals, he is to render the purification dues on it when a lunar year passes over it. He renders the dues based upon its value at the time that the purification dues are obligatory upon him. One does not consider price fluctuation—increase or decrease—at the head of the lunar year's passing and not after it. However, one is to consider it at the time that the purification dues are obligatory.

The explanation of that is the following: A man buys a horse for one hundred dinars. A lunar year passes over it and at the head of the lunar year, the value increases to one hundred fifty dinars. He is to render the purification dues from the one hundred fifty dinar. Similar is the case if a lunar year passes over it and the time for the purification dues occurs while the value is fifty dinars.

One is not obligated to render the purification dues from anything not in his possession. Rather, he is to render the purification dues on that which is in his possession based upon its value at the time that it is religiously obligatory upon his wealth because the value of wealth increases and decreases. The purification dues are simply obligatory at the head of the lunar year. Therefore, if the time for the purification dues occurs and the wealth's value increases, one calculates its value at that time. If decrease occurs, one takes from that which one has at that particular time.

Concerning the purification dues on wealth from camels jointly owned by two men

If two men owned eight camels with each person owning four, there are no purification dues owed by either one. If the both of them owned ten camels, each one of them owes a ewe. If the two of them owned sixteen, both of them only owe two ewes. Similarly, there is nothing else due from the both of them when there is less than twenty. When the amount reaches twenty, both owe four ewes—each owing two ewes. If the both of them have thirty camels, each one owes three ewes. If they own thirty-four or thirty-six, they do not owe anything other than three ewes. If they have forty camels, each one of them owes four ewes.

Even if they were to own forty-six camels, they do not owe anything else until the number reaches fifty. Afterwards, each owes a *bint makhāḍ*. If the two of them owns sixty camels, there is nothing due on them except a *bint makhāḍ* each. When the number reaches seventy-two, each owes a *bint labūn*. When the number reaches eighty or ninety, nothing is due other than a *bint labūn* each. When the number reaches ninety-two, each owes a *hiqqa*. Even if there were one hundred between them, they do not owe anything other than two *hiqqa*s. The same is the case whether it was one hundred ten or one hundred twenty.

When the number reaches one hundred twenty-two, each owes a *jadha'*. If the number is one hundred thirty, one hundred forty or one hundred fifty, they do not owe anything other than that. If the number increases to one hundred fifty-two, they owe four *bint labūn*s—each owing two. If the number is one hundred sixty, one hundred seventy or one hundred eighty, they do not owe anything other than that. When the number increases one hundred eighty-two, they owe four *hiqqa*s—each owing two. Afterwards, they do not owe anything else until the number reaches two hundred forty. At that point, they owe four *hiqqa*s—each owing two. If the number of camels increases beyond that, each owes a *hiqqa* for every fifty camels. What has been mentioned in this section is based upon the accounting that we have explained. So consider it—God willing—and aspire to that.

Concerning the purification dues on wealth from cows jointly owned by two men

If two men owned fifty cows, there are no purification dues owed by either one if they are equally divided between the two of them; neither owes the purification dues. If there were sixty, they owe two male or female calves. The calf refers to the yearling. If they were seventy, there is nothing due other than two calves. If there were eighty, each owes a full-grown cow. If they were one hundred or one hundred ten, there is nothing else is due. When the number reaches one hundred twenty, each owes two calves. Then, one does not owe anything else until the number reaches one hundred forty. When the number reaches one hundred forty, each owes a full-grown cow and a calf until the number reaches one hundred sixty. Afterwards, each owes two full-grown cows until the number reaches one hundred eighty. At that amount, each one of them owes three calves until the number reaches two hundred. When the number reaches two hundred, each owes a full-grown cow and two calves until the number reaches two hundred twenty. When the number reaches two hundred twenty, each owes two full-grown cows and a calf until the number reaches two hundred forty. When the number reaches two hundred forty, each owes three full-grown cows. What has been mentioned in this section is based upon the accounting that we have explained. So consider it—God willing.

Concerning the purification dues on wealth from sheep jointly owned by two men

If two partners owned forty, fifty, sixty or seventy ewes, there are no purification dues for them. However, if the number reaches eighty, each owes one ewe. If the number reaches two hundred, there is nothing due other than two ewes. Similarly, if the number reaches two hundred forty, there is nothing else due from them. When the number increases to two hundred forty-two, they collectively owe four ewes until the number reaches four hundred. When it reaches four hundred two, they collectively owe six ewes. When they have six hundred and the number of sheep increases, each owes a ewe for every two hundred. What has been mentioned in this section is based upon the accounting that we have explained. For eight hundred, eight ewes are due and for one thousand, ten ewes are due.

Concerning what two owners are to do when one has more than the other and the manner in which the purification dues are taken

An explanation of that is the following: There are seventy ewes between two men—one owns four-sevenths and the other owns three-sevenths. The dues collector takes a ewe from these sheep. They must settle the differences between them. The one to whom the dues are obligatory—the owner of the four-sevenths, which is the forty ewes—must return the difference to the one to whom the dues are not obligatory—the owner of the three-sevenths, which is the thirty ewes. The difference to be returned is three-sevenths of the ewe's value, which was his when the dues collector came to take from the owner of forty ewes.

Similarly, if the two of them own one hundred sheep—with one of them owning three-fourths and the other owning one-fourth—the collector takes a ewe from them. It is an obligation on the owner of the three-fourths rather than the owner of the fourth; he is to give its value or what contents him because the purification dues are only obligatory upon the owner of the three-fourths. This is because three-fourths are seventy-five ewes, which necessitates a ewe. The owner of the fourth is not obligated to render the purification dues because twenty-five ewes do not obligate the purification dues.

Similarly, if two men owned one hundred fifty sheep—with one owning two-thirds and the other owning a third—the collector is to take two ewes from them. The owner of the third returns a third to the owner of two thirds because the dues are obligatory on both of them. The owner of the one hundred ewes is obligated to give one ewe, and the owner of the fifty ewes is also obligated to give one ewe.

If the two of them had one hundred forty sheep—with one of them owning three-fifths and the other owning two-fifths—the collector takes two ewes. The owner of the two-fifths returns back a fifth to the owner of the three-fifths. Similarly, if the two of them own one hundred sixty ewes—with one of them owning three-fourths and the other owning one-fourth—the collector takes two ewes.

The owner of the fourth returns half back to the owner of the three-fourths because the purification dues are due on both of them. The owner of the fourth owes a ewe because he has forty ewes, and the owner of the three-fourths owes a ewe because he has one hundred twenty ewes. The owner of the one hundred twenty ewes says to the owner of the forty ewes "I owe a ewe and you owe a ewe. And the collector takes two ewes. I have three-fourths of them, which is a ewe and a half, and you extracted [the value of] a half ewe. I extracted for you a half a ewe, and you can return it to me."

Even if the owner of the forty sheep does not return the half ewe [i.e. its value] back to the owner of the one hundred twenty ewes, the dues are taken for the forty ewes except the half. This [i.e. the half] would not count. Similar is the case with all joint ownership of things other than livestock.

Concerning what one takes from camels of obligatory age

An explanation of that is the following: When a man has thirty-nine camels, it is obligatory for him to render a *bint labūn*. If he does not have a *bint labūn* but has a *bint makhāḍ*, the dues collector takes the *bint makhāḍ* as well as the money for the difference between the two.

There have been reports narrated regarding the monetary value between the two of them. There are also various statements regarding them, but we do not know of their authenticity. Rather, one is to take the amount that is known among the people who are just and rectify affairs.

Similarly, if one has fifty camels, it is obligatory for him to give a *hiqqa*. However, if he cannot find a *hiqqa* and has a *bint labūn*, it is to be taken as well as the monetary value between the two of them. Similarly, if he does not have a *bint labūn* and has a *jadha'*, it is to be taken and a just monetary value between the *hiqqa* and *jadha'* is to be given to the owner of the camels.

Concerning the delaying of the purification dues on cattle for two or three years

An explanation of that is the following: If a man had nine camels and he had not rendered the dues on them for two years, it would be obligatory for him to render the dues with two ewes now. Then, he is to resume rendering a ewe for each year. Even if he stops at ten, he would have to render two ewes each year.

If a man had one hundred twenty-one ewes and he delays his purification dues for two years, he is to render three ewes now—two ewes out of the one hundred twenty-one for the first year and one ewe out of the one hundred eighteen for the second year. If he had two hundred seven ewes and had not rendered the dues for three years with this number, he is to render three ewes for the first year, three ewes for the second year and three ewes for the third year. There should remain one hundred ninety-eight ewes. If another lunar year passes while he has these one hundred ninety-eight ewes, he is to render two ewes. Similar is the case for every other thing mentioned in this section regarding the one who delays paying the purification dues for two years.

If a man had forty-one cows and he had not rendered the dues for two years, it would be obligatory for him to render two full-grown cows now. If he had not rendered the dues for these forty-one cows for three years, it would be obligatory for him to render three full-grown cows and a calf at the head of the lunar year.

We only say that because the purification dues for the forty-one cows in the first year are one full-grown cow; this leaves forty. Then the second lunar year passes on the forty—to which one owes another full-grown cow. This leaves thirty-nine. When the third lunar year passes over the thirty-nine cows, one owes a male or female calf. One applies this same analogical reasoning to wealth that one delays in paying the dues or other things that we previously explained to you, God willing.

Concerning delaying the purification dues on gold

If a man had thirty mithqal of gold and delayed rendering the purification dues for two years, it is obligatory to render 2.5% of the thirty for the first year and 2.5% of the twenty-nine and a quarter for the second year.

Similarly, if a man had forty dinars and withheld paying the purification dues for a lunar year and a half and twenty go missing after the half of the second year has elapsed and he is not able to render the dues from that until the two lunar years has passed, he is to render the purification dues from the forty that the first lunar year passed over. The same is the case with the mithqal. Then, he is to render half a mithqal from the twenty that was missing that second lunar year. There is nothing due for the half of the lunar year in which the money was missing because the second lunar year had not passed over it. This is the case unless he found it during that time. Then, he is to render the dues for the past time that it was missing.

Concerning delaying the purification dues on silver

If a man had two hundred dirhams and three lunar years passed over it without him having rendered the purification dues on it, he is obligated to render the dues from it. He is to render five dirhams for the first lunar year, but there is nothing else due on him for the last two lunar years because after the five dirham was due on him from the two hundred for the first lunar year, there remained one hundred ninety-five dirhams. Two lunar years passed over that amount which does not obligate the purification dues.

If a man had two hundred five dirhams and two lunar years were to pass over it without him having rendered the purification dues on it, he is obligated to render five and an eighth dirham from it; he would not owe anything for the second lunar year. This is because when the second lunar year passed over it, the amount was less than two hundred by an eighth.

If he had one thousand dirhams and two lunar years were to pass over it without him having rendered the purification dues on it, he is obligated to render 2.5% of one thousand for the first lunar year. For the second lunar year, he is to render 2.5% of nine hundred seventy-five dirhams.

Concerning combining gold with silver

If a man had five dinars and one hundred dirhams and two lunar years were to pass over it without him having rendered the purification dues on it, it would be obligatory—according to us—to combine the value of the dinar and dirham. This is because the combination of the value of the dinar and dirham obligates the purification dues from the dirham. If the value of twenty dirham equals a dinar, this dirham amount would be considered two hundred dirhams. The amount of dinar would equal one hundred dirhams, and when this amount is joined with the initial one hundred dirhams, he would be obligated to render five dirhams for the first lunar year. However, he does not owe anything for the second lunar year because the amount was less than two hundred, which was depleted for the dues for the first lunar year. Similarly, if he had fifteen dinars and one hundred dirhams, it would be as if it was combined to equal twenty dinars. He would be obligated to render from it half a mithqal as dues.

Concerning the ruling regarding the people of the purification dues when the collector is delayed in collecting it from them and then later approaches them for it but they had already paid it to the poor and needy

He should inquire about it and ask them for clear evidence; he should thoroughly investigate it. If he has verified it, he passes over them for that lunar year. However, he is to scold them harshly for their ignorance and urge them to never do such action again. He is to also instruct them that if they were to repeat such action, it would not be valid and that he will take what is due from them. If they repeat it the coming year, it would be invalid after having cautioned them and he is to take from them the complete amount.

If they claimed that they had already distributed some of it and were not approached about it, he is to investigate their statement and ask for clear evidence. After verifying their statement, it would be considered valid but they are to be cautioned to not repeat such action again. However, if no evidence can be established or their statement cannot be verified, their statement is not acknowledged and the complete amount of the dues are to be collected from them.

Concerning what is collected from the Banu Taghlib, the Christians of the Peninsula

The Banu Taghlib are those who had made a fuss about the *jizya*[32] and were shown disdain. They asked that the dues be doubled for them and they were granted such. The condition upon them was that their children not be baptised. The meaning of 'their children not be baptised' is that they not enter their religion. Then, their children were baptised, and they violated their condition.

If Allah manifests the rightful imam to see that they invited them to Islam but they refused to enter it, he is to fight their fighters, capture their offspring and take their wealth because they violated their contracts with him. Similarly, it is narrated that the Commander of Believers, 'Ali b. Abi Ṭālib, upon him be peace, used to say: "Had Allah granted me mastery, I would be obliged to fight their men, capture their offspring and seize their wealth."[33] This is because they had violated their contracts and violated their condition that their offspring would not be baptised.

As for the one who does not manifest the word of justice and lowers the flag of truth, he is to take half of the wealth that he would take from the Muslims. Regarding gold and silver, he is to take half a tithe of twenty mithqals, which is a mithqal. From forty mithqals, he is to take two mithqals. For more, he is to calculate the same—half a tithe. Out of two hundred dirhams, he is to take ten dirhams. Out of four hundred dirhams, he is to take twenty dirhams—half a tithe.

Similarly, he is to take two ewes for every five camels as well as four ewes for every ten camels. He is to take two *bint makhāḍ*s for twenty-five camels, two *bint labūn*s for thirty, two *hiqqa*s for forty-six and two *jadha'*s for sixty-one. He is to take four *bint labūn*s for seventy-six, four *hiqqa*s for ninety-one. If there are more camels, he is to take two *hiqqa*s for every fifty.

Similarly, in regard to cows, he is to take two male or female calves for thirty cows. He is to take two full-grown cows for forty and four calves for sixty. He is to take two full-grown cows and four calves for one hundred. Any additional amount should be calculated thusly. For every thirty there is to be two calves and for every forty there is to be two full-grown cows.

Similarly, in regard to sheep, he is to take two ewes for forty sheep, four ewes for one hundred twenty-one, six ewes for two hundred one and six ewes for three hundred as well. If there are additional sheep, there are two ewes for every one hundred.

Similarly, in regard to that which is extracted from land, he is to take from them half a tithe and a tithe. Half a tithe is due for that which is watered by flowing water in the earth, streams or the heavens once it has reached five *wasq*s. A tithe is due on that which watered by buckets, camels, cows and other artificial means once the amount reaches five *wasq*s.

One is to not take any dues from their wealth until it reaches the amount that obligates the Muslims to render such—twenty mithqals, two-hundred dirhams, five camels, thirty cows, forty sheep, five *wasq*s of that which is measured and two hundred dirham worth of produce which cannot be measured. Once the amounts reach these limits, he is to take half of that which he takes from the Muslims.

That which is taken from the Banu Taghlib is booty that is religiously permissible for the Hashemites and others among the Muslims. This is not the same as the tithes and purification dues of the Muslims

---

[32] The term *jizya* is not to be understood as a penalty or fine for belonging to another religion; rather, it is a tribute that is paid not unlike that of other civilisations, such as ancient Rome and ancient Persia. We will address this in greater detail in a later footnote.

[33] Similarly narrated in ***Sunan Abu Dāwūd, Sunan al-Bayhaqi***

because the purification dues were made religious injunction upon the Muslims to purify and cleanse them by means of it as well as to raise their ranks in the hereafter. This *jizya* that is taken from these Christians is a substitute; it is a penalty and abjection for them so that they can remain in their religion just as Jews and Christians are made to pay a *jizya* so that they can remain in their religion.

For that reason, we say that everything taken from these Christians of Taghlib differs from that which is taken from the Muslims. We say that the *dhimmi* pays the *jizya* and does not pay the tithes of the people of the religion. However, he does not take the *jizya* from the heads of the Banu Taghlib because they had made a peace agreement that a tithe is taken from them. That which is taken from the *dhimmi* is less than what is taken from them.

Some have said that one does not take from the wealth of their children just as one does not take the *jizya* from the children of the *dhimmi*. According to me, this is nothing. Rather, I hold to the view that one is to take from their men, women and children because they rejected the *jizya* that is collected from the *dhimmi*. In order for them not to follow the Israelites, and they agreed to follow the Muslims in giving the tithes and giving much more than the tithe because they are not Muslims. With this, they have chosen the criteria for the people who give the tithe. The tithe is from whomever has capital among the Muslims including the men, women, or children. Therefore, we said that it is taken from whomever chooses the tithe criteria and not the criteria of the *jizya*. They should take from the Banu Taghlib that which is taken from the people of the tithe.

Concerning the fast-breaking dues (*zakat al-fiṭr*)

The fast-breaking dues are religiously obligatory on behalf of every dependent among the Muslims who is able. It is something that Allah's Messenger appointed, made an injunction upon the Muslims and commanded them to observe on the day of breaking their fast. Allah did such as appreciation to Him for what He has graced them of the deliverance of the Message to them as well as for completing the fast Allah made binding upon them and to purify their deeds from the previous months.

He, peace and blessings be upon him and his progeny, considered their poor[34] and wealthy on that great day and noble Eid. He intended that the wealthy Muslims be rewarded by the Lord of creation by means of their feeding and lightening the burdens of the people. He also intended that the poor be relieved on that day by means of their fast being broken by the rich just as the people of wealth are relieved of their excess wealth. Therefore, he, peace and blessings be upon him and his progeny, opened the opportunity by that for the needy and those in straitened circumstances insomuch that they can obtain relief from difficulty on that day. This was a mercy from him, peace and blessings be upon him and his progeny, for the slaves and a means to rectify the land.

Concerning the designation of the fast-breaking dues, its limit and those people for whom it is obligatory

The fast-breaking dues are religiously obligatory on behalf of the free and enslaved, the old and young

[34] In ***Al-Muntakhab***, al-Hādi explained in more detail those to whom the fast-breaking dues are to be given.

> I asked: "What do you say regarding the poor who do not have the fast-breaking dues to render? Must they accept it from others and then render it?" He replied: "No. How can one be obligated to render the fast-breaking dues that he does not have while he is among the poor who is supposed to take it?" "Explain to me: Who is the poor that is obligated to take the fast-breaking dues and not render it?" "He is the one who does not have a source of nourishment for ten days for him and his family. He takes the fast-breaking dues and does not render it." "If he were to have enough nourishment for ten days for him and his family, is he obligated to render the fast-breaking dues?" "Yes." "If he had not had a source of nourishment for ten days on the Fast-breaking Eid and fell into wealth a day or two after the Eid, is he obligated to render the fast-breaking dues?" "No. The fast-breaking dues are only obligated on the Fast-breaking Eid specifically. Once it is the day of breaking the fast while a man does not have what obligates rendering the fast-breaking dues, he is not obligated to render it after that. That should be sufficient, if Allah wills."

as well as the male and female Muslims.[35] It is religiously obligatory upon every Muslim for whom one is responsible to have the dues rendered on their behalf on the day of their breaking the fast. It is a *šā'* of wheat, barley, dates, corn, cottage cheese, raisins or anything else that can be used to support the recipient of the dues.

Concerning when the fast-breaking dues are collected and until when it is permissible for one to delay it

The dues are obligatory when it is obligatory to break the fast; it is in the first hour of the first day of Shawwāl [i.e. the month after Ramadan], the day of breaking the fast. It is encouraged for one to distribute something before they leave [for the prayer] even if they were to drink some water. Then they are to distribute it before their Eid prayer. These are the best times according to me.

However, there is no restriction on one who delays it to the middle or end of the day. Rather, we encourage one to hasten in distributing it to the one for whom it is due. Therefore, the wealthy distributors of the dues should give it to the poor Muslims of straitened circumstances for that day because it is a day of ease, festivity and happiness for the slaves.

One should not delay it to after the day of Eid nor should one withhold it from the people to whom Allah's Messenger, peace and blessings be upon him and his progeny, declared it unless such person is unable to distribute it to its people or knows who deserves it outside of his country. Then, he is to present it to them and not hesitate after it becomes possible for him to do so. If it is not possible for him to send a messenger to deliver it or accommodate, he is considered exempted from the command to accommodate because Allah—the Blessed and Exalted—says: **{Allah burdens not a soul except with what it can bear} (Q. 2:286)**.

Concerning the one who cannot find foodstuffs to distribute for the fast-breaking dues: Is it permissible to distribute money?

One should not distribute anything for the fast-breaking dues except foodstuffs. If the one distributing the dues cannot find any of the aforementioned foodstuffs, there is no problem in distributing the value of the foodstuffs in dirham. He is to collect from such people the value of a *šā'* of foodstuffs. It is to be the value of a *šā'* of foodstuffs that he and his family eats and take support from. However, if one desires to distribute the value of a *šā'* from the best of foodstuffs, it should be wheat—that is the best.

As for the obligation upon him, the only thing that is religiously obligatory is that from which he and his family eats and takes support. If he is not able to find someone deserving of the money or foodstuffs and he knows a place where someone who deserves the dues is, he is to send foodstuffs. If he is not able to send foodstuffs, he is to send money and order that the money be used to buy foodstuffs. Then, he is to have it distributed to the people most deserving of it.

We are simply prohibited from distributing dirham as dues unless out of necessity. We are obligated and encouraged to distribute a measured amount because a measured amount is easier and the best for the needy on the day of their Eid. Also, the dues collector is more able to request and seek out food than the poor and needy.

Concerning what the owner of the dues must do concerning the fast-breaking and preparation

The one upon whom the dues are obligatory should prepare and measure the fast-breaking dues ahead of time in case there is the fear of famine in the land. If one fears that one will not be able to find it on the fast-breaking day, one is to prepare for that and send someone to seek it out and buy it. He is to

[35] In ***Al-Muntakhab***, al-Hādi was asked "Is a man obligated to render the fast-breaking dues on behalf of a foetus?" He replied: "No. Others have said that, but we do not acknowledge that."

obtain that which is obligatory upon him preparing for that and seeking it out from the beginning of Ramadan. Otherwise, he is to prepare some of what he can for the one who ordered him. Even if he has a need to prepare for it before Ramadan, he should do so. This will bring him in proximity to his Lord and the greatest reward, God willing.

Concerning what one does with the wealth of one who is absent and not present during the time of the fast-breaking and concerning what is distributed from each dependent

Whoever has wealth and is capable of distributing the fast-breaking dues but is absent and not able to distribute it on the Eid, he should seek out an advance among his brothers who are able to take it from him and distribute his dues on his behalf. If he does not find a way and is not able to, it is a debt upon him until the time his wealth returns to him. When his wealth is to the amount that necessitates the dues, he is to extract it from it.

We simply command him to strive for the advance because he should make effort until it reaches the end. It is valid for him to do so even after he avoided distributing his dues until the time he is able. We therefore hold to the view that he should make effort to do such. If he is not able, it is as Allah says: **{Allah burdens not a soul except with what it can bear} (Q. 2:286)** and **{…except with what He hath given it} (65:7)**.

Concerning the one who has produce such as dates and other things that obligate the dues as well as when it is not possible to leave it until the time of drying for fear of spoilage

Whoever has fresh grapes and dates and needs to eat or sell them moist while it is not possible to dry and leave them until the point that it becomes obligatory for fear of ruin, there is no problem to distribute them at the time of their harvest completion. When there are no more dates and green herbs and it becomes the time that they can benefit their people, one is not exempt from distributed and paying them to their people. He computes by conjecture the quantity of fresh dates just as he would compute by conjecture the quantity on date palms because computing the quantity of fresh fruit by conjecture is different to computing the quantity of dried fruit by conjecture. Therefore, it is obligatory to distribute by conjectural computation the chief dates of the date palm. He does not distribute fresh dates as a measure; he is to take precaution in that.

Verily, it is only permissible for one to distribute that to the people who are mentioned by Allah based upon what we mentioned if there is no imam to take it. It is permissible for him to pay it to the deserving person directly. If there is an imam, he is responsible for that. If he wants to take fresh dates, he can take it. If he wants, he can order that it be left in the trees. If the imam orders one to save it, he must do so. If he sees fit to order one to sell it, he must do so.

We only prefer that, in the absence of the imam, one distribute fruit as dues in its fresh state and hand it over to its people at the time of its harvest because the distribution of dues of everything is from it. That has come in the Sunnah. If this tree were to produce fresh dates and the owner does not dry any of them, we prefer that he extract the dues from it.

Concerning an explanation of distributed dues and its meaning as well as its exposition from the Book, the Sunnah and language

The extraction of purification dues (*zakāt*) has three meanings in the language. First, it is the purification dues of the body. Its purification refers to that which brings one close to Allah as well as those pure and pleasurable deeds that bring one to Allah. It is purification for the believers and a cleansing from the contaminating impurities of the defiantly disobedient. That is based upon the statement of Allah: **{He has achieved who purifies (*zakāha*) it} (Q. 91:9)**. This means: the one who has achieved is he who cleanses it from disobedience to Allah until it is brought close to Allah by acts of obedience and ennobled by earning good deeds.

Included in that is the statement of the Glorified: **{He has achieved who purifies himself (*tazakka*) and mentions the Name of his Lord and then prays}** (**Q. 87:14-15**). When He says **{He has achieved who purifies himself}**, it means: the one who has achieved is he who purifies his soul by means of obedience to Allah and is brought close. He fears Him in his return and is secure by Him. He **{mentions the Name of his Lord and then prays}**. He obeys Allah and follows what he is commanded while being God-conscious. He refrains from acts of disobedience and he is cautious in what he is prohibited and he stays away from it.

The Glorified says when relating the account of His Prophet Moses, may Allah bless him and grant him peace: **{"Didst thou slay a pure (*zakiyya*) soul for other than a soul? Verily, thou hast done a thing objectionable"}** (**Q. 18:74**). The meaning of **{pure}** is a soul for whom no evil is known. Then, it was derived from the path of God-consciousness. He, may Allah bless him and grant him peace, called the youth **{a pure soul}** since his affair was concealed from him; he did not know what the other knew of his [i.e. the youth's] affair.[36]

Included in that is the statement of the Glorified: **{But the God-conscious shall avoid it—the one who gives from his wealth to purify himself}** (**Q. 92:17-18**). By that, the Glorified means that he will draw close to Allah by means of his spending, distribution of his wealth out of obedience to his Lord and loaning to his Creator out of purity for his body. It will be an increase for him due to sincerity in his religion. By this, the Most Gracious does not mean the obligatory purification dues. Have you not heard Him say in His Revelation of Light and Criterion: **{...and not for one who has a blessing to be recompensed except to seek the Face of his Lord, the Exalted}** (**Q. 92:19-20**)? If the purification dues are what was meant, He would not have said **{...and not for one who has a blessing to be recompensed}** because the purification dues are something that Allah appointed and made a source of ease for every poor person and an opportunity to ease for every person with the means.

The second meaning is that which Allah has made as an injunction upon creation in the observance of distributing wealth at its appointed time. That is based upon the statement of the Glorified **{...and give its due the day of its harvest}** (**Q. 6:141**) as well as His statement to His Prophet, peace and blessings be upon him and his progeny: **{Take from their wealth dues, wherewith thou may purify them and sanctify them}** (**Q. 9:103**). This means every portion of their wealth that is distributed. This is not the meaning of purifying one's soul by means of good deeds.

The third meaning is the Sunnah of the Messenger, peace and blessings be upon him and his progeny, which is religiously obligatory upon the Muslims—and that is the fast-breaking dues that are distributed on their Eid for every person—young and old, free and enslaved.

Concerning various issues regarding the purification dues

The purification dues of the slave are an obligation upon their masters. They are to extract it from what their slaves own or for what they own. That is, if they desire to do so, they are permitted to do so because whatever they own is for them. For that reason, we say that the purification dues are obligatory upon them. Similarly, the purification dues of the *umm walad*[37] and dependent are an obligation upon the master because he did not manumit them and they belong to him. If they belong to him, their wealth belongs to him.

---

[36] As a meaningful digression, we would like to point out here that Imam al-Hādi apparently held to the view that the 'youth' (*ghulām*) referenced in the Qur'an was a young man who had done something deserving of death unbeknownst to Moses. It is for that reason that Moses referred to him as a **{pure soul}**. This counters the view that the youth was a pre-pubescent boy who was killed for a sin that he would later commit, as is narrated in many accounts.

[37] We have chosen to leave this word untranslated since there is no equivalent in the English language. The words 'concubine' or 'courtesan' do not quite capture the full meaning of the term *umm walad* because according to Islamic law, the *umm walad* is freed upon having her master's baby. However, the terms 'courtesan' and 'concubine' do not carry such connotation.

As for the purification dues of the indentured labourer (*mukātab*) who works for his freedom after having formed a contract with his master and legally stipulated a price, there are no purification dues obligatory upon the indentured labourer until he is manumitted by his master at the agreed-upon stipulation or he is rendered incapable of fulfilling that by his master. If whichever situation were to occur, the wealth would belong to him [i.e. the indentured labourer] and he would have to render the dues for any years that passed. If the slave is freed and observed what was stipulated, then the wealth belongs to him and he is religiously obligated to render the dues. If he was incapable, then the wealth belongs to his master, and he [i.e. the master] is religiously obligated to render the dues.

We simply say that one does not render the dues until one's matter is clear. We obligate that the dues are rendered for any years that passed once it becomes obligatory on him because this wealth belonged to both of them and not one of them. Neither one can lay exclusive claim to owning it. This is because the master can say: "You are unable to own it and I own you." The slave can say "I have fulfilled what you have stipulated me to do without exception. You cannot take a dirham from my wealth." Therefore, whenever there is confusion regarding wealth, we do not obligate any one of them to render the dues from that in which there is confusion regarding whether it belongs to him or the other person. We do not hold to the view that one can deviate and falsify when it comes to the wealth of the purification dues. Consequently, we made this matter like the matter of a man who owes a debt to another. We have obligated that the owner fulfils his debt and then render the dues for the past years.

Regarding a man who grows crops on a property and then after harvesting it, sells its yield at random while it spikes and then the dues collector comes and finds that it was already sold—he is to take what is obligatory from it. The buyer is to return it to the seller with the value the collector took from it.

Others say that it is valid to take the obligatory value of crops from the seller but not take anything from the buyer. We do not hold to that view because it is obligatory for the owner of the crops to extract a tithe of his crops from it and not other than it. If he makes an error, he returns what he erred in, and whatever is not allowed for him is not allowed. This is because the yield that Allah makes obligatory is obligated upon its individual owner. It is that which belongs to the buyer, which was impermissible for him to buy. Therefore, it is obligatory for him to return it to the original owner; he is to return its value to the one who bought it.

If it were permissible for him to take a monetary tithe of what was extracted from the land from the buyer, it would be permissible to take a tithe of wheat from dates and a tithe of dates from wheat. If he were to take a monetary value of gold and silver for it, it would be contrary to the statement of Allah when He says: **{...and give its due the day of its harvest} (Q. 6:141)**. They extract from it that which is obligatory. Also regarding that, Allah's Messenger, peace and blessings be upon him and his progeny, said: ((Wheat is from wheat; dates are from dates; hooves are from hooves; and cloven hooves are from cloven hooves)).[38]

If the dues collector does not come until the purchased food spoiled, this differs from the first issue because the food was good initially but then spoiled. Therefore, he is to take a tithe from the seller at the value of the food. Similarly, if there is spoilage, the owner sells it and differentiates that which has spoiled and that which has not spoiled. The difference is clear to everyone with intellect and understanding.

Every form of wealth that ruined before the tithe is due on it—there are no purification dues on it. The time of the obligation of the purification dues occurs with seeding, safety from spoilage and manifestation of soundness. An example is the grape seed and date pit. When it produces a seed, it is obligatory to compute it by calculation. When it is time for harvesting, clipping or picking, take a tithe from what is computed.

---

[38] Similarly narrated in ***Musnad Imam Zayd, Ŝahīh Muslim, Sunan an-Nisā'i, Sunan at-Tirmidhi, Sunan Ibn Mājah, Sunan Abu Dāwūd, Sunan al-Bayhaqi, Sunan ad-Dārqutni***

If there is land or date palms watered by flowing water for half a year and by camels for the other half, it is obligatory for him to take the following values—a tithe for that which is watered by flowing water and half a tithe for that which is watered by camels.

The tithes of crops are taken before anything else is taken from it or removed from its provisions. It is not in a shovel, bucket, the earnings of labourers and anything that is needed from the earth. One is to begin with the tithe before anything else. My father related to me from his father that a man had land, grew crops on it and harvested it. "Is it permissible for him to remove the earnings of the labourers or some necessities and then extract the tithe from the rest of it?" He replied: "No. He is to extract the tithes from it before that."

It is impermissible for a man to be given purification dues by his father, mother or son because the Messenger, peace and blessings be upon him and his progeny, said: ((You and your wealth are for your parents)).[39] Consequently, this maintenance of theirs is obligatory upon the father and son in any case. For that reason, it is impermissible for the parent to be given the purification dues by the offspring and likewise. It is permissible for him to be given the dues by his brother or other relatives since there is no restriction to provide for them. It is not for him to escape from this right he owes or refrain from an obligation toward them.

Similarly, it is impermissible for him to pay any of the purification dues to his slave, dependent or *umm walad* except if he has manumitted them. Once he has manumitted them, they are similar to the rest of the Muslims in respect to the purification dues. They are most deserving than others because they were under his charge and he was responsible for their provision.

[39] Similarly narrated in ***Sunan Ibn Mājah, Sunan Abu Dāwūd, Sunan al-Bayhaqi, Mušannaf Ibn Abi Shayba, Al-Mu'jam al-Kabīr, Al-Mu'jam al-Awsaṫ, Ŝahīh Ibn Hibbān, Musnad Abu Ya'la***

The Book of Fasting

In the Name of Allah, the Most Gracious, the Most Merciful...

Concerning the obligation of fasting and its legalisation in the Book as well as an explanation of what Allah commands regarding it

Verily, Allah—the Blessed and Exalted—has made fasting as an injunction upon his slaves not out of need of their fasting or to benefit from any of their deeds. Rather, He created them as slaves to be commanded and prohibited. By that, He made them to choose. Then, He commanded and prohibited them and caused them to see misguidance and guidance as well as make possible their deeds and guided them towards their salvation. He made them capable to do all of that and commanded them to be obedient in their deeds **{...that those who perish would have perished upon evidence and those who live would have lived upon evidence. Verily, Allah is All-Hearing, All-Knowing}** (Q. 8:42).

They were commanded to perform the fast and given the injunction to act upon it just as it was given to the Children of Israel as an injunction before them. That is based on the statement of Allah: **{O ye who believe! Fasting has been prescribed for thee just as it was prescribed for those before thee so that ye may be God-conscious}** (Q. 2:183). The Glorified says: that you may be wary of opposing Me and that you may obey my commands and judgements as well as not substitute My injunctions just as those before you among the Children of Israel to whom I revealed of the Gospel. This is because Allah prescribed in the Gospel that the Children of Israel must fast the month of Ramadan. He also revealed that they not have intercourse in it as they would have intercourse with their wives outside of it. However, they changed and substituted it. They acted contrary to what they were commanded and rejected it. They were worried about its effect on them and the fierceness of its heat and coldness. Consequently, they moved the fast of Ramadan to other days and added twenty days to it as expiation of their claim. Allah cursed and disgraced them as well as destroyed them based on that. The statement of the Glorified **{just as it was prescribed for those before thee}** also means the Christians.[1]

Then, He says: **{a prescribed number of days}** (Q. 2:184). This means: the month of Ramadan in which the Qur'an was revealed. Allah made the month of Ramadan to consist of thirty or twenty-nine days. It is thirty days when it is complete but twenty-nine when it is deficient. If there is an excuse in the sky such as clouds, dust, fog or any other reason, one is to complete the fast for thirty days. Similar is narrated from Allah's Messenger, peace and blessings be upon him and his progeny, who said: ((Fast due to thc sight of it and break your fast due to the sight of it. If there is overcast on you, then complete the thirty days)).[2]

By 'complete,' he means from the day you first saw it and verified that it was the new moon. Similarly, it is narrated that Allah's Messenger, peace and blessings be upon him and his progeny, said: ((The month is such, such and such)). Then he said: ((And it may be such and such)). He held up all fingers three times in the first statement and all fingers three times while subtracting one finger in the second statement.[3] This is a proof from him, peace and blessings be upon him and his progeny, that a month may be thirty or twenty-nine days.

Allah says: **{They ask thee concerning the new moons. Say unto them: "It is a means of reckoning time for the people"}** (Q. 2:189). The Majestic says that the means of reckoning time is

---

[1] I was unable to locate any early or later references that corroborate what al-Hādi said about Ramadan being initially prescribed for the Children of Israel in the Gospels. All other authorities narrate that the Muslims fasted on Ashūra and three days out of every month before the fast of Ramadan was revealed.

[2] Similarly narrated in ***Sharh at-Tajrīd, Ŝahīh al-Bukhāri, Ŝahīh Muslim, Sunan an-Nisā'i, Sunan at-Tirmidhi, Sunan Ibn Mājah, Mušannaf Ibn Abi Shayba, Sunan al-Bayhaqi, Bihār al-Anwār***

[3] Similarly narrated in ***Ŝahīh al-Bukhāri, Ŝahīh Muslim, Sunan an-Nisā'i, Ŝahīh Ibn Hibbān, Sunan Ibn Mājah, Sunan al-Bayhaqi***

for their judgements as well as that which Allah has appointed as their religious obligations such as their fasts, purification dues, Hajj pilgrimages and other means.

Allah first made the fast a religious injunction upon the *Ummah* of Muhammad, peace and blessings be upon him and his progeny, just as He made it an injunction for those before them. They were to not eat, drink or have intercourse with their wives during the day until the conclusion of the month. They were to complete their fasts and not approach their wives night or day. They were to establish the fast of the day by that and eat during the time of breaking fast except if they slept. If they slept, it would be impermissible for them to eat or drink until the next day at the approach of night.

This was the case until the matter of an Anŝār took place. He was a man called Abu Qays; his name was Ŝirma b. Anas.[§] He worked in some of the outskirts of Medina. There he came across a *mudd* of dates and took it back to his wife while he was fasting. Then, she substituted it for him with a *mudd* of flour and prepared it for him by stirring it with butter (*'aŝada*). Then, he slept out of weakness and tiredness before his wife completed his meal. Then she came with it after it was completed and woke him up so that he could eat. He disliked that he should disobey Allah and His Messenger so he slept on an empty stomach that night. He woke up that morning after having fasted from the day before. He passed by Allah's Messenger, peace and blessings be upon him and his progeny, and he saw that he was pained. He said: ((You have awoken depraved, O Abu Qays!)). When he [i.e. Abu Qays] informed him of what happened, he, peace and blessings be upon him and his progeny, went silent.

'Umar b. al-Khaṫṫāb along with some men from the Companions used to have intercourse with their wives during the month of Ramadan, and they feared that their matter would be mentioned in the Qur'an alongside that of Abu Qays. 'Umar stood among those men and said: "Seek forgiveness for us, O Messenger of Allah! Verily, we have had intercourse with our wives!" Allah's Messenger, peace and blessings be upon him and his progeny, said to 'Umar: ((That is not befitting of you, O 'Umar!)). Then, Allah revealed what He revealed concerning Abu Qays, 'Umar and his Companions.[4]

This first type of fast was abrogated, and the Majestic said: **{Permitted for thee on the night of the fast is to go unto thy wives. They are a garment for thee and ye are a garment for them. Allah knows that ye used to deceive thyself, so He accepted thy repentance and pardoned thee. So, lay with them** [i.e. the wives] **and seek that which Allah has written for thee. Eat and drink until the white thread and black thread of dawn become clear unto thee. Then, complete the fast until night. And lay not with them whilst ye are secluded in the mosques. These are the limits of Allah so approach them not. Thus Allah makes clear His signs for the people that they may be wary} (Q. 2:187)**.

The Glorified permitted them to eat and drink every night—whether before they slept or after—until the white thread is distinguished from the black thread. The **{white thread}** refers to the establishment of dawn and its light. The **{black thread}** refers to the night and its darkness. He is saying: Eat and drink until the night and its darkness dissipate and the day and its light appear. The meaning of its appearance is its approach and descent as well as its drawing near and coming. Therefore, it is for the people to drink and eat until they fear the onset of morning. When the morning draws near, it is religiously obligatory to abstain and refrain from eating and drinking. It is permissible for them to have intercourse with their wives at night as much as they like until they fear the onset of the morning. When it approaches, they are to refrain from them and abstain from intercourse and approaching them.

Allah says regarding His slaves who are sick and are not able to fast due to weakness as well as the elderly person who is incapable of observing the fast: **{...and upon those whom are able is compensation of feeding a needy person. Whosoever does good it is better for him. However, to fast is best for thee if ye but knew} (Q. 2:185)**.

[4] Similarly narrated in ***Musnad Ahmed, Sunan ad-Dārimi, Ŝahīh al-Bukhāri, Sunan Abu Dāwūd, Sunan at-Tirmidhi***

The meaning of the Glorified's statement **{and upon those whom are able}** is: and upon those who are not able. Although the negative clause 'not' is missing, it is what is meant. The Qur'an is in clear Arabic. This exists in the Arabic language, and it appears in many verses in the Book. The Arab may use 'not' when he does not mean a negation and may not use it when he means a negation. As for an example in speech where a negative is denoted though the word 'not' is omitted, it is evident in the two forthcoming verses. It is also in the statement of the poet ['Amr b. Kulthūm] when he says:

You have descended to the position of guests from us.
So we hastened to entertain so you may abuse us.

Though he said "So we hastened to entertain so you may abuse us," the intended meaning is: So we hastened to entertain so you may not abuse us. Although the negative clause is missing, it is implied.

As for an example of speech where the negative clause 'not' appears but does not imply a negation, the poet [Qays b. Āsim al-Manqari] says:

With a day of good fortune, you have not shamed your fathers.
You have made them safe, and the horse bleeds from its bit.

Though he said "With a day of good fortune, you have not shamed your fathers," the intended meaning is: With a day of good fortune, you have shamed your fathers. The insertion of 'not' is for a different reason, it does not mean a relative clause in speech.

Another proof of that is in the Book of Allah when the Glorified says: **{...that the People of the Book may know not that they are not able to gain anything from the provision of Allah and that the provision is in the Hand of Allah. He grants it to whom He wills. And Allah is the Possessor of great provision}** (Q. 57:29). The intended meaning of **{that the People of the Book may know not}** is: that the People of the Book may know.

Another example is that of Moses, may Allah bless him and grant him peace: **{He said: "O Aaron! What prevented thee—when thou saw them going astray—from not following me? Didst thou disobey my order?"}** (Q. 20:92-93). Though He says **{from not following me}**, the intended meaning is: from following me. It is according to the language of the Arabs and the most eloquent in speech that the omission of 'not' in a phrase can mean a negation and the inclusion of 'not' in a phrase can mean an affirmation.

[...][5] Based upon that, one can derive the meaning of Allah's statement **{and upon those whom are able is compensation of feeding a needy person}** (Q. 2:185) to denote: and upon those who are not able. From the one who has weakness and would be ruined because of it, there is compensation of feeding needy people. He is saying that one is to feed lunch and dinner to thirty needy people for the whole month—a needy person for each day.

Then, He says: **{Whosoever does good it is better for him}** (Q. 2:185). By this, the Glorified means that if one increases, feeds two needy people each day and takes it upon himself to do so even at the expense of himself—this will be better for him.

Then, the Majestic says regarding the sick and traveller: **{The month of Ramadan is that in which the Qur'an was revealed—a guidance for the people and explanations of guidance and criteria. Therefore, whosoever witnesses amongst thee the month, let him fast. And whosoever is ill or on a journey—then a like number of other days}** (Q. 2:185). The sick person and traveller are permitted to refrain from fasting. The judgement on them is by the ruling of them to break the fast for a number of days.

[5] Here Imam al-Hādi engages in a discussion regarding Arabic grammar. Since it dealt with particularities in the Arabic language, which may not be appreciated by the English speaker, we refrained from translating it.

Then, the Glorified says: **{Allah desires ease for thee, and He desires not hardship for thee} (Q. 2:185)**. He informs them of His desire of ease for His slaves and His desire to lighten hardship for them by permitting them to refrain from fasting. He does not permit such abstention for the one who is a sound resident. Then, the Glorified says regarding the obligation for the traveller who refrained from fasting to make it up for those days he fasted: **{...and that ye complete the number of days and that ye may magnify Allah for guiding thee and that ye may be grateful} (Q. 2:185)**.

Then, the Glorified says regarding the prohibition of those in religious seclusion (*i'tikāf*) in the mosques of the Lord from having intercourse with wives: **{And lay not with them whilst ye are secluded in the mosques. These are the limits of Allah so approach them not} (Q. 2:187)**. The Glorified prohibited the one in religious seclusion from his wives day and night. It is impermissible for the one in religious seclusion to have intercourse with his wife, and one cannot be in religious seclusion except in the state of fasting. Religious seclusion refers to a man staying in the mosque and not entering a house other than it. He does not exit from it except for a need that is necessary for only him or for something that Allah is satisfied with. The fast during religious seclusion is a sunnah from Allah's Messenger, peace and blessings be upon him and his progeny. He appointed it for the one in religious seclusion.

Concerning what has come regarding the virtue of fasting the month of Ramadan

It has reached us on the authority of Zayd b. 'Ali from his fathers that 'Ali b. Abi Ťālib, upon him be peace, said:

> Allah's Messenger, peace and blessings be upon him and his progeny, ascended the pulpit and said: ((O people! Verily, Gabriel came to me, stood before me and said: "O Muhammad! Whoever reaches the month of Ramadan and does not seek forgiveness and dies will enter the Hellfire; Allah will curse him. Say: 'Ameen.'" And I said: 'Ameen.' Then he said: "Whoever encounters a just imam and does not seek forgiveness for him, Allah will curse him. Say: 'Ameen.'" And I said: 'Ameen.' Then he said: "Whoever encounters his parents and does not seek forgiveness for them, Allah will curse him. Say: 'Ameen.'" And I said: 'Ameen')).[6]

It has reached us that Allah's Messenger, peace and blessings be upon him and his progeny, spent the last ten days in religious seclusion giving life to the nights. He used to bathe himself, tie his sarong and strive hard until the completion of the month.[7] The meaning of 'tie his sarong' is stay away from his wives. The meaning of 'strive hard' is engage in worship of his Exalted Lord.

It has reached us on the authority of Zayd b. 'Ali from his fathers that 'Ali, upon him be peace, said:

> Allah's Messenger, peace and blessings be upon him and his progeny, said: ((For the faster are two reliefs: one relief when he breaks the fast and another relief on the Day of Judgement. A caller will sound off with the call: "Where are those whose livers were thirsty? By My Honour and Majesty, they will have their thirsts quenched today!")).[8]

It is narrated that 'Ali b. Abi Ťālib used to address the people during Ramadan by saying:

> Verily, this blessed month is that in which Allah obligated the fast. He has not obligated the supererogatory prayers (*qiyām*) in it. It has come to you. Do not let the fast be abstention from food and drink only but also from vain speech, lying and falsehood.[9]

---

[6] Similarly narrated in ***Ŝahīh Ibn Hibbān, Al-Mu'jam al-Kabīr, Al-Mu'jam al-Awsaṭ, Musnad Abu Ya'la, Ash-Shu'b al-Imān*** of al-Bayhaqi, ***Bihār al-Anwār***

[7] Similarly narrated in ***Musnad Imam Zayd, Ŝahīh al-Bukhāri, Ŝahīh Muslim, Sunan an-Nisā'i, Sunan Abu Dāwūd, Sunan Ibn Māja***

[8] Similarly narrated in ***Musnad Imam Zayd, Ŝahīh al-Bukhāri, Ŝahīh Muslim, Sunan an-Nisā'i, Sunan at-Tirmidhi, Sunan Ibn Mājah, Bihār al-Anwār***

[9] Similarly narrated in ***Mušannaf Ibn Abi Shayba, Ash-Shu'b al-Imān*** of al-Bayhaqi, ***Sunan al-Bayhaqi, Bihār al-Anwār***

Concerning the type of speech from which the faster and the one not fasting should refrain

Both the faster as well as the one not fasting should refrain, guard oneself and stay away from lying and false testimony. False testimony is greater than lying. It is a type of lie that Allah's Messenger, peace and blessings be upon him and his progeny, said ((Lying prevents one from faith)).[10]

Regarding these two types of lying as well as other than them that counters truth and establishes falsehood or that which harms a Muslim, Allah says: **{They only falsify lies—those who believe not in the signs of Allah} (Q. 16:105)**. Lies are of different ranks. The faster should refrain from all of such while fasting and the one not fasting should similarly avoid such. The Muslim should be on guard from such—whether sitting or standing.

The faster should refrain from obscene speech and looking at that which is impermissible. Such person should also refrain from listening to that which is impermissible—whether it is plucking string instruments, mandolins or flutes as well as other instruments that are prohibited for the faster and the one not fasting. It is also obligatory for such one to not walk where one should not walk. Neither should one join with groups that one is not permitted to join with. He should guard himself in his sitting and standing.

One should be on guard when rinsing the nose and mouth. One should be cautious when placing something in the mouth or nostrils insomuch that it reaches the throat. One should also be careful to prevent water from entering his insides during purification. He should be cautious of forgetfulness when waking up during the day out of fear of forgetting the fast. One should look to that which is impermissible of eating and drinking.

Concerning how a man should be careful from his family while fasting

The faster should not lie with his wife in one garment if he fears that he would be overcome by desire so that he is afflicted with trial by Satan. He should not kiss with desire nor should he touch with lust or look with desire.[11] One should not fool around with something that invites towards arousal. Rather, he should be careful in all of that, protect his fast, fear his Lord and increase in His remembrance.

Concerning that which is encouraged for the faster

It is encouraged for the faster to recite from the Qur'an in the morning; it is the best of acts of worship of the Most Gracious. For the rest of the day, one should increase in glorification and seeking forgiveness. One should also recite what one can from the Qur'an during the night, as well as glorify and magnify Allah. One is to also seek acceptance of that which is made binding on him of the fast.

Before the sun sets, one takes his tooth-stick and cleans his mouth with it. He should be cautious as to not let anything enter his mouth other than his own saliva. Whatever pieces of the tooth-stick mixes with his saliva—he should spit them out. Then, he washes his mouth and guards against water if the time for breaking the fast has not occurred.

When he sees stars, he says:

> Allah is the Greatest! Allah is the Greatest! **{Blessed be the One who made in the heavens constellations and made therein a lamp and an illuminating moon} (Q. 25:61)**. He has made it an ornament by means of lanterns for onlookers. He has made it a sign of the night for creation and a cessation point of the fast of Allah for those fasting.

---

[10] Similarly narrated in ***Amāli al-Murshid Billah***, ***Ash-Shu'b al-Imān*** of al-Bayhaqi, ***Sunan al-Bayhaqi***. This statement is also attributed to 'Ali in ***Bihār al-Anwār*** and ***Nahj al-Balāgha*** as well as Abu Bakr in ***Musnad Ahmed*** and ***Kanz al-'Ummāl***.

[11] According to ***Al-Muntakhab***, al-Hādi was asked: "If a man looked at his wife or anyone else with desire and ejaculated or emitted prostatic fluid, what is obligated for him?" To which he replied: "Making it up. Others say that he does not have to make up due to prostatic fluid. As for us, we say that he has to make up due to prostatic fluid."

When he intends to break his fast, he says:

> O Allah! Verily, You commanded us to fast during the day and we fasted. You have freed us to break the fast and we broke the fast. We fasted for You and observed Your injunction. We seek Your pleasure and break the fast by Your provision. Accept our fast, and forgive our sins! Allow us to attain the fast of all our month. Verily, You are Most Nigh and the Answerer of prayer!

After he breaks his fast, he says: "In the Name of Allah and with Allah! I have broken the fast by the provision of Allah—grateful to Him for it and praising Him for it."

When he has finished his food, he says:

> All praise is due to Allah, the Lord of creation, the Most Gracious, Most Merciful for providing us permissible provision and for feeding us from the good extracted for us in His land! O Allah, make us among those grateful to You and those who are ever praising of You, O Lord of creation!

Concerning fasting on the day of doubt

That which we have seen and heard from our elders and ancestors is that they used to fast on the day of doubt. Regarding that is what was narrated to me from my father from his father that 'Ali, the Commander of Believers, upon him be peace, used to say: "Fasting a day in Sha'bān is more preferable to me than not fasting a day in Ramadan."[12]

The faster on the day of doubt should intend: "If this is a day of Ramadan, I will fast on it as a Ramadan fast. If this is a day of Sha'bān, I will fast on it as a voluntary fast." If one did that and it was a day in Ramadan, he would have observed its fast based upon the belief of his intention. If it was not Ramadan, it would be decreed for him as a voluntary fast.

One should not have the understanding that he broke the fast during Ramadan because if it was Ramadan, he would not have violated it nor would he have to make it up. It is religiously permissible to be cautious regarding a day in Ramadan and seek out every reason to fast during it. If it was a day in Sha'bān, he would not have suffered a loss, and it would be considered a voluntary fast and he will receive a reward for it.

As for what many people have embellished regarding avoiding fasting on it, it is inauthentic and impermissible to hold to such view due to its being far from precaution and distant from that which is correct.[13] It is also due to its being near neglect of the fast and sin. Rather, the most authentic position is that in which there is no doubt. According to the one who is fair, fasting on the day of doubt and precaution regarding it is best and closest to Allah and security.

My father related to me that his father was asked about fasting on the day of doubt. He replied: "It is good and there is no problem fasting on it. It has been related to us that 'Ali, upon him be peace, said: 'Fasting a day in Sha'bān is more preferable to me than breaking the fast a day in Ramadan.'"

---

[12] Similarly narrated in ***Sharh at-Tajrīd, Sunan ad-Dārqutni, Sunan al-Bayhaqi, Uṣūl al-Kāfi, Bihār al-Anwār***

[13] Imam al-Mu`ayyad Billah, upon him be peace, says in his ***Sharh at-Tajrīd***:

> There is no disagreement that fasting on the day of doubt is permissible and encouraged. The only disagreement is regarding the nature of its fast. Ash-Shāfi'i encouraged it since he encouraged fasting the whole of Sha'bān or joining its fast [i.e. with that of Ramadan]. Abu Hanīfa encouraged it by having the intention to fast Sha'bān. That would mean that the encouragement to fast on it was agreed upon. If it is established as thus, we need only to clarify the meaning of the prohibition therein. We say that one is only prohibited from fasting on it [i.e. the day of doubt] with the notion that it was Ramadan. According to us, fasting on it from this perspective is what is impermissible. It is analogous to the idea that it would be encouraged to fast on it if it were the first of Sha'bān. Likewise, is the case with the day of doubt. Conceptually, if it were one of the days of Sha'bān, it would be permissible for people to fast on it with the idea of connecting it to that which came before it [i.e. the last day of Ramadan]. It would be permissible to fast on it by reason that it would be considered the first of Sha'bān.

Concerning the time to break the fast

According to us as well as those who are cautious in their religion and cognisant of the authentic actions of the Prophet, the time to break the fast is the darkness of night. Its darkness refers to its veiling. The sign of its entrance and the reality of its occurrence is that one sees a star of night that one would not see otherwise. As Allah says: **{When the night covered him, he saw a star...} (Q. 6:76)**.

As for the narrations reported by those of minimal perception and those ignorant of the time of night, there is no truth to them even if they were narrated by some scholars. How can such be attributed to the Chosen Messenger? They claim that Allah's Messenger, peace and blessings be upon him and his progeny, commanded them to break the fast before the darkness of night fell upon them. Many people break the fast based upon these narrations. The sun still shines its light when it sets, its radiance has not died, and the colour of its setting has not faded. Therefore, they have invalidated their fast on those days. They have confused themselves from the truth and mixed up the Muslims by means of their narrations.

My father related to me that his father was asked about the time for breaking the fast. He replied:

> The time that one should break the fast is the darkness of night and the departure of day as well as the appearance of a star in the heavens. This is because Allah says: **{When the night covered him, he saw a star...} (Q. 6:76)**.

Concerning the fasting on 'Āshūra, daily *(ad-dahr)*, on the white days and on the Day of 'Arafat

There is no problem with fasting on 'Āshūra; fasting on it is good. It has been narrated that the Prophet, peace and blessings be upon him and his progeny, specified the Banu Aslam with the command to fast on it and presented it to them.[14]

Similar is the case with the daily fast for the one who can and whose body will not be harmed by such. This is because Allah does not desire hardship for His slaves but only desires ease. That is based on His statement: **{Allah desires ease for thee, and He desires not hardship for thee} (Q. 2:185)**. Therefore, whoever is strong enough to fast should fast.[15] One should not fast on the Fast-Breaking Eid, the Eid of Sacrifice or the days of *Tashrīq* because Allah's Messenger, peace and blessings be upon him and his progeny, prohibited fasting on those days. He said: ((These are the days of eating and drinking)).[16] Whoever does not fast these days cannot complete a daily fast.

My father related to me that his father was asked about the fast of 'Āshūra and which day it is. He was also asked about fasting on the Day of 'Arafat [i.e. the ninth of Dhul-Hijja]. He replied:

> It is very good to fast on it and there is no harm if one refrained from fasting on it. There is much virtue that has come regarding fasting on the Day of 'Arafat. It is expiation for the previous year. 'Ashūra is the tenth day [of Muharram] and there is no disagreement concerning that.

My father related to me that his father was asked about the daily fast. He replied:

> There is no problem with it as long as he breaks the fast on the two Eids and the days of *Tashrīq*. Whoever does not fast these days cannot complete a daily fast. It has been related that Allah's Messenger, peace and blessings be upon him and his progeny, said: ((There is no

---

[14] Similarly narrated in ***Ŝahīh al-Bukhāri, Ŝahīh Muslim, Sunan an-Nisā'i, Sunan Abu Dāwūd, Al-Mustadrak, Musnad Ahmed, Sunan ad-Dārimi, Mušannaf Ibn Abi Shayba, Mušannaf 'Abdur-Razzāq, Sunan al-Bayhaqi, Majmu' az-Zawā'id, Al-Mu'jam al-Kabīr***

[15] The weakness that would prohibit one from the daily fast is that which would prevent one from performing an obligation or encouraged act. If any voluntary fasting would do that, it is discouraged for one to do so [Ref. ***At-Tāj***].

[16] Similarly narrated in ***Ŝahīh Muslim, Sunan Abu Dāwūd, Muwatta, Musnad Ahmed, Sunan an-Nisā'i, Sunan Ibn Mājah, Sunan ad-Dārimi, Ŝahīh Ibn Khuzayma, Sunan ad-Dārqutni, Mušannaf Ibn Abi Shayba, Bihār al-Anwār***

fasting or breaking the fast for the one who does a daily fast)).[17] It may be that Allah's Messenger, peace and blessings be upon him and his progeny, said this out of guidance, consideration and facilitation—not as a prohibition.

There is great virtue in fasting on the 'white days.' It has been narrated in traditions that there is much good for one who desires to fast on those days.[18] It refers to the thirteenth, fourteenth and fifteenth days of each month. It is not preferable that the one who can fast these days refrain from fasting.

My father related to me that his father was asked about fasting on the white days, Rajab, Sha'bān as well as Mondays and Thursdays.[19] He replied: "Fasting on all of these days is very good. It has been related that there is much virtue in fasting on the white days; however, it is not considered an obligation."

Concerning the faster cupping and applying kohl

There is no problem with the faster to have cupping done as long as he is secure from its weakness and sure of its strength. If one fears weakness, it is impermissible to take it upon oneself. My father related to me that his father was asked about cupping for the one who is fasting. He replied: "There is no problem for the one who is fasting to have cupping done as long as he does not fear harm for himself."

There is no problem with applying kohl because it is not among those things which break the fast. It is not considered a meal; rather, it is an apparent remedy. It does not enter the insides nor does it reach the throat. My father related to me that his father said: "There is no problem with kohl being applied to the one who is fasting."

Concerning the faster who has intercourse with his wife, eats or drinks out of forgetfulness during Ramadan

The most that one who eats or drinks out of forgetfulness is obligated to do is make it up on another day. It has been narrated that the Commander of Believers, 'Ali b. Abi Ťālib, said: "There is no make up for him."[20] Even if we considered it authentic, we would not act on it.

As for the one who has intercourse out of forgetfulness, it is said that he owes expiation for that just as there would be for one who did it deliberately. According to me, that is not the case because it is

---

[17] Similarly narrated in ***Ŝahīh Muslim, Sunan Abu Dāwūd, Sunan an-Nisā'i, Sunan at-Tirmidhi, Sunan ad-Dārimi, Ŝahīh Ibn Khuzayma, Ŝahīh Ibn Hibbān, Mušannaf Ibn Abi Shayba***

[18] Similarly narrated in ***Sharh at-Tajrīd, Amāli Abu Ťālib, Amāli al-Murshid Billah, Sunan Abu Dāwūd, Sunan an-Nisā'i, Sunan at-Tirmidhi, Sunan Ibn Mājah, Ŝahīh Ibn Hibbān, Musnad Ahmed, Sunan al-Bayhaqi, Kanz al-'Ummāl, Majmu' az-Zawā'id, Musnad al-Bazzār, Al-Mu'jam al-Kabīr, Al-Mu'jam al-Awsat.*** The following references mention fasting three days each month without specifying the thirteenth, fourteenth and fifteenth: ***Amāli al-Murshid Billah, Ŝahīh al-Bukhāri, Ŝahīh Muslim, Sunan at-Tirmidhi, Sunan an-Nisā'i, Sunan Abu Dāwūd, Sunan Ibn Mājah, Musnad Ahmed, Sunan ad-Dārimi, Mušannaf Ibn Abi Shayba, Mušannaf 'Abdur-Razzāq, Sunan al-Bayhaqi, Kanz al-'Ummāl, Majmu' az-Zawā'id, Al-Mu'jam al-Kabīr, Al-Mu'jam al-Awsat, Ušūl al-Kāfi, Bihār al-Anwār***

[19] Regarding the sunnah of fasting on Rajab, it has been narrated in the following hadith collections: ***Amāli al-Murshid Billah, Ŝahīh Muslim, Sunan Abu Dāwūd, Sunan an-Nisā'i, Sunan al-Bayhaqi.*** Regarding the sunnah of fasting on Sha'bān, it has been narrated in the following collections: ***Sharh at-Tajrīd, Amāli Ahmed b. 'Isa, Ŝahīh al-Bukhāri, Mušannaf Ibn Abi Shayba, Sunan an-Nisā'i, Sunan Ibn Mājah, Musnad Ahmed, Sunan al-Bayhaqi, Muwatta, Kanz al-'Ummāl, Majmu' az-Zawā'id, Al-Mu'jam al-Awsat, Ušūl al-Kāfi, Bihār al-Anwār.*** Regarding the sunnah of fasting on Mondays and Thursdays, it has been narrated in the following hadith collections: ***Al-Jāmi' al-Kāfi, Amāli al-Murshid Billah, Ŝahīh Muslim, Sunan at-Tirmidhi, Sunan an-Nisā'i, Sunan Abu Dāwūd, Musnad Ahmed, Mušannaf Ibn Abi Shayba, Mušannaf 'Abdur-Razzāq, Sunan al-Bayhaqi, Sunan ad-Dārimi, Kanz al-'Ummāl, Al-Mu'jam al-Awsat, Al-Mu'jam al-Kabīr, Bihār al-Anwār.***

[20] Similarly narrated in ***Ŝahīh Ibn Khuzayma, Ŝahīh Ibn Hibbān, Al-Mustadrak, Sunan ad-Dārqutni, Sunan al-Bayhaqi.*** There is a report in ***Musnad Imam Zayd*** in which 'Ali is narrated to have said: "Whoever eats and drinks out of forgetfulness has not invalidated the fast. Allah has provided for him." However, we say that this statement does not imply that the fast is not to be made up because the jurists are in agreement that even if one were to do something that invalidated the prayer out of forgetfulness, s/he would still be obligated to make up the prayer. If this is the case with the prayer, how much more so is the case for other than it? Rather, his statement "...has not invalidated the fast..." means that the fast has not been nullified completely, as he would be obligated to complete the fast for the rest of the day and not discontinue it. This same meaning is conveyed in other narrations as well. [Ref. ***Ušūl al-Ahkām***]

necessary that there is a differentiation between what is out of forgetfulness and what is deliberate. The most accurate statement according to me is that the most he owes is seeking forgiveness and making up the day.

Concerning the faster who has intercourse with his wife deliberately as well as kisses or looks at her and ejaculates during Ramadan

Whoever has intercourse with his wife deliberately during Ramadan is obligated to repent to Allah sincerely, make up a day in its place and repent to Allah from a major sin. Whoever kisses, looks or touches his wife and then ejaculates—such person does not owe anything more than making up a day in its place and repenting to Allah.

My father related to me that his father said regarding the faster who has intercourse deliberately during Ramadan: "It is obligatory for him to make up a day in its place, seek forgiveness from Allah and repent to Him from a major sin that he committed."

Concerning fasting while travelling

Allah—the Blessed and Exalted—says: **{Therefore, whosoever amongst thee is ill or on a journey—then a like number of other days} (Q. 2:184)**. Allah gives dispensation for the one travelling to refrain from fasting out of a mercy from Him and to make things easy for them. Allah appoints for the traveller the choice to refrain from fasting if he likes. However, if he fasts, it is better for him. This is based on the statement of Allah: **{...but if ye fast, it is best for thee} (Q. 2:184)**. He allows one to refrain from fasting out of mercy and dispensation from Him, and He informs the one who fasts and does not refrain of a virtue.

My father related to me that his father was asked about fasting while travelling. He replied: "We say that fasting during travel is better." It was then said to him that there is a tradition narrated from Allah's Messenger, peace and blessings be upon him and his progeny: ((It is not from righteousness to fast while travelling)).[21] He replied: "This means the voluntary fasts, not the obligatory fasts."

This tradition—if it is authentically attributed to Allah's Messenger, peace and blessings be upon him and his progeny—only means what my grandfather said, may Allah be merciful to him. And that is it refers to the voluntary fasts and not the obligatory fasts. How could Allah's Messenger, peace and blessings be upon him and his progeny, say that regarding the obligatory fasts when Allah says: **{...but if ye fast, it is best for thee if ye but only knew} (Q. 2:184)**? The one with intellect would not say this nor would one who has knowledge hold to this.

Concerning the man who fasts during some of Ramadan but then travels during some of it and concerning the distance that one is permitted to break the fast

Whoever fasts some of Ramadan and then travels afterwards, there is no problem for him to break the fast. It is obligatory for him to fast what he missed after becoming a resident in his city. It is only for him to break the fast once he enters the state of travel. He does not consider that the fast is obligatory upon him unless he is a resident because Allah simply says: **{And whosoever is ill or on a journey—then a like number of other days. Allah desires ease for thee, and He desires not hardship for thee} (Q. 2:185)**. When the traveller enters his journey, Allah makes religiously permissible for him to break the fast out of His mercy which was otherwise prohibited before. The breaking of the fast and the shortening are together, and their permissibility is equal to the one with intellect. That which makes the shortening obligatory makes the breaking of the fast permissible. It is according to us twelve miles, which is a *barīd*.

[21] Similarly narrated in ***Sharh at-Tajrīd, Ŝaḥīh al-Bukhāri, Ŝaḥīh Muslim, Sunan Abu Dāwūd, Sunan an-Nisā'i, Sunan Ibn Mājah, Sunan ad-Dārimi***

My father related to me that his father said regarding the man who went into Ramadan fasting but then travelled:

> When he is a resident, he fasts. When he travels, he breaks the fast and shortens [i.e. the prayers]. Breaking the fast is a dispensation and facilitation from Allah for His slaves because Allah says: **{And whosoever is ill or on a journey—then a like number of other days. Allah desires ease for thee, and He desires not hardship for thee}** (Q. 2:185).

My father related to me that his father said: "The faster breaks the fast when he shortens the prayer. It is—according to us—travelling a *barīd*, which is twelve miles."

Concerning the faster who wakes up in the state of major ritual impurity during Ramadan

There is no problem with that because Allah only burdens the slaves with what they can bear. He does not burden them with hardship in their affairs. When one wakes up in the state of major ritual impurity, he is to perform the purification wash. He does not owe anything.

It has been narrated that Allah's Messenger, peace and blessings be upon him and his progeny, departed during Ramadan with water dripping from his head and he prayed the dawn prayer with the people. It was the night of Umm Salama. When she was asked about it, she said: "Yes. He had intercourse and not a wet dream." Allah's Messenger, peace and blessings be upon him and his progeny, completed the day and did not make it up.[22]

My father related to me that his father said regarding the man who woke up in the state of major ritual impurity: "There is no problem with that. It is valid for him to fast. That has been narrated from Allah's Messenger, peace and blessings be upon him and his progeny."

Concerning the menstruating woman making it up

The menstruating woman makes up the fast but does not make up the prayer. We only say that because Allah decrees that the sick person makes up the fast but He does not decree that the sick person make up the prayer that he missed. We find that He—the Blessed and Exalted—decrees that the sick person and anyone else unable to fast make up the fast by His statement: **{And whosoever is ill or on a journey—then a like number of other days}** (Q. 2:185). Yet we do not find that He decrees that the one who is not able to pray due to sickness make up for the days he missed. Rather, the most that is obligated on that sick person is that he prays when he recovers; he prays the day prayers if he were to recover before the day ends and the night prayers if he were to recover before the night ends.

We find that menstruation is considered an illness and weakness that enters a woman until it makes her really sick. It can be as harsh as any other severe illness. That withstanding, that which we make binding on the menstruating woman is that which is equally applied to a sick person. We do not take into account whether it is a continuous sickness or severe nor do we take into account its ease or sparseness after it has been made clear to us that it is a sickness or weakness like any other weakness.

That which confirms what we said from the authentic narrations of the Prophet is that he never ordered any of his wives to make up the prayer as they were ordered to make up the fast. Similarly, based upon what we've seen from all of the elders from the Messenger's Progeny and their scholars, we've not heard from any of them that they obligated the menstruating woman to make up the prayer as they obligated her to fast for the missed days.

My father related to me that his father said: "The menstruating woman makes up the fast but not the prayer." Also, it has reached us that Abu Ja'far Muhammad b. 'Ali,§ upon them be peace, said:

---

[22] Similarly narrated in ***Musnad Imam Zayd, Amāli al-Murshid Billah, Ŝahīh al-Bukhāri, Ŝahīh Muslim, Sunan an-Nisā`i, Muwaṫṫa, Musnad Ahmed, Musnad Abu Ya'la, Mušannaf Ibn Abi Shayba, Sunan al-Bayhaqi, Al-Mu'jam al-Kabīr, Al-Mu'jam al-Awsaṫ***

> The Wives of the Prophet, the Mothers of Believers, observed what other women observed; they made up the fast but did not make up the prayer. Fāṭima, the daughter of Allah's Messenger, observed what other women observed; she made up the fast but did not make up the prayer.[23]

It has reached us from Zayd b. 'Ali from his fathers from 'Ali, upon him be peace: "Allah's Messenger, peace and blessings be upon him and his progeny, said: ((The menstruating women are to make up the fast))."[24]

The meaning of this narrated tradition is that they make up for the days that they refrained from fasting during their menstruation and the days that they were menstruating. If the days in which they menstruated continues and they know that the time of their normal bleeding has passed, the women with vaginal bleeding are to purify themselves, pray, fast, approach their husbands, insert cotton for the prayer and stuff it if the blood is overwhelming.

Concerning the one who intends a voluntary fast but breaks the fast

He does not owe anything except those obligations of Allah which he obligated himself with. Then, it would be a religious injunction on him imposed by the Glorified. If he were to do that, we do not prefer that he break the fast. If he were to break the fast afterwards, he is to make up the obligations of Allah that day which he obligated upon himself.

My father related to me that his father said regarding a man were to wake up after having intended a voluntary fast and then breaks the fast: "He does not have to repeat it unless it was something obligatory on him and he said it. It is not obligatory on him with an intention without stating it openly."

He meant by "It is not obligatory on him with an intention without stating it openly" that if he made a vow or a matter for which Allah that obligates on him by proof of the statement.

Concerning the one who breaks the fast while falsely assuming that the sun had set and concerning making up during Ramadan and its manner

Whoever breaks the fast while falsely assuming that the sun had set due to clouds or any other reason, he is not considered defiantly disobedient in the religion. However, it is obligatory for him to make up a day in its place. Similarly, if he were to eat the pre-dawn meal while falsely assuming the approach of dawn and then comes to know that he ate the pre-dawn meal after the dawn has entered, he does not owe anything more than making up a day in its place. The Muslims should be cautious from things like that; they should not be heedless of that.

If one were to break the fast during Ramadan, he is to fast for the day that he broke the fast. If he were to break the fast for consecutive days, he can make up the fast in every other day. If he were to break the fast in separate days, he can make it up in a different sequence of days. However, making it up every other day would be best.

My father related to me that his father said regarding the faster who falsely assumed that the sun set and ate after which the sun set: "He is to make up a day in its place when it becomes clear to him that he mistakenly ate during the day."

My father related to me that his father said regarding a man who ate the pre-dawn meal while assuming that it was night but then it turned out to be the dawn: "He is to complete that day and make up a day in its place if he ate and drank after the approach of the dawn."

---

[23] Similarly narrated in ***Ŝaḥīḥ al-Bukhārī, Ŝaḥīḥ Muslim, Sunan at-Tirmidhi, Sunan ad-Dārimi***

[24] Similarly narrated in ***Musnad Imam Zayd*** and ***Amāli Ahmed b. 'Isa***

My father related to me that his father said regarding a man who doubted the approach of dawn: "Did it come or not? Should I eat?"

> If one were to eat without knowing or be informed that he ate after the approach of dawn, he does not have to make up a day in its place. If it is confirmed that he ate after the approach of dawn, he is to make up for the day that he broke the fast. The dawn is the display of whiteness, and it is the white thread as Allah says.

My father related to me that his father said regarding making up the fast during Ramadan: "One makes it up just as he broke the fast. If he broke the fast consecutively, he makes it up consecutively. If he broke the fast interruptedly, he makes it up interruptedly."

This is the best that I've heard on this matter. It is nearest to balanced and divine guidance that one makes up the fast in the same way that he broke it.

Concerning religious seclusion and the fast of the Prophet

Religious seclusion cannot take place except with fasting. In it, one is to stay away from wives during the day and night until he departs from his religious seclusion. The minimum time for religious seclusion is a day. It is religiously obligatory for the one who does the religious seclusion for a day to enter the mosque before the approach of dawn. Then, he can exit from it in the evening.

It has been said that religious seclusion cannot take place except in a congregational mosque. However, this is not the case according to me. Rather, religious seclusion can take place in any mosque according to me. This is because Allah has not differentiated between them, but He has called all of them **{houses}**.

The Glorified says: **{...in houses where Allah allows to be raised and His Name to be remembered therein glorifying Him therein morning and evening—men whom are neither distracted by commerce or sale from the remembrance of Allah and establishing the prayer and rendering the purification dues. They fear the Day when hearts and vision shall turn about} (Q. 24:36-37)**. If Allah calls all of them **{houses}** and all of them are mosques, we therefore permit religious seclusion to take place in all of them together.

As for the fast of Allah's Messenger, peace and blessings be upon him and his progeny, it is narrated that he used to fast until one would say "He does not break the fast," and he used to break the fast until one would say "He does not fast." He used to increase fasting during the months of Sha'bān and said: ((Sha'bān is my month. Rajab is your month, O 'Ali. Ramadan is Allah's month)).[25]

There is no problem with the one in religious seclusion to depart the mosque if there is a need or if he must witness a funeral and then he returns to the mosque. My father related to me that his father was asked about religious seclusion. He replied:

> He is to seclude himself to a congregational mosque and does not depart from it except out of need. There is no problem for him to witness a funeral. Then he returns to the mosque and fast. There is no religious seclusion except with fasting. He is to not to infringe on anything that Allah has permitted for him regarding wives during the day or night until he departs from the religious seclusion that he obligated upon himself.

By 'congregational mosque,' my grandfather means any mosque in which there is prayer—two persons or more. It can be one in which a congregation prays [like a village mosque] or does not pray [like a small mosque in open land].

---

[25] Similarly narrated in ***Sharh at-Tajrīd, Uṣūl al-Kāfi, Bihār al-Anwār***

Concerning the time for the pre-dawn meal

The time for the pre-dawn meal—in which there is no doubt—is before the dawn. The Muslims should be cautious in their religion and not approach any of their matters with doubt. They should not approach the doubtful matters and should follow those clear signs. Whoever eats the pre-dawn meal with ample time—this is best for him in the religion.

As for what was said about delaying the pre-dawn meal, this only means that it should be delayed to the end of the night. Whoever eats the pre-dawn meal in the last third of the night has delayed it. He should be cautious about the approach of dawn with strenuous effort.

The pre-dawn meal is a virtue. Regarding that, it has reached us that Allah's Messenger, peace and blessings be upon him and his progeny, said:

> ((Verily, Allah and His Angels send blessings on the one who is mindful of the pre-dawn meal and those who eat the pre-dawn meal. Therefore, you should eat the pre-dawn meal even if it is just a swallow of water)).[26]

If one were to eat the pre-dawn meal for a day or more during Ramadan and assumed that he ate it in time but then comes to know that he ate it after the approach of dawn, he is obligated to make up for those days. However, he does not owe expiation for that because he did not know the time for the pre-dawn meal at the approach of dawn.

Concerning the one who breaks the fast a day or more intentionally during Ramadan

If a defiantly disobedient person breaks the fast intentionally a day or more during Ramadan, it is religiously obligatory for him to make up those days and repent sincerely to Allah for the evil he did. If there is a manifest imam, he is to instruct such person in his actions and urge him to repentance.

If he does not repent, he is to be put to death because he acted contrary to Allah's judgements, countered His commands and abandoned His injunctions. Whoever does that is considered blasphemous, and that which is obligated regarding an apostate is obligated regarding him—to call him to repentance. If such violator does not repent, he is to be put to death.

It is said that he is to manumit a slave [as expiation]; however, according to us, repentance is sufficient. Whoever desires to do so voluntarily and other acts of goodness, it would be good for him.

Concerning the faster who applies eye-drops, injections and salve to the urethra or the ears

Others discourage that, but we do not see a problem with it. Our proof is that Allah does not desire difficulty or ruin. He does not prohibit them from curative treatment during the state of affliction. He only subjects the slave to fast so that [the slave] can be patient during hunger and thirst. According to us, one does not make up for that which does not enter other than the mouth and throat.

The one who does the aforementioned has not invalidated his fast. However, inhalation of medicine is discouraged for the faster[27] because such person is not safe from some of it entering his throat and from the taste and remnants returning to his throat and mouth.

As for that which does not enter the throat such as drops and that which is not transported by the saliva to the insides—there is no problem with it. Kohl and other medicinal treatments for the faster are examples.

---

[26] Similarly narrated in ***Musnad Imam Zayd, Amāli Ahmed b. 'Isa, Amāli Abu Ťālib, Ŝahīh Ibn Hibbān, Al-Mu'jam al-Awsaṭ, Bihār al-Anwār***

[27] Although the word 'discouraged' is used here, the understanding is that it is prohibited. It is not unlikely for jurists to use the word 'discouraged to mean 'prohibited' and vice versa. When al-Hādi was asked about inhalation while fasting in ***Al-Muntakhab***, he replied:

> Inhalation is impermissible according to us, and we do not hold to its validity because inhalation enters his throat. And everything that causes something to enter the throat is not permissible for the faster to do.

Concerning the one who kisses or touches and then ejaculates

One should not embark on that. If he were to do that in error, he must fast a day in the place of the day in which he performed such error. Similarly, if he were to press her against him with desire and ejaculates, he is to repent for that and make it up.

Whoever has intercourse with his wife, he is to make up the fast for that day and repent to Allah for doing it and for his audacity. If he does such [intentionally have intercourse with his wife] and does not repent, he is to be put to death because of his audacity against his Creator.

It is said that he owes expiation for that. They make a slaughtered she-camel (*badana*) or the manumission of a slave as expiation for ejaculation—whether by intercourse or other than it. They make a cow as expiation for the emission of prostatic fluid and a sheep as expiation for the emission of penile discharge. It is also said that they are to fast for two consecutive months afterwards as expiation.

However, according to us, repentance is sufficient because we do not find these expiations in the Book of Allah nor in the Sunnah of Allah's Messenger, peace and blessings be upon him and his progeny.[28] If it were the case, Allah would have mentioned it as he mentioned the expiations for unlawful pronouncements (*žihār*), the Hajj pilgrimage and oaths.

Whoever desires to do so voluntarily as expiation, it is on him. It is a reward for him, as Allah says: **{Then whosoever does voluntary good, it is good for him} (Q. 2:184)**. These expiations—

---

[28] It is noteworthy that here Imam al-Hādi denies that such expiations are mentioned in the Prophetic Sunnah. Despite that, there are several reported traditions in which the Prophet, peace and blessings be upon him and his progeny, was related to have prescribed the aforementioned expiations for a person who had intercourse with his wife during the fast of Ramadan. Imam al-Mu`ayyad Billah addressed the existence of such reports in his ***Sharh at-Tajrīd***. After relating some of these narrations, he said:

> Discussion regarding these reports is of three aspects. One, the narrated reports regarding this subject are contradictory, and that which is contradictory is exempted and thus cannot be utilised as a proof. Two, the import of these reports indicates a recommendation and not an obligation. And the first aspect also indicates the second aspect. Three, this was the judgement of one who made an unlawful pronouncement, and the man who was commanded to do so [i.e. render the expiations] made an unlawful pronouncement.

As for the contradictory nature of these reports, in some of the narrations, the Prophet was said to have given the violator of the fast the choice between the three expiations; however, in other reports, he was said to have specified the order for the expiations—namely, freeing a slave; then fasting two consecutive months for the one without a slave and finally, feeding sixty hungry believers for the one who cannot fast two consecutive months. Thus, the narrations that obligate specific sequence of the expiations contradict those which indicate the choice between the expiations.

As for the proof of the recommendation for the expiations and not their obligation, this can be demonstrated from two perspectives. First, according to all the narrations, the Prophet, peace and blessings be upon him and his progeny, allowed the man who broke the fast to finally eat from the charity that he was to give to the poor. It is a matter of consensus that anyone who is obligated to give charity is not permitted to eat or use it. It is therefore concluded that this was a voluntary charity and not an obligatory expiation. Second, in some of the narrations, the sacrifice of a she-camel was prescribed in the place of fasting two consecutive months as expiation. Such substitution only serves to indicate the recommendatory nature of the expiation since an obligatory expiation cannot be substituted for anything else.

As for the proof that the reported instance refers to the obligatory expiation for an unlawful pronouncement and not for breaking the fast, in a narration related by Salama b. Ŝakhr, he says that he made an unlawful pronouncement on his wife during Ramadan but then violated this pronouncement by having intercourse with her. Then, the Prophet, peace and blessings be upon him and his progeny, prescribed the expiation on him until the end of the hadith. Therefore, it is probable that the other reported instances refer to this incident with Salama b. Ŝakhr and that he was commanded to render expiation—not because he broke the Ramadan fast but because he made an unlawful pronouncement.

What makes this interpretation likely is the fact that none of the reports relate that the Prophet told the violator to make up the fast he had broken. Making up a broken fast is obligatory according to the consensus of the scholars, so it would seem most likely that the Prophet, peace and blessings be upon him and his progeny, would have told the violator to make up the fast. However, such command does not appear in any of the narrations of this incident.

It may be argued that all three views contradict each other because one view dismisses the incident altogether due to the contradictions in the reports, the second view indicates that the expiations were recommendations for breaking the fast and the third view is that the expiations were obligations for the one who made an unlawful pronouncement to his wife. We reply by saying we do not hold to the authenticity of all three views; rather, we say that the existence of these different views disproves the obligation of expiation for intentionally breaking the Ramadan fast. Thusly, it confirms what Imam al-Hādi said—and that is, there are no obligatory expiations in the Prophetic Sunnah for breaking the fast.

according to us—are only mandatory in the case of the Hajj pilgrimage. Freeing a slave and fasting are the expiations in the case of unlawful pronouncements and in killing a believer unintentionally.

Concerning vomit from the faster and what breaks the fast by entering one's throat

The ritual ablution is invalidated by that which exits, but the fast is invalidated by that which enters. If the one who vomited is certain that something returned to the throat from the mouth, he has to make it up. If something had not returned from the throat or the insides, he continues with the fast and does not have to make it up.

My father related to me that his father said regarding the one who vomited while fasting or sudden vomiting: "It is not for the faster to induce vomiting. Whoever vomits or vomiting occurs suddenly and he is certain that it did not return to his insides, he is to continue fasting and does not have to make it up."

Whoever intentionally swallows a dinar, dirham, *fils*, glass, stone or other objects on the earth—he is to make it up and repent for what he did. Others allow this as a dispensation; however, that is not acknowledged according to us because it has entered the insides and has passed the throat. Allah has prohibited those fasting from inserting things into their throats to their insides. If it was permissible for them, it would also be permissible for them to swallow clay, mud or other things into their insides. He would have tasted them even though it was not considered food. Similarly, if he were to rinse the nose and mouth for the prayer and some water were to enter his insides, he has to make it up.

Regarding dust, smoke, fog and other things that cannot be prevented, he does not have to make it up but he should be cautious of that. My father related to me that his father was asked about dust that enters the throat of the faster. He replied: "It does not invalidate the fast."

The fast is not invalidated by tasting anything with the tip of the tongue because Allah only prohibits the faster from entering anything into his insides from the path normally travelled by his food. As for the mouth, the fast is not invalidated by that which enters it. If the fast was broken by anything that enters the mouth without entering his insides, the rinsing of the mouth would invalidate it. If rinsing the mouth invalidated the fast, one could not join the ritual prayer with the fasting; the ritual prayer would invalidate the fast and the fast would invalidate the ritual prayer. This is because there is no ritual prayer without the ritual ablution and no ritual ablution without rinsing the mouth. The ritual prayer is obligatory on every Muslim just as the fast. For that reason, we say that everything that enters the mouth but not the insides—such as honey, vinegar or water—does not invalidate the fast.

Concerning the one who vows a fast on himself for Allah

He is to act upon that which he intended. If he said twenty days and intended them to be consecutive, he is to fast them consecutively as he intended. If he obligated the number on himself but did not obligate that it was consecutive, there is no problem if he separates them when he fasts them. Similarly, if he vows it on himself to fast a year, he is to break the fast for the two Eids as well as the days of *Tashrīq* and then make those days up.

Similarly, I hold to the view that he is to make up the month of Ramadan because it wasn't a part of his vow. This is because the vow is only an obligation that he obligated. The month of Ramadan is an obligation from Allah on all the people. For that reason, we say that it is obligatory on him to observe his vow for the month until he completes it and what he obligates on himself for Allah. Therefore, if he intends that, he is not obligated to make it up. It is only a vow for a fast for eleven months and the fast of Ramadan is an obligatory injunction from Allah. It is not for him to intend to fast a complete year which includes Ramadan.

Concerning the menstruating woman who is purified in the middle of the day and had eaten in the beginning as well as the traveller who returns to his family at the end of the day after having eaten in the beginning

It is encouraged for both to stop eating for the rest of the day because both have transgressed the boundaries that permit them to eat.

Concerning the one who is permitted to refrain from fasting during Ramadan

It is permitted for the following women: the pregnant woman who fears that the fast would harm what is in her womb, the breastfeeding woman who fears that the fast would stop her milk and harm the baby, the menstruating woman, the woman with postpartum bleeding, the travelling woman, the sick woman with any type of sickness, the extremely thirsty woman who cannot endure without water and the elderly woman who cannot bear the fast. All of them can refrain from fasting and are to feed a needy person for each day.

It is permissible for four men to refrain from fasting: the extremely thirsty man who cannot endure without water, the elderly man who cannot bear the fast—both of whom can refrain from fasting and must feed a needy person each day—the sick person and the traveller.

It is obligatory for the man and woman with extreme thirst to feed a needy person for each day that he or she refrained from fasting. It is obligatory for both to take remedies for that which is the cause of the illness. If they are cured, they are to make up for all those days that they refrained from fasting. If their condition remained perpetually, their condition regarding the obligation of the fast is like that of the decrepit elderly person whose condition is too weak to fast. One is to feed just as the other is to feed; one is exempted from fasting just as the other is exempted from fasting. Those other than these two are obligated to make it up for every day that one experienced the illness that prevented them from fasting.

Regarding that, it has reached us from Allah's Messenger, peace and blessings be upon him and his progeny, that when the obligation of fasting for Ramadan was revealed to him, a pregnant woman came to him and said: "O Messenger of Allah, I am a pregnant woman. This month of Ramadan has been made an injunction, but I fear for that which is in my womb if I were to fast." He, peace and blessings be upon him and his progeny, said: ((You are exempted and may break the fast. But if you can, fast)). A breastfeeding woman came to him and said: "O Messenger of Allah, I am a breastfeeding woman. This month of Ramadan has been made an injunction, but I fear for that my milk will discontinue and the child would be harmed if I were to fast." He, peace and blessings be upon him and his progeny, replied: ((You are exempted and may break the fast. But if you can, fast)).[29]

As for the extremely thirsty person, he came to the Prophet and said: "O Messenger of Allah, this month has been made an injunction. However, I cannot endure an hour without water and I fear for myself if I were to fast." He, peace and blessings be upon him and his progeny, said: ((You are exempted and may break the fast. But if you can, fast)). An elderly man came to him being carried by two men and said: "O Messenger of Allah, this month has been made an injunction. However, I cannot fast." He, peace and blessings be upon him and his progeny, said: ((Go and feed a needy person half a *ṡā'* for each day)). It says that he, peace and blessings be upon him and his progeny, commanded them after that to fast a day or two and break the fast a day or two.[30]

It is necessary that his command to fast a day or two is for the one who can fast. As for the one who is unable, he does not have to fast. If it was obligatory for the one who is unable to fast a day or two, it would similarly be able to fast the complete the whole month. This is because the meaning of ability of ease for the one who is unable is like the meaning of the ability of much. Allah says: **{Allah**

[29] Similarly narrated in ***Musnad Imam Zayd, Amāli Ahmed b. 'Isa, Bihār al-Anwār***
[30] Ibid.

burdens not a soul except with what it can bear} (Q. 2:286) and **{Allah burdens not a soul except with what He hath given it} (65:7)**.

Also regarding that, it is narrated that Allah's Messenger, peace and blessings be upon him and his progeny, said: ((If a boy is able to fast three days, it is obligatory for him to fast the whole month)).[31] Similarly, it is obligatory for everyone with an illness. Also, it is obligatory for the pregnant and breastfeeding woman to fast a day or two and break the fast a day or two if she does not fear any harm to the baby.

Concerning the one who breaks the fast for Ramadan and then does not make it up until the coming month

If one avoided such due to a reason that prevented such person from making it up, such one is to fast for the subsequent month and feed a needy person for each day as expiation as a debt for the previous month.[32] He is to feed based upon the number of days that he refrained from fasting—whether many or few. When he has finished the injunction of fasting and completed Allah's command on him, he is to begin fasting what he missed after the Eid. This is the best view concerning that. If he fasted and did not feed, it is sufficient. Allah is the Bringer of every correct thing, and He is the only One who we ask for help, success and guidance.

Concerning the fast for unlawful pronouncements

Whoever makes an unlawful pronouncement to his wife, he is obligated by Allah to expiate. He is obligated to manumit a slave before he can touch her [i.e. his wife]. If he does not have a slave to free, it is obligatory for him to fast two consecutive months before he approaches her. If he cannot do that, he is to feed sixty needy people two *mudd*s each.

It is impermissible for him to discontinue his fast for an unlawful pronouncement—whether resident or traveller—unless there is a valid reason or fear of harm from the fast. It is therefore permissible for him to break the fast while the valid reason remains. If he finds relief from his affair, he is to fast. After he is secure from ruin due to the difficulty on himself in his matter and the severity of his illness is relieved and is able to fast to his Lord, he is to make it up for two months. This will be sixty consecutive days unless it is interrupted by any of the aforementioned reasons. If it is interrupted for any reason, one is to use as a basis the preceding days of fasting until the time of interruption due to the valid reason.

The fast of two months must be completed before a man can touch his wife. If his fast is interrupted by something that he can prevent or any other reason, he is religiously obligated to begin the fast anew for the two months consecutively until he completes it as Allah commands.

Others say that if the fast is interrupted by any reason—whether difficult or easy, whether able or unable to prevent it—he must begin the fast anew. According to us, that is not the case because this would be exceeding the bounds for the Muslims as well as an extreme difficulty for the believers. This is because not every person is safe from the burdens of sicknesses, and two months are not secure

---

[31] Similarly narrated in ***Sharh at-Tajrīd, Al-Jāmi' al-Kāfi, Kanz al-'Ummāl, Al-Jāmi' as-Saghīr*** of as-Suyūti, ***Uṣūl al-Kāfi***

[32] It has been noted by Imams Abu Ṭālib, Yahya b. Hamza, al-Mu`ayyad Billah and Ibn Murtaḍa that two different positions exist from al-Hādi regarding what is due on the faster who breaks the fast of Ramadan and then makes it up the following Ramadan. One view, which is presented here in the ***Ahkām***, is that one must feed a needy person for every day missed as well as make up the fast. However, the second view, which is presented in Al-Muntakhab, is that one only needs to make up the fast without feeding a needy person. Imam Abul-Abbās al-Hasani attempted to reconcile these two views in ***At-Tahrīr*** by stating that the ruling in ***Ahkām*** refers to one who broke the fast without a valid excuse and the ruling in ***Al-Muntakhab*** refers to those who broke the fast with an excuse. However, this interpretation is lacking due to the fact that al-Hādi explicitly stated 'due to a reason' in the ***Ahkām***. Instead, we say that a more plausible explanation is that the expiation mentioned in ***Ahkām*** is a recommendation and not an obligation. This view is supported by his later statement: 'If he fasted and did not feed, it is sufficient.' Such statement could not be made if expiation was obligatory [Ref. ***Al-Qawl al-Awwal***]

from the occurrences of mishaps. Rather, most people are subject to illnesses and sicknesses and are not able to fast for two months consecutively. Neither is everyone able to find the means to manumit a slave or feed for expiation as others are able.

Then, say to the one who is adamant about it and does not see that the faster has ample opportunities out of necessity: "What do you say about the man who makes an unlawful pronouncement to his wife while in straitened circumstances and he was not able to manumit a slave for expiation or able to feed someone due to the severity of his poverty or able to fast continuously for two months due to the calamities of his illness? Due to the strength of his difficulty, he must be able to fast for one month but not able to increase in that for one day. Isn't the severity of illnesses known and are not the afflictions that worsen circumstances familiar to the people? Have you prevented him from his wife perpetually since he is unable to counter what he said or do you say what the Exalted and Most High Lord says **{Allah burdens not a soul except with what it can bear} (Q. 2:286)** and **{Allah burdens not a soul except with what He hath given it} (65:7)**?"

If they say "Certainly! We say what Allah says and free him of this affliction that Allah frees him from," they have contradicted their original position, followed the correct matter, returned to that which we said and said what we have been saying. If they say "Certainly not! We say to the one who cannot find a means to manumit a slave or feed as well as to the one who has this affliction in his body perpetually and had fasted a month but broke the fast a day or two due to illness and straitened circumstances that could readily return if he were to fast for two months: Your wife will be prohibited from you until you are able to do what you cannot do and act upon that which is too difficult to act upon." They have acted contrary to the Book of their Lord and have been overly strict in a matter that their Creator has made easy. This is because Allah says: **{Allah burdens not a soul except with what it can bear} (Q. 2:286)** and **{Allah burdens not a soul except with what He hath given it} (65:7)** and **{...and slay not thyself. Verily, Allah hath been merciful unto thee} (Q. 4:29)** and **{And make not thine own hands contribute to destruction} (Q. 2:193)**. Whoever acts contrary to the command of Allah and makes difficult what Allah has made easy—this is in reality invalidation because one cannot follow anything of this doctrine.

Similarly, it is religiously obligatory for the one who made the unlawful pronouncement to manumit a slave. If he does not have the means to fast, he can fast some and then discontinue his fast and manumit a slave if he finds the means to manumit a slave. Similarly, if he is unable to fast due to an illness and then feeds some of the needy but afterwards regains health and is able to fast—such person is to fast and not count his feeding. This is because Allah only permits one to fast if he does not have the means to manumit a slave. If he finds a way—even if he was fasting—the fast is discontinued and he is obligated to manumit a slave. Similar is the case in the feeding when exempting the fast.

If one did not find the means to manumit a slave until after completing the fast, he is not obligated to manumit a slave. Similarly, if one could not fast until after feeding sixty needy people, he does not have to fast. We only say that because everything that one did completely does not have to be made up. If he did not have to make it up and has done what was better than it, it would not be permissible to do the first thing that was exempted while the second thing was obligatory.

It is analogous to the female who is divorced while she does not menstruate. She counts it by months. If two months pass from her waiting period (*'idda*) and she menstruates, it is religiously obligatory for her to proceed with three menstrual periods and not count the months that have passed. This is because she has become among those who menstruates; therefore, what is obligatory for her is what is obligatory upon him, and what is for her is for them.

Similarly, if the one who performs the joint pilgrimages (*al-mutamatu'*) does not find a sacrificial animal and fasts three days during the Pilgrimage but afterwards finds a sacrificial animal during the days of Mina and is able to sacrifice—it is religiously obligatory for him to sacrifice the animal. The fast that he did is not to be considered because he found the sacrificial animal during its time. The presence of the sacrificial animal invalidated the fast during that time. The sacrifice is then mandatory.

Concerning when the fast becomes religiously obligatory upon the male and female child

The fast becomes obligatory upon them both when they reach the age of fifteen years. If both are able to fast other than that, it is obligatory for the both of them to fast. It was narrated that the Prophet, peace and blessings be upon him and his progeny, said: ((If a boy is able to fast three days, it is obligatory for him to fast the whole month)).

We simply say fifteen years of age for the man or woman who has not reached maturity. As for the one who reached maturity [by the onset of puberty] at the age of nine or ten or eleven, the fast is religiously obligatory upon such one. There have been many different statements regarding that, but the best—according to us—is it is based on one's ability to fast or one who has reached maturity other than those of fifteen years of age. Otherwise, fifteen years of age is considered the age of maturity.

Concerning the witnessing of the new moon

When two witnesses witness the new moon for the fast and breaking the fast, their witness is sufficient and accepted as long as both are just, reliable and God-conscious. Similar has reached us from Allah's Messenger, peace and blessings be upon him and his progeny, that the people of Medina observed the dawn prayer fasting on the last day of Ramadan and some of them bore witness to Allah's Messenger, peace and blessings be upon him and his progeny, that they saw the new moon the night before. Allah's Messenger, peace and blessings be upon him and his progeny, ordered the people to break the fast and return to their prayer.[33] It has also reached us that the Commander of Believers, 'Ali b. Abi Ṫālib, said: "If two just men bear witness that they saw the new moon, fast and break the fast."[34]

If one man saw the new moon, that which is sufficient for him is between him and Allah. If he saw the new moon of Ramadan, he fasts. If he saw the new moon for Shawwāl, he breaks the fast. He should not manifest that to the people when it may be repulsive and there is disagreement concerning that.

Concerning the supplication one makes when witnessing the new moon

The one who sees the new moon should turn his face towards the *qibla* and say:

> My Lord and your Lord is Allah, the One with whom is no god except Him. He is the Ever Living and Self-Sustaining. He does not slumber nor does He sleep. He is **{the One who created the heavens and earth and made the darkness and light. Then, those who disbelieve in their Lord turn away} (Q. 6:1)**. We do not associate anything as partners with Allah nor do we take a god or protector in His stead. All praise is due to Allah, **{the One who made in the heavens constellations and made therein a lamp and an illuminating moon} (Q. 25:61)**. All praise is due to Allah, the One who made you a sign of night and appointed you as a stopping place. O Allah, verily, I ask You for the best of this month and I seek refuge from its evil. O Allah, make us among those who worship You!

If it is the new moon of Ramadan, one includes this supplication:

> O Allah, verily, this is a month that You have made great and have appointed the fast therein. We intend to observe Your injunction. Accept from us what we do for You, and do not have it pass from us except with Your pleasure, pardon and mercy. Verily, You are the Hearer of supplications.

---

[33] Similarly narrated in ***Sunan Abu Dāwūd, Sunan an-Nisā'i, Sunan Ibn Mājah, Sunan ad-Dārqutni, Mušannaf Ibn Abi Shayba, Sunan al-Bayhaqi***

[34] Similarly narrated in ***Sharh at-Tajrīd, Al-Jāmi' al-Kāfi, Mušannaf Ibn Abi Shayba, Sunan ad-Dārqutni, Sunan al-Bayhaqi***

It is narrated from the Commander of Believers, 'Ali b. Abi Ťālib, upon him be peace, that he used to say when he saw the new moon: "O Allah, I ask you for the good of this month: its opening, its victory, its light and its provision. I seek refuge in You from its evil and the evil after it."[35]

It has also reached us from him, upon him be peace, that he used to say when he saw the new moon of Ramadan: "O Allah, Lord of the new moon of the month of Ramadan. Have it come upon us with submission, security, faith, health from sickness as well as safety from being preoccupied from the prayer and the fast."[36]

Concerning various issues regarding the fast and religious seclusion

If a man intends a voluntary fast for a day but only fasts for half, he has the choice: he can continue fasting if he wants or he can break the fast if he wants. It is encouraged for him to complete it for Allah and not break the fast unless there is an illness or to make his Muslim brother happy [by accepting the latter's invitation]. Similar is narrated from the Prophet, peace and blessings be upon him and his progeny, that he commanded that to a Muslim brother.[37]

The one in religious seclusion departs for a need that is necessary, is present for the funeral rites and returns due to sickness. Whoever vows for himself that he will not talk during his religious seclusion—he should not do that and should feed ten needy people and then speak. This is because returning the greetings of peace is a part of speech and such is a religious injunction from the Possessor of Majesty and Nobility.

One should not obligate himself to avoid something that is an injunction upon him. If one were to obligate himself to fast a complete month for Allah, as well as two or three consecutive months—such person is religiously obligated to fast as he obligated. If he were to discontinue the fast for any day among those days, he is religiously obligated to renew the fast unless he contracted some type of illness during that time. He is not expected to continue the fast due to the weakness of his body and the continuance of his sickness. If he fears for himself, it is permissible for him to break the fast during a severe illness that prevents one from fasting. Then, when he recovers, he builds upon the fast that he missed.

Religious seclusion is when a man intends and stipulates a period of seclusion for particular days or says: "It is for Allah that I seclude myself such and such days." If he obligates that upon himself by stipulating his intention or by the aforementioned wording, he is to enter the mosque at the beginning of the time he stipulated upon himself and fast those days that he intended. Consequently, there is no religious seclusion without fasting.

Then, he is to be on guard from obscenity, lying, argument, debate and other forms of corrupt acts and speech. The one in religious seclusion is to increase in recitation of Qur'an, remembrance, seeking forgiveness and glorification of the Most Gracious.

He does not leave the mosque except for the reasons we mentioned: to fulfil a need, tend to one of the Muslims, follow the funeral bier of the believers, and in the case of a need to command or prohibit his family. He is to command and prohibit them while standing and not sit down before returning to the mosque.

It is impermissible for the one in religious seclusion to have intercourse with wives whether day or night. That which invalidates the religious seclusion invalidates the fast, and that which is permissible in it is permissible in the fast. If the one in religious seclusion invalidates the fast while in seclusion, he has likewise invalidated his religious seclusion.

If a man obligated a religious seclusion upon himself for a Friday, but does not specifically designate which Friday it is and which month it is, he can observe religious seclusion for any month and time he

---

[35] Similarly narrated in ***Amāli Ahmed b. 'Isa, Mušannaf Ibn Abi Shayba, Kanz al-'Ummāl, Ušūl al-Kāfi, Bihār al-Anwār***

[36] Similarly narrated in ***Amāli Ahmed b. 'Isa*** and ***Amāli Abu Ťālib***

[37] This incident regarding Salmān is mentioned and referenced in the next section.

wants. If he designates a specific Friday, he must observe religious seclusion on that day unless he is prevented from doing so on that day. He is to then observe religious seclusion on another Friday in its place when that which initially prevented him from the previous Friday has passed.

Whoever obligates religious seclusion upon himself for designated days and secludes himself and then has intercourse during his religious seclusion—his religious seclusion would be invalidated. He must begin his religious seclusion anew. He must be on guard against that which caused him to invalidate his religious seclusion until he observes his seclusion soundly.

Whoever says "It is for Allah that I seclude myself for twenty days" but intends the daylight hours and not the night, he is obligated to do what he intended. He must seclude himself as thus. It is obligatory for him to enter the mosque every day before the coming of dawn and not exit until the time for breaking the fast. The exception is what we previously mentioned—tend to the sick, be present at a funeral or exit for a need that is necessary for only him.

If a man obligated religious seclusion upon himself for a month after he recovers from an illness, he is obligated to fast within an hour after his illness has gone and is able to observe the injunction of seclusion upon himself. If he has recovered from his illness and Ramadan has come upon him suddenly while he is able to seclude himself at the end of Sha'bān, he is to begin with the obligation of Allah. When Ramadan has passed, he is to break the fast on the Eid because Allah's Messenger, peace and blessings be upon him and his progeny, prohibited the fast on that day. Afterwards, he begins with what he obligated upon himself and seclude himself for thirty days.

We only say that he is to seclude himself after Ramadan and not during it due to what he obligated upon himself. This is because he obligated upon himself to observe religious seclusion for a month and there is no religious seclusion without fasting. It is as if he obligated himself to fast for a month when he obligated himself to observe religious seclusion. He cannot observe another fast for a month when he has already been obligated to fast. There is that which he obligated himself, and there is that which his Lord has made as an injunction upon him. The religious injunction takes precedence over the voluntary because that which Allah has made as an injunction to His slaves is greater than offering that which he obligated upon himself. One draws near to Allah by that which He has obligated. This brings one nearer than the supererogatory acts that the slave has obligated upon himself.

There is no problem in applying kohl, oil or any scent that one wants, including musk or other scents. It is encouraged that he does not buy or sell. However, if he does that, it would not be considered invalidated.

If a woman obligates herself to observe religious seclusion for two months—more or less—she is obligated to observe what she obligated upon herself. While she is in religious seclusion, she is obligated to fast just as the man. That which invalidates it for her is the same as that which invalidates it for him, and that which makes it sound for her is the same as that which makes it sound for him. If she menstruates while in seclusion, she is to depart from the mosque. And once she is pure and has purified herself, she is to return to her religious seclusion. She then observes religious seclusion and the fast she obligated upon herself from the time she broke her fast until she completes the days she appointed for Allah.

Any person in religious seclusion—whether male or female—who fears for himself or herself in the mosque of their seclusion must depart that mosque and enter another. If one owes a religious seclusion that one obligated upon oneself and is close to death, such person is to bequest another to observe religious seclusion for such one for those days. He is to extract a third and pay a person for it as long as such person is among the people of Islam. He then observes religious seclusion on his behalf fulfilling the bequest of the deceased. It is religiously obligatory for the heirs and guardians of the deceased to maintain that which was bequeathed by the deceased.

There is no problem with the one in religious seclusion to marry; however, he cannot have sexual intercourse with his wife until he departs from his religious seclusion. There is also no problem for him to conduct the marriage of any Muslim or witness the marriage of those who marry in his mosque. There is no problem with him preventing the oppressors from the oppressed or assisting the weak against his oppressor. He is to prevent with his tongue. However, if he cannot do so except by his hand, then he is to do so by his hand.

If a man were to say "It is for Allah that I seclude myself for a day" and observes the seclusion that day but eats and drinks out of forgetfulness, his religious seclusion would be considered invalidated. He would have to make up a day in its place.

Concerning the one who swears by the religious seclusion

If a man says "I vow to observe religious seclusion for two months if I speak to so-n-so," he is not obligated to seclude himself until he speaks to that person. If he speaks to the person, he is religiously obligated to observe religious seclusion because he broke his oath. He is obligated to observe that with which he obligated himself. Similarly, if he said "I vow to observe religious seclusion on the Day of Breaking the Fast if I speak to so-n-so during Ramadan" and speaks to him before the completion of Ramadan, his oath is broken. However, he is to not fast on the Day of Breaking the Fast because Allah's Messenger, peace and blessings be upon him and his progeny, prohibited fasting on that day. Rather, he is to break the fast that day and observe religious seclusion on the day after the Eid.

If a slave obligates himself to observe religious seclusion on mutually understood days, he is obligated to observe that unless he is prevented by his master. It is the master's right to prevent his slave from doing so if he pleases. It is encouraged for the master to not prevent his slave from doing so if his only desire is nearness to his Lord. Similar is the case with subjects and female slaves. As for the indentured servant who obligated himself to observe religious seclusion, it is not for his master to prevent him. Rather, he is obligated to observe what he obligated upon himself because he is similar to a free man in his own house while under contract.

One must not fast uninterruptedly between two days—this refers to fasting day and night—while in religious seclusion or otherwise. Regarding that, it has reached us that the Commander of Believers, 'Ali b. Abi Ťālib, upon him be peace, said: "Do not fast uninterruptedly, and do not fast day and night."[38]

It has also reached us that he, upon him be peace, said: "Fasting three days is considered the continuous fast. They remove the impurity (*wahara*) of the breast." He was asked: "What is the impurity of the breast?" He replied: "His sin and rancour."[39]

He, upon him be peace, also used to say:

> Whoever desires to fast a day of the month should fast on Thursday and not on Friday because the latter is a day of Eid. Allah has joined together two great days—a day of fasting and a day of Eid—as a witness with the Muslims.[40]

It has reached us from him, upon him be peace, that he said: "You should not decide to fast on Friday unless it correlates to your fasting anyway."[41] It has also reached us from Allah's Messenger, peace and blessings be upon him and his progeny, that Salmān came to him one day and he invited the latter to eat.

---

[38] Similarly narrated in ***Musnad Imam Zayd*** and ***Amāli Ahmed b. 'Isa***. The following texts attribute the same statement to the Prophet: ***Sunan al-Bayhaqi, Mušannaf Ibn Abi Shayba, Mušannaf 'Abdur-Razzāq, Kanz al-'Ummāl, Al-Mu'jam al-Awsat, Ušūl al-Kāfi, Bihār al-Anwār***

[39] Similarly narrated in ***Musnad Imam Zayd, Al-Jāmi' al-Kāfi, Sharh at-Tajrīd***. The following texts attribute the statement to the Prophet: ***Sunan an-Nisā'i, Mušannaf Ibn Abi Shayba, Mušannaf 'Abdur-Razzāq, Kanz al-'Ummāl, Musnad al-Bazzār, Majmu' az-Zawā'id***

[40] Similarly narrated in ***Mušannaf Ibn Abi Shayba***

[41] Similarly narrated in ***Sharh at-Tajrīd, Al-Jāmi' al-Kāfi, Amāli al-Murshid Billah, Ŝahīh al-Bukhāri, Ŝahīh Muslim, Sunan Ibn Mājah, Sunan ad-Dārimi, Mušannaf Ibn Abi Shayba***

He replied: "O Messenger of Allah, I am fasting." He [i.e. the Prophet] then said: ((O Salmān, fast another day in its place. That would be best to do in order to cause happiness to enter your brother)).[42]

Concerning fasting for unintentional manslaughter

Allah—Glorified be He—says: {**If the slain belongs to a people hostile unto thee and he is a believer, a believing slave is to be set free. And if he belongs to a people between whom they and ye have a mutual covenant, then blood money must be paid unto his people and a believing slave must be set free. And whosoever hath not the wherewithal to do so must fast two consecutive months. It is a recompense from Allah. Allah is All-Knowing, All-Wise**} (**Q. 4:92**). Therefore, whoever kills a believer unintentionally must manumit a slave.

If he does not have the means to manumit a slave, he is to fast two consecutive months unless he has some valid reason that we previously recounted regarding the one who made unlawful pronouncements. In that case, he can break the fast. His situation in that respect would be the same as the one who made the unlawful pronouncement. It is not for him or the one who made the unlawful pronouncement to undertake a journey nor can the two of them break the fast while travelling if they are able to fast and have the strength. The both of them are to guard their religion and consider their own souls because Allah is not ignorant of their affair, nor are their secrets hidden from Him.

[42] Similarly narrated in ***Amāli Ahmed b. 'Isa, Amāli Abu Ťālib, Al-Jāmi' al-Kāfi, Al-Mu'jam al-Awsaṭ, Sunan ad-Dārqutni, Sunan al-Bayhaqi, Kanz al-'Ummāl***

The Book of the Hajj pilgrimage

In the Name of Allah, the Most Gracious, the Most Merciful...

The beginning of the chapters related to the Hajj pilgrimage

Verily, Allah—the Blessed and Exalted—enjoined his creation that they must perform their pilgrimage as a religious duty. He commanded them to observe their rituals and they are obligated with that which their Lord has obligated upon them. It was an obligation upon all of creation as a religious injunction to all believers. This is so that Allah could clearly differentiate the obedient from the disobedient, and separate the disbelievers from the believers. Regarding that, the Lord of creation says: **{And Allah has enjoined upon the people the pilgrimage to the House for whomsoever has the ability to find a way. Whosoever is ungrateful** (or **"disbelieves"**) **verily Allah is independent of creation}** (**Q. 3:97**). The Glorified also says: **{Observe the Hajj and 'Umra for Allah}** (**Q. 2:196**). The Blessed and Exalted is saying: Establish that which has been enjoined on you and observe that which you have entered from both. Establish the rituals of both which Allah has enjoined on the one who entered from them.

Regarding that, Allah—the Blessed and Exalted—said to His most forbearing Prophet, Abraham: **{And proclaim unto humankind the Pilgrimage. They shall come unto thee on foot and on every lean camel coming from every deep ravine}** (**Q. 22:27**). His Lord commanded him, upon him be peace, to perform the Hajj pilgrimage to His Sanctified House. He performed the Hajj pilgrimage just as Allah commanded just as his father, Adam, performed the Hajj pilgrimage. The Hajj pilgrimage of Abraham with his family and the believers was until it ended at the House of the Lord of creation. Allah commanded him to proclaim the Hajj pilgrimage; he proclaimed it and called to Allah. The one who believed in Allah listened, responded and followed. They all gathered to Abraham, upon him be peace, and he left with those with him to go to Mina.

It is said that the Devil confronted him at the halting place of al-'Aqaba. He [i.e. Abraham] hurled seven stones at him and declared Allah's greatness with each throw. He then confronted him again at the second halting place, and he did to him what he did at the first halting place. Then, he confronted him a third time at the third halting place. He hurled stones at him just as he had done at the second halting place. He finally despaired of him and accepted his response. It is also said that he resisted him and diverted him from the path of 'Arafat. He, upon him be peace, came to Dhul-Majāz and stopped there. However, he did not recognise it since he saw that he did not have a description of it. He left from there and the place was named—due to Abraham's attribution of that place—Dhul-Majāz. When Abraham, upon him be peace, came to the place to which he was commanded, he recognised it by the signs that were described to him. He, upon him be peace, then declared: "I recognised (*'araftu*) this place!" Afterwards, he named this place 'Arafat. He descended from there and prayed the noon and late noon prayers together. He stopped with the people and made Ishmael the leader. He then stopped and faced the House until the sun set. He then urged the people and they prayed the sunset and night prayers in Muzdalifa.

It is said—and Allah knows best—that it was named Muzdalifa because the people strolled (*izdilāf*) from there to Mina. The place is also called Jam'a because two prayers are joined (*jama'a*) there. He then woke up when the sun rose, stopped at a small hill and called it Quzah. The people stopped around it, and it is one of the holy landmarks in which Allah commands that He be remembered. Then he departed from there before sunrise. Afterwards, he stoned the halting place of al-'Aqaba with seven pebbles. He then departed for Mina, slaughtered an animal, shaved and performed what he performed of the Hajj pilgrimage. He showed the people their rituals, and the believers continued doing so with and after him. The Hajj pilgrimage is a religious injunction upon the one who can find a way. The 'way' refers to the provisions (*az-zād*), a riding beast and safety.[1]

Then, the Glorified and Exalted says as a proof for the time of the Hajj pilgrimage: **{The Hajj is in known months} (Q. 2:197)**. The months of the Hajj pilgrimage were Shawwāl, Dhul-Qa'da and the first ten days of Dhul-Hijja. Then the Glorified says: **{Whosoever undertakes the pilgrimage in those** [months] **shall abstain from lewdness, from all evil conduct and disputation while on pilgrimage} (Q. 2:197)**. The meaning of **{undertakes}** is: be obligated to assume and don the pilgrim garb (*al-ihrām*).

Concerning the entry points Allah's Messenger designated

Then, Allah's Messenger, peace and blessings be upon him and his progeny, appointed the people to assume the pilgrim garb at various entry points. The entry points for the people of Medina is Dhul-Hulayfa, for the people of the Levant is Al-Juhfa, for the people of Iraq is Dhāt 'Irq, for the people of Najd is Qarn and for the people of Yemen is Yalamlam. He then said: ((These are the entry points for their respective people and for the one who comes to them who are other than these people)).[2]

Concerning entering the Hajj pilgrimage

When you have—God willing—decided to undertake the Hajj pilgrimage and enter it by your action, it should be during the months of the Hajj pilgrimage. Then, you approach Dhul-Hulayfa, which is the place named after a tree under which Allah's Messenger donned the pilgrim garb. Afterwards, perform the purification wash intending the undertaking of the Hajj pilgrimage upon yourself. Your 'undertaking' is the entrance, and the entrance is the assumption of the pilgrim garb. That is based upon the statement of Allah, the Blessed and Exalted: **{Whosoever undertakes the pilgrimage in those** [months] **shall abstain from lewdness, from all evil conduct and disputation while on pilgrimage} (Q. 2:197)**.

When you perform the purification wash during the time of an obligatory prayer, pray that which Allah has made obligatory upon you. After you perform the final salutations, say:

> O Allah! Verily, I intend to observe the Hajj pilgrimage as a desire of mine concerning what You desire of it. I do so seeking Your reward and striving for Your pleasure. Therefore, facilitate it for me, and make me to reach my aspiration in this world and the next. Forgive me my sins and eliminate from me my evil deeds. Protect me from the evil of my journey and cause me to inherit a goodly inheritance for my children, family and wealth. Place me in Your safekeeping. I sanctify for You my hair, skin, flesh and blood as well as the earth that I traverse. That which I speak with my tongue is for You, and that which my heart contracts is for You.

Then, one says:

> *Labayk, Allahumma*! *Labayk*! *Labayk, lā sharīka laka*! *Labayk*! *Inna al-hamda, wa an-ni'mata laka wal-mulk. Lā sharīka lak*! *Labayk, Dhal-ma'ārij*! *Labayk*! *Wa ža'at li 'aḍamatika as-samawātu ka nafayha*! *Wa sabbaht laka al-aržu wa man alayha*! *Iyyāka qašadnā bi 'amālinā wa laka ahramnā bi hajjinā*! *Fa lā tukhayyib 'indaka amālanā*! *Wa lā*

[1] As a general principle, the absence of any of these three preconditions would exempt one from the Hajj pilgrimage. The term 'provisions' refers to adequate means for travel, supplies and other facilities, such as a servant for the one who needs it as well as a guide for the blind. The term 'riding beast' is general and refers to any animal or vessel that one owns or rents which allows the rider to travel if the distance between him and the furthest part of Mecca is at least the distance of a twelve miles. If one is unable to find such ride that can take him/her the distance of twelve miles, such person would be exempted from the Hajj—even if they are able to walk. The term 'safety' refers to the lack of fear for one's health, provisions or ride in terms of destruction or harm. [Ref. ***At-Tāj***]

[2] Similarly narrated in ***Sharh at-Tajrīd, Ŝahīh al-Bukhāri, Ŝahīh Muslim, Sunan an-Nisā`i, Mušannaf Ibn Abi Shayba, Musnad Ahmed, Ŝahīh Ibn Khuzayma, Sunan ad-Dārqutni, Al-Mu'jam al-Kabīr, Al-Mu'jam al-Awsat, Sunan ad-Dārimi, Sunan al-Bayhaqi***

taqiṭa' minka raja`anā! (Tr. "I'm at Your service, O Allah! I'm at Your service! I'm at Your service, You have no partners! I'm at Your service! Verily the praise and blessing is for You as well as dominion! You have no partners! I'm at Your service, O Possessor of ascensions! I'm at Your service! Your greatness placed the heavens in their atmosphere, and the earth and everyone on it glorifies You! It is only to You that we aim by means of our deeds! For You we assume our pilgrim garb on our Hajj pilgrimage! So, do not disappoint our hopes in You or cut off from You our expectations!")

Then, you embark towards Mecca. Similarly, if you had already prayed the obligatory prayers, pray two units in the Mosque and then say the aforementioned statement. Afterwards, be silent until you settle in the desert. You are to glorify Allah during your journey, declare His Oneness by saying *Lā ilaha ila Allāhu*, declare His greatness, recite the Qur'an, seek Allah's forgiveness, purify your intention to your Lord, repent to the Glorified for your misdeeds, as well as be cautious of lewdness, evil conduct, disputation and lying—which is from evil conduct.

Concerning the *talbiya*

When you have settled in the open desert, begin with the *talbiya* and raise your voice beautifully and moderately insomuch that it can be heard by the ones in front of you and behind you. You say:

> *Labayk, Allahumma*! *Labayk*! *Labayk, lā sharīka laka*! *Labayk*! *Inna al-hamda, wa an-ni'mata laka wal-mulk. Lā sharīka lak*! *Labayk, Dhal-ma'ārij*! *Labayk*! *Labayk*! *Lā yadhillu man wālayt*! *Wa lā ya'izzu man 'ādayt*! *Tabārakta Rabbanā wa ta'layt*! (Tr. "I'm at Your service, O Allah! I'm at Your service! I'm at Your service! You have no partners! I'm at Your service! Verily the praise and blessing is for You as well as dominion. You have no partners! I'm at Your service, O Possessor of ascensions! I'm at Your service! At your service! No one can debase the one to whom You associate. No one can honour the one from whom You disassociate. Blessed be You, our Lord, and highly exalted be You!")[3]

Concerning what is encouraged for the pilgrim whenever he wants to mount an animal after assuming the pilgrim garb in the desert

We encourage that when one intends to ride his riding beast, one says: "In the Name of Allah! And with Allah! All praise is due to Allah for Allah's blessings! May Allah's blessings be upon the Best of creation, Muhammad, the Messenger of Allah!"

And when he mounts the back of his riding beast or the saddle of his camel, he is to say: "**{Glorified be the One who subjugated these unto us. And we were not able to do so} (Q. 43:13)**. All praise is due to Allah, the Lord of creation!"[4]

Then, he recites the *talbiya*. One is to not yell the *talbiya* nor should one whisper it. Rather, one should seek a way between which is good. For every elevation on the land, one should say: "*Allāhu Akbar*! *Allāhu Akbar*! *Lā ilaha ila Allah*! *Allāhu Akbar*!" When one descends, one is to recite the *talbiya* the way we explained. One should not be heedless of the *talbiya* at any point.

---

[3] It is sufficient for one to recite the shortened version of this remembrance which consists of the wording: *Labayk, Allahumma*! *Labayk*! *Labayk, lā sharīka laka*! *Labayk*! *Inna al-hamda, wa an-ni'mata laka wal-mulk. Lā sharīka lak*! This has been narrated in the Musnad Imam Zayd from Imam Zayd—his forefathers—'Ali—the prophet, peace and blessings be upon him and his progeny. Afterwards, it is reported that Imam Zayd, upon him be peace, said: "If one wants, one can recite the condensed form. If one wants, one can add to that. All of such is good." It is also narrated in ***Al-Jāmi' al-Kāfi*** that Imam al-Hasan b. Yahya said:

> It is the consensus of the Prophet's Progeny, peace and blessings be upon him and his progeny, that one can add to the basic form of the talbiya which is narrated as: *Labayk, Allahumma*! *Labayk*! *Labayk, lā sharīka laka*! *Labayk*! *Inna al-hamda, wa an-ni'mata laka wal-mulk. Lā sharīka lak*! They permitted an addition and did not object to such addition being added. The basic wording is what is incumbent.

[4] The wording of this orison has been narrated by Sayyid Abul-Abbās al-Hasani with a complete chain to 'Ali.

Concerning that which is obligatory for the pilgrim to avoid

It is religiously obligatory for such one to avoid that from which Allah has prohibited him: **{…lewdness, from all evil conduct and disputation}**. The term **{lewdness (*ar-rafath*)}** refers to intercourse with women. That is based upon the statement of Allah—Glorified be He: **{Permitted for thee on the night of the fast is to go unto (*ar-rafath*) thy wives} (Q. 2:187)**. Another meaning of the term **{lewdness}** is: the slander of people. The word is ugly and denotes something that good people find repugnant.

The term **{all evil conduct}** refers to acts of disobedience, criminality, lying, oppression, misdeeds, tyranny against the slaves of Allah, repression, attacking Allah's associates, involvement with anything that complies to an enemy of Allah, ugly intolerance against a relative, as well as a lot of quarrels and disputations with such person.

There is to be no hunting, no pursuit of such and no pointing to it [to be killed]. There is to be no applying scents or wearing dyed clothing. There is to be no intercourse with wives or wearing a shirt after having performed the purification wash for the pilgrim state. One is to not cut any hair [or nails Ref. ***At-Tāj***] or apply any type of medicinal ointment with a scent. One is to not apply kohl [or henna to the hands or feet Ref. ***At-Tāj***] or kill any lice that may be in the clothing. If one wants to move the louse from one place to another, one may do that. If one kills it, such person must give food as charity. Also, one is to not marry or be given in marriage. One is to not eat meat that was hunted for him or anyone else.

The **{disputation}** that Allah prohibits refers to invalid arguments that nullify the truth. Among the disputations are fierce arguments that lead to obscenities which the perpetrator loses control of himself.

Know that the pilgrim not only avoids wearing clothes, intercourse with wives and applying scents, but he is to also avoid the aforementioned things we explained. They encompass all the meanings of **{lewdness}**, **{all evil conduct}** and **{disputation}**.

Concerning what is encouraged for the pilgrim to do when landing at the landing place

When the pilgrim disembarks at a landing place, he should say: **{"My Lord, cause me to disembark at a blessed site of disembarking. Thou art the best One who causes to disembark!"} (Q. 23:29)**.

Then, one is to bear in mind what one eats and drinks. One should not drink from nor eat any game animal—whether fowl, animal with cloven hooves or any other hunted land animal; this is the case whether one hunts it or someone else hunts it. That is based upon the statement of the Commander of Believers, upon him be peace, regarding game animals.[5] It is also the statement of his family afterwards. And it is they did not hold to the view that one can eat any game animals—whether one hunted it or it was hunted by someone else.

---

[5] 'Ali b. Bilāl reported in his ***Sharh al-Ahkām*** that Sayyid Abul-Abbās al-Hasani related with a complete chain of narrators to 'Abdullah b. al-Hārith al-Nawfal that his father prepared some food in a bowl for 'Uthmān b. Affān and brought a platter of partridge. 'Uthmān said: 'Eat, it was killed for me." It was said to him that 'Ali forbade that. 'Uthmān sent for 'Ali while the latter was shaking dead leaves from his forearms. 'Uthmān said to him: "You constantly disagree with us!" 'Ali replied: "I am reminding of Allah those who witnessed that a man came to the Prophet, peace and blessings be upon him and his progeny, and offered him donkey meat. He replied: ((I am in the state of pilgrim sanctity, so feed it to the people who are not in the state of pilgrim sanctity))." The people stood up and said that they bore witness to that. 'Ali then said: "I am reminding of Allah those who witnessed that a man came to the Prophet, peace and blessings be upon him and his progeny, and offered him five ostrich eggs. He replied: ((I am in the state of pilgrim sanctity, so feed it to the people who are not in the state of pilgrim sanctity))." The people stood up and said that they bore witness to that. Then, 'Uthmān stood up and went back inside his tent. The people then left the food for the people of the oasis who weren't in the state of pilgrim sanctity. This report is also narrated in ***Sharh at-Tajrīd, Sunan Abu Dāwūd, Musnad Ahmed, Al-Mu'jam al-Awsat, Musnad Abu Ya'la, Sunan al-Bayhaqi***.

In another narration, Sayyid Abul-Abbās al-Hasani related with other chains of narrators to 'Abdullah b. al-Hārith b. Nawfal that when 'Ali, upon him be peace, forbade eating game meat when offered by 'Uthmān, he recited the verse as his proof: **{Permissible for thee are the game of the sea and its food as provision for thee as well as for the wayfarers. And prohibited for thee are the game of the land as long as ye are in the state of pilgrim sanctity} (Q. 5:96)**.

Concerning what is permissible for the pilgrim to kill

There is no problem for the pilgrim to kill a kite, crow, rat, snake, scorpion or any other predatory animal if it is hostile. Also included is the mad dog if one fears for one's life and if the pilgrim fears its injury.[6] The flea, tick, bedbug, hornet and any other crawling animal that causes affliction and the Muslims fear injury from them—there is no problem for the pilgrim to kill any of them due to their harmfulness.

Concerning the pilgrim justifying the wearing of clothes due to some misfortune and extreme cold

If the pilgrim is justified in wearing clothing that he is otherwise prohibited from wearing due to some misfortune such as illness, sudden disease or any other thing from which he fears ruin for himself—examples include extreme cold, a persistent headache or other affliction of this world—then, he can wear the clothing due to such justifiable reason.[7] However, he owes a compensatory ransom. The compensatory ransom is what Allah declares when He states: **{And whosoever amongst thee are ill or hath an ailment of the head must pay a compensatory ransom of fasting or charity or sacrifice} (Q. 2:196)**. The **{fasting}** refers to fasting for three days. The **{charity}** refers to the feeding of six needy people. The **{sacrifice}** refers to the slaughter of a ewe. Whoever does more, it would be considered best for him according to his Lord.

Similarly, if he is justified in wearing an ointment with musk scent and the pilgrim takes it due to difficulty or not due to difficulty, he is obligated to pay the aforementioned compensation. Similar is the case for the one who has to wear leather socks due to some misfortune and he wears them. He is to pay the aforementioned compensation. Even if he wears leather socks, a turban and clothes at the same time, he only owes one compensatory ransom.

Concerning the pilgrim's entrance to the Sanctified Site (*al-Haram*)

When the pilgrim reaches the Sanctified Site, it is encouraged for him to descend, perform the purification wash and then enter the Sanctified Site. When he ties up his riding beast on the side of the Sanctified Site, he says:

> O Allah! This is Your Sanctified Site and Your place of safety as well as the place that You chose for Your Prophet. It is the place of pilgrimage that You made a religious injunction upon Your creation. Verily, those covetous of You have come to You regarding what You desire for us. They are hoping for the reward for it from You. To You belong the praise for the best attainment. It is only You that we ask the best companionship at the return. Do not disappoint our calls to You, and do not cut off our hopes in You. Forgive us and have mercy on us. Accept from us our strivings and reward our deeds. Grant us a goodly acceptance for our good and forgiveness for our mistakes. O Most Gracious of the merciful! O Lord of creation!

Concerning what the pilgrim says when viewing the Ka'ba

When the pilgrim reaches and sees the Ka'ba—God willing, he is to discontinue the *talbiya*. If he is on 'Umra, he is to do so when heading towards the Ka'ba. He is to not recite the *talbiya* afterwards

---

[6] In ***Al-Muntakhab***, the imam was asked about the permissibility for the pilgrim to kill a hyena. He replied:

> Others say that there is nothing due since it is a rapacious and wild animal. As for us, we know it in the Hejaz to not be a rapacious animal. The best statement according to me is that the pilgrim is to consider its case on the place. If it is rapacious towards him there, there would be nothing due on him [if he were to kill it]. If it is not rapacious in that place, one owes a ewe.

[7] In ***Al-Muntakhab***, al-Hādi was asked an interesting question regarding necessity, patience and their relation to the pilgrim.

> I asked: "What about the one [i.e. the pilgrim] who needs to apply medication or wear clothing but refuses to wear clothing and prevents himself from such out of seeking extra reward and patiently enduring it?" He replied: "The cases of patience are well-known. They are those cases in which there is not fear for one's life and ruin. If a person fears for his life due to the possibility of ruin, patient endurance would be prohibited for him and not permissible in that case. It is necessary for him in the religion of Allah to not avoid that which will assist in his recovery and to prevent that which would lead to his ruin."

until the end of the pilgrimage. Rather, he is to circumambulate the House seven times—jogging the first three times and walking the last four. One is to say at the beginning of his circumambulation and at the beginning of the Black Stone:

> *Bismillah ar-Rahmān ar-Rahīm. Wa lā hawla wa lā quwwata ila billahi al-'Aliyyi al-Aẓīm*! (Tr. "In the Name of Allah, the Most Gracious the Most Merciful. There is no strength and power except by Allah, the Most High, the Most Great!")

When he approaches the door of the Ka'ba, he says while facing it:

> O Allah! This House is Your house, this Sanctified Site is Your sanctified site and this slave is Your slave. This is place of protection—by means of You—from the Fire. O Allah, protect me from Your punishment and specify me for abundance of Your reward, as well as my parents and their offspring, the male and female Muslims! O Overpowering One of the lands and heavens!

Then when passing in his circumambulation, he says: "O Lord, forgive and have mercy! Pass over what You know. Verily, You are Allah, the Mighty, the Generous!"

He repeats this statement until he reaches the Black Stone. Once he reaches it, he greets it and says:

> O Allah! I believe in You and verify Your Book! I follow Your commands and imitate the Sunnah of Your Prophet, Muhammad, peace and blessings be upon him and his pure, chosen, truthful and righteous family! O Allah, forgive me my sins, and cover from me my evil deeds! Cause me to submit to Your obedience. Verily, You are the Hearer of prayers!

Then he passes until he reaches the second door and says and does what he said and did the first time. Then he is to greet all of the pillars. If one is not able to do so, such person is to point at them with the hand. He says when he greets the pillars: **{Our Lord, grant us in this world good and in the hereafter good, and protect us from the punishment of the Fire} (Q. 2:201)**.

Once one completes all seven circumambulations, one stands between the Black Stone and the door and supplicate saying:

> O Allah! You are the Truth! You are the God with which is no god but You! It is only You that We worship and it is only You that we seek help from! You are our Master in this world and the next. Therefore, forgive us our sins and pass over our evil deeds! Accept our striving and facilitate what is difficult in our affair! Cause us to act in accordance to Your commands, and make us among Your triumphant friends, O Lord of creation!

Then, one is to pass[8] and pray two units behind the *maqām*.

Concerning the two-unit prayer after the circumambulation behind the *maqām* and the entrance to Zamzam

Then, he is to approach the *maqām* of Abraham, upon him be peace, and pray two units behind it. He recites *Al-Hamd* (Q. 1) and **{Say: "O disbelievers…"} (Q. 109)** in the first unit. If he wants, he can recite **{Say: "He is Allah, the One…"} (Q. 112)** in the first unit and **{Say: "O disbelievers…"} (Q. 109)** in the second unit. If he wants, he can recite other smaller *surah*s from the Qur'an. However, we do not encourage one to recite any *surah* from the Qur'an except the small ones because one can carry it out and is not restricted in doing other than that. Also, there is no harm for the one who seeks out his desire.

---

[8] Although not mentioned in this text, al-Hādi was asked in ***Al-Muntakhab*** about the inclusion of the walled structure known as the *hijr* in the circumambulations.

> I asked: "Can one pass the hijr in his circumambulations?" He replied: "No." "If he were to circumambulate and pass the centre of the hijr, what does he owe?" "Others say that he would be obligated to repeat the circumambulation and sacrifice for that, but is is not as they say according to us. A man must not pass the hijr in his circumambulations nor should he enter it while circumambulating." "What if a man enters it while he is circumambulating/" "If he enters it ignorantly, there is nothing due on him as we previously said, and he does not have to repeat. If he enters it intentionally while cognisant of its prohibition, we obligate him to sacrifice for it."

Then, he is to rise, face the Ka'ba and say: "O Allah! Our Lord, forgive us of our sins and have mercy on us. Purify our deeds, and do not reject us as failures."

Afterwards, one is to go to the Zamzam from any place he desires. In it are blessings and much good. He is to drink from its waters and stare at its side and say:

> O Allah! You have manifested it and caused Your Prophet Ishmael to drink from it as a mercy from You by it, O Majestic One. You have placed in it blessings for his people. Therefore, I ask You to bless me in that which I drink from it and make it a remedy and healing. Benefit me—by means of it—from every ailment and cause me to be secure—by means of it—from every catastrophe. Verily, You are the Hearer of supplications, and You answer Your slaves as You please.

Concerning the departure to Ŝafa and Marwa and the actions that are to take place between them

Then, one is to depart to Ŝafa from between the two cylindrical columns (*al-asťawānatayn*) with it written on them. When one comes to Ŝafa, one should face the *qibla* and say:

> *Bismillah wa Billah wa al hamdulillah*! *Wa šalla Allahu 'ala Muhammadin an-Nabiyi wa alihi wa sallam*! (Tr. "In the Name of Allah and by Allah! All praise is due to Allah! May Allah send prayers and peace upon Prophet Muhammad as well as his Progeny!")

Then, one is to recite *Al-Hamd* (Q. 1) and the two *Surah*s of Protection (Q. 112 and Q. 113), as well as **{Say: "He is Allah, the One..."} (Q. 112)**, the Verse of the Celestial Chair (Q. 2:255) and the last verse of *Al-Hashr* (Q. 59:24). Afterwards, one says:

> There is no God but Allah, the One with whom is no partners! He gave victory to His slave and defeated the army! He has no partners! I bear witness that there is no God but Allah, the One with whom is no partners! And I bear witness that Muhammad is His slave and messenger. O Allah! Forgive me my sins and disregard my faults! Do not reject me as a failure, O Most Generous of the generous! And place me among the victorious!

Then, one descends from Ŝafa and walks until one is near the incline connected to the walls of the Mosque. Then, one should walk briskly (*harwala*) until one reaches the decline at the beginning of the two lamps. Afterwards, one is to walk until one reaches Marwa and say on the way: "Lord, forgive and have mercy! And disregard that which You know! Verily, You are Allah, the Mighty and Most Generous!"

One can repeat this statement, other beautiful remembrances of Allah or any supplication until the end of one's walking [between them]. When one reaches Marwa, he should turn towards the Ka'ba and recite the aforementioned supplication from Ŝafa. One can say that which he said on Ŝafa and other than that. Then, one is to return [to Ŝafa] and do what he did the first time on his way until he reaches Ŝafa. One is to then do the same thing until one did it seven circuits. Afterwards, one is to leave and cut the hair if on 'Umra.

One is to not shave the head completely if it is in the months of Hajj and one intends to perform the Hajj pilgrimage. After he has done all of the above, he is permitted to do that which is permissible, such as intercourse with his wife, the application of scents and the wearing of clothes.

Concerning beginning the Hajj pilgrimage on the Day of *Tarwiya* in Mecca

If it is the Day of *Tarwiya* [i.e. the eighth of Dhul-Hijja], one should begin the Hajj pilgrimage from the Holy Mosque. Also, he is to do and recite what one did and recited at the beginning of assuming the pilgrim garb. Then, one commences as a pilgrim reciting the *talbiya*. Afterwards, one stays in Mina and if it is possible, one should pray the noon and late noon prayers together there. If it is not possible to leave except a part of the night, one should leave when it is possible. All of that is possible after one reaches Mina for the dawn prayer.

As for the imam—if there is an imam—he should depart from Mecca at the half of the day when the sun reaches the zenith. After such, he prays the noon and late noon prayers in Mina. He is to stay there until he prays the sunset, evening and dawn prayer. Then, he heads to 'Arafat. Similarly, it is reported that the Prophet, peace and blessings be upon him and his progeny, prayed five prayers on the Day of 'Arafat with the last of them being the dawn prayer.[9]

Concerning the one who enters Mecca intending a solitary pilgrimage (*mufrida*) or performing the 'Umra pilgrimage

The one who intends to perform the 'Umra pilgrimage should begin at the entry point of 'Umra saying: "O Allah, I intend the 'Umra pilgrimage joined together with the Hajj pilgrimage. So please facilitate it for me." Then, he says what he said when assuming the pilgrim garb for the pilgrimage.

If he intends to perform a solitary Hajj pilgrimage, he is to say at the time of assuming his pilgrim garb: "O Allah, I intend the Hajj pilgrimage. So please facilitate it for me." He then declares what we explained at first and then says:

> *Labayk*! *Allahumma, Labayk*! *Labayk*! *Bi hajjatin tamāmuha wa ajruha alayk*! (Tr. "I'm at Your service, O Allah! I'm at Your service! I'm at Your service! With the Hajj it is complete and its reward is upon You!")

Then, he enters Mecca. One is to not discontinue the *talbiya* until he casts pebbles at the *Jamrat* al-'Aqba after the day of sacrifice from 'Arafat. That is the view of all the Ahl al-Bayt, and there is no disagreement regarding that.

If one wants to begin while entering Mecca and then circumambulate and walk [between Ŝafa and Marwa], one can do that and then remain in the pilgrim garb until the Day of *Tarwiya* or a night of 'Arafat. Afterwards, he should head to Mina. If he approaches it during the daytime, he remains there until he prays the dawn prayer a day on 'Arafat. If he approaches it during the night, the same is the case. If he approaches it the last part of the night, he spends the night there, prays the dawn prayer and then proceeds to 'Arafat.[10]

Concerning what the one who combines the pilgrimages (*al-qārin*) says and does as well as the manner in which they assume the pilgrim garb

If one wants to perform 'Umra and Hajj pilgrimages together simultaneously, it is impermissible according to us unless one drives a she-camel from the place where he assumed the pilgrim garb. When he intends to assume the pilgrim garb at the end of his prayer, he should say: "O Allah! I intend the Hajj and 'Umra pilgrimages, therefore facilitate it for me." Then he says what we have explained regarding the statement of the pilgrim at the beginning of his assuming the pilgrim garb. Afterwards, he recites the *talbiya* for the Hajj and 'Umra pilgrimages together.

When he approaches Mecca, he does a set of circumambulations and brisk walks between Ŝafa and Marwa twice: a set of circumambulations and brisk walks for his 'Umra pilgrimage and a set of circumambulations and brisk walks for his Hajj pilgrimage. There is no disagreement regarding this from the scholars of the Messenger's Progeny, peace and blessings be upon him and his progeny, in regard to the one who combines the Hajj and 'Umra pilgrimage.

---

[9] Similarly narrated in ***Ŝahīh Muslim, Sunan Abu Dāwūd, Sunan at-Tirmidhi, Sunan Ibn Mājah, Al-Mu'jam al-Awsat, Mušannaf Ibn Abi Shayba***

[10] In ***Al-Muntakhab***, al-Hādi was asked some questions about the pilgrim spending the night in Mecca.

> I asked: "Is it permissible for a man to spend the night in Mecca during the nights of Mina?" He replied: "That is impermissible." "What if he spent the night in Mecca during the nights of Mina?" "If he came to it at night and reached the dawn or came to it during the day and reached the night, he would owe a sacrifice."

If it is the Day of *Tarwiya* or the night of 'Arafat, one is to head towards Mina and do what one would do if s/he was performing the solitary Pilgrimage. He then heads towards 'Arafat on the eve of the Day of 'Arafat [i.e. ninth of Dhul-Hijja].

Concerning the declaration of Allah's greatness on the Days of *Tashrīq*

The first place that one begins the declaration of Allah's greatness on the Day of 'Arafat is after the dawn prayer from that day when the imam declares the final salutations. One is to say: *Allahu Akbar*! *Allahu Akbar*! *Lā ilaha ila Allah*! *Allahu Akbar*! *Allahu Akbar*! *Allahu Akbar kabīra*! *Wal-hamdulillahi kathīra*! *Subhana Allah bukratan wa aŝīla*

Then he is to recite the *talbiya* and then depart for 'Arafat. He must recite this declaration of Allah's greatness at the end of every obligatory prayer until the end of the Days of *Tashrīq* [i.e. the three days following the Eid of Sacrifice]. He will recite the declaration of Allah's greatness after the late noon prayer on the day of the last sacrifice and then discontinue the declaration. That will amount to twenty-three prayers.

My father related to me from his father that the latter said:

> The declaration of Allah's greatness starts from the dawn prayer on the Day of 'Arafat to the late noon prayer on the day of the last sacrifice. Similar is narrated from the Commander of Believers 'Ali b. Abi Ťālib, upon him be peace.[11]

Concerning the stopping points on 'Arafat and what one is to do there

When the pilgrim reaches 'Arafat, he is to descend and stand until he prays the noon and late noon prayers. After he prays the noon and late noon prayers, he is to stop and stand any place he wants on 'Arafat. The best place would be to stand near the place where the Prophet, peace and blessings be upon him and his progeny, stood between the mountains. If one is not able to do that because of the crowds, one can stand any place one wants except under trees. This is because Allah's Messenger, peace and blessings be upon him and his progeny, said: ((All of 'Arafat is a place of standing except under trees)).[12]

When one stands, one engages in the verbal remembrance of Allah—Glorified and Exalted be He above everything. He glorifies and praises Him as well as makes sincere intention to Him. One is to say:

> O Allah You are our Lord and the Lord of our ancestors! It is only to You that we aim and it is to You that we turn. Upon You is our reliance and it is in You that we hope. It is from You that we ask, so give us what we ask for. Remove from us our sins and unify our hearts. Establish us upon divine guidance and grant us our God-consciousness. Do not burden us. Accept our Pilgrimage and do not reject us as failures. Make us deserving of Your reward and safe from Your punishment. Protect us from Your wrath, O God of the heavens and earth.
>
> O Allah! To You belong the praise for Your blessings. To You belong the praise for Your beneficence. To You belong the praise for what You have given us and appointed for us. We enjoy due to Your blessings. Do not withdraw from us Your reward and blessings, O God of creation.

Then, one can supplicate for anything that one wants such as for oneself and one's parents. One can ask Allah for any provision one wants as well as anything else because He is the Hearer of supplications and grants the requests. He is Most Gracious and Most Generous.

---

[11] Sheikh 'Ali b. Bilāl reported in his ***Sharh al-Ahkām*** that Sayyid Abul-Abbās al-Hasani related with his chain of narrators to Zayd b. 'Ali from his ancestors that 'Ali, upon him be peace, said: "When Allah's Messenger, peace and blessings be upon him and his progeny, sent me, he said: ((O 'Ali, declare Allah's greatness at the end of the dawn prayer from the day of 'Arafat till the late noon prayer on the last day of sacrifice))." Similar is narrated in ***Musnad Imam Zayd, Al-Mu'jam al-Kabīr*** and ***Sunan al-Bayhaqi***

[12] Similarly narrated in ***Sharh at-Tajrīd, Mušannaf Ibn Abi Shayba, Al-Mu'jam al-Kabīr, Muwatta, Sunan al-Bayhaqi, Musnad Ahmed.*** It is narrated in ***Bihār al-Anwār*** as a statement of Ja'far as-Ŝādiq.

If the sun is eclipsed by a veil, one is to depart from 'Arafat reciting the *talbiya* towards Muzdalifa with tranquillity, dignity and reverence to Allah, the Overwhelming. On one's way, one is to increase in recitation of the Qur'an, seeking forgiveness, supplications, reciting *Allāhu Akbar* and *Lā ilaha ila Allah* as well as the exultation of Allah, the One and Majestic. If one has anything, one should donate charity to the weak and needy one sees. If it is possible for one to fast, one should do so.

One does not pray the sunset and night prayers until one reaches Muzdalifa. They are to be combined and one is to dismount for it and combine the sunset and night prayers. Due to its combination, it is called '*jama'a*'.

Concerning what one does in Muzdalifa

When one reaches Muzdalifa, one is to dismount and pray the sunset as well as the night prayers in the first third of the night with one call to prayer and two pre-prayer calls. Then one is to lodge there until the approach of dawn. After the dawn approaches, one should set out to leave. One is to continue without stopping until one reaches the Sacred Site (*al-Mash'ar al-Harām*). Such one should engage in the verbal remembrance of Allah—Glorified and Majestic be He!

Concerning what one does at the Sacred Site

When one approaches the Sacred Site, one should say:

> O Allah! This sacred site that you appointed for Your worship by Your beautiful mention and command is Your statement: **{When ye descend from 'Arafat, engage in the verbal remembrance of Allah at the Sacred Site} (Q. 2:198)**. There is no remembrance of You that is greater than declaring Your Oneness, establishing Your Divine Justice in all of Your affairs and confirming Your Divine Promise and Divine Threat.
>
> You are my God. There is no deity except You, and I do not worship other than You. Exalted are You from likeness to Your creation, and sanctified are You from having a likeness to Your slaves. You are the One who has no likeness, nor do You have an equal in justice. You do not beget nor are You begotten. You do not have an equal. You are the First before everything and the Last after everything. You brought into existence all that exists, and You are the Creator of the first things and the last. You are the One who will resurrect all of creation on the Day of Judgement. You are free from the actions of the slaves, and You are highly exalted from decreeing disobedience. You confirm the Divine Promise and Divine Threat. You are the Most Gracious and Most Merciful to the slaves.
>
> I ask You, O Lord of lords and One who frees the necks on the Day of Accounting, to ransom me from the Hellfire and appoint for me by Your power the best of domains, the Gardens under which rivers flow. Verily, You are One, Most Powerful and Overwhelming.

Then, one says:

> O Allah! Forgive me, my parents and what they parented. Also, forgive the Muslim men and women—the living among them as well as the dead. O Allah, to You belong the praise just as You began with praise. To You belong the thanks, and You are the Guardian of praise. To You belong the grace, O Possessor of grace and goodness. O Allah, give me what I ask for in this world and the afterlife. Verily, You are the Most Generous, the Most Kind.

Concerning pressing forward in multitudes (*al-Ifāḍa*) from the Sacred Site

Then, one is to return to Mina with reverence and humility. One is to recite what is easy from the Qur'an on one's way as well as supplicate for what one wants, engage in the verbal remembrance of Allah, seek forgiveness for one's sins and repent to Him for one's misdeeds. He does not forgive except the penitent, nor does He accept except from those who repent.

When one reaches the inside of Muhassir, a valley between Mina and Muzdalifa, such person is to continue hurriedly until stopping at the inside of the valley. It is narrated that Allah's Messenger, peace and blessings be upon him and his progeny, hurried in that place. However, hurrying in that place is not an obligatory tradition because Allah's Messenger, peace and blessings be upon him and his progeny, only did such due to an incident.[13] Even if one were to not hurry in that place, the avoidance of such does not invalidate or nullify one's Hajj pilgrimage.

When one reaches Mina, one is to continue until reaching the *jamrat* of al-'Aqaba in the middle of Mina. Then, one is to throw pebbles at it seven times, saying with each pebble: *Lā ilaha ila Allāh wa Allāhu Akbar kabīra. Wa al-hamdulillahi hamdān kathīra wa subhāna Allāhi bukratan wa aŝīla.*

One is to discontinue the *talbiya* with the first throw. Then, one is to approach one's dwelling and slaughter the extra animal. Otherwise, one owes a sacrifice. He should sever the neck of the sacrificial animal and say when placing the side of the blade on it: *Bismillah wa Billahi. Wa 'ala millati Rasūlillahi, salla Allāhu alayhi wa ala alihi. Lā ilaha ila Allāhu wa Allāhu Akbar.*

Afterwards, he severs the neck and says: *Allāhumma minka wa ilayk fa taqabbal min 'abdik ibni 'abdik.* (Tr. "O Allah! It is from You and to You. So accept it from Your slave the son of Your slave.")

Then, he portions it out. He and his brothers eat some of it. Then, he commands that some of it be given as charity to the needy. As for the needy, poor and destitute, the preference goes to those who are closest to his camp.

Then, he is to shave his head or cut it short. He can wear any clothing he wants and apply any scents he wants at that point. Everything would be lawful for him except intercourse (lit. "women"). When it is the last day or any day of the days of Mina, one is to approach the Ka'ba.

If he was alone and could not circumambulate for his Hajj or perform the walk between Ŝafa and Marwa, he is to circumambulate the Ka'ba seven times and perform the walk between Ŝafa and Marwa seven times. He is to do in every circumambulation and walk what we previously explained to you in the beginning of this chapter. He is to then return to the Ka'ba and circumambulate the circumambulation of women,[14] which is seven times also. He is to not trot in it. Then one is to pray two units for his circumambulation behind the station of Abraham, may Allah bless him.

If one had performed the circumambulation and walk [between Ŝafa and Marwa] seven times for one's Hajj before departing to 'Arafat, such one can circumambulate the circumambulation of women when he returns to the Ka'ba from Mina on any of the days of Mina one wants, or he can do so immediately after leaving from Mina. It is that which the people refer to as the circumambulation of visitation (*tawāf az-ziyāra*). It is the circumambulation of the Hajj pilgrimage which is mandatory, as Allah says: **{Then let them end their untidiness and render their vows. And let them circumambulate the Ancient House} (Q. 22:29)**. After that, women would be allowed for him.[15]

If his visitation was during the days of Mina and he entered Mecca on the first night, he is to depart from there that night. If he entered it during that day, he is to depart that day. If he entered on the first night and the morning approached or he entered during the day and the night approached, he owes a sacrifice. On the second day, he stones the *jamrat*.

---

[13] Similarly narrated in ***Musnad Ahmed, Musnad Abu Ya'la, Sunan at-Tirmidhi***

[14] This particular circumambulation is named such because after its performance, women—that is, intercourse with women—would be deemed permissible. [Ref. ***Sharh al-Azhār***]

[15] In ***Al-Jāmi' al-Kāfi***, it is related that Imam al-Hasan b. Yahya said:

> It is the consensus of the Prophet's Progeny, peace and blessings be upon him and his progeny, that the circumambulation of visitation is obligatory. The circumambulation of visitation is that with which there is no brisk walking, and intercourse with wives are not allowed until it is circumambulated.

Concerning the stoning of the *jamrats* and the actions regarding that

When it is the second day of the Day of Sacrifice, also named the Day of the Heads (*yawm ar-ru`ūs*), one is to set out to depart while in the state of ritual purity after the sun passes the zenith. One is to carry twenty-one pebbles that were taken from Muzdalifa, and they should be washed. That is narrated from Allah's Messenger, peace and blessings be upon him and his progeny.[16]

One is to approach the *jamrat* which is in the centre of Mina; it is the one which is closest to the mosque of al-Khayf. One is to then stone it with seven pebbles from the inside of the valley and say with each pebble: *Lā ilaha ila Allāh wa Allāhu Akbar kabīra. Wa al-hamdulillahi hamdān kathīra wa subhāna Allāhi bukratan wa aŝīla.*

Then, one is to face the *qibla,* turn his back to the *jamrat* he stoned and say:

> O Allah, I believe in You, confirm Your Book and follow the Sunnah of Your Prophet, Muhammad, peace and blessings be upon him and his progeny. O Allah, I am Your slave and the son of Your slave. I seek from You and submit to You. Therefore, cancel my slips by means of Your grace, forgive my errors and cover my nakedness. You are sufficient for all that causes me unease. From You do I seek, and to You do I aim. Do not cause me to err.
>
> Verily, You are my God. There is no God but You! In Your Hand is my forelock, and to You do I return. Make excellent my place in the hereafter and this life, and make me secure from my fear on the Day of Your meeting. Protect me from Your punishment, grant me from Your reward. For verily You are Most Kind, Most Generous, Most Clement and Most Gracious.

Then, one is to continue until he gets to the middle *jamrat*—the *jamrat* of 'Ali, upon him be peace[17]—and stone it with seven pebbles saying with each pebble: *Lā ilaha ila Allāh wa Allāhu Akbar kabīra. Wa al-hamdulillahi hamdān kathīra wa subhāna Allāhi bukratan wa aŝīla.*

Then, one is to face the *qibla,* turn his back to the *jamrat* and say:

> O Allah! Forgive me of the sins that counter blessings, and forgive my sins that produce regret. Forgive me of the sins that alter blessings, and forgive me of the sins that obstruct shares. Forgive me of the sins that uncover the covering, and forgive me of the sins that drive away supplication. Forgive me of the sins that obstruct heavenly aid, and forgive me of the sins that enter into caprice. O Allah, bring me in accordance to that which You love and are satisfied with. Protect me from error and mistakes. Verily You are One, Exalted and Most High.

Then one is to approach the *jamrat* of al-'Aqaba and stone it with seven pebbles while saying with each pebble: *Lā ilaha ila Allāh wa Allāhu Akbar kabīra. Wa al-hamdulillahi hamdān kathīra wa subhāna Allāhi bukratan wa aŝīla.*

Then one is to depart without stopping and say on his path:

> O Allah! Associate me with the one who associates with You. Pardon me with the one who seeks Your pardon. Bless me in what You have granted, and protect me from the bad that You have decreed. Verily, You decree and nothing is decreed upon You. You have blessed, our Lord, and You have exalted. The one You exalted cannot be debased, and the one You opposed cannot be ennobled. Glorified be You! There is no god but You. Strengthened is the one You have aided, and debased is the one You have abandoned. Victorious is the one You have helped, and diverted from the path is the one You have rejected. Guided is the one You have guided, and safe from destruction is the one You have accompanied and observed. I ask You to observe and accompany me in my journeys, stations and every one of my affairs. O God of the early ones and God of the later ones.

---

[16] Similarly narrated in ***Mušannaf Ibn Abi Shayba, Bihār al-Anwār***

[17] I was unable to find a reference to this *jamrat* being named after 'Ali or the reason.

Then he departs to Muzdalifa. If it was the following day and the sun has passed the zenith, he is to stone the *jamrat*s just as he did the previous day. Afterwards, if he wants to hasten departing to his family on this day after the sun passes the zenith and his stoning of the *jamrat*s, it is impermissible for anyone to depart. Also, he is to not stone on this day, which is the first day of the departure for Mina, unless it is after the passing of the sun from the zenith.

Concerning the first departure for Mina and the actions regarding that

Allah—the Blessed and Exalted—says: {**Therefore, whosoever hastens by two days—there is no sin upon him. And whosoever delays—there is no sin upon him. It is for the one who is God-conscious. Be wary of Allah and know that it is to Him that ye shall be gathered**} (**Q. 2:203**).

When one decides to depart for Mina, he is to approach the Ka'ba, circumambulate it seven circuits, pray two units, face the *qibla* and say:

> O Allah! The House is Your House, the Sanctified Site is Your Sanctified Site and the slave is Your slave. This place is Your protection from the Fire. O Allah, make it a praiseworthy walk, an accepted pilgrimage, forgiveness of sins and accepted action. O Allah, do not make it a delay in the obligation of Your Sanctified House which was made a *qibla* for the people of Islam and obligated as a pilgrimage for all people. O Allah, accompany us in our journey and be a Guardian and Protector for us.
>
> O Allah, verily we seek protection in You from the distresses of the journey, the evil of the hereafter, the obscenity of sight concerning our family, children, wealth as well as those who are connected to us from our relatives and the people under our care. O Allah, to You belong the praise for that which You have bestowed upon us of the observance of Your great obligation. To You belong the praise for good companionship and beautiful communication. O Allah, do not cause enemies to gloat over us, do not cause me to be vexed by friends and do not cause our souls to be weary.
>
> Our Lord, {**bestow upon us amongst our wives and offspring a coolness of the eye. And make us leaders for the God-conscious**} (**Q. 25:74**). {**Our Lord, divert from the punishment of Hell! Verily its punishment is painful. It is an evil settlement and station**} (**Q. 25:65-66**).

Then one enters Zamzam, drinks from its water, ascends and says:

> O Allah, You have caused it to emerge and placed water in it. You have made it a settlement in its land as a favour from You for Your creation by means of Your providing water for them. You have granted it to them by placing blessing in it.
>
> Therefore, provide us water from the cup of Muhammad, Your Prophet, peace and blessings be upon him and his progeny, on the day of thirst. Make us among Your and his party, enter us in his group, and grant us his intercession. Cause us to settle in his proximity, and grant us closeness to him in the hereafter. Cause us to gather upon his religion on the Day of Judgement. It is only You to whom we declare Divine Oneness, and it is to You that we attribute Divine Justice in all Your actions. We confirm all of Your Divine Promises and Threats. We follow the Sunnah of Your Prophet. It is only You from whom we seek help in the observance of all Your obligations. Therefore, assist us with Your assistance, open for us the gates of Your mercy, increase for us provisions and group us with the greatest of groups.

Then, one is to proceed to one's place, if Allah wills. However, if one has determined to proceed to the second departure for Mina, such person is to stay.

Concerning the second departure for Mina and the actions regarding that

If it takes place on that day, which is the fourth day of sacrifice and the last day of the *Tashrīq*, one is to depart for Mina when one has sacrificed. Such person is to stone the *jamrat*s at the time that he desires to rush to Mecca even if he wanted to stone the *jamrat*s and depart for Mina after the sun passes the zenith.

When one stones the *jamrat*s, one is to do in his stoning the same that was done the first time. He should supplicate with the supplications that were made the previous days. Then, such person is to proceed to Mecca until he performs the farewell circumambulations. Then, he is to pray two units, face the *qibla* and supplicate with one of the supplications we mentioned in the first departure for Mina. Afterwards, he enters Zamzam and drink seven handfuls of water as well as supplicate in the manner that was previously mentioned with the supplications from the first departure for Mina. If he has a place in Mecca, he should delay the departure to the day of his leaving and then depart and supplicate as we explained. Allah willing, the departure should not take place except on the day of departure.

It is encouraged for the pilgrim to—at the time of departing for Mina—give charity to whoever is present between Mecca and Mina. One should also donate charity to whoever is present on the day of his departure from Mecca and on his way back to his country.

Concerning the assumption of the pilgrim garb for 'Umra and Hajj pilgrimages together if one intends to join them

If the pilgrim desires that, such person should drive a she-camel with him. We do not hold to the view that one can combine the two except from the place where he assumed the pilgrim garb. If one cannot find a she-camel, such one cannot combine the two. This is the statement of all the scholars of the Progeny of Allah's Messenger, peace and blessings be upon him and his progeny. Others say other than that; however, we do not acknowledge their view nor do we rely upon it.[18]

When one readies the she-camel, he should place it on his entry point. Afterwards, he bathes, clothes himself with the two garments of pilgrim garb and then marks it by making a small incision in its right hump until it bleeds. Then, one has it wear a garland that contains a single slipper and wrap it with any cloak there is—whether it be wool, cotton or linen. Then, he prays two units and says:

> O Allah, I intend the Hajj and 'Umra pilgrimages together seeking thereby Your reward and desirous of Your pleasure; therefore, facilitate them for me. Realise for me my hope in this world and my hereafter. Forgive me my sins, and remove from me my bad deeds. Remove the evil of my journey, and leave behind goodness in my children, family and wealth. Settle me where You have confined me. I assume the pilgrim garb for You for Hajj and 'Umra together—my hair, person, flesh, blood and less than that in the earth from me. Also include that which my tongue speaks for You and that which my heart decides upon.

---

[18] The obligation of driving a she-camel and slaughtering it for the one who combines is also related as the opinion of Imams 'Ali b. al-Hussein Zayn al-'Abidīn, Muhammad b. 'Ali al-Bāqir and al-Qāsim b. Ibrāhīm, upon them be peace. The latter held to it as a precondition of the combined pilgrimages; if one neglected to do so, their combined pilgrimages would be considered invalid. Imam Abu Ṫālib even held it to be an essential Hajj ritual, and the neglect of such would necessitate a sacrifice. However, according to other scholars, such as Imams al-Mu`ayyad Billah, an-Nāsir, al-Murtaḍa, Yahya b. Hamza, Abul-'Abbās al-Hasani, Mālik as well as the Shāfi'ites and Hanifites—driving and sacrificing the she-camel is not considered an obligation or precondition for the soundness of the combined pilgrimages. Rather, they hold it to simply be a recommendation due to the claim of an apparent lack of textual proof of its obligation.

As is evident from the statement of al-Hādi here in the ***Ahkām*** as well as what was narrated from Imam al-Qāsim Rassi, there is consensus of Ahl al-Bayt regarding its obligation. This is coupled with the fact that it was later imams who held to its recommendation and not obligation; perhaps such judgement was due to their own individual scholarly efforts.

We say that the claim of consensus is more likely due to the following reasons: First, the Prophet, peace and blessings be upon him and his progeny, was said to have driven a she-camel for the combined pilgrimages without any contrary practice related from him. Second, it is narrated in the ***Musnad Imam Zayd*** that Imam 'Ali said: "Obligatory on the one who performs the combined pilgrimages and separate pilgrimages is the sacrificial animal…" This reference to the sacrificial animal implies that it must be driven and slaughtered in the cases of the combined and separately joined pilgrimages.

Then say:

> I'm at Your service, O Allah! I'm at Your service! I'm at Your service for 'Umra and Hajj together (*Labayk bi 'umratin wa hajjatin ma'an*)! I'm at Your service! You have no partners! I'm at Your service! Verily the praise and blessing is for You as well as dominion. You have no partners! I'm at Your service, O Possessor of ascensions! I'm at Your service! Your greatness placed the heavens in their atmosphere, and the earth and everyone on it glorifies You. O Allah, it is only to You that we aim with our deeds. It is for You that we assume the pilgrim garb for our 'Umra and Hajj pilgrimages (*wa laka ahramnā bi 'umratinā wa hajjinā*). Do not disappoint our hopes in You or cut off from You our expectations.

Then, one is to recite the *talbiya,* rise and depart so that he may be cautious and take care as to what we explained in the beginning of the chapter. He should also take care to not act upon what I forbade.

One is to not ride the she-camel or carry anything on it. One is to not ride one's servant on it except out of extreme necessity; in that case one can ride one's servant on it. One is to not wound or fatigue it. If one were to see a weak Muslim man who is too weary to walk, one can carry him on it on a steep road or two, a night or two. There is reward in that and goodness. The she-camel is for Allah, and it is necessary that one rides him upon it because he is a slave from the slaves of Allah.

When one gets to Mecca, such person is to perform the circumambulation of the House seven times. Then, one is to pray two units and intend by that circumambulation the circumambulation of his 'Umra. Then, he is to depart for Ŝafa and stop there. He is to then say what I explained in the first statement. Then he approaches Marwa, stop there and say what I previously explained in the first statement until he completes seven circuits between Ŝafa and Marwa. One is to not cut any of his hair. Then, such one is to return—if one likes to rush—to perform the circumambulation of the House seven times for one's Hajj pilgrimage. Then, he prays two units and then departs for the brisk walk between Ŝafa and Marwa seven circuits for one's Hajj pilgrimage. Then, one is still established upon one's pilgrim state and the assumption of such, and such one is to not abandon the recitation of the *talbiya*. If it is the Day of *Tarwiya*, one is to depart for Mina and 'Arafat and the pilgrim is to do what he is to do from the entry points, pressing forward and stoning. Then, one is to sacrifice the she-camel on the Day of Sacrifice and afterwards shave one's head. As Allah—Mighty and Majestic—says: **{Shave not thy heads until the sacrifice reaches its place} (Q. 2:196)**.

Then, one departs and visits the House performing the circumambulation of women once. After such, everything is religiously permissible for the pilgrim; however, he is still prohibited from women. This is the statement of all the scholars of the Messenger's Progeny, peace and blessings be upon him and his progeny. They hold to the view that there is no joint pilgrimage except by driving the she-camel. They also hold to the view that it is insufficient to perform less than two circumambulations and two brisk walks for the joint Hajj and 'Umra pilgrimages.

Those other than them say something else; they say that it is sufficient to perform one circumambulation and one brisk walking for the 'Umra and Hajj. This is—according to us—contrary to what must be done. We do not deem it permissible, hold to such view, license it or regard it.

Concerning what the one performing the separate joint pilgrimages (*al-mutamattu'*) does in his pilgrim state and leaving such state of 'Umra

When the one performing the 'Umra pilgrimage wants to assume the pilgrim garb for 'Umra, he is to bathe and put on the two pilgrim garments. Then, such person is to pray two units in his entry point just as the one who assumes the pilgrim state for his Hajj pilgrimage. Afterwards, one is to say:

> O Allah, I intend the 'Umra separate from the Hajj; therefore, facilitate it for me and be kind to me in its observance. Cause me to reach my hopes in it, and place me in Your safekeeping. I sanctify for You my hair, skin, flesh and blood as well as the earth that I traverse.

Then, one is to say:

> I'm at Your service, O Allah! I'm at Your service! I'm at Your service for 'Umra (*Labayk bi 'umratin*), at Your service! You have no partners! I'm at Your service! Verily the praise and blessing is for You as well as dominion. You have no partners! I'm at Your service, O Possessor of ascensions! I'm at Your service! Your greatness placed the heavens in their atmosphere, and the earth and everyone on it glorifies You. It is only to You that we aim by means of our deeds. For You we assume our pilgrim garb on our Hajj pilgrimage. Do not disappoint our hopes in You or cut off from You our expectations.

Afterwards, he is to rise in his journey proceeding on his way for His sake in his journey as I have explained and do what I commanded.

When such person sees the Ka'ba, he is to discontinue the *talbiya*. Then, he is to perform the circumambulation seven circuits for his 'Umra pilgrimage—jogging the first three circuits and walking the remaining four. He is to then depart and briskly walk between Ŝafa and Marwa. He is to cut his hair short and then depart from his state of pilgrim sanctity. Everything would then be permissible for him as it would be permissible for anyone else including women, scents and other things.

If it is the Day of *Tarwiya*, he is to assume the state of pilgrim sanctity for the Hajj pilgrimage from the Sanctified Mosque or from any other place one wishes in Mecca. He then departs for Mina and does similar to what the Hajj pilgrim does.

Concerning what the restricted person (*al-muhaŝŝir*) does

If the pilgrim is restricted by illness from travelling and obstructed from the journey, unable to mount [an animal] or move, fears for his life from an enemy ahead of him or is imprisoned by an oppressor and does not have the power to defend himself or is unable to liberate himself from his hand—such person is to send a sacrificial animal that he can afford. He then appoints his messenger to sacrifice it on one of the days of sacrifice.

He determines an exact time from that day for him [i.e. his messenger], then a lot or little time after this time. If it is after that time by a little, the restricted one is to shave his head and end his state of pilgrim sanctity. He is encouraged that if he appointed him in the morning, he is to shave in the middle of the day. If he appointed him in the middle of the day, he is to shave at the entrance of night. Caution regarding that is most suitable, if Allah wills.

If he is able to free himself from the restrictions until he reaches Mecca, he is considered to have performed the Hajj pilgrimage and can benefit from his sacrificial animal. He is not obligated to sacrifice or slaughter. But if the Hajj pilgrimage passes, he assumes the pilgrim garb for 'Umra. He then slaughters his beast for 'Umra. If he is unable to find a sacrificial animal, he is to fast for ten days—three in the Hajj pilgrimage and seven after the Days of *Tashrīq*. Finally, he removes his pilgrim state.

When the restricted one and others reach the Hajj pilgrimage

If the restricted one or anyone else reaches the stopping place in 'Arafat before the dawn in the night of the sacrifice—such person has reached the Hajj pilgrimage. He is considered like the one who reached 'Arafat by night. If the dawn approaches before the person has stopped in 'Arafat, he has missed the Hajj pilgrimage. There is no way at this point for the restricted person to use the sacrificial animal; he is obligated to sacrifice it.

Concerning what is permissible for the restricted person who is able to free himself in enough time to catch the Hajj pilgrimage

If the restricted person is able to free himself from his restriction and finds a fast mount that he knows will allow him to complete the Hajj pilgrimage on time, seeks to buy or rent it and the owner gives it to him for a price, it would be obligatory for him to do so as long as he is certain that he could reach to Hajj pilgrimage in time on it.

He is to buy or rent it by means of what he gave for it unless he fears for his life that he would perish by the depletion of financial maintenance. If he fears that, it is impermissible for him to contribute to his own destruction and share in killing himself; it is obligatory upon him to use his financial maintenance to preserve his own life. This is because Allah—Blessed and Exalted be He—says: **{And make not thine own hands contribute to destruction}** (Q. 2:193) and **{...and slay not thyself. Verily, Allah hath been merciful unto thee}** (Q. 4:29).

If he were to extract to purchase such riding beast without fearing that it would deplete his financial maintenance insomuch that he would fear for his own life by such depletion and he has extra to do so, it would be obligatory for him to extract such to use for a riding beast. Anything else would not be permissible because of its obligation of his extracting such to catch the Hajj pilgrimage. Such person would be able to catch it without any restrictions upon him. His situation would be similar to that of a traveller who cannot find water unless he were to buy it for an expensive price. He would be obligated to buy it for any price provided that by such purchase, he would be secure from destroying himself due to using his financial maintenance. It would be impermissible for him to avoid buying it if he has sufficient means to buy that water. It would be impermissible for a person in such situation to perform the dust purification because of the presence of the money for water. He would be considered one who has found the water that Allah has commanded him to use for purification.

If a man performs the Hajj pilgrimage with some of his female family members (*huram*) and he is restricted while his female family members are unable to go on their pilgrimage due to him staying behind and they fear for themselves, those females who accompanied him on the Hajj pilgrimage would be considered restricted by his restriction. It is obligatory upon him and them to send a sacrificial animal. The exception is if there was another male relative with them; then they are permitted to go with him and he would travel with them. As long as there is a male relative with them with whom it is permissible to travel, they would not be considered restricted. It is obligatory upon them to establish that which they intended while they have a male relative unless this restricted man had an illness and did not have any woman to benefit him and it was feared that he might be harmed if all of them left him. That withstanding, it would be permissible for some of the women to stay with and benefit him. She would be considered restricted due to her fear for him, and sending a sacrificial animal would be obligatory for her just as it is obligatory for him. She would do what the restricted man would do.

Concerning what is permissible for the pilgrim to do out of necessity

There is no problem for the pilgrim to pull out a thorn from his leg or squeeze a boil if he is harmed by its pus. If his two feet are hurt by being barefooted and is unable to find sandals, there is no problem cutting the leather socks from under the ankles and wearing them. There is no problem with the pilgrim assuming the pilgrim garb to wear pants and wrapped them as a belt if he cannot find a sarong. If he cannot find a cloak, he can wear the sleeves of a shirt or use the sides to wrap around himself.

If he has intercourse with wives before assuming the pilgrim garb at the entry point and is unable to find water at the entry point, he is to perform one dust purification intending by that purification from major ritual impurity and assuming the state of pilgrim sanctity. That would be sufficient to the Possessor of Majesty and Nobility. He is to then assume the pilgrim garb based upon whether he is assuming it for Hajj or 'Umra. He then puts on the two pieces of pilgrim garb and begins the *talbiya.* If he then finds water, he is to bathe with it once, and that would be sufficient for him.

My father related to me that his father was asked whether the purification wash is obligatory for the assumption of the pilgrim state of sanctity. He replied:

> It is from the Sunnah and it is from good character. Whoever assumes the state of pilgrim sanctity and had not washed—his state of pilgrim sanctity would still be valid and he would have to proceed to his Hajj pilgrimage or 'Umra in whatever state he is in.

Concerning the one who approaches his entry point ill, unconscious and unable to do anything

Whoever approaches his entry point ill in a state where he is unable to do anything in his pilgrimage—such person delays his assumption of the state of pilgrim sanctity until the last entry point between him and Mecca. When he reaches the last entry point between him and it, he is to assume the state of pilgrim sanctity before he passes to the end of the entry point.

If he is unable to assume the state of pilgrim sanctity and is unconscious unable to understand his affairs, someone else is to place the pilgrim garb on him for the Hajj pilgrimage and assume the state of pilgrim sanctity for him. His state of pilgrim sanctity by such is that one is to remove the clothes and pour water on him if he is able. Then, he is to say:

> O Allah! Your slave, so-n-so came out intending to perform the Hajj pilgrimage to Your Sanctified House following the statement of Your Prophet, peace and blessings be upon him and his progeny. He has attained sickness as You have seen. Then, we have removed his clothing and intended by it the state of pilgrim sanctity that he would have intended. He has assumed the state of pilgrim sanctity for You with his hair, skin, flesh, and blood.

Then, one is to recite the *talbiya* for him and then carry him. They should make him avoid all what should be avoided by the pilgrim, like scent, etc., but if he needed to wear garments, they make him do this, and he will be obligated to pay compensation. However, if he enters Mecca and recovers from his illness, he will have to complete those obligations of his Hajj pilgrimage. If his illness continues and his natural disposition is weak being unable to move or sit, then he is to circumambulate while being carried in the litter on the heads of men; everything that is obligatory for the one who enters it—from the state of pilgrim sanctity, the Hajj pilgrimage or the 'Umra pilgrimage—will similarly be obligatory on him.

Then, he is to be taken to 'Arafat and made to stop there. Afterwards, they are to press through the multitudes from 'Arafat with him at its time and then remain with him altogether there. They are to stand with him at the Sacred Site and then proceed to the *jamrat* of al-'Aqaba. They are to stone for him and shave his head. Then, they stone all of the *jamrat*s for him and he is to be brought back to the Ka'ba to perform the circumambulation of visitation. Afterwards, everything that was impermissible would be permissible for him.

If he were to die before the completion of his pilgrim sanctity, his head is to not be covered nor should scents be applied to him. Similar has reached us from Allah's Messenger, peace and blessings be upon him and his progeny, regarding a pilgrim who was crushed and died. Allah's Messenger, peace and blessings be upon him and his progeny, commanded that he be washed and that his head not be covered. He then said: ((Verily, he will be raised on the Day of Judgement reciting the *talbiya*)).[19]

Concerning what the pilgrim is to do—what is obligatory and impermissible

If the pilgrim were to dress in a shirt out of forgetfulness or assume the pilgrim garb with one out of ignorance, he should rip it near his chest until he comes out of it. Similar has reached us from Allah's Messenger, peace and blessings be upon him and his progeny, that he did such when he forgot.[20]

It is impermissible for the pilgrim to take a game animal, but if he takes it, he will be obligated to send it and give some of the food as alms which equals the fear that he causes to the animal. He must not cut green trees except if he did this to eat it or feed his riding camel.

The pilgrim is prohibited from marrying or marrying someone to another; if he were to do such, it would be considered invalid. His marriage contract would similarly be considered null and void.[21] If the pilgrim were to have intercourse with his wife, his state of pilgrim sanctity would be considered invalid and his Hajj pilgrimage would be cancelled. He would be obligated to sacrifice an animal in Mina as expiation for what he did. His Hajj pilgrimage until that point would be invalidated, and he would have to repeat it from the beginning. The woman's Hajj pilgrimage would also be invalidated. If she did so willingly and voluntarily, she similarly owes expiation in the way of sacrificing an animal. If she was forced by him and did so unwillingly, she does not owe expiation for such.

If they were to reach the point where they invalidated their Hajj pilgrimage in their next Hajj pilgrimage, it is religiously obligatory that they separate from that place. The term 'separate' does not mean the complete avoidance of a man from his wife or his leaving her; rather, 'separate' simply means that he does not ride with her or stay with her in the same dwelling. There is no problem with him riding on his own camel and her riding on her own camel either with her camel successively behind his or his camel successively behind hers.

It is impermissible for the pilgrim to eat the meat of lawful and unlawful game—whether the pilgrim slaughtered it or someone else did. It is religiously prohibited for him or anyone else; it is not religiously permissible for him or another to eat of it according to the ruling of the Possessor of Majesty. We simply say and hold to this as a command because Allah, the Glorified, says: **{O ye who believe! Kill not game whilst ye are in the pilgrim state. And whosoever kills it from amongst thee willingly—his recompense would be similar to what he killed of livestock} (Q. 5:95)**.

When Allah prohibited the pilgrims from unceremoniously killing game, it is similarly impermissible to slaughter them [i.e. for food] because unceremoniously killing is considered the same as

[19] Similarly narrated in ***Sharh at-Tajrīd, Ŝahīh al-Bukhāri, Ŝahīh Muslim, an-Nisā'i, Sunan Ibn Mājah, Sunan al-Bayhaqi, Sunan at-Tirmidhi, Musnad Ahmed, Sunan ad-Dārimi, Sunan ad-Dārqutni, Mušannaf Ibn Abi Shayba, Kanz al-'Ummāl, Al-Mu'jam al-Kabīr, Al-Mu'jam al-Awsat***

[20] Similarly narrated in ***Musnad Ahmed, Mušannaf Ibn Abi Shayba, Kanz al-'Ummāl***

[21] In ***Al-Muntakhab***, al-Hādi was similarly asked about the validity of marriage while in the state of pilgrim sanctity.

> I asked: "What if a pilgrim were to marry while in the state of pilgrim sanctity?" He replied: "His marriage would be considered null and void." "Some of the people of hadith narrate that the Prophet, peace and blessings be upon him and his progeny, married Maymūna bt. Al-Hārith while he was in the state of pilgrim sanctity." "This hadith is false and a lie upon Allah's Messenger, peace and blessings be upon him and his progeny. We do not hold to the view that the pilgrim can marry or give someone else in marriage."

As for those sources that narrate that the Prophet married Maymūna while he was a pilgrim, they include the following: ***Ŝahīh al-Bukhāri, Ŝahīh Muslim, Sunan at-Tirmidhi, Sunan an-Nisā'i, Sunan Abu Dāwūd, Musnad Ahmed, Sunan ad-Dārqutni, Al-Mu'jam al-Kabīr, Al-Mu'jam al-Awsat, Musnad al-Bazzār, Majmu' az-Zawā'id***. It is worth noting that even the jurists and hadith scholars of the Generality criticised this narration despite its appearance in their most authentic books.

slaughtering [in this case]. That which the pilgrim unceremoniously killed would be invalidated since it was not slaughtered in the correct way and it would not be religiously permissible or pure to eat of it. This is because the slaughterer has invalidated its slaughter and thus has not been slaughtered correctly. This is based upon his state of pilgrim sanctity and the prohibition from Allah upon him in that state. It would be similar to unceremoniously killing a domestic animal but not slaughtering it in the way that Allah commands; it would be impermissible to eat of that animal due to the way it was killed and due to that which occurred which is contrary to what Allah ordered to be done. Similarly, wild game that the pilgrim slaughtered would be religiously prohibited due to its being contrary to the slaughter ordained by his Lord. Therefore, the slaughter of game by the pilgrim which is religiously impermissible is like the unceremonious killing of a permissible animal. It is for that reason that we say that it is impermissible to eat lawful or unlawful game that a pilgrim slaughtered. This is because he is prohibited from slaughtering it, and it is unlawful for him to do so.

It is similar to what we said regarding the impermissibility of eating livestock that was unceremoniously killed by a hard blow, strike or other than that due to its being killed in that way. It would be unlawful for the killer or anyone else to eat of it[22] because that which is killed by hard blows has been made impermissible to eat by Allah. Similarly, that which has been struck by a staff until it was killed has been made religiously impermissible for the killer and other than him. It is simply impermissible because Allah has prohibited it. Similarly, game which the pilgrim killed by slaughter or any other method is unlawful due to the prohibition of Allah.

If the pilgrim was compelled to choose between eating either game or carcass, he is to choose carcass instead of game. If he fears for himself from eating the carcass, he may eat of the game to save his life. However, it would be impermissible for him to eat it unless he fears for his life.

If the non-pilgrim was compelled to choose between eating game that the pilgrim slaughtered or carcass, he can eat whichever one he wants to save his life due to the lack of prohibition for him.

Concerning the she-camel, cow or ewe for sacrifice and the sufficient amount

The she-camel is sufficient for ten people. The cow is sufficient for seven in the same family. The ewe is sufficient for one. The she-camel is also sufficient for ten performers of the separate joint pilgrimages from the same family.

If seven have jointly owned a she-camel or cow and it has wandered off or was stolen, they must substitute it. If they find it before sacrificing the one that they substituted, they may sacrifice whichever one of them they wish and benefit from the price of the one that they avoided. This is because it is only obligatory for them to sacrifice one of them and not both.

If they were to join in a voluntary sacrifice that is not obligatory upon them and it wandered off or was stolen and then they later found it after having chosen another to take its place, it would be obligatory for them to sacrifice both of them together. This is because this first sacrifice was voluntary and when it was lost, it was not obligatory for them to find another to take its place yet they did. It is as if they

---

[22] In ***Al-Muntakhab***, al-Hādi was asked a series of questions regarding the pilgrim who eats slaughtered game.

> I asked: "If he were to eat game meat while either knowing or not knowing it, what is due upon him?" He replied: "He would have to pay expiation if he knew that. The one who knows pays expiation." "If he knew that it was slaughtered before he ate it and ate it intentionally, what is due upon him?" "If he intentionally acted contrary to that which Allah commanded in His Book and persisted boldly in his deed and defiance to his Lord and His Prophet, peace and blessings be upon him and his progeny, such person is to be called to repentance by the imam. If he repents, he is to expiate." "What if he refuses to repent for eating game while in the state of pilgrim sanctity?" "If he refuses to repent, he is to be put to death because Allah—the Blessed and Exalted—had prevented him from slaughtering and eating it while in the state of pilgrim sanctity. It is impermissible for a pilgrim to kill game just as it is impermissible to consume usury or drink intoxicants. Whoever permits any of these three actions and not establish their prohibition as Allah has established their prohibition—it would be obligatory for such person to be put to death due to his declaring permissible what Allah has prohibited, refusing to repent for such and returning to that which Allah has commanded."

considered the other sacrifice as voluntary. Therefore, all of them relinquished their ownership by dedicating the both of them [i.e. sacrifices] to their Lord. It is for this reason that we say that it would be obligatory to slaughter both.

Concerning what a woman does if she were to approach an entry point or Mecca while in the state of menstruation

The menstruating woman is to be considered a pilgrim just as anyone else except that she is prohibited from praying. She is to purify herself, perform the purification wash if she likes, insert cotton to stop her flow and wear clean clothes. Then, she is permitted to perform the Hajj pilgrimage, assume the pilgrim state and do whatever the pilgrims do.

If she is pure before entering Mecca, she is to bathe herself for ritual purity and dress herself with her pilgrim garb. She can enter and perform the circumambulation and brisk walk between Ŝafa and Marwa similar to other women. If she enters Mecca while on her menses, she is to not enter the Mosque until she is purified from her menstruation. When she is pure, she completes her rites. Similar is the case if she was performing the solitary Hajj pilgrimage; she performs the circumambulations before departing to 'Arafat or after returning from it. She is not restricted in anything nor is anyone else.

Concerning a woman who enters 'Umra while in the state of menstruation and does not purify until departing for the Hajj pilgrimage

If she entered from the 'Umra pilgrimage and did not purify herself until the time comes for the departure to the Hajj pilgrimage, she avoids that 'Umra pilgrimage. Avoiding it means that she intends to delay it and is free from doing it as well as thinking about it; she will do something else other than it. Then she bathes and assumes her pilgrim garb that is free of impurity and the traces of filth. She assumes her pilgrim sanctity for performing the Hajj pilgrimage and walks to Mina and 'Arafat. She performs her religious duty of the Hajj pilgrimage and she establishes everything that one is to establish such as the stopping points in 'Arafat and stoning the *jamrāts*.

If she is purified in Mecca, she enters and performs circumambulation and brisk walk between Ŝafa and Marwa for her Hajj pilgrimage. Then she returns for the circumambulation of women; it is also called the circumambulation of visitation. Afterwards, everything that was previously prohibited for her would be permissible. She would be obligated to sacrifice in Mina for what she avoided of her 'Umra pilgrimage. She must make up that 'Umra pilgrimage that she avoided. She is to assume her pilgrim garb for it in the nearest entry point to Mecca. If she wants, she can assume it from the mosque of A'isha or the tree or Ju'urāna. Then she is to perform the circumambulations and brisk walk between Ŝafa and Marwa. Afterwards, she is to cut short her hair that has grown in each time a length that equals a fingertip for her 'Umra pilgrimage.

Concerning the garb of a woman in the state of pilgrim sanctity

A woman can wear a shirt, shirts, a coat, trousers, veil, cloak and a robe. She can also wear whatever else she likes. She is to not wear clothes dyed by saffron, wars or any other elaborately designed garment that manifests beauty in its colour. She is to also not wear a face veil (*niqāb*) or *burqa* because the pilgrim garb of a woman includes her face. There is no problem if she uses her garment to cover her face; however, she should cover it by having it hang over it.

She is to not wear any ornamentation for beauty. She is to refrain from everything that the other pilgrim refrains from. She should not intermix with the men in her circumambulations and brisk walks between Ŝafa and Marwa nor should she seek to greet the Black Stone with her hand while there is a crowd. Pointing to it from a distance is sufficient for her.

It is not obligatory for her to walk in a quick pace in her circumambulations and brisk walk between Ŝafa and Marwa, nor is she obligated to climb Ŝafa and Marwa. Standing at the bottom of both during the crowds is sufficient for her. Staying away from the crowds of men is more appropriate for her Hajj pilgrimage.

Concerning the child who reaches puberty, the slave that is freed and the *dhimmi* who embraces Islam during the days of Hajj

If the child reaches puberty, a slave is freed or a *dhimmi* embraces Islam during the nights of 'Arafat and it is possible for him to return to Mecca during those nights, he is to bathe for it, begin the pilgrim state at its Mosque and then catch up to his companions. Similar is the case with the *dhimmi* when entering Islam. He stops at 'Arafat with the people and continues with the rites for his Hajj pilgrimage. He performs what the other Muslims perform and observes what is obligatory upon him as an injunction from the Lord of creation.

If the aforementioned were in 'Arafat at the time of the sun's zenith or after it, they are to assume the state of pilgrim sanctity from there. They should proceed and stop at the stopping points with the people. Then they are to press forward and depart from 'Arafat when the other people do so. They observe all the rites that the pilgrim does. They would have completed their Hajj pilgrimage and observed their religious obligations.

If such were to take place among them on the night of sacrifice and it is possible for them to return to 'Arafat and stop there before sunrise, there is no problem to assume the pilgrim garb in Muzdalifa and afterwards hasten until they stop in 'Arafat. If they stop there before sunrise on the night of the sacrifice, they have caught the Hajj pilgrimage and completed that which others completed. They are obligated to finish the rest of their rites.

Concerning the time in which the pilgrim garb is assumed

The Muslim should not act contrary to the teaching of Allah nor that of Allah's Messenger in the assumption of the pilgrim garb for the Hajj pilgrimage outside of its months. Neither should he enter the state of pilgrim sanctity outside of its time.

The time of the assumption of pilgrim sanctity is during the months of the Hajj pilgrimage. That is based on the statement of Allah—Blessed and Exalted is He: **{The Hajj is in known months. Whosoever undertakes the pilgrimage in those** [months] **shall abstain from lewdness, from all evil conduct and disputation while on pilgrimage} (Q. 2:197)**. The months of the Hajj pilgrimage are Shawwāl, Dhul-Qa'da and the first ten days of Dhul-Hijja. It is the time that Allah has appointed for the Hajj pilgrimage to His Sanctified House.

They should not precede it; rather, it is obligatory for them to wait for it. Whoever assumes the state of pilgrim sanctity before it has erred, committed a misstep, rebelled and acted contrary to what they were commanded to do. That which has been made obligatory upon him is what he has obligated upon himself; otherwise, he has acted contrary to what his Lord taught him.

Allah has only appointed this time for them out of His consideration for them as well as a benefit for them. This is so that they not prolong their period of pilgrim sanctity and thereby make their good states abominable and aggravate their affairs due to the lengthening of their hair and nails. It is also so that they not avoid what Allah has made permissible for them of their spouses, delicious foods, nice clothing and pleasant scents. Allah has therefore facilitated it for them by shortening its period and not exceed the tribulation upon one's soul. Blessed be Allah, the Most Gracious of the merciful, the One who extends grace to creation!

Concerning mistakes in the wording of the *talbiya* with a different intention in the state of pilgrim sanctity

If someone intended to make the solitary Hajj pilgrimage but made an error and began reciting the *talbiya* for 'Umra while forgetting to recite the *talbiya* for his Hajj, its wording is not binding upon him/her. However, he must return and begin reciting the *talbiya* intending the obligatory Hajj pilgrimage. Similar is the case for the one who intended to make the joint pilgrimages but made an error and began reciting the *talbiya* for an obligatory Hajj pilgrimage; the mixed wording is not binding upon him/her. It is only binding for him to be bound to the intention of 'Umra. This is because Allah says: **{There is no sin upon thee regarding that in which ye erred. Rather, what is counted is whatsoever is in thy hearts. And Allah is Oft-Pardoning, Most Gracious} (Q. 33:5)**.

If one deliberately assumes the state of pilgrim sanctity to perform two obligatory pilgrimages together, he will be obligated to perform one of them. If he postpones the other pilgrimage for the next year due to avoiding it, he will be obligated to sacrifice an animal. If he decided to refuse and delay it for another year, he will have to sacrifice an animal the next year. He is obligated to observe what he avoided for the next year. According to us, it is only obligatory upon the one who intended as well as recited the wording for it intending the both of them together while remembering and not forgetting it.

As for the one who erred between the wording and intended meaning of one obligatory pilgrimage and then mentioned a second obligatory pilgrimage which he had not intended and had not obligated himself to positively do it, it is not binding for him except what he intended and he is not to be blamed for what he erred.

If one assumes the state of pilgrim sanctity to perform two 'Umra pilgrimages together but avoids one of them, he will be obligated to continue until he completed the first 'Umra pilgrimage that he obligated himself to perform. Then, he is to complete the second 'Umra pilgrimage that he avoided. Such person will have to sacrifice an animal for avoiding it. If it took place during the time of the Hajj pilgrimage, he is similarly obligated to complete the 'Umra pilgrimage he avoided before the Hajj pilgrimage or after it when his matter is clear. Such person would also be obligated to sacrifice what he is obligated to regarding the 'Umra pilgrimage in Jazārīn in Mecca because it is the place between two 'Umra pilgrimages just as Mina is the place between two Hajj pilgrimages.

Concerning the 'Umra pilgrimage and its months as well as the month in which one is to assume and relinquish the state of pilgrim sanctity for it

The Progeny of Allah's Messenger, peace and blessings be upon him and his progeny, agree that the 'Umra pilgrimage is in the month that one intends to perform it. One is to assume the state of pilgrim sanctity in it instead of any other month. It would be obligatory for such one to assume the state of pilgrim sanctity in that month and intend to complete one's 'Umra pilgrimage.

Have you not considered that if it is the time that one assumes the state of pilgrim sanctity, its restrictions will become binding and its pilgrim garb will become obligatory, one will be a performer of the 'Umra pilgrimage, it would be obligatory for such person to recite the *talbiya* using its designation [i.e. that of the 'Umra] and all of its rulings will be obligatory upon him? When we find that it is binding upon such person, then it would be obligatory upon him in the month in which he intended himself to perform it.

We say that it is in this month instead of any other month due to the proofs of the aforementioned statement that the month that one assumes the state of pilgrim sanctity is other than the month that one relinquishes one's pilgrim state. The least of what we mentioned should be sufficient to the people of fairness.

Concerning the performer of 'Umra and the time in which he separates the 'Umra and Hajj pilgrimages

The performer of the 'Umra pilgrimage cannot join it [to the Hajj pilgrimage] unless he assumed the state of pilgrim sanctity for 'Umra during the months of Hajj. If he assumes the state of pilgrim sanctity during the months of Hajj, he can join the two separately during his pilgrimage that year. He would be obligated to sacrifice because he would be among those whom Allah—the Blessed and Exalted—mentions: **{And whosoever joins the 'Umra to the Hajj pilgrimage separately[23] shall render the sacrifice as he can with ease} (Q. 2:196)**.

If a man were to perform 'Umra and assume the state of pilgrim sanctity in the month of Ramadan as well as perform the circumambulation and brisk walk between Ŝafa and Marwa in the month of Shawwāl and then settle in Mecca until assuming the state of pilgrim sanctity for the Hajj pilgrimage and perform the Hajj pilgrimage, he would not be considered as joining the two according to us. This is because his 'Umra was in the month of Ramadan since he began it in [Ramadan] and not Shawwāl. However, if he assumed the state of pilgrim sanctity in Shawwāl, he would be considered as joining the two separately, and we hold to the view that he would have to sacrifice for that.

If a person from the Levant or Yemen were to enter 'Umra outside the months of Hajj and complete it and then settle in Mecca until the months of Hajj and afterwards perform another 'Umra or two while in Mecca and settle in Mecca until he performs the Hajj pilgrimage that same year, his judgement would be the same as that of the people of Mecca. He would not be considered as joining the Hajj with the 'Umra separately nor would he be obligated to sacrifice as those who join the two.

If this person were to depart to the entry point of his country and go past a mile but then return assuming the state of pilgrim sanctity for 'Umra or return and assume the state of pilgrim sanctity in Mecca or in what is between that after having passed his entry point, he would be considered as joining the two [i.e. the Hajj and 'Umra] separately, and he would be obligated to sacrifice or fast.

Concerning the time that it is permissible and impermissible for the one who avoided the 'Umra pilgrimage to make it up

It is impermissible for the one who owes an 'Umra pilgrimage due to having avoided it to make it up until after the days of sacrifice. Similarly, whoever desires to perform an additional supererogatory 'Umra pilgrimage cannot do so until the completion of these days.

Whoever ignorantly assumes the state of pilgrim sanctity for 'Umra in Mecca, Mina or 'Arafat while performing a solitary Hajj pilgrimage must abandon this 'Umra pilgrimage for which he assumed the state of pilgrim sanctity and proceed with his Hajj pilgrimage. This is because the 'Umra pilgrimage is not included in the Hajj pilgrimage. When he completes his Hajj pilgrimage, he is then obligated to make up the 'Umra pilgrimage he abandoned after the days of sacrifice—the 'Umra pilgrimage for which he assumed the state of pilgrim sanctity and obligated upon himself.

Similar is narrated from the Commander of Believers, 'Ali b. Abi Ťālib, regarding the one who did such. He commanded that person who abandoned the 'Umra pilgrimage to make it up after the days of sacrifice. The person had to sacrifice due to his abandonment of the 'Umra pilgrimage.

Concerning the expiation due for the pilgrim who wears clothing during the times of prohibition

If a pilgrim were to wear clothes on his body such as a shirt, coat, pants, outer garment, tunic or any other garment that covers the body, he owes one expiation—whether for all of them together or separately. This is because he is only obligated to uncover his body and remove his clothes from his

---

[23] The verb used in the verse literally translates into "enjoy." The implication is that one who enjoys the period of break between assuming the state of pilgrim sanctity for 'Umra and that of the Hajj should sacrifice.

person. If he were to cover it due to any reason, covering with one garment is the same as covering with three, one time is the same as two and one day is the same as two.

If the pilgrim were to cover his head due to any reason and wear a cap, turban or helmet, he owes one expiation—whether he wears all of them together or separately. This is because all of them are worn on the head. Allah simply obligates him to uncover during his state of pilgrim sanctity. When he covers with one thing, it is the same whether he covered with multiple things or covered with only one. His covering would be the same whether he covered with all of that at one time or multiple times if this reason for which one covered it remains and he returns to what is due upon him in his first pilgrim state.

Similar is the case with leather socks and socks if one were to wear any of them. It would be the same as if one wore both of them together or not because one is simply obligated to uncover the feet. If one were to cover them for any reason, it is the same whether one covered them with one thing or two. One includes them in that so doing it one time would be the same as doing it multiple times as long as the reason for which one does it remains. Similarly, if one were to wear a shirt, turban, pants and leather socks all at the same time, he owes only one expiation and he can continue to wear all of such until after the reason has subsided.

If one were to wear a whole or partial head covering at one time and then wear a whole or partial body covering another time, he owes two expiations due to the differences in two times. Similarly, if he wears a feet covering on the third day or a third time, he would owe a third expiation. Then, he could wear all of such until after the reason subsides.

Concerning the shade of the pilgrim

There is no problem for pilgrims to shade themselves with a cover between them and the sun. The shade of camel litters and edifices are no less than that of parasols, houses and roofed shelters. If it were impermissible to seek shade from a camel litter, it would similarly be impermissible to seek shade from a house because seeking shade from either one is the same—whether it is for shelter or concealment.[24]

My father related to me that his father was asked about the pilgrim seeking shade from a parasol above a camel litter. He replied:

> I have not seen anyone from the Ahl al-Bayt of the Prophet differ regarding the pilgrim seeking shade. It is permissible as long as he does not cover his head with it. Verily, it is encouraged that he refrains from such as long as doing so does not cause any harm. The shade of a parasol on a camel litter is not more than the shade of tents and the roofs of houses—all of which are seen as being no problem by consensus.

Concerning the difference between the combined, solitary and separate joint pilgrimages

The best type of Hajj pilgrimage is the solitary pilgrimage[25] for those who performed the pilgrimage

---

[24] Al-Hādi repeats the same statement in ***Al-Muntakhab***; however, he also states: "Others say that one owes a sacrifice [i.e. for seeking shade]. However, this is not acknowledged." This statement of al-Hādi as well as the statement of Imam Rassi regarding the consensus of Ahl al-Bayt counters the statement of the Imami Shia that their imams prohibited the pilgrim from seeking shade. For example, they relate in ***Uṧūl al-Kāfi*** that when Imam Musa al-Kāžim was asked about whether the pilgrim can shade himself, he is related to have replied in the negative. Furthermore, it is also related that they prescribed the sacrifice for anyone who sought shade. However, as is evident from Imams al-Hādi and Rassi, such statements are falsely attributed to the imams of Ahl al-Bayt. Furthermore, it is related in ***Al-Jāmi' al-Kāfi*** that Imam al-Hasan b. Yahya narrated that the following imams used to seek shade while in the state of pilgrim sanctity: 'Ali b. al-Hussein Zayn al-'Abidīn, Muhammad b. 'Ali al-Bāqir, Zayd b. 'Ali and Ja'far b. Muhammad as-Ŝādiq, upon all of them be peace.

[25] Despite the explicit statement by al-Hādi regarding the solitary being considered the best type of Hajj pilgrimage, contrary has been related from him. It is said that he held the combined pilgrimage (*qirān*) to be the best type. Imam Yahya b. Hamza in his ***Al-Intiṧār***, as well as al-Mu`ayyad Billah and Abu Ťālib similarly note two different opinions from al-Qāsim and al-Hādi regarding the best type of Hajj pilgrimage. We reply that since al-Hādi's preference for the solitary pilgrimage is explicitly stated in both the ***Ahkām*** and ***Al-Muntakhab***, it is the most reliable position. [Ref. ***Al-Qawl al-Awwal***],

and for those who did not perform the pilgrimage. If the pilgrim wants to enter the separate joint pilgrimages, that is for him to do and it is good. If the joint pilgrimages were not less virtuous, Allah would not have obligated an expiation for the one who performs it. The one who is able to combine the two pilgrimages and bring a she-camel with him, that is a great virtue and better for his pilgrimage.

My father related to me that his father was asked about the combined, separate and solitary Hajj pilgrimages and which one is most preferable. He replied:

> If the joint pilgrimages were not less virtuous, Allah would not have commanded an expiation for the one who performs it. This is based on His statement: **{And whosoever joins the 'Umra to the Hajj pilgrimage separately shall render the sacrifice as he can with ease}** **(Q. Q. 2:196)**. Allah commands that the one who does it owes an expiation. Therefore, one holds to the solitary Hajj pilgrimage as best.

My father related to me that his father said regarding the separate, combined and solitary pilgrimages:

> The solitary is most preferable to me for the one who has not performed the Hajj pilgrimage. The separate pilgrimages are for him. The one who combines the two is to bring a she-camel with him to the place where he assumes the state of pilgrim sanctity, and that is best.

Concerning cupping for the pilgrim

There is no problem for the pilgrim to cup his shoulders, shins, back of the head, forearms or any other part of his body that he pleases. There is no expiation due upon him unless he shaves or cuts any hair. If he shaves any hair that is apparent from his head or nape, he owes a sacrifice for shaving some of his hair. As for that which is not apparent, he is to render charity if he can. As for cupping, there is no problem with it.

It has reached us that Allah's Messenger, peace and blessings be upon him and his progeny, had cupping done while he was in the state of pilgrim sanctity in Lahyi al-Jamal.[26] Kharāsh b. Umayya al-Khazā`i[§] performed the cupping with an animal horn covered in silver. Allah's Messenger, peace and blessings be upon him and his progeny, said when it was complete: ((How great is the trust of a man who stood on the jugular vein of Allah's Messenger with iron!))[27]

My father related to me that his father was asked about the pilgrim having cupping done, and he replied that there was no problem with that.

Concerning the pilgrim who kisses or hugs and then ejaculates

If a pilgrim kissed then ejaculated, then he will be obligated to sacrifice a she-camel. If he emits pre-ejaculatory fluid, he will be obligated to sacrifice a cow. However, if any of this happens and the kiss was with desire and a movement of pleasure, then he will be obligated to sacrifice a ewe. However, if he kissed or hugged without desire or movement, he will not be obligated to do anything.

My father related to me that his father said regarding the pilgrim who kissed or caressed and then ejaculated: "He owes a she-camel. If he emitted pre-ejaculatory fluid, he owes a cow. If it was with desire without ejaculation or pre-ejaculatory fluid, he owes a ewe."

If the pilgrim carried his wife from one place to another and experienced joy and desire, its judgment will be the same as the kiss regarding semen, pre-ejaculatory fluid and others. If there was movement and pleasure from bringing her to him and he emitted pre-ejaculatory fluid although he did not seek desire or pleasure in such, he is obligated, at most, to sacrifice. If he avoids it, the aforementioned would not be binding for him. It would be no problem for him to lift and carry her if he had no other option; however, expiation would be best for him and more rewarding because it is safer for one's

---

[26] This refers to a place between Mecca and Medina.

[27] Similarly narrated in ***Amāli Ahmed b. 'Isa, Ŝahīh al-Bukhāri, Ŝahīh Muslim, Sunan Abu Dāwūd, Sunan at-Tirmidhi, Sunan an-Nisā`i, Mušannaf Ibn Abi Shayba***

religion and more assuring to the Lord of creation. If he finds another option, he lifts her and places her while there is no need to do so and emitted pre-ejaculatory fluid, he must sacrifice.

My father related to me that his father said regarding the pilgrim who carries his wife and emits pre-ejaculatory fluid as a result:

> The most he is obligated to do is sacrifice. He should not go near her if he fears that. If it is the case and he is compelled to carry her, he owes what we mentioned regarding the expiation out of necessity. If it was due to play, then the expiation for the doer is a she-camel for the one who ejaculates and a cow for the one who emits pre-ejaculatory fluid.

Concerning the Hajj pilgrimage on behalf of the dead and the one who avoids the Hajj while not having the ability

The Hajj pilgrimage on behalf of the dead is a means to good, and the one who bequeathed someone else to do so on his behalf will get a reward. If one was not bequeathed to do so, the pilgrim who performed it on his behalf will be rewarded from his Lord based upon his intention.[28]

The one who avoids the Hajj pilgrimage while being unable due to a reason preventing him from such and he has the intention to perform the Hajj pilgrimage if the preventing reason is removed—such person will not be considered sinful. If the appointed person was negligent regarding the Hajj with which he was commanded and obligated by his appointee—such person's deeds would be considered sinful and unaccepted by his Lord.

My father related to me that his father was asked about the one who avoided the Hajj pilgrimage while being unable, and he replied:

> The one who makes the firm resolution to perform the Hajj pilgrimage [but is not able] is not like the one who intentionally avoided it. Capability regarding the Hajj pilgrimage is among those things which obligate it. They include the following: sufficient provisions, a riding beast, a sound body and safety in travel.

My father related to me that his father was asked about an elderly man and an infirmed person who cannot stay on a riding beast and who are unable to travel on them in a carriage. Is it permissible for one to perform the Hajj pilgrimage on their behalf although they are alive? He replied:

> The obligation of the Hajj pilgrimage is relinquished for these two because they are incapable of performing the Hajj pilgrimage. Allah only makes the Hajj pilgrimage an injunction on those who have the capability to perform it. This is because the Glorified says: **{And Allah has enjoined upon the people the pilgrimage to the House for whosoever has the ability to find a way} (Q. 3:97).**
>
> If they were to perform the Hajj pilgrimage themselves or one were to perform the Hajj pilgrimage on their behalf, it is good to do so. It has come in the hadith that a Khathami woman sought permission to perform the Hajj pilgrimage on behalf of her father, and she was permitted to do such.[29]

---

[28] It is narrated in ***Al-Jāmi' al-Kāfi*** that Imam al-Hasan b. Yahya said: "It is the consensus of the Prophet's Progeny, peace and blessings be upon him and his progeny, that performing the Hajj pilgrimage on behalf of the dead is permissible as well as bequeathing one to do so. The scholars of the Generality say the same thing."

[29] Similarly narrated in ***Amāli Ahmed b. 'Isa, Ŝahīh al-Bukhāri, Ŝahīh Muslim, Sunan Abu Dāwūd, Sunan at-Tirmidhi, Sunan an-Nisā'i, Sunan Ibn Māja, Bihār al-Anwār***

Concerning the pilgrim who has intercourse and shaves after stoning the *jamrat* of al-'Aqaba as well as the one who joins the pilgrimages and has intercourse before trimming the hair

If the pilgrim stones the *jamrat* and shaves but then has intercourse before performing the circumambulation of women, he owes a sacrifice. That Hajj pilgrimage is not considered invalid after having stoned and shaved his head. Similarly, if the one who has joined the two pilgrimages separately has intercourse with his wife before trimming the hair and has already performed the circumambulations and brisk walking, the most he is obligated to do is sacrifice.

My father related to me that his father said regarding the one who performed the joint pilgrimages separately who has intercourse with his wife before trimming the hair but had already performed the circumambulation and brisk walking: "The most he owes is a sacrifice. If he does not sacrifice, then I hope that it would not be a problem. However, sacrificing is most preferred to us as well as the safest according to his Lord."

Concerning the pebbles one uses for the *jamrats*, the place from which they take them and the time one stones the *jamrats* as well as stoning the *jamrats* while riding and stoning with multiple pebbles at once

It is encouraged for one to carry the stones for the *jamrats* from Muzdalifa. If one were to take them from some of the mountains and valleys of Mina, this would be sufficient. It is encouraged for one to wash them if one sees filth or traces on them. If one stones the *jamrat* while riding, this would be sufficient.[30]

One does not cast pebbles except one-by-one. One is to recite *Allahu Akbar* with each pebble. If he errs and throws more than one together, he repeats and casts seven pebbles separately one-by-one. He stones the *jamrat* of al-'Aqaba the first day in the morning, the second day at the sun's zenith and the third day at the sun's zenith. On the day of the great sacrifice, when the day reaches mid-morning, such one can stone for it until the night.

My father related to me that his father was asked about the man who stoned with seven pebbles at once. He replied: "It is preferred that he separate them." Also, my father related to me that his father was asked about the place where one collects the pebbles and whether they are to be washed. He replied: "It is encouraged that one carries them from Muzdalifa; however, it is no problem if he takes them from anywhere else. If he does not wash them, there is no problem as long as there is no visible filth on them."

My father related to me that his father was asked about a man who stones with seven pebbles altogether. He replied: "It is preferable to us that he separate them one after the other. That is the religious injunction upon him which is an obligation from Allah's judgement."

My father related to me that his father was asked about an ill person and whether someone can stone on his behalf. He replied:

> If he is overwhelmed and he is unable to stone due to his sickness, someone else can stone on his behalf. It is more of an obligation that someone else stone on his behalf when the latter is unable to stone. He is to also sacrifice on the other's behalf.

My father related to me that his father was asked about stoning the *jamrat* while riding. He replied: "It is valid. However, stoning while on one's feet is best and most resembling of the deeds of the righteous before him."

---

[30] In his ***Sharh at-Ahkām***, Sheikh 'Ali b. Bilāl reported that Sayyid Abul-Abbās al-Hasani related with a complete chain of narrators to Yahya b. Yamān that Imam Ja'far as-Ŝādiq used to stone the *jamrat* while on his riding beast. He similarly relates with a complete chain of narrators to Ibn Ḋumayra—his father—his grandfather that 'Ali used to stone while on a riding beast and on foot.

My father related to me that his father was asked about the time in which is best to stone the *jamrat*s. He replied: "The best time is at the sun's zenith except on the day of sacrifice. On that day, such one is to stone before the sun reaches its zenith."

My father related to me that his father was asked about that which a person should say when stoning the *jamrat*s. He replied:

> He should say with every pebble he casts: *Allahu Akbar*. Then he should stand in front of the first two *jamrat*s and stone them. He should supplicate with whatever supplication he has and engage in the verbal remembrance of Allah. As for the *jamrat* of al-'Aqaba, he should stone it and declare *Allahu Akbar* with each stone and not stand near it.

Concerning the stoning of the *jamrats* without the ritual ablution and stoning before sunrise

One should not stone the *jamrat*s except in the state of ritual purity because it is a noble site. However, if one were to stone them outside of the state of ritual purity unknowingly, this would not invalidate his rite. As for the stoning before sunrise, this is impermissible except for women due to their weakness. There is no dispensation for anyone in this regard except for them [i.e. women].

As for what is narrated in which the Prophet sent 'Abdullah b. 'Abbās with the women, it is said that he was a small child. One applies the idea that he was with them when they stoned before the dawn. Then, 'Abdullah b. 'Abbās departed with them to their homes. Afterwards, he returned and stoned at a time that it was permissible for him to stone after sunrise.

My father related to me that his father said regarding the one who stones without the ritual ablution:

> It is encouraged that the one who stones the *jamrat* does not do so except in the state of ritual purity. This is because it is a site of religious devotion and humility for Allah, glorified be He. It is among the rites of the worshippers. However, whoever stones it otherwise—his stoning is valid.

My father related to me that his father was asked about stoning the *jamrat*s before sunrise, and he replied: "It is a dispensation for the women. No man should stone the *jamrat*s except after the dawn sunrise."

My father related to me that his father was asked what one who sacrificed the first sacrifice should do if he still had pebbles on the third day. He replied:

> He should not do anything with them, and he should leave them and sacrifice because Allah—the Blessed and Exalted—says: **{Therefore, whosoever hastens by two days—there is no sin upon him. And whosoever delays—there is no sin upon him. It is for the one who is God-conscious} (Q. 2:203)**. If he is in a position to sacrifice, he is to leave the stoning of the *jamrat*s on the third day.

My father related to me that his father was asked about the manner that the menstruating woman completes her rites. He replied: "She is to complete all of her rites except for the circumambulation around the House."

My father also related to me that his father was asked about a woman who menstruates on the day of sacrifice and performed the circumambulation before praying. He replied: "When she completed her circumambulation, she prays after she is pure."

Concerning what is permissible and impermissible to slaughter as well as the shaving and trimming

It is valid to slaughter a lamb that is a yearling; however, it is invalid to slaughter a yearling of any livestock other than a lamb. It is valid to slaughter a two-year old camel as well as a two-year old cow and two-year old goat.

When it is healthy in eyes and ears, it is valid to slaughter. It is invalid to slaughter the lame, mutilated or any animal with a defect. If you were to buy an animal which is free of all of the aforementioned deficiencies such as lameness, mutilation and other defects, but then an accident occurs while it is in the custody of the owner after having bought it and the time of sacrifice approaches—it is no problem.

The camel is best if one can afford its price. Then after that, it is the cow and then the ewe. The lamb is also better than the goat.

When the pilgrim sacrifices or slaughters, he shaves or trims his hair. He does not shave or trim his hair before sacrificing because Allah—Glorified be He—says: **{Shave not thy heads until the sacrifice reaches its place} (Q. 2:196)**. Whoever ignorantly does that and shaves or trims his head before the slaughter, it does not invalidate his rites or his Hajj pilgrimage.

My father related to me that his father was asked about Allah's statement: **{shall render the sacrifice as he can with ease} (Q. Q. 2:196)**. He replied:

> It means what is easy and available. If a she-camel is easy, this is best. If a cow is available, that is best. Its ease and availability is its ability of independence and newness. The exception is the goat; it is that which is upon the common people.

My father related to me that his father was asked about the pilgrim slaughtering a sheep, cow and camel as well as whether one can cut plants for his riding beast. He replied that there is no problem with that. My father also related to me that his father said that the lamb yearling is valid to slaughter as well as the two-year-old goat.

My father related to me that his father was asked about the sacrifice as well as the number in Mina and the cities. He replied: "The sacrifice is to that which takes place on the day of sacrifice. Similar is the case in the cities."

My father also related to me that his father was asked about the number of she-camels that is valid for people. He replied: "The she-camel is valid for ten people, and the cow is valid for seven people of the same household."

My father related to me that his father was asked whether the man who enters Mecca for his 'Umra pilgrimage during the separate joint pilgrimages is supposed to shave or trim his hair. He replied:

> The one who enters Mecca for his 'Umra pilgrimage during his separate joint pilgrimages is supposed to trim his hair. He is to not shave until after he stones the *jamrat* of al-'Aqaba and after he slaughters on the day of sacrifice.

My father related to me that his father said regarding a pilgrim who plucks two or three hairs from his head:

> Whoever does less than that is to give charity for doing such. As for the one who takes more from his head insomuch that it is evident from his head—Allah appointed the following as compensation for that: fasting, charity or sacrifice.

Concerning the one who enters for the separate joint pilgrimages but cannot find a sacrificial animal as well as the one who vows to walk to the House of Allah

Whoever enters for the separate joint pilgrimages but cannot find a sacrificial animal—such person is to fast a day before *Tarwiya*, the Day of *Tarwiya*, the Day of 'Arafat and seven days after returning. As Allah—Glorified be He—says: **{Then whosoever cannot find such—he must fast three days in Hajj and seven days when ye return. That is ten complete days} (Q. 2:196)**.

Whoever fears that the three days will elapse in Mecca—there is no problem for him to fast before he enters Mecca in his state of pilgrim sanctity. If he were to fast but then find a sacrificial animal, he is to sacrifice. He does not take into account the days he fasted when there is time during the days of sacrifice.

Whoever vows to walk to the House of Allah but is then unable after having set out for his pilgrimage, he is to walk for what he is able and ride for what he is unable to walk; he is to sacrifice an animal for that [i.e. for the unfulfilled oath].[31] If he walks more than he rides, he owes a ewe. If he rides more than he walks, it is preferable that he sacrifice a cow. If he walks and rides the same distance, we prefer that he sacrifice a cow. If one is unable to find anything other than a ewe, it would be sufficient—God willing—due to his inability and scarcity in his possession.

My father related to me that his father said regarding the performer of the separate joint pilgrimages who fasts but then finds a sacrificial animal on the day of sacrifice or the second day: "If he finds it on any of the days of sacrifice, he is to sacrifice and not count his fasts."

My father related to me that his father said:

> There is no problem for one to fast three days on the way to Mecca if he fears that they would elapse in Mecca. There is also no problem for him to fast seven days on his way back to his family as long as he made the intention to fast on his way back. This is the case even if he fasts after having reached his family. He does so without there being a break in the days.

Concerning the times for the circumambulation, the shortening in the journey from Mecca to 'Arafat and the break in the circumambulation

There is no problem for a person to perform the circumambulation after the late noon and after the dawn to sunset. It is not discouraged to perform the circumambulation or prayer for it at any time except in those three times prohibited by the Prophet, peace and blessings be upon him and his progeny.[32] Also, there is no problem if a person performed some of the circumambulation, discontinued it and then returned to complete the rest of his circumambulation.

Whoever departs from the people of Mecca or others to 'Arafat, such person is to shorten the prayer. That is agreed upon according to the scholars of the Progeny of Allah's Messenger, peace and blessings be upon him and his progeny.

My father related to me that his father was asked about the number of prayers one is to perform after having performed seven circuits of the circumambulation twice or three times. He replied: "He prays two units at the completion of each seven circuits."

My father related to me that his father said regarding a man who performed the circumambulation after the morning or late noon to sunset: "Al-Hasan, al-Hussein and 'Abdullah b. 'Abbās used to perform the circumambulation after these two times as well as pray."

My father related to me that his father said regarding a person who breaks between his circumambulation and brisk walking:

> That's no problem as long as the break is for a valid reason until the end of the day or the next day. If it is slower than that, he is to avoid it more days. It is encouraged that he sacrifices for that. Others have extended that, but we do not hold to such view.

My father related to me that his father was asked about performing the complete prayer in Mina. He said:

> According to the Ahl al-Bayt, one does not perform the complete prayer whether he is on the Hajj pilgrimage or a journey unless he remains in a place for ten days. They say that the one who intends to remain in a place for ten days performs the complete prayer.

[31] Sheikh 'Ali b. Bilāl related in his ***Sharh al-Ahkām*** that Sayyid Abul-Abbās al-Hasani narrated with his chain of narrators to Zayd b. 'Ali—his ancestors that a woman came to 'Ali saying that she had vowed to walk to the House of Allah but was later unable to carry it out. He then passed the judgement that she is to walk the distance according to her ability and then sacrifice for what she was unable to. He also related similarly from Ibn Abbās that a man came to the Prophet with the same question and the Prophet responded similarly.

[32] Refer back to the **Book of Prayer** to identify those three times prohibited for one to pray.

My father related to me that his father was asked about a pilgrim who trims the moustache of a non-pilgrim. He replied: "There is no problem with that. It is only prohibited for him to trim his own moustache." Also, my father related to me that his father was asked the one who forgets to recite the *talbiya* until the end of his rites. He replied: "He does not owe anything. However, he should not avoid that intentionally."

My father related to me that his father was asked about the statement of Allah: **{So eat thereof and feed the contented and unfortunate} (Q. 22:36)**. He replied: "The **{contented}** refers to the one who refrains from asking for a necessity. The **{unfortunate}** refers to the beggar."[33]

Concerning a woman dyeing while in the state of pilgrim sanctity

If a woman were to dye in the state of pilgrim sanctity and her hands and feet are dyed at the same time, she owes one expiation. If her hands were dyed but she had not dyed her feet though she intended to dye them, she owes one expiation. If she were to dye her feet after that, she would owe another expiation.

If she dyed one of her fingers, she would have to give half a *šā'* of wheat in charity. If she were to extend it to the fingertip, she would have to give the value of a half *mudd* in charity. If she were to extend it to the whole palm, she would have to give two *mudd*s and a half in charity. She gives such charity to two needy people. Similarly, if she were to extend it to the fingertips of both hands, she would have to give a half *mudd* for each finger.

Concerning the expiation for the one who performs the combined and solitary pilgrimages

If any performer of the combined pilgrimages wears impermissible clothes, shaves his head or applies scented medicine—such person owes two expiations: an expiation for his 'Umra and an expiation for his Hajj. If he were to do such for a solitary Hajj or 'Umra, he owes one expiation. If he applies scented medicine in one or two spots, he owes one expiation. Similarly, if the performer of the solitary Hajj pilgrimage cuts a nail, we encourage him to give a *mudd* of food for charity. If the performer of the combined pilgrimages cuts a nail, we encourage him to give half a *šā'* of food for charity.

The penalty for killing game

Allah—the Blessed and Exalted—says: **{O ye who believe! Kill not game whilst ye are in the pilgrim state. And whosoever kills it from amongst thee willingly—his recompense would be similar to what he killed of livestock. The judges thereof are to be two possessors of justice amongst thee. It is a sacrifice to be brought to the Ka'ba or an expiation is to feed the needy or the equivalent thereof is fasting so that he may taste the consequences of his deed. Allah pardons that which occurred before; yet whosoever returns to it, Allah shall seek retribution from him. And Allah is the Most Great, the Possessor of retribution} (Q. 5:95)**.

The pilgrim who intentionally kills game is the one to whom Allah appoints a penalty. He is the one who desired to kill it intentionally—either by shooting it with an arrow, stabbing it with a spear or striking it with a sword intending thereby to kill it. The one who intended to kill it while forgetting that he is in the state of pilgrim sanctity is not like the one who remembered that he entered it for his pilgrimage. As for the one who killed it intentionally while remembering that he is in the state of pilgrim sanctity, it is necessary that he sincerely repent to Allah for that. It is considered a major sin that he should depart to Allah from it. Recompense is obligatory upon him for doing such. As for the one who intentionally killed it while forgetting that he was in the state of pilgrim sanctity, he is to only

[33] Sayyid Abul-Abbas al-Hasani related with a number of chains of narrations that Imam 'Ali, upon him be peace, said regarding the verse **{So eat thereof and feed the contented and unfortunate} (Q. 22:36)**: "The **{contented}** refers to the needy, and the **{unfortunate}** refers to the destitute."

pay a penalty just as Allah obligated upon him because he had not committed a major sin that obligated repentance. The penalty is like what he killed.

{The judge thereof are to be two possessors of justice amongst thee}. The term **{justice}** refers to insight in judgement regarding such with rectification in the religion and fear of the Lord of creation. The penalty for killing is a ewe. If one cannot find a ewe, he must feed ten needy people if he wants or fast for ten days. This is because the equivalent of a ewe is fasting, as Allah stipulates for the performer of separate joint pilgrimages to fast three days during the Hajj pilgrimage and seven days when he returns. Just as we find that Allah has established a ten-day fast to take the place of the minimum penalty—which is a ewe according to us—we say that the equivalent of every ewe is a ten-day fast.

We also say that the equivalent of a ewe is feeding ten needy people because we established that feeding ten needy people takes the place of the ten-day fast. Similar is established by the Ever-Living and Self-Sustaining when He says regarding the unlawful pronouncement (*až-žihār*): **{Whosoever cannot find one, then he fasts for two months continuously before they touch one another. Then whosoever cannot, he is to feed sixty needy people} (Q. 58:4)**. It is then established that feeding a needy person takes the place of fasting a day. Therefore, it is sound according to us that a ewe is equivalent to fasting for ten days or feeding ten needy people.

If a pilgrim kills a wild cow or ostrich, he owes a she-camel for the ostrich judged by a person of fair judgement. If a person dislikes the she-camel due to its heavy stock and prefers to judge its equivalence in feeding, we hold to the view that he is to feed one hundred needy people. If he prefers its equivalent in fasting, he is to judge it as equivalent to fasting for one-hundred days. It is the penalty, charity and fasting based upon whichever one chooses to do.

This is because Allah says: **{It is a sacrifice to be brought to the Ka'ba or an expiation is to feed the needy or the equivalent thereof is fasting} (Q. 5:95)**. It says {or} which indicates a choice. It does not say: "And if you cannot find it, do such-and-such and such-and-such." If it said that, it would mean that the one's penalty could not be feeding unless he could not sacrifice and that his penalty could not be fasting unless he could not feed. It is similar to Allah's statement regarding the unlawful pronouncement: **{Whosoever cannot find one, then he fasts for two months continuously before they touch one another. Then whosoever cannot, he is to feed sixty needy people} (Q. 58:4)**. The second is not valid until the first has been exhausted and the third is not valid until after inability.

We simply say that the equivalent of the she-camel is feeding one-hundred needy people or fasting one hundred days because we find that the she-camel takes the place of ten ewes, and we find that a ewe takes the place of a ten-day fast for the performer of separate joint pilgrimages in the judgement of Allah. We also find that Allah has made the feeding of a needy person take the place of fasting a day in the aforementioned statement regarding the unlawful pronouncement. Therefore, we say that the she-camel is analogously equivalent to ten ewes. If each ewe is equivalent to feeding ten needy people and there are ten ewes in this analogy of feeding, then one is to feed one hundred needy people.

Similar is the case with the one who wants to fast one hundred days based upon each ewe equalling ten days. It is as the Possessor of Majesty and Nobility says: **{And whosoever joins the 'Umra to the Hajj pilgrimage separately shall render the sacrifice as he can with ease. Then whosoever cannot find such—he must fast three days in Hajj and seven days when ye return. That is ten complete days} (Q. Q. 2:196)**. Similarly, the equivalent of a cow is the feeding of seventy needy people or fasting seventy days because it [i.e. the cow] takes the place of seven ewes.

Whoever kills an ostrich or wild cow, he owes a she-camel for the ostrich and a cow for the cow. Whoever kills a wild ass (or "zebra"), he owes a cow. Whoever kills a deer, he owes a ewe. Whoever kills a mountain goat, we obligate that such person owes a sheep. Whoever kills a fox, he owes a ewe. Whoever kills a pigeon, he owes a ewe.

Whoever kills a deer while he is a pilgrim in the Sanctified Site, he owes a penalty of ewe and the value of the deer. Similarly, if one were to kill a pigeon, he owes a penalty and the value of the pigeon. We simply say and obligate penalty due to Allah's statement: **{...his recompense would be similar to what he killed of livestock} (Q. 5:95)**. We also obligate its value due to the sanctity of the Sanctified Site.

If a pilgrim were to sick his dog on a game animal and the dog drives it into the Sanctified Site and kills it, it would be obligatory for him to extract the value of the game animal due to his dog killing it in the Sanctified Site. It would be obligatory for him to pay the equivalent for that and the penalty because he hunted it and he sicked his dog on it while he was a pilgrim. Similarly, if he were to sick his dog on a game animal in the Sanctified Site and it does not catch it until it is outside of the Sanctified Site and then kills it, he is obligated to pay both the value and the penalty. However, if a non-pilgrim was outside of the Sanctified Site and he had his dog attack and kill a game animal in the Sanctified Site, he is only obligated to pay the value of the game animal. If a non-pilgrim were to sick his dog on a game animal in the Sanctified Site but it killed it outside of the Sanctified Site, he is obligated to pay the value of the game animal because he sicked it on the latter in the Sanctified Site.

Regarding the performer of the solitary and separate joint pilgrimages as well as the non-pilgrim who share in the killing of a deer in the Sanctified Site, the performer of the separate joint pilgrimage owes two ewes and the value of the deer, the performer of the solitary pilgrimage owes one ewe and the value of the deer, and the non-pilgrim owes its value. Regarding the pilgrim that shows the non-pilgrim where the game animal is in the Sanctified Site and the non-pilgrim kills it, the pilgrim is obligated to pay the penalty of the game animal as well as its value. The non-pilgrim is only obligated to pay its value.

If the pilgrim frightens the game animal or scares it by gestures and signs but does not kill it, the pilgrim is to render charity for frightening the game animal. There is a ewe due on the killing of a partridge, quail, *dubsi* bird, turtledove or vulture. Similar is narrated from the Commander of Believers, 'Ali b. Abi Ťālib, upon him be peace. It is related that he made a she-goat the penalty for killing a jerboa or lizard based upon Allah's statement: **{...his recompense would be similar to what he killed of livestock} (Q. 5:95)**.[34] We also obligate the paying of its value due to its being killed in the Sanctified Site.

As for a pilgrim who breaks an ostrich egg or his riding beast steps on it, it has been related that the Commander of Believers, 'Ali b. Abi Ťālib, said that the offspring of the she-camel that stepped on it must be sacrificed.[35] I do not know how this narration could be authenticated!

It has also been related that Allah's Messenger, peace and blessings be upon him and his progeny, declared that the one is to fast a day for each egg or feed the needy.[36] This [i.e. the narration of the Prophet] is more authentically attributed to him, peace and blessings be upon him and his progeny, because it is more just, merciful, excellent and comprehensive.

Whoever kills a game animal in the Sanctified Site—whether he is a pilgrim or not—it is impermissible for him to eat it. It would not be religiously permissible for him or anyone else because Allah and His Messenger has made hunting in the Sanctified Site prohibited. If it is religiously impermissible to hunt it in the Sanctified Site, it is similarly impermissible to eat from that which is hunted. This is because hunting it is less than eating it, and eating it is greater than hunting it. That which is religiously prohibited to hunt is even more religiously prohibited to eat. Similarly, if the pilgrim hunted game and sold it to a non-pilgrim, it would be impermissible for the non-pilgrim to buy or eat it because it was impermissible for the pilgrim to hunt it.

---

[34] Similar is narrated on the authority of Ibn Abbās in ***Sunan al-Bayhaqi***.

[35] Similarly narrated in ***Amāli Ahmed b. 'Isa, Sunan al-Bayhaqi, Mušannaf Ibn Abi Shayba***

[36] Similarly narrated in ***Sharh at-Tajrīd, Mušannaf Ibn Abi Shayba, Sunan ad-Dārqutni, Sunan al-Bayhaqi***

Concerning the slaughtered animals that are permissible and impermissible for the pilgrim to eat

A pilgrim can eat from his she-camel if he performed the combined pilgrimages; he can also feed the needy and others. Similarly, the performer of the joint pilgrimages can do so with his sacrifice and the slaughterer can do such with his slaughter.

As for the penalty for hunting or the expiation for wearing clothing, shaving the head, coming into contact with scents and similar, the owner cannot eat anything from those nor can he take any benefit from them as well as be given the meat or skin from the one for whom it is permitted to have. This is because this is the meaning of charity. Consequently, Allah says: **{...must pay a compensatory ransom of fasting or charity or sacrifice}** (Q. 2:196). He therefore makes the sacrifice take the place of the charity. He clarifies by such that whoever gives anything in charity and Allah has ruled such to be charity, it would be impermissible for him to have any of it returned to him.[37]

Concerning the taming of wild livestock and domesticated livestock becoming wild

If a pilgrim kills a cow that was domesticated but then became wild, he does not owe anything. Similarly, there is no problem in the pilgrim killing and eating any domesticated livestock that becomes wild. As for the wild livestock that becomes tame and mingles among people, it is impermissible for the pilgrim to eat it. Examples include the wild ass, ostrich, deer and similar game animals. It would return to the basis of the ruling; it is impermissible for the pilgrim to violate any of the command.

Concerning the pilgrim buying game animals in the Sanctified Site

Whoever buys a game animal in the Sanctified Site must set it free; it is impermissible for him to bind or keep it. Similarly, if he buys it outside of the Sanctified Site, my opinion is that he is to set it free because the pilgrim should not capture or confine any game animal.

Similarly, if a pilgrim took a game animal and plucked it or cut its fur, it is obligatory for him to feed it and allow for its feathers to grow on its wings and then set it free. If he plucked off its hand, he owes expiation. If he plucked some of its feathers and wings, he is to feed for the feather that was plucked to the amount of the deficiency of its flight. Similarly, one is to extract the amount of deficiency of the wound to the amount of its traces.

Concerning the one who performed the circumambulation in the state of major ritual impurity or outside of the state of ritual purity

If one performed the circumambulation of the women while he forgot that he was in the state of major ritual impurity or if a woman performed the circumambulation while she was menstruating out of forgetfulness, it is obligatory for them to repeat it if they were in Mecca. However, if they had already returned to their families and reached their homeland and then remembered, each one of them would owe a she-camel. When they returned, they would have to make up that circumambulation.

If the person forgot to perform the circumambulation of women and did not perform it, he would have to return from wherever he was unless he feared ruin for his life. He then is to then wait and depart with the people. However, his condition would be that of a restricted person. Similar is narrated on the authority of the Commander of Believers, 'Ali b. Abi Ťālib, upon him be peace. He said: "The one who forgot the circumambulation of women must return to perform it even if such person came from Khorasan."[38]

---

[37] Therefore, any sacrifice offered as expiation or recompense would be impermissible to be eaten or used due to its resemblance to charity.

[38] Similarly narrated in ***Jāmi' al-Kāfi***

If a man had intercourse with his wife before returning and then performed that circumambulation, he owes a she-camel. Whoever performs the obligatory circumambulation and then remembers that he had not washed his right forearm [in the ritual ablution before such circumambulation], he is to repeat it by washing it and the left forearm and then wipe his head and wash his feet. Afterwards, he repeats his circumambulation.

Concerning the one who forgot the brisk walking between Ŝafa and Marwa

If it is possible to return to the brisk walking, one must return. If it is not possible, he owes a sacrifice as penalty and must make up that brisk walk when he returns to the Hajj pilgrimage. If he performs the brisk walk between them outside of the state of ritual purity and then remembers after leaving, he does not owe anything because there is no prayer in the brisk walk. However, one should not forfeit the ritual purity for the brisk walk between them because both are holy places, and the brisk walk between them is an act of worship to one's Lord. One should be ritually pure in one's act of worship. If it so happens that one's brisk walk is interrupted, it is no problem to return to where one discontinued and complete it.

Concerning the one who forgot to stone the *jamrats*

Whoever forgot to stone the *jamrat*s and then remembered on the last day of sacrifice, he must stone what he left and must sacrifice for delaying his stoning. If he had not remembered stoning them until the people left Mina, he owes a sacrifice and does not have to stone because the time for stoning and its days have passed.

If one forgot to stone by a pebble, two or three and then remembered the next day, he must stone and feed a needy person for every pebble. If he forgot to stone a *jamrat* by four pebbles and then stoned it the next day, he is to render charity for them by two *šā*'s of food. If he forgot four pebbles for every *jamrat* and he stones them with three pebbles, he owes a sacrifice for that. He is to return and stone them with pebbles as long as it is the days of stoning. If the time of stoning has passed, his penalty is the sacrifice.

Concerning the she-camel that gives birth, its milk and the time to sacrifice it in homelands

If a man drives a she-camel and it gives birth on the way, then it and what it gave birth to are considered a sacrifice and it is impermissible to drink any of its milk. His servant or helper cannot drive them either. He leaves it in its udder what her foal has left. But if he feared that leaving the milk in the udder may cause harm, then he is to milk it and give it as charity to the needy because it and its milk are for Allah, the Lord of creation.

If he or some of his servants drank some of it, then he is to give that which equals the value of her drink as charity to the poor. The same is the case with the cow and sheep one sacrifices as well as their babies.

The people of the cities should not sacrifice their animals until after sunrise; this is best and obligatory. If they sacrifice before sunrise, that would not be valid and they would have to return and sacrifice after sunrise as well as after the departure and return of the imam from the prayer.

As for the people of the villages, outskirts (*al-bawādi*) and places where there is no congregational prayer, there is no problem for them to sacrifice before sunrise and after dawn. We simply say that because the people of the cities are obligated to observe the Friday congregational prayer, depart for the prayer with the imam and the sermon. Since it is obligated upon them, it would not be valid for them to sacrifice until after they pray. The prayer is only obligatory after sunrise; therefore, this is how it is impermissible to perform the sacrifice until after it. Regarding that, Allah says: **{So pray to thy Lord and sacrifice}** **(Q. 108:3)**. He orders that the prayer take place before the sacrifice; the sacrifice after the prayer is best and preferable to us.

Concerning the pilgrim who delays the sacrifice until the days of sacrifice pass

If the performer of the separate joint pilgrimages delays the slaughter of his sacrifice until the days of sacrifice pass, he is obligated to slaughter the sacrifice that is with him as well as sacrifice another for delaying his sacrifice until the departure of its time. The performer of the separate joint pilgrimages can eat from the first sacrifice, but he cannot eat from the second sacrifice because it is an expiation.

If the performer of the combined pilgrimages delays the slaughter of his sacrifice, he is obligated to compensate as the performer of the separate joint pilgrimages did. He can eat from his sacrifice, but he cannot eat from his compensatory ransom.

Concerning the one who fears ruin for his sacrifice as well as substituting another for it

If a man drives his sacrificial animal and it becomes sick on the way and he fears its ruin, there is no problem for him to sell it and use its value to substitute another sacrifice from that place. If its price is less than the price of what he sacrificed, he is to increase it until he completes its price. But if the price of the sick animal was more than the price of that which he bought, then he must buy another sacrifice with the difference—whether a cow or sheep. If it was a sheep and the difference did not amount to a price of a sheep, then he is to buy food and to give it as charity to the needy in Mina after he slaughters his sacrifice.

After every sacrifice for 'Umra reaches the Sanctified Site and then it was feared that it would be ruined before it was killed—such would be considered valid and there is no compensation on its owner. Every sacrifice for the Hajj pilgrimage should be guaranteed until the day of sacrifice. However, its owner must pay a compensation if it was ruined before that day.

Concerning the one who vowed to sacrifice his son or anyone else in Mecca or Mina

Whoever says "I vow to Allah to sacrifice my son at the *maqām* of Abraham"—this is impermissible for him and not religiously permitted for him to do. He would have to sacrifice a ram in Mecca for doing that. He would also have to give its meat as charity to the needy. If he said "I will sacrifice him in Mina," he would have to sacrifice a ram on the day of sacrifice but he cannot eat from it—whether he was in Mecca or Mina. Similarly, if he were to say "I will sacrifice my brother" or "I will sacrifice myself," he would be obligated to sacrifice a ram. Allah had substituted a great sacrifice for Ishmael, upon him be peace, and that sacrifice was a ram.[39]

Whoever says "I vow to Allah to sacrifice my slave" or "...female slave" in Mecca or Mina, we hold to the view that he must sell him and use the price for a sacrificial animal to slaughter at the place that he mentioned—whether Mecca or Mina. This is because a slave is among his wealth, and it is impermissible for him to sacrifice him. Allah has obligated him to sacrifice for himself. He is obligated to extract its price and pay for his vow.

Similarly, whoever says "I vow to Allah to sacrifice my horse in Mina"—we say that the meat of the horse is impermissible for Muslims to eat. He therefore must sell it, buy a she-camel with its price and sacrifice the latter for the needy. That is the closest to the Lord of creation and most resembles the actions of the believers. It is also furthest from corruption and deviation as well as closest to excellence and God-consciousness.

Whoever says "I vow to Allah to sacrifice my *umm walad*..." or "...my indentured labourer if such-and-such happens," it would be obligatory for him to sacrifice what he sacrifice for his brother or

---

39 This is reference to **{and We ransomed him with a great sacrifice}** **(Q. 37:107)**. Although the Qur'an does not mention that the **{great sacrifice}** in the verse refers to a ram, some Qur'anic commentators identified it as such. Also, subsequent scholars used the implication of the verse to pass the ruling that a ram is to be used as a compensatory ransom for unlawful vows. 'Aṭā relates that a man came to Ibn Abbās and said; 'I made a vow that I would sacrifice myself!" Ibn Abbās then told him to sacrifice a ram and then recited: **{and We ransomed him with a great sacrifice}** **(Q. 37:107)**. [Ref. ***Uṣūl al-Ahkām***]

son—and that is a ram. This is because it would not be permissible to sell an *umm walad* or indentured labourer; they are not one's wealth whereby one earns a living that he can command, prohibit, gift or sell. That is the reason we do not command him to do the same as he would with a slave.

Concerning the man who says that he will use all his possessions in the way of Allah or that he will sacrifice everything he owns to the House of Allah or that he vows such or that he appoints everything to Allah

There is difference of opinion regarding that. There are no unified statements regarding that nor are there two statements that are the same. Others do not explain it in one way nor are there two explanations that are the same from them. The best statement according to us and that which we heard from our elders is that one is to extract a third of his wealth one designated and then render it. He is to keep the rest of it for his family and himself.

If he said that all his wealth is to be spent in the way of Allah, he must extract a third in the way of Allah. If he said that all his wealth belongs to Allah, he is to render a third of his wealth in the closest deeds to Allah. If he said "My wealth is a gift to the House of Allah" or "I gift it to the House of Allah," he is to buy a she-camel and food with a third of his wealth and distribute it among the people of need at the House of Allah.

My father related to me from his father that the latter said:

> Whoever appoints his wealth in the way of Allah or says that he will gift it to the House of Allah must extract a third of it and render it in the way that he said, and it is obligatory for him to extract it in that way. He also must keep two-thirds of his wealth for himself.

Concerning the one who vows to sacrifice for his brother, father, sons, non-marriageable relatives, any other relatives, slaves or anyone else from his wealth

Whoever says "I will sacrifice on behalf of my son, brother, sister or unrelated man at the House of Allah," he is prohibited by Allah to sell or slaughter it on the way. He is obligated to carry it and perform the pilgrimage with it until he fulfils the debt. Afterwards, he returns him to his homeland.

If he said "I vow to Allah to sacrifice for my slave or female slave," it would be obligatory for him to sell them and use the value for them to sacrifice at the Ka'ba. Then, he is to distribute it among the needy and feed those needy slaves of Allah because the male and female slave differ from the free man and free woman. Consequently, it is permissible to sell a male or female slave but it is impermissible to sell other than them. One's male and female slave is a part of one's wealth; one can make an earning from them and it is permissible for one to do such with them both.

Concerning the penalty for a slave or child who kills a game animal as well as the obligatory expiation due on them

If a male and female slave performs the pilgrimage with their master's permission, any expiation or penalty will be paid by the master—whether it be for wearing clothes or killing game intentionally or unintentionally while in the state of pilgrim sanctity. If he wants, he can sacrifice for him, feed or command him to fast.

If a slave kills a game animal while knowing that he is in the state of pilgrim sanctity and he does so defiantly and disobediently, it is not obligatory for his master to expiate for him due to his disobedience. He [i.e. the slave] would be in debt to him until he is freed and he would have to expiate by sacrificing, feeding or fasting. Similarly, if he applied scents or wore clothes that he did not need without any valid excuse defiantly and out of opposition, his master does not owe expiation on his behalf. It will be obligatory upon the slave until his freedom.

If a slave performs the pilgrimage without his master's permission, his master does not owe any expiation for what he does—whether intentionally or unintentionally. As for children, there is no penalty for him if they do anything because they are not obligated to do anything. If they accompany their guardians and observe what they observe, that is good. However, that is not obligatory upon them.

Concerning the one who sends his sacrificial animal with people and they promised to mark it with a garland on a day but then did not act upon it after days pass

If a performer of the joint, combined or separate pilgrimages sends a sacrifice with some people and commanded them to mark it with a garland on an exact day but was late, then he is obligated to assume the state of pilgrim sanctity the day they mark his camel with a garland. Similar is narrated from Allah's Messenger, peace and blessings be upon him and his progeny.[40]

Concerning a woman and slave who assumes the state of pilgrim sanctity without their guardian's permission

As for the woman who assumes the state of pilgrim sanctity without the permission of her husband, he has a choice: if he wants and if it is possible, he can continue with her until she completes what she obligated upon herself or if he wants, he can prohibit her from that and her pilgrimage would be nullified if it is not possible for him to go with her. He must send a she-camel on her behalf to be sacrificed. It must continue until it is the day that the sacrifices are made and it is sacrificed on her behalf.

If her assumption of the state of pilgrim sanctity is for the Islamic pilgrimage, he should not prevent her nor forbid her to do so unless there is a decisive reason that prevents him, her sons or any other non-marriageable male relative from travelling with her. If they are prevented from going with her or have a decisive reason for not travelling with her, then she is free of error and disposed from danger and objection. A sacrifice is made on her behalf. When it is possible for her due to her husband regaining health or a day when she is in charge of herself, she is obligated to continue from the place where she assumed the state of pilgrim sanctity for her Hajj pilgrimage.

As for the male and female slave, if they assume the state of pilgrim sanctity without their master's permission, they will be considered non-pilgrims and their pilgrim state will be invalidated. He will not be obligated to sacrifice on their behalf. When they are freed, they are to sacrifice what has passed due to what is obligated upon them for invalidating their pilgrim state.

---

[40] Sheikh 'Ali b. Bilāl reported that Sayyid Abul-Abbās al-Hasani related with a complete chain of narrators to Jābir b. 'Abdullah:

> I was sitting with Allah's Messenger, peace and blessings be upon him and his progeny. He took off his shirt from his pocket until it was taken from his feet. The people looked at Allah's Messenger, peace and blessings be upon him and his progeny, and he said: ((Verily, I was commanded that my she-camel I sent be garlanded today and sacrificed in this place. Then, I put on my shirt and forgot [about the state of pilgrim sanctity]. I did not remove my shirt from my head)). His she-camel was sent and settled in Medina.

It is also narrated in ***Sharh at-Tajrīd, Ŝahīh al-Bukhāri, Musnad Ahmed, Ŝahīh Ibn Khuzayma, Ŝahīh Ibn Hibbān***

The Book of Marriage

In the Name of Allah, the Most Gracious, the Most Merciful...

The beginning of the chapters regarding marriage and the explanation regarding what Allah has made permissible in marriage

Allah—Blessed and Exalted—says: **{And wed the solitary amongst thee and the righteous amongst thy slaves and bondwomen. If they are poor, Allah shall enrich them from His bounty. And Allah is All-encompassing, All-knowing}** (Q. 24:32).

The Glorified commands to marry single people if they desire to do so, when they are able to and when they are permitted to do so. The **{solitary}** are those women who are not married. The term **{amongst thee}** means: those free women among you including your daughters, sisters and all your women. And included in His statement **{And marry the solitary amongst thee}** is those men among you who have no wives. He therefore commands them to marry and allow the marriages of their women.

As for the statement of the Mighty and Majestic **{and the righteous amongst thy slaves and bondwomen}**, it is the freedom to conduct marriages between free and slave. He therefore commands such out of sympathy for all His creation and for one to marry His female slave.

Then, the Blessed and Exalted says: **{And wed those whom seem goodly to thee of women—two, three and four}** (Q. 4:3). That which is permissible for men to marry in respect to women is clarified. He informs that there are to be only four wives.

Therefore, it is impermissible for a Muslim to join in his marriage anything over four free wives except the Prophet, peace and blessings be upon him and his progeny. He was allowed to marry what he was allowed but then warned from adding any addition to the nine wives afterwards. It was prohibited for him to substitute any other women for any of them or add to them any other women. The Blessed and Exalted said to His Prophet, peace and blessings be upon him and his progeny, when he reached the limit of wives under him and as a warning to him against adding to them and substituting for them afterwards: **{It is impermissible unto thee women afterwards nor to substitute for them any wives even if thou art amazed at their beauty except those whom thy right hand owns. And Allah is over all things aware}** (Q. 33:52).

The daughters of paternal uncles and aunts as well as the daughters of maternal uncles and aunts are permissible. He says: **{O Prophet, We hath made permissible unto thee thy wives unto whom thou hast paid their dowers, and those whom thy right hand owns of those whom Allah hath given thee as spoils, and the daughters of thy paternal uncle and the daughters of thy paternal aunts, and the daughters of thy maternal uncles who emigrated with thee, and a believing woman if she gives herself unto the Prophet and the Prophet desires to ask her in marriage, specifically for thee in the stead of the believers. We are aware of that which We enjoined upon them concerning their wives and those whom their right hands possess that thou may be free from blame, for Allah is Oft-forgiving, Most Gracious}** (Q. 33:50).

Allah allowed him to marry those who are named the daughters of paternal uncles and aunts, daughters of maternal uncles and aunts as well as those female slaves whom the right hand possesses for the Messenger of the Lord of creation and all the Muslims. Then, He allowed him to marry the believing woman who gave herself to His Prophet, peace and blessings be upon him and his progeny. He warned other than him and made them specific for him instead of the believers. That is stated in His clear Book: **{...specifically for thee in the stead of the believers}**. The Blessed and Exalted permitted him to marry nine and joined them. However, He did not permit the Muslims to join more than four of any women—be they female slaves or far cut-off [i.e. not related].

Then, the One too majestic to be encompassed by words commanded them to be given a dowry of their pleasing: **{And those of whom ye seek pleasure, grant unto them their portions as a duty. And there is no sin for thee in what ye do by agreement after the duty. Verily, Allah is All-Knowing, All-Wise}** (Q. 4:24). He obligates that the dowry be given to their wives with His statement **{duty (*farīḍa*)}**. The word **{duty}** refers to Allah's judgement regarding the dowry for women upon the men.

Then, the Glorified says: **{And there is no sin for thee in what ye do by agreement after the duty. Verily, Allah is All-Knowing, All-Wise}** (Q. 4:24). By that, the Glorified means that there is no sin upon you for what you grant them while they are satisfied with the dowry they are rightfully given—whether you gave them all of it or some of it. That is, it would be valid for you to take it and you are no longer obligated to give it; you can consume it. As Allah, the Glorified, says: **{But if they remit unto thee any part thereof out of pleasure, take it cheerfully and happily}** (Q. 4:4).

He passed the judgement that those who had not entered and removed the cover from their wives would be permitted to take back half of the dowry if they divorced them. That is based on the statement of Allah, the Glorified: **{And if ye divorce them before having touched them and rendered unto them their duty, then unto ye is half the duty ye rendered except that which they pardoned and the one who contracted the marriage tie pardoned. To pardon it is nearer to God-consciousness. Forget not virtue amongst thyselves. Verily, Allah is ever seeing of what ye do}** (Q. 2:237).

He therefore obligates half the dowry for the one who divorces before entering unless she pardons and grants that half to her husband or her husband pardons the half that is due to him and he pays her the entire dowry. The husbands are urged to pardon and surrender it to them by the statement: **{To pardon it is nearer to God-consciousness}**.

The Possessor of Majesty and Nobility permitted marriage to female Muslim slaves for the one who has no means to marry free chaste women. He says: **{And whosoever is unable to afford to wed free believing women, then let him wed those believing maids whom thy right hand owns}** (Q. 4:25).

Then, He commanded that one not marry them without the permission of their people. Their 'people' refer to the ones who own the female slaves. He passed the judgement that the one who marries the female slave must provide a dowry that the wife and their guardians are satisfied with as an obligation. The Glorified made it a religious injunction and said: **{Therefore, wed them with the leave of their people and grant them their reward in kindness, they being chaste and not given to fornication and taking them as intimate companions}** (Q. 4:25). He is saying marry them with a sound and permissible marriage and do not fornicate with them impermissibly.

Allah's Messenger, peace and blessings be upon him and his progeny, prohibited marrying slave women over free women. He said: ((Do not marry female slaves over free women)).[1] He also said: ((If you marry a slave woman before a free woman and then marry a free woman after a slave woman, both marriages will be sound)).[2] By that, he, peace and blessings be upon him and his progeny, means when you come to know that a free woman as a slave woman and acquire her after being informed.

Concerning those from whom Allah prohibits marriage and the explanation of its judgement in the Qur'an

It is prohibited for the Muslims to marry any forbidden relative. That is based on the statement of the Mighty and Noble: **{Forbidden unto thee art thy mothers and daughters and sisters and paternal aunts and maternal aunts and the daughters of thy brothers and the daughters of thy sisters and thy mothers from whom ye nursed and thy sisters from nursing and the mothers of thy wives and thy**

---

[1] Similarly narrated in ***Musnad Imam Zayd, Mušannaf Ibn Abi Shayba, Sunan al-Bayhaqi, Sunan ad-Dārqutni, Ušūl al-Kāfi***

[2] Similarly narrated in ***Sharh at-Tajrīd***

stepdaughters in thy protection born of thy wives whom ye have entered upon. However, if thou hast not entered upon them, there is no sin upon thee [to marry the stepdaughters]. And forbidden art the wives of the sons from thy issue and to join two sisters save that which has previously transpired. Verily, Allah was Most Forgiving, Most Gracious} (Q. 4:23).

Therefore, Allah—the Blessed and Exalted—prohibited marrying mothers. He absolutely prohibited all who gave birth including grandmothers—the higher up it goes, the prohibition similarly goes with it. That is because they are grandmothers, and grandmothers are mothers. Also, Allah prohibited believers from their daughters as well as their offspring and their offspring's offspring, even successive generations of offspring. They would be daughters of grandparents in the judgement of Allah and it would be impermissible to marry them based upon Allah's prohibition from marrying mothers.

Similarly, Allah, the one too majestic to be encompassed by words, prohibited marrying sisters. He also prohibited by such prohibition their uncles from marrying their [sister's] daughters as well as their daughters and their daughters' daughters, even if there is a distance between sisters and their grandparents. This is because, even if they proceed their uncles in generations, the judgement regarding them would be that of their sisters from whom the Book prohibits. Consequently, they are like their daughters conceptually since they are their sisters' daughters.

Similarly, Allah prohibited marrying paternal and maternal aunts because they are counted as parents and mothers. Allah also prohibited marrying the nieces born from brothers and sisters because they are like daughters. This is out of His reverence for the nearness of familial ties and His confirmation for congenial connections for His slaves. Therefore, the judgement regarding the Muslim's niece is like the judgement of his own daughter. Similar judgement is the case with his sister's daughter.

Then the Glorified prohibited marriage between milk-mothers and those whom they nursed—whether they be offspring or their offspring's offspring—even if they did not birth them. This is because by their breastfeeding, they became their mothers even though they are not related.

Similarly, He prohibited marriage between the sisters and brothers of a milk-mother's relationship. He therefore also prohibited them from marrying the offspring of their [i.e. the milk-mothers'] siblings. And He prohibited one to marry the milk-mothers' nieces because he becomes their uncle, and it is impermissible for an uncle or aunt in a milk-mother relationship to marry a niece or nephew in such relationship as well as their offspring. Consequently, it is impermissible to marry a grandparent from a milk-mother relationship.

Then, the Glorified prohibited marriage with the mothers of wives due to their marriage with their daughters—whether they have intercourse with the daughters or not. It is impermissible for them to marry mothers. It is out of His reverence for the mothers from marrying their daughters and out of His prohibition from marrying thc mothcr aftcr hcr daughtcr.

Then, He prohibited marriage with the daughters of the wives one marries if he has had intercourse with the mother. He appoints the judgement of the stepdaughters prohibited for marriage. He establishes such due to the prohibition of marrying the mother similar to marrying her daughter. Stepdaughters are prohibited from men by the prohibition of the Possessor of power and majesty after they have intercourse with their mothers. It is prohibited to marry the grandparents of their stepdaughters just as it is impermissible to marry their daughters.

The One who is majestic in His praise and ennobles His associates prohibited men from marrying the wives of their sons from among their issue. He also prohibited sons from marrying those whom their fathers married due to the attachment the fathers had with their sons' wives being prohibited for them. He then makes the parents of their wives prohibited similar to the prohibition of their daughters, sisters and stepdaughters under their care. He makes the wives of their fathers forbidden for the sons due to His reverence of the right the fathers have over their sons. He also made the wives of their fathers like their mothers in the prohibition. He then says regarding that: **{And wed not among the women whom thy fathers wedded save whatsoever has previously transpired}** (Q. 4:22). He is saying: "…except what has happened in the past from the actions of the pre-Islamic era and the errors the sons used to make in marrying their fathers' wives."

Similarly, the Blessed and Exalted prohibited marrying two sisters at the same time out of His consideration for the slaves, rectification in the land and assistance for His slaves in attaining God-consciousness and righteousness. This is due to the enmity that may occur when marrying two sisters as well as the hatred that may occur between them. There should not be something that promotes the severing of familial ties nor that which contradicts the judgement of Islam. Due to the severity of constant alternating between them that one does with other wives, Allah has made a connection between two sisters out of consideration for them by prohibiting men from marrying the two of them at the same time.

The Glorified also prohibited marriage with idolaters and idolatresses until they believe. The Glorified says regarding that: **{Wed not idolatresses until they believe. And the believing bondwoman is better than an idolatress though she may amaze thee. Give not in wedlock to idolaters until they believe. And the believing slave is better than an idolater though he may amaze thee}** (Q. 2:221).

Concerning the invalidity of marriage without a guardian and two witnesses

It has reached us from Allah's Messenger, peace and blessings be upon him and his progeny, that he said: ((There is no marriage except with a guardian and two witnesses)).[3] It has also reached us on the authority of Zayd b. 'Ali from his ancestors from 'Ali b. Abi Ťālib, upon him be peace:

> There is no marriage except with a guardian and two witnesses. It is not by means of a dirham or two dirhams, not one day or two days. It would be similar to fornication. Nor is it valid with any other condition of marriage.[4]

It has also reached us that Allah's Messenger, peace and blessings be upon him and his progeny, said: ((There is no marriage except with a guardian and two just witnesses. Whoever cannot find a guardian for her, the sultan is her guardian)).[5]

The meaning of his statement ((…the sultan is her guardian)) is the imam of the Muslims for whom obedience is obligatory and disobedience is prohibited. In the absence of such, then [her guardian] is the best of the Muslims.

If a man marries a woman without being given in marriage by her guardian and it was witnessed by two witnesses, that marriage is considered invalid. This is because the marriage was not contracted by a guardian, and a marriage can only be contracted by her guardian, the imam of the Muslims when there is no guardian or a just male among the Muslims in the absence of a guardian or imam of the

---

[3] Similarly narrated in ***Musnad Imam Zayd, Amāli Ahmed b. 'Isa, Amāli Abu Ťālib, Sharh at-Tajrīd, Mušannaf Ibn Abi Shayba, Kanz al-'Ummāl, Sunan al-Bayhaqi, Al-Mu'jam al-Kabīr, Al-Mu'jam al-Awsaṫ, Sunan ad-Dārqutni***. The abbreviated form of the hadith ((There is no marriage except with a guardian)) without the added clause ((…two witnesses)) appears in ***Sunan at-Tirmidhi, Sunan Abu Dāwūd, Sunan Ibn Māja, Al-Mustadrak, Musnad Ahmed, Sunan ad-Dārimi, Sunan al-Bayhaqi, Kanz al-'Ummāl, Al-Mu'jam al-Kabīr, Al-Mu'jam al-Awsaṫ***

[4] Similarly narrated in ***Musnad Imam Zayd***

[5] Similarly narrated in ***Sunan at-Tirmidhi, Sunan Abu Dāwūd, Sunan an-Nisā'i, Al-Mustadrak, Musnad Ahmed, Sunan Ibn Mājah, Sunan al-Bayhaqi, Sunan ad-Dārimi, Mušannaf Ibn Abi Shayba, Majmu' az-Zawā'id, Kanz al-'Ummāl, Al-Mu'jam al-Kabīr, Al-Mu'jam al-Awsaṫ***

Muslims.[6] As for the case when there is a guardian, it would be impermissible to marry without his permission and one would not be able to contract a marriage with her except by his contract.

My father related to me on the authority of his father from Abu Bakr b. Abi Uways al-Madini from Hussein b. 'Abdullah b. Ḋumayra from his father from his grandfather from 'Ali b. Abi Ťālib, upon him be peace:

> Allah's Messenger, peace and blessings be upon him and his progeny, said: ((Do not marry a woman except with a guardian and two witnesses. If you were to marry, it would be invalid. If you were to marry, it would be invalid)) and he repeated it three times.[7]

It has reached us that the Commander of Believers, 'Ali b. Abi Ťālib, upon him be peace, said: "Don't marry a woman except with a guardian and two witnesses. Whoever marries, it would be invalid." Also, my father related to me on the authority of his father that he was asked about a man who marries a woman without a guardian, and a man is made the guardian and it is witnessed by two men. He replied:

> It is not for anyone to marry her except that she is given in marriage by her guardian. The guardian is to not prevent her or cause her harm. Whoever cannot find a guardian for her must appoint as guardian for her affair a man from the Muslims and he gives her in marriage. It is necessary that all marriages have two male witnesses.

The meaning of my grandfather al-Qāsim's statement regarding the guardian "…is to not prevent her or cause her harm" is that if she is prevented from marriage, the imam of the Muslims looks into her affair. He would be compelled to give her in marriage. In that case, only the imam can give her in marriage. If there is no imam, a man from the Muslims can be her guardian and contract her marriage for her.

Concerning the explanation of guardians

Guardians are those who are connected and joined to the woman by a familial linkage. They are in charge of contracting the marriage for a woman and giving her in marriage. They also assume the right of leaving her inheritance.

The most entitled is the son, and then the son of the son, the father, the paternal grandfather, the paternal/maternal brother, the maternal brother, the paternal/maternal nephew, the paternal nephew, the father and mother's paternal uncle, the father's paternal uncle, the son of the father's and mother's paternal uncle, the son of the father's paternal uncle, and then the freed slave.

It is encouraged that the father and grandfather contract the marriage rather than the son and the son's son because that is closest to modesty and excellence. Allah's Messenger, peace and blessings be upon him and his progeny, said: ((Modesty is from faith. There is no faith from the one who is not modest)).[8]

---

[6] This statement by al-Hādi prompted some imams to assume that he had two different opinions regarding the issue as to whether uprightness or justice (*'adāla*) is a precondition for guardianship. For example, Imam Yahya b. Hamza said in his ***Al-Intišār*** that two different statements exist from al-Hādi: one, open disobedience (*fisq*) invalidates guardianship and two, open disobedience does not invalidate guardianship. The same statement is echoed by Imam Ibn Murtaḍa in ***Al-Bahr***. It is plausible that the aforementioned imams compared this statement from the ***Ahkām*** with that of ***Al-Muntakhab*** in which al-Hādi stated "a man from the Muslims" without specifying that he is to be just.

In response, we say that the absence of al-Hādi's description in ***Al-Muntakhab*** does not necessarily imply its nonexistence, nor does it imply a contradiction. Rather, based on the jurisprudential methodological principle, the explicit mention of the description 'just' in the ***Ahkām*** takes precedence over its absence in ***Al-Muntakhab***. The dear reader should also take note that in the above passage, al-Hādi makes the precondition of uprightness for the non-related Muslim male to act as a guardian in the absence of a related guardian or just imam. However, in accordance with the most established position of the *madhhab*, uprightness is not a precondition for the guardianship of a male relative. And Allah knows best!

[7] Similarly narrated in ***Musnad Ahmed, Sunan ad-Dārimi, Musnad Abu Ya'la, Sunan ad-Dārqutni, Sunan al-Bayhaqi, Ŝahīh Ibn Hibbān,***

[8] Similarly narrated in ***Amāli Ahmed b. 'Isa, Ŝahīh al-Bukhāri, Muwaṫṫa, Ŝahīh Muslim, Sunan Abu Dāwūd, Sunan at-Tirmidhi, Sunan an-Nisā'i, Musnad Ahmed, Mušannaf Ibn Abi Shayba, Majmu' az-Zawā'id, Al-Mu'jam al-Kabīr, Al-Mu'jam al-Awsaṫ, Ušūl al-Kāfi, Bihār al-Anwār***

It is impermissible for any of the aforementioned men to contract a marriage for a woman when there is another person more entitled unless he is given permission and allowed to do so by the more entitled person. Then he would be permitted to do such, and the marriage contract between the two would be established as valid.[9] My father related to me that his father said that the guardians are those who contract marriage to the exclusion of appointees.

Concerning giving virgins in marriage and concerning the dowry and concerning two guardians giving in marriage to two men

It is impermissible for a guardian to give a woman in marriage without her permission once she reaches puberty—whether she is a non-virgin [i.e. divorcee or widow] or virgin. However, the father is permitted to give his young daughter in marriage; however, this does not apply in the case of an older daughter except by her permission. The Messenger of Allah, peace and blessings be upon him and his progeny, made the silence of a virgin a sign of her permission.[10] If she is silent, she is contented. If she is contented, this is sufficient to give her in marriage.

The dowry that is acceptable between them is ten dirham or more. As for that which is less than ten dirhams, it would not be considered a valid dowry according to us. The term 'acceptable' means that which the woman is satisfied to accept and that which the man is satisfied to designate as such as long as it is ten dirham or more.

Regarding the two guardians who contract a woman to marry two men, whichever of them is the closest to her in family relations is the one whose contract is most valid as long as she is satisfied to marry such man. This is because it is impermissible for a person further in her family relations to contract a marriage instead of one who is closer.[11]

If it is unknown which of the two contracted the marriage first and the two guardians are equal in family relations, the contract will go to whichever of the two potential husband she prefers. Then, she is married to him and it is considered a new marriage except in the case where she prefers the other one and rejects the first. Then, the marriage would be considered established between her and the one she prefers even if her guardian who contracted the marriage is not closest in family relations.

---

[9] The contrary is true as well. If a more entitled guardian were to object to the marriage contract of a less entitled guardian, the marriage would be considered invalid. This is exemplified in ***Al-Muntakhab*** in the following conversation:

> I asked about a woman who has a paternal grandfather and brother. He replied: "According to me, it is preferable that her grandfather contracts the marriage for her." "What if her brother contracts the marriage?" "If the grandfather is silent, it is considered sound." "What if the brother contracts the marriage but the grandfather refuses to agree?" "The marriage would be considered invalidated."

[10] Similarly narrated in ***Musnad Imam Zayd, Sharh at-Tajrīd, Ŝahīh al-Bukhāri, Ŝahīh Muslim, Sunan Abu Dāwūd, Sunan an-Nisā`i, Sunan Ibn Māja***

[11] Hypothetical situations of the above principle are mentioned as examples in ***Al-Muntakhab***.

> I asked him about a pubescent woman whose father contracted a marriage for her to a man and whose brother contracted a marriage for her to another man at night. "What if she objects to the one with whom her father contracted a marriage and is pleased with the one with whom her brother contracted a marriage?" He replied: "Neither contract of marriage would be considered sound because the father contracted a marriage with one with whom she was not contented and he was her guardian, whereas her brother contracted a marriage with one with whom she was contented while the father was most entitled. It is impermissible for the brother to contract the marriage while the father is alive and healthy. Therefore, both marriage contracts are invalid. However, the father should contract the marriage with the one with whom she is contented." "What if the father objects to the one with whom she is contented?" "He would be forced to accept. If he still objects, the matter will go to the imam of the Muslims." "What if both of them simultaneously contracted a marriage with two different men while she is pre-pubescent and each one objects to the choice of the other?" "It will be halted until she becomes pubescent. Once she reaches puberty, she can choose whomever she wants." "What if two of her brothers contracted a marriage for her while she is pubescent and both command her to marry him?" "The marriage contract will go to the first one." "What if she has a brother who contracts a marriage for her while she has not reached puberty? Can she object?" "Her objection would not be acknowledged since she had not reached puberty."

My father related to me that his father said regarding a man who wants to give his pubescent virgin daughter in marriage while she is unwilling:

> A virgin woman who has become pubescent cannot be given in marriage except after her permission even if her own father contracted the marriage for her. He gives her in marriage and does not force her to do so because the affair is her own to decide.

My father related to me that his father was asked about two guardians of a woman who contracted a marriage with one man and another. He replied:

> The contract is for the first one. If it is unknown who contracted the marriage first and she was already given in marriage by one of them but she prefers the second and not the first, then she is to be given in marriage to the one she prefers. There would be no contract with the one who she does not prefer.

My father related to me that his father said that his cousin contracted a marriage for the daughter of his brother, Muhammad b. Ibrāhīm. He married her to him and the latter sent the former four hundred dinars. He took a dinar for her and returned the rest to him.

My father related to me that his father said: "The minimum which is permissible regarding the dowry is what has been narrated from the Commander of Believers, 'Ali b. Abi Ťālib, upon him be peace—ten dirham."[12]

Concerning the *muta'* marriage and concerning the deputation of giving in marriage as well as the giving away in marriage by the appointee

According to us, the *muta'* is the marriage with and seeking pleasure from women in the way of a marriage contract with the guardians and the testimony of two just witnesses. Regarding that, Allah—the Blessed and Exalted—says: **{And those from whom ye seek pleasure (*astamta'tum*),[13] give unto them their portions as a duty}** (Q. 4:24). The intended meaning of **{those of whom ye seek pleasure}** is: by means of their guardians giving them in marriage **{grant unto them their portions as a duty}** (Q. 4:24). The word **{portions}** here refers to the dowry.

As for the statement of the people of dishonour who seek excuses and disgrace women, they say that it refers to women who contract their own marriages between them and their husbands without their guardians as Allah commanded. We do not acknowledge such statement nor do we rely on it because Allah has invalidated what they state. There is a violation in such statement based upon the clear ruling regarding the contracting of marriage by guardians as well as the clear prohibition on women [to contract their own marriages].

The Glorified says: **{And wed the solitary amongst thee and the righteous amongst thy slaves and bondwomen}** (Q. 24:32); **{Prevent them not from wedding their spouses}** (Q. 2:232) and

---

[12] The following sources report on the authority of 'Ali that ten dirhams is the minimum: ***Musnad Imam Zayd, Mušannaf Ibn Abi Shayba, Bihār al-Anwār***. The following sources report the same hadith from the Prophet on the authority of Jābir b. 'Abdullah: ***Sunan ad-Dārqutni, Sunan al-Bayhaqi, Kanz al-'Ummāl, Majmu' az-Zawā'id, Musnad Abu Ya'la.***

[13] The Arabic word for **{seek pleasure}** in this verse is a derivative of the word *muta'*. Here the imam is arguing for the denotative meaning of the word, which means 'to enjoy or seek pleasure,' rather than the legalistic meaning brought forward by the Imami Shia, which refers to a temporary marriage of sorts without the presence of a guardian or witnesses. Imam al-Mu`ayyad Billah said in ***Sharh at-Tajrīd*** regarding the verse's import:

> The permissibility of *muta'* is not proven by the verse because the word for 'seeking pleasure' (*al-istimtā'a*) linguistically means 'taking benefit'. The Exalted says **{"Ye squandered those good things in this world's life of thine and took pleasure (*astamta'tum*) therefrom..."}** (Q. 46:20) and **{...and they enjoyed (*astamta'uw*) their shares just as those before thee enjoyed (*astamta'tum*) their shares...}** (Q. 9:69). Therefore, the intending meaning of **{seek pleasure}** is 'take benefit from them by means of a sound marriage.' As for what is narrated from Ibn Abbās that he used to recite it as 'And those from whom ye seek pleasure until the appointed time', it is said that this narration is weak. Even if it was sound, it would apply to delaying the dowry. We permit the dowry to be delayed. And the verse states that if the narration is true, this would be considered permissible. The dowry is obligatory when the appointed term is due. Therefore, there is no evidence of *muta'* in it in any way.

{Therefore, wed them with the leave of their people} **(Q. 4:25)**. In all of that, Allah commands and prohibits. Allah appoints the marriage contract to the guardians. If it was as the invalidators say and falsely interpret attributing falsehood to Allah, the command and prohibition of women would be the same as the command to their guardians. Rather, Allah is merciful and kind, the Possessor of power, grace and nobility. How could He permit or command such as well as give them the freedom to do so? He says: **{Verily, Allah commands not obscenity. Dost ye say about Allah that which ye know not?}** **(Q. 6:28)**.

Which obscenity is greater than that of women giving themselves in marriage without men? When women are removed from the hands of their guardians, they can violate what Allah has stipulated upon them. A male fornicator can be found with a female fornicator and he could fornicate with her while falsely claiming that he was married to her. Consequently, the judgement of Allah regarding the prescribed punishment can be turned away due to such. If that is the case, they can make a false claim in front of witnesses and say that their testimony is correct. There would be no witness that could apply the punishment to them because the two sinners would not take measures against their act of disobedience. They would not take precaution from lying, nor would there be an investigation regarding the statement that they both know would entail a prescribed punishment on themselves. If that was permissible regarding the Muslims, then none of the judgements of the Lord of the creation would be established regarding the two disobedient fornicators, and no open sinner would take precaution from Allah. If that were true—highly exalted is Allah from that!—then the statement of the Glorified **{The fornicating woman and man found guilty of sexual immorality—scourge each of them with a hundred lashings. Let not thy compassion for them keep thee from this law (*dīn*) of Allah}** **(Q. 24:2)** would be affected. This is because no one would ever be considered a fornicator, and it would therefore necessitate disgrace and scandal among the Muslims. Indeed! He claimed to have married her and since she confirmed it, it would remove the punishment from him and her! Therefore, if it were as they say, their judgement of fornication would be considered the same as marriage! Certainly not! Verily Allah is most proper and fair in judgement to permit such impossibility and falsehood!

If a man deputised someone to give a female relative in marriage to another man, this would be permissible for the deputy. Thus is the judgement of the Majestic One. However, it is not for an appointee to give in marriage anyone who was placed under his charge because the guardians are more entitled to those female relatives under their charge than the appointees. The guardians among those connected by familial ties are the only ones who can contract a woman's marriage instead of any appointee. It would not be permissible for an appointee to do such unless he was permitted by an agnate and commanded to contract the marriage for those under his charge by a relative. As long as he was commanded to do such, it would be permissible for him to do it just as it is permitted for someone else who was deputised to contract a marriage.

My father related to me that his father was asked about the *muta'* marriage. The latter said:

> The *muta'* marriage is impermissible because the *muta'* was only during a journey of the Prophet, peace and blessings be upon him and his progeny. Then, Allah made it religiously prohibited on the tongue of Allah's Messenger, peace and blessings be upon him and his progeny. It has been authentically narrated to us from the Commander of Believers, 'Ali b. Abi Ťālib, that Allah's Messenger, peace and blessings be upon him and his progeny, prohibited it.[14]

---

[14] Similarly narrated in ***Musnad Imam Zayd, Sharh at-Tajrīd, Ŝahīh al-Bukhāri, Ŝahīh Muslim, Sunan al-Bayhaqi, Musnad Ahmed***

As for the one from the transgressing faction who uses the verse {**And those of whom ye seek pleasure, give unto them their portions**} (**Q. 4:24**) as a proof to permit obscenity, the 'seeking of pleasure' is to enter upon them in the sense of a sound marriage. The phrase {**grant unto them their portions**} means: give them their dowries except that which they relinquish out of kindness from themselves. The term {**by agreement**} means: by donation.

A marriage is impermissible except with a guardian and two witnesses because in that is an avoidance of what Allah made clear, a departure of women from the charge of their guardians and an invalidation of Allah's appointment of their guardians and the guardians' judgement upon them. Have you not heard how the One without partners says: {**And wed the solitary amongst thee and the righteous amongst thy slaves and bondwomen**} (**Q. 24:32**) and {**Wed not idolatresses until they believe**} (**Q. 2:221**) and {**Prevent them not from wedding their spouses**} (**Q. 2:232**)?

If the matter was the case concerning the women, it would invalidate the matter of them being under the charge of men, and mothers, daughters, sisters and other female relatives would depart from under the charge of the guardians. This and similar would be akin to the pre-Islamic era (*al-jāhiliyya*); it would lead to the shedding of blood among people, and there would be great corruption between guardians among men and women! How can it be when Allah has made Islam to rectify and not corrupt as well as fulfil the rights of family?

We have reached our elders among the Ahl al-Bayt and not one of them held to this view even until the end.[15] The despicable related it as hadith and narrated false narrations.

Verily, my father related to me from his father from Ismā'īl b. Abi Uways from Hussein b. 'Abdullah b. Ḋumayra from his father from his grandfather from 'Ali b. Abi Ťālib that Allah's Messenger, peace and blessings be upon him and his progeny, said: ((There is no marriage except by a guardian and two witnesses)).

It has also been related that Allah's Messenger, peace and blessings be upon him and his progeny, prohibited secret marriages. And it has been related that he, peace and blessings be upon him and his progeny, passed by the house of one of the *Anšār* one day. In it he heard a sound and asked ((What is this?)) It was said to him: "O Messenger of Allah, so-n-so got married." He replied: ((Praise be to Allah! This is a marriage not a whoredom! Celebrate the marriage!))[16]

My father related to me that his father was asked about a deputy and if he can give away in marriage. He replied: "The deputy is nothing compared to the related guardian. The guardians are only the people who share in kinship."

That which we and my grandfather mentioned regarding *muta'* is the truth. It is not as those who practice and advocate it say regarding the *muta'* from their conditions that they claim and stipulate which are at variance to the Book and Sunnah. They permit that which the Most Gracious prohibited and allow that which has been restricted by the Criterion.

The Glorified says regarding inheritors: {**Allah exhorts thee regarding thy offspring. To the male belongs a share like unto two females**} (**Q. 4:11**). He says regarding the inheritance between two spouses: {**Unto thee belong half of what thy wives leave even if they have no child. But if they have a child, unto thee belong a fourth of what they leave after any bequest they hath bequeathed or debt. Unto them belongs a fourth of what ye leave if ye have no child. But if ye have a child, then unto them belongs an eighth of what ye leave after any bequest ye hath bequeathed or debt**} (**Q. 4:12**).

[15] It is narrated that Imam al-Hasan b. Yahya said in ***Al-Jāmi' al-Kāfi*** that the consensus of the Prophet's Progeny holds to the prohibition of *muta'* marriage.

[16] Similarly narrated in ***Al-Mu'jam al-Awsaṫ*** and ***Bihār al-Anwār***

He says regarding the waiting period and that which Allah obligates after the completion of a spouse's divorce: **{O Prophet! When ye divorce women, divorce them for their waiting period and reckon the waiting period. And be wary of Allah thy Lord. Cast them not from their houses nor let them depart unless they commit an open obscenity} (Q. 65:1)**. Allah therefore obligates inheritance between children and parents as well as between spouses. He has also made the waiting period obligatory upon those who divorce. He obligates maintenance and enjoyment upon their husbands, and He adjudicates that for them in the Book.

The Imamites invalidate all of that by the *muta'* marriage and contradict the Book of Allah. They oppose Allah in His judgements and say: "The stipulations of men are more obligatory than the judgements of the Most Gracious!" They therefore invalidate kinship between child and parent and the inheritance between them. They say that there is no inheritance between the parents and a child. By that, they invalidate the judgement of the One, the Eternal Existent! They say that the wife does not inherit from her husband in the case of his death and that the husband does not inherit from his wife in the case of her death.[17] They also stipulate that there is no waiting period that she counts from the ejaculation of her husband as Allah has adjudicated upon her! They have contradicted the Book and acted contrary to Allah in all respects! They permitted what He prohibited and prohibited what He permitted! And this is one of the many reasons that we have explained in the introduction of this book of ours as well as explained what we have composed concerning the foundations of our religion.

Concerning the slave who marries without his master's permission and concerning the man who openly presents a dowry contrary to the agreement between them

Any slave who marries without his master's permission invalidates his marriage. It is impermissible, and the marriage of a slave is not established except by his master's permission. And whoever openly declares anything regarding the dowry and secretly gives something different must act upon what he openly declared unless he has proof for the witnesses of what he secretly presented.

An explanation of that is the following: A man marries a woman for one hundred dinars. He openly declared [that the dowry was] two hundred dinars, and the in-laws seek the two hundred that the witnesses testified to during the marriage and contracted in the contract. Then one objects to that saying: "You only married for one hundred dinars." Therefore, he would have to—based upon his statement and claim—provide proof for those who witnessed what the other person said. As an exception, he would be forced to act upon what was witnessed by the witnesses that witnessed in the marriage contract and heard what the apparent agreement between them was regarding the dowry. Otherwise, he would be obligated to swear an oath that negated what the other person claimed [regarding only paying half] and objected to what he heard.

My father related to me that his father said regarding a man who married a woman and then openly declared a dowry which was more than what he gave to her in secret. "Which one is taken?" He replied:

> He would be forced to present the dowry he openly declared unless there is evidence that what he declared openly is contrary to what he did secretly. Otherwise, he would have to swear an oath to the woman regarding it.

Concerning a woman whose husband dies without him having had intercourse with her and determined her dowry and concerning a man who marries a slave woman over a free woman and concerning a man who sleeps with a woman and then marries her

If a man marries a woman and then dies without having specified her dowry, the inheritance belongs

[17] Imam al-Hādi references an early opinion of the Twelver Shia jurists regarding the inheritance of a *muta'* marriage. One of the most prominent early Twelver Shia jurists, Sharif al-Murtaḍa says in his ***Rasā`il ash-Sharīf al-Murtaḍa*** **[1:295]**: "As for the one who practices the *muta'* marriage, there is no inheritance for her if that has been stipulated in that contract. But if it has not been stipulated, then she receives an inheritance."

to her and she is to enter the waiting period from the time her husband died. Similar is the case if he marries her and then divorces her before having intercourse with her without having determined the amount for her. The dowry would be for her based upon his ability and determination to pay it.

There will be no dowry for her because the dowry was not determined nor did he have intercourse with her.[18]

My father related to me that his father said regarding a man who married a woman and then died without having determined her dowry and had not had intercourse with her: "She would have to observe the waiting period from the time of her husband's death, and the inheritance would belong to her."

It is impermissible for a female slave to be married over a free woman. Whoever marries a slave woman over a free woman must be separated from the slave woman. Similar has reached us on the authority of Zayd b. 'Ali—his ancestors—'Ali that a man married a slave woman over a free woman and 'Ali separated them. He then said: "It is impermissible for you to marry a slave woman over a free woman."[19]

Whoever fornicates with a woman and then both of them repent to Allah sincerely, there is no problem for them to marry because their state after repentance is contrary to their state during the time of their disobedience. Allah only prohibits marriage between them in the state of disobedience and sin. Thus, they are free to marry in the state of obedience and belief.

My father related to me that his father was asked about the permissibility of a man marrying a woman he fornicated with. He replied:

> If he and she repent and return to the alliance (*al-wilāya*) with Allah, there is no problem for them to marry. This would be permissible even if they were idolaters, so how much so would it be for two people of the same religion? Ibn 'Abbās and others used to say "Fornication at first and marriage at the end."[20]

And he used to say: "Allah accepts them when they part but does not accept them when they join. This is an objection to the one who objects to such."

Concerning sexual impotence (*al-iynayn*) and concerning two *dhimmis* when one of them embraces Islam and concerning a man who owns two sisters as slaves as well as the withdrawal from a free woman

There is no problem withdrawing from a free woman when the husband withdraws out of fear of compressing her while suckling or feeding in utero (*al-ghīla*) or harming her. There should not be any harm to one's wife regarding that; that is out of his consideration.

---

[18] Two judgements have been narrated from al-Hādi. The first is what appears here in the ***Ahkām*** and that is there is no dowry for the woman with whom a marriage is contracted and her husband dies without having intercourse with her. The second judgement, which appears in ***Al-Muntakhab***, says that she is to get a dowry. Imam Abu Ťālib related these two opinions of al-Hādi in his ***At-Tahrīr***, as well as Ibn Murtaḍa in ***Al-Bahr*** and al-Mu'ayyad Billah in ***Sharh at-Tajrīd***. We resolve these two different statements by saying that the statement in the ***Ahkām*** is more correct and most likely the position of al-Hādi because of the following reasons. One, he later quotes the same judgement from his grandfather, Imam al-Qāsim from whom he took his own judgements. Two, it is narrated in the ***Musnad Imam Zayd*** that 'Ali said regarding the woman in the same situation: "She would get the inheritance and observe the waiting period. But there is no dowry for her." Three, in every instance that the dowry is mentioned in the ***Ahkām***, intercourse is mentioned in connection to it. That withstanding, the absence of one would necessitate the absence of the other. Four, al-Hādi's judgement in ***Al-Muntakhab*** does not explicitly state that the man refrained from intercourse with the woman before he died; rather, it simply says that he died without stipulating the dowry. It would therefore follow that his judgement in the ***Ahkām*** refers to a man who dies without consummating the marriage and stipulating the dowry; whereas, the judgement in ***Al-Muntakhab*** applies to a man who had intercourse but had not stipulated the dowry. [Ref. ***Al-Qawl al-Awwal***]

[19] Similarly narrated in ***Musnad Imam Zayd, Mušannaf Ibn Abi Shayba, Sunan al-Bayhaqi***

[20] Similarly narrated in ***Mušannaf Ibn Abi Shayba, Sunan al-Bayhaqi***

Any wife that is afflicted by impotence should be patient with what is afflicting her. We do not hold to the view that he is obligated to separate from her. Similar has reached us from the Commander of Believers, 'Ali b. Abi Ťālib, upon him be peace.[21]

It is impermissible for the Muslim male to be married to two free or slave sisters simultaneously. It is impermissible to sleep with one and sleep with the other insomuch that if he sends one away, it would be impermissible for him to bring the other one near even if he manumitted her or gifted her to another Muslim.

We do not hold to the view that he can gift her to his slave, neither can he marry her to him. He cannot give her in marriage to any other man because, in the situation where he gives her to his slave as his property, his slave and his slave's possesions would belong to the master. And we said that it would be impermissible to marry her to him because if the husband were to die, intercourse with her would be permissible for her owner. For that reason, we said that if she is relinquished from him, she would be more entitled to herself than he or someone else would be more entitled to her than he or she. For example, in the case of manumitting, selling or gifting her away to another Muslim, it would be permissible for him to sleep with the other one.

Regarding the two *dhimmis* who are married and then the man embraces Islam while the woman declines from entering Islam, to her belongs the dowry that made intercourse with her licit even if he had not entered Islam prior. However, we do not hold to the view that she is permitted for him. Later, we will mention the proof for the prohibition of marriage between Muslims and *dhimmis*, if Allah wills.

Similarly, if she were to embrace Islam and he did not, she would have the complete dowry and would have to undergo the waiting period from the time of his last ejaculation [during intercourse]. Then, if he were to embrace Islam after her waiting period, he would be more entitled to remarry her due to the first marriage.

Regarding two *dhimmis* in which the man has not had intercourse with the woman and then embraces Islam while she declines from becoming Muslim, she gets half of the dowry. Others say that there is no dowry for her; however, that is not the case according to us because she is established in a religion and it is impermissible to deprive her due to her departing from him.[22]

My father related to me that his father said regarding a Jew, Christian or Magian who marries a woman and then embraces Islam while she refuses to embrace Islam after having not had intercourse with her: "She gets some of the dowry just as any other." It is narrated that al-Hasan al-Bašri[§] said that she does not get any of the dowry. Others say that she gets half the dowry. Her judgement is similar to that of the other Muslims according to me.

My father related to me that his father was asked if one could marry two slave sisters simultaneously. He replied:

> One is to not marry two slave sisters simultaneously. That is the position of the Commander of Believers, 'Ali b. Abi Ťālib regarding it, upon him be peace.[23] The two female slaves are similar to two free women in that regard.

My father related to me that his father said regarding withdrawing from a slave woman and free woman: "There is no problem withdrawing from a slave woman, and there is no problem withdrawing from a free woman unless there is an objection from her."

---

[21] Similarly narrated in ***Sharh at-Tajrīd***

[22] That is to say that because even though the couple had not had intercourse, the marriage was not intentionally or unintentionally annulled on the part of the wife. Therefore, she is to get half the dowry. However, in cases where the wife mistakenly or wilfully engaged in an unlawful marriage and the couple had not had intercourse, she would not get any of the dowry. [Ref. ***At-Tāj***]

[23] Similarly narrated in ***Musnad Imam Zayd, Mušannaf Ibn Abi Shayba, Sunan al-Bayhaqi***

Concerning stipulation in marriage and a man who marries a man's widow and daughter

There is no problem for a man to join between a woman and a daughter in marriage; 'Abdullah b. Ja'far§ did that. He married a daughter of 'Ali and one of his widows. There is also no problem for one to marry the two daughters of two paternal uncles, the two daughters of two paternal aunts, the two daughters of two maternal uncles or the two daughters of two maternal aunts. Allah's Messenger, peace and blessings be upon him and his progeny, did that when he married the daughter of his paternal aunt, Umm Salama and the daughter of his paternal aunt, Zaynab bt. Jahsh.§

Any added stipulation in marriage is invalid unless the stipulation is permitted by Allah as a stipulation. This is the case even if a man marries a woman with a stipulation that he would not marry her. Nor does he remove her from her parents. That is not permitted for him to do in the judgement of Islam.

If a man marries a woman from another man and makes a stipulation for himself, that stipulation can be included in the dowry if the woman is contented for that to be so. If she is not contented to accept it from his possession, it will be owed to her in her dowry unless the husband prefers to give it as a gift. Then, it would not be owed to the wife. If he were to do that, it would be better between the Muslims and goodwill from the character of the believers. It would not be a judgement against him, nor will he be undone by leaving anything from his marriage.

My father related to me that his father was asked about a man who married a woman and a daughter of her husband, as well as two daughters of two paternal uncles and two daughters of two maternal uncles. He replied:

> 'Abdullah b. Ja'far married a daughter of 'Ali and a wife of 'Ali, upon him be peace. There was no problem with that because she was not her mother. As for the two daughters of two paternal uncles and two maternal uncles, Allah—the Blessed and Exalted—says: **{We hath made permissible unto thee…the daughters of thy paternal uncles and the daughters of thy paternal aunts, and the daughters of thy maternal uncles who emigrated with thee…} (Q. 33:50)**. And Allah's Messenger, peace and blessings be upon him and his progeny, was married to both Umm Salama, whose mother was a daughter of his paternal uncle, 'Abdul-Muṭṭalib, as well as Zaynab bt. Jahsh, whose mother was a daughter of his paternal uncle, 'Abdul-Muṭṭalib.

My father related to me that his father was asked about a man who married a woman and she stipulated that he would not take her from her town, village or house. He replied: "It is impermissible to stipulate these conditions in the marriage contract because these conditions are contrary to determined count and are not time-restricted."

My father related to me that his father said regarding a man who gave his daughter, sister or female relatives in marriage and stipulated on himself something that is not in her dowry: "He must observe what is in the marriage contract, and his stipulation is to be included in her dowry. That would be permissible for him as long as the woman is content with it."

My father related to me that his father was asked about a man who marries a woman and stipulated on her that he does not have to provide for her or that he can provide for her whatever he likes and that he can share whatever he wants with her day and night. He replied: "This is also an impossible condition. I do not prefer that anything be in a marriage except a stipulation that is known and determined."

Concerning the one who has four wives and divorces one of them and the time that it is permissible for him to remarry and concerning what is permissible for a man to do with his wife while she is menstruating

When a man has four wives and divorces one of them with a divorce in which it is possible for remarriage, he is not permitted to marry anyone else until she completes her waiting period which Allah appointed for her. If he divorces her with an irrevocable divorce in which she would be impermissible for him except after remarriage, it would be no problem for him to marry when he wants—even if it is during her waiting period.

It has been narrated from the Commander of Believers, ‘Ali b. Abi Ťālib that he said: “One does not join his semen in five.”[24] According to us, this is not authentically attributed to him because he simply discouraged that one remarries while he has a divorcee that he could remarry; then, he would be married to five. As for the one who does not have a divorcee that he could remarry, there is no problem with that [i.e. marrying another woman]. As for seminal fluid, there is no issue if it was in five or six woman as long as he is not married to (or has the ability to return to) more than four.

Everything except what is under the wife's sarong is permissible for a man during her menstruation. He should not approach her privates nor should he go near to the impurities that would soil him. As for that which is below or above her privates, there is no problem to approach anything but them. This has been narrated from Allah's Messenger, peace and blessings be upon him and his progeny.[25] It is said that he used to do that, and he is for us the best example. But if one were to avoid that out of fear and precaution for oneself, all of such would be good. The Muslims may not be able to control themselves just as Allah's Messenger, peace and blessings be upon him and his progeny, was able to.

My father related to me that his father was asked whether it was permissible for a man who had four wives and divorced one of them three times to marry a fifth before the divorcee completes her waiting period. He replied:

> If it was an irrevocable divorce or she died, there is no problem for him to marry the fifth when he wants. If the divorcee was in her waiting period for a divorce in which it is possible for remarriage, he cannot marry a fifth until the divorcee completes her waiting period. Similar is the case with a sister who is in her waiting period for a divorce in which it is possible for remarriage; he cannot marry her sister until her waiting period is over. However, if he divorces her with an irrevocable divorce, there is no problem for him to marry her sister.

My father related to me that his father was asked what was permissible for a man to do with his wife while she is menstruating. He replied:

> It is preferable that he not go near her or approach her. He should not have intercourse with her in clothing or under a blanket. This is based on the statement of Allah, the Mighty and Majestic: **{...and approach them not until they hath purified themselves} (Q. 2:222)**. It is from approaching the wives that we take precaution from these things even if it was only fondling. Traditions have been narrated in which the Prophet, peace and blessings be upon him and his progeny, used to engage with his wives except what was under the sarong when they were menstruating.[26] The Prophet, peace and blessings be upon him and his progeny, had more control, so precaution is preferable to us.

Concerning the wife of a missing person and concerning the meaning of the Glorified's statement {The male fornicator marries not save the female fornicator} as well as a man who marries the daughter of a woman and her mother without having had intercourse with either

The wife of a missing person is to never be remarried until she comes to know of his situation and is certain of his death. If she were to make an error and remarry under the assumption that he died and the news of his death turned out to be false and then he returned to her, the first husband would be more entitled to her than the last. However, the first husband would not be able to approach her until

---

[24] Similarly narrated in ***Ušūl al-Kāfi***

[25] Similarly narrated in ***Musnad Imam Zayd, Ŝahīh al-Bukhāri, Ŝahīh Muslim, Sunan Ibn Mājah, Musnad Ahmed, Sunan Abu Dāwūd, Sunan ad-Dārqutni***

[26] Similarly narrated in ***Sharh at-Tajrīd, Ŝahīh al-Bukhāri, Ŝahīh Muslim, Sunan at-Tirmidhi, Sunan an-Nisā`i, Sunan Ibn Māja***

she is free from the semen of the last [i.e. have completed the waiting period]. She would have the complete dowry from the last husband, which made intercourse with her lawful.

If she is pregnant from the last husband, the first husband cannot approach her until she delivers what is in her womb and is purified from her postpartum bleeding. Her child would be attributed to the last husband because the marriage was based on doubt. If she does not give birth until the first husband divorces her, then she is to wait until she delivers what is in her womb from the marriage in which there was doubt between her and the last husband. After she delivers and is purified from her postpartum bleeding, she is to count from the three menstrual cycles of the first marriage. If the first husband wants to return to her during this waiting period, he is more entitled to her. If he prefers to leave her until she completes this waiting period, it would be permissible for her to remarry whomever she wants of the two or anyone else.

As for the meaning of Allah's statement **{The male fornicator marries not save the female fornicator or idolatress. The female fornicator marries not save the male fornicator or idolater. And that is forbidden for the believers}** **(Q. 25:3)**, He conveys that one does not commit an indecency of fornication nor does the fornicator voluntarily approaches the private parts of women except the female fornicator from the religion or an idolatress who engages in fornication with idolaters. Similar is His statement regarding the female fornicator; no one has intercourse with her nor commits an indecency with her nor permits approaching that which Allah prohibited unless he is a fornicator from the same religion or an idolater that permitted himself to do so.

It is impermissible for a man to marry the mother of his wife with whom he contracted a marriage—whether he had intercourse with the latter or not. This is because she is prohibited, obscure and generally forbidden. That is based on the statement of Allah: **{Forbidden unto thee art…the mothers of thy wives}** **(Q. 4:23)**. It does not say "…if you do not have intercourse with them" or "…if you have not had intercourse with them." We have obfuscated what He has obfuscated and prohibited what He prohibited.

As for the daughter of the wife with whom he has had intercourse, it is impermissible to marry her because she is a stepdaughter who is under his charge since he had intercourse with and approached her [i.e. the mother]. Therefore, if he has not had intercourse with her, there is no problem to marry her daughter even if he had previously contracted a marriage with the mother as long as he had not had intercourse with or approached her [i.e. the mother]. That is based on the statement of Allah, the Mighty and Majestic: **{Forbidden unto thee art…thy stepdaughters in thy protection born of thy wives whom ye have entered upon. However, if thou hast not entered upon them, there is no sin upon thee [to marry the stepdaughters]}** **(Q. 4:23)**. He does not make it a sin to marry her as long as he has not had intercourse with her mother.

My father related to me that his father said regarding the wife of a missing person and what one does:

> It is not for the wife of a missing person to ever be remarried until she is certain that he is dead. If she remarries and he returns to her, the first husband is more entitled to her and she is to be considered freed from the last husband. That is the statement of the Commander of Believers, 'Ali b. Abi Ťālib, upon him be peace.[27]

My father related to me that his father said regarding the statement of Allah—the Blessed and Exalted **{The male fornicator marries not save the female fornicator or idolatress}** **(Q. 24:3)**:

> The word **{marries}** here refers to intercourse, and it can be contract and marriage. As for His statement **{save the fornicator and idolater}**, it is that one does not earn the wrath of Allah except the idolater or fornicator.

---

[27] Sheikh 'Ali b. Bilāl reported that Sayyid Abul-Abbās related with his chain of narrators to Shurayh b. Hāni that when he asked 'Ali about the action regarding a missing husband, he replied: "She is still his wife until he is judged as dead." Similar is narrated in ***Musnad Imam Zayd*** and ***Sunan al-Bayhaqi***

My father related to me that his father was asked about a man who married a woman and divorced her. "Is it permissible for him to marry her daughter or mother?" He replied:

> As for the mother, it is impermissible for him to marry her in any case because she is among the mothers of his wives and Allah says: **{Forbidden unto thee art…the mothers of thy wives} (Q. 4:23)**. As for the daughter, it is permissible for him to marry her if he had not had intercourse with the mother. This is based on the statement of Allah, the Mighty and Majestic: **{Forbidden unto thee art…thy stepdaughters in thy protection born of thy wives whom ye have entered upon. However, if thou hast not entered upon them, there is no sin upon thee [to marry the stepdaughters]} (Q. 4:23)**. He does not make it a sin to marry her as long as he has not had intercourse with her mother.

My father related to me that his father said regarding a man who married a woman and had intercourse with her before he gave her anything: "It's no problem as long as she is contented and the dowry has been determined." It is only valid to us when the dowry has been determined, and he and she know it. This is the case as long as she is contented with it and considered it before taking it. That is because if she was given all of it after it had been determined and she knew and accepted it, it would be a valid for him to give it to her. Whatever is valid for him to give to her, its consideration is even more permissible.

Concerning a prohibition not prohibiting a permission and whether it is permissible for a man to look at a woman he intends to marry and concerning when it is permissible for the divorced woman who has not had intercourse to remarry

The Progeny of Allah's Messenger, peace and blessings be upon him and his progeny, collectively agree that a prohibition does not prohibit a permission.[28] The explanation of that is the following: If a man fornicated with a woman and then intended to marry her mother, it would be permissible according to us. Similarly, if he fornicated with the mother, it is permitted for him to marry the daughter according to our position.

If a man intends to marry a woman, there is no problem to look at her with a glance permissible for Muslim males in regard to Muslim women when they intend what they intend. Regarding that, one does not look at any part of her nakedness; rather, he looks at her face.[29]

If a man divorces a woman before having intercourse with her, there is no waiting period for her and she can remarry in her own time. Similarly, if she married a second husband and he divorced her before having intercourse with her, she can return to the first husband in her time. This is because Allah—the Mighty and Majestic—says: **{O ye who believe, when ye wed believing women and then divorce them before having touched them, there is no waiting period on them for thee} (Q. 33:49)**.

My father related to me that his father was asked about a man who fornicated with the mother of his wife or her daughter. He replied: "A prohibition does not prohibit a permission; this is the statement of the people of tradition except Abu Hanīfa and others as well as a group of Iraqis who discourage it."

My father related to me that his father was asked about a man who intends to marry a woman and whether it is permissible to look at her once before that. He replied:

---

[28] This is narrated as an explicit statement of 'Ali by Sayyid Abul-Abbās al-Hasani with a complete chain of narrators.

[29] Regarding this lawful glance, it says in the ***At-Tāj al-Mudhhab***:

> Know that is not only permissible but encouraged for a man to look at the face and hands of a woman he intends to propose a marriage with. If he is able to accurate access her appearance in one glance, it is impermissible for him to repeat such. It would be permissible for him to do such as long as it does not incite the passions. If it incites the passions, it is impermissible for him to look at her. If he is unable to look at her, it would be permissible for him to send a woman to look at her on his behalf and describe her to him, even if she describes her body. The time of the look should be after the intention and before the proposal of marriage because if he were to decide to not marry her after the proposal, it would be difficult on her.

There is no problem with one look as long as he does not look at her nakedness and as long as the look is not prohibited for Muslims to see of her based on Allah's prohibition of those outside of their families or parents in the verse [i.e. **Q. 24:31**]. The Prophet, peace and blessings be upon him and his progeny, was asked about that and gave a dispensation.[30]

My father related to me that his father was asked about a man who divorced his wife once or twice and then she remarried. Then the second husband divorced her before having intercourse with her. "Would it be permissible for the first husband to remarry her?" He replied:

> There is no waiting period for her, and she can return to the first husband in her time if she wants. This is based upon the statement of Allah: **{O ye who believe, when ye wed believing women and then divorce them before having touched them, there is no waiting period on them for thee}** (**Q. 33:49**). The exception is if the first husband divorced her three times. Then, it would not be permissible for him to according to all people except after intercourse with the husband.
>
> Regarding that, there is a hadith of the wife of Rifā'i al-Quraḍi.§ He divorced her three times and when she wanted to return to Rifā'i, the Prophet, peace and blessings be upon him and his progeny, said: ((Not until her honey has been tasted)).[31] Allah's Messenger, peace and blessings be upon him and his progeny, prohibited her from that until the second husband had intercourse with her.

Concerning the exegesis of Allah's statement {or those without desire amongst men} and concerning the woman who marries during her waiting period and the explanation of suitability

The meaning of Allah's statement **{…or those without desire (*al-irba*) amongst men…}** **(Q. 24:31)** is 'those without a need.' It is from this that the Arabs say "I do not have a desire for such-and-such." The word **{desire}** is a derivative of the word for desirous. The ones who are **{those without desire amongst men}** are those who have no need to have intercourse with women nor do they have the means to fulfil their need with them. The one **{without desire}** could refer to one without intellect and one who is simple-minded and oblivious [i.e. mentally challenged].

It is impermissible for a woman to marry during her waiting period. Any woman who marries during her waiting period has automatically invalidated her marriage contract, and the magistrate can separate her and the man. The best thing to do in that situation is to educate him and her if he and she claimed ignorance of such and had little knowledge regarding what is permissible and prohibited in that. If he had intercourse with her, she keeps the dowry that made intercourse licit, but the marriage between him and her would be considered invalidated.

If she has a child greater than the six months from the day that the last husband had intercourse with her, the child belongs to the last husband and is attributed to him. But if she has a child less than the six months from the day that the last husband had intercourse with her, the child belongs to the first husband. It is counted from after the emission of semen of the last husband over the waiting period of the first husband that dissolved the marriage. When she completes her waiting period, she can marry whom she wants. If she wants to marry the other husband in a new marriage, her marriage would be considered valid.

Suitability refers to suitability in religion and rank only. Guardians are those who look into their affairs and seek what is best for their female relatives. If they force anyone, their force is not binding.

My father related to me that his father was asked about Allah's statement **{…or those without desire**

---

[30] Similarly narrated in ***Sharh at-Tajrīd, Sunan Abu Dāwūd, Musnad Ahmed, Mušannaf Ibn Abi Shayba***

[31] Similarly narrated in ***Ŝahīh al-Bukhāri, Ŝahīh Muslim, Sunan at-Tirmidhi, Sunan an-Nisā'i, Mušannaf Ibn Abi Shayba, Sunan al-Bayhaqi***. It is narrated in ***Bihār al-Anwār*** as the statement of Muhammad al-Bāqir.

(*al-irba*) **amongst men…}** **(Q. 24:31)**. He replied:

> The phrase **{those without desire}** are those people of doubt and those who do not have desire. They are also those in whom there is no certainty and those simple-minded men who do not have any intelligence in respect to women.

My father related to me that his father said regarding a woman who marries during her waiting period: "There is no contract for her and both she and the one that she married must be separated" My father also related to me that his father was asked about suitability and he replied: "Suitability refers to lineage and religion together."

Concerning the one who fornicates with a virgin and the meaning of the statement of Allah's Messenger ((A man does not propose against the proposal of his brother or bargain against the bargain of his brother))

Whoever fornicates with a virgin forcing himself on her—he is to pay her indemnity (*al-uqr*)[32] and the prescribed punishment is applied to him similarly. However, the prescribed punishment is not applied to her. If she was complicit in her fornication with him, there is no indemnity for her and the prescribed punishment is applied to them both.

As for the statement of Allah's Messenger, peace and blessings be upon him and his progeny, ((A man does not propose against the proposal of his brother…)),[33] it means that if a man is satisfied with a woman and she is satisfied with him and the said dowry was agreed upon, it is impermissible for another to entice her away from his brother with a larger dowry or veto him.

Similarly, one should not do that in the case of bargaining. It is when the owner of a commodity and buyer have agreed at something and are contented with its transaction. And then someone enters upon the bargaining after the owner of the commodity and buyer have already agreed and are contented and entices the seller by offering more than his brother insomuch that he turns to him and abandons what transpired with his brother, who was the original buyer.

My father related to me that his father was asked about a man who fornicated with a virgin and whether there is indemnity with the prescribed punishment. He replied:

> There is no indemnity paid to her unless he overcame her against her wishes. As for the mutually consensual fornication between them, the prescribed punishment is applied to the virgin and the prescribed punishment is applied to the male violator.

We only obligate the indemnity as a punishment for the infraction and as restitution for the woman because her virginity is that which most men desire from women. As for that which would be obligatory in another concept, it would not be obligatory because one does not join the dowry that is taken from a man with the prescribed punishment that is mandatory for what he did. Everything that necessitates the dowry by the command of Allah and the Sunnah of Allah's Messenger does not similarly necessitate the prescribed punishment. Everything that necessitates the prescribed punishment by Allah's command cannot have the dowry with it unless it is the aforementioned case of good in the sight of the scholars and that which differentiates two matters.

My father related to me that his father was asked about the meaning of the statement of Allah's Messenger, peace and blessings be upon him and his progeny: ((A man does not propose against the proposal of his brother or bargain against the bargain of his brother)). He replied:

> That is in the case of mutual contentment and satisfaction as well as discussion between them regarding the dowry. If there was a proposal here and another proposal there, there is

---

[32] It is understood by the context that the amount of the indemnity would be commensurate to the dowry. Also, in ***Al-Muntakhab***, when al-Hādi was asked about this indemnity, he replied that it would be the same as the dowry price.

[33] Similarly narrated in ***Sharh at-Tajrīd, Ŝahīh al-Bukhāri, Ŝahīh Muslim, Sunan Abu Dāwūd, Sunan Ibn Mājah, Sunan an-Nisā`i, Sunan al-Bayhaqi, Al-Mu'jam al-Kabīr***

no problem. Similar is the case with bargaining. There was a purchase of one who offered more money during the time of the Messenger, peace and blessings be upon him and his progeny. One man bargained against the bargain of his brother.

Concerning beating the hand drum (*ad-duff*) during a wedding

We do not encourage any type of musical entertainment (*al-lahw*) nor do we hold to its validity or choose such, whether it be a hand drum or any other musical instrument.[34] As for the hadith narrated in which Allah's Messenger, peace and blessings be upon him and his progeny, heard drums in some of the homes of the Anŝār and asked ((What is this?)) and it was said to him "So-n-so got married, O Messenger of Allah," to which he replied: ((Praise be to Allah! Celebrate the marriage! Celebrate the marriage!))—the intended meaning of ((Celebrate the marriage)) is simply that it should be mentioned and happily commemorated by initiating a festive gathering (*al-walīma*) and serving food. In that should be a joyous occasion for all people due to the marriage, and it is obligatory on the *Ummah* of Muhammad, peace and blessings be upon him and his progeny.

As for the matter of musical entertainment and instruments, it is impermissible to attribute that to him or claim that he supported such by his statement. My father related to me that his father was asked about beating the hand drum and musical entertainment at marriage celebrations. He replied: "Every form of musical entertainment and play is not that with which Allah is satisfied for His people nor is it allowed for them to engage in such."

Concerning a man who marries a woman on the judgement of one without intellect as well as a man who gives away his relative in marriage below the dowry of one like her

Anyone who marries or gives away in marriage on the judgement of one without intellect, there is no judgement for such person. The woman gets a dowry of one similar to herself, including her sisters, relatives, aunts and female servants.[35]

Whoever gives a female relative in marriage with less than the dowry of one similar to herself and she objects to it to her guardian and is dissatisfied with the one who contracted the marriage, she is to be given a dowry of one similar to herself. It is impermissible for her guardian to impose it on her unless the one who gave her in marriage is her father and she is a pre-pubescent girl. It would be permissible for him to impose it one her if she is a pre-pubescent girl.

Concerning a man who makes the manumission of his slavewoman her dowry and the statement regarding the waiving of a girl

If a man decided to manumit his female slave and make her manumission her dowry and she agrees to that, her agreement should be witnessed by witnesses. Then, they should be informed of that to which she and he agreed. When they hear his and her statement "I bear witness that I have made her manumission her dowry," she is considered free for the sake of Allah.

---

[34] It is understood by this statement of al-Hādi that he held to the impermissibility of hand drums and other instruments. Imam Ibn al-Murtaḍa narrated in his ***Al-Bahr*** that two different opinions from al-Hādi exist regarding playing the hand drum one, it is absolutely prohibited and two, it is discouraged. However, no narration exists to support the view that al-Hādi held to hand drums being discouraged. Perhaps Imam Ibn al-Murtaḍa interpreted the wording from the ***Ahkām*** to imply a 'discouraged' judgement. However, the wording in this entire section makes it clear to the reader that al-Hādi held to its impermissibility.

[35] A similar question was posed to al-Hādi in ***Al-Muntakhab***.

> I asked him about a sick man who married a sick woman for a thousand dirham, and the dowry of one similar to herself is one hundred dirhams. Then, she was irrevocably divorced and the man died without having anything other than one thousand dirhams. He replied: "We say in this regard that if it is a sickness in which the person maintains the intellect and not suffer from confusion, the marriage would be valid. If he marries for one thousand dirhams and his intellect is shown to be sound and there are witnesses, he would be obligated to give her the determined dowry. The witnesses would have to have heard such. One would not acknowledge the dowry of one similar to herself except in the case that the man does not know what amount to marry her for. In such case, he refers to the dowry of one similar to herself."

Similar was done by Allah's Messenger, peace and blessings be upon him and his progeny, with Ŝafiya,§ the daughter of Hayy b. Akhtab. He made her manumission her dowry and manumitted her.[36]

He should say "I make your manumission your dowry" before he says "I manumit you." This is because if he said "I make your manumission your dowry and you are free based on that," she would be bound by that which was established. However, if he were to say "I manumit you and I make your manumission your dowry," then he would have given her the choice. If she wanted, she could say "I do not agree [to marry]" because he began by manumitting her. When he said "I manumit you," she was then manumitted and she became the master of her own affair. His later statement "…and I make your manumission your dowry" is considered null and void, and she is free to either accept him or reject him.

If a girl's father waives her dowry from her husband and then she gets older and seeks her dowry from her husband, he is to pay it to her based on what he owes her. This is because the father permitted the waiving, but the girl had not permitted it. It was only her father who permitted it; however, the matter of her dowry does not belong to the father. Similar has reached us from the Commander of the Believers, 'Ali b. Abi Ťālib that he carried out such judgement.

If a slave boy of fifteen years gets married or is given in marriage, it is obligatory upon the one who gave him in marriage to pay the determined dowry.

If a man contracts a marriage with a woman upon the divorce of another woman and says "I contract a marriage with you upon the divorce of so-n-so" and her guardian permits that, the marriage will be considered valid and her dowry will be like the other. The first woman would be divorced from him. He should intend to divorce her and his wording [of such divorce] must be directed to his wife. This is because when he says "I divorce so-n-so" and he intended to divorce her when he married the other, his statement would be considered a divorce unless he did not intend to divorce her and did not observe by that wording the stipulations of divorce. If that were the case, there will not be a divorce for her nor a separation from her.

If he said "I contract a marriage with you upon me divorcing so-n-so" and she is satisfied and they marry, she would get her dowry. It is with the choice of divorcing the first wife; he can divorce if he wants or he can retain if he wants.

Concerning a woman who gifts her dowry to her husband as compensation

If a man contracts a marriage with a woman for a slave [as her dowry] which she takes from and gifts to him and then he divorces her before having had intercourse with her—the judgement regarding that would take into consideration the slave as her gift. If the gift to him was in the way of maintaining family ties in the case that they are related or if the gift was in the way of Allah or if the person did so seeking only reward from Allah, this will be considered an irrevocable gift for which one cannot take back.

The slave will belong to the husband and if he likes, he can return half of the slave's value to her. This is because the slave was her dowry yet she gifted the slave to him willingly in order to incline to his heart, curry his favour and seek his goodness. That withstanding, nothing is obligated to be taken.

It is her choice regarding her gift if she did not seek Allah's Countenance in doing so; if she wants, she can return it and if she wants, she can keep it. If she returned it, this would be similar to the one who

[36] Similarly narrated in ***Musnad Imam Zayd, Amāli Ahmed b. 'Isa, Sharh at-Tajrīd, Ŝahīh al-Bukhāri, Ŝahīh Muslim, Sunan an-Nisā'i, Sunan Ibn Mājah, Sunan at-Tirmidhi, Sunan Abu Dāwūd, Musnad Ahmed, Mušannaf Ibn Abi Shayba, Sunan ad-Dārimi, Ŝahīh Ibn Hibbān, Al-Mu'jam al-Kabīr, Al-Mu'jam al-Awsat, Sunan ad-Dārqutni, Sunan al-Bayhaqi, Bihār al-Anwār***

gifted a gift seeking compensation by such. That compensation for which one gifted would be prohibited to demand. It would therefore be for him to return his gift since it was prohibited for him to demand its compensation. If she gifted it to her husband seeking his goodness and to curry favour with him, the husband does not return any portion of the dowry to her. The slave—if she demands him/her from him—is returned to her and he will give to her half the slave's value; she would get half in the judgement of Allah.

Therefore, if he were to marry her for two hundred dirhams and she takes it from him and then gifts it to him but he divorces her before having had intercourse with her—whether the two hundred dirham is spent or not—all of such has the same ruling. Regarding the ruling, he would have to return one hundred dirhams to her even if she gifted her dowry to him seeking by such Allah's Countenance or seeking to maintain family ties. This is because she took the entire dowry from him and he separated from her before having intercourse with her. It would therefore only be permissible for her to keep half the dowry just as Allah has stipulated for her. The exception is if her husband pardons the remaining half; however, if he does not pardon it, it belongs to him. Her gift to her husband, which she takes back from him—whether it was used or not—will be like a gift to another. She would be obligated to return half of the dowry she took if the gift was given seeking Allah's Countenance and reward. If the gift was given to him seeking his goodness or to curry favour with him, she has the choice; she could return it to him and then take half the dowry from him.

If a man compels his daughter or son to marry and the two of them are pubescent, this would be permissible for the father to do. If the father increases the dowry of his son's fiancée and makes it more than her determined dowry and makes the dowry of his daughter lower than the dowry of similar to her, this would not be permissible for him to do. It would be permissible to give in marriage if the son gives the fiancée a dowry of one similar to herself or gives the daughter a dowry of one similar to herself. If the son's fiancée refuses to accept less than what was stipulated for her by her fiancé's father, his son has the choice: if he wants, he can permit all of what his father did or if he wants, he can nullify all of that. That withstanding, the marriage would be considered invalid.

Concerning one who marries a wife for something in particular and then it is destroyed before the marriage commences

If a man marries a woman for a slave or female slave and then they die, she gets the value of both on the day they died. If there was a delay in her acquiring them on her part and there was some type of confusion on his part, she would get the value of both on the day of the marriage.

If a man were to marry a woman for a date palm or house or land and then she demands it after that—according to us—she gets the value of the demand on the day of the marriage.

Concerning the girl who is given in marriage by her brother or uncle while she is pre-pubescent but then reaches puberty and chooses for herself

If she came to know that she had a choice in that but had not chosen until he had intercourse with her, she does not have the choice. If she had not known and then came to know that she had a choice, she could remain married if she wants or she could divorce herself from him if she wants. If he had intercourse with her while she was pre-pubescent, she has a choice when she reaches fifteen years old or menstruates before reaching fifteen years old. If one of them died before the girl reaches the time of her choice, one inherits from the other.

If a man marries a woman while her intellect is removed, the marriage is considered valid as long as the husband is sufficient for her, she is content with that and there is no objection from any of the guardians. We permit that action because he did what was permissible to do and did not act unjustly with the contentment of the woman in that. Moreover, one of the guardians permitted it and their contentment in what he did in marrying her is sufficient for her.

Concerning the one who is not permitted to be a guardian even if the person is a non-marriageable relative

It is impermissible to marry a Muslim woman to a *dhimmi* nor can he be her guardian—even if he is her son, father or brother. Similarly, Muslims cannot be guardians of *dhimmis* even if they are their sons, fathers or brothers. Likewise, *dhimmis* who are non-marriageable relatives cannot be guardians for Muslim women during travel even if they are sons or fathers. Similar is the case with a milk brother, milk son or milk father regarding marriage. Neither can a slave who is freed at his master's death (*al-mudabbar*), an indentured labourer or slave be guardians in marriage, even if they are fathers and sons. However, a milk brother, milk father and milk son can be guardians for a non-marriageable female relative during travel. A first cousin cannot be a guardian in travel but can be a guardian in marriage.

If a man wrote to another saying "Marry my female relative so-n-so to so-n-so, the son of so-n-so, based on the dowry you choose" and he marries him to her for less than the dowry of one similar to herself and similar to that of a mutual loss and gain between people in buying and selling, that would be permissible for him. If he marries her for less than the determined dowry not based on that which is a common loss and gain between people, she would get a dowry of one similar to herself if she objected and had not permitted that. If the husband wants, he can keep her or if he wants, he can separate from her. If he separates from her, he is obligated to pay half of what was stipulated on him. If he marries her for more than the dowry of one similar to herself, the marriage is considered valid and the dowry is hers to keep.

If a man gifted his daughter to another or a woman gifted herself to a man and the guardians permit that, their permission of her action would be considered a marriage for her; she would get a dowry of one similar to herself as long as the fiancé accepts that. Similar is the case with the one who gifts his daughter to another. If the fiancé says "I accept her," he is obligated to give her a dowry of one similar to herself.[37]

The witness of a slave regarding marriage is valid as long as he is an upright Muslim. The witness of a father for his son regarding marriage and the witness of a son for his father are valid confirming by their witness of the woman regarding the dowry and other things as long as they are upright and reliable. It is impermissible for a defiantly disobedient person to serve as a witness for a marriage or anything else.

Concerning a man who marries a virgin or non-virgin and how long he stays with each as well as concerning a wife who gives her days to another wife

A man spends seven days and nights with a virgin when he has intercourse with her. He spends three days with a non-virgin. Similar has reached us from Allah's Messenger, peace and blessings be upon him and his progeny. He said: ((Three for the non-virgin, and seven for the virgin)).[38]

---

[37] According to ***Al-Muntakhab***, when al-Hādi was asked whether a man could gift his daughter to another and whether a woman could gift herself, he replied with the following:

> As for gifting, it is impermissible because she is a free woman, and no one can gift a free person. However, if by gifting her to him he means that she gifts her dowry while she is pubescent and she is pleased with such, there would be no sin or problem if the man has intercourse with her based on such. But, it is preferable to me that he pay her at least the minimum dowry, which is ten dirhams.

Although, there seems to be a contradiction between the ***Ahkām*** and ***Al-Muntakhab***, this is easily reconciled by considering that a father who gifts his daughter to another does so with the understanding that she does not forgo the dowry. This is to distinguish the freewoman from the slave woman insomuch that if a man were to gift a slave woman to another, the latter is not obligated to give a dowry. His statement in ***Al-Muntakhab*** further emphasises what we said because a free woman cannot be gifted without the dowry.

[38] Similarly narrated in ***Musnad Imam Zayd, Sharh at-Tajrīd, Amāli Ahmed b. 'Isa, Ŝahīh al-Bukhāri, Ŝahīh Muslim, Sunan Abu Dāwūd, Sunan at-Tirmidhi, Musnad Abu Ya'la***

It has also reached us from him, peace and blessings be upon him and his progeny, that when he entered upon Umm Salama, he said: ((If you want, we can spend a week with you. If you want, I can circulate among you and them)). She then said: "No. Rather, circulate among us." He replied: ((If you want, I can spend a week with each of my wives, but I will not be able to spend a week with one of my wives)). Umm Salama then said: "I am only one of your wives; do what Allah wants you to, O Messenger of Allah."[39]

There is no problem with a wife giving her day to another of her husband's wives. Sawda bt. Zama'at b. 'Amr b. Lu'ay,[§] one of the Prophet's wives, would do that. She gave her day to A'isha because the former was an elderly woman.[40] At one point, Allah's Messenger, peace and blessings be upon him and his progeny, wanted to divorce her, but she said: "O Messenger of Allah, do not divorce me; I love to be included among your wives. I will give my day to A'isha." Allah's Messenger, peace and blessings be upon him and his progeny, accepted this from her.

Whenever a woman gives her day to one of the other wives of her husband and then takes it back, it is hers to do so. Similarly, if she gives her husband the choice to exchange whomever he wants and then takes it back, it would be obligatory for her husband to return to her or be generous to her with kindness.

Concerning a woman who owns her husband fully or partly

If a woman owns her husband fully or partly, it would be religiously prohibited for him and her. If she manumits him from her charge, they will have to recommence with a new marriage if they want to marry. This is because if she were in charge of her slave, she would be prohibited for him. She would nullify herself from his charge without there being a divorce. It is for that reason that we command them to renew the marriage.

Others say that when she manumits him from her charge, they will be considered married. We do not hold to that view nor do we act upon that. Rather, we invalidate that and are strict in that regard because if the marriage were valid after ownership and there was no nullification and such were permissible, it would permit a slave to marry his master in the first marriage and it would not be obligatory for the one that validates his marriage to separate from his wife.

Concerning the woman who is given in a suitable marriage by her guardian but her mother dislikes her marriage

If the woman is content as well as the guardian whom Allah appointed to contract the marriage and the husband is suitable, the marriage is valid even if the mother is dissatisfied with it. If the woman says "I am content with what my mother is content with," we do not consider the marriage to be valid unless the mother is content with it.

We encourage the mother to be consulted just as the pre-pubescent girl is consulted even though she does not have a say in the marriage. However, one should not avoid her consultation because she has a connection to her daughter. But, as long as the woman and the guardian are satisfied, the marriage is valid even if the mother is dissatisfied with it.

---

[39] Similarly narrated in ***Sharh at-Tajrīd, Ŝahīh Muslim, Sunan Abu Dāwūd, Sunan Ibn Mājah, Sunan an-Nisā`i, Sunan al-Bayhaqi, Musnad Ahmed, Sunan ad-Dārimi, Ŝahīh Ibn Hibbān, Mušannaf Ibn Abi Shayba, Al-Mustadrak***

[40] Similarly narrated in ***Sharh at-Tajrīd, Ŝahīh al-Bukhāri, Ŝahīh Muslim, Sunan Abu Dāwūd, Sunan Ibn Mājah, Mušannaf Ibn Abi Shayba, Sunan al-Bayhaqi, Majmu' az-Zawā`id, Al-Mu'jam al-Kabīr***

Concerning the man who marries a woman and stipulates that she financially maintains him and gives him her dowry as well as the woman who stipulates that she be given the right of intercourse and divorce

The stipulations of Allah take precedence over their stipulations. The right of divorce is his, the right of intercourse is his, the obligation of financial maintenance is his, the dowry is hers and she makes no such stipulation. If a man marries a woman and asks for her dowry and stipulates financial maintenance upon her and she does it, it would be considered a favour from her. If she does not go through with financially maintaining him then her financial maintenance would be obligatory on him: whether he keeps her or divorces her. Similarly, if he stipulates that she provide her own lodging, this cannot be carried out by him.

Concerning whether a woman can take responsibility for the marriage contract of another woman or not

It is impermissible for a woman to give another in marriage—whether the latter is related to her or a female slave. Rather, a Muslim man assumes responsibility of contracting the marriage.

Others say that a woman can give her female slave in marriage;[41] but we hold to the view that only a man can contract a marriage. This is because Allah, the Blessed and Exalted, has never commanded that anyone other than a man contract a marriage—whether the woman being married is free or a slave and [in the case of a slave] whether it is a male or female. If that were valid according the Glorified, He would have made it clear and mentioned it. This is because He has made known the status of the female slave compared to that of her master and her possessions in her slavery. He has not mentioned such command to her in His Book.

Concerning the one who marries with women as witnesses

If a man marries a woman with women as witnesses without a man among them, that marriage is invalid and void. The dowry that makes intercourse permissible will be hers [if they had already consummated the marriage]. They should firmly be taught proper protocol regarding this, and the husband must be instructed in this regard. The women who were witnesses without a man must also be instructed in this so that they cannot claim that they did not know what was obligatory on them in that. Similar is the case with the husband if he claimed ignorance in what he did so that he knows proper protocol, as well as the wife if she claimed ignorance. He may say: "I assumed that it was permissible." He and others must be taught proper protocol as well as that which is obligatory upon them regarding that.

Concerning the son's wife and the father's wife and concerning the woman who claims that a man married her while he objects to that and concerning a man who marries a woman and his son marries her daughter

When a man has a marriage contract with a woman, she is forever prohibited from his father—whether the former had intercourse with her or not. Similarly, when a father has a marriage contract with a woman, she is forever prohibited from his son—whether the former had intercourse with her or not. This is based on the statement of Allah, the Mighty and Majestic: **{And forbidden art the wives of the sons from thy issue} (Q. 4:23)** and **{And wed not among the women whom thy fathers wedded save whatsoever has previously transpired} (Q. 4:22)**.

If a woman claims that a man married her and he denies it, he is to swear an oath. If a man claims that a woman is his wife and the woman objects to such, he will be asked for proof and witnesses. Either he brings the witnesses or his claim is considered unsound. If he claims that they [i.e. the witnesses] had died, the woman is to swear an oath. We only ask the man for witnesses because it is necessary

[41] This opinion is said to be held by Abu Hanīfa and ash-Shāfi'i. [Ref. ***Al-Bahr***]

that the witnesses for the marriage be those who know the man's face and recognise him. The women do not bring witnesses, and her face cannot be ascertained by anyone. If she brings proof that involves identifying herself with her face[42] when she claims that he is her husband, then that which is binding on her is binding on him.

There is no problem with a father marrying the mother of his son's wife or the son marrying the daughter of his father's wife or the father's daughter or the son's mother.

If a man marries two Muslim women with one contract, has intercourse with them and then finds out that one of them is his milk sister or a non-marriageable relative, the marriage with the unrelated woman will be considered valid and the marriage with the relative will be considered nullified. The latter will keep her dowry that made intercourse lawful during the time of the confusion. Similar is the case with all women that are impermissible to marry.

Concerning a man and his son who marry two women and one of them mistakenly has intercourse with the other's wife

If a man and his son marries two women and each one mistakenly has intercourse with the other's wife, the ruling regarding that—according to me and all the scholars of the Messenger's Progeny—is each one of them is to return to her husband. This is the case whether they had intercourse or not because a prohibition does not invalidate a permission, and this was not done intentionally.

If this act of disobedience was done intentionally, each one of them would be charged with disobedience for sleeping with the other's wife and the prescribed punishment would be applied to them. Each woman would not be prohibited from her husband according to all the scholars of the Progeny of Allah's Messenger, peace and blessings be upon him and his progeny.

If it was done mistakenly and each of the women had intercourse with the other's husband, each wife keeps the dowry that made intercourse permissible and returns to her husband. He [i.e. the husband] does not have intercourse with her until she is free from the semen of the former. If they had not had intercourse, there is no dowry for her because he had not approached her private parts. Others prohibit them from their spouses due to disobedience and error; however, we do not see that as correct nor do we advocate for such.

If one were to divorce his spouse before having intercourse with her, she would get half of the determined dowry. It is impermissible for the father to marry the woman who his son had intercourse with because she was the wife of his son and Allah prohibited that by His statement: **{And forbidden art the wives of the sons from thy issue}** **(Q. 4:23)**. The same is the case whether the son had intercourse with her or not when he contracted a marriage with her and she is called his daughter-in-law.

Similarly, it is impermissible for the son to marry a woman with whom his father had intercourse after having divorced her because she would be his father's daughter-in-law. He had married her with the contractual marriage, and the contractual marriage in this case is like the marriage of one who had intercourse. As Allah says: **{And wed not among the women whom thy fathers wedded save whatsoever has previously transpired}** **(Q. 4:22)**.

When he contracted the marriage with her, he has married her. Regarding that, Allah, the One too majestic to be encompassed by words, says: **{O ye who believe, when ye wed believing women and then divorce them before having touched them, there is no waiting period on them for thee}** **(Q. 33:49)**.

---

[42] Imams al-Mu`ayyad Billah and Ibn Murtaḍa claimed in their works that Imam al-Hādi had two different opinions regarding the method in identifying the woman in her testimony. They said that the ***Ahkām*** delineates the face as the sole means of recognition while ***Al-Muntakhab*** includes the face, voce and other means. However, we do not see it as two contradictory statements. Rather, we say that the judgement in ***Al-Muntakhab*** applies in the case where one needs to ascertain certainty. Perhaps two women's faces may look alike; in that case, additional means can be used to identify her, such as the voice or other means, as stated in ***Al-Muntakhab***.

Then He says: **{...and ye hath appointed unto them a portion, then [render] half of whatsoever ye appointed...}** (Q. 2:237). Therefore, both of them are identified as married even if the one who married her had not touched her. They simply necessitate the name of contractual marriage because of the marriage contract with them and their contractual agreement with them only.

Concerning two men—one who contracts a marriage to a woman and the other who contracts a marriage with her daughter—and one is mistakenly given in marriage to the wife of the other

If two men contract a marriage—one with a woman and the other with her daughter—and one is mistakenly given in marriage to the other and each one has intercourse with the one to whom they were given, according to me and all of the scholars of the Progeny of Allah's Messenger, the judgement is that each one is to be returned to the rightful spouse. The woman with whom each had intercourse is to be given her dowry that made intercourse legal. The rightful husband is to not approach her until she is free from the semen of the one who mistakenly slept with her. A prohibition does not invalidate a permission. If one of them continued with intercourse with the other's wife even after knowledge, the prescribed punishment is to be applied to him. Similarly, if one of the women continued having intercourse with the other's husband after knowledge of the one with whom she had intercourse and she concealed it, the prescribed punishment is to be applied to her.

If each of them were to divorce his rightful spouse and intend to marry the wife to whom he was mistakenly given in marriage substituting the women he slept with for his rightful spouse, the one who was married to the mother and had not had intercourse with her before divorcing her would have the right to marry her daughter. She was the first wife of the other. This is because Allah, the Glorified, allows him to do such by His statement: **{Forbidden unto thee art...thy stepdaughters in thy protection born of thy wives whom ye have entered upon. However, if thou hast not entered upon them, there is no sin upon thee [to marry the stepdaughters]}** (Q. 4:23). Therefore, they are free to marry the daughters of their wives when their mothers are divorced before having intercourse with them.

As for the husband of the daughter whom he divorced before having intercourse her, it is impermissible for him to marry her mother to whom he was mistakenly given in marriage. This is because she is absolutely prohibited based on the statement of Allah: **{Forbidden unto thee art...the mothers of thy wives}** (Q. 4:23). Consequently, His statement **{the mothers of thy wives}** makes them prohibited absolutely—whether one has had intercourse with their daughters or not—when the marriage is contracted and their spouses have been determined by the contracting of the marriage.

Concerning the prohibition from marrying *dhimmis* as well as the explanation of that from the Book, Sunnah and intellect

My son, Abul-Qāsim, asked me about marrying them and I responded to him with an answer. I will write it here and it should be sufficient from any other explanation, if Allah wills. He asked me about marrying female *dhimmi*s and I said:

> You asked, O my son—May Allah guide you towards God-consciousness and make you among those who are guided and increase in guidance!—about an issue in which many people have gone astray and much confusion has occurred regarding it. The issue is marrying female *dhimmi*s among the Jews and Christians. By my life, Allah—the Mighty and Majestic—has made it clear to them in the Book He revealed to them by mention when He says: **{Wed not idolatresses until they believe. And the believing bondwoman is better than an idolatress though she may amaze thee. Give not in wedlock to idolaters until they believe. And the believing slave is better than an idolater though he may amaze thee. They art those who invite to the Hellfire}** (Q. 2:221).

There is no greater idolatry to Allah than the idolatry of one who has rejected Muhammad, peace and blessings be upon him and his progeny, as well as objected to the call of Islam with which he came! This is because when they rejected him, peace and blessings be upon him and his progeny, they have rejected Allah's design, and the one who rejects Allah's design regarding the sending of the Prophets is like the one who rejects His design regarding His creating creation. The one who rejects and objects to the verses (or "signs") with which Muhammad, peace and blessings be upon him and his progeny, came with is like the one who objects to the idea that Allah created the heavens and the earth. This is similar to the comparison between the one who objects to one verse of the Qur'an—whether a decisive or allegorical verse—and the one who objects to the whole Qur'an and that which Allah has revealed of the Criterion.[43] One cannot disagree with our statement regarding that nor can one doubt that which we said and explained—whether they possess intellect or are ignorant—unless by false testimony and calumny or such person is arrogant against the reality and stubborn against the truth. Therefore, know—O son—that it is never permissible for one to marry them until they acknowledge the truth of their Lord; recognise Him as their Creator; acknowledge the truth of their Prophet and that with which he came from their Lord, the Possessor of majesty and nobility; accept that which was sent to them; act upon that with which they were commanded and acknowledge the entire prescribed punishment of Islam. Then, it would be permissible to marry them and it would be legal to approach them.

They would be considered believing women, Muslims and the righteous about whom Allah says: {**O Prophet! If believing women come unto thee, taking an oath of allegiance unto thee that they will not ascribe any partner unto Allah and will neither steal, commit adultery, slay their children, come with a falsehood that they have devised between their hands and feet, nor disobey thee in what is right, then accept their allegiance and seek Allah's forgiveness for them. Verily, Allah is Oft-Forgiving, Most Gracious**} (**Q. 60:12**). Therefore, when they are, as Allah mentioned, among those who avoid ascribing partners to Allah, stealing, killing their children and refraining from slander and disobedience to Allah's Messenger, then they will be religiously permissible to marry and considered believing women. It would be obligatory to associate with them as well as ask forgiveness for them.

As for the one who is addicted to belying Allah and Allah's Messenger and rejects His verses and revelation, it is impermissible for a Muslim who believes in Allah to marry them. They would be considered prohibited for him and the one who follows his religion just as Allah, the Possessor of majesty and blessings, prohibits him. Therefore, understand and be guided by what we said. You will understand what we have explained until you are removed from deviance, God willing. You will be removed from ignorance regarding that. Have you not considered how the Possessor of majesty and nobility says {**Wed not idolatresses until they believe. And the believing bondwoman is better than an idolatress though she may amaze thee. Give not in wedlock to idolaters until they believe. And the believing slave is better than an idolater though he may amaze thee**} (**Q. 2:221**)?

As for the commentary of the ignorant regarding the statement of Allah, the Maker of the earth and heavens {**Today all good things are made lawful for thee. And the food of those who have received the Scripture is lawful for thee, and thy food is lawful for them as well as the chaste women of the believers and the chaste women of those who received the Scripture before thee when ye grant unto them their portions and live with them in chastity, not in fornication, nor taking them as secret mates. Whosoever rejects the faith, his deeds are in vain and he shall be in the Hereafter amongst the losers**} (**Q. 5:5**),

---

[43] The same argument—that is, idolatry is ascribed to those who reject the Qur'an—is brought forth and explicated by Imam al-Qāsim Rassi in his treatise ***Jawāb Mas`ala (fī at-Tawhīd) 'ala Rijlain min Ahl Tabaristān***. Refer to our forthcoming translation of ***Majmu' Imam al-Qāsim Rassi***.

the ignorant and those steeped in deviance who memorise the Revelation but are ignorant of its interpretation recite too quickly and overlook too hastily. He recites its revelation night and day yet does not carefully examine its interpretation or know much or a little of its meaning. He gropes about in his blindness and conceals himself in his ignorance. He considers its inner meaning as its outer meaning and judges its decisive verses as allegorical verses. He refers to the decisive verses over the allegorical verses that he finds and recites. Whenever he is asked or responds, he speaks that which is incorrect due to him not knowing. He speaks based on that which he does not understand. Due to the weakness of his knowledge and the greatness of his ignorance since he is duped by his interpretation, he readily assumes that he knows its hidden interpretation. It is as he has not heard what the Most Merciful says regarding him and others like him: **{He is the One who revealed unto thee the Book. In it are definitive verses; they are the basis of the Book. Others are figurative. As for those in whom are hearts of deviance, they follow the figurative thereof seeking thereby discord whilst seeking its interpretation. None knows its interpretation save Allah and those firmly grounded in knowledge. They say: "We believe in the Book; the whole of it is from our Lord." None shall grasp it except those of understanding} (Q. 3:7)**.

Therefore, they falsely assume that the food of the People of the Book that the Lord of lords made permissible for them includes their sacrificed meats that are slaughtered without facing the *qibla* of Islam. They also assume that the chaste women that they are free to marry refer to those who remain on their religion and disbelief. It is not as they imagine and falsely assume nor is it as they say and mention. Rather, the food that Allah makes permissible for the people of Islam refers to that food of theirs, which is not slaughtered, such as grains and other things that grow from the ground. Similarly, the chaste women from the People of the Book refer to the believing, penitent Muslim women who have returned to the truth; attributed the truth to the Messenger, peace and blessings be upon him and his progeny; entered into the faith and abandoned falsehood and disbelief. Allah therefore allows the believers to marry them after they repent and believe.

He ascribes **{the Book}** to them in this situation even though they believe in Allah and confirm the truth of Allah's Messenger just as He ascribes it to the one from the People of the Book who believed outside of this situation who was among the People of the Book at first. The Glorified says: **{And verily amongst the People of the Book is one who believes in Allah and that which was revealed unto thee and that which was revealed unto them—being wholly submissive to Allah—who hath not sold the signs of Allah for a paltry price. They art those who hath a great reward from their Lord. Verily, Allah is swift in account} (Q. 3:199)**. He calls them 'People of the Book' and attributes it to them even though they departed from that from which they repented, believed in Allah and confirmed the truth of His Messenger and that which Allah revealed on his tongue. This is the meaning of what Allah said, the One too majestic to be encompassed by words, regarding the food and the allowance to marry the chaste women from the People of the Book. It is not as the ignorant falsely assume or that to which those of falsehood ascribe.

Among the proofs against what these rabble say is that they are asked: "Inform us regarding these *dhimmi* wives—whether Jewish or Christian. Is it obligatory for her to receive the inheritance that Allah mandates on the husbands when He says **{Unto thee belong half of what thy wives leave even if they have no child. But if they have a child, unto thee belong a fourth of what they leave after any bequest they hath bequeathed or debt. Unto them belongs a fourth of what ye leave if ye have no child. But if ye have a child, then unto them belongs an eighth of what ye leave after any bequest ye hath bequeathed or debt} (Q. 4:12)**? Is it obligatory for her to receive inheritance in these situations while he is married to her and she is married to him?"

If they say "Yes," they invalidate the statement of Allah's Messenger, peace and blessings be upon him and his progeny, and contradict what he said when he said: ((Two people of different religions do not inherit from each other)).[44] Without a doubt, these two [i.e. a Muslim and *dhimmi*] are from two different religions. If they say "No; they do not inherit" based upon that which came from Allah's Messenger, they invalidate that which the Mighty and Majestic mandated upon spouses. And say to the one who says that: "What do you say? What is your belief regarding the Muslim who marries a *dhimmi* and he is graced with offspring by her and then her son dies and there is no one to inherit but her? Do you say that his inheritance is for her instead of the believers? Or do you say that it is for other than her?

If they say that it is for her and not for other than her, they contradict the *Ummah* by their statement. If they say that it is for the Muslims and not her, then say to them "Glorified be Allah! How can you say that and make the matter as thus while she is his mother who gave birth to him and he does not follow her religion? He remained on belief and she did not follow his religion, and she remained on *dhimmi* status and disbelief. His father simply married her while she was on disbelief and she gave birth while she was on her religion. Her son descended from her interior and was formed in her womb. His mother had not changed from her state that she was before nor did her son transition from the state that he was in. Yet, inheritance is prohibited from them both or for a reason after they joined?

It is known that Allah is just and not tyrannical in affairs both great and small. So how could Allah—in His justice, majesty, mercy and power—permit the father of this boy to marry his mother, extract him from her, make him her son and then prevent him from her inheritance and prohibit him from her wealth? How can that be the case while he does not change his religion nor does she change hers yet permit his father to marry her, make it legal to approach her and allow him to sleep with her, plant his seed in the place of her cultivation and justify such? How can He allow him to marry her and make it religiously permissible insomuch that when he does what Allah has permitted for him and takes advantage of the allowance that His Lord gives him, he acts unfairly to her by the command of his Creator and prevents her offspring which Allah graced her from her wealth and inheritance? How can it be that someone other than he inherits from his mother and makes for his mother a partner in his wealth? That has been revealed as an explanation in the Qur'an and a clarification in the divine revelation. He has provided its replacement and has prohibited it for another for whom he has illegalised it. Such is to not occur! Allah is exalted above what the ignorant say and what the invalidators attribute to Him!

Rather, according to their statement and the basis of their claim and doctrine, Allah allows and permits the father of this boy to marry someone who is not from the people of Islam. He then marries based on this allowance from Allah and plants his seed, which Allah extracts, in the place of cultivation that Allah granted and gifted him but then does not consider that which is commanded nor does he depart from that which he was warned or yield to that for which he is rebuked. Rather, he is on the straight path and in all of such in the Lord's pleasure. Would it be possible for Allah in His justice, generosity and greatness to allow His slave to marry a free woman and then prohibit him from her inheritance and prevent it from her child whom Allah caused them to parent? Would it be permissible for him to be excluded from that which he is commanded in marriage but not from that which

[44] Similarly narrated in ***Musnad Imam Zayd, Sharh at-Tajrīd, Sunan at-Tirmidhi, Sunan Abu Dāwūd, Sunan Ibn Mājah, Musnad Ahmed, Al-Mustadrak, Sunan al-Bayhaqi, Mušannaf Ibn Abi Shayba, Sunan ad-Dārqutni, Bihār al-Anwār, Ušūl al-Kāfi***. According to the last two sources referenced, Imam as-Sādiq is narrated to have said that the hadith means that the dhimmi does not inherit from the Muslim; however, the Muslim can inherit from the dhimmi. Provided its soundness, this does not weaken al-Hādi's statement because even the prohibition of one inheriting from the other contradicts the import of the Qur'anic verse.

prohibited in whoredom? Then he prevents him from that which He appointed for every slave other than him?

It is therefore necessary that they adopt one of three positions. As for the one who says that Allah allows and deems it religiously permissible for the Muslims to marry *dhimmis*—Jews and Christians, they would be obligated to inherit from their spouses and have their spouses inherit from them as well as inherit from their children and have their children inherit from them as Allah designated for them.

Or they would attribute oppression to their God and advocate such about their Creator if they claim that He allows them to marry *dhimmis*. He makes them like any other wives in that He obligates them to be given dowries and a waiting period yet Allah refrains their husbands and children from inheriting her wealth. However, He allows other than them to be inherited. Then, He prohibits them from inheritance without having committed a crime or act of disobedience. Rather, their husbands act upon that which Allah has permitted for them and allowed them to do. As for the children, He—Majestic and Mighty be He—created them and there is no sin on them for what others have done.

Or they would have to return to the truth and say that Allah does not allow or permit that which they say in regard to marriage with *dhimmis* just as He allowed and commanded marriage with Muslims. Then, they would be correct, and they would not have attributed tyranny to their Lord. Even if it was something that Allah allowed—Exalted be Him from such a matter!—He would have mentioned their inheritance in the Book by means of prohibition and reasons other than that, just as He mentioned other things so that there is no doubt. Also, the Messenger, peace and blessings be upon him and his progeny, would have mentioned such, legislated it and made it clear to the people of Islam. How is it—if the matter was as the ignorant say—that there is no explanation in the Book and Sunnah that anyone knows of?

Allah—the Possessor of majesty and authority—says regarding the proofs and criteria as He revealed to His Prophet: **{And We neglected naught in the Book. Then, to thy Lord shall ye be gathered} (Q. 6:38)**. The greatest of what one uses as a proof is in less than what we mentioned. By such, we establish our proof which is unnecessary to expound on in length. It is most sufficient and adequate for the one seeking the truth. It is guidance and truth to the one desirous of it. Praise be to Allah!

Have you not heard how the Most Gracious says regarding the Criterion He revealed to His Prophet: **{Ye shall not find a people who believe in Allah and the Last Day have mutual affection for the one who turns away from Allah and His Messenger—even though they art their fathers, their sons, their brothers or their kin} (Q. 58:22)**? My dear son, there is no mutual affection greater and more to the one with intellect than that of defloration, nearness, closeness, touching, intercourse and direct contact that brings happiness from a bed partner. This does not exclude the one who is either from the elite or from the common folk, especially when the husband receives from her the same and she is a supportive companion for him. Moreover, there is a mutual affection between them over the parent and others. There is no one who can compare in the matter of the two spouses insomuch that it is possible that the agreeable, obedient, generous, accommodating and affectionate wife could be more beloved to her husband than his mother, father, agnates, guardian, kin, wealth, children and siblings. Her husband cannot find any deviation, nor can she ever be separated from him—even if one strived to do so with every striving and struggled to one's utmost effort. That withstanding, how could there be any mutual affection greater than that which you see, hear, know or encounter?

We seek refuge in Allah from blindness and destruction! We ask Him for safety in both the hereafter and this life! The ignorant has reached the pinnacle of ignorance and committed the greatest of that which he does! He ascribes to Allah falsehood and slander, and such person will lose the most on the Day of Gathering!

One says that Allah—May His Names be sanctified and His allies be strengthened by means of the nobility of His alliance—allows the male to marry a female while knowing that marriage is a form of association. Then, He commands him to have dissociation and opposition while knowing that he is unable to hate her when he has already approved of her. Have you not heard how the Glorified says **{Ye art unable to deal equitably between wives, howsoever much ye wish. But turn not altogether away, leaving her as a hanging thing} (Q. 4:129)**. The Glorified is saying that you will never be able to deal equally between them in love—even if you made strenuous effort—since they differ in your eyes and hearts. Therefore, you are unable to be equal between them in terms of love just as you are unable to be equal between them in any other of their affairs. This is because the Glorified knows that this is not possible for them, and they will never be able to do so. Allah will never impose something on His slaves that they cannot do.

Have you not heard how the Possessor of majesty, nobility and might says **{Allah burdens not a soul except with what it can bear} (Q. 2:286)** and **{Allah burdens not a soul except with what He hath given it}** (65:7)? The Mighty and Majestic also says: **{Allah desires for thee ease, and He desires not hardship for thee} (Q. 2:185)**. The One too majestic to be encompassed by words also says: **{And strive for Allah with a striving that is His right. He hath chosen thee and hath not laid upon thee in religion any hardship—the path of thy father Abraham. He hath named thee Muslims…} (Q. 22:78)**.

By that, He means that He made ease for you in the religion and not strictness or restriction. By the lives of the blind confused and those of falsehood, there is no restriction, hardship or inability greater than this if it is as the ignorant say! He ascribes to Allah deviant oppression; however, the Glorified burdens with ease and grants the one who has less with more. He does not permit such matter for His slaves; rather, He prevents and prohibits them from such. Exalted be the Noble One, Possessor of omnipotence! He is the One who grants virtue, the Possessor of mercy and dominion! Praise be to Allah, the Lord of creation and the Finality for the God-conscious! Peace be upon the Messengers!

Concerning the woman who is with a husband while her son from another dies as well as concerning a woman who breastfeeds her husband within two lunar years

When a woman is with her husband and has a son from a previous marriage[45] and that son from the previous husband dies, he [i.e. the second husband] should refrain from intercourse with her until it becomes clear to him whether she is pregnant or not.

We simply say that because if she were pregnant at the time her son died, that baby would inherit from his maternal brother. If the deceased had a father, grandfather or son, the husband would not have to refrain from intercourse with his wife or stay away from her womb because all of the aforementioned would prevent the child in the womb from inheritance. This is because the child would be the brother of the deceased from the mother only, and such brother does not inherit with the existence of the four

[45] Although not mentioned in this text, al-Hādi was asked whether a woman with small children from a previous marriage could be prevented from raising them by her new husband in ***Al-Muntakhab***. He replied:

> That is impermissible. They can enter upon her and come to her to be raised. He should not prevent them from being raised. Similar was done by Allah's Messenger, peace and blessings be upon him and his progeny, regarding Umm Salama when he married her. Because of his love for her, he assumed responsibility for them [i.e. her children] with her consent.

we previously mentioned. It has similarly been related to us that the Commander of Believers, 'Ali b. Abi Ťālib[46] and al-Hasan b. 'Ali commanded one to refrain when there is no one among the four that we previously mentioned.

As for the woman who breastfeeds her husband in two lunar years, it is that a man has a woman who gives birth from him and then he divorces her. Then, the person lawfully in charge to marry her contracts a marriage between her and a small boy who has not reached two lunar years, and the woman breastfeeds him. If she did that, she would be prohibited from him because she became his milk mother, and Allah has prohibited one from his milk mother. There is no dowry for her because of the annulment caused by her. If her first husband decided to return to her, it would not be permissible for him to marry or remarry her if he divorced her three times. It would not be permissible for him until after the current husband had intercourse with her. Also, it is permissible for her to remarry without waiting because there is no waiting period for a child and because he had not had intercourse with her.

Concerning that which makes it permissible for a woman to remarry her first husband and the designation of defects for which a woman can be returned if she deceives him

When a man divorces his wife with an irrevocable divorce and she is married to a slave who is freed with the death of his master or an indentured labourer or a slave with the permission of their master and then one of the aforementioned three divorces her, it is permissible for him [i.e. the first husband] to remarry her after she had intercourse with her second husband. It would be permissible for her to remarry her first husband.

Even if any of those aforementioned marriages were valid, a woman's husband can return her if she deceives him and did not inform him of the following four things: leprosy, elephantiasis (*al-judhām*), insanity and femoral hernia (*al-qaran*). If he sends her back, he can take back his dowry unless he had intercourse with her. If he had intercourse with her, he does not return her dowry whether he remains with her or divorces her.

Concerning the one who apostatises from Islam

If a Muslim apostatises and reaches the domain of war (*dār al-harb*),[47] his wife is permitted to remarry after she menstruates three times. His wealth is then distributed among his heirs, including the wife. If the husband and wife apostatise together, their marriage would be considered valid until Islam is presented to them. If they embrace Islam, their marriage would be considered valid. If they reject, they are both killed. If only one of them embraces Islam, the other is killed and the Muslim inherits from the other.

The apostate is inherited from, and the Muslims inherit from him. However, he does not inherit from them because his judgement differs from their judgement since there is no judgement for him other than returning to Islam or death. If a Muslim apostatises and Islam is not presented to him until his wife

[46] Sheikh 'Ali b. Bilāl related in ***Sharh al-Ahkām*** that Abul-Abbās al-Hasani narrated with a complete chain of narrators to 'Ali, upon him be peace that he discouraged a man from having intercourse with a woman whose child from a previous marriage died. He discouraged that until she menstruates, and he said: "Either two menstruations or it is evident that she is pregnant."

[47] In classic Islamic legal theory, the domain of war (*dār al-harb*) or domain of disbelief (*dār al-kufr*) is defined as 'that territory which is under the power of the disbelievers and exhibits peculiarities of disbelief.' It is referred to as such even if there exists a treaty between its rulers and the rightful imam. [Ref. ***At-Tāj***] It is noteworthy that the term does not explicitly appear in the Qur'an or the Prophetic hadith collections. Rather, it is a terminology later adopted which reflected the political realities of the Prophetic era. Imam al-Manšūr Billah 'Abdullah b. Hamza said in his treatise ***Ajwaba as-Sā'il***:

> It is characterised by three traits: Either the statements and actions of disbelief are seen from its ruling authority (*sultān*), disbelief is openly manifested, or its people are overwhelming. The proof of that is Mecca—May Allah preserve it! It was the domain of disbelief before the Migration (*hijra*). In it, Allah's Messenger, peace and blessings be upon him and his progeny, and the Muslims openly manifested Islam but could not talk to anyone about it. They were overcome in some cases and verbally threatened by the disbelievers. In some cases, they [i.e. the disbelievers] acted on such threats.

menstruates three times and then Islam is presented to him and he rejects and is killed, his wife does not inherit from him. This is because she would have exited her waiting period before he was killed.

If the husband and wife apostatise together and they have a child less than six months from the time they apostatised, the judgement of the child is that of Islam. This is because he was a foetus in Islam and was in his mother's womb upon the truth. He inherits from them but they do not inherit from him because he is a Muslim. If they have him [i.e. the child] more than six months [from the time they apostatised], his judgement is their judgement and he is included in their apostasy. They do not inherit from him nor does he inherit from them.

If a man and his wife embrace Islam in the domain of war and one of them emigrates to the domain of Islam while the other remains behind, as long as there is a valid reason for remaining behind that prevents Emigration, one would have more right to the other. If the reason for remaining behind is desire for the domain [of war] and indifference towards Islam, the wife would be removed from his charge after she menstruates three times.

If the Muslim wife emigrates from the domain of war to that of Islam, she is to not remarry until she is purified. If she has a husband that is in an idolatrous country, her womb is purified by three menstruations. If she is a slave, her womb is purified by one menstruation. The slave woman who is captured in war is purified with one menstruation.

Concerning the one in the domain of war (*al-harbi*) who embraces Islam and emigrates while having a pre-pubescent wife in the domain of war

He is responsible for her as long as three months have not passed since her husband embraced Islam. If three months have not passed and one of her parents embraced Islam, such conversion would cause her conversion and she would remain his wife in this state. When she departs to the domain of Islam either pre-puberty or post-puberty, he is responsible for her.

Concerning the idolater who embraces Islam while having ten wives: among them are some he married with a joint contract and among them are some he married separately and concerning the one in the domain of war who departed to the domain of Islam in safety

If it is that the one who embraced Islam married them together with one contract, he separates from all of them and then chooses four among them. His separation from them is not considered an [Islamic] divorce because the marriage was invalid in its beginning. Then, he marries four with a marriage that is considered valid from its beginning. If he were to marry four with one contract and three in one contract, the marriage with four is considered valid and the marriage with three is considered null and void. If he were to marry two with one contract and three with one contract and two with one contract, the first two and last two marriages would be considered valid and the marriage to three would be considered invalid. If he were to marry one with one contract and six with one contract and two with one contract and one with one contract, the first marriage would be valid, the marriage to six would be invalid, the marriage to two would be valid and the marriage to the last one would also be valid. It is valid for him to marry up to four; anything other than is considered null and void.

As for the people from the domain of war—whether women or men—who enter Muslim lands in safety for business or other than that, the imam of the Muslims must inform them that it is impermissible for them to stay in the domain of Islam for more than a year. He must remove them if they stay for more than a year, and they mustn't remain but should return to their lands. They have two options [if they want to stay]: one, they embrace Islam and be among the Muslims with their wealth belonging to them and what is obligatory for them will be obligatory on them; or two, they impose the *jizya* on them and they will be considered *dhimmi*.

Concerning the apostasy of the pre-pubescent child and concerning one who embraces Islam and then apostatises before his wife embraces Islam

The apostasy of a pre-pubescent child is not considered apostasy until he is in a state whereby the judgements apply to him; it is that he grows pubic hair or has a wet dream. This is because his apostasy necessitates being put to death if he does not repent. If we adjudicate him with apostasy, we adjudicate that he engages in repentance. If we adjudicate that he engages in repentance, we adjudicate that he be put to death if he does not repent. The death penalty cannot be applied on him until he grows pubic hair or has a wet dream just as Allah's Messenger, peace and blessings be upon him and his progeny, did with the Jews of Bani Qurayḍa. He killed the ones who were pubescent due to the growth of pubic hair. It is for that reason we say that the apostasy of a pre-pubescent child is not acted upon.

If a man embraced Islam and then apostatised before his wife embraced Islam and he returned to the former religion of his wife or any other religion, his wife would be separated from him. This is because when he had entered the extent of Islam and then left from it, there is nothing for him except repentance or the sword. If he had intercourse with her, she would get the full dowry. If he had not had intercourse with her, she would get half the dowry because the separation came from him.

If a Magian embraces Christianity, a Christian embraces Judaism, or a Jew embraces Mazdaism, we hold the view that the connection between him and his wife is considered severed. In addition, she keeps the dowry that made intercourse with her lawful.

We do not say that all idolatry is the same religion as others say and declare the marriage between them as sound. How can they all be considered one religion when some of them are more blasphemous and extreme according to others? How can it be when each one declares the other as disbelievers and dissociates from him and his religion? And then one joins such people in their disagreement? Rather, we differentiate them by their religion just as they differentiate themselves by their schools of thought. Even though they are disbelievers according to us and we judge them as idolaters by the judgement of Allah, have you not heard how Allah informs you that some of them declares the disbelief of others? Moreover, have you not seen such from them with your own eyes and heard their statements and their disagreements in their religion with your own ears? Regarding that, Allah—the Mighty and Majestic—says: **{The Jews say: "The Christians are upon nothing!" And the Christians say: "The Jews are upon nothing!"} (Q. 2:113).**

It is for the reason we mentioned of their disagreement and differences in their religion that it is impermissible for a Jewish man to marry a Christian woman or a Christian man to marry a Jewish woman, nor is it permissible for any other group of idolaters opposed to another group to marry the other.

Concerning the *dhimmi* or his wife who embraces Islam and then divorces during her waiting period as well as a female *dhimmi* who embraces Islam while she has a pre-pubescent husband

If a female *dhimmi* embraces Islam while having a *dhimmi* husband, the connection between them is considered severed and she must undergo the waiting period from his last ejaculation. If he divorces her during her waiting period, the divorce is valid and she undergoes a waiting period from the time of her divorce. This is because her Islam does not constitute an [Islamic] divorce; it is simply a separation and void. If her ex-husband embraces Islam at any point in time and wants to remarry her, she can return to him with two divorces remaining.

If a pubescent female *dhimmi* marries a pre-pubescent male *dhimmi* and then embraces Islam afterwards, she is withheld from him until the judgements apply to him. Then, he is invited to Islam. If he embraces Islam, he remains married to her. If he rejects, he is separated from her. Similarly, if the husband was old and then he embraces Islam while his wife rejects Islam, it is impermissible for them to remain married. Islam renders the relationship between them null and void according to us.

Regarding our earlier statement, it is not that if she embraced Islam during her waiting period, they would still be considered married. As for what is narrated regarding that and what is said that the Commander of Believers, ‘Ali b. Abi Ṭālib, upon him be peace, permitted the marriage to female *dhimmis*—this is not truly attributed to him nor do we advocate for such.[48] This is because they are idolatresses, and Allah has said: **{Wed not idolatresses until they believe} (Q. 2:221)**.

Concerning the one who owns a non-marriageable relative and one who owns a marriageable relative

It has reached us that Allah’s Messenger, peace and blessings be upon him and his progeny, said: ((Whoever owns a non-marriageable relative—such relative is considered manumitted)).[49] If a man owned his daughter, sister, mother, paternal aunt, maternal aunt, the daughter of his son, the daughter of his daughter, the daughter of his sister, the daughter of his brother—even if they are lower in descent—paternal grandmother, maternal grandmother or great grandmother; they are all considered manumitted from the time he owned them with any ownership.

If he jointly owned a share of any one of them, such share would be considered manumitted. He is to reimburse the partner with the value of his wealth. If it is a relative who sold to him knowing that he is to manumit the one he owned, he is responsible to give the remaining price value to his partner. Similarly, if he substituted any men [relatives] for these women, he is to manumit them due to his relations with them if he owned them.

If he owned a marriageable relative, he is free to exchange, sell or buy them. Examples include the daughter of a paternal uncle, the son of a paternal uncle, the son of a maternal uncle, the son of a maternal aunt, the daughter of a maternal aunt, the son of a paternal aunt, the daughter of a paternal aunt, his milk brother, his milk daughter, his milk sister, his milk maternal aunt, his milk paternal aunt and his milk grandmother by his father and mother. All of the aforementioned are permissible for him to buy, sell and exchange. However, it is impermissible for him to have intercourse with any of his milk relatives.

Concerning the slave girl of two men who gives birth to the child of one of them

If there is a slave girl of two men and she gives birth to the child of one of them, the father of the child is responsible for half the value of slave girl on the day of her pregnancy, half the value of the child on the day of birth as well as half the indemnity. The prescribed punishment is to be applied to him because of what he had taken part in with her. We do not hold to the view that he is exempted from the indemnity because he forced himself on her, and it was impermissible for him to force himself on her. If he was exempted from paying her indemnity, he would be exempted from paying half the value of her child because the indemnity preceded the child.

There is collective agreement that if he had intercourse with her but had not impregnated her, he would have to pay half her indemnity. If it is binding for him to pay half her indemnity, it is binding

---

[48] Among the texts that report Imam ‘Ali’s permission to marry female *dhimmis* is the ***Musnad Imam Zayd***:

> Zayd b. ‘Ali related to me on the authority of his father from his grandfather from ‘Ali, upon them be peace: “The Muslim can marry a Jewess and Christian but cannot marry a Magian or idolatress (*al-mushrika*).” He also discouraged the marriage to a non-Muslim in the domain of war and Arab Christians. He said: “They are not the People of the Book.”
>
> Zayd b. ‘Ali related to me on the authority of his father from his grandfather from ‘Ali, upon them be peace, that he said that if a Jew were to embrace Islam and his wife were to embrace Islam, they will still be considered married. And if he were to embrace Islam but his wife does not, they will still be considered married.

These reports explicitly denote that Imam ‘Ali, upon him be peace, permitted marriage to female *dhimmis*. However, as is evident from the statement of Imam al-Hādi, such reports are attributed with falsehood.

[49] Similarly narrated in ***Musnad Imam Zayd, Sharh at-Tajrīd, Sunan at-Tirmidhi, Sunan Ibn Mājah, Sunan al-Bayhaqi, Sunan Abu Dāwūd, Al-Mu’jam al-Kabīr, Al-Mustadrak, Musnad Ahmed***

for him to pay half the value of the child. If it is binding for him to pay half the value of the child, it is binding for him to pay half the indemnity. This is because both of them are the same, and both are for the doer of the same action. It is an offense against his partner regarding two equal offences. If he was exempt from one of them, he would be exempted from all of them. If one of them is established, all of them are established.

If the partner of this person who fornicated with the slave girl was his brother, he is obligated to pay half the value of the slave girl, half the value of her indemnity but is exempted from paying half the value of the child. This is because the child is considered manumitted due to the ownership of his uncle. This is also because the one who is owned by a non-marriageable relative is considered manumitted.

Concerning the purification of a slave woman at the time of buying and selling as well as concerning the man who marries a slave woman and then buys her

It is obligatory for the one who sells a slave woman to have her free of her menses before selling her. Similarly, it is obligatory that the buyer have her free of her menses before having intercourse with her. If she is a pre-pubescent girl or an older woman who no longer menstruates, he should have her free of such a month before selling her or having intercourse with her. If he buys her while she is pregnant and she delivers while with him, she is permissible for him after she has completed her postpartum bleeding and is purified from her blood flow.

If a man marries a slave woman and then buys her before having intercourse with her, ownership invalidates the marriage. However, it is not invalidated by divorce. It is for the buyer to have intercourse with her due to ownership. It is not for her first master to seek out her husband for half the dowry that was stipulated for her at first. If he likes, the one who buys her can gift her, marry her or sell her; that is permissible for him.

If it is that she is married by her first master and he has intercourse with her before buying her and then he buys her, ownership invalidates the marriage also. He can have intercourse with her due to ownership. The one who sells her is to pay the full dowry because he had intercourse with her due to his ownership of her and before he sold her. If the buyer wants to marry her or sell her, this would not be permissible until she is purified from three menstruations. If she gives birth from him before he bought her and then he buys her, his marriage is considered null and void and his ownership is considered valid and established.

If a free man marries an owned slave woman, his children would be considered owned slaves unless it was stipulated that his children would be free. Then his stipulation on them would be binding.[50]

Concerning marriage to slaves and their divorce

The slaves—in terms of marriage, divorce and the waiting period—are like free people. There is no difference between them in that. This is because Allah does not differentiate between them in His Book and has made known the position of the slaves. If He wanted to differentiate between them in terms of marriage or divorce or the waiting period, He would have made it clear in His Book or the tongue of His Prophet, peace and blessings be upon him and his progeny. Nothing has come in the Book of Allah regarding any difference nor has any difference between slaves and free people been narrated from His Prophet, peace and blessings be upon him and his progeny.

---

[50] This topic is expanded a bit more in ***Al-Muntakhab***.

> I asked him about a free man who marries a slave woman with her mater's permission: "What would his offspring be considered?" He replied: "Slaves." "Would her husband be obligated to provide financial maintenance?" "It would be as per the condition." "What services does her family do for her? And do they have to financially maintain her and clothe her?" "If there is a marriage between them and they send her to him, he is to financially maintain her. However, if they employ her services, they are to financially maintain her unless they stipulate a precondition otherwise. Then, the stipulation takes precedence."

Concerning the women one is permitted to marry

It has reached us that Allah's Messenger, peace and blessings be upon him and his progeny, said: ((You should have women with ample hips, for they breed and in them is good fortune)).[51] The meaning of his statement ((breed)) is have children, and the meaning of ((good fortune)) is blessings and benefit.

It is permissible for a man to marry his slave to his *umm walad* if he frees her with her agreement. He can also marry his slave woman who is freed at his death as well as his female slave even if both of them dislike that. Similarly, he can marry his female indentured labourer if she permits him to do that. The dowry for the female indentured labourer is for her as support for her in indenturement. What applies to her is similarly applied to her child. Once she completes her contracted labour, they are manumitted when she is manumitted. If she is unable to repay, they remain enslaved as she remains enslaved. Similarly, the children of a slave who is freed at the master's death are manumitted when she is manumitted.

If she gives birth to them after the indentured labour contract or agreement to enslavement until the master's death and a man marries off his slave woman or slave who is freed at her master's death, the two of them have a choice when they are manumitted—either themselves or their husbands. They can choose for separation if they want, or they can marry if they want. Similar has been narrated from Allah's Messenger, peace and blessings be upon him and his progeny, regarding Barīra,[§] the slave girl bought by A'isha.

There were four traditions from the Prophet, peace and blessings be upon him and his progeny, regarding that. The first is that A'isha bought her and the one who sold her stipulated upon her that the clientage (*walā*) belonged to him. Upon this, the Prophet, peace and blessings be upon him and his progeny, said: ((The inheritance belongs to the one who sold her)).[52]

The second is that Barīra received charity, and A'isha mentioned that to the Prophet, peace and blessings be upon him and his progeny. Thereupon, he said: ((It is charity for her and a gift for us)).[53]

The third is that she had a husband, and Allah's Messenger, peace and blessings be upon him and his progeny, gave her the choice [to remain married] after manumission.[54] This exemplified the *sunnah* of giving the choice to the slave woman after her manumission. If she chooses for separation, that would nullify the marriage between her and her husband. If she chooses to remain married, the marriage between them would be valid.

The fourth is that he did not consider her being sold as a divorce. If he considered her being sold as a divorce he would not have given her the choice in her and her husband's affairs after she was manumitted. Therefore, the *sunnah* was exemplified in these four by the Messenger, peace and blessings be upon him and his progeny. Muhammad b. Yahya [the transmitter of this book] says: "It is the same whether the husband is a slave or free man."

If a man said to another man "I permit you to have intercourse with my slave girl" and he has intercourse with her or he said "That is a woman for her husband" or "…mother for her child" or "...for any man from among the people," such would not be permissible for him nor would it be licit. If anyone had intercourse based on this statement believing it to be permissible without knowing that

---

[51] Similarly narrated in ***Uṣūl al-Kāfi*** and ***Kanz al-'Ummāl***

[52] Similarly narrated in ***Sharh at-Tajrīd, Ṣahīh al-Bukhāri, Ṣahīh Muslim, Sunan an-Nisā'i, Sunan Ibn Mājah, Musnad Ahmed, Muwatta, Sunan al-Bayhaqi, Uṣūl al-Kāfi, Bihār al-Anwār***

[53] Similarly narrated in ***Ṣahīh al-Bukhāri, Ṣahīh Muslim, Sunan an-Nisā'i, Ṣahīh Ibn Hibbān, Muṣannaf Ibn Abi Shayba, Sunan al-Bayhaqi, Bihār al-Anwār***

[54] Similarly narrated in ***Ṣahīh al-Bukhāri, Ṣahīh Muslim, Sunan an-Nisā'i, Ṣahīh Ibn Hibbān, Sunan ad-Dārqutni, Sunan al-Bayhaqi, Al-Mu'jam al-Kabīr***

it is religiously impermissible, such person is exempted from the prescribed punishment due to uncertainty. However, he would have to pay her the dowry for having intercourse with her. If he had intercourse with her while knowing that this was not religiously permissible and licit, the prescribed punishment would be obligatory upon him.

Concerning an absentee who was announced as dead and his inheritance is distributed but then he returns

When an absent man is announced as dead and his wealth is distributed and then he returns, he takes it back from everyone who has it. If any of his heirs manumitted some of his slaves, his slaves are to be returned to him. If any of his heirs sold some of his slaves or property, he is to take back that which he finds and that which was in the possession of the buyer is returned to him. If there was a slave that was to be manumitted at the master's death and she is found, she is to be taken back even if she had married. He takes her indemnity and the value of her child from her husband. The child would be considered free and attributed to his father. If the heirs found some of the property that was damaged or ruined, that which is ruined is returned to them and sought out.

If a slave married a free woman without the permission of his master and the free woman did not know that he had not had permission but then the master arrives and nullifies the marriage between them, he can do that and take the dowry that the slave gave the woman. On the day that the slave is freed, the woman can seek out the slave for a dowry of one similar to herself.

Concerning the marriage of an indentured labourer and his purchase of his wife

When an indentured labourer buys his wife after marrying her with the permission of his master, his purchase is not invalidated even by the marriage. He is permitted to have intercourse with her due to the first marriage that was permitted by his master. When his contract of indentured labour is complete, the marriage is invalidated but he is permitted to have intercourse with her based on ownership.

Similarly, if an indentured labourer buys a female slave, he cannot have intercourse with her. If he marries her after buying or manumitting her, he cannot have intercourse with her due to marriage or ownership until he observes the completion of his contract of indentured labour. Then, it would be permissible for him to have intercourse with her due to ownership at that point. If he wants to manumit, he can because there is no ownership of her before he observes the completion of his contract of indentured labour. His matter regarding her would then be permissible. Haven't you considered that if he were unable, all of such would be binding upon his master?

Concerning what obligates the dowry

When a wife enters upon her husband and is secluded with him and the curtain is lowered and the door is closed, the dowry is obligatory upon him. This is whether he has intercourse with her or not. Similar has been narrated from the Commander of Believers, 'Ali b. Abi Ťālib, that he said: "When he lowers the curtain and closes the door, he is obligated to pay the dowry."[55]

If he lowers the curtain or closes the door while there are others in the house with him—such as his sister, mother, mother-in-law her sister and he does not touch her, he is not obligated to pay the dowry to her. He is only obligated to pay the dowry to her when she is secluded with him. If he divorced her after having lowered the curtain upon them both and the aforementioned relatives are with them, he is only obligated to give her half the dowry.[56]

---

[55] Similarly narrated in ***Bihār al-Anwār***. It is also narrated in ***Mušannaf 'Abdur-Razzāq*** as a statement of 'Umar.

[56] In ***Al-Muntakhab***, there is a discussion around disagreement regarding the claim of intercourse and the dowry.

Concerning one who gives a manservant, maidservant or more in marriage as a dowry

There is no problem with a man giving a manservant, maidservant and servants as a dowry in marriage as long as it was stipulated in terms of their number, colour and gender. He would be obligated to provide the servant that which he described. If he had not described the manservant to her, she could take the average of that. If there is a disagreement between them regarding that, they should consult a slave trader who is knowledgeable of such to value him. However, it is preferable to us that he and she not marry with a manservant or maidservant as a dowry because of the disparity and disagreement that can occur as well as a restriction that is not agreed upon. If someone decides to do that, he should do what we previously described.

If a man marries a woman for a free woman or free man as dowry without being aware that such person is free, she is to get a dowry of one similar to herself. If he marries her for a slave that is manumitted at the master's death, an indentured labourer or *umm walad* as dowry without her being aware, she is to get the value of what she married him for on the day that the marriage contract occurs.

If he marries her for something that is impermissible to buy or sell as dowry, such as intoxicants or pigs or the killing of humans, that would be impermissible as dowry and she would get a dowry of one similar to herself.

Concerning a man who marries a woman for a slave woman as dowry specifically and then has intercourse with the latter before she is given to her

If a man marries a woman for a slave woman that belongs to him and stipulates her [i.e. the slave woman] as a dowry for her and then has intercourse with her before he gives [the slave woman] to her, he is exempted from the prescribed punishment due to uncertainty because she was his responsibility afterwards.

If she [i.e. the slave woman] has a child, she [i.e. the wife] would have the following choice. If she wants, she can take her, her indemnity and her child. If she wants, she can take the dowry of one similar to herself. If she wants, she can take her value and the value of her child. If he divorces her before having intercourse with her, he is obligated to pay half the indemnity of the slave girl and the slave girl would belong to him and her. Half the value of the child would be given to her and the child would not be attributed to his father because he had intercourse with his mother unlawfully. The slave woman would not be considered an *umm walad* because she gave birth from him in an invalid way.

If a man married a woman for a slave girl, horse, or she camel as dowry and had not given it to her until the slave girl, horse or she camel gave birth, she is to take her and the child. If the child dies before she assumes possession of it and prefers to take the slave girl or animal with deficiency, it is permissible for her to do. If she wants, she can return her [i.e. the slave girl or animal] and take her value on the day the marriage occurs.

Concerning deputation (*al-wikāla*) in marriage

If a man writes to another man saying "Marry me to so-n-so for one thousand dirhams" and he marries him to her for two thousand dirhams with the permission of the husband, this would be permissible. If the husband said "I am dissatisfied with what you did and I do not permit it" and then the woman says "I am satisfied with one thousand dirhams," that marriage would not be considered valid. This is because he nullified it with his statement "I am dissatisfied and I do not permit what you did."

I asked: "If a man and woman disagree about intercourse with the husband saying 'I did not have intercourse with you' and the wife saying 'You did have intercourse with me' and neither has evidence, which one would get the dowry and upon whom would be the obligation of evidence?" He replied: "The obligation would be upon the woman because she is the plaintiff, and the man would be obligated to swear an oath."

If what the deputy did reached him and the latter said "I permit the marriage contract but I do not permit what was designated as the dowry," that is to be proposed to the woman. If she is satisfied with one thousand dirhams, the marriage would be valid. If she was not satisfied except by what the deputy stipulated, the marriage would be considered null and void.

We would only permit it if the woman was satisfied with one thousand because we established that the second one-thousand is a gift that the woman gave to the husband from her dowry and because the husband had said "I permit the marriage contract" and then spoke about the dowry after that. Then, his statement regarding the dowry would be considered contradictory. His seeking a decrease in the dowry from him while he is satisfied with the marriage would establish the contract as sound.

Concerning an old man who had intercourse and died because of his wife

If he is having intercourse with her and she pushes him or punches him in the chest or tightly embraces him or does something similar and then he dies, she is obligated to pay his indemnity. Similar has reached us from the Commander of Believers, 'Ali b. Abi Ťālib, upon him be peace. He made a judgement regarding a weak elderly man who died. He was having intercourse with his wife and when he ejaculated, he squeezed her tightly out of his passion and she squeezed him very tightly. By her squeezing him tightly, he suffocated and died. He [i.e. 'Ali] passed the judgement that she was obligated to pay indemnity.

Concerning the one who contracts a marriage with a woman and then her sister is deceptively given to him as well as what is binding upon her regarding her husband

It has reached us that the Commander of Believers, 'Ali b. Abi Ťālib, upon him be peace, passed a judgement regarding a man who proposed to a woman from her father. Her mother was an Arab woman, and her father married her to him. She had a sister whose mother was a non-Arab. When the time of consummation came, the non-Arab woman was made to enter upon him. When the morning came, the man objected to her and the Commander of Believers and just imam, 'Ali b. Abi Ťālib, upon him be peace, was informed about it. He passed the judgement that the dowry was to be given to the non-Arab daughter with whom he had intercourse. He also passed the judgement that the Arab daughter belonged to the man and made the dowry obligatory upon her father.[57]

The Commander of Believers, upon him be peace, necessitated that he pays the dowry to his daughter because there cannot be intercourse except by the dowry, and the first wife and her dowry that was binding belonged to her. The imam must rectify the behaviour of her father and prevent him from repeating the offence.

Concerning the child of a free woman from a slave

A free woman has more right to her child as long as their father is a slave. When he is manumitted, he has more right to them than she does if they were to divorce and the children are able to bear instruction.

Concerning a slave woman who escaped, claimed that she was free, was married to a free man, had children and then was caught

If a slave woman escaped and used deception about herself claiming that she was a free woman and then married someone who was ignorant of this and had children but then was caught by her master afterwards, he [i.e. the husband] would have to return her to her master as well as the value of her children. However, nothing is to be taken from the dowry that was paid to her because he had intercourse with her.

[57] Similarly narrated in ***Amāli Ahmed b. 'Isa***

The husband would then claim restitution from her master to the degree of her offense. Her offense here would be that which is binding of the value of her child that the master took. If her value is less than their value, the value of the child is exempted from him. The rest of their value is to be given to the master by the slave woman.

If the husband seeks out her remaining restitution, it is his. If her value is more than their value, the slave's master can seek out the value of her child. The husband can demand it from her master due to her offense; it is the value of the child that is taken from him. This is because she concealed it from him because of her deceiving him. The slave woman is to be flogged with fifty stripes as the prescribed punishment because she fornicated in her marriage without her master's permission.

Others have said that the child would be considered a slave and that it would not be obligatory for the offended to pay for her offense. They narrated that from the Commander of Believers, upon him be peace. However, we do not attribute that to him nor do we authenticate that from him because it would be impermissible to distress this oppressed person with a child and remove these slaves from his possession. Similar would not be invalidated due to an offense. Wouldn't it be binding for the slave woman's master to return dirham if he concealed it from a Muslim? The minimum of what would be obligated upon this oppressed person regarding his child is that which is obligated for the one who bought the slave woman from the market and then she had a child and was reclaimed. Everyone holds to the view that the child belongs to the father and that their value is for her master and that their father returns its value to the one who sold her and was tricked by her.

To the one with intellect and fairness, there is no difference between the one who unknowingly bought a stolen slave woman from the market and one who unknowingly married an escaped slave woman who claimed she was free. Rather, the right of confirmation for the buyer is to ascertain her for marriage. This is because the buyer must investigate the background of the slave woman as well as her buying and selling. He must also consider her matter carefully before buying her for fear that she was stolen and will be reclaimed afterwards.

As for marriage, there is more of an obligation when finding a woman upon his religion in a town. He must ask if she has a guardian in town. If he does not know of her guardian for marriage, the imam of the Muslims or a believing man can contract a marriage for him. It is not for one to avoid her fearing that she may be a slave. Even if it is an obligation upon people, it is impermissible for one to marry a woman except in her town. It is prohibited for the Muslims to marry any unknown woman or give her in marriage. Allah does not obligate this excess upon His slaves so that none of the aforementioned things occurs or happens suddenly. Therefore, it is prohibited to marry her, and his children will belong to her master to own as slaves. The prescribed punishment would be applied to him for having intercourse with a slave woman without her master's permission.

Concerning a woman who is deceived by a slave and she marries him assuming that he is a free man

If his master comes to know, his master is obligated to give her the dowry. The choice is hers. If she wants, she can remain married to him. If she wants, she can separate herself from him. If the master did not know about it but then later comes to know about it, it would be valid. The matter is the same, and the choice belongs to her even if he does not permit it. If there is separation, it is obligatory for the slave to give her the dowry when he is manumitted provided that she demands it.

Concerning marriage to a eunuch

If a woman marries a eunuch and is content with that, the marriage is considered valid. If his penis and testicles were castrated (*majbūb*), he cannot be married to her. However, if only his testicles were extracted (*maslūl*), he can be married to her.

Similar has reached us from the Commander of Believers, 'Ali b. Abi Ťālib, upon him be peace. He passed a judgement regarding a eunuch that he could not be married.[58]

Concerning *shighār*

Shighār is that a man gives his female relative to another to marry while he marries the other's female relative and neither one pays the dowry to the other because each one mutually forfeited the dowry of the other. This is religiously prohibited and impermissible. Marriage is impermissible except by means of a well-known dowry between Muslims, which is ten dirham or more.

Concerning two men who have intercourse with a slave woman during the same period of purity and she gives birth without knowing the identity of the father

If all of them come to know of the pregnancy at the same time and then one of them claims [the child] while the other is uncertain, it belongs to the one who made the claim. If both of them claim it together, [the child] inherits from them both, and both of them inherit from [the child]. It will belong to the remaining one among them.

If one of the two men is a slave and both of them claim it together, it shall belong to the free man because the claim of both of them is equal yet freedom increases the claim of the free man. This is because if the child is connected to the slave, it will be considered a slave. But if it is connected to the free man, it will be free.

Similarly, if one of the claimants is a *dhimmi* and the two made the same claim, [the child] would belong to the Muslim because although the claim of the both of them is equal, Islam increases the claim and proof of the Muslim. This is because if the child is connected to the *dhimmi*, it will be considered a *dhimmi* because its mother is a slave. If it is connected to the Muslim, it will be considered as a Muslim. The garment of Islam is preferred over that of disbelief.

Each man must be properly educated regarding intercourse with their slave woman between the two of them. The *dhimmi* must also be properly educated that, if the slave woman was Muslim, there are two points of discipline. One, he fornicated with a Muslim woman and two, he fornicated with a slave woman he did not exclusively own.

Concerning the narration of the Prophet regarding the reward for having intercourse with one's wife

It has reached us that Allah's Messenger, peace and blessings be upon him and his progeny, said to a man: ((Have intercourse with your wife, for verily in that is a reward for you)). The man asked: "How can I get reward for something done in my passion?" He replied: ((You get reward in that you avoid that which Allah has prohibited for you and fulfil that which Allah has permitted for you)).[59]

Allah's Messenger, peace and blessings be upon him and his progeny, has spoken the truth! How can there not be reward? One obligates one's soul to depart from disobedience to Allah as well as deters one's heart from wandering thoughts regarding Allah's prohibitions by fulfilling his burning desire and having his soul influenced by his sensual delight.

It has reached us that Allah's Messenger, peace and blessings be upon him and his progeny, saw a woman that amazed him. He then entered upon Umm Salama and fulfilled what a man fulfils with his

[58] Similarly narrated in ***Musnad Imam Zayd, Amāli Ahmed b. 'Isa, Mušannaf Ibn Abi Shayba***

[59] Similarly narrated in ***Ŝahīh Muslim, Musnad Ahmed, Ŝahīh Ibn Hibbān, Sunan al-Bayhaqi***

wife and then left. He then said: ((Whenever a man is amazed by a woman, let him enter and fulfil his need with his wife. She is simply a woman like his wife)).[60]

By that, Allah's Messenger, peace and blessings be upon him and his progeny, meant that one can turn one's sensual delight to his wife and deter one's soul from the thought of that which does not belong to him. Otherwise, perhaps such thought will bring him close to sin.

Concerning the prohibition of women's anuses from their husbands

It is impermissible for men to have anal intercourse with their wives; it is not permitted or allowed for their husbands. This is because Allah—the Blessed and Exalted—says: **{When they have purified themselves, come unto them where Allah has ordained for thee}** (**Q. 2:222**). By His statement **{where Allah has ordained for thee}**, the Blessed and Exalted proves that they have places that Allah has prohibited them and forbade that one should enter them through such place. A woman only has two openings; therefore, if Allah has permitted that they be approach from the place He has ordained for them, then He commands that they be approached from one of the two places. If He permitted that they be approached in one place, it would be impermissible to approach them in the other place.

And Allah says: **{Thy wives are as a tillage (*harth*) for thee. Go into thy tillage as thou please}** (**Q. 2:223**). The **{tillage}** is only a place of cultivation; the place of cultivation can only be the frontal private part not the rear because the child is only sought in the vagina. As for the statement **{as thou please}**, it simply means 'when you please.'

Regarding that, it has reached us that Allah's Messenger, peace and blessings be upon him and his progeny, said: ((Anal intercourse with women is disbelief (*kufr*)!)).[61] It has also reached us that he, peace and blessings be upon him and his progeny, said: ((Allah is not shy in respect to the truth. Do not have anal intercourse with your women, for the one who has anal intercourse with their women has disbelieved [or "committed a grave offense"])).[62]

It has also reached us that he, peace and blessings be upon him and his progeny, said: ((Allah does not look at the one who has anal intercourse with a woman)).[63]

It has reached me that a man came to a scholar and ask him about that. He grumbled and said: "Do you want to do something that the people of Lot did?" What he [i.e. the scholar] said is correct; Allah has showed through him that which is correct.

Concerning a man who marries a woman and another woman says "I am the mother of them both" in that she breastfed him and his wife

If a man marries a woman and another woman says that she breastfed him and his wife, we hold to the view that he should refrain from her and let her go for fear that the matter is as [the claimant] mentioned. Precaution in that is best.

Similar has reached us from Allah's Messenger, peace and blessings be upon him and his progeny. 'Uqba b. al-Hārith[§] came to him and said: "O Messenger of Allah, I married a woman and had intercourse with her; then, a black woman claimed that she breastfed me and my wife. O Messenger of

---

[60] Similarly narrated in ***Mušannaf Ibn Abi Shayba, Sunan ad-Dārqutni, Sunan ad-Dārimi, Kanz al-'Ummāl, Bihār al-Anwār.*** Similar is transmitted in ***Ŝahīh Muslim, Sunan an-Nisā'i, Sunan Abu Dāwūd, Musnad Ahmed, Sunan at-Tirmidhi, Al-Mu'jam al-Kabīr, Al-Mu'jam al-Awsat*** except that the wife Zaynab is mentioned instead of Umm Salama.

[61] Similarly narrated in ***Sharh at-Tajrīd*** and ***Al-Mu'jam al-Awsat***

[62] Similarly narrated in ***Sharh at-Tajrīd, Sunan at-Tirmidhi, Sunan Ibn Mājah, Musnad Ahmed, Sunan ad-Dārimi, Ŝahīh Ibn Hibbān, Al-Mu'jam al-Kabīr***

[63] Similarly narrated in ***Sunan at-Tirmidhi, Sunan Ibn Mājah, Musnad Ahmed, Sunan ad-Dārimi, Ŝahīh Ibn Hibbān, Al-Mu'jam al-Awsat***

Allah, I fear that she may be lying." Allah's Messenger, peace and blessings be upon him and his progeny, then said: ((What if it is as she said?)) Then, the man separated from her based upon what Allah's Messenger said to him.[64]

Concerning the wife of one imprisoned in the domain of war

His situation is like that of a missing person. His wife is to not be married until it is confirmed that he died and that Allah has taken him.

Concerning equity between wives

There is to be equity between them in both days and nights.[65] A man mustn't show favouritism of one over the other in terms of the night or day. He must show equity between them regarding that which is not concealed from them, such as clothing, financial maintenance and gifts. However, there is no problem if he secretly does something special for one of them out of love, as long as it is not a source of injustice or harm to the rest of them.

Regarding equity, it has reached us that Allah's Messenger, peace and blessings be upon him and his progeny, used to be carried in a garment during his sickness and would circulate among his wives—equally distributing his days and nights between them.[66]

Concerning the choice of a boy between his mother and paternal uncle

If a boy gets older and his mother marries and he is educated and dispenses with the education but has not reached puberty though he has intellect and understanding, he has a choice. If he wants, he can stay with his mother. If he wants, he can stay with one of his paternal relatives, like a paternal uncle or another.

However, if his mother is not married, she is most responsible for him; she belongs to him and he stays with her—whether he likes it or not. He sticks to her in his youth, and she sticks to him in his old age. He is to support her, show kindness and righteousness to her as well as be gentle with her in all matters.

Concerning that which is obligatory on the husband and wife regarding service and maintenance in matters of their home

It is obligatory upon the man to consider those things outside of the home, maintain it and provide for its upkeep. It is obligatory upon the woman to maintain those things that are inside the home—all of its affairs and rectification of all its matters.[67]

---

[64] Similarly narrated in ***Sharh at-Tajrīd, Ŝahīh al-Bukhāri, Sunan Abu Dāwūd, Sunan at-Tirmidhi, Sunan an-Nisā'i, Sunan ad-Dārimi, Ŝahīh Ibn Hibbān***

[65] According to ***At-Tāj***, this equity in terms of the nights refers to the amount of time that the husband spends with each wife at night. He is to equally divide his nights with them even though he may not have sexual intercourse with them on those nights. This also entails that he spends that time with his wife secluded while no other person is present with them unless it is with her permission. If she permits someone to be with them, it would be considered religiously permissible. The same applies to the days. If something prevented the man from spending an equal amount of time with one wife due to some sort of necessity, he is to make up that time with her unless she permits him to do otherwise.

[66] Similarly narrated in ***Amāli Ahmed b. 'Isa***

[67] In ***Al-Muntakhab***, al-Hādi provides a bit more detail in the expectations of the husband and wife.

> I asked him: "What is obligated for the man in regard to his wife?" He replied: "He is to look into that which is outside [the house] as well as maintain it and provide for its upkeep." "What is an example of that?" "An example would be providing financial maintenance, clothing and other things that would not be appropriate for her to leave for." "What is obligated for the wife in regard to her husband?" "She is to maintain those things that are in the home as well as all of its affairs and rectification of all its matters." "What is an example of that?" "An example would be serving the house, preparing the food, cooling the water, shaking the bed, and other household services. Thusly, Allah's Messenger, peace and blessings be upon him and his progeny, decreed between 'Ali and Fātima, peace be upon them. He decreed that his daughter, Fātima, should serve the house, and he decreed that 'Ali, may Allah be pleased with him, rectify that which is outside as well as maintain its upkeep."

Similar has reached us that Allah's Messenger, peace and blessings be upon him and his progeny, charged that his daughter, Fātima, with the housework and charged 'Ali with the rectification and maintenance of everything outside.[68]

Concerning what a man should do when approaching his wife

The one who approaches his wife should mention Allah's Name before having intercourse with her. He should also recite prayers upon Muhammad and seek refuge in Allah from the rejected Satan as well as ask Allah that He make the intercourse blessed and provide a child that is God-conscious, pure, blessed and upright.[69]

They should not strip completely naked insomuch that there is nothing covering their nakedness. It has reached us from Allah's Messenger, peace and blessings be upon him and his progeny, that he said: ((When one of you approaches his wife, they should cover. They should not strip completely naked)).[70]

Concerning a man who has intercourse with his wife with someone else in the room

A man should not approach his wife while someone else is in the room. That is simply the actions of beasts without intellect or modesty. Similar has reached us from Allah's Messenger, peace and blessings be upon him and his progeny, that he prohibited a man from having intercourse with his wife while someone else was in the room—even if it was a baby in the cradle.[71]

---

[68] Similarly narrated in ***Mušannaf Ibn Abi Shayba***

[69] Sheikh 'Ali b. Bilāl reported in his ***Sharh al-Ahkām*** that Sayyid Abul-Abbās al-Hasani related with a complete chain of narrators to Musa b. Ja'far—his father—his grandfather that the Prophet, peace and blessings be upon him and his progeny, said:

> ((O 'Ali, when you go to have intercourse with your wife, say: "In the Name of Allah: O Allah, prevent me from Satan and prevent Satan from me! And if it is decreed that we have a child, do not cause Satan to harm him!")).

[70] Similarly narrated in ***Sunan Ibn Mājah, Al-Mu'jam al-Kabīr, Al-Mu'jam al-Awsat, Musnad al-Bazzār***

[71] Similarly narrated in ***Sunan al-Bayhaqi*** and ***Usd al-Ghāba*** by Ibn Athīr. In the latter reference, the author related on the authority of al-Hasan al-Basri that he heard from fifty Companions that the Prophet, peace and blessings be upon him and his progeny, prohibited a man from having intercourse with his wife while another is present—even if it were a baby in a cradle. Ibn Athīr added: "This was also related by Ibn Manda and Abu Nu'aym."

The Book of Divorce

In the Name of Allah, the Most Gracious, the Most Merciful...

The beginning chapters regarding divorce as well as an explanation of what Allah commands regarding it and the proof for it

Divorce consists of three divorces as Allah—the Blessed and Exalted—says. The three divorces do not take place except one after the second and the third after the second. That is based on the statement of the Blessed and Exalted: {**Divorce is twice and then hold fast to her with that which is good or release her with excellence**} **(Q. 2:229).**

The intended meaning of the statement of the Mighty and Majestic {**then hold fast to her with that which is good or release her with excellence**} is the third. He is saying that when one divorces her twice and then returns to her, he can either hold to that which is good forever or release her with excellence. She would not be religiously permissible after that unless she married another husband.

Concerning the sunnah divorce and it being a divorce of the waiting period

Allah, the Blessed and Exalted, says: {**O Prophet! When ye divorce women, divorce them for their waiting period and reckon the waiting period. And be wary of Allah, thy Lord. Cast them not from their houses nor let them depart save they commit an open indecency. Such are the limits of Allah. And whosoever transgresses Allah's limits, such one verily wrongs his own soul. Thou know not: it may be that Allah shall cause a new matter to occur afterwards**} **(Q. 65:1)**.

The Glorified demonstrates to His slaves guidance for their affairs, and He commands them to rectify their deeds. By such, they come to know the error that they used to commit. He then commands them to {**reckon the waiting period**}. The {**waiting period**} refers to menstruations as well as that which Allah has appointed as a waiting period for women. Then, He prohibits from expelling them from their houses until they complete their waiting period.

Then, the Glorified says: {**Such are the limits of Allah. And whosoever transgresses Allah's limits, such one verily wrongs his own soul**}. He is saying that Allah decrees that that they not be expelled from their houses. His decree is His command, and His command is His limits that one should not transgress. Therefore, the one who acts contrary to Allah is the one who expels them and disobeys.

Then, the Mighty and Majestic says: {**Thou know not: it may be that Allah shall cause a new matter to occur afterwards**}. This means: it may be that Allah may renew the man's love for her after he decided to divorce her and he may return to her. After the divorce and disagreement, there may be affection and mercy. Therefore, if the divorcee wants to divorce, he should divorce by the sunnah divorce that Allah demonstrated and chose for him. Such person should not transgress, for if he transgresses, it would be an error. It would necessitate the divorce that he necessitated on himself which was contrary to that with which he was commanded.

The sunnah divorce is that when he wants to divorce her, he avoids his wife until she is pure from her menstruation, departed from her menses and has performed the purification wash from her menstrual cycle. Then, he says to her when she is pure with no intercourse "You are divorced" (*anti tāliq*) or "You are to observe the waiting period" (*a'taddi*) and intends divorce by that. Afterwards, he avoids her allowing her waiting period to pass—until she menstruates three times.

If it becomes evident that he wants to return to her during the third menstruation, he has more right to her than she and her guardian as long as it is during her waiting period before she is purified. If he desires such, there should be two witnesses that he returned to her. Then, she will belong to him. However, if he delays returning to her until she completed three menstruations and washed from her third menstruation with water, she has more right to herself than he has and he will have to propose a new marriage contract with her. If she wants, she can remarry him; if she wants, she can marry another. If he wants to return to her, he would have to renew the marriage proposal to her guardian, pay a new dowry and contract it with two witnesses.

If he decided to divorce her another time after having divorced her the first time, he would divorce her just as he did the first time when she is pure with no intercourse. He is to say to her: "You are divorced" or "You are to observe the waiting period" and intend divorce by that. Then he avoids her during the waiting period of this second divorce.

If it becomes evident to him just as it was evident to him before that they want to nullify her waiting period before completion of the three menstruations, he has more right to her than she and her guardian. There should be two witnesses that he returned to her. Then, he would have taken possession of her, and there would be only one divorce left for him. However, if he delayed until she completed the waiting period for this second divorce, he would have to propose marriage again. If she wants, she can remarry him; if she wants, she can avoid such. If she remarries him, he remarries her with a guardian, two witnesses and a new dowry. Then there would remain only one more divorce for him and no other because he already divorced with two divorces, and he remarried her with two remarriages. This would constitute the third as Allah said: **{then hold fast to her with that which is good or release her with excellence} (Q. 2:229)**.

If he were to divorce her a third time, it would not be permissible for him to remarry her unless she married someone else. She should not marry another person until she menstruated three times and purified herself from the blood of the third time. If she married at any point during her waiting period, the marriage would be invalid and not sound for her.

For each divorce, the one who pronounced the divorce should—if the waiting period is observed in his house and her house—take precaution from looking at her hair, body or any part of her nakedness. He should seek her permission if he wants to enter upon her either by loudly clearing his throat or by his voice or speech. He should take precaution, and she should increase her clothing. It is impermissible for him to discontinue his financial maintenance of her or her servants. If she needs any clothing for her nakedness, he is to clothe her.

He should have his divorce witnessed. If he wants, it can take place during the pronouncement of the wording the first time; if he wants, it can take place during the dissolution of her waiting period and her departure from his house. It should be witnessed by two just witnesses. This is the waiting period divorce and its meaning regarding a woman.

If a man desires to divorce a woman whose menstruation discontinued or a young female who never menstruated, I encourage him to refrain from intercourse with her until a month passes in which there is no intercourse. Then, he says to her at the head of the month "You are divorced" or "Observe your waiting period" intending by such divorce. If he divorces her before the month passes, there is no restriction on him because there was no observance of menstruation by which she would have to be purified. Then, she would have to observe her waiting period. Her waiting period would be three months as Allah says: **{And those who are beyond the age of menstruation amongst thy wives—if thou have any doubt, their waiting period is three months—as well as those who have not menstruated} (Q. 65:4)**.

Allah makes the waiting period three months for those who discontinued menstruation as well as for those who never menstruated. If he wants to return to her before the completion of the three months, he has more right to than she and her guardian. Two witnesses should witness the return, and then she belongs to him. However, if he delays until three months pass, she has more right on herself and he would have to propose anew to her. If she wants, she could remarry him; if she wants, she could marry another. All her matters will be as they were at first, and the statement from us regarding her would be just as the statement from the first.

The one who wants to divorce his wife with a sunnah divorce while she is pregnant should delay and refrain from intercourse with her until a month passes. Then, he can pronounce the divorce. However, if he divorces her before that, it would be permissible for him if he were cautious by refraining from her for a month. It would be for him to divorce her when he likes before that because he did not observe menstruation from her while she was pregnant and purified herself after intercourse with him.[1] When she delivers that which is in her womb, she has more authority on herself than he. As Allah says: **{As for those who are laden with child, their period shall be till they deliver their load}** (Q. 65:4). If she delivers her child on the following day, she is in charge of her own affair and has more authority over herself than her husband. If he wants to return to her, he has to propose. She can return to him if she wants.

If he divorces her while she is pregnant and desires to return to her during her pregnancy, he has more right than she and her guardian. It is not for him to expel her from his house until she delivers that which is in her womb.

To her belongs financial maintenance and lodging, as Allah says: **{Lodge them wherein ye lodge from thy wealth, and harm them not so as to straiten them. If they are laden with child, maintain them till they deliver their load}** (Q. 65:6). Therefore, every divorcee who divorces his wife should house her with him and should not house her with other than him in restricted housing. Allah has prohibited him from restricting her; rather, He commanded him to do the opposite regarding her. That is based on the statement of the Exalted: **{and harm them not so as to straiten them}**. It is impermissible for a man who maintains his wife during the observance of her waiting period to harm and commit excess to her—even if he does not desire her. Rather, it is obligatory on him upon the completion of her term to maintain her with goodness if he desires her or divorce her with goodness if he wants to divorce her. As Allah, the Glorified, says: **{When ye divorce women and they hath reached their term, hold to them with goodness or release them with goodness. Hold not to them as to harm them lest ye transgress. Whosoever does such hath wronged his own soul}** (Q. 2:231).

The **{term}** that is to be reached refers to their completion of the third menstruation in the first and second divorces. Allah says regarding the permissibility of remarriage between a husband and wife after an irrevocable divorce due to it being the third divorce after which remarriage is impermissible until marrying another spouse: **{And when ye have divorced women and they reach their term, harm them not in the way of their marrying their husbands if there is contentment between them in goodness. This is an admonition for whosoever amongst thee who believeth in Allah and the Last Day}** (Q. 2:232).

My father related to me from his father regarding the sunnah divorce:

> It is that one divorces her in the state of purity from not having touched her. He then says to her: "Observe your waiting period." Then her waiting period passes until she completes three menstruations. If there is no completion of menstruations or there is an interruption of her waiting period, he would have more right to her than she has on herself. If he wants to return to her, he can return to her even without her permission. There should be two males to witness the return. If he wants to divorce her, he should maintain her until she completes her waiting period of three menstruations. Then, she has more right to herself after that.

[1] In ***Al-Muntakhab***, al-Hādi was similarly asked about divorcing a pregnant woman. He replied: "It is said that he is to leave her for a month and then divorce her. As for me, I say that he can divorce her when he wants if she is pregnant."

As for the pregnant woman, her husband can divorce her when he wants to divorce her. Her waiting period is until she delivers what is in her womb. That is based on the statement of Allah: **{As for those who are laden with child, their period shall be till they deliver their load} (Q. 65:4)**. They refer to the divorcees.

My father related to me from his father that the latter was asked about a man who is divorced without being witnessed and remarried without being witnessed. He replied: "It is necessary that there be witnesses. This is due to the fear that there may be disagreement and dispute between them both."

Concerning that from which a woman in her waiting period should refrain and concerning the one whose menstruation is delayed

If her waiting period was during the death of her husband, she should not apply henna or perfume, wear elaborately patterned clothing, style her hair nicely, travel to Hajj or 'Umra or wear ornaments for beauty. Neither should she apply kohl unless she fears some eye sickness. She can observe the waiting period anywhere she wants—whether it is her father's house or her husband's house.

As for the waiting period of one with a revocable divorce, there is no restriction in beautifying herself or applying perfume. Rather, she can apply perfume, beautify herself and manifest such to her husband in order to entice him back to her. She is to observe her waiting period in her husband's house until the completion of her waiting period.

As for the woman who is divorced and always waiting on her menstruation, it is impermissible for her to observe her waiting period without menstruation as long as she is an age in which she menstruates. This is because perhaps the menstruation is prevented due to some defect or illness that occurred in the woman. If it is delayed due to her illness, one does not consider (alternatively) the waiting period (using only the time period) months until she reaches the age in which there is no longer menstruation; that is sixty years old. When she reaches this, then the months are counted as the waiting period. This is a trial and she must be patient with this.

If she or her husband dies before she menstruates or no longer menstruates, she inherits from him and he inherits from her. If he desired to return to her at any point after a little of lot, he is considered returned and has more right to her during her waiting period than she.

My father related to me that his father was asked regarding the one who no longer menstruates or never menstruated and how they are to be divorced and observe their waiting periods. He replied:

He is to divorce her in time periods and she is to observe her waiting period in time periods as Allah says: **{their waiting period is three months} (Q. 65:4)**. Similar is the case with a woman who has continuous vaginal bleeding. When the blood comes and ends, he divorces her.

My father related to me that his father said regarding the divorced woman from whom the menstruation is discontinued from her: "The waiting period is observed with menstruation, even if it is extended or removed. If she no longer menstruates, her waiting period is three months."

By his statement 'If she no longer menstruates,' my grandfather means 'when she reaches the age in which menstruation is discontinued and she does not menstruate after that.'

My father related to me that his father was asked about the divorced woman and the widow as well as where the both of them are to observe their waiting period. He replied:

The both of them are to observe their waiting period in the house of the divorcee and the deceased except in the case of the widow; she has the choice. This is the statement of the Commander of Believers, 'Ali b. Abi Ṭālib, upon him be peace.[2] She can observe her waiting period where she wants.

[2] Sheikh 'Ali b. Bilāl related the following reports in his ***Sharh al-Ahkām***:

Concerning the one who divorces before having intercourse and concerning the waiting period of the woman who initiated divorce and the *umm walad*

Whoever divorces his wife before having intercourse with her—she gets half the dowry and there is no waiting period for her. According to us, the same is the case whether he were to pronounce the divorce on her once, twice or thrice. We hold to the view that three [pronouncements of divorce] return to one even when they are uttered together—whether she was divorced after he had intercourse with her or not had intercourse with her. We will elaborate the proofs regarding that—if Allah wills—in the place where we mention it.

It has reached us that Zayd b. ʿAli, may Allah bless him, said regarding a man who divorces his wife three times but had not had intercourse with her:

> It is an irrevocable divorce by the first [pronouncement], so the rest are done and do not count for anything. She gets half the dowry and there is no waiting period for her. If he says to her before having intercourse with her "You are divorced. You are divorced. You are divorced" three times, this is considered divorce. It is confirmed by the statement of the one who declares the divorce "You are divorced" three times in one statement. It is better that it be made clear by it.

My father related to me that his father said: "For every divorce before intercourse in which the dowry has been determined for her, the divorced woman is to get half the dowry."

My father related to me that his father said: "For every divorce after intercourse in which the dowry has been determined for her, the divorced woman is to get the full dowry."

My father related to me that his father was asked about the divorce being declared three times to a woman before intercourse with her. He replied: "It is considered an irrevocable divorce, and he would have to propose a new marriage."

As for the woman who initiated divorce, her waiting period is obligatory and her husband is to financially maintain her unless there was a precondition placed on her by her husband that there would be no financial maintenance or lodging for her. If it is the case that there is a mutual agreement between them regarding this precondition, it will be permissible based on what was agreed between them. As for the waiting period of the *umm walad*, it is the same as the waiting period of the female slave.

My father related to me that his father was asked about the waiting period of the woman who initiated divorce and the place where she is to observe her waiting period as well as whether there is lodging and financial maintenance for her. He replied:

> Lodging and financial maintenance is to the extent that it was a precondition of her husband for her in her initiation of divorce. If that is the case, her waiting period would be the waiting period of any divorcee.

Sayyid Abul-Abbās reported to us [with a complete chain of narrators to] Zayd b. ʿAli—his father—his grandfather that ʿAli, upon him be peace, said: "The divorcee who is divorced thrice does not leave her house—whether night or day—until her appointed time permits her. The widow can leave during the day but not spend the night elsewhere. None of them can beautify themselves or apply perfume unless the pronouncement of divorce was pronounced on them once or twice. If that is the case, they can apply perfume and beautify themselves."

Sayyid Abul-Abbās also reported to us [with a complete chain of narrators to] Ibn Ḍumayra—his father—his grandfather that ʿAli, upon him be peace, said regarding the widow that she is to not wear elaborately patterned clothing nor touch anything with perfume. However, she can comb her hair but without perfume. She is to not apply kohl on her eyes unless out of medical necessity; she can then apply kohl with *ithmid*, but she is to not wear any ornaments.

It is narrated with the same chain of narrators to ʿAli, upon him be peace, that he used to say: "The widow can observe the waiting period in her house and not the house of her deceased husband."

My father related to me that his father said regarding the waiting period of the *umm walad* when her master dies: "Her waiting period is that of the female slave."

Concerning the waiting period of the *dhimmi* and the female apostate

The waiting period of the female apostate is like that of any other woman. If she is free, it is that of the free woman; if she is a slave, it is that of the slave woman. Her waiting period is that of the free woman. The waiting period of the female *dhimmi* if she embraces Islam, is divorced by a *dhimmi* or the latter dies is like the waiting period of Muslim women.

My father related to me that his father was asked about the waiting period of the female apostate. He replied:

> Her waiting period is like that of any other women. If she is free, her waiting period is that of a free woman; if she is a slave, her waiting period is that of a slave woman. The waiting period of the slave woman is the same as the waiting period of the free woman.

My father related to me that his father said regarding the female *dhimmi* that is divorced or embraces Islam during her waiting period after her husband dies: "She is to observe her waiting period until it is complete."

Concerning the declarations of freedom (*al-bariyya*), release (*al-khaliyya*), separation (*al-bāyin*), settlement (*al-batta*), prohibition (*al-harām*) and "Your rope is upon your own withers"

These narrations have been narrated from the Commander of Believers, 'Ali b. Abi Ťālib, upon him be peace; however, they are not authentically attributed to him nor are they firmly established according to us. It is simply said that it was from him.[3]

The best of what we hold to regarding that is that it counts as one, and he has the right to return to her as long as it is during her waiting period. However, once she completes her waiting period, he must propose to her anew just as the proposal of anyone else.

My father related to me that his father was asked about the declarations of separation, settlement, freedom, release, prohibition and the statement "Your rope is upon your own withers." He replied:

> It is narrated from 'Ali that he used to consider such as three [divorces]; however, that is not authentically attributed to him according to us. That is because they allegedly found it from him claiming that it was in a book. The minimum regarding that—according to us—is that it counts as one [divorce].

Concerning the statement "Your affair is in your hands" and concerning choice and divorce before marriage

If the man says to his wife "I have left the matter to you, so choose," it would be permissible for her affair to be hers. If she wants, she can divorce herself; if she wants, she can remain married to her husband. This is—according to us—from his action and her action; this is a form of deputation. When he says "Your affair is in your hands," it is like he deputised her with her own divorce. If she wants, she can divorce.

It would be permissible for him to do such to her just as it would be permissible for him to do such to someone else. If he were to deputise someone to divorce her and says to him "If you want to divorce her [from me] then divorce her," that would be permissible for the one who was deputised since her

---

[3] It is related in the ***Musnad Imam Zayd*** as well as the ***Amāli Ahmed b. 'Isa*** that Imam 'Ali was asked about a man who says to his wife "You are free" or "You are released" or "You are separated" or "You are prohibited from me" or "Your rope is upon your own withers" intending divorce. He supposedly replied that such declaration of any of the aforementioned phrases would be considered as three divorces or an irrevocable divorce. That withstanding, the man who wanted to remarry his wife could only do so after she has married another. Imam al-Hādi, upon him be peace, also declared the inauthenticity of this report in ***Al-Muntakhab***.

husband appointed her affair to such person. Thus and based on that is it derived that the husband can appoint the affair of divorce to her. It would be as though he deputised her to divorce herself and permitted her to actualise it when she wants.

The matter of appointing her to divorce herself and permitting her to do so would be as if he deputised another wife to divorce his wife from him and permitted the other wife to divorce him from her if she wants. If the wife wanted, she could divorce him from her and actualise the divorce he appointed to her. From that it is derived that it is permissible for her since he appointed this to her. We therefore permit that she can divorce herself with his permission just as we permit that someone else can divorce her from him with his permission. In all the cases of deputation and its judgements, women are just like men. Whatever is obligatory on one is obligatory on the other, and whatever is established for one is established for the other.

Have you not considered that if a man said to his female slave "I appoint the matter of your manumission to you; therefore, manumit yourself whenever you want. I have placed it in your hands, and given you permission to have say in the matter" and the slave girl says "I manumit myself with your permission, and I am free for the sake of Allah," that would be permissible for her master? She would be manumitted based upon her statement. No one with intellect would dispute that nor would the ignorant doubt that! Likewise, if he were to say to her "Verily, I appoint the manumission of your children to you; I permit you to do that and manumit. Therefore, manumit them when you want" and she says "Verily, I manumit them with your permission and free them for the sake of Allah," that would be permissible for him and they would become free and not owned slaves. They would be considered free and manumitted based upon her statement.

If a man said to his wives "Choose me or yourselves" and they choose him, that would not be considered a divorce according to us, nor would it necessitate separation based on his statement or theirs. If they choose themselves, this would be considered a divorce. Regarding that is what took place from the action of Allah's Messenger, peace and blessings be upon him and his progeny, when he gave his wives a choice by the command of Allah. That is based on the statement of Allah: **{O Prophet, say unto thy wives: "If ye desire the life of this world and its beauties, come and I shall content thee and dismiss thee with a beautiful dismissal. But if ye desire Allah and His Messenger and the abode of the afterlife, verily Allah hath readied for the right-acting ones amongst thee a great reward!"} (Q. 33:28-29)**. Then, Allah's Messenger, peace and blessings be upon him and his progeny, did what Allah commanded him in giving them the choice and they chose him. That was not considered a divorce from him, peace and blessings be upon him and his progeny.

If a man divorces before contracting a marriage, that would not be considered a divorce according to us. If a woman was designated specifically and then he says "On the day I marry so-n-so, she is divorced" this would not necessitate that she is divorced because he had not contracted a marriage with her. Similar has been narrated from the Commander of Believers, 'Ali b. Abi Ṭālib, upon him be peace. He used to say: "There is no divorce or manumission unless previously contracted."[4]

My father related to me that his father was asked about a man who said "On the day I marry so-n-so, she is divorced" and "When I am married to a woman, she is divorced," or if he said: "If I am married to so-n-so, she is divorced." He replied:

[4] Similarly narrated in ***Musnad Imam Zayd, Sharh at-Tajrīd, Sunan Ibn Mājah, Sunan Abu Dāwūd, Sunan ad-Dārqutni, Al-Mu'jam al-Awsat***. It is also narrated as the statement of Imam Ja'far as-Sādiq in ***Bihār al-Anwār***.

It has been narrated from the Commander of the Believers, 'Ali b. Abi Ťālib that he said: "There is no divorce except after marriage, and there is no manumission except after ownership—even if she was named."[5]

It is also narrated that a man from the Anŝār insulted his nephew and argued with him. Then, his nephew swore to him that he would divorce and not marry his daughter and that she would be divorced if he married her. The father asked Allah's Messenger, peace and blessings be upon him and his progeny, and he commanded him to marry her and did not necessitate that he divorce her before marrying her.[6]

My father related to me that his father said regarding a man who gives his wife the choice between him and themselves: "Allah's Messenger, peace and blessings be upon him and his progeny, gave his wives the choice and their choice of him was not considered a divorce."

My father related to me that his father was asked about a man who said to his wife "Your affair is in your hands." He replied:

It is narrated that the Commander of Believers, 'Ali b. Abi Ťālib used to say: "When her affair is placed in her hand, he has removed from his hand what was previously in it. Only one divorce occurs. The statement 'Your affair is in your hands' confirms that it is my choice." That is—according to us—not the same because Allah's Messenger, peace and blessings be upon him and his progeny, gave the choice to his wives and that was not considered a divorce. This is also the position of the Commander of Believers, 'Ali b. Abi Ťālib, upon him be peace.[7] He [i.e. 'Ali] was most knowing of what he [i.e. the Prophet] said.

If a man says to his wife "Your affair is in your hands" without specifying what her affair is and she does not accept what he has appointed to her until she leaves that specific meeting, her affair will not belong to her after that. This is because she avoided acceptance of such and she did not accept until after divorce. Her affair was permitted and negated. However, if she accepted her affair and actualised the right of divorce that was appointed to her, it would be obligatory upon him and her as well as binding upon them both.

If she were to divorce herself with his permission three times, our statement regarding that is just like our statement regarding three [pronouncements of divorce]. It simply returns to one [divorce] in our statement, choice and opinion. He can return to her during her waiting period.

Concerning unlawful pronouncements

For anyone who declares an unlawful pronouncement[8] to his wife, it is impermissible for him to approach her after that unless he expiates with those expiations that Allah has obligated upon him. He is to free slaves before he touches her. If he cannot find such, he is to fast two consecutive months before he touches her or has intercourse with her. Whoever cannot fast is permitted to feed; he is to feed sixty needy, free Muslims compelled by need. Then, his wife would be religiously permissible for him after that.

---

[5] Similarly narrated in ***Amāli Ahmed b. 'Isa, Mušannaf Ibn Abi Shayba, Sunan al-Bayhaqi, Majmu' az-Zawā`id, Al-Mu'jam as-Saghīr***. In the following sources it is related as a hadith from the Prophet: ***Al-Mustadrak, Sunan ad-Dārqutni, Mušannaf Ibn Abi Shayba, Sunan al-Bayhaqi, Kanz al-'Ummāl, Majmu' az-Zawā`id, Al-Mu'jam al-Kabīr, Al-Mu'jam al-Awsaí, Musnad al-Bazzār***

[6] Similarly narrated in ***Amāli Ahmed b. 'Isa***

[7] Similarly narrated in ***Sharh at-Tajrīd, Ŝahīh al-Bukhāri, Ŝahīh Muslim, Sunan at-Tirmidhi, Sunan Ibn Mājah, Sunan Abu Dāwūd, Sunan an-Nisā`i***

[8] For the Arabic word *žihār,* we have opted for the translation unlawful pronouncement' due to its more encompassing connotation. The Arabic word is derived from the word for 'back,' as the pre-Islamic Arabs used to say as a form of divorce: "You are to me as my mother's back!" This is to imply that the wife was allegorically equated to the husband's mother and would therefore declare the woman impermissible for him to marry and have intercourse with—thus, necessitating divorce.

Regarding that is what Allah—the Blessed and Exalted—says when He revealed to His Prophet regarding the unlawful pronouncement of Aws b. as-Sāmit al-Anŝāri[§] to his wife Khawla bt. Tha'laba.[§] He was looking at her while she was praying and was aroused by her. He then commanded her to come to him, and she refused. After she completed her prayer, he was angry with her and said: "You are to me as the back (*žahr*) of my mother!" This was the method of divorce in the pre-Islamic era of ignorance and an unlawful pronouncement. He regretted doing so, and she regretted. She approached Allah's Messenger, peace and blessings be upon him and his progeny, and mentioned that to him. She said: "Look. Is there repentance for him?" He replied: ((I do not see that there is repentance for him in returning to you)). She raised her hands to Allah and said; "O Allah! Verily Aws divorced me while I am old in age, weak in my body, frail in my bones and the desire of men has left me!" Allah had mercy on her and revealed the expiation. Allah's Messenger, peace and blessings be upon him and his progeny, summoned him and said: ((Free a slave)). He replied: "I do not have one." The Prophet, peace and blessings be upon him and his progeny, then said: ((Fast two consecutive months)). He replied: "O Messenger of Allah, if I do not eat three times a day, I could not withstand it!" He, peace and blessings be upon him and his progeny, then said: ((Feed sixty needy people)). He replied: "I do not have anything to give in charity unless Allah and His Messenger gives it to me." Allah's Messenger, peace and blessings be upon him and his progeny, helped him with an *araq* of dates. An *araq* is a large bucket. In it was thirty *ŝā'* of dates for charity. He said: "O Messenger of Allah, by the One who sent you as a Prophet in truth, there is no family more in need than us!" The Prophet, peace and blessings be upon him and his progeny, then said: ((Go ahead and eat—you and your family. Have sexual intercourse with your wife)). Then, Allah revealed what He revealed regarding these two Anŝāris: **{Those who make an unlawful pronouncement to their wives and then goes back on what they said, they are to free a slave before they touch one another. That is for thee to take exhortation. And Allah is aware of what ye do. Whosoever cannot find one, then he fasts for two months continuously before they touch one another. Then whosoever cannot, he is to feed sixty needy people} (Q. 58:4)**.[9]

Others have said that the slave to be manumitted in unlawful pronouncements can be a disbeliever. They claim that their proof of such is that the verse does not specifically say 'believer' as He says 'believer' elsewhere.

Allah forbid that such statement is correct! Nor is it even close to the truth or right statement! We seek refuge in Allah that we should ever advocate for such! How can it be permissible that one free the disbelieving idolaters in manumission and utilise the expiations due to the believers' shortcomings for the people of rejection amongst the disbelievers? How can it be that one actualises the manumission of those who object to the Messenger of the Lord of creation instead of freeing Muslim slaves and those whose gnosis of Allah is perfect and who has established the truth of the trustworthy Messenger? Rather, we say that it is impermissible for one to do such; it is not religiously permissible for one to manumit disbelieving slaves. This is because the manumitter does not manumit except out of affection, love and adoration. Adoration is affection, affection is mercy, and mercy is love and compassion. Allah has commanded contrary to that for disbelievers and hypocrites.

He said as is revealed in His Clear Book and commanded Muhammad, the Seal of the Prophets: **{O Prophet, strive against the disbelievers and hypocrites and be harsh against them. Their resting place is Hell, an evil destination!} (Q. 9:73)**. Allah commanded him to be harsh against the one who disbelieves in the Book and rejects the Messenger of the Lord of lords. It is not harshness against the one who associates partners with the Most Gracious and stubbornly rejects the Light and Proof that was revealed when one does good to him while the latter is arrogant and when one manumits him from slavery while the latter transgresses and associates partners with Allah, the Exalted. Rather, it is obligatory for one to manifest contempt against such people and similar among creation. He is to also

[9] Similarly narrated in ***Sunan Abu Dāwūd, Sunan al-Bayhaqi, Al-Mustadrak, Sunan ad-Dārimi, Musnad Ahmed, Bihār al-Anwār***

demonstrate diminution and remoteness for them as well as restriction to the extent of permissible restriction against them. The clear superiority of the Muslims due to such good action regarding them must be clearly demonstrated so that they can recognise the virtue of Islam and its people. Such must also take place so that they can be desirous of the path and religion of Muhammad, peace and blessings be upon him and his progeny. Insomuch that they can be with the Muslims and included among them instead of other than them from the people of disbelief and opposition. Never in the land of Islam should the Muslim slave be relegated secondary status.

Therefore, whoever is in straitened circumstances but does not find it difficult to purchase a Muslim slave and cannot find one in any city close to him or with any people, we hold to the opinion that one is to not overstep the Muslims and manumit any idolater. If he wants to speedily return to his wife, we hold the opinion that he must fast. If he is unable to fast, he is to feed. This is because if he cannot find slaves that are permissible to manumit—even if he can afford one—he is not considered as one who has [a slave]. It is similar to one who finds a slave but does not find the price; such would be considered as not having found one due to the absence of his/her price. Similar is the case with one who finds his/her price in the absence of himself/herself. This is—according to me—considered not having found such one. It is not considered as having found one until s/he is found as well as his/her price. At that point, one is considered having found him/her and such one would be obligated by Allah to manumit him/her. This is the same as the case with a traveller according to me.

Have you not considered that the one who finds water but does not find its price is not considered as one who found it and the dust purification would be obligatory upon such person? Have you not considered that if he found the price but had not found the water with which to purify himself, he would not be considered as having found water despite the existence of the price and would be obligated to perform the dust purification with the high earth with which he is commanded?

As for the one who says that one can manumit a disbelieving slave despite the presence or absence of a Muslim slave, I do not advocate that. The likeness of that—according to me and anyone who is fair to his intellect and abandons the arrogance of his own understanding—is a man who has an excess of wealth but then looks for water. He cannot find it but can find milk, vinegar, honey, rose water or vinegar drink (*sikanjibīna*). If it were permissible for him to buy any of those things and perform the ritual ablution with it, it would be permissible for him to buy and manumit a disbeliever if he cannot find a Muslim. Rather, manumitting a disbeliever—according to me—is a major objectionable action and a sin of the body because such person is not safe from his misconduct if he were to escape and separate from slavery. Nor would such person be free from the bonds of the slave himself. Rather, leaving him as a slave is in more proximity to the Most Gracious and more resembling righteousness and excellence.

Similarly, we heard from the people of knowledge regarding the discouragement of manumitting disobedient Muslims. All of the scholars from the Messenger's Progeny agree that Muslim slaves should not be freed unless one is safe from their misconduct in religion. How much more so should one discourage manumitting idolaters who oppose Allah at every stage and ascribe falsehood to the Book that Allah revealed to His Prophet, those who do not incline to Islam and the Muslims out of insanity but rather earn loss and an evil end?

3

The unlawful pronouncement is when a man says to his wife "You are to me as the back of my mother" or "...like her womb" or "...like her thighs" or "...like her legs" or "...like her shins" or "...like her privates" or "...like her hand" or like anything else intending by such divorce. If he says that intending divorce but not intending an unlawful pronouncement, it is considered a divorce. It would be permissible for him to return to her during her waiting period, and expiation would not be obligatory for him.

If he were to say "I do not intend divorce or an unlawful pronouncement. I simply intended a vow," others say that he is a false swearer who is obligated to expiate. However, we do not advocate that because a false swearer is not obligated to expiate, and expiation is not obligatory except on one who swears by Allah.

If a man says to his wife "You are to me as my mother" or "...like my mother," he is asked about his intention. If he intended divorce, it would necessitate divorce. If he intended an unlawful pronouncement, it would necessitate an unlawful pronouncement. If he says "I did not intend that" or "...not that," it would be considered a lie because she is not like his mother nor could she ever be considered as his mother. One who utters an unlawful pronouncement by his milk mother, milk sister, milk daughter or a woman connected by milk relationship is not considered as one who utters an unlawful pronouncement. It is not considered an unlawful pronouncement except if it is by his mother and not other than her as Allah said.[10]

Concerning the oath of abstention (*al-ilā`u*) and the statement regarding it

According to us, the oath of abstention is when a man swears by Allah that he will not touch his wife four months or any number of months more than that. As for the one who swears for less than four months—beit a Friday, two Fridays, a month or two months—he would not be considered one who swore an oath of abstention.[11]

If a man swears an oath of abstention and completes the time period of his oath but does not return to his wife and expiates for what he swore, we hold to the view that the imam is to stop him and say: "Compensate your wife." If he chooses to compensate, he expiates for his oath and returns to his wife. If he refuses to compensate, the imam can separate them both. His separating them can be a command for them to separate, or he can force him to divorce.

We do not hold to the view that the imam should stop him until after the passing of four months. As for before it, we do not hold to the view that he should stop him. Rather, he is to delay and allow him to look into his own affair so he can return to what he should do. Otherwise, if the time that Allah has given him has passed, then the imam should stop him. If the man does not approach the imam and wasn't stopped after a year or two, the imam must stop him and his wife will not be considered divorced until he is stopped. When he is stopped, he returns to consummation; otherwise, the imam

---

[10] This concept of unlawful pronouncements is expanded more in ***Al-Muntakhab***.

I asked him about a man who says to his wife "You are to me like my sister's back!" or "...like my aunt's back!" or "...like your sister's back!" or "...like your mother's back!" or ...like the back of any unmarriageable relative other than his mother. He replied: "Neither of those would be considered an unlawful pronouncement. Others say that all such statements are unlawful pronouncements, but we do not acknowledge such. According to us, it is not other than when a man says to his wife: "You are to me as the back of my mother!" Then, he would be considered one who declared an unlawful pronouncement as Allah says: **{Those amongst thee who make an unlawful pronouncement to their wives—they are not their mothers...} (Q. 58:2).** He does not mention anyone but the mothers." "What if he says 'You are to me like my sister's back!' or '...like the back of some unmarriageable relatives!' Does he intend by such?" "No. This is because these are lies." "What if he intends by such divorce or refraining my wife from me? What is one to do?" "That divorce which he intended would then be considered binding."

[11] Two different opinions are said to exist from al-Hādi regarding whether one is considered a swearer of the oath of abstention if such person had not specified the time period that he would not have intercourse with his wife. One opinion—which is said to be in the ***Ahkām***—says that such person would be considered a swearer of the oath of abstention. The other opinion—which is in ***Al-Muntakhab***—is that he would not be considered such. Imam Abu Ṭālib reported these two different opinions of al-Hādi in his ***At-Tahrīr***, as well as ***Al-Intiṣār*** of Imam Yahya b. Hamza and ***Al-Bahr*** of Imam Ibn Murtaḍa.

However, a closer reading of the two opinions does not reflect a contradiction because al-Hādi's statement in the ***Ahkām*** is not related to specifying or not specifying a time. This issue of time specification is not mentioned in the ***Ahkām*** at all. Rather, in ***Al-Muntakhab***, he was specifically asked: "What if a man swears an oath that he will not have intercourse with his wife but had not specified a time?" Al-Hādi replied: "He would not be considered a swearer of an oath of abstention..." [Ref. ***Al-Qawl Awwal***]

seperates them. It is similar to the statement of the Commander of Believers, ‘Ali bin Ťālib, upon him be peace, that he used to stop it after two years.[12]

Regarding the oath of abstention, the Lord of creation says: {**Those who swear an oath of abstention upon their wives shall delay four months. If they return, verily Allah is Oft-Pardoning, Most Gracious. But if they are determined to divorce, verily Allah is All-Hearing, All-Knowing**} (**Q. 2:226-227**).

The imam stops him when the matter is brought to him and says: “Retain your wife and expiate for your oath! Return to her; otherwise, divorce her.” Then he returns upon the determination of the imam and divorces. If he refuses to divorce and refuses to return, the imam can detain and restrict him indefinitely until he returns or divorces.

My father related to me that his father was asked whether the one who swore an oath can be stopped after four months or not. He replied:

> The best I heard regarding it is that he is to be stopped. This is the statement of the Commander of Believers, ‘Ali b. Abi Ťālib, as well as that of the scholars of the Messenger’s Progeny, upon them be peace.[13]

My father related to me that his father said: “There is no oath of abstention on the swearer except four months or more. Whoever swears for less than four months is not considered a swearer of an oath of abstention.”

My father related to me that his father was asked about the oath of abstention and its manner. He replied: “The oath of abstention is when one swears to his wife that he will not have intercourse with her or go near her.”

The term ‘compensate’ refers to intercourse itself. However, the one who is unable to do such, he can do so by his statement and his compensation is witnessed. If a man swears an oath of abstention to his wife and then desired to return to her before the passing of four months but was defective and could not have intercourse, it is permissible for him to compensate her with his statement. He then says: “Bear witness that I went back on my oath and returned to my wife.”

If he is healthy and is able to have intercourse, it is obligatory for him to approach her as long as he is able and is possible for him. It is impermissible for him to leave that after he has the ability. This is because his oath of abstention and oath can only take place by intercourse and approach.

If someone who is defective and unable to have intercourse swears an oath of abstention to his wife but then desires to return to her after four months, it is sufficient for him to compensate by means of his statement and have that witnessed. If he is healthy after that and able to have intercourse, there is no problem for him to leave off intercourse for a day, two days or more after having obtained ability. This is because the months in which he swore had already passed. Similarly, if he swore for ten months, the matter in those would be like the matter in four months.

If he swore an oath of abstention that he would not go near her for four months and then divorced her the day after the period of his oath, it would necessitate divorce; this would be considered one divorce. Her waiting period is completed after the four months or before it similarly according to us. This is because we do not hold to the view that her divorce was necessitated by his oath of abstention at the completion of the four months without stopping even if a year or more has passed. For that reason, we

---

[12] It is narrated in ***Musnad Imam Zayd*** and ***Amāli Ahmed b. ‘Isa*** that ‘Ali stopped it after four months to a year without specifying two years.

[13] Sheikh ‘Ali b. Bilāl reported in his ***Sharh al-Ahkām*** on the authority of Sayyid Abul-Abbās al-Hasani with a complete chain of narrators to Zayd b. ‘Ali—his father—his grandfather that ‘Ali, upon them be peace, said:

> The oath of abstention is considered an oath and a swearing. If a man were to swear by Allah that he will not go near his wife for four months or more, he would be considered a swearer of an oath of abstention. If it is less than four months, he would not be considered a swearer of an oath of abstention.

say that the passing of the months is not required of him in divorce; whether its departure was before the completion of the waiting period or afterwards.

We do not say what others say regarding that. They hold to the view that one is to observe the completion of the four months before the divorce waiting period firstly, and then one is to observe the completion of the divorce waiting period secondly. This is invalid according to us and we do not hold to that view, nor do we advocate it or acknowledge it.

If a man swears an oath of abstention and divorces his wife before compensating but then returns to her before the completion of the waiting period but still does not compensate and continues to observe his oath of abstention from her until the passing of four months, we hold to the view that he would have the choice after the completion of the four months. If he compensates, then that is that. But if he does not compensate, he would be compelled to divorce another divorce after having returned to her after the first divorce. He would have two divorces at that point, and he will have one remaining divorce.

My father related to me that his father was asked about 'compensation.' He said: "Compensation refers to intercourse. If one is not able to touch due to illness, defect or travel, compensation is by his tongue. It would be sufficient for him to say it unless his reason departs."

Concerning divorce of slaves and concerning divorce of the severely inflicted, child, compelled, person with pleurisy and intoxicated

Buying a female slave does not constitute a divorce for her, nor is it religiously permissible for the purchaser to marry her until her husband divorces her. This is the statement of the Commander of Believers, 'Ali b. Abi Ṫālib, upon him be peace: "The right of divorce is for the one who holds the shin [i.e. for the husband]."[14] Similar is narrated from the Prophet, peace and blessings be upon him and his progeny, regarding Barīra. He did not consider her purchase as her divorce [from her husband].[15]

If a slave divorces his wife, it is impermissible for him to return to her until after her master marries and has intercourse with her. She will not be permissible to her husband simply by the intercourse of her master because a woman is impermissible for the husband who divorced her except after marriage to another. She is not religiously permissible until her husband has intercourse with her out of desire for her.

As for intercourse with her owner, this is impermissible for him.[16] She would not be permissible for him except in the case of a revocation, such as the revocation of a completed divorce. Thus, she would not be permissible for him until after divorce. It is not for the master and owner to divorce [his slave women]; rather, divorce is only for spouses.

Divorce of the insane and severely inflicted takes place at the time of their recovery. If they recover at any point in time, it is permissible. If they do not recover at any point, there is no divorce for them.

We say similarly regarding a person with pleurisy. There is no divorce for such person while their intellect is gone. There is no divorce until his intellect returns to him. There is no divorce of children until they attain intellect and know what is necessary for them and obligatory upon them. Regarding that, Allah's Messenger, peace and blessings be upon him and his progeny, said: ((The pen is lifted

[14] Similarly narrated in ***Amāli Ahmed b. 'Isa***. Similar is narrated on the authority of Ibn Abbās from the Prophet in ***Sunan Ibn Mājah, Sunan ad-Dārqutni, Sunan al-Bayhaqi, Al-Mu'jam al-Kabīr***

[15] Similarly narrated in ***Ŝahīh Muslim, Sunan an-Nisā'i, Sunan ad-Dārimi, Ŝahīh Ibn Hibbān***

[16] That is, it would be impermissible for the husband to remarry a slave after an irrevocable divorce due to intercourse with her master. It is only the intercourse of a spouse that makes remarriage permissible.

from three: the sleeper until he awakes, the insane until he recovers and the child until he attains puberty [lit. "has a wet dream"])).[17]

My father related to me from his father that the latter was asked about a man whose slave married a slave woman and then bought her. "Does the purchase constitute a divorce?" He replied: "His purchase of her does not constitute a divorce; it is a divorce when the husband does so himself."

My father related from his father that the latter was asked about divorcing an insane person. He replied:

> Divorce of an insane person is permissible on the condition that such person is recovered. It is impermissible to divorce when his intellect is removed. This has been narrated from the Commander of Believers, 'Ali b. Abi Ťālib, upon him be peace.
>
> As for the divorce of children and one afflicted by pleurisy, there is no divorce of a child until they attain intellect. As for the divorce of one afflicted by pleurisy, there is no divorce of such person. Similar is the case with anyone else who is delirious in his illness and has no intellect.

Similar is the case with the forced person; when he is forced to divorce, it does not constitute a divorce. The same is true with belief and other things. The divorce of an intoxicated person is permissible; he shoulders the responsibility because he did that to himself and caused it to enter his intellect.

Concerning that which one writes to divorce his wife what he does not say

If a man writes a letter to his wife and it says "When this letter reaches you, you are considered divorced," she would be considered divorced when the letter reaches her. If the letter is lost or destroyed or her husband regretted writing it and withheld it, she would be considered married to him and not divorced. This is because the letter had not reached, as was stipulated by the man.

If he wrote in his letter "You are divorced" but does not stipulate that such is the case when it reaches nor does he state a specific time that the divorce occurs, she would be considered divorced whether the letter reaches her or not.

My father related to me that his father was asked about a man who writes a letter of divorce to his wife and does not state such with his mouth. He replied:

> The divorce occurs as he wrote it when his letter comes to her. If he does not send the letter, the divorce does not occur. The divorce only occurs the day that the letter comes to her and it says "When this letter of mine reaches you, you are divorced." If it says "You are divorced" and it is not present, she would be considered divorced as was written in the letter even if the letter had not reached her.

Concerning one who has four wives and divorced one of them without it being known which one he divorced and without the clear intention as to which one it was

Whoever has three or four wives and divorces one of them without it being known which one of them and without the intention of specifying which one, it is obligatory for him to divorce all of them with one divorce each. If he would then like to return to all of them or some of them, we do not know of any impermissibility regarding that.

My father related to me from his father that the latter was asked about a man who had two, three or four wives and he said: "One of you are divorced." What would be binding in that case? He replied:

> If the divorcer did not specify the woman and the divorce occurs without there being a doubt that the divorced woman is unknown, it is preferred to us that he divorces each one with one

[17] Similarly narrated in ***Musnad Imam Zayd, Amāli Ahmed b. 'Isa, Sunan Ibn Mājah, Sunan Abu Dāwūd, Sunan an-Nisā`i, Sunan at-Tirmidhi, Ŝahīh Ibn Hibbān, ad-Dārqutni, Al-Mustadrak, Musnad Ahmed, Sunan ad-Dārimi, Sunan al-Bayhaqi, Mušannaf Ibn Abi Shayba, Majmu' az-Zawā`id, Al-Mu'jam al-Kabīr, Al-Mu'jam al-Awsaṫ, Bihār al-Anwār***

divorce and then return to the one he wants afterwards. Then, the confusion he caused would be made clear to him.

Concerning when a woman with two children in her womb can marry after being divorced

The waiting period of a woman is not complete until her womb is empty and she has delivered all of her load. Her husband can return to her until she delivers all that is in her womb because that which remains in her womb constitutes her waiting period. Allah has said: **{As for those who are laden with child, their period shall be till they deliver their load} (Q. 65:4)**. He makes the delivery of the child the end of the waiting period. The delivery of some of her load is not the delivery of all of it, nor is the delivery of all of it the delivery of some.

My father related to me that his father was asked about a woman who was divorced with two children in her womb and she delivers one of them. He was asked whether her husband can return to her before she delivers the second one. He replied: "The waiting period is not over until she delivers all of her children that are in her womb."

Concerning the financial maintenance of a woman whose husband has died and when it is counted—when she comes to know of his death or from the day he died?

The financial maintenance of a woman whose husband died will always be from the capital until her waiting period is completed—whether she is pregnant or not. If the [financial maintenance of the] pregnant woman and anyone else is different—the financial maintenance of the pregnant woman being in the inheritance of the baby and the financial maintenance of the non-pregnant woman being from the wealth—the judgement would differ in that. The truth is that there is no difference in its judgement; such perceived difference is invalid.

The proof against the one who says that the financial maintenance of the pregnant woman is from the wealth of what is in her womb is that it is said to him: "Since you claim that the financial maintenance of this woman is counted based upon that in her womb, tell us what your opinion is if the baby is underdeveloped and she miscarries or it dies after development in her womb and she delivers it dead? Or what if it is completely developed and she gives birth to it completely formed and then it dies? Would it not be permissible for one to return the remaining inheritance for the financial maintenance of that woman who was not inherited by her baby?"

If they say that it is not returned, they have proved that the financial maintenance of the pregnant woman and that of another is from the capital wealth of the dead. If they necessitate her financial maintenance and calculate it from its inheritance, they have unfairly oppressed her and acted contrary to Allah's judgement concerning her because Allah, the Glorified, says: **{If they are laden with child, maintain them till they deliver their load} (Q. 65:6)**. He obligates financial maintenance for the spouses during their lifetimes as well as inheritance upon the offspring and dead upon the husband. That is based on the statement of the Glorified: **{...and upon the heir is the likeness of that...} (Q. 2:233).**

That maintenance which is therefore obligatory upon the heir is similarly obligated upon the child and the one who breastfeeds it. When it is binding for the child, it is binding for the wife of the deceased because financial maintenance of the child outside of the womb is like the financial maintenance of it inside of the womb. Similarly, its financial maintenance while in her womb and Allah's nourishment for it while in her womb is like the financial nourishment while it is breastfed.

As for the husband who died, it is to be counted from the day death reached him and not from the day that his death was confirmed for her. Among the proofs for that is that Allah does not permit her to do the following things immediately after his death: beautify herself, apply perfume, dress in ornate clothing, dye with henna for beauty and celebrate. Rather, she is obligated to manifest sadness and mourning for her husband out of respect a wife has for her husband and recognition of the sanctity between husband and wife.

If that is the case and her husband died in the beginning of the year without her knowing while she engages in an action that is prohibited for her such as beautification and perfume for the whole year without manifesting sadness or preventing herself from those things that are permissible for a widow until the end of the year when she comes to know that he died in the beginning of the year, she will begin from the time that she came to know of her husband's death, marry another husband, enter upon him after some days, as well as beautify and perfume herself for him! Where is the grief and sadness? Where are those things that Allah obligates she refrains from to the one who said that she counts from the day her husband died? Such one does not obligate grief on her or the abstention from beautification or refraining from marriage for the waiting period that Allah obligates upon her. Rather, he holds to the rejection of grief, sadness, concern as well as the prevention of her waiting period and frees her to marry at that point.

This is at variance with that which Allah intended from her regarding the avoidance of those beautiful things in life when her husband died. Whoever allows her to do such and permits her to count from the day that she verified the day of his death—such person would have invalidated the meaning that Allah intended for a wife when her husband died and he would prevent her from that which she is prevented.

If one permitted such for her, the widow would be in two situations according to the Book of Allah and the Sunnah: the situation of misfortune and the situation of delight. As for the situation of misfortune, it is when she comes to know of the death of her husband. As for the situation of delight, it is when she knows of her husband's death after four months and ten days. She would not be obligated to refrain from anything that others could refrain. This would be impossible to hold to and considered obscene to do according to one with intellect and understanding. It would also be an invalid analogy from all respects.

Concerning the one who divorces three times simultaneously and one who divorces contrary to the sunnah divorce

Some of our brothers asked me about one who divorced contrary to the sunnah divorce and whether such divorce is valid or not. "Allah has said: **{When ye divorce women, divorce them for their waiting period} (Q. 65:1)**. What about the one who divorced contrary to the divorce of the waiting period?" I answered him and proved to him this issue. I will repeat in this book that which I responded to him—if Allah wills:

> Know that Allah appointed us and you that when He makes the truth a law, it is to be followed. When He makes clear the truth, it is to be benefited from. Allah has shielded us and you from the paths of deviants—those whose concern is being the chiefs of the pre-Islamic era and stubbornly cling to that which they know of it from their teaching and statement—even if it may differ from the foundations of their religion and the statements of the scholars of the Ahl al-Bayt of their Prophet. The latter are those upon whom they are supposed to rely and those whom the slaves are commanded to obey. Yet they, due to their deference to the treasure house of knowledge, rebel and allow themselves to be seduced.
>
> They allow their false assumptions to fill their hearts and persist in them. They trample along in their ignorance regarding it without any concern for their opinion. They reckon that the truth is with no one but themselves, and Satan has confused them regarding their truth and correctness. They give edicts with mistakes and call the people to errors and corrupt passions. They come between them and their guidance and prevent them from asking their scholars—those who they are supposed to ask among the Ahl al-Bayt of their Prophet. They confuse them in their matters and falsely assume that the truth is in their statements. Due to their ignorance, they permit every prohibition and they prohibit that which Allah has permitted.

They have taken upon themselves the responsibility of the people in their affairs and means; therefore, they have earned from Allah their bad deeds along with their own. They are as Allah, the Lord of creation, says regarding them and their early brothers: **{But they shall bear their own loads and other loads beside their own, and they shall be questioned on the Day of Resurrection concerning that which they invented} (Q. 29:13)**.

They do not imitate the one who they are commanded to imitate. They are obligated to ask them and commanded to seek them out. They are to go to the Ahl al-Bayt of their Prophet in every one of their affairs. That is based upon the statement of Allah, Glorified be He: **{Ask the People of the Remembrance if ye know not} (Q. 16:43)**. The **{People of the Remembrance}** are the Progeny of Muhammad who are the inheritors of the Book.

The judgements were sent down among them. They also made clear to those who resembled cattle everything that is permissible or prohibited. They are the interpreters of the ambiguous of the Book. They are in agreement to the correct path Allah that which will not deviate from their understanding. It is impermissible to take anything except from their scholars. They are the summation of every light and argument. They are the clarification of every matter for the one who seeks it since they are the ones whom Allah entrusted of His creation. They are the successors in His earth and land as well as the custodians of all His creation and slaves. They are the inheritors of His clear Book and made them the scions of the Seal of the Prophets. Regarding that, the Lord of creation says: **{Then, We have caused to inherit the Book those whom We have chosen amongst Our slaves. Amongst them is he who oppresses himself, amongst them is he who is moderate, amongst them is he who is foremost in good by the permission of Allah. That is a great virtue!} (Q. 35:32)**.

Therefore, among them, as they are humans, are those who oppresses himself, and those who are moderate in their statements and actions and those who are foremost in approaching and rushing to their Lord. The latter is one with whom no one can join with neither can anyone else come close to his precedence.

Know that the whole of creation among the people of truth and falsehood have undoubtedly agreed that whoever divorces his wife has made her prohibited from him except after revoke. No one disagrees with this, and no one differs—Praise be to Allah!—with the fact that a divorce occurs at the pronouncement of such. However, they disagree as to the meaning and manner of divorce. A small group, the Imamite Rafidites, says in deference to the truth of the meaning of the Book and Sunnah that whoever divorces his wife while she is impure from other than intercourse or divorces her with three pronouncements together—such is not a divorce and they remain married. They say that if he divorced her with two or three pronouncements every year until he pronounced the divorce thirty times in ten years, they would remain married and the divorce he pronounced on her does not apply unless he divorced her in a state of ritual purity from other than intercourse.

All the scholars of the Progeny of Allah's Messenger, peace and blessings be upon him and his progeny, differ with them in this. Also, all the scholars of the Muslims follow them in their disagreement regarding this. They say: "One should divorce with the sunnah divorce when she is pure from everything but intercourse. Therefore, he should divorce her for her waiting period as Allah had shown him and taught as well as guided to the right way. If there is a divorce contrary to that, we obligate for him what he obligated on himself even if it is contrary to what His Lord has instructed him." We have therefore considered the affair and disagreement of the Imamites, and there is no proof with them nor is there a narrated tradition in their possession from the Messenger on this.

There is no intellectual proof other than what they advocate from the interpretation of the verse: **{...divorce them for their waiting period and reckon the waiting period} (Q. 65:1)**. Then we will consider the statement of those that differ from them in the exegesis of the verse. If the logical truth is with them, it is that if a divorce is invalidated from one pronouncement, then it should be invalidated multiple times continuously. If that is the case, then divorce would be just play and jest, and the number will be unknown! If the wording is invalidated, its number is invalidated. If its number is invalidated, that which Allah has set as a limit and what He mandated by His statement **{Divorce is twice and then hold fast to her with that which is good or release her with excellence} (Q. 2:229)** will also be invalidated. It would necessitate the meaning of the third divorce in terms of language and grammar.

They also have a proof from the narrated traditions and consensus that which is narrated regarding the Prophet and Ibn 'Umar. It is that the latter divorced his wife while she was menstruating. 'Umar came to the Prophet, peace and blessings be upon him and his progeny, and said: "O Messenger of Allah, 'Abdullah b. 'Umar[§] divorced his wife while she was menstruating!" The Prophet, peace and blessings be upon him and his progeny, said to him: ((Go to him and have him return to her! When she is purified, he can separate from her based on purity from other than intercourse)). When he said ((Go to him and have him return to her)),[18] we, as well as everyone with intellect and comprehension, know that return and revoke cannot take place unless there was an irrevocable divorce just as there could be no divorce without a man being married to women.

We find a proof from the Book of the Lord of creation that is stronger than the interpretation of the verse **{divorce them for their waiting period} (Q. 65:1)** forwarded by the Imamites. It is established by other than the Imamites that the meaning of this verse is a demonstration of proof, instruction and recognition to rectify affairs of the slaves. It is not that which is a complete prohibition or invalidation of what took place! This statement of Allah is similar to other statements in many other places.

Among that which proves the exposition, explanation, rectification, right guidance and excellence of what is commanded and mentioned in His Book that one is not restricted from doing an action and one's deeds are not invalidated by such action and that Allah does not consider the one who acts contrary as disobedient or blameworthy is the statement of Allah: **{And when ye art free of the state of pilgrim sanctity, hunt} (Q. 5:2)**. If they do not hunt after exiting the state of pilgrim sanctity, they would not be considered defiant nor would they be considered disobedient to Allah.

Similar is His statement regarding wives, eating and drinking in fasting: **{Allah knows that ye used to deceive thyself, so He accepted thy repentance and pardoned thee. So, lay with them** [i.e. the wives] **and seek that which Allah has written for thee. Eat and drink until the white thread and black thread of dawn become clear unto thee} (Q. 2:187)**. If they were not to have intercourse every night of Ramadan and refrained from it, they would not be considered defiant according to all the Muslims. Neither would they be considered disobedient. Similarly, if they were to not eat and drink, they would not be blameworthy.

Similar is the case with His statement regarding fasting: **{Therefore, whosoever amongst thee is ill or on a journey—then a like number of other days} (Q. 2:184)**. If the sick person or traveller were to endure and fast seeking thereby the reward and earnings, they would not be considered sinners or transgressors.

---

[18] Similarly narrated in ***Sharh at-Tajrīd, Amāli Ahmed b. 'Isa, Ŝahīh al-Bukhāri, Ŝahīh Muslim, Sunan Abu Dāwūd, Sunan at-Tirmidhi, Sunan an-Nisā`i, Sunan Ibn Māja***

Another example is His statement to His Prophet, peace and blessings be upon him and his progeny, regarding the supererogatory prayers: {**...and a part of the night, establish a night vigil prayer as supererogatory for thee**} (**Q. 17:79**). If he or anyone else had not prayed it as a supererogatory prayer or observed the prayers Allah mandated, they would not be considered disobedient for not praying the supererogatory prayers.

Another example is His statement regarding the Friday congregational prayer: {**When the prayer is completed, disperse within the earth and seek from the bounty of Allah**} (**Q. 62:10**). If they do not disperse on that day and leave from the mosque, they would not be punished based on the consensus of the Muslim *Ummah*. Rather, they would be rewarded by Allah for engaging in remembrance and praying an additional voluntary prayer. Similar is narrated that Allah's Messenger, peace and blessings be upon him and his progeny, said about it: ((That is the stronghold (*ar-ribāt*)! That is the stronghold!))[19]

Another example is the statement of the Mighty and Majestic: {**Then when they have fallen to their sides, eat thereof and feed the contented and unfortunate**} (**Q. 22:36**). If one does not eat from that and instead gives all of it as charity, it would not be considered a sin to Allah. Those who do such will not be punished for doing so, neither will they be taken to task for such in the hereafter.

Similar to that is His statement regarding divorce of pregnant women: {**If they are laden with child, maintain them till they deliver their load. If they suckle for thee, grant them their due and consult amongst yourselves in kindness**} (**Q. 65:6**). The term {**kindness**} refers to extra and surplus for them which is more or less compensation and support upon which the common people rely. If he does not give this extra amount and compensation which is not obligatory upon him, he would not be punished nor would he be considered an oppressive sinner or defiantly disobedient to Allah.

Similar to that is the statement of the Mighty and Majestic: {**And wed those whom seem goodly to thee of women—two, three and four. If ye fear that ye could not be just, then one or that which thy right hand owns**} (**Q. 4:3**). If a man does not marry but abstains and rather endures that and restrains and if one avoids marriage to two, three or four women who are permissible for him to marry and prevent himself from taking a wife and slave woman, he would not be considered disobedient to Allah by that nor would he be considered a defiant rebel due to such.

There are many other examples similar to these in the Book that resemble Allah's statement: {**O Prophet! When ye divorce women, divorce them for their waiting period and reckon the waiting period**} (**Q. 65:1**). By such, He intends for His slaves that which is best and proper for them and not that it would invalidate what they did by such.

Due to their ignorance of the Book, the Imamites falsely assume that this command from Allah is similar to His statement: {**Shave not thy heads until the sacrifice reaches its place**} (**Q. 2:196**). If a man without an excuse shaves his head outside of Mina, the consensus of the Muslim *Ummah* says that would be impermissible.

They also falsely assume that it is like Allah's statement: {**Then, press forward from whence the people press forward**} (**Q. 2:199**). Everyone is prohibited from pressing forward from Muzdalifa and they are commanded to halt and press forward from 'Arafat.

They liken it to His statement: {**O ye who believe, when ye stand for the prayer, wash thy faces and thy hands to the elbows, wipe thy heads and** [wash] **thy feet to the ankles**} (**Q. 5:6**). This is an obligation to perform the ritual ablution before the prayer, and there is no

[19] Similarly narrated in ***Ŝahīh Muslim, Musnad Ahmed, Ŝahīh Ibn Khuzayma, Ŝahīh Ibn Hibbān***

disagreement in that. They also liken it to His statement: **{When one of thee comes from relieving oneself or thou touch women, if thou dost not find water, take to high, pure earth...} (Q. 5:6)**. The one who cannot find water is obligated to perform the dust purification with high, pure earth and this obligation is upon all the slaves.

They liken it to the statement regarding travellers: **{When ye have settled then, establish the prayer, for the prayer is decreed upon the believers at established times} (Q. 4:103)**. He commands them to complete the prayer when they have settled as residents. Similarly, they liken it to the command to obey Him and His Messenger, peace and blessings be upon him and his progeny, in His statement: **{O ye who believe, obey Allah and obey His Messenger} (Q. 4:59)**.

They liken it to His statement: **{Fight those who are near unto thee amongst the disbelievers and let them find in thee harshness} (Q. 9:123)**. Also, they liken it to His statement regarding women and the dowry that is to be given to them: **{Give unto women their dowries as a bestowal. But if they remit unto thee any part thereof out of pleasure, take it cheerfully and happily} (Q. 4:4)**. That is a firm command for one to observe regarding their dowries. And if they want to give it as a gift to him out of their kindness, that would be permissible. According to the entire Muslim *Ummah*, there is no disagreement regarding that.

When we find that everyone agrees that divorce occurs—and we do not find any disagreement among them concerning that—we find that there is simply a disagreement on the meaning of divorce, its manner, time and the exegesis of these verses and not other than them. Then, we find that for the one who differs with the evidence of the Imamites that which we have mentioned, said and explained. Then we have come to know that the verse is contrary to what we find of the verses likened unto it and that the Imamites have erred in their interpretation. If the verse is contrary to what they say, then there will be no disagreement among the Muslim *Ummah* regarding it just as there is no disagreement regarding other verses.

They have invalidated the divorce that takes place, which is contrary to the sunnah divorce and not held to it when the person has made it binding on himself. They invalidate the divorce of the one who pronounces the divorce three times to the pure or impure woman. They have acted contrary to the entire Muslim *Ummah* and spoken regarding that out of blindness, false assumption and caprice.

My father and two uncles, Muhammad[§] and al-Hasan,[§] the sons of al-Qāsim b. Ibrāhīm, related to me from their father, al-Qāsim b. Ibrāhīm—may Allah be satisfied with him and them—that he was asked about divorcing a menstruating woman and he replied: "It is wrong, but that which he made binding on himself is binding."

My father and two uncles related to me from their father that he said regarding a woman who was divorced while she was menstruating and whether the waiting period is observed in that menstruation: "Her divorce is binding and he returns to her until he divorces her with a Sunnah divorce when she is pure without having touched her or being intimate."

My father and two uncles related to me on a reliable authority from Ahmed b. 'Isa b. Zayd[§] that he was asked about pronouncing divorce three times together and replied: "She is divorced by one pronouncement and it is not as the Rafidites say." By that, he means that they invalidate that.

They also related to me on a reliable authority from Musa b. 'Abdullah[§] that he was asked about a man who divorces his wife with three pronouncements at once and replied: "He divorces his wife although it is contrary to His Lord's instruction."

They also related to me on a reliable authority from Muhammad b. Rāshid§ from Nasr b. Mazāhim§ from Abu Khālid al-Wāsiti§: "I asked Abu Ja'far Muhammad b. 'Ali [al-Bāqir] about one who divorced his wife with three pronouncements at once and he replied: "It is considered as one."

They related to me from their father, al-Qāsim b. Ibrāhīm from a reliable man from Ja'far b. Muhammad from his father from his ancestors from 'Ali b. Abi Ṭālib said regarding one who divorced with three pronouncements at once: "He divorces with one statement and it is revocable unless the period of revocability in divorces have passed."

Abu Muhammad al-Qāsim b. Ibrāhīm, upon him be peace, said: "There are two statements: the statement of the one who invalidates that the divorce took place and the statement of the one who says that it occurs with the three pronouncements. The latter is my statement. It is narrated from Zayd b. 'Ali and Ja'far b. Muhammad from many places that the one who divorces three times together at once divorces by one."[20]

To me, the proof that the three divorces resort to one is strong and clear. That is based on the statement of Allah, the One and Most-Merciful: **{Divorce is twice and then hold fast to her with that which is good or release her with excellence} (Q. 2:229)**. We know that three is

---

[20] In ***Al-Muntakhab***, al-Hādi reiterated the position of the imams and scholars from Ahl al-Bayt and the Generality regarding the three pronouncements of divorce counting as one. He said:

> Many narrations have been related regarding that—some of which are from the scholars of the Prophet's Progeny and some of them which are from the Generality in their reports from those considered reliable by them. They have abandoned what their reliable narrators have narrated; they blindly follow their whims and abandon that which has been narrated from their reliable scholars that state that three pronouncements of divorce are counted as one pronouncement. Among those is that which was narrated by Ahl al-Bayt, such as my grandfather, al-Qāsim b. Ibrāhīm—all of his sons—their father—Abu Hārūn al-'Abadi—Ja'far b. Muhammad—his father—his grandfather—'Ali b. Abi Ṭālib, upon him be peace. Therefore, whoever pronounces three pronouncements of divorce at one time will still have the chance to return to her as long as she is in her waiting period. Similar has been narrated by 'Abdur-Razzāq al-Yamani on the authority of Mu'ammar—Abu Tāwūs—his father—Ibn Abbās that the three pronouncements of divorce during the times of Allah's Messenger, Abu Bakr and half the Caliphate of 'Umar counted as one divorce. This hadith was also narrated by Ahmed b. 'Abdullah b. an-Naba`--Muhammad b. 'Abdullah b. al-Qāsim al-Hashāsh—'Abdur-Razzāq. Muhammad b. Ubayd al-Kindi al-Kufi narrated on the authority of Muhammad b. Ishāq az-Zuhri—Ibn Uyayna—'Umar—Atā—Ibn Abbās that the three pronouncements of divorce during the times of Allah's Messenger, Abu Bakr and 'Umar counted as one divorce. Muhammad b. Ubayd related on the authority of Ahmed b. Subayh—Yahya b. Ya'la—Sufyān b. 'Abdullah—Anas b. Mālik: "A man was brought to 'Umar b. al-Khattāb who had divorced with three pronouncements in one sitting. He struck his stomach and back." Muhammad b. Ubayd related on the authority of 'Uthmān b. Abi Shayba—Ibn Idrīs—Layth—Tāwūs—Atā, Jābir b. Zayd and Abu Musa al-Ashari: "Whoever pronounces divorce three times—it is to count as one when she is pure from other than intercourse." 'Abdur-Razzāq narrated on the authority of Ibn Jurayj—some of the sons of Rāfi'—Ikrima—Ibn Abbās: "A man divorced his wife with three pronouncements during the time of Allah's Messenger, peace and blessings be upon him and his progeny. The Prophet commanded him to return to her. He said: 'But I divorced her thrice.' He replied: ((I know. Allah says to His Prophet: **{O Prophet! When ye divorce women, divorce them for their waiting period and reckon the waiting period} (Q. 65:1)**))." 'Abdur-Razzāq narrated on the authority of Mu'ammar—Ibn Tāwūs—his father—Ibn Abbās that the three pronouncements of divorce during the times of Allah's Messenger, Abu Bakr and some of the Caliphate of 'Umar counted as one divorce. 'Umar said: "The people have hastened in a matter in which they had complaints. So, if we fulfil it on them, then it will be fulfilled for them." 'Abdur-Razzāq narrated on the authority of Ibn Jurayj—Ibn Tāwūs—his father—Abu as-Sahbā said to Ibn Abbās: "You know that three pronouncements of divorce during the times of Allah's Messenger, Abu Bakr and a third of the Caliphate of 'Umar counted as one divorce?" Ibn Abbās replied: "Yes." 'Abdur-Razzāq narrated on the authority of 'Umar b. Hawshab—'Amr b. Dīnār—Tāwūs: "I entered upon Ibn Abbās and his freed slave, Abu as-Sahbā, was with me. Abu as-Sahbā asked him about a man who pronounced the divorce on his wife three times altogether. Ibn Abbās said: "We used to consider that as one divorce during the times of Allah's Messenger, Abu Bakr and some of the time of 'Umar's government until 'Umar addressed the people and said: 'Many of you are increasing in this divorce, so whoever says such will be as one says." These reports are authentic and agree with the Book of Allah. We have only relayed these reports in this section and used them as a proof because it is from the reports of the Generality who transmitted them from their reliable narrators that none can object to except the arrogant. Therefore, we presented their proofs in this section by that which they narrate as authentic reports from reliable narrators.

real, and the number three cannot be except that there is a first, middle and last. There cannot be a second pronouncement unless after a revoke. Similarly, a third cannot take place by two pronouncements except after two revokes.

Haven't you considered how the Most Gracious distinguishes between them both in that which He clearly revealed from His Criterion after He mentioned the two pronouncements of divorce by saying: **{...hold fast to her with that which is good or release her with excellence} (Q. 2:22)**? He proves by such that there is an opportunity to revoke after two pronouncements of divorce. By the phrase **{...hold fast to her with that which is good or release her with excellence}**, it shows that there is no revocation after it until she marries a spouse after him. For that reason, we say that three cannot take place in one statement since the number is simply joined to that which Allah mentioned of the limitation of divorce. There cannot be a second pronouncement of divorce except that there was a first pronouncement before it. And there cannot be a third pronouncement of divorce except that there was a second pronouncement before it just as there cannot be a two unless there is a one before it, nor can there be a three except that before it is a two. Whoever pronounces three together is simply pronouncing a numbered amount in the wording but not in the meaning of what Allah dictated as the number of divorces. This is without doubt and uncertainty!

One of the proofs of those who join the number of something in one statement without carrying out that number by consensus is the glorification (*at-tasbīh*) which has come from the Prophet in the prayer. It is three glorifications in the bowings and three in the prostrations. Does anyone say: "Whoever joins them in one statement has carried it out"? This is binding on him by analogy. So, if he permits such, he must say "Glorified be Allah the Great and may He be praised three times" in the bowings and "Glorified be Allah the Exalted and may He be praised three times" in the prostrations. If this is the case, it would be sufficient for him to say "...three times" rather than repeat the glorifications three times in the bowings and prostrations. If he agrees to this, his flawed logic should be evident to himself and others. However, if he does not permit that, he must say that it is impermissible to pronounce the divorce three times together nor is it permissible to join them in one statement. It would be necessary for him to carry it out just as Allah has appointed them—one after the other and three after two. When one knows that, one knows that the second pronouncement of divorce cannot take place unless there was the first revocation before it and that a third divorce cannot take place unless there is the second revocation before it. When one knows that, one knows that one cannot approach the three pronouncements that Allah mentioned until there is between them revocations that divide them. This is because it would not be possible for the one who divorces his wife once to divorce her a second time unless he remarried her after the first revocation. Afterwards, there can be a second pronouncement of divorce. Similar is the case with the third pronouncement of divorce.

Another proof against them regarding that is if it is permissible for a separation to be joined by one statement and bring them together by means of a part, then by rule of analogy, one could say that the one who says "Glorified be Allah a million times!" or "May Allah bless Muhammad and his progeny a million times!" is the same as one who repeats "Glorified be Allah" one million times until he dies or one who repeats "O Allah, bless Muhammad and his progeny" one million times until he dies. This statement would be considered loathsome, invalid and impossible.

Similarly, it would be binding for one who advocated for that to say that it is permissible for one to stone the *jamrāt*s with seven pebbles together at once without stoning them with individual pebbles one-by-one and that it would not be obligatory for such one to stone them individually. However, this is impermissible, and none of the scholars or ignorant say this. It is considered loathsome, invalid and impossible.

We have clarified and explained with proofs in this treatise of ours that the meaning of Allah's statement **{divorce them for their waiting periods}** is a demonstration and urge to His slaves to that which is best and closest to correctness. This is because a command is that which one should not avoid nor is it permissible for one to act contrary to it. Therefore, such one would have blasphemed and acted contrary to his Lord if one were to act contrary to it and avoided it.

Similarly, by such, one departs from the statement of the Most-Compassionate, Most Merciful, Mighty, Most Kind and Most Generous: **{divorce them for their waiting periods and reckon the waiting period}**. He commands them by that command and demonstrates the best action to them; however, it is not invalidated by one who does the opposite. Rather, the Messenger, peace and blessings be upon him and his progeny, has obligated it as we have clarified and explained in the beginning of our treatise. If it were a prohibition from Allah and the divorce would not take place except otherwise, then Allah's Messenger, peace and blessings be upon him and his progeny, would have said to 'Umar when asked about his son's divorce that it wasn't a divorce and would have gone to him and made him retain his wife. He would not have said: ((Go to him and return him to her)). Therefore, Allah's statement **{divorce them for their waiting periods}** was out of consideration for them and the best action from Him to them by proving to them its revocability as long as it is within the waiting period. It is possible for them after the completion of the waiting period. If one acted on the revocation by renewing the marriage, one has followed the right path and righteousness.

It is that the sunnah divorce is when one divorces her while she is pure from other than intercourse. Then he says: "Observe your waiting period" or he pronounces the divorce. Then, he stays away from her and she completes her waiting period. If he returns to her before the passing of three menstruations, he is more entitled to her than herself and her guardian. Then, he can return to her.

She will remain with him with two [divorces] remaining; the third has been done as one. If he does not see fit to stay with her and leaves her and her menstruations pass, she shall be more entitled to herself than him. If she and he want, he can return to her with a new dowry, guardian and witnesses. If he returns to her and then wants to divorce her, he divorces her while she is pure from other than intercourse. If he sees fit to stay with her, he will be more entitled to her than herself and her guardian as long as she is in her waiting period. He can return to her without a dowry or guardian. Two witnesses must witness the revocation. There would be two [pronouncements] used and one remaining. If he sees fit to divorce her and divorces her, he would not be able to return to her unless she marries another man who has 'tasted her honey' as the Prophet stated, peace and blessings be upon him and his progeny. Then, she can remarry the first husband.

Regarding the benefit of the sunnah divorce for the people, the Commander of Believers, 'Ali b. Abi Ťālib, upon him be peace, said: "If people performed it correctly (i.e. divorce), no one would have regret for the wife."[21] By that, he means that if a man were to do it, he would not have regret due to the length of time of the waiting period and he could return to her. He is saying that if one does that within her waiting period and he regrets and then returns to her or if he completes it because of his determination to keep away from her, this would be considered the sunnah divorce due to this long time. This is an assistance for him and a recognition of error if he were to do it. Allah informs them about it, commands them towards proper etiquette and shows them its virtue. However, it is not a difficult matter in that the divorce is invalidated, nor is such separation binding on the one who acts contrary to such.

[21] Similarly narrated in ***Amāli Ahmed b. 'Isa, Mušannaf Ibn Abi Shayba, Sunan al-Bayhaqi***

Know—May you be guided—that a divorce will occur in any situation is binding for any man who declares it. The exception is the one who divorces his wife while she is menstruating; one does not count that menstruation as a part of her waiting period, and it resumes with three future menstruations. I do not know of anyone who narrates or says contrary to that other than this party of Satan who are destroyed losers according to Allah. They are those who are tyrannical due to corrupt passions, followers of lusts and those who permit the prohibited and command obscenities. They are the party who ascribes to the weak slave the qualities of the One Majestic and attributes the impossible to Allah. They are the party blinded by the deviance and those who deny the doctrine of Divine Oneness. They are the party that likens Allah the Praiseworthy to the defects of slaves. They are those who invalidate the waiting period of the wives and reject the connections and inheritance that Allah ordered. They are those who oppose the Book of Allah in all matters. They are those who stubbornly reject truth then follow sinfulness and disobedience. They are the party of the Imami Rafidites who reject the truth and its people as well as criticise the associates of Allah, the warriors who command what is good and forbid from evil and oppression. It is the statement of those Imamites who halted jihad and manifested corruption in the lands and between the slaves, who assured the oppressors of their safety and that they will not be overthrown, who allowed them to rule and became their support and obtained from their riches but at the same time declared blasphemy on those who rebelled against the rulers.

The opinion of this deviant party is not acknowledged because of their blasphemy and extremism as well as their lying and disobedience. They lie against Allah and His Messenger, peace and blessings be upon him and his progeny, in every matter and oppose them. They openly and flagrantly disobey them and rebel against them with audacity and transgression. They openly permit obscenities and evil as well as become enemies of those who command the good and forbid the evil. They are enemies of the guided imams of the purified Ahl al-Bayt of the Messenger, peace and blessings be upon him and his progeny. Woe unto them! They violated what is sacred, concealed all good and incited against truth. Then they opposed the Book, abandoned the correct and permitted forbidden sexual relations, giving birth to lying and chaos.

Regarding them is what my father and two uncles Muhammad and al-Hasan, related to me from their father, al-Qāsim b. Ibrahim from his father from his grandfather from Ibrahim b. al-Hasan from his father from his grandfather, al-Hasan b. ‘Ali from ‘Ali bin Abi Ťālib from the Prophet, peace and blessings be upon him and his progeny: ((O ‘Ali, at the end of time, there will be a people who will be called ‘Rafidites.’ If you ever live to meet them, kill them—May Allah destroy them—for they are idolaters!)).[22]

We—may Allah aid you and guide you to that which He is most satisfied with!—find that by their consensus and the consensus of other than them among the people of truth and falsehood, divorce occurs without a waiting period and ritual purity. We also find that by their statement as well as that of other than them that it occurs whether the wife is menstruating or not menstruating. That is a divorce of a man from his wife when he has not had intercourse with her. Both they and other than they obligate it based upon the statement of her husband to her based upon the verse in whatever state she is. No one doubts that she can marry during her

[22] Similarly narrated in ***Musnad Abu Ya'la, Al-Mu'jam al-Kabīr, Musnad Ahmed.*** It must be understood that the command to kill the Rafidites was contextual and it referred specifically to those Shia who held to heretical beliefs. Similarly, the author's grandfather, Imam al-Qāsim Rassi, upon him be peace, countered the claims of the Rafidites in two of his treatises in which he ascribed to them the belief in idolatry and extremism. As was stated in a previous footnote, the ‘Rafidites’ are not to be understood as the lot of Twelver and Ismaili Shia of our time. Rather the term encompasses those who held to deviant and heretical beliefs during the time of the said imams. Please refer to our forthcoming translation ‘The Luminary of the Prophet's Progeny: The Collected Works of Imam al-Qāsim Rassi’ for a complete detail of the Rafidites.

waiting period and that there is no waiting period for her. That is the statement of Allah—Mighty and Majestic: **{...there is no waiting period on them for thee} (Q. 33:49)**.

If they say that a divorce does not occur except in the state of ritual purity, then they are mistaken. The statement of the Muslim *Ummah* is contrary to theirs, and their ignorance will be manifest to other than them. If they say that the divorce does occur with the statement of her husband, then they have established that divorce can occur in any state. Consequently, they necessitate that it can take place by the statement of men and that there is no difference in the occurrences of divorce. They thus necessitate the divorce of the one who has intercourse with her and that of one who has not had intercourse with her to the one who recognises the permissible and prohibited. This would be in accordance with the religion of Muhammad, peace and blessings be upon him and his progeny, and that of the people of belief and Islam. This is because the woman who had intercourse and the one who had not had intercourse are the same in regard to divorce. It is only due to the fear that she may be pregnant. The pregnant woman would not be exempted from the statement of divorce by her husband because the pregnant woman, in regard to divorce, is the same as other than her other than the fact that their waiting period is longer than three courses and three months. That is based on the statement of Allah, the Exalted: **{As for those who are laden with child, their period shall be till they deliver their load} (Q. 65:4)**. The Glorified makes the end of the period of pregnant women the time that they deliver what is in their wombs—whether their delivery is days after divorce or consecutive months afterwards.

Ask the one who says that a divorce does not take place except in the state of ritual purity from other than intercourse: What do you say regarding a man who allows his wife to enter, lowers the curtains, close the doors and then approaches her? Afterwards, he divorces her before intercourse. Since he lowered the curtains on her, is he obligated to give her the dowry? Do you say to him that he should return it to her and no divorce took place since—according to you—she was outside of the state of ritual purity? You are basically necessitating that as the basis of your statement!

If they say "Yes," we say that he has erred and we hold to the view that he has acted contrary to His Creator and Maker. Say to them: If it is as you say and claim, then you would be more knowledgeable about Allah, His Book and its permissions and prohibitions than His Messenger and Seal of the Prophets!

If you claim such, it would be impermissible. Allah's Messenger, peace and blessings be upon him and his progeny, did such and permitted it when his wife Asmā bt. al-Nu'mān b. al-Aswad b. al-Hārith al-Kindi§ came to him. When she came to him, A'isha bt. Abi Bakr said to her: "If you want to gain the favour of Allah's Messenger, say 'I seek refuge in Allah from you!' when he stretches his hand to you." She did what was suggested, and he turned his face from her and said: ((From whom do you seek refuge in Allah? Return to your family)).[23]

Similarly, Allah's Messenger, peace and blessings be upon him and his progeny, did the same with his wife, Juwaynib, the daughter of Abu Usayd when Abu Usayd as-Sā'idi came with her. A'isha and Hafsa§ took responsibility to comb her hair and tend to her. One of the two said to her that the Prophet, peace and blessings be upon him and his progeny, would be pleased with a woman who said to him when visiting her: "I seek refuge in Allah from you!" When he entered upon her, lowered the curtains, closed the door and stretched his hand to

[23] Similarly narrated in ***Amāli Ahmed b. 'Isa, Ŝahīh al-Bukhāri, Sunan an-Nisā`i, Sunan Ibn Mājah, Al-Mustadrak, Sunan ad-Dārqutni, Sunan al-Bayhaqi, Al-Mu'jam al-Kabīr, Bihār al-Anwār***. It is interesting to note that in all the Sunni references to the incident, A'isha is not implicated as the one who suggested it to Asmā. However, in the ***Tabaqāt*** of Ibn Sa'd, the author relates the incident as Imam al-Hādi does imprecating A'isha and Hafsa while using al-Bukhāri's chain of narrators. [Ref. ***Subul as-Salām***]

her, she said: "I seek refuge in Allah from you!" Whereupon he covered his face with his sleeve and said ((You sought refuge?)) three times. He then left and commanded Abu Usayd to take her back to her people and gave her two cotton garments as post-divorce compensation. It is narrated that she died of grief. May Allah be merciful to her![24]

If they say that it is permissible for him and that there is no problem with divorcing her outside of ritual purity, then they are saying that it is valid for the doer and that divorce is valid in all states. This is the correct statement and it returns to what we said. They would have abandoned arrogance and disagreement as well as entered the truth and agreement.

Among the proofs that divorce occurs even outside of the state of ritual purity from other than intercourse is that if a man were to have intercourse with his pregnant wife in the morning and divorced her at night, there would not be disagreement among the people of knowledge and proof. They would agree that the divorce was binding even though he consummated with her for a short period of time before divorcing her. Therefore, why would they say that the divorce was not binding on the one who declared it only after they are ritually pure without intercourse?

We seek refuge in Allah from innovation and engaging in innovations as well as from acting contrary to the truth and the truthful and from the blindness of the deviators' deviance! Know that divorce occurs in all states with all women with whom a contract of marriage is made when the man declares a divorce—even if it is contrary to the etiquette of His Lord and at variance to the right action that Allah has shown him. That is the statement of my father, the Chosen, peace and blessings be upon him and his progeny; my grandfather, 'Ali b. Abi Ṭālib; my forefathers before me as well as myself.

Concerning involuntary divorce

If a man fears for himself from an oppressive tyrant or inimical oppressor and his enemy makes him swear an oath by divorce on a matter that is impermissible for the oppressor, he would not be considered divorced by such oath nor would he have to observe that which a divorcee observes. Similarly, if he says to him "Divorce your wife" and if he does not do it, he would fear of harm or loss to himself due to beatings, killing or imprisonment—then he divorces her although it would not be considered a divorce, and separation would not be binding on him.

Similarly, if an oppressive tyrant makes him swear to help him and forces him to swear allegiance to him and he swears to do so by divorcing his wife, such oath of allegiance would not be considered binding on him and he would not be considered one who broke a valid oath. It would be upon him to not consider such obedience as binding on him.

My father related to me that his father was asked about swearing an oath to these oppressors by divorce, manumission and charity of what he owns. He replied:

> Whatever a person is involuntarily forced to do and unwillingly compelled to do—such would not be binding on him. Whatever he does without being involuntarily forced—it would be binding on him. There is no disagreement among the scholars of the Progeny of Allah's Messenger, peace and blessings be upon him and his progeny, concerning that.

Concerning one who says to his wife: "Observe your waiting period!"

If he says to her "Observe your waiting period owed by you", he would be asked his intention in saying that. If he intends by that what is normally intended—that is, divorce—it would be considered one

[24] This incident is also recorded and authenticated in Sunni texts such as ***Al-Mustadrak, Musnad Ahmed***, ***Majmu' az-Zawā'id***, ***Al-Mu'jam al-Kabīr*** and ***Al-Mu'jam al-Awsaṭ***. In these reports, the woman is known simply as 'a woman of Jawn' or 'a Kilābi woman.' There is disagreement about her name, but in some narrations her name is given as Asmā bt. an-Nu'mān, as in the first report. Such actions on the part of A'isha and Hafsa should not be considered unlikely because the exegetes agree that the condemning verses of ***Surah Tahrīm*** **(Q. 66)** were revealed about them both.

revocable divorce. However, if he said "I intended dirham" or "I intended walnuts"[25]—divorce would not be binding on him. If he was accused, he must swear an oath that what he intended was not what he said and that he had not intended divorce.

Concerning a man who says to his wife "You are not my wife" or "You are released" or "You are free"

If a man were to say any of that to his wife intending divorce, it would be considered a divorce pronouncement. If he had not intended divorce, it would not be considered divorce. If it is claimed that he intended other than what he said, he must confirm such or he will be made to swear if he was accused.

If a man said to his wife "You are not my wife," he is to be asked his intention. If he intended divorce, she is divorced. If he had not intended divorce, then he lied and he should not return to anything like such.

Concerning the stating of exceptions in divorce

If a man says to his wife "You are divorced unless your father wants to keep you" and the father says "I want to keep her but do not divorce her," he does not have to divorce her. If her father said "I want you to divorce her," he has to divorce her.

If a man says to his wife "You are divorced once but not once," she would be considered divorced once. If he said to her "You are divorced once unless your father wants it to be thrice," he would be asked his intention. If he said "I meant that it would not be binding if he wants it to be thrice" and the father wanted it to be thrice, the wife would not be considered divorced. If the father wanted it to be once and not thrice, she would be considered divorced once.

If the husband said "I meant in my intention that it would be thrice if the father wants it to be thrice as he said," it would be obligatory on him to divorce her thrice according to the statement of the proponents of three. According to the position of those who say that three resorts to one, it would be considered once because this is not confirmed from the statement of the husband who says to her: "You are divorced thrice." Its reversion to one is the more correct of the two positions according to me. This is based upon that which I proved in the beginning of this section.

Concerning continuation between divorces

If a man said to his wife "You are divorced. You are divorced. You are divorced," nothing would be binding for her except one divorce. This is because at the time that he said "You are divorced," she was divorced from him and then there occurred the second and third pronouncement on the wife. However, she was not married to him at that point so that there did not occur another divorce according to our position.

As for the proponents of three, they hold to the view that the divorce would be binding upon her even if it were in her waiting period. However, we do not take that view nor do we hold to that.

Concerning a man who calls out to one of his wives by name and another wife answers and then he divorces her

If a man calls out to one of his wives with the determination and intention to divorce her and another one answers him and he says "You are divorced" while assuming that the one he called to was the one who he intended to divorce, the one who responded would not be considered divorced. The one whom he intended to divorce would be considered divorced. The one who he had not intended to divorce would not be considered divorced because if he simply said "You are divorced" following the wording to the pronoun in his heart, that statement would follow his intention.

---

[25] The Arabic phrase "Observe your waiting period" also carries the connotation of "Count…" Therefore, one could argue that he meant "Count the dirham" or "Count the walnuts."

Concerning one who divorces with part of the pronouncement

If a man said to his wife "You are divorced with a tenth of a pronouncement" or "...a third of a pronouncement" or "...a fourth of a pronouncement" or "...a sixth of a pronouncement" or "...a ninth of a pronouncement," all of such would be considered one full pronouncement of divorce. This is because a divorce cannot be a fraction, and any fraction in it is compulsory. Similarly, if a man said to two of his wives "There is a pronouncement of divorce and a half for each of you," each wife would have a full pronouncement of divorce.

If a man said to the two of them "There are two pronouncements of divorce and a half for each of you," there would be a full pronouncement of divorce for each based upon the position of the one who reverts three to one. As for those who hold to three [i.e. three pronouncements of divorce constitute three divorces], he would say that there are two pronouncements of divorce for each one. However, the first position is the one to be acted upon according to us.

Similarly, if one said to two of his wives "There are five pronouncements of divorce for each of you," the opinion of the one who says that three resorts to one is that there would be only one divorce for each. As for the one who opines for three, there would be three divorces for each and she would not be permissible for him until she marries another husband.

Concerning one who swears by divorce and unknowingly breaks the oath

Whoever swears an oath by divorce that he would not leave or buy ten *raṫls* of sugar but then buys ten *raṫls* of sugar and finds a *raṫl* of a crystallised piece after leaving, we hold to the view that he broke his oath. Similarly, if he swore that he would not leave until so-n-so loans him ten dirhams and the man loans him ten dirhams but he found included two dirham made from iron after he left, we say that he broke his oath.

Concerning one who swears by divorce of different wives or all of them collectively

If a man says to his wives "You all are divorced if you strike so-n-so's child," he is to be asked his intention. If he intended and desired that they are to not strike him altogether and that he had not sworn that they should not strike him separately, there would be no divorce unless they all strike him together. If he intended that they are to not strike him individually, the oath is broken whether they struck him individually or collectively.

Similarly, if he were to say to each one individually "You are divorced if you enter so-n-so's house," he would be asked his intention. If he swore that they are to not enter altogether and they enter individually, the oath is not considered broken. If he intended that they are to not enter in any case—collectively or individually—and they enter, then the oath is considered broken. This is the case whether they entered individually or collectively. If he intended that he would not divorce any one of them unless all of them entered together, then he would have to divorce all who entered the house. If he meant by his intention and statement that each one who entered the house would be divorced due to her entrance, it would be as he intended. Anyone who entered the house would thusly be divorced. If they all entered the house together, they would all be divorced. If some of them entered and some of them did not, those who entered would be considered divorced and those who had not would not be considered divorced.

Concerning an unlawful pronouncement of a slave woman

An unlawful pronouncement of a slave woman is the same as an unlawful pronouncement of a free wife; it is for a husband or owner. If a man declares an unlawful pronouncement to a slave woman, he does not owe expiation. If a man declares an unlawful pronouncement to an *umm walad*, that unlawful pronouncement is considered to not be an unlawful pronouncement. This is because Allah—the Mighty and Majestic—only mentioned unlawful pronouncements in connection to wives, not slave women. The Glorified says: **{...those who declare unlawful pronouncements amongst thee of their women} (Q. 58:2)**. He means: 'their wives'; slave women are not referred to as wives.

If a man says to one of his wives "You are to me like my mother's back if you do not do such-and-such" and that thing is done, the oath is not broken and the unlawful pronouncement had not occurred. The unlawful pronouncement in this situation is like oaths; if he fulfils it, it is not broken and if it does not fulfil it, it is broken. If he appointed a certain time, it is permissible at that time and he does not act upon that which he swore. The oath would be broken and the unlawful pronouncement would occur. If he had not appointed a certain time, there is no breaking of the oath as long as there was agreement on what he sworn and there was determination to fulfil one's oath. If one enters it avoiding fulfilling one's oath and not intending to fulfil one's oath, it is considered an unlawful pronouncement and he must expiate.

If a man said "When I marry so-n-so, she will be to me like my mother's back," there would not be an unlawful pronouncement binding on him when he marries her. This is because there can be no unlawful pronouncement before there is a marriage. Similarly, there can be no divorce before there is a marriage.

Similarly, if a man said "Any woman I marry in a year or two years will be to me like my mother's back," there would be no unlawful pronouncement for him because there is no unlawful pronouncement except after a marriage contract. Similarly, if he said "Any slave woman I purchase is to me like my mother's back," that would not be binding on him because there is no unlawful pronouncement for a slave woman.

Concerning one who declares an unlawful pronouncement on two, three or four wives

If a man declares an unlawful pronouncement on a number of wives—three or four, it would be obligatory for him to expiate for each one. He has a choice of expiation. If he is not able to manumit a slave for each of them, he can manumit a slave for some and fast for some. If he is not able to fast, he is to feed. If he cannot find a way to feed for each of them or fast, then he is to feed in what he is able, fast if he can and manumit a slave if he finds one.

Concerning one who declares an unlawful pronouncement on his wives twice, thrice or four times

If a man declares an unlawful pronouncement on his wife twice, thrice or four times and had not expiated for the first and second, one expiation is sufficient. If he expiated and declared an unlawful pronouncement after expiating, he is obligated to expiate again.

Similarly, if he declared an unlawful pronouncement five times and expiated for every two, he would still be obligated to expiate. After having expiated for the first and then declared an unlawful pronouncement, he would have to expiate again. Then, if he returns after expiation and declares another unlawful pronouncement, he must expiate for that unlawful pronouncement based on this analogy and so on.

Concerning one who swears an oath of abstention and then divorces his wife during this abstention

If a man swears that he will not come near his wife for four months and then divorces her before he returns, the answer to that is if she completes her waiting period before he returns, it is considered an irrevocable divorce. He will not be able to go back to her except with a new marriage with a guardian, two witnesses and a new dowry.

If he wants to return to her like that, he must observe the oath of abstention until its completion and expiate. If it is completed before the end of her waiting period, he must expiate for his oath. He would then be able to return to her without a guardian or dowry. However, two just witnesses must witness the revocation and then he can return to her.

If he swears an oath of abstention to her while she is pregnant and then divorces her, it is for him to return when he wants. If she delivers what is in her womb, she will be irrevocably divorced from him. The divorce invalidated the oath of abstention. If he does not return to marry her (i.e. after the divorce is finalised), the oath of abstention returns to him when this revocation happens before the completion of the period in which he swore to not come near her. So, understand that.

If he marries her after that with a guardian, witnesses and a new dowry, he must expiate for his oath if he wants to go near her. If he returns to her before the delivery, he is more entitled to her than herself and her guardian. He is to expiate for his oath and she will be with him because the return after a divorce is a revocation.

Unlike others, we do not say that the divorce and oath of abstention are like two horses running for a wager (*ka farasay rihān*).[26] This is because we do not hold to the view that the passing of the four months obligates divorce. We say that separation is not binding until after he stops and returns or divorce—whether after such or when he comes closer (i.e. does not divorce).

Concerning one who divorced a pre-pubescent girl and she menstruates before the completion of three months in which she observed her waiting period

If a man divorces a pre-pubescent girl who has not menstruated and she observes the [three] months for her waiting period but then two months—more or less—passes and she menstruates in the third month, it is obligatory for her to begin her waiting period from her menstruation and not consider those months that passed. She is to count three menstruations from the beginning.

We simply say that because Allah made months the waiting period for those who do not menstruate. However, when this pre-pubescent girl then menstruates before the completion of three months, she is considered among those who menstruate and the waiting period of pre-pubescence is removed from her. She is then mandated by Allah's statement: **{And the divorced women shall wait by themselves three courses} (Q. 2:228)**. We thus obligate on her that her waiting period begins at her menstruation because it would not be permissible for her to establish her waiting period with months while Allah has mandated it as the waiting period for the one who does not menstruate and she menstruates.

Concerning the divorce of male slaves and the waiting period of female slaves

All pronouncements of divorce are for men, and the waiting periods are for women because Allah mandated divorce for men as well as commanded them regarding it and prohibited them. He mandated the waiting period for women as well as commanded them regarding it and prohibited them. Men were not commanded anything regarding a waiting period just as women were not commanded regarding divorce. It is based upon what we find Allah stating in His Book **{O Prophet! When ye divorce women, divorce them for their waiting period and reckon the waiting period} (Q. 65:1)** and **{O ye who believe! When ye wed believing women and then divorce them before touching them…} (Q. 33:50)** and **{When they hath reached their term, hold to them with goodness or release them with goodness} (Q. 65:2)**.

---

[26] According to **Lane's Arabic English Lexicon**:

> It was said by a man who swore that he would abstain from his wife for four months and then divorced her; for the period during which a woman may be taken back after a first or second divorce is that of three menstruations or three periods of purity from menstruation; and if it ended in this case before the end of the four months during which he swore to abstain from her, she became separated from him by that divorcement: so he likened the two periods to two horses running for a wager.

We find in all that the command and prohibitions regarding divorce are given to the men. By that, we know that the matter of divorce is for men—whether free or slave—and the matter of the waiting period is for women—whether free or slave. One does not consider anything from their command; rather, one simply considers that from their husbands.

Similarly, we find that Allah—the Blessed and Exalted—says: **{When they hath reached their terms…} (Q. 65:2)**. He conveys that the waiting period is for them. And the Blessed and Exalted says: **{And the divorced women shall wait by themselves three courses} (Q. 2:228)**. The Glorified says **{And those amongst thee who perish and leave behind wives, they should bequeath unto their wives a provision for the year without turning them out. But if they go out, there is no sin upon thee in whatsoever they do of themselves within their rights. Allah is Mighty and Wise} (Q. 2:240)** and **{As for those who are laden with child, their period shall be till they deliver their load} (Q. 65:4)** and **{...those who no longer anticipate menstruation from thy women—if thou are in doubt, their waiting period is three months, as well as those who have not menstruated} (Q. 65:4)**. In all of that, He mandates that the waiting period is for women and not men; He commands and prohibits them regarding it in all cases. When we find such to be the case, we say that the waiting period is a matter for women—whether free or slave—and that the matter of divorce is for men—whether free or slave.

An explanation of that is the following: If a slave is married to a free woman and he divorces her with one pronouncement, he is more entitled to her as long as she has not menstruated three times. If he returns to her and then pronounces a divorce on her a second time, similar would be the case. If he pronounces a divorce on her a third time, she would not be permissible for him until after she married another husband. She would have to observe three menstruations as her waiting period. He mandated the matter of his divorce that made her prohibited from him until after marrying another husband with three divorces. He also mandated that her waiting period be three menstruations because she is free.

Similarly, if a free man is married to a slave woman, he is more entitled to her as long as she has not menstruated three times. When she is pure from the third one, her master is more entitled to her than her husband and she would not be prohibited from him [i.e. her first husband] until after three menstruations. Similar is the case with a slave woman—whether she is under a free man or slave.

We simply say that the waiting period for the slave woman is the same as that of a free woman and that the divorce of a slave with three divorces is like that of a free man because Allah has made known the status of the slave but had not differentiated between their divorce and that of anyone else; this principle is for both the free and the slave. If there was a distinction between the two, He would have made that clear and explained it in His Book. The divorce of a slave and free man is the same—three divorces.[27]

Concerning one who swears by divorce that he would do such and such but then dies before he is able to do it

If a man swears by divorcing his wife that he will do such and such and then dies before he does it while intending to do his action and had not avoided it, the divorce would take place at the time of his death and she will inherit from him because she would be considered in her waiting period.

---

[27] In ***Al-Muntakhab***, al-Hādi was similarly asked about divorcing slave women. He replied:

> Others amongst the Generality as well as some specified groups have said that the slave is to divorce twice and the slave woman is to observe two menstruations as a waiting period. That has been narrated from the Commander of Believers, 'Ali b. Abi Ṭālib and other jurists of theirs. However, this is not authentically attributed to 'Ali nor do we find that to be correct by the proofs of the intellect.

Such judgement is attributed to 'Ali in texts such as ***Bihār al-Anwār*** and ***Musnad Imam Zayd.*** The judgement is also narrated from 'Umar, Ibn 'Umar and A'isha in ***Muwaṭṭa***, ***Sunan ad-Dārqutni***, ***Muṣannaf 'Abdur-Razzāq***, ***Sunan al-Bayhaqi***, ***Kanz al-Ummāl***

If he specified a time and said that he would divorce if he did such and such on this day or this month but dies after specifying the time, the specified time the oath was broken would be considered outside of that time and his wife would be considered divorced before his death. When she is declared divorced within the time of its revocation, she would be able to inherit from him during her waiting period. If it was outside of her waiting period, she does not inherit from him.

Similarly, if he broke his oath and she was divorced from him with this pronouncement and he had already declared two pronouncements of divorce, she would not inherit from him because this would be the third pronouncement of divorce in which she would not be permissible for him until she married another. For that reason, we say that she would not inherit from him in that case and if he were to die the day after the broken oath.

My father related to me from his father that the latter was asked about a man who swore to divorce if he were to strike his servant boy or marry or approach such and such town and then died before marrying, striking his servant boy or approaching such and such town. He replied:

> If there was no intention concerning striking his slave and he had not appointed a specific time for breaking his oath, there would be no breaking of oath. Similar is the case with marriage and approaching the town.

Concerning the one who deserves the child and concerning the compulsion of the guardian to financially maintain the pre-pubescent child

The mother or maternal grandmother is more entitled to her daughter's child. If there is no grandmother, his father is more entitled.[28] If there is no father, the maternal aunt is more entitled because she is the sister of his mother. Then, the other relatives are more entitled.

My father related to me that his father was asked regarding the guardians: "Out of the siblings, aunts, uncles and grandparents, who is more entitled to a child?" He replied:

> The grandmother is most entitled to the child after the mother, and she is the mother's mother. If there is no mother or maternal grandmother, the father is more entitled. If there is no father, the maternal aunt is more entitled because she is in the place of the mother.

It is obligatory on the father of the pre-pubescent child to provide its financial maintenance and all its necessities. The financial maintenance is for the mother who breastfed it if he married a woman who had not breastfed it in the case that its father divorced the latter. He would have to pay compensation to the nurse mother who breastfeeds the one who is breastfed.

It is impermissible for its father or mother to be made to suffer because of it, as Allah—the Blessed and Exalted—says: **{A mother should not be harmed because of her child, nor should he to whom the child is born be harmed because of his child. And upon the heir is the likeness of that} (Q. 2:233).** The meaning of that is the husband should not make the mother suffer if he were to divorce her and prevent her from breastfeeding her child and prevent the like of her from compensation. Rather, it is obligatory upon him to let her breastfeed it and give her compensation for

[28] Regarding the care of the child after the death of the mother and grandmother, there are two different opinions attributed to al-Hādi. One view, which is narrated here in ***Ahkām***, is that the father is more entitled than the maternal aunt; whereas ***Al-Muntakhab*** relates that he held to the view that the maternal aunt is more entitled than the father. Al-Mu'ayyad Billah related these two different views from al-Hādi in his ***Sharh at-Tajrīd*** and Ibn al-Murtaḍa in his ***Al-Bahr***. The author of ***Al-Qawl al-Awwal*** argues that the judgement in ***Al-Muntakhab*** represents al-Hādi's most recent and therefore authoritative position. He based it on its adherence to the report in which the Prophet assigned the daughter of Hamza b. 'Abdul-Muttalib to her maternal aunt to care for her and said: ((The maternal aunt is like the mother)). However, we favour the judgement in the ***Ahkām*** over that of ***Al-Muntakhab*** for two reasons. The first reason is that it mirrors the view of al-Hādi's grandfather, al-Qāsim, whose judgements al-Hādi held to be authoritative. Refer to the Translator's Introduction. The second reason is that the narrated report does not preclude the precedence of the father over the maternal aunt because the father, Hamza, was already deceased when the discussion regarding his daughter took place.

breastfeeding it.[29] Similarly, it is impermissible for her to harm its father regarding it by giving it to him without breastfeeding it until another nurse mother can be found.

Similarly, it is impermissible for the heir to harm the *umm walad* regarding it; it is obligatory that he provide assistance to the pre-pubescent child as well as financially maintain the nurse mother just as it would be obligatory upon its father if he were alive.

My father related to me that his father said regarding the statement of Allah—the Blessed and Exalted **{A mother should not be harmed because of her child, nor should he to whom the child is born be harmed because of his child. And upon the heir is the likeness of that} (Q. 2:233)**:

> It is obligatory upon the heir of the pre-pubescent child who inherited it when its father dies to do similar to the father regarding financial maintenance of the nurse mother. The harm of the mother regarding the child is that she does not breastfeed it while she is able in order to harm the father by means of that. It is also upon the father to not harm the mother in that she should be allowed to breastfeed her child when she wants to without anyone else. Similar is upon the heir in regard to harming the child and providing the financial maintenance that the parents would provide.

Concerning the one who says to his wife "You are divorced to this month" or "...this year"

If a man says to his wife "You are considered divorced at the beginning of the year" or "...at the beginning of the lunar year" or "...at the beginning of the month," he is permitted to have intercourse with her until the time he appointed for the divorce. He would be obligated to observe the divorce he obligated on himself. According to us, this is the best statement regarding that and the closest to truth. He does not mandate on his wife other than what he mandated on himself.

As the people of Medina say, if he mandated that verbally stipulating a specific time, then he is obligated to observe that which he verbally stipulated and not delay until that time. Rather, that would be considered oppression from him if he were to divorce his wife before that stipulated time he originally intended and determined.

Concerning mutual cursing (*al-li'ān*)

Mutual cursing occurs between a man and his wife when he denies her child, accuses her of infidelity and there are not four witnesses for his claim. Then, the magistrate brings them both and says to him and her: "Fear Allah, your Lord! Be wary of your Creator! Do not proceed with the mutual cursing!" If the husband desists, he is to be flogged with eighty lashes and she is divorced from him; this is the prescribed punishment for false accusations of infidelity. If she desists, she is to be stoned.

If they go through with the mutual cursing, the magistrate says to him: "Say: By Allah, the Most Great! I am truthful in my accusations of her and my denial of the child! The child is a ward of its mother!" And the husband is to point to it with his hand and repeat that four times. When he swears by Allah four times, he says the fifth time: "May the curse of Allah be upon me if I am lying in my accusations against you regarding my denial of this child!"

---

[29] Regarding the obligation for the mother to breastfeed the child, more detail is given in the conversation between al-Hādi and Muhammad b. Suleiman al-Kufi in ***Al-Muntakhab***.

> I asked him about a man whose wife has just had a baby and his wife says that she will not breastfeed it. "Is she obligated to breastfeed it?" He replied: "If it is during the period of colostrum, she is obligated—whether she likes it or not." "How long is the period of colostrum?" "A day. At the most, three." "What if the wife were to say to her husband after three days: "I will not breastfeed it until you hire me to breastfeed your child."? "It is for her to do so. He can hire her to breastfeed his child or hire someone else to do so." "What if he hired a wet-nurse to breastfeed the child but then the baby's mother says "I have more right to my child. Hire me and I'll breastfeed the child."? "That is for her to do." "What if the father says: "I do not want you to breastfeed it!"? "That would not be for him to do, nor would his statement be acknowledged."

Then he [i.e. the magistrate] says to the woman "Swear by Allah four times that he is lying in his accusations against you regarding his claim of infidelity and the denial of this child!" The woman then says: "By Allah, the Most Great! He is lying in his accusations against me regarding the denial of my child!" When she says this four times, she says on the fifth: "May Allah's anger be upon me if he is truthful!" When the two of them perform the mutual cursing, the magistrate divorces them and they are to never remarry.

Concerning the one who says to his wife: "You are divorced if Allah wills"

Whoever says to his wife "You are divorced if Allah wills," it is said that he has an exception, and it is also said that there is no exception clause in divorce. As for me, I hold to the view that if the man is righteous and his wife accepts turning the matter of Allah regarding her husband to her husband, it is considered an exception for her husband regarding her. If that is the case, it still stands as we have mentioned. This is because Allah says regarding those women after their waiting period: **{When they hath reached their term, hold to them with goodness or release them with goodness} (Q. 65:2)**. He also says: **{Cast them not from their houses nor let them depart unless they commit an open obscenity} (Q. 65:1)**.

Regarding that, a tradition is narrated from the Prophet, peace and blessings be upon him and his progeny: ((Allah has not prohibited or permitted anything more hated to Him than divorce)).[30] Holding on to a good wife—if the husband is good to her—is the best of good deeds. Allah has commanded the most virtuous of deeds and excellence when He says **{Forget not virtue amongst thyselves} (Q. 2:237)**. A man's wife is most entitled to his virtuous deeds and excellence. I say that a man who is sinful will not deal with excellence, and an ignorant will deal with his wife unfairly and oppressively. He will not observe the command of Allah regarding her neither will he be fair towards them. For such person, there is no exception clause regarding her and there will instead be a pronouncement of divorce against her. This is because he would be considered an oppressor to her as well as one who has contravened Allah's command regarding her.

If that is the case, Allah wills that there be a separation and commands such to be a divorce. That is based on the statement of Allah, the Glorified and Exalted: **{hold to them with goodness or release them with goodness} (Q. 65:2)**. The One too majestic to be encompassed by words says: **{then hold fast to her with that which is good or release her with excellence} (Q. 2:229)** and **{harm them not so as to straiten them} (Q. 65:6)**.

In all of that is the command to do good to them as well as the prohibition of treating them unjustly. He commands the one who is not able to act upon that to divorce them because oppression is not from excellence. If there is no excellence and fairness, then Allah obligates him to divorce. Everything that Allah commands is what He wills, and what He wills is what He desires. So understand what we said regarding that about which you asked and contemplate the meaning of what we have mentioned. The truth has been made clear to you, and your heart has been illuminated by the truth if Allah wills. And strength is by Allah and for Him!

You asked about one who says to his wife "You are to me like a carcass!" or "…like blood!" or "…like pork!" and what must be done in the case of any other similar matter stated by the people of Islam. It necessitates that the one who says that to his wife is saying: "You are prohibited for me!" This is because he is simply saying by such prohibitions that he is making his wife prohibited like these things and that he is prohibiting her from himself like he would these other prohibitions. Similar is the case with one who says to his wife "You are to me like so-n-so" and mentions a woman prohibited for him to marry. There are many statements that have been made regarding this prohibition as well as abundant interpretations.

---

[30] Narrated by ***Mušannaf Ibn Abi Shayba***, ***Sunan ad-Dārqutni, Sunan al-Bayhaqi, Ušūl al-Kāfi***.

I say that which is obligatory—according to us—is that it is one. He is able to revoke and return to her as long as it is during her waiting period. It has been narrated that the Commander of Believers, 'Ali b. Abi Ṭālib, may Allah's mercy and blessings be on him, that such person must be held accountable for such. Then he said "If you intended one, then it is one."

Concerning a man who divorces a slave woman with three divorces and then buys her afterwards

If a man divorces his slave woman with three divorces and then afterwards buys her, she would not be permissible for him until after she has married someone else. This is because of the statement of the Exalted: **{And when he hath divorced her, she is impermissible for him until after she hath wedded another}** (Q. 2:230).

If a free man divorces a slave woman with three divorces and she is free from his semen and her master has intercourse with her, she will not be permissible to her first husband due to the intercourse of her master. Similarly, if a male slave divorced a female slave with three divorces and then her master has intercourse with her, she would not be permissible for him due to the intercourse of her master because it is the intercourse of an owner.

The woman would not be permitted for her first husband after three divorces until another husband marries her, as Allah says: **{And when he hath divorced her, she is impermissible for him until after she hath wedded another}** (Q. 2:230). Allah shows the position of the master although He has not mentioned it and the husband specifically. This is what the Commander of Believers, 'Ali b. Abi Ṭālib, said, upon him be peace, meant when he said: "...until she is permitted the same way as she became forbidden."[31] By that, he means 'by the husband.' It is like that which prohibits her from the husband.

Concerning a woman whose husband dies in absentia and when she observes the waiting period

The waiting period of a woman whose husband dies in absentia and then she comes to know of it—more or less—is to be counted from the day the news of his death reaches her and she is informed of it. Others say that she is to count those days that passed from his death in her waiting period. However, we do not say that because the one who advocates for such view would mandate that she would be divorced by the time the news of his death reaches her along with the time that actually passed, and this waiting period could amount to the four months and ten days! When that is the case, the meaning of Allah's intent regarding the wife whose husband dies will be lost. This would include the respect due for his death, the momentousness of his calamity, the hampering of herself and the rejection of happiness and beautification until Allah's judgement of four months and ten days for her waiting period passes.

Then we say: What do you say about a man who dies in Kufa and his wife is in Mecca, and she does not come to know about it until after five months since the day he died? Would it be permissible for her to remarry at the time she came to know about it? If they said yes, we say to them: "O Glory be to Allah! Where is that in relation to Allah's statement **{And those who perish amongst thee and leave behind wives, they shall wait and keep themselves apart four months and ten days. And when they have reached their term, there is no sin upon thee regarding whatsoever they did themselves in goodness}** (Q. 2:234)?" You know that the probationary period does not take place by the marriage to other than her husband except after she comes to know of her situation. This is because prior to it reaching her, she was captivated by what she knows; that her bridal price is with a man. It would not be permissible for her to undergo a probationary period or anything else. However, you have judged and obligated that she marries without going through the probationary period for

[31] Similarly narrated in ***Sharh at-Tajrīd***

herself at the point she heard about the death of her husband. Thereby, the probationary period had already taken place.

This is contrary to what Allah commands; rather, the statement regarding this is that she would be obligated to observe the probationary period since the day her affair belonged to her. She would be considered in the probationary period. She would be obligated to manifest grief for her husband and be inactive for four months and ten days for her own sake. Otherwise, she would be similar to anyone else in that which Allah has mandated on her due to the heavy loss experienced by her for her husband. This is not the meaning of the probationary period that Allah mentioned.

Concerning the waiting period of the *umm walad* regarding manumission and death

If a man manumits an *umm walad* and her womb is cleansed by two menstrual cycles, she is permitted to marry. Others say that one menstrual cycle is sufficient; however, this [i.e. the former view] is more precautionary regarding an *umm walad*.

If her master dies and he had not manumitted her, her waiting period would be three menstrual cycles from his death. Then, she would be permitted to marry, and two menstrual cycles would be sufficient although three is more precautionary and preferred.

If he freed her then married her but afterwards died, her waiting period would be that of the free woman in case of death, which is four months and ten days.

Concerning the post-divorce compensation which is binding on the slave

If a slave is married to a free woman with his master's permission and then divorces her, he [i.e. the master] is to give her a post-divorce compensation that Allah commanded similar to the dowry He commanded. If he marries without his master's permission, it is not binding for his master to pay any post-divorce compensation. However, it would be considered a debt that he owes after he is manumitted.

It is only for him to pay it to her if she had not known that he was a slave or that his master had not given him permission to marry yet she married him knowing that he was a slave but was then informed by that slave who gave her the impression that he had his master's permission. Such would be considered a grave offense on the part of the slave against his master for the woman.

If she knew that the master had not given him permission, there would be no post-divorce compensation for her unless she claimed ignorance of the ruling that the marriage to a slave without the permission of his master is considered invalid.

If a free man divorces a slave woman, the post-divorce compensation belongs to her. Similar is the case with a slave who marries a slave woman with his master's permission. It is obligatory for the latter to pay the post-divorce compensation.

Concerning the waiting period for the woman with vaginal bleeding

The waiting period for the divorced woman with vaginal bleeding is when she knows the completion of her menstruation periods for herself. It is similar to what she does for the prayer. When the time of her ritual purity comes, she knows it for herself.

If she is divorced during her menstruation and during the time that she is exempted from the prayer, she performs the purification wash and begins to calculate just as she would for the prayer. She then prays during the time that she knows she is pure, and she refrains from the prayer during the time she knows she is menstruating. She refrains from the prayer three times and then performs the purification wash on the third. She would have completed her waiting period, and three periods would have passed. She observes her waiting period and its timing based upon the calculation of the days of her menstrual periods just as she would for the prayer. This means that the prayer and the waiting period are the same in regard to the woman with vaginal bleeding. Her waiting period is counted from the days she knows of her menstrual cycles until the completion of three menstrual cycles.

Concerning the *khula'* divorce and when it is permissible for a man to declare a *khula'* divorce

It is impermissible for a man who performed a *khula'* divorce from his wife to take any portion of it from her unless he begins to seek that from her while she is unfair. She may say "I will not honour you in anything!" or "I will not have intercourse with you!" or "I will not obey any of your commands!" If that takes place from her and she does not repent for that which is obligatory regarding him, it would be permissible for him to perform the *khula'* divorce from her and take back what he gave her. It would be impermissible to take anything more than what she took from him.

It is necessary that the *khula'* divorce is pronounced as a divorce because every marriage between a man and a woman cannot be annulled except by divorce. This is my position and that of the one who holds to the view. Therefore, it is necessary that the divorce be stipulated before any wealth is taken or pronounced after the wealth is taken. If one does not do that in the beginning or end, the woman will still be considered married to him and anything he takes from her would be considered hers and not his.

As for the stipulation before the wealth is taken from her, it is that he says to her: "When you give me such-and-such or relinquish me from your dowry which is obligatory upon me, you will be considered divorced." If he does that and the amount for the dowry is relinquished or the stated amount of wealth is given to him, she will be considered divorced by the first statement. He does not have to repeat the divorce. It is similar to a man who says: "If you do such-and-such, you will be considered divorced." If she were to do it, she is considered divorced.

As for the wording after taking the wealth, it is that the one who took the wealth says when taking it: "You are divorced." It is to be witnessed by two witnesses. If that does not take place like this, I do not hold to the view that a divorce took place because the husband did not stipulate nor add it as a condition first or last.

If he said to her "Give me such-and-such and I will divorce you with a *khula'* divorce" or he says to her "Give me such-and-such and I will divorce you" and she gives it to him, he has a choice. He can divorce her and take it if he wants, or he can remain married and return what he took. This does not obligate divorce on him because this was only a promise, and a separation had not occurred.

The statement "If you did such-and-such, I will divorce you" is different from the statement "If you did such-and-such, you are considered divorced." To the people of knowledge and understanding, the distinction is clear.

Concerning the woman who was *khula'* divorced

When a woman is *khula'* divorced from her husband, she is irrevocably divorced. He cannot return to her except with a guardian, two witnesses and a new dowry. The man should not *khula'* divorce her unless he fears that he cannot establish the prescribed punishment of Allah regarding her or that she cannot establish it regarding him. If her rebellion is apparent and he admonishes her but she does not repent regarding that which is obligatory on her regarding him, it would then be permissible to *khula'* divorce her. He should not take anything from her, which is more than the dowry he gave her.

When he takes it from her based upon the *khula'* divorce, he should say to her: "Go, for you are divorced." Then she is considered irrevocably divorced by the pronouncement. He cannot return to her except with a new marriage with a guardian, witnesses and a new dowry.

If he also says to her "I have released you based upon what I took from you," that would be permissible as a divorce because the meaning of the statement "I have released you" is the same as "I have divorced you" if he intended such. If one claims contrary to that, his claim is taken into consideration by swearing and further investigation regarding that.

The Book of Suckling

In the Name of Allah, the Most Gracious, the Most Merciful...

The beginning of the chapters regarding suckling

Allah—the Blessed and Exalted—says: {**Forbidden unto thee art thy mothers and daughters and sisters and paternal aunts and maternal aunts and the daughters of thy brothers and the daughters of thy sisters and thy mothers from whom ye nursed and thy sisters from nursing and the mothers of thy wives and thy stepdaughters in thy protection born of thy wives whom ye have entered upon. However, if thou hast not entered upon them, there is no sin upon thee [to marry the stepdaughters]. And forbidden art the wives of the sons from thy issue and to join two sisters save that which has previously transpired. Verily, Allah was Most Forgiving, Most Gracious**} (**Q. 4:23**). Allah has prohibited the milk mothers and milk sisters without mentioning anyone else but them.

Then, many reports have come from the Prophet, peace and blessings be upon him and his progeny, which were transmitted by reliable narrators who were not criticised by the Progeny of Allah's Messenger, peace and blessings be upon him and his progeny. Among them is what was narrated from the Messenger, peace and blessings be upon him and his progeny: ((That which is prohibited for milk relations is prohibited for blood relations (*nasb*))).[1]

Also among them is what was narrated from the Commander of Believers, 'Ali b. Abi Ťālib, upon him be peace:

> He said: "O Messenger of Allah, I notice that you yearn for the women of the Quraysh. Isn't the daughter of al-Hamza b. 'Abdul-Muťťalib the most beautiful girl among the Quraysh?" He replied: ((O 'Ali, do not you know that she is the daughter of my milk brother and that which Allah has prohibited for milk relations is prohibited for blood relations?)).[2]

These reports have come and were transmitted by reliable narrators.

We do not hold to the view nor do we encourage anyone to enter into a marriage with any relative by milk relations due to doubt and confusion it may cause as evident by these reports. Refraining from entering into such doubtful matters is preferred to us than to leave room to enter it and other similar matters for the one with intellect. Such would also prevent the occurrences of confusion and doubtful matters.

There have been different statements regarding that and many narrations with consensus agreeing to its transmission by reliable narrators. Allah—the Blessed and Exalted—says: {**Whatsoever the Messenger gives thee, take it. Whatsoever he prohibits thee from, leave it. And be wary of Allah. Verily, Allah is severe in punishment**} (**Q. 59:7**) and {**Obey Allah and obey the Messenger**} (**Q. 64:12**).

Concerning what is prohibited from suckling—more or less

A suckle or two sucklings of breastmilk make prohibited just as many sucks make prohibited. Similar has been narrated to us from the Commander of Believers, 'Ali b. Abi Ťālib, upon him be peace, that a woman came to him and said: "My nephew came to me, and I gave him my breast; he suckled from it once. Then I mentioned it to his relatives and he was prevented from continuing. I want him to marry my daughter when he reaches puberty." The Commander of Believers, upon him be peace, said: "One suckle is like one hundred suckles. She will never be permissible for him."[3]

---

[1] Similarly narrated in ***Sharh at-Tajrīd, Ŝahīh Muslim, Sunan an-Nisā'i, Sunan Ibn Mājah, Ŝahīh Ibn Hibbān, Sunan at-Tirmidhi, Musnad Ahmed, Bihār al-Anwār***

[2] Similarly narrated in ***Musnad Imam Zayd, Sharh at-Tajrīd, Ŝahīh al-Bukhāri, Ŝahīh Muslim, Sunan an-Nisā'i, Sunan al-Bayhaqi, Bihār al-Anwār***.

[3] Narrated ***Sunan ad-Dārqutni*** and ***Sunan al-Bayhaqi***.

Similarly, if a baby does not suckle from the breast but it is given milk and it is placed in its mouth for medicine or drink, that which is prohibited in terms of suckling would be prohibited likewise; such and suckling are the same.

My father related to me that his father was asked about suckling and what it makes prohibited. He replied:

> That suckling which makes prohibited—more or less—is one suckle or two. This is what is narrated from the Commander of Believers, 'Ali b. Abi Ťālib, upon him be peace.
>
> It is narrated on the authority of Ibn az-Zubayr[§] that the Prophet, peace and blessings be upon him and his progeny, said: ((One or two sucklings do not make prohibited)).[4] However, this is not authentically attributed to him according to us. Nor would it be possible because he, peace and blessings be upon him and his progeny, would not say anything contrary to the Book of Allah. This is from the one who narrated it and therefore invalid and impossible.

Concerning milk relations after weaning

There are no milk relations after weaning, and weaning is after two lunar years. That is based on the statement of Allah: **{...and the mothers may nurse their children for two complete lunar years for the one who desires to complete the nursing}** **(Q. 2:233)**. Allah makes that the time for nursing, and He makes its completion the time for the completion of nursing.

The Glorified says: **{And he was borne and dependent for thirty months...}** **(Q. 46:15)**. The minimum time for pregnancy is six months, and the remaining time of thirty months is for nursing. Therefore, the remainder time after six months would be two years. Allah makes two years the time for suckling. Therefore, whoever suckles or is suckled during that time is considered milk relations. That which takes place afterwards and after weaning is not considered prohibited milk relations.

Thus, we say that if a man has his son breastfed after weaning and after the completion of two lunar years from the time he was a baby, we do not hold to the view that he would be considered prohibited even if suckling took place after weaning and the completion of two lunar years.

As for the hadith that was narrated in which the Prophet said to Sahla, the wife of Abu Hudhayfa, when she asked him about her adopted son, Sālim, being allowed to enter upon her while she is uncovered due to the revelation of the prohibition of attributing adopted sons [**(Q. 33:5)**] ((Nurse Sālim ten times so he can enter upon you as he used to))[5]—this is not authentically attributed to him according to us. We do not hold to the view, and it is nothing according to us

Regarding that, it has reached us that a man came to 'Ali and said: "O Commander of Believers, I have a wife and a son from her. I also took charge of a slave woman and concealed her. She said 'Bring her to me' and promised not to anger me in her regard. I then brought her to my wife and she later said: 'I breastfed her' [attempting to make her impermissible for him]. What do you say regarding that?" 'Ali, upon him be peace, said to him: "Go and punish your wife for what she did, and take your slave girl as you please. There are no milk relations except by that which grows flesh and strengthens bones. There are no milk relations after weaning."[6]

My father related to me that his father was asked about milk relations after weaning. He replied: "There are no milk relations after weaning."

---

[4] Similarly narrated in ***Ŝahīh Muslim, Sunan at-Tirmidhi, Sunan Abu Dāwūd, Sunan an-Nisā'i, Sunan ad-Dārqutni, Mu'jam al-Kabīr, Musnad Ahmed*** and ***Sunan al-Bayhaqi***.

[5] Similarly narrated in ***Sharh at-Tajrīd, Musnad Ahmed, Ŝahīh Muslim, Sunan Abu Dāwūd, Sunan Ibn Mājah, Sunan an-Nisā'i, Sunan al-Bayhaqi***

[6] Similarly narrated in ***Sharh at-Tajrīd.*** It is narrated in ***Uŝūl al-Kāfi*** as a hadith of the Prophet.

My father related to me that his father said:

> A little suckling is like a lot when it takes place within two lunar years. This is based on the statements of Allah {**And he was borne and dependent for thirty months…**} **(Q. 46:15)** and {**…and the mothers may nurse their children for two complete lunar years for the one who desires to complete the nursing**} (**Q. 2:233**).

My father related to me that his father said:

> That which is prohibited by milk relations is similarly prohibited by blood relations. This is narrated from Allah's Messenger, peace and blessings be upon him and his progeny, as well as from the Commander of Believers, upon him be peace.[7]

Concerning the 'milk of the man' (*laban al-fahl*)

The 'milk of the man'[8] prohibits based upon what was narrated from the Prophet, peace and blessings be upon him and his progeny, regarding the daughter of al-Hamza b. 'Abdul-Muttalib when he said: ((She is the daughter of my milk brother…)). Similar is the case with impregnation. Therefore, the woman's milk is due to impregnation just as the 'milk of the man' is. So the 'milk of the man' is like impregnation.

Concerning the suckling of the People of the Book

One should not suckle from a disbeliever because she is considered ritually impure as Allah—the Glorified and Exalted—says: {**Verily, the idolaters are impure**} (**Q. 9:28**). There is no idolatry greater than one who rejects the signs [or "verses"] of Allah, His Messengers, His Prophets, His Books and claims another God along with Him.

If one is compelled, she can suckle the child until another woman is found. One should not delay finding another. Rather, I hold to the view that if he does not fear ruin for the child, he should give it sheep milk to drink by dripping it into his mouth like medicine and not the milk of a disbelieving idolatress except out of necessity. It is similar to eating carcass; when one is free of such situation, carcass is prohibited. Similar is the case with the suckling of a Muslim child by an idolatress.

Concerning a boy and girl being given the milk of two different children from the same nurse mother with two years or more between

If a nurse mother suckles a boy with the milk of one child and three years pass and then a girl is suckled with the milk of another child of hers [i.e. the nurse mother], the boy will not be permitted for the girl because the both of them are considered milk siblings even if there was a stretch of time between their sucklings from the same nurse mother. A sibling relationship due to the suckling of a nurse mother is like a sibling relationship due to birth.

My father related to me that his father was asked about a slave boy and slave girl who were suckled by a nurse mother with the milk of two different children with a year or more between their sucklings. "Would the boy be permitted to marry the girl?" He replied:

> Know—may Allah be merciful to you—that the both of them would be considered siblings due to the same nurse mother. This is just like the sibling relationship due to birth from the same womb. They all would be considered as the same offspring even if they were nursed by a different woman, as they would be considered as siblings.

A little suckling is like a lot as long as it is before the completion of two lunar years. Regarding that, Allah says {**…and his weaning is within two years**} (**Q. 31:14**) and {**…and the mothers may nurse their children for two complete lunar years for the one who desires to complete the nursing**} (**Q. 2:233**).

---

[7] Similarly narrated in ***Musnad Imam Zayd, Sharh at-Tajrīd, Sunan at-Tirmidhi.***

[8] This term amongst jurists refers to the husband of the milk mother acquiring the status similar to that of the father due to his contribution towards inducing lactation. [Ref. ***Al-Bidāyat al-Mujtahid***]

Regarding a little and a lot, since Allah mentions nurse mothers when He says **{...and thy mothers from whom ye nursed and thy sisters from nursing...} (Q. 4:23)**, the Glorified refrains from mentioning a limit when mentioning suckling—whether a little or a lot. Therefore, suckling is by the consensus of the people, and there is no limit for a little or a lot. Yet, it is narrated that Allah's Messenger, peace and blessings be upon him and his progeny, said: ((One and two sucklings make prohibited as well as one and two nursings)).

Allah does not mention suckling with a little or a lot; He simply mentions suckling generally. Regarding the prohibition of marrying a nurse mother and milk siblings, He says: **{...and thy mothers from whom ye nursed and thy sisters from nursing...} (Q. 4:23)**. Everyone connected by the designation of nursing is prohibited for marriage. The designation of nursing applies to whether suckling is once or twice and whether nursing is once or twice. It is similar to whether the nursing is for a month, two months, a year or two years. The one with intellect cannot reject that, nor can the people of understanding ever object.

Concerning a woman who gives her husband her breastmilk to drink without him knowing

Any woman who gives her husband any of her breastmilk desiring to make herself prohibited from him would not be considered prohibited from him. It would be permissible for him to instruct her in proper etiquette and consider her to be contemptuous for doing so.

The Book of Financial Maintenance (*an-Nafaqāt*)

In the Name of Allah, the Most Gracious, the Most Merciful...

Concerning the financial maintenance of a pregnant woman whose husband has died

If a man dies and his wife is pregnant, she is to be financially maintained with all of his wealth. Others have said that she is to be financially maintained from a portion allotted from what is in her womb. According to us, that is nothing because it is a weak, invalid statement that is not acknowledged.

That is because that which is in her womb inherits if it cries (and then dies) and it does not inherit if it dies without crying. Also, the baby does not inherit if it is miscarried. So what does the one who holds to the view that her financial maintenance is to be taken from the baby's inheritance say if the baby is born dead? Does it necessitate financial maintenance for her or is it calculated from the entirety of his wealth? In this case, it would be inevitable for this person to admit that it is taken from all his wealth. For that reason, we say that her financial maintenance is taken from the entire wealth.

If one were to say that it is calculated from her inheritance from her husband, we reply by asking: "What if she was an *umm walad* and she did not have a child other than the one in her womb and then it died before crying? Upon whom will be the financial maintenance?" He would have no choice but to accept our statement that the financial maintenance is taken from the entire wealth.

Concerning a slave who marries a free woman that has children from him and who financially maintains the children

Their financial maintenance is upon their free mother because she inherits from them and they inherit from her. It is not obligatory for their father to financially maintain them because they do not inherit from him nor does he inherit from them. If their mother does not have the wealth to financially maintain them, the judgement of financial maintenance falls on her relatives or paternal relations. This is because they inherit from her children. Their financial maintenance is upon those who inherit from them. Whoever does not inherit from them is not obligated to financially maintain them.

Concerning the financial maintenance of a divorcee who is impermissible until after remarriage

If a man divorces his wife with three divorces that do not make her permissible for him until after her remarriage, he does not provide lodging for her but financially maintains her. We simply say that he financially maintains her because she is prohibited from marriage until the completion of the waiting period. Therefore, as long as she does not remarry, we obligate her to be patient until the completion of her waiting period. We make financial maintenance for her until she is permitted to remarry; otherwise, she may die or suffer from hunger. Her financial maintenance and lodging are together for the husband who can still revoke the divorce of the wife with whom he is married if he likes.

My father related to me that his father was asked about one who divorced his wife with a divorce in which it would be impermissible to remarry until she married another. "Does he provide lodging and financial maintenance for her?" He replied:

> If he divorced her with an irrevocable divorce thrice, there is no lodging for her. Regarding that, there is a hadith of Fāṭima bt. Qays[§] that is narrated in which her husband divorced her three times and the Prophet, peace and blessings be upon him and his progeny, did not appoint that she received lodging. The majority of the people deny that she does not receive lodging.

There is no lodging provided except for the wife with whom one can revoke, as long as it is during her waiting period or if there is a way for him to return to her before marriage to another. We simply say that because we find that lodging is something that Allah has appointed out of consideration for His slaves. Consequently, they can contemplate their matters, repent for any errors committed and return to their wives after having declared divorce on them. If they desire to do so, a man can return to his wife while she is in his house without her leaving and without her going to the house of another.

Regarding that, Allah says: **{Thou know not: it may be that Allah shall cause a new matter to occur afterwards} (Q. 65:1)**. The **{matter}** refers to returning and revocation. If there was a divorce that one could not revoke, this **{new matter}** that Allah causes would be nullified. This is because the Glorified has prohibited her from this situation until she marries another husband, and this lodging would be exempted from him.

Haven't you considered how Allah prohibited the one for whom He wants to **{cause a new matter to occur}** in terms of revocation from removing her from his house? Rather, He commands that she be given lodging. He says: **{Cast them not from their houses nor let them depart save they commit an open indecency. Such are the limits of Allah. And whosoever transgresses Allah's limits, such one verily wrongs his own soul. Thou know not: it may be that Allah shall cause a new matter to occur afterwards} (Q. 65:1)**.

Allah links lodging with the command regarding the **{new matter}**; the 'matter' refers to revocation. If there is no revocation for the husband, then there cannot be a **{new matter}** for Allah to cause for him. This is because Allah has prohibited one from that except for after marriage. If there is no command, then there is no lodging because the both of them are joined together and linked in the verse. The presence of one establishes the presence of the other, and the absence of one establishes the absence of the other. Therefore, if you negate the revocation that Allah mentions causing anew, you similarly negate the lodging. If that is the case, then lodging is not necessitated.

Concerning a man who is unable to financially maintain his wife

Whoever is not able to financially maintain his wife, such person is not obligated to divorce her. He is obligated to make strenuous effort regarding the affairs of his wife as well as her financial maintenance to the extent of his own financial maintenance. He is not obligated to separate from her unless such person judges by something other than Allah's judgement regarding himself and her. There is nothing due on him more than strenuous effort. If he extends himself in his provisions, he is not obligated to do more than that in his affair.

Regarding that, Allah says: **{Let he who has ample provisions spend to the extent of his means and let he whose provision is measured spend of that which Allah hath given unto him. Allah hath not burdened a soul beyond what it can bear} (Q. 65:7)**. Allah also says: **{Allah burdens not a soul except with what it can bear} (Q. 2:286)** and **{...the rich according to his means and the straitened according to his means—a just proportion—a right upon those who do good} (Q. 2:236)**.

With today is tomorrow, and with hardship is ease. Regarding that, Allah says: **{For verily, with hardship is ease. Verily, with hardship is ease} (Q. 94:5-6)**.

If a man marries a woman and does not have intercourse with her, he is obligated by Allah to financially maintain her if the abstinence was from him and not her. However, if the abstinence was from her, he is not obligated to financially maintain her.

My father related to me that his father was asked about a man who was unable to financially maintain his wife. "Is he forced to divorce her?" He replied:

> If there is a trial for the wife due to the destitution of her husband, that does not remove her from his charge. **{For verily, with hardship is ease. Verily, with hardship is ease} (Q. 94:5-6)**. Allah has said: **{If there be those in need, Allah shall enrich them from His bounty. And Allah is All-Encompassing, All-Knowing} (Q. 24:32)**.

My father related to me that his father said regarding a man who marries a woman who seeks financial maintenance from him before having intercourse: "If the abstinence was on his part, he is obligated to provide financial maintenance. If the abstinence was on her part, he does not have to provide financial maintenance for her."

A wife inherits from her husband if it is during the waiting period in which he is permitted to revoke the divorce. As for the period outside of the waiting period in which he is not able to revoke the divorce except after she marries another, there is no inheritance between them.

As for the parents who command their son to divorce his wife, it is impermissible for him to obey their command in that regards. His disobeying them in this would be acceptable to Allah because that would be considered undue oppression on the wife.

As for the man who has four wives and he divorces one of them but then dies without it being known which of the wives he divorced, an eighth will be distributed among them or a fourth if none of them had children or grandchildren. All of them are to observe their waiting periods from him to the furthest of their appointed times.

My father related to me that his father was asked about a man who divorced a woman while he was sick, and he died while she was in her waiting period. Do both inherit from each other? He replied:

> If the woman dies during her waiting period or her husband dies while he is able to revoke the divorce, he inherits from her and she from him. If it is an irrevocable divorce, there is no inheritance between them according to us.

My father related to me that his father said regarding a man with four wives who divorced one of them and then died without it being known which one he divorced: "All of them inherit a third from him and it is distributed among them based upon their number."

If a man said to his wife "You are divorced if I do not strike you with a hundred lashings," it would be impermissible for him to strike her violently. If he intended by that severe strikes, he is to divorce her and then return to her. However, he is to not strike her because Allah does not permit him to do that to her.[1]

Concerning a disbeliever who embraces Islam—either he or his wife—and whether he is obligated to financially maintain her

If a disbeliever embraces Islam and his wife does not, he is not obligated to financially maintain her. However, if she embraces Islam but he does not, he is obligated to financially maintain her because of the position of Islam. This is because when she embraced Islam, she would be obligated to enter upon that that which he would enter. If she did not do that, it would be a divorce on her part. Financial maintenance would therefore not be obligatory upon him.

Similarly, if she were to embrace Islam but he had not, it would be a divorce on his part. This is because she had entered that which Allah has commanded her and he had not. Therefore, the divorce would be on his part. He would thus be obligated to provide financial maintenance for her as long as she is in her waiting period. Once her waiting period is over, there is no financial maintenance for her.

If she embraced Islam and he embraced Islam while she is in the waiting period, both of them would be considered married. If he embraced Islam later after the completion of the waiting period, they would have to conduct a new marriage if they want to reunite after separation.

---

[1] It should be noted here that Imam al-Hādi denounces the act of physically abusing one's wife. This is notwithstanding the existence of the Qur'anic verse: **{...those [i.e. wives] from whom ye fear their rebellion, admonish them and then forsake them in the beds and then strike them...} (Q. 4:34)**. The parameters of such disciplinary actions have been legislated and not left to the whims of husbands to act on such as they please. Imam Ibn Murtaḍa related in his ***Al-Bahr*** that such strike should not induce bleeding or lead one to fear loss of life and limb. Additionally, one must avoid striking the face and/or neck.

Concerning the financial maintenance of a slave's wife

If a slave is married to a slave woman with the permission of his master, the responsibility of her financial maintenance is upon his master if he gives her to the slave and she is not in his [i.e. the master's] service. However, if she is in his service and he does not hand her over to the slave and she is not situated in his house, there is no financial maintenance or dowry due to her by his master.

If he marries her without his master's permission, it is permissible for his master to annul the marriage and the dowry will be from the service of the slave unless it is voluntarily donated by his master.

Concerning the judgement that financial maintenance of the one in straitened circumstances is upon the abled heir

It is obligatory upon the related heir of the one in straitened circumstance to provide financial maintenance to the extent of his inheritance—whether the inheritance is small or large. This is based upon the statement of the Blessed and Exalted: **{…and upon the heir is the likeness of that…} (Q. 2:233).**

If inheritance is commanded with financial maintenance, the one who inherits is responsible for financial maintenance. Any living person who is prevented by another from inheritance is not responsible for financial maintenance.

An explanation of that is the following: A man in straitened circumstances has a paternal brother and paternal sister who are both abled. The mother and the father's paternal uncle are both in straitened circumstances. Financial maintenance would thus be obligatory upon the abled heirs. A fourth of the financial maintenance responsibility would be on the paternal brother, and a three-fourths would be the responsibility of the paternal sister. The mother and the uncle are both in straitened circumstances so there is no obligation on them; rather, they are both obligated to receive financial maintenance. The paternal sister is to financially maintain the uncle, and the paternal brother is to financially maintain the mother in straitened circumstances. We appoint a fourth for the paternal brother because he and the paternal sister who was obligated three-fourths of the financial maintenance both inherit those same amounts. The sister inherits half of six—which is three, the paternal brother inherits one out of six and that total would equal four. So, we consider what inheritance is in their possession if the abled were to die; it would be four parts. Therefore, we say to the sister: "You have three-fourths, so you are responsible for three-fourths of the financial maintenance." And we say to the brother: "You have a fourth, so you are responsible for a fourth of the financial maintenance." Thus, whatever amount it is, one is obligated to render that same amount as we mentioned. Then, each one is required to do what s/he is required to do in that respects.

If a person in straitened circumstances has two paternal/maternal sisters in straitened circumstances as well as two paternal sisters and a mother who are abled, the responsibility of financial maintenance would be on the mother alone. The two paternal sisters would be exempted from financial maintenance even though they are abled because there are also the paternal/maternal sisters and they are exempted from inheritance. If they do not inherit, they are not responsible for financial maintenance. Thus, anyone who is exempted from inheritance by another is not responsible for the financial maintenance of the one who exempted them while alive.

Similarly, if the one in straitened circumstances has a maternal brother and grandfather and mother but his grandfather is also in straitened circumstances, the financial maintenance is upon the mother because the maternal brother does not inherit along with the grandfather. Similarly, if the one in straitened circumstances has a father and grandfather and mother but the father is in straitened circumstances, the responsibility for financial maintenance would be on the mother. Nothing would be due on the grandfather because the father exempts him from inheritance.

Similarly, if a woman in straitened circumstances had a daughter in straitened circumstances and three different sisters who were abled, the responsibility of the woman's financial maintenance would be on her paternal/maternal sister. This is because she and her daughter inherit from the remainder after the half is taken. The responsibility of the daughter's financial maintenance would be on her three maternal aunts. Three-fifths of the financial maintenance will be the responsibility of her father's and mother's maternal aunts: one-fifth of the financial maintenance responsibility would be on each aunt. If her mother had died, there would not be any heirs for the daughter except her aunts; they are those relatives who inherit. If that is the case, they are to financially maintain her as we explained about financial maintenance.

Concerning the Muslim who has a poor relative who is a disbeliever

A Muslim is not responsible to financially maintain a disbeliever except if the disbeliever is the Muslim's father or mother; one is obligated to financially maintain any one of the parents. This is based upon the statement of Allah: **{Accompany them both in this world acceptably (*ma'rūf*)} (Q. 31:15)**. It is not considered **{acceptably}** if they are thirsty and hungry; neither are they to be left naked.

Concerning that which is binding upon the abled regarding a relative in straitened circumstances

Financial maintenance is binding upon the abled as well as clothing, lodging and servants for relatives in straitened circumstances if such one is not able to serve themselves. This might be due to a defect or sickness that prevents one from establishing his command and sufficiency from serving himself.

The Book of Sales (*al-Buyū'*)

In the Name of Allah, the Most Gracious, the Most Merciful...

The beginning of the chapters regarding sales

Allah—the Blessed and Exalted—says: **{O ye who believe! Consume not thy wealth amongst thee in falsehood except that it be a transaction by mutual consent between thee, and slay not thyself. Verily, Allah hath been merciful unto thee}** **(Q. 4:29)**. The Glorified means that one should not consume usury, ill-gotten wealth, oppression or bribery so that it becomes invalid.

As for His statement **{except that it be a transaction by mutual consent between thee}**, the term **{mutual consent}** refers to the seller's agreement to pay back the value of commodity with the same price without increasing it for the delay of payment.

One of the consensual agreements is that one sells it himself without its sale being forced or compelled. The One majestic in His praise says: **{O ye who believe! When ye contract a debt for a fixed term, write it down. Let a scribe record it in writing amongst thee equitably. Let not a scribe refuse to write as Allah hath taught him. So, let him write, and let him upon whom is the debt dictate. And let him be conscious of Allah, his Lord, and diminish naught thereof. But if he upon whom is the debt is one of minimal understanding or weak or unable to dictate, let his guardian dictate equitably. And let two witnesses amongst thy men bear witness. And if there not be two men, then a man and two women amongst those of whom ye are satisfied as witnesses. So that if one errs, the other shall remember. And the witnesses must not refuse when they are called. Refuse not to write down whether it be small or great, to the fixed term thereof. That is more just to Allah and surer for testimony and the best way of avoiding doubt save only in the case when it is a present transaction that ye transfer amongst thyselves. Then, it is no sin upon thee if ye write it not. And have witnesses when ye sell one to another, and let no harm be done to scribe or witness. If ye do, verily, it is an act of open disobedience for thee. Be conscious of Allah. And Allah teaches thee. And Allah is of all things most knowing}** **(Q. 2:282)**.

As for His statement **{and let him upon whom is the right dictate. And let him be conscious of Allah, his Lord}**, it simply means that the debtor who buys has to declare of what he owes to the creditor so that the witnesses testify to what they hear from his self-affirmation.

As for the statement of the Mighty and Majestic **{and diminish naught thereof}**, it means that one should not be deficient due to any personal bias, and he [i.e. the debtor] has to declare all of that which he owes.

As for the statement **{But if he upon whom is the right is one of minimal understanding or weak or unable to dictate, let his guardian dictate equitably}**, the term **{minimal understanding}** refers to a deficiency in intellect due to either youth or weak intellect. As for the statement of the Glorified and Exalted **{weak}**, it refers to inability due to lack of intellect or inability due to illness or inability of one to dictate speech due to a disability.

Similar is His statement—Mighty and Majestic is He: **{or unable to dictate}**. It is that which is due to an incapability of expressing himself or due to young age also or due to any reason that prevents him from that. If that is the case, it is obligatory for the guardian to dictate that which is obligatory for his companion. He should explain and clarify it in the presence of the owner of the commodity as well as establish it for him in the presence of two witnesses.

As for the statement of the Mighty and Majestic **{And let two witnesses amongst thy men bear witness}**, it simply means by this: the reliable people of your religion with whom you are satisfied with their justice and uprightness.

As for His statement **{And if there not be two men, then a man and two women amongst those of whom ye are satisfied as witnesses}**, Allah has two women take the place of a second male witness due to any weakness in them both [i.e. the two males] or any lack of knowledge on their part regarding that which is obligatory upon them. Do you not hear how He says: **{So that if one errs, the other shall remember}**? By that, He means the erring of forgetfulness or any other matter of deficiency that the two women cannot rely upon. Therefore, He means that one can remind the other of that and encourage her to fear her Lord in case the latter wants to intentionally falsify her witness.

Then the Glorified says: **{And the witnesses must not refuse when they are called}**. He is saying that they should not refuse to act as witnesses based upon what they know of that in which they are called upon to witness. It is obligatory upon them to act as witnesses in the presence of the imam based upon what they know. This is in order to extract the rights of the one for whom they are testifying.

As for the statement of the Mighty and Majestic **{Refuse not to write down whether it be small or great, to the fixed term thereof}**, He is saying 'Do not hesitate to write down whether it be small or great, to the appointed time.'

As for His statement of the Mighty and Majestic **{...and the best way of avoiding doubt...}**, it means: so that you are not uncertain about it, its number, weight or appointed time. When there is a scribe to write it down in the presence of witnesses, that is the best way to instruct the witnesses and for them to recognise when they see the writing. Therefore, they can remind, refer back to and know all that they witnessed.

As for the statement of the Mighty and Majestic **{...save only in the case when it is a present transaction which ye transfer amongst thyselves. Then, it is no sin upon thee if ye write it not}**, the meaning of **{present}** here is 'you are physically present in your city and its monetary transaction while you are physically present.' There will be no sin on you in that case if it is not written down or if there are no witnesses.

Then the Mighty and Majestic says **{And have witnesses when ye sell one to another}**. The Glorified is saying to have witnesses with the approval of the seller and buyer so that there is no revocation or withdrawal from any of them. As for the statement of the Glorified **{and let no harm be done to scribe or witness}**, it is a prohibition from Allah that the scribes be prevented from writing as Allah has taught them and that the witnesses be prevented from bearing witness to the truth when called as Allah has commanded them. Then, He declares that the one who does that has committed **{an act of open disobedience}**.

As for the statement of the Glorified **{and surer for testimony}**, it means: more just and more established in the case of the scribes and in the case of the debtor that is present. Then the debtor cannot deny nor detract what he owes to the creditor.

As for the statement of the Mighty and Majestic **{And if ye are on a journey and find not a scribe, then pledge in hand} (verse 283)**, He is saying: if you are on a journey and cannot find a scribe or writing material, such as an inkwell or paper, a pledge with the hand takes the place of witnesses and scribes. The **{pledge in hand}** refers to the pledge of the recipient to the owner of the commodity.

As for the statement of the Mighty and Majestic **{And conceal not testimony}**, He is prohibiting witnesses from concealing the testimony that they know. Concealment has a number of meanings and reasons such as the denial of testimony, a witness's pretext with a reason not authorised by Allah or a preoccupation from establishing testimony due to a matter not considered valid by his Creator.

As for the statement of the Mighty and Majestic **{And if one of thee entrusts another, let he who is entrusted return his trust} (verse 283)**, this verse is abrogated by the statement of Allah **{O ye who believe! When ye contract a debt for a fixed term, write it down. Let a scribe record it in writing amongst thee equitably} (verse 282)**.

Its abrogation is not considered prohibited due to the existence of other abrogated verses in which a command was repealed by a more established judgement that substituted it. This is because the establishment of trusts between Muslims regarding their wealth was considered good, and goodness is not considered worthless to the One, Most Gracious. Rather, the Glorified abrogated it by demonstrating the better and substantiated between them and furthest from all corruptions. Therefore, He demonstrated to them the establishment of scribes and witnesses out of His consideration for all His slaves. Whoever considers and follows the good, Allah will reward such one and not punish him.

Whoever desires to undergo a business transaction must obtain understanding of it in the religion. He must look into the permissible and prohibited from the Book of Allah so that he saves himself from errors and mistakes in partnerships, selling and buying.

Regarding that, it has reached us that a man came to the Commander of Believers, 'Ali b. Abi Ťālib and said: "O Commander of Believers, I want to engage in business. So, supplicate to Allah for me." The Commander of Believers, upon him be peace, asked him: "Have you acquired a thorough understanding in Allah's religion?" He replied: "A little." Then, he [i.e. 'Ali] said: "Woe unto you! Thorough understanding first and then business. Verily, whoever sells and buys but then not ask about the permissible and prohibited will fall into usury and then fall."[1]

It has reached us that the Commander of Believers, upon him be peace, said: "Allah's Messenger, peace and blessings be upon him and his progeny, said: ((Verily, Allah loves the slave who is lenient in selling, buying, issuing judgements and demanding back payment))."[2]

It has reached us that the Commander of the Believers, upon him be peace, said: "Allah's Messenger, peace and blessings be upon him and his progeny, said: ((Verily, I curse the imam who engages in business with his flock))."[3]

Concerning profit, merchandise and strictness regarding usury

There is no problem for the Muslim to engage in business in order to free his family and relatives from the subjugation of begging. His business should minimise the possibility of gain by oppressors and tyrannical rulers as well as prevent harm from the Muslims. It would be impermissible to engage in such business and profit from the sale of weapons, mounts as well as male and female slaves if such would increase the gain of oppressors or strengthen the power of the openly disobedient. He should engage in business in other than these things—to minimise their gain and remove their association.

It is encouraged for the one who engages in business and needs something of that which was mentioned to increase the price of those things for him and others so much that they would not accept the price. He does not do what the disobedient and evil traitors do, such as trade relations (*ta'ammul*) for their own benefit and exclusive ownership for themselves and no others as well as buying what is suitable for them. They invalidate their profit by that and obligate Allah's major punishment.

I surely know of a business; its achievement is due to Allah. It provides gain for its merchant and happiness to the one seeking it. It grants success to the one who buys it and blessings to the one who owns it. It restrains the one who enters it and facilitates the one who engages in it.

---

[1] Similarly narrated in ***Musnad Imam Zayd, Ušūl al-Kāfi, Bihār al-Anwār***

[2] Similarly narrated in ***Musnad Imam Zayd***, ***Amāli Ahmed b. 'Isa,*** and ***Sharh at-Tajrīd***. Similar appears in ***Ŝahīh al-Bukhāri, Majmu' az-Zawā'id, Sunan Ibn Mājah, Sunan at-Tirmidhi, Al-Mu'jam al-Awsat***

[3] Similarly narrated in ***Musnad Imam Zayd, Amāli Ahmed b. 'Isa.***

Business saves one from painful punishment; however, no one seeks it out, so I will mention it. No one desires it, so I will explain it. No one prefers it, so I will expound on it. However, perhaps **{For, verily, with hardship is ease. Verily, with hardship is ease}** **(Q. 94:5-6)**. Perhaps, Allah will facilitate His path and empower His associates and debase His enemies.[4]

The Mighty and Majestic says: **{Perchance Allah shall grant victory or a command from His presence. Then they shall regret of what they secretly had in themselves}** **(Q. 5:52)**. Regarding that, the Messenger of the Lord of creation, peace and blessings be upon him and his progeny, said: ((When difficulty increases, there will come a relief)).[5] Also regarding that, my grandfather, al-Qāsim b. Ibrāhīm said:

> Perhaps by proximity to the naked, you will dress yourself.
> And by the debasement of the seizers, you will gain victory.
> Perhaps it is a drink unsullied that will replenish a thirst.
> And the thirst will be prolonged by a murky watering spring.
> Perhaps a bonesetter of broken bones due to his kindness
> May bring some relief to the broken bone and set it aright.
> May you not despair of Allah, for He is lenient in the mighty.
> Perhaps the images of yesterday have injustices hidden in them.
> A bright justice will revive them and manifest. Perhaps the prisoners
> Will be released with chains below them as a nailed nail of iron
> Perhaps a type of ease will come from Allah sooner.

As for usury, no one deals with it or concerns himself with it except the openly defiant and disobedient as well as those who wage war against Allah and who are disbelieving enemies. This is because it is a command of great importance and a weighty matter. Allah declared it to be war even for even a small amount [i.e. the remains], let alone a large amount. He says: **{O ye who believe! Be conscious of Allah and give up whatsoever remains of usury if ye are indeed believers! If ye do not do so, know that ye are at war with Allah and His Messenger. But if ye repent, for thee is the principal of thy wealth. Ye shall do no wrong nor will wrong be done unto thee}** **(Q. 2:278-279)**.

The designation of belief and God-consciousness cannot be applied to them if they hold on to the remains of usury without leaving it altogether. Then, He declares to them that there is war with Allah and His Messenger if they keep what remains of it as well as if they refrain from leaving from it altogether. War refers to warfare, and warfare refers to encountering and striking. The striking is that which removes doubt and uncertainty, and there occurs killing, punishment, dying and captivity for the people of war insomuch that they return to obedience and truth as well as turn from disobedience and wickedness.

Regarding usury, Allah's Messenger, peace and blessings be upon him and his progeny, said: ((Whoever refrains from the purification dues and consumes usury has waged war on me in this world and the hereafter)).[6]

Regarding that, it has reached us from the Commander of Believers, upon him be peace:

> Allah's Messenger, peace and blessings be upon him and his progeny, cursed usury, its consumption, the one who consumes it, the one who sells it, the one who buys it, the one who records it and the one who acts as a witness to it.[7]

---

[4] Sayyid Abul-'Abbās al-Hasani related with his chain of narrators to Zayd b. 'Ali form his father from his grandfather from 'Ali, upon them be peace, that a man came to Allah's Messenger, peace and blessings be upon him and his progeny, and asked: "O Messenger of Allah, what is the best type of earning?" He replied: ((A man who labours with his hands and a righteous business transaction)).

[5] Reported in ***Kanz al-'Ummāl***

[6] Similarly narrated in ***Musnad Imam Zayd, Amāli Ahmed b. 'Isa***

[7] Similarly narrated in ***Musnad Imam Zayd, Ŝahīh Muslim, Sunan Abu Dāwūd, Sunan at-Tirmidhi, Sunan an-Nisā'i, Sunan al-Bayhaqi, Al-Mu'jam al-Awsat, Musnad Ahmed, Mušannaf of Ibn Abi Shayba, Ŝahīh Ibn Hibbān, Bihār al-Anwār***

My father related to me from his father on the authorities of some of his elders and ancestors from 'Ali b. Abi Ťālib, upon him be peace:

> Allah's Messenger, peace and blessings be upon him and his progeny, said: ((A dirham of usury is worse to Allah than thirty-four acts of fornication and more detested than a man who has intercourse with his mother)).[8]

Concerning that which is weighed or measured when one sells to another

Gold is for gold in similarity—beit its dinar or ore. Silver is for silver in similarity—beit its raw material or dirham. Whoever adds to that has engaged in usury. Similarly, dates are for dates, wheat is for wheat, corn is for corn and barley is for barley.

Each type is for that type, and one thing is with its like. Whoever adds to that has engaged in usury—whether there is a quantitative difference in the two colours, tastes and measures or not. It is impermissible to sell one *mudd* of wheat for two *mudds* of wheat, one *mudd* of dates with two *mudds* of dates, one *mudd* of corn with a *mudd* and a half of corn or even a *mudd* of barley with a *mudd* and one-fourth of barley. Rather, a like is to be sold with a like hand-to-hand. A dirham and *dāniq*[9] cannot be sold for a dirham, nor can a dirham and broken *dāniq* be sold for a sound dirham. A mithqal and a sixth cannot be sold for a fixed-rate dirham.

Regarding that is what has reached us from the Commander of Believers, 'Ali b. Abi Ťālib, upon him be peace:

> A date was gifted to Allah's Messenger, peace and blessings be upon him and his progeny, and he did not partake in it. He said to Bilāl: ((Stay away from this date until I ask about it)). Bilāl left and gave away the date for two similar dates. On the next day, he said to him: ((O Bilāl, give us our item that we gave to you)). Bilāl came with the date, and Allah's Messenger, peace and blessings be upon him and his progeny, asked him: ((What is this item we gave to you?)). He then informed him of what he did, and Allah's Messenger, peace and blessings be upon him and his progeny, said to him: ((This prohibited thing is impermissible to consume. Go and return it to its owner. Tell him that this transaction was invalid)). Then, Allah's Messenger, peace and blessings be upon him and his progeny, said: ((Gold is for gold, like for like; Silver is for silver, like for like; dates are for dates, like for like. Barley is for barley, like for like; wheat is for wheat, like for like; and corn is for corn, like for like. Whoever increases in that has engaged in usury. Similarly, salt is for salt, like for like)).[10]

My father related to me that his father was asked about exchange, and the latter said:

> Reliable people narrated to us with the chain reaching to Allah's Messenger, peace and blessings be upon him and his progeny: ((Do not sell gold for gold unless it is like for like. And do not increase some of it over another part. And do not sell present money for absent money)).[11]

My father related to me that his father was asked about selling a restored silver dirham for a good silver dirham. He replied:

---

[8] Similarly narrated in ***Mušannaf of Ibn Abi Shayba, Sunan ad-Dārqutni, Musnad Ahmed***

[9] This refers to an ancient coin whose worth was a sixth of a dirham. [Ref. **Lane's Arabic English Lexicon**]

[10] Similarly narrated in ***Sharh at-Tajrīd*** and similar is narrated on the authorities of Abu Hurayra and Abu Sa'īd al-Khudri in ***Ŝahīh al-Bukhāri, Ŝahīh Muslim, Sunan at-Tirmidhi, Musnad Ahmed, Sunan an-Nisā'i, Sunan Ibn Mājah, Ŝahīh Ibn Hibbān, Sunan al-Bayhaqi, Sunan ad-Dārqutni, Sunan Abu Dāwūd***

[11] Similarly narrated in ***Sharh at-Tajrīd, Muwatta, Ŝahīh al-Bukhāri, Ŝahīh Muslim, Musnad Ahmed, Ŝahīh Ibn Hibbān, Sunan al-Bayhaqi, Sunan an-Nisā'i***

As long as no unlawful quantitative disparity (*at-tafāḍul*) takes place in it, there is no problem with that. It is simply as what has come from the Prophet, peace and blessings be upon him and his progeny: ((...like for like, hand-to-hand)).[12]

Concerning that which is discouraged in sales

It is impermissible to have two stipulations for a sale, sell what one does not have, lend on the condition of a sale or profit from what one does not possess. Similar has reached us that Allah's Messenger, peace and blessings be upon him and his progeny, prohibited such.[13]

He also prohibited a transaction that becomes binding simply by touching it (al-*mulāmasa*)[14], a transaction in which the seller obligates it by throwing pebbles at the potential buyer (*al-hasāt*)[15], the selling of a tree before it bears fruit[16] as well as the selling of dung (*al-a'dhira*). He said of the latter: ((It is considered as carcass)).[17]

He, peace and blessings be upon him and his progeny, also prohibited the consumption of predatory animals with fangs and birds with talons.[18] He prohibited the consumption of domesticated donkey meat[19] and sexual intercourse with a pregnant slave women until they deliver—whether they were bought or acquired as booty—if they were impregnated by someone else.[20] Allah's Messenger, peace and blessings be upon him and his progeny, said: ((Fluid intermixes with fluid, strengthens the bones and grows the flesh)).[21]

He similarly prohibited the prostitute's dowry;[22] by that, he means paying a fornicating woman. He similarly prohibited the consumption of stallion stud fees;[23] this refers to payment for stallions to mate with mares. He prohibited the price for carcass as well as the price for intoxicants.[24] He prohibited the sale of the purification dues until after it was acquired as well as the sale of the fifth-dues until after it was acquired.[25]

---

[12] Similarly narrated in ***Sharh at-Tajrīd, Sunan an-Nisā'i, Ŝahīh Muslim, Musnad Ahmed, Sunan Ibn Mājah, Ŝahīh Ibn Hibbān, Sunan al-Bayhaqi, Sunan ad-Dārqutni, Sunan at-Tirmidhi, Sunan Abu Dāwūd***

[13] Similarly narrated in ***Musnad Imam Zayd, Sharh at-Tajrīd, Sunan an-Nisā'i, Ŝahīh Muslim, Musnad Ahmed, Sunan Ibn Mājah, Ŝahīh Ibn Hibbān, Sunan al-Bayhaqi, Sunan at-Tirmidhi, Al-Mustadrak, Sunan Abu Dāwūd, Al-Mu'jam al-Awsaṫ, Al-Mu'jam al-Kabīr, Mušannaf Ibn Abi Shayba, Sunan ad-Dārqutni, Bihār al-Anwār***

[14] Similarly narrated in ***Musnad Imam Zayd, Ŝahīh al-Bukhāri, Ŝahīh Muslim, Sunan al-Bayhaqi, Sunan an-Nisā'i, Ŝahīh Ibn Hibbān, Sunan Ibn Mājah, Musnad Ahmed***

[15] Similarly narrated in ***Musnad Imam Zayd, Al-Mu'jam al-Awsaṫ, Sunan al-Bayhaqi, Musnad Ahmed, Ŝahīh Ibn Hibbān, Sunan ad-Dārimi, Sunan ad-Dārqutni***

[16] Similarly narrated in ***Musnad Imam Zayd*** and ***Sunan ad-Dārqutni***

[17] Similarly narrated in ***Musnad Imam Zayd*** and ***Sharh at-Tajrīd***

[18] Similarly narrated in ***Musnad Imam Zayd, Sharh at-Tajrīd, Ŝahīh Muslim, Sunan abu Dāwūd, Sunan Ibn Mājah, Ŝahīh Ibn Hibbān, Sunan ad-Dārimi, Sunan al-Bayhaqi, Sunan an-Nisā'i, Musnad Ahmed, Bihār al-Anwār, Ušūl al-Kāfi***

[19] Similarly narrated in ***Musnad Imam Zayd, Ŝahīh al-Bukhāri, Ŝahīh Muslim, Musnad Ahmed, Al-Mu'jam al-Kabīr, Mušannaf Ibn Abi Shayba, Sunan an-Nisā'i, Sunan at-Tirmidhi, Sunan Ibn Mājah, Sunan Abu Dāwūd, Sunan ad-Dārqutni, Bihār al-Anwār***

[20] Similarly narrated in ***Musnad Imam Zayd, Sharh at-Tajrīd, Sunan ad-Dārqutni, Sunan Abu Dāwūd, Sunan at-Tirmidhi, Musnad Ahmed***

[21] Similarly narrated in ***Musnad Imam Zayd*** and ***Sharh at-Tajrīd***. Similar is narrated in ***Ŝahīh Muslim, Sunan 'Abd Dāwūd, Al-Mustadrak, Sunan ad-Dārqutni, Mušannaf Ibn Abi Shayba, Sunan ad-Dārimi, Sunan al-Bayhaqi, Bihār al-Anwār***

[22] Similarly narrated in ***Musnad Imam Zayd, Amāli Ahmed b. 'Isa, Ŝahīh al-Bukhāri, Ŝahīh Muslim, Sunan Ibn Mājah, Sunan at-Tirmidhi, Sunan an-Nisā'i, Sunan Abu Dāwūd, Muwaṫṫa, Musnad Ahmed, Mušannaf Ibn Abi Shayba, Al-Mustadrak, Sunan ad-Dārimi, Sunan al-Bayhaqi, Kanz al-'Ummāl, Majmu' az-Zawā'id, Al-Mu'jam al-Kabīr, Al-Mu'jam al-Awsaṫ, Ušūl al-Kāfi, Bihār al-Anwār***

[23] Similarly narrated in ***Musnad Imam Zayd, Al-Mu'jam al-Awsaṫ, Mušannaf Ibn Abi Shayba, Sunan an-Nisā'i, Musnad Ahmed, Sunan Abu Dāwūd, Sunan at-Tirmidhi, Sunan ad-Dārimi, Sunan ad-Dārqutni,***

[24] Similarly narrated in ***Ŝahīh al-Bukhāri, Ŝahīh Muslim, Sunan Abu Dāwūd, Sunan at-Tirmidhi, Sunan an-Nisā'i, Sunan Ibn Mājah, Musnad Ahmed, Sunan al-Bayhaqi, Kanz al-'Ummāl, Majmu' az-Zawā'id, Al-Mu'jam al-Kabīr, Al-Mu'jam al-Awsaṫ, Ušūl al-Kāfi, Bihār al-Anwār***

[25] Similarly narrated in ***Musnad Imam Zayd. Amāli Ahmed b. 'Isa, Sharh at-Tajrīd, Al-Mustadrak, Sunan al-Bayhaqi, Majmu' az-Zawā'id, Al-Mu'jam al-Awsaṫ, Mušannaf Ibn Abi Shayba, Mušannaf 'Abdur-Razzāq***

It has reached us that the Commander of Believers, upon him be peace, said: "The hoarding of food is a sin of the disobedient."[26] He used to circulate and check on the butchers so they were prohibited from over-inflation. He also used to say: "Over-inflation is from Satan; therefore, do not over-inflate the price of food and drink nor this"[27]—meaning sheep at the time of slaughter.

My father related to me that his father said regarding the hoarding of food while food is scarce:

> If its purchase is not due to the weakness of the people of Islam and if it is not a means of harm for the Muslims, there is no problem in it. The meaning of hoarding simply refers to restraining something out of harm.

Hoarding is impermissible for the merchant seeking exploitation. Also, the one in straitened circumstances is to not hoard beyond his need nor the need of his family at the time of price fluctuation, problematic affairs [i.e. market instability], extreme hunger, death threats and fear. This is because there is threat of harm for the Muslims in that, and it is the centre of their attention. When they do not see food in their markets, they would fear for themselves. When they do not see displays in the possession of their merchants, it is a harm and source of harm for all. This is prohibited by Allah and forbidden by the One, the Overwhelming.

Concerning uncertainty and protecting one's family from it

Uncertainty, its display as well as that of which enters upon humankind are whisperings from Satan that enter upon the lorded. This is so that he can distance them from the Lord of creation. That is because there is disobedience to Allah in uncertainty as well as an act of deference to Him for the one who partakes in it.

There are many matters of this regard, such as that which Satan causes to enter man regarding his wife and his slave. He makes him falsely assume that he divorced when he had not divorced insomuch that the ignorant would have possibly divorced their wives illegally. They say: "We divorced them" when they had not divorced them due to the uncertainty that Satan causes to enter their hearts. That withstanding, it comes to reside in the people of uncertainty and ignorance so that they divorce their wives ambiguously due to the uncertainty. Then, she marries another man while she is still married to him because of an illegal divorce. Such person would be among the destroyed according to Allah, the Mighty and Majestic. He gives authority of his wife to another man due to the whispering of Satan and the occurrence of uncertainty in the heart of humankind.

Similarly, such uncertainty occurs to him regarding his male and female slaves until he falsely assumes that he manumitted him when in fact he had not. He declares this judgement upon him and perceives that he removed him from his ownership and freed him of his servitude. He says that he manumitted him and removed him from his ownership and possession while lying to himself and acting in deference to the judgements of his Lord. Such person [who was assumed to be manumitted] would still be considered an owned slave according to Allah but manumitted according to another.

Consequently, that uncertainty would grant him the status of a free person to the owners. However, in the judgements of Allah, he would still be considered a slave from the clear statements of the Truthful as well as by the judgements of the One who has more right. In the laws of retaliation, marriage, inheritance and judgements, he would be considered on equal footing with other free people among the Muslims. However, that would be contrary to the judgements of the Most Gracious and would grant him that which Allah has removed from him.

---

[26] Similarly narrated in ***Musnad Imam Zayd***, ***Amāli Ahmed b. 'Isa***. Similar is narrated as a hadith from the Prophet in the following texts: ***Ŝahīh Muslim, Al-Mustadrak, Sunan at-Tirmidhi, Sunan Ibn Mājah, Sunan Abu Dāwūd, Sunan ad-Dārimi, Musnad Ahmed, Sunan al-Bayhaqi, Kanz al-'Ummāl, Mušannaf 'Abdur-Razzāq, Al-Mu'jam al-Kabīr, Al-Mu'jam al-Awsaṭ, Bihār al-Anwār, Ušūl al-Kāfi***

[27] Similarly narrated in ***Amāli Ahmed b. 'Isa***

He would inherit the wealth of the free Muslims while he is considered an owned slave to Allah. In the judgements of Allah, the inheritor is not the same as the inherited. If he were to commit adultery, he would be killed for fornication [due to the false assumption that he is free]; however, he is to not be stoned according to the judgements of Allah and his blood is to be spared [due to his slave status]. Rather, he takes ownership of what is his responsibility and he becomes humiliated in his sin and wrongdoing.

That is why we say that the one who has uncertainty in himself and acts upon it while Satan has manifested it to him has sinned. It is that uncertainty which enters such person that is considered greater than the fear to remove it from himself.

Allah has clarified the difference between uncertainty and certainty in that which differentiates the two in name as well as their judgements in their two meanings. When there is clear difference between two judgements, then there is a difference in their actions in all things. According to the one with intellect, understanding and the ability to clearly differentiate between two matters, there is a clear difference between the two analogously and conceptually. If one necessitates uncertainty by that which one necessitates certainty, then certainty and uncertainty would be considered the same even though they differ in name and concept. That withstanding, whoever has doubt in his actions will be like the one who has certainty.

Uncertainty is confusion and conjecture in humans; whereas certainty is firm establishment, truth, veracity and clarity. Regarding the difference between uncertainty and conjectures on one side and certainty, truth, veracity and clarity on the other side is as stated by the Majestic Lord of creation: **{O ye who believe! When there comes unto thee a disobedient person with news, verify it lest ye afflict a people ignorantly and then become regretful for what ye hath done} (Q. 49:6)**. The Glorified also says: **{O ye who believe! Refrain much from conjecture; verily, in some conjecture is sin} (Q. 49:12)**.

He commands that one firmly establishes, and it is to seek out certainty whenever there is a statement from disobedient people. He also commands that one refrains from conjecture, and He conveys that some conjecture is sin. Conjecture is doubt. Uncertainty and conjecture are both considered blameworthy, and truth and certainty are both considered praiseworthy. This is because uncertainty and certainty are mutual opposites that remain contrary.

Regarding that, the Most Gracious says in the Light and Evidence He revealed: **{Verily conjecture avails not against the truth a bit} (Q. 53:28)**. If a judgement of conjecture, uncertainty, certainty and truth were the same in concept, they would differ in something. If it does not differ, one of the two would avail over the other. If that is the case, it would be contrary to the statement of Allah because He says: **{Verily conjecture avails not against the truth a bit} (Q. 53:28)**.

Therefore, if there is a difference in acting on truth and acting on conjecture, then there would be a difference in the judgement of certainty and that of uncertainty according to everyone. It is for that reason that we say that it is religiously obligatory for one in whom there is uncertainty about something to refrain from and avoid that thing as well as not act upon it. The avoidance of a doubtful matter and the refraining from acting on it is more precautionary and safer to the one who is afflicted by Satanic whisperings and has allowed Satan to reside in his heart and soul.

Regarding that, it has reached us that Allah's Messenger, peace and blessings be upon him and his progeny, said: ((Verily, Allah has forgiven my *Ummah* for that which may occur to their souls or that which may be suggested as long as they do not act upon it or speak on it)).[28] The meaning of "or speak on it" refers to a matter that one talks about.

---

[28] Similarly narrated in ***Amāli Ahmed b. 'Isa, Ŝahīh al-Bukhāri, Ŝahīh Muslim, Sunan Abu Dāwūd, Sunan at-Tirmidhi, Sunan an-Nisā`i, Sunan Ibn Mājah, Musnad Ahmed b. Hanbal, Sunan al-Bayhaqi, Mušannaf Ibn Abi Shayba, Al-Mu'jam al-Awsaṭ, Bihār al-Anwār***

My father related to me that his father was asked about a man who has a lot of uncertainty and doubts in prayer and other things. He doubts as to whether he swore or not swore. He doubts as to whether he had not prayed any of his prayers. And he would assume that he had not prayed even though he had performed the prayer and he would assume he said more, even though he had not said a thing. He replied:

> All of this is uncertainty and conjecture that one cannot establish a judgement upon. Nor does one acknowledge any judgement of truth in that which there is conjecture. It is impermissible for anyone to establish a judgement in manumission or anything else in the religion unless there are no doubts and uncertainties in it.
>
> The one with knowledge and understanding does not equate certainty with uncertainty and doubts in a matter. It is from the most ignorant of ignorance and the most distant of anyone with knowledge that one passes a judgement on another with uncertainty and doubt in the matter of manumission. How can your judgement on that in which you have uncertainty and doubt be similar to the judgement in which you have certainty and knowledge? No! How can it be according to one with knowledge and intellect but not to the majority of those who are ignorant?
>
> The difference between uncertainty and certainty proves the difference between the two in their judgements in the religion. If one necessitates emancipation due to uncertainty regarding one in which Allah has caused him to own, there would be a distinction between certainty and uncertainty. Allah has clearly distinguished uncertainty and conjecture from certainty in the judgement of truth when the Glorified says: **{Verily conjecture avails not against the truth a bit} (Q. 53:28)**.
>
> If one passed a judgement with it, it would avail. Then, the one who Allah has caused to own a slave or anyone else will not have possession removed from him either by an oath or anything else unless by that which Allah caused to be removed out of fact and certainty. This is from Satan and his whisperings, and it is in this situation, the prayer or anything else. It is simply that you are uncertain and doubtful so that he leads them away from truthfulness to something else and their delusions. Instead, they are in the wrong from their apprehensive and doubtful behaviour and in this is a sin and wrongness that only Allah knows.

It has reached us that Allah's Messenger, peace and blessings be upon him and his progeny, said: ((Verily, Satan comes to one of you and asks: "Who created the heavens?" One replies: "Allah." Then he asks: "Who created the earth?" One replies: "Allah." Then he asks: "Who created Allah?" When one of you encounters that, say: "I believe in Allah and His Messenger."))[29]

It has also reached us from him, peace and blessings be upon him and his progeny, that a man came to him and said: "O Messenger of Allah, I find something in my soul that striking my neck would be preferred to me than to talk about it!" He replied: ((That is clear faith)).[30]

Abul-Hasan [i.e. 'Ali b. al-Hasan b. Ahmed b. Abi Harīša, the compiler of the ***Al-Ahkām***] says:

> Although this chapter consists of those affairs of the son of Adam, such as the prayer, manumission, divorce, transactions and other things—we saw fit to place it here. And with Allah is success!

---

[29] Similarly narrated in ***Musnad Abu Ya'la, Musnad Ahmed, Al-Mu'jam al-Awsat, Al-Mu'jam al-Kabīr, Majmu' az-Zawā'id.*** A similar hadith with slightly different wording is related in the following texts: ***Ŝahīh al-Bukhāri, Ŝahīh Muslim, Sunan Abu Dāwūd, Musnad Ahmed, Kanz al-'Ummāl***

[30] Similarly narrated in ***Ŝahīh Muslim, Sunan Abu Dāwūd, Ŝahīh Ibn Hibbān, Musnad Abu Ya'la, Musnad Ahmed, Majmu' az-Zawā'id, Al-Mu'jam as-Saghīr, Kanz al-'Ummāl***

Concerning the choice of a transaction

Two people involved in a transaction have the right to annul the agreement as long as they do not separate, as was stated by Allah's Messenger, peace and blessings be upon him and his progeny. According to me, the 'separation' here refers to a mutual disagreement that takes place between buyer and seller as well as after the contract was concluded between them and witnessed by witnesses. When that is the case, the commodity belongs to the buyer and the sale is for the seller. The buyer becomes more entitled to it unless he relinquishes it from him. Then his relinquishment would be considered a good deed from him.

Some people say that the 'separation' refers to the physical separation of bodies. If it was as they said, then as long as the seller and those with him are confined to his house, the sale would not be binding and the buyer would not be obligated to buy anything. Similarly, if there were two gathered in a small area and then they conducted a business transaction, the sale would not be obligatory between them nor would the matter be concluded between them. The buyer would be able to annul the buying and the seller would be able to annul the sale perpetually until they physically leave from the confinement or area.

What is obvious to the intellect is the ruin and destruction of the commodity. If the thing that is bought is an animal or something else and then it dies or is ruined before the buyer and seller physically separate, who would be responsible? And who would be obligated to suffer the loss of value of that commodity? It would therefore necessitate that those who hold to this position analogously remove the responsibility from the buyer even if he bought it and concluded the transaction between them. However, this is unacceptable to the intellect, and no one would advocate for such unless such person is mentally dull, heedless and slow-witted!

My father related to me that his father was asked about the meaning of the hadith of Allah's Messenger, peace and blessings be upon him and his progeny: ((The transaction between two is subject to annulment as long as the two do not separate)).[31] He replied:

> The two have the right to annul as long as they do not separate in terms of agreement and disagree about the commodity. When they agree, the commodity belongs to the buyer unless there is a withdrawal or the seller withdraws the price.

As for those camels and other livestock that are milked, if one buys it for its milk, the buyer can annul the transaction until he can induce its milk for one day and one night. If he is satisfied, the transaction is considered complete. If he is not satisfied, he can return it along with a compensation for its milk. That has been narrated from Allah's Messenger, peace and blessings be upon him and his progeny. He said: ((Whoever buys a she-camel with tethered teats has the option: he can either milk it to retain it or he can return it with a *ŝā'* of dates)).[32]

The 'she-camel with tethered teats' refers to a camel whose milk has been restrained due to its udders and cannot be milked at that time as she was milked before. Her udders are restrained, and her milk is collected. Then, the onlooker who is seeking such is easily deceived and hopeful that it wasn't unattended [i.e. so that it looks like it has a lot of milk].

Also, among the options are the stipulations of choice on everything that is bought and sold. If that buyer stipulates and says "I have the choice regarding what I stipulate for a day, two days or three to the extent of what was stipulated" and the two stipulate that, the two of them would be bound to observe that to the end of the period based upon that which they stipulated.

---

[31] Similarly narrated in ***Sharh at-Tajrīd, Ŝahīh al-Bukhāri, Ŝahīh Muslim, Sunan at-Tirmidhi, Sunan Abu Dāwūd, Sunan an-Nisā`i, Sunan al-Bayhaqi, Musnad Ahmed, Sunan ad-Dārqutni, Ušūl al-Kāfi, Bihār al-Anwār***

[32] Similarly narrated in ***Musnad Imam Zayd, Sharh at-Tajrīd, Ŝahīh al-Bukhāri, Ŝahīh Muslim, Sunan Abu Dāwūd, Sunan at-Tirmidhi, Sunan Ibn Mājah, Sunan al-Bayhaqi, Bihār al-Anwār***

Concerning the sale of a slave who is freed at the master's death as well as the *umm walad* and concerning the one who buys something but then notices that it has a defect

An *umm walad* is not sold, and this is impermissible for one to do so because they would be manumitted from their masters due to the sale. The right of intercourse would remain for their masters due to their slavery; however, if they are manumitted from all ownership, it would be impermissible for their masters to have intercourse with them except due to marriage. Their manumission simply means the judgement that prevents their masters from selling them until they bear their master's child.

That has been narrated regarding Allah's Messenger, peace and blessings be upon him and his progeny. He said regarding the mother of his son, Ibrāhīm when he was born, while she was a slave gifted to him by a Copt: ((Her son has freed her)).[33]

Therefore, Allah's Messenger, peace and blessings be upon him and his progeny, passed the judgement that the child prevents his father from selling his mother even though he had owned her. Had this ownership not been considered valid, it would not have been considered permissible for her master to make her dowry her manumission if he wanted to manumit her and marry her. This is because sexual intercourse is impermissible except by the dowry.

If she were not under his ownership, it would be impermissible to make her manumission her dowry. Her manumission, therefore, would take the place of her bridal price. Have you not considered that if he said to her "You are manumitted and I make your manumission your dowry" and they agree upon that and he manumits her based on that but then desires to marry her afterwards and she refuses, the judgement would be in his favour against her by means of confusion regarding her bridal price? This is because of the treachery, contradiction and breach of contract that came before it.

As for what the riffraff narrate in which the Commander of Believers, upon him be peace, permitted the sale of them [i.e. *umm walad*],[34] it is not truthfully from him nor would anyone who knew him attribute that to him. Regarding that, my father related to me that his father was asked about the sale of the *umm walad* and he said:

> This is impermissible, nor can one pass such judgement on them. As for what the people of ignorance narrated from the Commander of the Believers, upon him be peace, one does not accept that from them, and it is not truthfully attributed to him.

That being the case, his progeny would know best.

As for the slave that is freed upon his master's death, if the owner is compelled to do so because he needs the money and there is no overstepping of bounds in the sale, there is no problem to sell him out of necessity. He acts on such judgement based on what necessitates it of the religion and what relieves himself. Therefore, if one finds an overstepping of bounds in such sale, it is preferable to us that he compensates that which he was given and that the slave is given a third of what Allah has given him after his [i.e. the master's] death as stipulated in his will and testament.

As for the one who buys a commodity and finds a defect in it which was unknown to him prior, he has the choice. If he wants, he can return it due to being deceived about its defect. If he wants, he can keep it and subtract an estimated value of the defect from the price.

Similarly, if he buys a slave woman and has intercourse with her but then notices a defect after having intercourse, he can take an estimated value of the defect from the sale. However, if he notices the defect before having intercourse with her and then has intercourse with her anyway after having

---

[33] Similarly narrated in ***Musnad Imam Zayd***, ***Al-Mustadrak***, ***Sunan Ibn Mājah, Sunan al-Bayhaqi, Sunan ad-Dārqutni, Al-Mustadrak***

[34] The permissibility of selling the *umm walad* has been narrated from 'Ali in ***Musnad Imam Zayd***. The Imamites also relate that 'Ali permitted it and hold to the judgement that it is permissible. The conflicting accounts in this regard have been discussed in the Translator's Introduction.

known about the matter, his intercourse with her is his acceptance of her and there is nothing else due for her sale. This is because at the moment he saw the defect, he had a choice. It would not be permissible for him to have intercourse with her until after he becomes her owner. Neither would he be able to return her, subtract the defect from the price or seek pardon from the owner. He could have either returned her and not owed anything from her or he would have kept her and covered the difference, or he could have forgiven the seller and accepted what he had taken and bought. When he had intercourse with her after noticing the defect, that defect enacted the sale because one does not have intercourse with someone with whom one is not satisfied. That which is agreed upon on returning is the same as it being sold.

Similarly, if a person buys a commodity with a defect he had not seen and then another person tells him about the defect before the first person saw it, he has the choice. If he wants, he can return the commodity and return the estimated value of the defect. If he wants he can keep it and subtract the estimated value of the unknown defect. We make it the buyer's choice because he was deceived and wasn't informed about the defect in the commodity. According to us, it therefore necessitates that he has the choice.

If a man buys many commodities in one transaction as one bargain—beit slaves or anything else—and then finds defects in some of them, it is for him to either keep all the bought goods or return all of them.

My father related to me that his father was asked about selling an *umm walad*. He replied: "I do not hold to that view. We do not see that which has been narrated from the Commander of the Believers in which he permitted their sale, to be authentically attributed to him."

My father related to me that his father was asked about selling a slave who is freed upon his master's death. He replied:

> There is no problem selling the slave who is freed upon his master's death if the owner is compelled to do so. It is narrated that Allah's Messenger, peace and blessings be upon him and his progeny, allowed a man to sell his slave who is freed upon his master's death. He said: ((If the master of the slave freed at his master's death were to die, then he [i.e. the slave] is counted from one-third of his property, which is considered as a will)).

My father related to me that his father was asked about a man who buys a commodity but then finds a defect and protests the sale. "Can he return it to the seller after protesting it?" He replied: "Some say that he cannot return it and must keep it. However, the position according to us is that he can return it if he wants."

My father related to me that his father was asked about a commodity that was bought with a defect which was unknown to the buyer until another told him about it. Does he return it or keep it? He replied:

> Some have said that if he was informed about the defect, he simply deducts the estimated value of the defect from the commodity. However, according to us, the one who had not known about the defect prior to being told by another has a choice.

My father related to me that his father was asked about sexual impotency and whether one could return the one [i.e. a purchased slave or slave woman] who has it. He replied: "Sexual impotency is a defect for which one could return as long as the one who bought the slave was not aware of the defect before."

My father related to me that his father was asked about a man who bought two slaves, two riding beasts or other goods and one of the two has a defect. He replied:

> If it was contractually agreed that he purchase all of them at once, he either takes all of them or returns all of them. If it was contractually agreed that he purchase each individually, he returns the one which has the defect. The rest would be permitted for him.

If two men sell a commodity to one man and one of the sellers says "It is free of any defects" but it does have defects that the buyer was not aware of until after the purchase, the seller who had not said

"It is free of any defects" is not innocent from knowing of the defect in the commodity since he may have feared for the sale had he told the buyer. The buyer has a choice. If he wants, he can take the value of the defect. If he wants, he can return it.

If the seller objects to anything being deducted from the price, then he is judged to take back the product and return its value as a judgement.

My father related to me that his father was asked about a man who sold a commodity and said "It is free of any defects" and did not mention the defects. He replied:

> If he did not mention the defects, he is not innocent of being aware of the defect before selling it and what is similar. He is to follow it. If he knew of the defect before selling it, he must inform him of the defect prior to the sale. If the defect was there when the product was with him [i.e. the seller] and he had not known, some people say that it is not binding on him and others say that it is. We hold to the view that it is binding on him and it is returned to him because there was a defect on the item before he sold it.

Concerning the sale of a copy of the Qur'an, recitation and instruction

According to us, there is no problem selling a copy of the Qur'an, transcribing it for profit or making such a business. This is because one can take payment from its labour, transcription and handiwork. As for the one who takes payment for teaching its memorisation, there is no good in that.

It has come on the authority of the Commander of the Believers, 'Ali b. Abi Ťālib, upon him be peace: "Allah's Messenger, peace and blessings be upon him and his progeny, said: ((Whoever takes payment for teaching the Qur'an will not have its share on the Day of Judgement))."[35]

My father related to me that his father was asked about buying and selling copies of the Qur'an. He replied: "There is no problem with buying or selling copies of the Qur'an, nor in transcribing it for payment."

It is obligatory upon the one who teaches for a monthly salary or anything else to not specify the Qur'an itself in the payments. Rather, the payment should be based on other things such as instruction in etiquette, handwriting, calligraphy, recitation of other books and so forth. The Qur'an should only be included in the instruction fee without it being stipulated specifically. If it is out of the kindness of the student and a reward for such, the teacher can accept it and it would be permissible for him to take it.

My father related to me that his father said regarding teaching the Qur'an for payment:

> There is no problem in that as long as it is not stipulated for the Qur'an specifically. It has been narrated that an expedition sent out by Allah's Messenger, peace and blessings be upon him and his progeny, happened to pass by a Bedouin neighbourhood. Their chief was stung, and he asked them if there was someone among them who performed incantations (*ruqya*). One of them performed the incantation reciting *Fātiha* (Q. 1) and he was healed. They gave thirty sheep as payment. When they came to the Prophet, peace and blessings be upon him and his progeny, they informed him of what happened. He said: ((Allocate a share for me along with your share)).[36]

Concerning increase in a delayed sale and concerning a sale of unknown weight and measure as well as concerning an oath during a sale

There is no good in any type of increase in a delayed sale; it is considered usury and credit for future payment (*al-i'yna*) according to us. An explanation of that is the following: A man buys ten *makaki* of food with a dinar of money. Someone buys it from him for nine with a delayed

---

[35] Similarly narrated in ***Sharh at-Tajrīd, Musnad Imam Zayd, Amāli Ahmed b. 'Isa***. Similar is related in ***Kanz al-'Ummāl*** and ***Bihār al-Anwār***

[36] Similarly narrated in ***Šahīh al-Bukhāri, Šahīh Muslim, Sunan Abu Dāwūd, Sunan Ibn Mājah, Sunan at-Tirmidhi, Sunan al-Bayhaqi, Mušannaf*** of Ibn Abi Shayba, ***Musnad Ahmed, Sunan ad-Dārqutni, Šahīh Ibn Hibbān***

sale. This would be considered unlawful increase in the transaction. He has increased in the transaction, and this increase is considered usury according to us.

Similar is the case with all commodities impermissible to sell when their price differs [i.e. same product, different prices] and there is a condition of cash and condition of deferment; it would be considered impermissible for the increase as well as that which is increased.

My father related to me that his father said regarding a man who sold food to a known delayed time for less than the price on the day he originally sold it:

> This is discouraged according to us and those scholars among us who hold to our opinion. It is considered credit for a future payment, an unlawful increase and usury. It has been narrated from 'Abdullah b. al-Hasan§ that his uncle, 'Ali b. al-Hussein§, used to say: "Unlawful increase is simply usury."

Usury is not that a debtor says to the indebted: "Hurry and repay my right before the appointed time commences and I will disregard some of it from you." Usury is simply when a debtor says to the indebted: "Delay your repayment and I will increase it because of your delaying it." This is undoubtedly considered usury according to us.

There is no problem with the sale of a certain item without a measure or weight (*juzāf*) as long as there is no one among the two of them who knows the measure or weight of the object. If one of the two actually knows, it would be considered deceit on the part of the person [who knows] and the transaction between them will be considered invalid.

There is no good in oaths regarding buying and selling; we discourage it. However, if it is truthful, there is no sin on such person. As for the sin of the liar, he will be considered a disobedient ingrate of Allah's blessings. Regarding that is what has reached us from Allah's Messenger, peace and blessings be upon him and his progeny: ((There are three that Allah will not look at or purify on the Day of Judgement and they will incur punishment: a man who gives the oath of allegiance to a just imam who is for him only if he gives him something of this world but is not for him if he does not give him anything, a man who has extra water while travelling but prevents it from another traveller and a man who swears an oath that he was truthful in taking payment for giving such and such commodity yet lied about it)).[37]

Concerning selling a slave's services, the merchandise of the idolaters and selling a slave without his master's permission

There is no problem with a master selling a slave's services for a period of time if he wants, as long as it is a determined time. According to me, that would be considered similar to renting him out.

There is no buying or selling a slave without his master's permission. If one buys or sells anything without his permission, it would be considered invalid unless the slave is one that he permitted to be bought and sold absolutely. If that is the case, the buying and selling of the slave would be binding due to his master.

There is no problem buying and selling from idolaters as long as one does not sell them weapons or military equipment (*karā'a*). This is because Allah has permitted buying and selling without mentioning idolatry or anything else as a precondition. Allah's Messenger, peace and blessings be upon him and his progeny, was sent to some of the idolaters that raised livestock and he used to buy from them. He used to also buy weapons and other things from them.

---

[37] Similarly narrated in ***Musnad Imam Zayd, Sharh at-Tajrīd, Ŝahīh al-Bukhari, Ŝahīh Muslim, Sunan an-Nisā'i, Sunan Abu Dāwūd, Mušannaf*** of Ibn Abi Shayba, ***Musnad Ahmed, Sunan al-Bayhaqi, Sunan Ibn Mājah, Sunan at-Tirmidhi, Bihār al-Anwār***

There is no problem with a buyer buying an idolater's son, brother or anyone else from the idolater—even if some of them he bought are war captives. This is because Allah has permitted them to take captives or kill them; the one that is permitted as a war captive is similarly permitted to be purchased.

My father related to me that his father was asked about buying slaves taken as war captives from idolaters. He was also asked about a man among them who sold his son and whether it was permissible for a Muslim to buy one from him. He did not see a problem with such and said: "That which Allah permits in the way of his blood and capture is even greater than buying him."

He [i.e. Imam al-Qāsim Rassi] also used to say regarding the merchandise of the idolater: "There is no problem with that as long as they do not sell them weapons or military equipment." He also used to say:

> During the time of Allah's Messenger, peace and blessings be upon him and his progeny, livestock was raised and Allah's Messenger used to buy from them as well as weapons and other things in their possession. Also, Allah says {**Allah has permitted trade and prohibited usury**} (**Q. 2:275**) but does not specify the buyer or seller as an idolater or Muslim.

War captives can be separated from each other except the mother from her child. It is narrated that when a group of war captives was brought before Allah's Messenger, peace and blessings be upon him and his progeny, he stood up and looked at their faces. He saw a woman crying and asked her: ((What are you crying about?)). She replied: "My son has been sold." He then commanded that he be returned to her.

Abu Usayd§ came to him with war captives and placed them before him. He [i.e. the Prophet] stood and looked at them. He saw a woman crying and asked her: ((What are you crying about?)). She replied: "My son has been sold in Bani Absin." The Prophet, peace and blessings be upon him and his progeny, said: ((You must ride out and bring him back just as you sold him for a price)). Abu Usayd rode out and brought him back.[38]

Concerning the purchase of fresh clovers, herbs, cucumber and melon

One does not buy fresh clovers, fresh herbs, cucumbers, melons, eggplant or any other thing that comes one after the other unless it can be counted or openly manifested, extracted and known. As for that which is in a tree or the earth which cannot be extracted, it cannot be purchased because it is considered unknown. It is not known whether it is a little or a lot, suitable or unsuitable. There can be disagreement regarding uncertainty in it, and the uncertain sale among Muslims is impermissible. That is the judgement of the Lord of creation.

My father related to me that his father was asked about the sale of fresh clovers and fresh herbs. He replied:

> We do not permit it for fresh clovers, fresh herbs or anything else that is bought which is unknown and can change. It cannot be bought unless by weight, number or amount. Nor can a specified amount be bought of that which is extracted monthly or yearly because all of such is subject to change and can increase or decrease. All of that is considered uncertain, and Allah's Messenger, peace and blessings be upon him and his progeny, prohibited uncertain purchases.[39]

---

[38] Similarly narrated in ***Musnad Imam Zayd, Al-Mustadrak, Sunan al-Bayhaqi.*** In the ***Majmu'***, the Companion is identified as Zayd b. Hāritha and not Abu Usayd. Also, the report in the same text relates that both parents were crying due to being separated from their child. The variants in the reports indicate the possibility of these being two separate instances.

Regardless, the two principles that are established from these reports is that parents cannot be separated from pre-pubescent children and that such transaction would be considered invalid otherwise. This is exemplified in similar variant reports in which the Prophet, peace and blessings be upon him and his progeny, was narrated to have said ((Whoever separates parents from their children will be separated from the one he loves on the Day of Judgement)) and ((Do not separate parents from their children)).

[39] Similarly narrated in ***Musnad Imam Zayd, Sharh at-Tajrīd, Ŝahīh Muslim, Sunan Abu Dāwūd, Sunan at-Tirmidhi, Sunan Ibn Mājah, Sunan an-Nisā'i, Musnad Ahmed***

Similarly, it is impermissible to sell milk in the udders of an animal and that which is in its womb. Nor can one sell that which is on its back, such as the wool, fur or hair. It is impermissible to sell fish in a bowl or pond. All of this is considered something based on uncertainty, and an uncertain sale is impermissible. This is because it can increase or decrease, and it can be sound or unsound. Similar is the case with the sale of a runaway slave, lost livestock or any other similar case of an uncertain sale.

Concerning one who buys a commodity and returns it with extra

The explanation of that is a man buys a slave or commodity and benefits from it by means of milk or anything else. Then, he dislikes it and seeks revocation from the owner. However, he refuses to revoke it unless something is deducted from the price due to what was taken from it; so, the buyer deducts from the price. In this case, it would not be permissible according to us.

It is simply revocation and good etiquette or avoidance due to that which is in people's possession. It is instead a gift, donation and leaving what he has if it was left as a donation from the giver not asked or required by the receiver. If that is the case, it would similarly be righteousness and goodness, and there is no problem with righteousness and goodness. As for the case of it being due to coercion, that would impermissible for the seller.

My father related to me that his father was asked about a man who purchased a commodity, used it and returned it along with extra dirham based on its purchase. He replied: "All of such is discouraged. It is simply a cancellation or sell. If it is taken, it is taken by necessity. If one is compensated by means of it, it is considered only compensation."

Concerning one who buys a slave woman and comes to know that she is his *umm walad*

If a man buys a slave woman who comes to live with him or a wife for a period of time and then he comes to know with certainty that she gave birth from him, the transaction is considered abrogated. He is obligated to return the money and the slave woman.

If he bought her from another man and had intercourse with her and she bore him a son and the first master mentioned that he had intercourse and had a baby with her, the slave woman would belong to the first with whom she bore a child. He would be obligated to return the money to the one who bought her from him and take the *umm walad* from him. The child of the second master would belong to his father, and the child of the first master would belong to his father when he establishes it as his child. The two children would inherit as brothers due to sharing the mother. The first master cannot approach her until she is pure from the semen of the other.

Concerning one who hires out a slave or riding beast and then another hires them out for more than what was hired out to him

There is no problem for a man to hire out a slave or riding beast for a day or two, a month or two and then another hires the two of them out as long as it does not go beyond that for which the both of them were hired out to him in terms of work and progression. If the one who hired them out goes beyond that which their owner stipulated or violates anything of their affair and are damaged as a result, the one who hired them out would be held responsible. In the case of the owner of the riding beast who hired it out, he would be compensated for the value of the riding beast.[40]

---

[40] Imam Abu Ṭālib stated in his ***At-Taḥrīr*** that two different opinions from al-Hādi exist regarding the permissibility of a hireling hiring out another's slave without the master's permission. He says that al-Hādi permitted it in his ***Ahkām*** but declared it impermissible in ***Al-Muntakhab***. We say that there is no disagreement and it stems from a misunderstanding of al-Hādi's statement in the ***Ahkām***: "...and then another hires the two of them out as long as it does not go beyond..." The hiring out of another does not preclude that it took place without the master's permission. This is evident by his later statement: "If the one who hired them out goes beyond that which their owner stipulated..." Such transfer of hire can only take place with the owner's permission. [Ref. ***Al-Qawl al-Awwal***]

Concerning what is discouraged of uncertain sales

If a man buys a horse or a slave and then says to another man "Take it and sell it. Whatever is extra over such-and-such dinar will be split between you and me," this matter would be considered invalid because the fee of the seller would be based on uncertainty due to its being unknown.

Concerning resale for profit (*al-murābaha*)

If a man purchases a commodity for a price and sells it but then wants it back and the buyer increases its price and resales it to the initial buyer, we do not see it as a resale for profit based on the price the other person bought it for or based on the increase that the owner applied to its value due to the other's desire. Rather, it would be considered a bargaining transaction. It should not be considered as a resale for profit because the increase was due to the desire for it and not a sum of its price and value.

Concerning a commodity resold for profit by two partners and the manner in which it is resold for profit

If two men bought a commodity for fifty dinars and argued among each other on fair terms that it is sixty dinars but then one of them pays the other a profit of five dinars and he accepts it, it would be obligatory for the one who wants resale it to calculate its profit based upon the fifty-five and not the sixty because the commodity was only bought for fifty-five. Once he informs the buyer of this, it shall be considered permissible for him to resale it for profit as he likes—whether a little or a lot—if both are satisfied and know about it.

Concerning a commodity taken by a man to show it and then if the one who is shown it likes it, he buys it

If a man takes a commodity from its owner to show it to a potential buyer and the owner had not made any stipulations to return it and it is damaged or lost on the way, it is not the responsibility of the one who was carrying it. However, if he stipulated that it is to be returned, he [i.e. the carrier] will be responsible for it and will have to incur its cost because its owner stipulated that the responsibility is on him.

Concerning the sale of price-marked clothing (*ar-ruqūm*)

The sale of price-marked clothing is invalid and impermissible unless the owner price-marked it correctly after coming to know what it cost him of commodity costs, transportation costs and other things. If he were to price-mark it and inform the potential buyer afterwards and the latter accepts it as well as the increase in price, it would be no problem with that transaction.

Concerning the sale of that of which one does not take possession

For every sale of that which one does not own or take possession of, the sale is considered invalid. If a man bought a horse from another man for a hundred dinar and then sold it to a third man for a hundred and twenty dinars before actually taking possession of it, the sale would be considered null and void. Only after taking possession and ownership of it would it be permissible to sell.

If one were to buy a slave woman from another for fifty dinars and then sell her to another man before the seller concluded the sale and took ownership of her and then the buyer manumitted her, the manumission would be considered invalid because her purchase was invalid.

If a man were to buy a slave from another and the seller concluded the transaction but then the buyer says to him "Send him to me tomorrow" and leaves the slave with him after having taken ownership of him and concluded the transaction and then the buyer sells him before the original seller sends [the slave] to him—this transaction would be considered permissible because he took ownership of him, concluded the transaction and then left him with another afterwards and hid him away.

Concerning the option of one who buys something and takes possession of it but does not look at or inspect it

If a person buys a garment, weapon or any other commodity from another person at a determined price and then concludes the transaction with the seller but does not inspect it, look at it or exonerate the buyer from any possible defect it may have—the buyer has a choice after looking at, inspecting and investigating it. If he wants, he can keep it. If he wants, he can return it if he is not satisfied with it.[41]

Similarly, if he buys barley or wheat or dates or raisins and orders that it be delivered to his house without looking at it, he has the choice when looking at it. If he wants, he can take it. If he wants, he can return it to the seller. Similar is the case with all things that are bought and not inspected or scrutinised by the eyes—whether it is bought in the night or day—the buyer has the choice in that which he bought and must be able to inspect it.

Concerning the partner's sale from his partners or others that was not shared by them

If a man and his partners bought a package of leather, package of sandals or a warehouse of food and then he sold his share to another man who is not one of his partners before equally distributing it among them that was agreed upon, that would be considered invalid and impermissible for him to sell. This is because he deceived the buyer when he did not allow him to investigate it or inform him of such. However, if he and his partners had investigated that item and examined it, there will be no problem for him to sell his share before dividing it among some of his partners because they had examined it and came to know about it.

It would be discouraged for him to sell it to his partners if they had not examined that item with the fear that they would return it after investigating it if they did not like it or sell their portion. It would be considered like an uncertain sale or something unknown to him. The partner who buys his share from him may return the share he had not bought from him or he may return to his partner that which he took from him. This sale would be considered invalid.

Therefore, if the partners are aware of it, a partner can only buy the share that he saw from his partner. Then, it would be no problem to sell it to a partner before having divided it. That would be impermissible for anyone who is not a partner.

Concerning one who wanted to buy a commodity, postponed its payment and then bought it from its owner for less than its price

This would not be considered permissible for either one of them, nor is it appropriate for their religious life. An explanation of that is the following: A man buys a slave woman from another for one hundred dinars. He then postponed either some of the one hundred or all of it. The slave woman comes to settle with the buyer for a period of time, and then he sends her out and displays her for sale. She becomes worth seventy or eighty dinar to him. The first seller then says: "I bought her for what she was worth." That would be considered discouraged for him due to the fear of favouritism due to postponement.

If something were to happen to the slave woman in which her value was diminished or increased without any trickery involved, we hope that there would be no problem with either and the transaction would be sound.

---

[41] According to Imam al-Mu'ayyad Billah in his ***Sharh at-Tajrīd*** as well as Imam Ibn al-Murtaḍa in his ***Al-Bahr***, Imam al-Hādi had two different statements on this issue. The first—which is stated here in the ***Ahkām***—is that if a buyer notices a defect after purchasing an item, s/he has the choice to retain or return the item. The second—which is narrated from al-Hādi in ***Al-Fanūn***—is that if a buyer is informed of the defect in the commodity prior to purchase but notices that it is contrary to the way it was described, he does not have the choice and must return it. However, we do not find any disagreement between the two rulings because they reflect two very different circumstances. The case mentioned in ***Al-Fanūn*** refers to a commodity that does not have a defect but is not in accordance to what the buyer and seller agreed upon. In this case, the sale would be considered completely annulled. [Ref. ***Al-Qawl al-Awwal***]

Concerning one who bought something and then it was damaged before he could take possession of it

If a man wants to buy an item from another and pays for some of the item and then the owner of the item says "I will not let you leave with my good until you complete the rest of the payment" and keeps it but then it is damaged, it is considered the seller's responsibility because he rejected the completion of the sale. If there is no completion of the sale, the buyer does not own it; if the buyer does not own it, then the responsibility is on the seller because he rejected the completion of the sale.

If he took possession of the item when he bought it and agreed to pay security deposits (*rahana*) for some or all of it until completion and then it is damaged, they must reassess its value as a security deposit and depositee.

If a man buys something from another and leaves it with a just man to look after until its payment is completed but then it is damaged, it would be considered property of the seller not the buyer because the payment was not completed and [the buyer] had not taken possession of it.

Concerning the option when there was a stipulation of three days, more or less

If a buyer stipulates that he has the option to terminate the transaction in three days and the purchased slave woman or male slave dies within that three days, the buyer is obligated to pay the full price. This is because the sale was binding, and the commodity was ruined while in the buyer's possession. He would not be considered exempt nor can he be refunded.

If the option [to terminate the sale] was given to the seller and the good was ruined while in the possession of the buyer without any breach in his option, it would be considered the property of the seller because the transaction was not completed for the buyer as a valid sale. It is also because [the seller] gave himself the option [to terminate the sale] during a determined period. If he wanted, he could carry out the sale or return it.

Similarly, if the option [to terminate the sale] was both of theirs together and both or one of them dies, the sale would be binding on the seller and the option [to terminate the sale] would be invalidated. If the time in which the both of them could make the option [to terminate the sale] was given to them but they were both silent and had not stated the option, the option would be considered invalidated and the slave would belong to the buyer. If the option was given to the buyer and he died within the three days before choosing, the sale would be binding on the heir to pay the full price and the option would be invalidated because the option is something that is not inherited.

Similarly, if the commodity is rendered deficient while in the possession of the buyer, he is to keep it with the deficiency and the option [to terminate the sale] is invalidated if the sale had been discontinued based on his choice after days. If there was no amount paid and the sale was discontinued, the purchase of the commodity would not be binding.

If the option [to terminate the sale] was from the seller for three days and it was more than that, the option would be his. If it were less than that, the option would belong to the buyer and not the seller.

Concerning working for a third or fourth of something

If a man gave another man iron and said "Make some knives for me and you can have a quarter of them" and the latter loses that iron, our view is that it would be his [i.e. the welder's] responsibility because the owner hired him for a quarter of it and not as a partner.

Concerning that which is damaged by the manufacturer

If any hired manufacturer spoils that which he is hired to fix, he is considered responsible for it. An explanation of that is the following: If a person paid a carpenter to repair a door and it is damaged, the carpenter has to pay the value of the door if it is completely ruined. However, if it is not completely ruined, he would only have to pay the value of the damage he caused.

Similar is the case with a tailor, weaver, fuller or any other manufacturer that damages that which they are hired to repair; they would be responsible for what they damaged.[42] If the damage was less than half the value of the damaged item, the value of the damage must be paid to the owner. If the damage was more than half the value, the owner has the option: if he wants, he can either take the value of what was damaged or he can take the complete value and conclude it with the manufacturer.

If it was damaged while he was there and the work had already been complete, the owner has the option. If he wants, he can take the item, subtract the value of the damage and pay the repair person for the amount that he was hired to repair or he can give it to him and take from him its value from the day he priced it. If there is disagreement regarding the value, the evidence is on the owner, and the oath is upon the manufacturer.

Concerning one who acts contrary to another's command regarding his wealth

If a man gives another some wealth and commands him to buy some food for the owner to gain profit from and the latter acts contrary to that and buys a camel or cow or slave, the man who acted contrary is considered responsible—whether he was appointed, hired or a partner. All of them would be considered responsible if they acted contrary to what they were commanded to do unless the proprietor decided to take what they bought for him. In that case, it would be considered his.

If he does not take it and the one who acted contrarily is responsible and sells it, we do not hold to the view that the profit is his if he were to make profit for it. Rather, we hold to the view that it would go to the public treasury of the Muslims.[43]

Concerning the meaning of the Prophet's statement: ((No city-dweller should sell for a Bedouin))

This report has been narrated,[44] but we do not know how it could have been authenticated! It may be that someone comes with a commodity and presents it to a village. A [Bedouin] woman may not want to intermingle for buying and selling, and there may be weak people who may not be good at buying and selling. This is not among the authentic reports because Allah's Messenger, peace and blessings be upon him and his progeny, was merciful. This is a way that people could benefit each other. If harm were to come to the people or some type of harm between buyers and sellers, the imam would have to look into that.

---

[42] This concept is expanded and elucidated more in ***Al-Muntakhab*** where al-Hādi was asked about the liability of a weaver.

> I asked: "What if a man gives his yarn to a weaver and the latter's house is broken into with the man's yarn and the yarn of others being taken?" He replied: "It would be the responsibility of the weaver." "What if a fire occurs in the weaver's house and the house and everything in it is burned?" "The weaver would not be held responsible for that." "Why would the weaver be responsible in the case of the theft but not responsible when his house is burned?" "It is because he had the ability to prevent the theft but did not have the ability to prevent the fire."

From this dialogue, we learn that the manufacturer or repair person who can prevent damage to the item is held liable for it. However, any unpreventable damage to the item does not necessitate liability on the part of the manufacturer or repair person.

[43] Imam Yahya b. Hamza in his ***Al-Intiŝār*** as well as Imam Ibn Murtaḍa in his ***Al-Bahr*** stated that al-Hādi had two different views regarding what is to be done with the surplus wealth earned by one who acted contrary to the command of the owner. They said that one view was that the surplus is to be given to the Muslim public treasury, as indicated here in the ***Ahkām***. The other view, which is related in ***Al-Muntakhab***, is that it is to go to the owner of the wealth. We say that such 'disagreement' is resolved when one reads the entire context of the ***Ahkām*** and notices the differences between the two cases. The text states that the wealth is to be given to the Muslim public treasury if the owner decides not to take it. However, if he does decide to take it, it is considered his. [Ref. ***Al-Qawl al-Awwal***]

[44] Similarly narrated in ***Sharh at-Tajrīd, Ŝahīh al-Bukhāri, Ŝahīh Muslim, Sunan Abu Dāwūd, Sunan Ibn Mājah, Ŝahīh Ibn Hibbān, Sunan an-Nisā'i, Musnad Ahmed, Mušannaf Ibn Abi Shayba, Ušūl al-Kāfi***

Concerning the Messenger's prohibition of intercepting cattle drivers (*al-jalūba*)

City-dwellers should not intercept outside Bedouins from the village to buy their livestock from them, bring them in and then sell it for themselves. This is because in that is deception on the part of the people of livestock. Rather, it should be avoided until they [i.e. the Bedouins] bring it to their market and sell from their own transactions.

Concerning something in which some differ in designation from others

If there are some things that are joined with others under one designation and they are considered recombinant in the same sense, it would be considered the same class, even if there are things with different designations. It would not be permissible for the buyer or seller to compare between them for preference.

An explanation of that is the following: All of the dates are the same, even if they differ in colour and designation. It would therefore be impermissible for one to break them up into two different groups; this is the case even if they differ in designation. For example, a *makūk* of *barni* dates would be impermissible to exchange for a *makūk* and a half of *šayhāni* dates and one could not exchange two *makūks* of *jama'* dates for a *makūk* of *adhāq* dates. All dates carry the same judgement; one is like the other. Whoever goes beyond that has engaged in usury.

Similar is the case with wheat, corn and raisins; all of these categories are the same. It is impermissible to make one cup of Maysāni wheat the same as a cup and a half of white wheat. It is impermissible to make one cup of white corn the same as a cup and a half of black corn. It is impermissible to make a cup of white raisins the same as a cup and a half of black raisins.

Similar is the case with all types of fruits and other things. Whoever goes beyond in any of that has engaged in usury and has invalidated what he bought and sold. This [judgement] pertains to that which is measured and not other than that.

Concerning difference in two types and what is permissible in terms of sales

There is no problem equating one thing with two things and two things with one thing if the two things are different. An example would be making a cup of wheat the same as two cups of barley, a cup of raisins the same as two cups of corn or a cup of dates the same as two cups of barley. There is no problem in buying and selling any of that. Similarly, if there is disagreement regarding its type and genus, it would be considered hand-to-hand. Therefore, if there occurs in it delay of payment, the buying and selling would be invalidated.

Concerning the sale of an animal for another

There is no problem in selling one animal for two or two animals for one—whether they are the same type or different types—as long as it is hand-to-hand and there is no delay of payment. There is no problem in buying a camel with two camels, a cow with two cows, a sheep with two sheep, a bird with two birds, a horse with two horses, a donkey with two donkeys or a mule with two mules.

There is no problem in buying a horse with two camels, a camel with two cows, a slave with two slaves, a female slave with two male slaves as long as it is hand-to-hand. Whoever delays payment in any of that has invalidated the sale and engaged in usury.

Concerning additional money with two animals

There is no problem for a man to pay additional dirham or dinar with a head and buy another head. An explanation of that is the following: A man buys a horse with another horse plus five dinars, a camel with three dinars plus another camel, a cow with a cow plus a dinar or a sheep with two sheep plus a dinar. All of that in terms of animals would be considered permissible as long as it is hand-to-hand.

There is no problem to buy a slave woman with ten dinars plus a slave woman or to purchase a slave boy with another slave boy plus one hundred dirhams.

Concerning the sale of meat for an animal

It is impermissible to sell a sheep for twenty *raṫl*s of meat or more or less. It is impermissible to sell ten *raṫl*s of meat for a sheep—whatever the meat may be. It is impermissible to buy an edible animal with it because Allah's Messenger, peace and blessings be upon him and his progeny, prohibited the sale of animals for meat.[45]

Concerning the purchase of one meat with other types of meat

There is no problem for a buyer to buy a *raṫl* of sheep meat with two *raṫl*s of cow meat or two *raṫl*s of cow meat with three *raṫl*s of camel meat. This is because camels differ from sheep, and cows differ from camel. Similar is the case with all dissimilar pairs. Their differences permit quantitative disparity between their meats, and it is because the same types cannot be joined together.

As for all the types of sheep, it is impermissible for its meat except in the case of its like, hand-to-hand. Similar is the case with its milk and fat.

There is no problem to buy three *raṫl*s of cow fat for two *raṫl*s of sheep fat. There is also no problem to buy a portion of camel milk for a portion of sheep milk as long as it is hand-to-hand. Whoever delays payment in any of that has invalidated the sale.

Concerning the purchase of dates with their receptacles

Whoever buys dates which is a determined amount of *raṫl*s for a dinar, one does not weigh it with its receptacle—whether it is a palm-leaf receptacle (*julal*) or sack—unless that is included in the stipulated price. It may be that one sees the receptacles and realises it, or it may be described to him and he comes to know of it. As for that which is not stipulated, the purchase would not be binding because he simply desired to buy the dates and not the receptacle.

Whoever buys a sack full of dates and is satisfied with what he apparently sees but then opens it and discovers that which is contrary to what he initially saw, he has a choice. If he wants, he can keep it and subtract the estimated value of the defective ones or if he wants, he can return it and reclaim the full amount he paid for it.

If the buyer of the dates says to the seller or the seller says to the buyer "I deduct such-and-such *raṫl*s in this sack," this would not be considered permissible because it would be something unknown and uncertain. It is impermissible to deduct that which is uncertain just as it is impermissible to buy or sell something that is uncertain. The exception is if it is shown to the buyer and he is satisfied with including the weight of the receptacles along with the weight of the dates.

Concerning a slave being permitted to buy and sell in business

If a master gives his slave permission to engage in a business transaction, that which the latter buys and sells is considered binding on his master—whether it be inexpensive or expensive. Similar has reached us from the Commander of Believers, 'Ali b. Abi Ṫālib in which two men in dispute came to him. One of them said: "O Commander of Believers, this slave of mine purchased such-and-such item, but I did not want it and decided to return it." The Commander of Believers, upon him be peace, said to him: "Did you send your slave with dinar to buy meat for you?" He replied: "Yes." He then said: "Then, I make his purchase binding on you."

---

[45] Similarly narrated in ***Sharh at-Tajrīd*, *Muwaṫṫa*, *Al-Mustadrak*, *Sunan ad-Dārqutni*, *Sunan al-Bayhaqi***.

Concerning one who sells himself or commands another to sell him

Whenever a freeperson sells himself or commands another to sell him, it is obligatory to observe proper etiquette if he understood what constitutes proper etiquette. The one who buys him should observe proper etiquette if he bought him with knowledge of such and should not impose slavery on him. He should continue to take steps in that which he took from him until he returns it to him. If someone else is the one who sold him, his price must be returned to him.

If the seller sold himself or if the one who sold himself was a pre-pubescent child or mute (*'ajam*) fearing for his fortune, he should not receive any portion of the price for which the person was bought if the one who bought him knows such person's situation. This is because the buyer bought him with the intentional insight that it was impermissible for him to do so.

Similar has reached us that a man sold himself during 'Umar's government. When his affliction worsened, he came to 'Umar and said: "I am a free man." 'Umar replied to him: "May Allah curse you! You are the one who sold yourself!" 'Ali b. Abi Ťālib, upon him be peace, said: "There is no ownership of a freeperson." Then, he started striking him severely and the one who sold him. Also, he ordered the buyer to give the seller the amount. If he knew in any way, he made him work for his freedom. I only say that because he is of age. If he was a child or a mute who did not understand, he would not be punished and asked to work for his freedom. He did not punish the buyer because he did not know that he was free when he bought him.

Concerning that which is impermissible regarding buying and selling as well as that which is permissible to buy and sell for the other

As for every category of that which is weighable and measureable as well as that which is not weighable or measureable of that which is worn but not an animal product, one cannot sell two like things for one like thing of the same category. That is impermissible unless one sells a like thing for a like thing, hand-to-hand and it does not differ in categories. If it differs in categories, it would be no problem to sell two things for one thing, hand-to-hand.

It is impermissible to delay payment if all of it is weighable or all of it is measureable. If one thing is measureable and the other thing is weighable, it would be no problem to delay payment in such as long as there is no usury accrued nor a daily increase in price due to the delay.

There is no problem in buying two *raťls* of *qali'* lead for one *raťl* of black lead, hand-to-hand; it is impermissible to delay payment in that. There is no problem in buying a *raťl* of copper for two *raťl*s of lead, hand-to-hand. There is no problem buying a *raťl* of iron for two *raťl*s of brass, hand-to-hand; it is impermissible to delay payment in that. This is because all of such is weighable.

If one of the categories is weighable and the other is measureable, there is no problem in buying two for one and one for one with delayed payment because it departs from the judgement of prepayment (*as-salam*).

There is no problem with buying five *raťl*s of iron for three *makāki* of wheat in delayed payment. It is as prepaying iron for wheat. We prefer that the one who does that specifies the time frame, specifies the type of wheat and specify the weight exactly.

It's impermissible for a man to buy a crop of wheat harvested in an abandoned field for a known measure of wheat—whether a tenth portion or more or less. This is because this is an unknown amount of wheat due to its being in its harvest. If there is an extra or deficient amount of wheat that is measured, it would be considered usury because it is impermissible to sell wheat for anything but its like, hand-to-hand. Whoever increases in that has engaged in usury.

It is encouraged for the one who sells something that can be measured by price to not buy something else with that money until he has received the money; then, he could buy using that money. This is because if he were to buy what can be measured with that money, then the payment would be considered delayed due to them both being both measureable. However, there is no problem if he buys what is weighable using the amount of what is measureable before getting the payment and vice versa.

It is impermissible to buy meat with an animal and buy thirty *raṭl*s of meat with a sheep because Allah's Messenger, peace and blessings be upon him and his progeny, prohibited the purchase of meat with animals.

It is impermissible to sell curdled milk for butter (*zubda*) unless the butter in the milk is less than the butter the buyer wants to buy. Then, the butter that is in the milk would be considered similar to the other butter, and the excess butter would be considered the same price as the excess butter that is mixed with milk.

It is impermissible to sell three *raṭl*s of butter for two *raṭl*s of fat because that would constitute a difference between the excess and deficiency of butter compared to the derived fat. The transaction would be considered invalid. I dislike that butter be considered the same as fat because there are also differences and deficiencies between them.

Muzābana is prohibited because Allah's Messenger, peace and blessings be upon him and his progeny, forbade it due to its differences. It is when a man sells fresh dates for dried dates, and it is the selling of fresh dates on the heads of date-palms for dried dates by measure. This is because it decreases when it is dried and quantitative disparity occurs in it. Similarly, it is impermissible to sell two *makūks* of fresh dates for a *makūk* of dried dates or a *makūk* of such for a *makūk*. It is impermissible to sell more or less than that.

Similarly, one cannot exchange unripe dates for dried dates or dried dates for unripe dates. One can sell any category for its like, hand-to-hand and like for like. Each dried date is to be considered the same—whether *barni* dates, *šayhān* dates or *alwān* dates. It is impermissible to sell two *makūk*s of *alwān* dates for *barni* dates or four *ṣā'* of *šayhān* dates for five *ṣā'* of mixed dates.

Similarly, each type of grape is to be considered the same. It is impermissible for some of them to be sold for an increase in others. It is impermissible to sell one *raṭl* of grapes for three *raṭl*s of grapes of the same colour. That withstanding, it is impermissible to sell a *raṭl* of grapes for two *raṭl*s of raisins because of the deficiency and the state of the fresh date versus the state of the dried date.

It is discouraged [i.e. prohibited] to sell a *makūk* of wheat for a *makūk* of flour because they differ from one another in deficiency and addition due to the grinding process. This is the case even if the wheat and flour are the same measure. There is no problem for a kneader to sell kneaded dough for more than the wheat or flour of the kneader. Similarly, there is no problem for a baker to sell a *makūk* of bread for two *makūk*s of flour because both kneaded dough and bread have then departed from their ability to be measured to their ability to be weighed.

It is impermissible to sell a *makūk* of wet wheat for a *makūk* of dry wheat or anything else because they vary and the dry would be more than the wet.

There is no problem in buying pomegranates, quince and other fruits that are not measured, weighed or sold by number one for two, two for one, as long as it is hand-to-hand.

It is impermissible for a buyer to buy a commodity and say "I have bought this from you for what you are selling to other people" because this would be considered deceptive and erroneous. One is not aware of that because the seller may have investigated some sellers and sold it for a cheaper price. Maybe he would have been permissive and sold it for a more expensive price. Whoever bought or sold it for that may have made its value binding on the buyer and may give him its value around the people without considering his stipulation because that stipulation may be invalid without him being aware of it.

One should not sell a garment for two garments of the same type at a deferred time. In the case of different types, there is no problem with selling a garment for two garments at a deferred time. The explanation of that is the following: Selling a *qūhi* garment for two *qūhi* garments is impermissible at a deferred time. Selling a *daybaqi* garment for two *daybaqi* garments is impermissible at a deferred time. Selling a *shatawi* garment for two *shatawi* garments is impermissible at a deferred time. Selling a brocade garment for two brocade garments is impermissible at a deferred time. Selling two silk wool blend (*khazz*) garments for a silk wool blend garment is impermissible at a deferred time. Similar is the case with each type: it is impermissible to sell two garments for one at a deferred time. However, it is permissible hand-to-hand.

However, in the case of different types, there is no problem selling one garment for two garments at a deferred time. One stipulates an understood length and width amount is at a deferred time. There is no problem for one to buy a *daybaqi* garment for two *marwi* garments, hand-to-hand and at a known deferred time. Similarly, there is no problem for one to buy a *washi* garment for two silk wool blend garments hand-to-hand but not at a deferred time because the two types differ. It is impermissible to buy a washi garment for two *washi* garments at a deferred time, but there is no problem for one to buy one garment for two hand-to-hand. Similarly, everything similar to this will be rendered as we mentioned, God willing.

It is impermissible to sell curdled milk for buttermilk and fresh milk for buttermilk because there is water in the buttermilk. If one were to sell that which has water for that which does not have water, one would not be selling a like for its like. The milk that has water in it is less milk than that which does not have water. It is impermissible to sell milk for milk unless it is the same.

If a man buys a camel on behalf of another man and was placed in charge of that camel, it is not for the buyer to hand it over to anyone else except by the order of the one for whom he bought it. If he handed it over to another without his permission or the issue of a ruler, the buyer has the option: if he wants, he can give him permission or if he wants, he does not have to give permission. The transaction would not be binding, and he would not have to return the money he spent for it because the commodity was handed over without his permission or the issue of a ruler.

If a man says to another man "I'll sell you all the clothes in my house for two garments and a dinar" and the buyer agrees, that transaction would be considered invalid. It would be for the buyer to reclaim that from the seller if he were to see it and not be pleased with it because he was sold something about which he had not known. He did not know whether it was good or bad and whether it was cheap or expensive. Similarly, if he came across a basket and there were pomegranates or citrons in it and was told "I will sell you five citrons for a dirham," this transaction would not be considered valid until he is able to differentiate the five, separate them and see what he bought. Once he examines what he bought, he can purchase what he saw. Similar is the case with watermelons and other things that can expire.

If a buyer bought some type of fruit or other things with the assumption that it was good and broke a piece of it but then found a defect in it that he did not know about, he is to consider the commodity if the defect was not known until after the break. If it was purchased with the defect after the break or if it had a break after being priced, the purchase would then be binding but the seller would have to return the difference in value between the defective and non-defective commodity.

If the commodity was such that it would be worthless after the break and the defect is evident, it is to be returned, like a rotten egg or similar; it is to be returned and the paid value is returned to the buyer. However, whoever buys a defective item with the knowledge of such defect, such person does not have the choice after the purchase.

It is impermissible for a man to sell something he bought—whether it is measured or weighed—if he had not taken possession of it or received its full weight. Similarly, if he received its full weight and then intends to sell it or take ownership, he should not sell it until he completes its payment or weighs it again before selling it or giving it away. Similar is narrated from Allah's Messenger, peace and blessings be upon him and his progeny: ((With every conclusion of a transaction is a measure of weight)).[46] According to us, revocations, assumptions and transactions regarding that are the same in that it is necessary for them to be reweighed.

If a buyer bought anything not knowing its measure, he can sell it, rescind it or assume it without knowing its measure just as he bought it. Similarly, if he wants to sell some of it with measure and some of it without measure, he can do so.

Concerning exchange as well as substituting silver for silver, gold for gold, gold for silver and silver for gold

It is impermissible to exchange a debt while the exchange is hand-to-hand. An explanation of that is the following: A man buys dirham with dinar, and the exchanger agrees to twenty. All of it is not with the exchanger, and there remains a dirham or dinar from the twenty. Then he says to him: "Return to me when you are ready" and the owner of the remaining dinar takes it and leaves it. He returns after a while and then takes it. This is prohibited and impermissible. It would be obligatory for the one who exchanged the dinar for dirham and the dirham for dinar to not divide the demanded portion from his companion. That would not be for him whether a lot or a little.

If one is afflicted with any of that, let him calculate the amount of dirham and then calculate the value of the dinar. He is to then pay it to the owner of the dirham and become a partner in the dinar by the remaining carats or *hubba*. Either he breaks a piece of the dinar or leaves a deposit with the owner until he returned to him and then gives what was left for him or he cuts a piece from him—that which he wanted to do. If that is the case, he may leave what remains of his carats with its owner.

It is impermissible to buy some gold for gold without knowing its measure as well as buy any silver for silver without knowing its measure because that is considered excess by the increase of one of them against its owner. It is impermissible to exchange gold for gold or silver for silver except like for like, hand-to-hand. Similarly, it is impermissible for him to buy any sum of gold with ten mithqal while ignorant of its weight. Also, it is impermissible to buy any sum of silver with twenty weighed dirhams while ignorant of its weight because it is that which is not weighed; perhaps it would be increase or decrease, and usury will be due to any increase or decrease.

However, there is no problem for a man to buy a sum of silver with ten mithqal of gold while ignorant of its weight. Similarly, if one were to buy a sum of gold with a thousand dirham while ignorant of its weight, it would be permissible. Thus, if one buys gold for silver while ignorant of its weight or silver for gold while ignorant of its weight, this would be permissible because these two types differ.

It is impermissible to include silver with gold for gold in order to increase it as many ignorant people have done. Neither is it permissible to include iron with silver for silver in order to increase it as many people of this time have done. This is because Allah, the Mighty and Majestic, does not deceive and He knows the secret and hidden. This is simply the fraud of the fraudsters, and it is impermissible for them who are lorded. How much more so is it for the Lord and Creator of creation!

If a man buys a dirham from another for a dinar and the former does not have all the dirham and then takes a complete loan from him, he is to fulfil all of his right before separating. Then, the exchange would be considered complete and sound. If he does not complete it with him, the exchange between them will be considered null and void. He bought the dirham he had in dinar at the same exchange rate and took the rest of his dinar. This action—according to us—would not be considered permissible otherwise.

---

[46] Similarly narrated in ***Mušannaf Ibn Abi Shayba***

Regarding a sword or copy of the Qur'an that is embellished with silver and bought with dirham, it would not be considered permissible according to us unless the weight of the embellishment is known in terms of dirham. One can then buy the embellishment by its weight and then purchase the sword or copy of the Qur'an with the excess if he wants.

Similar has reached us that Allah's Messenger, peace and blessings be upon him and his progeny, commanded a man who bought a gem-studded, gold necklace on the Day of Khaybar to separate the gems from the gold. The man took it apart until he came to know what was in it. He then purchased it by its weight of gold and said: "I only purchased it by the excess of the weight difference." He, peace and blessings be upon him and his progeny, replied: ((Not until you have separated them)).[47]

Whoever buys any of that, he and the owner are to not separate and there remains between them an action that is hand-to-hand. It is impermissible to buy a gold necklace for ten dinars at a deferred time. Similarly, one cannot purchase silver embellishment by its weight at a deferred time. If one buys an embellished sword for one hundred dirhams and the weight of its embellishment is fifty dirhams, there is no problem as long as the blade of the sword equals fifty dirham. If it equals less than fifty, it would be impermissible because the excess simply occurs in the embellishment due to the owner increasing it because of its manufacture. This would not be permissible or valid even if one did not know whether the weight of the silver was fifty dirhams.

If a man buys dirham with dinar, it would not be permissible for him to buy dinar with dirham until he takes possession of the dinar. It is impermissible to buy the dust of gold minerals in gold or the dust of silver minerals in silver. It is similarly impermissible to buy the dust of those who engage in goldsmithing and silversmithing in gold or silver. This is because that may lead to excess or deficiency and makes possible uncertainty. In terms of gold for gold, it is impermissible except in the case that there is like for like and hand-to-hand. In terms of silver for silver, it is impermissible except in the case that there is like for like and hand-to-hand. Whoever engages in such transaction, it will be considered invalid and impermissible.

Whoever buys the dust of gold minerals in silver or the dust of silver minerals in gold, he and the seller will have the choice once it is made clear as to how much was extracted. If they want, it can be considered terminated or if they want, it can be considered binding. This is because this transaction is considered uncertain and invalid from the beginning. Whoever buys or sells anything with uncertainty—such transaction is considered invalid.

The dirham during the era of Allah's Messenger, peace and blessings be upon him and his progeny, is similar to our dirham today. The minting of the dirham and dinar did not occur during the era of the Prophet nor during the pre-Islamic era for the Arabs. They used to simply buy and sell with the known raw material (*tibr*) of the dirham as well as understood *awāq*. The first *raṫl* during the time of Allah's Messenger in Medina was twelve *awāq*, and each *awāq* was forty dirhams. Therefore, their *raṫl* was four hundred and eighty dirham of the dirham that is in the people's possession today. He, peace and blessings be upon him and his progeny, established the value of their *raṫl* based on that.

The proof of what we advocate regarding that is his statement: ((There are no purification dues on that which is below five *awāq* of silver)).[48] Then, according to the consensus of the Muslim *Ummah*, he said: ((There is no purification dues on that which is below two hundred dirham)).[49] From that, we know from his statements ((There are no purification dues on that which is below five *awāq* of silver)) and ((There is no purification dues on that which is below two hundred dirham)) that the *awāq*s were

---

[47] Similarly narrated in ***Ŝahīh Muslim, Sunan Abu Dāwūd, Sunan an-Nisā`i, Sunan at-Tirmidhi, Al-Mu'jam al-Kabīr***. The narrator of the report and the one who purchased the necklace in the report is identified as Fuẑāla b. 'Ubayd al-Ansāri.

[48] Similarly narrated in ***Ŝahīh al-Bukhāri, Ŝahīh Muslim, Al-Muwaṫṫa, Sunan an-Nisā`i, Sunan at-Tirmidhi, Sunan Ibn Mājah, Sunan Abi Dāwūd, Ŝahīh Ibn Hibbān, Musnad Ahmed, Sunan ad-Dārqutni***,

[49] Similarly narrated in ***Musnad Imam Zayd, Mušannaf 'Abdur-Razzāq, Bihār al-Anwār***

considered forty of these dirham for which there is no disagreement from the Muslim *Ummah*. The purification dues are obligated for two hundred dirhams.

It is said that the first to mint the dirham in Islam was 'Abdul-Malik b. Marwān.[§] This dirham was the one that was used for the purification dues. It is the dirham that the people of Iraq call 'the weight of seven' (*wazna sab'a*). They call it 'the weight of seven' because it is the weight of seven tenths of the mithqal. The proof of that is that if you were to increase three tenths of this dirham, it will become a mithqal. Due to that, ten dirham becomes seven mithqal.

The dinar was from the Caesar, the ruler of Rome. The dirham was from the *baghliyya* of the Persian rulers. It was brought to the Arabs in Mecca during the Pre-Islamic era. They did not buy and sell with it; rather they would refer to the raw material they knew over the weight of a mithqal and the dirham. They utilised *awāq* and *raṫl*s. Their *raṫl* was like the *raṫl* of Medina—four hundred eighty dirhams. Also, their *awāq* was forty dirhams.

The Book of Prepayment (*as-Salam*)

In the Name of Allah, the Most Gracious, the Most Merciful...

The beginning of the chapters regarding prepayment

The permissible and valid prepayment is that a man pays another in advance for a known thing with a known weight or measure as well as a known description to a known appointed time that was designated. He also pays it in advance in a known place. If he pays that wealth in advance and adheres to these preconditions, this prepayment will be considered valid. I do not know of any disagreement among the scholars of the Prophet's Progeny or others regarding this.

It has been authentically narrated to us that Allah's Messenger, peace and blessings be upon him and his progeny, took a prepayment of dinar from a Jew. It was for dates whose species was known to a known appointed time in a known measure. Similarly, it has been narrated to us that the Commander of Believers, 'Ali b. Abi Ṭālib, upon him be peace, did not see a problem with prepayment. Similarly, my grandfather, al-Qāsim b. Ibrāhīm said that prepayment was permissible given its soundness. Likewise, all the scholars among the Progeny of Allah's Messenger from the descendants of al-Hasan and al-Hussein used to say that. Regarding the permissibility of prepayment, we do not know of any disagreement from any of them if it is sound.

The valid prepayment consists of five things. When they are recalled and stipulated, the prepayment would be considered valid for the people of Islam. It is that a man pays another man some wealth with a known measure or known weight; it is such-and-such *raṭl*s for a dinar or such-and-such measure for a dinar or dirham and stipulated by a known category and known colour if that which differentiates its colours is to a known appointed time. He can hand it over in a specified country without necessarily specifying an area or land within its boundaries.

If that for which he prepaid was anything that grows or taken from trees, such as dates, wheat, barley, rice or anything else which is measured or weighed, it would not be permissible for him to prepay for an enclosed fruit garden of a known limit such as grapes and others that can be weighed. Similarly, it would be impermissible to prepay for raw silk (*qazz*) to be cultivated and woven by a specific person. If one prepays for a garment or silk to be manufactured, this would be considered discouraged and impermissible because there is uncertainty in it. This is because it is possible that the fruit could be spoiled by that garden and would therefore ruin the item that was prepaid for. Similar is the case with woven silk; it is possible that it could be ruined. Perhaps the person who was hired to work on the prepaid item may die before working on it; then the prepayment would be considered invalid. For this reason, it is impermissible to prepay for an enclosed fruit garden itself or for labour itself.

Therefore, whoever establishes in his prepayment a known measure, known appointed time and known description without stipulating an enclosed structure itself or human labour itself as well as stipulates that the prepaid item would be paid for at a known place—such action would be considered a valid prepayment between them both before they separate and the transaction is concluded with sound money.

A way that a prepayment would be considered invalid and impermissible is that the one who is prepaid and the one who prepays are the same in that they both have hope and fear while there is no chance for only one of them that indicates safety from invalidity. Rather, the both of them would be the same in such with each of them hoping that he would be content with that which the other took and that there would be some type of profit and not loss in its buying and selling. That is because there may be a gain or loss in value at the time that the one who is prepaying collects the prepaid item, and that would be an unknown gain for one and not the other. Perhaps the one who prepaid would have a greater chance for gain when the prepaid item changes in value.

It's possible that a man may prepay another ten dinars for twenty *qafīz* of wheat, rice or dates so that he could collect it at the time of its harvest in a known month on a known day. That being the case, the appointed time takes place, and the value changes resulting in two and a half *qafīz* for a dinar. People buy and sell that food item at that value at that particular time. The one who is prepaid loses, and the one who prepaid gains based upon the changed value of that prepaid item.

Perhaps there is a case with increase and decrease. When we find a prepayment situation like that without any difference and there is no loss in profit for the prepaid item due to there being both profit and loss, this transaction would be considered valid according to us. This would be considered the same situation since there would be contentment for both the one who prepaid and the one who was prepaid. It would be similar to an estimated sale of unknown measure and weight (*al-juzāf*) about which none of the Muslim *Ummah* disagrees regarding its permissibility.

The sale of unknown measure and weight is when a man buys a house filled with dates, wheat or barley from another man. He examines it, looks at it and then buys it from him without knowing the measure or weight. The two of them agree on the price taken by the owner of the house, and it is prepaid for to the owner of the purchased item.

Similar to that is when a man goes to the date palm of another and buys fresh dates from it with a price to which both of them agree. He then pays him the price and gains possession of the dates at the head of the date palm. The buyer allows the dates to dry and then takes the dates. Then, perhaps there is an increase in value and an excess in the price for which the seller sells the dates at that time. Perhaps there is a loss in value when the dates were clipped and allowed to dry. It would be considered an increase in the value at that time, and the buyer would gain while the seller would lose. That transaction would not be considered permissible, and its establishment is disagreed upon by the *Ummah* of Muhammad, peace and blessings be upon him and his progeny.

The prepayment is more just and clearer than this because the prepayment is not for the date palm itself nor for the planting itself. Rather, the purchase is of the fruit itself. Someone may ask: If the sale of the fruit itself is permissible when it is shown to be sound, what about if it is shown to be spoiled? It is replied to him that similar would be the case in that prepayment. One only takes the sound product from the one who was prepaid based upon how the item was previously described and stipulated.

One may liken the prepayment to a delayed purchase in which increase and excess occur for the seller in any case and in every time or likeness. Or he may assume that it is like the advanced loan which leads to profit about which Allah's Messenger, peace and blessings be upon him and his progeny, said: ((Every advanced loan (*salaf*) which leads to profit is prohibited)).[1]

However, such likening is an error and defect in analogy because the advanced loan that leads to profit is the advanced loan that secures the advance from loss and ensures gain in every situation. The debt cannot be out of deceit where one person is always the loser while the other is always the winner by gaining profit for his capital due to delayed payment.

An example is that a man loans another ten dinars in advance and stipulates that he is to be repaid twelve dinar or more. These twelve dinar which are taken will be considered unlawful gain in his advanced loan, and there would be no fear of loss. This is what is impermissible, and it is the usury that is prohibited. Or if a man buys food from another while waiting on daily reduction in the price, it would be like the wheat is twelve *makūk* for a dinar. He then says to him: "Sell me this wheat and wait for me until the price is a dinar for ten *makūks*." Or the seller may say: "I will sell you this wheat and subtract two *makūk*s from its rate. Then it will be a dinar for ten *makūk*s." Or he may say "I will sell you this ten for a dinar," while both he and the buyer know that this rate decreased that day and that

[1] Although I could not find the hadith with the exact same wording, I did find one with similar wording: ((Every loan which leads to profit is considered usury)). This appears in ***Amāli Ahmed b. 'Isa, Sunan al-Bayhaqi, Mušannaf Ibn Abi Shayba, Kanz al-'Ummāl***

this decrease only took place due to delay. If he were to do that and wait for its price, this would be considered usury according to us and an unlawful transaction which is impermissible and not allowed. It would be an advanced loan which delays payment because its owner and the owner of the initial ten dinars that was paid with the extra usurious two dinars were safe from the usurious fluctuation due to the cheapness of the rate and not the expense. This is because only the dinar was taken and the profit had not changed. The owner did not fear loss and took it from him while being certain that it was a loss for the latter. It was not marketed sincerely—whether in means or conceptually.

The prepayment is not such that the one who prepays has the hope of unlawful increase and release from the one who is prepaid. Similarly, the one who is prepaid should not hope for such release and unlawful increase from the one who prepays. This is because the one who paid dinar in advance took the food item that was designated with a known measure to an appointed time while not knowing what the rate would be at the time he collected the food item. Then, he would be given the food item with fear and dread in his heart that the item would be more expensive at that time and he would have engaged in unlawful usurious gain. He would also fear that the food item decreased in value and would therefore lose. This would be contrary to the situation of the one who was prepaid and who would not have such hope or fear.

The analogy of the prepayment is that of the purchase of unknown measure and weight without the mutual agreement of the seller and buyer. If the measure and weight of the two of them are unknown, there is no disagreement among the *Ummah* that—when the transaction of unknown measure and weight takes place and neither of them know the exact weight or measure—the transaction between them would be considered valid and permissible once it is measured and weighed. It will be a gain for the one who gains and a loss for the one who loses as long as the buyer had seen it with his eyes.

The analogy of a prepayment with a profit which we mentioned as impermissible according to us is that of a person who sells something of unknown measure and weight to another person while [the seller] knows its measure and weight. It would be transferred to the buyer with the assumption that he [i.e. the seller] did not know the measure and weight. This would be an invalid transaction that is impermissible for the seller to engage in because he was certain of unlawful usurious gain, knowing what would be paid.

Therefore, the difference in permissibility and impermissibility between these two cases should be clear. It should similarly be clear regarding the difference between the prepayment for which one of the two involved in the transaction is confident of gain while safe from loss and the transaction in which there is a delay in profit that is known and understood; the difference is clear.

By my life! Even if Allah's Messenger, all the scholars of his Ahl al-Bayt and the other Muslim scholars had not agreed that prepayment is permissible and that it is not like other than it and that it does not resemble an invalid transaction, logic would support our statement regarding the difference between the two. That should be sufficient as a proof. Therefore, how could there be narrated that there is a difference in that from Allah's Messenger while there is no disagreement among any of the scholars of Ahl al-Bayt or other than them regarding that? All of them say that prepayment is permissible given the soundness of its characteristics as well as the establishment of its restrictions and preconditions. If anyone were to abandon any of its restrictions and preconditions, the prepayment would be considered invalidated and impermissible for one to engage in.

If anyone were to prepay and abandon any of the aforementioned preconditions of prepayment but then it is mentioned to him and the other person before the transaction is concluded, the restrictions and preconditions of the prepayment should be recalled and confirmed. If he is not reminded of any of the preconditions before the transaction is concluded, the prepayment between them would be considered invalid. The capital that he used to pay for it will belong to him unless he wants to renew the prepayment. Then, he should take his capital back from the other person and repay it to him observing all of the preconditions of a valid prepayment transaction. Then, the prepayment would have begun.

If the one who was given prepayment found a defective dirham in the money used, such person should return it and take a substitution for it. The prepayment would be considered valid. Others say that such prepayment between them would be considered invalid; however, we do not hold to such view that the prepayment between them would not be sound.

If a man prepays for dates, then he should describe the particular type of date. He should say: '[I want] pure *barni* dates which are good quality without inferior-quality dates." Similar is the case if he were to prepay for *šayhāni* dates and says: "*Šayhāni* dates will be taken from you which are pure without inferior-quality dates." Or he may say: "Pure *šayhāni* dates will be taken." Similarly, regarding wheat, one must specify by saying "white wheat" or "tan wheat" specifically. Likewise, every prepayment must have its characteristics and type specified as preconditions.

He cannot say "It is the best ever" because this cannot be specified. If one stipulates that which is not fully specified, the prepayment will be considered invalidated. If one prepays for something but is given other than that—such person will only be obligated to take that for which he prepaid.

Prepayment is permissible in everything that consists of measure, weight and breadth whose attributes are fully specified. The description must be mentioned and not subject to many differences. Therefore, I do not hold to the view that it is permissible to prepay for animals because their bodies are subject to many differences with time. An example is a man who prepays for a two-year old or three-year old camel, horse, cow or sheep. He is able to establish the age, species and description; however, he is unable to establish the grading. This is because the two-year old to three-year old may be better than other animals the same age. The two-year old to three-year old may not be the same as two *jadha's* in terms of body, swiftness and speed regarding camels and horses; this is something that is not specified.

Similar is the case with male and female slaves because they diminish in body, grade, character, intellect and limbs (*al-juzāra*). The defect of animals invalidates it from prepayment, which makes it null and void according to us.

It is impermissible for one who prepays to use that which is measurable to prepay for that which is measurable and to use that which is weighable to prepay for that which is weighable except in the case of gold and silver. It is permissible for one to use that which is measurable to prepay for that which is weighable and likewise. If there is a difference in kind of that which is measurable, it is impermissible to use that which is measurable to prepay for that which is measurable.

It is impermissible for one to use barley to prepay for rice, and impermissible for corn to be used to prepay for legumes (*al-bāqillā'i*) because the basis of such is a measure. Likewise, it is impermissible for one to use sugar to prepay for *qubbāt*[2] because the basis of such is a weight.

We simply prohibit such because the prepayment is deferred until an appointed time. It would therefore be impermissible for one to buy that which is measurable with that which is measurable if they differ in categories—whether one for one or two for one—unless it is hand-to-hand. It would simply be impermissible for a *makūk* of barley to be exchanged for a *makūk* of wheat except in the case that it is hand-to-hand. It would be impermissible for it to be deferred because it is a measure, and every measure is impermissible to use in prepayment because prepayment is a deferment. Similar is the case with the proof for weight.

There is no problem if one prepays for that which is unmeasurable or unweighable if they differ in kind. There is also no problem if one uses an ornamental garment to prepay for a silk-woollen garment

[2] This refers to a light pastry made from almonds, coconut and pistachios. (Ref. ***Al-Qāmūs al-Wasīt***)

or likewise. Neither is there a problem with using a *Qūhi* garment to prepay for a *Daybaqi* garment or likewise. We simply permit prepayment for that which is unmeasurable and unweighable when there is a difference in kind because it is permissible to buy two garments with one garment of a different kind in the case of delay (*nasā*).

It is permissible to buy one kind of item with two of a different kind whether unmeasurable or unweighable. However, it is impermissible to use one kind of item to buy two of the same kind of a measurable or weighable item in the case of delay. This is because there is no mixture or confusion in that which is unmeasurable or unweighable insomuch that this would not be known from that. It would therefore permit delay in it because of its being able to be returned itself—that is, its owner can reclaim it from the buyer. If it was a case of insolvency while the item was present or there was some type of imperfection in the purchased item, the owner could reclaim that garment as his garment.

If there was some type of mixture of garments and it is possible for one to be known by means of some piece of cloth or a mark on its side, it would be impermissible for there to be a delay in that which is measurable or weighable. This is because if there occurred some type of imperfection in the purchased item and it was mixed with like items that are measurable and weighable, he would not be able to see it with the eyes or know if it were ruined. He would be obligated to pay its value in dirham. Dirham differs from that which he paid for in advance. Nothing else is to be used for prepayment. Consequently, this is the meaning of any difference that occurs between them.

Concerning the one who prepays for a damaged good and concerning when the one who was prepaid considers that for which he prepaid to be ruined

If a man prepays another dirham or dinar for a ruined good to an appointed term and then comes to know about its damage, he can take an equivalent in money and weight in the case that the one prepaid wants it returned and finds the one who used it. Similarly, if one prepaid for an item that is measurable or weighable, he is to take an equivalent of its measure and weight from the category of that which was prepaid.

If the prepaid item is an unmeasurable or unweighable commodity (*arḍ*), he is to take its value and not take its equivalent. This is because the like can differ in the case of unmeasurable or unweighable commodities, and one could hardly notice that they are not the same. However, the value of such is more just and reliable.

If one prepaid for an animal and it is ruined, its value is to also be taken. It is impermissible to take its like because a likeness cannot be found. It necessitates that they differ in some praiseworthy or blameworthy characteristics in body or other things. If there is disagreement regarding the value and the one who prepaid claims that his commodity equals something but the one to whom it is paid claims that it is equal to something else, the one who prepaid must provide evidence since he would claim more. If he does not come with evidence, he must swear an oath to the one he paid that his statement is correct. If he declines from taking such oath, the claim of the other will be considered binding.

It is impermissible for the one who was prepaid to use the prepaid item if he knows that their prepayment transaction was invalidated.

If the one who prepaid for an item says "I do not know what equals my unweighable and unmeasurable commodity" and the one who was prepaid says "I do not know what it equals either," it is to be described to one who can assess the value and knows its price. Then, he is to establish its value utilising diligent effort to reach the truth and adjudicate that between them. He is to not consider the value of the price that was prepaid because the value is only the value that the purchaser paid to the one who was prepaid. If that were the case, the one who was prepaid would have to return what he paid to the purchaser, and the latter would be obligated to take it back. However, in the case that it was ruined, it would be obligatory for the one who ruined it to return the value [of the ruined item] instead of the value of anything else. This is because something other than that was not the property of the one who prepaid due to the imperfection of the prepaid item.

If he also came to own it due to the soundness of the prepayment and then the one who was paid could not do so—perhaps due to some impediment or other valid reason—it would not belong to the one who prepaid. The only thing that would belong to him is that for which he prepaid or the capital he used or the value of that for which he paid.

If it were an unmeasurable or unweighable commodity, it would not be the value of that which was prepaid for because if one were to take the value of that which was prepaid, it would be considered invalid due to any possible addition or deficiency in that which was paid. If any addition were to occur in similar, it would be considered impermissible because perhaps one paid ten dinars in advance for ten *qafiz* of wheat and when the appointed time came, the one who prepaid was hindered (*a'iq*) from paying the price in advance and did not apply the payment because of that impediment. Then, if the one who prepaid says "Return my prepayment to me," it would be obligatory for the ten dinar to be returned to him and not the value of that ten *qafiz* at that time because its value at that time exceeded ten dinars. It would be impermissible for him; the dinar must be returned to him. It would not be allowed for him to take any additional amount with it because it is impermissible for him to pay ten dinars in advance and then take eleven or twelve dinar back due to this being considered unlawful usury. This is because gold is only taken for gold, hand-to-hand, and silver is only taken for silver, hand-to-hand.

Similarly, if the value of that thing at that time is eight dinars, it would be impermissible for him to return eight dinars if he had taken ten. That is why we say that one should not consider the value of the thing for which he prepaid and that nothing belongs to the one who prepaid except the same amount he paid particularly or the capital that is returned to him. The situation of the unmeasurable or unweighable commodities when prepaid is like the situation of credit (*naqd*) in this case. This concept is simply that he does not get anything except that thing—if it is still valid—whether it is itself or the value it was on the day it was prepaid to him.

There is no problem if a man prepays for wool, cotton, linen, hair or fur with a known description and known weight to a determined time. However, one does not stipulate the particular item as a requirement in the case of lamb's wool, livestock fur, camel's hair, linen or old cotton (*kursuf*). If one were to stipulate the particular item as a requirement in the case of any of the above, the prepayment would be considered invalidated and the prepaid item must be returned.

Concerning prepayment for that whose value varies in itself and whose measure differs in itself, such as pomegranates, citrons, quince, pears, melons, cucumbers, bananas as well as eggs such as ostrich eggs and chicken eggs, the Indian nut (*rānij*) and the like

The best viewpoint I see regarding such is that the one who wants to prepay for any of the above—along with the one who is prepaid—should attempt to weigh it until the measure of such is clearly demonstrated. If the two of them attempt to weigh it and agree to the measure of the item, then one can prepay the other after such attempt. The prepayment of such is based on the known weight to the determined time with a known description and genus.

One does not prepay for a fruit from a specific category nor for an egg from a specific chicken. If he prepays for a known weight after attempting to weigh any of the categories of the purchase, the prepayment will be considered valid. This is the best viewpoint I see and hold to regarding prepayment.

For those things whose value is subject to variation, one is to refer to the weight after attempting such due to that which is agreed upon by the one who prepays and the one who is prepaid. I do not hold to the view that one can similarly prepay based on number because one could make a banana take the place of two bananas, a citron takes the place of two citrons, a pomegranate takes the place of two pomegranates and a melon take the place of two melons. Whoever prepays for such based on number has bought and sold based on uncertainty. A transaction of uncertainty between Muslims is impermissible. However, if one refers to the weight of all the above after the attempt of the buyer and seller, no uncertainty will enter it and neither will invalidation. It would be established on justice, truth and correctness.

As for those fruits that can be measured and weighed, such as dates, grapes, apples, pears, figs, almonds and apricots—there is no problem for them to be prepaid for based on measure or weight. None of the aforementioned items can be prepaid for except before it appears on the tree or before one reaches the time of its sale. Priority regarding that is preferable to me.

As for firewood and reed, it is impermissible to prepay for it based on the number of loads and bundles because its value varies. If one intends to prepay for any of the aforementioned items or similar, the only way to do that is he can prepay based on a known weight and known description to a determined appointed time. One does not prepay for firewood or reeds based on a determined number.

Concerning prepayment for meat, heads and roasted meat (*ash-shiwā*)

I do not hold prepayment for any of that to be permissible except if one prepays for meat with very little fat (*manqiyyi*). If the seller gives him meat that is fattier than what was mentioned to him, it would be considered surplus from the one who was prepaid. If the seller gives him the meat with very little fat, it would be considered his right. If he gives him less than that, he must return it to him and does not take anything except what was originally stipulated.

Similar is the case with his stipulation regarding roasted meat. If he says that the roasted meat is from a lamb with very little fat, we simply permit it for the one who stipulated meat with very little fat because the very little fat is a known limit and no lesser except in the case of a lean animal. In the case of a lean animal, one does not pay attention to such [case].

Prepayment is impermissible for meat that is without a specific description because when it is without a specific description and one says "I want to prepay for meat" without describing it, it is rendered deficient by the avoidance of describing some of the preconditions for the prepayment. This is because it is necessary that one describe the meat of livestock with such-and-such description just as one who prepays for *barni* dates must describe them with such-and-such description or wheat with such-and-such description or a blended garment with such-and-such description. Then one must come with the specified description that the one who prepaid stipulated. Whenever one does not describe it with a description that distinguishes it from other than it from what is above or below it, the preconditions of the prepayment would be deficient. The prepayment with any deficient preconditions is considered invalid.

It is only permissible to describe with a description in which one is able to clearly know the limits and established meaning. For that reason, we discourage prepayment for meat unless it is described as having very little fat only. This is because if he had not prepaid for lean meat and set it as a precondition, he could prepay for meat in general without specifying its description. If any of the preconditions of the prepayment are deficient, it would be considered invalid.

To me, it is impermissible to prepay for anything from an animal. There is no problem prepaying for anything from an animal that is not subject to variation in measure or weight. One can prepay for a camel or horse for its labour or anything else from an animal regarding food, clothes or anything else for which one wants to prepay.

The proof for the soundness of prepayment related from the Prophet

It has reached us from Allah's Messenger, peace and blessings be upon him and his progeny, that a Jew came to him and said: "O Muhammad, if you want, I can prepay you for a known measure of known dates with a known weight to a determined time from a known plantation." Allah's Messenger, peace and blessings be upon him and his progeny, replied: ((No, O Jew! Rather, if you want, I can be prepaid for a known measure of known dates with a known weight to a determined time. I will not designate to you a plantation though)). The Jew agreed and then prepaid him. When the appointed time came, the Jew came to Allah's Messenger, peace and blessings be upon him and his progeny, to demand his right. Allah's Messenger, peace and blessings be upon him and his progeny, said to him: ((O Jew, we still have some time remaining)). He replied to him: "You sons of 'Abdul-Muṭṭalib are a procrastinating people!" 'Umar then started to use harsh and rude words towards him. But Allah's Messenger, peace and blessings be upon him and his progeny, said to him [i.e. 'Umar]: ((Go with him to such-and-such place and give him his right. And give him such-and-such extra for what you said to him)).[3]

Whoever wants to prepay for milk should prepay for milk that is known by its genus; it should be attributed to what the milk came from. If one wanted to prepay for camel milk, he must mention that and designate it. He is to say 'fresh camel milk' or 'sour camel milk' with a known measure until a determined time. He is to pay him such-and-such in a known place every day if he were to prepay him for it on consecutive days. If he prepays him at one time, he must stipulate its measure, designation and appoint for him the determined time.

Baby camel milk is not prepaid for and then designated in particular; rather, one prepays for camel milk that is designated while mentioning the specific camel. Then the owner can bring the one who prepaid from anywhere he wants—whether it is his or anyone else's camel—and milk it whenever he wants. Similar is the case with one who prepays for cow milk; it would be obligatory for him to do what the one did with the camel milk.

Likewise, if one prepaid for sheep milk, such person should designate the milk with any condition he pleases—buttermilk, sour milk or fresh milk—and then establish all the stipulations of the prepayment when he prepays the owner before they separate. If he avoids any of the prepayment stipulations or designations of the milk and then separate, the prepayment will be considered invalid. However, if they are reminded about what they forgot before separating and then mention it, the prepayment will be considered valid.

Similarly, it would be religiously obligatory that the one who prepays for oil, vinegar or fat to designate the oil by saying 'Sarawi oil' or 'Palestinian oil' or 'Maghrebian oil' or 'Eastern oil'—whether clarified or not clarified. Likewise, one says regarding vinegar: 'wine vinegar' or 'date vinegar,' sharp-tasting and pure or any other known designation agreed upon by them.

Similar is the case with fat. One designates it by known descriptions, such as 'cow fat' or 'sheep fat' and 'well-cooked.' The designation of all sheep is the same—whether lambs or goats. That is, if the one who prepays makes a claim to the one who is prepaid, it is sufficient for him unless he stipulates the fat of a goat or the fat of a lamb. Then, that which he stipulated would be for him. If he does not establish the type of sheep fat at the time of the prepayment between them, their prepayment transaction will not be considered invalidated because lambs and goats are considered sheep. However, it is preferable to us that one clearly designate the type of sheep in a prepayment for its fat. This is the same in the case of milk according to us.

If one prepays for anything in particular and then specifies something else after the completion of the determined time, it would not be considered valid and would be necessary for them to disregard that which they had not agreed to in the prepayment.

[3] Similarly narrated in ***Sharh at-Tajrīd***, ***Sunan al-Bayhaqi***, ***Al-Mu'jam al-Kabīr***, ***Sunan Ibn Mājah*** and ***Al-Mustadrak***.

It is impermissible for one who prepaid for something to take other than what was originally designated from the genus of that thing and consider such as credit—even if it was less. As for the one who prepaid for a designation of a genus such as dates and the one who was prepaid gave him dates which are better than that which was originally designated, he has a choice. He can either take it if he wants or he can only take what he originally designated if he wants.

Concerning that which is impermissible in prepayment in regard to time and days

It is impermissible for a man to engage in a prepayment transaction with another using the following as deadlines: until the time of the approach of an absent person, the departure of a present person, the health of a sick person, the walking and speech of a baby, the puberty of a child or the death of a living person. This is because all of such are times that are subject to difference and is not clearly known; one cannot pinpoint such days. Any prepayment transaction for which its time cannot be pinpointed specifically and determined by day, month or year is considered invalid and impermissible.

Similarly, if one engages in a prepayment transaction to a determined year, it is obligatory for a specific month to be designated for the completion of the prepayment. It is preferable to us that one even designate a specific day out of that month—whether it be the tenth, fifteenth, twentieth or any other specified day.

It is impermissible for one to engage in a prepayment transaction until the arrival of the pilgrims or the arrival of the first of them or the arrival of the last of them. Similarly, it is impermissible to engage in a prepayment transaction until they return or until they leave because these times cannot be pinpointed. Maybe there is a delay, or maybe there is a rush.

Therefore, whoever engages in a prepayment transaction until any of the aforementioned times or any other time that cannot be properly pinpointed—such prepayment will be considered invalidated and must be returned to its owner. However, if one engages in a prepayment transaction until a determined time and mutually understood day, the prepayment will be permissible and sound.

Concerning that which is permissible in prepayment in regard to time and days

If one desires to prepay then let him prepay to a mutually understood determined time. If he desires to engage in a prepayment transaction to a specific year, he is to say: "Give me my prepaid item in such-and-such month in such-and-such year." If he does that, then his prepaid item would be compulsorily due in that month.

It is encouraged for one to say: "I have prepaid you such-and-such for such-and-such to such-and-such day in such-and-such month in such-and-such year." It is the most reliable prepayment transaction and the best method for one who engages in such in a determined year. Whoever prepays to a certain month out of the year and says "...to such-and-such day out of such-and-such year," he has taken the best precaution in that practice of prepayment.

It is impermissible for the one who prepays for dates to say "...to the time of clipping" and one who prepays for a crop to say "...to the time of harvest." This is because these times may be delayed or rushed. They have a beginning, a middle and an end, and all of such is subject to change.

However, if one intends to engage in a valid prepayment transaction, such person and its owner must find a flexible period, specifying the exact time that it would take to complete the prepayment transaction so that both may be informed of the exact time that it is possible for the one engaging in such to observe it. Thereby, the both of them should fix a determined time so the two of them can take precaution for themselves. If the one who prepays says "...to such-and-such day from such-and-such month," the month should be that for which one knows that dates or crops usually dry in it.

There is no problem for the one engaging in a prepayment transaction to say "…to the Fast-breaking Eid" or "…to the Eid of Sacrifice" or "…to the Day of 'Arafat" or "…to the day of *at-Tarwiya*" or "…to the day of the major sacrifice" or "…to the day of the minor sacrifice" or "…to the start of the month" or "…to the start of the year."

Whoever engages in a prepayment transaction to the start of the new moon, it would be obligatory for his prepayment to last from that night to sunrise. Whoever engages in a prepayment transaction to the start of the year, his prepayment would be from the sighting of the new moon of Muharram to the sunrise of the first day of Muharram. There is no restriction for them to conclude the prepayment transaction during the day of the first of Muharram. Similar is the case with the entrance of the first of any day of the month for the one who engaged in a prepayment transaction stipulating the start of the month.

As for the Day of 'Arafat, *Tarwiya*, the sacrifices, Fast-breaking Eid or the Eid of Sacrifice—if the determined time is the entire day, concluding the transaction in the beginning of the day would be the same as concluding it at the end of the day. The exception is if the determined time was specified as the beginning of the day, the middle or the end. Then, the determined time for the both of them would be the time the both agreed to.

If one engaged in a prepayment transaction for fatty meat characterised by fat, one should not designate it as fatty meat. Fat is something that is subject to change or an alterable description. And a prepayment transaction should not be with a description that is subject to change. If the description is subject to change, the prepayment transaction would be considered invalidated. The description of 'fatty' is subject to change because the amount of fat cannot be pinpointed by the eye. Thusly, any fat that is below the designated amount would be considered less, and any fat that is above the designated amount would be considered fattier. For that reason, we say that designating the fat cannot be adequately observed against the limited description.

Haven't you considered that if one prepaid for meat with very little fat but the owner claimed that it was fatty and the one who prepaid said "I did not prepay for this; I prepaid for meat which was fattier than this," there would not be a designated limit to the prepayment transaction or description by which they could judge?

Similarly, if the one who was prepaid said to the one who prepaid while having two types of meat—meat with a generous amount of fat and meat with a moderate amount of fat—"I'll only give you the one with a moderate amount" and the other said "I'll only take the meat with the extra amount" and the one who was prepaid said to him "You only prepaid me for fatty meat, and this is fatty meat. So take it" but yet the one who prepaid objects and brings the case to the magistrate and the two of them relate their individual accounts, there will be no designated limit stipulated for their prepayment transaction that the magistrate can base his ruling on.

It is for this reason that the prepayment transaction for meat would be considered invalidated unless a designated limit was mutually known. If there was an additional amount or deficient, the addition or deficiency must be known—similar to what we said regarding the stipulations of lean meats.

Roasted meats are similar; the position regarding that is that one does the same according to us. Likewise is the case with heads; it is impermissible to prepay for them except that one stipulates lean heads and that the prepayment transaction take place with scales after viewing them. It is similar to what one does with fruits that are subject to change. This is because its meat is subject to change—whether big or small and additional or deficient. Therefore, its subjection to change would be a matter of disagreement. We discourage a prepayment transaction for it unless there is a known weight because there will be no disagreement or subjection to change regarding weight.

If one were to say "If the head is measured as big, it is due to the heaviness of the bones," reply by saying: The same is the case. If it grows, its meat increases just as one may say when its bones decrease that its meat decreases. The owner understands that the bigger the bones, the more the meat. This is because the measure of meat is based on the bone. If there are large bones, there will be a lot of meat. If there are small bones, there will be a little meat. Weighing such would therefore be a more just way of extracting that so that there is no disagreement or subjection to change in it. Therefore, one would weigh it just as one would weigh roasted meat.

Concerning prepayment for clothes, outer garments, furnishings and other things from that category

There is no problem with prepaying for any of the above. The one who prepays for that should describe what he prepays for with the following: type, description, colour, piece of cloth, width and length to a known determined time to the owner in a mutually understood place.

Similarly, if one prepays for a cotton garment, he is to say: "I'll buy from you a Baghdadi garment," "...a Kufan garment," "...Mervi garment," "...a Balkhi garment," "...Tabaristani garment," "...Qūhi garment," or any other type of cotton garment. "...with such and such piece of cloth." He is to describe it by the thinness and thickness of its tailoring as well as such-and-such length with such-and-such width.

Similarly, if someone prepays for a linen garment, he is to say: "...Shatawi garment," "...Daybaqi garment," "...Qasabi garment," "...Ma'afiri garment," or any other type of linen garment. He should describe it with a description, and he should mention the type and pinpoint the length and width.

Similar is the case with outer garments; he is to describe the types, colours, length and width. Likewise, with furnishings, he should describe the type, number, pieces, colours as well as the length and width of any pieces. He should specify whether it is Tabaristani, Armenian, Messeni, Sousi, Sanjardi, Barnawi, or any type of furnishing.

Similarly, if someone prepays for a silk wool blend (*khazz*) garments, he must describe the silk wool blend. He should describe what he intends by it and what he prepays for with a description that is mutually understood between him and the owner. He must also describe its width, length and number.

Similarly, if someone prepays for embroidered garments, he must describe them with descriptions that are mutually understood by him and the owner. They must agree to their boundaries, and their tailoring must be mutually understood. Then he must describe the length and width of each garment as well as their pieces of cloth and imprints with mutually understood descriptions and obvious characteristics. Its type must also be described. Then he must say whether it is an embroidered garment from Kufa, Sanā'a, a silk wool blend from Kufa if it is from Kufa or a silk wool blend from Sous. It is not required that the work be done by a specific manufacturer or manufacturers in that place nor does one have to stipulate people by their names.

Similar is the case with a silk wool blend; one is not required to stipulate the work of a specific manufacturer or manufacturers in that place nor does one have to stipulate people by their names. However, he must mention the place specifically and does not have to mention the work of a specific manufacturer by name.

Likewise, it is permissible for the one who engages in a prepayment transaction for food and other things to stipulate the dates of a place specifically. However, he does not stipulate dates in an enclosed structure of a place specifically. He can prepay for *Šayhāni* dates of the city and Barni dates; but, he does not have to specify a plantation of dates of these places. He should therefore prepay for specific dates and not others from an enclosed plantation of that place.

Concerning one who prepays for an item to an appointed time and then the one he prepaid asks to take some of the item as food and return the rest in money

If a person prepays another person fifty dinar for a hundred *qafīz* of food in a valid prepayment transaction and the appointed time occurs and the one who was prepaid says "Take fifty *qafīz* of your prepaid item and I will return twenty-five dinars" and the owner agrees, this is considered permissible for them both in our opinion. This is because it is permissible for one to gift some of his prepaid item. Whatever is permissible for an owner to gift is similarly permissible for him to revoke. Others discourage that, but we do not discourage it; rather, we see it as good and permissible.

Concerning the one who engages in a valid prepayment transaction to an appointed time but the one who is prepaid or the one who prepays says "Hurry for me…" or "Allow me to hurry…" or "Delay for me and I'll give you more" or the one who prepays says "I will delay for you if you give me more"

If a person prepays another in a valid prepayment transaction to the known appointed time and the one who prepays says to the one who is prepaid "Hurry for me with my wealth that you are withholding based on the description I described to you and I will pay you a designated amount from it" and the one who is prepaid agrees to it and hurries with his right while taking a portion of it for himself—that would be considered permissible for them both, and we do not see a problem with it.

Similarly, if the one who is prepaid says to the one who prepaid "Subtract an amount for me from your wealth that I am withholding which I described to you and I will hurry to give it to you" and the one who prepaid agrees to give it to him and take his right—that would be no problem for them both when he gives him that prepaid item based on that description of a general food item or harvest. Whichever of the above two categories by which the prepayment transaction takes place—it would be impermissible for him to give him anything other than those two.

Therefore, if he pays him a portion of the prepaid item and he hastens it before its appointed time, there is no problem with that. It would only be considered unlawful usury if the creditor were to say: "Delay for me and I'll increase it for you." It would not be considered unlawful usury if one were to say: "Subtract a portion for me and I will hurry to give it to you."

Similar has reached us from 'Ali b. al-Hussein[§], upon him be peace. He used to say "Unlawful usury is in delayed payment." He also used to say: "Unlawful usury is not in 'Subtract a portion for me and I will hurry to give it to you.' Rather, unlawful usury is in 'Delay for me and I'll increase it for you.'"

If the one who was prepaid says to the one who prepaid at the appointed time "Delay your prepaid item for me and I will increase it for you," that would not be permissible for them to do. It would be considered unlawful for them both.

Similarly, if the one who prepaid said to the one who was prepaid at the appointed time "I will allow you to delay it after the appointed time if you give me more," that would also be considered unlawful and impermissible for them both. This would not be allowed in their religion because this type of usury is the essence of usury.

Concerning the surrender of some wealth by the one who prepays and the one who is prepaid from one another

If a man prepays another twenty dinars for one hundred classes of dates or wheat in a valid prepayment transaction and then the one who is prepaid relinquishes a portion of the twenty dinar before or after taking possession of it, that is considered permissible. There would be no problem with that.

Similarly, if the one who prepaid relinquishes a portion of the hundred classes from the one who was prepaid before or after taking possession of it, that is considered permissible for them to do and not invalid. This is because it would be considered righteousness and excellence on the part of one to the other in buying and selling. Allah, the Mighty and Majestic, has commanded towards excellence and generosity when He says **{Demonstrate excellence just as Allah has demonstrated excellence to thee} (Q. 28:77)** and **{And forget not generosity amongst thyselves. Verily, Allah sees whatsoever ye do} (Q. 2:237)**. Also, Allah's Messenger, peace and blessings be upon him and his progeny, said: ((Verily, Allah, the Glorified, loves the slave who is lenient in buying, selling, demanding payment and demanding repayment)).

Others say that it would not be permissible for them to do after taking possession of it but permissible before taking possession of it. According to us, there is no difference between the two, and they are the same conceptually. Consequently, we hold to the view that after taking possession, it is permissible and lawful for the one who relinquishes and the one for whom it is relinquished. This is because at the moment that one owns it, it is permissible for him to sell it or gift it if he wants to the one whom he wants. There is no problem with that—according to us—if there are no instances of unlawful usury involved in it between them both as well as no wilful deceit and confusion.

Concerning a man who prepays two categories for one category

There is no problem with a man prepaying dinar and garments for a known measure of food. There is also no problem with someone prepaying a camel, cow, sheep or slave for a known measure of food to a known appointed time in a valid prepayment transaction.

There is no problem if a man prepays wheat and barley for garments as long as he prepays for a known measure of a known type of garment with a known piece of cloth of a known and mutually understood length and width. There is also no problem if a man prepays a horse for a known measure of food or a known category of garments or known weight of oil, fat, sugar or crystallised sugar (*qand*). Also, there is no problem if he prepays crystallised sugar and sugar for wheat and barley.

There is no problem prepaying almonds for sugar. However, one does not prepay almonds for wheat, rice or anything else that can be measured because the basis of almonds is a measurable commodity. One cannot prepay a measurable commodity for a measurable commodity as we have previously proven.

Similarly, one cannot prepay grapes for crystallised sugar or sugar, nor can one prepay the two of them for grapes because the basis of all such is a weighable commodity.

Concerning the one who prepays another with a debt or deposit (*al-wadī'a*)

If a man has a debt of twenty dinars over another man and he intends to prepay it to him for food, it is not considered permissible for them because this is a like measure for a like measure. Allah's Messenger, peace and blessings be upon him and his progeny, has prohibited that because it is exchanging a debt for a debt.[4]

It is also impermissible for one with a twenty-dinar deposit to engage in a prepayment transaction with it for food before taking possession of it. We simply discourage that because if the owner of the deposit were to object to it, he would not be responsible for it nor would the one who used it as a deposit. It is impermissible to engage in a prepayment transaction until one takes possession of it. Once its owner takes possession of it, it is permissible to engage in a prepayment transaction with it.

Others say that engaging in a prepayment transaction with it would be permissible before one takes possession of it. However, we do not hold to that view nor do we advocate for such based on the evidence we mentioned.

Similarly, if a man owes another ten dinars and pays him another ten while saying to him "This ten, which is in addition to the ten that I owe you, is a prepayment for food," this would be considered a

[4] Similarly narrated in ***Sunan ad-Dārqutni***, ***Sunan al-Bayhaqi***, ***Al-Mustadrak***

valid prepayment transaction by the share of the ten that was given but it would be invalid due to the previous loan.

Similarly, if someone had a deposit of twenty dinars and paid an additional twenty while saying "This twenty, which is in addition to the twenty owed to you, is a prepayment for food," I hold to the view that it is valid for him to use it as a prepayment but invalid to be used to pay as a deposit based on the evidence we previously mentioned.

Concerning the man who partners with another in a prepayment agreeing on the rate and amount

If a man prepays another twenty dinars for forty *qafiz* and another man comes to him and says "Partner with me in your prepayment transaction with so-n-so and budget for me half of what you prepaid him" and the other man agrees by saying "I have partnered with you in it," that is considered invalid and impermissible because his partnership was in something that he had not taken possession of and owned. A partnership can only take place in something that was owned and in possession due to a transaction. As for that which had not been taken in possession, a partner can only be a seller and it would be impermissible for one to sell something he had not taken possession and ownership of.

When a man prepays another and then partners with someone else in the prepayment transaction, the one who prepaid is considered the one who engaged in the prepayment transaction and the two of them can engage in a transaction of that which he claimed to be a partner of. It is impermissible for him to sell that of which he has not taken possession.

Similarly, if the one who prepaid bargained with the one he prepaid for food and they agreed on it but he had not paid money for it yet and then he said to him "Partner with me" and he partners with him, it would also be considered invalid. The matter is the same—whether he paid him or not—when they agreed on the known rate.

Likewise, if a man said to one who was prepaid "Let me partner with the one who prepaid you and bargain from me half the money he bargained with you which I will pay to you later and you can return half of what he paid to you" and the latter says "I will partner with you," that would also be considered invalidated because he had partnered in a transaction which he engaged in with another and the buyer was more entitled than he is.

If the one who prepaid took possession of the item from the seller and then a man says to him "Let me partner in your prepayment transaction" and he partners with him after the latter had taken possession of it, that would be considered permissible and he would have to pay half of what the one who prepaid paid for that food.

Similarly, if a man says to the one who was prepaid "Let me enter into your prepayment transaction and you can take half the food he owes you and give me half of what you took from the one who prepaid" and he agrees to that, it is permissible for them both.

Concerning when the one who prepaid and the one who was prepaid disagree in claims

If the one who prepaid and the one who was prepaid disagree and the one who was prepaid says "You prepaid me for dates" and the one who prepaid says "I prepaid you for wheat" or one of them says "I prepaid you for ten *qafiz*" and the other says "You prepaid me for five *qafiz*" or they disagreed about the place in which the one who prepaid is to take possession of the item, they both have to swear an oath.

If each of them swears an oath against the claim of the other, the prepayment transaction between them will be considered void. That is the case if there is no clear evidence for the claimant, who is the one who prepaid. If there is clear evidence for his claim, it would be judged in his favour on the basis of such.

If the both of them swear an oath or establish clear proof for what they swore, the claim would be in favour of the one who was prepaid due to his proof because the claimant is more entitled to provide evidence. This is because the evidence could be against the claimant. When he establishes it, it would be judged in his favour on the basis of such.

If the one who prepaid says "I engaged in an invalid prepayment transaction with you without a condition or appointed time" and the one who was prepaid says "You engaged in a valid prepayment transaction with me to a known appointed time with known conditions," the claim will be in favour of the one who was prepaid with evidence. In the case that there is no evidence for him and the one who was prepaid comes with evidence against his claim, the claim will be in favour of the latter with his evidence.

If both of them come with evidence, the claim will be in the favour of the one who engaged in a valid prepayment transaction. If neither one of them have clear evidence, then the claim will be in favour of the one who swore an oath. If the both of them swore an oath, the claim would be in favour of the one who established the valid prepayment transaction. If one of them swore an oath and the other refused to swear (*nakala*), it would be judged in favour of the one who swore over the one who refused to swear. If both of them refused to swear, the prepayment transaction between them would be considered void and the one who prepaid must return the prepaid item to the one who was prepaid.

Concerning a guarantee and taking a security deposit (*rahn*) in the prepayment transaction

There is no problem if the one who prepaid takes a guarantee or security deposit from the one who was prepaid as long as the preconditions and descriptions are met in its appointed time and that it is not witnessed or recorded. However, if it is witnessed and recorded, there is to not be a guarantee or security deposit taken.

According to me, a valid prepayment transaction is simply like an advance payment of a trustee. Allah—the Mighty and Majestic—has commanded that a security deposit be taken in the absence of reliable witnesses or scribe. This is because the scribe without witnesses is of no use, and the witnesses without a scribe are of no use. There cannot be a scribe without witnesses, and there cannot be witnesses without a scribe. That is based on the statement of Allah, the Mighty and Majestic: {**If ye are on a journey and find not a scribe, then a deposit in hand. And if some amongst thee entrust something to another, let he who is entrusted deliver up that which is entrusted unto him and let him be conscious of Allah, his Lord**} (**Q. 2:283**).

Concerning the one who borrowed something

Whoever borrows dinar, dirham, food or anything else that can be weighed or measured must return the like of what he took unless there is a facility between them both regarding what is between the values of money and types of food.

Whoever borrows something and returns more than that, there is no problem with that. However, it must not be a precondition in that nor should the one who loaned it do such for an additional amount. Allah's Messenger, peace and blessings be upon him and his progeny, borrowed dates and returned more than that.[5] There is no problem if it is done out of generosity as long as there is no deceit in cause or concept.

As for the one who borrows animals, we discourage that based on its assessing of worth. This is because if the two of them were to take their disagreement to a magistrate, he would not be able to pass an accurate judgement for them since he does not know the original value of what was borrowed in terms of its fatness, additions or defects.

[5] Similarly narrated in ***Al-Mu'jam as-Saghīr***

The Book of Pre-Emption (*ash-Shufa'*)

In the Name of Allah, the Most Gracious, the Most Merciful...

The beginning of the chapters regarding pre-emption: Concerning pre-emption

It has reached us that Allah's Messenger, peace and blessings be upon him and his progeny, said: ((The neighbour of a house has more right to it)).[1] It has also reached us that the Commander of Believers, 'Ali b. Abi Ťālib, upon him be peace, said: "If a place is being sold, the neighbour has more right to it when the price has been established as he likes; otherwise he is free to give it up."

Concerning what is obligatory regarding pre-emption

Pre-emption is obligatory in four things: partnership in something that is sold, partnership in a watering source, partnership in a road and an adjacent neighbour. It is obligatory for the pre-emptor for whom pre-emption is obligatory to take his pre-emption from the buyer who comes to him—whether present or absent at the sale. The seller should be present when he takes the pre-emption from the buyer out of precaution and fear that he may claim that he had not sold the property after the day.

Pre-emption is for the old, the young, the present, the absent, the male and the female. Every possessor of pre-emption can seek out his pre-emption whoever he is. It is for him to take anything that was sold with his pre-emption—whether it is in possession of the seller or in the possession of the buyer. The purchase and contractual guaranty (*uhda*) shall be written for the one who owns the property, and the price shall be paid to the initial owner or buyer if the latter is in possession of it.

If the owner of the house is in possession of the price and the buyer is in possession of the property and then the pre-emptor comes to seek out his pre-emption, it shall be taken from the buyer's possession and he shall be paid the weight of its value. Then a contractual guaranty shall be written for him instead of the initial owner who sold it.

Concerning distinguishing the pre-emptors: the first and then the foremost

When land or an enclosed date plantation or house is sold and there is a partner in it and a partner in the road to it, the right of pre-emption shall belong to the partner in it and not the partner in the road to it.

If land is sold and its owner has a partner in the road to it and a partner in its watering source, the right of pre-emption shall belong to the partner in its watering source instead of the partner in the road to it. If there is a partner in the road to it for the owner of this land and he has a neighbour, the partner in the road to it shall be more entitled than the neighbour.

The partner in it is more entitled to pre-emption than the partner in its watering source. The partner in its watering source is more entitled than the partner in the road to it—then the partner in the road to it and then the neighbour. The partner in the road to it cannot be except a neighbour; therefore, he is more entitled than the neighbour who is not the partner in the road to it.

Concerning the choice of pre-emptor as well as what is permissible and impermissible

It is permissible for the pre-emptor to take his pre-emption from an entire estate when all of it is sold. Similarly, if two or three people seek to buy from the owner, it is permissible for the pre-emptor to take pre-emption over all of them if he likes. Or he can take two portions of it as pre-emption and leave the remaining third to his partner. Likewise, it is permissible for him to take a portion as pre-emption from whatever he likes and leave his remaining two portions for the two partners.

---

[1] Similarly narrated in ***Sharh at-Tajrīd, Sunan Abu Dāwūd, Sunan at-Tirmidhi, Musnad Ahmed, Sunan al-Bayhaqi, Al-Mu'jam al-Kabīr, Ŝahīh Ibn Hibbān***.

It is permissible for him to release the purchase to whomever he wills rather than the ones he does not want, and the purchase to him may be released to the exclusion of others. It is also permissible for him to seek out pre-emption when he gets older if he is young. It is also permissible for him to seek out and demand pre-emption if he had been absent and had not known about the selling of that land until approaching or he found out while travelling and his demand for his pre-emption was witnessed.

If his partner sold his right, it would not be permissible for him to say to his partner "I am seeking pre-emption for half of this right and sell half" or "...some of it and sell some" because in that is a harm for the transaction. This is because his sale would be considered more valuable to him and more abundant in his right. Therefore, if his partner wanted to take his right, he could take it completely and if he wanted to hand it over to the one who buys it, he could hand it over. It is impermissible for him to harm his partner and anyone else because Allah's Messenger, peace and blessings be upon him and his progeny, said: ((There is no harming or reciprocating harm in Islam)).

It is not permissible for him to sell his pre-emption nor to take it from the hand of the purchaser and give it to another man if he is not the one who buys it nor seeks it for himself.

Concerning the one who buys a garden or house and then part of it is damaged or added to and then the pre-emptor seeks its pre-emption

If a man buys a garden or house for a hundred dinar and then its gates and wood and iron are damaged but then he sells it for fifty dinars and the pre-emptor seeks out its pre-emption after that and it is judged in the latter's favour, it is obligatory for him to pay that fifty dinar in his possession as well as account for the other fifty dinars he sold it for.

Similarly, if he buys a productive date palm and then sells some of its fruit but then a pre-emptor seeks out its pre-emption, it is obligatory for him to calculate the value of the fruit he sold and then hand over the rest of the fruit to him [i.e. the pre-emptor].

If he buys it while it has no fruit but then he tends to and waters it and then the time comes for it to bear fruit and it does bear fruit but then the fruit is damaged at the time the pre-emptor comes to seek out his pre-emption, it would be obligatory for the pre-emptor to hand over everything that was extracted in it and not count the fruit that was damaged. This is because the initial purchase occurred when there was no fruit and then Allah caused it to produce fruit while it was under his ownership.

Therefore, anything that newly occurred after he bought it and before the pre-emptor sought it out shall belong to the former because the buyer was the owner. He was responsible for his property until another came into ownership of it. Have you not considered that if some damage occurred to a date palm, the damage would be considered the property of the buyer and he would not refer it back to the pre-emptor who comes into possession of it or the sale? It is for that reason that we apportion to him that which newly occurred while under his ownership and responsibility.

If it produces fruit due to the pre-emptor, he would be more entitled to what is on his date palm since he was established as its source and would be responsible for any losses that may occur while under his ownership.

If a man buys a house from another while ignorant that there is a pre-emption on it and adds to it by building on it and construction occurs but then he was sought after for pre-emption by a pre-emptor when returning from his absence or when he [i.e. the pre-emptor] becomes an adult, the judgement according to us would be that the house would be for the pre-emptor and the value of what was built upon it would be for the one who had it built on the day the pre-emption removed it from his possession.

If a man bought a house and it was damaged by rain or wind or any other reason for which he is not held liable while in his possession or bought a tree and it was torn because of the wind or storm and the pre-emptor seeks it out, he has a choice. If he wants, he can take it as is in the state of damage and then pay full price to the one who owned it for anything that was extracted from it. Or if he wants, he can just leave it in the owner's possession and disregard his pre-emption. According to us, nothing else would be for him because the buyer is to not be held liable for any damage that occurred to it.

Concerning the one who sells and then cancels it and what is incumbent on the pre-emptor

If a man sells land or a date palm or any other type of immovable property in a valid transaction but then a buyer purchases it from him and comes to own it and the pre-emptor seeks it out from the buyer who is told to cancel it by the original owner and he does so and returns it to him, that will not be permissible for the both of them to do.

The pre-emptor would be more entitled to take it from the buyer's possession, and it would not be for the original owner to have it cancelled. This is because the pre-emptor has more right at the moment that the transaction occurred and at the point that the buyer took possession of it from the seller. He becomes more entitled to it than the first seller, so it would not be for the buyer to cancel it or sell it because cancellation is fundamentally and conceptually the same as the transaction. If it were permissible for him to cancel it while the pre-emptor established his right over it, it would similarly be permissible for him to buy it from its owner or anyone else; however, this would be considered impermissible.

Likewise, if the original owner buys it from a man for a price and he is content with it and undergoes the transaction with the two of them separating on that and the buyer had not assessed the value at that time but then cancels it while the pre-emptor establishes his right over it, it would not be for the latter to cancel it. Rather, it would be for the pre-emptor to do so instead of him.

It is impermissible for a *dhimmi* to have pre-emptive right over any village that the Muslims inhabit, started, built or constructed—even if he was a neighbour or partner. This is because the Muslims are more entitled to their village than he is. Any village that belongs to villagers is their pre-emptive right. Some can exercise their pre-emptive right over others; however, they cannot pre-empt Muslims. Muslims are more entitled to that which is in their possession than others among the disbelievers.[2]

Concerning a man who sells a house or estate for a price and the pre-emptor increases it and then reverts it to another price without knowing the original price until after the transaction

If a man sells a house or estate for one hundred thirty dinars and the pre-emptor increases it saying "I do not want it at that price" and the buyer asks for a discount of thirty and buys it for one hundred but then the pre-emptor comes to know about it after that, it would be for the latter [i.e. the pre-emptor] to take the one hundred from the buyer. This is because he simply avoided it the first time considering one hundred thirty to be too expensive and then reverted it to one hundred as the price at the end. It was a choice just as the first price was a choice. He decided to avoid it due to its expensiveness and take it due to its affordability.

Similarly, if a seller sells an enclosed plantation for one thousand dinars and excluded part of it and the pre-emptor says "I do not want it for one thousand" and had excluded something from it but then he sells it to another and adds to it and increases it with that which was excluded from the enclosed

---

[2] Imam Abu Ťālib narrated in his ***At-Tahrīr*** that Imam al-Hādi had two different opinions as to whether a dhimmi could pre-empt a Muslim in respect to land. Similarly, Imams Ibn al-Murtaḍa and al-Mu'ayyad Billah related the two different opinions from al-Hādi in ***Al-Muntakhab*** [its permissibility] and the ***Ahkām*** [its impermissibility]. We say that there is no conflict between the two opinions because the reference in the ***Ahkām*** clearly indicates that the Muslims are more entitled to pre-empt *dhimmis* in Muslim villages. However, it does not preclude dhimmis from having pre-emptive rights over Muslims in *dhimmi* villages because of the established principle: "Any village that belongs to villagers is their pre-emptive right." Al-Hādi's statement "Some can exercise their pre-emptive right over others; however, they cannot pre-empt Muslims" can be inferred to mean that the *dhimmi* cannot pre-empt Muslims; however, the intended meaning is clarified by the previous statement: "It is impermissible for a *dhimmi* to have pre-emptive right over any village that the Muslims inhabit, started, built or constructed—even if he was a neighbour or partner." Thus, the prohibition is restricted to that which another people own.

plantation and the pre-emptor comes to know about it, it would be for the latter [i.e. the pre-emptor] to take it from the buyer and have the one thousand dinar handed over to him. This is because he simply avoided it due to what its owner excluded. When he handed it over, the pre-emptor had the choice just as he had the choice initially.

Likewise, if something was excluded from it with the rest being sold for one thousand and then the pre-emptor says "I will not agree to the transaction unless it is everything together for me specifically and I do not want what my partner has for me" and the owner sells it to another for one thousand one hundred and includes that which was excluded and hands over all of it to him but then the pre-emptor seeks out his pre-emptive right from it, it would be judged in the favour of the pre-emptor. This is because he simply turned away and avoided it due to that which was excluded.

Concerning an estate or house that is bought for a price and sold for more than that before its pre-emption is sought

If a man buys land from another for one thousand dinars and sells it for one thousand five hundred dinars and then pre-emption is sought from it, it shall be judged in the latter's favour. It shall also be judged that he would have to pay one thousand dinars to the one who took it for the initial price. He is to refer to that which was taken from his possession over that extra five hundred which it was sold for and that was added to the initial price.

Similar is the case if it was constantly successive and was sold for one thousand and then sold for one thousand two hundred and then sold for one thousand five hundred and then the pre-emptor came. It would be judged in his favour and he would have to pay the initial price for it. He is to pay the price it was when it was taken from his possession. The one who took it from his possession returns it to the one who sold it for the five hundred surplus, and the one who took back the five hundred returns it to the one who sold it for the two hundred.

If a man sells another a date palm for a hundred dinar while it has fruit and then the new owner takes all the fruit and sells it [i.e. the date palm] for one hundred dinars without fruit and the second buyer cultivates it until it produces fruit while in his possession and then he eats it and sells it to a third buyer for one hundred dinars who cultivates it until it produces fruit and then he eats it and the pre-emptor seeks it out, it shall be judged in his favour. He would have to pay one hundred dinars to the one who initially owned it and then sold it; he would not include the value of the fruit as well as what was eaten from it; this would be his sole responsibility.

Similar is the case with the fruit that was eaten by the second (lit. "middle") person; it was his. He [i.e. the pre-emptor] is to not seek that out because he [i.e. the second owner] was simply responsible for the upkeep of the date palm, and the fruit occurred while under his ownership. He refers to that which was taken from his possession with the value of the fruit over the hundred that he sold it for. The second person goes to the first owner of the date palm who sold it to him for one hundred with the value of the fruit he ate. This is because he bought it along with what was on it for one hundred. He was responsible for what occurred with the fruit during the purchase because the pre-emptor was obligated to take the date palm and the land upon which was the fruit from his possession just as he bought it.

If this first buyer had not sold it until it bore fruit while under his ownership and then it bore the same fruit for another who bought it which was also eaten and then sold, the fruit which occurred under the ownership and responsibility of the second person is to not be sought after. Rather, it is only the fruit that occurred at the time of the purchase along with the date palm during the days of its purchase from the first one who sold it which is to be sought after.

Concerning the man who buys land but then stipulates that he has the option of three days or the seller stipulates that on him or the two of them stipulate that the both of them have the option of three days

If a man buys a date palm or land or house and stipulates that the seller has the option of three days and the pre-emptor comes during those three days, it shall be judged in the favour of the pre-emptor. He would have to pay the price to the one from whom he took possession; a contractual guaranty and purchase must be written for him.

Similarly, if three days pass and the buyer does not have the intention, the statement regarding it would be the same as the first.

If the seller stipulates three days and the pre-emptor comes during the three days, the owner of the house has a choice: he can keep it if he wants and the pre-emptor will not have the right of pre-emption, or he can pass over the sale and the pre-emptor would be more entitled to the purchase than anyone else would.

If the buyer stipulates the choice of three days and the seller also stipulates the choice of three days and then the pre-emptor comes during those three days, he would have to wait for the passing of three days for the judgement regarding that. If the seller hands the sale over to the buyer, the pre-emptor shall be considered more entitled to it than anyone else shall. If he does not hand over the sale, he shall be considered more entitled to what is in his possession. If the three days pass and the seller had not clarified the matter or mentioned that he had not begun the transaction, the transaction shall be obligatory on him and it shall be incumbent for him to dispense with what he has from his appointed time. The pre-emptor would then be considered more entitled to the house than anyone else would.

Concerning a transaction in which a pre-emptor takes for a price but then another pre-emptor who is more entitled comes to claim pre-emption

If a man sells a house or land and a partner in watering source seeks pre-emption but then a partner in the sold item comes and seeks pre-emption, the judgement shall be in favour of the latter and he would have to pay the one who had it in his possession because he would be most deserving of pre-emption.

Similarly, if it is sold and the pre-emptor who is a partner in the road seeks out pre-emption and buys a piece of land and then the partner in watering source comes and seeks pre-emption, it shall be judged in the latter's favour. He would have to pay the one who had it in his possession the same value that was dispensed on the day the purchase occurred.

Likewise, if a man buys a house from another and the neighbour seeks pre-emption but then the partner in the road to it seeks pre-emption, the partner in the road to it would be more entitled to it than the neighbour. After him, the neighbour would be more entitled to it than anyone else would.

Concerning one who buys a house with a house or land with land or a gifted item from that and the seeking of an equivalent for a particular item and the statement regarding a gift or charity

If a man uses a date palm to buy a date palm or uses a house to buy a house or uses land to buy land and one of the pieces of land is sought after by the pre-emptor, that land shall be judged in his favour and he would be mandated to pay the value of the land that was given as an equivalent. A contractual guaranty must be written for the one from whom he took possession.

If there is a pre-emptor for every piece of land, the judgement shall be in favour of each pre-emptor regarding that which is sought. Each would be mandated to pay the value of the land to the one from whom he took possession.

Similarly, if a man gifts land to another on the condition that he gives him an equivalent of a specified house or if he gifts him a house on the condition that he gives him an equivalent of a specified land and then the pre-emptor establishes his claim to it, it shall be judged in the latter's favour. He would have to pay the one who took it from his possession the value of that equivalent the owner desired—whether a lot or a little, big or small—unless he is forced to leave it and hand it over to the owner. He would then hand the equivalent of what was desired to the owner.

To me, exchange is just like a purchase—whether land for land, date palm for date palm or house for house. There is no difference or contradiction between the two in my opinion.

As for the one who gifts another without seeking an equivalent or gives charity seeking Allah's Countenance thereby, the pre-emptor is to not demand that which the charitable gives as charity or gift because pre-emptive right is simply something demanded from its owner. And he would be obligated to hand over that which was dispensed by means of pre-emptive right. That which is given as a gift and charity is not something that the pre-emptor can reclaim.

Similarly, the one who gives a gift and the one who gives in charity does not take anything from the wealth of this world. The pre-emptor reclaims the like of what is taken, or he is more entitled to what was dispensed. Therefore, the gift and charity are simply due to righteousness and generosity from the one who gifted to the one who was gifted. And pre-emption is simply a right for the pre-emptor due to the judgement of Allah and the imam of the Muslims.

It is not for a man's partner in something who gifted that man with his portion or gave it as charity out of generosity to be judged as a partner in that gift or charity. Every act of generosity that is done by a generous person is not considered as a compulsion similar to the compulsion on a transaction involving pre-emption. This is because people are more entitled to their wealth; they can give it as a gift to whomever they want, and they can give it as charity to whomever they want. There is no partner with them in that, and no one else can seek pre-emption in that which they give as a gift.

Concerning the obligation of seeking pre-emption between seller and buyer

If a man buys a house or date palm or land from another and then the pre-emptor comes and seeks out pre-emption, he seeks it out from the buyer and not the seller because there is no seeking out between the two of them. It was simply the buyer who opposed him because he came to him regarding his pre-emption. So, he seeks it out by what he purchased which he was more entitled to. He writes a writ for him and pays him the price.

If he does not seek it from the buyer by force but seeks out the seller for pre-emption instead of him, there shall be no pre-emption for him over the other because he was dispensed from his opposition to him by avoiding seeking what he sought. Therefore, the buyer is dispensed from it by his refraining from it by force and then avoiding it. This would be a handing over by him due to his seeking out his pre-emption.

His seeking it out would be considered null and void due to the transaction because he did not have any opposition or a means. It would simply be for him to take his right from the one whose possession he found it in. If he seeks it out from anyone else and disregards him, he would be dispensed from his opponent due to his disregarding him and he would be dispensed from the other person due to his oppression of him.

It is impermissible for him to seek it out if he does not have the desire for such. The exception is if his claim to the seller was out of ignorance of the ruling. If this is the case, his ignorance does not forfeit his right, and he may demand it from the buyer after that.

He is to write a writ in the presence of the buyer and mention in the writ that he had sought out pre-emption of this house from the possession of so-n-so son of so-n-so because he bought it from so-n-so son of so-n-so. "The pre-emption is for me, so I demanded my pre-emption and took it with the judgement of Allah. I handed over its price to so-n-so, and it was such-and-such dinar in cash in the presence of so-n-so son of so-n-so who sold it."

We simply prefer that he be present at the time of the witnessing, writing and payment of the price out of precaution that the first owner of the house may say that the seller had not written: "The house is my house and it is in my possession in its condition. It was not sold to other than me, nor was it dispensed from my ownership for any reason." It would then be invalidated at its pre-emption.

As for the one who buys it from him and a writ as well as a contractual guaranty were written for its purchase and witnesses witnessed it, he should take the writ and pre-emption. He should write another writ for the pursuit of its pre-emption and the handing over of its price to him. If that is the case, it would not be binding on him and the first seller does not have to be present.

Concerning pre-emption

Pre-emption is for every partner or neighbour—the nearest and then the next nearest. If the pre-emptor is present at the buying and selling and the seller takes the price from the buyer without any statement or claim of pre-emption from the pre-emptor and he does not object to the buyer or seller, he shall have no pre-emptive right after they conclude the sale.

The exception is if he was prevented from speaking and seeking his pre-emptive right at that time due to fear for his life from an oppressor or tyrant—whether from the buyer or seller or anyone else. If fear prevents him from seeking out his pursuit, he shall have the pre-emptive right. If that is not the case however, he shall not have any right in that regard.

If the seller is his partner or neighbour of the commodity that was sold and the pre-emptor was not present, he shall have pre-emptive right when he comes to know about it. He can demand it against the buyer and would be more entitled to it.

Even if he were in a faraway place, the pre-emptive right would belong to him after the news of it reached him, if he was seeking it out. The actions of the buyer and seller are to be objected to, and his seeking of pre-emptive right should be witnessed. He would also be obligated to dispatch that with full knowledge to the buyer and seller as fast as he can.

If he were to refrain from it and not mention it as well as avoid seeking it out without any objection to it, there would be no pre-emption for him. If he were ignorant of what was obligatory on him regarding that—whether the witnessing or dispatching to the owner his knowledge of such—and he agrees to his seeking out his right and then seeks it out when he returns from his journey, it shall belong to him.

If it were assumed that he was content and refrained from seeking it out since he was ignorant of the obligation of having witnesses and it wasn't witnessed and then he claimed that he agreed to seek out his right, he would be obligated to swear an oath by Allah that he had not refrained from such and still agreed to demand it. Then, if the buyer had made any new additions to a building he bought or tree he planted or anything else and it was judged in favour of the pre-emptor, it would be obligatory for the buyer to relocate what he added to that property that was pre-empted. He [i.e. the buyer] would be more entitled to it and would have to hand it over in the same state in which he bought it unless there was an agreement between the two of them that the pre-emptor would also purchase any of the additions to the property. In that case, if there is contentment between the two of them, it is considered permissible.

If land belonged to two men and one of them sold his portion to another without the knowledge of his partner and then the other man sold his portion to another without the knowledge of the partner who first sold his portion, there would be no pre-emptive right for the second partner or the person who bought it from the first partner. This is because it was a sale without the knowledge of his partner, and that was not for him to do. Then, if he came to know of what his partner did and had removed the pre-emptive right of ownership from his possession and placed it in the possession of the one who bought it without the permission of the second partner, such would invalidate all their pre-emptive rights according to us.

If the pre-emptor took an amount of money to relinquish his pre-emptive right or sold his pre-emptive right, that would not be for him to do and the price for such would have to be returned.

Every child who has an established pre-emptive right is to demand it when older, even if all his paternal relatives permitted him to do so [i.e. seek out pre-emption while he is a child]. The exception is if it is something that his father or any other paternal relative gifted to him. Then, it would be permissible for the one who gave the gift to permit it specifically as long as it was in a will and the child was under his charge and in his residence. If it were an inheritance left by his mother or any other of his relatives, it would not be for any of his paternal relations to say anything about it.

Pre-emption is obligatory in all things—whether estates, garments, slaves or anything else.[3] Pre-emption is obligated for anyone who inherits an asset from the owner in the inheritance.

According to me, pre-emption is based on the amount per head and not the proportion of shares. I simply say this because I have found that the owner of a large share is considered the same is the owner of a small portion. I have also found that the owner of a small portion demands his pre-emptive right on an entire land just as the owner of a large portion would seek out pre-emptive rights on his large portion. That withstanding, I do not see the difference between them in terms of the concept of pre-emption, nor do we find a distinction between them in terms of inherent value of property.

An explanation of that is the following: Three men share a plot of land between them. One owns half of it, another owns an eighth, and the other owns three-eighths. The owner of the half sells it, and the owner of the eighth says "I want to pre-empt it" while the owner of the three-eighths says: "I want to pre-empt it." Then we will investigate the judgement between them. If it were for each one of them to take what is in his possession, pre-emption would not be able to be demanded even if it would be extra in their possessions because the owner of the eighth would be permitted to seek pre-emptive right on all of it from his partner if he were to sell it. The latter would be more entitled to it than anyone else due to what he owns. Similarly, according to us, the owner of the three-eighths would be equally deserving of it and while owning some of the pre-emptive amount. Therefore, we do not find a conceptual difference between the large amount one owns and the small amount that the other owns in terms of their measure against the seeking of pre-emptive right. This is because the one who owns a small portion of the land would have pre-emptive right to it in its entirety just as those who own larger portions of the land. It is for that reason that we said what we said about it and declared about it what we declared. And Allah helps towards all good!

If the pre-emptor hands over his pre-emptive right to a buyer and gives him permission in a purchase and the buyer buys it and then returns it to him after the purchase, we do not acknowledge such as return of pre-emptive right. This is because he had given him permission for a pre-emption that had not occurred when his property was in his possession. Pre-emption would only occur for him after his property leaves his possession and gives him the right of his pre-emption. As for when it takes place before the sale, there would be no pre-emption for him.

---

[3] This concept is further elucidated in ***Al-Muntakhab***.

> I asked him about the right of pre-emption on slaves, animals and other goods. He replied: "Pre-emptive right in all of such belongs to the partner and no one else." "What if the partner is a Jew or Christian?" "Similarly, the right of pre-emption is for the Jew and Christian in everything except those estates in which the purification dues are obligated. Then, such person shall not have the right of pre-emption in that. And he does not allow the dhimmis to buy anything from the estate unless they are from those who are in a treaty with us and we wrote between us and him the same writ that we wrote regarding Najran or from those who heard it and were satisfied with it."

Also concerning pre-emption

Pre-emption is for the shareholder (*qāsim*) and neighbour. A shareholder is a partner and more entitled to it than a neighbour is. The neighbour is more entitled than anyone else is. Regarding that, it has reached us from Allah's Messenger, peace and blessings be upon him and his progeny; ((The neighbour of a house has more right to it)).

The seeking of pre-emption can be delayed for three days[4] as long as he [i.e. the pre-emptor] comes within that time. Otherwise, the seller would be free to sell it. It would be impermissible for there to be any harm nor should it be a source of harm among the Muslims. This is because Allah's Messenger, peace and blessings be upon him and his progeny, said: ((There is no harming or reciprocating harm in Islam)). Delaying the price for the seller is a harm if it is more than three days unless the judging authority (*al-hākim*) sees that the pre-emptor is incapable or unable due to his absence or financial inability.

If a man gifts another with land, there would be no pre-emption for a partner or anyone else regarding a gift. Similarly, if a woman is married for land and it was paid to her and a partner or anyone else seeks out pre-emption, there would be no pre-emption for him because pre-emption can only take place in a sale. The dowry is simply a gift and bestowal, as Allah says: **{Give unto women their dowries as a bestowal} (Q. 4:4)**. The meaning of **{bestowal}** is gift or present. It is for that reason we say that pre-emption is not sought from a dowry.

My father related to me that his father was asked about the neighbour and whether pre-emption belongs to him. He replied:

> There has been disagreement regarding that. The statement according to us is that he gets pre-emptive right. A shareholder is more entitled than he is if there is a shareholder. The neighbour is more entitled than anyone else if there is no shareholder.

[4] Imam Ibn Murtaḍa related in his ***Al-Bahr*** that two different opinions from al-Hādi exist regarding the period in which the delay of pre-emption can occur. He says that the maximum period mentioned in the ***Ahkām*** is three days but ***Al-Muntakhab*** states that a month is the maximum time. We say that a closer reading of the texts reveals that there is no disagreement between them. When Imam al-Hādi was asked about delay in pre-emption in ***Al-Muntakhab***, he replied:

> It has been narrated from Zayd b. 'Ali and others among the Ahl al-Bayt that the maximum is a month. Others say three. But as for me, my statement is that the judging authority is to look into the pre-emption to the extent of rectification and what is possible…

It is clear that the view of the maximum being a month is not related as an opinion of al-Hādi; rather, it is a view that was narrated from Imam Zayd and others from the Ahl al-Bayt. It is also noteworthy that al-Hādi counters what was narrated from Imam Zayd and the Ahl al-Bayt by saying "As for me, my statement…" This further emphasises the idea that al-Hādi did not regard everything transmitted as the opinion of Imam Zayd or any other imam from Ahl al-Bayt to be authentically attributed to them because he held to the view that there is no disagreement among the Ahl al-Bayt. It is also noteworthy that according to the ***Musnad Imam Zayd***, Imam Zayd held to the view that three days is the maximum, not a month.

The Book of Partnership

In the Name of Allah, the Most Gracious, the Most Merciful...

Concerning partnership: A co-partnership (*al-mufāwaḍa*)

If two men decided to form a co-partnership, each one of them must dispense with everything he owns and then measure the amount of wealth of each. Each one of them must know the amount of dinar and then mix it together after each one understood the amount of his wealth. Neither one of them should leave any part of their wealth except that he dispenses with it. There can be no co-partnership or valid co-partnership unless it is all of the wealth. It can only be as such out of fear of confusion from anyone of the owners. If it is mixed together, then they can use it and buy and sell with both of them joined together. Each one will be able to spend the entire amount of wealth using his opinion as well as buy and sell with the money and debt.

Whenever anyone of them contracts a debt, it shall be binding on his partner. Whoever among the partners is absent when a debt is sought after in their business transaction shall be obligated whenever his partner is obligated except if it is in the case of a crime committed or marriage to a woman.

They will both financially maintain themselves and families from their collective wealth when their financial maintenance is the same. If the financial maintenance of one of them is greater than that of the other and the partner is agreeable with that, it is considered no problem. If he is not agreeable to it, that extra amount is considered a debt on his partner. However, neither he nor his partner should take it until the conclusion of their partnership and discontinuation of their mixed wealth. He would then pay that extra amount back to the other because when he pays it back, he would have an amount that is different to that of his partner. This would invalidate the co-partnership.

As for those immeasurable and unweighable commodities (*al-urūḍ*) that belong to both of them, such would not invalidate their partnership unless one of them sells some of it and then it becomes ready money contrary to co-partnered wealth. At that point, the co-partnership is considered invalidated.

As for that which maintains their valid co-partnership, it is that both of them are equally partners. If the both of them prefer to write down a contract, they must designate their wealth in it as well as have their partnership witnessed. They should write the following:

> In the Name of Allah, the Most Gracious, the Most Merciful: This is the partnership between so-n-so son of so-n-so and so-n-so son of so-n-so. It is a partnership based upon God-consciousness and His obedience, as well as sincere worship to Him. It is the observance of trust between both and good deeds in their transaction. It is a co-partnership in their ready money—whether little or lot, small or large, gold or silver. It is in such-and-such month and such-and-such year.
>
> Moreover, they can buy and sell whatever is necessary for them with their wealth and reputation (lit. 'faces') in cash and credit—whether combined or parted. And each one of them should act upon that with his opinion, executing his command in everything that is in their possession of any other credit they took with their reputations or one of them took without his owner's reputation. So whatever extra provision Allah has given them in all of that shall be divided into half for each and whatever loss of this wealth that occurs shall be shared by both.

If they would like to mention the wealth and designate the wealth of each one, they can say at the end of their contract:

> And the sum of this wealth is two thousand dinars, and for each one of them is one thousand dinars. Therefore, whatever they gain in that would be two halves for both, and whatever they lose in that would be two halves from both. So-n-so and so-n-so have witnessed this contract.

Therefore, if they were to initiate a partnership in their transaction, each one of them would be able to take from a debt that which is binding on his partner and seek out the debt that is his from the debtors.

If one of them buys a good to an appointed time but then is absent, it shall be up to the partner in the wealth to take it up on his partner's behalf at the end of the appointed time. Similarly, if one of them had a debt to someone from their business transaction to an appointed time but then the owner of the debt is absent at the time of the appointed time's conclusion, it would be obligatory for his partner to demand that on his partner's behalf. Also, if one of them sells a commodity and is then absent when the purchased item is shown to have a defect, it shall be refunded by the present partner. Likewise, everything that is binding on one of the partners in a business transaction shall be binding on his partner.

Concerning a partnership that is other than a co-partnership

If two men decide to form a partnership other than a co-partnership, it shall be for them to form a partnership based on what they want from their money—whether it is a little or a lot. They cannot form a partnership except based on ready money. And the profit is between them according to what they agree upon, and the condition is based on the amount of capital. The loss will depend on the amount of capital.

Therefore, if the both of them buy something for a hundred dinar and the two of them agree that one of them will have two-thirds of the profit and the other will have one-third and the they work together in buying and selling, their agreement is considered permissible in that case. The loss will depend on the amount of capital, and they will have—in this situation—two halves.

If the capital of one of them was two hundred dinars and the capital of the other was one hundred dinars and both agree that the profit between them will be two halves and the loss will depend on the amount of capital of their collective wealth, that would be considered permissible for them and the stipulation would be considered valid.

However, if they stipulated that the profit between them is split in two halves and the loss between them is split in two halves, such would be considered an invalid stipulation. Their stipulation regarding the profit would be valid, but their stipulation regarding the loss would be invalid. Their loss should depend on the amount of capital of their collective wealth.

If the both of them stipulated that one of them would get two-thirds of profit and the other would get a third and the owner of the two-thirds is the one who engages in trade with it and has it at his disposal, this would be no problem. However, if both of them stipulated that the one who does not engage will have two-thirds of the profit and the one who engages will have one-third of the profit, it would not be considered permissible. The profit between them must be based on the amount of their capital.

If they make their capital equal and then agree that the one who gets a third of the profit is the one who has the wealth at his disposal and engages and that the one who gets two-thirds of the profit is the one who does not have it at his disposal or engage, it would not be considered permissible because the profit here will simply occur with the partner who does not engage. And the wealth of the owner does not earn benefit for his partner due to his stipulation unless it will have some type of gain from the partner's wealth. However, in the case that it [i.e. the capital] is equal and one of them engages in business, the inactive one will have precedence over the one who engages, which would resemble unlawful gain.

If their capital is the same and then they stipulate that the one who engages gets two-thirds and the inactive one gets a third of the profit, this is considered permissible because a third is equal to a third. And the remaining third is for the pay for his body and compensation for his labour.

If they prefer to write a contract regarding their partnership and stipulations between them, they should write:

In the Name of Allah, the Most Gracious, the Most Merciful: This is the partnership between so-n-so son of so-n-so and so-n-so son of so-n-so. It is a partnership based upon God-consciousness and His obedience, as well as following that which pleases Him. It is in observance of trust and rejection of treachery. It is based on strenuous effort and sincere advice in every one of their actions from that which is in their partnership. It is with the collective wealth of such-and-such amount for so-n-so son of so-n-so and such-and-such amount for so-n-so son of so-n-so in a partnership and combination.

With such, they can, based on their opinion, buy and sell in cash and credit—whether combined or parted. And each one of them should act upon that with his opinion. So whatever extra provision Allah has given them in all of that shall be such-and-such amount for so-n-so and such-and-such amount for so-n-so. That is the case whether it is loss or profit. It shall be based on the amount of their collective capital. So-n-so and so-n-so have witnessed this contract.

Concerning two men who form a partnership but have no wealth to buy and sell with their reputations

There is no problem if two men form a partnership in order to take unweighable and immeasurable commodities or anything else with their reputations and then buy and sell it. They should write a contract between them if they want. If they decide to write a contract, it should say:

In the Name of Allah, the Most Gracious, the Most Merciful: This is the partnership between so-n-so son of so-n-so and so-n-so son of so-n-so. It is a partnership based upon God-consciousness and His obedience, as well in observance of trust. It is that they may take cash and commodities with their reputations and buy together and separately with cash and credit. And each one of them can sell and buy based on his opinion with cash and credit. They can buy and sell together and separately.

So, whatever extra profit Allah has given them in all of that shall be divided into two halves for them both, and whatever loss that occurs shall be incurred in two halves by both. This partnership of theirs has transpired based on that in such-and-such month from such-and-such year. And it was witnessed by so-n-so and so-n-so.

If they form a partnership based on such and then one of them is better than the other in buying and selling and the two intend to give him more of the income as a profit, it is considered impermissible for them both. This is because it is impermissible for a man to be responsible for something and have another consume the gain that he is responsible for. This is because they would be equal in responsibility for what they took from debt. Likewise, the gain between them should be the same unless it is made clear from the beginning of the partnership.

Therefore, whatever is taken from the debt should be made clear to his partner that two-thirds is due on one and one-third is due on another. At that point, extra profit would be permissible for the one who is responsible for two-thirds of the debt. Then, to him will belong two-thirds of the profit, and one-third will be for the other. Therefore, the two of them should be equal in profit just as they will be equal in responsibility. When that is the case, it is considered permissible. And any loss that is incurred on both of them shall be based on the amount under their responsibility. Two-thirds would be the responsibility of the owner of two-thirds, and one-third would be the responsibility of the owner of one-third.

Concerning two carpenters, two tailors, two farmers, two cuppers, two weavers and other manufacturers who share in what they manufacture

There is no problem if two manufacturers share in what they manufacture and divide the shares of what they earned from what Allah has provided them as long as they are advised about it and observe their trusts. Any gain they acquire in that shall be divided into half for each, and any loss or ruin that occurs shall be borne by both with a half for each.

If they stipulated that both their works are accepted and that one-third profit would be for one and two-thirds would be for the other, it would be considered invalid and impermissible for both. Any profit that is earned should be divided into half for each because the responsibility for each is the same.

If the both of them intend to give more to one of them, it should be established at the beginning of the partnership and it should be made clear to all that accepts the work. It should be said to such one that one-third of the responsibility is for one and two-thirds is for the other. If they do it like this, the profit shall be divided according to the responsibility. This is because responsibility is similar to capital.

If the both of them intend to write a contract for their partnership, they should write the following:

> In the Name of Allah, the Most Gracious, the Most Merciful: This is the partnership between so-n-so son of so-n-so, the carpenter and so-n-so son of so-n-so, the carpenter. It is a partnership based upon God-consciousness, sincerity in His worship and His obedience, as well in observance of trust. It is a partnership for the acceptance of work. So whatever earnings Allah has given them in all of that shall be divided into two halves for them both, and whatever loss that occurs shall be incurred in two halves by both—whether the labour is done or accepted together or separately. And it was witnessed by so-n-so and so-n-so.

Similar is the case if their manufacturing was different; there would be no problem for them to partner based on what we have mentioned regarding partnership and explained regarding its restrictions and matters. If two partners disagree on any of that, their partnership is considered invalidated.

The Book of Speculative Partnership (*al-Muḍāraba*)

In the Name of Allah, the Most Gracious, the Most Merciful...

Concerning a speculative partnership

A speculative partnership is when a man gives another either gold or silver money but does not give him a commodity by its value. Neither does he give him a slave, good, garment nor anything else other than money. If a man wants to engage in a speculative partnership with another, he gives him the money he wants and the two of them make a designated stipulation regarding the profit with which they are pleased. It can be that the profit between them is split in half for each or it can be that the proprietor gets two-thirds of the profit and the speculator (*muḍārib*) gets one-third. Or it can be any other arrangement they like and are pleased with.

If they want, they can write up a contract between them or if they want, they can avoid the contract—all of such would be fair for them. However, the contract is considered more reliable. If they want to write a contract, they can write the following:

> In the Name of Allah, the Most Gracious, the Most Merciful: This is a contract between so-n-so son of so-n-so and so-n-so son of so-n-so. Verily, you have given me such-and-such dinar in kind and good money as a speculative partnership venture between you and me so that I can have it in my disposal and engage in trade with it in both land and sea as well as buy with it something on credit (*dayn*) and something of real value (*'ayn*).
>
> So whatever profit Allah has given shall be divided into half for me and half for you. I will take from you this designated amount of wealth in this contract of ours. It shall come to me provided that I advise concerning it and observe the trust regarding it in such-and-such month in such-and-such year.

And it should be witnessed.

If the proprietor does not appoint the speculator to sell credit for his wealth, this should be stated in his contract. Likewise, if he does not allow him to travel with it, this should be stated in the contract.

The profit between them is based on what the two of them agreed to, and the loss is based on the capital specifically. The speculator must not mix the wealth of the speculative partnership venture with his own wealth nor should he pay it to someone else in order to engage in another speculative partnership venture. He also must not loan any of this wealth to anyone.

If the proprietor were to say to him "Act on your opinion and do whatever you want with it," it would be permissible for him to do anything with it except engage in a loan. Neither would he be permitted to lend it to someone in one country in order for it to be repaid to the lender or his deputy in another country (*suftaja*) unless the proprietor gave him permission regarding these two specific cases. Then it would be considered permissible.

If the speculator does business with the wealth in another village, whatever he spends for his own financial maintenance shall be from his own wealth. Whatever he spends for the financial maintenance of the business shall be from the profit. If he profits, then he uses the profits. If he does not profit, whatever he spends for financial maintenance shall be from the capital.

If one of them were to stipulate that he would get such-and-such dirham as profit and the other would get whatever remains, this would be considered an invalid and impermissible stipulation because it would be uncertainty on the part of the owner of extra. Perhaps the wealth would not incur any profit except for the original amount of dirham, and the one who stipulated will take what was his and the other will not have any profit or extra. This uncertainty is invalid and impermissible because the amount of dirham was specified and designated for one but not designated and specified for the other.

If the two of them stipulate that one of them would take a fourth or tenth or half a tenth or an eighth of a tenth or more or less after they decided to allocate a portion of the profit to be distributed and it becomes a portion that they made, it would be considered permissible for them both. This is because it is inevitable that the both of them will take some profit even if the profit is one dirham. And it is because it was simply stipulated as a condition that he gets a portion of the profit and not stipulated that he gets a designated amount of dirham. Therefore, the potential harm and benefit in that would be for both; one of them would not be happier and sadder than the other.

It is impermissible for the speculator to be given a garment (*bazz*) to the value of that which he is entrusted with because it is a commodity, and a commodity is impermissible to be used in a speculative partnership venture.

If a man gave another cash with the understanding that it was a speculative partnership but there was no stipulation between them regarding the distribution of profit or what is to be done with it, it would be considered an invalid speculative partnership. Whatever profit is gained would be for the proprietor, and whatever loss occurs would be incurred by him. The like would be for the speculator due to his buying and selling.

Likewise, if he gives wealth as well as stipulates that the profit be shared between them and claims exclusive right to five dinar of the profit or two dinar or more or less, this speculative partnership would be considered invalid. This is because the wealth may not go beyond that which he stipulated, and this would be a harm for the speculator (*muḍārab*). Similarly, if the speculator stipulated that he gets exclusive right to a dinar or two, it would also be considered an invalid speculative partnership. The earnings of the buying and selling is for the speculative partner, and any loss incurred is upon the proprietor.

Everything that the speculator buys before he takes the wealth of the speculative partnership venture is not considered part of the speculative partnership. It is not considered part of a speculative partnership unless that which he bought was from the wealth of the speculative partnership after having taken possession of it.

An explanation of that is the following: A man buys a commodity for a hundred dinar and then goes to another man and says: "I have bought such-and-such for a hundred dinar. Give it to me so I can invest it for you." He gives him the one hundred dinar and the latter invests it as the value of the commodity. That would not be considered a speculative partnership according to us; it would simply be a loan. Any profit or loss will be upon the one who purchased the commodity, and the one hundred dinar would be a debt owed by him to the one who paid it.

The valid speculative partnership venture is that he takes the dinar before he buys something and that they stipulate the profit in a determined stipulation. The proprietor commands him to do business with it in a known way specifically in a known village or he allows him to act by his opinion. Then, the latter does business with it how he likes and has it at his disposal as he likes. At that point, this speculative partnership venture would be considered valid, and the profit between them would be based on what they agreed upon.

Similarly, if he engages in a speculative partnership venture with one hundred dinars and says "Contract a loan of another hundred with the one hundred" and gives him the dinar permitting him to contract a loan of a designated portion and then the speculator contracts a loan as he is commanded and does business with the one hundred and the loaned amount and subsequently makes a profit, the entire profit and loss shall be shared between them based on what they agreed to. The profit shall be split in half.

If he gives him a hundred dinar and says "Contract a loan from the wealth with whatever you want" without designating the specific amount, the profit he makes from the one hundred shall be shared between them based on what they agreed to. Whatever loss that occurs shall be from the one hundred.

Whatever profit is made from the loan shall belong to the proprietor, and whatever loss incurred from it shall be upon him also. This is because the speculative partnership venture regarding this loan was invalid due to him not specifying the amount, and a speculative partnership can only take place with a specified amount of wealth.

If a speculator buys a commodity with fifty dinars of that speculative wealth and concluded the purchase of the commodity with the fifty and it is sold for that with complete agreement but then the proprietor requested more money for the sold commodity and is given more money, the additional money would be for him and not the speculator.

If a man gives another man wealth in a valid speculative partnership venture and the speculator buys a commodity with that wealth and makes a profit from it with the permission of the proprietor, it would be no problem for him to buy and sell the item for himself. However, if he buys it himself, the purchase would be considered invalidated and impermissible. It is based on its situation in which it is sold in the state of the speculative partnership. Whatever profit occurs shall be based on what was stipulated, and whatever loss occurs shall be from the capital.

There is no problem if the proprietor assists the speculator in buying and selling and then buys and sells; that speculative partnership between them would be considered valid. This assistance would not invalidate the speculative partnership for the proprietor.

Others have said that it is impermissible for him to sell but he can buy. We do not advocate for that; rather, selling and buying are the same. There is no problem if he wants to help his brother if the latter seeks it out and buys and sells with him. However, we do not hold to the view that the proprietor can authorise him. The act of authorisation, commanding and prohibiting is for the speculator who took the wealth from his proprietor based on the speculative partnership.

If a man paid another man one hundred dinar or more or less in a valid speculative partnership venture and then the speculator engages with it insomuch that there is a profit gain of one hundred dinars but then engages with it a second time and there is a loss of fifty dinars, it would be impermissible for him to gain any profit until he pays a hundred dinar and separates it from the capital, which is one hundred dinars. Then the remaining profit must be divided between them based on what they agreed upon. And that is if the first profit had not been divided between them insomuch that they both lose what was lost in the second purchase.

However, if the first profit had been divided between them so that there was a share of profit for each and then the speculator had engaged with the capital afterwards and then lost fifty dinars, the proprietor of the wealth would not be able to claim any of the speculator's profit and the loss will be taken from the capital. This is because the proprietor of the wealth had already divided the profit and then left the capital in the other's possession after that. So, the speculative partnership venture would have begun.

If the speculator had been given wealth by the proprietor and buys something with it and loses but then gets access to another commodity with it and makes a profit in it, he shall not get any of the profit until he regains the complete capital he took from the proprietor and then divides the extra profit made from the capital.

This issue is not the same as the first because the both of them had already divided the profit in the first case and then began the speculative partnership venture. The speculator had not encountered the loss that was present in the second speculative partnership venture. In the first case, the two of them had not divided the wealth and began it. Therefore, the capital would be binding on the speculator even if he engaged with it twenty times and made profit gain and loss in each.

If a man gives another man one thousand dinar in a valid speculative partnership venture and stipulates a specified profit that they agree to and then the speculator buys an enclosed plantation with it and afterwards sells it for one thousand and one hundred and another was offered for sale but then the speculator wants to buy it for himself and take it by pre-emptive right, that would be for him to do so based on the profit gain of one hundred from the price of the enclosed plantation he bought for one thousand. This is because he had become the partner of the proprietor by means of his share of the profit. However, if the enclosed plantation was made equal at the time that the enclosed plantation next to it was sold for only one thousand or less or there was some loss, then the speculator would not have pre-emptive right over that property as a neighbour because he had not owned anything in it due to not having any profit. The pre-emptive right would therefore belong to the proprietor, if he wanted to demand it, because the capital had been in this enclosed plantation.

If a man had a speculative partnership with another man's wealth and he were to die, the judgement would be as follows: If that wealth was designated at the time of his death as well as mentioned and made clear to his partner—whether isolated in particular or known by its weight, it would be for the owner. Otherwise, his partner would be most similar to the debtors and he could join his portions along with their portions [in the debt claim process].

If he did not have a debt and the wealth of his partner was made known to him, the judgement would be in his favour. Otherwise, it would be obligatory for his partner to provide evidence for it so that he can claim it from the possession of the heirs. If he does not have evidence of that and the heirs object to it, they must swear an oath to him that they were no aware of any money owed to him. It would be considered impermissible for the heirs—if they know of anything of such matter—to deprive him of his right irrespective of any reason or predicament whether he had proof or not.

It has reached us that the Commander of the Believers, 'Ali b. Abi Ťālib, upon him be peace, said regarding a man who died while having the wealth of a speculative partnership: "If he designated in particular before he died and said 'It is for so-n-so,' then it shall be for him. However, if he died and had not mentioned him, he would be most similar to the debtors."

Concerning speculative partnership

A slave who is permitted to do business as a free person can engage in a speculative partnership venture with the wealth that he is paid and stipulated unless that wealth is ruined while in his possession. His master would then take over his sell and continue the sell that the slave engaged in using the master's wealth until the proprietor's right is fulfilled.

If a man gave someone's slave wealth in a speculative partnership venture and the latter did not have permission to engage in business, this would be considered impermissible. If the slave were to engage in business with that wealth and make a profit, the entire profit would belong to the proprietor and nothing would belong to the master or the slave. It would be obligatory for the proprietor to pay the slave for the business he did on his behalf with the wage that one similar to him would be paid.

If the wealth is ruined while in possession of the slave, the master would not be responsible for any damage caused by his slave because the proprietor had given the slave the wealth to engage in business without his master's permission. However, if the slave were manumitted on that day, he would owe the proprietor the property that was ruined.

Similar is the case with the pre-pubescent child if he has the permission of his father, guardian or his father's executor in business. His case would be the same as the slave who has permission to engage in business. He would get the profit based on what was agreed upon in the speculative partnership. If the property were ruined, he would be obligated to replace the property that was ruined while under his possession. Otherwise, his offense would have to be paid by his clan.

If the speculator is given wealth and engages in a speculative partnership venture without his guardian's permission, he would be obligated to get a wage similar to his like. However, he is to not be considered responsible for any of the wealth if it is ruined while in his possession because the owner gave it to him without his guardian's permission.

Concerning that for which the speculator is not responsible

If a man gives another man wealth to engage in business and stipulates that he get half the profit, he would not be held responsible for any damage to the property. However, if he stipulates responsibility, he will not get any profit from that wealth. The businessperson does not join responsibility for the wealth with any of its profit. Even if the proprietor is content with the speculator having responsibility, that responsibility and his contentment will be considered invalid.

The Book of Security Deposits *(ar-Rahn)*

In the Name of Allah, the Most Gracious, the Most Merciful...

Concerning security deposits: the depositor and the depositee

The depositee of the security deposit does not own any part of the security deposit, so he cannot sell it or deposit it for himself. He is to protect that which has been placed in his possession.[1] In the case of an animal, he is to feed it with what the depositor owns. [However, the depositee is to not take any benefit from the animal, such as riding it or using it to carry anything. Ref. ***Al-Muntakhab***]

If the security deposit is lost or destroyed while in the possession of the depositee, he and the depositor are to refer to credit. An explanation of that is the following: A man gives another a security deposit of that which is valued at twenty dinars for fifteen dinars. Then, the deposited item is destroyed while with the depositee. It will be for the depositor to seek out that credit of five dinars from the depositee. Similarly, if he were to leave a deposit of something valued at fifteen dinar for a loan of twenty dinar and it was destroyed while in the possession of the depositee, it would be for the depositor to seek out the remaining five dinar from his wealth based on the value of the deposited item.[2]

It is not for the depositee to seek out any return from him until the completion of the appointed time, nor is it for the depositor to use any portion of the asset for contracting labour or selling in the case of a slave or anyone else. Nor can it be used for charity, a gift, manumission by death (*tadbīr*), marriage or hiring.

If the depositor deposited an item to an appointed time and said to the depositee "I came to you with your right to this appointed time; otherwise, the deposit would belong to you by your right," this statement would be considered invalid. It would be obligatory for them to reclaim the surplus between them, and the precondition stipulated by them would be considered invalid.

If a depositor deposits a female slave or she-camel and the female slave or she-camel gives birth, the offspring would be considered a deposit along with the mother until he compensates for that which is owed by the mother. The depositee would not be able to alter anything nor would he be able to deposit any of it without the permission of the depositor. So, if the depositor borrowed from the depositee, the depositee would be considered free from his responsibility. Consequently, the depositee would become more entitled than the depositor.

If the depositor dies while owing debts, the depositee would be more entitled to the entire deposit that was in his possession. If there was credit due on him, the credit is to be return to the creditors. If the depositee had credit over the depositor, the depositee would take the deposit by what is in it as well as share the remaining wealth with any creditors.

---

[1] The topic of security deposits is similarly dealt with in ***Al-Muntakhab***. However, the imam mentions the textual basis of such there which is not mentioned in the ***Ahkām***

> I asked him about security deposits: "Can it be forfeited?" He replied: "A security deposit cannot be forfeited. Similar has been narrated from Allah's Messenger, peace and blessings be upon him and his progeny: ((A security deposit cannot be forfeited. Any increase is for the recipient, and any loss is borne by him)). According to us, this is the most authentic report that has been narrated regarding security deposits. Out of the statements, it is the most preferred to us." "What is the meaning of ((Any increase is for the recipient, and any loss is borne by him))?" "He means by this that the depositor and recipient are to refer to credit between them if the deposit is lost."

The narrated report exists in texts such as the ***Muwatta, Mustadrak, Sunan Ibn Māja, Sunan ad-Dārqutni, Mušannaf Ibn Abi Shayba, Mušannaf 'Abdur-Razzāq, Sunan al-Bayhaqi*** and ***Kanz al-'Ummāl***.

[2] Ibn Rushd, the author of ***Al-Bidāyat al-Mujtahid***, attributes this view to Imam 'Ali b. Abi Ťālib. He also says that the jurists differ as to whether the depositor can take the complete deposit if the item is destroyed or if the depositor can simply take the surplus between the deposit and value of the deposited item.

Similarly, if the depositor declares insolvency and the appointed time of the depositee comes, the deposit is given to the latter. We simply say that it is given to the depositee because he was liable for the deposit and because if it were destroyed while in his possession, it would have invalidated the right of the depositee to the depositor.

If the depositor and depositee disagreed regarding the deposit and the depositee said "You deposited an embroidered garment with me" and the depositor said "I deposited a blended garment with you," the claim would belong to the depositor with him swearing an oath. The exception is if the depositee presented evidence of his deposit that was witnessed.

The deposit cannot be that which is public property (*mushā'a*)[3] neither can it be anything other than that which is clearly determined, known and mutually understood in itself and its boundaries.

Concerning security deposits

If a depositor deposits a date palm or fruit tree or married female slave and the trees bear fruit and the female slave gives birth, the produce of the trees is considered a deposit along with the tree based on what the owner took. Similarly, all that is birthed by the female slave is considered a deposit along with her based on what was obligatory on her. If anything were to happen to the produce or children or palm itself or female slave herself while in the possession of the depositee, the depositor would assume the responsibility for the value of that which was damaged. The remaining portion of the deposit shall be borne by the one who damaged it.

All of the responsibilities of the tree's upkeep, watering and the like shall be borne by the depositor's wealth. Similarly, the financial maintenance of the deposited male and female slave shall be the responsibility of the depositor. If there is any addition to that deposit, it shall be for the owner. It would be impermissible for the depositee to sell the dates of the palm, fruit of the tree or have intercourse with the female slave unless he has the permission of the owner, who is the depositor. The exception is if he fears spoilage of the fruit while the owner is absent. Then the depositee would be able to sell that in good trust and after strenuous independent consideration.

Also concerning security deposits

If a man deposits a golden crown to another and it breaks into pieces while in the depositee's possession without it being his or anyone else's fault and it was due to a house or wall falling on it, the depositee shall not be fined for any part of it because the same crown is intact as well as its gold without anything being deficient from it. However, if any portion of it is deficient in weight or there was a jewel in it that was broken, the depositee would be considered liable for what was deficient in it.

If there was no deficiency in it but the depositee was at fault for its damage, he would be fined for its loss of value due to damage. If it were someone else's fault, the owner of the deposited item would seek it out from the depositee while the depositee would seek it out from the one who was at fault. The depositor has a choice: he can take back his deposit as well as the value of the damage if he wants or he can hold the depositee responsible for the cost of the unbroken crown and leave the broken crown with him and the depositee would owe it to the depositor.

---

[3] Imam Yahya b. Hamza says in his ***Al-Intišār***: "As for the deposit of public property, there has been disagreement. Abu Hanīfa and his companions hold to its impermissibility as well as a narration in the ***Ahkām***. It is the soundest. Ash-Shāfi' held to its permissibility as well as a narration from ***Al-Muntakhab***."

Likewise, Imams Abu Ṫālib and Ibn Murtaḍa pointed out the disagreement between what is narrated from al-Hādi in the ***Ahkām*** and ***Al-Muntakhab*** regarding the issue. We reply by saying that the possible reason for the disagreement is that the narration in the ***Ahkām*** addresses the deposit of a publicly-owned item explicitly. However, the issue in ***Al-Muntakhab*** is a bit more ambiguous because al-Hādi was initially asked about the permissibility of selling shares. Then the questioner asked him about shares as a security deposit. Finally, he was asked: "[Is it permissible] if it was inseparable?"—to which al-Hādi replied: "Yes." It is possible that what al-Hādi approved of was the selling of that which is public property. This is because the initial inquiry was about selling and the pronoun 'it' in the question could easily refer to the sale in general. [Ref. ***Al-Qawl al-Awwal***]

Concerning disagreements between the depositor and depositee

If the depositor and depositee disagree and the depositee says "You deposited twenty dinars with me" and the depositor says "I deposited fifteen dinars with you," the depositee shall be asked to bring proof for his claim. If he brings evidence, the judgement shall be in his favour by his claim. If he does not bring evidence, the right of claim shall belong to the depositor with him swearing an oath because the depositee made a claim and the depositor objected.

My father related to me that his father was asked about the depositee and depositor who disagree—the depositor saying that the deposit was ten and the depositee saying that it was twenty. He replied:

> The right of claim shall belong to the depositor, and the depositee cannot establish his claim except by clear evidence. The most of what is obligated on the depositor is that he is to swear an oath. This is because the evidence is due on the plaintiff and it is upon the defendant to swear an oath.

The Book of Suretyship (*al-Kafāla*), Guaranty (*aḍ-Ḍamān*), Debt Transfer (*al-Hawāla*) and Deputation (*al-Wakāla*)

In the Name of Allah, the Most Gracious, the Most Merciful...

Concerning suretyship and guaranty

Everything for which a man is made guarantor is a right upon the man, and he would be a guarantor for that right when sought after. It would be impermissible for there to be a guaranty in the case of the prescribed punishment (*al-hudūd*). The guaranty of the slaves who are permitted to engage in business is considered permissible and binding upon them.

If a guarantor is made liable for wealth with the permission of the principal (*maḍmūn 'anhu*), the wealth shall be for the guarantor. It would be for the guarantor to take the principal with his payment because he agreed to it. If the debtor relinquishes the guarantor from his guaranty, the one who owes the wealth cannot be relinquished by the principal. The owner would then return back to the one who he owes. If the principal gifted it to the guarantor, he would have more of a right than the one who initially had it. He can pay it to the guarantor as a gift.

If the owner of the wealth relinquished a portion from the principal, he would have also relinquished it from the guarantor. Or his gifting it would also be considered as the guarantor relinquishing it from him.

If a man makes another man a guarantor for his wealth without the latter's permission, the guarantor would be held responsible (*makhūdh*) for what is guaranteed. If the guarantor covers the debt from the principal without his permission, the principal has a choice: he can accept such from him if he wants or he does not accept such from him if he wants. This is because he is not bound to do so. His obligation regarding that is between him and Allah when he knows that it is not a gift for him and that he is simply observing the claim from him so that he is required to return it to him. This is because Allah says: **{Is the recompense for excellent naught save excellence?}** **(Q. 55:60)**. It would not be permissible for him to imprison him. It is a must that every debtor, when made liable for wealth by a guarantor, stipulate between him and the guarantor that the principal is relinquished and that the guaranteed is not liable.

If someone owed another person ten dinar or more or less and he transferred that debt to another person and the latter agreed to it, this would be considered permissible. The first debtor would not owe anything, and his wealth would be due on the person who agreed to the debt transfer. So, if the one who did the debt transfer were to die, he would be similar to the creditors regarding that wealth. Similarly, in the case of insolvency, the first debtor would not owe anything because his debt was transferred and became due on the other person based on this transference. That which was due on the first debtor would be due on the insolvent or deceased.

Haven't you considered that if the one who transferred his debt to the insolvent were to ask for what was originally due on him after he transferred it to another and attempted to ask anyone other than him, he would not be able to do so? It would be impermissible for him to seek out that which was transferred to another. If it is impermissible for the first debtor to ask for his debt based on what was transferred to another debtor, it shall also be considered impermissible for the responsibility to be transferred to the first debtor after the latter absolved it from him to be transferred to another.

Concerning deputation

If a man appoints a deputy (*wakīl*) in his general or specific affairs, everything that the deputy makes binding would be considered binding and obligatory upon the one who appointed him as such. If the deputy wants to appoint a deputy, he cannot do so unless he gets the permission of the one who appointed him as a deputy. Then, he can do what he was permitted to do.

The Book of Misappropriation (*al-Ghašb*) and Confessions

In the Name of Allah, the Most Gracious, the Most Merciful...

Concerning the misappropriation of living property

If a man misappropriated another's living property—such as a camel, cow, sheep or slave—and the aforementioned living property gave birth while with him, it shall be for the victim of misappropriation (*al-maghšūb*) to take back all of such as well as that which they gave birth to. Also, if the misappropriator sold the offspring or mothers, the victim of misappropriation could take the value of the mothers and offspring that were sold. Similarly, it would be for such person to take back what was sold and return the money to the one who paid for it.

If the mothers were to die and the offspring remained, he could take back the offspring and demand the value for the mothers. If the offspring were to die and the mothers remained, he could take back the mothers but not demand the value of the offspring if he [i.e. the misappropriator] was not responsible for their death. However, if he were responsible for the death of the offspring, their value could be demanded from him.

We simply obligate that he can take the offspring and demand the value of the mothers when the mothers die because the mothers themselves were unlawfully misappropriated from him. Therefore, we obligate on him [i.e. the misappropriator] the value of what he misappropriated and do not obligate upon him the value of the offspring because they occurred while he was liable for their mothers. If he were not responsible for their death, their value cannot be taken from him after their deaths because he had not misappropriated them. They were simply an addition that occurred while he was liable for their mothers. Similarly, if they and their mothers were stolen while with him or if something was stolen from them, it would be for the victims of misappropriation to take back the value of what was stolen from them.

Concerning one who misappropriates livestock and then slaughters it

If a man misappropriated a camel or a cow or any other type of livestock or bird or any other animal and then slaughtered it, the owner has a choice: he can take it back in its slaughtered state if he wants or he can take the value of it had it been alive if he wants.

Concerning one who misappropriates dates, date pits, any type of fruit or eggs

If someone misappropriates any of the aforementioned things and then harvests it and then it grows and similar, the owner of such can only take back the value of that which was destroyed among them. Similarly, the owner of the egg—if it were to hatch and a chick emerged from it—can only take the value of the egg that was misappropriated from him.

Concerning one who misappropriates a small or large date palm or tree

Regarding the one who misappropriated a large or small tree—whether a date palm or anything else—and cultivated and watered it until it grew, there is a difference of opinion. Some say that it is considered ruined for him based on the additions that occurred in it, and he can demand its value and not uproot it. Others say that he can demand the value of it itself and not for any addition that occurred afterwards such as a tree that was cultivated; it would belong to the cultivator. This is because it is valued in and of itself and not any additions due to his using it all completely.

According to me, the second statement is the better of the two and the closest to the truth because it is something that is valued in and of itself, and its additions took place while in the possession of the cultivator and not the victim of misappropriation. It would be similar if there were any deficiencies; the victim of misappropriation would still take it back with deficiencies as long as it is alive because it is valued in and of itself. Similarly, he would take it with any additions if any occurred since it is valued in and of itself.

To me, this is similar to a goat kid, weaned camel or foal that was increased while in the possession of the victim of misappropriation. According to me, any addition to an animal or anything else is the same when that thing is valued in and of itself. The small is the same as the large. The owner can take it back whenever he wants unless there was a sound agreement between them.

Concerning one who misappropriates an enslaved minor, lamb or baby animal

Any of these which are misappropriated when they are small can be taken back by the owner when they are older. If it is misappropriated while it is emaciated, it can be taken back when it is fat. If it gives birth while in his possession, one can take its offspring. If it dies, one can take its value.

Concerning one who misappropriates a garment, cotton, wool or hair

Whoever misappropriates a garment and cuts it into a shirt, collar, trousers, sleeves or anything else—the owner has a choice: he can take it back stitched or unstitched if he wants, or he can take the value of it before it was cut if he wants.

Others say that if it is stitched, it is considered ruined and he can only demand the value. However, we do not hold to that view or advocate for such because its stitching is not an addition to it rather it is a diminishing in its value. Therefore, the owner is given the choice in all cases: he can take it if he wants or he can take the value of it if he wants. According to us, this is not the case with something that is considered ruined.

As for cotton and hair, if they are manufactured, they are considered ruined. This is because when cotton is manufactured into a garment or hair is manufactured into a sack or thread, they are considered permanently altered from their original state as well as ruined due to their manufacture. Their owner can take their value from the day they were taken from him and that is it.[1]

Concerning the misappropriated item

If a man misappropriated land and then built on it, he would have to demolish his building if he built on it without permission. If he built on it with permission, the financial maintenance that takes place in his building would belong to him.

If a man misappropriated a female slave who is freed at the death of her master and she gave birth, her child would be considered manumitted with her manumission. Their lineage would not be tied to the one who unlawfully raped their misappropriated mother.

Concerning one who buys something and uses it but then its right is demanded afterwards

If a man buys a slave and utilises him but then the slave is demanded back from the original owner, the judgement shall belong to the one who demands the right. The buyer should return to the seller to refund him for the purchase as well as for that which the slave produced while he was employed on his property and his liability.

---

[1] A similar topic is mentioned in ***Al-Muntakhab*** but not covered here in the ***Ahkām***.

> I asked: "What if he misappropriated leather that has not been tanned but the misappropriator tanned it to a like of its price and then the rightful owner establishes evidence against him?" He replied: "The owner is to take it tanned." "Why is it that the owner of the leather takes the tanned leather but the owner of the yarn takes its value?" "It is because the value of the leather still remains the same and does not change even after it is tanned; it is still leather whether tanned or not tanned. It would not be considered ruined if it were. As for yarn, if it is used to make a garment, the yarn is not a garment and the garment is not yarn. It is for that reason that it would be considered ruined due to it no longer holding the same meaning."

Concerning one who takes an animal or any other unmeasurable and unweighable commodity without the owner's permission and then it is ruined

If someone ruins another person's animal or any other unmeasurable and unweighable commodity without the other's permission, we hold to the view that he is obligated to pay the value of such, and two just witnesses are to arbitrate between them.

If the two of them were to quarrel or disagree about the value, the owner of the commodity is to swear an oath regarding the value of the commodity he bought as well as for any addition or subtraction. He is to also establish such based on the present state of the thing he bought. That would be considered the value of the ruined good.

It would be impermissible for another animal or unmeasurable and unweighable commodity to be given to him in its place because it was not free of disharmony and disagreement. If there occurs disagreement in a like commodity, it would be considered invalid and subject to complaint. Therefore, paying the value of the commodity is safest due to collective agreement. The value of such would be calculated from the day that the commodity was ruined.

Concerning one who confesses a right that necessitates the prescribed punishment

Everything for which one confesses a right shall make that for which he confessed binding—whether large or small. Similarly, every truth for which one confesses to Allah or the slaves regarding that which necessitates the prescribed punishment or anything else is considered binding. Therefore, the one who confesses four times to committing fornication shall obligate the prescribed punishment upon himself after the imam looks into his affair, as we will explain in the Book of Prescribed Punishments. Similar is the case with theft and keeping what was stolen.

Everything to which one confesses shall necessitate the prescribed punishment except in the case of fornication. Therefore, whoever retracts from his confession shall not obligate the prescribed punishment upon himself.

Whoever confesses that the child of a female slave is his is considered connected to the child, and familial connection is thereby established.

Whoever confesses to the debt to an inheritor or anyone else and it is considered correct—such confession is permissible and binding. Similarly, if one confesses to a debt while sick and then recovers from the sickness, such confession is considered binding if the one who confesses demands that for which s/he confessed.

If a man confesses that someone is his brother and the rest of his family denies it, it shall be for him to make the subject of confession a partner in inheritance of his sole portion. Familial connection cannot be established by the lone testimony of the confessor. It shall be binding upon the confessor and the subject of confession to inherit from one another and be inherited from one another in the position of complete brotherhood. As for the confession of a captive for one another, we do not consider it as evidential while he is a dependant or the like.

Concerning the confession of the slave

When an owned slave makes a confession against himself which necessitates any type of retaliatory penalty regarding his body, his confession is considered valid regarding that which is related to his body among the retaliatory penalties for injury or the like. However, if he confesses to anything that obligates his master for a debt, such as loss or anything else, his confession is not considered binding.

Similarly, if a slave confesses to anything that would ruin himself, his confession would be considered invalid because he is the responsibility of his master and not himself. He would make binding on the slaves that to which they confess among the rights and other matters. When they are manumitted, they can demand it when there is confession for or against them.

Similar is the case for a ward (*al-mahjūr alayh*) regarding his wealth. Whatever he claims—whether a cause or confession regarding an obligatory right in respect to wealth or felony, his confession is considered obligatory and binding. The guardian cannot prevent him from that unless such person [i.e. the ward] is insane with his intellect gone or if such person is a small child without intellect. If it is the case that these two situations are non-existent, the confession of such person is considered binding—whether he is a ward or not—because the guardian would not have a sound basis due to the wealth belonging to the former once he has reached maturity and sound intellect.

Concerning that for which a person is permitted to confess

There are five things for which a man can make a confession: when he says "This is my son," "This is my wife," "This is my father," "This is my master/freed slave," or "So-n-so owes me such-and-such." When he confesses to any of these five categories, his word is to be taken. Inheritance is to take effect after his death unless there is evidence from his heirs that he wanted to redistribute any portion of it.

Likewise, that which is permissible for a man is permissible for a woman. Others say that her claim of childhood is not accepted. However, her claim regarding childhood is even more binding than his regarding other than that because childhood from her is more certain. She has more connection than a man in that regard because if a man were to fornicate with a woman and she were to give birth, that child may not be connected to the one who fornicated with her and would therefore not necessitate inheritance. However, if a woman were to fornicate and give birth to a child, she would be connected to the child and would necessitate inheritance. It is for that reason that we say that her confession is sound and even more than the confession of the man.

The Book of Insolvency (*at-Taflīs*)

In the Name of Allah, the Most Gracious, the Most Merciful...

Concerning one who becomes insolvent while having a creditor's commodity

If a man becomes insolvent while having a creditor's commodity valued in and of itself, the owner of the commodity is more entitled to it than other creditors.[1] That is the judgement of Muhammad, the Messenger of Allah, peace and blessings be upon him and his progeny.

It has reached us that he, peace and blessings be upon him and his progeny, said: ((Whoever has left his wealth with an insolvent person is more entitled to it than anyone else is)).[2] It has also reached us that he, peace and blessings be upon him and his progeny, said: ((Whenever a man dies or is insolvent, the owner of the commodity is more entitled to it once he finds the exact item)).[3]

If he finds it valued in and of itself, he can take an additional or less amount if he likes. If he wants, he can be like other creditors and it is for him to do so. It is not for the other creditors to be included with him in that commodity of his, neither can they take part in any portion of it. This is because Allah's Messenger, peace and blessings be upon him and his progeny, passed the judgement that it is for him instead of them.

An explanation of that is the following: A man buys land from another man and there are crops on it. He excludes those crops and then the buyer becomes insolvent and they are harvested when his creditors come to him. Then, the landowner can take back his land along with the crops.

If it was harvested before his insolvency and he ate its fruit and then he became insolvent, the landowner would be more entitled to its legal deed. He can take part in the rest of the insolvent person's property along with the other creditors by the value of the crops on the days that the land was bought.

If he were to buy the land from him while there were no crops on it and then crops grew on it and he became insolvent afterwards, the landowner would be more entitled to the legal deed of his land. He may say to him: "Be patient until the crops are harvested. And when they are harvested, the creditors can take it and you can take your land." Even if he decided not to wait, he would be compelled to do so because Allah's Messenger, peace and blessings be upon him and his progeny, said: ((There is no harming or reciprocating harm in Islam)). This means the harming of the creditors and insolvent person. Therefore, he cannot abandon that.

Similarly, if a man bought a palm from another while there was fruit on it and he fecundated it and excluded it from being bought and then ate from it and completely consumed it but later became insolvent, the owner of the palm would be considered more entitled to the palm and similar to other creditors regarding the value of the dates on the day the palm was bought until the remainder of the insolvent person's wealth. He would have a share in it just as they [i.e. the other creditors] have a share, and they can divide the shares of what they take.

---

[1] Although not stated in this text, an important condition to consider when reclaiming the property of the insolvent is whether the insolvent person and his family are dependent upon that property for survival. This principle is exhibited in ***Al-Muntakhab*** in the following conversation:

> I asked: "What is it that can be sold from the wealth of the insolvent person?" He replied: "That which he can do without." "What if he has two garments that are valued at ten dinars?" "He can sell them and buy what he needs from its price. The remainder is to be given to his creditor." "Similarly, what if he has a house? Would he be obligated to sell some of it and leave a portion for him and his family to live in?" "Yes." "Similarly, what if he has a ring? Is he obligated to sell it?" "Yes, because it is not a necessity." "What if he has a two- or three-month amount of financial maintenance for his family?" "If he has anything other than the amount used for financial maintenance of his family that equals the amount of financial maintenance once or twice, he is to sell that which is other than the amount for financial maintenance. That which is left as financial maintenance is to be used for him and his family to live off of."

[2] Similarly narrated in ***Ŝaḥīḥ al-Bukhārī, Ŝaḥīḥ Muslim, Al-Mu'jam al-Awsaṭ***

[3] Similarly narrated in ***Sharh at-Tajrīd, al-Muwaṭṭa, Sunan Abu Dāwūd, Sunan Ibn Māja***

Likewise, if he were to buy a date palm with no dates on it and then fecundate it but then become insolvent before they mature, the owner of the date palm would be more entitled to his palm. However, he would have to wait until the dates ripen and then, he can take from the base value he bought.

Similarly, if he bought land or a fruit tree such as pomegranate or the like and the fruit tree produces fruit and that fruit was excluded but then he became insolvent and had sold it and completely consumed it, the tree would belong to the owner if he wants and demands it. He, along with the other creditors, can demand the value of the fruit on the day the tree was bought. Its value would simply be from the base value of the purchase. The price would be equally divided based on the enclosed plantation [in the case of the land] and fruit [in the case of the fruit tree]. The value of the fruit would be considered from the base value of the purchase on the day the tree was bought.

Similar is the case with everything we previously mentioned, such as date palms, trees and crops. If one buys it and excludes the fruit and does not make its good condition clear, the value of this fruit will be the value of one-sixth of the price of the enclosed plantation. The tree and the enclosed plantation would be included as five-sixth of the price. He can demand one sixth of the price along with the other creditors. Similar is the case if the price of the fruit was an eighth or more or less; it would be the same.

If he were to sell it as a small palm or small tree and then become insolvent, the landowner can take back the land along with what is on it including that tree—whether large and mature or small—or a part of it. It would be for him to take the land and what is on it. He can demand it from him along with the creditors that which was damaged from what was sold. It would be determined that he would get its value on the day it was sold.

Similarly, if he sold a young slave girl and she grows and matures but then he became insolvent, it would be for the owner of the slave girl to take the slave girl in her condition of increase because she is his property specifically. Likewise, if he bought her while in good condition with perfect and complete characteristics but then he became insolvent and her condition worsened or she became defective or chronically ill, he would have to take her back in her deficient condition just as he would take her in perfect condition.

Concerning one who buys a slave girl from another man and she gives birth while with him and then he becomes insolvent

If a man buys a slave girl from another man to an appointed time and then that slave girl gives birth from another while she is with the buyer and then the buyer becomes insolvent, it would not be for the original owner of the slave girl to take back anything but her herself. He takes her and leaves her offspring because this thing occurred while in the possession of the buyer and under his responsibility. Nothing would belong to the owner of the slave girl except the slave girl herself.

The owner can only take her when the buyer becomes insolvent. He leaves her offspring if the offspring is from other than the insolvent man due to intercourse. If the offspring are from the insolvent man, her first master who sold her would not be able to take her from the insolvent man's possession because he would consider her ruined. Her situation would be similar to other things that are considered ruined. The seller would not have found her in the same situation he paid for her in because he sold her to him as a slave but found her as an *umm walad*.

Concerning one who becomes insolvent while having a slave for which he had not paid and was given wealth as a gift

If a man bought a slave from another man and he gave the buyer some wealth as a gift and clothed him with a garment but then became insolvent, it would be for the owner of the slave to take back the slave only. He would not be able to take back that which he gifted to the insolvent person.

The creditors can take what is in his possession [including the gift] and distribute it amongst themselves.

Similarly, if a man bought a slave who had wealth or garments and the buyer excluded the wealth that belonged to the slave but then considered the slave ruined after the purchase and then became insolvent, the owner of the slave can take him back and then divide the shares of the rest of the insolvent person's wealth with the other creditors to the value of that wealth that was with the slave on the day of his purchase.

If he bought a slave woman from him and then became insolvent while the slave woman was pregnant from someone else, the slave woman and that which is in her womb would return to the possession of the one who initially sold her to him. This is the difference between a connected and disconnected addition.

Similarly, if he bought a camel or sheep from him and some of them were destroyed but then he became insolvent, it would be for the owner to take from it and divide the rest of insolvent's extra wealth as shares among the creditors.

Concerning one who buys barren land but then harvests date palms on it or constructs on it but then becomes insolvent

If a man bought land from another and harvested date palms on it or constructed on it but then became insolvent, the creditor has a choice. He can take the land and give him the value of the harvest if he wants, or he can assign it to the other creditors and give him what he sold it for if he wants.

If he decides to not take the land and pay the value of what was harvested on it and the other creditors prefer to uproot what was harvested and pay him for the land, they can uproot it. That which is judged in his favour shall not be against them. If he decides to not give them the value and they decide to not uproot the harvest, the judgement shall be in his favour by that for which the land was sold. The land will be assigned to the creditors along with what is on it. The judgement would be against him and if he decides to refuse such judgement, it shall be forced upon him.

Concerning one who sells something and takes possession of some of its price but then the buyer becomes insolvent while he owes the remainder of the price

If a man sold a slave to another man and took half the price and delayed the other half and then became insolvent, ownership of the slave would be between the latter and the other creditors. It would not be judged that he could take him and return the part of the price he took because he had part of the price in his possession. The slave would remain in his possession due to the portion of the price he took. It would be for the other creditors to sell the other half based on his value that day—whether a little or a lot. If the one who had owned half of him wants, he can take his value on that day.

Concerning one who leaves a security deposit that is more or less than its value and then he becomes insolvent

If a man leaves another man a security deposit that equals a hundred dinar for something that is fifty dinars and then he becomes insolvent, the remaining value of the deposit shall be returned to the other creditors because the recipient has already fulfilled his right and therefore refers the surplus to the creditors. However, if a man leaves another man a security deposit that equals fifty dinars for something that is one hundred dinars and then the depositor becomes insolvent, the security deposit shall belong to the recipient by its value and the latter can demand the rest of his right from the remaining wealth of the insolvent along with the other creditors. He shall have a share in it, and they can divide the other shares.

If the security deposit were two male slaves or female slaves and one of them died while in the possession of the recipient and then the depositor becomes insolvent, the judgement would be that he must consider their value. “How much were they? How much was she?” If their value was greater than what he owes, the recipient shall return the surplus value to the creditors. The value of the destroyed is considered binding on him and included in his wealth. If their value was less than what the insolvent owes, he shall take their value from his wealth, and the remaining value of his right from the wealth of the insolvent shall be divided amongst the creditors.

If the security deposit were a date palm and it produced yield for two or three years and then the depositor becomes insolvent, that which is due upon the owner of the palm is considered as well as the value of the yield for those years. If the value of the yield is included with what he owes, it shall be assigned to him and he can take the original date palm. If that which he owes of the date palm is greater than the value of the yield, it is considered fulfilled when he and the creditors sell the base value of the asset and he assigns the entire remainder to them. If it is the case that the yield and date palm are uprooted, it would belong to him. If all of that does not cover the value of his owed assets, it would be considered as such and the remainder of such assets shall be considered the assets of the insolvent person as well as the creditors.

Concerning a man who buys a house, demolishes it, builds another one and then becomes insolvent

If a man buys a house from another man and demolishes it but then builds a new house and becomes insolvent, the judgement regarding that would be that he shall say to the owner “If you want to take it back and return the rest of its value today from the surplus of its first value, you can do so. If you decide not to, you can be like the rest of the creditors.”

We simply give him the choice in that because the lot of the house has a value in and of itself and other than that based on what is on it, such as stones, wood, and other benefits. If there is a change in its initial state, it is considered open land and there is no alteration in most of its wood and stones. If it is as we mentioned valued in and of itself, it would be the house that was sold and its construction before and after would be considered altered between its initial state and second state. They would differ, and their description would be subject to change. Quantitative disparity between the first and latter state would appear in it. It is for that reason that we necessitate that the owner, if he wants it, extracts the surplus value that occurred in it to the time that the second building was constructed on it. Therefore, if he constructs a building on it instead of the first building, the wood and stones on it would be considered extra, and the owner can take it as well as divide the shares of any deficiency from his house among the other creditors regarding the rest of the insolvent’s wealth.

Concerning debt

If a man has a hundred-dinar debt to the people and bequests from it fifty dinars, this is considered impermissible because he owes a debt and the debt takes precedence. The proper action in that regard is that he is to pay the fifty-dinar debt to its people by dividing their shares to the extent of their debts. He is to pay each one with half of their debt because he left fifty dinars and owes one hundred dinars.

If a man dies and leaves wealth as an inheritance but then a claimant claims that he owes him a debt and this claim is witnessed by some of the inheritors such as two men or a man and two women, the judgement shall be in favour of the claimant based on what he claimed which was witnessed by the inheritors. That would be excluded from the capital.

If the claimant of the debt was witnessed by one man from among the inheritors, his testimony would be considered valid in respect to his right only, and he would be obligated to observe the debt to the value of that which he made binding regarding his right. The same is the case with two women; their obligation regarding their rights would be the same as that of one man.

An explanation of that is the following: A man dies and leaves six sons and six hundred dirhams. Another man claims that he owed him one hundred dirhams, and it was witnessed by one of the sons but rejected by the others. It would therefore be obligatory for that witness to pay the one for whom he witnessed sixteen and two thirds dirham from the hundred. This is because he said: "Our father owed one hundred of the six hundred dirham to this man, and there remains five hundred. Our individual portions are eighty-three and a third for each."

We [i.e. the man who is owed] say to him [i.e. the son that witnessed]: "You have confessed to this one hundred and that there remains for you eighty-three and a third from your father's inheritance based on your confession. Therefore, I will take it and pay it towards the debt that your father owed me which you have readily witnessed."

Similarly, if there were five sons and their father left them six hundred dirhams and one of them witnessed that their father owed a man one hundred dirham, it would be said to this witness: "You claim that your father owes this man one hundred dirham and that five hundred of this inheritance remains after the hundred. You also claim that after this hundred is paid, there remains one hundred for each of you. Therefore, you are to take your hundred and pay what remains in your possession after your one hundred to the one who is owed."

Concerning imprisonment for debt

Creditors can imprison a person for delay in repaying a debt after employing much effort and after the elapse of the appointed time. As for the poor person in difficult circumstances, he cannot be imprisoned when his difficulty and lack are evident. One is to delay it until the time of his ease, as Allah—the Exalted and Majestic—says: **{And if the debtor is in straitened circumstances, then postponement till ease} (Q. 2:280)**.

The most of what is obligatory upon the person in difficult circumstances is that he should pay in instalments with an arrangement that is suitable for him and the one he owes.

The Book of Settlements (*aš-Šulh)*

In the Name of Allah, the Most Gracious, the Most Merciful...

Concerning the making of settlements between Muslims

Every settlement that Muslims make with each other is considered permissible except in four things: a settlement that prohibits what Allah permits, a settlement which permits what Allah has prohibited, a settlement regarding a prescribed punishment that Allah has obligated its establishment after reaching the imam of the Muslims or a settlement regarding the payment of a debt.

An example of a settlement regarding a debt, which is impermissible, is when a man owes another man ten dinar and when he demands it, he is rejected and prevented from such. Then, a settlement is made between them in which it is reduced to five dinars, and he accepts the five. Afterwards, the creditor settles and is content with that but then he waits for the five for a long time. Such settlement would be considered impermissible and invalid.

Whoever claims something and settles for an amount greater than that—such settlement would be considered invalidated. Whoever claims something and settles for an amount less than that—such settlement would be considered permissible based on what we previously said regarding rushing that for which they settled.

If a settlement occurs between two creditors for something that is obscure or random for which one does not know its weight or measure, it is considered permissible just as it is permissible to purchase something with an unknown weight, measure or number.

Likewise, a settlement between people is permissible regarding blood money, compensation, payment, debts and everything else that is transacted and claimed between them unless it is from one of those aforementioned four things. Settlements are valid whether it is between Muslim men and women or the *dhimmi*. There can be no settlement except among those who are recognised as mature by law—and that is the person who is fifteen years old or has reached puberty.

Concerning settlements of gold for silver and silver for gold in repayment

There is no problem in that when it is hand-to-hand. An explanation of that is the following: A man owes another one hundred dirhams and exchanges the like of that with twenty for each dinar. He gives him five dinars and says: “This is the amount that I owe you, take it in exchange.” This would be considered permissible for them hand-to-hand.

Similarly, if he owed him five dinars and gives him one hundred dirhams, it would be considered permissible for him to repay him by exchanging hand-to-hand.

The Book of Oaths, Vows and Expiations

In the Name of Allah, the Most Gracious, the Most Merciful...

Concerning the judgement of expiations for oaths and concerning one who swears invalidly while knowing that

Whoever swears an oath invalidly and violates a Muslim's right by such or intends transgression and sin—such person would be considered openly disobedient, a flagrant sinner and oppressor. Regarding these type pf people and similar, the Most Gracious says in the revelation of the Qur'an: **{Verily, those who purchase Allah's covenant and their oaths with a measly gain shall have no share in the Hereafter. Allah shall neither speak to them nor look at them on the Day of Judgement, nor shall He purify them. To them shall belong a painful punishment} (Q. 3:77)**.

The statement of the Blessed and Exalted **{shall have no share in the Hereafter}** means that there will be no portion of Allah's reward for them in the Hereafter. As for His statement **{Allah shall neither speak to them}**, it means that Allah will not give them the good news of His Mercy nor will He specify them for His forgiveness or look at them with His grace. As for His statement **{nor shall He purify them}**, it means that He will not award them with purity nor will He seal them with mercy or blessing; He will not judge them as purified or triumphant.

This verse was revealed regarding a man who swore a false oath to Allah's Messenger, peace and blessings be upon him and his progeny, as a sinner. Allah's Messenger, peace and blessings be upon him and his progeny, said: ((Whoever swears an oath regarding his brother's wealth in order to cut it short oppressively—such person will meet Allah on the Day of Judgement dejected)).[1]

Allah, the Glorified, says: **{And make not Allah an excuse for thy oaths that ye may be righteous and God-conscious and that ye may make peace between people. And Allah is All-Hearing, All-Knowing} (Q. 2:224)**. This means that if a man were to swear that he would not be righteous or reconcile between the Muslims due to Allah's command **{And if two parties of believers fight, then make peace between them. And if one party of them doeth wrong to the other, fight those who doeth wrong till they return unto the command of Allah. Then, if they return, make peace between them justly and act fairly. Verily, Allah loveth the fair} (Q. 49:9)**, the man should not disobey the command towards righteousness and reconciliation due to his swearing of such oath. If it is said to him "Make peace between them" and he says "But I swore that I would not do that, and I cannot go back on my oaths or that which I swore!", Allah—the Mighty and Majestic—prohibits such.

When He says **{And make not Allah an excuse for thy oaths that ye may be righteous and God-conscious and that ye may make peace between people. And Allah is All-Hearing, All-Knowing} (Q. 2:224)**, the Glorified is saying that you should not make your oaths a reason for disobedience to Allah in maintaining your family ties and reconciliation between your brothers. Rather, you should be righteous and God-conscious, pursue good and reconciliation as well as expiate for your oaths.

Included in the exegesis of this verse is that Allah prohibits His slaves from falsely swearing regarding any truth and falsehood. It is also that He makes an object for one's oath regarding anything. Allah says: **{Allah shall not take thee to task for that which is unintentional in thy oaths, but He shall take thee to task for the oaths that ye swear intentionally. The expiation thereof is the feeding of ten needy persons…} (Q. 5:89)**. Then, the Glorified says: **{Allah shall not take thee to task for that which is unintentional in thy oaths. Rather, He shall take thee to task for that which thy hearts hath sought} (Q. 2:225)**.

---

[1] Narrated with similar wording in ***Ŝahīh al-Bukhāri, Ŝahīh Muslim, Ŝahīh Ibn Hibbān, Sunan at-Tirmidhi, Sunan Abu Dāwūd, Musnad Ahmed, Al-Mu'jam al-Kabīr, Al-Mu'jam al-Awsaṭ, Sunan al-Bayhaqi***

Oaths are of three types: unintentional, the seeking of the hearts and the intentional oath. As for the unintentional, it is an oath that one swears with the assumption that he is truthful regarding it. It will be that which he swore as he swore. This is the unintentional oath; there is no expiation for it. However, one should not return to the like of it, and one should be cautious when swearing an oath by Allah unless such person has certainty. Then, there is no sin in it.

As for the seeking of the hearts, it is when one falsely swears while he knows that he is lying and is intentional in that. It can be in buying, selling or anything else involving discussion of things. There is no expiation for it. However, there is repentance to Allah, seeking forgiveness, returning from transgression back to Allah as well as trembling (*al-istiqāla*).

As for the intentional oath, it is when a man swears that he will not do something while having the firm determination to fulfil his oath but then he sees that it is better to do it and then does it. He owes an expiation for that, which is feeding ten needy people their lunch and dinner—the moderate amount that he would feed his family as well as providing them a moderate amount of condiments for their bread (*al-idām*).[2] He is to feed each one a half *šā'* of flour, dates, barley, corn or any other foodstuff that he and his family eats.

Or [the expiation is] that he clothes them with a garment that covers the whole body of each of the needy people. It can be a long and loose-fitting shirt, draping dress (*milhafa*) or a long, outer cloak. The garment can only be that which covers the whole body; it would be impermissible to clothe any of them with one turban or one pair of pants.

Or [the expiation is] that he manumits a Muslim slave, whether young or old. These are the three forms of expiation for which one can choose to do as s/he wants. Clothing is better than feeding, and manumission is better than clothing. If one does not have the means to do any of the above or is unable to do it, he is to fast three consecutive days [as expiation].

Then, the Glorified says: **{...and preserve thy oaths} (Q. 5:89)**. His saying 'preserve them' means: expiate for them and establish that which We have obligated upon you regarding them. Then the Glorified says regarding the exception: **{And say not of anything "Verily, I shall do that tomorrow" without saying "...if Allah wills." And remember thy Lord when thou forget, and say: "It may be that my Lord shall guide me unto a way nigh unto this truth"} (Q. 18:23-24)**.

He commands him to use an exception when speaking or when he hopes to do an action on the next day. Then, He says: **{And remember thy Lord when thou forget, and say: "It may be that my Lord shall guide me unto a way nigh unto this truth"} (Q. 18:24)**. By such, He means: You should use an exception when you remember after you forgot in the beginning of your affair, so do not let your exception be at the end of your speech after you speak.

It is necessary that the feeding of ten needy people be the expiation for oaths and the feeding of sixty needy people be the expiation for unlawful pronouncements for the one who cannot manumit a slave or fast. It is impermissible to refrain from doing so for some of them if one cannot find all of them. It is necessary that one feed the number of people mentioned by Allah even if he cannot find some of them; he is to wait until he finds them. If he feeds some of them, he would have to wait until he finds all of them.

---

[2] We found the Arabic word *al-idām* difficult to translate since it denotes a category of edibles that has no equivalent in English. We rendered the word as 'condiments' based on the lexicons we consulted; however, the word encompasses more than that. Perhaps, a clearer definition of the word can be seen in the exchange of al-Hādi with Muhammad b. Suleiman al-Kufi in ***Al-Muntakhab***:

> I asked him about a man who swore that he would not use condiments, and he ate with salt, roasting, oil or vinegar. He replied: "As for vinegar, it is considered a condiment, but salt is not considered a condiment." I asked: "What about roasting, broth, sesame oil, onions and similar things which are eaten with bread?" "All of such would be considered condiments except salt and water."

My father related to me that his father was asked about the expiation of oaths and how much should be given to each needy person. He replied:

> It is two *mudd*s of wheat or flour for each needy person along with any condiments that may be there or the equivalent value of it for their lunch and dinner. Similar has been narrated from the Commander of Believers, 'Ali b. Abi Ṭālib, upon him be peace.

My father related to me that his father was asked about feeding the needy for expiation when he cannot find sixty or ten of them. Would it be permissible to refrain from doing so altogether? He replied: "He does not refrain from doing so; rather, he is to wait until he finds the number mentioned by Allah—whether it be sixty needy people or ten needy people."

Concerning repetition of an oath regarding one thing

If a man repeats the same oath regarding one thing—falsely swearing regarding the same thing and not anything else—he would only owe one expiation. However, if he falsely swears regarding something else and then breaks the oath, he shall owe two expiations.

My father related to me that his father was asked about a man who repeats an oath for one thing. He replied: "If it is regarding an oath for the same thing—that he will not do something and then he does it—he only owes one expiation."

Concerning what is to happen for the one who swears the oath

Whoever says "I swear by Allah, I did not do such and such!" or "I swear by Allah, I will not do such and such" or "I swear by the right of Allah…" or "I swear by my Lord…" or "I swear by the Lord who created everything that was and will be…" or "Upon me is Allah's covenant!" or "I swear an oath by Allah!"—all of such would necessitate expiation for the one who falsely swears an oath by such.

My father related to me that his father was asked about a man who says "Upon me is Allah's covenant!" He replied: "I do not see a difference in whether a man says 'Upon me is Allah's covenant!' or 'I swear an oath by Allah!' All of such is considered an oath."

If a man says "I swear that I will not do such and such," he shall be asked his intention. If he intended that he swore by Allah, that would be considered an actual oath and he would owe expiation for it. If he intended that he swore by other than Allah, there would be no expiation for him because people swear by other than Allah regarding many things.

My father related to me that his father was asked about that which a needy person should be clothed with for expiation. He replied: "He is to be clothed with a garment, shirt or its equivalent value if one cannot find a complete garment. There is no specific value."

Concerning which slaves are valid to be used as expiations

The following slaves are valid to be used as expiations for both unlawful pronouncements and oaths when one cannot find otherwise: pre-pubescent, blind, defective, lame, paralyzed, mute and insane. However, if one finds a healthy Muslim slave, it is preferable to use such person.

As for the expiation for unintentional manslaughter, it is only permissible to use a healthy and pubescent slave known for Islam as well as acting upon it. This is because Allah says: **{…he is to manumit a believing slave} (Q. 4:92)**. The believer is one who is known for faith and acting upon its dictates; the judgements shall then apply to such person.

As for that regarding vows, that which one obligates upon oneself would be considered binding. If one intended a sound slave, such person would owe a sound slave. If one intended an old slave, such person would owe an old slave. A person would have to observe that which he vowed to his Lord just as he appointed it to Allah upon himself.

It is permissible to use the slave freed upon his master's death (*al-mudubbar*) as expiation for oaths and unlawful pronouncements; however, it is discouraged for such one to be used as expiation for unintentional manslaughter.

My father related to me that his father was asked about the statement of Allah **{...he is to manumit a believing slave} (Q. 4:92)** and whether it is permissible to use a pre-pubescent, blind, defective, lame, paralyzed, mute and insane slave for such. He replied:

> There is disagreement regarding that; however, all of them are permissible according to me. The sound Muslim slave is preferable unless in the case of expiation for unintentional manslaughter.
>
> The believing slave is one who is known for the practice of Islam and prays, and this is the only one that can be used for unintentional manslaughter. It is therefore valid for a child and the like to be used as expiation for unlawful pronouncements unless such person intended that a sound slave be used. In that case, no other would be valid except a sound slave because the value would be more. He would owe the vows he appointed to Allah upon himself if he made a vow.

Concerning a man who swears an oath and then makes an exception after ending his statement

If someone swears an oath regarding something and makes an exception in his gathering before completing his speech while still standing, then he shall be excused based on such exception. However, if he made an exception after he completed his speech and finished what he said regarding an oath he swore, there would be no excuse for him in that and he would owe expiation if he broke his oath.

My father related to me that his father was asked about a man who swore an oath and made an exception after completing his speech or while in the presence of the people. He replied:

> If he made an exception while still in his gathering before completing his speech, he would be excused. However, if he did not make an exception until after completing his speech and stood from his place, he would owe expiation for his oath and would have no excuse.

Concerning one who swears by other than Allah

Whoever swore by Allah's House or by a *surah* from Allah's Book or by the grave of Allah's Messenger or by the right of any of Allah's Prophets that he would not do something but then sees good in doing such thing as well as sees it as a means of attaining nearness to Allah by doing such, he should do it. There would be no expiation for him because expiation is only due for one who swears by Allah alone.

It would not be due on one who made any of the aforementioned things the object of one's oath. He must fulfil what he swore unless there is something else in which there is good from it and nearness to Allah. Then he must act on what he swore, but there would not be any expiation due on him. Others say that expiation would be due on such person, but we do not hold to that view or say that expiation is due for that.

My father related to me that his father was asked about a man who swore by the entire Qur'an, a *surah* or a verse or by the Sanctified House. He replied: "Swearing by the House or the Qur'an is not an oath that necessitates expiation. Expiation is only due on one who swears by Allah."

There is no problem in manumitting a slave woman's child of fornication for any of the expiations, whether it was for unlawful pronouncements, unintentional manslaughter or oaths. It is impermissible to manumit an indentured labourer as well as any offspring that was contracted along with her or born during her indentured servitude. Her offspring has the same position as she.

If a man were to say "I swore by Allah regarding such and such" and he had not sworn or if he said "I am under oath" and he was not under oath, that would be considered a lie and that which he lied about would not make anything binding on him even if he uttered such oath and said such. That which is not is not binding on him, and he would not be obligated to observe that which he has not made binding on himself.

My father related to me that his father was asked about a man who falsely said: "I swore by Allah" or "I am under oath." He replied: "Such would be considered a lie, but he would not be obligated with that which is not from him."

Concerning one who must observe expiation but cannot find needy Muslims and whether it is permissible to feed or clothe the needy *dhimmi*

It is impermissible to exchange the expiations of the Muslims for the *dhimmi*s. Rather, he would have to consider the poor Muslims until he exchanges it among them and assigns it to them and no others. Others have said that it would be permissible to do so with the poor *dhimmi*s, but we say that it would only be permissible for the poor of the same religion for whom the purification dues are paid by their wealthy. It is by this that Allah passes the judgement regarding their wealth. Therefore, when the purification dues of the Muslims are permitted for them, it would equally necessitate that their expiations and charity would be permitted for them.

My father related to me that his father was asked about a man who intended to feed the needy for expiation of a broken oath but could not find needy Muslims. "Is it permissible to feed the needy among the *dhimmi* Jews and Christians?" He replied: "The idolaters are to not be fed from the expiations; rather, only the needy among the Muslims are to be fed."

Concerning one who was forced to swear a false oath and concerning one who confesses that a child is his but then denies it

Whoever is forced to swear an oath is not considered an oath breaker unless his oath is a means of oppression to the Muslims or if it is out of disobedience to the Lord of creation. If that is the case, he is an oath breaker.

An explanation of that is the following: Someone takes a Muslim's wealth or kills him and takes it. Afterwards, he is forced to swear an oath that he had not taken the wealth or killed. He would be considered as an oath breaker because he is an oppressor. This is because he swore to an act of oppression that was impermissible to swear to. Rather, it is obligatory that he repudiate such act or confess to it.

Whoever confesses to a child being his at one point but then later denies it—it shall not be accepted from him. It would be considered his, and he would be flogged as the prescribed punishment. If it was his *umm walad* with whom he copulated, she would be considered manumitted.

Concerning one who swore an oath to a particular time

If a man swore by Allah to come to someone in the evening time, he would be asked his intention. If he intended by such that he would come to him at the beginning of evening time during its obligatory time and then he comes after that time in the quarter or third of the night, he would be considered an oath breaker. If he had not intended the beginning of the night and then comes before the dawn of the next day, he would not be considered an oath breaker because that is the time of its prayer for one who has a valid reason to delay the prayer, such as the unconscious person who comes to at the end of the night or the menstruating woman who becomes pure at the end of the night.

Similarly, if he swore to come to you after the night prayer, he would be asked his intention. If he intended by that the moment after the completion of his prayer, he would be considered an oath breaker if he delayed. If he had not intended such, he would have the entire night.

Likewise, if he swore to repay a debt to a creditor at a time of day or night, the matter would be as we previously explained to you.

Similarly, if a man swore an oath of divorce so that another person would speak to him or come to him at the outset of the year or the outset of a month, he would be obligated to come to him at the beginning of that next year and end of the previous year. And he shall speak to him on the first night of the coming year between it and the dawn. If the dawn comes before he speaks or comes to him, he would be considered an oath breaker because the night of that coming year had already passed and thus, the end of the previous year had passed. Similar is the case with months. So, understand these two concepts, and utilise sound analogous reasoning with what has come to you, if Allah wills.

Concerning one who swore an oath while he was a minor and then breaks the oath while still a minor or after maturing and concerning the breaking of an oath by a slave

If a pre-pubescent child swears an oath and then breaks it, there shall be no expiation due because the oath is not binding during the time of his youth when he swore it. Similarly, if he swore as a minor that he would not speak to someone and then spoke to him after maturing, there would be no expiation for such in his maturity because he contracted the oath while he was a minor and the initial contracting was not binding. Since he would not be obligated to observe that which he contracted, he would not be obligated to expiate for it.

Similarly—according to me—if a man were to swear an oath of divorce or manumission while he was a minor and then does what he swore he would not do, I do not hold to the view that he would be obligated to observe that which is due by an oath breaker in respect to divorce or manumission. Similar is the case whether he were to do it as a minor or adult since such person swore an oath that he would not do something while he was ten years old or around that age. Consequently, he was not considered mature at the time.

As for the slave, if he were to swear an oath and break it, he would owe expiation if he were mature. The expiation for his broken oath would be to fast three consecutive days, and nothing else would be valid. If his master were to feed or manumit on his behalf, it would not be considered valid. Similar is the case whether it was the expiation for an unlawful pronouncement or unintentional manslaughter; nothing would be valid for him [i.e. the slave] except to fast two consecutive months.

This is because Allah—the Blessed and Exalted—has made these expiations due upon the one who sinned in terms of their wealth and possessions as well as that for which they are responsible as a way to instruct them in etiquette. He also did such so that they may be reprimanded by means of a fine so that they do not return to such action. However, the slave does not own property nor the property of his master. Therefore, he cannot be instructed or reprimanded for such except by that which he can observe himself. It is for that reason that we obligate him to fast, and we do not validate any action from his master whether it is manumission, clothing or feeding.

Concerning one who swore an oath that he would not buy something, sell something or marry

If a man swore an oath that he would not buy or sell something and then he conducts an invalid sale or purchase, it would be permissible for him to gift it, give it as charity or manumit. He would be obligated with that of an oath breaker.

For example, if he sold a gold handle that was six mithqal for five dinars and took the dinar and then gifted it or gave it as charity, this gift and charity would be considered permissible. Similarly, if he sold a slave and freed him, this manumission would be considered valid.

If the transaction between him and the one who took the golden handle for the dinar was void due to him taking less than the weight of the handle, he would be obligated to return the handle he bought until he takes the like of the handle's value—whether in mithqal or gold. This is because the gold must be of like value, and no quantitative disparity must exist between them. The judgement of the transaction is that the amount of five dinars be returned to him similar to the dinar he paid, and he would not be obligated to return the same five dinars that was given in charity or used to manumit a slave.

Similarly, if he bought a slave in exchange for two slaves but made a one-year condition for the sale to be completed and manumitted him before the year's completion, this manumission would be considered binding because he bought him. It shall be judged that he be compensated for his [i.e. the slave's] value on the day he sold it to him, and it shall not be judged upon him for the two slaves because of the delay and debt that occurred since the time he bought him until the time the judgement was passed.

It is impermissible to sell animals, two for one to an appointed time; however, it would permissible to do so from hand-to-hand. A day and two days regarding that is like a month and two months. The slave is to not be returned to him because the buyer had ruined him by manumitting him. Therefore, there is no judgement that something should be returned specifically. Such action of taking something would be considered permissible when it is not returned. The like of it would simply be demanded in the case of credit, or its value would be demanded in the case of a commodity.

The one who swore the oath would be considered an oath breaker because he had ruined the value of the thing, and he would not be judged to return the item specifically and not something else. Therefore, he would be obligated by ruining the value of something in a designated transaction. And when the transaction is binding on him, the penalty for breaking the oath is similarly binding on him.

If a man swore an oath that he would not marry and later engaged in an invalid marriage, he would not be considered an oath breaker because the marriage was not a valid marriage. This is also because a divorce cannot occur with such marriage; it is simply void. In every valid marriage, a divorce can occur. And for one who cannot divorce, there would be no marriage to women.

The marriage in which there is no breaking of an oath is when a man marries his milk sister or a woman who unknowingly shared a milk mother with him or a woman whom he did not know was his wife's mother. It would be similar to a remote land that he does not know of. Therefore, there would be no penalty for oath breaking due to such marriage because a divorce would not be possible nor would she be obligated to have intercourse with him based on such.

Concerning one who is obligated to expiate a number of times when he can only find ten needy people

It is not preferable that he give expiations for a number of oaths to the same ten needy people unless he is unable to find others for any reason. The most that he can give to the same ten people is two expiations—an expiation of feeding and an expiation of clothing. He is to pursue others in the case of additional amounts. However, if he cannot find others, he is to pay it to them at different times. He can feed them every day as expiation.

If he finds a way to send it to the poor and needy in another place, we permit that for him. We simply prefer him to pay it to them when he cannot find others after searching day after day. He is to not pay it to them in total for fear that they may eat three days' worth of expiation in a day and a half or two days instead of three days. This is because it is obligatory for each oath-breaking expiator to feed ten needy people with each expiation of feeding taking place each day.

If he were to feed as expiation for three oaths in two days, it would then be considered two expiations; thus, it would be impermissible for him to feed them for three expiations in two days. Each needy person could be fed three *mudd*s and alternatively a *mudd* and a half each for their lunch and dinner in his house until the three expiations are completed for ten needy people.

It would also be impermissible for him to feed them in their houses by giving all of it to them at once because he would not know how much of it they ate or exchanged it for. Although I would prefer it for myself and those who take care of me, whoever expiates for an oath can invite the needy to his house in order to feed them their lunch and dinner.

If the needy are women in their houses who are unable to leave and come to him, he can send a bowl of bread crumbles (*maftūt*) with condiments to them. I would simply consider that as him feeding them—even if he provides bread crumbles and condiments before sending it to them—because Allah says: **{…and feed ten needy people…} (Q. 5:89).**

He obligates either feeding, manumission or clothing. If he were to invite them to his house or send bread crumbles to them, it would be necessary for them to eat it and not exchange it for other than its worth. If he were to send it to them as grains, he would not be sure that they would not exchange it for anything else but food and eat it.

And if they were to do that, it would not be considered as them being fed. And if they are not considered fed, then it cannot be that he has fed them because feeding is only by food. It would not be sound for him to have fed them until he feeds them food, just as it would not be sound for him to have given them drink until he gives them drink. It would not be sound for him to have hit them until they find the point of contact that he hit, nor could it be considered sound that he addressed them until they hear his statement and understand his command. It would not be sound for him to have perfumed them until they demonstrate the effects of the perfume and find its scent; otherwise, they cannot be considered to have been perfumed.

Similarly, they would not be considered as fed by him until they are fed by his food and their hunger is driven away by such. Otherwise, one would not have observed that which Allah commands regarding the feeding of ten needy people. How could they be considered fed if one had not driven away their hunger by means of feeding them food? Allah simply obligates the manumission of a complete slave or the complete clothing or feeding. Feeding cannot take place unless a person is fed, and such person cannot be fed except by eating.

If he were to assign to them expiations and they were to buy a garment with it or go into a partnership and buy a donkey with it or take a container or leather bottle (*shi'ār*) with it, he would not have observed that which Allah commanded him—whether manumission, clothing or feeding the needy. It is for that reason that we say what we said and explained what we stated.

If it were permissible to feed them for two days by feeding them a *ṣā'* each day and counting that as two expiations in one day, it would be similarly permissible to feed them one expiation in two days. He would then feed the ten a *mudd* each day. This is because the additional amount is the same as a deficient amount in that regard. Then the expiation would be removed from its intended purpose for which it was made.

Concerning that for which none can swear

There are three things for which one cannot swear: fornication, theft and drinking intoxicants. Whoever is implicated for any of the above when the plaintiff does not have evidence for his claim—there would be no prescribed punishment for such person as long as there is no evidence of such which is established.

Whoever claims that a man or woman was a fornicator, he would be asked for evidence of what he said and charged the person of. If he were to come with three witnesses with him being the fourth, the prescribed punishment shall be applied to the accused. If there were not four witnesses, he [i.e. the accuser] would be flogged as the prescribed punishment because he was a slanderer.

The Book of Claims

In the Name of Allah, the Most Gracious, the Most Merciful...

Concerning oaths and evidence as well as for whom they are obligated

Evidence is obligatory upon the one who makes a claim, and oaths are obligatory upon the one who objects.[1] If a man claimed something in the possession of another man, the evidence is upon the plaintiff. No evidence is required from the one who has the item in his possession. If the plaintiff establishes evidence for the item with just witnesses, he shall have more right to it.

If something is in the possession of two men and each one claims it for himself and both bring evidence, the item shall belong to both. If neither one has evidence, both shall be asked to swear to their claim; the item shall belong to both also.

Whoever has a claim against him that necessitates the prescribed punishment of Allah, he would not be adjudicated to swear an oath nor would the prescribed punishment be applied to him. As for the one who has a claim of injury while there is no evidence of such by the plaintiff, we hold to the view that the plaintiff is to swear an oath. That which is for Allah is not like that which is for the slave. This is because the slaves demand their rights, and Allah only obligates the prescribed punishments for that which requires evidence and just witnesses. Because of His compassion for them, the Blessed and Exalted objects to the establishment of such on any of His slaves without just witnesses.

Concerning a woman who claims family ties against a man

Any woman who claims that a man is her paternal/maternal uncle or brother and the man objects to what the woman claimed, the woman shall be asked for evidence of her claim. If she brings evidence, the family ties shall be established, and he would be obligated to financially maintain her. If she does not come with evidence, he shall be asked to swear an oath. If he swears an oath, he shall not be bound to anything regarding her. However, if he refuses to swear an oath, he shall be obligated to financially maintain her. Actual familial ties would not be established between them because familial ties cannot be established by uncertainty. Rather, family ties can only be established by clear evidence.

---

[1] This fundamental jurisprudential principle permeates throughout the ***Ahkām***. It would therefore seem rather implausible that al-Hādi would contradict this principle in his other works. Indeed, Imams Abu Ťālib, Ibn al-Murtaḍa and al-Mu`ayyad Billah noted in their works that a contradictory statement exists in ***Al-Muntakhab*** in which al-Hādi purportedly said that the plaintiff is not obligated to present evidence and the one against whom the claim is made is not under obligation to swear an oath. It is evident that such report from ***Al-Muntakhab*** is an error on the part of a narrator or scribe. Imam al-Mu`ayyad Billah acknowledges this in his ***Sharh at-Tajrīd*** when he said: "As for what has been related from him [i.e. al-Hādi] in ***Al-Muntakhab***, it contradicts his fundamental principle and issue. Therefore, it is not to be ascribed to him. It is possible that it is an error of the narrator."

Imams Abu Ťālib and Ibn al-Murtaḍa also stated in their works that this contradictory statement is due to a mistake on the part of the copyist. It should also be borne in mind that all existent manuscripts of ***Al-Muntakhab*** do not contain this purported statement of al-Hādi. On the contrary, the extant copies of ***Al-Muntakhab*** record al-Hādi as saying that evidence is upon the plaintiff. However—he says—if the plaintiff is unable to provide evidence, he is to swear an oath. [Ref. ***Al-Qawl al-Awwal***]

The Book of Sharecropping (*al-Muzāra'a*)

In the Name of Allah, the Most Gracious, the Most Merciful...

Concerning sharecropping and what is related

There is no problem if a man gives another a date palm or fruit tree to care for, water and cultivate so that he can own a portion of it that was designated at the beginning—whether a little or a lot. Similarly, if he gives another man land to cultivate and grow crops and water and harvest, he can give him a designated portion of it to own—whether a fourth, third, more or less—when he gives it to him or hires him to work on it.

As for giving him some of the fruit for labour, we do not permit that between them due to the uncertainty on the part of the labourer and the oppression against him. Similar is the case with financial maintenance from the landowner or between them.

The most preferable thing to me is that there be financial maintenance from the landowner and that there be an amount of seed shared between the landowner and labourer to the extent of what was stipulated for the labourer. A designated amount of seed is to be extracted for him based on what was stipulated regarding the yield. The matter between them regarding partnership would be based on what we explain in the Book of Partnership.[1]

Concerning the yard of wells and streams as well as their surroundings

The best statement and concept that we have seen and heard regarding this is that the judgement of the source of a spring is that which is five hundred cubits from every direction: the east, west, south and north. One is to not enter it without the owner's permission nor dig in any of the land that it surrounds. The surroundings for a well during the pre-Islamic era was fifty cubits in all directions, and the surroundings for a well during the Islamic era is forty cubits. This is the best of what I have seen and heard regarding that.

Concerning one who constructs a building on an estate without or with the landowner's permission

If a man builds on a people's land without their permission and they come to him seeking to retain their land, the judgement shall be in their favour against him by demolishing what he built on their land and removing his demolished materials from their lot. However, if he builds on their land with their permission and stipulates to them that he and his offspring never be removed from this place, we hold to the view that they are not to remove him unless there is an event that alters his situation.

If that was from him and they had stipulated on him what they stipulated, they are to pay him for what he spent for his house, and that which was from his house would belong to him.

If he had not stipulated on them a place on their land to any specific time and he simply sought their permission to build on it and they give him permission and he builds on it but then they require their land back, they shall pay him the value of his building on the day they required it.

Concerning two partners in regard to the lower level and upper level

If a man owned a house on a lower level and another man owned a place above it and had it demolished but the owner of the lower level objected to building on his lower level and the owner of the upper level intended to restore his home, the judgement shall be in favour of the owner of the lower level. He can seek the value from the owner of the upper level because there could be no upper level without a lower level.

---

[1] Although the original Arabic text in all manuscripts has the word for 'Sharecropping,' it is the translator's humble opinion that from a contextual perspective, the word should be 'Partnership' since Imam al-Hādi is referring to a previous reference.

In the case of financial insolvency, the owner of the upper level would be free to build over the lower level, and the owner of the lower level would not be able to object to his building until [the former] is able to pay his debt.

Similar is the case with the owners of springs. If some of them gave life to it, it would not be permissible for the others to cultivate with it until they repay the cost to the same value that their partners had.

Concerning roads, streets and alleyways that come from every direction when their people dispute regarding their capacity and narrowness

If the people of the roads and streets and alleyways dispute about their alleyways when there is no outlet, I hold to the view that the breadth of the road should be made seven cubits. The breadth of an alleyway in which there is no outlet should be based on the breadth of the widest gate in it. Allah's Messenger, peace and blessings be upon him and his progeny, passed this judgement regarding roads with outlets and roads without outlets.[2]

As for a large road that allows large and overbearing camel litters, I hold to the view that the minimum one should make its breadth is a spear's length (*rumh*), which is about twelve cubits. There is no explanation or measurement narrated from Allah's Messenger, peace and blessings be upon him and his progeny, regarding the roads for camel litters because they did not exist during his time. However, we simply say that this is the measure based on independent judgement from our opinion as well as from what we have observed as the most moderate amount of our measurements. Regarding that, we follow his statement: ((There is no harming or reciprocating harm in Islam)). We therefore made that the proper measure.

We did not make the street wider since the people could quarrel for wider than twelve cubits but then we would have to restrict it for the homeowners who would quarrel. We did not make it less than that since it would be too narrow and restrictive for travellers or others who use the road.

It is the duty of the imam to inspect the roads and streets of the Muslims, as well as their markets and cities. He must illuminate the roads for the pilgrims and build streets, as well as establish waterways and purify the places from which water is drawn. He must facilitate any difficulty he can, as well as cut off any part of a tree that may inflict harm on the passer-by and must destroy tall silos in the cities that overlook into Muslims' homes and display their women to the one who stands on top of them. That is the most appropriate of actions because in their tallness, the one who is in them could dishonour the sanctity of the Muslims and shame the Muslim neighbours of the mosques.

Similarly, he must widen the paths of their roads and protect the people to the right and left from the harm of the passer-by as well as the restriction of the one going to and fro. He must also order them to inspect the lanes and command their owners to clean them and prevent them from becoming too restrictive and narrow. This is because Allah's Messenger, peace and blessings be upon him and his progeny, ordered the cleaning of inner courtyards and commanded that lavatories be moved to streets and roads as well as transferred to the inside of homes.[3]

Concerning two partners who share land and one of them digs a well on the other's land

If two partners jointly own land and one of them digs a well on his partner's land, the former cannot prevent the latter from entering and drinking from it. If there is some harm in it due to agriculture that

---

[2] It is narrated in texts such as ***Ŝahīh Muslim*, *Sunan Ibn Mājah*, *Sunan Abu Dāwūd*** and ***Sunan at-Tirmidhi*** that the Prophet, peace and blessings be upon him and his progeny, said; ((If you disagree on a road, make its breadth seven cubits)).

[3] As for the command to clean inner courtyards, there are reports in ***Sunan at-Tirmidhi***, ***Musnad Abu Ya'la*** and ***Al-Mu'jam al-Awsaṭ***. As for those reports in which the people were commanded to move the lavatories to the sides of roads and inside the houses, it is reported in the ***Mušannaf 'Abdur-Razzāq*** from 'Ali, upon him be peace.

he planted or any other reason that occurred, their proportions must be mutually cancelled and redistributed to a new proportioning. The well and its immediate surroundings will not be included by the owner in the new agreement.

The Book of Gifts, Charity, Life Grants (*al-'Umra*), *Ruqba*, Loaned Items (*al-Ā'riya*) and Entrusted Items (*al-Wadī'a*)

In the Name of Allah, the Most Gracious, the Most Merciful...

Concerning what is permissible and impermissible regarding gifts

Whoever gives someone a gift and it is witnessed that it is for the recipient and the recipient accepts it while it is known specifically as such—such gift is considered permissible. It would be impermissible for the giver to request it back even if the recipient had not taken possession of it but rather accepted it. This is because the witness of its acceptance is greater than taking possession of it.

It is impermissible for people to give other people a gift in an unknown way. If one were to give another a gift in an unknown way without a mutual understanding [that it is a gift], it would be considered invalid and the giver could request it back whenever he wants.

It is impermissible for a Muslim to give some of his offspring gifts to the exclusion of the rest of his offspring unless the recipient is one who spends his wealth very generously on his father, and the majority of them take benefit from such person. Then, he can be given a gift to the exclusion of the others based on his actions and generous spending of his wealth on his father because Allah says: **{Is the recompense for excellent naught save excellence?} (Q. 55:60)**.

As for those who are equal in obedience and generous spending, it would be impermissible to give some of them gifts to the exclusion of others. This is based on a hadith that was related to me from Allah's Messenger, peace and blessings be upon him and his progeny, regarding an-Nu'mān b. Bashīr.[§] He came to Allah's Messenger with his son saying: "Verily, I have gifted this son of mine with a slave that belongs to me." Allah's Messenger, peace and blessings be upon him and his progeny, asked him: ((Do all of your sons have the same gift?)). He replied: "No." Allah's Messenger, peace and blessings be upon him and his progeny, then said: ((Then, reclaim it from him)).[1]

If a man gave another man a gift without seeking any type of divine reward for it and then the recipient died, the gift would be inherited in his house and it would be impermissible for the giver to reclaim it. If a man gave another man a gift without seeking any divine reward or mercy or nearness to Allah and that thing is valued in and of itself and the recipient accepts it while being witnessed but then the giver dies before the recipient is able to take possession of it, that thing would be considered his [i.e. the recipient's]. The giver would not be able to prevent it from being included in the other's inheritance because the witnessing took place as well as the acceptance from the recipient. This is greater than taking possession of it according to us.

Whoever gives someone a gift out of mercy and nearness, it shall be impermissible for him to reclaim it after he has gifted it to him.

Concerning gifts for the slave

If someone gave a slave a gift of a slave girl or house or slave or a riding beast and the slave says "I accept," it would belong to him and his master would be the owner of the slave and what he owns. If the master said "Don't accept it" and the slave said "I accept," the statement would be that of the slave. If the slave said "I do not accept it" and the master said "Accept it," the statement would be that of the slave and the thing would not belong to him. The master would only own something if the slave accepted it.

---

[1] Similarly narrated in ***Sharh at-Tajrīd, Ŝahīh al-Bukhāri, Ŝahīh Muslim, Sunan Abu Dāwūd, Sunan an-Nisā'i, Sunan Ibn Mājah, Sunan al-Bayhaqi, Musnad Ahmed, Ŝahīh Ibn Hibbān, Muwaṭṭa***

Similar is the case if someone bequeathed something to the slave: the matter would be the same. If he accepted it, it would be his. If he did not accept it, it would not be his.

Concerning gifts and charity when they are known, recognised and determined

According to us, there is no problem if a man said to another man: "I have gifted to you this house of mine in such and such place." The gift would be considered permissible according to us. Similar is the case with charity that has not been taken into possession once it is determined, known, mutually understood and witnessed. There is no disagreement regarding that according to the scholars of the Prophet's Progeny. This is also the statement of the Commander of Believers, 'Ali b. Abi Ťālib, upon him be peace.

Its being determined is when one says: "I have gifted you this house of mine that is in such and such place, and its determined boundaries are such and such." Similar is the case with charity. Likewise, if someone said to him "I have gifted this slave girl of mine to you named so-n-so" or "I have gifted this slave of mine to you named so-n-so" or "…this horse of mine" or "…this camel of mine," that would be considered permissible as long as the recipient is present.

Concerning donating a house, land or wealth as charity to a man and he does not take possession of it

Everything that is given in charity to a minor or adult and the charity in his possession is paid with him being informed of it and it is witnessed by the recipient, it would be considered permissible for the one who gave it after it is witnessed and accepted by the recipient. There is no disagreement regarding that according to the scholars of the Prophet's Progeny.

My grandfather, al-Qāsim b. Ibrāhīm, may Allah have mercy on him, said:

> My view regarding that is that the witnessing when it is established is considered more reliable than taking possession of it unless the recipient did not accept it. If it were the case that he does not accept it, the gift and charity would not be considered valid. No evidence regarding that would be useful because maybe the recipient accepted or maybe he had not. If he accepts it with evidence, it shall belong to him. If he does not accept it, it will not belong to him.
>
> As for the minor, that which is donated to him shall be held for him until he is old enough to accept or not accept it.

If it is held for him, its yield and work are also halted on it. If he has a guardian, like a father or grandfather, and he accepts it on his behalf, such acceptance would be valid and permissible.

Concerning one who gifts something seeking an equivalent and concerning an indentured labourer being bought as a slave with what remains

If a giver gifts something seeking an equivalent in value and is not given that equivalent, he can reclaim his gift. If he does not reclaim his gift until after the equivalent of his gift he was seeking was ruined, he can reclaim his gift the moment he comes to know that the item was ruined. If he extends the time after coming to know of the damage an hour or two or a day or two and then he reclaims the gift, it would be impermissible for him to do that because he would have left the gift in the possession of the recipient after that equivalent item was ruined. His leaving that item after having come into the knowledge is a type of contentment with it.

Similarly, if a man gifts another man a dirham but then it is destroyed or mixed with other dirhams to the extent that he does not know his dirham from the others, he would not be able to reclaim it because he was unable to establish which was his. Likewise, if a man were to give another man a gift of paying his debts, he would not be able to reclaim it because the wealth was already used without him being able to establish what was his.

Everything that is gifted for the sake of Allah or to secure family ties shall not be for the donor to reclaim it for any reason.

There is no problem if a man buys an indentured labourer as a slave with the remaining value of his indentured contract as long as the indentured labourer approves of it and his clientage (*al-walā*) is stipulated as belonging to him.

Concerning reclamation of charity

Whoever donates charity to a relative or unrelated person or his young offspring—it is impermissible for him to reclaim it because charity is only for the sake of Allah. Its situation is not like that of gifts. Whoever gives a gift to his young offspring is permitted to reclaim it. However, he would not be permitted to reclaim charity.

Concerning life grants and *ruqba*

Ruqba and life grants are considered gifts when a giver gives them to a recipient saying: "This is for you and your successors" or "...offspring." When the giver says to him that it will belong to him and his offspring, they would be considered more entitled to it than the giver would. The recipient would also have it included as his and his family's inheritance forever.

If he says to him "Verily, I give this house to you as a life grant as long as you live," he can live in it as long as he lives. If he says to him "I give this date palm to you as a life grant as long as you live," he can eat from it as long as he lives. It would belong to him during his lifetime; however, when he [i.e. the recipient] dies, it shall return to the giver's heirs because the believers are obligated to their stipulations.

Regarding that, it has been related in a hadith on the authority of Jābir b. 'Abdullah[§] that the Prophet, peace and blessings be upon him and his progeny, said: ((Whenever a man gives a life grant to another and his successors, it shall belong to the recipient. The one who gave it cannot reclaim it because he gave it as a grant, and it has become inheritance)).[2]

The meaning of his statement ((...it has become inheritance)) is that it has become that which is inherited based on the statement of the giver "...for you and your successors." It is for this reason that this life grant cannot be returned to the giver. As for the giver who does not mention successors, people are obligated to their stipulations.

Concerning a guarantee of loaned items and concerning a man who dies while owing the dowry to his wife

A loaned item that is taken with a guarantee is considered a guaranteed item. If it is not taken with a guarantee, it is not considered a loaned item with a guarantee. Allah's Messenger, peace and blessings be upon him and his progeny, borrowed armour from Šafwān b. Umayya al-Jamhi[§] and was asked: "Is it a guaranteed loaned item or usurped?" He replied: ((Rather, it is a guaranteed loaned item)).[3] Therefore, the Prophet, peace and blessings be upon him and his progeny, guaranteed it and would have paid for it had it been ruined.

---

[2] Similarly narrated in ***Ŝahīh Muslim, Sunan at-Tirmidhi, Sunan an-Nisā'i, Sunan Abu Dāwūd, Muwatta, Musnad Ahmed, Mušannaf Ibn Abi Shayba, Sunan al-Bayhaqi, Jāmi' al-Ušūl, Kanz al-Ummāl, Al-Mu'jam al-Kabīr, Al-Mu'jam al-Awsat***

[3] There are some differences in this report between the hadith texts of the Generality and what was reported by Imam al-Hādi. First, in the hadith of the Generality, the report is on the authority of Ya'la b. Šafwān instead of Šafwān. Second, in the texts of the Generality, the Prophet, peace and blessings be upon him and his progeny, was reportedly asked if it was a guaranteed loaned item or loaned item to be paid back instead of the choice between a guaranteed loaned item and a usurped item as mentioned above. Third, in the texts of the Generality, the Prophet replied to the question ((A loaned item to be paid back)) instead of his answer of ((A guaranteed loaned item)) as was reported by Imam al-Hādi. (Cf. ***Sunan Abu Dāwūd, Sunan an-Nisā'i, Musnad Ahmed, Ŝahīh Ibn Hibbān***).

As for the woman, she would be similar to other creditors regarding her dowry. She would take a share with their shares from her husband's wealth.

My father related to me that his father was asked about loaned items and whether they were guaranteed or not guaranteed. He replied:

> The loaned item is guaranteed when the loaner takes it with a guarantee. Anything other than that which people take as a loan amongst themselves will not be considered a guaranteed loan. The exception is if he differed regarding a riding beast that was loaned to him; he would be held liable for anything that happens to it if he transgressed in that.

And he, may Allah have mercy on him, said: "The wife is similar to other creditors regarding her dowry."

Everything one loans without a guarantee and there is a difference of understanding regarding it—such as one who loans a donkey to a city and rides the donkey to a city which is further than that city or loans it to someone else and it is ruined under his charge—he [i.e. the loaner] would be obligated to pay for it.

Similar is the case with things such as garments and jewellery that are loaned because of the confusion regarding the city. Then, he travelled to another city or loaned it to other people and it was destroyed; it would be obligatory for the loaner to pay for it due to the difference in understanding.

Concerning entrusted items and what Allah commands regarding it

Allah, the Glorified, says: **{And if some amongst thee entrust something to another, let he who is entrusted deliver up that which is entrusted unto him and let him be conscious of Allah, his Lord. Conceal not testimonies; whosoever conceals it shall verily be sinful at heart. And Allah is of what ye do most knowing}** (Q. 2:283).

If a man entrusts an item to another man and it is destroyed, the latter shall not be liable for it unless it was destroyed due to some felonious offense on the part of the entrusted. Then, he shall be held liable. The felonious offense for the loaned item, deposited item or borrowed item or similar between one and another refers to that which is without the loaner's permission. Then, such person would be held liable for it.

If the entrusted person claimed that the item was lost, he would not be held liable for it. His statement would be accepted unless the one who entrusted him accused him; then, he would have to swear an oath.

If two men entrusted a man with an item and the latter did not know which of the two entrusted him and each one of the two claimed it for himself, there is a difference of opinion regarding this issue. The best viewpoint that I hold to is that the entrusted item is to be withheld until its owner brings evidence.

If both were to establish clear evidence and their witnesses are equal in describing the entrusted item and its embellishments, the entrusted item would be divided between them. If neither one of them has evidence, then both are to swear an oath. If one of them refuses to swear and the other one swears, the item shall be given to the swearer. If both of them swear, it shall be divided between them as well.

If a man entrusts another man with a credited item and then dies afterwards and his heir does not know about the entrusted item, he would not have a right to it over them unless he accuses them and swears an oath to them. He must not do anything other than that to them because the deceased had not guaranteed what was entrusted. It is for this reason that he cannot obligate them when they did not know about it or establish that the deceased entrusted what he claimed.

The Book of Lost and Found Items

In the Name of Allah, the Most Gracious, the Most Merciful...

Concerning lost and found items

It is for the imam to appoint a storehouse (*mirbad*) for the lost items of the Muslims. Therefore, everyone who picks up a lost item is to take it to this storehouse, and they [i.e. the riding beasts] shall be foddered from the Muslims' public treasury. Every lost item that is claimed by a Muslim with evidence shall be given to him.

If there is a time in which there is no imam to do such and one takes the lost item, I hold to the view that he must keep it because he has assumed responsibility for it by taking it. He is to cause it to be known and proclaim it. Then, if its owner were to come for it, such person would be liable to the one who kept it for anything that was spent on its upkeep. However, if it were to remain in his possession, it would be a trust for him.

If it were ruined, the liability would be on its owner when it is sought out. If it were destroyed due to a felonious offense, then he [i.e. the one who kept it] would be held liable; he would have to pay the owner its value when the latter comes to seek it out. If it were destroyed without felonious offense from him or anyone else, he would not be held liable for it.

Similar is the case with found items according to us that it is binding upon the one who found it. It would be impermissible for him [i.e. the finder] to utilise or completely use it. He must make it known whether it remained with him for a long time or not. This is because if he wanted to, he could leave it, and no one would be obligated to take it. And if he were to completely use it until it is ruined, he would be held liable for it.

Concerning male and female foundlings when they are found

When people find a male and female foundling, they are to raise them until they are older. They are to not sell them or give them as gifts. They are to be considered free, and one is to financially maintain them. One cannot reclaim what was spent on them; that would be considered voluntary for him.

If a man found a slave girl, he is to raise her and not have intercourse with her except by way of marriage. If he is ignorant of such and has intercourse with her, they are to be separated and he would be obligated to provide a dowry for her to the value of her like. If he wanted to marry her, he would have to marry her with a sound marriage and a new dowry.

Similarly, if the one who found her sold her and a man bought her but the former had intercourse with her, the matter would be brought before the magistrate who will judge in favour of the buyer over the seller with the price being returned to the one who took from it. It shall be judged that the one who had intercourse with her would have to pay the dowry to the value of her like, and they would be separated. It is the best thing to discipline the seller and buyer unless they claimed ignorance of what is obligatory upon them. If he wanted to marry her, he would have to marry her with a sound marriage and a new dowry likewise.

Similar has reached us from the Commander of Believers, 'Ali b. Abi Ťālib, upon him be peace. A woman came to him seeking his assistance against a man. He bought a slave girl from her, and he still owed money for her. She said: "O Commander of Believers, I have a right over this man!" The man said: "I bought a female foundling from her." She replied: "The woman, yes! O Commander of Believers, I left for the mosque to pray the dawn prayer, and a girl was on the street. I took her and hired a wet nurse for her. I financially maintained her until she reached puberty and then sought to benefit from her." 'Ali said to the woman: "May Allah reward you for taking care of her!" He asked the man: "Did you have intercourse with her?" He replied: "Yes." He [i.e. 'Ali] then said to the woman: “You do not have a right over her. Seek from her your asset before that. Give the woman a dowry of one similar to herself.” He then said: “There cannot be intercourse without a dowry.”

The Book of Prescribed Punishments *(al-Hudūd)*

In the Name of Allah, the Most Gracious, the Most Merciful...

Concerning the prescribed punishment for fornication in the Book

Allah—the Blessed and Exalted—says regarding fornicators: {**The fornicatress and fornicator—flog each one of them one hundred stripes. And let not pity for them twain prevent thee from Allah's religion if ye truly believe in Allah and the Last Day. And let their punishment be witnessed by a party of believers**} (**Q.** 24:2).

He obligates one hundred lashes upon the fornicators when they are free and pubescent. And there should be four just witnesses from the Muslims. They must establish their testimony to the imam regarding the withdrawal and penetration; the magistrate must also have knowledge of the soundness of their intellects. At that point, each one of them is to be lashed one hundred times as Allah commands.

As for His statement {**And let not pity for them twain prevent thee from Allah's religion**}, the word {**pity**} refers to mercy, compassion, kindness and weakness regarding their matter when it comes to lashing them if they are able to withstand the pain. As for the party that Allah commands to witness it, it refers to a group of believers—more sometimes and less sometimes. It has been said that the minimum of a party is six: the imam, four witnesses and the flogger.

As for two unmarried persons (*al-bikrān*), each one is to only be flogged one hundred times and nothing else. As for two married persons (*ath-thayyābān*), it has been authentically narrated that Allah's Messenger, peace and blessings be upon him and his progeny, ordered that the both of them be stoned. There is no disagreement among the narrators regarding the stoning that he stoned Mā'iz b. Mālik al-Aslami and that the Commander of Believers, 'Ali b. Abi Ťālib stoned Shurāhat al-Hamadhāni.[1]

The judgement of stoning continued after Allah's Messenger, peace and blessings be upon him and his progeny, and no two people disagreed about it, nor did any two people debate about it. 'Umar b. al-Khaťťāb stoned while there were many of the Prophet's Companions, including the Commander of Believers, 'Ali b. Abi Ťālib, yet no one objected to him doing that. The Commander of Believers, upon him be peace, used to flog and then stone. He used to say: "Flogging is in the Book of Allah, and stoning has come from Allah through Allah's Messenger, peace and blessings be upon him and his progeny."[2]

The greatest of proofs regarding the obligation of stoning is that Allah's Messenger, peace and blessings be upon him and his progeny, used to stone and order stoning.[3] He, peace and blessings be upon him and his progeny, is the model and example to follow. Allah has said: {**Verily there is for thee in Allah's Messenger a great model for the one who hopes for Allah and the Last Day**} (**Q. 33:21**) and {**Obey Allah and obey the Messenger**} (**Q. 4:59**) and {**Whatsoever the Messenger gives thee, take it. Whatever he prohibits thee from, leave it**} (**Q. 59:7**).

So, if an objector would like to object or an inquirer would like to inquire and seek guidance, he may say: "We do not find stoning mentioned in the Book of Allah as an obligation upon the fornicator; rather, we only find the judgement of one hundred lashes for the fornicator. Where can we find evidence for the obligation of stoning?"

---

[1] It is related in ***Al-Jāmi' al-Kāfi*** that Imam al-Hasan b. Yahya said:

> It is the consensus of the Prophet's Progeny that Allah's Messenger, peace and blessings be upon him and his progeny, obligated the stoning for the married man and woman and that it is incumbent for the imam to act upon that without neglecting or acting contrary to it as a judgement.

[2] Similarly narrated in ***Musnad Ahmed, Al-Mustadrak, Al-Mu'jam al-Awsaț, Sunan al-Bayhaqi, Sunan ad-Dārqutni***

[3] Similarly narrated in ***Ŝahīh Muslim, Sunan Abu Dāwūd, Sunan at-Tirmidhi, Sunan Ibn Mājah, Musnad Ahmed, Sunan al-Bayhaqi***

We reply to him: Glorified be Allah! Did Allah neglect anything for which He did not make its basis in the Book? The basis of stoning can be found in the Qur'an to the one with thorough understanding. And Allah's Messenger, peace and blessings be upon him and his progeny, observed it by the order of Gabriel from Allah, the Mighty and Majestic. Is it not the case that Allah commanded him upon the tongue of Gabriel to do it just as He commanded him to perform other rudimentary actions whose basis is in the Book? He detailed and explained its rudimentary actions upon the tongue of Gabriel, upon him be peace. This includes the prayer, the number of its obligations and bowings, as well as the purification dues, an explanation of what Allah desires to be taken and the minimum and maximum of wealth that necessitates it. He establishes the basis of the command with His statement **{Establish the prayer and render the purification dues} (Q. 73:20)**. The believers would not know what he has obligated them of their wealth nor when they are obligated to pay the purification dues from what is in their possession unless Allah differentiates and explains it after stating its basis and obligation in the Book. He explained the details to His Prophet, peace and blessings be upon him and his progeny, upon the tongue of Gabriel, upon him be peace. Gabriel then commanded the Messenger, peace and blessings be upon him and his progeny, and the Messenger commanded his *Ummah* to do so just as Allah commanded him. He made the noon prayer four units, the late noon prayer four units, the sunset prayer three units, the night prayer four units and the dawn prayer two units. However, the numbers of units and details did not come in the Book.

Similar is the case with the purification dues. Allah's Messenger, peace and blessings be upon him and his progeny, commanded that five dirhams be paid from two hundred dirham of silver, half a mithqal be paid from twenty mithqal of gold, a lamb be paid from five camels, a male or female calf be paid from thirty cows and a lamb be paid from forty sheep. Regarding that which is extracted from the earth, a tithe is taken from that which is watered naturally, and a half tithe is taken from that which is watered artificially once it reaches the measure of five *wasq*s. A *wasq* is sixty *šā's* from the *šā'* of the Prophet, peace and blessings be upon him and his progeny. The Blessed and Exalted pardoned that which was below five *wasq*s. None of such was explained in detail in the Book; it was simply that which came from the trustworthy Messenger from the One, the Manifest Reality.

Had it not been for the detailed explanation and explication upon the tongue of the Messenger, one would assume that one could be taken from a lamb, camel and cow or that one dinar, dirham and *makūk* could be taken. Similar is the case with the prayer; had Allah not explained it upon the tongue of the Messenger, such as its details, restrictions the number of units and its obligations—one would pray one or two units or even one hundred units. The people would not be able to determine the restrictions of the prayer and the purification dues.

Allah has done likewise with the stoning just as He has done with the prayer and purification dues. He has mentioned its performance for those who engaged in anal fornication among the people of Lot, as well as the prescription of stoning for them based on their acts of fornication. He passed a judgement, and we do not do other than what He passed as a judgement. We would never pass a judgement that he Himself had not done. It is established that He passed such judgement so one does not act contrary to His judgement. Similarly, the Glorified says: **{This is the tradition (*sunnah*) of Allah regarding those who passed from aforetime. Never shall ye find for Allah's tradition a substitute} (Q. 33:62).**

The front and rear private parts as well as their judgement are considered the same according to the one who knows about judgements as well as the determination of what is permissible and prohibited. This is because one who engages in illicit anal intercourse with a woman is like one who commits illicit vaginal intercourse with her. This is considered the same to all the people of Islam; the judgement of both is considered equal. Therefore, if it is established as sound that the judgement of the front and rear private parts is the same, then the judgement of stoning is also established as sound to the one of intellect and fairness based on Allah's stoning the people of Lot for what they did.

That is derived from His statement: {**He said: "What then is thy errand, O Messengers?" They replied: "Verily, we have been sent unto a people most wicked that we may send upon them stones of clay marked by thy Lord for those who exceed the bounds**} (**Q. 51:31-35**).

Therefore, if the Glorified prescribed stoning for those who engaged in fornication among the people of Lot, the mention of stoning establishes its basis as Allah's Judgement in the Qur'an. And that which Allah has done—the One too majestic to be encompassed by words—was obligated upon the Messengers so that they did it, passed its judgement and appointed it. By doing so, they imitated the action of Allah. Whatever the Messengers did was obligatory for the imams to do and imitate.

If an objector objects by saying "We have found that Allah obligated that the fornicator be lashed one hundred times," say to him: That is obligatory upon the unmarried person specifically. It is also obligatory upon the married person along with stoning. The unmarried person is to be lashed one hundred times, and the married person is to be lashed one hundred times also as Allah commands in His Book. Then, the latter is to be stoned as Allah commanded upon the tongue of his Prophet, peace and blessings be upon him and his progeny. Had it not been a command from Allah to His Prophet, then Allah's Messenger, peace and blessings be upon him and his progeny, would not have done it out of his consideration for the shedding of Muslims' blood and taking their lives without Allah's command. He would not have passed such judgement upon them for fornication.

Allah distinguishes between one He has favoured with a blessing and allows him to get married, own a slave, permit intercourse and suffices him from that which He has prohibited him. However, such person is not content with that until he pursues the prohibited and abandons the permissible that Allah has graced him with. Then, he was exempted from the women of the Muslims after having been sufficed with that by the Lord of creation. Afterwards, he sinned with them and transgressed after his chastity and sufficiency. He then corrupted cultivation and progeniture by such. Allah has enriched him and preoccupied him with permissible sexual relations.

Allah distinguishes between such person and the one who slips into carnal needs due to the stirring of lower desires and imprinting of acting upon it. Such person is given to sexual desires (*maj'ūl*) to the one who has not married so that he has not refrained from intercourse with his wife nor has he been provided with riches as another was provided. He is thereby stirred by a need that stirs a similar person to act upon his lower desires with a similar person. Therefore, Allah obligates that such person who slips and fornicates out of carnal need and is overcome and afflicted is lashed one hundred times.

Also, Allah obligates flogging and stoning for the one who commits adultery and fornicates recklessly and insolently as well as acts ungrateful to Allah's blessings, commits tyranny and desires the corruption of Muslims' cultivation and progeniture as well as the illegal attribution of offspring to those to whom the offspring do not belong. Rather they would be considered the offspring of sinning fornicators insomuch that noble lineage is degraded recklessly, and corruption is allowed to enter the Muslims' progeniture and offspring insolently. Consequently, brotherhood would be between those who are not brothers. Muslim women would be considered the aunts of those for whom they are not actually aunts, grandmothers for those for whom they are not actually grandmothers and sisters for those for whom they are not actually sisters. The wealth of the Muslims would be invalidly inherited to those who are not their sons and daughters. Oppression, transgression, blindness and iniquity would take place after there had been sufficiency and abstinence by Allah. Such flogging and stoning would be suitable punishment for the one who sinned and transgressed as well as corrupted progeniture and lineage.

There is just as much clear distinction between the sinner who sins after carnal need and intense affliction and the one who does such without carnal need, compulsion, affliction or the drive to urge himself to that which summons him as there is a clear distinction between one who is compelled to do something and one who is not compelled in everything. For the ignorance of the blind there is a clear distinction between these two fornicators, and the wisest would clearly distinguish between these two.

How could there not be a clear distinction between them to the ignorant when the distinction is as clear and illuminated by the light of shining certainty?

The objector may persist in his objection and say: "Maybe it is authentically attributed to Allah's Messenger, peace and blessings be upon him and his progeny, that he stoned Mā'iz b. Mālik al-Aslami in successively transmitted reports and narrations. If that were indeed the case, then it would not be permissible to reject or invalidate them. Perhaps, Allah's Messenger, peace and blessings be upon him and his progeny, stoned Mā'iz b. Mālik due to personal opinion that was specific to him. That withstanding, such action of his would not be binding on the *Ummah* and anyone else other than him. It would be like anything else that would not be binding on the people to do that was based on his own personal opinion; it would not be binding on his *Ummah* nor anyone else from his religion."

If he were to say that, say to him that such was not based on his own personal opinion, nor would it be permissible to attribute such to a Prophet who was sent as a guide or the imam after him who is to be imitated. This is because it would be the wanton shedding of Muslim blood, and Allah has said regarding the one who kills a believer **{And whosoever slays a believer intentionally—his recompense shall be Hell therein to abide forever. And Allah's anger shall be upon him as well as His curse. And he shall ready for him a great punishment}** **(Q. 4:93)** and **{Whosoever slays a soul—save for manslaughter or corruption in the earth—it shall be as if he had slain all humankind. And whosoever saves a life, it shall be as if he saved all humankind}** **(Q. 5:32)**. Allah does not excuse the shedding of blood for any of His Prophets unless it is due to a right that is obligated upon the killer by means of Allah's judgement.

Allah prohibits the shedding of blood except after caution, warning and the response to such by His statement: **{And if thou should fear from the people treachery, then throw back unto them [the treaty] so as to be equal. Verily Allah loves not the treacherous}** **(Q. 8:58)**. It wasn't permitted for the Prophet, peace and blessings be upon him and his progeny, to kill the idolaters and those at war with him until after warning and caution. Therefore, how could it have been permissible for him to kill Muslims, and how could it have been valid for the Messenger of the Lord of creation to act contrary to Allah's command in that? It is impossible that Allah's Messenger, peace and blessings be upon him and his progeny, be attributed to such due to his repulsion to shedding Muslims' blood. Allah forbid that His Messenger would do such or act contrary to any of Allah's commands!

Whoever says that Allah's Messenger, peace and blessings be upon him and his progeny, acted on his own personal opinion and killed any of the Muslims contrary to Allah's command has slandered Allah's Messenger with the greatest of the major sins. Such person must repent to Allah from the obscenity of his statement and show remorse to Him for his bold insolence against Allah's Messenger, peace and blessings be upon him and his progeny. Otherwise, he would be among the destroyed who insolently slandered Allah's Messenger with one of the greatest of major sins! This would be the case whether it was an Arab who said it or non-Arab. Such statement would be considered grave, unjust and a transgression against him. It would be impermissible for any Muslim to say such about any other Muslim; how much more so would it be impermissible to say about the Messenger of the Lord of creation? Has not the one who uttered this obscenity not heard what the Most Gracious has said regarding His Messenger in the Qur'an: **{Verily, he follows not save that which was revealed unto him…}** **(Q. 10:15)**?

The obstinate may return to his obstinacy and say: "It is clear to me that Allah's Messenger, peace and blessings be upon him and his progeny, would not be permitted to do something unless it was by Allah's command. It has come in authentic narrations that he had Mā'iz b. Mālik al-Aslami stoned. Perhaps he stoned him due to a reason other than fornication."

If he were to say that, say to him: This is an arrogant statement and an impossibility from you because the narrations that were authenticated establish that Mā'iz confessed himself to Allah's Messenger that he committed fornication just as it was authentically established that he was stoned. No one who is fair would doubt that he was stoned for the fornication for which he confessed.

Do you have anything to bring forth in which the people agree with you that he was stoned without confessing to fornication just as there is agreement that he was stoned for confessing to Allah's Messenger that he committed fornication? If so, bring it forth. Otherwise, you would have to return to the truth and say farewell to the arrogance, transgression in deviance, connection to impossibilities and invalid obscenity in your statement.

Stoning remained during the time of Moses and before him until Allah sent it to His Prophet, peace and blessings be upon him and his progeny. Gabriel commanded it just as he commanded other things that have come to the Prophet, peace and blessings be upon him and his progeny, from his Lord that have their basis in the Clear Book. One of the proofs that stoning was an earlier judgement from Allah against married persons is Allah's statement through His Prophet to the Jews and their repulsion from the Torah and distorting Allah's judgement: **{...and of the Jews, those who pay heed to falsehood, listen to other people who hath not come unto thee—distorting words from their places...} (Q. 5:41)**. He intends by that their distorting the judgement of stoning in the Torah.

This verse was revealed regarding the matter that occurred with Busra, the Jewess. This is because Allah revealed to Moses b. Imrān the judgement of stoning for the adulterer. The Jews then altered that and substituted flogging in its place. They flogged with forty lashes using a cord with tar and used to darken their faces. They placed him on a donkey and faced him backwards on the donkey with him facing its tail. They continued to do that until the Prophet, peace and blessings be upon him and his progeny, emigrated to Medina. A Jewish woman named Busra was brought with a man. The Jews desired to flog her, but they feared that the Prophet, peace and blessings be upon him and his progeny, would expose them for changing the judgement from the Torah. The rabbis among them said out of derision: "We will go to Muhammad and ask him about the prescribed punishment for fornication. If he says that he should be flogged, we will accept it from him. If he commands that he be stoned, we will object to that and not accept it." They came to the Prophet, peace and blessings be upon him and his progeny, and asked him. He replied: ((There is to be stoning if he was married)). They replied: "Moses commanded that the married person be flogged." The Prophet, peace and blessings be upon him and his progeny, said to them: ((You lied! He commanded you to stone, and he stoned)). They said: "Certainly not!" He then said to them: ((Appoint an arbitrator between you and me)). They said: "Choose who you would like." Gabriel came to him and said: "Appoint a tall, one-eyed young man from the people of Khaybar named 'Abdullah b. Šūriya." The Prophet, peace and blessings be upon him and his progeny, called them and asked ((Do you know a man from the people of Fadak?)) and then described him to them. They replied: "Yes." He then asked: ((How is his knowledge of the Torah among you?)). They replied: "He is the most knowledgeable of the Torah among us." He said: ((He can arbitrate between you and us)), and they agreed to that. They sent for him and he came to the Prophet, peace and blessings be upon him and his progeny, with the Jews. The Prophet, peace and blessings be upon him and his progeny, asked him ((Are you Ibn Šūriya?)), and he replied: "Yes." He then asked ((Are you the most knowledgeable Jew regarding the Torah?)), and he replied: "Yes." The Prophet, peace and blessings be upon him and his progeny, then said: ((I implore you by Allah, the Most Merciful who revealed the Torah to Moses b. Imrān and drowned the people of Pharaoh while you were looking—what did Allah reveal to Moses about fornication?)). His body began trembling with fear, and he replied: "Stoning." The Jews then started to say to him: "Why did you tell him?!" He replied: "He made me swear an oath! If I had not told him what he asked of me, the Torah would have engulfed me in flames!" The Jews said: "Ibn Šūriya is a liar! That is not in the Torah!"

'Abdullah b. Salām[§] said to the Prophet, peace and blessings be upon him and his progeny: "Appoint the Torah as an arbitrator between you and them. It is written inside." The Prophet, peace and blessings be upon him and his progeny, said: ((Let the Torah arbitrate between you and me!)). They replied: "Yes." The Prophet, peace and blessings be upon him and his progeny, rode to the teacher's house on his donkey along with his Companions. He said to them: ((Do not initiate the greetings of peace to the Jews. If they greet you with peace, say: "And the same to you.")). The Prophet, peace and blessings be upon him and his progeny, came to the teacher's house and entered. He said ((Bring the Torah)), and they brought it. The one who was present was Judayy b. Akhtab and not Huyayy b. Akhtab. 'Abdullah b. Salām sat with him and said: "Read the section on prescribed punishments." He did so but when he came to the passage about stoning [Deuteronomy 22:23-24], he covered it with his thumb. 'Abdullah b. Salām said to him "Lift your hand!" and he did so. He said: "Read it!" He read in the Torah that stoning was clearly stated by Allah.[4]

As for His statement **{So if they come unto thee, judge thou between them or turn away from them} (Q. 5:42)**, it is an abrogated verse that was abrogated by the statement of Allah: **{Judge thou between them with that which Allah has revealed, and follow not their caprices} (Q. 5:49)**. He is obligated to judge between the People of the Book by the judgements Allah has revealed in the Book and upon them. Therefore, Allah's Messenger, peace and blessings be upon him and his progeny, was commanded by these verses that were revealed regarding the two fornicating Jews and he therefore had them stoned.

Similar has been stated by Allah when He says: **{And for those who are guilty of an open indecency from amongst thy women, call to witness against them four from amongst thee. If they bear witness, confine them to their houses till they are taken by death or till Allah appoints a way for them} (Q. 4:15)**. This was the first to be revealed to the Prophet, peace and blessings be upon him and his progeny, regarding the matter of two fornicators before He revealed to him what He revealed regarding the prescribed punishments. That is the **{way}** that Allah mentioned that He would appoint.

The imam should not reprimand or use harsh words against the accused in order to get a confession because it has been narrated that there is no prescribed punishment on the one who confesses after an affliction.

Also, the imam must not strike or stone until it is clear to him that she is not pregnant due to her being free from such by the menstruation Allah has made for her. Allah only made it as a way for her herself and not any child in her womb. This is because there would be no ensuring for her that she would not lose the child in her womb if she were to be flogged while pregnant. Similarly, if she were to be stoned to death, it would kill what is in her womb. It is not from the judgements of the Lord of creation that the imam kills two souls for one. Rather, it is obligatory that the imam of the Muslims allows her to be free from what is in her womb. Once she is free from the foetus, then the judgement of the Lord of creation is to be applied to her. If she is pregnant with her foetus, he must wait for her to deliver her child and then wait for her child to be naturally separated and independent of her. Once her child becomes independent of her, the prescribed punishment is to be applied to her unless one cannot be found to feed the child. If someone can be found to feed the child who is reliable, the prescribed punishment would be applied to her and guardian would take responsibility for all the child's affairs.

Similar has reached us from the Commander of Believers, 'Ali b. Abi Ṭālib, upon him be peace. During the government of 'Umar, a woman was brought to him. He asked her, and she confessed to fornication. He then ordered her to be stoned. Then, 'Ali, upon him be peace, met her and asked: "What's wrong with her?" He was told: "'Umar ordered that she is to be stoned." 'Ali, upon him be peace, sent her back and asked: "Did you order for her to be stoned?" He [i.e. 'Umar] responded by saying: "Yes. She confessed to me that she fornicated." 'Ali said: "This is your judgement on her, but what is your judgement on that which is in her womb?" 'Umar replied: "I did not know that she was pregnant!" 'Ali said: "If you do not know, then she is to be free of what is in her womb." Then 'Ali said: "Perhaps, you strongly reprimanded her or used harsh words against her." 'Umar replied that this was the case. 'Ali said: "Haven't you heard Allah's Messenger, peace and blessings be upon him and

---

[4] Similarly narrated in ***Ŝaḥīḥ al-Bukhāri, Ŝaḥīḥ Muslim, Al-Muwaṭṭa, Sunan Abu Dāwūd, Sunan al-Bayhaqi, Ŝaḥīḥ Ibn Hibbān***

his progeny, say: ((There is no prescribed punishment on one who confesses after an affliction))? Perhaps, she confessed because you threatened her." Then, 'Ali, upon him be peace, asked her about that, and she replied: "I did not confess except out of fear!" He then ordered for her to be released. Afterwards, 'Umar said: 'Women are too inadequate to give birth to the like of 'Ali! Had it not been for 'Ali, 'Umar would have perished!"[5] It is also narrated that 'Umar used to say: "May Allah not cause me to be in a difficulty for which I cannot ask the son of Abu Ťālib!"[6]

The Commander of Believers, 'Ali b. Abi Ťālib, upon him be peace, was not a fool in position, small in state, a shirker of command, less in patience, distant from mercy, ignorant of what the Qur'an says, lacking in compassion for the subject or confused regarding the order upon humankind. He was the brother of the Chosen Messenger, the guardian of the one who believes and is guided, the helper of the Religion, the one who established the proof of the Lord of creation, the one who ruled by the Clear Book, the one who sacrificed himself for Allah and His Messenger, the one who brandished his sword for the truth of others, the killer of the opponents, the one who re-routed the warriors from every aspiration with might, the one who broke through enemy lines, the keeper of family bonds (*al-ayāšir*), and the one was related to wield the sword that brings benefit. He was the father of the Two Pure Grandsons, al-Hasan and al-Hussein, the sons of Allah's Messenger, peace and blessings be upon him and his progeny. He was the foremost warrior in the way of Allah with whom there was no one else to precede him. He was the first of the Muslims and the noblest of followers and emigrants. He was designated with 'belief' in the Qur'an, as well as judged with guardianship and spiritual excellence. That is from the statement of the One, the Most Merciful **{Is the believer like unto him who is disobedient? Nay! They are not equal} (Q. 32:18)**[7] and **{The forerunners are the forerunners! They are those who art brought nigh} (Q. 56:10-11)** and **{Verily, thy only Guardian is Allah, His Messenger, and those who believe—those who establish the prayer and render the dues whilst bowing} (Q. 5:55)**. This is only a fraction of what is mentioned about him in the Qur'an of which those who feign ignorance are not ignorant or unmindful of except the treacherous oppressors! **{And those who oppress shall come to know what reversal of fate shall befall them} (Q. 26:227)**.

Concerning when the prescribed punishment is obligated upon the married and unmarried by witness

The prescribed punishment is not obligated upon the fornicator until the act of fornication—penetration and withdrawal—was witnessed by four just witnesses.[8] When the four witnesses witnessed such, the imam must ask about the justice of the witnesses, their intellects, their Islam and their vision. Perhaps there is a *dhimmi* among them for which his testimony is impermissible based on religion. Perhaps there is a blind man among them for which his blindness is not apparent except to the one who knows him; it may be cataracts. That might not be apparent to the imam unless he asked about his sight.

Once that is the case, he is to inquire as to whether there is some type of animosity between the witnesses and the accused [lit. "witnessed"] so that he may dismiss such. The imam must not accept the witness of an enemy who has animosity for another due to bias, the mixing of issues as well as the

---

[5] Similarly narrated in ***Musnad Imam Zayd* و *Farā`id as-Simtayn, Bihār al-Anwār***. The same is narrated in texts such as the ***Mušannaf Ibn Abi Shayba*, *Sunan ad-Dārqutni*** and ***Sunan al-Bayhaqi***, except the name of 'Ali is substituted with Mu'ādh b. Jabal.

[6] Similarly narrated in ***Fađā'il as-Sahaba, al-Isti'āb, Usd al-Ghāba, Tārīkh Dimashq, Farā`id as-Simtayn, Bihār al-Anwār***

[7] Many texts dedicated to Qur'anic exegesis narrate that this verse was revealed regarding 'Ali b. Abi Ťālib, upon him be peace. One of which is ***Asbāb an-Nuzūl*** by al-Wāhidi. He narrates: "The term **{believer}** refers to 'Ali b. Abi Ťālib, and the term **{disobedient}** refers to al-Walīd b. 'Uqba."

[8] In ***Al-Muntakhab***, al-Hādi was asked: "Why is it that Allah necessitates four witnesses for fornication but only two witnesses for manslaughter?" He replied:

> It is because fornication is the action of two fornicators, and Allah appoints two witnesses for each of the two fornicators. There is no prescribed punishment for less than two witnesses. As for manslaughter, Allah only appoints two witnesses because the both of them testify against the killer on behalf of the victim.

lack of accurate and true testimony. The imam must be cautious of that as well as careful, astute, standing off the middle of his soles[9], intellectual, fervent regarding Allah's command, judge in Allah's judgements, one who does not act upon doubts and one who does not delay from proper application.

Regarding that, Allah—the Mighty and Majestic—says: **{O ye who believe, if a disobedient person comes to thee with news, verify it lest ye afflict a people ignorantly and become regretful for what ye did commit} (Q. 49:6)**. Allah's Messenger, peace and blessings be upon him and his progeny, said: ((Refrain from the prescribed punishments in the case of doubtful matters)).[10] The Commander of Believers, 'Ali b. Abi Ṫālib, upon him be peace, said: "A mistake in pardon is more preferable to me than a mistake in punishment."[11]

When we mentioned the statement of Allah and His Messenger and the Commander of Believers, what we are saying is that the imam of the Muslims must be cautious in the affairs of people. We are also saying that abstention in the case of a doubtful matter is better than acting on an error.

Once the imam has confirmed the matter of the witnesses, he must inquire about the accused in order to establish the soundness of his intellect and intelligence. Then he must inquire as to whether such person is free or a slave. Then he must inquire as to whether such person is married or not. If two just witnesses bear witness that he is married, the imam is to ask them both the basis of his marriage. If the two of them establish his marriage itself, they must inform him that he had gathered his wife and family. Then, he is to establish the prescribed punishment for adultery: he is to be flogged a hundred times and then stoned. The priority of stoning him goes to the four witnesses, then the imam after them, then all the Muslims or whoever is present at the stoning from them.

If he were to inquire about him and it was mentioned that he was unmarried and it is proven that he is not married to a woman who is currently pregnant or divorced, he is to be flogged with one hundred lashes. One is to not have any compassion or mercy on him just as their Lord commands them.

Similarly, the imam must be cautious in the affairs of the woman just as he is cautious in the affairs of the man because their matter is the same regarding their crime according to Allah. The prescribed punishment and its various judgements are the same for both according to the Glorified.

Concerning when the prescribed punishment is obligated upon the one who confesses to fornication

In the case of one who confesses to fornication, it is obligatory for the imam to divert himself from him, rebuff him and not act upon what he said. If he were to leave and not return to him [i.e. the imam], the imam is to not inquire about him. However, if he refuses and persists in repeating his statement and bringing up his charge on himself, he [i.e. the imam] is to continue to rebuff him with each easy and non-distressing confession until he confesses against himself four times.

Once he has maintained his confession and testimony against himself for committing fornication, the imam must ask him about fornication, its meaning and manner. When it is proven that he knows the meaning, he must inform him of the prescribed punishment for fornication and that his sexual relations with the woman was religiously prohibited just as sexual relations with his wife is permissible. Then, he must ask [the confessor] about his intellect as well as research the extent of his understanding.

Once his intellect is shown to be sound, he is to inquire as to whether [the confessor] is free or a slave. Then, he is to command that he be flogged. He is to be flogged with one hundred lashes if he is free and fifty lashes if he is a slave. The Muslims are to not have pity or mercy on him. If he is unmarried,

[9] An Arabic epithet used to describe good and noble qualities. [See **Lane's Arabic English Lexicon**]

[10] Similarly narrated in ***Sharh at-Tajrīd, Amāli Ahmed b. 'Isa, Sunan al-Bayhaqi, Kanz al-'Ummāl, Bihār al-Anwār***

[11] Similarly narrated in ***Sharh at-Tajrīd, Sunan at-Tirmidhi, Sunan ad-Dārqutni, Sunan al-Bayhaqi, al-Muwaṫṫa, Mušannaf Ibn Abi Shayba***

then the flogging is sufficient. If he is married and free, he is to be stoned after the flogging. The priority of stoning after confession goes to the imam and then after him, the Muslims.

If the one who confesses is a woman, it would be obligatory to do to her what is done with the man, such as rebuffing her and diverting oneself away from her at first. If she leaves, she is to not be inquired about. If she establishes it as well as brings four witnesses against herself, the imam is to inform her that she is to be stoned if she was married and flogged if she was unmarried.

He must say to her: "Perhaps you did so out of fear. Perhaps you were raped. Perhaps you did so because you were forced." If she were to admit to any of the above, she is to be released and the prescribed punishment is to not be applied to her. She is to not be asked about the one who raped her because it would not be obligatory for the prescribed punishment to be applied to him based on her lone testimony. But, if she were to deny any of the above, she would be asked about her intellect just as anyone else would be asked about his/her intellect. If her intellect and understanding are shown to be sound, the same prescribed punishment is to be applied to her—whether married or unmarried. She is to be flogged if she is unmarried or stoned after flogging if she is married. Similar has been narrated to us that the Commander of Believers, upon him be peace, flogged and then stoned.

The man sentenced to be stoned is to be buried to his navel, and the woman sentenced to be stoned is to be buried to her breasts. Their arms are to be left so they can guard themselves with them.

My father related to me that his father was asked about the confession of fornication and the number of times they should be rebuffed. He replied: "It has been narrated from the Prophet, peace and blessings be upon him and his progeny, that he rebuffed Mā'iz four times. After the fourth time, he commanded that he be stoned."

If a person is sentenced to be stoned due to evidence, the first to stone should be the witnesses. However, if the person confessed, the first to stone should be the imam and then the people afterwards. Similar has been narrated from 'Ali, upon him be peace.

Regarding flogging, 'Ali used to say that all the body parts can be struck except the face. He also used to say that one should leave the hands of the punished person free so that he can guard his face and eyes. As for the one sentenced to stoning, he is to be buried in a hole to his navel. As for the woman, she is to be buried to her breasts. Then, the congregation is to stone her one by one until they are done. The whip that is used for flogging the sentenced person should be a whip that is neither too thin nor too thick.

It has reached us that the Commander of Believers, 'Ali b. Abi Ťālib, upon him be peace, stoned a woman in Kufa. He had her buried to her breasts. He stood and the people formed one line. Then, he took two large stones and threw one with his right hand and the other with his left hand. Then the people threw.

It is narrated that when Mā'iz b. Mālik al-Aslami came to Allah's Messenger, peace and blessings be upon him and his progeny, he said: "O Messenger of Allah, I fornicated!" But he [i.e. the Prophet] turned away from him. He repeated "I fornicated!" but he turned away from him again. He repeated "I fornicated!" but he turned away from him again. He then said: I fornicated!" The Prophet turned to him and asked: ((Did you sleep with her?)) He replied: "Yes." He asked: ((Insomuch that this of yours entered that of hers similar to a collyrium stick enters a kohl container and a rope enters a well?)) He replied: 'Yes." He asked: ((Do you know what fornication is?)) He replied: "Yes. I had prohibited sexual relations with her just as a man has permissible sexual relations with his wife." He asked: ((What do you want by your statement?)) He replied: "I want Allah to purify me, O Messenger of Allah!" He then ordered him to be stoned. Two men passed by and one of them said to the other: "Look at this man who had his affair concealed by Allah but would not leave it alone himself! Now, he was stoned like a dog!" Allah's Messenger, peace and blessings be upon him and his progeny, did not say anything to them until they passed by a donkey's rotting carcass.

Allah's Messenger, peace and blessings be upon him and his progeny, said to them both: ((Go down and eat from this rotting carcass!)). The two of them said: "May Allah forgive you, O Messenger of Allah! Should we eat from this rotting carcass?" He replied: ((The disdain you two showed to your brother is graver than what you would eat of this rotting carcass! Verily, he is now in the rivers of Paradise submerging in them)).[12]

Concerning the establishment of the prescribed punishment on the slave by his master

If a slave fornicates, the imam has more authority to establish the prescribed punishment on him than his master does. This is because he is more entitled due to Allah commanding him to do so and not commanding his master. If there is no imam, there is no problem for the master to apply the prescribed punishment on his slave. A hadith has been narrated from the Prophet regarding that. There is also a hadith related from 'Ali b. Abi Ṭālib, upon him be peace. However, we do not know of their authenticity.

As for the hadith narrated from the Prophet, peace and blessings be upon him and his progeny, it is that he purportedly said: ((Establish the prescribed punishments on the one whom your right hand possesses)).[13] As for the hadith that is narrated from the Commander of Believers, upon him be peace, it is related that a man came to him and said: "O Commander of Believers, my slave woman fornicated." 'Ali told him: "Flog her with half, which are fifty lashings. If she repeats it, repeat it." He was asked: "Do I send her to the ruler?" 'Ali replied: "You are her ruler (*sulṭān*)."[14]

My father related to me that his father was asked about the male and female slaves who fornicated and who is to establish the prescribed punishment on them. He replied: "The imam of the Muslims and not their master."

Concerning what takes place with a man and woman of consummative marriage

A man is considered consummative married (*yuhšan*) with a free woman and slave woman as long as they are not insane or neither one is a pre-pubescent wife with whom he does not have intercourse. As for when he can have intercourse with her, it is when she is able to in the place of cultivation or when she is fifteen years old.[15] Then, she would be considered consummative for him and the judgements would then apply to her.

---

[12] Similarly narrated in ***Amāli Ahmed b. 'Isa, Musnad Imam Zayd, Sunan an-Nisā`i, Ŝahīh Ibn Hibbān, Sunan ad-Dārqutni, Sunan Abu Dāwūd, Sunan al-Bayhaqi, Musnad Abu Ya'la, Kanz al-'Ummāl***

[13] Similarly narrated in ***Sharh at-Tajrīd, Sunan Abu Dāwūd, Sunan Ibn Mājah, Musnad Ahmed, Mušannaf Ibn Abi Shayba, Sunan ad-Dārqutni, Al-Mu'jam al-Awsaṭ, Bihār al-Anwār***

[14] Similarly narrated in ***Al-Mu'jam al-Kabīr, Sunan al-Bayhaqi, Kanz al-'Ummāl***

[15] This judgement of al-Hādi is further elaborated in ***Al-Muntakhab*** in which he was asked about the age which is suitable for intercourse. He replied by saying:

> It is said to be nine years old or more or less. However, according to us, this is not a definitive time. Rather, one is to consider what the women and just people say about such. When they say that she is of the age that similar to her is suitable for intercourse, one would be free to have intercourse with his wife when he has paid her dowry.

Therefore, according to Imam al-Hādi, Islamic Law does not justify intercourse with a child whose body would be harmed by such. It is unfortunate that news reports exist in which an unfortunate underage girl dies or is permanently injured by pelvic damage caused by her adult husband. What is even more unfortunate is the justification used to make such intercourse licit! Regarding such 'justifications,' Imam al-Mu`ayyad Billah states in his ***Sharh at-Tajrīd***:

> If it is said that the Prophet, peace and blessings be upon him and his progeny, consummated his marriage to A'isha while she was nine years old and subsequently made such age permissible for such, we reply by saying that there is nothing in the report in which the Prophet, peace and blessings be upon him and his progeny, made that the age of consummation. It simply proves that nine happened to be the age for which it was permissible to consummate with her [i.e. A'isha]. And this is something that we do not object to.

Furthermore, even if the reports about the Prophet marrying A'isha at the age of six and consummating at the age of nine weren't plagued by contradictions and inconsistencies, it would beg the question as to why he waited three years to consummate the marriage if marriage makes intercourse licit. We say that he waited for some indicator of pubescence or other signs of bodily maturity before consummating the marriage. Such knowledge of indicators is well-known amongst just women and qualified health care professionals. And Allah knows best!

As for the People of the Book, such as the Jewish and Christian women, they are not considered as consummative marriage with men according to us because marriage with them is invalid and impermissible. We do not hold to the view that a Muslim can marry an idolater. The *dhimmi* women are considered idolaters specifically, disbelievers in their Lord and rejecters of their Prophet. They object to the Book of the Lord of creation and reject the obligations of the Most Gracious.

My father related to me that his father was asked about a free man who marries a slave girl and then fornicates and whether he would be considered in a consummative marriage with her. He replied:

> The slave girl would be considered a consummative marriage with the free man in our view with the consummative marriage of free woman. His prescribed punishment when he fornicates would be the prescribed punishment of a consummative married person. There is disagreement as to consummative marriage. Some say it refers to the contract, while others say that it refers to sexual contact.

According to us, there is no consummative marriage except by intercourse or closing the curtain on her and being in seclusion with her. He would be obligated to pay her dowry. That which obligates the entire dowry similarly obligates the designation of consummative marriage and the prescribed punishment for each person.

Concerning some witnesses who retract

When four witnesses testify against a man for fornication and confirm their testimonies but then some of them retract after having testified and before the prescribed punishment is applied, the retractor is to be flogged because he slandered and then retracted from his slander. It would then be binding to apply the prescribed punishment on the false accuser and not on the rest because the testimony of the four was initially completed before the retractors retracted.

If the first of the witnesses testifies against someone for fornication but then the remaining witnesses refuse to testify and do not testify, the one who initially testified is to be flogged, and the accused and the one who refused is not to be punished. This is because the testimony is incomplete without four witnesses as Allah says, and the initial witnesses are considered false accusers.

They would be obligated to bring four witnesses for their claim and accusation, or two witnesses would be required to corroborate the witness of the other two witnesses against the one who committed fornication if those who testified were the first two. If those who set out to testify were three, they would have to bring a fourth witness who witnessed with his eye what they witnessed. If the one who set out to testify was one, he would have to bring three witnesses who witnessed what he witnessed at that particular time and place. Insomuch that all of them would have to have witnessed that they all saw the act of fornication being committed at the same time it was taking place. If the witnesses who testify do not number to four as Allah mentions, they would be considered false accusers based on the statement of the Glorified: **{And those who accuse chaste women yet bring not four witnesses, let them be flogged eighty lashes}** (**Q. 24:4**). Also regarding that, the Commander of Believers, ʻAli b. Abi Ṫālib, upon him be peace, said: "I do not wish to be the first of the four witnesses." This proves that if some of them retract, the first of them must be flogged.

If four witnesses testified that a man committed fornication and he is stoned as a result but one of them retracts his statement after the stoning, the retractor would be asked if he intentionally had the person put to death by his testimony. If he says yes and confesses that he intentionally had the person put to death by such, his testimony shall be invalidated and he shall be put to death.

If he denies that he had the person put to death intentionally and says "I did not know of this penalty on him!" claiming to have made a mistake, he shall pay a fourth of the compensation for the lashings and a fourth of the indemnity (*ad-diya*); that would be considered his bloodwite (*ʻaqila*). If he intentionally had him put to death and confessed to that and the victim's guardians accept his indemnity he paid to them whether small or large, it shall be paid from his own personal wealth and not his bloodwite. He would also have to be flogged as a prescribed punishment for his slander. There would be no sin on the other three that testified and had not retracted because the prescribed punishment had already taken place due to the complete testimony by the imam's judgement.

Concerning the retraction of one witness regarding the marriage state of the punished

If a man were accused of fornication by four witnesses in front of the imam and the latter asked about his marriage state with two of the witnesses confirming his marriage state but then one of the two retracted his statement before the prescribed punishment, there would be no prescribed punishment applied. The imam should instruct such person in proper conduct until he is established in his affair and witness. The aforementioned witness would not owe anything because he had not slandered in his testimony insomuch that he would be considered a false accuser. He simply testified to a marriage state and had not retracted his initial testimony [i.e. fornication]. He must be properly educated on such conduct.

Concerning one who hires, is loaned or given a slave woman as a deposit and then he has intercourse with her and says "I thought that she was permissible for me"

I hold to the view that the one who has intercourse with a hired or loaned slave woman is considered a fornicator; it would be obligatory for the prescribed punishment to be applied to him. As for the owner of a slave woman who was given to him as a deposit but then he has intercourse with her and claims that he assumed that it was lawful for him due to her being a deposit for him, he shall be exempted from the prescribed punishment. There is no disagreement regarding this.

We simply make a distinction between him and someone else in terms of whether she was ruined while with him. If so, he would be considered liable for her due to the deposit. The exception is in the case of any additions; then he should settle it between them. If he does not claim ignorance of what he did, the prescribed punishment is to be applied to him like anyone else.

Similarly, if someone misappropriated a slave woman and her children and had intercourse with her, the prescribed punishment would be applied to him. The slave woman and her children would be returned to the owner. If the slave woman were to die while in the possession of the one who misappropriated her, the owner could seek out her value from the day she was misappropriated as well as take back her children. If some of the children were to die, the one who misappropriated them would not be considered liable for their value because it was accidental except in the case of the rape.

Concerning a man who was accused of fornication but was later discovered to have been insane after the prescribed punishment was applied

If a man was accused of fornication by four witnesses while in a consummative marriage and then he was stoned and later discovered to have been insane, the imam would be obligated to pay the indemnity from the Muslim public treasury because this was the imam's error. The imam is obligated to inquire about the soundness of the accused's intellect just as he is obligated to inquire about other matters.

If he [i.e. the accused] was not in a consummative marriage and was flogged because of their testimonies, the imam would be obligated to pay compensation for the lashings from the Muslim public treasury. Similarly, if they testify against a man and he was subsequently stoned but it was later discovered that he was a slave, his value is to be paid to his master from their wealth if they testified that he was free. However, if they had not testified that he was free and the imam had him stoned but then it was later discovered that he was a slave, this would be considered the imam's error and he would have to pay indemnity from the Muslim public treasury because it is obligatory upon the imam to inquire as to whether he is free or a slave.

Concerning a woman who was accused of fornication but was later discovered to have had a closed-up vagina (*ratqā*) or to have been a virgin after the prescribed punishment was applied

If four witnesses accused a woman of fornication and the prescribed punishment was applied to her but then women looked at her and discovered that she was a virgin or had a closed-up vagina, the imam or witnesses would not owe anything because this is one of the prescribed punishments and the testimonies of women that is not acceptable in the case of a prescribed punishment.

Also, if they were to look at her before the prescribed punishment was applied and they mentioned it, the witnesses would not be subject to the prescribed punishment for slander. This is because the witnesses nullify what the women said, and the prescribed punishment is not established on men by the testimony of women. The prescribed punishment is exempted from an accused woman due to any doubtful matters that may occur with her.

Concerning men and women accused of fornication who were husband and wife but not in a consummative marriage

If a man and woman were accused of fornication and accused to be in a consummative marriage but then the imam looked into the matter of the accused people's marriage and discovered that one of them was a minor who does not have intercourse or insane or comatose or the wife of the man is a *dhimmi*, he is to not stone any of them if both are in that situation. Neither is he to flog the virgin with one hundred lashes.

We simply say that the insane man and woman are not considered in a consummative marriage because the prescribed punishment cannot be applied to them. Anyone to whom the prescribed punishment cannot be applied could not be used to apply the prescribed punishment. Similarly, anyone to whom the prescribed punishment cannot be applied could not have the prescribed punishment applied for him. Anyone to whom the prescribed punishment for a consummative marriage cannot be applied could not be considered in a consummative marriage.

Concerning a witness who was discovered to be a *dhimmi*, blind or insane

If four witnesses testified against a man for fornication and some of the witnesses were discovered to be a *dhimmi* or blind or insane without intellect, the accused would be exempted from the prescribed punishment. Also, the witnesses would not be charged with the prescribed punishment of slander since they did not know the state of the fourth witness nor understood that such person's testimony is unacceptable.

If the prescribed punishment was applied due to their testimony, the indemnity is to be paid from the Muslim public treasury because this was the imam's error. He was supposed to have looked into it and investigated the matter of the witnesses.

Concerning the *umm walad*, female indentured labourer and female slave who is freed upon her master's death when they fornicate

If the female indentured labourer or female slave who is freed at her master's death or *umm walad* were to fornicate, my statement is that neither one of them would be stoned. The *umm walad* and female slave freed at her master's death are to be flogged with fifty lashes each, and the female indentured labourer is to be flogged to the value of her manumission.

Similar has reached us from the Commander of Believers, 'Ali b. Abi Ṫālib, upon him be peace, regarding that.[16] If she has reached the middle of her indentured labour contract, she is to be lashed seventy-five times. If it is more or less than that, it is to be calculated thusly.

Concerning *ta'zīr* and whether it is permissible

Ta'zīr is impermissible to take the place as a prescribed punishment. It is when one is free and is lashed less than one hundred times with one whip or two, and when one is a slave and is lashed less than fifty times with one whip or two. Similar has reached us from the Commander of Believers, 'Ali b. Abi Ṫālib, upon him be peace, that he said: "Allah rejects that a prescribed punishment is applied except by witnesses."

It is also narrated from him, upon him be peace, that a man was lashed ninety-nine times for raping a slave girl. The witnesses testified that they saw him mount and cover her, and 'Ali, upon him be peace, said: "If you have not witnessed the penetration and withdrawal, Allah prevents that the prescribed punishment be applied except by four witnesses."[17] He means by such: witnessed penetration and withdrawal.

It is for the imam to consider situations like this. May Allah give him success and rectify him! Perhaps the one that the Commander of Believers, upon him be peace, flogged was unmarried. I hold to the view that if he were married and then I brought him myself and the imam consulted with me, I would have thought that he should punish him with imprisonment for a long time. Likewise is my opinion in a similar case.

If a fornicator fornicated with a female *dhimmi* or idolater, he is to have the prescribed punishment applied to him similarly: he is to be stoned if he was in a consummative marriage and flogged if he was unmarried. Likewise, the prescribed punishment is to be applied to her as well.

Concerning one who fornicated with an unmarriageable relative

If a man were to fornicate with an unmarriageable relative, the prescribed punishment would be applied to him and her—whether they are in a consummative marriage or unmarried. The imam is to consider that, such as the issues of abuse or denial. As for Allah's judgement, their judgements are considered the same. They would be considered sinning fornicators.

Concerning a woman who claimed that a man forced her

If four witnesses testified against a man and woman for fornication and the woman said "He forced me against my own wishes," she would be exempted from the prescribed punishment based on her proof.

If the witnesses testified that she was complicit, the witnesses would be asked: "Were you present for their affair and the beginning of their seclusion insomuch that you heard their conversation and the manner of their affair?" If they reply by saying "Yes. We witnessed from the beginning of their affair, and we know the manner of their deed as well as heard the beginning of their conversation," her statement would be disregarded and the prescribed punishment would be applied to her.

If they were to say "We weren't present at the beginning of their affair but we entered in on them while they were fornicating without knowing about the initial affair," their testimony about her complicity with what was done to her would not be considered. She would be exempted from the prescribed punishment by the doubtful matter that was presented, but the prescribed punishment would be applied to the fornicator.

---

[16] Similarly narrated in ***Musnad Imam Zayd, Amāli Ahmed b. 'Isa, Mušannaf 'Abdur-Razzāq***

[17] Similarly narrated in ***Sharh at-Tajrīd, Amāli Ahmed b. 'Isa, Mušannaf 'Abdur-Razzāq, Shu'b al-Imān*** of al-Bayhaqi, ***Bihār al-Anwār***

Concerning one who married invalidly and whether he would be considered in a consummative marriage or not as well as concerning the minor and insane person who fornicates

If a testimony is established against a man for fornication and the matter of his consummative marriage is investigated and it was shown that he engaged in an invalid marriage to someone that he was forbidden to marry such as a milk sister, other milk relations, unmarriageable relative, his wife's sister, his wife's mother, his father's ex-wife, his son's ex-wife—that marriage would not be considered a consummative marriage and would therefore not obligate that he be stoned. However, the prescribed punishment of one hundred lashes would be applied to him.

As for the minor and insane person who has not recovered, there would be no prescribed punishment applied to them. The prescribed punishment is only applied to the one who fornicates unless such person is a minor or insane.

Concerning a man who fornicated with three or four women

Regarding that, the prescribed punishment is to be applied for each one. As long as it can be repeated after the prescribed punishment, it would be repeated. If he were in a consummative marriage, he would be stoned. If he were unmarried, he would be flogged. Similar is the case with the women; the prescribed punishment would be applied to them thusly.

Concerning an infirmed person against whom a testimony is established for fornication as well as the slave who testifies against himself for fornication

If a testimony was established and four witnessed testified against an infirmed person for fornication, the infirmed person would be stoned if he were in a consummative marriage. This would be the case even if he had a serious illness because the obligation to put him to death is considered greater than his illness. If he were unmarried and his illness was serious, I hold to the view that he should postpone it [to give a chance to recover] and clear him of such [if the illness is perpetual] because his prescribed punishment of flogging is considered less than his ruination.

Similarly, if four witnesses were to testify against two disabled or blind persons for fornication, they are to be stoned if they are in a consummative marriage or flogged if they are not in a consummative marriage. If they were to testify against an emaciated ill person or one with ascites who cannot tolerate the prescribed punishment, he would be stoned if he were in a consummative marriage. If he were unmarried, the imam is to consider the establishment of the prescribed punishment on him. If he considered the matter and joined ten whips and flog ten lashes with them, he can do so. If he considered other than that, he should use independent judgement in such consideration.

It has been narrated from Allah's Messenger, peace and blessings be upon him and his progeny, that a sick man was brought to him with a swollen and leaking abdomen and he was close to death according to some of the hadith. He had fornicated, and the Prophet, peace and blessings be upon him and his progeny, called for a cluster of one hundred palm stalks and flogged him once with it.[18]

If a slave were to testify against himself four times for fornication, such testimony would be valid. He is to be flogged with fifty lashes whether he was in a consummative marriage or not.

Concerning the prescribed punishment for the *dhimmi*

The prescribed punishment for the *dhimmi* is like the prescribed punishment for the coreligionist; the one in a consummative marriage is stoned and the unmarried person is flogged. Similar is the case with the prescribed punishment of their slaves; it would be the same as the prescribed punishment of the Muslims' slaves.

---

[18] Similarly narrated in ***Amāli Ahmed b. 'Isa, Musnad Ahmed, Sunan an-Nisā'i, Sunan Ibn Mājah, Al-Mu'jam al-Awsat*** of at-Tabarāni

Concerning the prescribed punishment for the one who fornicates with a woman in her anus

The one who fornicates with a woman in her anus is like the one who fornicates with a woman in her vagina because both of them are private parts. Entering either one is fornication, and the same prescribed punishment would be for both. The punishment for the married is the punishment for the married, and the punishment for the unmarried is the punishment for the unmarried.

Concerning the prescribed punishment for homosexual acts

Homosexual acts are considered fornication; his prescribed punishment is the prescribed punishment of the fornicator when he enters the anus. It is considered the greater sin of the two fornications. Similar has been narrated from the Commander of Believers, 'Ali b. Abi Ṭālib, upon him be peace: "The prescribed punishment for the homosexual is like the prescribed punishment for the fornicator.[19]"

The prescribed punishment of the man who enters another man's anus is like that of the fornicator. He is stoned if he was in a consummative marriage, and he is flogged if he was unmarried. Similar is the case with the men who allowed themselves to be penetrated.

It has been narrated from Allah's Messenger, peace and blessings be upon him and his progeny, in successively transmitted reports and numerous narrations that he said: ((Kill the one who does it and the one to whom it is done)).[20]

My father related to me that his father was asked about one who committed homosexual acts. He replied: "The prescribed punishment for such is the prescribed punishment of the fornicator. He is to be stoned if he were in a consummative marriage and flogged if he were unmarried."

Similar has been narrated from the Commander of Believers, upon him be peace, regarding a man who was brought to him who did such. [He had him stoned and said:] "Allah stoned the people of Lot from the heavens for such.[21]" [Ref. **Q. 11:82** and **51:32-34**]

Concerning the prescribed punishment for slander

Allah, the Blessed and Exalted, says regarding the prohibiting his slaves from slandering others for what they have not done and stating that for which they are not certain: **{And pursue not that for which ye have no knowledge. Verily, the hearing, sight and heart are all of those that shall be questioned} (Q. 17:36)**. The meaning of **{And pursue not that for which ye have no knowledge}** is do not say or do not slander chaste women of that which you do not know. His statement **{Verily, the hearing, sight and heart are all of those that shall be questioned}** is informing him that his hearing, sight and heart will be asked on the Day of Judgement whether he uttered that for which he knew or did not know.

The Glorified also says: **{And those who accuse chaste women yet bring not four witnesses, let them be flogged eighty lashes} (Q. 24:4)**. The meaning of that is whoever slanders a free Muslim woman or man of fornication and does not bring four witnesses is to be flogged with eighty lashes just as Allah commands. Such person is considered a liar among the disobedient according to Allah, and his testimony is to never be accepted unless such person repents for his act of disobedience. Through such remorse and repentance to Allah, he will be considered among the acceptable when he makes a sincere repentance.

---

[19] Similarly narrated in ***Musnad Imam Zayd, Amāli Ahmed b. 'Isa, Bihār al-Anwār, Uṣūl al-Kāfi***

[20] Similarly narrated in ***Sharh at-Tajrīd, Amāli Ahmed b. 'Isa, Sunan Abu Dāwūd, Sunan at-Tirmidhi, Sunan Ibn Mājah, Musnad Ahmed, Sunan al-Bayhaqi, al-Mustadrak, Sunan ad-Dārqutni, Kanz al-'Ummāl, Al-Mu'jam al-Kabīr***

[21] Similarly narrated in ***Amāli Ahmed b. 'Isa***

It is as Allah, the One too Majestic to be encompassed by words, says: **{And never accept a testimony from them—and they are the defiantly disobedient—unless they repent afterwards and rectify. Verily, Allah is Most Forgiving, Most Gracious}** (Q. 24:4).

The Glorified says regarding the actions of the Pre-Islamic Arabs who used to force their female slaves to fornicate so that they could sell their offspring: **{And compel not thy handmaidens to whoredom when they desire chastity, that ye may seek the desires of this world's life. And whosoever compels them—verily, Allah is Most Forgiving and Most Gracious after they are compelled}** (Q. 24:33).

He therefore prevents them from utilising them [i.e. the slave women] for fornication due to their seeking out their hire and the selling of their offspring. Then He informs them that He is forgiving and merciful to those who are afterwards forced against their will to do what their masters commanded them. Allah informs them that He will not punish them for that which they are not complicit and are forced to do out of fear for their lives. Then, He promises them that He will forgive them for that and will remove His punishment from them by having mercy if they are forced to do it.

He says: **{And whosoever compels them—verily, Allah is Most Forgiving and Most Gracious after they are compelled}**. He therefore obligates forgiveness for those Muslim slave women who are forced. It is said that this verse was revealed about a Muslim slave woman who belonged to 'Abdullah b. Ubayy b. Salūl.[§] He commanded her to fornicate with a man and then produce children for him to sell. She refused and went to the Prophet, peace and blessings be upon him and his progeny. She informed him of that, and he freed her and married her off.[22]

Concerning the explanation of slander and when the prescribed punishment is obligatory

When a man says to a Muslim man "O, fornicator!" or "O, son of a fornicating woman!" or "O, son of a fornicator!" and the slandered excuses him and does not bring it to the imam, he can do so. If he does bring it to the imam, the imam is to inquire for evidence for the accusation. If he brings evidence, the imam is to ask the accuser about his evidence for what he claimed. If four witnesses are brought forward to establish the testimony of the fornication of the slandered, he is to leave him and establish the prescribed punishment on the slandered. If he does bring four witnesses, he is to bring him [i.e. the accuser] out and flog him with eighty lashes as Allah says: **{And those who accuse chaste women yet bring not four witnesses, let them be flogged eighty lashes}** (Q. 24:4). The slandered is to be present for the imam's flogging of the accuser.

Concerning the son who slanders the father and the father who slanders the son

If a man slanders his son for fornication himself by saying "O, fornicator!", the prescribed punishment is to be applied to him because Allah says **{And those who accuse chaste women…}** (Q. 24:4) and does not make an exception for a parent or anyone else. Others say that he is to not be flogged, but we do not acknowledge such.

If he were to kill him, he would not be put to death for such unless he killed him out of rebelliousness, recklessness against Allah or corruption. Then, the imam would have to consider the matter. Similarly, if he [i.e. the father] were to take some of his [i.e. the son's] wealth out of preservation, he is to not have his hand severed for it because Allah's Messenger, peace and blessings be upon him and his progeny, said: ((You and what you own belong to your father)).[23] The father would have to repent to Allah for saying something about his son that he did not know.

---

[22] Similarly narrated in ***Ŝaḥīḥ Muslim, Muŝannaf Ibn Abi Shayba, Sunan al-Bayhaqi, Asbāb an-Nuzūl***

[23] Similarly narrated in ***Sharh at-Tajrīd, Amāli Ahmed b. 'Isa, Sunan Abu Dāwūd, Sunan Ibn Māja, Musnad Ahmed b. Hanbal, Muŝannaf Ibn Abi Shayba, Muŝannaf 'Abdur-Razzāq, Sunan al-Kubra*** of al-Bayhaqi, ***Jami' al-Uŝūl*** of Ibn Athīr, ***Kanz al-Ummāl, Majmu' az-Zawā'id, Musnad al-Bazzār, Al-Mu'jam al-Awsat, Al-Mu'jam al-Kabīr, Bihār al-Anwār***

If a son were to slander his father, he would be flogged eighty times as the prescribed punishment. If a father said to his son "O, son of a fornicating woman!", he would be asked to bring four witnesses to substantiate the fornication of his wife, the mother of his son. If he brings them, she is to be flogged and then stoned. If he does not bring them, they will be called to do a mutual cursing. If he refuses, the prescribed punishment would be applied to him and his wife would be left alone. If they perform the mutual cursing, the imam is to separate them, and they are to never be joined again.

My father related to me that his father was asked about a man who slandered his son. He replied:

> The prescribed punishment is to be applied to him because Allah commanded that the prescribed punishment be applied to one who slandered a chaste person. The father who slandered his son is among those whom Allah commands to apply the prescribed punishment because of the fact that they committed their crime.

Concerning one who slanders a group

If a man slanders a group and says "O, you sons of fornicating women!", he is to be brought to the imam and flogged for each person as a prescribed punishment. He should seek out the prescribed punishments for each of the mothers of the slandered people. If some of them were dead, their guardians are to seek out what is obligatory for her in that.

If a man said to two or three men "O, sons of a fornicating woman!", the prescribed punishment would be applied to him if their mother was the same woman. If their mothers were different, the prescribed punishment would not be applied to the false accuser because he slandered all of them with one mother; however, they all had different mothers. One cannot be three just as three cannot be one.

Concerning a Muslim who slanders a *dhimmi* or slave

If a Muslim were to slander a *dhimmi*, there would be no prescribed punishment applied to him for his slander because Allah, the Blessed and Exalted, only obligates the prescribed punishment regarding the believing free women, and the *dhimmi* is not a believer. Similarly, if he were to slander a slave, there would be no prescribed punishment applied to him.

My father related to me that his father was asked about a Muslim who slanders a *dhimmi* and about a free person who slanders a slave. He replied:

> As for the *dhimmi*, there is no prescribed punishment applied to the Muslim because Allah, the Blessed and Exalted, says: **{Verily, those who accuse chaste, oblivious believing women…} (Q. 24:23)**. The *dhimmi* is not considered a believer. Nor do we hold to the view that the prescribed punishment is applied to the free person who slanders a slave.

If a Muslim were to slander a *dhimmi* by saying "O son of a fornicating woman!" and the *dhimmi*'s mother had embraced Islam, he would be asked to bring evidence for what he said. If he brings evidence, the prescribed punishment shall be applied to the Muslim mother of the *dhimmi*. If he does not bring evidence, the prescribed punishment shall be applied to him due to his slander of her because he slandered her after she embraced Islam.

Concerning a man who says to another "O one who fornicates with his mother!" or "O sinner!" or "O openly disobedient one!"

If a man said to another "O one who fornicates with his mother!", this would be considered the greatest of slander. The prescribed punishment is to be applied to him.

As for the statements "O sinner!" or "O openly disobedient one!", he would be asked the meaning and intention of his statement. If he meant slander regarding fornication, the prescribed punishment is to be applied to him. If he intended a sinner in religion or an openly disobedient person in those matters in which Muslims are to not be disobedient, he would be exempted from such and the prescribed punishment would not be applied to him. The imam would have to instruct him in proper etiquette.

If a man slandered and was asked for evidence but the evidence was not present, he must delay it till an appointed time for which it is possible for the evidence to be brought forth. If he comes with it, then no prescribed punishment would be applied.

My father related to me that his father was asked about a man who said to another "O one who fornicates with his mother!" or "O sinner!" or "O openly disobedient one!" He replied:

> As for the one who said "O one who fornicates with his mother!", that which is applied to the slanderer is applied to him. As for the one who said "O sinner!" or "O openly disobedient!", he is to be asked the intended meaning of his statement. If he meant fornication, he is considered a slanderer. If he meant any other sin or act of disobedience in the religion, he would not be considered a slanderer. But, he would have to be reprimanded.

Regarding the most and least of *ta'zīr*, it is said that *ta'zīr* cannot take place except that it is less than the minimum of every prescribed punishment. Some of them also say that *ta'zīr* is based on the amount that the imam considers from every free person or slave—the most of which or least.

My father related to me that his father was asked about a man who slandered and claimed that his evidence wasn't present. He replied: "He is to wait till an appointed time regarding his claim."

Concerning one who is flogged for slander and then slanders again before his flogging is complete

If he is flogged for slander and some of the prescribed punishment remains, the prescribed punishment that remains is to be completed. This would be considered sufficient for the punishment for his second slander if it is between the two punishments. Then, if he were to slander again, he would be punished for the first slander and then after the second slander. It is similar narrated that the Commander of Believers, upon him be peace, carried out two prescribed punishments in the same event.

Concerning the *dhimmi* who slanders a Muslim

If a *dhimmi* slanders a Muslim male or female, the prescribed punishment is to be applied on their behalf because Allah says: **{And those who accuse chaste women yet bring not four witnesses, let them be flogged eighty lashes} (Q. 24:4)**. The term **{chaste women (*muhšanāt*)}** refers to believing women because belief is the chastest. Regarding that, Allah willing, is the most definitive of proofs.

Concerning the *dhimmi* who is slandered by a Muslim but then embraces Islam afterwards as well as a slave who is slandered by a free person but then is manumitted or slanders a free person

If a Muslim slandered a *dhimmi* and then the *dhimmi* embraced Islam after being slandered by the Muslim and seeks him out for slander, there would be no prescribed punishment applied because he slandered him while he was a disbeliever and not a Muslim. Similar is the case with a free person who slandered a slave and then the slave was manumitted and seeks him out for slander. There would be no prescribed punishment on him because he slandered him while he was a slave and not free.

If a slave slandered a free person and is manumitted a moment after he slandered him and then the free person seeks him out for slander, the prescribed punishment is to be applied to him. The prescribed punishment for the slave would be forty lashes because he slandered him while he was a slave. The prescribed punishment would be obligated on him at the moment he uttered the slanderous statement.

If a free man slandered a minor or slave or slave woman or a slave freed at his/her master's death or the son of an *umm walad* from other than her master or an indentured labourer, there would be no prescribed punishment applied to such person. However, the imam must instruct that person in proper etiquette regarding that.

Concerning the man and woman confirmed each other's statements

If a man said to a woman "O, fornicating woman!" and she said to him "O, fornicator!" and then he said "I fornicated with you!", there would be no prescribed punishment applied to either one of them. This is because when she slandered him, she confirmed his statement "I fornicated with you" and exempted her from the prescribed punishment due to his confirmation of her statement. He would also be exempted from the prescribed punishment because he testified against himself one time, and the prescribed punishment is not binding on one who testifies against himself one time without the testimony of four witnesses to the imam.

Similarly, if he said to her "O, fornicating woman!" and she said "I fornicated with you!" and then he said "O, fornicating woman!" and she said "You fornicated with me!", the prescribed punishment would be applied to both of them because both of them slandered.

Likewise, if he said "O, daughter of a fornicating woman!" and she said "You fornicated with her!", the prescribed punishment would be applied to both of them. If he said "O, daughter of a fornicating woman!" and she said "She fornicated with you!", the both of them slandered the woman's mother and the prescribed punishment would be applied to both of them.

If she said to him "O, son of a fornicating woman!" and he said to her "You are right!", she would be considered a slanderer. If he responded to her by saying "You are right; she is a fornicating woman!", both of them would be considered slanderers.

If he said to her "O, daughter of fornicating parents!" and she said "If they are fornicating parents then your parents are fornicators!", the prescribed punishment would be applied to him and not her because she had not applied the slander to his parents absolutely.

If a man said to his slave "Whoever sold you is a fornicator" or "Whoever bought you is a fornicator" or "The mother of the one who sold you is a fornicator" or "The mother of the one who bought you is a fornicator", it would be obligatory to look into the mother of the one who bought or sold him. If she was a slave, the prescribed punishment would not be applied to him. If she was free, the prescribed punishment would be applied to him because he slandered her.

If he said "The mother of the one who sold you..." or "The mother of the one who bought you..." without indicating the person specifically, the prescribed punishment would not be applied to him because he had not slander anyone. The prescribed punishment is simply applied when the slanderer is sought; however, no one seeks him out because he had not indicated anyone by his slander.

Concerning the man and child who slanders

If a man said to a girl "O, fornicator!", the prescribed punishment would not be applied on him because the prescribed punishment would not be applied if she were to have slandered him. The imam would have to instruct him in proper etiquette. And if a woman says to a boy "O, fornicator!", the prescribed punishment would not be applied on her because the prescribed punishment would not be applied on him if he were to have slandered her.

If a boy said to a man "O, son of a fornicating woman!" the prescribed punishment would not be applied to him. And if a man said to a boy "O, son of a fornicating woman!", the prescribed punishment could be applied on behalf of the boy's mother if she sought it out.

If a man said to a woman who was the daughter of an *umm walad* "O, daughter of a fornicating woman!", there would be no prescribed punishment applied on her behalf because her mother is a slave. If her mother had been manumitted before the slander and the slander took place while she was a free Muslim, the prescribed punishment would be applied on her behalf if she seeks it out. However, if she was manumitted after the slander and sought it out, there would be no prescribed punishment on her behalf because she was considered a slave when he slandered her.

If a man said to a man who was the son of an *umm walad* from other than her master "O, fornicator, son of a fornicating woman!", there would be no prescribed punishment applied on their behalf because the two of them are considered slaves. If he slandered him while the latter's mother was manumitted, the prescribed punishment would be applied to him on her behalf and not his [i.e. the son's] behalf because she is considered free and he a slave. If he slandered the both of them after they were manumitted, the prescribed punishment would be applied on his and her behalf if they sought it out.

Concerning the one who slandered the son of an *umm walad* from her master or slanders her

If a man said to the son of an *umm walad* from her master "O, fornicator!", the prescribed punishment would be applied to him if the son of the *umm walad* was a pubescent man. If he said to him "O, fornicator, son of a fornicating woman", the prescribed punishment would be applied to him and the imam would have to look into the affair of his mother. If his father had manumitted her before the slander, the prescribed punishment would be applied on her behalf also. If she had not been manumitted, there would be no prescribed punishment applied to him on her behalf.

If a man said to him "O, fornicator, son of two fornicators!", two prescribed punishments would be applied to him on his [i.e. the slandered] and his father's behalf. And if the mother was manumitted before that, a third prescribed punishment would be applied to him on her behalf.

Regarding that, we do not advocate the statement of those of combine the prescribed punishments of a group into one prescribed punishment. Rather, we advocate that separate prescribed punishments be applied to one who slanders a group of people separately or together. This is because each slandered person is not partnered with another, and Allah orders that every slandered person has the prescribed punishment applied to the slanderer on the behalf of each. He does not mention in His Book that two or three slandered people are to be partnered in the eighty lashes. Therefore, we advocate that when a group is slandered by one statement, the prescribed punishment would be applied to him on each slandered person's behalf.

The Blessed and Exalted simply says: **{And those who accuse chaste women yet bring not four witnesses, let them be flogged eighty lashes} (Q. 24:4)**. He therefore obligates that each male or female slanderer be punished on behalf of each slandered man or woman by eighty lashes. We imitate the Most Gracious's judgement in that, and we articulate that which the verses of the Qur'an articulate. If it were permissible to partner two slandered people in one prescribed punishment, there would always be eighty lashes for one slander. If that were the case, it would not be permissible to flog one slanderer eighty lashes on behalf of one slandered person.

Concerning the testimony of women

A woman's testimony is inadmissible in any case involving the prescribed punishments that Allah obligates upon creation—whether a lot or few. However, their individual testimonies are permissible for other than that, such as those situations in which men cannot act as witnesses and those cases that permit their testimonies when coupled with the man's testimony.

As for those situations for which they can testify individually, an example is the midwife's testimony regarding the child's inception as long as she is reliable and trustworthy. Another example is their testimony regarding those things related to a free woman and slave woman that only women can act as witnesses for, such as any defect in their private parts that may deter a slave woman from being sold or bought. Examples include a prominent bone in her privates (*al-qarn*), a closed-up vagina (*ar-rataq*), rounded breasts (*al-falak*) and other female medical issues. If the women who act as witnesses to such are just, upright, truthful, pure and trustworthy—one can adjudicate based on their testimonies because they relate to those matters for which no one else can testify.

As for those situations in which their testimonies are permitted when coupled with that of a man, they are those things that people do which are to be witnessed. Examples include bequests, gifts, buying and selling, charity and other things excluding the prescribed punishments.

My father related to me that his father was asked about the testimony of women. He replied:

> Women's testimonies are inadmissible regarding any of the prescribed punishments of Allah. An individual woman's testimony is admissible regarding those things for which no one but a woman can act as a witness, such as midwifery, as long as she is truthful and just.

Concerning the *dhimmi* who fornicates with a Muslim woman and concerning when she is forced against her will

If a *dhimmi* forces a Muslim woman against her will, the prescribed punishment would be applied to him just as it is applied to any Muslim. Then, the imam would see to it that he is punished with a punishment that differentiates him from the Muslims, such as lengthy imprisonment or exile.

Others say that he is to be put to death, but we do not advocate for such because if it were mutually assumed that the *dhimmi* fornicated with her while she was complicit, then there would be no prescribed punishment greater than that which would be applied to similar. Then, we say to them that similarly, it would necessitate the prescribed punishment on the Muslim for similar—whether in a consummative marriage or the unmarried. The *dhimmi* could not be asked to swear that he did not fornicate with her complicity or without it. If you obligate that he be put to death in the case of coercion, it will obligate that he is put to death in the case of complicity. This is because Allah prohibits the Muslims from fornication just as He prohibits such from the *dhimmi*, and He prohibits it from the *dhimmi* just as He prohibits it from the Muslims. If the prescribed punishment for the *dhimmi* who fornicated with a Muslim woman weren't considered the same as the prescribed punishment for the Muslims who fornicated with her, the prescribed punishment for the Muslim woman who fornicated with the *dhimmi* would be different from her prescribed punishment if she were to have fornicated with a Muslim fornicator. If it would be obligated to put him to death, it would be obligated upon her as well. If it were exempted from him, she would be exempted also. This may be required of the one who said to put the *dhimmi* to death if he fornicated with the Muslim woman. It would also necessitate by analogy that she be put to death if she fornicated with a *dhimmi*.

Rather, the *dhimmi* breaks his contract by committing an act of deeds openly amongst the Muslims and reject them with apparent discredits, such as war and other things that if a Muslim were to do them, it would make his blood licit to shed after inviting him to repentance or similar actions Muslims may commit openly.

As for that which she was forced to do, there would be no prescribed punishment applied to her because she was overcome against her will and she had not committed fornication with complicity.

My father related to me that his father was asked about a woman who was forced against her will. He replied:

> Every woman who is forced against her will is to not have the prescribed punishment applied to her. Similar has been narrated from the Prophet, peace and blessings be upon him and his progeny, as well as narrated from 'Ali, upon him be peace.[24]

---

[24] Similarly narrated in ***Sunan at-Tirmidhi, Sunan Ibn Mājah, Musnad Ahmed, Al-Mu'jam al-Kabīr, Mušannaf Ibn Abi Shayba, Sunan al-Bayhaqi***

My father related to me that his father was asked about a *dhimmi* that forced himself on a Muslim slave woman. He replied: "That which is obligatory upon him is that which is obligatory upon any Muslim that was to force himself on someone because Allah obligates the same prescribed punishment on all fornicators."

Concerning the one who attempts magic and the cuckold (*duyūth*)

It has reached us that Allah's Messenger, peace and blessings be upon him and his progeny, said: ((Kill the cuckold when you find him)).[25] According to us, the meaning is: after he was called to repentance. If he is called to repentance and does not repent, he is to be put to death. If he repents, he is to not be put to death. It is said that he is to be killed and not called to repentance; however, we do not hold to that view or advocate for that.

My father related to me that his father was asked about the one who attempts magic[26] and what the prescribed punishment for such is. He replied:

> His prescribed punishment is that he is to be put to death after being called to repentance and does not repent. If he repents, he is not put to death. Mālik b. Anas[§] and the people of Medina say that he is to be put to death and not called to repentance. However, that is not our position.

Concerning the prescribed punishment for heretics and apostates

The heretic and apostate are not put to death except after being called to repentance. If they repent, they are to be left alone. If they do not repent from their disbelief, their necks are to be cut.

I prefer that they or anyone else who is called to repentance not be put to death until they are called to repentance three times in three days. They are to be called to repentance once each day and then put to death on the third day if they refuse repentance and belief and choose to remain on disbelief and rebellion.

My father related to me that his father was asked about what should be done to the apostate. He replied: "The apostate is put to death if he remains on his rebellion. His death sentence is to not be waived unless he repented."

My father related to me that his father was asked about heretics and what their prescribed punishment is. He replied: "The heretics are to be put to death if they do not repent and not put to death if they repent."

Concerning the prescribed punishment for women who have intercourse with women

If a woman were to have intercourse with another woman, their prescribed punishment would be the same as the prescribed punishment of a man who had intercourse with another man without anal penetration, as well as the prescribed punishment of a man who had intercourse with a woman without penetration and withdrawal. In all such cases, the punishment would be *ta'zīr* to the extent the imam sees fit.

---

[25] Similarly narrated in ***Musnad Imam Zayd, Sharh at-Tajrīd, Sunan at-Tirmidhi, Al-Mu'jam al-Kabīr, Mušannaf 'Abdur-Razzāq***. In ***Al-Muntakhab***, al-Hādi was asked about this hadith.

> I asked: "What if someone says that this is a narration and we do not know whether it is authentically attributed to Allah's Messenger or not? Explain to me from where is the death penalty obligated?" He replied: "It is from the statement of the Allah, the Blessed and Exalted: **{Verily, the recompense of those who make war against Allah and His Messenger and those who strive to spread corruption in the land is that they are to be put to death or crucified…} (Q. 5:33).** He obligates the death penalty for the one who spreads corruption in the land. What corruption is greater to Allah than causing one who is not one's son to inherit and facilitates illegitimate children? This includes corruption that leads to a brother marrying his sister."

[26] We have opted for the translation 'attempts magic' as opposed to 'practices magic' because of the scholarly disagreement as to whether magic has a reality and effect. Those who argue that it does say that the fact that the Qur'an advises that one seek refuge from the 'blower of the knots' in **Q. 113:4** points to the reality and effect of magic. However, those who say that magic does not have a reality refer to a Qur'anic passage in which the so-called 'magic' of Pharaoh's magicians was said to **{appear to (*yukhayyalu ilayhi*)}** Moses as something that it wasn't (**Q. 20:66**). The Arabic word *khiyāl* can only denote something that is imaginary and not real. This is coupled with the fact that their 'magic' was referred to as falsehood in **Q. 7:117** and **Q. 20:69**.

This is because Allah does not establish the prescribed punishment except when there is penetration and withdrawal, and a woman does not engage in penetration and withdrawal. Rather, the imam is to utilise *ta'zīr* in their regards. He can flog them ninety-eight lashes if they are both free women or forty-eight lashes if they are both slave women. He is to also add to that by imprisonment to the extent he sees fit.

My father related to me that his father was asked about a woman who has intercourse with another woman. He replied: "*Ta'zīr* is to be applied to them by the imam to the extent that he sees fit."

Concerning the prescribed punishment for the thief and what Allah obligates upon him in the Qur'an

Allah, the Blessed and Exalted, says: {**The male thief and female thief—sever their hands as recompense for what they have earned as an example from Allah. And Allah is Mighty and All-Wise**} (**Q. 5:38**).

[This is applied] if a thief stole ten dirham or its value[27] from a protected place. A protected place refers to a person's house, pasture and storehouse that are protected. Similar has been narrated to us regarding Allah's Messenger, peace and blessings be upon him and his progeny, that he amputated for a shield, which was worth ten dirham.[28]

The one who has a limb amputated for theft and then dies without repenting is considered among the people of the Hellfire because the amputation is not considered repentance in and of itself; it is simply a punishment in this life. He would still be obligated to repent to Allah for committing an evil deed. If he repents, we hope that he receives forgiveness from Allah. Haven't you considered how Allah says: {**Then whosoever repents after wrongdoing and rectifies—verily, Allah shall turn unto him**} (**Q. 5:39**)? He is saying: Whoever repents after stealing and rectifies his deeds and does not return to his offense—Allah will accept his repentance.

Regarding that, it is narrated that a man who stole was brought to Allah's Messenger, peace and blessings be upon him and his progeny, and the latter asked: ((Did you steal?)). The man replied: "Yes." The Prophet, peace and blessings be upon him and his progeny, said: ((Amputate him)). When he was amputated, the Prophet said to him: ((Repent to Allah)). He replied: "Verily, I repent to Allah!" The Prophet then prayed: ((O Allah, accept his repentance!)).[29]

Concerning the thief who is amputated but then repeats

If a thief steals ten dirham or its value, his right hand is to be amputated from the wrist. If he repeats and steals a second time, his left foot is to be amputated from the ankle. If he repeats a third time and steals, we hold to the view that he is to be imprisoned from the Muslims.

No other hand or foot is to be amputated because such amputations would be a cause for his destruction. Such would also be a hindrance of his performing his purifications and prayers because there is no prayer without the purification. Moreover, it would also be considered a type of mutilation (*al-muthl*), and Allah's Messenger, peace and blessings be upon him and his progeny, prohibited the mutilation of an animal.[30] How much more so in the case of a human being?! Also, if both feet and hands were amputated, he would remain defiled because he would not be able to clean himself from filth or properly fulfil his needs. Therefore, imprisonment would protect him from his incitement and prevent his destruction. Allah is most merciful to His creation!

---

[27] This is said to be valued at about 25.2 grams of silver.

[28] Similarly narrated in ***Musnad Imam Zayd, Sharh at-Tajrīd, Sunan an-Nisā'i, Sunan Abu Dāwūd, Mušannaf 'Abdur-Razzāq, Sunan ad-Dārqutni***

[29] Similarly narrated in ***Al-Mu'jam al-Kabīr, Sunan ad-Dārqutni, Mušannaf 'Abdur-Razzāq, Shu'b al-Imān***

[30] Similarly narrated in ***Sunan an-Nisā'i, Sunan Ibn Mājah, Musnad Ahmed, Mušannaf Ibn Abi Shayba***

My father related to me that his father was asked about where the thief is to be amputated. He replied: "From the wrist." He also said: "One is to be amputated for ten dirham or its value in commodities when one steals from a protected place."

Concerning the one who confesses to theft

If a thief confesses twice to the imam, the imam must ask him about the theft: What did he steal? How much was it? How was it? From where did he steal it? Once the theft is established as well as its meaning and manner and he informed him that he stole from a protected place, he must be asked about his intellect. If his intellect was shown to be sound at the time he confessed to the theft, his hand is to be amputated from the wrist.[31]

If there is anything in his statement or explanation or confession that would exempt him from the prescribed punishment, he is to be exempted from it. That which he confessed to stealing would be withheld and returned to the place from which it was stolen.

If he were to confess and when the knife is close to his hand, he denies and belies himself regarding what he confessed, he is to be freed and not amputated or held liable. He would be in the position of witnesses who retracted. Similarly, the statement of a confessor to fornication—if he were to retract at the time of the stoning or prescribed punishment—he is to be freed and the prescribed punishment is to not be applied to him. He would similarly be in the position of witnesses who retracted.

Regarding that, it has been narrated from Allah's Messenger, peace and blessings be upon him and his progeny, concerning Mā'iz b. Mālik al-Aslami, that when the latter was being stoned and felt the effects of the stoning, he started to flee from the hole. Some of the people threw the bone of a camel's foreleg at him and killed him. Allah's Messenger, peace and blessings be upon him and his progeny, was informed of it and said: ((Why could not you have left him alone?)).[32]

He [i.e. the Prophet] would not have said that unless he knew that if he [i.e. Mā'iz] had retracted from his own testimony, he would have been exempted from the prescribed punishment. It is as if he had considered his fleeing from the stoning as a retraction.

If confessors retract their confessions, the imam must instruct them in proper etiquette so that they and others do not repeat such actions.

Concerning the testimony of two witnesses of theft against the thief

If two witnesses testify against a thief, the imam must ask them what he stole as well as what it was they found with him that they witnessed he stole. If they mentioned anything that is ten dirham or a commodity that is its value, he is to ask them where he stole it from, how he took it and from which place he was able to take it. If they reply by saying that he took it from a protected place from such and such place and that they saw him exit from such place, the imam is to inquire about their uprightness. If they are upright and reliable, he is to inquire about the intellect of the thief. If his intellect is shown to be sound, he is to amputate.

---

[31] The punishment for theft is the prerogative of the imam of the Muslims and no one else. The victim of theft is not to take matters in his own hands when it comes to amputating the thief. In ***Al-Muntakhab***, al-Hādi was asked about this issue.

> I asked him about a man who found a thief who stole an item from a protected place in his house and the man amputated his hand before bringing him to the imam. "What would be obligatory upon the amputator if he is brought before the imam?" He replied: "If the one who amputated claimed ignorance and said 'I did not know that I wasn't supposed to amputate him', he would be declared ignorant of amputation but he would have to pay half the complete indemnity."

When al-Hādi was asked if the indemnity is to be paid to the amputee, he replied; 'No. It is to be paid to the Muslim public treasury." He also said that the indemnity is to be paid by the amputator's clan since it was an action that was done out of ignorance.

[32] Similarly narrated in ***Sharh at-Tajrīd, Sunan Abu Dāwūd, Musnad Ahmed, Al-Mustadrak, Mušannaf*** of 'Abdur-Razzāq, ***Mušannaf Ibn Abi Shayba***

If the two witnesses mentioned that he had not left with it from the protected place and that he took it from somewhere else, the stolen item is to be returned to its owner and the thief is to be instructed regarding what he stole. Similarly, if it is mentioned to him [i.e. the imam] that the thief lost his intellect and was insane, the prescribed punishment would be exempted from him—whether he stole it from a protected place or any other place.

Concerning the one who climbs the wall of a house or opens its door and takes an item from it

If a thief enters a house from its door or scales the wall or pierces a hole in the wall and then takes an item from it that equals ten dirham and then exits from the door or throws it over the wall and he is discovered by witnesses who saw him with it and witnessed him take it from its protected place, the imam is to amputate the thief's hand.

If he is found with it on the inside of the house but had not left with it or departed, there is to not be a prescribed punishment applied to him. Rather, the imam is to apply *ta'zīr* to him and instruct him in proper etiquette because the thief's hand is simply amputated for theft when he departs with it from its house. As for the one who does not leave the house with it, he is to not be amputated.[33]

My father related to me that his father was asked about the thief who was seized before he departed with the item from its protected place and whether he is to be amputated. He replied: "There is no amputation applied to him unless he left with the stolen item from its protected place. If he is seized before leaving with it from its protected place, there is no amputation applied to him for it."

Concerning a group of thieves among whom some enter, some transport the stolen item and some keeping watch

If there were thieves who opened the door or scaled the walls and then there were some who collected the stolen item in the house and some who transported it from the inside of the house to the outside and some on the outside who were keeping watch, the ones who transported it from the inside of the house to the outside would be amputated. Those who collected it in the house and those on the outside keeping watch would have to be taught a good lesson.

If there were two thieves with one of them standing at the door from the outside and the other taking the stolen item from the inside and then witnesses saw what they were doing and said that the one on the inside came close to the stolen item and placed it at the doorstep from the inside and the other extended his hand and took it out, the hand of the one who took it outside is to be amputated, and the other is to be taught a good lesson. If they witnessed that the one on the inside placed it on the other side of the door or threw it to the other from above the wall, the hand of the one on the inside is to be amputated and the one on the outside who caught it is to be taught a good lesson.

If the one on the inside gathered it in a big bundle and then pulled it until he reached the door of the house and then placed his hand at the door of the house and took it from one side of the bundle while the one on the outside took it from another side and the two of them carried it until it is brought out and then they are seized while having what they did witnessed, the hands of both of them must be amputated because both of them brought it out of its protected place.

---

[33] A similar principle is exhibited in ***Al-Muntakhab*** regarding a thief who steals from another thief.

> I asked him about a man who stole a garment from someone and then another thief stole it from him. "If it equals ten dirhams, would it be obligatory to amputate the second thief" He replied: "It would be obligatory to amputate the first thief because he took it from the property and protected place of its owner. It would not be an obligation to amputate the second thief because he stole it from one who does not own it nor did he steal it from the first protected place."

Concerning one for whom amputation is not obligatory when bringing it out to one for whom amputation is obligatory

If a group of thieves entered a man's house and some of them gathered the stolen item inside the house and then brought it out to an insane person or pre-pubescent child insomuch that he leaves with it and the thief and insane person or pre-pubescent child carries it out and then they are seized while having what they did witnessed, neither one of them are to be amputated.

However, the man on the inside is to have a severe *ta'zīr* applied to him and is to be imprisoned for a long time but not amputated because he had not taken the stolen item out from its protected place. It would be obligatory for the pre-pubescent child to be instructed in proper etiquette to the extent that the imam sees fit but not amputated because the prescribed punishment is to not be applied to one for whom there is no judgement. The same is the case for the insane person.

Concerning the number of times the one who confesses to theft is to confess before being amputated

The thief is to not be amputated until he confesses twice in front of the imam. His two confessions take the place of two witnesses just as there is no prescribed punishment applied to the fornicator who confesses until he confesses four times. This is because the latter takes the place of four witnesses. If he retracts his confession against himself, his denial is to be accepted and the prescribed punishment is to not be applied to him.

My father related to me that his father was asked about a thief who confesses to theft and the number of times he should repeat such. He replied: "It is narrated from 'Ali, upon him be peace, that the thief should repeat it twice."[34]

Similarly, if the thief were to confess, he is to be amputated unless he retracts from that and objects. Then, he is to be exempted from the prescribed punishment because of his retraction from his initial confession.

Concerning one who stole something from a protected place but then returned it before he was brought to the imam

If a thief stole something from a protected place that required amputation and he was witnessed and brought to the magistrate but then had returned the stolen item before being brought to the magistrate, the magistrate is to amputate and not acknowledge that he returned it since it was witnessed that he took it from its protected place. This is because amputation is obligated by Allah's decree at the moment he departed with it from its protected place. Allah makes it clear by his taking it, and it would not be for the imam to do anything when such was witnessed except to amputate his hand.

If the witnesses and owner of the stolen item pardoned him before he is taken to the magistrate, it would be for them to do so and it would not be for the magistrate to pursue him afterwards. The owner had pardoned him since he had not taken him to him [i.e. the magistrate], and the witnesses had not testified in front of him.

Others have said that if the thief were to return the stolen item to the owner before reaching the magistrate, he is to be exempted from amputation. They claim is that he would not be considered a thief at that point. However, this is out of the arrogant overestimation of their intellects and invalidity of their understanding. It is as if they have not heard Allah say: **{The male thief and female thief—sever their hands…} (Q. 5:38)**. They know that he had stolen and that the decree of Allah must be applied to him for what he did since he took the stolen item from its protected place. It is also as if they have not heard the supplication of Allah's Messenger, peace and blessings be upon him and his progeny, that Allah will not pardon the magistrate who pardons the one for whom the prescribed punishment is due.[35]

---

[34] Similarly narrated in ***Sharh at-Tajrīd, Sunan al-Bayhaqi, Mušannaf Ibn Abi Shayba***

[35] Similarly narrated in ***Al-Mu'jam al-Kabīr and Mušannaf 'Abdur-Razzāq***

Concerning the slave who steals his master's property

If a slave were to steal anything from his master's property that would necessitate amputation, he is to not be amputated because he is considered [his master's] property who stole property. However, if a slave were to steal from the property of other than his master, which would necessitate amputation, he is to be amputated. This is based on what has reached us regarding the Commander of Believers, 'Ali b. Abi Ťālib, upon him be peace, that a man came to him and said: "O Commander of Believers, my slave stole from my property!" He replied: "That which you own stole from that which you own. He is to not be amputated."[36]

If he were to steal from the joint property of his master and someone else and it [i.e. the other's property] is either less than what belongs to his master or equal, he is to not be amputated since it is communal and it is not known which portion belongs to whom. However, if he steals more than what belongs to his master, which necessitates amputation, he is to be amputated.

Concerning one who steals intoxicants from the *dhimmi*

If a Muslim were to steal an intoxicant from a *dhimmi*, which was in a protected place that is permissible for a *dhimmi* to live and build their places of worship, he is to be amputated if he stole that which equals ten dirhams. However, if it was stolen from a *dhimmi* in a Muslim village in which it is impermissible for him to live or built places of worship, it would not be considered a protected place for him because he did not have a house there and due to the impermissibility for him to live there. This is because Allah's Messenger, peace and blessings be upon him and his progeny, commanded us to oust the *dhimmi* from the places of the Muslims.[37] The places of the Muslims refer to their towns that they have established and built. So, they [i.e. the *dhimmi*] should have their own villages in which they inhabit and live in, such as al-Hira or other places similar.

If a Muslim were to steal intoxicants from him in al-Hira or any other of their villages in which it is permissible for them to manifest their religion, he is to be amputated. If it was stolen in a Muslim city, he is to not be amputated because it is not for the *dhimmi* to enter the places of Islam with intoxicants or settle there.

It is obligatory for the imam to prevent the *dhimmi* from manifesting anything of their affair in the places of Islam, such as the buying and selling of intoxicants, its manufacture or the outward display of their festivals. This is because the *dhimmi* is to not be given the chance to manifest any of their affairs nor should their religions be given esteem. The *dhimmi* is to simply be subjugated and humbled, and that which contradicts the religion of Islam is to be concealed from what they remain firm against.

The imam must oust them and command them to build their own villages on the outskirts of the Muslim towns so as to not hear the clamour, music or other objectionable things to the extent of two miles or more. Their people must settle there and return there at night. There is no problem for them to do business in the villages of the Muslims. The imam must prevent them from slaughtering the meats they may sell in the markets because their meats are impermissible for Muslims to eat; rather, they are prohibited.

---

[36] Similarly narrated in ***Musnad Imam Zayd, Sharh at-Tajrīd, Mušannaf Ibn Abi Shayba***

[37] Similarly narrated in ***Ŝahīh al-Bukhāri, Ŝahīh Muslim, Sunan Abu Dāwūd***

Concerning one who steals a slave child or free child

Whoever steals a slave child from a protected place is to be amputated. If he were to steal a free child, he is to not be amputated.[38] However, *ta'zīr* is to be applied to the extent that the imam sees fit because the free person is not the property of anyone. The slave belongs to an owner, and amputation is only applied to one who steals property.

Likewise, if he were to misappropriate an adult slave in a protected place as well as bind him in chains and carry him until he takes him from the protected place, he would have to be amputated according to us.

If he [i.e. the thief] were to drive him from the front with the adult slave following him, he is to not be amputated since the slave followed him voluntarily. However, if he [i.e. the slave] were forced out of fear for his life insomuch that he would be killed otherwise, his situation according to us would be like that of an animal such as a camel or any other animal who was taken by force—whether being led or driven. The thief would be subject to amputation for leaving with him.

If the thief is caught with the slave and brought to the imam, the latter should ask the witnesses: "Did you witness that the slave was complicit? Did you see him at the time that he was taken?" If they were to testify that they saw him when he was stolen and that the slave was complicit without any fear for his life, [the thief's] hand is to not be amputated for taking him from a protected place because he followed him and did not force him. If they were to testify that he forced him and the latter feared for his life, the imam is to amputate his hand. If they had no idea, the imam is to exempt the thief from amputation due to it being a doubtful matter.

If the slave were to claim that the thief forced him, one is to not act on that. If the thief confessed that he forced him, he is to be amputated unless he retracts his confession. The imam must not amputate him until he confessed twice, and it is known that his confession is established; then, his hand is to be amputated. If it is established, then his hand is to be amputated after he confessed twice.

Concerning one who steals an animal

The one who steals an animal from the wilderness or open field is to not be amputated. He is to only be amputated if he stole it from a private pasture or protected place. If he were to steal it from a private pasture or house or fenced property, he must be amputated for what he stole as long as it equals ten dirhams.

Concerning one who steals agriculture or dates

If a thief were to steal fruit or agriculture such as wheat or barley or dates or fruit as well as cut it from its tree and then take it before its harvest and clippings, he is to not be amputated for that.[39] He is to only be amputated if the owner had already harvested, clipped, cut, transferred it to a barn or placed it in a protected

---

[38] A contrary opinion is narrated from al-Hādi in ***Al-Muntakhab***. According to the text, the imam was asked about whether the thief of a free child is amputated to which he purportedly responded: "Yes. It is obligatory to amputate in that case. In fact, it would be even more obligatory to amputate because by means of such act, the thief made the one who Allah has declared 'free' a slave and considered him by such as property."

This point of disagreement between the two texts was noted by Imams Ibn Murtaḍa, al-Mu'ayyad Billah and Abu Ṭālib in their works [Ref. ***Al-Qawl al-Awwal***]. We say that the ruling in the ***Ahkām*** is stronger and more authoritative than that mentioned in ***Al-Muntakhab*** for the following reason. If it is prohibited to relegate the status of a free person to that of a slave—as is mentioned in ***Al-Muntakhab***—how much more so should it be prohibited to apply the same punishment to someone who steals a free child and one who steals a slave child? That is to say that if we were to apply the same principle mentioned in ***Al-Muntakhab***, applying the same punishment to both would be equating the status of the slave and that of the free person. We see that in most, if not all, cases in the *Sharia'*, the penalties of affecting a free person are differentiated from those of the slave due to the difference of their statuses. Therefore, it is necessary that the penalty for the theft of a free child be differentiated from the theft of a slave child.

[39] This would also include any branches and twigs from the said trees. This principle was exemplified in ***Al-Muntakhab***.

I asked: "What if a tree or date palm does not produce fruit and a thief enters, cuts off a branch of the date palm or tree which equals ten dirhams and leaves with it from the gate? Is he to be amputated?" He replied: "No." "Why not since it is equal?" "It's because it is a branch and it hit the ground. It would be similar to a fruit."

place. If he were to steal it in any of the aforementioned situations, he is to be amputated.

As for that which hangs on the heads of trees, he is to not be amputated for it. Regarding that, Allah's Messenger, peace and blessings be upon him and his progeny, said: ((One is not amputated for produce or the spadix of palm trees)).[40] Produce for which one is not amputated is that which hangs from trees, and the spadix of palm trees is pith taken from the heads of palm trees. As for the palm pith in a protected place which is stolen and it equals ten dirhams, one is to be amputated for it.

My father related to me that his father was asked about a man who steals livestock or cows or fruit or dates or agriculture. He replied:

> He is to not be amputated for any of the above things except if he stole from a barn, fenced property, private pasture or protected place. It has been narrated through Rāfi' b. Khudayj[§] that the Prophet, peace and blessings be upon him and his progeny, said: ((One is not amputated for produce or the spadix of palm trees)). The spadix of palm trees refers to palm pith.

Concerning one who confesses that the stolen item is with him

Whoever confesses that the stolen item is with him—the judgement is that he must return it. If it were ruined while with him, the judgement is that he must compensate for it. If the owner were to establish proof that it belongs to him, it is to not be sold or given as a gift unless the one who has it has established proof that he bought it. Then, the judgement would be that it is to be reclaimed from the one who sold it. The owner who establishes the proof is considered more entitled to it. A similar judgement has reached us from the Commander of Believers, 'Ali b. Abi Ṭālib, upon him be peace.

Concerning the prescribed punishment for the grave robber (*an-nabāsh*)

The grave robber is the one who unearths a grave and takes the shrouding of the deceased. He is to have his hand amputated if he steals that which similarly necessitate the amputation, which is that which equals ten dirhams. This is because the grave robber is similar in judgement as the thief; he is even greater in disobedience and more severe in his crime. Similar has been narrated to us that the Commander of Believers, 'Ali b. Abi Ṭālib, upon him be peace, said: "The grave robber is like the thief, but he is the greatest of them in his crime!"[41]

My father related to me that his father was asked about the grave robber who is found with the shrouding of the deceased. He replied: "His hand is to be amputated when he exits the grave. The grave is considered the protected place of the dead."

Concerning snatching (*al-khulsa*)

If a man were to snatch another person's garment from off his shoulders or any other part of his body, he is to not be amputated. The imam must teach him a good lesson and ensure that he does not repeat such action.

Similarly, if someone were to steal a saddle from the back of a riding beast on the road or sever its stirrups or steal a sword from its owner while he is travelling on the road, he is to not be amputated. However, he is to be instructed in proper etiquette and have the *ta'zīr* applied.

Concerning one who violates a trust or pilfers in buying and selling

One is not amputated for violating a trust because the violator was entrusted, and everyone who violates a trust is to not be amputated for such. When it is clear that he violated it, the judgement is that he must return it and be instructed in proper etiquette regarding such.

---

[40] Similarly narrated in ***Sharh at-Tajrīd, Amāli Ahmed b. 'Isa, Sunan Abu Dāwūd, Sunan at-Tirmidhi, Sunan an-Nisā'i, Sunan al-Bayhaqi, Musnad Ahmed, Mušannaf 'Abdur-Razzāq***

[41] Similarly narrated in ***Sharh at-Tajrīd*** and ***Amāli Ahmed b. 'Isa***

Similar is the case with pilfering against the Muslims in a sale; one is to not be amputated for pilfering. Once it is established, the imam must instruct such person in proper etiquette.

The judgement for a cutpurse (*aṭ-ṭarrār*) who slits the garment of a person and steals while the victim is unaware is that he is to be amputated for that and similar.

Concerning one whose left hand is mistakenly amputated

If the imam ordered that the thief's hand be amputated and the amputator mistakenly amputated his left hand or he ordered him to extend his hand and the left hand was extended ignorantly or intentionally and was amputated, the prescribed punishment would be considered as carried out and nothing would be owed by such. This is because Allah, the Blessed and Exalted, did not specify the right hand or left hand. However, one should not intentionally do that or deliberately amputate the left hand instead of the right.

Similar has reached us from the Commander of Believers, 'Ali b. Abi Ṭālib, upon him be peace, that he ordered a thief's hand to be amputated. He extended his left hand, and it was amputated. When he came to know, he said: "The prescribed punishment has been carried out."[42]

My father related to me that his father was asked about the thief who was ordered to have his right hand amputated but instead extended his left hand and it was amputated. He replied: "That would suffice in his amputation because Allah had not specified the right or left."

Both hands of the thief are to not be amputated. If he were to steal twice or thrice or four times, his right hand is to be amputated the first time, and then his left foot on the second time. After that, he is to be imprisoned if he were to repeat such theft until it becomes clear to the imam that he repented, can be trusted and regretted what he did.

Similar has reached us from the Commander of Believers, 'Ali b. Abi Ṭālib, upon him be peace, that a thief was brought to him who had his hand and foot amputated. The people came to him and said: "Amputate his other hand!" He replied: "How would he eat?" Then, they said: "Amputate his other foot!" He replied: "How would he walk?" Then, he commanded that he be imprisoned, and he financially supported him from the Muslim public treasury.[43]

Women and slaves are considered the same in respect to amputation.

Concerning those who make war

Allah, the Blessed and Exalted, says regarding those who make war against Allah and His Messenger as well as those who rob highways and strive to spread corruption in the land: {**Verily, the recompense of those who make war against Allah and His Messenger and those who strive to spread corruption in the land is that they are to be put to death or crucified or have their hands and feet severed from opposite sides or be banished from the land. That is for them a recompense in this world, and to them shall belong a great punishment in the hereafter**} (Q. 5:33).

This verse was [said to be] revealed regarding the people of Bajīla, who were the last of the Bedouins to embrace Islam. They embraced Islam, emigrated and established themselves in Medina. They started to become sick due to settling there. Their bellies began to swell, they started to become pallid [lit. "yellow"] in colour and their conditions worsened. They asked Allah's Messenger, peace and blessings be upon him and his progeny, to give them camels as charity so that they can drink their milk and urine; he gave them permission to do so. When they did that and started to regain their health and when their conditions improved, they began to fight

[42] Similarly narrated in ***Amāli Ahmed b. 'Isa***

[43] Similarly narrated in ***Musnad Imam Zayd, Sharh at-Tajrīd, Amāli Ahmed b. 'Isa.*** Similar has been related in ***Mušannaf 'Abdur-Razzāq, Sunan al-Bayhaqi, Mušannaf Ibn Abi Shayba***

and kill the keeper of the camel. They took the camels and left with them. When the news reached Allah's Messenger, peace and blessings be upon him and his progeny, he had them pursued and captured. He also commanded that their hands and feet be amputated as well as their eyes gouged out. He then left them to languish in the sun until they died. The Prophet, peace and blessings be upon him and his progeny, was censured for their affair.[44]

Allah knows best regarding the truthfulness of this report![45] Regardless, Allah revealed the judgement regarding those who do similar to what they did when He says: **{Verily, the recompense of those who make war against Allah and His Messenger and those who strive to spread corruption in the land is that they are to be put to death or crucified or have their hands and feet severed from opposite sides or be banished from the land. That is for them a recompense in this world, and to them shall belong a great punishment in the hereafter} (Q. 5:33)**.

One is obligated by the judgement of Allah and His Messenger to expel from the land those who carry weapons and terrorise the Muslims. If he simply seized them and instructed them in proper etiquette or applied *ta'zīr* to them, he would not have acted upon Allah's judgement as we mentioned. He [i.e. the perpetrator] is to be followed on horseback by men until he is driven out and banished. However, the one who terrorises the roads and steals property [but does not kill] must have their hand and foot amputated from the opposite sides—that would mean the right hand and left foot. Then, he is to be left to go where he pleases.[46]

As for the one who terrorises the roads and steals property and kills, he is to be put to death and crucified after he is killed. This is because it is impermissible for a living person to be crucified. [The crucified person is to not be naked; rather, he is to have his nakedness covered. Ref. ***Al-Muntakhab***]

The meaning of **{they are to be put to death or (*aw*) crucified}** is '...and crucified.' It [i.e. the Arabic word for 'or'] is used as a conjunction of inclusion that does not carry the meaning of choice. This is what the Arabs do in their speech.[47] Regarding that, Allah says: **{...and We sent unto him one hundred thousand or (*aw*) more...} (Q. 37:147)**. By that, the Glorified means "...and more..." It is used as a conjunction of inclusion here just as it is used in the verse **{...or crucified...}**. If it were a conjunction of alternative in the phrase **{...or more...}**, it would imply uncertainty. And Allah—the Blessed and Exalted—is free of such, and the Glorified is highly exalted from such! Rather, He is the most knowing, and there is nothing hidden from Him—whether it be in secret or in the open. It is as He says **{He knows the treachery of the eyes and whatsoever the breasts conceal} (Q. 40:19)** and **{He knows the secret and what is more hidden} (Q. 20:7)**.

That which Allah mentions is that He knows what is more hidden than a secret, so there is nothing that is a secret to Him nor anything concealed from Him in the breasts. It may not be apparent in their thoughts or reach their hearts or imprisoned in their breasts. They may not even make it aware and may secretly desire it. Yet, Allah had known that from them and knew all of the words and deeds that will transpire in their hearts because He encompasses all things. He knows all that will exist before it even comes into existence. Glorified be the One who has no limits that can be breached nor a likeness for which He can be likened to! He is the One, the Possessor of authority and majesty, and He is the One who is exalted from taking consorts or offspring! He is too holy to decree oppression and corruption, and He is too distant to have a share in the deeds of the slaves! Therefore, His actions are

---

[44] Similarly narrated in ***Asbāb an-Nuzūl*** of al-Wāhidi, ***Sunan an-Nisā'i, Sunan Abi Dāwūd, Sunan Ibn Māja***

[45] The imam seemingly doubts the details of the report. This is the reason we rendered the beginning of the report with the additional wording "said to be."

[46] In ***Al-Muntakhab***, al-Hādi was asked about the punishment for the one who terrorises the road and causes fear to the Muslims but does not steal any property nor kills anyone. He replied: "He is to be banished from the land."

[47] The Arabic word for 'or' is generally said to have twelve different meanings—one of which corresponds to the conjunction 'and.' See the entry for '*aw*' in the **Lane's Arabic English Lexicon**. Such interpretation of the imam is more reasonable since it would be rather nonsensical for the verse to present crucifixion as an alternative to 'putting to death' if crucifixion itself is a method of putting one to death.

not like the actions of His creation, and the actions of His creation are not like His actions! This is because His actions are perpetually existent, and the actions of His slaves are accidental from non-existence. That which is non-existent can never be likened to that which is perpetually existent just as that which is living can never be compared to that which is dead. Glorified be the Possessor of the Divine Threat and Divine Promise, the Truthful! Glorified be the Possessor of might and praise, the One who is exalted from what the falsifiers say and the deviants attribute to Him!

If this one who made war were to come to the imam repenting for what he had done before the imam overpowers him or before the Muslim forces gain victory over him, it is obligatory for the imam to accept his repentance if he came to him seeking amnesty. He must also ensure the safety for such one in terms of his life and wealth.

Similarly, if the one who made war were to write to the imam and ask for amnesty from the one affected by what he did in terms of wealth and life, the imam must grant him amnesty if it is good for the overall Muslim community. Therefore, if he were to come to the imam seeking amnesty, the imam is to not inquire as to that from which he is seeking amnesty. If anyone were to come to the imam regarding anything related to that from which amnesty was sought, the imam is to not count it against him and must prevent him from being sought after. If anyone were to kill [the one seeking amnesty] due to his killing of someone while he was in the state of war, the imam is to put such person to death because he had insured his life by the protection of Allah, His Messenger and the imam.

If the imam were to seize him in a part of the city before the latter wrote to him seeking amnesty or giving himself up and then the captured person asks for amnesty while [the imam] is informed of his repentance and that he came to him after having repented, he is to not accept the claim of his repentance and must apply Allah's judgement against him. This is because a repentance like this cannot take place except by his coming voluntarily to the imam after having prevented himself from doing so. It is only then that his repentance would be accepted. As for the one who was caught or had not reached a place of refuge and had claimed repentance, such would not be accepted from him in that case.

My father related to me that his father was asked about the one who made war and how he is to be exiled. He replied: "He is to be exiled from city to city."

Concerning intoxicants and its prohibition from the Book of Allah

Allah, the Blessed and Exalted, says regarding the prohibition of intoxicants: {**O ye who believe! Verily, intoxicants and games of risk and idolatrous altars and divining arrows are but impurities from the works of Satan. So, eschew them that ye may prosper**} (**Q. 5:90**).

The term {**intoxicants**} refers to anything that colludes and corrupts the intellect. If a lot corrupts it, then even a little is prohibited. For that reason, it is called 'intoxicants' (*khamr*) due to its colluding and falsifying the intellect. The same is the case whether it is from grapes, dates, honey, corn, barley, wheat, fruit of palm or anything else.

The term {**games of risk**} refers to backgammon (*an-nard*), chess (*ash-shaṭranj*) and all wagers (*al-qimār*). It is that which distracts one from the remembrance of the Most Merciful as well as preoccupies one from obedience and faith.

The term {**idolatrous altars**} refers to Pre-Islamic altars that were constructed from stone so that they could worship other than Allah. They exist today and are present in the ravines of the earth and their traces. They are erected in their states and have remained during their ages.

The term {**divining arrows**} refers to arrows that were used in the Pre-Islamic era. These arrows were divided and used as arbitrators for their affairs. There were different signs and markers written on them. Whenever one would extract an arrow with these markers and signs on them, they would base their decisions on such.

Allah, the Blessed and Exalted, informs them that all of such actions from them diverts them away from Allah and prevents them from His obedience. They also may preoccupy them from observing the obligatory prayers during their respective times. That is based on His statement: {**Verily, Satan only desires to cause enmity and hatred amongst thee regarding intoxicants and games of risk, as well as divert thee away from the remembrance of Allah and from the prayer. Wilt thou not refrain?**} (**Q. 5:91**).

Concerning the prescribed punishment for intoxicants

The prescribed punishment for the one who drinks a little or many intoxicants is eighty lashes when two male witnesses witnessed him drinking it. If they were to simply see him drinking or smell its scent on him, it would be obligatory for the prescribed punishment of eighty lashes to be applied on him.

Similar has reached us from the Commander of Believers, 'Ali b. Abi Ťālib, upon him be peace. He said to 'Umar b. al-Khaťťāb that there was a matter between him and Qudāma b. Maž'ūn al-Jamhi[§]. When Qudāma drank intoxicants, Abu Hurayra[§] had the prescribed punishment applied to him in Bahrain. Since Qudāma was placed in charge of Bahrain by 'Umar, he was brought to 'Umar. He raised a complaint against Abu Hurayra, and 'Umar sent for him to represent himself. Abu Hurayra came along with witnesses who testified to Qudāma drinking intoxicants. One of those who came with him was al-Jārūd al-Abadi[§]. When Abu Hurayra came to him, he asked him about the matter with Qudāma and the latter informed him that he lashed him for drinking intoxicants. 'Umar asked him for evidence, and he [i.e. Abu Hurayra] came with witnesses. 'Abdullah b. 'Umar met al-Jārūd al-Abadi and asked him "Are you the one who witnessed my uncle drinking intoxicants?" He replied: "Yes." He [i.e. 'Abdullah] then said: "Your witness against him is impermissible!" Al-Jārūd became angry and said: "By Allah, either your uncle is to be lashed or your father is to be considered a disbeliever!" They entered upon 'Umar and bore witness that he lashed him for intoxicants. Qudāma said: "There is no hardship to be applied to me for intoxicants because I am simply among those for whom Allah says: {**There is no hardship upon those who believe and perform righteous deeds regarding that which they have eaten when they are God-conscious, believe and perform righteous deeds and then are God-conscious and believe and then are God-conscious and do good. And Allah loves those who do good**} (**Q. 5:93**)." Qudāma fought in Badr, and 'Umar was afraid to do anything based on what he said. He then sent for 'Ali b. Abi Ťālib, upon him be peace, and said to him: "Didn't you hear what Qudāma said?" He informed him of what he recited from the Qur'an. 'Ali, upon him be peace, then said: "Verily, when Allah prohibited intoxicants, the believers complained to the Prophet, peace and blessings be upon him and his progeny, saying: 'How much more so with our fathers and brothers who died before us and were killed while drinking intoxicants? How much more so are our prayers that we prayed while they drank? Will Allah accept from us and them or not?' Then Allah revealed regarding them: {**There is no hardship upon those who believe and perform righteous deeds regarding that which they have eaten when they are God-conscious, believe and perform righteous deeds and then are God-conscious and believe and then are God-conscious and do good. And Allah loves those who do good**} (**Q. 5:93**). That was an excuse for those in the past and a proof for those in the present. O 'Umar, he drinks intoxicants. When he drinks, he becomes intoxicated. When he becomes intoxicated, he speaks irrationally. When he speaks irrationally, he slanders. Therefore, establish the prescribed punishment of one who slanders; the one who slanders is flogged with eighty lashes."[48]

---

[48] Similarly narrated in ***Sunan Abu Dāwūd, Mušannaf 'Abdur-Razzāq, Bihar al-Anwār***

Similar has reached us from the Commander of Believers, upon him be peace, that he used to flog the one who drinks alcohol with eighty lashes. He used to say: "Everything that intoxicates is considered an intoxicant."[49] It has also reached us that he used to flog for a little amount just as he would flog for a lot.[50]

My father related to me on the authority of his father:

> Abu Bakr b. Abi Uways related to me from al-Hussein b. 'Abdullah b. Ḋumayra—his father—his grandfather—'Ali b. Abi Ťālib, upon him be peace, used to flog the one who drank a lot of intoxicants just as he would flog the one who drank a little.

My father related to me that his father was asked about intoxicants, and he replied: "Everything which intoxicates by a lot of it, even a small amount is prohibited. Similar has been related from the Prophet, peace and blessings be upon him and his progeny."[51]

Whatever Allah prohibited to drink—the one who drinks it is subject to the prescribed punishment. My father related to me that his father said:

> It has reached us from the Commander of Believers, upon him be peace: "I did not find anyone who drank intoxicants or intoxicating date juice (*nabīdh*) except that he was flogged eighty lashes as the prescribed punishment."

Concerning what the imam should do with the prescribed punishments

The imam should avoid clothing the one being punished with only one garment; neither should he strip him of all his clothing. Also, he should not fetter any of the Muslims; the term 'fetter' means to bind one's hands to one's neck.

As for what has been narrated from the Commander of Believers, upon him be peace, in which he supposedly allowed the punished person's hands to be free to protect himself, this is not authentically attributed to him according to me. This is because if he allowed one's hands to be free, there is a possibility that such one could prevent himself from a portion of the eighty lashes for his sin.

Binding his hands would be more useful for him and better suited to protect him from his foolishness because that would be more painful. And when his pain teaches him a lesson, it is over. No prescribed punishment that does not hurt or cause pain to the punished will deter one from doing that which is impermissible. I hold to the view that the prescribed punishments are simply to teach a lesson.

It has reached us from the Commander of Believers, upon him be peace, that a drinker of intoxicants was brought to him and he flogged him with eighty lashes.

Concerning various points related to the prescribed punishments

The prescribed punishment is applied to the perpetrator when it is testified to in front of the imam—whether it was done in the past or not. As for the statement of the people that the prescribed punishment is exempted if it was done in the past, their statement is unacceptable, and we do not acknowledge it from them. This is because it is an obligatory command from Allah; whenever it has been established by just witnesses in front of the imam, it is obligatory for him to apply the prescribed punishment.

They say that it is exempted in the case of a past theft, fornication or intoxication. However, they agree with us in the case of slander. They say that when one brings proof for slander, it is accepted whether it occurred in the past or not. They also say that it is because it is from the rights of the people. By my life! The right of the Most Gracious, to the one with intellect, is more obligatory than the right of the people.

---

[49] Similarly narrated in ***Sharh at-Tajrīd, Amāli Abi Ťālib, Ŝahīh Muslim, Sunan Abu Dāwūd, Sunan at-Tirmidhi, Musnad Ahmed, Al-Mu'jam al-Kabīr***

[50] Similarly narrated in ***Mušannaf Ibn Abi Shayba***

[51] Similarly narrated in ***Musnad Imam Zayd, Sharh at-Tajrīd, Sunan Abu Dāwūd, Sunan at-Tirmidhi, Sunan an-Nisā'i, Sunan Ibn Mājah, Musnad Ahmed, al-Mustadrak***

'Ali b. Abi Ťālib, upon him be peace, established the prescribed punishment for intoxication on al-Walīd b. Uqba§ during the government of 'Uthmān b. Affān. He did not hold to the view that it is to be abandoned, and he took responsibility for that in his own hands. They narrate that 'Uthmān said: "Whoever would like to establish the prescribed punishment on him can do so. But as for me, I will not command anyone to do so." The Commander of Believers, upon him be peace, said: "By Allah! The prescribed punishment of Allah will not be nullified as long as I am in Islam!" Then, he stood and flogged him eighty lashes.[52]

That prescribed punishment was for something done in the past because he [i.e. al-Walīd] used to drink in Kufa. It is said that he prayed four units for the dawn prayer and vomited alcohol in the mosque! He then lifted his head and said: "Do you want more [units]?" They witnessed him drinking and brought this up to 'Uthmān, and the matter was as we explained earlier in the account.

It has reached us that the Commander of Believers, upon him be peace, said:

> There are three things that I have never done and will never do: I have never worshipped an idol, and that is because I cannot worship something that cannot harm or benefit me. I have never committed fornication, and that is because I dislike in the wife of another that which I dislike in my wife. I have never drunk intoxicants, and that is because I prefer that which increases my intellect over that which nullifies it.

Concerning the one who slanders his wife who is a pre-pubescent girl

Whoever slanders his wife who is a pre-pubescent girl will not be obligated to perform a mutual cursing with her because if he were to belie himself, there would be no prescribed punishment applied to him. Also, it is because if she were to slander him, there would be no prescribed punishment applied to her on his behalf.

Similarly, if someone else were to slander her, there would be no prescribed punishment applied to him on her behalf. However, her husband and anyone else who slandered her must be taught proper etiquette and cautioned against such.

Concerning the man who slanders his wife with a slave, Jew, Christian or Magian

If he were to slander her with any of the above, he would be required to engage in a mutual cursing. If he belied himself before completing the mutual cursing with her, the prescribed punishment would be applied to him on her behalf and the woman would be left as she is.

There is to be no prescribed punishment applied if one slandered a slave, Jew, Christian or Magian because Allah—the Mighty and Majestic—only obligates the prescribed punishment upon the one who slanders a believing free man (*muhšan*) or woman. There is no prescribed punishment on the one who slandered a slave.

If he were to slander her [i.e. his wife] and then divorce her, she is to observe her waiting period and then they are to engage in a mutual cursing. If her waiting period had already passed, the prescribed punishment is to be applied to him on her behalf and there is to be no mutual cursing between them.

Concerning the man who slanders his wife and then dies before performing the mutual cursing with her or she dies

If he were to slander her and then die before engaging in a mutual cursing or she died, she would inherit from him and he would inherit from her because the both of them had not gone through the mutual cursing and would thus be considered married. If her husband were to refuse to swear, the

[52] Similarly narrated in ***Sharh at-Tajrīd, Ŝahīh al-Bukhāri, Ŝahīh Muslim, Sunan Abu Dāwūd, As-Sunan of al-Bayhaqi, Mušannaf 'Abdur-Razzāq***

prescribed punishment would be applied to him on her behalf. There would be no dissolution of marriage between them and they would not resume with a new marriage.

Concerning the slave who slanders a free woman or slave woman when she is married to him and concerning a free man who slanders his wife who is a slave

If a slave is married to a free woman and slanders her, they are to engage in a mutual cursing. However, if his wife were a slave woman and he slandered her, there would be no mutual cursing between them. He [i.e. the slave that slandered his free wife] is to be flogged with forty lashes as a prescribed punishment, and his children would be considered connected to him.

If a free man slandered his wife who is a slave, there is to be no mutual cursing between them. The mutual cursing would be exempted from them because if he belied himself, there would be no prescribed punishment applied to him on her behalf due to her being a slave and him a free person.

Concerning one who said to the son of a woman who engaged in a mutual cursing "You are not the son of so-n-so" meaning the one who engaged in the mutual cursing with his mother and concerning one who slandered his wife by a specific man

Whoever says to the son of a woman who engaged in a mutual cursing "You are not the son of so-n-so" meaning the one who engaged in the mutual cursing with his mother, it is obligatory that the prescribed punishment be applied to him on behalf of the woman who engaged in the mutual cursing if she demands it. This is because if the said person were to negate that the man who engaged in the mutual cursing was not his [i.e. the accused's] father, he would have falsely accused his mother of unlawful fornication. This is because a child can only be from a man except in the case of Jesus, the son of Mary, upon him be peace.

Anyone who slanders must either engage in a mutual cursing or prescribed punishment. The mutual cursing takes place between spouses, and the prescribed punishment takes place between non-spouses. The exception to the above cases is if four witnesses testify to what the accuser said.

As for the one who slandered his wife designating a specific person, they are to engage in a mutual cursing. If he refuses to swear before the mutual cursing, he and his wife would be considered married and the prescribed punishment would be applied to him on her behalf. And if the man he slandered demanded it, the prescribed punishment would be applied to him on his behalf. Likewise, if the spouses go through with the mutual cursing and then the man he slandered demands it, the prescribed punishment would be applied to him on his behalf unless the accuser came with four witnesses to testify to the fornication.

Concerning one who said to his wife "I found you to not be a virgin"

Whoever said to his wife "I found you to not be a virgin", there is no prescribed punishment applied to him for such because the hymen can be ruptured [lit. "virginity can be removed"] from a number of things other than intercourse. Some examples include rigorous washing, tearing during menstruation due to excessive insertion, riding an animal bareback, as well as other reasons. For that reason, we do not assign the prescribed punishment for such.

However, if he were to mention to her that it was due to fornication, he would be considered a slanderer and the prescribed punishment for slander would be applied to him.

Concerning the proofs of the one who claims that there is no prescribed punishment for intoxication and the refutation of the one who claims that the Commander of Believers revoked the prescribed punishment for such

There are those who say that there is no prescribed punishment applied for intoxication. They narrate a false hadith that is not authentically attributed to the Commander of Believers, 'Ali b. Abi Ṭālib, upon him be peace, in which he flogged a person for intoxication and the person died. He then paid indemnity for him from the Muslims' public treasury. Ibn al-Kawwa[§] came to him and said: "O Commander of Believers, why did you pay indemnity for him?" He replied: "I did so because we flogged him for intoxication and he died, and this prescribed punishment was not commanded by Allah. Rather, it was the opinion that was held by ten Companions. Whoever dies as a result of an opinion of ours must be compensated by us from the Muslims' public treasury." [Ibn al-Kawwa] replied: "What is this that you are claiming? Are you saying that you held to a view that was not from the Book of Allah and paid indemnity for it from the public treasury of the Muslims?" Then, the narrators of this so-called hadith claimed that the Commander of Believers, upon him be peace, abandoned the prescribed punishment for intoxication from that day.[53]

This is a falsehood against Allah, as well as a lie against Him, His Messenger and the Commander of Believers! This entire "hadith" is false and impossible. It is an obscene lie, and no one with intellect would accept it nor would any believer believe it to be true.

The one who was foremost in the obligation of dealing with intoxicants and establishing the prescribed punishment for it was Allah's Messenger, peace and blessings be upon him and his progeny. He is the one who made eighty lashes an obligation and compulsory judgement for the one who drinks it.[54]

As for that which is narrated from the Commander of Believers, upon him be peace, in which he said "We obligate eighty lashes upon the one who drinks it because when he drinks, he becomes intoxicated. When he becomes intoxicated, he speaks irrationally. When he speaks irrationally, he slanders," it is possible that this statement of his was transmitted from the Messenger, peace and blessings be upon him and his progeny. This is because the Commander of Believers, upon him be peace, does not mention anything from himself. The proof that it was from Allah's Messenger, peace and blessings be upon him and his progeny, is that it has been narrated from him [i.e. 'Ali] without any disagreement from the people of knowledge and narrations:

> A man who drank intoxicants was brought to [the Prophet] and he had him flogged with eighty lashes. Then he said: ((If he repeats it, put him to death)). The man repeated it and we waited for the command to put him to death. Then [the Prophet] commanded that he be flogged a second time, and he was flogged.[55]

So how can you say and narrate from the Commander of Believers, upon him be peace, that he said the prescribed punishment for intoxication was his opinion and that of other Companions while Allah's Messenger, peace and blessings be upon him and his progeny, did it, obligated it and carried out its judgement and he is the exemplar and model?

Among the proofs for the obligation of the prescribed punishment for intoxication is that intoxication is a prohibition from Allah by the consensus of the *Ummah*. This is based on the statement of the Glorified and Exalted: **{O ye who believe! Verily, intoxicants and games of risk and idolatrous altars and divining arrows are but impurities from the works of Satan. So, eschew them that ye may prosper} (Q. 5:90)**. He prohibited it from the slaves by forbidding them to drink it and commanding them to avoid it. Then, he informed them that it is ritually impure, and ritual impurity is prohibited from the believers.

---

[53] Similarly narrated in ***Musnad Imam Zayd*** in a condensed form:

> Zayd b. 'Ali related to me—his father—his grandfather—'Ali, upon them be peace, said: "Whoever dies from the prescribed punishment for fornication and slander will not have to pay indemnity; the Book of Allah puts him to death. Whoever dies from the prescribed punishment for intoxication will have to pay indemnity from the Muslim public treasury; it is something from our opinion."

[54] Similarly narrated in ***Sharh at-Tajrīd, Ṣaḥīḥ Muslim, Sunan at-Tirmidhi, Sunan Ibn Hibbān, Al-Mu'jam al-Awsaṭ, Mušannaf 'Abdur-Razzāq***

[55] Similarly narrated in ***Sunan Abu Dāwūd, Sunan at-Tirmidhi, Sunan an-Nisā'i, Mušannaf 'Abdur-Razzāq, Sunan Ibn Mājah, Al-Mu'jam al-Kabīr***

From that is the statement of the Lord of creation: {**Say: "I find not in what has been revealed to me any food forbidden to be eaten save that it be carcass or blood poured forth or swine flesh—for verily, it is an impurity** (*ar-rijs*)**—or an act of disobedience sacrificed to other than Allah..."**} (**Q. 6:145**). The Glorified mentions that every prohibited item is considered impure. If it is established as sound that every prohibited item is impure, it is similarly established as sound that every impurity is prohibited from the believers due to it being declared prohibited by Allah, the Lord of creation.

If there is no doubt to anyone that they [i.e. intoxicants] are prohibited by Allah, the judgement of drinking such is like the judgement regarding eating that which is prohibited to eat, such as swine meat, blood and carcass. If anyone were to eat carcass or blood while it is forbidden by Allah's declaration of its prohibition, it would be obligatory for the imam to discipline such person as well as teach him a lesson and urge him towards repentance. If the person were to repeat such action, he [i.e. the imam] must repeat the disciplinary action. And if the person were to repeat it, he must repeat it. For every repetition of the action, there must be a repetition of the disciplinary action.

However, it would not be permissible for him to put him to death for such because it is prohibited by Allah, and Allah never commanded the death penalty for one who were to eat any of the above. It would be for the imam to decide on what to do for such action; however, he would not be allowed to put such person to death because Allah has not commanded him to do such, neither has He passed such judgement against such person. When such prohibition from Allah has not been permitted and one says that Allah has declared such as prohibited, such person declares himself that he would be considered disobedient to Allah if he were to do it.

Similarly, it would be obligatory for the one who drinks intoxicants to be disciplined once its prohibition has been acknowledged and established. Likewise, the judgement of one who considers that which Allah has prohibited as permissible and declares Allah's prohibition of drinking it as permissible would be like the judgement of one who similarly declares the consumption of carcass and blood to be permissible despite Allah prohibiting such.

If a man were to say that carcass and blood are permissible and not prohibited as well as believe that and advocate for such, it would be obligatory for the imam to urge him towards repentance for such. If he repents, he is to be left alone. If he does not repent, he is to be put to death. Similarly, if he were to say that intoxicants are permissible and not prohibited as well as believe that and advocate for such, it would be obligatory for the imam to urge him towards repentance for such. If he repents, [he is to be left alone]. Otherwise, he is to be put to death because he has openly opposed Allah by declaring that which Allah has prohibited as permissible and that which Allah permitted as prohibited. The one who permits what Allah prohibited is like the one who prohibits what Allah permitted. And the one who permits what Allah prohibited and prohibits what Allah permitted is ignorant of Allah and has rejected Him. This is because the one who objects to an action of Allah in terms of His permissions or prohibitions and says that which He has prohibited is not prohibited is like the one who objects to His action of sending Messengers and says that He has not sent Messengers. Whoever objects to His action of sending Messengers is like the one who objects to His action of creating the heavens and earth. And whoever says that Allah has not created the heavens or anything else does not know of Him or worship Him because he worships one who has not created the heavens, and Allah created and formed them.

Likewise, whoever says that Allah has not prohibited blood and intoxicants has objected to and does not worship Allah. Neither does such person know of or acknowledge Him because he says that the one who prohibited intoxicants is not Allah and that Allah has not prohibited it. Fundamentally, such person worships, by his own statement, one who has not declared carcass, intoxicants, blood and swine meat as prohibited while Allah has declared such as prohibited. And if he does not worship the One who has declared carcass, intoxicants, blood and swine meat as prohibited, he worships other than Allah. Whoever worships other than Allah is like the one who disbelieves in Allah and commits idolatry. In judgement, such person would be considered to have become an idolater; the process regarding that would be like the process regarding apostates. If they were to repent and show remorse and retract, they would be left alone. However, if they were to not retract and repent, they would be put to death.

Therefore, since the judgement of the one who permits intoxicants and carcass and blood and swine meat despite Allah prohibiting such is that he is to be put to death if he does not repent, the judgement of the one who partakes in such is punishment and disciplinary action. This is for the one who at least acknowledges that Allah has prohibited such. It is considered the same, and there is no disagreement in that.

Since it is sound according to us and proven by our intellects, we know that it is necessary that there be some type of disciplinary action for such. Then, we found that there was a disciplinary action for drinking intoxicants which was demonstrated from the Messenger, peace and blessings be upon him and his progeny, as a prescribed punishment during his lifetime. Therefore, we imitate his action in that and make it binding for the one who drinks intoxicants just as the Messenger, peace and blessings be upon him and his progeny, made such binding. There is no disciplinary action or prescribed punishment for one who consumes carcass, blood and swine meat because no one consumed it during his lifetime or afterwards until today as far as we know. If it were to occur, the imam would have to exercise his own independent judgement regarding a disciplinary action for such.

Whoever does not obligate a disciplinary action for the drinking of intoxicants similarly does not obligate a disciplinary action for one who consumes carcass, blood and swine meat because all of such is considered the same in the judgement of Allah, the Exalted and Most High. Whoever obligates a disciplinary action for all of that and anything else, such person must hold to the opinion that the establishment of such is an obligation upon the imam. It would not be obligatory to consider such as objectionable if he were to develop his own disciplinary action because it would simply be his own independent judgement. His desire is its rectification and preventing one from Allah's disobedience to His obedience.

The imam is simply in a custodianship like the druggist and healer who is known by insightful healing and treatment. If the healer sees that the defect requires a medicine, he is to utilise his own independent judgement in its treatment and seek the permission of the patient's relatives. If the defect worsens or the patient dies, the healer is to not be considered blameworthy or compensate after having utilised independent judgement and sought the relative's permission. Similar is the case with the imam; he is to utilise independent judgement regarding that which would rectify his subjects and prevent disobedience and rebellious acts from them. That is what Allah commands him.

Allah commands him to observe such against any mistakes that they may commit and frees his hand from such. This is considered greater than the permission of the patient's relatives to treat such patient. If the imam utilises his own independent judgement in the rectification of the *Ummah* by disciplinary actions in order to prevent them from disobedience and rebelliousness to their Creator and anyone of them worsens or is destroyed, no one can hold him responsible for any of that. He is obligated to uphold and investigate in terms of a disciplinary action as well as utilise independent judgement for the sake of Allah in order to rectify the affairs of the people and places.

If he were to ruin creation greatly for which only he can be responsible or do that which Allah had not permitted for him, he would be obligated to pay indemnity and be considered blameworthy. The one who unintentionally does something that s/he is not permitted to do and commits an error thereby—such as two witnesses who testify against a man for stealing something from a protected place and the imam amputates him but then one of them was discovered to be blind or insane or when four witnesses testify against a man for fornication and he is stoned but then one of them was discovered to be blind—this would be considered his [i.e. the imam's] error and he would be obligated to pay indemnity for such.

As for that which is necessary for him to do and impermissible for him to avoid regarding disciplining the *Ummah*, he would not be considered blameworthy for such because blameworthiness is simply due to an objectionable action on the part of the one who erred so that he does not return to such act. If compensation is due on the imam on behalf of the disciplined person because he permitted something in a disciplinary action that was impermissible for him to do, that would be considered an objectionable action for him for disciplining the *Ummah*. If he were to shirk from disciplining them, he would be punished in the Hellfire by the Possessor of Majesty and Nobility greater than the punishment of the imam's disciplining. If there were no imam to properly discipline the *Ummah* to the extent of their sins, they would be destroyed in all respects and some of them would consume others. However, Allah is the best at decrees, the most merciful to His creation and the most compassionate to His slaves!

Regarding that which we mentioned, it should be most sufficient to the people of knowledge and understanding. Praise be to Allah, the Most Exalted and Most High! May the prayers and peace of Allah be upon Muhammad and his Ahl al-Bayt!

My uncle, al-Hasan b. al-Qāsim related to me:

> It has been related to me with the most reliable of chains to the Prophet, peace and blessings be upon him and his progeny, that Daylam al-Himyari§ came to him from the people of Yemen. He said: "O Messenger of Allah, we live in a land that is extremely cold and we do very hard labour. We drink a drink from wheat that gives us strength for our labour and helps with the cold of our land." The Prophet, peace and blessings be upon him and his progeny, asked: ((Does it intoxicate?)). He replied: "Yes." [The Prophet] responded: ((Keep away from it)). Al-Himyari then brought it in front of him and said the same thing. He, peace and blessings be upon him and his progeny, asked: ((Does it intoxicate?)). He replied: "Yes." He, peace and blessings be upon him and his progeny, replied: ((Keep away from it)). [Al-Himyari] then asked: "What if the people do not abandon it?" He replied: ((If they do not abandon it, fight them!)).[56]

This hadith agrees with the hadith in which he, peace and blessings be upon him and his progeny, said ((Every intoxicant is prohibited)) as well as the hadith in which he, peace and blessings be upon him and his progeny, said: ((Everything which intoxicates by a lot of it, even a small amount is prohibited)).

Regarding another hadith ((Even a taste of it is prohibited)), it agrees with the hadith that was narrated regarding the man who drank intoxicants and was flogged. Then he said: ((If he repeats it, put him to death)). Then he repeated it and he commanded to flog him eighty times. The differing of his initial command and acting on the other proves that Allah appointed for him a command and adjudicated flogging as a judgement. Therefore, Allah's Messenger, peace and blessings be upon him and his progeny, did not consider his initial command to put to death.

My uncle, al-Hasan b. al-Qāsim related to me:

> It has been related to me with the most reliable of chains to the Prophet, peace and blessings be upon him and his progeny: ((Intoxicants were made prohibited from us, and there were no intoxicants for us except from dates)).[57]

The intoxicants that were prohibited were simply that which was cultivated in Medina by the people of Yathrib. The people of Yathrib were the people of date palms and dates. There were no grapes for them except in small amounts. I assume that it was considered a new occurrence, and it was new after having not previously been.

---

[56] Similarly narrated in ***Sunan Abu Dāwūd, Musnad Ahmed, Al-Mu'jam al-Kabīr, Mušannaf Ibn Abi Shayba, Sunan al-Bayhaqi***

[57] Similarly narrated in ***Amāli Ahmed b. 'Isa, Ŝahīh Muslim, Sunan an-Nisā'i***

The Book of Indemnity, Injuries and Offences

In the Name of Allah, the Most Gracious, the Most Merciful...

Beginning of the judgement regarding indemnity in the Book and what Allah decrees against the one who intentionally kills a soul

Allah—the Blessed and Exalted—says: **{And whosoever slays a believer intentionally—his recompense shall be Hell therein to abide forever. And Allah's anger shall be upon him as well as His curse. And he shall ready for him a great punishment}** (Q. 4:93).

The term **{intentionally}** refers to the intention to oppress and act with audacity in shedding the blood that Allah has prohibited. Allah simply obligates that the threat of His Hellfire, punishment, anger and curse be upon the one who intentionally kills a believer wrongly and act with audacity against Allah by killing. As for the one who intentionally kills rightfully, there is no punishment on such person.

I hold to the view that the one who is killed rightfully is not considered a believer because the right does not obligate that a believer is killed except if he committed a crime and repented before being stoned or committed manslaughter but repented sincerely to his Lord before being put to death. This is because killing is only obligated in Allah's judgement in ten situations.

The first is the killing of idolaters after inviting them to Allah and they refuse to either embrace Islam or a contractual relationship. The second is the killing of the apostate from Islam after such person refuses repentance. The third is the killing of the Muslim "magician" after such person refuses repentance.[1] The fourth is the killing of heretics after they refuse repentance. The fifth is that which Allah commanded through Allah's Messenger, peace and blessings be upon him and his progeny, regarding the killing of a cuckold if such person persists after being called to repentance.

The sixth is the killing of a rebellious faction of Muslims if they rebel and oppose the believers, as Allah commands in His statement: **{And if two factions of believers fight, seek rectification between them both. Then, if one of them rebels against the other, fight the one who rebelled until they return to the command of Allah}** (Q. 49:9). This would include those who invite to that which is not for them to do and claim that they are imams, those who seek to invalidate the judgements and disgrace Islam, as well as those who oppose the Most Gracious and manifest disobedience and wickedness. They are those about whom Allah says: **{O ye who believe! Fight those near unto thee amongst the disbelievers and let them find in thee harshness. And know that Allah is with the God-conscious}** (Q. 9:123). Then, He clarifies who they are specifically when He says: **{And whosoever judges not by that which Allah hath revealed—they are the disbelievers}** (Q. 5:44).

---

[1] As for why we placed the term 'magician' in quotations, please refer back to our previous footnote regarding the prescribed punishment for magic. A common objection to the view that magic does not have a reality is that if it does not have a reality, they say, then how could a person be punished for it? Imam al-Mu`ayyad Billah addresses this in his ***Sharh at-Tajrīd***:

> Know that magic is simply imaginary and a type of illusory sleight of hand. Perhaps they assume that they give life to the dead, alter creation, transmorph some animals to others or cause people to ride on inanimate objects. It is narrated that Pharaoh's magicians used to make leather cords appear as snakes, place mercury in them and put them out in the sun. By such they would twist the imaginations of the people so that it would appear to them that they were living snakes. Therefore, whoever did such or similar in order for it to appear as reality—such person would be considered an apostate magician who is permitted to be put to death. The imam is obligated to put him to death just as he is obligated to put the apostate to death because the majority of such that the person appears to do is that which only Allah can do. So, anyone who claims that he can do any of the aforementioned—by that, I mean giving life to the dead, altering creation and transmorphing men into some animals—such person thereby claims Divine Lordship and disbelieves in Allah. Such person becomes an apostate who must be put to death. However, whoever does such actions with the acknowledgement that they are simply illusions and sleight of hand tricks—he would simply be considered an illusionist and not a magician who is permitted to be put to death. It would be for the imam to discipline him how he sees fit.

As for His statement **{those near unto thee amongst the disbelievers}**, this means 'those among you who are more harmful to you than others.' Then, He obligates you to 'fight those who are close among the disobedient until there remains none on the earth that will oppose Me.'

Likewise, descriptive prepositions can be used interchangeably with each other. The word 'near' can take the place of 'among' so that the phrase 'among you' can be intended by the statement **{near unto thee}**. In the Arabic language, they all mean the same.

An example of that is the statement of the Lord of creation relating the declaration of the accursed Pharaoh when he said: **{"...I shall crucify thee in (*fī*) the trunks of palm trees..."} (Q. 20:71)**. The phrase **{in the trunks of palm trees}** means 'on (*'ala*) the trunks of palm trees' insomuch that 'on' takes the place of 'in.' Also, Allah—the Glorified—says: **{...and whatsoever is sacrificed upon (*'ala*) stone altars...} (Q. 5:3)**. The meaning is simply '...sacrificed to (*li*) stone altars...' because the word 'upon' can be substituted with the word 'to.' Thus, descriptive prepositions can be used interchangeably with each other. Regarding that, the poet [i.e. Abu Dhu'ayb] says: "They drank from the water of the sea, then rose / to the sea expanse with them having a sound of commotion." When he says "...rose to (*lada*) the sea expanse...", it means '...rose above (*'ala*) the sea expanse...' He is describing the clouds and mentions that they rise above the sea expanse.

The seventh [situation] in which Allah commands that one is put to death is regarding those who commit highway robbery against the Muslims. They are those who make war against Allah, the Messenger and the believers when they steal their wealth and kill them. That is based on the statement of Allah: **{Verily, the recompense of those who make war against Allah and His Messenger and those who strive to spread corruption in the land is that they are to be put to death or crucified or have their hands and feet severed from opposite sides or be banished from the land. That is for them a recompense in this world, and to them shall belong a great punishment in the hereafter} (Q. 5:33)**. The eighth is the killing of one who intentionally kills a believer. Allah adjudicates that such person be put to death because of His statement **{...a soul for a soul...} (Q. 5:45)** as well as **{Slay not a soul which Allah has prohibited save by right. And whosoever is slain wrongly—We shall grant authority to his heir} (Q. 17:33)**. The authority that Allah grants to his heir is that he can put [the killer] to death.

The ninth is that the one who curses, verbally abuses, negates the right of or discounts Allah's Messenger, peace and blessings be upon him and his progeny, can be put to death. This is based on the statement of Allah's Messenger, peace and blessings be upon him and his progeny: ((Whoever verbally abuses me is to be put to death)).[2] The tenth is that the one who fornicates after being in a consummative marriage is to be put to death. Similar was done by Allah's Messenger, peace and blessings be upon him and his progeny; he had such person stoned to death.

Eight out of these ten are to be left alone and not put to death if they repent. One of the situations in which one is to be put to death whether he repents or not is the adulterer in a consummative marriage. The other situation is when the heir commands that the one who unlawfully killed his relative be put to death; if he wants, he can have him killed or leave him alone.

Whoever verbally abuses Allah's Messenger, peace and blessings be upon him and his progeny, is to be called to repentance. If he were to repent and return to that which Allah has obligated upon him, the repentance to his Lord would be held as sincere, and I hold to the view that he is to be left alone. However, the one who maintains that [i.e. the verbal abuse of the Prophet] is to be put to death. The verbal abuse of Allah's Messenger, peace and blessings be upon him and his progeny, is not greater than the verbal abuse or rejection of Allah. Whoever holds such to be licit regarding Allah is to not be killed until he is called to repentance. If he repents, he is left alone; if he refuses, he is put to death.

---

[2] Similarly narrated in ***Sharh at-Tajrīd, Amāli Ahmed b. 'Isa***

These ten situations in which one is permitted to shed a person's blood are an obligation from Allah in their judgement and determine the designation of the one who does it. Similar has been narrated from Allah's Messenger, peace and blessings be upon him and his progeny, that he said: ((The fornicator does not fornicate while he is a believer, and the thief does not steal while he is a believer)).[3] A proof of this is that the judgement of Allah against such person is Hellfire and punishment; however, the one who is a believer is not among the people of punishment. It is impermissible to attribute such person to punishment because the designation of belief necessitates Allah's reward. That is why we say that the people who act audaciously against Allah with open disobedience are not considered the people of belief according to His judgement.

Then, we say after this that *kufr* has two meanings. One of the meanings is the *kufr* of idolatry and disbelief in Allah, the Prophet and the Criterion [i.e. the Qur'an]. The one who objects to Allah in His Essence or objects to His creating His heavens or rejects His Prophets and Divine Messages are considered the same because the one who objects to any of His actions has objected to His creating. This is because the one who says that Allah has not done what He did has claimed and necessitated that someone other than Allah has done it. And whoever says that someone other than Allah did what Allah has done—such person has rejected Allah by his statement because he worships one who has not done that which the One he rejects did, and Allah is the One who did it. Therefore, it is sound that the one who rejects an action of Allah has rejected Allah, and the one who does not acknowledge His creating has disbelieved in Him.

The second meaning of *kufr* is ingratitude by means of disobedience to the One, Possessor of nobility and excellence. Whoever shows ingratitude to the blessings (*kafara ni'ma*) of Allah is considered disobedient in Allah's religion due to his ingratitude of Allah's blessings. Whoever is in such state is considered far from the designation of belief and near to the designation of sin, wickedness and disobedience.

Have you not heard how Allah distinguishes the believers from the disobedient and how the Most-Wise does not join the two in deeds and designation? Rather, He conveys that the two are distinct and their designations are opposite and clearly different in concept. The believer is attributed to His judgement of reward, and the disobedient is attributed to His judgement of painful punishment. He says in the Book He revealed: **{Is the believer like unto him who is disobedient? Nay! They are not equal. As for those who believe and perform righteous deeds, for them shall be Paradise as a destination, a welcome for what they used to do. As for those who commit acts of disobedience, their destination shall be Hellfire. Whenever they desire to exit therefrom, they shall be hurled back into it. And it shall be said to them: "Taste ye the Fire which ye used to belie!"} (Q. 32:18-20)**.

Also regarding that, Allah—the Blessed and Exalted—says: **{And [recall] when thy Lord declared: "If ye art grateful, We shall increase thee. If ye art ungrateful (*kafartum*), We shall punish thee severely."} (Q. 14:7)**. When the Glorified says **{And [recall] when thy Lord declared…}**, it means: When your Lord issued the judgement, "If you are grateful to Me and perform acts of obedience and seek My pleasure, I will increase you in My virtue and increase for your My reward. However, if you are ungrateful of My blessings and disobey My commands and turn away from My obedience, I will punish you with a severe punishment!"

Concerning what Allah mentions about retaliatory compensation (*al-qišāš*)

Allah passed the judgement of retaliatory compensation regarding the Children of Israel, and there will be no indemnity for them absolutely. The Glorified says: **{And We decreed for them therein: A soul for a soul, an eye for an eye, a nose for a nose, an ear for an ear, a tooth for a tooth and injuries as retaliatory compensation. But whosoever forgives it as charity—it shall be for him an expiation. And whosoever judges not by that which Allah hath revealed—they are the wrongdoers} (Q. 5:45)**.

[3] Similarly narrated in ***Sharh at-Tajrīd, Amāli Abu Ťālib, Ŝahīh al-Bukhāri, Ŝahīh Muslim, Sunan Abu Dāwūd, Sunan at-Tirmidhi, Sunan an-Nisā`i, Sunan Ibn Māja***

The Glorified clarifies that which we said at the end of the verse **{But whosoever forgives it as charity—it shall be for him an expiation}** that there was no indemnity between them. There was only retaliatory compensations or gifts.

The Glorified passed the judgement that a man's life can be given for a woman's life, a man's eye can be given for a woman's eye, a man's nose can be given for a woman's nose and all of the man's injuries are like the injuries of a woman. He did not make one more than the other, as He says: **{And We decreed for them therein: A soul for a soul...}**. Then He says later in the verse: **{...and injuries as retaliatory compensation}**. The meaning of His statement **{And We decreed for them therein}** is that He decreed such in the Torah. He made the judgements of their slaves in all that like their judgements.

Then Allah lightened that and pardoned the *Ummah* of Muhammad, peace and blessings be upon him and his progeny. He changed their judgements and differentiated between their indemnities based on their statuses and virtues out of His mercy. He says about the judgements He revealed to their Prophet regarding retaliatory compensation among the people of Islam: **{Retaliatory compensation has been decreed upon thee regarding manslaughter: the free for the free, the slave for the slave and the female for the female. As for the one who is pardoned by his brother for anything, it is to be followed by goodness and payment to him in kindness. That is a lightening from thy Lord as well as mercy. Then, whosoever transgresses after that—for him shall be a painful punishment} (Q. 2:178)**.

Therefore, Allah decrees that the free is for the free, the slave is for the slave and the female is for the female. Based on such judgement, it was prohibited for a male to be put to death for a female or a free person for a slave. The Glorified differentiates the Muslims from the Israelites except in the case that there is a man who has killed women and slaves for causing corruption in the earth, tyranny, veering from the path or disbelief. Then the imam of the Muslims would have to look into that. If he wants, he can put such person to death for his great sin; if he wants, he can do other than that among those actions in which is Allah's success.

Then, the Mighty and Majestic says: **{And there is life for thee in retaliatory compensation, O people of understanding, that ye may be God-conscious} (Q. 2:179)**. The **{life}** that is mentioned regarding retaliatory compensation refers to the fear of retaliatory death that occurs to the oppressors. This is so that they can turn from such when they come to know that they would be put to death for manslaughter. It is also so that they can lengthen their lives when they turn away from their disobedience and withdraw from killing one for whom they are put to death and transgressing Allah's judgement. That is Allah's judgement regarding retaliation (*qawad*) between His slaves and retaliatory compensation for the one He mentions in His Book—death for those who commit manslaughter or compensation for limbs. Similar is the case for the retaliatory compensation for injuries.

Then, the Blessed and Exalted says: **{It is not for a believer to slay another believer unless it be without intent. And whosoever slays a believer without intent—he is to manumit a believing slave and compensate his family unless they remit it as charity} (Q. 4:92)**. The Glorified appoints the manumission of a believing slave as a compensation for the one who unintentionally kills another as well as the payment of indemnity to his family unless they forgo it as charity. The **{charity}** here refers to a gift and forgiveness for his sins as well as refraining from taking indemnity from his clan.

Then, the One too Majestic to be encompassed by words, says: **{And if he belongs to a people who are at war with thee whilst he is a believer, then ye are to manumit a believing slave} (Q. 4:92)**. He does not appoint indemnity for a believer who lives among the idolaters. If a man embraced Islam while he lived among his people and concealed it from them insomuch that they did not know he was a Muslim and then the Muslims encounter him in war at the land borders and kill him assuming that he was an idolater but then come to know that he was a Muslim, Allah makes an expiation for him and not indemnity. This is because Muslims inherited it instead of him being attributed to the idolaters while they are the ones who would pay his bloodwite. If he were injured, Allah would make them more entitled to pay his indemnity since they would pay him the indemnity and not to his clan who are not his coreligionists.

The Glorified then says: {**And if he belongs to a people between whom they and ye have a mutual covenant, then blood money must be paid unto his people and a believing slave must be set free. And whosoever hath not the wherewithal to do so must fast two consecutive months. It is a recompense from Allah. Allah is All-Knowing, All-Wise**} (**Q. 4:92**). He made indemnity for the one who had a contract between him and the idolaters. That is because when one had a contract and agreement between them, the payment of indemnity was assigned to them. When there was Allah's contract and agreement between them [i.e. the Muslims], the Glorified appointed an expiation because he was a believer. Then, He appointed a consecutive two-month fast as expiation for the one who could not find a believing slave. There was no difference between the two except in the case of a major reason. If there was a major reason, then there was a difference between the two and the fast would be based on the removal of the reason. Then, the fast would be considered the expiation.

The Muslims remained upon that until Allah, the Blessed and Exalted, revealed ***Barā`at*** (**Q. 9**). The contract between them and the idolaters was then nullified. Allah's Messenger, peace and blessings be upon him and his progeny, withdrew them from their contract and informed them of what Allah commanded regarding those at war with them. The first to have their contract reneged was the idolaters among the Quraysh specifically because they were the formulators of the agreement. Then, the Blessed and Exalted made an exception and said: {**...save those who seek refuge with a people with whom is a covenant between ye and them**} (**Q. 4:90**). This verse was revealed concerning Hilāl b. Uwaymir.§ There was a contract between him and the Prophet, peace and blessings be upon him and his progeny, and Hilāl had not violated the contract between him and the Prophet, peace and blessings be upon him and his progeny. The idolaters from Quraysh came from Mecca to Hilāl, and the Companions of Allah's Messenger, peace and blessings be upon him and his progeny, wanted to kill the idolater who came to Hilāl. Allah's Messenger, peace and blessings be upon him and his progeny, prevented them from doing so by mentioning His statement: {**...save those who seek refuge with a people with whom is a covenant between ye and them**} (**Q. 4:90**).[4]

When Allah completed His blessing upon the Muslims and gave dominance by His granting the Seal of the Prophets victory, He abrogated these two verses as well as repealed the contract between Him and the idolaters. He then said: {**Slay the idolaters wheresoever ye find them and seize them and besiege them and lie in wait for them at every place of ambush. But if they repent and establish the prayer and render the purification dues, leave them on their way. Verily, Allah is Oft-Forgiving, Most Gracious**} (**Q. 9:5**). He commanded the Muslims to fight the idolaters wherever they found them, wait in ambush for them and not to spare any of the idolaters unless they repent from their misdeeds and return to Allah from their evil.

Then the Mighty and Majestic says in warning the believers and as a confirmation of His protecting them that when they travel on the earth, they should be careful as to not kill other believers. He says: {**O ye who believe! When ye set out in the way of Allah, be careful to discriminate and say not unto the one who offers thee peace: "Ye art not a believer!" seeking the displays of the life of this world. With Allah is abundant booty!**} (**Q. 4:94**).

It is said that this verse was revealed regarding Usāma b. Zayd§ when Allah's Messenger, peace and blessings be upon him and his progeny, dispatched him to the land of Ghatafān. He was not ordered to be secretive and was informed of them and they fled. They ran away, and a man from Ghatafān named Mirdās b. Nahīk§ trailed behind. When he saw them, he was afraid and stored his booty in a mountain cave. Afterwards, he headed towards them and greeted them with the greetings of peace

[4] Similarly narrated in ***Tafsīr at-Tabari, Tafsīr al-Jalālayn***

reciting the testimony of faith. Usāma attacked him, stabbed him to death and took his wealth. Gabriel then descended and informed the Prophet, peace and blessings be upon him and his progeny, of what happened. When they came back to the Prophet, peace and blessings be upon him and his progeny, the leader of the war campaign started to praise Usāma. Allah's Messenger, peace and blessings be upon him and his progeny, turned away until the man started to become afraid. Allah's Messenger said to him: ((O Usāma! The man said: "There is no God but Allah" and you killed him?! How could you have done that with "There is no God but Allah"?!)). He [i.e. Usāma] replied: "O Messenger of Allah, he only said that to protect himself from us! He said it with his tongue, but he did not really mean it in his heart." The Prophet, peace and blessings be upon him and his progeny, replied: ((Did you open his heart to see what was inside?!)). He said: "His heart is only a part of his body." Allah's Messenger, peace and blessings be upon him and his progeny, said: ((I have only been commanded to fight the people until they say: "There is no God but Allah." When they say it, their blood and wealth are protected from me, and their accounting is with Allah)).[5]

Concerning indemnities and injuries

If a Muslim male is killed, the complete indemnity is due. The indemnity is a hundred camels for the owner of camels, one thousand sheep for the owner of sheep, two hundred cows for the owner of cows, one thousand dinars for the owner of dinar, and ten thousand dirhams for the owner of dirham.

The exchange in that dirham is regarding that which we mentioned: ten dirhams for one dinar. Half the indemnity is due for one eye, and the complete indemnity is due for both eyes. Half the indemnity is due if one ear is destroyed, and the complete indemnity is due for both ears. Half the indemnity is due for one leg, and the complete indemnity is due for both legs. Half the indemnity is due for one hand, and the complete indemnity is due for both hands. There are ten camels due for every finger. The complete indemnity is due for the tongue. If the penis is cut from its base, the complete indemnity is due. The complete indemnity is due for the back. If the nose is removed from its base, the complete indemnity is due. The complete indemnity is due for two testicles. Five camels are due for each tooth.

There are five camels due for the head wound in which the whiteness of the bone is apparent (*al-mūḍiha*) and ten camels due for a head wound in which the bone is broken (*al-hāshima*). There are fifteen camels due for a head wound in which some of its bones are removed (*al-munaqqila*). A third of the indemnity is due for a stab wound that reaches the body's interior (*al-jā`ifa*), and a third of the indemnity is due for a stab wound that reaches the brain.

According to us, all of such traditions and judgements are authentically attributed to Allah's Messenger, peace and blessings be upon him and his progeny, based on what he said.[6] It has also been narrated from him, peace and blessings be upon him and his progeny, that he appointed indemnity for nose cartilage.[7]

---

[5] Similarly narrated in ***Ŝahīh al-Bukhāri, Ŝahīh Muslim, Sunan Abu Dāwūd, Mušannaf Ibn Abi Shayba***. Far from understanding the verse **{Slay the idolaters wheresoever ye find them…} (Q. 9:5)** and this hadith as a general command for Muslims to subject all non-Muslims to the sword, the imams of Ahl al-Bayt restrict it contextually to apply only to the Arab idolaters. Differentiating the engagement with the *kitābi* [i.e. the Jews and Christians] and the non-*kitābi*, Imam Ibn Murtaḍa says in his ***Al-Bahr***:

> There is nothing accepted from the non-*kitābi* except Islam or the sword due to his statement, peace and blessings be upon him and his progeny: ((I have only been commanded to fight the people…)). There is nothing accepted from the *kitābi* except Islam or *jizya* due to the statement of the Exalted: **{…till they render the *jizya* willingly…} (Q. 9:29)**.

As for the verse **{Slay the idolaters wheresoever ye find them…} (Q. 9:5)**, he said that it proves that "Nothing is to be accepted from the Arab idolaters but Islam or the sword."

[6] Similarly narrated in ***Sharh at-Tajrīd, Amāli Ahmed b. 'Isa, Sunan at-Tirmidhi, Sunan an-Nisā`i, Sunan Ibn Mājah Mušannaf Ibn Abi Shayba.***

[7] Similarly narrated in ***Sharh at-Tajrīd, Sunan ad-Dārqutni, Mušannaf 'Abdur-Razzāq, Mušannaf Ibn Abi Shayba, Sunan al-Bayhaqi***

Concerning how the indemnity is to be taken

The indemnity is to be taken in four age categories[8] for each life and other than it, such as head wounds and more. One of the fourths is a goat kid, a fourth is a *hiqqat*, a fourth is a *bint labūn* and a fourth is a *bint makhāḍ*. Similarly, the indemnity of a woman is to be taken in four age categories based on what we mentioned. The indemnity of a woman is half the indemnity of the man.

Concerning the delineation of the indemnity and its designation from wealth

The indemnity of a man in gold for the owner of gold is one thousand mithqal [i.e. 4000 grams]. The owners of gold are the people of the Levant, Egypt, the Maghreb, Iraq, the Hejaz, Bahrain and Yemen. The indemnity of the people of dirham is ten thousand dirhams; they are the people of Khorasan and other regions who only use dirham.

The indemnity for the people of the wilderness among the Bedouins and others is one hundred camels. The indemnity for the owners of cows, such as the people of Tihama in Yemen and the rural areas of Kufa and others, is two hundred cows. The indemnity for the owners of sheep where they are, such as the mountain people of the east and west and Yemen and the Levant, is one thousand sheep.

Whoever belongs to the aforementioned categories will not have the indemnity taken except from his/her wealth. The people of the indemnity shall not be responsible for the indemnity except from their wealth. The indemnity is to be taken from all who owes it in span of three years with a third being paid each year.

Concerning injuries for which there is no retaliation

There is no retaliation for the stab wound that reaches the brain, the head wound in which some of its bones are removed, the stab wound that reaches the body's interior, nor the bone that is broken in the middle, such as the upper arm, shin, thigh or forearm which is cracked in the middle. Similar has been narrated that Allah's Messenger, peace and blessings be upon him and his progeny, said that there is no retaliation for that.[9]

He simply invalidated the retaliation in all that because it is something that the owner of such cannot accurately assign. If he were to attempt to do so one after another, one cannot fully consider such or accurately retaliate against the one who did it. That is because the like cannot be done, retaliated or compensated for unless the perpetrator is declared free of such. If he declared such person free of such, he would demand his right. If the other person died as a result, it would then be a situation of manslaughter. Even if he were to live from the result of such retaliated injuries and someone else were to seek retaliation from him, he would not be safe from destruction due to it. A life would be killed due to an injury. For that reason, retaliation is invalidated for it due to the fear of such and its enormity.

---

[8] Regarding the number of age categories of camels from which indemnity is to be taken, Imam al-Mu`ayyad Billah attributes two different opinions from al-Hādi. Four categories are mentioned here in the ***Ahkām***, but five are mentioned in ***Al-Muntakhab***. Imam Abu Tālib also mentioned this disagreement in his ***Sharh at-Tahrīr***. We say that the opinion mentioned here in the ***Ahkām*** is the soundest for the following reasons. One, it has been related in ***Musnad Imam Zayd*** from 'Ali on the authority of Imam Zayd b. 'Ali through his ancestors. Two, it has also been related in the ***Amāli Ahmed b. 'Isa*** that 'Ali said that the age categories are four. Three, it has also been related by other than the Ahl al-Bayt that 'Ali held to the view that the age categories are four. Ibn Rushd said in his ***Al-Bidāyat al-Mujtahid***:

> It has been related that our master, 'Ali, passed the judgement that it is to be four categories excluding from it twenty-five *banu labūn*. This opinion was adopted by 'Umar b. 'Abdul-Azīz…He [i.e. the well-known Māliki scholar, Ibn 'Abdul-Barr] said: "'Ali's report is more preferable to me [than a contrary report of Ibn Mas'ūd narrated in ***Ŝahīh al-Bukhāri*** and ***Sunan at-Tirmidhi***, which states five as the number of categories] because there is no dispute regarding the narration attributed to 'Ali. However, there is dispute regarding the narration attributed to Ibn Mas'ūd.

[9] Similarly narrated in ***Sunan Ibn Mājah, Sunan al-Bayhaqi***

Concerning the indemnity for the one upon whom it is obligatory

Whoever intentionally commits manslaughter, breaks another's limb or causes an injury—such person must be retaliated against. Whatever he did must be similarly done to him unless the injured person is content with indemnity for the injury. Then the matter would be for them to decide.

Any indemnity or restitution due to an intentional act must be paid from the wealth of the person who committed the intentional act and not from the wealth of his clan. However, any unintentional act regarding a life or anything else shall be paid from the wealth of his clan, and they are responsible for such. The clan refers to the relatives.

It is necessary that the indemnity be taken up by close relatives and distant relatives if the close relatives are not able to take up the indemnity. If none are able to take it up, the closest relative must take it up to the extent of their ability and would owe the remaining amount as a debt.

If the clan were people of the registry who receive provisions from the imam along with other Muslims who receive such, the indemnity is to be extracted from what they receive for three years. A large or small portion is to be taken from each man every year to the extent of their large or small amounts and to the extent of what they can take on from what they are given.

Concerning the numbers of indemnity for the people

There is indemnity for the following: a life, the sight, the hearing of one who is made deaf, dumbness which is the result of a man striking another, the voice of a person whose voice was cut, the tongue, the intellect, the nose, the back that was beaten and not set, the penis, the urethra and bowels of one who was struck so hard that they are incontinent, the two legs, the two hands, the two ears that are severed, the lips, the testicles and the teeth.

As for the hair of the beard and the hair of the head, others say that there is indemnity due on both if they were not pulled out due to the actions of their owner; however, we do not hold to that view. Rather, there is to be a severe judgement passed that is approximate to indemnity. Similarly, others say that indemnity is to be paid on eyelashes and eyebrows; however, we do not hold to that view or advocate it. Rather, we say that there is to be a judgement passed which is less than half the indemnity. That is the view we hold to, and it is closest to the truth according to us.

Regarding a head wound in which the bones are broken but not removed, the indemnity would be a tenth less than that of the same head wound in which some of its bones are removed. Regarding the thin skin above the skull (*as-simhāq*) that is bruised less than a head wound in which the whiteness of the bone is apparent, four camels are to be paid as indemnity. It has been said that less or more of that is due for skull fractures; however, we do not hold to such view regarding something that is predetermined. Rather, regarding all of such are judgements that have been thoroughly considered with the help of Allah.

Concerning the free person who kills a slave and a man who kills a woman out of rebellion and causing corruption in the land

If a free person kills a slave in any of those situations, the imam must look into the affair. If he sees fit to put such person to death, he can do so. Similar is the case with a man who kills a woman in any of those situations. It would be for the imam to put him to death on her behalf. Similar has reached us from the Commander of Believers, 'Ali b. Abi Ṭālib, upon him be peace, that he put these two people to death in these situations.

My father related to me that his father said: "Any free person who kills a slave or man who kills a woman rebelliously and unjustly causing corruption in the land—it is for the imam to put such person to death on their behalf."

Concerning the kinds of manslaughter

Manslaughter has two kinds according to me: intentional and unintentional; there is no third kind. It has been said that there is a third kind: almost intentional. Traditions have been narrated about it from the Commander of Believers, 'Ali, upon him be peace. However, we do not see such reports as authentically attributed to him according to us. We hold to the view that there is either intentional or unintentional.

If it is intentional, there is to be retaliation unless the guardians of the victim want indemnity. The matter would be as they command and say. If it is unintentional, there is to be indemnity and expiation.[10]

My father related to me that his father was asked about indemnity for the unintentional death and 'almost intentional.' He replied:

> There is no position between intentional and unintentional. Every act of manslaughter is either intentional or unintentional. For that, Allah has appointed retaliation or indemnity.
>
> Others have said that 'almost intentional' is neither intentional nor unintentional and that the indemnity for it is a severe bloodwite. It is narrated that 'Ali, upon him be peace, said that 'almost intentional' is that which was committed by a staff[11] and projected with a large stone. But this is not authentically attributed to him according to us.

Concerning a one-eyed person who gouged a healthy eye

Reports regarding such have been narrated from the Commander of Believers, upon him be peace. However, we do not see them as authentically attributed to him. That which is obligatory, according to us, is that one retaliates for it because Allah says: **{...an eye for an eye...} (Q. 5:45)**. The exception is if one demands indemnity for it. That would be best for him and, he would have to pay half the indemnity.

My father related to me that his father was asked about a one-eyed person who gouged a healthy eye. He replied: "He is to be retaliated against; it is simply an eye for an eye. If he is demanded indemnity, he is to pay half the indemnity."

Concerning the nail and tooth that are blackened

If a tooth is blackened, it is considered the same as a tooth that was knocked out. Their judgements are the same: five camels.[12] If it is chipped, its judgement would be based on the extent of the deficiency. As for the nail, there is an independent judgement to be passed for its blackening. Such has been narrated from the Commander of Believers, 'Ali b. Abi Ťālib, upon him be peace.[13]

---

[10] Imam Abu Ťālib stated in his ***At-Tahrīr*** that two different opinions exist from al-Hādi regarding the penalty for intentional and unintentional manslaughter. Here in the ***Ahkām***, the penalty is mentioned as retaliation or indemnity but not expiation. Whereas, in ***Al-Muntakhab***, he is said to say that expiation is rendered for both intentional and unintentional manslaughter. This disagreement was also noted by Imams al-Mu`ayyad Billah and Ibn al-Murtaḍa in ***Sharh at-Tajrīd*** and ***Al-Bahr*** respectively. We say that the judgement in the ***Ahkām*** reflects the more correct view because a close reading of the judgement in ***Al-Muntakhab*** reveals no contradiction between al-Hādi's views. In fact, ***Al-Muntakhab*** confirms the judgement from the ***Ahkām***. In ***Al-Muntakhab***, al-Hādi was asked whether expiation is to be rendered for intentional and unintentional manslaughter. He replied with the following: "Regarding a man who killed a man intentionally or unintentionally and then he later came to know that his father was killed intentionally, there is nothing [i.e. no expiation] due on him. Similar is the case whether he killed a brother."

[11] Similarly narrated in ***Musnad Imam Zayd, Mušannaf 'Abdur-Razzāq, Al-Mu'jam al-Kabīr, Mušannaf Ibn Abi Shayba***

[12] Two different judgements regarding the indemnity for blackening the tooth have been narrated from al-Hādi. Here in the ***Ahkām***, the penalty is judged to be a pre-determined amount—five camels. However, in ***Al-Muntakhab***, when he was asked the indemnity for a blackened tooth was to be determined by the judging authority. This point of disagreement was noted by Imams Abu Ťālib and al-Mu`ayyad Billah. We reconcile these two seemingly contradictory statements by saying that the indemnity on the blackened tooth should be based on whether the tooth is still functional or not. If the blackened tooth is no longer useful, the judgement of the ***Ahkām*** is to be followed. However, it is also possible that the tooth could be blackened but still maintain its use. In that case, the judgement in ***Al-Muntakhab*** is to be followed. Imam al-Mu`ayyad Billah reflects our sentiments in his ***Sharh at-Tajrīd*** when he said: "It is necessary that one look into its affair. If it is blackened to the point that its beauty is removed and is without beneficial use, the correct statement is that narrated in ***Al-Muntakhab***." This interpretation is in line with much of what al-Hādi has related regarding indemnity in the rest of the ***Ahkām***.

[13] Similarly narrated in ***Musnad Imam Zayd, Sharh at-Tajrīd***

My father related to me that his father was asked about the tooth that is blackened. He replied: "If the tooth is blackened, there is to be five camels paid for it. If it is chipped, it is to be paid based on the value of its deficiency—whether a half, fourth, less or more."

Concerning the two ovaries

It has been said that two-thirds of the indemnity is due for the left ovary and a third is due for the right. Such person claims that the child is from the left ovary. However, he has not brought any proof for that from the Book or Sunnah. According to us, the indemnity for both is the same.

My father related to me that his father was asked about the two ovaries. He replied:

> For both is the complete indemnity, and for each one is half the indemnity. For every pair in human beings—whether eyes, ears or feet—indemnity is due. For every singular of the pair, half the indemnity is due.

Concerning the blind eye, lame hand or leg and mute tongue

Regarding that, the judgement of such is based on the extent to what occurred in it as well as based on the extent to the benefit the person gets from these limbs. The imam is to pass a judgement based on what Allah causes his heart to agree to.

My father related to me that his father was asked about the blind eye, lame hand and mute tongue. He replied: "There is a judgement based on all of that. There is no predetermined indemnity for any of them."

Concerning the injuries by a child and slave and concerning a herniated bladder

An injury by a slave is incumbent on him and his responsibility. There is nothing obligatory upon his master greater than paying it in its entirety. His master has a choice in the case of an unintentional injury: he can pay it in its entirety if he wants or he can ransom him with the indemnity of his injury if he wants. As for intentional injury, he must hand him over unless the guardians of the injured want to accept the slave's value from the owner or any other form of settlement on his behalf.

As for the injury by a child, it is due on his clan just as anything else would be due on his clan. However, that which a child does is not considered intentional; rather, all of his actions are considered unintentional.

As for the herniated bladder, if it was due to a wound that reaches the body's interior, it would be considered such and one would owe a third of the indemnity. If it were not due to such, one would have to look into it and apply a judgement.

My father related to me that his father was asked about the injury by a child and slave. He replied: "As for the injury by a child, it would be due on his clan. As for the injury by a slave, it would be his own responsibility."

Concerning a man and child who share in intentional manslaughter or injuries together

If they share in the intentional manslaughter of a Muslim, the man is to be put to death because of his intentional killing the man. The indemnity of injury would be due on the clan of the child because any injury caused by a child in the state of pre-pubescence is considered unintentional until such child attains intellect. Then, the judgements would apply to him.

My father related to me that his father was asked about a man and child who shared in manslaughter. He replied: "The adult is to be put to death, and the indemnity is to be paid by the child's clan."

Concerning the injuries by men and women as well as concerning the injuries of the foetus of a free woman, slave woman, livestock, slaves and children

All of the injuries of women—the lot of them and the least of them—are considered half the injuries of men. The bloodwite of women and men are not considered the same in terms of injuries.

Regarding the foetus of a free woman, it has been narrated that a male or female slave is given as compensation for injury if she gave birth to a stillborn. However, if she were to give birth to a living child and then it dies afterwards as a result of the injury, one would have to pay the complete indemnity. Likewise, if she were to give birth to two foetuses or more, the complete indemnity is to be paid for each. Their indemnity would be just like any other indemnity in that it is to be collected in three years with a third being paid each year.

If she were to give birth to a living foetus and a stillborn and then the living foetus died afterwards, a male or female slave would be due for the stillborn and the complete indemnity would be due for the living foetus as well as the manumission of a slave.

As for the foetus of a slave woman, it is half the tenth of her value if it was born alive. That would be due on the clan regarding the free woman and the slave woman.

As for the foetus of livestock, if it is struck in its stomach and it gives birth to a living foetus and then it dies afterwards due to injury, its like value is to be paid. If it miscarried, one would owe half a tenth of its value.

If the one who struck the stomach of a free woman or slave woman were a slave or woman or child, the injury of the child and woman is due on their clan and the injury of the slave is his own responsibility. If it is more than his value, there is nothing obligatory on his master greater than handing him over. If it is less than his value, he has a choice: he can hand him over or pay his indemnity.

My father related to me that his father was asked about the injuries of women. He replied: "It is half the injuries of men, just as the indemnity of a woman is half the indemnity of a man. That has been narrated from 'Ali b. Abi Ťālib, upon him be peace."[14]

He was asked about the foetus of a free woman and replied:

> Regarding the foetus of a free woman, a male or female slave is due if the injury caused it to be born a stillborn. That has been narrated from the Prophet, peace and blessings be upon him and his progeny, and from 'Ali, upon him be peace.[15]

He was asked about the foetus of a slave woman and replied: "It would be based on the extent of her value just as the foetus of the free woman is based on the value of her indemnity."

He was asked about the foetus of livestock and replied: "It is similarly based on the value of its price." He was also asked about injuries and which one is to be retaliated for. He replied: "It is that which he can accomplish and that which is in his ability without fear of his own ruin."

Concerning the injuries by an *umm walad*, a slave freed upon his master's death and an indentured labourer

The injuries by an *umm walad* and slave freed upon his master's death are to be borne by their master based on their value between him and them. There is nothing due on him which is greater than their value in regard to an unintentional injury by them both. Neither is he to assign the injuries to them if it is greater than their value because their actions and injuries were unintentional. Nothing regarding the unintentional injury by a slave is considered greater than his value.

The person who mistakenly committed manslaughter is not to be put to death for an unintentional act. The slave's indemnity is simply to be paid for [by the master] in its entirety. It is not for the guardians of the victim to put him to death for his unintentional act.

---

[14] Similarly narrated in ***Musnad Imam Zayd, Sharh at-Tajrīd, Mušannaf Ibn Abi Shayba***

[15] Similarly narrated in ***Musnad Imam Zayd, Sharh at-Tajrīd, Ŝahīh Muslim.*** Similar has been related in ***Ŝahīh al-Bukhāri, Sunan Abu Dāwūd, Sunan Ibn Mājah, Sunan an-Nisā'i***

The slave freed upon his master's death and the *umm walad* are not owned. That is why we say that they are to not be handed over.[16] Rather, they are to have it paid off based on their value; the extent is paid off on their behalf by means of manumission due to childbirth [in the case of the *umm walad*] or the master's death [in the case of the slave freed upon the master's death]. If their master was in straitened circumstances, he must hand over the slave freed upon his master's death for his crime, and the *umm walad* must work to pay off her value [i.e. the value of her indemnity].

As for the indentured labourer, injuries caused by him are to be his responsibility. He is to take steps towards paying it along with his contracted labour.

If the injuries by the *umm walad* and slave freed upon his master's death are intentional and lead to death, they are to be given up to be put to death and not given up to be temporarily enslaved. This is because the temporary enslavement of an *umm walad* is impermissible because enslaving her would allow intercourse with her by the one who temporarily enslaved her. It would be impermissible for anyone other than her master to have intercourse with her unless her master manumitted her and another married her.

Concerning the free person who injured a slave and the injuries by slaves

As for the eye of a slave, if a free person were to injure it, it would be half its value. Every injury by a slave is calculated based on his value. A third of its value is due for a stab wound that reaches the body's interior.

Concerning that for which the clan (*al-'aqila*) does not pay the bloodwite

The clan does not pay the bloodwite for a slave, intentional act, confession or settlement; they pay the bloodwite for other than these. Similar has come in narrations from the Prophet, peace and blessings be upon him and his progeny.[17]

Many people have said that the meaning of the hadith ((The clan does not pay the bloodwite for a slave)) is that the clan does not pay the bloodwite on behalf of their brother slave if he killed one of their brothers. Neither do they pay the bloodwite for the injury caused to one of their slaves by another of their slaves.

That is not the case according to me. Rather, according to me, it is that they do not pay the bloodwite for an injury caused by one of their slaves against anyone. This is because the slave is to be handed over for what he committed, and it is obligatory for his master to hand him over for his offense. As for the one who unintentionally caused an injury and the slave killed some of those to whom he was handed over, they must share in the bloodwite as they do with others. This is because in this case, he is owned and they are obligated to support him if it was done unintentionally. That is the meaning of the statement of Allah's Messenger, peace and blessings be upon him and his progeny, which is closest to the truth and fairness.

Concerning a slave who strikes the stomach of his master's wife and she gives birth to a living foetus or stillborn

If a slave were to strike the stomach of his master's wife and she were to give birth to a stillborn, it would be upon his master to pay the wife a sixth of the value of a slave if the child belonged to them. If they do not have a child, he would have to pay her the value of a third of a slave woman. A slave woman would be due in the case of a miscarriage.

---

[16] According to ***Al-Muntakhab***, al-Hādi was asked whether an *umm walad* could be given as expiation for unintentional manslaughter. He replied in the negative.

[17] Similarly narrated in ***Musnad Imam Zayd, Sharh at-Tajrīd***

If she were to give birth to a living child but then it died, he would be obligated to pay his wife a third of his slave's value due to the injuries caused by him unless he chooses to ransom him. Then he would ransom him with a third of the indemnity for injury to the living foetus if he assumed it was a third of his value. This is the case if there was no child. If they had two children or more, it would necessitate that she is paid a sixth of the indemnity because the offspring prevents the mother from the third. This is because if the indemnity were due on other than the father with an injury from other than his slave, a third would be due to her if she did not have a child and a sixth if they had a child. The slave would have to fast two consecutive months if the wife gave birth to a living foetus.

Concerning the indemnities of slaves who have skills

If a man were to buy a slave for twenty dinars and then teach him skills whose knowledge would make his value to equal ninety dinars but then a person kills him, the killer would be obligated to pay the slave's value on the day he was killed.

Similar is the case with a female slave who has skills unless those skills she was taught are impermissible, such as singing, musical instruments, lute-playing, loud mourning and all such other actions prohibited by Allah's Messenger, peace and blessings be upon him and his progeny.

Concerning the one who castrated a slave

Whoever castrates a slave child must pay his value twice if he severed his penis and once if he severed his testicles. One is to not consider that as an increase or decrease in value, nor should one consider the statement of the one who says that there is no indemnity paid for the owner who injures a slave because castrating him increases his value or that if he wants, he could subtract his value before castrating him or he could leave him if he wants.

Such a statement is invalid according to us and is to not be acted upon because indemnity is due and obligated for every body part severed from a person. It is therefore necessary that indemnity be paid for severing a part of this child whether it increases or decreases his value. This is because Allah and His Messenger decreed indemnity, and it is necessary that one adhere to what Allah and His Messenger decreed.

If a free person misappropriated a slave and kept him until the slave reached a state in which no one could get any benefit from him, it would be for the rightful slavemaster to take his value and pay it to the injured.

Concerning a man who kills a woman intentionally

The woman's guardians have a choice: they can have the killer pay them half the indemnity and put the killer to death on behalf of the woman or they can accept five hundred dinars, which is half the indemnity and let the killer live. This is the statement of ʻAli b. Abi Ṫālib, upon him be peace.[18]

Concerning a *dhimmi* who kills a Muslim

If a *dhimmi* killed a Muslim intentionally, he would be put to death on his behalf. If he were to kill him unintentionally, he would have to pay the complete indemnity. It would be taken from him for three years.

If a free person killed a slave, he would have to pay the value of the slave irrespective of the cost—whether a lot or a little. That is the statement of the Commander of Believers, ʻAli b. Abi Ṫālib, upon him be peace.[19]

---

[18] Similarly narrated in ***Sharh at-Tajrīd, Mušannaf Ibn Abi Shayba***

[19] Sheikh ʻAli b. Bilāl reported in his ***Sharh al-Ahkām*** on the authority of Sayyid Abul-Abbās al-Hasani who related with his chain of narrators to ʻAli, upon him be peace: "A freeperson is not put to death for a slave because a slave's indemnity is his value. A slave is not put to death for a freeperson because the indemnity of the freeperson is more than that of the slave." Similar is narrated in ***Musnad Imam Zayd, Amāli Ahmed b. ʻIsa, Mušannaf ʻAbdur-Razzāq*** and ***Mušannaf Ibn Abi Shayba***

Concerning a Muslim who kills a *dhimmi*

A Muslim is to not be put to death on behalf of a disbeliever; however, the complete indemnity is due on a Muslim if he were to kill one with whom is contracted protection. This is based on the statement of the Mighty and Majestic: **{And if he belongs to a people between whom they and ye have a mutual covenant, then blood money must be paid unto his people…} (Q. 4:92)**. And he owes expiation for the one he killed, and Allah obligates the expiation on the killer.

Others say that the indemnity of the Jews and Christians is four thousand dirhams, and the indemnity of the Magian is eight hundred dirhams. However, we do not hold to the view because Allah mandates a complete indemnity to the victim's family with whom is a contract and covenant, as well as the expiation on the killer afterwards.

My father related to me that his father said:

> The Muslim is not killed on behalf of the disbeliever—whether he kills him in confrontation or assassination. This is because Allah only appoints indemnity and expiation for that. This has been narrated from the Prophet, peace and blessings be upon him and his progeny, as well as from 'Ali, upon him be peace. Some say that he is to be killed on their behalf, but this is nothing.

My father related to me that his father was asked about the indemnity of the Jews, Christians and Magians. He replied:

> The indemnity of the Jews, Christians and whoever has a contracted protection is that which is stipulated in the contract, the complete indemnity. It has been said that their indemnity is half the Muslims' indemnity, and it has also been said that it is four thousand dirhams for them and eight hundred for the Magians.
>
> However, according to us, the indemnity of all who have a contracted protection is the same as the indemnity of the Muslims. There is to be expiation paid by the killer as Allah commands. It is to be the manumission of a slave or fasting two consecutive months for the one who does not have a believing slave.

Concerning the one who removes something from his borders and it injures a person and concerning a riding beast that injures its leg

If a man removes something from his borders to the roads and pathways of the Muslims and digs a hole in it for a well or an accident occurs in it that would not have otherwise occurred in the roads and pathways of the Muslims, he would be considered liable for any damage that occurred in it to the passer-by.

The meaning of 'of no account' (*jubār*) in the narration of Allah's Messenger, peace and blessings be upon him and his progeny, ((The well is of no account, and the riding beast is of no account))[20] is when the two situations occur in the home of the owners and within its borders and not in the paths and roads of the Muslims.

As for the riding beast who stops in the roads of the Muslims, the owner is considered liable for any accident that occurs in their roads and marketplaces due to its forelegs and hind legs.

My father related to me that his father was asked about a man who removes something from his borders and a person is injured as a result. He replied: "If that which he removed is placed in the road of the general population, he would be fined due to any harm that occurred to a life or wealth."

[20] Similarly narrated in ***Musnad Imam Zayd, Amāli Ahmed b. 'Isa, Ŝahīh al-Bukhāri, Ŝahīh Muslim, Sunan Abu Dāwūd, Sunan at-Tirmidhi, Sunan an-Nisā'i, Sunan Ibn Māja, Uŝūl al-Kāfi, Bihār al-Anwār***

My father related to me that his father said:

> It has been narrated that 'Ali b. Abi Ťālib, upon him be peace, said: "Whoever leaves his riding beast in the roads of the Muslims or their marketplaces—he will be liable for anything that were to occur by its forelegs or hind legs."[21]

Concerning a man who kills his son and a son who kills his father

The killer does not inherit from the one he intentionally killed—whether from his indemnity or wealth. The killer does not inherit from the indemnity of the one he unintentionally killed; however, he does inherit from his wealth. Others say that he is to not inherit from the wealth or indemnity. This is considered unjust according to us.

It is not sound regarding injustice for the one who narrate such narration nor is such statement established as proof. This is because it is necessary that there be a difference between intentional and unintentional acts. The killer may have unintentionally killed someone who if given the choice between putting him to death or ruining his wealth and life the choice of whether to ruin his life and wealth before stretching forth his hand to kill him would be given to his parent, child, brother or relative. Whereas the intentional killer may only be killed for his intention by those who agree on his being put to death desiring to ruin and destroy him.

This has been derived from the statement of the Commander of Believers, 'Ali, upon him be peace: "The killer does not inherit from the killed."[22] He means by this intentional manslaughter, not unintentional manslaughter. It also applies to the when referring to the indemnity, he is to not inherit from it. This would include both the intentional and unintentional killer.

Concerning the indemnity that one who killed unintentionally is to not inherit

The unintentional killer is simply prevented from inheriting anything from indemnity because the indemnity is a fine to be paid and a form of discipline for the unintentional killer. It is also an urging from Allah for precaution and a deterrent. It is for that reason that he is to not inherit from it since it is a warning of vigilance and a compensation for leaving one dead in error.

If that is the case, it would be considered impermissible for one who is compensating to share with others among the guardians or be included along with any of the relatives. This is because if he were included along with them in the indemnity just as he was included with them in the wealth, he would falsely assume that he is the same with them in all cases. It is necessary that there be a distinct and clear difference between the correct and mistaken in a situation.

A proof for that is the indemnity for an unintentional act is due on the clan of the person who killed unintentionally instead of him and that they are the ones who pay it. If he were to take some of the indemnity along with them and did not pay it out, the unintentional killer would be given more virtue than the one who paid it and served as his guardian! If that were considered permissible for the killers, they would be considered more fortunate and greater than those who paid for them! That would be a virtue for him greater than the one who had not killed anyone since the one who had not killed would have to pay the indemnity and fine and the killer would be able to take from it and benefit!

Concerning the killer who is pardoned by some of the guardians when he intentionally killed

If a man killed another man intentionally and some of the victim's guardians pardoned him, the death penalty would be waived from him due to their pardon. He is to not be put to death even if other

---

[21] Similarly narrated in ***Musnad Imam Zayd, Sharh at-Tajrīd***

[22] Similarly narrated in ***Musnad Imam Zayd, Sharh at-Tajrīd, Sunan Ibn Mājah, Sunan at-Tirmidhi, Mušannaf 'Abdur-Razzāq, Sunan al-Bayhaqi, Sunan ad-Dārqutni***

relatives demanded that he be put to death. He would have to pay the complete indemnity unless the pardoners pardoned the indemnity along with the death penalty. If that is the case, he would be exempted from a share of the indemnity of the one who pardoned him. He would have to pay the rest of it to the remaining guardians, and he must pay expiation for his crime as well as repent to Allah for his obscene sin.

My father related to me that his father was asked about a man who killed someone and was pardoned by some of the victim's guardians. He replied:

> When some of the guardians pardon the killer, the death penalty is waived from him. If some of the remaining guardians accept, he is to pay the indemnity. If others among them were to pardon him from the death penalty and indemnity together, he would be exempted from the share of the indemnity of those who pardoned him. However, he is to not be put to death if some of the guardians pardoned him.
>
> Other people say other than this; it is an odd statement. They claim that the killer's blood can be shed for any of the guardians who demand it, even if he were pardoned by some of the guardians. That is not correct according to us.

Concerning one who confessed to manslaughter—whether intentional or unintentional

Anyone who confessed to unintentional or intentional manslaughter must pay the indemnity because the clan cannot pay the bloodwite for a slave, intentional killer, settlement or confession. A confession is that which a person readily confesses against himself for manslaughter.

Concerning a group who kills a person unintentionally or intentionally

If a group killed a man intentionally and all of them shared in his killing, all of them are to be put to death. If they all killed him unintentionally, their share of the indemnity must be paid by their clans when evidence has been established against them from the people of Islam and the judgement has been passed on them by the imam.

Concerning the pardon of an enslaved killer

If a slave killed a free person and his master turned him over to the victim's guardians, they can have him put to death if he killed intentionally. They can also enslave him, manumit him, sell him, give him as a gift or pardon him.

If they pardoned the master from turning over his slave and forgave him of his sin, the slave would return to the ownership of his master as he was before. If they pardoned the slave and manumitted him, he would be considered free and his master would have no right over him. This is because when his master turned him over to them, he became their property and their judgements applied to him. Others say other than this, but we do not hold to that view or act on it.

Concerning taking indemnities for an injury

The complete indemnity is taken in three years with a third being taken each year. In the case of a half indemnity, such as the indemnity for an eye or hand, it is to be taken in two years. Similarly, two-thirds of the indemnity is to be taken in two years. Three-fourths of it is to also be taken in two years. In the case of a third of the indemnity, it is to be taken in one year. Similar is the case with anything less than a third of the indemnity.

Concerning swearing an oath

The swearing of an oath is obligatory regarding the victim who is in a village or city when none of his guardians can rightfully claim the identity of the killer. If that is the case, the guardians of the victim must gather fifty men from all of the men of that village and the latter must swear by Allah: "We did not kill him, nor do we know the killer." If all of them swear such, they are to be left alone, and the indemnity must be paid by the clans of the villagers or the tribe in the place where the victim was found.

If some of the fifty men were to decline from swearing the oath, they would have to be imprisoned until they either swear or confess. If one confesses, he is to be seized for his crime. If they swear, the indemnity would be due on all the clans of the villagers—those among them who swore and those who had not sworn.

The one who was absent from the people of that place does not have to swear an oath, nor does such person have to pay indemnity if he was absent at the time of the murder. The swearing of the oath is only obligatory on those men who were present at the time of the murder; this excludes the women, children and slaves. The same is the case whether there is a stranger in that tribe or a non-stranger and whether such person is a resident in a rented house or a purchased house. It is necessary that paying indemnity and swearing an oath is due on them if they were present at the time of the murder.

If the murder took place in a village without fifty men in it, the men in it would be considered and the oath would be repeated by them until it reached fifty oaths. If there were only twenty-five men, each one would be asked to swear twice. If there were only thirty men, they would be asked to swear thirty oaths and the victim's guardians would choose twenty from the thirty to repeat their oaths until the number reached fifty oaths.

Regarding the swearing of oaths, it has reached us that a man came to Allah's Messenger, peace and blessings be upon him and his progeny, and said: "O Messenger of Allah, I found that my brother was killed among the tribe of so-n-so." He, peace and blessings be upon him and his progeny, replied: ((Gather fifty men from them and have them swear by Allah that they did not kill him or know who did)). The man asked: "Is anything to be done for my brother other than this, O Messenger of Allah?" He replied: ((Indeed. One hundred camels)).[23]

If a man found the murder victim between two villages and did not know which of the two the killer is in, he is to compare the distance between the victim and two villages. Swearing the oath would be obligator upon the village that was closer to him. Fifty men from the villagers should swear that they had not killed or know who did. Then, the indemnity paid to the guardians of the victim is obligatory on the clans of that village.

If a man were to die due to being trampled by the people in a mosque or on a road and no one knows who killed him, the indemnity would be paid from the Muslim public treasury.

It has reached us that a murder victim was found between two villages, and Allah's Messenger, peace and blessings be upon him and his progeny, ordered that the distance between the victim and both villages be compared. Whichever one was the closest was the one who had to pay the indemnity. They were compared and one of the villages was found to be closer than the other. They were then made liable for the indemnity.[24]

It has similarly been narrated to us that the Commander of Believers, 'Ali b. Abi Ťālib, upon him be peace. It has been narrated to us that when a murder victim was brought to him from the middle of a village, the indemnity was imposed on that tribe in which the victim was found. When a murder victim was found at the gate of the village or the village square, he imposed the indemnity on all the villagers.

Concerning a pregnant woman who is killed

If a woman was killed while she had not delivered what is in her womb, there is nothing due but the indemnity for her. If she delivered a stillborn, a slave is to be given by her killer. If she delivered a live baby and then it died after being delivered, there is indemnity paid for it and her by the killer.

---

[23] Similarly narrated in ***Sharh at-Tajrīd, Sunan ad-Dārimi, Ŝahīh Ibn Hibbān***

[24] Similarly narrated in ***Sharh at-Tajrīd, Musnad Ahmed, Sunan al-Bayhaqi***

Concerning a murder victim who was found among a people who were declared innocent by the victim's guardians but then they claimed that it was someone else

If a murder victim was found in the place of a people and those people were declared innocent by the victim's guardians and then they claimed that someone else killed him, those who were declared innocent would be exempted from swearing an oath and the indemnity. Swearing the oath would also be exempted from those who were claimed to have done it because the victim was not found among them. There is nothing due upon them greater than the oath: "We did not kill the victim." Only the one among them who is accused has to swear an oath. If no person is accused specifically, no one is obligated to swear an oath.

Concerning one who plucks out all a person's teeth

Whoever plucked out all a person's teeth must pay the indemnity, half the indemnity and a tenth of the indemnity. This is because there are thirty-two teeth in the mouth. For each one, five camels are due. That would be one-hundred sixty camels. This is because there are four central incisors, four lateral incisors, four canines, four first bicuspids, four second bicuspids and twelve molars. That equals thirty-two teeth.

If a man removed another's hands or feet or nose, he would have to pay the complete indemnity for the nose and a half indemnity for each hand and half for each foot. That is to be taken from him in three years. This is the best view we hold to regarding its timing.

Concerning a man who commits a number of injuries

If a man gouges out the eye of one man and severs the hand of another and severs the foot of another and cuts off the nose of another, it is obligatory that he be retaliated for all such injuries. His eye is to be gouged out as well as his hand, leg and nose are to be severed. Similar is the case if he were to have killed someone; he is to be put to death after the other retaliatory punishments.

Concerning that which the clan is to be fined

The clan is to pay the bloodwite for injuries—five camels or more—for things such as a tooth and head wound in which the whiteness of the bone is apparent and above that. As for that which is below five camels, it shall be paid from the man's wealth.[25] If he is well off, he is to extract it from his wealth. If he is in straitened circumstances, he is to seek it out from near and distant relatives. If they want, they can give it to him; if they want, they can prevent it from him.

Concerning the doctor, circumciser and healer who ruined what they were supposed to treat

If they are innocent and employed much effort and sincere advice, they are to not be held liable. If they were accused of deceptive practices, they are to be made to swear an oath that they were not negligent in their treatment. If they rushed headlong into medical treatment and harms as a result, they would be held liable.

[25] Imams Abu Ťālib, Ibn al-Murtaḍa and al-Mu`ayyad Billah said in their works that al-Hādi differed in his judgement regarding who is to pay the bloodwite for a head wound in which the whiteness of the bone is apparent. According to what is narrated from him in the ***Ahkām***, the clan is to pay it if it is more than such injury. However, in ***Al-Muntakhab***, it is narrated that he said that the clan is to pay it even if it is less than that. We say that the judgement in the ***Ahkām*** is considered more authoritative because it states an explicit limit—five camels. Whereas, the reference in ***Al-Muntakhab*** simply says: "It is sufficient for you that the clan is to pay the bloodwite for everything other than these four things [i.e. a slave, intentional killer, settlement or confession] whether more or less."

The phrase 'whether more or less' is vague and needs explanation. Furthermore, the explicit mention of five camels in the ***Ahkām*** serves as an explicator of the limit that necessitates whether the clan or offender pays the bloodwite.

Similar has been narrated that the Prophet, peace and blessings be upon him and his progeny, said: ((Whoever practices medicine without being known for such before that and a person is harmed as a result, he shall be held liable)).[26] It is also narrated that the Commander of Believers, 'Ali b. Abi Ṭālib, upon him be peace, said:

> Whoever is a doctor and treats someone will be innocent of anything that occurs by his hand. Witnesses must testify to his innocence. Then he is to treat and employ much effort and sincere advice as well as fear Allah his Lord regarding the one he is treating.

Concerning a leaning wall that collapses on a person and concerning one who dies as a result of retaliation

If a wall was known to be leaning and damaged and a source of fear and the owner leaves it that way, he would be held liable for any damage that occurs under it. If it was not known to be leaning, he would not be held liable.

The one who retaliated against another for an injury and the latter died as a result will not be held liable for such because he had not died from his action; rather, he died from the judgement of his Lord. He was seized for his crime and died by the judgement of his Lord.

Whoever urges his horse to go on a street that the Muslims pass and travel on and someone is injured by the horse—the rider would be held liable for any damage caused by the injury. If he were to urge his horse in an open field of land off the streets where no one passes and someone is killed or injured, the rider would not be held liable.

My father related to me that his father was asked about a leaning wall. He replied; "If the owner leaves it that way after it is clear to him that it is a source of fear, he would be held liable for any damage it caused."

My father related to me that his father was asked about a man who had a retaliatory penalty applied to him and died as a result. He replied: "There is nothing due for such. He was simply killed by the judgement of Allah upon him. This has been mentioned by the Commander of Believers, upon him be peace."[27]

Concerning a man who was killed but has small children and concerning a woman who was forced by a sinner against her will and she killed him

If a man who was killed has small children, the killer is to be imprisoned and must wait until they mature. Once they are adults, he would be surrendered to them. If they were to pardon him, their pardon would be permissible. If they were to have him put to death, that would be for them to do. If some of them were to pardon him, the death penalty would be exempted from him and he would have to pay indemnity.

If a sinner or rebellious whoremonger were to force himself on a woman against her will and she did not have a way to repel him except by killing him and she killed him intentionally, there is to be no retaliation or indemnity paid by her. This is because he sought from her that which Allah has prohibited and commanded her to stay away from, and she wasn't able to avoid his advances except by killing him.

My father related to me that his father was asked about a man who was killed and had small children. He replied: "He is to wait until he is pardoned by the victim's children and they are to retaliate against him once they become mature."

---

[26] Similarly narrated in ***Sunan Abu Dāwūd, Sunan an-Nisā'i, Sunan Ibn Mājah, Mušannaf Ibn Abi Shayba, Sunan ad-Dārqutni, Sunan al-Bayhaqi***

[27] Similar has been narrated in ***Mušannaf 'Abdur-Razzāq***

My father related to me that his father was asked about a man who forces himself on a woman against her will and she killed him. He replied:

> If that is correct, she is to not be retaliated against or pay indemnity. This is the case as long as killing him was the only way that she could prevent him from what he wanted to do and as a means to protect herself from him.

Concerning swearing oaths and a rabid dog

Swearing an oath is obligatory upon the defendant, and evidence is obligatory upon the plaintiff. If there is no evidence, fifty men must swear against the defendant. It is not as the people of Medina say—that is, the oath is obligatory upon the plaintiff. How can the plaintiff be deserving of a claim without evidence of murder? Is he deserving of even a dirham against a Muslim without evidence? This is what is not sound regarding the truth, nor would anyone with intellect advocate such!

As for the dog, if its owners know that it is rabid and its rabidity is well known but its owners still leave him after having knowledge of this, they would be held liable for whatever injuries it caused. If they had not known about this from their dog, they would not be obligated regarding that which their dog causes unless they depart with it to the roads and streets of the Muslims. Then, they would be held liable for what occurs in them, and his case would be similar to the case of other animals.[28]

My father related to me that his father was asked about swearing oaths and the way it is to be done. He replied:

> Swearing an oath regarding a death is obligatory upon the defendant. If they swear, they free themselves from the claim of the one who makes a claim of murder against them.
>
> No one is to be put to death by a swearing, as the people of Medina advocate. There is no disagreement among the Prophet's Progeny regarding that. The plaintiff does not deserve even a dirham in swearing an oath, so how can he be deserving of a death?!
>
> Fifty men are to swear against the defendant fifty oaths by Allah that they did not kill the victim or know who did it.

My father related to me that his father was asked about the rabid dog and what is due for the one he bit. He replied: "If the dog is known to be rabid, its actions in its rabidity would be considered the liability of his owner. If it is not known to be rabid, there is nothing due on him if it were to attack someone."

Concerning various issues regarding indemnities

If a man were to sever an extra sixth finger or toe, a judgement would apply to him. There would be no predetermined indemnity due on him. Similarly, if an extra tooth were to be plucked, a judgement would be applied to him. Regarding retaliation, one is to retaliate from injuries to the extent of the length and width of the injury.

Regarding the one who hires a child—whether free or slave—without the permission of his guardians and he is injured, such person would be responsible for his value if he were enslaved and his indemnity if he were free.

---

[28] A similar topic is discussed in ***Al-Muntakhab*** regarding injuries caused by riding beast.

> I asked him about riding beasts that were neglected in the pastures and they gored or bit each other. "Is the owner of the animal that gored or bit considered liable?" He replied: "If this animal was known to gore and bite and then its owner sent it while cognizant of that, its goring or biting would be the responsibility of its owner. If the animal is in the property of its owner and another animal comes to it and enters into the property of its owner and it is gored, its owner will not be held liable." "What if this riding beast is not known for goring before then and it gores other animals and one of them die as a result?" "If that is the case, its owner will not be held liable because of the statement of Allah's Messenger, peace and blessings be upon him and his progeny: ((…and the riding beast is of no account))."

Concerning one who inherits from indemnity

Indemnity is like inheritance that is inherited by everyone who inherits from the wealth of the dead; their judgements are the same. Whoever inherits from wealth inherits from indemnity. Similar has reached us from Allah's Messenger, peace and blessings be upon him and his progeny, that he passed the judgement of indemnity from inheritance and bloodwite upon the relations.[29]

If a *dhimmi* were to have a Muslim son and the latter died and left Muslims' inheritance but then his father were to embrace Islam after the death of his son, he is to get a little of the inheritance. There will not be a designated obligatory portion for him because inheritance is due to one's family at the time of death. It would be the same whether they were to distribute a portion for him from that day or if they were to leave it for ten years. It would be for the one for whom it is obligatory at the time of death; it would not be for them to share it with one for whom it is not obligatory.

Similar has been narrated to us that the Commander of Believers, 'Ali b. Abi Ťālib, upon him be peace, gave a judgement regarding a man who died whose mother was a Christian and then she embraced Islam after his death before inheritance was distributed. The Commander of Believers, 'Ali b. Abi Ťālib, upon him be peace, said that she would have no right to the inheritance; however, they could give her a small portion of her son's wealth. They gave her a small portion of his wealth and did not distribute a portion of his inheritance to her.[30]

Concerning one who bit a person's hand and removed a chunk of hand from his mouth along with his own tooth or teeth

Whoever bit his Muslim brother in an act of wrongdoing and aggression and then removed a chunk of hand from his mouth along with his own teeth—there would be no indemnity for him nor retaliation. Similar has reached us from Allah's Messenger, peace and blessings be upon him and his progeny, that he passed a judgement regarding that.[31] It has also reached us that the Commander of Believers, 'Ali b. Abi Ťālib, upon him be peace, did such.[32]

Concerning one who brands his slave with fire

It has reached us from the Commander of Believers, 'Ali b. Abi Ťālib, upon him be peace, that he manumitted a slave who was branded in the face by his master.[33]

This obligation, according to me, is related to a punishment that touches him on his body because no one is represented by another. However, the imam of the Muslims should look into the affair of his subjects by what Allah has facilitated: **{Verily, Allah is with those who are God-conscious and those who do good} (Q. 16:128)**. 'Those who do good' from the entire *Ummah* are the thoughtful, as Allah's Messenger, peace and blessings be upon him and his progeny, said: ((Everyone who does good is thoughtful)). If that is for those who do good among the Muslims, then their imam would be considered more so.

---

[29] Similarly narrated in ***Mušannaf 'Abdur-Razzāq, Mušannaf Ibn Abi Shayba, Sunan al-Bayhaqi***

[30] Similarly narrated in ***Mušannaf Ibn Abi Shayba***

[31] Sheikh 'Ali b. Bilāl reported in his ***Sharh al-Ahkām*** on the authority of Sayyid Abul-Abbās al-Hasani related with a complete chain of narrators to Imrān b. Hušayn:

> A man bit the hand of another man, and when the man removed his hand from the other's mouth, two of his incisors came out. They took their dispute to Allah's Messenger, peace and blessings be upon him and is progeny. He said: ((When one of you bites his brother like the biting of a male camel, there is no indemnity for such)).

Similar has been narrated in ***Ŝahīh al-Bukhāri, Ŝahīh Muslim, Sunan at-Tirmidhi, Sunan an-Nisā'i, Musnad Ahmed, Al-Mu'jam al-Kabīr, Al-Mu'jam al-Awsat.***

[32] Similarly narrated in ***Musnad Imam Zayd*** and ***Sharh at-Tajrīd***

[33] Similarly narrated in ***Musnad Imam Zayd, Sharh at-Tajrīd, Ŝahīh al-Bukhāri, Ŝahīh Muslim, Sunan Abu Dāwūd, Sunan an-Nisā'i, Sunan Ibn Māja***

Concerning one who did an action that causes damage without the intention of the doer

If a man were to spray the door to his house while it is in the street of the Muslims and another man slipped on it and broke his hand or leg, the one who sprayed while in the street of the Muslims would have to pay the indemnity.

Similarly, if a man threw a stone in another man's house and the stone passed through to the house of another without the thrower intending it to do so and then the stone caused an accident, the indemnity for that accident would be due on the thrower. Similar is the case with one who shot an arrow at a bird on the wall but then the arrow missed the bird and injured or killed the person behind it; the one who shot the arrow would be held liable for the accident caused by his arrow.

Likewise, if a man were to shove another man onto a garment and the garment ripped as a result, the one who shoved the other would be held liable. The shoved person would take the place of the stone. That is the case if there was no action or injury on the part of the shoved person.

If a man had a well dug on his property by another man and someone was injured by it, there would be no blame on the owner or the digger because he was simply digging on his own property and not in a place where someone else could pass or in the path that any of the Muslims take. However, if he had digging done in any of the roads and paths of the Muslims and someone was injured as a result of the digging, the blame would be on the digger and not the one who had the digging done if the former knew. If he were a free person, his clan would have to pay the indemnity. If he were a slave, his injury would be his responsibility.

If the slave master gave his slave permission to hire himself out to dig holes or anything else, the injury of the slave would be his responsibility. His master would not have to pay anything to the one who commanded him to dig the hole. If the slave did not have his permission to be hired to work on the hole by his master or he dug that hole in the streets of the Muslims and someone was injured as a result, the blame would be on the slave. He would be assigned to his master, and the slave master can seek the value of the slave's work from the one who ordered him to dig the hole because he was hired to dig a hole without his master's permission.

If a man lent another man a wall and the borrower built on it and placed the wood of his building on it but was then was demanded to vacate it, the judgement regarding that would be that the borrower must ask the lender. If the wall was lent to him for a designated and mutually-appointed time to build upon it during this designated time and he built on it during that time and the owner requested that the borrowed item be returned to him, it would be for him to do so. The judgement would be for the builder to demolish his building since he was permitted until a specific and stipulated time. However, if the owner lent it to him to build on it without designating a specific time and the borrower built on it and the owner of the wall requested that the wall be returned, the judgement would be in favour of the owner of the wall in terms of the wall but against him and for the borrower in terms of the value of the building. The owner of the wall would have to pay the expenses of the building.[34]

The same is the case regarding the judgement of lending land until an appointed time or non-appointed time and then the borrower builds on it or an accident occurs or charges a fee in it.

Concerning two ships that collide with each in the sea

If they collide with each other with their masts or sides or fronts, each person would be held liable for the destruction of the other. However, if only one of them collided with the other or one is blown by the wind to the other insomuch that it collides into the side or portion of it, the one who collided into the other would be held liable for what was destroyed on the collided vessel.

---

[34] It would seem that the aforementioned judgements regarding borrowing and lending are out of place here. However, as evidenced by the following principle, the issues related to lending and borrowing relate to ownership and consequently, liability.

The Book of Inheritance Shares

In the Name of Allah, the Most Gracious, the Most Merciful...

The beginning of the chapters regarding inheritance shares

There are seventeen inheritance shares referenced in the Book of Allah. They include thirteen that are specifically named and four that are not. As for the inheritance shares that are named, one of them is the inheritance share for the daughter which is half based on the statement of Allah, the Mighty and Majestic: **{And if there be only one, then half for her}** (Q. 4:11). The inheritance share of two daughters is two-thirds based on Allah's statement: **{And if there be women more than two, then two-thirds of what he left}** (Q. 4:11). The inheritance share for the two parents is one-third (lit. "two-sixths") for both based on the statement of the Exalted: **{And for his parents, there is to be for each of them a sixth of what he left behind if he has a child}** (Q. 4:11). The inheritance share for the mother is a third based on Allah's statement: **{...and his parents are the heirs, then for his mother is a third...}** (Q. 4:11). The inheritance share for the sister is half based on the statement of the Exalted: **{If a man were to perish without child and has a sister, then unto her shall be half of what he left}** (Q. 4:176). The inheritance share for two sisters is two-thirds based on the statement of the Exalted: **{If there are two sisters, unto both shall belong two-thirds of what he left}** (Q. 4:176). The inheritance share for the maternal brother or sister is a sixth based on the statement of the Exalted: **{And if a man or woman who is inherited has no direct heir but has a brother or sister, then for each of them twain is a sixth. And if they be more than that, then they shall be sharers in the third}** (Q. 4:12). The inheritance share of the husband with the offspring is a fourth and his inheritance if there is no offspring is a half. That is based on the statement of the Exalted: **{And unto thee shall belong a half of what is left by thy wives if they are without child; but if they are with child, then unto thee shall belong a fourth...}** (Q. 4:12). The inheritance share of the wife is a fourth if there is no offspring and an eighth if there is offspring based on the statement of the Exalted: **{And unto them belong a fourth of what ye leave behind if ye have no child. But if ye have a child, then unto them shall belong an eighth}** (Q. 4:12). These are the inheritance shares that are specifically named in the Qur'an; they are thirteen inheritance shares.

As for the four that were not named, they are in the Book. One is the inheritance share of the offspring based on the statement of the Exalted: **{Allah enjoins thee regarding thy offspring. For the male is like the portion of two females}** (Q. 4:11). The inheritance shares of the father when there is no child is based on the statement of the Exalted: **{...and if he has no son and his parents are his heirs, then to his mother belong a third...}** (Q. 4:11). This inheritance of the father was not designated. The inheritance share of the brother from his sister is based on the statement: **{...and he would have inherited from her had she died without child}** (Q. 4:176). The inheritance share for brothers and sisters is based on the statement of the Exalted: **{...and if they be siblings, men and women, unto the male is the equivalent of the share of two females}** (Q. 4:176).

Concerning the inheritance shares from the sunnah and what is agreed upon

The inheritance shares from the sunnah are seven inheritance shares not mentioned in the Qur'an; however, it has come in the sunnah and is agreed upon. The inheritance share of the son's daughter is a half if there is no son. The inheritance share of the son's daughters is two-thirds if there is no son. The inheritance share of the son's daughter with his own daughter is a sixth; it is from the inheritance shares that were narrated from the Prophet, peace and blessings be upon him and his progeny. He gave that as a judgement.[1] The inheritance share of his son's daughters with his own son is a sixth—two-thirds of the entire property; that is agreed upon. The inheritance share of the paternal sister is half, and the inheritance share of the paternal sisters is two-thirds. The inheritance share of the paternal

[1] Similarly narrated in ***Sharh at-Tajrīd, Ŝahīh al-Bukhāri, Sunan Abu Dāwūd, Sunan at-Tirmidhi, Sunan Ibn Māja***

sisters with a paternal/maternal sister is a sixth—two-thirds of the entire property. One does not consider their number in that—whether one or many. The inheritance share of the grandfather with the offspring is a sixth; there is no disagreement regarding that according to us. The inheritance share of the mother with the husband and father is a third. The inheritance share of the mother with the wife and father is also a third. That which remains after the half is for the husband and a fourth for the wife.

Concerning those men who have inheritance shares allotted to them and concerning one who inherits from his paternal relatives and others

Those men for whom Allah allots inheritance are four. A sixth is allotted to the father with the son based on His statement: **{And for his parents, there is to be for each of them a sixth of what he left behind if he has a child}** (Q. 4:11). The inheritance share of the husband is half if there is no offspring with him and a fourth if there is an offspring. The inheritance share of the maternal brother is a sixth if he is the only one; however, if he has brothers or sisters, they all are to share in a third. The inheritance share of a brother from his sister is not named, as He says: **{...and he would have inherited from her had she died without child}** (Q. 4:176).

As for the male heirs, they are fifteen men. They include thirteen paternal relatives and two that are not. As for the paternal relatives, they are the son; the son's son, even if he is further down in descent; the father; the grandfather; the paternal/maternal brother; the paternal brother; paternal/maternal male cousin; the father's male cousin; the father's and mother's maternal uncle; the father's maternal uncle; the father's and mother's male cousin; the father's male cousin; and the manumitted slave. Those are considered the paternal relatives, and they are thirteen men.

As for the two men who inherit that are not a part of the paternal relatives, they are the maternal brother and the husband.

Concerning those women who have inheritance shares allotted to them and how much is inherited from them

Those women for whom Allah allots inheritance are seven and none other than them. He allots a half for one daughter, a third for daughters, a sixth for the mother if there is offspring or brother or sisters, a half for the sister, two-thirds for two sisters, a sixth for a maternal sister, an eight for a wife with offspring and a fourth for her if there is no offspring.

There are nine women who are inherited from; three are inherited from in all situations and six that are exempted in some situations. As for the three that are inherited from in all situations, they include the daughter, mother and wife. As for the six that are exempted in some situations, they include the grandmother, the paternal/maternal sister, the paternal sister, the son's daughter, the maternal sister and female slave.

The designation of those men and women who do not inherit

As for those men who do not inherit, they are ten: the daughter's son, the sister's son, the son of the mother's brother, the mother's paternal uncle, the son of the mother's paternal uncle, the paternal aunt's son, the maternal aunt's son, the maternal uncle, the maternal uncle's son and the grandfather of the mother's father.

Those women who do not inherit are ten: the daughter's daughter, the sister's daughter, the brother's daughter, the daughter of the paternal uncle, the daughter of the maternal uncle, the paternal aunt, the daughter of the paternal aunt, the maternal aunt, the daughter of the maternal aunt, the grandmother of the mother's father's mother.

The designation of family inheritance shares and what has come regarding urging the study of inheritance

It has reached us that Allah's Messenger, peace and blessings be upon him and his progeny, said: ((Learn the Qur'an and teach it to the people. Learn the laws of inheritance shares and teach it to the people. For verily, I am a mortal man that will be taken in death. Consequently, the knowledge of such will perish and controversy (*fitan*) will manifest insomuch that two people will dispute regarding inheritance shares and not be able to find anyone who can settle it between them)).[2]

It has reached us that some narrators said:

> The one who learns the Qur'an should learn the laws of inheritance shares. He should not be like a man whom a Bedouin came to and asked: "O Emigrant, can you teach the Qur'an?" The man replied: "Yes." He then said to him: "Verily, human beings are among the people who will die, and the inheritance would therefore be due upon him. If it were to occur, he would be negligent of the knowledge of that which Allah has taught and addition that Allah has increased him by even if he had not done well." He then said: "By what are our unique virtues, O fellow Emigrants?"

Concerning the inheritance shares of the two parents

Know—may Allah bring you to success!—that the father inherits from everything that the son leaves. If the deceased did not have children or grandchildren or husband or wife or a maternal grandmother or mother and it was anyone else other than these six, the father would inherit exclusively. No one would inherit with the father if they be brothers, sisters, grandfather, grandmother or any of the paternal clan or relatives.

If a man were to die leaving behind a father and son, the father would get a sixth and the remainder would go to the son. If he were to leave behind a father and two sons and two daughters, the father would get a sixth and the remainder would be distributed amongst the offspring with the males getting twice the shares of the females. If he were to leave behind a father and sibling, the wealth would belong exclusively to the father.

Similarly, if he were to leave behind a grandchild, s/he would be considered the same as his child. The male would be considered the same as a male and the female the same as a female. The males would give the father a sixth that Allah has mandated. If the deceased had a daughter, she would get half and the remainder would go to the father after receiving the sixth. If a father and two daughters were left behind, two-thirds would be left to the daughters and the remainder would be left to the father.

Concerning the one whom the mother exempts and the one who exempts her from the third

The mother exempts each of the grandmothers from inheritance. She is exempted from receiving a third by four: the offspring, grandchildren, brothers and sisters.

If a man were to die leaving behind both parents, his mother would get a third and the remainder would go to the father. If he were to die leaving behind both parents and a daughter, the daughter would get half and the mother and father would get a sixth each and any remaining wealth would go to the father.

The grandson would exempt the mother from receiving the third, as Allah says: {**And for his parents, there is to be for each of them a sixth of what he left behind if he has a child**} (**Q. 4:11**). The brothers and sisters—whether from the father and mother or the father or the mother—exempt the mother from receiving a third, as Allah says: {**And if he has a brother, then there is to be for his mother a sixth**} (**Q. 4:11**).

---

[2] Similarly narrated in ***Sunan Ibn Mājah, al-Mustadrak, Sunan ad-Dārimi, Sunan ad-Dārqutni, Sunan al-Bayhaqi, Al-Mu'jam al-Awsat***

If he were to leave behind a grandson and both parents, the parents would get a third and the remainder would go to the grandson. If he were to leave behind both parents and a granddaughter, the granddaughter would get half and the parents would get a third. The remainder would then go to the father.

If he were to leave behind two granddaughters and both parents, two-thirds would go to the two granddaughters and the parents would receive a third. If he were to leave behind both parents and a son and a daughter, a third would go to the parents and the remainder would be distributed among the offspring with the son getting twice as much as the daughter's share.

The mother would not exempt anyone but the grandmothers. If he were to leave behind a daughter and mother and both grandmothers, the daughter would get half, the mother would get a sixth and the remainder would go to the paternal relatives. The grandmothers would be exempted—both the maternal grandmother and paternal grandmother. The mother exempts both from their sixths. If he were to leave behind a grandfather, the mother would get a third and the remainder would go to the grandfather.

Concerning the inheritance of the offspring and with whom s/he inherits and does not inherit as well as which of the offspring exempts the paternal relatives and does not exempt them

If a man were to die leaving behind a son, his wealth would go to his son. If he left behind a daughter, half of it would go to her and the remainder would go to his paternal relatives. If he left behind two daughters, two-thirds would go to the two daughters and the remainder would go to the paternal relatives. If he were to leave behind sons and daughters, the wealth would be distributed among them with the males getting twice the shares of the females.

If he were to leave behind a daughter and his paternal/maternal brother, his daughter would get half and the remainder would go to his paternal/maternal brother. If he were to leave behind two daughters and three different brothers, two-thirds would go to the two daughters and the remainder would go to the paternal/maternal brother. The maternal brother would be exempted because the offspring [of both father and mother] exempts the mother's offspring—whether female or male. The paternal brother would also be exempted while there is a paternal relative because the paternal/maternal brother has a closer paternal relationship than [the paternal brother] does.

If he were to leave behind daughters and a paternal brother and a maternal brother, the daughters would get two-thirds, and the remainder would go to the paternal brother. If he were to leave behind two daughters and six different sisters [i.e. two maternal sisters, two paternal sisters and two paternal/maternal sisters], two-thirds would go to the two daughters and the remainder would go to the paternal relatives. The latter would consist of the two paternal/maternal sisters. If he were to leave behind two daughters and a mother and a paternal/maternal brother, two-thirds would go to the two daughters, the mother would get a sixth and the remainder would go to the paternal/maternal brother. If he were to leave behind a son and a paternal/maternal brother or a paternal brother or maternal brother or sisters, the wealth would go to the son and the brothers would be exempted from it because the male offspring exempts the brothers and sisters.

If he were to leave behind two sons and a mother and six brothers, the mother would get a sixth and the remainder would go to the two sons. If he were to leave behind two sons and two daughters and both parents and a grandfather, the parents would get a sixth each and the remainder would go to the offspring with the sons getting twice the shares of the daughters; the father would exempt the grandfather. If he were to leave behind a mother and grandfather and son and daughter, the grandfather and mother would each get a sixth and the remainder would go to the son and daughter with the son getting twice the share of the daughter. If he were to leave behind a daughter and two grandfathers—a paternal grandfather and maternal grandfather, the daughter would get half and the remainder would go to the paternal grandfather; the maternal grandfather would be exempted because he is not from the paternal relatives and is among those ten who do not inherit.

If one were to die leaving behind a daughter and four grandmothers—the mother's mother and the father's mother and the mother of the father's father and the mother of the mother's father, the daughter would get half, the two grandmothers—the father's mother and mother's mother—would get a sixth. The mother of the mother's father would not get anything because she is among those ten who do not inherit. As for the mother of the father's father, if the paternal grandmother is present, the latter would be considered closer than the former so she would not get anything in that case.

Concerning paternal/maternal brothers and sisters as well as who exempts and who is exempted and the grandfather

The other offspring of the father and mother [i.e. a brother] are exempted by four—the son; the son's son, even if he is further down in descent; the father and the grandfather in the statement of the one who makes the grandfather the same as the father. That is nothing according to us. The grandfather in the statement of the Commander of Believers, 'Ali b. Abi Ṭālib, upon him be peace, cannot exempt anyone except the mother's offspring.

The offspring of the father and mother exempts the offspring of the father when they are females and completed two-thirds of the entire property unless he is with a paternal male offspring. He would then get the remainder, and it would belong to the brothers and sisters with him. If it is the male offspring of the father and mother, they would exempt the offspring of the mother—whether they are male or female. They would not be exempted by them in the inheritance shares in the Book and Sunnah.

If a man were to die leaving behind two paternal/maternal brothers and two paternal brothers, the wealth would go to the two paternal/maternal brothers. If he were to leave behind a mother and a paternal/maternal brother and a paternal brother, a sixth will go to the mother and the remainder would go to paternal/maternal brother.

If he were to leave behind two maternal brothers and two paternal/maternal brothers and a mother, the mother would get a sixth, the maternal brother would get a third and the remainder would go to the paternal/maternal brother. The offspring of the paternal/maternal offspring would not exempt the maternal offspring because they are possessors of shares.

If he were to leave behind four grandmothers and two maternal brothers and a paternal/maternal brother, the two grandmothers we explained would get a sixth between them, the maternal brothers would get a third and the remainder would go to the paternal/maternal brother. If he were to leave behind two paternal/maternal sisters and two paternal sisters, two-thirds would go to the two paternal/maternal sisters and the remainder would go to the paternal relatives. The father's offspring would exempt because they simply inherit when the paternal/maternal offspring had not completed two-thirds. When they have completed the two-thirds, they would exempt. If he is with a male paternal offspring, the issue would be as is; two-thirds would go to the two paternal/maternal sisters and the remainder would go to the paternal brother and sister with the male getting twice the share of the female.

If he were to leave behind a paternal/maternal sister and two paternal sisters, the paternal/maternal sister would get half and the two paternal sisters would get a sixth between them—two-thirds of the entire property. The remainder would go to the paternal relatives.

If he were to leave behind six different sisters, the two maternal sisters would get a third and the two paternal/maternal sisters would get two-thirds. If he were to leave behind a mother and a maternal sister and two paternal/maternal sisters and two paternal sisters, the mother would get a sixth, the two paternal/maternal sisters would get two-thirds and the maternal sister would get a sixth.

If he were to leave behind a mother and a maternal sister and a paternal/maternal sister and two paternal sisters, the mother would get a sixth, the paternal/maternal sister would get half and the two maternal sisters would get a sixth—two-thirds of the entire property—and the maternal sister would get a sixth.

If a woman were to die leaving behind six different brothers and a husband and a mother, the husband would get half, the mother would get a sixth and the two maternal brothers would get a third. The two paternal/maternal brothers and paternal brothers would be exempted based on the statement of 'Ali b. Abi Ṭālib, upon him be peace. His proof for that is that he said:

> I never found inheritance shares for two paternal/maternal brothers in the Book; however, I found inheritance shares for two maternal brothers. The possessor of inheritance shares is more deserving that the one not assigned inheritance shares in the Book of Allah.

He also used to say: "Just as there is no amount greater than a third for the maternal offspring, they are to not be exempted from it ever."

If she were to leave behind three different sisters with each one having a brother, the maternal sister and her brother would get a third. The remainder of it would go to the paternal/maternal brother and sister. The paternal brother and sister would be exempt.

If she were to leave behind three different sisters and a mother, the paternal/maternal sister would get half, the paternal sister would get a sixth—two-thirds of the entire property. The mother and the maternal sister would each get a sixth.

Concerning an explanation of the inheritance of brothers and sisters from the father and with whom they inherit as well as concerning the one who exempts them from inheritance

Five exempts them—the son; the son's son, even if he is further down in descent; the father; the paternal brother and the maternal brother. It has been said that the grandfather also exempts them based on the statement of the one who makes the grandfather the same as the father. However, this is nothing according to us. The correct statement regarding that is the statement of the Commander of Believers, 'Ali b. Abi Ṭālib, upon him be peace: "The grandfather exempts no one except the mother's offspring."

If a man were to die leaving behind a paternal brother, the wealth would belong to him. If he were to leave behind two paternal sisters, they would get two-thirds and the remainder would go to the paternal relatives. If it were only one, she would get half and the remainder would go to the paternal relatives.

If a man were to die leaving behind paternal brothers and sisters, the wealth would be distributed between them with the males getting twice the share of females. If he were to leave behind two maternal sisters and a paternal sister and his mother, the mother would get a sixth, the maternal sister would get a third and the paternal sister would get half. If he were to leave behind his mother and his maternal sister and a paternal brother and sister, his mother would get a sixth, the two maternal sisters would get a third and the paternal brother and sister would get the remainder with the male getting twice the shares of the female.

If he were to leave behind two maternal brothers and sisters and two paternal brothers and sisters, the two maternal brothers and sisters would get a third, and the remainder would go to the paternal brothers and sisters. If he were to leave behind two grandmothers and two paternal brothers and two maternal brothers, the two grandmothers would get a sixth, the two maternal brothers would get a third and the remainder would go to the two paternal brothers. If he were to leave behind two daughters and two paternal brothers, the two daughters would get two-thirds, and the remainder would go to the two paternal brothers.

If he were to leave behind two maternal sisters and two paternal sisters, two-thirds would go to the two paternal sisters and a third would go to the two maternal sisters. If he were to leave behind three different sisters, the maternal sister would get a sixth, the paternal/maternal sister would get half, the paternal sister would get a sixth and the remainder would go to the paternal relatives.

If he were to leave behind a maternal sister and three paternal brothers with a sister for each, the maternal sister would get a sixth and the remainder would go to the paternal siblings with the males getting twice the shares of the females. If he were to leave behind a wife and paternal brothers and sisters, the wife would get a fourth and the remainder would go to the siblings with the males getting twice the shares of the female.

If a woman were to die leaving behind her husband and a brother and her paternal sister, the husband would get half and the remainder would go to the brother and sister with the male getting twice the share of the female.

Concerning an explanation of the inheritance of the mother's offspring as well as the amount they can exempt from the inheritance and the amount of their inheritance

The mother's offspring is exempted from the inheritance by four: the son; the son's son, even if he is further down in descent; the father and the grandfather. There is no disagreement among them that the grandfather exempts the mother's offspring.

If a man were to die leaving behind a maternal brother, he would get a sixth and the remainder would go to the paternal relatives. If he were to leave behind two maternal brothers, they would get a third and the remainder would go to the paternal relatives. If he were to leave behind more than that, they would have equal shares in the third, as Allah says: **{And if they be more than that, then they shall be sharers in the third} (Q. 4:12)**.

If he were to leave behind a maternal sister, she would get a sixth. If he were to leave behind two sisters, they would get a sixth and the remainder would go to the paternal relations. If he were to leave behind his mother and wife and two maternal brothers and sisters and five paternal/maternal brothers, a fourth would go to the wife, a sixth would go to the mother, the two maternal brothers and sisters would get a third and the remainder would go to the paternal/maternal brothers.

If he were to leave behind two paternal sisters and two maternal sisters, a third would go to the two maternal sisters and two-thirds would go to the two paternal sisters. If he were to leave behind six different sisters, the maternal sisters would get a third and the two paternal/maternal sisters would get two-thirds; the two paternal sisters would be exempted due to the entire two-thirds being inherited by the offspring of the father and mother.

If he were to leave behind his wife and two paternal/maternal brothers and two maternal brothers and two paternal brothers, the two maternal brothers would get a third, the wife would get a fourth and the remainder would go to the two paternal/maternal brothers.

If he were to leave behind his mother and six paternal brothers and three maternal brothers and three maternal sisters, the maternal brothers and sisters would get a third, the mother would get a sixth and the remainder would go to the paternal brothers.

If a woman were to die leaving behind her husband and three maternal brothers and four grandmothers, the maternal brothers would get a third, the husband would get half and the grandmothers would get a sixth between them. If a woman were to die leaving behind her mother and four grandmothers and three paternal brothers and sister, the mother would get a sixth and the remainder would go to the paternal brothers and sister. The grandmothers would be exempted because they do not inherit anything along with the mother.

If she were to die leaving behind her mother and daughter and husband and two paternal/maternal brothers and three paternal/maternal sisters and a paternal sister, the daughter would get half, the husband would get a fourth, the mother would get a sixth and the remainder would go to the paternal/maternal brothers and sisters.

Concerning all the brothers and sisters as well as the brothers' offspring and an explanation of their inheritances

If a man were to die leaving behind his paternal/maternal brother and a paternal brother and maternal brother, a sixth would go to the maternal brother and the remainder would go to the paternal/maternal brother; the paternal brother would be exempted because the paternal/maternal brother is closer than he is. If he were to leave a paternal/maternal brother and paternal brother, the wealth would go to the paternal/maternal brother instead of his paternal brother because the latter is closer than the former. If he were to leave behind a paternal/maternal brother and a maternal brother, the maternal brother would get a sixth and the remainder would go to the paternal/maternal brother.

If he were to leave behind six different brothers, the two maternal brothers would get a third and the remainder would go to the two paternal/maternal brothers. If he were to leave two maternal brothers and two paternal brothers, a third would go to the maternal brothers and the remainder would go to the two paternal brothers.

If he were to leave behind six different sisters, the two maternal sisters would get a third and the two paternal/maternal sisters would get two-thirds; the two paternal sisters would be exempted. If he were to leave behind a paternal/maternal sister and a maternal sister and three paternal sisters, the maternal sister would get a sixth, the paternal/maternal sister would get a half, the paternal sisters would get a sixth between them and the remainder would go to the paternal relatives. If he were to leave behind a maternal sister with her brother and a paternal/maternal sister and a paternal sister with her brother, the maternal brother and sister would get a third, the paternal/maternal sister would get half and the remainder would go to the paternal brother and sister with the male getting twice the shares of the female.

If he were to leave behind three different sisters with the paternal sister accompanying her brother, a sixth would go to the maternal sister, half would go to the paternal/maternal sister and the remainder would go to the paternal brother and sister with the male getting twice the shares of the female. If he were to leave behind three different sisters with each one being accompanied by the son of her brother, the maternal sister would get a sixth, the paternal sister would get half, the paternal sister would get a sixth and the remainder would go to the nephew[3] who accompanies the paternal/maternal sister.

If he were to leave behind the paternal sister with her nephew but there was no nephew with the paternal/maternal sister, he [i.e. the paternal sister's nephew] would get the remainder of the inheritance shares after it was distributed.

If he were to leave behind three different sisters with the maternal sister being accompanied by the son of her brother, the maternal sister would get a sixth, the paternal/maternal sister would get half, the paternal sister would get a sixth and the remainder would go to the paternal relations. The nephew who accompanied the maternal sister would be exempted because he is among the ten who do not inherit anything along with the paternal relatives.

If he were to leave behind three different sisters with each one of them being accompanied by her brother, the maternal brother and sister would get a third and the remainder would go to the paternal/maternal brother and sister with the male getting twice the share of the female. The paternal brother and sister would be exempted.

If he were to leave behind a paternal/maternal nephew and a paternal brother, the wealth would go to the paternal brother because the paternal brother is closer in relation and over the paternal/maternal nephew. If he were to leave behind a paternal/maternal nephew and maternal nephew, the wealth would go to the paternal/maternal nephew instead of the paternal nephew because he is closer in relation.

[3] The nephew mentioned in this section refers exclusively to the brother's son and not the sister's son.

If he were to leave behind three different nephews—a paternal/maternal nephew, a maternal nephew and a paternal nephew—the wealth would go to the paternal/maternal nephew. If he were to leave behind three paternal nephews and three maternal nephews, the wealth would go to the paternal nephews and nothing would go to the maternal nephews because the maternal nephews do not inherit anything.

If he were to leave behind three different nephews with each one being accompanied by his sister, the wealth would go to the paternal/maternal nephews. As for the daughters of the brother who accompany the paternal/maternal nephews, they are to not inherit any wealth. The wealth would go to their brothers instead of them. The maternal offspring and paternal offspring would be exempted.

If he were to leave behind two paternal/maternal nephews with whom are their two sisters, the wealth would go to the two men and not their sisters. If he were to leave behind a paternal nephew with his sister, the wealth would go to the man and his sister would be exempted. If he were to leave behind a maternal nephew with his sister, the wealth would go to the paternal relatives. Nothing would be for the both of them, and they would be exempted from inheritance completely. If he were to leave behind three paternal/maternal nephews and their sisters, the wealth would be for the males and not the females.

If he were to leave behind three different brothers and five grandmothers and four wives, a sixth would go to the maternal brother, a fourth would go to the wives, a sixth would go to the grandmothers, the remainder would go to paternal/maternal brother and the paternal brother would be exempted. If he were to leave behind three different brothers and a mother and a wife, the mother would get a sixth, the wife would get a fourth, the maternal brother would get a sixth and the remainder would go to the paternal/maternal brother.

If he were to leave behind three different sisters with each one having three different sisters, the maternal sister with her maternal sister as well as the paternal/maternal sister from her mother would get a third between them. The sisters from one mother would be four. Nothing would be for her paternal sister along with them. The paternal/maternal sister with her paternal/maternal sister would get two-thirds, but her paternal sister as well as all her father's offspring would be exempted because when the paternal/maternal sisters complete the two-thirds, there would be nothing for the father's offspring as long as there were no males. However, if there are males among them and some remaining amount, it would be distributed between them with the male getting twice the amount of the female.

If he were to leave behind three different sisters with each one having a nephew with three different paternal aunts, the paternal/maternal sister along with the aunt of her paternal/maternal nephew—who is in fact her paternal/maternal sister—would get two-thirds. The remaining third would be distributed among the four maternal sisters.

If he were to leave behind a paternal brother and sister as well as a paternal/maternal sister, the paternal/maternal sister would get half and the paternal brother and sister would get the remaining amount with the male getting twice the share of the female. If he were to leave behind a paternal/maternal brother and sister and two paternal brothers and a mother, the mother would get a sixth and the remaining amount would go to the paternal/maternal brother and sister; nothing would go to the two paternal brothers.

If he were to leave behind a paternal/maternal sister and a maternal sister and five paternal sisters, half would go to the paternal/maternal sister, a sixth would go to the maternal sister, the paternal sisters would get a sixth—all of which would complete two-thirds—and the remaining amount would go to the paternal relatives. If there were any brothers included in the remainder, they would get twice the amount of the females.

Concerning the sharing among the paternal/maternal brothers and maternal brothers regarding the third as well as who among them does not share

If a woman were to die leaving behind her mother and husband and six different brothers, the mother would get a sixth, the husband would get half and the two maternal brothers would get a third. The paternal/maternal brothers and paternal brothers would be exempted based on the statement of the Commander of Believers, 'Ali b. Abi Ťālib, upon him be peace. It is agreed upon that this is on the authority of 'Ali b. Abi Ťālib, upon him be peace.

One can use it as a proof and say that just as they are not given more, they are not given less than the third that is for them in the Qur'an. Haven't you considered that even if they were a hundred, they would not be given more than a third. Therefore, how can they be given less than that? The paternal/maternal offspring would all share in the third. There is no inheritance share for the paternal/maternal brothers mentioned in the Book; they are simply like the one who takes booty (*ghānim*). He can take it one time and not take it another time. Therefore, if there is extra from the holder of shares, he can take it; otherwise, there is nothing for them, as Allah does not appoint anything for them.

They disagree in that regarding what is narrated from 'Abdullah [b. Mas'ūd]§ and Zayd [b. Thābit].§ Some of them narrate from the both of them that the paternal/maternal brothers and maternal brothers share in a third. They said that father does not increase them except in paternal relations. Others narrate from them that the two are to not share, and they use as a proof that the two of them say that the designated shares in the Qur'an are completed. That is the statement of the Commander of Believers, 'Ali b. Abi Ťālib, upon him be peace. This issue is called collectivism (*al-mushtarika*). It has reached us on the authority of 'Ali b. Abi Ťālib, upon him be peace, that he used to not allot shares of the mandatory inheritance.[4]

It is narrated on the authority of Hakīm b. Jābir§:

> A woman died among us and left behind her husband, her mother, paternal/maternal brothers and maternal brothers. That was brought to 'Ali b. Abi Ťālib, upon him be peace, and he said: "Her mother is to be given a sixth, her husband is to be given half and her maternal brothers are to be given a third. That is the completion of the shares. As for her paternal/maternal brothers, they are like those who take booty—they can take one time and not take."[5]

Those who do not share use as a proof against those who share by asking them the question that was asked in this section. It is that a woman died leaving behind her husband, mother, maternal brother and four paternal/maternal brothers. They would all say regarding this issue that the husband gets half, the mother gets a sixth, the maternal brother gets a sixth, and the remainder goes to the paternal/maternal brothers. They would say to them that the share of the maternal brother is greater than the share of the paternal/maternal brothers. We do not see deficiency in them except from the paternal side since the maternal brother himself would be considered the same as them in totality—even if they were to reach a large number, they are those from the paternal and maternal sides. Had it not been for the father, they and the maternal brothers would be considered the same in inheritance law.

They can also use as a proof against them that the maternal brothers simply inherit in this issue with the inheritance designated in the Qur'an. It was spoken of in the Book, and that is the statement of Allah: **{And if they be more than that, then they shall be sharers in the third} (Q. 4:12)**.

As for the paternal/maternal brothers, there are no inheritance shares for them in the Book. The remaining shares are simply for them. Therefore, those who are not allotted inheritance shares in the Book do not share with those who are allotted shares in the Book. This is because the people of inheritance shares are more deserving of the inheritance shares than those for whom there are no inheritance shares. These are all the proofs, and these are the proofs of the Commander of Believers, 'Ali b. Abi Ťālib, upon him be peace.

---

[4] That is to say that in the case that there are remains left behind, there are shares allotted. However, in the case where there are no remains, there are no allotments shared amongst inheritors.

[5] Similarly narrated in ***Sunan al-Bayhaqi***

Concerning the inheritance of paternal uncles

If a man were to die leaving behind his mother's and father's paternal uncle and his father's paternal uncle, the wealth would go to his mother's and father's paternal uncle and nothing for his father's paternal uncle. If he were to leave behind his father's paternal uncle as well as his mother's and father's paternal cousin, the wealth would go to his father's paternal uncle because he is closer.

If he were to leave behind three different paternal uncles—one belonging to the father and mother, one belonging to the father, one belonging to the mother—the wealth would go to the father's and mother's paternal uncle. The father's paternal uncle would be exempted because the father's and mother's paternal uncle is closer. As for the mother's paternal uncle, he is one of the ten men who do not inherit, and he is not among the paternal relatives.

If he were to leave behind three different paternal uncles with each having three different sisters, the wealth would go to the father's and mother's paternal uncle and the sisters would be exempted as well as the other heirs. If he were to leave behind four paternal uncles and four paternal aunts of the mother and father, the wealth would be for the males and not the females because the paternal aunts are among those who do not inherit anything.

Concerning the inheritance of paternal cousins

If a man were to die leaving behind two paternal cousins—one of whom is the son of the father's and mother's paternal uncle and the other one is the son of the father's paternal uncle—the inheritance would be for the son of the father's and mother's paternal uncle. If he were to leave behind two sons of the father's and mother's paternal uncle—one of whom is the mother's brother—the mother's brother would get a sixth, and the remainder would be split between them as two halves. This is the statement of the Commander of Believers, 'Ali b. Abi Ťālib, upon him be peace.

As for the statement of 'Abdullah [b. Mas'ūd], it is that the wealth would be only for the paternal cousin which is the mother's brother. However, that is nothing according to us. The correct statement is that of the Commander of Believers, 'Ali b. Abi Ťālib, upon him be peace.

If he were to leave behind the son of the father's brother as well as the father's and mother's paternal uncle, the inheritance would be for the son of the father's brother and nothing would be for the paternal uncle because the son of the father's brother is closer.

If he were to leave behind a son of the father's and mother's paternal uncle as well as the father's and mother's paternal uncle and the mother's paternal uncle and a grandfather, the wealth would go exclusively to the grandfather. If he were to leave behind the son of the son of the father's and mother's paternal uncle as well as the son of the son of the mother's paternal uncle, the inheritance would be for the son of the son of the father's and mother's paternal uncle.

If he were to leave behind a father's and mother's paternal uncle and three grandmothers and a grandfather, a sixth would go to the two grandmothers—the mother's mother and the father's mother—and the remainder would go to the grandfather.

If a woman were to leave behind four paternal cousins through the mother and father as well as a husband and the mother's brother, the mother's brother would get a sixth, the husband would get half and the rest would go to the four. If a woman were to die leaving behind two sons of a paternal uncle and a husband and the mother's brother with each with a brother taking his place, a third would go to the two maternal brothers, half would go to the husband and the remainder would go to the four.

If he were to leave behind two sons of the father's and mother's paternal uncle as well as their two sisters, the wealth would go to the two men and not the two women. And if he leaves behind cousins from the paternal uncle of the same mother and father and their sisters, then the inheritance is for the males and not the females. If the ruling is passed down from the deceased son of the brother or uncle from generation to generation, the females would not have inherited anything with males. So, understand and use analogous reasoning regarding what I explained to you, Allah willing.

Concerning the inheritance of nieces and nephews

It has reached us that the Commander of Believers, 'Ali b. Abi Ťālib, upon him be peace, said:

> Allah's Messenger, peace and blessings be upon him and his progeny, said that when someone has no daughter along with his son's daughter, the son's daughter would get half. If there was a daughter along with her, she would get a sixth.[6] If there was a son's daughter and a son's daughter lower in descent along with her or greater than that after that from their relatives, the son's daughter that is of the highest descent would get half and those who follow her would get a sixth—whether it was one or many—which completes the two-thirds. They would get a sixth. The position of the inheritance of the son's daughters is like the position of the inheritance of one's own daughters when there are no daughters to inherit or exempt.

Know that the son's son cannot exempt one from inheritance except the son. None can inherit with him except seven: female offspring, the wife, the husband, the father, the mother, the grandfather and grandmothers when there is no mother. The one who does not inherit with him is one who is lower than him in descent from the son's son. He would be in the position of the son, and their son's daughters would be in the position of the daughters in their inheritance shares. If there is only one, she would get half. If it is two females, they would get two-thirds.

If one were to leave behind a son's son and a son of a son's son that is lower than him in descent, the wealth would go to the one who is closest to the deceased. If he were to leave behind three of his son's daughters—some of whom are lower in descent than others, half would go to the one who is higher in descent, those who follow would get a sixth and the remainder would go to the paternal relatives.

If he were to leave behind three of his son's daughters—some of whom are lower in descent than others—as well as a boy who is even lower in descent than all of [the granddaughters], half would go to the granddaughter who is higher in descent, those who follow would get a sixth and the boy would get the remainder of what is obligatory from his paternal aunt, with the males getting twice the shares of the females according to the statement of the Commander of Believers, 'Ali b. Abi Ťālib, upon him be peace. As for the statement of 'Abdullah [b. Mas'ūd], it is that the remainder would go to the male only.

If he were to leave behind three of his son's daughters—some of whom are lower in descent than others—along with a sister for each and a boy who is even lower in descent, the two of them [i.e. the granddaughter and her sister] which are the highest in descent would get two thirds. The one that follows her as well as her sister, including those others who are lower in descent—there would be nothing for them, and they would be exempted by the completion of the two-thirds that was given to the two girls of higher descent. The remainder would be for the boy; he can refer it to the lowest daughter and her sister as well as the middle daughter and her sister, with the male getting twice the shares of the female.

If he were to leave behind three of his son's daughters—some of whom are lower in descent than others—along with three different sisters for each and a boy who is even lower in descent, the one of highest descent and her paternal/maternal sister and the latter's paternal sister would get two-thirds. The remainder would be for the boy; he can refer it to the lowest daughter, her paternal/maternal sister and paternal sister as well as the middle daughter, her paternal/maternal sister and her paternal sister with the male getting twice the shares of the female.

---

[6] Similarly narrated in ***Sharh at-Tajrīd, Ŝahīh al-Bukhāri, Musnad Ahmed, Al-Mu'jam al-Kabīr, Al-Mu'jam al-Awsat, Al-Mustadrak, Sunan ad-Dārqutni, Musnad Abu Ya'la, Mušannaf Ibn Abi Shayba, Sunan at-Tirmidhi, Ŝahīh Ibn Hibbān, Sunan Ibn Māja***

If he were to leave behind a son's daughter and the daughter of the son's son that is lower than she is in descent as well as three grandmothers, the son's daughter would get half and the one that follows her would get a sixth, which completes the two-thirds. The grandmothers would then get a sixth between them, and the remainder would go the paternal relatives.

If he were to leave behind a wife and grandfather and three grandmothers, the father's paternal grandmother would be exempted because he is her son according to the statement of the Commander of Believers, 'Ali b. Abi Ṭālib, upon him be peace. As for the paternal grandmother and maternal grandmother, they would inherit a sixth, the wife would get a fourth and the remainder would go to the grandfather.

Regarding the inheritance of the indirect heirs (*al-kalāla*)

Allah, the Glorified, says: **{They ask thee for an edict. Say: "Allah passes an edict unto thee regarding indirect heirs. If a man were to perish without child and has a sister, then unto her shall be half of what he left. And he would have inherited from her had she died without child} (Q. 4:176)**.

Some of the scholars say that the **{indirect heirs}** refer to those without offspring, and they use as their proof this verse **{Say: "Allah passes an edict unto thee regarding indirect heirs. If a man were to perish without child…}**. Others say that the **{indirect heirs}** refer to those without offspring and parents based on the statement of Allah earlier in the *Surah*: **{…and his parents are the heirs, then for his mother is a third…} (Q. 4:11)**. The Glorified mentioned the brothers but does not appoint a thing for them along with the father.

Have you not considered that the Mighty and Majestic caused them to inherit regarding indirect heirs, and the Blessed and Exalted says in the *Surah*: **{And if a man or woman who is inherited has no direct heir but has a brother or sister…} (Q. 4:12)**? This verse makes it clear that the father was not included in the indirect heirs. Regarding their proof for the offspring, they use the verse at the end of the *Surah*: **{Say: "Allah passes an edict unto thee regarding indirect heirs. If a man were to perish without child and has a sister, then unto her shall be half of what he left. And he would have inherited from her had she died without child} (Q. 4:176)**.

Regarding that, it is narrated from Allah's Messenger, peace and blessings be upon him and his progeny, that a man asked him about indirect heirs. He replied: ((Haven't you heard the verse that was revealed in the summer: **{They ask thee for an edict. Say: "Allah passes an edict unto thee regarding indirect heirs. If a man were to perish without child and has a sister, then unto her shall be half of what he left. And he would have inherited from her had she died without child} (Q. 4:176)**? The one who does not leave behind offspring and parents, the indirect heirs inherit)).[7]

It is narrated that the Commander of Believers, 'Ali b. Abi Ṭālib, upon him be peace, said: "The indirect heirs refer to those without offspring and parents." That is correct according to us. Praise due to Allah, the Lord of creation! Peace be upon the Messengers! May Allah's prayers and peace be upon Muhammad and his Ahl al-Bayt!

It has reached us that a man asked: "O Messenger of Allah, who are the indirect heirs in **{They ask thee for an edict. Say: "Allah passes an edict unto thee regarding indirect heirs} (Q. 4:176)**?" He replied: ((Haven't you heard the verse that was revealed in the summer: **{They ask thee for an edict. Say: "Allah passes an edict unto thee regarding indirect heirs} (Q. 4:176)**? It is the one who does not leave behind offspring and parents)).

[7] Similarly narrated in ***Sunan at-Tirmidhi, Al-Mustadrak, Musnad Abu Ya'la, Sunan al-Bayhaqi, Musnad Ahmed***.

Concerning the *munāsakha*

The *munāsakha* is when a man dies and leaves behind an inheritance, but their inheritance is not distributed until some of them also die leaving inheritance. This is the closest and primary *munāsakha*. It is that the inheritance of the dead is perhaps not distributed until the second, third and fourth heir dies. I will explain how the *munāsakha* is begun, dispensed, imposed, accounted and how shares are accurately accounted, Allah willing.

An explanation of that is that a man died leaving behind his wife and two sons, but the inheritance is not distributed until one of the two sons died. Then the first inheritance is established. It is properly accounted from sixteen shares: the wife would get two shares, which is an eighth. The remainder would go to the two sons, which is fourteen—with seven for each. When one of the two sons dies and leaves behind his mother and brother, a third would go to the mother and the remainder to the brother. That which is in the possession of the deceased would be seven shares, and it cannot be divided into thirds. Three shares would be for her, and the remaining brother would get two.

The inheritance shares would be out of three: the third that goes to the mother is one, and the remainder that goes to the brother is two. The inheritance of the second would not correlate with anything in the possession of the inheritance of the first. If it had correlated, it would have been a multiple that was imposed in the first inheritance. When it has not been correlated, one would multiply the shares together. Then it would be three times sixteen and would result in forty-eight shares. Then he is to count and divide the forty-eight shares at the beginning of the inheritance. So, the first left forty-eight shares as well as left his wife and two sons. Then the wife would get an eighth, which amounts to six, and the remainder would go to the two sons, which is forty-two—twenty-one shares for each. Then, one of the sons died leaving behind twenty-one shares, and his mother would get a third of that—which is seven—and the remainder would be for his brother, which is fourteen shares. Thirteen shares would then go to the mother's possession—six on the part of her husband and seven on the part of her son. Thirty-five shares would go to the living brother's possession—twenty-one shares on the part of his father and fourteen on the part of his brother. That which has come to you from this chapter analogously presents what we explained to you whether the *munāsakha* is long or short.

Concerning the *'awl* regarding inheritance shares

The *'awl* regarding inheritance shares is sound according to us. It is impermissible unless the inheritance shares exceed; otherwise, some of those who Allah and His Messenger, peace and blessings be upon him and his progeny, imposed it on will be deducted. Similar has been authentically attributed to us from the Commander of Believers, 'Ali b. Abi Ṭālib, upon him be peace, that he used to apply *'awl* to inheritance shares.

An explanation of that is the following: A man dies and leaves behind both parents, a wife and two daughters. The two daughters would get two-thirds, both parents would get one-third (lit. "two-sixths") and the wife would get one-eighth. This would exceed its amount—its base number being twenty-four but exceeded to twenty-seven. The two daughters would then get sixteen, the two parents would get eight and the wife would get three. It would start for them as twenty-four but then later become twenty-seven.[8]

From that, a woman dies and leaves behind her husband, mother, two maternal sisters and two paternal/maternal sisters. The husband would get half, the mother would get a sixth, the two maternal sisters would get a third and the two paternal/maternal sisters would get two-thirds. This would be an increase, as it started out as six but then became ten [10/6 or 5/3]. This is called *umm furūkh*, and it is an increase that exceeds the inheritance shares.

---

[8] This means that the shares, whose original number was twenty-four, would be re-divided into twenty-seven shares and then divided among the heirs in the mandated proportion.

How would the one who does not hold to the view of the *'awl* act in this case of inheritance shares? Would he subtract from the shares of the two paternal/maternal sisters while they are to get the shares allotted to them by their sister in the Book? Or would he subtract from the inheritance shares of the two paternal sisters mentioned in the Book? Or would he subtract from the inheritance shares of the mother mentioned in the Book? How would such person act in their affair? What would such person say regarding the injunction Allah obligates upon them?

The Glorified has obligated two-thirds for two paternal/maternal sisters, a third for the two maternal sisters, a sixth for the mother and half for the husband. The wealth is completely exhausted by a third and two-thirds. Therefore, from where can an additional sixth and half be paid if the *'awl* is not imposed in the base amount unless each one is deprived of the shares that Allah has obligated for them? This proves the establishment of the *'awl*. No one who is fair and with intellect will reject it, and only the arrogant and ignorant would abandon it.

Concerning redistribution (*ar-radd*)

Our statement regarding redistribution is the statement of the Commander of Believers, 'Ali b. Abi Ťālib, upon him be peace. That is because I found that Allah says in the Qur'an: **{And those possessors of kinship are closer one to another in the decree of Allah…} (Q. 33:6)**. According to me, that means that those kin have more right to receive the excess after the shares have been designated. This is because they and others from the Muslims share an affinity in Islam, and this sanguine relationship increases in terms of relations and familial connections. It is for that reason that such person is more entitled to the excess than the Muslim public treasury.[9]

An explanation of that is the following: A man dies and leaves behind his daughter and mother. The daughter would get half, and the mother would get a sixth. The remainder would also be given to them to the extent of their shares. The first inheritance share would be from six, in which the mother would get a share and the daughter would get three. When the excess is then redistributed to them, it would return to the four. The mother would get a share from the four, which is a fourth of the wealth, and the sister would get three shares from the four, which is three-fourths of the wealth.

Similarly, if he were to leave behind a daughter only, she would get half based on Allah's statement: **{And if there be only one, then half for her} (Q. 4:11)**. She would also get half of the remainder based on Allah's statement: **{And those possessors of kinship are closer one to another in the decree of Allah…} (Q. 33:6)**. We redistribute it to her because she is most entitled to her father than anyone else.

Similarly, if he were to leave behind only his mother or only his sister or any other heir who receives shares in the Book and Sunnah, it would be for such person to take their share and then have the remainder redistributed to him/her due to his/her familial relationship with the deceased when there is no other paternal relative along with him/her.

Concerning the inheritance shares of the grandfather

The grandfather does not receive anything more than a sixth with the offspring or offspring's offspring unless they are females; then he would get something extra. If there were no one else with him, then it would belong to him.

An explanation of that is the following: A man leaves behind a son and grandfather. The grandfather would get a sixth, and the remainder would go to the son. Similar is the case if it were a son's son and grandfather. However, if he were to leave behind a daughter and grandfather, the grandfather would

---

[9] Some jurists are of the opinion that any excess of the inheritance after it has been distributed to the respective recipients is to be given to the Muslim public treasury. [Ref. ***Al-Bidāyat al-Mujtahid***]. However, the imams of Ahl al-Bayt hold to the view that the excess is to be redistributed amongst the living heirs.

get a sixth, the daughter would get half and the remainder would then be redistributed to the grandfather. This is because he is the paternal relative of the deceased, and the paternal relatives are to get the remainder after the distribution of shares. Similar would be the case if it were the son's daughter and her grandfather.

The grandfather shares with the brothers and sisters. When there are no offspring, there is no sharing. He would have a choice of the sixth. If there is a sixth, he has a choice from the shares to take the sixth.

An explanation of that is the following: A man dies and leaves behind his grandfather, four paternal/maternal brothers or paternal brothers. The wealth would be shared between the grandfather and brothers in fifths. If he were to leave behind six paternal/maternal brothers and a grandfather, the grandfather would get a sixth and the remainder would go to the brothers because the sixth is his choice from the shares. This is the statement of the Commander of Believers, 'Ali b. Abi Ťālib, upon him be peace.

It has reached us that a man came to the Prophet, peace and blessings be upon him and his progeny, and said: "O Messenger of Allah, my son's son has died. Do I have a share in his inheritance?" He replied: ((You get a sixth)). When he turned away to depart, he called back for him and said: ((Then you get another sixth)). When he turned away to depart, he called back for him and said: ((The other sixth is an additional portion from me to you)).[10]

To the one who holds to the view that the meaning of this is that the grandfather is to receive a third, they forget that Allah's Messenger, peace and blessings be upon him and his progeny, said that it was an additional amount from him. It is for that reason that the Commander of Believers, 'Ali b. Abi Ťālib, upon him be peace, said:

> I remembered and you forgot that the second sixth was an additional amount from Allah's Messenger, peace and blessings be upon him and his progeny. To him. It is not an obligatory amount allotted to him for inheritance.

It has also reached us that he used to say: "Whoever would like to be charred in the main levels of Hell, let him issue a *fatwa* from his opinion regarding the grandfather."[11] Then we see him issuing a *fatwa* regarding him. From that, we know that he would not give a *fatwa* unless he heard it from Allah's Messenger, peace and blessings be upon him and his progeny.

The grandfather shares with the brothers and sister when they are together, but the grandfather does not share with the sisters when it is just them alone with no male with them. This is because they have inheritance shares for them mentioned in the Book, which are apportioned to them.

An explanation of that is the following: A man dies and leaves behind three sisters and a grandfather. The sisters would get two-thirds, and the grandfather would get the remaining portion. However, if he were to leave behind two sisters and a brother and a grandfather, the wealth would be shared between the grandfather, the brother and the two sisters. The males would get twice the portions of the females. It would be derived from six: each sister would get a share, the brother would get two shares and the grandfather would get two shares.

Concerning the inheritances of the drown victim, burn victim, demolish victim and missing altogether as well as the inheritance shares for similar

If relatives were to drown together or a building were to collapse on them or they were burn victims or they were missing and it is unknown as to whether they died before, some would inherit from others as if one of them died and others remained. They would inherit with the heirs

---

[10] Similarly narrated in ***Musnad Ahmed, Sunan Abu Dāwūd, Sunan at-Tirmidhi, Sunan ad-Dārqutni, Sunan al-Bayhaqi, Mušannaf Ibn Abi Shayba***

[11] Similarly narrated in ***'Iddat al-Ušūl*** of Sheikh at-Ťūsi

as if they are among those who inherit with them. If there are some who lived among those presumed dead and one of the relatives presumed to be living were to die, they would inherit with the heirs just as those who inherited from his wealth the first time.

Similar would be done with all of them—whether a lot or a little—until some of them inherit from others. Then it would be as though they died altogether, then the living would inherit what is in their possession which was then part of the inheritance they initially inherited as well as that which was part of their wealth. This is the statement of the Commander of Believers, ʻAli b. Abi Ṭālib, upon him be peace.

This is the truth according to us because the one who does not allow some to inherit from others may not know that he passed them over. That is because he may not know whether some died before others, and the delayed may inherit from the wealth of the rushed. It would therefore be obligatory for the one who does not know that and does not pass over their deceased to take precaution so that some of them inherit from others. That way, everyone would be able to inherit from everyone else since confusion and then doubt may occur.

An explanation of that is the following: A group of brothers drown together without it being known which of them died first. Each one of them left behind two daughters. The proper thing to be done is that one of them is to be presumed to have died before the other so that it would seem as if the one who died left behind his two daughters and his brother. The two daughters would get two-thirds and the brother would get the remainder. Then the one who was presumed to have died would be considered living, and the one who was presumed to have lived would be considered dead. He would be treated as if he left behind two daughters and his brother; the daughters would get two-thirds and the brother would get the remainder. Then both would be considered dead altogether, and each one would inherit the wealth of the other brother.

Concerning the accounting of inheritance shares and its summation

When the inheritance shares come to you and you want to know how much is properly accounted, establish the following as its basis: If there is a half in it and a remainder, it will be out of two. If there is a third in it and a remainder, it will be out of three. If there is a fourth in it and a remainder, it will be out of four. If there is a sixth in it and a remainder, it will be out of six. If there is an eighth in it and a remainder, it will be out of eight.

An explanation of the half and a remainder is that when the deceased leaves behind a daughter and brother, the daughter gets half and the brother gets the remainder.

An explanation of the third and a remainder is that when a man dies and leaves behind his mother and father, the mother gets a third and the father gets the remainder. It is out of three so that the mother gets a third, which is one, and the father who gets the remainder, which is two.

An explanation of the fourth and a remainder is that if a man dies and leaves behind his wife and brother, the wife gets a fourth and the brother gets the remainder. It is out of four so that the wife gets a fourth, which is one, and the brother gets the remainder, which is three.

An explanation of the sixth and a remainder is that if he leaves behind a mother and son, the mother gets a sixth and the son gets the remainder. It is out of six so that the mother gets one, and the son gets five.

An explanation of the eighth and a remainder is that if he leaves behind a wife and son, the wife gets an eighth and the son gets the remainder. It is out of eight so that the wife gets one and the son gets seven.

In the case of any issue in which there is a third and half, its base number will be out of six. Similarly, a third and a sixth would be out of six. In the case of any issue in which there is a fourth and a third or a fourth and a sixth, its base number will be out of twelve. In the case of any issue in which there is an eighth and a half, its base number will be out of eight. In the case of any issue in which there is an eighth and a sixth or a third, its base number will be out of twenty-four.

When an issue comes to you and you want to know whether its accounting is proper, establish this as its base number and then consider how much goes to each person. If you know how much goes to each person, distribute it between them.

Whoever does not divide what is in his possession and establishes it and whoever divides what is in his possession must consider how much is in their possession as well as know its number and the amount per head. Then one is to consider whether the number in their possession agrees with the amount per head. If the number of what is in their possession agrees with the amount per head by a tenth, a tenth would be paid as a base number of the inheritance or any other kind of inheritors. If it is divided among them, he pays it to all of them as a base number of the inheritance. Similarly, if it correlates to a ninth, he pays a ninth. If it is an eighth, he pays an eighth. If it is a seventh, he pays a seventh. If it is a sixth, he pays a sixth. If it is a fifth, he pays a fifth. If it is a fourth, he pays a fourth. If it is a third, he pays a third. If it is a half, he pays a half.

Similarly, if it is divided into a tenth and it correlates into portions, the portions will be paid which correlate with them. I am explaining to you how it is; therefore, use analogous reasoning based on everything I have mentioned to you.[12]

If a man were to die leaving behind eight daughters and two grandmothers and a sister, the daughters would get two-thirds, the two grandmothers would get a sixth and the sister would get the remainder. The base number would be six, so the daughters would get four out of six, the grandmothers would get one out of six and the sister would get one out of six.

Then, four is divided among the eight daughters, and one is divided among the two grandmothers. The four would be in the possession of the daughters, which correlates with the amount per head by a fourth. This is because a fourth of four is one, and a fourth of eight is two. Therefore, each would be paid two, which correlates with the amount per head and what is in their possession from the base number of the inheritance, which is six. It [i.e. the base number of six] would then become twelve. Then it would be apportioned similarly to the amount of the two grandmothers because they are two. It is that which correlates to the number of daughters by two; a half of two is a portion. The daughters would therefore get eight out of twelve—which is two-thirds—with each getting one, and the grandmothers would get two out of twelve—which is a sixth—with each getting one. And the remaining portion would go to the sister.

If he were to leave behind twelve daughters and four grandmothers and three sisters, the base number would be six. The daughters would get two-thirds, which is four; the grandmothers would get a sixth, which is one; and the sisters would get the remainder. Four shares would be divided among the twelve, one would be divided among the four grandmothers, and one would be divided among the three sisters.

Therefore, there would be four shares in the possession of the daughters. The amount per head would then correlate with what is in their possession by fourths. One would take a fourth of their number, which is three. Then, one would pay that regarding the amount per head of grandmothers, which would be four. Then, that would be three times four, which is twelve. The number of sisters is three, and three would be included in the twelve. That way, twelve would be paid as the base number of the inheritance, which is six.

It would be easier to bring it to seventy-two and become properly accounted, if Allah wills. The daughters' shares of two-thirds would be forty-eight, with each one getting four shares. The grandmothers' shares of a sixth would be twelve, with each getting three shares. The sisters' shares of a sixth would be twelve, with each getting four shares.

[12] The following section deals with apportioning the inheritance when the number of heirs and amount of the inheritance are figured as fractions. The imam here is explaining how one can properly divide the shares so that each heir is able to get a whole number rather than a fraction.

If that same issue were the case and there are four sisters, a portion would be derived from the initial amount, and its accounting would be like the accounting in the first case. Similarly, if it were six or twelve, it would be derived from the initial amount.

If he were to leave behind eight daughters and four grandmothers and four wives and seven sisters, the base number would be twenty-four. The daughters' shares of two-thirds would be sixteen, the wives' shares of an eighth would be three, the grandmothers' shares of a sixth would be four, and the sisters' shares of the remainder would be one. Consequently, the sixteen shares among the daughters would not have to be apportioned; it would simply be two shares given to each. The eighth, which is three shared between the four wives, would have to be apportioned as well as the sixth between the four grandmothers. The portions would then have to be properly apportioned between them. The remaining portion of one between the seven sisters must be apportioned.

The daughters and grandmothers would be excluded because their portions were properly applied to them, so there is no need to multiply them. Rather, one would multiply those shares that are not proportionate with each other. Four would be multiplied by seven, and that would result in twenty-eight. It is for that reason it would be twenty-eight as the base number of the inheritance. The [new total] would be six hundred seventy-two shares. The daughters' share of two-thirds would be four hundred forty-eight shares, with each one getting fifty-six shares. The grandmothers' shares would be one hundred twelve, with each getting twenty-eight shares. The wives' share of an eighth would be eighty-four shares between them, with each getting twenty-one shares. The sisters would then get the remaining portion of twenty-eight shares between them, with each getting four shares.

If that same issue were the case and there were eight sisters, the wives would be included with the eight sisters. Then reconfigure the eight into the base value of twenty-four and you will get one hundred ninety-two. The daughters' share of two-thirds would be one hundred twenty-eight, with each getting sixteen. The wives' share of an eighth would be twenty-four, with each getting six. The grandmothers' share of a sixth would be thirty-two, with each getting eight. The sisters' share of eight would then be divided with each getting one.

Whatever situation comes to you like that, simply seek out a way to reconcile it. That which is reconciled must be distributed as is. However, that which is not reconciled must be reconfigured so that the amount per head is reconciled with the base number of the inheritance, if Allah wills.

Concerning the inheritance of the hermaphrodite

The judgement regarding the hermaphrodite is based on how such person urinates. If the urine comes out of his penis, he is considered a male. If it comes out of an opening, he is considered a female.

The proper course of action regarding that would be that such person would have to go close to a wall and then be ordered to urinate; it is to be examined. From whichever place that the urine falls against the wall first, the judgement would be based on that. If any doubt occurs as to which one happened first and both come together at the same time, the judgement of the person would be considered as a half male half female when it comes to inheriting in two cases.

An explanation of that is the following: A man dies and leaves behind two sons, with one of them being a hermaphrodite. If the urine comes out of an opening, he is considered a female, and the inheritance would be out of three: [the hermaphrodite] would receive one and the male would get two. However, if the urine comes out of a penis, he is considered a male.

If any doubt occurs, though, such person would get half the share of a male and half the share of a female. Their inheritance is out of twelve with the female getting five and the male getting seven. So, if a man were to die leaving behind his daughter and his paternal/maternal hermaphrodite brother with doubtful gender, the daughter would get half and the hermaphrodite would get half the shares of a female and half the shares of the male. The remainder would go to the hermaphrodite because in the worst-case scenario, if he turned out to be female, the sister would be with the daughter in paternal relations.

If he were to leave behind a paternal/maternal sister and a paternal sister and a maternal hermaphrodite sister, the paternal/maternal sister would get half, the paternal sister would get a sixth which completes the two-thirds, and the maternal hermaphrodite sister would get a sixth in any case because the shares of the male and female from the mother's offspring would be the same. The remainder would go to the paternal relatives. If there are no paternal relatives, those leftover shares would be redistributed among the heirs based on their shares. The paternal/maternal sister would get three-fifths, the paternal sister would get a fifth and the maternal sister would get a fifth. This leftover amount would be derived from five.

If he left behind a hermaphrodite paternal uncle and a sister, the sister would get half and the paternal uncle would get the remainder if he were considered a male and nothing if he is considered a female. If there were doubt regarding gender, he would get only a half of the male share because he would be in a situation in which he would not inherit had he been a paternal aunt. It is for that reason that we do not give him the shares of a female. Its derivation is from two if he was male: the sister would get a share and he would get a share. Its derivation is also from two if he was female: the sister would get a share and the paternal relatives would get a share. If there were no paternal relatives, the shares would be redistributed to the sister. Its derivation would be from four shares if there were doubt regarding the gender: two would go to the sister and he would get half the share of the male. Then, there would be half of two remaining; the remaining portion would be for the paternal relatives. If there are no paternal relatives, it would be redistributed to the sister and him based on the amount of their respective shares.

If a woman were to leave behind three paternal/maternal nephews and one of them is a husband and the other is the maternal brother and another is a hermaphrodite, half would go to the husband, a sixth would go to the maternal brother and the remaining shares would be split between the three of them if the hermaphrodite is a male. If he were a female, the remaining shares would be split between the male nephews instead of him because the niece does not inherit anything along with the nephew. If there were doubt regarding the gender of the hermaphrodite, he would get half the portion of the male only. The remaining portion would be shared among the nephews equally. Everything that I have brought you in this chapter can be analogically based on what I have mentioned to you, if Allah wills.

Concerning the one who dies and leaves behind a pregnant woman and heirs and then they rush to distribute it before knowing that she is pregnant

If a man were to die leaving behind a pregnant woman and heirs and the heirs rush to distribute the property, it would be incumbent for them to leave a share that is greater than that for the pregnant woman—it would be for four males. When the baby is born, they would have taken the proper precaution and there would be no deficiency in such. However, if other than that occurs [i.e. a miscarriage], they can simply redistribute any extra amount.

An explanation of that is the following: A man dies and leaves behind three sons and a pregnant wife. In such case, it would be obligatory for the inheritance to be out of eight. The wife would get one out of eight and that would leave seven. They are to then set aside four shares for four males and take three shares for themselves. When the baby is born as such, they would have taken proper precaution and each one could then take his right of the shares. However, if other than that occurs, they would redistribute the extra amount. Similarly, if the baby born is a female or females, they would give her share to her from the entire wealth. Then, they would redistribute any extra amount afterwards.

Concerning the inheritance of a missing person

The missing person's wealth is to not be distributed or inherited until the news of his situation is known. Similarly, his wife is to not be remarried. If his heirs rush or the news of his situation comes to them and it turns out to be a lie and they had already distributed his wealth and his wife had already remarried and he returned, he would be more entitled to his wife. However, he must wait until after she is free of the semen of the one who remarried her before he [i.e. the initial husband] can come near her. Also, anyone who took from his wealth is to return it to him. If any of his heirs inherited a slave from him and manumitted such person, the manumitted slave must be returned to his ownership.

Concerning bequests

In the case of any deceased person who bequeaths more than a third of his/her wealth, the matter regarding that would be for his heirs. If they want, they can permit the bequeathed person to keep what the deceased bequeathed to them. If they want, they can redistribute it until it reaches a third.

An explanation of that is the following: A man bequeaths a third of his wealth to someone and half of it to someone else. If the heirs permit that, it is considered permissible. However, if they choose to redistribute it, they will have to do so until it is a third between the both of them based on five portions. The person who was bequeathed a third of the deceased's wealth would get a fifth of the third. The person who was bequeathed a half would get three-fifths of a third. It would be that portion that the heirs cannot take anything from. Whatever I have brought you in this chapter can be analogically based on what I've mentioned to you, if Allah wills.

Similarly, if he were to leave behind sons and daughters and bequeath to a man the like of one of them and more or less, it would be based on what I've previously mentioned to you. If the bequest was more than a third, the matter would be for his heirs. If they want, they can permit it. If they want, they can redistribute it until it reaches a third. It would then be distributed based on the amount that was bequeathed. However, if the bequest were less than a third, the bequest would be permitted for the one who was bequeathed by the deceased.

Concerning confessions and denials

The fundamental of confessions and denials—according to us—is that for everything that is confessed to will be binding regarding that which is in one's possession. If he were a partner, he would share. If he were one who is exempted, everything in his possession would be assigned to him. If he confessed against another, his confession against the other would not be binding.

An explanation of that is the following: If a man were to die leaving behind two sons and one of the two claimed that there was another son, it would be said to the claimant: "You claim that you are three, and you say 'A third of the wealth belongs to me.' Therefore, take what you claim to be yours and pay the remaining amount to the one you claimed." It would be a sixth of the wealth.

The basis of their inheritance in the first case would be two in a denial and three in a confession for the second case. Therefore, three would be paid to two because there is no agreement between the two inheritances. It would also be two paid to three, which would then become six. The one who denies says: "It [i.e. the inheritance] is between you and me; I get three and you get three." However, the one who confesses would say: "It is between us three; you get two, I get two and this person gets two." The denier may object to affirming that. Then, it would be said to the one who claimed: "You claimed that you get two, and you confessed that this brother of yours gets a share. Therefore, pay him his share and the two shares for them shall be taken for you."

If a denier confesses to be one who is exempted, it would be obligatory for him to assign over everything in his possession. An explanation of that is the following: Two brothers confess that one of them is the son of the deceased and the other objects. It would then be obligatory for it to be said to the one who confessed: "Pay with what is in your possession—half the wealth—to the one you confessed because he exempted you."

Concerning the maternal relatives

The maternal relatives are those who are not obligated to receive inheritance in the Book and Sunnah. They are ten males and ten females—those whom we designated in this chapter of ours—as well as those who are like them and from them. The proper course of action regarding them is that they are to be raised to the status of their parents until it ends with them to the point of the one among them who inherits from their grandparents.

An explanation of that is the following: A man dies and leaves behind his paternal aunt and maternal aunt. The maternal aunt would get a third and the paternal aunt would get two-thirds. This is because if we were to raise the two of them to the status of heirs, we would raise the maternal aunt to the status of the mother and the paternal aunt to the status of the father. It would be as if he left behind his mother and father. The mother would get a third, and the father would get the remaining shares. We therefore assign the paternal aunt to the position of the father and the maternal aunt to the position of the mother.

We would simply raise the status of the maternal aunt to that of the father and not that of the paternal uncle in this case because the inheritance of the father and uncle is the same. Also, the mother would inherit a third with both of them. When there is a female heir with two males, the father and paternal uncle would be the same in that. We would then, assign the maternal aunt to the position of the mother.

If he were to leave behind a daughter from the paternal uncle of the father and a daughter from the paternal uncle of the mother, the wealth would belong to the daughter from the paternal uncle of the father instead of the daughter from the paternal uncle of the mother. That is because if we were to raise the status of the daughter from the paternal uncle of the father to that of the paternal uncle of the father as well as the status of the daughter from the paternal uncle of the mother to that of the paternal uncle of the mother and the paternal uncle of the mother does not inherit while the paternal uncle of the father does inherit, we would assign the inheritance to the daughter of an heir and exclude the daughter of the non-heir.

Similar is always done in the case of maternal relatives; they would be raised to the status of their parents. The one who precedes the other to the point of an heir would then inherit instead of the other.

Likewise, if a man were to leave behind his brother's daughter and his paternal uncle's daughter, the wealth would go to his brother's daughter. This is because if you raise the status of the paternal uncle's daughter to that of the paternal uncle and the status of the brother's daughter to that of the brother, it will be as if he left behind his uncle and brother. The wealth would then go to the brother instead of the paternal uncle.

If he were to leave behind a paternal uncle's daughter and the son of the brother's daughter, the wealth would go to the paternal uncle's daughter instead of the son of the brother's daughter. This is because if you were to raise the status of the paternal uncle's daughter to that of the paternal uncle and the status of the son of the brother's daughter to that of the brother's daughter, it would be as if he left behind his paternal uncle and brother's daughter. The wealth would then go to the paternal uncle. That is why we give it to his daughter instead of the son of the brother's daughter due to her preceding him in familial relations regarding inheritance.

If he were to leave behind a daughter's daughter and a paternal uncle's daughter, the daughter's daughter would get half and the paternal uncle's daughter would get the remaining amount. This is because if you were to raise the status of the daughter's daughter to that of the daughter and the paternal uncle's daughter to that of the paternal uncle, it would be as if he left behind his daughter and paternal uncle. The daughter would get half and the paternal uncle would get the remaining amount. Therefore, we give both their daughters the inheritance in this way.

If anyone invalidates the inheritance of the other, we would assign the inheritance of one instead of the other because she preceded her in inheritance. An explanation of that is the following: If he were to leave behind the daughter of a paternal uncle's daughter and the daughter's daughter, the inheritance would go to the daughter's daughter because she would be the closest in relations to the one who leaves inheritance if their statuses were raised.

Similarly, if he were to leave behind a paternal uncle's daughter and the daughter of a daughter's daughter, the inheritance would be for the paternal uncle's daughter because she would be the closest in relations to the one who leaves inheritance if their statuses were raised.

We would do likewise with all the maternal relatives. Therefore, understand this well, if Allah wills! Apply analogical reasoning regarding them and the truth will be made manifest to you. To and by Allah belongs the power!

Concerning the inheritances of the Magians

The basis regarding the inheritances of the Magians is that they inherit from two sides by familial connection and not by marriage because marriage is impermissible. That is the view and statement of the Commander of Believers, 'Ali b. Abi Ṫālib, upon him be peace.[13] I do not know of anyone who disagreed with him in that.

The explanation of their inheriting from two sides is the following: A Magian mates with his daughter and she gives birth to three daughters. Then, he dies—May Allah curse him!—and leaves two-thirds inheritance to his four daughters and the remaining portion goes to the paternal relatives. Then, one of the three daughters dies and leaves behind her paternal/maternal sister and paternal sister—the latter being her mother. The mother would then get a sixth and her paternal/maternal sister would get two-thirds. If one of the two remaining sisters were to die, the paternal/maternal sister would get a half and her paternal sister who is her mother would get a sixth, which completes the two-thirds. She would also get a sixth because she is her mother. She gets a third because she is her mother as well as a sixth because she is her paternal sister.

She therefore inherits from two sides and exempts herself from a third of the mother's inheritance because she is the second sister of the deceased woman along with the remaining sister. It would be as if she left behind a paternal/maternal sister and a paternal sister.

Similarly, if the Magian were to mate with his daughter and she gives birth to a son and then the son were to die after the death of his father, the inheritance from her son would be a third because she is his mother and a half because she is his paternal sister. They have then inherited from two sides. If he were to have an heir other than her, they would inherit the remaining sixth. If he were to not have an heir other than her, the remaining sixth would be redistributed.

Concerning the inheritance of the son of a couple that performed a mutual curse

The son of a couple that performed a mutual curse does not inherit from the one who performed such with his mother, nor is he attributed to him. His paternal relatives would be the paternal relatives of his mother; he would inherit from them and pay the indemnity for him. He would be considered similar to their offspring.

---

[13] Similarly narrated in ***Musnad Imam Zayd, Sharh at-Tajrīd, Mušannaf Ibn Abi Shayba, Mušannaf 'Abdur-Razzāq, Sunan al-Bayhaqi***

Concerning the inheritance of the People of the Book

The basis regarding them, according to us, is that Jews do not inherit from Christians and Christians do not inherit from Jews. This is because—according to us—even if they are all disbelievers, they differ in their religions. Some of them ascribe disbelief to others, and one does not view the other upon his religion and negates the other from his religion. If the people of different religions are thus, they do not inherit from one another according to us. Since they differ in their religions in our statement, if a Christian were to die leaving behind a Jewish son, we hold to the view that he does not inherit from him. Rather, his wealth would be for those heirs who are his coreligionists.

Similarly, if the Jewish son were to die, his Christian father would not inherit from him because they are—according to us—upon two clearly distinct religious paths. Allah's Messenger, peace and blessings be upon him and his progeny, has said: ((Two people of different religions do not inherit from each other)).

Concerning the inheritance between Muslims and *dhimmis*

The Muslim does not inherit from the *dhimmi*, and the *dhimmi* does not inherit from the Muslim. If a Jewish or Christian man were to have two sons and one of them embraced Islam and the other one had not and then their Jewish father died, his inheritance would only go to the Jewish son and not the Muslim son. Similarly, if his Muslim son were to die, his inheritance would go to the Muslims excluding his father and brother. This is because the Muslims are more entitled to it due to their being upon the same religion. They can also pay indemnity on his behalf and leave him inheritance because people of two different religions cannot inherit from one another.

Concerning the inheritance of the apostate

If someone were to apostatise from Islam and then die in his apostasy, he would inherit from the Muslims and they inherit from him to the exclusion of others. This is the case even if they [i.e. others] were with him in his religion and in his apostasy because the apostate's judgement is the judgement of the Muslims since he is not granted dispensation in his apostasy. There is nothing for him except the sword or repentance. It is for that reason that he is inherited by and inherits from the Muslims. His judgement in that is the judgement of the Muslims.

Concerning the inheritances of the free and the slaves

The free do not inherit from slaves, nor do slaves inherit from the free because the wealth of the slave belongs to his master. It is for that reason that the free do not inherit from them nor are inherited by them. This is because if they were to be inherited from, that would be taking from his master's wealth. And if one were to inherit, the master would take their wealth. This is because the slave does not own anything of his own; rather, all of his wealth belongs to the one who owns him.

An explanation of that is the following: A slave dies and has a free son. There would be no inheritance from him for his son, and his [i.e. the slave's] wealth belongs to his master dead or alive. Similarly, if the free son were to die leaving behind his slave father, there would be no inheritance left by his son for him because he does not have wealth of his own; everything he inherits would be for his master.

Since that is the case, it is impermissible for his master to inherit anything from anyone who is not his direct relative. The wealth of the free deceased person would then go to the Muslim public treasury instead of his father. The exception is if there are free heirs; then, they would inherit if they were among those who inherit along with the father, such as the son, the son's son, the mother, the wife and the mother's maternal grandmother.

So, if a free person were to die leaving behind a son who is a slave and does not leave behind anyone else, the wealth would then go to the Muslim public treasury. If the son is manumitted before the wealth is distributed, he would inherit it. Similar is narrated from the Commander of Believers, upon him be peace, that he said: “One can be bought and manumitted and afterwards inherit the assets of his father. He would then count the amount from his father’s assets as an obligation on him.”

Also, the Commander of Believers, upon him be peace, passed a judgement regarding a man who died leaving behind wealth and a slave mother but had not left behind paternal relatives. He ruled that the mother can be bought and manumitted by that wealth. And his mother would be given her inheritance from that wealth of his. The remaining amount would then be redistributed among the relatives.

If a slave is partially manumitted[14] and then dies, his wealth would be divided into two parts: one part for the heirs at the point of his partial freedom and the other part for his master based on what is left of ownership. A similar judgement has reached us from the Commander of Believers, upon him be peace.

One is to give the payment of debt precedence over everything else, then bequests afterwards and then inheritance from what is left. Therefore, if a man were to die and he owed a debt and made a bequest and left behind an heir, he would first begin with the debt which would be extracted from his wealth. Then, a third from what remains of his wealth after the debt would be used for his bequest. Afterwards, the inheritance shares would be distributed from what remains.

If a man were to leave a bequest to an absent man but then both the one who bequeathed and the one who was bequeathed were to die, the bequest would then go to the heirs of the one who was bequeathed. Similar is the case with the bequest of an indentured labourer; if he were to observe some of his indentured labour, the bequest would be permissible based on the amount of his indentured labour that he has already observed.

Regarding the indentured labourer’s indentureship that is contracted on his behalf and the behalf of his father and then he bequeathed wealth but then the father died before observing anything, the indentured service shall be binding on the son. He would have to observe it on his behalf as well as on behalf of his father based on the contract of indentureship. Then, he can inherit from his father.

Similarly, if the contract of indentureship were on the behalf of an indentured labourer and a group of his offspring, they would have to observe it on his behalf and would inherit from him. They would then assign the clientage over to the one to whom they are contracted because they had entered into the indentured contract with their father and no one else from their father’s children outside of their mother.

Concerning clientage and manumitted slaves as well as an explanation of the inheritance of the freed slave and those who inherit from him

If a freed slave were to die leaving behind his former master’s paternal relatives, the inheritance would go to the oldest relative of the deceased. An explanation of that is the following: A freed slave leaves behind the son of his paternal master’s paternal cousin’s son as well as leaves behind the son of the son of a paternal/maternal master’s paternal cousin’s son. The inheritance will go to the son of his paternal master’s paternal cousin’s son because he is the closest to the father and the oldest.

If he were to leave behind his former master’s three different nephews who are the same age, the inheritance would go to the paternal/maternal nephew. And if he were to leave behind three daughters from his master’s son—some of them lower in descent than others—with each having a cousin, the wealth would go to the cousin that is highest in descent which is the son of his former master’s son. He would be in the position of the highest of the three. Moreover, the clientage would belong to the men instead of the women.

[14] This partial manumission refers to an indentured labourer who fulfils half his contractual obligation with his master and was granted freedom with the payment of the other half.

If he were to leave behind three daughters of his former master's son—some of them being lower in descent than others—along with each is a son of her grandfather's brother, the wealth would go to the son of her middle grandfather's brother. That is because he is the son of the manumitter's son and has the highest position in descent from the daughters.

If he were to leave behind three daughters of his former master's son—some of them being lower in descent than others—along with each is her grandfather, the inheritance would be for the grandfather of highest descent. He is the client of the deceased who he freed.

If he were to leave behind three daughters of his former master's son—some of them being lower in descent than others—along with each is her father's grandfather, the inheritance would go to the grandfather of the middle father; he is the one who manumitted the deceased.

If he were to leave behind three daughters of his former master's son—some of them being lower in descent than others—along with each is the son of the maternal aunt of the daughter of her paternal aunt, the wealth would go to the son of the maternal aunt of the daughter of her paternal aunt of highest descent because he is the son of the manumitter's (*mu'tiq*) son as well as the highest brother of the daughters. Therefore, he would get the inheritance instead of her because the clientage would belong to the men instead of the women.

Concerning clientage and manumitted slaves in family relations (*as-ŝulb*)

Regarding a man who manumits another man and then the manumitted slave (*al-mu'taq*) died after the death of his manumitting master and left behind the two sons and daughter of the master who manumitted him, it would be as if he left behind two sons and daughters of his master. However, the inheritance would be for the two sons and not their sister because women do not inherit from clientage except from those she manumitted and those who the manumitted has manumitted.

If this manumitted slave were to die leaving behind two daughters of his and two daughters of his master, two-thirds would go to his daughters and the remaining amount would go to the paternal relatives of his master and not his daughters. If his master does not have paternal relatives, he would redistribute it among his own two daughters and not his master's daughters. However, if he were to leave behind a son and daughter of his and his master's son, the wealth would go to his son and daughter, with the male getting twice the shares of the female. And nothing would go to his master's son.

If the manumitter was a woman who freed a slave and then she died as well as the manumitted slave after her and she left behind a daughter and son, the inheritance would go to his mistress' son and not her daughter. Also, if he were to leave behind his mistress' daughter and paternal cousin, the inheritance would go to her paternal relative—that is, her paternal cousin—and not her daughter.

If he were to die leaving behind the son of his mistress' son, the inheritance would go to him. Similarly, if he were to leave behind the son of the son of his mistress' son, the inheritance would go to him. This is because the male offspring inherits from clientage even if they descend very low in descent, but the offspring of the daughter does not inherit—whether male or female. That is because if their mother does not inherit, how can they inherit? Therefore, understand this well and you will be guided. Apply analogical reasoning to what we explained to you, if Allah wills.

Concerning an explanation of one who manumits one who was manumitted by a woman

If a woman were to manumit a slave and then the slave manumitted the slave but her master were to die and then his master died leaving behind his daughter and his master's daughter and the daughter of his master's mistress, his daughter would get half and the remaining amount would go to the paternal relatives of his master's mistress. However, if there are no paternal relatives for his master, there would be no paternal relatives for her, and the paternal relatives are men. He would then redistribute it among his daughter and not his master's daughter or the daughter of his master's mistress.

If he were to leave behind his daughter and the paternal cousin of his master's mistress, his daughter would get half and the remaining amount would go to his master's paternal cousin and not the paternal cousin of his master's mistress. That is because his master's paternal relatives are closer than the paternal relatives of his master's mistress are.

If he were to leave behind his daughter and his master's daughter and the daughter of his master's mistress and her paternal cousin, his daughter would get half and the remaining amount would go to the paternal cousin of his master's mistress and not her daughter or his master's daughter.

If he were to leave behind his master's daughter and the maternal grandfather of his master's mistress and her paternal cousin, the inheritance would go to the paternal cousin of his master's mistress and not his master's daughter or the maternal grandfather of his master's mistress. This is because the maternal grandfather is not a paternal relative, and he does not inherit due to that. If the situation is as thus but with her paternal grandfather instead of her maternal grandfather, the inheritance would go to her paternal grandfather and not her paternal cousin.

If a man were to die leaving behind his daughter and his master's son and his sister, half would go to his daughter, the remaining amount would go to his sister and the master's daughter would be exempted. Also, if he were to leave behind three daughters of his son—with some of them being lower in descent than others—and his master's son, the one of highest descent would get half, a sixth would go to those who follow and the remaining amount would go to the master's son.

If he were to leave behind his master's son and his paternal brother's son and his maternal brother, his maternal brother's son would get a sixth and the remaining amount would go to the paternal brother's son and not his master's son.

If two men were to manumit a slave and then he died after them and one of the two left behind a son and the other left behind a daughter, half of the inheritance would go to his master's son and the other half would go to the paternal relatives of the other. However, nothing would go to the daughter. If there were no paternal relatives, he would return to his daughter regarding the amount for maternal relatives.

Concerning the hermaphrodite in clientage

If a man were to manumit a slave and then the manumitter died and the manumitted slave died after him and left behind his master's two daughters and a hermaphrodite son, the judgement regarding that would be based on the manner of urination. If the urine comes out of his penis, he is considered a male. If it comes out of an opening, he is considered a female. If any doubt occurs as to which one happened first and both come together at the same time, the person would be given half the portion of the male and not half the portion of the female. This is because the only one who can receive half the male's portion and half the female's portion from a hermaphrodite is the one who inherits in both cases.

As for the one who does not inherit in a case where he is considered female, he would not be given half the female's portion. And this is because if he is considered a female, there would be nothing for him due to him being considered a female that's not a sister. However, if he is considered a male, the master would inherit from his father and not his daughter. However, if doubt were to occur, he would get half the share of the male, which is half the wealth, and the remaining amount would go to the paternal relatives of the deceased if there are paternal relatives. But, if his master does not have any paternal relatives, the hermaphrodite would be given half the wealth and the remainder of the wealth would be redistributed to him due to the assumption that he is a male and not a female. Therefore, understand this well and apply analogical reasoning to what we explained to you, if Allah wills.

If he were to leave behind his master's hermaphrodite son and his master's hermaphrodite paternal cousin and there is doubt regarding the gender of both, the master's hermaphrodite son would get half the male shares, which is half the wealth, and his master's paternal cousin would get the remaining half. That is because if his master's paternal cousin were considered male, he would get the remaining half after half was given to the son. Since there is doubt regarding the gender, he would be given half of the remaining half, which is a fourth. The remaining portion would then go to the paternal relatives. It would be derived from four shares: a share for the cousin, two shares for the son and the remaining share for the paternal relatives.

The basis of that is that the inheritance is established as the base number for the first and then for the other and one of them is divided into the other. If the number does not divide into the other as a whole number, a half portion would be paid as two in inheritance shares. If it is divided into threes, it would be paid as a third in inheritance shares. If it were divided into fours, it would be paid as a fourth in inheritance shares. The exception is if the amount per head is less than that. Then, we would make the first inheritance share the base number and it would be out of two. That is because we consider the minimum amount of his wealth as half since two is the minimum [i.e. number of shares]. Then we would consider the other inheritance share and make it out of two with the remaining half. In so doing, the least asset for him would be half of two. We would then multiply the first [two] with the second and this would be four. The son would get half of that, which is two and two would remain. We would then give the paternal cousin half of the remaining value, which is one. We only give to the paternal cousin of doubtful gender because the son was also of doubtful gender and we gave to him. This is because it can be said that the son was possibly a female.

Therefore, if he were to leave behind three paternal cousins of his master and one of them is a hermaphrodite with doubtful gender, this hermaphrodite would get half the male's shares, which is a sixth. The remaining portions would be divided in half between his two brothers. It would be derived from twelve shares with the hermaphrodite getting two out of the twelve shares and his two brothers getting the remaining ten out of twelve—each getting five. This is because if we considered that the hermaphrodite was female, it would be out of two. If he were considered a male, it would be out of three. We would then take that three and multiply it times two to equal six, and the hermaphrodite would get one out of six. If we divide that five of each male into half, each one of them would get two and a half out of six. However, if we were to make the base number twelve, we would make the share of the hermaphrodite half the male's share, which would be two out of twelve.

That is because if he were a male, we would divide the portion between them as four-twelfths each. Therefore, we subtract two from the portion due to the doubtful gender and do not subtract the portion of half a female's shares because if he were a female, he would not inherit anything because women do not inherit from clientage except in the case we explained. Therefore, understand if Allah wills. The remaining ten would then be distributed among the paternal cousins, with each getting five.

If he were to leave behind a hermaphrodite son and his master's hermaphrodite son and the son of his master's cousin and the urine comes out from his hermaphrodite son's opening, he would be considered a female and would get half. If the urine were to also come from the opening of his master's hermaphrodite son, he would also be considered a female and would not get anything. The remaining portion would go to the son of his master's cousin. However, if his hermaphrodite son's urine were to come out of a penis, he would get the wealth and without anything going to his master's hermaphrodite son—even if urine were to also come out of his penis.

If doubt were to occur regarding the gender of both hermaphrodite sons, his hermaphrodite son would get half the male's share and half the female's share. If urine were to come out of the opening his master's son, he would not get anything. But, if urine were to come out of his penis, he would get the remaining amount. If doubt were to occur regarding the gender of his master's hermaphrodite son, his master's hermaphrodite son would get half the male's shares only, and the remaining amount would go to the son of his master's cousin. Its derivation would be out of eight: the hermaphrodite son would get six, his master's hermaphrodite son would get one and one would go to the son of his master's cousin. That is because his hermaphrodite son would get half of two shares, which is six and would leave two as the remainder. His master's hermaphrodite son would get half the male's share only, which is one. And the remaining one would be given to the son of his master's cousin.

Concerning the maternal relatives in clientage and its explanation

The manumitted slave's paternal relatives are more entitled to his inheritance than the paternal relatives of the one who manumitted him are. The manumitter's paternal relatives are more entitled to the manumitted slave's inheritance than the maternal relatives of the manumitter are. The manumitted slave's maternal relatives are more entitled to his inheritance than the maternal relatives of the manumitter are.

If a man were to manumit a slave and die and then his manumitted former slave died after him and left behind his master's daughter and his own daughter's daughter, the inheritance would go to his daughter's daughter. That is because she would get half the portion of her mother. As for the remaining portion, it would be redistributed to her just as it would be redistributed to her mother. His master's daughter would not get anything. So, therefore, realise that. This is because women do not inherit anything from clientage.

If there were maternal relatives and no paternal relatives with them, they would inherit to the measure of the maternal relatives related to his master. If he does not have maternal relatives and his master had maternal relatives, they would be considered as his maternal relatives.

His maternal relatives would be more entitled than his master's maternal relatives would because Allah says: **{And those possessors of kinship are closer one to another in the decree of Allah...} (Q. 33:6)**. By that, He means 'the judgement of Allah.' So, understand and apply analogical reasoning to what we explained to you, if Allah wills.

If he were to leave behind the daughter of his master's son and the daughter of his master's daughter, it would be as if he left behind his master's son and his master's daughter. The wealth would go to the daughter of his master's son and not the daughter of his master's daughter.

If he were to leave behind the daughter of his master's maternal uncle and the daughter of his master's sister, the inheritance would go to the daughter of his master's sister because she is the closest heir to his master. Moreover, if he were to leave behind the daughter of the son of his master's sister and the daughter of his master's maternal uncle, the daughter of the son of his master's sister would get half, the daughter of his master's maternal uncle would get a third and the remaining portion would be redistributed between them with each getting her respective shares. Three-fifths would be in the possession of the daughter of the son of his master's sister, and two-fifths would be in the possession of the daughter of his master's maternal uncle. The derivation would be from five.[15]

If he were to leave behind the daughter of his master's daughter and her brother as well as the daughter of his master's sister and her brother, half would go to both the daughter of his master's daughter and her brother without any extra for the brother over the sister. The remaining portion would go to the daughter of his master's sister and her brother without any extra for the brother over the sister. The derivation would be from four: the two offspring of the daughter would get two with each getting one, and the remaining amount of two would go to the two offspring of the sister with each one getting one. We simply make the males from the maternal relatives equal to the females because their inheritance is the same.

An explanation of that is the following: A man leaves behind his daughter's daughter and his sister's daughter. His daughter's daughter would get half and his sister's daughter would get half. Similarly, if he were to leave behind his sister's son and his daughter's son, his sister's son would get half and his

[15] This is because if we set six as the minimum amount of inheritance, half would be three and one-third would be two. That would set five as the new base number. Then, the portions could be divided respectively as three out of five and two out of five.

daughter's son would get half. Likewise, if he were to leave behind his brother's daughter and his daughter's son, his brother's daughter would get half and his daughter's son would get the remaining half. The derivation would be from two.

When we see the shares of the female from the maternal relatives, it is the same as the male's shares in that situation. We do not make any of the shares between them as more than the other in regard to maternal relatives. We assign their shares based on the shares of the mother's offspring. There is no extra amount for the males over the females, and the mother's offspring are made equal in inheritance because Allah has not granted extra to their males over their females. If both were singular, he would inherit a sixth and she would inherit a sixth. If it were two males, they would get a third and if it were two females, they would get a third. Similarly, if it were a man and woman, they would get a third, with each getting a sixth. He would not get more than her. So, understand and apply analogical reasoning to what we explained to you in this chapter, if Allah wills.

Concerning a missing person and concerning pregnant woman in clientage

Know that the missing person's wealth is to not be distributed until the news of his affair is known. Similarly, his wife is to not be remarried until his affair is known. If it is evident that he has died leaving behind a pregnant wife and his master's pregnant wife as well as his daughter and his master's daughter and they rush to pay out the distribution, a ninth of the wealth is paid to his daughter and eight out of nine would be the majority left for the pregnant wife. It would be for four males. If that is the case and his wife were to deliver four males, she would take her portion. If she delivers less, she will take the remaining portion for her.

Nothing would be paid to his master's son until his wife gives birth. If she were to give birth to a male or males, there would be nothing for him. However, if she were to give birth to a female or females, they would get two-thirds along with their sister. Then, one would wait with the rest of the wealth for the baby of his master's wife. If the master's son were to rush and desire to distribute the third he took from the extra inheritance of his father, a fifth of a third would be paid to him and he would leave behind more shares for the pregnant wife, which would be four-fifths of a third. If the pregnant woman were to deliver as thus, he would have secured his right. However, if she were to deliver less than four males, he would return to get the rest of his right along with them. If the pregnant woman were to deliver a female or females, he is to take what was set aside, which is four-fifths of a third. Nothing would be for the females from the inheritance of the master. So, understand what has been explained to you in this chapter, for it is from the excellent chapters as Allah wills. Apply analogical reasoning to everything we explained to you in this chapter.

Concerning clientage regarding the drown victim, burn victim, demolish victim as well as similar deaths for which one does not know who died before his companion

If a former slave and his master were to die by drowning and each one left behind two daughters without knowing which one died first and the slave left behind wealth, it would be assumed that the manumitter died first and his two daughters would be given two-thirds and the remaining amount would be given to the paternal relatives. Then, it would be assumed that the slave died and the manumitter lived. Afterwards, the two daughters of the manumitted slave would be given two-thirds of their father's inheritance, and the remaining amount of one-third would go to their master. Then, his [i.e. the master's] daughters would get a third of his third, and the remaining amount would go to the paternal relatives and not returned to the two of them. The two daughters of the slave would remain with the two-thirds of their father's inheritance, and the two daughters of the manumitting master would get a third of a third due to their father having a paternal relative. In the case of their father not having a paternal relative, it would be redistributed among them both. A third of the slave's wealth would belong to them both along with their inheritance from the wealth of their father.

If the situation was as thus and the master's son is included with the freed slave's two daughters with neither one of the two being paternal relatives and there are no other previously mentioned heirs, the freed slave's two daughters would get two-thirds of their father's wealth in all cases.

In the situation where the master died first, the remaining third would go to his master's son instead of his two daughters. However, in the situation where the freed slave died first, his two daughters would get two-thirds and the remaining third would go to his master. Then, that third would be divided between the master's son and the freed slave's two daughters in four shares. The son would get two, and the daughters would each get one. So, understand what has been explained to you in this section and apply analogical reasoning to everything we explained to you in this chapter based on this analogy.

Similar is the case with the inheritance of the demolish victim as well as those burn victims and the like. The matter and analogy in these cases are the same.

Concerning the apostasy of the manumitter and manumitted

If a man were to manumit his slave and apostatise and then move to the domain of war while leaving behind sons and daughters in the domain of Islam but then the manumitted slave died while the manumitter survived in his state of apostasy, the inheritance of the freed slave would go to the sons of the manumitter and not the daughters. Also, nothing would go to the manumitter himself because the inheritance would belong to his sons and not him.

If a slave were to apostatise and move to the domain of war and die in the state of apostasy while leaving behind his master and daughter, the daughter would get half and the remaining amount would go to his master. If he were to apostatise while having a son also and the father died in the state of his apostasy, the inheritance would then be divided into three shares: the son would get two shares, and the daughter would get one share.

This is specific to the apostates only. People of two different religions do not inherit—as Allah's Messenger, peace and blessings be upon him and his progeny, said—except in the case of apostates. That is because their judgement is the judgement of Muslims. If the imam were to present to them the option of repentance and returning to Islam or the death penalty, it is inevitable that they would either have to choose the sword or Islam. The judgement of the Muslims against them is similar: Muslims inherit from them, but they do not inherit from Muslims. So, understand this difference, if Allah wills. And all power belongs to Allah!

Therefore, if a manumitted slave were to apostatise and leave behind his son and master who manumitted him and then his son died leaving behind his father in the state of his apostasy, his entire inheritance would go to his father's master and not the father. If both he [i.e. the slave] and his son were to apostatise in the same case but one of the apostate's sons—the brother of the deceased—embraced Islam before his death, the entire inheritance would go to the brother and not his father or master.

If a slave were to apostatise and leave behind his son and his master's daughter and the son died while his father was in the state of apostasy and had not left his son as an heir, his master's daughter would inherit as an 'other relative' because one who is related is more entitled than the one who is not related.

If he were to leave behind his daughter's daughter and his master's daughter, his daughter's daughter would get the wealth because the slave's relatives are more entitled than his master's relatives are. Nothing would be for the father who apostatised as long as he remained in the state of apostasy. So, understand that and apply analogical reasoning to everything we explained to you in this section.

Concerning the clientage of the People of the Book and the Magians

It has been said that all of these religions are the same, and it has been said that the people of each religion are in opposition. The latter is what we hold to and our view. How can a person from your own religion declare you a disbeliever? Haven't you considered that the Jews declare the Christians disbelievers, and the Christians declare the Jews disbelievers? Allah says: **{The Jews say: "The Christians are upon nothing!" And the Christians say: "The Jews are upon nothing!" Yet, the both of them recite the Scripture. Even thus speak those who know not similar to their word. But Allah shall judge between them on the Day of Judgement concerning that wherein they differed}** **(Q. 2:113)**. Don't you see that Allah says that some of them declare others as disbelievers?

Then the Glorified testifies against them regarding dissension and disagreement by His distinguishing them from one another in His statement: **{Thou wilt find that the most vehement of people to those who believe art the Jews and those who commit idolatry. And thou wilt find that the most nigh to them in mutual affection towards those who believe art those who saith "We are Christians." That is because amongst them art priests and monks, and they art not those who exult themselves}** **(Q. 5:82)**.

Allah makes it clear that they differ and are upon different doctrines. This is from the statement of Allah, and it confirms what we say and the truth we hold to. It also belies the statement of the one who makes them the same in Islamic Law and not different in deviance and doctrine. So, praise be to Allah, the Lord of creation!

If a Jew were to manumit a slave who converted to Christianity along with his master's paternal cousin and then the slave died upon Christianity, his inheritance would go to his master's paternal cousin and not his master because he [i.e. the cousin] is upon his religion, and his master is upon a different religion. The people of two different religions do not inherit from one another. They are not like the apostates because they are not bound by Islam due to their paying the *jizya*. Therefore, understand the difference between them and those who apostatise from Islam.

Similar is the case with a Christian who becomes a Jew or a Magian who becomes a Christian or a Jew who becomes a Magian. Each one of these religions differs from each other and does not agree. One denounces the other, and one curses the other. Likewise, the Muslims do not inherit from the Jews, Christians, Magians star-worshippers or anyone else; they are not inherited by them either.

Concerning clientage in claims and denials

If a man were to manumit a slave and die and the slave died after him leaving behind his daughter and his master's daughter but then each one of them claimed a brother, the slave's daughter would be affirmed and the wealth would be divided between them based on three shares. She would get one share, and her brother would get two shares. She is affirmed because she confessed against herself and no one else because, otherwise, half would be for her according to the Book and the second half would have been redistributed to her. As for the daughter of the manumitting master, she would not be affirmed because she confessed against someone else and had not confessed to something that would disadvantage (lit. "harm") her.

If the master's daughter were to confess to having a brother and the slave's daughter had not confessed to such, the slave's daughter would get half and the remaining portion would be redistributed to her. If the slave's daughter were to confess to her father's master having a son but the master's daughter had not confessed, her confession would be permitted because she would have confessed against herself; she would get half the inheritance and the remaining portion would go to the one whom she confessed was the son of her father's master.

If he were to leave behind his own daughter and his master's son, his daughter would get half and his master's son would get the remaining half. However, if the daughter confessed to having a brother and the master's son confessed to having a sister, the daughter would get half and the remaining portion would go to the master's son.

It would be impermissible for her to confess against the master's son for his half because she would be confessing for his right to be taken from his possession. She would give a third of her possession to the one for whom she confessed, which would be a sixth of the entire wealth. This is because when she made her confession, she appointed for him two-thirds of the entire wealth and a third for herself. Then we would say to her: "Take what you claimed as his for yourself and pay him with what remains of your right based on your confession and his confession of sisterhood which would be incumbent on him regarding inheritance." If he were to die, she would inherit as his sister. As for the portion of the manumitted slave's inheritance that is in his possession, she would not have a right to it.

If this manumitted slave were to leave behind his mother and daughter and the mother confessed that the son of her son's master is hers, her confession would not be accepted or permissible unless it is against herself because she would have confessed against someone other than herself so that the daughter would be deprived of her right in regard to redistribution. This for which she confessed is to be countered by that which is against her after the sixth; it would be half a sixth. Its derivation would be out of twenty-four, so that it would be said to her: "Take her fourth, which is six. Then take a sixth from the total, which is four. Then, pay two to the one for whom you confessed." Afterwards, eighteen would be paid to the daughter, which is hers from her father's inheritance after three-fourths of the remaining third is redistributed. So, understand this principle and apply analogical reasoning to that which we explained to you in this section, if Allah wills.

Concerning a Magian's clientage for a Magian

Regarding a Magian who manumitted a Magian and died leaving behind a son and daughter from his mother and then the freed slave died after his master leaving behind his daughter from his mother, his daughter would get half and the remaining amount would go to his master's son. His daughter would exempt herself from the sixth of the maternal sister.

If a manumitted slave were to leave behind three daughters of his master's son—some of them lower in descent than others—and each one of them is accompanied by the nephew of her father's paternal uncle and his sister, the wealth would be for the middle nephew of her father's paternal uncle because he is the son of the manumitting master's son. He would be in a higher position than the daughters, but she would not inherit along with him because no woman in clientage inherits except those we designated earlier in this chapter.

If a manumitted slave were to die leaving behind three daughters of his master's son—some of them lower in descent than others—and the highest one is accompanied by the nephew of her father's paternal uncle from his grandmother, the slave's wealth would go to the highest nephew of her father's paternal uncle because he is the son of the deceased's brother as well as his paternal uncle through his mother. The heir of inheritance would be on the part of the brother's son because he is a paternal relative. Inheritance would not be on the part of the paternal uncle through the mother; the paternal uncle through the mother does not inherit anything with the nephew.

Concerning clientage

Clientage is for the one who manumits not for one who purchases or is gifted a slave. If one buys or is gifted a slave, that [i.e. clientage] would be invalid. It is a relationship that is not like family relations. This is the judgement of Allah's Messenger, peace and blessings be upon him and his progeny.

When a slave is manumitted, the relationship of clientage exists for his son. Also, clientage is for men and not women, it is from the sons of the freed slave and the son's sons.

Clientage is appointed for men and not women because men always attribute their offspring to the manumitted slave, so clientage would always be referred to him. If women were to share with him in that, then their [the women's] offspring would share in it as well as their offspring's offspring. They would be considered from the same womb as the manumitted slave.[16]

If clientage were permissible to be with other than the paternal relatives of the manumitted slave, clientage would also be permissible for one who was not manumitted. And if it were permissible to make inheritance for those other than the paternal relatives of the manumitted slave, it would be permissible to buy and gift the one he manumitted to someone else.

Clientage cannot be for women except for the one she manumitted or the one who the manumitted or when clientage is granted to the one she manumitted.

Clientage is for the oldest of the paternal relatives,[17] and the oldest are those who are closest to the manumitted slave. Clientage is like wealth; whoever keeps the wealth of the deceased from the male paternal relatives will similarly keep the wealth of clientage.

[16] Although not present in this text, the same statement is made in ***Al-Muntakhab*** as a hadith related from the Prophet. The hadith is related in texts such as ***Sunan ad-Dārimi*** and ***Sunan al-Bayhaqi*** except with the addition ((…except that which she does as indentured labour or manumits)). Furthermore, it says in ***Al-Muntakhab*** regarding this hadith:

> I asked him about the explanation of the statement of Allah's Messenger, peace and blessings be upon him and his progeny: ((Clientage is for men and not women)). He replied: "It means that clientage is appointed for men and not women because clientage is a kinship like lineage. Allah simply makes clientage for men and not women because they are agnates; therefore, clientage is for them. It is because men will always attribute their children to them, so clientage would always return to them. It is for that reason that clientage is for men. And if women were to share in it, then their children and the children of their children would share in it. And they may be from a womb other than the womb of a freedman, so clientage was not given to women."

[17] Similarly, this statement of al-Hādi in ***Al-Muntakhab*** presents this statement as a hadith from the Prophet: ((Clientage is for the oldest)). However, I was unable to find this report attributed to the Prophet in the texts of hadith. Instead, it is presented as the statement of 'Ali, Zayd b. Thābit, 'Umar, 'Uthmān, Ibn Mas'ūd and Tāwūs in texts such as ***Al-Jāmi al-Kāfi, Sunan ad-Dārimi, Mušannaf Ibn Abi Shayba*** and ***Sunan al-Bayhaqi***.

The Book of Hunting Game (*as-Ŝayid*)

In the Name of Allah, the Most Gracious, the Most Merciful...

Beginning of the chapters regarding hunting game and its explanation in the Book

Allah—the Blessed and Exalted—says: {**They ask thee what is permissible for them. Say: "Permissible for thee are the pure. And whatsoever of those animals which ye have trained as dogs—ye teach them that which Allah has taught thee—eat of that which they catch for thee and mention Allah's Name upon it, and be God-conscious. Verily, Allah is swift in account!**} (Q. 5:4).

This verse was revealed to Allah's Messenger, peace and blessings be upon him and his progeny, regarding the matter of Zayd al-Khayr at-Ṫā`i§ and Adi b. Hātim.§ That is because they came to Allah's Messenger, peace and blessings be upon him and his progeny, and said: "O Messenger of Allah, Allah has made carcass prohibited for the one who eats it. We have dogs that we hunt with. We are able to reach the game animal [i.e. to pronounce Allah's Name on it] with some of them, and we are not able to reach the prey with others." Then Allah revealed this verse to His Prophet, peace and blessings be upon him and his progeny, and he pronounced it to them. He then said: ((If you pronounce the Name before sending your dogs and the dogs take the game animal and it dies in their mouths, you can eat it)).[1]

If a trained dog is sent upon a game animal and the sender pronounces Allah's name and then the dog kills the game animal, it would be considered properly sacrificed and permissible to eat. Even if the dog were to eat some of it and its owner reached it, there would be no problem in eating its leftover. Similar has been narrated from the Prophet, peace and blessings be upon him and his progeny.

As for the hawk, falcon, Shahin and other birds of prey—that which they kill would not be considered properly sacrificed because they do not do as they are commanded, nor do they come when they are called for other than food or go when commanded. However, dogs come when they are called and go when they are sent because they are trained as hunting dogs specifically which entail commandability. We do not use such label for birds of prey because they do not act upon commands. They simply go to food when they see it and fly towards the game animal when they are hungry and have the need to eat. When it is satiated, it does not go when it is sent nor does it return to its owner when it is called. That withstanding, they cannot be considered as an animal that can be commanded. If there is no commandability, there is no trainability.

As for the lynx, if it is similar to a dog in that it can be commanded, sent, returned, incited and trained in both states of hunger and satiety—the case of its game animal would be like that of the dog. However, if it differs from the dog in terms of trainability and commandability, eating what it kills would be incorrect.

My father related to me that his father was asked about the killing of game by a dog and hawk. He replied:

> That which a trained dog killed is considered permissible to eat according to me. That which was sacrificed properly by the killing of a trained dog can be eaten, even if only a small amount was eaten. I do not know of any answer among the people that is contrary to what I replied to you except something related from Ibn 'Abbās.[2] It is narrated that he said that one cannot eat from that game animal eaten by a trained dog; it is only a game animal when it eats it for itself and not for the one who sent it. We assume that Ibn 'Abbās said that based on his interpretation of Allah's statement {**eat of that which they catch for thee**}.

---

[1] Similarly narrated in ***Ŝaĥīĥ al-Bukhārī, Sunan at-Tirmidhi, Sunan an-Nisā`i, Sunan al-Bayhaqi***

[2] It is also related in ***Al-Muntakhab*** that al-Hādi, upon him be peace, said:

> If a dog is trained and it eats some of it [i.e. the game animal], one may eat from the rest. This is my statement and the statement of the scholars of the Prophet's Progeny, upon them be peace. It is said that Ibn 'Abbās said that if a dog were to eat some of it, one cannot eat the rest. But I do not know if this is authentically attributed to Ibn 'Abbās or not.

Therefore, according to Ibn 'Abbās, one can eat from other than that which was caught for the one who sent it. According to me, the catching refers to the killing of it. It is also well-known that Adi b. Hātim and Abu Tha'laba al-Khushani§ asked Allah's Messenger, peace and blessings be upon him and his progeny, about eating from that game animal which a trained dog ate, and he permitted them to eat the leftover from the dog.

The Companions of Allah's Messenger, peace and blessings be upon him and his progeny with the exception of Ibn 'Abbās, held to the position that one can eat from the leftover of a trained dog even if there only remains a small portion of meat.

As for that which was killed by a hawk or falcon, the best thing said to me about it is that it would not be considered properly sacrificed because Allah says: **{those animals that ye have trained as dogs (*mukallibīn*)}**. He did not say "those animals which you trained as hawks." The dog can be incited, and the most canine of dogs is the one who can be incited the most. Dogs can only be incited through the use of calls and commands. However, the hawk cannot be commanded, called or incited.

In the case of a lynx that cannot be incited or commanded or called, it would not be permissible to eat the leftover of what it eats. However, if it can be trained to act on commands and calls and incitements, it would be considered similar to a dog. One could eat what it leaves behind, and its killing of game would be considered properly sacrificed.

This has reached me as the statement of 'Ali, upon him be peace, Ibn 'Abbās and Ibn 'Umar. It has also been narrated that Tāwūs§ used to say: "Neither the hawk, lynx nor tiger are among those animals from which Allah permits one to eat the leftover portion of the game animal." However, others have said that all of these animals are like the dog in what it hunts and eats.

Concerning hunting game with the dogs of the Magians, Jews and Christians

If a Jew or Christian or Magian sent his dog to hunt a game animal and it killed it, we do not hold to the view that it can be eaten. Similarly, we do not hold to the view that one can eat the sacrificed meats of any one of the aforementioned groups.

If a Muslim were to send a *dhimmi*'s dog and pronounce Allah's Name when he sent it, there would be no problem in eating the game animal because the dog was not sent by the owner when someone else sent it.

My father related to me that when his father was asked about the game animal caught by the trained dog of a Magian, he replied: "There is no problem in eating its game as long as the one who sent it was Muslim, the Name of Allah was pronounced, and the dog was trained."

Concerning hunting at night

There is no problem with hunting at night or day because Allah makes it permissible absolutely. He does not restrict His slaves from doing such during the night or day. It is simply prohibited to hunt at night that which comes to its nest by night so that it is taken from its place of safety. For that reason, it is impermissible to take it, and we do not hold to the view that it can be hunted. Regarding that, it is narrated that Allah's Messenger, peace and blessings be upon him and his progeny, said: ((The birds are protected by Allah in their nests)).[3]

My father related to me that his father was asked about hunting at night. He replied:

> It is simply prohibited in the case of that which goes to its nest at night. As for that which departs and goes out in the open, there is no problem in hunting by night or day because Allah permits hunting without specifying a time in the day or night.

---

[3] Similarly narrated in ***Sharh at-Tajrīd*** and ***Al-Mu'jam al-Kabīr***

Concerning the caught fish of the Magians and idolaters

There is no problem eating the fish they catch as long as it is washed from their filth and that which their hands touch is cleaned of the impurity of their touch. This is because fish is not something that is sacrificed by slitting its throat or severing its jugular vein. Allah simply makes it permissible by catching it and not slitting its throat. For that reason, it is a permissible game animal.

We say that it can be eaten, but it has been narrated from the Commander of Believers, 'Ali b. Abi Ṭālib, upon him be peace, that he prohibited it.[4] However, this is not authentically attributed to him according to us.

My father related to me that when his father was asked about the caught fish of the Magians and idolaters, he replied: "One is to wash what their hands touch, but there is no problem in it because it is considered properly sacrificed itself."

Concerning the one who shoots an arrow at a game animal or sends one's dog on it then it is hidden from sight and one later finds it

If a person were to shoot a game animal with an arrow or send his trained dog to catch it and it escaped his sight for a period of time only to later find it with his arrow in it and nothing else and he is certain that it died when it fell by his arrow or trained dog and he had not seen any other signs of death but by his arrow or his dog, it would be no problem to eat it when he understood that he was the one who killed it. This is because Allah permits that without saying whether it is hidden or not hidden. One does not remove certainty except by certainty; if he is certain that he killed it when he shot his arrow or that his dog killed it when he sent it, eating that game animal would be considered permissible.

My father related to me that his father was asked about a man who shot a game animal and it fell but disappeared from sight due to darkness or falling behind a mountain and then found it dead and with his arrow in it. He replied:

> If he does not see any other traces but his own arrow or dog and he knows it with certainty, he can eat it. It would be permissible for him to eat it whether it fell in the night or day and whether it was on the coast or a mountain.

Concerning fish that died and were not caught game

Fish that are considered properly sacrificed are those taken alive. As for those that are found floating or washed ashore dead, it is no good. It is narrated that the Commander of Believers, 'Ali b. Abi Ṭālib, upon him be peace, prohibited it.[5]

If a man were to cast a net in the water and fish were to enter it and the one who threw the net drew it in and discovered dead fish floating on the top of the water in the net, they would be considered carcass and no good due to their floating on top of the water. As for those who remain on the ground outside of the water in the net, there would be no problem eating them whether they were living or dead because they were captured, taken out of the water and they remained in a place that permits them to be caught.

My father related to me that his father was asked about fish that are found floating, washed ashore or victims of one another. He replied:

> These would all be considered carcass, and we do not permit that they be eaten.[6] It has been narrated that 'Ali, upon him be peace, prohibited fish found floating and that they are considered carcass among fish. Similar is the case with carcass prohibited by Allah whether beasts of the land or fish of the sea.

---

[4] Similarly narrated in ***Mušannaf Ibn Abi Shayba***

[5] Similarly narrated in ***Amāli Ahmed b. 'Isa, Sunan Abu Dāwūd, Sunan Ibn Mājah, Al-Mu'jam al-Awsat, Sunan al-Bayhaqi***

[6] It is related in ***Al-Jāmi' al-Kāfi*** that Imam al-Hasan b. Yahya declared the consensus of Ahl al-Bayt regarding the prohibition of eating dead fish found floating.

Concerning the game caught by an untrained dog as well as that game that is shared between a trained and untrained dog

If one were to send an untrained dog upon a game animal and it catches it and brings it back to the sender but had not killed it, it would be no problem eating it; it would be considered permissible for the owner. However, if it brought it back to him after having killed it, we do not hold to the view that it can be eaten. This is because it would be considered the game animal of the dog and Allah does not permit one to eat what it killed for itself because it was not trained.

If one were to send a trained dog upon a game animal but it is intercepted by an untrained dog and it assists in killing it and puts some aside for itself or takes a portion, it would be impermissible to eat it. The untrained dog invalidated the proper sacrifice when it assisted the trained dog.

If two men were to send two trained dogs upon a game animal and both dogs killed it, that game animal would be considered properly sacrificed when Allah's Name is pronounced. The game animal would be considered permissible for both of them whether both dogs killed it or ate some of it.

Concerning the use of a bow and arrow to shoot a game animal and the statement regarding an arrow with no feathers or head (*al-mi'rād*)

If you shoot your arrow from your bow and then strike it and cause it to bleed, you can eat what you killed with your arrow after bleeding and piercing it. However, if you were to not cause your game animal to bleed and it died after being hit by your arrow, you cannot eat it because it died by a blunt object.

Similar is the case with an arrow with no feathers or head. One cannot eat what was killed by it unless one comes up to it to sacrifice it correctly. This is because he had not pierced it with iron and sacrificed it correctly.

It has reached us from Allah's Messenger, peace and blessings be upon him and his progeny, that Adi b. Hātim said: "O Messenger of Allah, we are people who shoot game animals." He replied: ((That which you pronounce Allah's Name over and shoot and then pierce—you can eat it)). He asked: "What about an arrow with no feathers or head/" He replied: ((Do not eat from that which you kill with featherless and headless arrows except what you sacrifice)).[7]

Concerning hunting with clay pellets (*al-julāhiq*)

Whatever is knocked down by clay pellets and then encountered and sacrificed—it would be no problem to eat it. However, that which is killed by such is impermissible to eat because it was not sacrificed properly. Similar has reached us from Allah's Messenger, peace and blessings be upon him and his progeny: ((Do not eat that which was hunted by clay pellets unless it was encountered and then sacrificed correctly)).[8]

Concerning a game animal that is thrown to the ground or falls into water

If a game animal is thrown into a mountain and thrown down when the arrow hits it, it is to not be eaten because of the fear that it was killed by being thrown down. Similarly, if it were thrown into the water, we prefer that it not be eaten because of the fear that it died by drowning. A precautionary measure like this is preferable in the religion and safer for the Muslims.

Concerning properly sacrificing the game animal

If a man reached the game animal while it moves its foot or glances with its eye or moves its tail and he sacrificed it, it would be considered sacrificed correctly. Similarly, if it were to not move any of these things except after slitting its throat, it would be considered sacrificed correctly. It would be considered the same whether it moved before slitting its throat or if it moved afterwards. If it does

[7] Similarly narrated in ***Ŝahīh al-Bukhāri, Ŝahīh Muslim, Sunan Abu Dāwūd, Sunan at-Tirmidhi, Sunan Ibn Māja***

[8] Similarly narrated in ***Amāli Ahmed b. 'Isa*** and ***Musnad Ahmed***

not move any of those things after having its throat slit, it would not be considered sacrificed correctly. Consequently, it would be considered carcass and impermissible to eat.

The Book of Sacrificed Meats (*adh-Dhabā`ih*)

In the Name of Allah, the Most Gracious, the Most Merciful...

The beginning of the chapters regarding sacrificed meats and its explanation in the Book

Allah says: **{Eat not from that upon which Allah's Name was not mentioned, for that would be open disobedience. Verily, the devils inspire their associates to wrangle with thee. But if ye were to obey them, ye would indeed be idolaters}** (Q. 6:121).

This verse was revealed regarding Qurayshi idolaters because they used to say to the believers: "You claim to follow Allah's command while you leave that which Allah has sacrificed for you and do not eat it! Yet, that which you sacrifice you eat! Carcass is simply that which Allah has sacrificed!" Then, Allah revealed: **{Eat not from that upon which Allah's Name was not mentioned}**. By that He prohibited carcass as well as that which was sacrificed for other than Allah in the pre-Islamic era. Then, He says: **{...for that would be open disobedience}**. He means that eating that upon which Allah's Name was not mentioned will be considered an open act of disobedience.

Then, He says: **{Forbidden unto thee is carcass, blood, the flesh of swine, that which hath been dedicated unto other than Allah, the strangled, that which was beaten to death, that which died by falling from a height, that which hath been killed by horns, that devoured by wild beasts save that which ye hath sacrificed, and that which hath been sacrificed unto idols. And (forbidden is it) that ye swear by the divining arrows. This is for thee open disobedience. Today, those who disbelieve despair of thy religion, so fear them not but fear Me. Today, I have perfected for thee thy religion and completed upon thee My favour and am pleased for thee with Islam as thy religion. Therefore, whosoever is compelled to hunger to sin unwilfully—verily, Allah is Oft-forgiving, Most Gracious}** (Q. 5:3).

As for **{that which hath been dedicated to other than Allah}**, it refers to that upon which the name of other than Allah was mentioned. As for **{the strangled}**, it refers to an animal that has its throat choked between two rods, by a rope or anything else that it is strangled with until it dies. As for **{that which is beaten to death}**, it refers to shooting it with a blunt object or hitting it with one until it dies. As for **{that which died by falling from a height}**, it refers to throwing it from a mountain, the top of a deep well or anything else similar until the animal falls and dies and then one is not able to sacrifice it correctly. As for **{that which hath been killed by horns}**, it is that which was gored by a bull or ram and then it died. As for **{that devoured by wild beasts}**, it refers to a wild animal that eats it without one being able to go to it and sacrifice it correctly. Allah prohibits all of that unless one is able to go up to it to sacrifice it correctly and slit its throat before it died. At that point, it would be considered permissible to eat and not prohibited. In the pre-Islamic era, they used to consider all of that as properly sacrificed and not carcass. Then, Allah says: **{and that which hath been sacrificed unto idols}**. Those **{idols}** refer to their idol gods that they used to sacrifice for and in their names.

Then, the One too mighty and majestic to be encompassed by words says: **{And Allah hath not appointed anything of *bahīra* or *sā`iba* or *waŝīla* or *hām*. Rather, it was those who disbelieve who falsely attributed it to Allah. Most of them do not use their intellect!}** (Q. 5:103).

That is because Qusayy b. Kilāb was the first to slit the ear of the newly born she-camel (*bahhara*), leave a she-camel to pasture alone and unburdened as a dedication for their gods (*sayyab*), leave a sheep that bore consecutive females to roam freely and unburdened as a dedication for their gods (*waŝala*) and leave a male camel who just copulated to roam freely and unburdened as a dedication for their gods (*hamā*). Afterwards, the Quraysh followed him in this as well as the Bedouins who followed their religion. They used to do this as a vow and claimed that Allah appointed this as His Judgement. Allah belies their statement as well as the statement of their brothers, the Coercionists, who falsely attribute every enormity to Allah. The latter say that Allah decrees upon them every act of disobedience and places in them every obscenity!

He says: {**And Allah hath not appointed anything of *bahīra* or *sā`iba* or *waŝīla* or *hām***}. He negates thereby that He created such in them or decrees that upon them. He declares the one who assigns this action to Him as a liar as well as the one who falsely attributes this evil deed to Him. He is therefore negated from that and He attributes that to the people. He then says that they attribute a lie to Him. Allah confirms that He is innocent from their actions. He is highly exalted from their acts of wrongdoing and corruption! He is distant from decreeing upon them that which He has not commanded them as well as placing in them that from which he has prohibited them!

The term *bahīra* refers a she-camel that would consecutively give birth to five camels and then would be freed at the birth of the fifth one. If the baby were a male, it would then be sacrificed and given as a gift to those who served their gods. If the baby were a female, it would be left alone to freely graze, and its ear would be slit. It would then be given the name '*Bahīra*.' Afterwards, no one would be permitted to use her as payment for indemnity, milk her or shear her hair. One would only be allowed to milk her if they feared that her udders would drag otherwise. If they were to shear her, they would do so on a windy day and scatter her dander in the wind. Also, they would not ride her back and would leave her to walk wherever she wanted. If she were to die, both men and women would share her milk and then eat her.

As for the term *sā`iba*, it refers to a she-camel. The men used to seek healing from her when they fell sick, seek her assistance when they travelled or ask her for something. One set the she-camel free when they desired to thank Allah; they therefore called it a *sā`iba*. They left it to go wherever it wanted, similar to the *bahīra*; it was not prevented from eating, drinking or grazing.

As for the term *waŝīla*, it refers to a sheep. Whenever it gave birth to five lambs and the fifth was a male lamb, they would sacrifice him or both in the case of two male lambs. If it gave birth to two females, they would be allowed to live. If it gave birth to a male and female, they would leave the male and not sacrifice him because of his sister. They said: "She is connected to him (*waŝalat hu*), so it is impermissible to sacrifice him because of her." As for the mother, among the offering of the sheep is its milk. Its milk would be shared among the men and not the women. If it were to die, the men and women would eat it and share in such.

As or the term *hām*, it is a camel-stud. When it reaches ten years and its child gives birth, they say: "Its back has become prohibited (*hamā*)." Then they leave it to bear offspring for them, they call it a '*hāma*' and leave it to go its own way. They do not prevent it from going anywhere similar to a *bahīra* and *sā`iba*. Afterwards, no one would be permitted to use her as payment for indemnity or ride on her back. These three types of livestock are those whose backs are prohibited.

The Glorified says: {**...eight pairs—twain of sheep and twain of goats. Say: "Hath He forbidden two males or two females or whatsoever is contained in the wombs of the female? Inform me if ye art indeed truthful." And twain of camels and twain of oxen. Say: "Hath He forbidden the two males or the two females, or that which the wombs of the two females contain, or were ye witnesses when Allah appointed this unto thee? So, who is greater in wrongdoing than he who attributes such lie to Allah, that he may lead humankind astray without knowledge? Verily, Allah guides not the wrongdoing people**} (**Q. 6:143-144**).

The Glorified mentions that which they have declared prohibited, such as the *bahīra*, *sā`iba*, *waŝīla*, *hām* and others. Such person makes the male a pair and the female a pair. He is saying: "You make two males from eight prohibited on yourself or two females."

Then, He says: {**"Bring forth thy witnesses—those who hath borne witness that Allah has forbade such!"**}. They said: "We bear witness!" Then, the Glorified says: {**If they bear witness, bear not**

witness with them. Follow not the whims of those who belie Our signs and those who believe not in the hereafter and make with thy Lord equals} (Q. 6:150).

Then, the Glorified informs them of what is prohibited for them when He says: {**"I find not in that which is revealed unto me anything prohibited for an eater to eat thereof save carcass or blood poured forth or the meat of swine. For, verily that is impure or open disobedience which was dedicated to other than Allah. But whosoever is compelled, without craving or transgressing, verily thy Lord is Oft-Forgiving, Most Gracious"**} (Q. 6:145).

The term {**poured forth**} refers to that which flows or drips. As for the phrase {**For, verily that is impure**}, He is saying that it is prohibited. As for the statement {**open disobedience which was dedicated to other than Allah**}, the term disobedience refers to sin and act of insolence against Allah by sacrificing for other than Allah. As for His statement {**But whosoever is compelled, without craving or transgressing**}, it means: without the desire to do it, commit an act of disobedience by eating it or transgress the command of his Lord; rather, he is forced to do it. It would be permissible for him to eat it if he fears dying of hunger. He could then eat enough of it to save himself and enliven his body so that he finds spaciousness in his affair.

Everything that Allah has permitted for the Muslims in His Book is clarified in the Book of the Lord of creation. And that which He prohibits from them is also clarified for them in His Book {**...that those who perish would have perished upon evidence and those who live would have lived upon evidence. Verily, Allah is All-Hearing, All-Knowing**} (Q. 8:42).

Concerning a woman's sacrifice as well as that of a child, person in the state of major ritual impurity and a menstruating woman

There is no problem with the sacrifice performed by a woman if she is a righteous Muslimah and knows the proper method of sacrifice, respects its boundaries severs its jugular vein and faces the *qibla*. Similar is the case with a child; there is no problem with him performing the sacrifice if he understands the proper method, can sever its jugular vein and knows its boundaries and restrictions.

Also, there is no problem with the sacrifice performed by a person in the state of major ritual impurity or a menstruating woman in the state of their impurity. This is because both are Muslims, and there is nothing restricted from them in the state of impurity except the prayer and recitation of the Qur'an. As for the remembrance of Allah as well as the glorification and praise of Him, it is obligatory upon them and anyone else whether in that state or any other state.

Sacrificing is simply beautified by the religion and pronouncement of the Name. If they were restricted from Allah's remembrance in the case of their sacrifice, they would be restricted from it at other times as well. When it comes to Allah's remembrance, there is no restriction on His slaves. It is a religious injunction for them whether in the state of purity or impurity. For that reason, their sacrifice is permitted.

My father related to me that when his father was asked about the sacrifice performed by a woman, he replied: "There is no problem with her sacrifice if she is from the people of religion and knows the place of sacrifice." He was asked about the sacrifice of a child and replied: "There is no problem as long as he knows the manner and is a Muslim." He was asked about the sacrifice performed by a person in the state of major ritual impurity and the menstruating woman and replied: "There is no problem with that."

Concerning sacrifice with a sharp stake, nail, stone or bone

It is impermissible to perform the sacrifice with a sharp stake, nail or bone. There is no problem with a sharp pebble or stone as long as the jugular is severed, the blood flows and the aorta is opened just as a knife would do. One cannot use this unless one cannot find an iron blade.

Similar has reached us from Allah's Messenger, peace and blessings be upon him and his progeny, that a shepherd came to him and asked: 'O Messenger of Allah, can I perform the sacrifice with a bone?" He replied: ((No)). He then asked: "Can I perform the sacrifice with a sharp stake?" He replied: ((No)). He then asked: "Can I perform the sacrifice with my nails if I feared that it would precede me in doing it itself?" He replied: ((No. Rather, you should get a sharp pebble and perform the sacrifice with it. As long as it severs, you can eat it. However, if it does not, you cannot eat it)).[1]

Concerning the sacrifice performed by the mute, runaway slave and uncircumcised

There is no problem with the sacrifice performed by any of the aforementioned as long as they are people of religion and knowledgeable of the manner of sacrifice. If the uncircumcised avoided circumcision based on a valid excuse that can be presented to Allah as a proof, the one who permits marriage with him will similarly permit his sacrificed meats.

My father related to me that his father was asked about the sacrificed meats of the uncircumcised, runaway slave or mute. He replied: "There is no problem with their sacrificed meats as long as their religion is sound, and they are of its people."

Concerning the sacrifice of a foetus and what has been narrated that its sacrifice is the sacrifice of its mother

It has been narrated in reports that the sacrifice of a foetus is considered sound by the sacrifice of its mother.[2] However, this is not authentic according to us. We do not consider such in our analogical reasoning because proper sacrifice is not considered sound except for that which was properly sacrificed. That which exits the mother's womb would also have to be properly sacrificed because the sacrifice should be for one and then another just as one life is taken and then another.

It may be that it dies in its mother's womb before it is sacrificed just as it would die at the time of its sacrifice. It may be that it survives in its mother's womb and is extracted alive after her death. That is possible in respect to livestock and other females of living things.

One does not perform the sacrifice on that which is in the womb except after it has been delivered alive. Its sacrifice would be similar to the sacrifice of its mother. Therefore, just as its being delivered alive and subsequent sacrifice would necessitate its designation as proper sacrifice, a woman's child being delivered alive and its initiation would necessitate the judgements of inheritance and prayer. Not everything that has been narrated is correct, and that which was narrated regarding it from Allah's Messenger, peace and blessings be upon him and his progeny, is not true.

My father related to me that his father was asked about the narrated hadith that stated the sacrifice of the foetus is considered sound by the sacrifice of its mother. He replied:

> The foetus is to be properly sacrificed with its mother if it is alive. This is because her life is different from its life and her death is different from its death. It may be that it died in her womb, and Allah has prohibited carcass—whether it is young or old.

---

[1] Similarly narrated in ***Musnad Imam Zayd***. Also, a similar report appears in ***Ŝaħīħ al-Bukhāri, Ŝaħīħ Muslim, Sunan Abu Dāwūd, Sunan at-Tirmidhi, Sunan an-Nisā'i, Ŝaħīħ Ibn Hibbān***. A contrary report appears in the ***Muwaťťa*** of Imam Mālik in which the Prophet is narrated to have permitted the sacrifice with a sharp stake.

[2] Similarly narrated in ***Musnad Imam Zayd, Musnad Ahmed, Ŝaħīħ Ibn Hibbān, Sunan Ibn Mājah, Sunan Abu Dāwūd, Sunan at-Tirmidhi***

Whoever slits the throat of a sacrificed animal and the head was decapitated—there would be no problem with eating it. It is said that this is called a quick sacrifice. Similar was said by my grandfather, may Allah have mercy on him.[3]

If a camel or cow were to fall in a well and it was impossible to remove them alive, it would be obligatory for their owners to demand one to sacrifice the camel or cow. If one is not able to do that, one is to stab and pierce it whenever they can. After removing it from the well, it can then be eaten.

Concerning that which is permissible and impermissible in respect to sacrifice

It is impermissible for the sacrificed animal to be one-eyed, blind, mutilated or with a broken horn. It is impermissible in respect to camels, cows and goats except that which is in its second year.

A lamb younger than a year is permissible, and the best sacrificed animal is the fattest. The castrated among them is permissible and is generally the fattiest and choicest. It has been narrated that Allah's Messenger, peace and blessings be upon him and his progeny, sacrificed a castrated ram.[4]

My father related to me that his father was asked about the sacrifice of an animal with a slit or pierced ear as well as one with a broken horn. He replied:

> Any defective animal that is one-eyed or mutilated is impermissible to sacrifice unless one is unable to find any other animal in the land. There is no problem with a castrated animal because it is fatty and it is narrated that Allah's Messenger, peace and blessings be upon him and his progeny, sacrificed a castrated ram.

It has reached us on the authority of Zayd b. 'Ali—his ancestors—'Ali b. Abi Ţālib, upon them be peace:

> Allah's Messenger, peace and blessings be upon him and his progeny, ascended the pulpit on the Eid of Sacrifice, and he praised and extolled Allah. Then, he said: ((O people! Whoever has the means, let him honour the signs of Allah. Whoever does not have it, Allah does not make a soul responsible for other than what it can bear)). Then he descended, and a man from the Anŝār came to him and said: "O Messenger of Allah, I sacrificed my animal before I left, and you commanded them to do it. Perhaps you can honour me today?" He, peace and blessings be upon him and his progeny, replied: ((Your lamb is just mutton. If you have anything other than it, you can sacrifice it)). He said: "I only have a she-goat kid." Then, he replied: ((Sacrifice it, but it would not be permissible for anyone after you)).[5] He then said: ((If it is a fatty young lamb younger than one year, there is no problem in sacrificing it. However, if it is a goat kid, it would not be sound)).

The meaning of his statement ((…it would not be sound)) is that it would not be sound if he sacrificed a goat kid younger than a year. As for his statement ((Whoever has the means, let him honour the signs of Allah)), it means to let him make it the best if he is able to sacrifice a fat lamb or goat (*jazūr*)--that would be better. If he is able to sacrifice a cow, that would be better than a lamb. However, if he is only able to sacrifice a lamb, let him choose a fat one that is free from defects and imperfections.

As for his statement to the Ansari ((Your lamb is just mutton)), it means that since the Ansari sacrificed in Medina before the imam came out and whoever sacrificed before the imam came out, his sacrifice was not considered valid. This is because the people of the cities are to only sacrifice after their imam comes out. By such, the Sunnah is exhibited, and the evidence is established for the people.

There is no problem if the owner of the sacrificed meat to extract what he wants and store away what he wants. Similar has been narrated from Allah's Messenger, peace and blessings be upon him and his

---

[3] The same judgement is narrated from Imam 'Ali, upon him be peace, in ***Musnad Imam Zayd***.

[4] Similarly narrated in ***Sharh at-Tajrīd, Amāli Ahmed b. 'Isa, Musnad Ahmed, Sunan Ibn Mājah, Sunan Abu Dāwūd***

[5] Similarly narrated in ***Musnad Imam Zayd, Ŝahīh Muslim, Sunan Abu Dāwūd, Ŝahīh Ibn Hibbān, Musnad Ahmed, Al-Mu'jam al-Kabīr, Sunan al-Bayhaqi***

progeny, that he used to prohibit the storage of sacrificed meat for more than three days. Then, he said after that: ((Before, I used to forbid you from storing sacrificed meats for more than three days, but now you can store it as you wish)).[6]

He alleviated them from what he restricted for them, and now there is no set number of days. A fat sheep or goat suffices for ten family members of one house, and a cow is sufficient for seven. A lamb is sufficient for three; but one is preferred to us.

My father related to me that his father was asked about the length of time sacrificed meats could be stored. He replied: "The owner can store it for as long as he wants; there is no set number of days." When he was asked about how many family members are sufficient for camels, cows and sheep—he replied: "A camel is sufficient for ten, a cow is sufficient for seven, and a lamb is sufficient for three."

Regarding the Muslim male who forgot to pronounce Allah's Name at the time of sacrifice, he used to say: "He can eat the meat. Intention and religion are sufficient from pronouncing the Name." If he avoided it unintentionally, he can eat it. However, if he avoided it intentionally, he cannot eat it or give it away.

Concerning one who steals a lamb and sacrifices it

Whoever steals a lamb from its owner and then sacrifices it without its master's permission would not be permitted to eat it or feed it to another because Allah has made it prohibited. If he were to get the owner's permission after having sacrificed it or its price was agreed upon, there would be no problem with eating it afterwards.

My father related to me that his father was asked about a man who stole a lamb and sacrificed it without the knowledge of its owner. He replied: "It is impermissible for him or anyone else to eat it if it were stolen. It is impermissible for him to sacrifice that which Allah has prohibited."

Whoever unknowingly sacrifices without facing the *qibla* can eat his sacrificed meat. Whoever sacrifices without facing it intentionally cannot eat his sacrificed meat.

The camel is to be sacrificed standing while facing the *qibla*. Its forelegs are to be tied and the one who sacrifices it should do so while standing. Then, he is to strike its neck with the blade until its jugular is severed. **{When they have fallen upon their sides} (Q. 22:36)**, as Allah says, they are skinned and eaten. The term 'fallen' denotes tumbling and collapsing.

Whoever unknowingly sacrifices using the blunt end of a blade (*qafā*) can eat the sacrificed meat. However, whoever does so intentionally cannot eat the meat. The best course of action is for him to be taught the proper etiquette.

Every animal that is sick, fallen or gored and then sacrificed but then it moves its tail, head, foreleg, foot, limb or blinks its eyes—such animal would be permissible to eat and considered properly sacrificed, as Allah says: **{...save that which ye hath sacrificed} (Q. 5:3)**. The meaning is "...except that which you have slit its throat." Sacrifice cannot occur except on that which was previously alive.

Concerning the *aqīqa*

The *aqīqa* is a sunnah from the Messenger, peace and blessings be upon him and his progeny. It is a lamb that one sacrifices on behalf of a child on the seventh day. Then, one prepares it and his family eats from it. They then feed it to whomever they want and give it away as charity.

It is encouraged for them to shave its [i.e. the baby's] head and donate the weight of its hair in gold and silver to charity. It has been narrated that the Prophet, peace and blessings be upon him and his progeny, performed the *aqīqa* on behalf of al-Hasan and al-Hussein, upon them be peace. He gave

[6] Similarly narrated in ***Musnad Imam Zayd, Musnad Abu Ya'la, Sunan Abu Dāwūd, Ŝahīh Muslim, Ŝahīh Ibn Hibbān, Sunan al-Bayhaqi***

some away as charity, ate some of it and fed others from their *aqīqa*.[7] This is a sunnah of the Muslims that none should avoid unless one is unable to find one.

My father related to me that his father was asked about the *aqīqa* for boys and girls. He replied:

> One is to perform the *aqīqa* on behalf of a baby that is born—whether it is a boy or a girl. Similar has been narrated from Allah's Messenger, peace and blessings be upon him and his progeny. It is encouraged for one to donate the weight of the infant's hair in silver and gold to charity. Similar has been narrated from Fãtima, the daughter of Allah's Messenger, peace and blessings be upon him and his progeny, that she used to do that.[8]
>
> A lamb is for both the boy and girl.[9] One performs the *aqīqa* on the seventh day. It is called the *aqīqa* due to the shaving of the infant's head on the seventh day as well as the sacrifice on behalf of the newborn. It is simply the shaving of the head.

If a man wants to sacrifice a goat or any other type of livestock and it escapes from him and he is not able to catch it and sacrifice it and he throws his sword or arrow or spear at it to stun and kill it and is able to pierce it when he threw the projectile, there is no problem in eating it if he was unable to slit its throat. However, if he were to do such rebelliously, he cannot eat it. He must be taught proper etiquette for mutilating an animal and acting contrary to the sunnah in his sacrifice.

---

[7] Similarly narrated in ***Ŝahīh al-Bukhāri, Ŝahīh Muslim, Sunan at-Tirmidhi, Sunan an-Nisā`i, Musnad Abu Ya'la, Mušannaf Ibn Abi Shayba, Sunan al-Bayhaqi***

[8] Similarly narrated in ***Mušannaf Ibn Abi Shayba, Al-Mustadrak, Al-Mu'jam al-Kabīr, Sunan al-Bayhaqi, Ušūl al-Kāfi***

[9] In ***Al-Muntakhab***, al-Hādi states: "Others say that there are two lambs for the boy and one lamb for the girl. But as for us, we say that it is a lamb for each." Some narrations exist in which the boy is said to have two lambs sacrificed on his behalf and the girl is said to have one lamb. See ***Sunan ad-Dārimi, Ŝahīh Ibn Hibbān, Sunan at-Tirmidhi, Sunan an-Nisā`i, Sunan Ibn Mājah, Al-Mu'jam al-Kabīr, Al-Mu'jam al-Awsat, Musnad Abu Ya'la, Mušannaf Ibn Abi Shayba, Sunan al-Bayhaqi***

The Book of Foods, Drinks and Clothing

In the Name of Allah, the Most Gracious, the Most Merciful...

The beginning of the chapters regarding foods and the explanation of what is prohibited regarding them in the Book and Sunnah

Allah—the Mighty and Majestic—says regarding what He prohibited for His slaves: {**Say: "I find not in that which is revealed unto me anything prohibited for an eater to eat thereof save carcass or blood poured forth or the meat of swine. For, verily that is impure or open disobedience which was dedicated to other than Allah. But whosoever is compelled, without craving or transgressing, verily thy Lord is Oft-Forgiving, Most Gracious"**} (Q. 6:145).

The Glorified also says: {**Forbidden unto thee is carcass, blood, the flesh of swine, that which hath been dedicated unto other than Allah, the strangled, that which was beaten to death, that which died by falling from a height, that which hath been killed by horns, that devoured by wild beasts save that which ye hath sacrificed, and that which hath been sacrificed unto idols. And (forbidden is it) that ye swear by the divining arrows. This is for thee open disobedience. Today, those who disbelieve despair of thy religion, so fear them not but fear Me. Today, I have perfected for thee thy religion and completed upon thee My favour and am pleased for thee with Islam as thy religion. Therefore, whosoever is compelled to hunger to sin unwilfully—verily, Allah is Oft-forgiving, Most Gracious**} (Q. 5:3).

Allah prohibits everything mentioned in these two verses for all Muslims except for the one who is {**compelled to hunger**}. The term {**hunger**} refers to hunger at the time of necessity and need to the point where the spirits would leave the bodies otherwise. If that is the case, it would be permissible for one to eat some of that which Allah has prohibited. One should only eat that which is below satiety to the extent that life is preserved to that which Allah has made easy. He says: {**For verily, with hardship is ease. Verily, with hardship is ease**} (Q. 94:5-6). The Glorified also says: {**And there is not a beast in the earth but that the sustenance thereof depends upon Allah. He knows its dwelling and repository. All is in a manifest decree**} (Q. 11:6).

Allah's Messenger, peace and blessings be upon him and his progeny, prohibited the meat of all fanged predatory animals or birds with talons.[1] The Muslims should therefore avoid everything that Allah's Messenger, peace and blessings be upon him and his progeny, prohibited because Allah—the Mighty and Majestic—says: {**Whatsoever the Messenger gives thee, take it. Whatever he prohibits thee from, leave it**} (Q. 59:7). The exception is that which is necessary and incurs a need.

Then, the Glorified says as a way for His slaves to realise His grace upon them and desire for their success: {**Say: "Who hath forbidden the ornaments of Allah which He has brought forth for His slaves as well as the good of provision?" Say: "They are for those who believe during the life of this world, exclusively on the Day of Judgement." Thus, do We detail the signs for the people who know**} (Q. 7:32).

The Glorified also says: {**O Messengers, eat of the good and do righteous deeds, for verily I am of those who perform deeds All-Knowing**} (Q. 23:51). Therefore, the Glorified allows His believing slaves and Prophets to eat the good of His provision and does not prevent them from any of it out of His beneficence. He makes everything that He created on the face of the earth as provision for them. He allows them to eat it in a permissible way and not eat from that which was unlawfully misappropriated from any of His slaves. The Glorified says regarding that: {**Consume not thy wealth amongst thee in falsehood**} (Q. 2:188).[2]

---

[1] Similarly narrated in ***Musnad Imam Zayd, Ŝahīh Muslim, Sunan Abu Dāwūd, Ibn Mājah, Ŝahīh Ibn Hibbān, Sunan ad-Dārimi, Sunan Bayhaqi, Sunan an-Nisā`i, Musnad Ahmed***

[2] It is related that Imam al-Hasan b. Yahya said in ***Al-Jāmi' al-Kāfi***:

Concerning washing the hands before eating

One should wash and clean the hands before partaking in a meal because that is the healthiest, most wholesome and closest to righteousness and God-consciousness. Also, before one partakes in a meal, the one eating should say: "In the Name of Allah and by Allah and all praise is due to Allah for our provision that He facilitated and our meal that He graced us with!" When he completes his meal, he should say: "All praise is due to Allah for what He provided us with! All praise is due to Allah who fed and satiated us! He has facilitated for us our sustenance and bounty! All praise is due to Allah for that with thankfulness! There is no partner with Him!"

No one is to eat with his left hand unless some ailment prevents him from eating with the right hand. The one eating should eat that which is closest to him in front of him unless it is from dates. Then, one can eat whichever one likes.

It has come from the Sunnah of Allah's Messenger, peace and blessings be upon him and his progeny, that he used to eat the closest food and what was in front of him. He did not stretch forth his hand to anyone else's. However, when dates were placed in front of him, he would reach his hand anywhere in the container.[3]

Concerning the virtue of the table spread (*mā`ida*) of Muhammad's Progeny as well as the virtue of the one who eats with them

The table spread of Muhammad's Progeny has more virtue than the table spread of anyone else. The one who eats from it has more virtue than the one who eats from anyone else's. It is a virtue Allah grants to them due to them being offspring of His Prophet, peace and blessings be upon him and his progeny. This is also due to the Glorified making clear their virtue as well as completing and manifesting His grace upon them.

Regarding that, my father related to me from his father with the chain going all the way to the Prophet: ((When the table spread of Muhammad's Progeny is laid down, the Angels surround them sending blessings and seeking forgiveness for them as well as for the one who eats their food with them)).

That is a proof for them from Allah that there is virtue from Him to them. If they are grateful, they are increased, and if they are ungrateful, they are punished. Therefore, we ask Allah to make us grateful for His grace, remember His favours and fearful of Him! We ask Him to grace us with gratefulness for appointing us as His associates and giving us the best gift of being the offspring of the Master of Messengers and Chosen of creation!

When those eating finish from eating their food, they are to wash their hands and thoroughly clean them. Do not mimic the actions of the tyrants who avoid it; rather, washing them is among the actions of the righteous and a form of purity for the praying slaves of Allah.

Concerning flies, beetles, mice and similar that fall in the food

If flies or beetles were to fall in the food, one is to simply remove them and eat it because it is not prohibited or ruined. Regarding that, it has reached us from Allah's Messenger, peace and blessings be upon him and his progeny, that a bowl of meat broth was brought to him and there were beetles in it. He commanded that they be removed and said: ((Pronounce Allah's Name over it and eat it, for there is

---

It is the consensus of the Prophet's Progeny, peace and blessings be upon him and his progeny, that wealth should be spent liberally (*al-iqtiṣād*) on food and that one should spend from one's permissible financial maintenance and not be restrictive in such. According to them, such is not considered excessive unless it was spent impermissibly. Then, it would be considered excessive, whether a lot or a little.

[3] Similarly narrated in ***Sunan at-Tirmidhi*** and ***Sunan Ibn Māja***

nothing prohibited in it)). Then, some food was brought to him and he found flies in it. He removed them and said: ((Eat it, for there is nothing prohibited in it)).[4]

If a mouse were to fall in it and it is removed alive, there is no problem in eating the food that it fell in. However, if it were dead and removed, one is to remove the portion of the food it touched and eat the rest as long as nothing was contaminated by it. If it were to fall in a container of clarified butter or oil and then die in it while it was solid, one simply removes it and that portion that was around it. However, if it was not solid and its scent or colour or taste were altered due to the dead mouse in it, one is to dispose of all of it.

Concerning eating lizard

It is discouraged to eat lizard but not prohibited. Regarding that, it has been narrated that Allah's Messenger, peace and blessings be upon him and his progeny, entered upon his wife, Maymūna b. al-Hārith[§], along with 'Abdullah b. 'Abbās and Khālid b. al-Walīd[§]. She had some lizards and an egg. He asked her: ((From where did you get this?)). She replied: "My sister Hurayna b. al-Hārith[§] gave it to me as a gift." Allah's Messenger, peace and blessings be upon him and his progeny, said to 'Abdullah b. 'Abbās and Khālid b. al-Walīd: ((Eat it)). They replied: "We do not eat it." Allah's Messenger, peace and blessings be upon him and his progeny, also did not eat it. He said: ((There are visitors from Allah who visit me)). Then, Maymūna asked: "Would you like to drink some of our milk, O Messenger of Allah?" He replied: ((Yes)) and after drinking some, he asked: ((From where did you get this?)). She replied: "My sister gave it to me as a gift." Allah's Messenger, peace and blessings be upon him and his progeny, then said: ((Do you see your slave-girl whom you asked me for permission to manumit? Give her to your sister and bring her to take care of her. That would be better for you)).[5]

It has also reached us that a man called out to Allah's Messenger, peace and blessings be upon him and his progeny, and said: "O Messenger of Allah, what is your view regarding eating lizards?" He replied: ((I do not eat them, but they are not prohibited)).[6]

Concerning that which is discouraged to eat

It is prohibited[7] to eat floating dead fish as well as that which was washed ashore unless it reaches you while alive or died in a fishing net. It is prohibited to eat sea snakes (*al-jira*) and catfish eels (*al-mārmāhi*). Similar has been narrated from the Commander of Believers, upon him be peace.[8]

It is discouraged to eat many digging animals (*al-harashāt*) such as the hedgehog and lizard. We consider it discouraged and loathsome, but it is not prohibited in the Book and Sunnah. Similar is the case with rabbits; we consider eating them loathsome but not prohibited. It is related that Allah's Messenger, peace and blessings be upon him and his progeny, considered them loathsome and did not eat it when it was given to him as a gift. However, he permitted his Companions to eat it.[9] It is among those land game animals that Allah permits to hunt.

It is prohibited to eat cat—whether domestic or wild—just as it is prohibited to eat other predatory animals. It is discouraged to eat spleen; it has been narrated to us from 'Ali b. Abi Ťālib, upon him be peace, that he said that it is the morsel (*luqma*) of Satan.[10]

---

[4] Similarly narrated in ***Sharh at-Tajrīd, Musnad Ahmed, Sunan Abu Dāwūd, Sunan Ibn Mājah, Musnad Abu Ya'la, Sunan ad-Dārimi, Sunan al-Bayhaqi***

[5] Similarly narrated in ***Muwatta***

[6] Similarly narrated in ***Ŝahīh al-Bukhāri, Ŝahīh Muslim, Sunan an-Nisā'i, Sunan al-Bayhaqi***

[7] Although the Arabic word typically translates into 'discouraged', we opt for the word 'prohibited' to conform to the ruling from the previous chapter as well as interchangeability between the words for 'prohibited' and 'discouraged' based on the context.

[8] Similarly narrated in ***Al-Jāmi' al-Kāfi, Uŝūl al-Kāfi, Bihār al-Anwār***.

[9] Similarly narrated in ***Mušannaf 'Abdur-Razzāq, Musnad Abu Ya'la, Sunan al-Bayhaqi***

[10] Similarly narrated in ***Mušannaf 'Abdur-Razzāq, Mušannaf Ibn Abi Shayba***

It is similarly prohibited to eat the cheese of the People of the Book and Magians because they make it using the stomach lining of carcass. It is prohibited to eat the fat of the Magians, Jews and Christians just as it is prohibited to eat their sacrificed meats due to their contamination and ritual impurity.

It is prohibited for a man to eat while lying on his back or stomach as well as to eat with the left hand. Regarding that, it has reached us from Allah's Messenger, peace and blessings be upon him and his progeny, that he prohibited a man from eating with his left hand and from eating lying on his back or stomach.[11]

It is discouraged to eat turtle because it is not among those whom Allah specified to be permissible as He specified other game from the land and sea. Some people permit it, but we do not encourage that. We typically discourage those land animals that we do not know about.

As for the eating of the meat of a cow, sheep or bird who feeds upon dung (*al-jallāla*)—there is no problem with it as long as the amount of fodder it feeds upon in a stall exceeds the amount of dung. It is encouraged for the one who intends to eat the animal to set it aside for some days until its insides are clean.

My father related to me that his father was asked about the eating of the meat of a cow, sheep or bird who feeds upon dung. He replied: "There is no problem with it. It may be prohibited, but one is to refer to whether it feeds on more fodder. If so, there would be no problem in eating it."

Concerning the blessing (*baraka*) of that from which Allah's Messenger ate and drank

It has reached us that there was a man from the Companions of Allah's Messenger, peace and blessings be upon him and his progeny, whom some say was Jābir and others say was Abu Ṭalha[§] and that each one of them prepared a *ṣā'* of food. Then, they invited Allah's Messenger, peace and blessings be upon him and his progeny. Then Allah's Messenger, peace and blessings be upon him and his progeny, got up and went to them along with everyone with him. He entered and that food was ordered to be placed in front of him. Allah's Messenger, peace and blessings be upon him and his progeny, was saying something and then said: ((Allow ten people to come)). Ten people were allowed to enter, and they ate until they were satiated. He then said: ((Allow ten people to come)). Ten people were allowed to enter, and they ate until they were satiated. The number of men there were seventy or eighty![12] His 'saying something' over the food was a supplication that placed blessing in it.

Concerning one who is compelled to eat carcass and the amount he is to eat as well as whether he can take it as provisions

The one who is compelled to eat carcass must only eat enough that will preserve his life. He can take some of it as provisions if he fears that he will not be able to find anything else. It is impermissible for him to be satiated by it; rather, he should only eat it before satiety and then not eat any more until the hunger and need returns to him as the first time.

My father related to me that his father was asked about eating carcass. "How much can one who is compelled eat?" He replied:

> He can eat as much as would suffice him, and he can take some as provision if he feared that he would not be able to find anything else to eat. When he does eat it, he is to eat to the point before satiety and not exceed the bounds.

Concerning eating clay and vinegar

It is impermissible for anyone to eat any clay that would harm him/her because it is said that it could kill one. Allah has prohibited that one's hand contribute to one's destruction. The Glorified says {**And make not thine own hands contribute to destruction**} (Q. 2:195) and {**...and slay not thyself. Verily,**

---

[11] Similarly narrated in ***Sunan Ibn Mājah, Musnad Ahmed***

[12] Similarly narrated in ***Ṣahīh al-Bukhāri, Ṣahīh Muslim, Muwaṭṭa, Musnad Abu Ya'la, Sunan at-Tirmidhi***

Allah hath been merciful unto thee} (**Q. 4:29**). Anything that assists in destruction is impermissible for the Muslim to eat.

It has been narrated that Allah's Messenger, peace and blessings be upon him and his progeny, prohibited one from eating clay. He said that it hardens the stomach and assists in killing. It has also reached us that Allah's Messenger,[13] peace and blessings be upon him and his progeny, said: ((Whoever eats clay until the point that it reaches his insides and dies—such person should not be prayed over!)).

There is no problem in eating vinegar that was made from grapes and is called 'wine vinegar.' This is because Allah simply prohibits wine and not vinegar. Plus, vinegar does not collude the intellect so that it would be forbidden wine.

My father related to me that when his father was asked about eating vinegar, he replied: "There is no problem because vinegar is not wine. Allah simply forbade wine and not vinegar."

Concerning accepting an invitation and what is encouraged regarding festive gatherings (*al-walīma*)

A believer is to accept the invitation of a believer even if it is just a morsel of food. A festive gathering for a marriage and circumcision are traditional practices of Allah's Messenger, peace and blessings be upon him and his progeny. One should not avoid them if one is able.

Regarding that, it has reached us that Allah's Messenger, peace and blessings be upon him and his progeny, said: ((If one of you is invited to a festive gathering, you should go)).[14] It is also narrated that he, peace and blessings be upon him and his progeny, said to a man from the Anŝār: ((Have a festive gathering even if it is just with one lamb)).[15]

Concerning eating with the left hand

It is impermissible for the Muslim to eat or drink with the left hand unless for a valid reason. Regarding that, it has reached us that Allah's Messenger, peace and blessings be upon him and his progeny, said: ((When any of you eat, eat with the right hand and drink with the right hand. Verily, Satan eats and drinks with his left hand)).[16]

Concerning the intestines of the disbeliever

It has reached us from Allah's Messenger, peace and blessings be upon him and his progeny: ((The believer eats in one intestine, and the disbeliever eats in seven intestines)).[17] Similarly, it has reached us that Allah's Messenger, peace and blessings be upon him and his progeny, invited a disbeliever to eat. He ordered that a sheep be milked, and the disbeliever drank the milk. He then ordered that it be milked again, and he drank the milk seven times. Afterwards, he accompanied him and embraced Islam. Allah's Messenger, peace and blessings be upon him and his progeny, ordered that a sheep be milked for him. He drank it, and then he ordered that it be milked again. However, he did not drink it this time. Allah's Messenger, peace and blessings be upon him and his progeny, said: ((The Muslim eats in one intestine, and the disbeliever eats in seven intestines)).

---

[13] Some manuscripts attribute this statement to 'Ali, upon him be peace.

[14] Similarly narrated in ***Ŝahīh al-Bukhāri, Ŝahīh Muslim, Muwatta, Sunan Abu Dāwūd, Ŝahīh Ibn Hibbān***

[15] Similarly narrated in ***Ŝahīh al-Bukhāri, Ŝahīh Muslim, Sunan at-Tirmidhi, Sunan Abu Dāwūd, Sunan Ibn Māja, Sunan al-Bayhaqi, Majmu' az-Zawā'id, Al-Mu'jam al-Kabīr, Al-Mu'jam al-Awsat***

[16] Similarly narrated in ***Ŝahīh Muslim, Sunan Ibn Mājah, Sunan ad-Dārimi, Musnad Abu Ya'la, Mušannaf 'Abdur-Razzāq, Mušannaf Ibn Abi Shayba, Bihār al-Anwār***

[17] Similarly narrated in ***Ŝahīh al-Bukhāri, Ŝahīh Muslim, Sunan Ibn Mājah, Muwatta, Sunan at-Tirmidhi, Bihār al-Anwār***

Concerning drinks

Allah's Messenger, peace and blessings be upon him and his progeny, said: ((The consumer of alcohol is like the worshipper of idols)).[18] The 'consumer' here is the one who is always found drinking it—even if it was the beginning of each year. Such person persists in his drinking without making an attempt to stop it or repent to his Lord for it.

'Alcohol' refers to anything that colludes and corrupts the intellect—whether it is from grapes, raisins, honey, dried dates, unripe dates, wheat, barley, corn or anything else. It has reached us that 'Ali b. Abi Ťālib, upon him be peace, said:

> Allah's Messenger, peace and blessings be upon him and his progeny, said: ((Paradise is forbidden for three: the consumer of alcohol, the one who constantly reminds that he gave (*al-mannān*) and the backbiter)).[19]

It has also reached us that 'Ali, upon him be peace, said that Allah's Messenger, peace and blessings be upon him and his progeny, cursed alcohol, the one who presses it, the one for whom it is pressed, the one who buys it, the one who sells it, the one who pours it, the one who drinks it, the one who consumes its price, the one who carries it and the one for whom it is carried.[20]

No one can take any benefit from alcohol in reason or concept. It is impermissible to use vinegar after it has fermented because Allah has prohibited its purchase and taking benefit from it. Since the price is prohibited—and it is simply a dirham—it would mean that it in itself is prohibited. If it is exchanged, it is even more prohibited.

As for Allah's statement **{In both is great sin, and benefit for men; but the sin of them is greater than their benefit} (Q. 2:219)**, the **{benefit}** here refers to benefit they used to get from it in the pre-Islamic era due to buying and selling it as well as from the profit they would gain. Then, Allah—the Blessed and Exalted—prohibited them from it and caused them to know that its sin is greater than the benefit of its price and profit.

My father related to me that his father was asked about vinegar that becomes intoxicating. He replied:

> The Progeny of Allah's Messenger, peace and blessings be upon him and his progeny, do not hold to the view that there is benefit in its vinegar or anything else from it. This is because Allah's Messenger, peace and blessings be upon him and his progeny, ordered them to burn it and prohibited its ownership on the day alcohol was prohibited.[21]

Concerning the intoxicants and intoxication

It has reached us that the Commander of Believers, 'Ali b. Abi Ťālib, upon him be peace, said: "Allah's Messenger, peace and blessings be upon him and his progeny, said: ((Every intoxicant is prohibited))." It has also reached us on the authority of Zayd b. 'Ali, upon him be peace, from his forefathers that the Commander of Believers, upon him be peace, came to a man who was drinking intoxicants and applied the prescribed punishment by lashing him eighty times. Also, it has reached us on the authority of Zayd b. 'Ali from his forefathers that 'Ali, upon him be peace, said: "Intoxicants are the same as alcohol."

My father related to me from his father—Abu Bakr b. Abu Uways—al-Hussein b. 'Abdullah b. Ḋumayra—his father—his grandfather that 'Ali b. Abi Ťālib used to lash the one who indulge in a small amount of intoxicants just as he lashed one who indulged in a lot.

---

[18] Similarly narrated in ***Sunan Ibn Mājah, Ŝahīh Ibn Hibbān, Al-Mu'jam al-Kabīr, Mušannaf 'Abdur-Razzāq, Mušannaf Ibn Abi Shayba, Ušūl al-Kāfi, Bihār al-Anwār***

[19] Similarly narrated in ***Sunan an-Nisā'i, Musnad Ahmed, Sunan al-Bayhaqi, Al-Mu'jam al-Kabīr, Al-Mu'jam al-Awsaṫ, Bihār al-Anwār***

[20] Similarly narrated in ***Sunan Ibn Mājah, Ŝahīh Ibn Hibbān, Sunan Abu Dāwūd, Sunan at-Tirmidhi, Al-Mu'jam al-Kabīr, Al-Mu'jam al-Awsaṫ, Musnad Abu Ya'la, Mušannaf Ibn Abi Shayba, Mušannaf 'Abdur-Razzāq***

[21] Similarly narrated in ***Ŝahīh al-Bukhāri, Sunan Abu Dāwūd, Sunan at-Tirmidhi, Sunan ad-Dārqutni, Musnad Abu Ya'la, Sunan al-Bayhaqi, Al-Mu'jam al-Kabīr***

My father related to me that his father was asked if intoxicants were considered the same as alcohol. He replied:

> It has been narrated in traditions and reports that every intoxicant is considered alcohol and that the prescribed punishment and basic concept for both are the same though they differ in name. Anything that intoxicates a lot—even a little is considered prohibited.

Human beings (*al-insān*) are simply designated as such because of their natural capacity for forgetfulness (*an-nisyān*). The heavens (*as-samā*) are designated as such due to their being elevated (*sumuwwi*), raised, exalted and lifted. Wind (*ar-rīh*) is designated as such due to the refreshment (*ar-rawh*) that is in it. The jinn are designated as such because of their being hidden (*istijnān*) from sight. Similar is the case with all things; they are not designated as such except by their meaning. For example, growth (*at-tal'a*) is designated as such due to its growth from its initial state. Likewise, fresh dates are designated as *rutab* due to its being moist (*rutūba*). Similarly, alcohol (*al-khamr*) is designated as such due to its colluding (*mukhāmara*) and corrupting the intellect. Therefore, anything that colludes and corrupts it is considered 'alcohol.' This is the case whether it be from grapes, dates, raisins, wheat or anything else.

It has reached us that the Commander of Believers, 'Ali b. Abi Ṭālib, upon him be peace, said: "That which intoxicates a lot—even a little is prohibited." Also, it has reached us on the authority of Ja'far b. Muhammad, upon him be peace, from his forefathers: "There is no dissimulation (*taqiyya*) in three things: drinking fermented date wine, wiping over the leather socks and reciting *Bismillah ar-Rahmān ar-Rahīm* audibly."

It has reached us that the Commander of Believers, upon him be peace, said: "We are prohibited from giving the greetings of peace to an intoxicated person." And it has reached us that 'Ali b. Abi Ṭālib, upon him be peace, said: "Allah's Messenger, peace and blessings be upon him and his progeny, said: ((That which intoxicates a lot—even a little is prohibited. O Allah! I do not permit intoxicants!))."[22]

My father related to me that his father was asked about the juice of raisins, honey or anything else which is boiled until two-thirds of the liquid has evaporated (*at-tilā'i*). He replied: "That which does not intoxicate in large amounts is permitted in small and large amounts. That which intoxicates in large amounts is prohibited in small amounts."

When he was asked about the third that was boiled until half of it evaporated and does not intoxicate, he replied: "This is also that which intoxicates in large amounts; therefore, it is impermissible in small amounts. That which does not intoxicate in large amounts is pure and permitted."

My father related to me that his father said:

> It has reached us that the Commander of Believers, upon him be peace, said: "I do not find anyone who drinks alcohol or intoxicating date wine except that I lashed him eighty times for the prescribed punishment."

Concerning drinking out of gold and silver containers

According to us, it is impermissible to drink out of gold and silver containers as well as gold-coated and silver-coated containers. There is no problem with eating and drinking out of as well as taking benefit from containers made out of anything else—whether copper, lead or any other container.

My father related to me that his father was asked about drinking out of copper, lead, brass or silver-coated containers. He replied: "There is no problem drinking out of any of that, but drinking out of silver-coated containers is prohibited."

---

[22] Similarly narrated in ***Musnad Imam Zayd, Sharh at-Tajrīd, Sunan Abu Dāwūd, Sunan at-Tirmidhi, Sunan Ibn Mājah, Musnad Ahmed, Mustadrak, Sunan ad-Dārqutni***

Concerning the one who drinks and wants to give some to his companions

If a man drinks water or milk or rose water or anything else and wants to give his companions to drink, then he is to pass the drinking container to the one on his right first and continue passing it round until it reaches the one to the left of the original person.

Regarding that, it has reached us that Allah's Messenger, peace and blessings be upon him and his progeny, was brought and drink and drank from it. There was a boy [i.e. 'Abdullah b. al-'Abbās] to his right and elders to his left. He asked the boy: ((Do you permit me to pass it to them?)). The boy replied: "No. By Allah, I will not give my share from you to anyone!" Then, Allah's Messenger, peace and blessings be upon him and his progeny, placed it in his hand.[23]

Concerning what has been narrated regarding the prohibition of drinking from golden and silver containers

It is impermissible to eat and drink from golden and silver containers. I do not hold to the view that one can eat or drink from any container that is adorned with them. Regarding that, it has reached us that Allah's Messenger, peace and blessings be upon him and his progeny, said: ((The one who drinks from silver or gold containers will kindle the Fire of Hell in his belly)).[24]

Allah's Messenger, peace and blessings be upon him and his progeny, prohibited blowing into drinking containers.[25] If a drinking person sees something in his drinking container he wants to blow, he should take it with his hand and remove it from his drink or pour it out from it.

Concerning the chapters related to clothing

Wearing silk is impermissible for men unless in wars. In that case, the garment should not be entirely silk but rather a silk blend with something else. It is also impermissible for them [i.e. men] to wear a gold ring. Similar has reached us from the Commander of Believers, 'Ali b. Abi Ťālib, upon him be peace, that he said: "Allah's Messenger, peace and blessings be upon him and his progeny, was gifted silk garments. He then commanded me to distribute it among the women."[26]

I do not prefer one to pray in anything made of unknown skins because I am not sure if there is anything in it made of carcass due to the corruption of era and the idiocy of its manufacturers. As for silk, there is no problem for a man to wear a garment that comprises of silk and another material other than silk as long as the non-silk material is more than the silk—this would be more than half.

My father related to me that his father was asked about men wearing silk. He replied:

> There is no problem with it as long as the garment is entirely made of it and the majority of the non-silk material exceeds the amount of silk. However, if one chooses to avoid it altogether, his avoidance of wearing such is better. This is based on what has been narrated from the Prophet, peace and blessings be upon him and his progeny.

Concerning concealing oneself in water and bathhouses

One should not uncover one's nakedness when entering the water or a bathhouse because Allah commands him to cover nakedness. Allah's Messenger, peace and blessings be upon him and his progeny, has said: ((The nakedness of a believer is prohibited from another believer)).[27] It is recommended that the one who enters it cover his nakedness also. However, it is obligatory for the one who enters it with someone to cover himself.

---

[23] Similarly narrated in ***Ŝahīh al-Bukhāri, Ŝahīh Muslim, Musnad Ahmed, Muwatta, Sunan al-Bayhaqi***

[24] Similarly narrated in ***Ŝahīh Muslim, Sunan al-Bayhaqi, Musnad Ahmed, Mušannaf 'Abdur-Razzāq, Al-Mu'jam al-Kabīr, Ŝahīh Ibn Hibbān***

[25] Similarly narrated in ***Sunan Ibn Mājah, Ŝahīh Ibn Hibbān, Al-Mu'jam al-Kabīr, Al-Mu'jam al-Awsat, Musnad Abu Ya'la, Mušannaf 'Abdur-Razzāq, Mušannaf Ibn Abi Shayba***

[26] Similarly narrated in ***Musnad Abu Ya'la, Mušannaf Ibn Abi Shayba, Mušannaf 'Abdur-Razzāq***

[27] Similarly narrated in ***Musnad Ahmed, Sunan Ibn Khuzayma, Mustadrak, Ušūl al-Kāfi, Bihār al-Anwār***

Concerning one who wears fox skin, tiger skin and other predatory animals

Everything that is prohibited to eat is similarly prohibited to wear their skins, take any benefit from them or anything else. My father related to me that when his father was asked about wearing tiger skin, he replied:

> One is to not wear the skins of that which is prohibited to eat. Similarly, one is to not wear the skins of carcass—whether tanned or not. It is impermissible for one to use the skin, horn, bone or sinews of a carcass.

There is no problem in wearing the fur of livestock unless it is from the skin of carcass. Then, it is considered impermissible and not allowed to take benefit from any of it.

Concerning a woman who weaves her hair with another's hair and concerning changing grey hair

There is no problem with a woman weaving hair extensions or wool from the hair of livestock to her hair. As for human hair, it is impermissible for her to weave any of it to her hair. Regarding the weaving of human hair extensions to her hair, it is narrated that Allah's Messenger, peace and blessings be upon him and his progeny, cursed both the one who has false hair applied and the one who applies it.[28]

There is no problem with changing grey hair; however, it is best to leave the Lord's creation as it is. It has been narrated from the Commander of Believers, 'Ali b. Abi Ťālib, upon him be peace, that he had a lot of grey hair and someone said to him "If only you would change the colour of your beard!" He replied: "I dislike altering the adornment that Allah has adorned me with!"

Concerning that which one should avoid wearing

We prefer that men not wear garments completely saturated in yellow dye nor that which is flashy with many colours unless in war. We prefer that one not wear anything made from carcass—whether sandals or leather socks. However, there is no problem with its hair, wool or fur as long as it has been washed and cleaned. This is because it is not necessary to sacrifice it properly while it can be taken from a living animal.

One should not wear anything with pig hair because it is a forbidden animal in all states, whether living or dead. That which Allah has prohibited in all cases is considered prohibited to take any benefit from it.

My father related to me that when his father was asked about wearing pig hair, he replied: "It is objectionable, and avoiding it is best." He was also asked about the hair and fur of carcass and said: "There is no problem with any of that as long as it has been washed and cleaned because it is not necessary to sacrifice it properly while it can be taken from a living animal."

My father related to me that his father was asked about wearing a garment dyed with urine stains. He replied:

> If he were to wash it until it was clean but was not able to completely remove the traces, there would be no problem with that. He would not be able to pray in it except after washing and cleaning it until it was as it was before.

My father related to me that his father was asked about the skins of carcass were tanned. He replied:

> The hadith regarding that differs. Its prohibition has been narrated from Allah's Messenger, peace and blessings be upon him and his progeny, in his letter to the Muzayna [tribe]: ((Do not take any benefit from carcass—whether its skin or sinews)).[29] It is impermissible to take benefit from its skin and sinews just as it is impermissible to benefit from its meat or anything else.

---

[28] Similarly narrated in ***Sharh at-Tajrīd, Ŝahīh al-Bukhāri, Ŝahīh Muslim, Sunan Abu Dāwūd, Sunan an-Nisā'i, Sunan Ibn Mājah, Sunan at-Tirmidhi, Musnad Ahmed, Uŝūl al-Kāfi, Bihār al-Anwār***

[29] Similarly narrated in ***Sharh at-Tajrīd, Sunan an-Nisā'i, Sunan at-Tirmidhi, Sunan Abu Dāwūd, Sunan Ibn Mājah, Musnad Ahmed, Uŝūl al-Kāfi, Bihār al-Anwār***

My father related to me that when his father was asked about wearing yellow and clothes died with safflower (*al-mu'aŝfar*), he replied:

> Men are not to wear clothes that ornately patterned similar to curtains (*al-muqarram*). It refers to that which is completely dyed with red. We do not prefer that one wears anything that is overly flashy. We do not grant dispensation for anyone to wear it unless in war.

It is impermissible to wear anything that is thin and shows the form of the body in the prayer—in the case of both women and men—unless such garment is under another article of clothing that covers it.

My father related to me that his father was asked about women wearing a thin, delicate cloth (*as-sābiriyyi*) or a Shaṫawi garment or Egyptian linen. He replied: "There is no problem as long as it adequately covers and does not show that which is forbidden to uncover as well as that display that which is impermissible for one to see. Otherwise, it is impermissible to be worn." By that, he means that it is impermissible for them to wear such in the presence of people. As for in seclusion or in the presence of their husbands, it would be no problem with that.

My father related to me that his father was asked about men wearing a ring. He replied: "There is no problem with that as long as it is not gold. That which is emphasised by the Ahl al-Bayt of the Prophet, peace and blessings be upon him and his progeny, is the wearing of rings on the right hands."

It has come in the narrated traditions that the Prophet, peace and blessings be upon him and his progeny, used to wear his ring on the right hand,[30] as well as 'Ali, al-Hasan, al-Hussein and the chosen nobles of the Prophet's Progeny. That would be considered obligatory according to me because if the Name of Allah was engraved on the ring, it should be farthest from the left hand due to the possibility of it getting soiled by excrement and the like.

My father related to me that his father was asked about children wearing golden anklets. He replied: "There is no problem with girls and women wearing such, but it is considered prohibited for male children just as it is prohibited for male adults."

Concerning allowing the sarong to drag

A woman must allow it to hang an arm's length and lower her sarong until it covers her feet and everything else. Regarding that, it has reached us from the Prophet's wife, Umm Salama that she said to the Prophet, peace and blessings be upon him and his progeny, after he mentioned the sarong: "And what about the women, O Messenger of Allah?" He replied: ((Allow it to hang a handspan)). She asked: "What if it leaves her uncovered?" He replied: ((Then the length of a forearm but no more than that)).[31]

A woman must lower her hems and cloaks until it covers her ankles and feet. This does not apply to men; the most of what men should lower their garments is the tops of their feet [i.e. their ankles].

Concerning beautifying oneself with nice clothing

The one whom Allah has provided clothing and adorned with attire should clothe oneself with it and not exhibit lack while Allah has protected him from such. Regarding that, Allah—the Blessed and Exalted—says: **{O children of Adam, take thy adornment at every place of prostration. And eat and drink but be not prodigal. For Allah loves not the prodigal} (Q. 7:31)**.

---

[30] Similarly narrated in ***Sharh at-Tajrīd, Sunan at-Tirmidhi, Sunan Abu Dāwūd, Sunan an-Nisā'i, Sunan Ibn Mājah, Musnad Ahmed, Bihār al-Anwār***

[31] Similarly narrated in ***Muwaṫṫa, Sunan an-Nisā'i, Sunan Abu Dāwūd, Ŝahīh Ibn Hibbān, Al-Mu'jam al-Kabīr, Sunan al-Bayhaqi***

The **{prodigal}** here refers to one who is wasteful against himself by spending in disobedience to Allah as well as squandering that with which Allah is pleased from the affairs where the spender is punished by Allah. Allah prohibits His slaves from wastefully spending His provision in disobedience and insolently spending of what is punishable.

As for a person spending on behalf of his brothers and feeding them while showing hospitality to the one who seeks aid, it would not be considered wasteful excess even if such person does so preferring others over oneself. How could this be considered wasteful excess? Or how could it be other than what we said regarding the prodigality of one who spends in disobedience to Allah? How could it be impermissible for one of Allah's slaves who loves Him to do that which Allah has granted Him the opportunity to do and praised him for it?

That is based on Allah's statement regarding the Anŝār when they preferred others to themselves and used their provisions to nourish others. They took them in despite the poverty of their families and children as well as spent their wealth on those who emigrated to them. Then Allah says: **{...and they give preferring others to themselves even though they were in poverty. And whosoever is saved from the stinginess of his soul—they shall be the successful!}** (Q. 59:9). He therefore praised them for spending in obedience to Him and showed gratitude to them despite their poverty and the poverty of their families, as well as for their sacrifice for others. There was no censure of their actions.

And regarding that is what He says in praise of Muhammad's Progeny due to their sacrificing for others over themselves as well as for patience in hunger, feeding the needy, the orphan and the freed prisoner for the sake (lit. "Face") of Allah. The Glorified and Exalted says regarding that: **{...and they feed out of His love the needy and the orphan and the prisoner [saying:] "We simply feed thee for the Countenance of Allah. We desire not from thee recompense or thanks! We simply fear from our Lord the Day of frowning and distress!" Therefore, Allah hath warded off from them the evil of that Day and hath bestowed upon them brightness and joy. And He hath rewarded them—due to their patience—with a garden and silk}** (Q. 76:8-12).

Then the Glorified connects their virtues in that as well as what He has given them in the Surah to His statement: **{Verily, We hath revealed unto thee a revealed Qur'an}** (Q. 76:23). Regarding that and the like is what Allah has made clear—All praise is due to Allah for those who whom He has made it clear! And it is that the one who spends from what the Lord of creation has given him is not to be considered wastefully excessive. Rather, such person who spends is considered virtuous and righteous in the judgement of the Most-Wise.

If one were to say out of miserliness or slanderous transgression that he may go out and spend from that on those who do not deserve it, it is said to him that if the recipient does not deserve it, the giver is deserving to do good to his people and others. He would therefore observe what is obligatory on him to his people. He would perform that which he is obligated to for the people [i.e. those who deserve it] and provide from what is given to other than those [who deserve it] from him and make them more favourable to his religion.

Allah's Messenger, peace and blessings be upon him and his progeny, used to do that and enjoin others to do so. Regarding that, he said: ((One should do favours for one's people and those who are not from his people. If it makes it to those who deserve it, they are most deserving of it. If it makes it to those who do not, they can share in a part of it.[32] He, peace and blessings be upon him and his progeny, used to feed the Jews and give them gifts while they were disbelievers and rejecters of the truth he came with! He is the best of role models for all the believers, as Allah—the Mighty and Majestic—says: **{Verily there is for thee in Allah's Messenger a great model for the one who hopes for Allah and the Last Day}** (Q. 33:21).

[32] Similarly narrated in ***Bihār al-Anwār***

Therefore, all of the above are clear proofs that **{prodigality}** simply refers to that for which people are punished in respect to spending in excess and disobedience. It does not refer to those acts of excellence for which Allah shows appreciation.

The one who interprets the verse contrary to what we say does not guard himself from stinginess as if to exempt himself from the blame from his Lord. Rather, he distorts the interpretation and acts contrary by restraining his wealth, eating alone, preventing his assistance as well as depriving his guests and neighbours. Then, he considers himself as correct in doing such and assumes the one who does contrary to him to be ignorant and uncouth. Such person and those like him are as His Lord says: **{Say: "Shall we inform thee as to who are the greatest losers? They are those whose efforts go astray in the life of this world yet imagine that they are doing good works!"} (Q. 18:103-104)**.

Concerning clothing as well as which clothing and other things are prohibited to wear

Allah's Messenger, peace and blessings be upon him and his progeny, prohibited a man from wrapping one garment over one of his shoulders and that he sits with his legs drawn up with only one garment so that there is nothing covering his private parts.[33] He also prohibited one walking in one sandal,[34] reciting Qur'an while bowing, wearing gold rings as well as wearing clothes died with safflower or any other ornately dyed clothing for men unless they do so among their families.

Allah's Messenger, peace and blessings be upon him and his progeny, simply prohibited wrapping the garment over one shoulder because doing so would uncover one's private parts and upper thighs. Those Bedouins who were uncouth used to dress this way as well as the obscene people from the lower villages.

---

[33] Similarly narrated in ***Ŝahīh al-Bukhāri, Ŝahīh Muslim, Muwatta, Sunan Abu Dāwūd, Sunan at-Tirmidhi***

[34] Similarly narrated in ***Ŝahīh Muslim, Muwatta, Sunan an-Nisā`i, Sunan Abu Dāwūd, Sunan at-Tirmidhi, Sunan Ibn Mājah, Musnad Ahmed, Bihār al-Anwār***

The Book of Bequests

In the Name of Allah, the Most Gracious, the Most Merciful...

Concerning what the living can do on the dead's behalf, such as Hajj, manumission, charity and other acts of righteousness

This has come in narrated reports, and there is disagreement regarding it. It has been narrated that one can do such on one's behalf. Allah knows best regarding the truthfulness of what was narrated about it.

The best view is that it is authentic and the view that I hold to is that everything that the living dispenses with on behalf of the dead is for the living instead of the dead. This is because righteousness is for the righteous, manumission is for the manumitter and the Hajj pilgrimage is for the pilgrim. Every good thing one does is only a means of reward for such person except in the case of a dead person who bequests it or commands it or requests it from a close relative. If that is the case, Allah will reward such person.

It is encouraged that Muslims establish in their bequests that which I was encouraged to establish in my bequest. I ordered my family to do the same. Whoever would like Allah to grant him every good when writing his bequest, he says:

> In the Name of Allah, the Most Merciful the Most Gracious. All praise is due to Allah, the Lord of creation! May Allah send prayers upon Prophet Muhammad and his Pure Ahl al-Bayt! A testimony from Allah witnessed by Yahya b. al-Hussein b. al-Qāsim. He bears witness to that upon which Allah bears witness for himself. He bears witness **{that there is no god save He, and so do the Angels and the possessors of knowledge, as well as that He is the Maintainer of justice. There is no god save He, the Mighty, the All-Wise} (Q. 3:18)**. O Allah, it is from You and to You and in Your grasp and Your power that Your slave and the son of Your slave, this is what Yahya b. al-Hussein bequests.
>
> He bequests that he bears witness that there is no god but Allah, the One with whom is no partner. And he bears witness that Muhammad was his Slave and Messenger that He sent **{with guidance and the religion of truth that He may cause it to prevail over all religion though the idolaters may hate it} (Q. 9:33)** and **{to warn whosoever lives and that the word may be fulfilled against the disbelievers} (Q. 36:70)**. And he bears witness that the Commander of Believers, 'Ali b. Abi Ťālib, upon him be peace, was the brother of Your Messenger and Your Guardian as well as the Establisher of Your truth after Your Messenger, the one who called to Your obedience, the one who struggled against those who deviated from Your call and from following the sunnah of Your Prophet, the one who sacrificed his soul and wealth for You, the one who unsheathed his sword for nothing less than Your right and command and in defence of Your Prophet, the one who was patient for Your sake, the one who persevered in Your obedience—whether in good days or bad days and whether in difficulty or ease. He was the most preferred of people to You and Your Messenger as well as the greatest of them in adhering to Your command and path. By means of his association and mutual affection as well as the association of those who associate with him and opposition to those who oppose him, he brings such person near to You. He [i.e. Yahya b. al-Hussein] bears witness that he [i.e. 'Ali] was the most deserving to take the place of Your Messenger out of all Your creation and that he was most deserving to be Your caliph after him [i.e. the Prophet] out of all Your slaves. You chose him for them and mandated on them obedience to him after Your Messenger **{...that those who perish would have perished upon evidence and those who live would have lived upon evidence. Verily, Allah is All-Hearing, All-Knowing} (Q. 8:42)**.
>
> O Allah! I call You to witness, O Lord—and You are sufficient as witness!—as well as the bearers of Your Divine Throne, the people of Your heavens and earth and those whom You created that You are Allah, the One with whom is no other god but You alone, the One without

partners. I also call You to witness that Muhammad is Your slave and Messenger, the Hour is undoubtedly coming, and that Allah will resurrect the dead from the graves.

I call You to witness that You are One and eternal and that You do not beget nor are You begotten and that there is no equal to You; You have no likeness or equivalent, neither do You have a rival nor one on par with You (*'adīl*). There is nothing like You nor does anything share a likeness with You. You are the All-Hearing and All-Seeing. You are not encompassed by directions or hidden by the seas, nor are secrets concealed from You. The heavens and earths cannot strike a glance at You, neither can You be imagined by the restriction of the imaginers. You cannot be indicated by the indicators except by that which You indicate Yourself. This is because You are the Glorified, the One, the Majestic, and creation is the only indicator of You.

You do not decree corruption, nor do You force acts of disobedience upon the slaves; You are free of their actions. Rather, You decree the good and command towards it as well as prohibit sin and rebellion; You punish for it. You affirm the reality of the Divine Threat and Divine Promise, and You are Most Gracious and Most Merciful towards Your slaves.

I say about You that which You have mentioned regarding Divine Justice and Divine Oneness as well as the affirmation of the Divine Threat and Divine Promise. My statement is with the statement of the one who says similar, and it is sufficient against the one who rejects its acceptance. There is no strength or power except by Allah, the Mighty and Great!

O Allah! Whoever bears witness to that which I bear witness should write his testimony along with mine. However, whoever objects should write his testimony in the place of mine and make for me a contract. On that Day I will meet You alone, and You do not act contrary to Your promise!

Then, Yahya b. al-Hussein bequests—after bearing witness to Allah from the testimony of truth to every parent and child who is connected to him and knows him as well as those who do not know him—that one has consciousness of Allah, the One without partners. He also bequests that one obeys Him and struggle for His sake in both ease and difficulty as well as fear Him and have a conscious awareness (*al-marāqaba*) of Him. For verily, He knows the secret and hidden, and He knows the treachery of the eyes and what the breasts conceal. He bequests that one promotes the greater good and prevents oppression and vice as well as observes Allah's affair.

Whoever knows that he has the right to establish Allah's command, there are preconditions that are obligatory upon him regarding the establishment and imamate. Among them are religiosity, scrupulousness, knowledge of what Allah has permitted and prohibited in the Book, forbearance, bravery, generosity, mercy and compassion for his subjects, inspector of their affairs yet refraining from monopolising them and allowing them to observe their affairs that Allah has appointed over them, rightly taking from their possessions that which Allah has commanded and spending it based on its intended purpose, establisher of His judgements and prescribed punishments as well as one who has the firm resolution to worship His Lord. He should therefore establish his obligations for Allah as well as call people to himself and jihad against His enemies. He must call to command the good and prohibit the evil. He must not tire, wear out or fall short in this because this is an obligation of Allah on him that he cannot abandon. Neither is it permissible for him to reject that which is obligatory upon him whether in the state of fear or safety, prosperity or distress.

Whoever does not have firm resolution nor completes every affair—he should fear his Lord and not enter in any of this because it does not belong to him. Let him observe the enemies of Allah and prepare his weapons and that which he is able to prepare, and let him wait for Allah to establish a proof (*hujja*) from the Ahl al-Bayt of His Prophet who has these conditions. He should rise with him and be willing to sacrifice himself and his wealth for him. For that is the closest thing that brings him to the Most Gracious and assists him in fleeing from the Hellfire.

And whoever dies among the believers waiting for that will die a pious martyr, who will be honoured by Allah.

Then, Yahya b. al-Hussein asks his parents, children and children's children to the Day of Judgement, brothers, paternal uncles, paternal cousins, everyone who acknowledges his loyalty, partisans, people of mutual affection as well as all who loves righteousness or at least, those who draw close to Allah who have a relationship with him during his lifetime and after his death—to gift a donation on his behalf that would be accepted from them in his lifetime and after his death in what they are able. They [i.e. those things to be gifted on his behalf] include an act of righteousness, a gift, the maintenance of family ties, the manumission of a righteous believing slave from whom nothing but good is known and no accusation exists, any possible expiations for their oaths or any possible charity of clothing, food, money or water to a praiseworthy citizen. He asks them to not despise him for anything between a speck and more because Allah accepts little but grants much. Therefore, whoever is able to do what Yahya b. al-Hussein asked—whether a little or a lot, let him say when he does such on his behalf: "This is what Yahya b. al-Hussein, may Allah have mercy on him, ordered. I have gifted and spent it on his behalf as he ordered and requested me based on its intended purpose by which he draws closer to Allah, the Mighty and Majestic. O Allah, benefit him by that and grant him his desire! And allow him to attain his hope in the place of his afterlife! You are the Mighty, the All-Wise!"

Yahya b. al-Hussein does not choose any of those who love righteousness among his designated parents, children, children's children to the Day of Judgement whose lineage remains to him, brothers, paternal uncles, paternal cousins, all his relatives, partisans and people of mutual affection except the most righteous and pure.

Yahya b. al-Hussein asks those he designated and sought righteousness to—if Allah causes such person to reach the appearance of a just imam—to assist him in establishing the obligations of Allah and stand with him, if Allah wills. He asks that one supplicates for him, asking for divine mercy, forgiveness, pleasure, acceptance and good. Yahya b. al-Hussein asks those men who are present to partner with him in standing with the imam, fighting jihad with him, defending him, helping him inspire fear to the oppressors and doing good to the believers.

Then Yahya b. al-Hussein asks Allah to grant reward to the one who does what he has asked. He also asks Allah to bestow upon such person the best of bestowals, for He is the Most Nigh and Responder to supplication. **{Our Lord, grant us good in this world and good in the hereafter, and protect us from the punishment of the Hellfire!}** (**Q. 2:201**). As Allah wills! There is no power or strength except by Allah, the Mighty and the Great! **{And sufficient for us is Allah! How excellent is He as a Protector!}** (**Q. 3:173**). **{How excellent is He as a Master! How excellent is He as a Helper!}** (**Q. 8:40**).

Then, he bequeathes a bequest after that as he likes regarding his wealth, his children and all his things. He does not neglect to give what he wants from his fortune. He may present it in front of him and save it for a day when he needs it and not be extravagant in his bequest. He should remember the one from his family who is left behind, and only a third of what he left is permissible for such person. Anything more than that is for him, and the statement and matter regarding that is permissible for him.

Concerning the bequest of the sick, pregnant and those engaged in fighting

The sick person in the initial stages of sickness should manumit a slave and give a gift from his wealth as he likes. He should not—at the point that his sickness intensifies—give a third of his wealth. If he were to give a third, the matter of the third would then go to his heirs. They can permit it for him if they want, or they can redistribute it if they want.

Similar is the case for the pregnant woman. She would be permitted to do so at the initial stages of her pregnancy if she had the first full-term pregnancy from the time she gave birth, which would be six months. That is based on the statement of Allah, the Exalted: **{…and she bore him and weaned him for thirty months…} (Q. 46:15)**. The weaning is two lunar years based on the statement of Allah, the Glorified: **{And the mothers shall suckle their children for two whole years for those who desire to complete the suckling} (Q. 2:233)**.

That which is excess over the two lunar years is less than a full pregnancy in which a woman can give birth to her child completely, which is six months. This is because two lunar years is twenty-four months, and the remaining portion is the six months that Allah mentions. If a woman has exceeded six months, it is impermissible for her to allocate anything more than a third of her money unless the heirs permit such after her death. They will have the choice after she dies: they can permit more than a third to be given based on her request, or they can redistribute the third.

Similar is the case with a person in a military campaign. He can do what he wants with his wealth as long as he is not actively engaged with the enemy or marching to fight. If he marched to fight and approached the opposing forces of men and lives were being lost while the battle heated up and the peers engaged in battle, he would have no right to bequest more than a third of his wealth. If he were to bequest more than that, his heirs would have the choice: they can permit it if they want, or they can redistribute the third.

Concerning the bequest to the heir

Allah's Messenger, peace and blessings be upon him and his progeny, passed the judgement that there is no bequest to one heir.[1] This is authentic according to me because it is the closest to right guidance and truth as well as furthest from oppression and falsehood. This is because he, peace and blessings be upon him and his progeny, had prevented a man from donating a donation to one son without the rest of his sons. There is no disagreement regarding this narration. The bequest is not more substantiated than a donation; therefore, it is to not be done without him.

Allah's Messenger, peace and blessings be upon him and his progeny, simply meant by his statement ((There is no bequest to one heir)) that all heirs are to be considered the same and that each heir must be accounted in the inheritance as per Allah's judgement. As for the third, it is for him to bequest it to anyone he wants among his near or distant relative. If the bequest is permissible for the distant relative, the near relative is more deserving of it.

Allah's Messenger, peace and blessings be upon him and his progeny, is simply prohibiting one from bequeathing his property to some of the heirs and not others. That is in the case when it exceeds a third. As for a third of one's property, it would be permissible for him to do that and carry out its judgement. He would be able to bequeath it to whichever near or distant relative he wants because Allah has allowed him to bequeath it to whomever he wants.

Maintaining near family ties is dearer to Allah than maintaining distant ties. Allah's Messenger, peace and blessings be upon him and his progeny, commanded that family ties be maintained in order to affirm them and urge one to increase in such. It is considered more appropriate than for him to prohibit such, so one cannot derive that from his statement: ((There is no bequest to one heir)). It would only be permissible according to us when it does not exceed a third of his property as we have explained.

An objector may say that it would also be impermissible for one to bequeath to a non-heir with other than a third; otherwise, what is the meaning of his statement ((There is no bequest to one heir))? To that we reply by saying that the near relative differs from the distant stranger. For example, there is no fear of severing family ties with a distant stranger if one does not bequest a third to such person. However, if one were to bequest more than a third without the permission of the near relative, there could be a fear of estrangement and severing family ties between them. Indeed, this is without a doubt!

---

[1] Similarly narrated in ***Sunan Abu Dāwūd, Sunan at-Tirmidhi, Sunan an-Nisā'i, Sunan Ibn Mājah, Musnad Ahmed, Sunan al-Bayhaqi, Al-Mu'jam al-Kabīr***

Therefore, Allah's Messenger, peace and blessings be upon him and his progeny, prohibited that in the case of near relatives specifically in that it would be prevented from the Muslims out of fear that there would severance between them as we mentioned. Therefore, he emphasised it to them for that reason. The same fear would not apply to the unrelated stranger, and he would not be as was mentioned. The third is for the deceased, and no one else can claim it—whether near relative or distant. This is the difference between what the questioner asked and the reply to it. And may Allah bring agreement to the good!

If the deceased sought permission regarding inheritance in his bequest to bequeath to his heirs or non-heirs more than a third and they permit him to do so, he would be allowed to do so to the amount that they permitted for him. It would not be permissible for them to redistribute it after his death. Others have said that it is impermissible; however, we do not acknowledge such statement. If some were to allow him to do so and some object, it would be permissible to the amount of the share for the one who allowed it in the bequest.

Concerning the bequest

If a man were to bequeath something to another man in his bequest and it was accepted but then desired to be exempted from it during his lifetime and before his death, that would be considered permissible for him. However, if it was accepted during his lifetime and he desired to be exempted from it after such, it would not be permissible for him to do so.

Similarly, if the deceased were to bequeath something to an absent person and the latter rejected the bequest after having reached him, it would be permissible for him to do. However, if it were accepted when it reached him and he desired to be exempted from it after that, it would be impermissible for him to do so.

Whoever bequeaths something by a bequest, it is permissible for him to negate it, affirm it, invalidate it, add to it and subtract from it. All of such would be considered permissible for him if he does such in his bequest.

Whenever a man bequeathed a bequest to another man and the one who was bequeathed died before the one who bequeathed, it is not for the heir of the bequeathed person to carry out the bequest. It would return to the heirs of the one who bequeathed. The bequest of the *dhimmi* to the Muslims is permissible, and the bequest of the Muslims to the *dhimmi* is permissible.

Concerning the deceased's gesturing with his head in the bequest

If man is close to death and is mute and he is asked by some of his heirs "O so-n-so, do you want to manumit your slave, so-n-so?" and he gestures 'Yes' with his head, he would be asked "Do you confirm such and such from your property?" He would then indicate "Yes."

It has been narrated that al-Hasan and al-Hussein, upon them be peace, did that with Umāma bt. Abil-'Ās b. ar-Rabi' al-Umawi§ and her mother, Zaynab,§ the daughter of Allah's Messenger, peace and blessings be upon him and his progeny. 'Ali b. Abi Ťālib, upon him be peace, married her after the death of Fātima, the daughter of Allah's Messenger, peace and blessings be upon him and his progeny. That is because Fātima, the daughter of Allah's Messenger, peace and blessings be upon him and his progeny, asked him to marry her while she was the daughter of her sister. [Al-Hasan and al-Hussein asked her] and she then gestured 'Yes' with her head, and they accepted that and carried it out.

And I do not think that they, may Allah bless them both, did that when he proposed to her at that time, but we are certain that she was of sound mind. If that is the case, it is sound and permissible for one to gesture.

Concerning the act of bequeathing

If a man were to bequeath another man or three absent men and one of them accept it while the other two reject it when it reached them, the acceptor would be considered the executor of all the wealth and would take responsibility of the entire bequest in place of them all.

If one were bequeathed to give a woman in marriage from the one he bequeathed, it would be considered permissible if she does not have a paternal guardian. However, if she has a guardian, it would be impermissible for one to bequeathed that without the permission and authorisation of her guardian.

And if a man bequeathed two men to his small son and he owes people debts and deposits, then there is no problem with one of the executors doing that if he is a witness and the owner is absent. Whatever he does from taking something from his possession or giving something to its owner, it is considered permissible for him if he did not transgress the right and did not allow what is necessary. Others have said that he is responsible for what was discharged without the owner's permission; however, we do hold to that view or advocate it.

Whether the heirs are minors or adults, it is permissible for the executors to sell that which was for the deceased and carry out the bequest except that which is left as commodity, such as immovable property, estate and slaves. Then it does not take place except by the permission of the adult heirs.

If the young heirs had immovable property they inherited from their mother and then their father died and bequeathed to them an executor, the executor would not be allowed to sell anything from that nor take it out of their property. This is because their father did not have the right to sell it, so how can the executor appointed by their father do so? He must be careful in his building structures on it and strive to reform it so that his yields return to them and make them independent of selling it. And if their estates differ and the stream of their fruits is cut off from them and the executor fears their destruction, then there is no problem with reviving them using a portion of their wealth with goodness as long as it is necessary and needed.

Concerning the man who bequeaths some of his wealth to another man

If a man were to bequeath an entire third of his wealth to another man—whether in hard cash or immovable property or anything else, his executor would be a partner with them in that wealth, whether hard cash or immovable property. He would share with them the third with it being equally distributed among them. That which is not possible to be equally distributed shall be sold and then redistributed among them or it can be left as is while some of them can take its value and the executor takes his right from that which the deceased left whether it is little or a lot.

The heirs do not have the right to give the executor hard cash in the place of immovable property nor immovable property in the place of hard cash unless he wants that. Therefore, he can sell them his right to sell for a price that he is satisfied with, and he takes it in cash. Or he can buy the immovable property from them with his share of the cash. If he wants, that would be permissible for him and they would be obligated to buy and sell from him.

And if he bequeathed to him money of known weight or number, then he is their partner in what is weighed and counted from the amount and not a partner in the immovable properties. They have to sell from it until the bequeathed money is fulfilled by the deceased.

Concerning the bequest of the child, idiot, insane and weakling

Every bequest that is bequeathed from someone's wealth is permissible except in the case that one is devoid of intellect, such as a child of five, six, seven or below ten years old. Other examples include the insane who does not recover or the idiot who does not recover his senses. As for the insane and idiot who recovers in time, they can be left a bequest in the time that they recover.

The Muslims are to not bequeath more than a third of their wealth. Regarding that, it is been narrated that a man asked Allah's Messenger, peace and blessings be upon him and his progeny, whether he can bequeath a two-thirds of his wealth. He replied: ((No)). He then asked: "What about half?" He replied: ((No)). He then asked: "What about a third?" He replied: ((A third is the most that you can give. To leave your heirs rich is better than to leave them poor and begging from people. You would never incur an expense seeking Allah's Countenance but that you would be rewarded for it)).[2]

[2] Similarly narrated in ***Ŝahīh al-Bukhāri, Ŝahīh Muslim, Sunan an-Nisā'i, Sunan Ibn Mājah, Ŝahīh Ibn Hibbān, Musnad abu Ya'la, Musnad al-Bazzār, Mušannaf 'Abdur-Razzāq***

The Book of the Contract of Indentureship, Slaves Freed by Their Master's Death, Manumission, the *Umm Walad* and the Like

In the Name of Allah, the Most Gracious, the Most Merciful...

Concerning the contract of indentureship and its mention in the Book

Allah—the Mighty and Majestic—says: {**...and if any amongst those whom thy right hand possesses seek a writ, write a writ for them if ye see in them goodness and bestow upon them with some of the wealth that Allah hath bestowed upon thee**} (Q. 24:33).

Allah permits that a contract of indentureship be written for one in whom goodness is known, who seeks such contract from owners. The term {**goodness**} here refers to righteousness, God-consciousness, excellence, religiosity, Islam, gnosis of Allah, certainty and obedience to the one who contracts him. The term {**writ**} is an agreement reached by the slave and master which is known and paid in instalments to a known time, month, two months, two years. Every instalment is such-and-such dinar according to what they agreed upon and wrote down in the contract as stipulated by the master upon the labourer. If he is unable, he is not obligated to accept it, and such person would return to slavery.

He would have to stipulate that his custodianship and the custodianship of his slave with a known stipulation. When it is agreed upon as thus and the two of them record it as thus, the slave will be considered an indentured labourer who can engage in any work he wants and can do what he likes. He would have to observe that which was stipulated in instalments. Once he completes that, he is considered free and his custodianship shall be for his master if that was stipulated. However, if he is unable to meet the demands in his contract, such person will return to slavery. That which he took from his master would return to his master, and nothing would go to him unless he [i.e. the master] permitted.

Similar is the case with the slave woman also. If a contract of indentureship is made for a male or female, it is contracted on such person's behalf as well as that of his/her offspring. They would be considered the same as the parent: when such person is considered manumitted, they would be considered manumitted also. If he is enslaved, they would be considered enslaved also.

The one born as offspring to one for whom a contract of indentureship was written will not have to observe any portion of it on their own behalf nor is it upon their mother to observe it on their behalf. They would have to observe it until their mother has a contract of indentureship written for them. Then, they will be considered manumitted. Otherwise, they would be considered enslaved if she was unable to observe that which is obligatory upon her.

If the person who was contracted for indentureship were to be killed or have a limb severed, the indemnity would be based on the amount observed from his contract and the remaining value of it.

Similar is the case with all of the prescribed punishments when they are binding. That is the statement of the Commander of Believers, 'Ali b. Abi Ṭālib, upon him be peace. If his master who has a contract of indentureship written were to die, it is not for his heirs to seek out his contract of indentureship. He would be in the same situation he would have been with his master until he is incapable or is paid indemnity.

Concerning the one under the contract of indentureship

If the one who is contracted with indentureship sought out a reduction or resignation in slavery without any disadvantage to his master nor any reason that may occur, such would be considered permissible. If he were returned to the state of slavery, everything that he used to aid himself in his indentureship that is taken from him would be referred to the imam of the Muslims and the rest of the Muslims. That which he uses in the state of slavery is impermissible for him to use or from which take benefit. If the slave were to earn anything by his hand and not utilise it in the state of his emancipation, it would be considered permissible for his master to take it and derive benefit from it because he and what he owns belong to his master.

Concerning the contract of indentureship

I do not hold to the view that the man who forms a contract of indentureship with his slave woman can have intercourse with her under such contract. If he were to approach her for such, he would have to pay the dowry of one similar to herself. While she is under the contract of indentureship, he is exempted from the prescribed punishment if he were to have done so out of ignorance or ambiguously.

If she is unable [to fulfil the preconditions of the contract], she returns to the state of slavery. And everything that she earned or utilised from Allah's property in the state of her emancipation shall not belong to him, nor would it be permissible for him to take it.

If he wants to marry her off to someone after she has observed a sound marriage, it must be with her permission and approval along with a dowry and two witnesses. He would be considered her guardian after her permits her to marry.

If a man were to have intercourse with his indentured labourer with or without her permission while ignorant of what is incumbent in that, she would have the choice. She can remain in that indentureship if she wants or nullify it if she wants. Similarly, if she were to give birth from him during her contract of indentureship, she has the choice. She can remain in that indentureship if she wants or nullify it if she wants. If she chooses to remain in the indentureship, she would be entitled to the dowry due to his having intercourse with her. If she nullified the indentureship, her master would not be obligated to give her the dowry since she was his slave woman.

If an indentured labourer were to buy an *umm walad* and she gave birth from him and he died while there remained more time in his contract, the situation of the *umm walad* and her children would be the same. If she were to observe the remainder of the contract on her master's behalf or some of the children observed it on her behalf, she would be considered manumitted as well as her children. If she does not or they do not observe it, she would return to slavery as well as them. Consequently, their father's master would not be able to return them or their mother to slavery unless they had not observed the remainder of the deceased's contract.

If some of them were to say "We prefer to remain in slavery and not observe the remainder of the contract" and others were to say "We prefer to observe the contract and not remain in slavery," those who observe more than their father's contract would be considered manumitted as well as their siblings and mother based upon their observance of extra.

If a man were to say to his slave "You will be free if you pay me a hundred dinar" or "You will be free when you pay me one hundred dinars" and he pays him fifty or sixty but then his master died, the slave would then belong to his master's heirs. They would not be obligated to take the remainder of the amount and manumit him because his master simply stipulated that the amount be paid, and it was less. He had not paid him the entire amount during his lifetime. Therefore, the precondition was nullified. Its judgement is not the same as the judgement of the indentureship, nor can the one with intellect consider them to be equal.

Concerning the slave freed upon his master's death and manumission in health and illness

If a sick man were to decree that his slave is free upon his death—whether male or female slave—the latter would be free upon his master's death. If he decided to sell him before his death, he would be free to do so. If she were a female slave, he would be free to have intercourse with her.

If the master were to die, the slave freed upon his master's death would take effect from a third [i.e. of the master's property]. He can form a contract of indentureship or manumit him due to an expiation of a broken oath or for an unlawful pronouncement.

If a man manumitted a slave or slaves while he was sick and he has property that they can extract from a third, that manumission would be considered permissible. If he does not have property other than them, it would be permissible for his heirs to manumit them. If they refuse to manumit a third of each and each has worked a third of his value, they would be manumitted even if he has recovered from his illness.

Concerning manumission

If a man were to say "The first that you give birth to will be free" and she gives birth to twins, both would be considered manumitted. This is because he simply meant the first to be born from the womb. That would be based on his intention without his being aware that she would give birth to twins. He simply assumed that she would give birth to one similar to what is done by the majority of people. That was not specifically designated, and the first was not made an exception from twins since both were born from the same womb.

Concerning a slave that is owned by two people and one of them manumitted his share

If there is a slave owned by two people and one of them manumits him with the permission of his partner, he would not have anything over the other. The manumitter would not be responsible for his partner's property because he was manumitted by his permission, and it is impermissible for the one who has ownership to take such with his own property because he is not a partner with Allah, but the slave was considered half his value.

If the partner were to manumit the slave without his partner's permission, the manumitter would be responsible for half the value of the slave if he were in a state of financial ease. If he were in straitened circumstances, the slave would have to work to the extent of half his value without any excess.

If two men owned a child slave and one of them manumitted half and the other did not, the boy would remain a slave until he reaches maturity. The judgement of such is that he is to continue working for the one who still owns half of him to the extent of half his value while he was a child during the time that half of him was manumitted. If the partner that manumitted him were in straitened circumstances, the responsibility shall be on his partner for half the slave's value while he was a child during the time that half of him was manumitted.

If a man were to say to his male and female slaves while they are married "Your wife will be free if she gives birth to a girl, and you will be free if she gives birth to a boy," the father is considered manumitted if she gives birth to a boy and the mother is considered manumitted if she gives birth to a girl. If she were to give birth to male and female twins with the boy coming first and then the girl afterwards, the father would be considered manumitted from the time the boy was born and the mother would be considered manumitted from the time the girl is born. Although the male and female slaves would be considered free, their children would be considered slaves.

If she were to give birth to the girl first and then the boy, the male slave as well as the female slave and the boy would be considered manumitted. However, the girl would still be considered a slave. This is the case because after the girl was born, the female slave is considered manumitted and becomes free. Then, when she gives birth to the boy while she is free, he is considered free also as well as the father due to the stipulation of their master is. The boy is considered free because the mother gave birth to him while she was declared manumitted and free; this is because a free woman can only give birth to a free baby. That which a slave woman gives birth to is considered a slave, and that which a free woman gives birth to is considered free.

If a man were to say to his slave "Serve my offspring in their estate for ten years and when the ten years is complete, you will be considered free" and his offspring sell their estate after a year or two, he [i.e. the slave] would have to serve them in other than their estate for the completion of the ten years. Once the ten years have elapsed, he would then be considered manumitted.[1]

If some of his offspring were to say "I exempt you from my service which my father obligated upon you" and others were to say "I do not exempt you from it," he would be obligated to serve those who had not exempted him from service for each year to the extent of their share. And he would be exempted from the service of those who exempted him to the extent of their share. However, he should not count them by years so that he subtracts from the ten years by calculating those that were given to him because he was stipulated to serve ten years and because his master made his manumission after ten years. He made the completion of such a stipulation for his manumission, and he would therefore not be manumitted in any time less than that which his master appointed for him.

This is similar to a person who says to his slave "You will be considered free at the head of the year" or "…at the head of two years" or more. The slave would be considered a slave till that time. Once that time has come, he would be considered manumitted since the stipulation was fulfilled. It is for that reason that we hold to the view that the slave who was stipulated for ten years must serve his master's offspring for each year to the extent of their share as they like.

If he [i.e. the master] had six offspring and three of them exempt him from service, he would have to serve the remaining three halves of each year until he completed ten years. He would then be considered manumitted since the stipulated time that his master appointed has been fulfilled and the appointed time has elapsed.

Concerning a slave that is manumitted and joins the disbelievers as an apostate but then is acquired as war booty by the Muslims

If a slave—Byzantine or otherwise—joins the disbelievers as an apostate but then is acquired as war booty by the Muslims after having been acquired by the idolaters, his matter should be considered. If at the time of his manumission he were a Muslim or embraced Islam after being manumitted and then returned to the domain of war as an apostate and was acquired, he would be called to repentance. If he were to repent, he would be left alone. If he objects, he is to be put to death. However, if at the time of his manumission he left the domain of Islam as a disbeliever without having embraced Islam, he would be considered a slave that can be distributed as war booty; his manumission would not be considered. Similar has reached us from the Commander of Believers, 'Ali b. Abi Ṫālib, upon him be peace, that he gave such judgement.

Concerning a slave who is sold while owing a debt

If a man sells a slave with a debt, the debt is to be included in his price. It would be upon the seller to repay it because he [i.e. the slave] acquired a debt while under his ownership. It would therefore be incumbent for the owner to repay it.

---

[1] Al-Hādi was asked a similar question in ***Al-Muntakhab***.

> I asked him about a man who said to his slave: 'If you serve my child for many days, you will be manumitted.' "When would he be considered manumitted?" He replied: "He would be considered manumitted when he serves him for a year. This is because we consider the minimum number of days, which is three. Then, we consider the maximum number of days, which are multiples of a few; such days are designated as many. Such is possible from ten days to one hundred, two hundred, three hundred days, more or less. We therefore consider that the completion of days would be the completion of an entire year. This is because the completion of what is termed 'many days' would be a year due to the fact that every year has a completion of its days. Afterwards, another year begins. Therefore, every year has known months and numbered days. This is the best view that we hold to regarding it."

Concerning claim of liability (*'uhda*) for a runaway slave

It has reached us from the Commander of Believers, 'Ali b. Abi Ṭālib, upon him be peace, that he used to say: "There is no claim of liability in the case of a runaway slave unless otherwise stipulated by the purchaser."

The meaning of his statement "There is no claim of liability in the case of a runaway slave" is that there is no liability on a runaway slave during the days that he is designated as such except if it was stated as a precondition by the buyer. The precondition could be: "I will take responsibility after three days—more or less—during his escape. If he runs away within that time, it will be your responsibility. If he runs away after that time, you will be free of responsibility."

However, if one were to not make a stipulation and purchase him while knowing that he is a runaway slave and the latter runs away from him the same day or after that day and the purchase was concluded with the seller taking the price and they separated, there would be no liability on the seller.

Concerning the indentured labourer and manumitted slave left behind by their master without any other property except them

If a man died and left behind an indentured labourer or a slave that he manumitted during his illness and had not left behind a debt, the manumitted slave would be considered free and the indentured labourer would go to his [the deceased's] heirs with two-thirds his value. If they do not allow his manumission because the slave was manumitted in a state of burden on him and in the depths of illness, then it will be considered similar to a bequest. If the heirs allow him, it will be considered permissible. If they refuse, he must work for them until two-thirds of his value is complete.

If a man were to manumit his slave after his death and died while owing a debt but did not have any property other than the slave and the value of that slave was less than the debt, he [i.e. the slave] is to work until his value is completed. If his value is the same as the debt, he is to work until all the debt is repaid; afterwards, he would be considered manumitted. If his value was more than the debt, he is to work until all the debt is repaid as well as work two-thirds extra of his value for the heirs if they had not allowed him to be manumitted.

An explanation of that is the following: A man leaves a slave behind that equals the value of thirty dinars and he owes fifteen dinars. He manumits him after his death but leaves nothing else behind as property. However, his heirs disallow the slave to be manumitted. The slave would be obligated to work to pay off the fifteen-dinar debt, and fifteen dinars would remain. It would be as if he died while leaving behind fifteen dinars and had not left behind a debt. It would also be as if another man that was bequeathed and the heirs did not allow it. He would then be obligated to hand over two thirds of it to them and take a third due to the bequest of the original owner.

Concerning one who makes an exception in manumission

If a man were to say to his slave "You are free if Allah wills," the latter would be considered free. If the same man mentioned manumission after death, the slave would be manumitted after he died. If he had not mentioned death, the slave would be considered free at the moment the manumitter said: "You are free if Allah wills." This is the case if the slave is an obedient and righteous Muslim because Allah—the Blessed and Exalted—loves excellence and wills manumission such as this. He establishes manumission on the manumitter even if he does not want to manumit.

As for the openly disobedient wicked sinner against Allah, he is to not be manumitted by the statement "You are free if Allah wills" or "You will be free after I die if Allah wills" because Allah does not will such manumission. The proof that Allah does not will that such person be manumitted is that Allah does not reward the person that manumits such person. Rather, He punishes him for loosening the binds of his slavery and enabling him to commit open indecencies since he knew of his wickedness, disobedience lack of religiosity and faith but still released him from his bondage. By such, he enabled him to commit evil deeds and strengthened him to sin and evil. Therefore, it would not be permissible to manumit such person because by manumitting him, he would be condoning and enabling him to disobedience, and Allah obligates people to restrain others from acts of disobedience if they can and prevent them from defiance to the Lord of creation if they are able.

Whoever says to his slaves during illness "A third of you will be free" and he does not own anything else other than them, each one would have to work for the heirs until two thirds of their value is completed. However, if he were to say the same thing to them while he is healthy and permitted in such situation, each one of them would be considered manumitted if he has property other than them. If he does not own anything other than them, each one would have to work until two thirds of their value is completed.[2]

His situation is like that of two partners who own slaves and one of them freed his share of the slave. The judgement would be that if he were in the state of ease, he could pay his partner the value of his share of them because he manumitted them for Allah and thereby invalidated his partner's ownership of them. This is the case since Allah made them partners and Allah—the Blessed and Exalted—does not share partnership in anything. However, if he [i.e. the partner] were in straitened circumstances, the judgement would be that they would have to work for the owner who had not manumitted them until their value is completed.

Concerning the *umm walad* of a *dhimmi* or his slave woman who embraces Islam

If an *umm walad* of a *dhimmi* were to embrace Islam, she would have to work for him until her value is completed and not be returned to him. If his slave woman were to embrace Islam, the judgement is that he would have to sell her to the Muslims.

Concerning one who manumits a part of his slave

Whoever manumits a body part or limb of a slave, the whole slave would be considered manumitted. Similar has reached us that the Commander of Believers, 'Ali b. Abi Ťālib, upon him be peace, said that when a man manumitted the limb of a slave, the entire slave was considered manumitted.[3]

If a man were to say to his slave "Your leg is free" or "Your hand is free" or "Your thigh is free" or "Your chest is free," the entire slave would be considered free. Likewise, if a man were to say to his slave woman "That which is in your womb is free," it would be considered free while the slave woman would be considered a slave. If he were to say "You are free and that which is in your womb is a slave," both she and that which is in her womb would be considered free because every child born to a free woman is considered free.

If a man were to manumit his slave when he died and he owed a debt, the slave would have to work until his value is completed if nothing else was left behind but him.

If a man in a partnership were to purchase a slave and later came to know after the purchase that the slave was a relative of his, the slave would be considered manumitted at the moment that he bought him. The buyer would be responsible for the price accrued by his partner if he was in a state of ease.

---

[2] A similar question was posed to al-Hādi in ***Al-Muntakhab***.

> I asked him about a man with three slaves, and a conversation took place between him and one of them. Then, he said: 'One of my slaves will be manumitted if I do not do an action.' But then he dies without doing it. "What would be the judgement on that?" He replied: "Each one of them would be manumitted to a value of a third, but each one would have to work two-thirds of his value." "What if the master had not died but rather survived and not done the action?" "It would be said to him: 'Choose which of the three you want to manumit,' and such person would be considered manumitted." "What if the man said 'Half this slave of mine is manumitted, a third of this slave of mine is manumitted and a sixth of this slave of mine is manumitted,' and he has wealth other than them or no wealth other than them?" "All of them would be considered manumitted based on what he said. This is because if he were to say 'Half of my slave is manumitted,' the whole slave would be considered manumitted." "They would not have to work for the remainder of the amount?" "No. There would not remain for them any slavery because when he said 'Half of my slave is manumitted,' the whole slave was considered manumitted. Similar is the case with the rest of them. Working only takes place if he [i.e. the master] had a partner. If he does not have a partner, then no."

[3] Similarly narrated in ***Ŝahīh al-Bukhāri, Mušannaf Ibn Abi Shayba, Sunan al-Bayhaqi***

However, if he were in straitened circumstances, the slave would have to work to the value of the partner's share without inconvenience to him or exhausting him.

If two men owned a slave and one of them manumitted his share and the other partner stipulated manumission upon his death, the stipulation of manumission upon his death would be considered invalid. The manumission of the one who manumitted him would take precedence, and the responsibility for ensuring the value of the other partner's share would fall upon the first partner who manumitted the slave if he is in a state of ease. However, if he is in straitened circumstances, the slave shall have to work for the second partner until his share of value is completed.

Similarly, if two men owned a slave and one of them stipulated manumission upon his death before the other partner manumitted his share, the manumission of the second partner would be considered invalid. Moreover, the stipulation of manumission upon the first partner's death would take precedence, and the responsibility for ensuring the value of the other partner's share would fall upon the first partner who stipulated manumission upon his death.

If a man had a slave and stipulated manumission of a part of the slave upon his death, the whole slave would be considered freed upon his master's death. He would work for him during his lifetime and he would be considered manumitted after his death from a third.

If a slave was owned by two men and one of them testified against the other that he manumitted his share while the other objected to such, the judgement would be that it shall be said to the witness: "You have testified against your partner that he manumitted his share, so you have no share of the slave because you claimed that his portion is free. By Allah, you have no partnership, so you have no share of the slave and nothing else except the value of your right. If you are in straitened circumstances, the slave will work for him on your behalf."

If the judgement is against the witness by such, it shall be said to the objector: "The slave has been manumitted based on your partner because he testified against you regarding the manumission of this slave. Therefore, based on his testimony against you, he has relinquished his ownership. You have a right over him to pay his value to you if he is in a state of ease. If he is in straitened circumstances, the slave will work for you until his value is completed just as he will work for the other until his value is completed during the latter's straitened circumstances."

If two men testify against another that his slave was manumitted by him and the slave says "You had not manumitted me! Those two men are lying in their testimonies," the judgement shall be that the slave will remain under ownership due to his own confession, and the testimonies of the two witnesses are considered invalid. It is impermissible for his master to claim that he enslaved him if he had manumitted him, and he cannot claim ownership of him after having manumitted him. This would be between him and Allah [if he is lying].

If two just witnesses testify that a slave woman was manumitted, their testimonies shall be accepted and the slave woman will be considered manumitted even if she objected. [While she is enslaved] her master is not prevented from having intercourse with her. This is not like the situation with the male slave because he cannot have intercourse with the male slave but can with the slave woman. The prescribed punishment for intercourse with her is not the same as the prescribed punishment for other than her.

Concerning the one who manumits his slave to an appointed time

If a man were to say to his slave "You will be considered free for the sake of Allah when so-n-so returns from his journey" or "...if such and such happens" or "...if we return safely from the sea" or "...at the head of the year" or "...on the Day of 'Arafat," the slave would be considered manumitted at the time that the aforementioned happens. However, if the aforementioned were to happen or appointed time came after having sold him, the manumission would not be considered binding.

All of such would be considered the same if he sold him before that—whether in scarcity or abundance—as long as he sold him out of necessity and need. We do not permit him to sell him except out of need and necessity. His selling him would be considered a means of escape from that which Allah has appointed and spoken by his tongue regarding the manumission of his slave. That would not be considered permissible or binding. His situation would be similar to that of the one who manumits a slave upon his death according to us. It would be impermissible for him to sell [the slave] except out of necessity.

Concerning a man who says to his slave that does not belong to him: "You are free from my ownership"

This statement is considered nothing. One cannot manumit one he does not own, and one cannot divorce one to whom he is not married.

Concerning manumission by announcement

If a man or woman were to say to their slaves "Whoever announces such-and-such to us is considered free" such as the death or birth of a person and similar and one of the slaves announces that and then another announces it afterwards, the first one would be considered free because he was the one who gave the announcement. The second one would not be considered manumitted because he simply gave the announcement that the first one gave. As for that which is already known, there is no announcement for him.

The Book of the Magistrate, Magistrates and Testimonies

In the Name of Allah, the Most Gracious, the Most Merciful...

Concerning that which is obligatory for the magistrate to do

When two litigants come to the magistrate for judgement, he must not judge on behalf of one of them until he hears the statement of the other, understands both of their meanings as well as establishes the evidence of both. Regarding that, it has reached us that Allah's Messenger, peace and blessings be upon him and his progeny, said to 'Ali: ((When two litigants come to you for judgement, do not judge in favour of one until you hear the statement of the other)).[1]

The magistrate should not judge between Muslims while he is angry, nor should he judge between them while he is extremely hungry. He should not greet one of the litigants without greeting the other even if he were friends with one of them. This is because if he were to do that, he could frighten his friend's opponent.

He should seat the two litigants at an equal level and begin with the weak over the strong. He should listen to his [i.e. the weak person's] statement and evidence first unless the strong person is assaulted by the weak. However, if both are equal in litigation, he should begin with the weak. He should do likewise with women and men.

He should not pass a judgement while his heart is preoccupied with other matters. One should not seek out to be a magistrate or ask to be one because it is a great danger in doing so. Regarding that, it has reached us that Allah's Messenger, peace and blessings be upon him and his progeny, said: ((Whoever has been appointed as a magistrate has been slaughtered without a knife)).[2] It has also reached us that he, peace and blessings be upon him and his progeny, said: ((Whoever asks to be a magistrate will be left to his own devices)).[3]

The magistrate should not go into any of his matter with the litigant nor refer to him with an opinion unless he commands him to fear Allah and warn him as well as to leave injustice in all his affairs and to do justice to his opponent only.

It has reached us that Allah's Messenger, peace and blessings be upon him and his progeny, said: (('Ali is the most knowledgeable of people and the best in judgement)).[4] It has also reached us the 'Ali, upon him be peace, said:

> By Allah! If you were to come to me to judge between you using the Torah, the Torah would say: "O Allah, he has judged by me!" And if you were to come to me to judge between you using the Gospels, the Gospels would say: "O Allah, he has judged by me!" If you were to come to me to judge between you using the Qur'an, the Qur'an would say: "O Allah, he has judged by me!" However, you will not do it! By Allah, you will not do it!

It is also narrated that he, upon him be peace, said:

> Allah's Messenger, peace and blessings be upon him and his progeny, sent me to Yemen. I found a Bedouin neighbourhood there in which a hole was dug on an elevated plain (*zubya*) for a lion. They caught one in it and when they went to look at it one of them fell in while holding on to the other who was holding on to another who was holding on to another until all four of them fell in. The lion injured all of them. One of them was able to kill it, but all of them died from their injuries. The guardians of one of the men took up arms to go kill the guardians of the first one. 'Ali came to them and asked: "Do you intend to kill them while Allah's Messenger is

---

[1] Similarly narrated in ***Musnad Abu Ya'la, Musnad al-Bazzār, Sunan al-Bayhaqi***

[2] Similarly narrated in ***Sunan Abu Dāwūd, Sunan at-Tirmidhi, Sunan al-Bayhaqi, Sunan Ibn Mājah, Sunan ad-Dārqutni***

[3] Similarly narrated in ***Sunan Abu Dāwūd, Sunan at-Tirmidhi, al-Mustadrak, Musnad Ahmed, Sunan Ibn Mājah, Sunan al-Bayhaqi***

[4] Similarly narrated in ***Sunan Ibn Māja***. A hadith with variant wording but similar meaning appears in ***Tārikh ad-Dimashq, Fadā'il as-Sahāba*** by Ahmed b. Hanbal, ***Musnad Ahmed, Majmu' az-Zawā'id***.

alive and I am here with you?! If you were to kill them, you would have killed more than those for whom you differed about! I will judge between you with a judgement with which you will be pleased. I will not prevent any of you from going to Allah's Messenger, peace and blessings be upon him and his progeny, so that he judges between you as thus. Then, whoever differs after that shall have no right. Gather for me from the tribes of those who fell in the hole a fourth, third, half and complete indemnities. A fourth of the indemnity will be for the first one who fell in because he led to the death of the other three above him. A third of the indemnity would be for the one who died second because he led to the deaths of the two above him. The third person would get half the indemnity because he led to the death of the other one above him. The fourth person would get the whole indemnity." They refused to accept that and went to Allah's Messenger, peace and blessings be upon him and his progeny. They met him at the *maqām* of Abraham in the Sanctified House and related the account to him. He said: ((I will pass a judgement between you)) and wrapped himself in his cloak. One of the men said: "'Ali passed a judgement for us." When they related the account to him regarding 'Ali's judgement, he confirmed that and they acted on it.[5]

It has reached us that the Commander of Believers, 'Ali, upon him be peace, found his armour with a Christian. He went to a magistrate named Shurayh[§], who would judge between the Muslims, and took his complaint to him. When Shurayh saw him [i.e. 'Ali], he stood up from his seat for him. ['Ali] said to him "Stay in your seat" and sat next to him. He then said: "O Shurayh, had my opponent been a Muslim, I would have sat in the same place as the opponent. However, he is a Christian. Allah's Messenger, peace and blessings be upon him and his progeny, said: ((If you and they are on the same road, restrict them to the narrow sides of it. Debase them as Allah has debased them without oppressing them))." Then, he said: "O Shurayh, this is my armour; I have not sold or gifted it." Shurayh said to the Christian: "What do you say regarding the statement of the Commander of Believers?" The Christian said: "The armour belongs to none but me. I am not saying that the Commander of Believers is lying though." Shurayh turned to 'Ali and said: "O Commander of Believers, is there proof?" 'Ali, upon him be peace, laughed and said: "Unfortunately Shurayh, I do not have proof." So, he judged that the armour belonged to the Christian. The Christian stood up and departed. He returned and said: "As for me, I bear witness that this is the judgements of the Prophets! The Commander of Believers came to the magistrate to be judged and the magistrate judged against him! I bear witness that there is no God but Allah, the One with whom is no partners and that Muhammad is His slave and messenger! By Allah, the armour is yours, O Commander of Believers! I followed your army when you went to Ŝiffīn. You dropped it from your camel, and I took it." The Commander of Believers said: "Since you have embraced Islam, it belongs to you." He then placed him [i.e. the former Christian] on his horse. He fought alongside the Commander of Believers in the Battle of Nahrawān.[6]

May Allah have mercy on 'Ali, the Commander of Believers! Whoever is ignorant of his right is ignorant of his virtue. Whoever deviates from the intended objective deviates from one's intended right. How much more so is the case when one deviates from his right after hearing the statement of the Allah when He says about him, may Allah be satisfied with him: **{Verily, thy only Guardian is Allah, His Messenger, and those who believe—those who establish the prayer and render the dues whilst bowing} (Q. 5:55)**?! Allah appoints Guardianship to Himself, His Messenger and the believer who rendered the charity while bowing. This refers to the Commander of Believers and no one else from the rest of the Muslims. No one can remove him from this or deprive him from such regarding Allah's judgement for him.

---

[5] Similarly narrated in ***Musnad Imam Zayd, Mušannaf Ibn Abi Shayba, Sunan al-Bayhaqi***

[6] Similarly narrated in ***Amāli al-Murshid Billah, Sunan al-Bayhaqi, Hilayat al-Awliyā, Tārikh al-Khulafā, Subul as-Salām, Kanz al-'Ummāl, Bihār al-Anwār***. The account appears with variant wording but with the same general gist.

His statement regarding him and others is {**The forerunners** [in faith] **are the forerunners. They are the ones brought nigh** [to Allah] **in Gardens of Paradise**} (**Q. 56:10-12**). He was the forerunner to his Lord and not preceded by anyone else.

Also, the Blessed and Exalted speaks about him and al-'Abbās b. 'Abdul-Muttalib when they differed with one another about virtue. Al-'Abbās said: "I provide water for the pilgrims." 'Ali replied: "I am the forerunner to Allah and His Messenger." Then, Allah revealed regarding that: {**Dost ye make the providing of water to the pilgrim and the maintenance of the Sacred Mosque equal to that of the one who believes in Allah and the Last Day and struggles in the way of Allah? Those who believe and emigrated and striven with their wealth and their lives in Allah's way are greater in rank to Allah. These are they who are victorious. Their Lord giveth them glad tidings of mercy from Him and pleasure and Gardens wherein shall enduring pleasure be theirs to abide therein forever. Verily with Allah is a great reward!**} (**Q. 9:19-22**). The reason for its revelation was that al-'Abbās b. 'Abdul-Muttalib mentioned a virtue of his in respect to providing water for the pilgrims and tending to the Sacred House. The Commander of Believers mentioned his precedence in Islam and Emigration as well as struggling against his Lord's enemies in jihad and sacrificing himself for the sake of Allah and His Messenger. The Most Gracious judged between them and the comparison of their virtues in His Book.[7]

Even if someone were to describe what is for the Commander of Believers, upon him be peace, which has been clearly revealed from the beautiful Reminder, he would have had difficulty remembering it and would have to explain it for a long time. Therefore, praise be to Allah, the Lord of creation and recompense for the God-conscious. May Allah's prayers be upon Muhammad, the Trustworthy, and his righteous and pure Progeny!

Concerning magistrates and the one who claims hearing loss

If a person were to claim hearing loss, one should employ the use of trickery against him. He should attempt to frighten [the claimant] from behind by striking something when he is unaware. If he is frightened by the sound, such person is declared a liar. If he is not frightened, such person is declared truthful even if the accused were to swear an oath against his claim. The striking of fear in him while he is unaware will undoubtedly bring out his true conscience.

Concerning magistrates and a stream of water divided among estates

It is for the owner of agriculture to allow the water to the two sandal straps and for the owner of a date palm to the ankles. Then, the water is to be allowed to flow to the one that is lower than them. Similar is to be done to the lower ground till the stream has run out to the last of the estates—whether a lot or a little after having depleted to the lower ground. However, the higher ground should be given priority with a little water.

Similar has reached us from Allah's Messenger, peace and blessings be upon him and his progeny, that he passed the judgement between the people of Medina regarding the stream of Mahzūr. It used to flow in it till it changed. The people at the bottom of the valley used to say: "The people at the top of the valley are depriving us of water!" Allah's Messenger, peace and blessings be upon him and his progeny, then passed the judgement that it is for the owner of agriculture to allow the water to the two sandal straps and the owner of the date palms to the ankles. Then they are to allow it to flow to those below them.[8]

Concerning judgements between the people of the marketplaces and setting up

It has reached us that the Commander of Believers, upon him be peace, went out to the marketplace one day. When stores were being raised and built, he said:

> This marketplace is only for the black and white. Whoever comes first in the morning shall have

[7] Similarly narrated in ***Asbāb an-Nuzūl, Tafsīr at-Tabari, Tafsīr Ibn Kathīr, Bihār al-Anwār***

[8] Similarly narrated in ***Sunan Ibn Mājah, Sunan Abu Dāwūd, Sunan al-Bayhaqi, Musnad Ahmed***

that space until the evening. Whenever we go to a man with whom we have engaged in a transaction in one place, we find someone else in his place the next time!

This is regarding those who set up in the middle of the roads. It does not refer to those storekeepers in houses and shops. It is only those who set up on the road in front of the owners of houses and shops. They are the ones about whom the Commander of Believers is referring. As for the owners of houses and shops, they are more entitled to their homes and shops. No one can deprive them of this nor does anyone have more right to them than they.

Concerning those characteristics that a magistrate must have

The magistrate must be knowledgeable of that for which he is judging and understand what is related to him. He must be scrupulous in his religion and innocent from the wealth of the Muslims. He must be forbearing when approached by constant ignorance and must be reliable in intellect. He must be excellent in distinguishing matters and firm in Allah's affairs. If he is lacking in any of the aforementioned qualities, he would be considered deficient.

The magistrate must assume responsibility for those who are brought before him for judgement. If he were to prolong their custody while abandoning their needs and justice, he would be considered a violator of their rights and an irresponsible magistrate who cannot even raise his head to them!

The magistrate must strive towards a peaceful settlement between the masses when the truth is not readily evident to him. As for those cases in which the truth is evident, there is to be no settlement. It has reached us that Allah's Messenger, peace and blessings be upon him and his progeny, said: ((The magistrates are three: two are in the Hellfire and one is in Paradise. As for the one who is in Paradise, he is the one who passes judgement while knowing the truth and then judges by it. He will be in Paradise. As for the two magistrates that are in the Hellfire, one is he who passes judgement while knowing the truth but intentionally avoids it and the other is he who passes judgement without knowledge and is too shy to say: "I do not know." These two will be in the Hellfire)).[9] Also, the magistrate must be impartial to the two litigants in giving them his attention and speaking to them.

Concerning granting the magistrate provisions for his office of judgement

It is necessary that the magistrate be provided for so that he and his family do not die as well as ensure that his heart is not preoccupied. Similar has reached us that the Commander of Believers, 'Ali b. Abi Ṫālib, upon him be peace, used to provide Shurayh with five hundred dirham.[10]

Concerning judgements with oaths accompanied by a witness

According to us, there is no disagreement regarding judgements with oaths accompanied by a witness; that has come from the Prophet's sunnah. If any were to object to that, ask him: "What do you say regarding a man who claims the wealth of another without evidence and matters are not clearly distinguishable?" Is there not consensual agreement between us and you that the defendant would have to swear an oath that the plaintiff's claim is invalid and that he is not true in what he presented? If he relinquishes the oath and does not take an oath, the plaintiff shall swear and have the right over the defendant. If he says yes, he will be asked: "Then if you hold to the view that this is a right that he is entitled to with only his oath, so how can it not be the case if there is a witness with the oath?

An explanation of that is the following: A man claims a right over another man and includes a reliable and just witness with his claim. If he were to do that, he would be asked to swear an oath with his witness and a judgement will be passed concerning his right.

---

[9] Similarly narrated in ***Sunan Ibn Mājah, Sunan al-Kubra*** of al-Bayhaqi, ***Al-Mu'jam al-Kabīr, Al-Mu'jam al-Awsaṭ, Mušannaf*** of Ibn Abi Shayba

[10] Similarly narrated in ***Al-Jāmi' al-Kāfi*** and ***Mušannaf 'Abdur-Razzāq***

However, a judgement passed with an oath and witness can only apply to rights and wealth. As for other things, it is not the case. Judgements with an oath and witness are consensually agreed upon by the Progeny of Allah's Messenger, peace and blessings be upon him and his progeny.

Concerning the testimony of newly pubescent youths against each other in cases of head wounds and bodily injuries

The testimony of newly pubescent youths against each other in cases of head wounds and bodily injuries is permissible as long as they do not differ. If they differ, their testimony is not accepted unless it is corroborated by a reliable witness before they differed. We simply say that their witness is not acceptable if they differ because newly pubescent youths do not fully know that which is permissible or prohibited for them. That being the case, such person would not be safe from errors in testimony; they could easily add to or take away from it due to the lack of knowledge regarding that which his Lord makes obligatory upon him.

Concerning those from whom testimonies are not accepted and those for whom testimonies are permitted

The testimony of *dhimmi*s, the openly disobedient Muslims, minors or someone with personal interest is not to be accepted if they are litigants. The slave's testimony can be accepted if he is a pure and upright Muslim. The testimony of the son for his father, father for his son, brother for his brother or husband for his wife can be accepted as long as they are just and believing Muslims. The testimony of a lone woman is not accepted except in the case of those things for which none but her can testify, such as stillbirths and genital defects.

If the ruler were informed about the corruption of a people or the sinning of witnesses, he is to make the witnesses swear an oath out of precaution in religion. That is for him to do because he is entrusted to the Muslims and their wealth. Therefore, precaution in that is for the Muslims.

It has reached us that Allah's Messenger, peace and blessings be upon him and his progeny, said: ((Whoever deprives a Muslim of his right by his oath—Allah will make Paradise prohibited for him and Hell obligatory for him)). He was asked: "O Messenger of Allah, even if it were for a trivial thing?" He replied: ((Even if it were for a twig from the Arak tree)). He repeated that three times.[11]

It has also reached us that he said: ((Whoever swears a false oath on this pulpit of mine will take his seat in the Hellfire)).[12]

Concerning some testimonies

There is no problem with two men testifying on behalf of one man regarding rights. As for the prescribed punishments, it is discouraged in the case of a prescribed punishment and severing a limb. This is because if the imam were to command the witnesses to lash him or sever his limb, they would be obligated to obey him, and it would not be preferred for them to establish a prescribed punishment for that which they had not witnessed the perpetrator do. It can only be established by the testimony of other than them.

As for stoning, it is impermissible absolutely because the witnesses are more entitled to stone and it is impermissible for them to be the first of people to stone someone for something that they had not seen him do.

I simply declare it to be discouraged in the case of the prescribed punishments, severing and lashings because the person could possibly die as a result. If a person were to die due to the testimony of one person, the witness would be held liable for his blood and indemnity if the testimony was invalid or the witnesses lied.

---

[11] Similarly narrated in ***Ŝaḥīḥ al-Bukhārī, Ŝaḥīḥ Muslim, Sunan an-Nisā'i, Sunan al-Bayhaqi, Al-Mu'jam al-Kabīr, Al-Mu'jam al-Awsaṭ***

[12] Similarly narrated in ***Muwaṭṭa, Sunan Ibn Mājah, Ŝaḥīḥ Ibn Hibbān, Al-Mu'jam al-Kabīr, Al-Mu'jam al-Awsaṭ, Musnad Abu Ya'la, Sunan al-Bayhaqi, Mušannaf*** of Ibn Abi Shayba, ***Musnad Ahmed, Sunan Abu Dāwūd, Sunan an-Nisā'i***

Concerning bribery in court cases, the prostitute's hire, the pay to a fortune-teller (*al-kāhin*), the contracting of a mercenary and the price of a dog

Whoever bribes in his court case—such person is considered to have forbidden and ill-gotten wealth (*suhtun*) and is cursed by Allah as a disobedient sinner. The hire of a prostitute, price for a dog and pay to a fortune-teller are all considered ill-gotten wealth.

It is impermissible to contract a mercenary in the way of Allah; he is the one who would not go out to fight unless he was paid. According to us, that is considered an impermissible earning. Similar has been narrated to us from the Commander of Believers, 'Ali b. Abi Ťālib, upon him be peace.

Concerning dispersing witnesses

There is no problem in dispersing witnesses if they are accused. Rather, I say that it is obligatory on the imam. If they are accused, he is to ask them one by one and separate them until some of them do not know others. If their testimonies are the same, pass a judgement by them. If they differ in their statements, their testimonies are considered invalid.

Concerning the testimony of a child when he gets older and the disbeliever when he embraces Islam

When a child who attains puberty or a disbeliever who embraces Islam testifies to something about which they know, their testimonies would be considered valid.

The Book of Expeditions (*as-Siyar*)

In the Name of Allah, the Most Gracious, the Most Merciful...

Introductory statement regarding expeditions

The first thing that we should discuss and mention is the description of the imam obligatory for the *Ummah* to obey and aid as well as the one who is prohibited to abandon.

Concerning the description of the imam and the statement regarding that

The imam who is obligatory to obey must be from the offspring of al-Hasan and al-Hussein, may Allah bless them both. He must also be scrupulous, God-conscious, diligent in Allah's affairs, inimical towards this world's life and its people, understanding of that which is required of him, knowledgeable of confusing matters that come to him, courageous, valiant, generous, liberal, compassionate with his subjects, merciful, pardoning, sympathetic, forbearing, have a sense of equality to them, and participatory with them in affairs without controlling them. He must not be one who rules by other than what Allah decrees and must be sober in intellect and distant from ignorance. He must be able to take Allah's wealth from its places and distribute it for its intended purposes appointed by Allah. He must establish Allah's judgements and prescribed punishments as well as carry them out on those for whom it is obligatory—whether relative or non-relative (lit. "near or far"), noble or commoner. He must not be blamed for that which Allah has made blameworthy. He must be one who establishes His right, brandishes his sword for His sake, calls to his Lord, be diligent in his call, raises His banner, distributes callers throughout lands, and not fall short in solidarity with the slaves.

He must be a source of fear to the oppressors and a source of security for the believers. The defiantly disobedient should not feel safe and secure with him; rather, he should seek them out and they should seek him out. He should manifest them, and they should manifest him. He should be hostile against them, and they should be hostile against him. Thereby, they would establish their treachery against him and seek to destroy him, rebel against him and muster the tribes to fight him. But they should fear that he would exile them, and he must be a source of fright for them. He must not renege his call towards Allah's affair or change due to fear. He must not shrink from his struggle against them out of trembling. He must rally all of his forces and not fall short of that.

If the aforementioned is the case for a descendant of the two Grandsons—al-Hasan and al-Hussein, he is the imam religiously obligatory to obey, and it is an obligation upon the Muslims to help him. Whoever falls short of that and does not connect himself to Allah, does not make his sword known, does not expose the oppressors and they him, does not manifest his affair, does not raise his banner so that the perfect evidence of his Lord is visible for all to see, and does not demonstrate a good example—it will not be obligatory for the Muslims to obey such a one, emigrate to him or be patient with him.

Whoever amongst the Muslim *Ummah* does that after it has been made clear to them that he is their guardian, and he has aspired towards his Lord, made his sword known and uncovered the manifestations of the oppressors, his call to Allah is religiously obligatory. Whoever falls short of that would have Allah's proof against him, which is firm, established, decisive and manifest. His proof is decisive {**...that those who perish would have perished upon evidence and those who live would have lived upon evidence. Verily, Allah is All-Hearing, All-Knowing**} (**Q. 8:42**).

Concerning the imamate which is established by an imam

The imamate is established for an imam for whom it is obligatory upon the people, which was established by Allah as long as the aforementioned preconditions exist. Whoever for whom this is the case—Allah has judged that it is so, whether the people like it or not.

It is not for the people to establish the imamate as the ignorant claim, as the imamate can only be established by the agreement of some of them as they allege. However, this is the most impossible of impossibilities and the most loathsome of their statements! Rather, the imamate is established by the establishment of the Most Merciful for the one whom He deems as fit, whether the people like it or not. The one for whom Allah establishes the imamate is obligated to be obeyed by the *Ummah*. The one for whom Allah has not established the Guardianship upon the Muslims is considered sinful and punished as well as the one who follows him. This is because he has followed one to whom Allah has not given the right as well as made a covenant with one for whom Allah has not made a covenant.

The matter and choice regarding that is due upon the Most Merciful and it is not the choice of the people. As Allah says: {**And thy Lord creates what He wills and chooses; they do not have a choice. Glorified be Allah and exalted from what they associate!**} (Q. 28:68). The Glorified also says: {**It is not for the believing man or believing woman to—when Allah and His Messenger have decreed a matter—claim a choice in their affair. Whosoever disobeys Allah and His Messenger has clearly gone astray**} (Q. 33:36).

Allah has confirmed the deviance of the one who chooses other than His choice and passes a judgement with that which is contrary to His judgement. The judgement is for Allah. Whoever He is pleased with, we are pleased with. Whoever the Glorified places over us, we will obey him. Whoever the Mighty and Majestic turns us away from, we turn away from him.

The Glorified has made clear to us the one whom He decrees to be appointed over the *Ummah* and the one who is distracted from commanding the good and prohibiting the evil from the subjects. Therefore, He has appointed as the right-acting successors (*khulafā ar-rāshidīn*) and safeguards of the believers those chosen ones whom we have described and explained regarding an imam. And He informed us that whoever was otherwise among them would not, by Allah's judgement, be an imam over them.

Regarding that, Allah says: {**Is the one who guides to the truth worthier to be followed or the one who cannot guide unless he is guided? What aileth thee? How doth thou judge?**} (Q. 10:35). He therefore prohibits them from the judgement of one who falls short of guidance to the truth. And He establishes the judgement of the one among His slaves whom He has chosen who guides to the truth and is God-conscious. He prefers them to the rest of His slaves and makes them the heirs of the Clear Book. They are those who are rulers by the judgement of the Lord of creation. He seals the Messengers by means of them and makes their path the best of paths. They are the Progeny and Offspring of the Messenger, peace and blessings be upon him and his progeny. They are the fruit of his heart and beloveds as well as Allah's appointed successors and guardians.

Regarding that, the Mighty and Majestic whose words cannot be encompassed, says: {**Then, We have caused to inherit the Book those whom We have chosen amongst Our slaves. Amongst them is he who oppresses himself, amongst them is he who is moderate, amongst them is he who is foremost in good by the permission of Allah. That is a great virtue!**} (Q. 35:32). He makes their quality of being foremost their matter as well as their judgement over the rest of the Muslims and slaves of the Lord of creation.

My father related to me that his father was asked about the establishment of the imam's imamate without the agreement of the Muslims and without the oath of allegiance of two or more. He replied:

> Know—may Allah guide you—that the imamate can only be established by Allah alone with that which He has made obligatory, such as the complete perfection about which one should know and not be ignorant. Whoever is complete in knowledge and is not ignorant of what is required of him from the religion—the Muslims are obliged to contract with and accept him. It is impermissible for them to do otherwise, and they are not allowed to do but that.

Concerning two men from the Prophet's Progeny who share in these qualities

If two men share in the quality of knowledge but differ in the quality of scrupulousness, the imamate will go to the one who is more scrupulous. If the both of them share in the qualities of scrupulousness and knowledge, the imamate will be necessitated for the one who is more indifferent towards this world's life. If they both share in that, the imamate will be for the one who is more generous. If they both share in that, the imamate will be for the one who is more courageous. If they both share in that, the imamate will be for the one who is more merciful and compassionate towards the subjects. If they both share in that, the imamate will be for the one who is humbler. If they both share in that, the imamate will be for the one who is more forbearing and excellent towards the people.

If they both share in that or any other of the aforementioned preconditions for the imamate—no two could ever share in all of that. Even if one were to make strenuous effort in that, there cannot be agreement in all of them and there must be differences in some of the preconditions of the imam. However, for the sake of precaution, we must say that if the both of them share in all of these [i.e. the preconditions for the imamate], the imamate will be for the older of the two. If the both of them are the same age, the imamate will be for the one who is more handsome. If the both of them are the same in handsomeness, the imamate will be for the one who is cleverer. If both of them are the same in cleverness, the imamate will be for the one who is more eloquent and articulate. If the both of them are equal in all that, the imamate will be for the one who was given the oath of allegiance first. It is not for anyone who shares in all of the aforementioned qualities to be given the oath of allegiance when the other person was already given the oath before him.

My father related to me that his father said:

> If two men share in the qualities and they are the same in every one of them, the oath of allegiance will be to the one who came first. It is not for the one who possesses these qualities to be given the oath after the first one has been given it. The exception is if any one of them is deficient in any of the qualities or has more than the other. As for when the both of them are equal and the same in the qualities, the imamate will go to the one who was given the oath first even if only one person did so. This is because the oath is only obligatory upon him by means of his precedence and qualities we described. When his state is complete and there is contentment with his actions, it is binding for everyone to be pleased with him as the choice.

If one were to ask "Why do you obligate the oath of imamate to the one who was approached first but not obligate it for the other who has the same qualities?", we reply by saying that it is due to the precedence and initiative in the oath. However, there is no deficiency in the other candidate for imamate after it is shown that he equally deserves it due to his qualities.

Concerning the removal of the imam from the imamate

The imamate is removed from the imam when he commits a major sin, persists in it and does not repent for it. If that is the case, the imamate is to be removed from him, his reliability (*'adāla*) is considered invalid and the *Ummah* is no longer obliged to obey him. According to Allah, he would be considered among the disgraced, the cursed, the wretched and the wicked whose enmity is obligatory and whose alliance is forbidden.

My father related to me that his father related with his chain to the Prophet, peace and blessings be upon him and his progeny, that Allah's Messenger, peace and blessings be upon him and his progeny, said: ((Allah said to Gabriel, upon him be peace: "O Gabriel, remove aid from him and them, for I am not pleased with this action of this seed (*zaru'*) of this Prophet!")).

This statement and hadith simply refer to the offspring of Allah's Messenger, peace and blessings be upon him and his progeny, who does not act by the right. As for the one who acts by the right, he is considered agreeable, a guide, guided, accepted and aided by Allah.

Concerning what is permissible for the imam to do regarding his subjects as well as when it is permissible to depart from his command and refrain from him

The imam is permitted to do that which Allah permits and is prohibited from that which Allah prohibits in His Book. He cannot depart from the oath of allegiance that he has entered, nor can he reject that which he was pledged to do.

They are to be helpers in that which Allah commands and seekers in that with which Allah is pleased. They rise with him if he rises, strive with him if he strives, and depart with him if he departs, and descends with him if he descends. They are to sacrifice themselves and their wealth as well as imitate him in all of his states. If he finds helpers in this way, he will obtain with them that which he desires and come out with them against oppression, and the religion of Muhammad, peace and blessings be upon him and his progeny, will be manifested little by little. He increases them every day in the land, and they advise him to fight those who oppose him from among the slaves. Therefore, it is impermissible for him to depart from them, and it is not allowed for him to step aside and be alone from them as long as they are established on that and they are with him in thus.

As for he whose command is constantly disobeyed and whose judgements are treated stubbornly and whose call to jihad against Allah's enemies is not obeyed while he called them to rise but rather they call him to sit down and he asks them to console their Muslim brothers and to spend some of their money in striving for the sake of the Lord of creation yet they are stingy with their spending and do not travel with him in the way of Allah to the horizons and their ambitions are shortened, their breaths became small and their obedience worsened, and he does not find anyone to lead them to the truth and strike them with it for the word of truth—it would be impermissible for him to remain established over them. It would be impermissible—according to Allah—for him to preoccupy himself with them instead of others.

It would be obligatory for him to observe that which Allah commanded his Messenger when the latter called but was not obeyed and commanded but was not followed during the days he was established in Mecca and before the Emigration (*al-hijra*). Allah commanded him to abstain from the transgressors and stay away from the enemies. Then, the Glorified says: **{Turn away from them and thou shalt incur no blame. And continue to warn, for warning benefits the believers} (Q. 51:54-55)**.

Therefore, Allah commanded him to turn away from those who disobeyed him and abstain from those who rejected him. He informed him that after diligent effort, he would not incur any blame for abandoning them nor would he be punished for their rejection. Then, He informed him that he should warn the people and invite all of the lorded (*al-marbūbbīn*) as well as informed him that this would be beneficial for the believers. Everything that is a means of benefit to the believers in terms of admonition and reminder is Allah's proof against the disbelievers and disobedient. If he is afflicted by this from his followers and fears them for the religion of his Lord, then let him withdraw from them to others so that he should strive in seeking for his purpose. It is for God that he delegates and not falter, slack or weaken in Allah's command. Allah says **{And if ye aid Allah, He shall aid thee and establish thy feet} (Q. 47:7)** and **{…so that Allah may aid those who aid Him. Verily, Allah is Powerful and Mighty} (Q. 22:40)**.

Similar was done by al-Hasan b. 'Ali, upon him be peace, when he was opposed, disobeyed and could not find anyone to follow him in truth. He departed when he was removed and left when he was abandoned. Then, after that, he was lying in wait, hoping and desiring that the right helpers would carry out what Allah required him to do of jihad against the oppressors. If the imam becomes aware of the people's betrayal of him and the rejection of his order as well as the lack of supporters on his right to that, he must do as al-Hasan, upon him be peace, did before him.

Concerning that which is narrated from the Prophet: ((Whoever dies without knowing the imam will die the death of the pre-Islamic era))

If there is an imam of the age who has arisen, is righteous, God-conscious, knowledgeable and pure but yet one does not know him or aid him and instead abandons him and dies in that state—such person would have died the death of the pre-Islamic era.

However, if there were no manifest imam who is known by name or who has not arisen, the imam would be the Messenger, Qur'an and Commander of Believers. Whoever follows that example and is from his offspring who fits the description—it would be obligatory for the people to know such person by the aforementioned characteristics. If there is no imam known in the land at that time, it would be obligatory for them to know that this matter is specific to the offspring of the Messenger, peace and blessings be upon him and his progeny, and no one else. It is also obligatory for them to know that there is no era devoid of Allah's proof: an imam from them that commands the good and forbids the evil.[1]

When all of the aforementioned is known and the matter is as we have explained and the person dies, he would be saved from dying the death of the pre-Islamic era. Such person would have died the death of a Muslim. However, the one who is ignorant of and does not hold to such would have departed from the death of Islam and died the death of the pre-Islamic era. This is the explanation and meaning of the hadith.[2]

Concerning what Allah obligates upon the imam: anger in His affair, establishment of His proof and diligent effort in His obedience

Allah obligates the imam to establish His command, command by it and prohibit what He prohibits. He obligates him to establish His prescribed punishments on all for whom it is obligatory—whether noble or ignoble, distant or near relative. He is to take Allah's wealth from those for whom he is obligated and distribute it to those for whom he is obligated. He is to increase in anger against those who disobey the Most Gracious even if it may be his father, brother, uncle or son. He does not treat one unfairly, favour one or fall short in Allah's command. He does not make any exceptions towards the disobedient but acts severely against them. He is close to the believers and easy on them but shows harshness towards the hypocrite. He is agreeable to the one who agrees. As Allah says to Muhammad, peace and blessings be upon him and his progeny, and his Companions {**Muhammad is the Messenger of Allah. And those who art with him are severe against the disbelievers and merciful amongst themselves. Thou see them bowing and prostrating, seeking favour from Allah and His pleasure…**} (Q. 48:29) till the end of the *Surah*. The imam must be angrier for the sake of Allah than he is for himself.

---

[1] This doctrine regarding the impossibility of the absence of Allah's proof on Earth is not to be confused with the Imami Shia concept, which posits this 'proof' (*hujja*) as a succession of physical entities from the time of Adam till now. Al-Hādi's grandfather, Imam al-Qāsim Rassi, refuted this 'Shia' doctrine in his ***Radd 'ala Rāfiḍa***. Please refer to our upcoming translation: "The Luminary of the Prophet's Family: The Collected Works of Imam al-Qāsim b. Ibrahim Rassi."

Instead, Imam al-Hādi's concept regarding the perpetual existence of Allah's proof is as he articulated: Allah's proof is the imam; and in the latter's absence, Allah's proof is the Qur'an, Prophetic Sunnah and 'Alawi tradition.

[2] The purport of this hadith has undergone various interpretations on either side of the Islamic spectrum. One side—as represented by the Generality—proposes that the hadith imposes the collective obligation of appointing a universal caliph to govern the affairs of the Muslims. Otherwise, they say, the whole *Ummah* incurs the sin. The other side of the Islamic spectrum—as exemplified by the Imami Shi'ites—says that the collective Muslim community is obligated to identify their hidden imam as the leader in order to be save from the death of *kufr*.

Both views posit a theological problem as they impose an unbearable burden upon the Muslim community. In the first instance, the Muslims are charged with the impossible task of seeking out and establishing a caliph that satisfies the entire global Muslim community. The implausibility of this can readily be seen throughout the tattered history of the Sunni caliphate in which the caliph's authority was challenged by the existence of contending ruling authorities and caliphates as well as the failed attempt on the part of the Sunni activists to restore it at the 1931 Caliphate Conference. As for the discrepancy of the Imami Shi'ite interpretation of the hadith, it places the onus of belief in an unseen and unknown personality who is not forthright or public in his claim of imamate. See the previous footnote.

Al-Hādi's interpretation of the hadith is a lot more reasonable since it abandons the two sides of the spectrum as well as the inherent theological impossibilities of both. Instead, it presents the collective obligation upon the Ummah to know those qualities that qualify one for the imamate.

Concerning what is narrated regarding the Mahdi

We hope that Allah brings him close and soon because we see that the objectionable has been manifested and the truth has been effaced and altered. Allah has said: {**For, verily, with hardship is ease. Verily, with hardship is ease**} (**Q. 94:5-6**). He also said: {**...till when the Messengers despaired and assumed that they were belied. Then, there came unto them Our victory and We saved whom we willed. And Our punishment shall not be warded off from the criminals**} (**Q. 12:110**).

Allah's Messenger, peace and blessings be upon him and his progeny, said: ((When difficulty increases, there will come a relief)). He, peace and blessings be upon him and his progeny, also said: ((…because being in difficulty awaiting prosperity is more beloved to me than being in prosperity awaiting difficulty)).

The difference between the hereafter and this world is the ephemerality and finality of this world as well as the eternality of the hereafter. Everything in this world is subject to passing, and that which is in the hereafter is forever. It is as if the relief has approached, and the bliss has risen, and the victory has descended, for the temptations have accumulated, and most of what we are in is the disruption of the Book and the Sunnah, the open display of fornication, indifference towards marriage, the appearance of unqualified spokespeople (*ar-ruwaybiđa*), the drinking of alcohol, the committing of evils, the consumption of usury, the acceptance of bribes, the frolicking in the fields of corrupt passion, the abuse of authority, the traversing of the path of Satan, the abandonment of enjoining good and forbidding the evil as we may see and consider. All of this in our present age which we have readily seen.

Then, it is as a chief of religion had been afflicted by his sin and strove to his Lord, so Allah answered his supplication, had mercy on his state of need, revealed his grief, revealed his victory, manifested his wisdom, revived him after his destruction, enlivened him after his death, and strengthened him after his weakness by means of a man from the Ahl al-Bayt of his Prophet. He will manifest him in some of his land, establish the pillars of religion by him, honour the believers, reduce the unbelievers, humiliate the transgressors and rule by the Book of the Lord of creation. Allah will enable him to trample on His land, manifest His word, dignify His call, fill hungry stomachs by means of him, clothe the naked, strengthen the weakness of the weakened, and remove the oppression of the oppressors by means of him. By means of him, darkness will be repelled, immoralities will be negated, the fire of open disobedience will be extinguished, the light of truth will be raised, he will be supported with victory, he will be aided by means of terror, His allies will be dignified, and His enemies will be humiliated.

So whenever anger possesses someone who owns a land, it impels him to seek another, until he owns all the lands so that he can control the whole country and tread on all nations with Allah's help, conciliation, victory and support. He will fill the earth with justice and equity just as it was filled with tyranny and injustice.[3] The blame of a blamer will not be taken by Allah to the one with whom his helpers and supporters will gather from the lands of the earth just as the autumn cumulus gathers in the sky.

It is as if by means of him, thousands will be presented, the noses of his enemies will be severed, and he will rush boldly to death while penetrating the ranks of danger with large armies. In them will be lions of protection valiantly fighting, flying with the strikes of claws and cuts with the shield the meteors of events until the cavalries are called back, the call of the Most Gracious is manifested, every person is called to the truth, the enemies are fought, the objective is met, the insulted are defended, the barriers are brought down, the people are intermixed, Islam is victorious, and the call of Muhammad, peace be upon him, and victory is manifested. This is for the believers, and the disbelievers as well as those who rebelled against him will be met with disappointment. This is so that Allah will help him. Verily, Allah is Strong and Mighty!

---

[3] This function of the Mahdi has been mentioned verbatim by the Prophet, peace and blessings be upon him and his progeny, in a well-known hadith. He is related to have said: ((If only one day were to remain in this world, Allah will send a man from my Ahl al-Bayt who will fill it with justice and equity just as it was filled with tyranny and injustice)). This narration appears in texts such as ***Sunan Abu Dāwūd, Al-Mustadrak, Musnad Ahmed b. Hanbal, Mušannaf Ibn Abi Shayba, Jāmi al-Ušūl*** of Ibn Athīr, ***Kanz al-'Ummāl, Majmu' az-Zawā`id, Al-Mu'jam al-Kabīr, Al-Mu'jam al-Awsaṭ, Ušūl al-Kāfi*** and ***Bihār al-Anwār***.

At that time, Allah's victory for the righteous will be completed, His betrayal and destruction of the transgressors will be perfected. Allah will uproot the misguided imams of oppression and revive, by means of His blessing of the pure Mahdi,[4] the call to truth. He declares the word of truth and provides by such, is kind to him, is well supported and conciliated in it.

Noble, Hashemite, Fatimid, one who gathers the heart,
Compassionate, praiseworthy, fearless of death in war.
You see his enemies wary of him with distress of death.
He is brave, destroying the spirits in battle by means of striking,
Merciful to my brother in piety, severe to my brother in sin,
Wise out of piety and very decisive in judgement and affairs,
By means of the justice of the Mahdi, succour of east and west!

It has reached us from Zayd b. 'Ali, may the prayers of Allah be upon both of them: "We are the resurrected and we are the seekers of blood. The pure soul is from the son of al-Hasan, and the one who is helped is from the son of al-Hussein. It is as if I am the youth of the pure soul and he is leaving Medina, desiring Mecca. If the people kill him, there is no helper left for them on earth, nor is there in heaven there an excuse. At that, the Riser (*al-Qā'im*) of the family of Muhammad, may Allah's prayers and peace be upon him and his progeny, will rise with his back to the Ka'ba. Between his eyes is a bright light that only the blind of the heart will be blinded to in this world and the hereafter." Abu Hāshim asked: "Verily, O Abul-Hussein, what is that light?" He said: "His justice regarding you and his argument against creation."

It has reached us from Allah's Messenger, peace and blessings be upon him and his progeny:

> ((Sedition will continue to pile up in the plains (*jarāthīm*) of the Arabs insomuch that 'Allah' will not be uttered. Then Allah will send a people who will gather as the autumn cumulus gathers, and there will Allah revive truth and destroy falsehood)).[5]

Concerning seeking assistance from enemies against the oppression of the disobedient

There is no harm in seeking the help of the transgressors and sinners against the immoral disbelievers as long as the rulings of the rightful are applied to them, and the prescribed punishments of the Lord of creation are established on them, and they were not reluctant to do so. With the imam should be a group of the righteous in the military, who enjoin the good and forbid the evil as well as frighten those who oppose that. And if that were impermissible, then the victory of the truth and the righteous would not have been an obligation from the Lord of creation against all disobedient immorality and jihad against them. Therefore, it is the best obligation from the Lord of creation.

And if the obligation of jihad on the part of the sinners with the guiding imams were exempted, then those deeds of the workers which is below it, such as prayer, fasting, and other acts of the people, would also be exempted from them. Rather, the statutes of the Most Merciful are obligatory for every human being in a state of disobedience and benevolence, and all of Allah's rulings are clearly established upon them. And the imam must exhort them and command them all to obey their Lord and towards jihad. Therefore, the best of His obligations, Glory be to Him, is to command them and exhort them to it, even if they are in opposition to the truth and deviate from the path of righteousness when the rulings are imposed on them and on the height of their falsehood is the light of Islam.

---

[4] The term 'Mahdi' is universally understood by all Muslims to refer to a messianic figure who is to appear at the end of time in order to restore justice and revive the pure religion of Allah. Although the name and title of this personality is consensually agreed-upon, the other details regarding him and his abilities are rather varied and have taken on, as it were, even mythical proportions. Moreover, the idea which places the Mahdi in this light as a sort of supernatural saviour figure is what I would call 'Mahdi-ism.' Such doctrine serves as the firewood for the flames of Shi'ite and Sufi theology. Moreover, such doctrine is not present in the writings of al-Hādi or the consensus of the Ahl al-Bayt.

[5] Similarly narrated in ***Ŝahīh Ibn Hibbān, Al-Mu'jam al-Kabīr, Al-Mu'jam al-Awsaṭ, Musnad Abu Ya'la***

Allah's Messenger, peace and blessings be upon him and his progeny, used to call for jihad against the disbelievers and command all servants to do it as well as seek help from many immoral, hypocritical, unjust, and disobedient ones. Likewise, the Commander of Believers, 'Ali b. Abi Ťālib, upon him be peace, used to fight those who fought with his people, and among them were many disobedient, unjust, hypocritical and traitorous people.

Regarding this is what was narrated from him, upon him be peace, of his saying after he returned from Ŝiffīn while he was delivering a sermon on the pulpit in Kufa, and some of the Kharijites said: "There is no ruling except for Allah, and there is no obedience to one who disobeys Allah." He, may Allah have mercy on him, replied:

> I await Allah's ruling upon you! As long as you have three things over us, we will have three things over you. We will not prevent you from praying in our mosques although you are not upon our way, we will not initiate war against you unless you initiate it against us first, and we will not prevent you from any of the war booty. Your hands are with our hands.[6]

The meaning of his statement "Your hands are with our hands" is regarding 'the war against our enemy.' So this proves that he sought the assistance of the enemies, as long as the rulings of the Lord of creation were imposed on them.

My father related to me that his father said regarding seeking assistance from the disobedient against rebels:

> They can seek assistance from them against them if they help, and then especially if they submit to the rule of truth and remain calm, because Allah—Glory be to Him—has enjoined upon them to assist the righteous, even if they are disobedient, wicked, and sinners, just as He has enjoined upon them the prayer and other obligations of the religion even if they are openly disobedient. And that which Allah has enjoined upon them from His obligations and if they transgress is more of an evidence and clear explanation. How can they not seek assistance from the disobedient against them while assistance is an obligation from Allah on the sinners among them? How is it impermissible in the religion of Allah for a believer to refrain or leave doing such but not for a disobedient one? According to Allah, leaving and refraining from such is a means of curse and destruction.

If someone asks "How about that which they do not believe in from the immorality and injustice that Allah has forbidden?" we respond by saying: If they reached a point regarding that matter, a judgement was passed upon them according to what was necessary for them in that judgement. If it were forbidden to seek assistance from them for the sake of what they fear of that in the transgressors, then it would also be forbidden to seek their assistance to fight the idolaters because of the fear of their immorality and deceit is the same as fear from the transgressors.

Allah, the Blessed and Exalted, has mobilised the hypocrites to fight for His cause and condemned them for not fighting behind His Prophet, peace and blessings be upon him and his progeny, and the believers. Allah's Messenger, peace and blessings be upon him and his progeny, fought the idolaters alongside the hypocrites. However, the hypocrite is more entitled and deserving of fear than a monotheist who commits open disobedience and sin. And if the believers were forbidden to help them, the believers would be obliged to expel and fight them. And if they were to assist them, all the oppressors would be destroyed, but if they were to abandon their assistance, all the Muslims would be destroyed.

If it were impermissible for the believers to seek help and assistance from the openly disobedient nor right for the disobedient to respond to and support the believers, then how would such one who advocates for this opinion view Allah's Messenger himself if he were alive today among the people of his religion and the various nations that remain today and he called them to do similar to what was done then while they held to the same view?

[6] Similarly narrated in ***Al-Mu'jam al-Awsaṫ, Mušannaf Ibn Abi Shayba, Sunan al-Bayhaqi***

Rather, if he called them, a group of them from misguidance would respond to him until he establishes the right of Allah regarding them and the common people. Does that require him to judge between them according to the rulings that Allah has commanded him to do, or does he not judge by the rulings of Allah over them?

Why does he have disobedience and misguidance among them, or does he remain with and among them as long as they have permanently established their misguidance and disobedience? How can that be when Allah says: {**Verily, we hath revealed unto thee the Book with truth that thou may judge between humankind by that which Allah hath shown thee. And be not for the treacherous a pleader**} (**Q. 4:105**)? And if he were to abandon the wrongdoers while he can find a way for them and the Muslims to change their wrongdoing and crimes and that which displeases Allah, then pleading on their behalf would be one of the greatest causes of Allah's wrath.

Allah has also said regarding the appointment of injunction upon His Messenger: {**And plead not on behalf of those who deceive themselves. Verily, Allah loves not the one who is treacherous and sinful**} (**Q. 4:107**). The Blessed and Exalted prohibits that one argues on behalf of the treacherous or the enemies. Arguing on their behalf is considered even less beneficial and weaker than abandoning them due to treachery and neglecting the application of Allah's judgement on them regarding it.

What we have said suffices as a proof and evidence since it contains a path of guidance for the one who is fair. That which is in this section is clear and illuminating. Allah is praised that such interpretation can be counted!

Concerning one who refuses to pledge allegiance to a just imam or is discouraged from him

The least that should be done to a person who refuses to pledge allegiance to a just imam is that his testimony be discarded, and his reliability removed. Also, he is to be refused the war booty which is given to others, and he is to be given the least in regard to his standing.

As for the one who withholds obedience, it is obligatory for them that he teach them their etiquette until they stop. Otherwise, they must be imprisoned and prevented from discouraging Muslims from the greatest obligation of the Lord of creation, or they are to be exiled from Muslim lands; this is the least thing to be done with them. They are like those who withheld and were {**the fearmongers in Medina**} (**Q. 33:60**).

They are those about whom Allah says: {**If the hypocrites and those in whose hearts is a disease and the fearmongers in Medina do not cease, We shall verily urge thee on against them. Then, they shall not be thy neighbours therein save a little while. Accursed [are they]! They shall be slain with a mighty slaughter wheresoever they are found as an established practice (*sunnat*) of Allah regarding those who hath passed from aforetime. And never wilt ye find a change in Allah's established practice**} (**Q. 33:60-62**).

So Allah, Glory be to Him, has declared that this is an established practice for the first and the last, as well as for all those who withheld obedience. This statement from Allah, the Mighty and Majestic, is specific to the chosen Prophet and general to all the imams of guidance.

My father related to me that his father was asked about the one who refuses to pledge allegiance to a just imam. The latter replied: "The least that should be done is that his share of the war booty must be prevented from him and that his testimony not be accepted."

Concerning that which is obligatory for the just imam regarding the subjects and what is obligatory for them regarding him

It is obligatory for the imam's subjects to listen to him, obey him and implement what he commanded them to implement. They are to leave what he commanded them to leave, rise when he calls them to rise, to sit down when he commands them to sit, fight when he commands them, be at peace with those with whom he is at peace, and be hostile to those with whom he is hostile. They are to advise him in secret and in public. They are to be loyal to him and show mutual affection with him, and love the one who loves him, and hate the one who hates him. They are to not conceal something that he needs to know nor are they to incline towards something that he dislikes out of enmity. They are to observe that which Allah has obligated upon them in respect to him, and they are to be behind him in preserving the unseen just as they are in his face.

They are to help him though it be against their own interests and that of others, even if they are their fathers, sons, brothers or clan. They are to prevent him from what they prevent from themselves, their families, children and their money. They are to support him in secret and public, as well as in hardship, prosperity and comfort. They are to fulfil to him that which they promised and that for which they pledged allegiance to him.

And if they did that and they were for him, then they would have fulfilled that which Allah has enjoined upon and decreed for them. And they will be—according to Allah—among the pious, pure, and noble believers who will have no fear on the Day of Judgement, nor will they have trepidation when meeting Him on the Day of Resurrection. Rather, they will be as the Most Generous describes them: **{…as brethren on couches facing one another}** **(Q. 15:47)** **{The great terror shall not grieve them. And the Angels shall welcome them: "This is thy day which ye were promised!"}** **(Q. 21:103)** **{Verily, the God-conscious shall be in shade and springs and fruits which they desire. "Eat and drink for what ye used to do!"}** **(Q. 77:41-43)** **{The God-conscious shall be in a secure place amidst gardens and springs, adorned in silk and brocade facing one another—thus, shall it be. And We shall pair them with mates of clear eye (*hūri'ayn*), therein they shall be calling for every fruit whilst in security. They shall not taste therein death save the first death, and they shall be protected from the Hellfire as a bounty of thy Lord. That is the great achievement!}** **(Q. 44:51-57)**.

It is obligatory for the subjects' imam to guide them to the truth, forbid them from immorality, enjoin the greater good, forbid injustice and evil, judge by Allah's judgement regarding them, fulfil Allah's judgements over them, be fair between them in his judgement, be equal among them in the division of their war booty, lead them to the Book of their Lord, give them understanding in the religion, bring them closer to the Lord of creation, save the wealth of the rich, enrich the wealth of their Lord for the poor, fill those with hungry bellies, clothe those who are naked, pay off their debts, marry those who cannot find the means of marriage among them according to capacity and existence, bring them near and not alienate them, honour them and not insult them, appear to them and not hide from them, care about them and not reject their matter, check on them with kindness, bestow grace upon them, is merciful and forgiving to them, is severe against those among them who oppose the Most Gracious until he restores such person to goodness and benevolence as well as deters him from injustice and disobedience.

Furthermore, he is to not monopolise them with the wealth of their Lord nor spend it on anything other than them. Rather, he is to return the wealth of Allah when He commanded him to return it as well as spend it on that which Allah has appointed him to spend on from the neediest aspects of the Muslims' affairs and to the benefit, good and righteousness for the *Ummah*.

And he must not force himself upon them or raise himself above what is obligatory upon them. For the sons, he should be better than their fathers and for the parents, he should be better than their sons in terms of showing sympathy, care, concern, mercy, patience and forbearance.

If he were to do such, he would have observed his trust to Allah, advised his subjects, demonstrated his justice, unloosened the shackles from his neck, confirmed for Allah his proof, and imitated the action of his grandfather about whom Allah says: **{There has come unto thee a Messenger from amongst thy selves, grievous to him that ye suffer, full of concern for thee, merciful and compassionate towards the believers}** **(Q. 9:128)**.

And it is obligatory for the *Ummah* to obey, support, unite with, help, and aid him. Also, it is forbidden for them to leave and abandon him. It is impermissible for them—according to Allah—to reject him, turn away from his group, or refrain from the oath of allegiance to him. And whoever dared to do any of that against Allah will be considered among the sinners deserving of a humiliating torment about whom Allah, the Glorified, said: {**"Ye shall be called against a people of great might. Ye shall have to fight them [till death] or till they surrender. And if ye obey, Allah shall give unto thee a good reward; but if ye turn away as ye did turn away aforetime, He shall punish thee with a painful punishment!"**} (**Q. 48:16**).

Allah has obligated such upon us insomuch that as long as they demonstrate such to us, we will be such for them by our strenuous efforts.

Concerning the one who breaks the oath of allegiance to a rightful ruler

Whoever breaks the oath of allegiance to a rightful ruler—such person is considered one of the wicked according to Allah and punished in Allah's judgement. Regarding that, the Lord of creation says about them: {**Verily, those who pledge allegiance to thee hath simply pledged allegiance to Allah. Allah's Hand is above their hands. So, whosoever breaks the oath has simply broken the oath to their own harm. And whosoever honours his pledge with Allah—unto him shall bestow a great reward**} (**Q. 48:10**).

Regarding that, it has reached us from Allah's Messenger, peace and blessings be upon him and his progeny:

> ((There are three that Allah will not look at or purify on the Day of Judgement and they will incur punishment: a man who gives the oath of allegiance to a just imam who is for him only if he gives him something of this world but is not for him if he does not give him anything, a man who has extra water while travelling but prevents it from another traveller and a man who swears an oath that he was truthful in taking payment for giving such and such commodity yet lied about it)).

It has also reached us that the Commander of Believers, 'Ali b. Abi Ṭālib, upon him be peace, said:

> Allah's Messenger, peace and blessings be upon him and his progeny, said: ((O fellow men! Whoever among you takes the oath of allegiance to me just as women would take the oath of allegiance to him and dies—Paradise will belong to him. Whoever commits something that is prohibited for him, and the prescribed punishment is applied to him—it would be considered expiation. Whoever commits something that is prohibited for him, and it is concealed—it would be for Allah. He can punish him if He wills, or He can pardon him if He wills)).[7]

The meaning of his statement, peace and blessings be upon him and his progeny, ((...and the prescribed punishment is applied to him—it would be considered expiation)) is that the expiation would be due on him after repentance, refraining from the sin and returning to obedience.

Concerning acting as a scribe for an oppressor and causing fear to the tyrants

It is impermissible to act as a scribe for oppressors and to sympathise with them with a writing or something else for the believers because due to the writing for them, we are reassured and sympathetic to them as well as that which invites affection between them. However, Allah has said: {**Ye shall not find a people who believe in Allah and the Last Day have mutual affection for the one who turns away from Allah and His Messenger—even though they art their fathers, their sons, their brothers or their kin**} (**Q. 58:22**) to the end of the *Surah*.

The exception is the believer who is compelled to write for an oppressor out of fear. If he were to be killed for refusing to write for him, he should write for him at the time of the necessity and not write for him when such necessity is over. He is to apologise to Allah for that based on the reason that is known by the Glorified. He is to be on guard against writing that which is impermissible for him to write. He should not incline towards [such oppressor] in his writing at all, for Allah says: {**Incline not towards those who do wrong lest the Fire shall touch thee. And ye shall have against Allah no allies. Then, ye shall not be helped**} (**Q. 11:113**).

---

[7] Similarly narrated in ***Ŝaḥīḥ al-Bukhāri, Ŝaḥīḥ Muslim, Sunan an-Nisā'i, Sunan ad-Dārimi, Sunan at-Tirmidhi, Sunan ad-Dārqutni, Sunan al-Bayhaqi***

My father related to me that his father said that al-Ma`mūn asked a man from the descendants of Abu Ťālib whom he respected to write a correspondence between him and al-Qāsim b. Ibrāhīm, may Allah have mercy on him, and to appoint a certain amount of money for him for a grave matter. So that man came to him and asked him if he should write a letter to al-Ma`mūn or assure him that if he were to write al-Ma'mun's letter, he would respond to it. Al-Qāsim b. Ibrāhīm, may Allah be satisfied with him, said to the man: "No, by Allah! Allah will never see me doing that!"

Whoever causes fear to an oppressive ruler and tyrant in this world will be granted safety by Allah in his hereafter. By the One who has the soul of Yahya b. al-Hussein in His Hand! I am not contented to be safe from the oppressors for one night even if I were to possess everything that the sun rose on! This is because if were to be so, we would have been dependent on them and loyal to them, and Allah has forbidden that to the believers.

It has reached me that some of the ancestors used to say: "Whoever among them made him [i.e. an oppressor] afraid of them and they became afraid of him, Paradise will be obligatory for him."

Concerning what is obligatory upon the believers who cannot change the oppressor's actions that they see

It is obligatory for the believers to object to the objectionable with their own hands if they are able to do so. If they are unable to do it, then they must object it with their own tongues. And if they cannot do that, they must emigrate on their behalf. They must also have objection and hostility to the oppressors in their hearts and not remain in the place among them or be close to them.

Whoever among the believers is not able to do that due to the abundance of his family size and their need for him and is not able to take them with him, then let him stay with them for a while until he earns for them what will benefit them for a few days of their lives. Then, he is to emigrate in Allah's land far enough from the oppressor so that if he fears loss on the part of his family, he could return to fulfil their needs and then rush from them. Thus, he should not remain with the oppressors, nor should he cause loss to the one with him until Allah makes a way out for him from his affair.

Concerning what the imam should do before fighting the enemy

The imam must write a letter to the rebels before sending an army to them and invite them to the Book of Allah and the Sunnah of His Messenger in it, peace and blessings be upon him and his progeny. He must enjoin what is right and forbid what is wrong, revive the truth and put an end to falsehood. He must teach them that if they were to enter into that agreement and respond favourably to his call, they will have what the other Muslims have and will be treated the same in terms of virtue and goodness. They are subject to what they have from a judged ruling or a determination from Allah in decided matters.

If they accept that, he can give them what he gives them. If they do not accept that and do not respond favourably, he is given permission to wage war against them and cast them out. Allah does not guide the plots of the treacherous, so seek Allah's help against them as well as urge the believers to jihad against them. Therefore, fight them until there is no persecution and so that the religion, judgement and affair are for Allah alone. As the Glorified says: **{Fight them till there is no persecution and the religion is for Allah. But if they cease, then let there not be hostility save against the wrongdoers} (Q. 2:193)**.

Concerning what the imam of truth does when he marches towards jihad against the enemies and meets the disobedient

It is preferable for the imam to, if he goes to meet his enemy, write a letter of second invitation and send a messenger with it ahead so that he precedes to his enemy, inviting him to what he first called him. So, when the imam descends into the camp in which he meets his enemy facing him, he will send to him one, two or three men who have knowledge, understanding, reason, opinion, religion, manliness, cunning, acumen and piety.

If he is safe from them, they will come to and call him to the Most Gracious. And they are to prevent him from obeying Satan and instil fear of Allah in him as well as His torment and punishment. He is to be reminded of Allah and the domain of the hereafter. They are to ask him to spare bloodshed and enter into the goodness and guidance into that which the Muslims have entered. If he responds to them favourably, then he is to be considered one of them. If he refuses to do so, they should return his news to their leader.

If the imam wants to mobilise his soldiers and arrange his companions, then let him arrange them row by row just as people line up for prayer, levelling their shoulders and keeping them tightly aligned. Allah, the Glorified, says: **{Verily, Allah loves those who fight in His way in ranks as if they were a solid structure} (Q. 60:4)**.

So, if he lined them up row after row, the length of their rows should be according to the capacity of their camp. He places in the first row their best and protectors, and on his right hand is a brave, courageous man, and on his left is a similar type of man as well. He is to be in the heart or between the two rows in a critical position of horses and men who are trustworthy and reliant in their religion and their men. If he wants to be somewhere else, he can do so.

A group of equestrians is to remain behind all the ranks and repel everyone who is deviated from the army or turns away from the enemy. He is to put in the first row two wings as dense as the number of those with him and their number. If an opportunity or surprise from their enemy were to occur, they can seize it, take advantage of it, and come behind them if they can. If they are able, let them come from behind them, and the first row should be carried over them from their front, and the rows should follow it slowly, crawling, without separation or mixing.

And if the two wings do not see the situation as an opportunity or chance, they should remain steadfast and not leave their position. If the right wing is overwhelmed, extend it to the right wing below it. Likewise, if the left flank is attacked and overshadowed, extend it to the left wing that is closest to it and do not falter. Likewise, if the centre is overtaken and the right and left wings increase in some of its men, the imam should advise his companions to speak less and not shout or roar.

So if he establishes his ranks and spreads his wings and stops those who repel the perversions of the soldiers from behind them and sets the people on their banners and takes charge of all the horses and the men who are the commanders and the order of his army, then let him order the Qur'an to be spread or hung on the spears and let a group of people emerge between the two rows shouting: "O people, we call you to what is in these copies of the Qur'an! So, respond to it, obey Allah and enter into the truth the Muslims have entered into! Do not break the staff of the believers! Spare your blood and ours and return to the truth that Allah has shown to you and us! Do not be deceived by Satan or this person who calls you to war with us and wants to cause damage between you and us! O people, we call you to that which Allah has called you! We invite you and forbid what Allah has forbidden! We permit what Allah has permitted, take the right and give it, negate oppression and injustice, feed the hungry, clothe the naked, reform the country, do justice to the slaves, place the Book in front of us and before you and follow His judgement! We warn you and ourselves of Allah!"

If they respond favourably or some of them answer, they are to be considered close, honourable, best, and respected. If they persist in misguidance and follow the immorality ignorantly, then let the group carrying the Qur'an say with the loudest of their voices "Oh Allah, we call You to witness against them!" three times. Then, he is to let them return to their camp.

And if the imam is able to give up their war on that day and perceives a way to that insomuch that he did not fear deception for himself or his companions from his enemies, he can do so. Therefore, if on the next day, he should mobilise his army as it was the day before and then have the callers between the two rows bring out the Qur'an with them and command that the Book that was read the day before should be read on that day so that they can respond favourably. Otherwise, Allah, His Angels and Messengers will bear witness against them. Then, he is to let them go to their camp.

If the imam is able and sees a reason to desist that day, then that is the most complete argument for them and closer to Allah's victory over them. So, when he leaves, let him make vanguards and spies over them and fortify them during the day and night in a trench if he can. They should surround all his soldiers and plant caltrops (*hasīka*) around if they have any. If he is not able to do any of that, he is to order the commanders to mobilise their companions and be careful during their nights and days, as well as be on guard without being negligent. They should be commanded to use anticipation and fear to plot the movements of their enemy. He should also order them, if they are attacked by a group, to not speak. No one from the army should shout except to those who were in that flank. If it is something like that, it will extend the place of shouting and crowding with men and kindle for them a great fire on the side of the camp so that they can take comfort and know their leader's plan for it.

On the third day, he is to appear to his enemy, arrange his soldiers, mobilise his armies, deliver sermons, admonish them, and tell them what Allah has prepared for the patient. Then he is to command the callers to go out, stand between the two rows and do with the Qur'an what they did previously in terms of spreading it with spears raised. He is to command that something be written in which the call is given, so that it is read to the enemy and they are called to what is in it.

If they respond favourably, they are to be accepted. If they refuse, Allah's callers are to testify against them three times, then they are to be allowed to return to their camp. Then, Allah willing, it will become clear that they had betrayed them, and victory was required for the believers over them; so let the imam's army go to them in an expedition together with intention, insight, knowledge, and a noble argument with dignity, reverence, remembrance of Allah, and submission while reciting *Allahu Akbar* repeatedly. If horses came out for them, horses came out to them, and if men emerged, men came out to them. If nothing came out of that, the people are to march together until they fight against their enemy, show their banners and brandish their swords against the enemies of Allah and asked Allah for victory and help against them.

If Allah helps and supports them as well as subdues their enemy and humiliates their positions, then let them beware of temptation to enter them or enmity with them. And let them increase in the remembrance of Allah, thanking and praising Him.

If those who fought them had a faction to which they would return and an imam they would defend against and he was not with them and was in a country other than their camp to which they would return and be repelled, the Muslims would follow their ruler and allow their wounded to be investigated in the demand for them. They would kill those who pursued and take captives of those they loved until they separated them, dispersed their group and secured their return.

And if they do not have a group to which they can return and he is the chief to whom they take refuge and turn back after their defeat against him, they are to not be pursued and their wounded are to not be punished. However, if they are expelled and scattered and dispersed, it is impermissible for them to be killed if they turn away and are defeated. If Allah defeats, humiliates, punishes, and kills them, the imam is to order the collection of their spoils and include everything that was in their camp. He is to urge the people to fulfil the trust in it and inform them of what Allah, the Mighty and Majestic, has enjoined on those who transgress in any of that. If he collects and investigates it, he is to command that it be distributed among the people of the army and that arrows be drawn for them.

Concerning the distribution of war booty among the army

The booty is to be collected—whether they are few or more, whether they are small or great. If all of it is collected and combined, the imam will have the choice as to anything that he wants from it—either a horse, sword or shield. Similar was done by Allah's Messenger, peace and blessings be upon him and his progeny, regarding war booty. It was designated as *as-ŝafi*.

Regarding that, my father related to me that his father used to say:

> It is for the imam to choose from the war booty the portion that he wants or a known thing for himself, just as was done by Allah's Messenger, peace and blessings be upon him and his progeny, in respect to the spoils of war. He can choose from the spoils that which he wants, and he be permitted to do that according to his own independent judgement and opinion. This is because he simply takes, gives and judges by what he sees of the spoils before they are divided. That which Allah judges regarding its judgement is that it is for Allah and His Messenger specifically. This has been narrated as the judgement of the Qur'anic verse regarding the spoils of war.
>
> It is narrated that Allah's Messenger, peace and blessings be upon him and his progeny, could take for himself the portion that was designated as *as-ŝafi*. This name proves he had the choice and could take from the entire war booty, and it is a clear evidence of such. This is because if *as-ŝafi* were about distribution and equal sharing, then it would be designated as such. If it were to be distributed equally, it would not be permissible to call it *as-ŝafi* or *Mustafa* while all of such could be equally divided.

The imam has the right to all the booty before it is divided as he likes because Allah, the Blessed and Exalted, has made the matter of the spoils to belong to Allah's Messenger, peace and blessings be upon him and his progeny. The rights and judgement regarding that which belongs to Allah's Messenger, peace and blessings be upon him and his progeny, similarly belongs to the rightful imams of his Ahl al-Bayt who follow him and his path, peace and blessings be upon him and his progeny, as well as judge by his judgement and Sunnah.

My father related to me that his father said:

> When the war booty is collected, it is permissible for the imam to divide the spoils according to his opinion. He can do what Allah's Messenger, peace and blessings be upon him and his progeny, used to do. He can divide the spoils according to his opinion based on the amount that he sees fit. He can divide a portion of it based on the one who was fiercest against the enemies of Allah. If he were to do that, he would have established that which is obligatory upon him regarding those people of strenuous effort in fighting. It is also based on the judgement of Allah when He says in *Surah al-Anfāl*: **{They ask thee about the spoils. Say: "The spoils belong to Allah and His Messenger. So, be conscious of Allah and rectify amongst thyselves. And obey Allah and His Messenger if ye art indeed believers"} (Q. 8:1)**.
>
> Therefore, if there were no spoils among the entire war booty, then there would be nothing to say about it. When the believers asked about it and started speaking about what Allah's Messenger, peace and blessings be upon him and his progeny, did with it, Allah—the One with whom are no partners—declared that it belongs to Him and His Messenger with Him. He and His Messenger have the authority over it, as well as the judgement and decision in its matter. It is not for any believer after him to say anything about it, nor is there religion and Islam for anyone who disagrees with Allah regarding it. And that which Allah has appointed for His Messenger of that is for the just and rightful imam after him.

If the war booty is collected and the imam chooses what he wants for himself as well as distributes what he wants to the people of strenuous effort if he sees fit, he is to command that the war booty be divided into five shares. One share is removed from the five shares; it is one fifth of the spoils for those whom Allah has designated and appointed. Then, the imam is to divide and distribute the remaining four-fifths of the war booty among the soldiers who fought and were present: two shares will be for the cavalryman and one share for the foot soldier.

There is only an additional share for the horse. Others say that there are two additional shares for the horse, but we do not hold to that view regarding the war booty. One is to appoint shares for the non-Arabian horses (*al-barādhīn*) just as one would do for Arabian horses. However, shares are not appointed for the mule, donkey or camel.

Once four-fifths of the booty is divided among the free, adult Muslim soldiers who attended it, the imam orders the fifth, which was at his disposal. It is then divided into six parts and distributed among those whom Allah has made for him from among his family whom he has been placed in charge.

Concerning the distribution of the fifth of the war booty

The fifth is commanded, and it is divided into six parts: one for Allah, one for His Messenger, one for the relatives of His Messenger, one for orphans, one for the wayfarer, and one for the poor. Regarding that, Allah says: **{And know that whatsoever ye take as booty, verily a fifth thereof is for Allah, and for the Messenger and for the kin and orphans and the needy and the wayfarer}** **(Q. 8:41)**.

As for the share that belongs to Allah, the imam spends it on the affairs of Allah and that which brings him close to rectification for His slaves, such as repairing their roads, digging their wells, providing supplies for their mosques, rebuilding dilapidated mosques, completing their repair projects and other things that he strives for according to his opinion, which Allah grants success for which no one else can help him.

As for the share that belongs to Allah's Messenger, peace and blessings be upon him and his progeny, it is for the rightful imam. He can spend it on his family, horse, servants as well as that which benefits the Muslims generally and provide extra to their collective wealth.

As for the share that belongs to the relatives of the Prophet's Progeny, peace and blessings be upon him and his progeny, it is for those whom Allah has designated. They are those from whom Allah has prohibited charity and who has been given this as a substitute. They are the progenies of 'Ali, Ja'far, Aqīl and al-'Abbās. It is to be equally distributed to them—whether male or female. It is to never be removed from any of them because Allah has simply appointed that it be given to them due to their relations to Allah's Messenger, as well as their struggles and strenuous efforts with him. It will not be removed from them as long are relatives, and their relationship with him will never be removed nor will it be given to anyone other than them.

These four relatives are those among whom Allah's Messenger, peace and blessings be upon him and his progeny, distributed the fifth dues. It has been narrated to us that he gave the fifth dues to the Bani al-Muṭṭalib. It has also reached us on the authority of Jubayr b. Mut'im[§]:

> When Allah's Messenger, peace and blessings be upon him and his progeny, distributed the shares to the relatives among the Banu Hāshim and Bani al-Muṭṭalib. 'Uthmān and I came to him and said: "O Messenger of Allah! They are the Bani Hāshim, and we cannot deny their virtue due to your position that Allah has placed you in in respect to them. However, have not you considered that you gave to our brothers from the Bani al-Muṭṭalib and deprived us? Verily, are not we and they the same?" The Prophet, peace and blessings be upon him and his progeny, said: ((They have not separated from us in the days of the pre-Islamic era nor Islam. The Banu Hāshim and Banu al-Muṭṭalib are simply like this)) and he held up two fingers together.

It is for that reason that we say that it is impermissible to distribute to anyone other than these four sets of relatives. This is because Allah's Messenger, peace and blessings be upon him and his progeny, did not mention that it is to be distributed to other than them unless they are from the Banu al-Muṭṭalib.

It is possible that he distributed it among the Banu al-Muṭṭalib as a gift from him, peace and blessings be upon him and his progeny, to them due to the appreciation for their past actions and patiently striving with him and not that he made it an obligation to distribute a share to them. The imam is to consider such in agreement with Allah's guidance.

That which Allah mentions as the sixth of the fifth dues of the war booty is simply obligatory for those whom Allah designated among the relatives of Allah's Messenger, peace and blessings be upon him and his progeny. They are those four sets of relatives whom we designated that follow, obey and aid the imam. As for those who do not obey or strive with the imam and are stubborn against the truth due to their turning away from the rightful imam, there is no right or share for them unless they repent to Allah for their sin and manifest such repentance to the imam. Then, they would be an example set by him for others regarding Allah's judgement and wealth.

As for the share of the orphan and the needy and the traveller, it refers to the orphans, needy, and travellers among the progeny of Allah's Messenger, peace and blessings be upon him and his progeny. They are to be given priority over other than them. If there are no orphans, needy, or travellers from the progeny of Allah's Messenger, then it is to be given to the descendants of those who emigrated to Allah's Messenger, peace and blessings be upon him and his progeny. When those who are close to Allah's Messenger are sufficiently enriched, then one is to refer to those people other than them who are close to the Messenger. When the descendants of the Emigrants are sufficiently enriched, then the closest in relation to the Messenger is the Anŝār. This is due to their aiding and striving with Allah's Messenger, peace and blessings be upon him and his progeny. One is to begin with those who strive the most in jihad as well as provide the most aid for Allah and Islam. When the Anŝār are sufficiently enriched, one is to refer to the remaining Muslims among the Arabs and others. This would be for the orphans, needy, and travellers.

Whoever amongst the descendants of the Emigrants and Anŝār and the remaining Muslims rebel against the right and the rightful imam as well as express hatred for the Ahl al-Bayt or oppose or refrain from helping the imam of the believers, there will be nothing for them just as there is nothing for those who oppose the Progeny of Allah's Messenger and others.

We simply say that the orphans, needy, and travellers among the Prophet's Progeny are most deserving of the fifth dues than other orphans, needy and travellers because the latter can take what they want from the tithes and charity and the former cannot; the latter can take benefit whereas the former cannot. Because of that, they [i.e. the orphans, needy and travellers from the Prophet's Progeny] are given more priority in the shares of the fifth dues than others. They are in more need of it as long as there are those orphans, needy and travellers whom Allah mentions among them.

Regarding that, it has reached us from 'Ali b. al-Hussein b. 'Ali, may Allah bless them all, that he used to say regarding the statement of Allah, the Blessed and Exalted **{And know that whatsoever ye take as booty, verily a fifth thereof is for Allah, and for the Messenger and for the kin and orphans and the needy and the wayfarer} (Q. 8:41)**: "They are our orphans, our needy and our travellers."

We say that when they are sufficiently enriched, then one is to refer to closest in relations among the descendants of the Emigrants due to the virtue that Allah affords those who struggled with His Messenger. After that, we appoint such to those Anŝār due to their struggles and patience. Likewise, the imam of the Muslims must be cognisant of those who endured hardship in Islam. That is because of the most benefit towards the religion and the claim of restitution from the Muslims.

If the imam needs to spend the entire fifth dues to rectify the affairs of the Muslims, he can do so and not distribute it. This is similar to what was done by Allah's Messenger, peace and blessings be upon him and his progeny, in the Battle of Hunayn as well as the Commander of Believers, upon him be peace, in the Battle of Ŝiffīn; he took the fifth dues and declared it lawful. It is for the imam to do such only out of necessity and need and not during times of ease. If the needy are more deserving of all of it, all of it is to be spent on them; similar is the case with travellers.

The proof for what we said regarding the shares of the orphans and needy from the war booty which Allah allows to be given to the soldiers and that it is to be given to the descendants of the Emigrants after the Prophet's Progeny and then the Anŝār once the Emigrants are sufficiently enriched and then the remaining Muslims after the Anŝār are sufficiently enriched is the statement of Allah, the Blessed and Exalted: **{Whatsoever Allah giveth as spoils unto His Messenger from the people of the townships—it is for Allah and His Messenger and the near of kin and the orphans and the needy and the wayfarer, that it not be a rotating wealth between the rich amongst thee. Whatsoever the Messenger gives thee, take it. Whatsoever he prohibits thee from, leave it. And be wary of Allah. Verily, Allah is severe in punishment. And it is for the poor emigrants who have been driven**

from their homes and their wealth, who seek bounty from Allah and who help Allah and His Messenger. They are those who are the truthful. And [it is for] **those who entered the domain and belief before them. They love those who flee unto them for refuge and find not in their breasts a need for that which hath been given them but prefer them above themselves though poverty was their lot. And whosoever is saved from his own avarice, such are they who are the successful. And those who came after them say: "Our Lord Forgive us and our brethren who were before us in the faith, and place not in our hearts any rancour toward those who believe. Our Lord! Thou art the Kind, the Merciful} (Q. 59:7-10)**.

Concerning those women, children, slaves and *dhimmi*s who are present in war and the distribution of war booty

If any of the aforementioned are present during the fighting, one is to not do with them what one would do with the men. Rather, it is for the imam to reward them to the extent of their assistance, benefit and fighting for the Muslims and efforts to obedience to the Lord of creation.

Concerning the captives who should not be killed

If a captive is captured and shackled so that he is prevented from escape, it is impermissible to kill him after that. Rather, he is to be imprisoned and shackled if he fears any matter from him or senses that he is a cause for harm for the Muslims. If there manifests from the captive any clear matters that indicate continued aggression during war after having been captured and the Muslims are unable to imprison him, the imam may choose to kill him. This is similar to the course of action with the Commander of Believers, 'Ali b. Abi Ťālib, may Allah have mercy on him, regarding the captive of 'Ammār[§] when there manifested from him a plot against the Commander of Believers while the war with the enemy was ongoing.

My father related to me that his father was asked about those captives who are impermissible to kill. He replied: "They are those who are weakened and subdued and deserve to be imprisoned and shackled due to their captivity." Then we asked him: "What is a captive?" He said: "He is the one who is shackled and forcefully inclined, just as Allah's Messenger, peace and blessings be upon him and his progeny, said: ((…not till you seize the hands of the wrongdoer and forcefully incline him towards the right way)).[8] He was asked: "What is the forceful inclination?" He replied:

> It is fastening and binding, just as Allah says: **{…and We fortified their vigour (*asra*)} (Q. 76:28)**. The interpretation is: We fastened their knot and frame. The Glorified makes the fortification of **{their vigour}** the tying of their ring. It is known in the Arabic language and speech that whoever fastens a tie has subjugated another. This is the captive that the Commander of Believers, 'Ali b. Abi Ťālib, upon him be peace, forbade from killing.
>
> It is not for the believer to take a captive—disbeliever or disobedient Muslim—in fetters, ropes or anything else even if such captive comes to him in humble submission unless it comes to the attention of the Commander of Believers. Then he can grant such favour afterwards or imprison such captive. It is impermissible for the imam who fears treachery and an assassination plot to release such person from prison even if it occurred to his soul to do so. How could it be considered a sound judgement to release one from whom the most righteous of the Muslims and one charged by Allah to assist the religion is not safe from assassination? How can one for whom is the fear of escape be released? How can such be the case when he could assist the wrongdoer in his wrongdoing and open disobedience? If they were to consider the imprisonment of the indecent for his indecency even though he is not a soldier, they would say that it would be necessary for the imam to exercise his right to keep the indecent imprisoned for such.

[8] Similarly narrated in ***Sunan at-Tirmidhi, Sunan Abu Dāwūd, Sunan Ibn Mājah, Musnad Ahmed***

One may say that 'Ali, may Allah be merciful to him, obligated release while he feared killing and fighting against the believers and that he released and set them free. However, he simply did such because it seemed good to him for the believers to cease fighting and to form a settlement with them. Allah says to His Messenger: **{And if thou fear treachery from any people, then cast it back to them equitably. Verily, Allah loves not the treacherous}** (**Q. 8:58**). The statement of the Glorified **{equitably}** simply means 'based on evidence.'

How can disbelieving captives be released while there is the fear of difficulty from him? How can he not imprison him while he assumes evil from him and the manifestation of his impudence against Allah? Allah, the Mighty and Majestic whose Names are sanctified, says: **{When ye meet those who disbelieve, strike their necks till ye hath subdued them, fastening their bonds. Thereafter, either grant them favour or a ransom till the war lays down its burdens}** (**Q. 47:4**). There should not ever be favour or ransom until after capture and imprisonment without doubt.

A hadith from Allah's Messenger, peace and blessings be upon him and his progeny, has come regarding them in which he housed captives in a stronghold and prison one night during the Battle of Badr. Allah's Messenger, peace and blessings be upon him and his progeny, had some anxiety that night concerning his uncle. 'Umar said to him regarding what was said and mentioned: "O Messenger of Allah, why is it that I see worry and anxiety in you insomuch that you cannot sleep?" He, peace and blessings be upon him and his progeny, replied: ((How can I not be concerned when I heard moaning from my uncle that night while he was in prison?))[9] If the matter were that it was not correct for him to imprison the captives after capture then he would have commanded that his uncle be released. If it were impermissible to imprison the captives—since he was not safe a whole year, it would have been impermissible to imprison him for the entire night rather than just a moment. It would not be for the believers to capture them until they debase and thrash them by killing and manifesting power over them. Then, if they were to be fought and conquered, they could be captured and imprisoned.

If the wrongdoers submit themselves to judgement or enter into a settlement after taking position in the ranks with the hopes of bringing them to the right or settlement without joining with a faction or group involved in the fighting, stop in this case and refrain from taking them as property.

Whenever there is established evidence that a captive killed the Muslims, he is to be killed. If he caused an injury, he is to be charged for it. If there is no proof of killing or causing injury and he repents with a manifest repentance, it is obligatory for the imam to release him. However, if there is reason to fear from such person, he is to be imprisoned. Similarly, if he fears for anyone else, such person must be imprisoned.

Concerning fighting the people of the *qibla* in their towns

The people of the *qibla* must not be housed in their towns, nor should their catapults be situated near them inside their fortresses. They should not be deprived of supplies nor from drinking. The sea should not be channelled to drown their towns, nor should their towns be burned down out of fear that women, children and others who are not to be affected will unknowingly be affected as well as innocent travellers to their towns.

Regarding that, Allah says to his Prophet, peace and blessings be upon him and his progeny, regarding the expedition of al-Hudaybiyya: **{And had it not been for believing men and believing women, whom ye know not—ye would tread them under foot and thus incur guilt for them without knowledge. It is so that Allah might bring into His mercy whom He will. If they were clearly separated, We could punish those who disbelieved with a painful punishment}** (**Q. 48:25**).

[9] Similarly narrated in ***Sunan al-Bayhaqi*** and ***Kanz al-'Ummāl***

Concerning attacking by night (*al-bayāt*)

It is impermissible for soldiers to engage in a sudden attack by night if there are among them those who would not be safe, such as travellers, business owners, women or children. Similarly, it is impermissible to suddenly attack a village or town by night.

As for those camps and military campaigns in which those who are impermissible to kill are safe or not present, there is no problem in suddenly attacking them by night and fighting them—whether a lot or a little—as long as there was an initial invitation [for peace] before that and they were given protection yet rejected such after it reached them. If there is a sudden attack by night after that, the war spoils would be for the one who attacked suddenly by night and there would be the fifth dues.

Concerning spoils and its explanation

The spoils are all lands that were opened by sword, treaty or seized and left as is, such as the dominions of Iraq and other places. It also includes that which is taken as *jizya* from the *dhimmi*s. Those spoils are distributed amongst the free Muslims, whether young or old, noble or any other similar state unless the imam needs to spend it or a portion of it to rectify the affairs of the Muslims. It would then be for him to do so because it would be out of his consideration for them. It is an obligation upon him by Allah to make strenuous effort in all their affairs as well as provide from such wealth and other types of Allah's wealth due to their fighting. However, the Progeny of Allah's Messenger, peace and blessings be upon him and his progeny, are to not be provided with charity and tithes; he can provide others with such though.

Concerning how the imam should admonish his forces when dispatching them or his soldiers when addressing them

When the imam addresses them while confronting the enemy, it is obligatory for him to admonish with everything that he is able, such as obedience to Allah, kindness, good dealings, excellence and firmness in his affair. Then, he is to say the following:

> In the Name of Allah, by Allah, for the sake of Allah and based upon the path of Allah's Messenger, peace and blessings be upon him and his progeny. Do not fight the people until you establish a proof against them. If they respond to you favourably by entering into the truth and departing from falsehood and open disobedience as well as by entering into your affair, they are your brothers. What belongs to them belongs to you and what is upon them is upon you. If they object to such and fight you, seek Allah's help against them. Do not kill a child, woman or elderly man who is not able to fight you. Do not drain springs or chop down any trees unless the trees are a source of harm for you. Do not make it into the shape of a man or animal. Do not go to the extremes or transgress.
>
> Whenever a man comes from your fortresses and gestures to another and he accepts the gesture, he is to be granted safety until he can hear the Speech of Allah, which is His Book and Proof. If he accepts, he is your brother in religion. If he objects, he is to be returned to his place of safety and you should seek Allah's help. Do not grant the people the status of Allah's protection (*dhimma*) nor that of His Messenger's protection or my protection. Rather, grant the people your protection and fulfil your covenant you granted them.

Much of what was mentioned above was that which Allah's Messenger, peace and blessings be upon him and his progeny, addressed to his soldiers.

If the forces are sent to fight a group of people from the domain of war, they are commanded to invite them to bear witness that there is no god but Allah and that Muhammad is Allah's Messenger, peace and blessings be upon him and his progeny. They are to be informed that if they respond favourably to such, their blood will be considered sacrosanct, and their wealth protected. They shall be admonished with that which the rebellious faction is admonished.

Concerning one who carries out a military expedition for hire

Whoever goes out for the sake of Allah is considered for hire even if he is not dispatched. He is to get the reward of his military expedition. However, everything obtained from the military expedition will be for the one who hired him with his wealth to join the expedition.

Concerning that which is in the possession of the oppressors and their helpers

When the imam overcomes the imams of oppression and tyranny, he can take everything from their possessions and belongings—whether a lot or a little, large or small, commodity or otherwise. The exception is if he owned a slave girl with whom he has had children. She cannot be taken with bearing his children because this would be considered a complete exhaustion of her.

As for other than that—such as estates, wealth, and other things acquired during their rule---all of such can be taken which was acquired from the wealth of Allah as well as any other type of wealth acquired during their rule, such as crops, if they were theirs before their sultanate because that which they fully consumed from Allah's wealth is more than what is taken from them.

The same judgement applies to their followers and those who help them in their oppression. If one of the Muslims establishes evidence on a specific thing that does not change and is not fully consumed and then evidence is established against him that it was misappropriated by force and taken from him unjustly, it is to be handed over to him and returned after being misappropriated from his possession.

My father related to me that his father was asked about the wealth, estates and slave girls in the possession of oppressors after the just imam overcomes them. He replied: "All his possessions can be taken." When he was asked: "Do you hold to the view that his slave girls and their children can be taken?" He replied: "This would be considered a complete exhaustion of them [and therefore impermissible]." He was then asked: 'What is your view on other things that they inherited or were gifted?" He replied: 'Only that which they fully consumed from Allah's wealth which was more than that."

Concerning the judgement of rebels regarding their *jizya* and herds

Their judgment is acknowledged, that which is the right is established, and that which is false is repelled. Rather, we have established what their ruling was in agreement with the right because it is a right. That which is a right is the judgement of Allah and not the judgement of the one who makes the judgement.

As for their herds and *jizya*, it is established from that as long as it is not extravagant and as long as they give it to those who gave it to him without helping them to extinguish the light of truth or suppress the word of truth. And it is licit as long as their giving it to him was for the good of the Muslims or for the right of an obligation from the Lord of creation. As for what they gave for unlawful amusements, music, evil, lying, opposing the truth and the rightful and its facilitating the killing the believers and destroying the Muslims, that which is taken from their possessions is not to be returned to them.

My father related to me that his father was asked about its judgement regarding oppressors. He replied: "That which is in accordance with the judgement of Allah is approved, and that which angers Allah, the Mighty and Majestic, is disapproved."

Concerning mercantile wealth of rebel soldiers

When there is mercantile wealth from among the rebel soldiers, which they did not bring against those in the right in terms of weapons or mounts, it is impermissible or lawful for those in the right to take it. However, whatever horses or weapons they brought, it would be permissible for the Muslims to take it and divide it into spoils if they were to obtain such.

As for other than that, it is to be returned over to them as long as there is nothing in their disobedience that was used to aid those of falsehood because of their goods they brought, which would be permissible for what they did not bring from their money.

My father related to me that his father was asked about the wealth of the merchants among the rebellious soldiers and whether it would be permissible or impermissible for the Muslims to distribute it as spoils if they were to overcome them. He replied:

> Whenever merchants are in their military or for others and its people do not bring it to use against the Muslims or set up what is in their possession to fight the believers, it is impermissible for the believers to take or distribute it as spoils. Rather, the believers are to return it to its owners because their merchandise is for them in such case and their kindness to them by means of the facility of their trade. Even if they were disobedient, Allah did not make their wealth permissible or rightful spoils for the believers due to their disobedience. Even if the believers say that they oppose that and harass them, they would not be permitted to do such. However, if they say that they brought it, their wealth can be distributed as spoils.

Concerning the wealth of women and children who were among the soldiers of wrongdoers and transgressors

Whatever was in their military that was not brought against those in the right would not be permissible for the believers to take, but whatever a boy or woman or merchants brought would be considered permissible as spoils for the Muslims.

My father related to me that his father used to say regarding taking spoils of those things among those who had them from the wives, children and women that whatever was not brought by its owner to fight those in the right, it is considered the belongings of the owners. However, that which was brought by a man or woman which was used against those in the right—it is to be included among the spoils of those in the right and booty for the Muslims.

Concerning the imam who says to a man: "If you kill so-n-so, you can have his plunder"

If the imam were to say to one of his soldiers "If you kill so-n-so, you can have his plunder" regarding an enemy combatant and he kills him, he can have his apparent and well-known plunder of clothes, belt, armour, sword, horse, saddle, jewellery, and other apparent equipment. However, if he [i.e. the enemy combatant] has a jewel or property under his clothes or some of his travel items, this would not be considered a part of his plunder. Consequently, it would be impermissible for him to take it because plunder is what he apparently wears or rides armed with among war equipment.

And if he had said "If you kill so-n-so, then you can have his plunder" and he and others killed him, the plunder would not belong to him or the one with him because he simply appointed him to kill him and he killed him along with someone else. That withstanding, he did not appoint for him his plunder.

If the imam said in a general statement "Whoever kills so-n-so will have his plunder" and someone and others kills him, the plunder would be for him and for those who killed him along with the killer.

My father related to me that his father was asked about an imam who said to a man: "If you kill so-n-so, you can have his plunder." Does the killer get the plunder of the killed? He replied:

> Every apparent thing from his plunder is not unknown. I say that if there is any jewellery on him whether pearls or rubies or whether he has any wealth of silver or gold of great value, he is to get nothing of that except that plunder which can be apparently seen and is not hidden, such as clothing, weapons, vehicles, horses and other things that are on his person. This is because all of such is a gift from the imam, and the imam does not have the right to withhold anything from what he has appointed, and no one can repay it on his behalf.

He was asked: "What if someone else helped the killer? Is there anything that is due upon that person?" He replied:

> No, unless the imam said a literal statement that did not single out the man who killed so-n-so indicating who can have his plunder. Therefore, whoever helped kill him would be the same as the one who received his plunder because he was killed by one, two or more. As a result, their

situation would be the same in killing him. And if he said, "If you kill him, O So-n-so…" meaning a specific man, and he did not kill him except with someone else, then the plunder would not be for him nor for the one who killed him along with the killer.

He was asked: "Why would it not be permissible to be shared between them? If it was a retaliation to which all of them would be bound, then why should they not share its plunder between them all?" He replied:

> It is because he did not appoint it for them but made it for him without them on the condition that he kill him alone and not with others. So, when all of them killed him, they were all nullified since all of them had joined him to kill him. Had it been in retaliation, all of them would have been killed for it and would be bound to observe retaliation just as he would. The judgement of all of them would be the same as his judgement.

Also, if the imam had said to a man who was occupied in killing so-n-so "If you kill him, you can have his plunder" then he was tempted to seek the help of someone else with him or hire someone to help him in doing so and then killed him with others, the obligation of the imam upon him would be for him rather than anyone else.

Concerning that which the imam can appoint for the killer

If the imam were to say to a man "If you kill so-n-so, you will get a thousand dirham or less and more" and he killed him, the imam could give him what he appointed for him from the booty if there was any. If there is no booty, he can give him from the spoils. If there are no spoils available, he can give him from the Muslims' charity and tithes because Allah—the one who cannot be encompassed by words—makes the charity of Islam and its people a means of benefit and aid.

Concerning the wealth of dominions and other places that were conquered

Whatever is collected from the collection of a land that was conquered or a country with whom is a peace treaty—one-fifth is taken from it and distributed to those whom Allah has designated.

Concerning what is required regarding fulfilling the trust of the imam

One of the greatest obligations of Allah is the fulfilment of the trust to the imam. The fulfilment of the trust is advice to him, honesty in every report conveyed to him, informing unknown news to him and the investigation on his behalf in all its causes.

This includes fulfilling the trust regarding the wealth collected by the tax collectors, as well as that given to the worker in his work, so he must fulfil the trust in it and raise it to the imam. If he permits such, it is considered permissible for him; and if he prevents such from him, it is considered forbidden to him; and if he permits some of it, that which he permits is considered permissible for him.

Regarding that is what has reached us from the Commander of Believers, 'Ali b. Abi Ṭālib, upon him be peace, that he hired a man to do some work. When it was the following year, he dismissed him. He brought a cash advance of dirham that he carried until he put it in the hands of 'Ali. He said: "O Commander of Believers, this is given to me by the people of my work. It is for them to give it to me before you hired me or after you dismissed me. If I had it, I would take it; otherwise it is up to you." So, the Commander of Believers, may Allah have mercy on him, said: "Well done! If I had held on to it, it would have been considered unlawful." And he ordered that it be taken to the treasury.

Concerning partiality towards a group who is advancing

It is impermissible for Muslims to turn away and take sides from their enemy if they meet, unless it is a strategic manoeuvre in fighting or to join ranks with a group from whom they seek help or resort to. Regarding that, Allah says: {**O ye who believe, when ye meet those who disbelieve advancing, turn not thy backs to them. Whosoever turns his back to them unless as a stratagem for battle or as a**

means to join another company—such person would incur the Anger of Allah. His destination shall be Hell, a wretched destination!} (Q. 8:15-16).

Regarding that is what has reached us from a group of the Prophet's Companions:

> We were in a detachment expedition and met the idolaters. The people wheeled round, and we were among those who were wheeled round in flight. When we returned to ourselves, we asked: "How can we look at the faces of the Muslims when we were filled with Allah's anger?" One said: "We entered Medina at night." We replied: "We will leave Medina while Allah's Messenger, peace and blessings be upon him and his progeny, is there." We did not meet him, so we went to him while he departed to the dawn prayer. When we saw him, we said: "O Messenger of Allah, we are the ones who fled!" He replied: ((No. You are the ones who fought and returned. I am the main body for every Muslim)). Then we kissed his hand.

Concerning waiting for the rightful imam

Waiting for the rightful imam is like the one who struggles in the way of the Lord of creation. Regarding that, it has reached us that Allah's Messenger, peace and blessings be upon him and his progeny, said: ((Whoever devotes himself (*habasa nafsahu*) to our caller, Ahl al-Bayt, or wait for our riser—such person would be like one whose sword and shield were smeared with his own blood in the way of Allah)).

Concerning whether there is a fifth paid from plunder

If the imam says in the war "Whoever kills a man can have his plunder," then the plunder of every person he killed would belong to him. He would be obligated to pay the fifth dues from it because it is booty from Allah for him, just as the fifth dues is due from that which comes out of the sea, minerals and treasures.

Concerning commanding the good and forbidding the evil and concerning one who takes control of the Muslims' affairs

Commanding the good and forbidding the evil is an obligation from Allah that cannot be abandoned, and it is impermissible to reject it. Regarding that is what Allah says: **{…those who, if We were to give them authority in the land, establish the prayer, render the purification dues, command the good and forbid the evil. And to Allah is the end of all affairs}** (Q. 22:41).

Regarding that is what has reached us from Allah's Messenger, peace and blessings be upon him and his progeny:

> ((You should command the good and forbid the evil or Allah will allow oppressors to rule over you. And they will afflict you with the worst torment insomuch that even when the best of you supplicate, they will not be answered until when the decree reaches its term. Then, Allah will grant Himself victory. Afterwards, it will be said: "What prevented you from being angry for My sake when you saw Me being disobeyed?!)).[10]

Also, regarding that is what has reached us from him, peace and blessings be upon him and his progeny:

> ((Verily, Allah sent me with mercy and warfare. He made my livelihood in the shadows of my spear and not made me a ploughman or merchant. Although the worst of Allah's slaves is the ploughman or merchant unless he gives the right and takes the right)). **{O Prophet, struggle against the disbelievers and hypocrites, and be harsh against them. Their destination is Hell, a most evil destination!}** (Q. 9:73).

---

[10] Similarly narrated in ***Musnad Imam Zayd, Amāli Ahmed b. 'Isa, Sharh at-Tajrīd, al-Mu'jam al-Awsaṫ, Majmu' al-Bazzār, Mušannaf Ibn Abi Shayba***,

Also, regarding that, it has reached us that he, peace and blessings be upon him and his progeny, said: ((The feet that are dusty from fighting in the way of Allah will not be touched by the Hellfire)).[11] It has also reached us that he, peace and blessings be upon him and his progeny, said: ((Sleeping after fighting in the way of Allah is a better act of worship than sixty years of standing your nights in prayer without faltering and fasting your days without breaking the fast)).

It has reached us from Hassān b. Thābit al-Ansari: "I have ten thousand [dirham]. If I spend it, will I have the reward of one who fought in the way of Allah?" He, peace and blessings be upon him and his progeny, said: ((How about the saddles and riding beasts?)) [i.e. it is not comparable].

Woe unto the one who is placed in charge of the affairs of the Muslims! What a difficult task to undertake! Whoever is placed in charge of any of the affairs of the Muslims, let him know that it is between a painful punishment and a noble reward. Then, he must be fair with his effort and must incite to his Lord, for if he finds every good and evil that has taken place before, let him prefer the eternal hereafter over the transient world. Let him deal with Allah, for tomorrow he will meet Him, and perhaps it will be like that, so let him consider himself well.

Regarding that, it has reached us from Allah's Messenger, peace and blessings be upon him and his progeny:

> ((Whoever is in charge of any of the affairs of the Muslims will come on the Day of Judgement with his hands tied to his neck, so that his justice will be that which frees him or the injustice will be that which binds him)).[12]

By Allah, had it not been for the dignity of Allah and the love of what Allah loved, altruism would not have been desired, nor would the necessity of the argument, the fulfilment of the obligation, the knowledge from myself of what no one else knows from me, and the desire for what Allah gave of the profitable price.

As the Blessed and Exalted says: {**Verily, Allah hath purchased from the believers their lives and their wealth because the Garden shall be theirs. They fight in the way of Allah and slay and art slain. It is a promise that is binding on Him in the Torah and the Gospel and the Qur'an. Who fulfils His covenant better than Allah? Glad tidings then in thy transaction that ye hath made, for that is the great victory**} **(Q. 9:111)**.

And with that, he sought the ranks by which Allah favoured the Emigrants over those who remained behind, when He said: {**Those amongst the believers who remain, other than those who have a disabling harm, are not equal with those who strive in the way of Allah with their wealth and lives. Allah hath awarded upon those who strive with their wealth and lives a rank above those who remain. Unto each Allah hath promised good, but He hath bestowed on those who strive a great reward above those who remain—ranks from Him as well as forgiveness and mercy. Allah is ever Oft-Forgiving, Most Gracious.**} **(Q. 4:95-96)**.

And we hope that, by means of us, Allah will rectify the affairs of the Muslims, heal the disharmony of the believers, guide the slaves, make the lands safe, fill hungry bellies, clothe the naked, repay grievances to the oppressed, strengthen creation in truth, humiliate the wrongdoers, honour the righteous, and that we follow the path of the Angels of the Lord of creation and His Messengers, may the blessings of Allah be upon them all. We hope to be reminded by our biography of the most virtuous of our forefathers who passed away, afflicted the enemies of truth and beheld the word of truth. We aim to please the Most Merciful and anger Satan so that I may water its end by its beginning and that I may turn the face of its beginning onto its end.

---

[11] Similarly narrated in ***Ŝahīh al-Bukhāri, Sunan an-Nisā'i, Ŝahīh Ibn Hibbān, Al-Mu'jam al-Kabīr, Al-Mu'jam al-Awsat, Musnad Abu Ya'la, Mušannaf Ibn Abi Shayba, Sunan al-Bayhaqi***

[12] Similarly narrated in ***Al-Mu'jam al-Kabīr, Al-Mu'jam al-Awsat, Mušannaf Ibn Abi Shayba, Sunan al-Bayhaqi***

And I let the few remaining ones catch up with the first of the past so that the ignorant and the suspicious may know from the misguidance that their worldly life, to me, is easier and more despised to Yahya b. al-Hussein than the skin of the date pit. Rather, what obscures from that and prevents us from being like what we have described, said, and mentioned is the dignity of the Lord of majesty and authority we desire, as well as the desire to accompany the righteous in Paradise, the mercy of Muslims, the victory of truth and religion, and to follow the example of the most resolute of the Prophets.

Therefore, we ask Allah for good in all affairs and to repel every source of fear in religion or something that is forbidden and to have us reach what we hope for of obedience to our Lord and Master. Praise be to Allah, Lord of creation! There is no power or strength except by Allah, the Exalted, the Great and Manifest Truth. Allah, the Exalted and Generous, is sufficient for us, and we rely upon Him; He is the Lord of the Great Throne! May the prayers of Allah be upon Muhammad, the Seal of the Prophets, as well as upon his righteous Ahl al-Bayt!

Concerning the virtue of a just imam

Whoever rules by Allah's judgement, is just among the slaves, and is the fittest of the land from the Ahl al-Bayt of the chosen Prophet—he is the caliph of Allah, the Exalted and the Most-High as long as he fulfils the conditions of the Imamate, as well as its signs, prescribed punishments and attributes. Regarding that, it has reached us that Allah's Messenger, peace and blessings be upon him and his progeny, said:

> ((Whoever commands the good and forbids the evil from among my descendants—such person is the caliph of Allah in His land, the caliph of His Book and the caliph of His Messenger, peace and blessings be upon him and his progeny)).

It has also reached us that he, peace and blessings be upon him and his progeny, said:

> ((The just and humble ruler is in the shadow of Allah and His mercy. Whoever sincerely advises him regarding himself and the slaves of Allah—such person will be gathered by Allah in his delegation on the Day in which there will be no shade but His. Whoever cheats him regarding himself and the slaves of Allah—such person will be abandoned by Allah on the Day of Judgement)).[13]

He, peace and blessings be upon him and his progeny, also said: (([The deeds] of the just and humble ruler are raised every day and night like the deeds of sixty truthful people—all of whom are diligent workers in themselves)).[14]

It has also reached us that Allah's Messenger, peace and blessings be upon him and his progeny, said: ((It shall be said to the just imam on the Day of Judgement in his grave: "Good news, for you are the intimate friend of Muhammad!")).

It has also reached us that Allah's Messenger, peace and blessings be upon him and his progeny, said:

> ((Whoever gives life to my sunnah that was dead after me—such person will have the reward of the one who does such action without decreasing anything from the reward of the doer. Whoever innovates with an innovation that Allah and His Messenger are not pleased with—such person will carry the sin of the one who does such action without decreasing anything from the sin of the doer)).[15]

Also, Allah's Messenger, peace and blessings be upon him and his progeny, said:

> ((There are three who are complete the qualities of faith: The one who, even if he is able, does not deal with what does not belong to him; the one who, even if he is satisfied, is not led into

[13] Similarly narrated in ***Kanz al-'Ummāl***

[14] Ibid.

[15] Similarly narrated in ***Ŝahīh Muslim, Sunan Ibn Mājah, Sunan ad-Dārimi, Ŝahīh Ibn Hibbān, Al-Mu'jam al-Kabīr, Al-Mu'jam al-Awsaṭ, Mušannaf Ibn Abi Shayba, Sunan al-Bayhaqi***

falsehood by his contentment; and the one who, even if he is angry, is not taken out of the right by his anger)).

Concerning the code of conduct regarding the rebels

It is obligatory to fight those who transgress against a group of believers or against a rightful imam from among the righteous, so it is obligatory to fight them if they refuse the rule and are not satisfied with the right. As Allah says: {**And if two parties of believers were to fight, make peace between them. And if one party of them doeth wrong to the other, fight the one who doeth wrong till it returns unto the matter of Allah. Then, if they return, make peace between them justly and act equitably. Verily, Allah loveth the equitable**} (Q. 49:9).

So, it was obligatory to fight one who oppresses the Muslims against a group of believers, so how about fighting one who oppresses the Lord of creation, goes against the rule of the righteous and refuses to obey the guided imams whom Allah commands to be obeyed?

Therefore, whoever refuses to do that, opposes the Most Gracious and manifests open defiance to Allah and disobedience, it is obligatory for the Muslims to fight him forever until he complies with Allah's command and rules by Allah's judgement, and the matter is handed over to Allah's allies until the religion is purely for Allah. As the Mighty and Majestic says in His Book and Criterion: {**And fight them until persecution is no more, and religion is solely for Allah. But if they cease, then let there be no opposition save against the wrongdoers**} (Q. 2:193).

It is obligatory upon the one who fights the rebellious oppressors to bring evidence against them before fighting them and to invite them to the Book of their Lord. If they respond favourably, it is forbidden for them to kill them, fight them, and take their money. If they refuse from the right, it is permissible for the Muslims to kill them and fight them and take spoils from what they brought into their military expedition. It is impermissible for them to take them captive, and that is not permitted among them.

The Commander of Believers, 'Ali b. Abi Ťālib, peace be upon him, did likewise in Basra on the day of the Camel. He killed those who fought him and took what was among the army. He did not allow any of the retreating soldiers to be pursued or the wounded to be killed, and he did not allow anyone to be taken captive. So, some of his companions spoke about that and asked: "You made their blood and money lawful for us, and you forbade us from taking them captive?" He replied: "That is Allah's judgement on them and regarding them and on others besides them who do what they did."

So, when they increased in numbers to him regarding that, he stood up to deliver a sermon and praised and exulted Allah and prayed for the Prophet, peace and blessings be upon him and his progeny. He then said: "O people, you have increased with gossip and talk about that which is impermissible from us. Who among you would take A'isha as spoils?!" All of them replied: "None of us." He then replied: "How is that the case when she was the greatest of people in crime?" When he said that, they woke up from their ignorance and perceived from their blindness and woke up from their sleep. He was patient in what he said, and they followed him in his command. They knew that he was correct and placed away doubt and suspicion.[16]

So, whoever opposes the truth and stubbornly opposes it, it is obligatory to fight him, and his blood becomes lawful. And whoever is allowed to take his blood, it would be booty for the Muslims' soldiers, and his captors are forbidden and is impermissible.

Concerning spies and concerning the code of conduct of warfare in the domain of war

If it is proven that the spy killed one of the Muslims with his spying, he shall be killed; otherwise, he is to be imprisoned.

---

[16] Similarly narrated in ***Musnad Imam Zayd, Kanz al-'Ummāl, Sunan al-Bayhaqi, Al-Mustadrak***

According to us, it is impermissible for us to fight the people of the domain of war except with a just and rightful imam with whom it is permissible to shed their blood, take their wealth, and take their children into captivity. As for a situation in which there is no rightful imam, then no.

And he should call to Islam and to the testimony that there is no god but Allah, One without partner, and that Muhammad is His slave and Messenger. If they respond favourably to that, then they are considered Muslims. They have what the Muslims have, and what is upon one is upon the other. After that, it is impermissible to kill them, take their wealth, or take them captive. If they refuse to do that, it is offered to them that they become *dhimmi* and that they pay the *jizya* to the Muslims and that the rulings of the Muslims are applied to them and that the rulers of the Muslims take over their lands, and they will be left to their religion as the other *dhimmi*s are left. If they respond favourably to that, the *jizya* will be imposed on them as it is imposed on others. Forty-eight dirham will be taken from their wealthy and kings, twenty-four dirhams from their middle-class and merchants, and twelve dirhams from their lower classes and poor. If they refuse to do so, they shall be fought against, and Allah's help is sought against them. [17]

If they are defeated, the sword is placed among them, and they are to be killed or captured and enslaved. Their lands are considered liberated after killing their men. Then their spoils are to be collected and divided into five parts. A fifth of them would be given to those whom Allah designated from among the people of the fifth dues. The remaining four-fifths is to be divided among those who attended the battle among the cavalrymen and foot soldiers. The cavalryman is to get two shares, and the foot soldier is to get one share. Then he divides a fifth to the one whom Allah has appointed for him according to what we have explained and mentioned in the beginning of this book of ours.

For the idolaters, the fulfilment and security of the covenant is the same for the Muslim rebels, except that the imam should not grant anyone of them security who enters him unless he informs him and tells him that it is impermissible for him to reside in the Muslim lands for more than a year. He is to also inform him that if he finds him in the domain of Islam after the year, he will not leave him to depart from it; rather, he will be forced to pay the *jizya* and he will be considered a *dhimmi*. If he is found, he will be judged as such.

Concerning the imposition of taxes upon conquered lands and then it was left and not divided, as what was done with dominions and other parts of the Levant, Egypt, and so on

If the land was conquered and the imam decided to leave it and not divide it and assigned those who had it first or others with half, less or more, then he may agree with them on something that is determined.

---

[17] In the dialogue featured in ***Al-Muntakhab,*** al-Hādi clarifies the purpose and parameters of the *jizya* in more detail:

> I asked: "And their children?" "He replied: "It is not taken from them until they reach puberty, nor is anything taken from their women." "Why is it not taken from their women, slaves or children if they are idolaters?" "The *jizya* is simply a compensatory exemption from fighting. That is based on the statement of Allah, the Mighty and Majestic: **{Fight those who believe not in Allah and the Last Day and hold not that which Allah and His Messenger prohibit to be prohibited neither do they adhere to the religion of Truth—though they be amongst those who have been given the Book—till they render the *jizya* willingly after having been subdued} (Q. 9:29)**. Therefore, whoever is able to fight and engage in war must have the compensation imposed on him. But whoever is not able to fight and is not from its people, there is no compensation imposed on him. As for the women, Allah's Messenger, peace and blessings be upon him and his progeny, prohibited them from being fought because they are weak. Neither are they to be among them or carry weapons among them. As for children, the judgements of Allah do not apply to them and they are to be exempted from fighting since it is one of Allah's judgements. Since they are exempted from all of such, they would be exempted from the jizya as well, neither would it apply to them. As for slaves, they are simply their property and their situation is like that of any other property since they are compelled to follow as they are commanded by others regarding their masters' wishes and cannot act contrary to that. That being the case, they have no free choice. Since they do not have a choice, they must carry it out for them. And they were subject to the choice of their masters, so they were exempted from fighting and became booty for the Muslims to seize. Therefore, when the fighting was exempted from them, the *jizya* is exempted from them."

As for the lands of dominion, it is narrated from the Commander of Believers, 'Ali b. Abi Ṫālib, upon him be peace, that when he was placed in charge, he sent a man from the Anŝār to four of the border districts (*rasātīq*): al-Bihqubādhāt, Shīr river, al-Mulk river and Juwayn river. He commanded him to impose a dirham and a half upon every sixty-by-sixty cubits (*jarīb*) of thick farmland, a dirham upon every sixty-by-sixty cubits of middle farmland and two-thirds of a dirham for every sixty-by-sixty cubits of thin farmland. And he commanded him to impose ten dirhams upon every sixty-by-sixty cubits of date palm orchards, ten dirhams upon every sixty-by-sixty cubits of humid palm—which is the reed, and ten dirhams upon every sixty-by-sixty cubits of vineyard and orchards that gather the palms and trees. And he commanded him to throw every palm straying from the villages to any of those who pass by. He also commanded him to impose forty-eight dirhams upon each of the feudal lords (*ad-dahāqīn*) who ride non-Arab horses and wear gold rings, twenty-four dirhams upon their middle-class and merchants, and twelve dirhams upon their lower class and poor. Therefore, he did that and collected from those four border districts eighteen million sixty thousand dirhams and surplus.

Concerning the people of Islam granting safety to the people of idolatry

The people of Islam may grant safety to one of them over all of them. If a man were to grant safety to one of the soldiers of the idolaters or one of their villages and then the imam learns of that, it is impermissible for him [i.e. the imam] to accost them until they leave the protective status that the Muslim has secured from them.

If one, two or three Muslims were to grant safety to a hundred idolaters which includes their lives and property and then their village is conquered, it is impermissible for the imam to do anything to those who were granted safety by the group of Muslims, nor can he do anything with their property. Everything other than that is considered permissible booty.

If one of the villages of the idolaters was conquered and the wealth or men or slave women are taken as booty and then a group of Muslims came afterwards and said to the imam "We had granted safety to the people of this village for their lives and property," that would be considered nothing and the imam is to not accept it even if the group who made this claim was among those present in the conquering, fighting, captivity and seizing of their property. Since they did not say anything at the time of its conquering and only spoke after that, their words are to not be acknowledged. If they were from the people of honesty, loyalty and religion, they would not have remained silent after having granted them safety, nor would they have fought them, killed them, seized their property and shed their blood. No one who permits that in his religion deserves to be declared truthful by another.

If they were absent from the military at that time and then came and spoke about it, they must establish evidence for it confirming that. Then, everything in the possession of the Muslims must be returned to them.

And it is impermissible for anyone to grant safety to anyone from the idolaters for an extended period of time. And it is impermissible to guarantee them perpetual safety because the security of the idolaters is only for a period of time, and then the obligation of Allah is to be established on them by striving against them and inviting them to the religion of Islam.

If the imam sends an army and seizes a city and then when the captives and wealth are brought to him, the imam says "I did not command you regarding this town and that town. I have granted their people safety until a period of time," his statement would be considered truthful, and it would be obligatory to return them to their city and grant them safety. His situation regarding claims is unlike that of others.

If a people from the domain of war entered the domain of Islam in safety, it is impermissible for the imam to allow them to buy a weapon or armour to take with them, nor should he let them leave the domain of Islam to go to the domain of war with any weapon or armour unless they originally came with it; they can only take such out specifically. If they enter with a weapon in order to exchange it, then there is no problem with them exchanging the good for the bad from the Muslims and taking the extra of what is between them.

Concerning a Muslim captive who is granted safety in the domain of war by someone

If a Muslim is taken prisoner and the people of idolatry enter their domain with him and he asked some of them to grant him safety and they grant it to him, it would be impermissible for the Muslims because he is captive in the hands of their warriors and their judgments are applied to him in their domain.

Concerning a Muslim who enters one of the villages of the idolaters after being granted their safety and then they are suddenly attacked and captured while he is among them: Is he permitted to buy them?

When a Muslim enters one of the villages of the idolaters with their grant of safety and they are suddenly attacked while he is among them and they are taken captive, it is preferable that he not buy them if it was a precondition for them when he entered upon them that he would not do so. If it was not a precondition for them to do so, then there is no problem with him buying them outside from the domain in which he entered with their grant of safety.

There is no problem with him buying something from the people of the domain he entered with the grant of safety if they were taken captive by others. Also, there is no problem with the idolaters buying some of them from others—even if it entails buying the son from the father and the brother from the brother. This is because if it is permissible for him to take and misappropriate it against himself, then the whole price would be considered a wage for which the one who took it was hired

Concerning a man from the domain of war and the *dhimmi* who embraces Islam at the hand of a Muslim man

If the one from the domain of war (*al-harbi*) were to embrace Islam at the hand of a Muslim, then the latter would be considered his client (*mawla*) and he inherits from him if the one from the domain of war dies without Muslim heirs. If a *dhimmi* were to embrace Islam at the hand of a Muslim and were to die without a Muslim heir, all the Muslims would inherit from him. His inheritance would be taken to the Muslim public treasury because a *dhimmi* covenant is not like that of the one from the domain of war.

Concerning a slave who embraced Islam in the domain of war

If a slave were to embrace Islam in the domain of war and then emigrate to the domain of Islam, he would be considered free. If his master were to embrace Islam after that and enter the domain of Islam, he would have nothing over him because Islam freed him before his master embraced Islam.

If his master had embraced Islam in the domain of war and then the Muslims suddenly attacked that domain and took the people captive, the Muslim slave would not be included in the spoils of the Muslims because of his previous conversion to Islam. Likewise, if the slave had embraced Islam and then his master had embraced Islam in the domain of war, they would have no right over the master, the slave, nor their wealth except that which cannot be carried, like real estate and property. The slave would be considered the property of his master because both embraced Islam in the domain of war; therefore, they would be considered the same.

Concerning the one in the domain of war who embraces Islam and then emigrates to the domain of Islam while having children in the domain of war and then the Muslims take over that domain: What is to happen to his children?

If a man from the people of the domain of war were to embrace Islam and emigrate to the domain of Islam and then the Muslims were to take over that domain while his son was in it, all of those sons who had not attained puberty at the time of their father's conversion to Islam would be considered Muslims following their father. Therefore, the Muslims would not be able to take them as spoils. However, the one who had attained puberty by the time of his father's conversion would be considered spoils for the Muslims [if such person had not similarly converted].

We simply make his pre-pubescent sons his followers in such because Allah's Messenger, peace and blessings be upon him and his progeny, said: ((Islam takes precedence in the offspring)). And if one of the parents of the pre-pubescent child embraces Islam, their Islam would imply his Islam and they would be considered Muslims. They were snatched from the hand of the disbeliever and became in the hand of the Muslim.

Likewise, if a person from the domain of war married a young girl in the domain of war and then her husband converted to Islam while he had consummated the marriage with her and then one of the woman's parents converted to Islam before the woman had completed her waiting period of three months [after the pronouncement of divorce]—even if by one day—and then her father took her out to the domain of Islam after three years or more, she would be considered as belonging to her husband because her father embraced Islam before the end of her waiting period and her Islam had been established. So, although she became a Muslim with the Islam of her father and her marriage ties were established, it was not forbidden for her husband to hold her protective status. However, if her father had embraced Islam after her waiting period, her husband would not have a right over her except through a new marriage.

Concerning the people from the domain of war who embrace Islam while there are Muslim slaves in their possession whom they took as booty from the Muslims prior to their embracing Islam

If the people of the domain of war were to embrace Islam while having Muslim slaves in their possession, they would still be considered as slaves in their possession because they embraced Islam while they had the slaves in their possession. Whoever embraced Islam while owning something he took from the domain of idolatry—it would belong to him.

Concerning an indentured labourer and *umm walad* who are captured by idolaters and then the latter embrace Islam while owning both

If a person from the domain of war were to embrace Islam while owning a Muslim's *umm walad* or indentured labourer, the imam would pay the *umm walad*'s ransom to her master from the Muslim public treasury if the latter is in straitened circumstances. However, if he is in a state of ease, the imam can force him to ransom her by her value.

It is impermissible for a Muslim who embraced Islam while she [the *umm walad*] was in his possession to have intercourse with her because she is the *umm walad* of another Muslim. If the one who embraced Islam while she was in his possession had intercourse with her in the domain of war and then entered it [i.e. the domain of war] along with him while she was pregnant by him, the child would be attributed to him because he had intercourse with her in a condition in which it is impermissible to have intercourse with her. Therefore, the *umm walad* is to be returned to the one who originally owned her along with her value. He is to not have intercourse with her until she delivers what is in her womb and is purified from her menses (lit. 'blood').

As for the indentured labourer, he is to work for the one who owns him to the extent of his value. After he completes his value for the one who embraced Islam, the clientage would be for the one who originally contracted the indentured labourer. If the labourer refused to work for the one who embraced Islam until his value is fulfilled, he would be considered a slave in his possession. The situation of the one who refuses to work for the one who embraced Islam is like that of one who refused to work for the one with whom he initially contracted himself. In such case, he would be considered a slave. Likewise, whatever comes to you from this chapter, it will be explained according to this statement, if Allah wills.

Concerning a Muslim slave who is captured by the people of the domain of war and then apostatises from Islam in the domain of war but some of them embraces Islam and departs with him to the domain of Islam

If a Muslim slave were taken captive and then apostatised from Islam but then some of them who departed with him became Muslim, he is to be invited to return to Islam. If he chooses to embrace Islam, he is considered owned by the one who embraced Islam and entered the domain of Islam with him. If he refuses to embrace Islam, he is to be put to death.

Likewise is the case with the indentured labourer; he is to be offered Islam. If he chooses to embrace Islam, he shall observe the contract of indentureship with the one who embraced Islam similar to the first statement. However, if he does not choose to embrace Islam, he is to be put to death.

Likewise, if the *umm walad* were to apostatise in the domain of war and then some of them [i.e. the people of the domain of war] embraced Islam and entered into [the domain of Islam] with the apostate, Islam is to be offered to her. If she embraces Islam, the father of her child is to pay her ransom if he is in the state of financial ease. However, if he is in straitened circumstances, the imam is to pay her ransom. If she refuses to embrace Islam, she is to be put to death.

If she is pregnant, she is to be spared so she can deliver. Once she delivers, her child is to be breastfed. The father is to facilitate the breastfeeding. If he is in straitened circumstances, the imam is charged with facilitating the breastfeeding. Then, she is to be offered Islam or death. If one is unable to find one to breastfeed her child, she is to be spared until the child is weaned. This is because two cannot be killed by the death of one. Once the baby is weaned, she is to be offered Islam; if she refuses, she is to be put to death.

Concerning one from the domain of war who accepts the *dhimmi* status and agrees to pay the *jizya* while he owns Muslim slaves from the slaves of the Muslims

If people from the domain of war agree to be *dhimmi*s and pay the *jizya* upon entering the domain of Islam while owning Muslim slaves, it shall be said to their leader: "If you want to ransom them, you will be paid their value in ransom. Otherwise, you will be commanded to sell those in your possession." This is because it is impermissible for a *dhimmi* to own a Muslim.

Similarly, if they were to enter with indentured labourers, it would be said to them: "Your indentured labourers is considered as having observed their term, and those who originally contracted the indentureship would be considered the owners." If he refuses to grant it to the one with whom he entered into the indentureship, he shall be commanded to sell him because it is impermissible for a *dhimmi* to own a Muslim.

Similarly, if one of them entered into the *dhimmi* status while having a Muslim slave-woman with him and she had become pregnant from him in the domain of war, he would be told: "Withdraw from her, for she is impermissible for you to approach. That which is in her womb is considered a Muslim because of her Islam."

If the *dhimmi* who had intercourse with her were to become Muslim while she was in her waiting period, then she would be considered his *umm walad*. However, if she were outside of her waiting period, he would not be permissible for her except by a new marriage proposal, a dowry, witnesses and her acceptance. He would be considered his [i.e. the child's] guardian because she is his *umm walad* due to his embracing Islam. She would be with him until three complete divorces, and the first separation would not be considered a divorce.

The Book of Asceticism (*az-Zuhd*), Etiquette and Other Matters Related to Ennobling Character

In the Name of Allah, the Most Gracious, the Most Merciful...

Concerning disagreements among Muhammad's Progeny

There is no disagreement from the Progeny of Muhammad, peace and blessings be upon him and his progeny, except in the case of negligence. So, whoever of them neglects the knowledge of his forefathers and does not follow the knowledge of his father's family from his father until it ends with 'Ali b. Abi Ṭālib, may Allah bless him, and the Prophet, peace and blessings be upon him and his progeny, and shares with the Generality in their sayings and follow their interpretations—such would necessitate disagreement. This is the case especially if such one has no insight and discernment and does not refer what has been reported to him back to the Book nor refer the allegorical (*al-mutashābih*) to the decisive (*al-muhkam*).

As for those of them who quote from their forefathers—father from father—until they end up to the foundation while neither considering what others have said nor drawing attention to the opinion of others with a distinct understanding based on what came to him from the Book and agreed-upon Sunnah and the intellect which Allah appointed as a proof regarding it and refers all his affairs to the Book referring the allegorical to the decisive, it will never be a source of misguidance, nor will it contradict the truth in the first place.

Concerning the virtue of visiting the Prophet's grave

My father related to me that his father said:

> A man from the Banu Hāshim who used to fast and pray a lot related to me from his ancestors with the chain of narration going to the Prophet that Allah's Messenger, peace and blessings be upon him and his progeny, said: ((Whoever visits me during my lifetime or visits my grave after my death, the Angels of Allah will pray for him for twelve thousand years)).[1]

It has reached us from al-Hussein b. 'Ali, upon them be peace, that he asked the Prophet, peace and blessings be upon him and his progeny: "O Messenger of Allah, what is for the one who visits us?" Allah's Messenger, peace and blessings be upon him and his progeny, replied: ((Whoever visits me alive or dead, your father alive or dead, your brother alive or dead, or you alive or dead, has a right upon Allah to save him on the Day of Judgement)).

It has also reached us that he, peace and blessings be upon him and his progeny, said: ((Whoever visits my grave will have my intercession)).[2]

Rather, all of this is obligatory upon Allah's Messenger peace and blessings be upon him and his progeny, and he does such for those who love him and his family and are not hostile to them, are not loyal to their enemies, and do not bear the guilt of their offender over their benefactor. As for the one who was an enemy to them and did not establish the obligation of Allah on him regarding them, then his intercession would not be necessitated for him nor is his generosity granted to him. If intercession and generosity were obligatory for their enemies who visit them, then the reward will be obligatory for the one who prayed and fasted but did not acknowledge Muhammad, peace and blessings be upon him and his progeny. This is because action does not benefit without acknowledgement, just as acknowledgement does not benefit without action.

---

[1] Similarly narrated in ***Al-Jāmi' al-Kāfi, Sunan ad-Dārqutni*** and ***Ash-Shu'b al-Imān*** by al-Bayhaqi

[2] Similarly narrated in ***Al-Jāmi' al-Kāfi***

Concerning the urging towards obedience to Allah, the Mighty and Majestic

It has reached us on the authority of Zayd b. 'Ali from his ancestors from 'Ali, upon them be peace:

> I heard Allah's Messenger, peace and blessings be upon him and his progeny, say: ((There are seven that will be under the shade of the Throne on a Day when there is no shade except His shade: a young person who spends his youth in the worship of Allah, the Mighty and Majestic; a man who, when enticed by an [unrelated] woman to come to her, says: "I fear Allah, the Lord of creation!"; a man who exits his house, completes his purity [i.e. ablution], then walks to one of the houses of Allah to establish one of the obligations of Allah, and then dies between that and him; a man who leaves for the Hajj pilgrimage or 'Umra pilgrimage; a man who dies as a warrior in the way of Allah; a man who roams the earth seeking Allah's bounty, is satisfied with what is sufficient for him, and returns with it to his family; and a man who wakes up in the middle of the night while other eyes are heavy, completes his purification, then stands in prayer in one of the houses of Allah, and then dies between that and him)).[3]

Concerning seeking forgiveness

It has reached us on the authority of Allah's Messenger, peace and blessings be upon him and his progeny, that a man complained to him about his condition, and he said: ((Where are you in seeking forgiveness?)) Then, Allah's Messenger, peace and blessings be upon him and his progeny, said to him:

> ((Whoever seals his day by saying ten times "I seek Allah's forgiveness, the One with whom is no god but He! The Ever-Living and Self-Sustaining! I repent to Him! O Allah, forgive me and turn to me! Verily, You are Most Oft-Turning, Most Merciful!" Allah will forgive him of what he committed that day. If He says it at night, Allah will forgive him from what he committed that night)).

This refers to the one who sincerely repents. As for the one who persists in acts of disobedience and does not sincerely repent to Allah—even if he were to seek forgiveness every day and night one hundred million times—Allah will not forgive him. How can He forgive him when he persists in them? How can it be that one returns to Allah while he is immersed in them? Have you not considered what Allah says: **{Verily, Allah only accepts from the God-conscious} (Q. 5:27)**?

Therefore, the judgment for repentance and forgiveness is the one who departs to Allah with repentance from acts of disobedience. As for the one who persists in acts of disobedience and seeks forgiveness for that which he persists in—this is in contradiction to the Most Gracious and the One. That would be an example of Allah deceiving Himself, which contradicts what is right. One would be saying what one does not do and would be seeking Allah's forgiveness. **{They think to beguile Allah and those who believe, and they beguile none save themselves; but they perceive not. In their hearts is a disease, and Allah increases their disease. A painful doom is theirs because they lie} (Q. 2:9-10)**.

Have they not heard the Glorified say to them as well as those of sins similar to them: **{Forgiveness is only upon Allah toward those who do evil in ignorance then repent quickly to Allah. These are they toward whom Allah turns. Allah is All Knowing, All Wise. Forgiveness is not for those who do evil deeds until, when death approaches one of them, he says: "Verily, I repent now;" nor for those who die while they are disbelievers. For such, We have prepared a painful punishment} (Q. 4:17-18)**? This statement from Allah should be sufficient as light and guidance for the one who desires guidance and the truth.

[3] Similarly narrated in ***Musnad Imam Zayd, Ŝahīh al-Bukhāri, Ŝahīh Muslim, Sunan an-Nisā'i, Ŝahīh Ibn Khuzayma, Sunan al-Bayhaqi, Musnad Ahmed, Ŝahīh Ibn Hibbān, Sunan at-Tirmidhi***

Concerning seeking permission

When a Muslim seeks permission to enter the house of Muslims, he should seek permission at the door and must not look beyond the door, beyond the house or at what is in the house. Asking permission is simply for fear of looking at that which the owner of the house does not like others to see.

Seeking permission should be done three times either by greeting the people of the house or by saying "We would like your permission to enter upon you." The first seeking of permission is a warning and precaution to those in the house. The second is when people get ready and take their clothes. The third is when they either answer by saying that one can enter or not enter. If he is allowed to enter, he can enter, and if he is told to come back, he comes back.

Regarding that, Allah says: {**O ye who believe! Let those whom thy right hand possesses and those amongst thee who have not attained puberty ask leave of thee at three times: before the dawn prayer, when ye lay aside thy raiment for the heat of noon, and after the night prayer. There are three times of privacy for thee. It is no sin for them or for thee at other times when some amongst thee go round attending to others**} (**Q. 24:58**).

Allah simply made seeking permission at these three times and urged them to do so because they are times when Muslims at that time would choose to go to their wives so they can purify themselves for prayer and from the state of major ritual impurity. A man should not enter upon his mother, daughter, sister, paternal aunt, maternal aunt or grandmother until he asks their permission.

Concerning weeping out of fear of Allah and concerning visiting one's brothers in Allah

It has reached us on the authority of Allah's Messenger, peace and blessings be upon him and his progeny: ((Whoever out of humility to Allah, sheds a tear from his eye the size of a fly's wing, Allah will make him secure on the Day of Great Distress)).[4] Allah's Messenger, peace and blessings be upon him and his progeny, meant by such those who adhere to the command of Allah and who refrain from Allah's prohibition, the pious, righteous and guided believers.

It has reached us on the authority of Salmān al-Farsi, may Allah be merciful to him, that he said:

> I went out with Allah's Messenger, peace and blessings be upon him and his progeny, to visit some Yemeni people out of politeness. They had taken the oath of allegiance to Allah's Messenger, peace and blessings be upon him and his progeny, to accept Islam. He entered upon them and shook their hands one-by-one. When we left, he said: ((O Salmān, shall I give you good news?)) I replied: 'Certainly, O Messenger of Allah!' He said: ((A Muslim does not leave his house to visit his Muslim brothers except that he is immersed in the Mercy of Allah and accompanied by 70,000 Angels. When they meet and shake hands, it would be as though one hand will wash the other. They will be forgiven for previous sins and will be given what they ask for)).[5]

They are those who are guided among the believers. Do you not hear how he says: ((A Muslim…))? And a Muslim is not a Muslim until he comes out of Allah's disobedience to his obedience.

Concerning the will of the Commander of Believers, 'Ali b. Abi Ťālib

It has reached us on the authority of 'Ali, upon him be peace, that he called his sons to him. They were eleven men: al-Hasan b. 'Ali, al-Hussein, Muhammad al-Akbar, 'Umar, Muhammad al-Asghar, 'Abbās, 'Abdullah, Ja'far, ''Uthmān, 'Ubaydullah, and Abu Bakr. They are the sons of 'Ali b. Abi Ťālib, upon him be peace. When they gathered round him, he said:

> O my sons, the youngest of you should behave with righteousness towards the oldest of you. The oldest of you should behave with mercy towards the youngest of you. And do not be like

[4] Similarly narrated in ***Sunan Ibn Mājah, Al-Mu'jam al-Kabīr, Musnad al-Bazzār***
[5] Similarly narrated in ***Al-Mu'jam al-Awsaṭ***

the deceitful and ungodly likes who did not have understanding of the religion and were not given certainty from Allah similar to a crack in an egg in an ostrich nest.[6] Woe be unto the chicks of Muhammad's Progeny from the self-made caliph and self-indulgent (*mutraf*) oppressor who will kill after me and after that![7]

By Allah, I have been taught the conveyance of the divine messages, the perfection of words and the fulfilment of promises. And Allah has bestowed His grace upon you, O Ahl al-Bayt![8]

He then said to al-Hasan and al-Hussein, upon them be peace:

I exhort the both of you to be God-conscious and to not hanker after the life of this world nor be sorry for anything from it which you have been denied. Speak the truth and be merciful to the orphan. Be an enemy to the oppressor and helper to the oppressed.[9] Act by the Book and do not be amongst the blameworthy of the blamers regarding Allah.

Then, he looked at Muhammad b. 'Ali al-Hanafiyya and said: "Do you understand my exhortation to your brothers?" He replied: "Yes." He then said: "I exhort you with the same thing. Also, I exhort you to honour your two brothers, magnify their rights, beautify their affairs and do not decide on any matter without them."

He then said: "I exhort the two of you regarding him [i.e. Muhammad al-Hanafiyya]. He is your brother (*shaqīq*) and the son of your father. You know his status to your father and that he loves him, so love him."

The last thing he spoke afterwards or exhorted to al-Hasan what he wanted was "There is no god but Allah." He repeated it until he died, may Allah's prayers and peace be upon him. He passed away on Monday night, the twenty-first of Ramadan in the fortieth year of the Prophet's eEmigration to Medina. Al-Hasan b. 'Ali, may Allah have mercy on him, recited *Allahu Akbar* over him five times [i.e. in the funeral prayer].

Concerning inciting animals to fight

It has reached us that Allah's Messenger, peace and blessings be upon him and his progeny, said: ((The one who incites animals to fight is cursed)).[10]

Concerning the acts of the people of Lot which Allah's Messenger prohibited

It has reached us on the authority of Zayd b. 'Ali from his fathers that 'Ali b. Abi Ṭālib, upon them be peace, said:

Allah's Messenger, peace and blessings be upon him and his progeny, said: ((There are ten actions from the people of Lot from which one should be cautious: elongating the moustaches,

---

[6] This portion appears in sermon #166 from ***Nahj al-Balāgha***.

[7] The term *mutraf* used by Imam 'Ali is a Qur'anic allusion mentioned in verses such as: **{And We sent not unto any village a warner, but its self-indulgent (*mutrafūha*) said: "Verily, we are to that which ye bring unto us disbelievers!"} (Q. 34:34)**. This is undoubtedly a reference to Mu'awiya, Yazīd and the successive oppressive and self-indulgent caliphs who viciously pursued the Prophet's Descendants. In one of his letters to Mu'awiya, 'Ali explicitly said to him "...because you are self-indulgent (*mutraf*)..." The passage "Woe be unto the chicks..." is a reference to a lengthy hadith from the Prophet, peace and blessings be upon him and his progeny, in which he is reported to have said the same. See ***Kanz al-'Ummāl*** hadith #31061.

[8] This portion appears in sermon #120 from ***Nahj al-Balāgha***.

[9] This portion appears in letter #47 from ***Nahj al-Balāgha***.

[10] Similarly narrated in ***Sunan Abu Dāwūd, Sunan at-Tirmidhi, Al-Mu'jam al-Kabīr, Musnad Abu Ya'la, Sunan al-Bayhaqi***. The act of inciting animals to fight is not only condemned but also punishable at the discretion of the imam. In the chapter dealing with the prescribed punishments, it says in ***At-Tāj*** regarding this act:

Inciting animals to fight is the same—whether they are owned by someone or someone else or not owned at all, such as dogs and the like. It is considered an act of disobedience that necessitates *ta'zīr* for it. As for the one who does not incite animals to fight but does not separate them, such person's reliability in testimony and the like (*'adāla*) would be nullified.

sectioning the hair, chewing with loud smacking sounds,[11] opening the buttons of a shirt, letting the sarong hang, flying pigeons, shooting clay pellets (*julāhiq*), whistling, gathering to drink and fooling around with each other)).[12]

It has also reached us on the authority of Zayd b. 'Ali from his fathers to 'Ali b. Abi Ťālib, upon them be peace:

I heard Allah's Messenger, peace and blessings be upon him and his progeny, say: ((There are three who will not be granted my intercession on the Day of Judgement: one who has intercourse with animals, one who restrains from charity and one who has intercourse with men as he would with women)).[13]

Concerning memorising the Qur'an and the virtue of reciting the Qur'an

It has reached us on the authority of Zayd b. 'Ali from his fathers that 'Ali b. Abi Ťālib, upon them be peace, said:

Allah's Messenger, peace and blessings be upon him and his progeny, said: ((The Qur'an will come on the Day of Judgement and will have a tongue that is free and articulate saying, confirming and interceding. It will say: "O Lord, Your slave, so-and-so, gathered me in his belly but did not act in Your obedience, nor did he refrain from disobedience or stayed within Your limits." He will say: "You have spoken the truth!" So, there will be darkness between his eyes, another to his right, another to his left, and another behind him. One will leave him, and another will push him until he takes him to the bottom of the fire. Then, he will come and say: "O Lord, Your slave, so-and-so, gathered me in his belly and acted in Your obedience, refrained from disobedience and stayed within Your limits." He will say: "You have spoken the truth!" Then, he will have a light that shines between the heavens and earth until he is admitted into Paradise. Then, it will be said to him: "Recite, for you will be raised in rank for every letter until you reach the same as that of the Prophets and martyrs like this!")) And he joined his index finger and middle finger.[14]

---

[11] The narration in some sources includes the phrase ((…chewing resin (*maďghu al-'ilk*)…)) instead of our rendering ((…chewing with loud smacking sounds (*tanqīďu al-'ilk*)…)). Both phrases appear in the various manuscripts of the ***Ahkām***. However, since there is no offense in chewing resin, gum or anything else, we opted for the narration variant in the above text.

[12] Similarly narrated in ***Musnad Imam Zayd, Amāli Ahmed b. 'Isa***. We saw fit to explain the offensiveness of some of the seemingly innocent actions mentioned in this narration. The practice of 'elongating the moustaches' is generally condemned because of its prevalence among the disbelievers. The term 'sectioning the hair' here refers specifically to shaving part of the head and allowing another part to grow long. Such practice is condemned by the Prophet, peace and blessings be upon him and his progeny, in well-known reports. The practice of 'chewing with loud smacking sounds' among the people of Lot seems to be considered blameworthy due to the men intentionally doing such to resemble women. The term 'opening the buttons of a shirt' refers to wearing only a shirt and leaving it unfastened so that one's nakedness is shown. It is related that when the Prophet, peace and blessings be upon him and his progeny, was asked whether one could pray in just a shirt, he replied: ((Yes. It should be fastened even if it is with a thorn)). As for 'letting the sarong hang,' this is considered blameworthy for men due to it being among the actions of the arrogant. This practice has been condemned by the Prophet in several well-known authenticated reports. As for 'flying pigeons,' this can refer to the act of pigeon racing in order to gamble, or it can refer to using the direction that the pigeons fly to base a decision or action on, or it can refer to the belief that pigeon flying can bring benefit or avert harm. Regardless, all such actions are forbidden by the Qur'an and Prophetic statements. As for the prohibition of 'shooting clay pellets,' the implication here is that one should refrain from playfully shooting animals with these clay pellets in order to inflict unnecessary injuries on them. It is narrated by al-Bukhāri, Muslim, Abu Dāwūd, and others on the authority of 'Abdullah b. Mughaffal that Allah's Messenger, peace and blessing be upon him and his progeny, prohibited casting pebbles at humans and animals. He said: ((It neither kills game animals or enemy soldiers; rather it simply gouges out the eye and breaks the tooth)). As for 'whistling,' the import of its blameworthiness is when such action is used to distract people from prayer and worship as well as a means of mindless entertainment. Such view is substantiated by the Qur'an when Allah says: **{…and their prayers at the House are naught save whistling and clapping…} (Q. 8:35)**. The prohibition of 'gathering to drink' and 'fooling around with each other' is self-explanatory. [Ref. ***Ar-Rawďat an-Naďīr***]

[13] Similarly narrated in ***Musnad Imam Zayd***

[14] Ibid.

It has reached us on the authority of Zayd b. ‘Ali from his fathers that ‘Ali b. Abi Ťālib, upon them be peace, said:

> A man from among the Anŝār was teaching the Qur’an in the mosque of Allah’s Messenger, peace and blessings be upon him and his progeny, and a man who he was teaching came to him with a horse and said: “This is for you. I will carry you on him in the way of Allah.” Then, the Prophet, peace and blessings be upon him and his progeny, came to him and asked him about that. Allah’s Messenger, peace and blessings be upon him and his progeny, asked him: ((Do you want it to be your property tomorrow?)) He replied: “No, by Allah.” And he returned it to him.

Concerning righteousness towards parents and maintaining family ties

It has reached us on the authority of Zayd b. ‘Ali from his fathers that ‘Ali b. Abi Ťālib, upon them be peace, said:

> Allah’s Messenger, peace and blessings be upon him and his progeny, ascended the pulpit and said: ((O people, Gabriel came to me and said: “O Muhammad, whoever allows both his parents or one of them to come to nothing (*adrak*) and dies, he shall enter Hell, and Allah will be distant from them! Say Ameen!” And I said: “Ameen!”)).[15]

It has reached us from ‘Ali, upon him be peace:

> If a man were to be righteous towards both his parents during their lifetimes and then they die without him seeking forgiveness for them—Allah will declare him to be disobedient. If a man were to not be righteous towards both his parents during their lifetimes and then they die with him seeking forgiveness for them—Allah will declare him to be righteous.[16]

It has reached us on the authority of Zayd b. ‘Ali from his fathers that ‘Ali b. Abi Ťālib, upon them be peace, said:

> Allah’s Messenger, peace and blessings be upon him and his progeny, said: ((Whoever wants to prolong his life, expand his provision, have his prayers answered, prevent himself from an evil ending—let him obey his parents in obedience to Allah. Also, let him maintain family ties. He should know that family ties are connected to the Divine Throne. It will come on the Day of Judgement with a tongue that is free and articulate saying: “O Allah, form ties with the one who formed ties with me! And sever ties with the one who severed ties with me!” Allah—the Blessed and Exalted—will answer it by saying: “Verily, I have answered your supplication! Verily, a slave may be upright and sees that he is on a good path until the womb of family ties comes to him and takes him by his head to the lowest level of Hell due to his severing ties with it while he was in this world)).[17]

It has reached us on the authority of Zayd b. ‘Ali from his fathers that ‘Ali b. Abi Ťālib, upon them be peace, said: “Allah’s Messenger, peace and blessings be upon him and his progeny, said: ((Verily, it is from the respect of Allah’s honour that one honours the parents in Allah’s obedience)).”

It has reached us that Allah’s Messenger, peace and blessings be upon him and his progeny, said: ((Looking into the Book of Allah is worship. Looking at the Sanctified House is worship. Looking into the faces of parents out of respect and honour for them is worship)).[18]

It has reached us from al-Hussein b. ‘Ali, upon them be peace:

> Allah’s Messenger, peace and blessings be upon him and his progeny, said: ((If a man were to maintain family ties and there only remained for him three more years of life, Allah will make it thirty-three. If a man were to sever family ties and there only remained for him thirty-three years of life, Allah will make it three)).

---

[15] Similarly narrated in ***Ŝahīh Ibn Hibbān, Musnad al-Bazzār, Ash-Shu’b al-Imān, Al-Mu’jam al-Kabīr***

[16] Similarly narrated in ***Kanz al-’Ummāl***, ***Ušūl al-Kāfi, Bihār al-Anwār***

[17] Similarly narrated in ***Ŝahīh al-Bukhāri, Ŝahīh Muslim, Mušannaf Ibn Abi Shayba, Musnad Abu Ya’la, Sunan al-Bayhaqi***

[18] Similarly narrated in ***Mušannaf Ibn Abi Shayba*** and ***Kanz al-’Ummāl***

It has reached us that Allah's Messenger, peace and blessings be upon him and his progeny, said:

> ((Whoever guarantees me one thing I will guarantee him four things: Whoever maintains family ties will be loved by his family, have his wealth increased, have his life prolonged and will be admitted to his Lord's Paradise)).[19]

Concerning the right of a Muslim on another Muslim and the right of a neighbour

It has reached us on the authority of 'Abdullah b. al-Hasan—his father—his grandfather: "Allah's Messenger, peace and blessings be upon him and his progeny, said: ((Verily, among the things that make forgiveness obligatory is causing happiness to enter your Muslim brother))."[20]

It has reached us on the authority of Ja'far b. Muhammad—his father—his ancestors, upon them be peace:

> Whoever fulfils a need for a believer, Allah will fulfil many needs for such one—one of which is Paradise. Whoever relieves a believer of distress, Allah will relieve such person of the distress of the Day of Judgement. Whoever feeds the one who is hungry, Allah will feed such one from the fruits of Paradise. Whoever gives drink to the one who is thirsty, Allah will give such one a drink from the sealed nectar on the Day of Judgement. Whoever covers one with a garment, such one will be under Allah's protection as long as a thread of that garment remains. By Allah, fulfilling the need of a believer is better than a month of fasting and religious seclusion.[21]

It has reached us that a man once came to al-Hussein b. 'Ali, upon them be peace, concerning a need. He asked him to fulfil his need, and [al-Hussein] said: "I am in the state of religious seclusion." He then went to al-Hasan b. 'Ali, upon him be peace, and informed him saying: "I went to Abu 'Abdullah to fulfil a need I had, and he said: 'I am in the state of religious seclusion.'" Then, al-Hasan fulfilled the man's need and made his way to al-Hussein. He said to him: "O brother, what prevented you from fulfilling the need of your brother?" He replied: "I am in the state of religious seclusion." Al-Hasan said: "Fulfilling the need of a Muslim brother is more preferable than religious seclusion for a month."[22]

It has reached us from al-Hasan b. 'Ali, upon them be peace:

> Allah's Messenger, peace and blessings be upon him and his progeny, said: ((He does not believe in Allah!)). They asked: "Who is the one who does not believe in Allah, O Messenger of Allah?" He replied: ((The one who eats until he is satiated but his neighbour remains hungry while he is aware)).[23]

It has reached us that Allah's Messenger, peace and blessings be upon him and his progeny, said: ((Righteousness, good etiquette and neighbourliness increases one in provisions and aids in building community)).[24]

My father related to me that his father said:

> Abu Sahl b. Sa'īd[§] related to us on the authority of al-Faḍl[§]—al-Hasan [al-Basri]—his brother ['Abdullah b. Sa'īd al-Maqburi[§]]—his father [Sa'īd b. Abu Sa'īd al-Maqburi[§]]—Abu Hurayra: "Allah's Messenger, peace and blessings be upon him and his progeny, said: ((He does not believe in Allah!)). They asked: 'Who, O Messenger of Allah?' He replied: ((The one whose neighbour is not safe from his evil))."[25]

---

[19] Similarly narrated in ***Ŝaḥīh al-Bukhāri, Ŝaḥīh Muslim, Ŝaḥīh Ibn Hibbān, Sunan al-Bayhaqi, Musnad Abu Ya'la***

[20] Similarly narrated in ***Al-Mu'jam al-Kabīr, Al-Mu'jam al-Awsaṭ***

[21] Similar is narrated in ***Ŝaḥīh al-Bukhāri*** and ***Ŝaḥīh Muslim*** on the authority Sālim from his father.

[22] Similarly narrated in ***Amāli Ahmed b. 'Isa*** on the authority of Muhammad al-Bāqir, upon him be peace. Similar is narrated in ***Al-Mu'jam al-Kabīr*** from the Prophet, peace and blessings be upon him and his progeny.

[23] Similarly narrated in ***Al-Adab al-Mufrad, Al-Mu'jam al-Kabīr, Al-Mustadrak, Sharh Ma'āni al-Athār, Mušannaf Ibn Abi Shayba***

[24] Similarly narrated in ***Musnad Ahmed***

[25] Similarly narrated in ***Sharh at-Tajrīd, Ŝaḥīh al-Bukhāri, Ŝaḥīh Muslim, Musnad Ahmed, Musnad Abu Ya'la, Al-Mustadrak, Ŝaḥīh Ibn Hibbān, Mušannaf Ibn Abi Shayba***

My father related to me that his father said:

> Al-Maqburi related to us on the authority of al-Fadl from al-Hasan: "Allah's Messenger, peace and blessings be upon him and his progeny, said: ((He does not believe in Allah!)). They asked: 'Who, O Messenger of Allah?' He replied: ((The one whose neighbour is not safe from his oppression and tyranny))."

It has reached us that a man came to the Prophet, peace and blessings be upon him and his progeny, complaining about his neighbour. Allah's Messenger, peace and blessings be upon him and his progeny, said to him: ((Go and remove your things into the road)), and he removed them. Then, the people passed by and began to curse him since he blamed it on his neighbour. The neighbour came to the Prophet, peace and blessings be upon him and his progeny, and said: "O Messenger of Allah, I found something odd from the people." He asked: ((What did you find from them?)). He replied; "They are cursing me!" He replied: ((Allah has cursed you before the people)). He replied: "O Messenger of Allah, I will not repeat what I did." Then, the man who complained against his neighbour came to the Prophet, peace and blessings be upon him and his progeny, and the latter said to him: ((You can pick up your things now; you are safe and sufficient)).[26]

Concerning reliance upon Allah

Verily, Allah, the Blessed and Exalted, provides His slaves with his provisions and expand their blessings. He singles out those who rely upon Him and those who are confident in what he has. So that from Him, Glory be to Him, is a blessing and a reward for them and an argument against the disobedient and a favour upon them [i.e. the reliant]. He is the Provider of creation from where they know and from where they do not know.

And most of Allah's provision is for the one who trusts in and fears Him from where he never expected it and did not hope for it. Regarding that, Allah says: **{And whosoever is conscious of Allah, Allah will appoint a way out for him and will provide for him from whence he does not expect. And whosoever places his trust in Allah, He will suffice him. Verily, Allah bringeth His command to pass. Allah hath made a measure for all things} (Q. 65:2-3)**.

Concerning those who love one another for the sake of Allah

It has reached us that Allah's Messenger, peace and blessings be upon him and his progeny, said: ((I am an intercessor for any two brothers who love each other for the sake of Allah—from the time I was sent until the Day of Judgement)).[27]

It has reached us on the authority of Zayd b. 'Ali from his fathers that 'Ali b. Abi Ťālib, upon them be peace, said:

> Allah's Messenger, peace and blessings be upon him and his progeny, said: ((Allah—Blessed and Exalted—said: "By My honour, My greatness, My pride and My existence, I will admit to My house and accompany among My friends, marry the clear-eyed mates of Paradise (*hūra ayn*) to those who love each other for My sake, form fraternal bonds for My sake and show love to My creation.")).

Concerning men who resemble women and women who resemble men

Cursed is the woman who imitates men in any situation, as well as the man who imitates women. Regarding that, it has reached us that Allah's Messenger, peace and blessings be upon him and his progeny, cursed the one who commits it and the one for whom it is committed.

---

[26] Similarly narrated in ***Al-Adab al-Mufrad, Sunan Abu Dāwūd, Al-Mustadrak, Al-Mu'jam al-Kabīr, Kanz al-'Ummāl***

[27] Similarly narrated in ***Kanz al-'Ummāl***

He, peace and blessings be upon him and his progeny, said: ((The masculine woman will not enter Paradise. Allah and His Angels curse the man who has intercourse with men or animals or a man who resembles women or a woman who resembles men)).[28]

Allah's Messenger, peace and blessings be upon him and his progeny, cursed the woman who applies false hair, the one for whom the false hair is applied, the woman who tattoos and the one for whom the tattoo is applied unless there is a disease to justify it. He also cursed the woman who plucks facial hair and the one who is plucked.[29]

He, peace and blessings be upon him and his progeny, said: ((I dislike seeing a woman who has not dyed herself with henna)).[30] He, peace and blessings be upon him and his progeny, also said: ((What prevents you from changing the colour of your nails?))[31]

It is also narrated that he, peace and blessings be upon him and his progeny, used to command them [i.e. the women] to wear henna dye as well as command them to wear necklaces around their necks and ornaments or anything else on their hands or feet if they are able. He also disliked that a woman would refrain from wearing ornaments as a man would. Also, he, peace and blessings be upon him and his progeny, disliked that a woman would pray without wearing a necklace or anything else.

He, peace and blessings be upon him and his progeny, used to say: ((If any of you were to say when approaching his spouse "O Allah, protect us from Satan and protect what You provide for us from Satan!" if he were to have a child, Satan will have no power over him)).[32]

Concerning seeking the best choice (*al-istikhāra*)

Muslims should not do any of their affairs from their travels or from all their occasions except after seeking the best choice from Allah, the Mighty and Majestic, regarding that matter. One should say: "O Allah, You know, and we do not know! You have the power, and we do not have the power! We intend such-and-such. O Allah, if there is good for us in that, facilitate it for us and make it easy. Protect us upon it while I am in it. If there is not good in it for us, divert it from us, O our Lord, in well-being, for You are the Guardian of all good and the Preventer from all harm."

Regarding that, it has reached us that Allah's Messenger, peace and blessings be upon him and his progeny, used to teach his Companions the method of seeking the best choice just as he taught them a chapter of the Qur'an. He used to say:

> ((Whenever one of you intends a matter, let him name it and say: 'O Allah, I seek the best choice from You regarding it by Your knowledge and I seek Your power regarding it by Your power. Verily, You know, and I do not know. You have the power, and I do not have the power. You know the unseen. O Allah, if there is good in this matter of mine, then provide me with it, facilitate it for me, assist me in it and make me pleased and content with it, and bless me in it. If there is evil in it, divert it from me, and facilitate good for me in its place.')).[33]

---

[28] Similarly narrated in ***Sunan Ibn Mājah, Sunan Abu Dāwūd, Al-Mu'jam al-Kabīr, Al-Mu'jam al-Awsaṭ, Mušannaf Ibn Abi Shayba***

[29] Similarly narrated in ***Ŝahīh Muslim, Sunan Abu Dāwūd, Sunan an-Nisā'i, Ušūl al-Kāfi, Bihār al-Anwār***. According to ***At-Tāj***, this prohibition of plucking applies to faces of both women and men—whether it is the eyebrows, moustache, beard or any other facial hair. The only exception are the nose hairs, which are permissible to pluck.

[30] Similarly narrated in ***Sharh at-Tajrīd, Ŝahīh al-Bukhāri, Ŝahīh Muslim, Sunan Abu Dāwūd, Sunan an-Nisā'i, Sunan Ibn Mājah, Sunan at-Tirmidhi, Musnad Ahmed, Al-Mu'jam al-Kabīr***

[31] Similarly narrated in ***Sharh at-Tajrīd, Sunan al-Bayhaqi, Kanz al-'Ummāl***

[32] Similarly narrated in ***Ŝahīh al-Bukhāri, Ŝahīh Muslim, Ŝahīh Ibn Hibbān, Al-Mu'jam al-Kabīr, Al-Mu'jam al-Awsaṭ, Sunan Abu Dāwūd, Mušannaf Ibn Abi Shayba, Sunan at-Tirmidhi, Bihār al-Anwār***

[33] Similarly narrated in ***Ŝahīh al-Bukhāri, Al-Mu'jam al-Kabīr, Al-Mu'jam al-Awsaṭ, Mušannaf Ibn Abi Shayba, Ŝahīh Ibn Hibbān, Sunan al-Bayhaqi, Sunan at-Tirmidhi, Sunan an-Nisā'i, Sunan Ibn Mājah, Sunan Abu Dāwūd, Musnad Ahmed, Bihār al-Anwār***

It has reached us that Allah's Messenger, peace and blessings be upon him and his progeny, said: ((It is from the increase in seeking the best choice that there is blessing for a person. It is from the avoidance of seeking the best choice that there is wretchedness for a person)).[34]

It has reached us that the Commander of Believers, 'Ali b. Abi Ťālib, upon him be peace, said: "I do not mind the outcome either way when I seek Allah for the best choice."

Concerning the virtue of worship during the pre-dawn

It has reached us that Allah's Messenger, peace and blessings be upon him and his progeny, said:

> ((Verily, in the last hour of the night, Allah—Majestic is He—commands an Angel to call out so that all between east and west can hear among the men and jinn: "Is there anyone who seeks forgiveness so that he can be forgiven? Is there anyone who repents so that he can have his repentance accepted? Is there anyone who calls for goodness so that will be answered? Is there a beggar so that he can be given that for which he begs? Is there a desiring person so that he can be given that which he desires? O performer of good, be accepted! O performer of evil, be cut off! O Allah, grant everyone who spends wealth successors, and grant everyone who withholds wealth destruction!")).[35]

It has reached us that Allah's Messenger, peace and blessings be upon him and his progeny, said: ((Whoever has the door of supplication opened for him has the door of reply and mercy opened for him. That is based on the statement of Allah: **{"Call unto Me and I shall answer!"} (Q. 40:30)**)).[36]

The one for whom the door of supplication is opened refers to the one who increases in his supplication to Allah. He asks for His pleasure and contentment as well as to enable him to fight jihad in His way and achieve martyrdom. That is the best thing that one can ask for.

Concerning good character and the virtues of prayers upon the Prophet and the virtues of the Friday congregational prayer

Good character is a means of closeness to Allah and a means of closeness to people. Good character and softness of people's affection is able to attain that which the one who gives wealth without good character cannot be attain. Whoever is of good character, let him thank Allah and know that it is the greatest of Allah's blessings upon him.

It has reached us that Allah's Messenger, peace and blessings be upon him and his progeny, said: ((Verily, by means of good character, a man can attain the rank of the one who fasts during the day, stands in prayer during the night and fights jihad for the sake of Allah. Due to evil character, he will be declared a tyrant even if the only thing he owns is permissible for him)).[37]

Whoever increases in the prayers upon Allah's Messenger, peace and blessings be upon him and his progeny, Allah will increase His mercy to him, raise his rank and erase his bad deeds. The best time for the prayers upon the Prophet, peace and blessings be upon him and his progeny, is Friday. The best hour of Friday is the time that the sun passes the zenith. Friday is the best and greatest of days according to the Possessor of Majesty and Nobility. The night before Friday is best of nights. Good deeds are increased during the day of Friday and the night before. Friday is simply called *Jumu'a* because people congregate (*ijtimā'a*) on it to perform the obligatory prayer as Allah commands them when He says: **{O ye who believe, when the call is made for the prayer on the day of congregation, rush towards the remembrance of Allah and leave commerce. That is best for thee if ye but knew} (Q. 62:9)**.

---

[34] Similarly narrated in ***Sunan at-Tirmidhi, Musnad Ahmed, Musnad Abu Ya'la, Musnad al-Bazzār, Al-Mustadrak, Ash-Shu'b al-Imān***

[35] Similarly narrated in ***Ŝahīh al-Bukhāri, Ŝahīh Muslim, Ŝahīh Ibn Hibbān, Musnad Ahmed, Bihār al-Anwār***

[36] Similarly narrated in ***Mušannaf Ibn Abi Shayba, Sunan at-Tirmidhi, Bihār al-Anwār***

[37] Similarly narrated in ***Al-Muwatta, Musnad Ahmed, Sunan Abu Dāwūd, Al-Mu'jam al-Kabīr, Al-Mu'jam al-Awsaț, Ušūl al-Kāfi, Bihār al-Anwār***

It is from Allah's glorification of that day that He made it a festival (*Eid*) for Muslims. Regarding it, it has reached us from the Prophet, peace and blessings be upon him and his progeny, from Gabriel that he said ((“Friday is the Day of Judgement, and the Last Hour will be established on it”)).[38]

Ever since I recounted this hadith, fear and apprehension has entered me every Friday. This is not out of my evil opinion of my Lord, nor my lack of knowledge of the mercy of my Creator. Rather, it is due to fear of meeting Him without me having done what He commanded me to do. I arise with what I was encouraged to arise in it and made it the greatest of His obligations upon me and the best for me and my son in opposing the transgressors, striving against the oppressors and supporting the religion of the Lord of creation. And I hope that Allah does not cause my shortcomings in seeking that to be known, nor in my eagerness to be like that, but rather cause it to be known that I am neither desirous of the truth nor seeking it from creation, nor a helper for me in it, nor a supporter for me in it. I hope that it is said that I called to that but was disobeyed and that I arose to do so but was abandoned and left. I called to the Most Merciful and struggled to revive what had died of faith, so the ears of this creation were deafened to my call, and they were indifferent to what they were told of the rights of my life. And I was involved in the command of Allah but was not followed and was disobeyed when I called to Allah. I said: “O Lord, I own nothing but myself! I bought it from Him, and my wealth is in the side of the Ka'ba, the Sanctified House by the price He gave me.” The Possessor of Majesty and Nobility says: **{Verily, Allah hath purchased from the believers their lives and their wealth because the Garden shall be theirs. They fight in the way of Allah and slay and is slain. It is a promise which is binding on Him in the Torah and the Gospel and the Qur'an. Who fulfils His covenant better than Allah? Glad tidings then in thy transaction that ye hath made, for that is the great victory} (Q. 9:111)**.

Then I waited for Allah's command and stood aside for that until Allah opens and permits what I sought—reviving His right, permission with His help and payment and reconciliation for that as well as the rectification between the hearts of the slaves who are hoped to reform the land or that we meet Him, Glory be to Him, resolute and holding fast to it.

Concerning humility, patience and gratitude

Humility is the ornamentation of the believer, and the one who shows humility to Allah and the Muslims will be raised by Allah. It is like the earth that is watered, shaken, nurtured, and sprouted to produce every pair. Its plant is lofty, its side is green, its fruit is ripe, its water is abundant, and its blessing is great. It is better for someone in need to have humility in the face of a just imam according to Allah as long as his humility is for Allah and in Allah. Whoever humbles himself for the sake of Allah will be raised by Allah. Whoever is arrogant and forceful in Allah's earth will be abased. Whoever is raised by Allah will not be humbled, and whoever is abased by Allah will not be raised.

The best way to exercise Allah's blessings is to show gratitude to Allah, and the best way to show gratitude to Allah is to praise Allah, carry out with His command, strive in obedience to Him, and not simply thank Him with the tongue without action. Gratitude is in deeds and the tongue. So, whoever shows gratitude to Allah obeys Him, and whoever obeys Him has shown gratitude to Him.

Patience is the symbol of the believers, and it is a means to overcome the disobedient. The noblest of patience is patience in obeying Allah, persevering in His pleasure, as well as refraining from disobeying Him, and carrying oneself to what pleases Him. The most beautiful of patience is endurance in that which counters the corrupt passions and perseverance in asceticism regarding this world. Regarding that, the Most Exalted says: **{As for the one who transgresses and prefers this world's life, Hell is his final resting place! As for the one who fears the position of his Lord and prevents the soul from corrupt desires, Paradise is his final resting place!} (Q. 79:37-41)**.

---

[38] Similarly narrated in ***Amāli Ahmed b. 'Isa, Amāli Abu Ṫālib, Musnad Abu Ya'la, Al-Mu'jam al-Awsaṫ, Mušannaf Ibn Abi Shayba, Al-Mustadrak, Ušūl al-Kāfi, Bihār al-Anwār***

The one who does not restrain his soul from disobedience to Allah or is not patient in Allah's obedience is not considered among the people of patience. Regarding that, it has reached us that Allah's Messenger, peace and blessings be upon him and his progeny, said: ((Verily, when Allah loves a slave, He afflicts him with trial. And when He afflicts him with trial and the person is patient, it is sufficient for him)).[39]

Regarding that, it has reached us from the Commander of Believers, 'Ali b. Abi Ťālib, upon him be peace:

> Allah's Messenger, peace and blessings be upon him and his progeny, said: ((There are three for whom Allah will make their flesh protected from the Hellfire and will have Paradise: the one who engages in repentance when afflicted by trials, the one who praises Allah out of gratitude when Allah grants him a blessing and the one who seeks Allah's forgiveness when he sins)).

It has reached us that the Commander of Believers, 'Ali b. Abi Ťālib, upon him be peace, said:

> Allah spoke by inspiration to Moses b. Imran saying: "Do you know why I chose you over the rest of creation and spoke to you?" He replied: "Why, O Lord?" He said: "Because I looked at the hearts of my slaves, and I did not find among them anyone humbler than you."[40]

Concerning generosity, deeds for Allah and stinginess

Generosity is a means of closeness to people and a source of closeness to Allah. Such is beloved to Allah and beloved to people as long as the person is a believer. Regarding that, it has reached us that Allah's Messenger, peace and blessings be upon him and his progeny, said: ((Allah loves the generous, so love him, and He hates the stingy, so hate him)).[41]

It has also reached us that Allah's Messenger, peace and blessings be upon him and his progeny, said:

> ((Generosity is a tree whose roots are in Paradise, and its branches are in this world. So, whoever takes a hold of it, that branch will lead him to Paradise. Stinginess is a tree that is fixed in the Fire, and its branches are in this world. So, whoever takes a branch from it, that branch will lead him to the Fire)).[42]

Also, it has reached us that Allah's Messenger, peace and blessings be upon him and his progeny, said:

> ((Whoever prays eight units of prayer in the middle of the night and prays *witr* and continues to do so until Allah meets them, Allah will open for him twelve gates of Paradise, and he will enter through whichever one he wants)).[43]

It has reached us that Allah's Messenger, peace and blessings be upon him and his progeny, also said: ((The prayer in secret is seventy times more excellent than the prayer in open)).[44]

Concerning kindness

Whoever shows kindness to his brothers will cause their mutual affection to last. Whoever shows it to his family will win their hearts. Whoever shows it to his enemies will decrease their enmity towards him. Whoever shows it to his servants will perpetuate their sincerity. Whoever shows it in his sustenance without falling short nor diminishing—his chivalry will perpetuate the grace of his Lord.

---

[39] Similarly narrated in ***Amāli Ahmed b. 'Isa, Amāli Abu Ťālib, Al-Mu'jam al-Awsaṭ, Musnad Ahmed, Sunan at-Tirmidhi, Sunan Ibn Māja, Uṡūl al-Kāfi, Bihār al-Anwār***

[40] Similarly narrated in ***Bihār al-Anwār***

[41] Similarly narrated in ***Musnad Ahmed, Sunan al-Bayhaqi, Kanz al-'Ummāl***

[42] Similarly narrated in ***Kanz al-'Ummāl, Sunan ad-Dārqutni, Ash-Shu'b al-Imān, Hilayat al-Awliyā, Uṡūl al-Kāfi, Bihār al-Anwār***

[43] Similarly narrated in ***Sharh at-Tajrīd***

[44] Similarly narrated in ***Mušannaf Ibn Abi Shayba, Al-Mu'jam al-Kabīr, Sunan al-Bayhaqi***

It is a good deed for the one who spends and destruction for the one who withholds, as Allah's Messenger, peace and blessings be upon him and his progeny, said.[45] Therefore, one should not spend his provision that was provided by Allah in disobedience to Allah. Neither should he restrain it from Allah's obedience while it was out of Allah's generosity.

My father related to me from his father—his grandfather—his ancestors, upon them be peace, that Allah's Messenger, peace and blessings be upon him and his progeny, said: ((Kindness is prosperity, and stupidity is misfortune)).[46] Also, it has reached us that Allah's Messenger, peace and blessings be upon him and his progeny, said: ((When Allah desires good for a family, He guides them to kindness)).[47]

Being kind to one's soul is closer to Allah than being kind with his money and not being kind to his soul. Whoever does not protect it from stinginess and turns away from it the occurrence of meanness and removes the miserable miserliness from it while negating the shame of scorn. If he does not do that, he will not be protected by its stinginess. According to Allah, such person is not among the successful. The one who is not among the successful, according to Allah, is considered among of the destroyed. Regarding that, the Most Truthful says: **{And whosoever is saved from the stinginess of his soul—they shall be the successful!} (Q. 59:9)**.

Concerning aiding the oppressors

Whoever helps an oppressor, even by handwriting a letter, lifting an incandescent device, or placing it down and then meets Allah—the Mighty and Majestic—for that without being forced to do so out of fear for himself, he will meet Allah on the Day of Judgement with His anger upon him. The one with whom Allah is angry will have Hellfire as his destination.

As for me, I do not say that this applies to one of the wrongdoers without anyone else. Rather, I say that it is impermissible to aid the oppressor, assist him, benefit him or serve him—whoever it may be, whether from the family of Allah's Messenger or anyone else. Every oppressor is accursed, and every helper of an oppressor is accursed.

Regarding that, it has reached us that Allah's Messenger, peace and blessings be upon him and his progeny, said: ((Whoever collects a dirham for an unjust ruler, will be thrown by Allah into the Hellfire by his nostrils)). Also, regarding that, it is said that the one who helps the oppressor is like the one who helped Pharaoh against Moses.[48]

Regarding that, it has reached us that Abu Ja'far Muhammad b. 'Ali, upon them be peace, used to relate a narration and say:

> On the Day of Judgement, Allah will make a pavilion of fire and place the helpers of the oppressors in it. He will make for them nails of iron with which they will rub their bodies until their hearts appear, and they will say: "Our Lord, did we not worship You?" It will be said: "Yes, but you assisted the oppressors!"[49]

It has reached us that Allah's Messenger, peace and blessings be upon him and his progeny, said: ((Whoever gains dominance over us has shared in shedding our blood)). The term 'gains dominance' here means to overcome in number. Therefore, whoever overcomes in number in terms of person, statement or aiding with one's wealth against the rightful ruler from the Prophet's Progeny—such person has shared in shedding his blood and committing a crime against Allah's Messenger, peace and blessings be upon him and his progeny, regarding his offspring. He, peace and blessings be upon him and his progeny, would be angrier regarding the anger of his offspring and more pleased regarding the pleasure of his offspring than the rest of the people.

---

[45] Similarly narrated in ***Ŝaḥīḥ al-Bukhāri, Ŝaḥīḥ Muslim, Ŝaḥīḥ Ibn Hibbān, Al-Mustadrak, Al-Mu'jam al-Awsaṭ***

[46] Similarly narrated in ***Amāli Ahmed b. 'Isa, Amāli Abu Ťālib, Al-Mu'jam al-Awsaṭ, Ušūl al-Kāfi, Bihār al-Anwār***

[47] Similarly narrated in ***Amāli Ahmed b. 'Isa, Amāli Abu Ťālib, Al-Mu'jam al-Kabīr, Musnad Ahmed, Ušūl al-Kāfi, Bihār al-Anwār***

[48] Similarly narrated in ***Al-Jāmi' al-Kāfi*** and ***Bihār al-Anwār***

[49] Similar is narrated in ***Ušūl al-Kāfi***.

This misguided *Ummah* bears the guilt of the sinners from the Progeny of Allah's Messenger, peace and blessings be upon him and his progeny, against the pure righteous one from them, who is angrier and more hateful. By that action, the wrongdoer, like all other people, faces a situation before Allah, where Muhammad, Allah's Messenger, peace and blessings be upon him and his progeny, contends with him, and Allah judges between them with the truth. {**And they find whatsoever they did presented unto them. And thy Lord is not unjust to anyone**} (Q. 18:49).

Woe be to the one who does that from this *Ummah*! Does he not hear the words of Allah, glory be to Him, when He says about that {**One shall not bear the burdens of another**} (Q. 35:18) and {**And for every human, We hath fixed his fate upon his neck. And We shall bring forth for him on the Day of Judgement a book which he shall find opened. "Read thy book! Sufficient is thy soul against thyself this Day as an accountant!"**} (Q. 17:13-14)?

Indeed! They heard and understood it, but they were stubborn in that truth and shunned the truth with injustice, deceit, rebellion and tyranny and hostility to Allah, His Messenger, peace and blessings be upon him and his progeny, and his offspring. It is as if they had not heard how Allah commands His Prophet to convey to the *Ummah* the obligation of mutual affection when He says: {**Say: "I ask thee for no reward but only affection toward the kin."**} (Q. 42:23).

Indeed! They have heard that with their ears and understood Allah's mandate upon them with their hearts. Then they rejected and left it after that out of enmity and envy towards the family of Allah's Messenger, peace and blessings be upon him and his progeny. They were as the Most Gracious said in what was revealed from the verses of the Qur'an about those who were before them who knew the same as what they knew and then denied as they denied: {**But when there came unto them Our visible signs, they said: "This is manifest sorcery!" And they denied them, though they were certain of its truth, out of wrongdoing and arrogance. So, behold what the consequence is for the corruptors!**} (Q. 27:13-14).

Concerning commanding the good and forbidding the evil as well as supplicating to Allah

Whoever supplicates to Allah and is responded to, he will have the same reward as everyone who is answered, without detracting from the reward of those who do good. And supplication to Allah is the greatest of deeds. Regarding that, the Possessor of Majesty and Nobility says: {**Recite what has been revealed unto thee from the Book and establish the prayer. Indeed, the prayer prevents from obscenity and the objectionable. Verily, the remembrance of Allah is greatest. And Allah knows what ye do**} (Q. 29:45).

The {**remembrance of Allah**} mentioned here refers to supplication to Allah. Regarding that, my father related to me that his father used to say about the statement of Allah, the Glorified {**Verily, the remembrance of Allah is greatest**}: "The {**remembrance of Allah**} mentioned here refers to supplication to Allah."

And with that, the remembrance of Allah includes the preoccupation of the heart with contemplating Allah's majesty, power, greatness and authority, as well as the remembrance of Him with that with He reminded Himself of His Divine Oneness, His Justice, and the truthfulness of His Divine Promise and Divine Threat.

It has reached us that Allah's Messenger, peace and blessings be upon him and his progeny, said: ((It is impermissible for an eye that sees Allah being disobeyed to turn away until you change it or move)).[50] This obligation is incumbent on the one who can bear the change. The one who cannot bear the change must emigrate from that place where the Most Gracious is disobeyed and Satan is obeyed to one of the places in Allah's land where the sinners are not seen and the judgements of the unjust are not applied to him from its plains or mountains. Allah, the Glorified, says: {**Verily, as for those whom the Angels**

[50] Similarly narrated in ***Sharh at-Tajrīd, Amāli Ahmed b. 'Isa, Bihār al-Anwār***

take in death while they wrong themselves, [the Angels] shall ask: "In what state wert thou?" They shall say: "We were oppressed in the land." (The Angels) shall say: "Was not Allah's earth spacious that ye could have emigrated therein?" As for such, their resting place shall be Hell, an evil destination!} (Q. 4:97).

Concerning observing trusts, fulfilling covenants and being truthful in speech

This is one of the characteristics of the believers. Regarding this, it has reached us that the Messenger of the Lord of creation, peace and blessings be upon him and his progeny, said:

> ((Guarantee for me six, and I will guarantee you Paradise by Allah: fulfil a promise when you make it, observe a trust when you are entrusted, be attentive when you speak, guard your private parts, lower your gaze and maintain your family ties)).[51]

This is confirmed in the Book of Allah: **{Fulfill the covenant of Allah when ye hath made a covenant}** (Q. 16:91) **{...and those who keep their covenant when they make one, and the patient in tribulation and adversity and time of stress. Such are the sincere. Such are the God-conscious}** (Q. 2:177).

Allah says regarding the observance of trusts: **{And if one amongst thee entrusts to one another, let he who is entrusted fulfil that which is entrusted unto him and be God-conscious}** (Q. 2:283) **{Indeed, Allah orders thee to render the trusts to their owners and when ye judge between the people to judge with justice. Indeed, excellent is what Allah advises thee with! Indeed, Allah is All-Hearing All-Seeing}** (Q. 4:58).

He says regarding truthfulness **{Verily, the men who surrender unto Allah and women who surrender, and the men who believe and women who believe, and the men who obey and women who obey, and the men who speak the truth and women who speak the truth...}** and then says at the end of the verse **{...Allah hath readied for them forgiveness and a vast reward}** (Q. 33:35). He declares that He had prepared such for those who were like that which Allah mentioned.

Regarding that, it has reached us that Allah's Messenger, peace and blessings be upon him and his progeny, said: ((Honesty brings sustenance, and treachery brings poverty)).[52]

Concerning backbiting and arrogance

Backbiting and arrogance are among the actions of the disbelievers and not among the character of believers. Regarding backbiting, Allah says: **{Do not backbite one another. Would anyone amongst thee like to consume the flesh of thy dead brother? Thou wouldst abhor it! Be God-conscious. Verily, Allah is Oft-turning, Most Gracious}** (Q. 49:12).

Regarding that is what Allah's Messenger, peace and blessings be upon him and his progeny, said to az-Zubayr[§] and his companion when they said "Look at this man who had his affair concealed by Allah but would not leave it alone himself! Now, he was stoned like a dog!" Allah's Messenger, peace and blessings be upon him and his progeny, did not say anything to them until they passed by a donkey's rotting carcass. Allah's Messenger, peace and blessings be upon him and his progeny, said to them both: ((Go down and eat from this rotting carcass!)). The two of them said: "May Allah forgive you, O Messenger of Allah! Should we eat from this rotting carcass?" He replied: ((The disdain you two showed to your brother is graver than what you would eat of this rotting carcass! Verily, he is now in the rivers of Paradise submerging in them)).

---

[51] Similarly narrated in ***Musnad Ahmed, Ŝaḥīḥ Ibn Hibbān, Sunan al-Bayhaqi, Al-Mustadrak, Biḥār al-Anwār***

[52] Similarly narrated in ***Kanz al-'Ummāl, Uṣūl al-Kāfi, Biḥār al-Anwār***

Regarding arrogance, Allah says: **{Thus Allah sets a seal over every heart of an arrogant tyrant} (Q. 40:35)**. Regarding that, it has reached us that the Commander of Believers, upon him be peace, and Abu Dharr asked Allah's Messenger, peace and blessings be upon him and his progeny: "What is the greatest sin to Allah after idolatry?" He replied: ((Arrogance! Arrogance!)).

Concerning major sins and their explanation

The major sins are all those actions for which Allah has obligated the Hellfire upon the one who does without repentance and departing from such, such as idolatry, likening him to His creation, attributing injustice to His action, deliberately killing a believer, fleeing from the battlefield except to reroute the attack or regroup, consuming usury after warning, consuming the wealth of the orphan, homosexual acts, fornication, slandering chaste and oblivious believing women, perjury, deliberately lying against Allah, deliberately lying against His Messenger, deliberately lying against the just imam, unjustly consuming people's wealth, and returning to the desert (*at-ta'arrub*) after the Emigration.[53] Allah promised the Hellfire to all who do such.

Concerning charity

Charity in secret extinguishes the wrath of the Lord. The best charity is that which takes place in later years. That is what Allah has made a steep path that only the patient can attain. Regarding that, Allah, the Blessed and Exalted, says: **{But he hath not attempted the steep path. And what has reached thee regarding the steep path? It is to free a slave, to feed on the day of hunger an orphan near of kin or the needy in the dust of misery}** (**Q. 90:11-16**).

Charity is what Allah praises the Progeny of Muhammad for when He says: **{...and they feed food out of love for it [or "love for Him"] to the needy and the orphan and the captive. "Verily, we simply feed thee for the Countenance of Allah! We desire not from thee any reward nor gratitude!"} (Q. 76:8-9)**. Also, regarding that, Allah says: **{...and the man who gives charity and the woman who gives charity...} (Q. 33:35)**.

Verily, charity brings about provision and prevents an evil death. Regarding that, it has reached us that Allah's Messenger, peace and blessings be upon him and his progeny, said: ((Increase your provision by means of charity)).[54]

Concerning constantly doing favours

Constantly doing a favour is one of the greatest benefits of Muslims, and in it is a great reward from the Lord of creation. Its doer is not neglected in this world nor in the Hereafter. Regarding this, a wise poet [i.e. Jarwal b. Aws b. Mālik al-'Abbasi] said: "Whoever does a favour will not lack in reward. / The favour will not vanish between Allah and the people."

Also, it has reached us that Allah's Messenger, peace and blessings be upon him and his progeny, said:

> ((One should constantly do favours for one who is deserving and one who is not deserving. Verily, if you were to do a favour for someone who deserves it, he would be deserving of it. But if you were to do a favour for one who does not deserve it, you will be deserving of it)).

It has reached us that Allah's Messenger, peace and blessings be upon him and his progeny, said to A'isha: ((Can you recite a poem of Ibn Urayđ, the Jew [i.e. as-Sumawal b. Adiya]?)). She said: "No." Umm Salama said: "But I can recite it." He said to her: ((How?)). She said: "He said: 'I reward you if he praises you and / Whoever praises you for what you did is rewarded.'" Then Allah's Messenger, peace

[53] The returning to the desert after the migration is a metonym that refers to Muslims committing apostasy. Such was symbolised by Bedouins returning to the desert after having answered the call to migrate (Ref. ***Lisān al-Arab***). The same phrase is narrated and listed among seven major sins by Allah's Messenger, peace and blessings be upon him and his progeny, in texts such as ***Al-Mu'jam al-Kabīr*** and ***Al-Mu'jam al-Awsaṭ***.

[54] Similarly narrated in ***Shu'b al-Imān, Sunan Ibn Mājah, Sunan al-Bayhaqi, Uṣūl al-Kāfi, Bihār al-Anwār***

and blessings be upon him and his progeny, said: ((Gabriel said: "O Muhammad, for those who give you a hand, let him suffice him and if you are not able, praise him.")).

Concerning apologies and the urging its acceptance

It is obligatory for the one to whom is apologised to accept the apology and show its acceptance to the one who apologised, whether the one who apologised was right or wrong. This is because such is more like the actions of the people of faith and a means of closeness to the Most Gracious for the one who did it.

Regarding that, it has reached us that the Commander of Believers, 'Ali b. Abi Ťālib, upon him be peace, said:

> Allah's Messenger, peace and blessings be upon him and his progeny, said: ((Whoever does not accept an apology—whether the one who apologised was right or wrong—such person will not meet me at the Basin)).[55]

Also, regarding that, it has reached us that al-Hasan b. 'Ali, upon them be peace, said: "If someone insulted me in this ear and apologised to me in the other ear, I would accept it."

Concerning one who is compelled or forgets

Whoever is compelled to do something without having power over the one who compelled him and whoever fears ruin to himself in his disobedience of such—such person will not be punished for what he is forced to do and made to enter into unless s/he was afterwards pleased with what he entered into. However, if his heart is not satisfied with it, then there is nothing upon him regarding that.

Regarding that is what Allah said about the incident of 'Ammār b. Yāsir, may Allah be satisfied with him, when the Quraysh did to him what they did: **{Whosoever disbelieves in Allah after his belief—save he who is forced thereto whilst his heart is still content with belief—but opens his heart to disbelief, upon them is the wrath of Allah. For them shall be a great punishment} (Q. 16:106)**.

Regarding that, it has reached us on the authority of Zayd b. 'Ali from his forefathers from 'Ali, upon them be peace:

> Allah's Messenger, peace and blessings be upon him and his progeny, said: ((I have been given three things: a mercy from my Lord, an expansion for my *Ummah* under compulsion until he is satisfied insomuch that a man says that an unjust ruler hates him unless he is satisfied with the injustice that he is upon, and an excuse for error until he does so deliberately and for forgetfulness until he is reminded of it)).[56]

Concerning the sanctity of Medina

It has reached us that when Allah's Messenger, peace and blessings be upon him and his progeny, climbed the mountain of Uhud, he said: ((This is a mountain that loves us, and we love it. O Allah, Abraham sanctified Mecca, and I sanctify what is between its two plains)).[57]

It is impermissible for game to be hunted, nor to prop up trees with something from the two plains of Medina. They are its two enclosed, stony areas in which hunting is forbidden.

---

[55] Similarly narrated in ***Amāli Ahmed b. 'Isa, Amāli Abu Ťālib, Al-Mu'jam al-Awsaṫ, Bihār al-Anwāri***. In the last reference, the hadith ends with the wording ((…will not receive my intercession)).

[56] Similarly narrated in ***Al-Mu'jam al-Kabīr, Al-Mu'jam al-Awsaṫ, Mušannaf Ibn Abi Shayba, Sunan Ibn Mājah, Ŝahīh Ibn Hibbān, Sunan ad-Dārqutni, Sunan al-Bayhaqi***

[57] Similarly narrated in ***Ŝahīh al-Bukhāri, Ŝahīh Muslim, Musnad Ahmed, Sunan al-Bayhaqi, Sunan at-Tirmidhi, Al-Muwaṫṫa, Musnad Abu Ya'la, Sunan Ibn Māja***

Concerning the virtue of Medina

It has reached us that Allah's Messenger, peace and blessings be upon him and his progeny, said when departing from Mecca: ((O Allah, the Quraysh ousted me from the city that is most beloved to me, so cause me to stay in a city that is most beloved to You!)).[58] Allah caused him to settle in Medina.

It has also reached us that Allah's Messenger, peace and blessings be upon him and his progeny, said: ((Between my house and pulpit is a garden from the gardens of Paradise, and my pulpit is upon my Basin)).[59]

Concerning shyness

The best of what the believers can behave with is shyness, and the best shyness is the shyness that is shy of Allah. The one who is not ashamed of Allah will openly disobey Him. The one who is not ashamed of Allah cannot be designated by the name of shyness. The one who is ashamed of Allah will not disobey Him deliberately.

Regarding that, it has reached us that Allah's Messenger, peace and blessings be upon him and his progeny, said: ((Shyness is from belief, and there is no belief for the one who is not shy)).[60] It has also reached us that he, peace and blessings be upon him and his progeny, said: ((For everything is a character, and the character of human beings is shyness)).[61]

Concerning anger

Self-control for the Lord's pleasure when anger calls and repressing anger is praiseworthy according to Allah because it is from excellence. Regarding that, the Most Merciful says: **{…those who suppress their wrath and are forgiving towards humankind. And Allah loves those who do good} (Q. 3:134)**.

One of the cures for anger if it is severe is to recite the prayer upon Muhammad, peace and blessings be upon him and his progeny. If the angry person is standing, he should sit, and if he is sitting, he should stand. Regarding that, it has reached us that a man came to Allah's Messenger, peace and blessings be upon him and his progeny, and said: "O Messenger of Allah, teach me some words that I can live by and do not make them too much for me." Allah's Messenger, peace and blessings be upon him and his progeny, replied: ((Do not be angry)).[62]

It has also reached us that he, peace and blessings be upon him and his progeny, said: ((The strong man is not the one who is good at wrestling. Rather, the strong man is the one who can control himself when angry)).[63]

Concerning the fortune-teller, physiognomist, astrologer and soothsayer

One is to not accept the statement of any of these people, nor does one act upon it or rely on it, for whoever accepts something from that has wronged himself and committed evil in his act. Similar has reached us from the Commander of Believers, 'Ali b. Abi Ťālib, upon him be peace.[64]

---

[58] Similarly narrated in ***Al-Mustadrak***

[59] Similarly narrated in ***Ŝahīh al-Bukhāri, Ŝahīh Muslim, Musnad Abu Ya'la, Al-Muwaťťa, Musnad Ahmed, Sunan al-Bayhaqi, Al-Mu'jam al-Kabīr, Al-Mu'jam al-Awsaṭ, Sunan at-Tirmidhi, Ŝahīh Ibn Hibbān, Mušannaf Ibn Abi Shayba, Sunan an-Nisā'i***

[60] Similarly narrated in ***Amāli Ahmed b. 'Isa, Amāli Abu Ťālib, Ŝahīh al-Bukhāri, Ŝahīh Muslim, Musnad Ahmed, Mušannaf Ibn Abi Shayba, Musnad Abu Ya'la, Sunan Abu Dāwūd, Al-Mu'jam al-Awsaṭ, Sunan at-Tirmidhi, Ŝahīh Ibn Hibbān, Al-Muwaťťa, Sunan an-Nisā'i, Sunan Ibn Māja, Ušūl al-Kāfi, Bihār al-Anwār***

[61] Similarly narrated in ***Al-Mu'jam al-Kabīr, Al-Mu'jam al-Awsaṭ***. Similar wording is narrated in ***Amāli Ahmed b. 'Isa, Amāli Abu Ťālib, Sunan Ibn Mājah, Musnad Abu Ya'la, Al-Muwaťťa, Mušannaf Ibn Abi Shayba, As-Su'b al-Imān***

[62] Similarly narrated in ***Ŝahīh al-Bukhāri, Musnad Ahmed, Ŝahīh Ibn Hibbān, Al-Mu'jam al-Kabīr, Al-Mu'jam al-Awsaṭ, Sunan al-Bayhaqi, Sunan at-Tirmidhi, Musnad Abu Ya'la, Mušannaf Ibn Abi Shayba, Al-Muwaťťa, Al-Mustadrak***, ***Ušūl al-Kāfi, Bihār al-Anwār***

[63] Similarly narrated in ***Ŝahīh al-Bukhāri, Ŝahīh Muslim, Musnad Ahmed, Al-Muwaťťa, Mušannaf Ibn Abi Shayba, Sunan al-Bayhaqi, Sunan Abu Dāwūd, Ŝahīh Ibn Hibbān, Musnad Abu Ya'la, Ušūl al-Kāfi, Bihār al-Anwār***

[64] Similarly narrated in ***Sunan Abu Dāwūd, Sunan Ibn Mājah, Sunan at-Tirmidhi, Sunan ad-Dārimi, Sunan al-Bayhaqi***

Concerning discouraged speech

Muslims must beware of speaking as they guard against other actions, and speaking less than what is true is better than speaking a lot. If there were one good thing in many words other than that which pleases the Possessor of Majesty and Nobility, there would have been many different kinds of good in its lack.

Regarding that, it has reached us that Allah's Messenger, peace and blessings be upon him and his progeny, said: ((He whom Allah saves from the evil of these two things will enter Paradise)). A man said: "O Messenger of Allah, do not tell us." Allah's Messenger, peace and blessings be upon him and his progeny, was silent and then repeated what he said initially. Then a man went to speak, but a man next to him silenced him. Allah's Messenger, peace and blessings be upon him and his progeny, said: ((He whom Allah saves from the evil of these two things will enter Paradise: the evil of that between his two jaws and the evil of that between his two legs)).[65]

It has reached us that Allah's Messenger, peace and blessings be upon him and his progeny, said:

> ((A man speaks what is pleasing to Allah while he does not assume that it will have the result that it does, and Allah will write for him His good pleasure for it until the Day he meets Him. And a man speaks what excites Allah's anger while he does not assume that it will have the result that it does, and Allah will write His anger for him for it until the Day he meets Him)).[66]

It has reached us the Jesus Christ, son of Mary, upon him be peace, used to say to the Children of Israel: "Do not increase in much speech without the mention of Allah, for you will harden your hearts. A hard heart is far from Allah, though you do not know."[67]

Concerning a Muslim staying away from his Muslim brother

It is not from the character of believers to stay away from each other. Staying away from each other is simply the character of the disobedient. Believers are, as Allah says, **{brothers upon couches facing one another} (Q. 15:47)**. Regarding that, it has reached us that Allah's Messenger, peace and blessings be upon him and his progeny, said:

> ((It is impermissible for a Muslim to stay away from his brother more than three days with one turning one way and the other turning to the other way when they meet. The better of the two is the one who is the first to greet the other)).[68]

It has also reached us that Allah's Messenger, peace and blessings be upon him and his progeny, said:

> ((Do not harbour hatred towards one another, and do not be envious of each other. Do not show your backs to each other. Be slaves of Allah as brothers. It is impermissible for a Muslim to stay away from his brother more than three days)).[69]

Concerning identifying the needy

It has reached us that Allah's Messenger, peace and blessings be upon him and his progeny, said: ((A needy person is not the one who goes from door to door, begging and is turned away with a date or two or with a morsel or two)). They asked: "O Messenger of Allah, who is the needy?" He replied: ((He is the one who does not have enough to live on, and neither is it apparent from his appearance that he is

---

[65] Similarly narrated in ***Al-Muwatta, Musnad Ahmed, Sunan at-Tirmidhi, Sahīh al-Bukhārī, Al-Mu'jam al-Awsat, Ash-Shu'b al-Imān, Al-Mustadrak, Musnad Abu Ya'la, Sahīh Ibn Hibbān, Bihār al-Anwār***

[66] Similarly narrated in ***Sunan al-Bayhaqi, Al-Mu'jam al-Kabīr, Al-Mustadrak, Musnad Ahmed, Al-Muwatta, Sunan at-Tirmidhi, Sunan Ibn Mājah***

[67] Similarly narrated in ***Al-Muwatta, Sunan at-Tirmidhi, Muṡannaf Ibn Abi Shayba, Ash-Shu'b al-Imān, Uṡūl al-Kāfi, Bihār al-Anwār***

[68] Similarly narrated in ***Sahīh al-Bukhārī, Sahīh Muslim, Al-Muwatta, Al-Mu'jam al-Kabīr, Al-Mu'jam al-Awsat, sunan Abu Dāwūd, Sahīh Ibn Hibbān, Sunan at-Tirmidhi, Muṡannaf Ibn Abi Shayba, Bihār al-Anwār***

[69] Similarly narrated in ***Amāli al-Murshid Billah, Sahīh al-Bukhārī, Sahīh Muslim, Musnad Ahmed, Muṡannaf Ibn Abi Shayba, Musnad Abu Ya'la, Sunan al-Bayhaqi, Sunan Abu Dāwūd, Al-Muwatta, Sahīh Ibn Hibbān, Al-Mu'jam al-Awsat, Bihār al-Anwār***

needy and should be given alms, nor does he beg anything from others)).[70]

Concerning seeking protection and invocations (*ar-ruqya*) for illness

It has reached us that Allah's Messenger, peace and blessings be upon him and his progeny, used to recite the verses of protection [i.e. **Q. 113** and **114**] as invocations for himself while he was ill and then blow upon himself. [71]

He, peace and blessings be upon him and his progeny, used to say to one of his Companions who felt pain: ((Rub seven times over the place of pain with your right hand and say: "I seek refuge in Allah's might and power from the evil that I experience.")). And that which he experienced would be removed from him.[72]

He, peace and blessings be upon him and his progeny, also used to say: ((A disease does not descend without the cure likewise descending)).[73] He also used to command the feverish one to cool his fever with water and say: ((Fever is from the heat of Hell, so cool it with water)).[74]

He, peace and blessings be upon him and his progeny, would similarly say: ((Whoever settles somewhere and says "I seek refuge in the perfect words of Allah from the evil of what He created!" nothing will harm him until he leaves that place)).[75]

Concerning dreams

It has reached us that Allah's Messenger, peace and blessings be upon him and his progeny, used to say: ((A good dream from a righteous man is forty-sixth part of prophecy)).[76]

He, peace and blessings be upon him and his progeny, also used to say: ((None shall remain after me except the conveyors of good news (*al-mubashshirāt*))). They asked: "O Messenger of Allah, what are the conveyors of good news?" He replied: ((The good dreams that the righteous slave sees or those that are seen for him. They are forty-sixth part of prophecy)).[77]

He, peace and blessings be upon him and his progeny, also used to say:

> ((A good dream is from Allah, and a bad dream is from Satan. When one of you sees something in a dream that he dislikes, he should blow thrice on his left when waking up and then seek Allah's refuge from its evil. Then it will not harm him if Allah wills)).[78]

---

[70] Similarly narrated in ***Amāli al-Murshid Billah, Ŝahīh al-Bukhāri, Ŝahīh Muslim, Musnad Ahmed, Musnad Abu Ya'la, Sunan an-Nisā'i, Sunan Abu Dāwūd, Ŝahīh Ibn Hibbān, Sunan al-Bayhaqi, Al-Muwatta***

[71] Similarly narrated in ***Ŝahīh al-Bukhāri, Ŝahīh Muslim, Musnad Ahmed, Ŝahīh Ibn Hibbān, Sunan Ibn Mājah, Sunan an-Nisā'i, Al-Muwatta, Sunan Abu Dāwūd, Bihār al-Anwār***

[72] Similarly narrated in ***Amāli al-Murshid Billah, Ŝahīh Muslim, Musnad Ahmed, Sunan at-Tirmidhi, Al-Mustadrak, Al-Mu'jam al-Kabīr, Al-Mu'jam al-Awsat, Sunan Abu Dāwūd, Al-Muwatta, Ŝahīh Ibn Hibbān, Sunan Ibn Mājah, Mušannaf Ibn Abi Shayba, Bihār al-Anwār***

[73] Similarly narrated in ***Amāli al-Murshid Billah, Ŝahīh al-Bukhāri, Al-Muwatta, Sunan Abu Dāwūd, Sunan al-Bayhaqi, Musnad Ahmed, Mušannaf Ibn Abi Shayba, Al-Mustadrak, Al-Mu'jam al-Kabīr, Sunan Ibn Māja, Bihār al-Anwār***

[74] Similarly narrated in ***Al-Muwatta, Ŝahīh al-Bukhāri, Ŝahīh Muslim, Sunan at-Tirmidhi, Sunan Ibn Mājah, Ŝahīh Ibn Hibbān, Musnad Ahmed, Al-Mu'jam al-Kabīr, Al-Mu'jam al-Awsat, Mušannaf Ibn Abi Shayba, Al-Mustadrak, Musnad Abu Ya'la, Sunan ad-Dārimi, Ušūl al-Kāfi, Bihār al-Anwār***

[75] Similarly narrated in ***Amāli al-Murshid Billah, Al-Muwatta, Ŝahīh Muslim, Sunan at-Tirmidhi, Ŝahīh Ibn Hibbān, Al-Mu'jam al-Kabīr, Al-Mu'jam al-Awsat, Musnad Ahmed, Mušannaf Ibn Abi Shayba, Sunan Ibn Mājah, Sunan Abu Dāwūd, Musnad Abu Ya'la, Bihār al-Anwār***

[76] Similarly narrated in ***Ŝahīh al-Bukhāri, Al-Muwatta, Sunan Ibn Mājah, Ŝahīh Ibn Hibbān, Musnad Ahmed, Bihār al-Anwār***

[77] Similarly narrated in ***Ŝahīh al-Bukhāri, Al-Muwatta, Musnad Ahmed, Al-Mu'jam al-Kabīr, Sunan at-Tirmidhi, Ŝahīh Ibn Hibbān, Ash-Shu'b al-Imān, Bihār al-Anwār***

[78] Similarly narrated in ***Ŝahīh al-Bukhāri, Ŝahīh Muslim, Al-Muwatta, Sunan ad-Dārimi, Musnad Ahmed, Al-Mu'jam al-Awsat, Ŝahīh Ibn Hibbān, Sunan at-Tirmidhi, Sunan Abu Dāwūd, Mušannaf Ibn Abi Shayba, Sunan Ibn Mājah, Bihār al-Anwār***

Concerning greetings

It has reached us that Allah's Messenger, peace and blessings be upon him and his progeny, said: ((The one riding should greet the one walking. If one from a group greets, it is sufficient for all of them)).[79]

Returning the greetings is obligatory because Allah says: **{When ye are greeted with a greeting, greet with a greeting better than it or return it} (Q. 4:86)**.

It has reached us that Allah's Messenger, peace and blessings be upon him and his progeny, said: ((If the Jews were to greet you with "Poison be upon you! (*as-sām alaykum*)," respond to them saying: "And upon you (*wa alaykum*)!"))[80]

Concerning images

It has reached us that Allah's Messenger, peace and blessings be upon him and his progeny, said: ((The Angels will not enter a house in which there are statues or images unless they are designs on a garment)).[81]

I discourage it out of its closeness to it as it were unless the owner of such finds no other choice. Allah's Messenger, peace and blessings be upon him and his progeny, simply made an exception for the designed images as a mercy for their owners and as a dispensation to them. However, when one is able to find a better choice, it is best for one to refrain from it altogether.

Concerning owning a dog

A dog is ritually impure, and whoever becomes unclean from it is even more ritually impure. It is impermissible to own a dog except for agriculture, stock farming or hunting. Regarding that, it has reached us that Allah's Messenger, peace and blessings be upon him and his progeny, said: ((Whoever owns a dog except for guarding agriculture, guarding livestock or hunting—such person will lose two *qīrāṭ* of good deeds each day)).[82]

Concerning calamity one should fear

It has reached us that Allah's Messenger, peace and blessings be upon him and his progeny, said: ((Calamity (*ash-shu`m*) is in the house, woman and horse)).[83] It has also reached us that he, peace and blessings be upon him and his progeny, mentioned that in a woman and horse is a source of blessing (*yumna*) and goodness.[84] It has reached us that a man came to him complaining about poverty, so he commanded him to marry. Once he married, things started to open up for him.

It has reached us that he, peace and blessings be upon him and his progeny, said: ((Goodness is tied to the forelocks of horses until the Day of Judgement. And their masters are helped by them)).[85]

In such is both calamity and blessing. The calamity is calamitous, and the blessing is a blessing.

---

[79] Similarly narrated in ***Ŝaħīħ al-Bukhārī, Ŝaħīħ Muslim, Al-Muwaṭṭa, Sunan at-Tirmidhi, Sunan Abu Dāwūd, Musnad Ahmed, Sunan ad-Dārimi, Mušannaf Ibn Abi Shayba, Mušannaf 'Abdur-Razzāq, Kanz al-Ummāl, Al-Mu'jam al-Kabīr, Ash-Shu'b al-Imān***

[80] Similarly narrated in ***Ŝaħīħ al-Bukhārī, Ŝaħīħ Muslim, Ŝaħīħ Ibn Hibbān, Musnad Ahmed, Al-Muwaṭṭa, Sunan Abu Dāwūd, Sunan at-Tirmidhi, Sunan Ibn Mājah, Sunan ad-Dārimi, Bihār al-Anwār***

[81] Similarly narrated in ***Ŝaħīħ al-Bukhārī, Ŝaħīħ Muslim, Al-Muwaṭṭa, Musnad Abu Ya'la, Musnad Ahmed, Sunan al-Bayhaqi, Al-Mu'jam al-Kabīr, Sunan an-Nisā'i, Sunan at-Tirmidhi***

[82] Similarly narrated in ***Ŝaħīħ al-Bukhārī, Ŝaħīħ Muslim, Sunan an-Nisā'i, Sunan al-Bayhaqi, Mušannaf Ibn Abi Shayba, Sunan at-Tirmidhi, Ŝaħīħ Ibn Hibbān, Musnad Ahmed***

[83] Similarly narrated in ***Ŝaħīħ Muslim, Musnad Ahmed, Al-Muwaṭṭa, Sunan an-Nisā'i, Sunan Abu Dāwūd, Bihār al-Anwār***

[84] Similarly narrated in ***Al-Mu'jam al-Kabīr, Al-Mu'jam al-Awsaṭ, Sunan Ibn Māja***

[85] Similarly narrated in ***Ŝaħīħ al-Bukhārī, Ŝaħīħ Muslim, Musnad Ahmed, Al-Mu'jam al-Kabīr, Al-Mu'jam al-Awsaṭ, Sunan ad-Dārimi, Mušannaf Ibn Abi Shayba, Sunan an-Nisā'i, Sunan al-Bayhaqi, Ŝaħīħ Ibn Hibbān, Sunan Ibn Mājah, Sunan at-Tirmidhi, Sunan Abu Dāwūd***

Concerning playing chess

It is impermissible to play it because it is an accursed thing that diverts people from the remembrance of Allah, establishing the prayer, and goodness. Instead, it calls to sin, lying, swearing, argumentation and bitterness. It is the sister of dice and is gambling by name; it joins the two of these together. The one who plays it should be disciplined, and such one should not be greeted. This should be sufficient as an insult and offense.

It has reached us that the Commander of Believers, upon him be peace, came across people who were playing it and did not greet them. Then, he ordered one of his equestrsians to descend, break it [i.e. the chessboard], burn the pieces, and bind each one of the men who were playing it. They stood up and said: "O Commander of Believers, we will not do it again!" He replied: "If you return to it, we will return!"[86]

Concerning names that are discouraged

The best and greatest of names are a blessing. Regarding that, it has reached us that Allah's Messenger, peace and blessings be upon him and his progeny, said: ((Who will milk this camel for us?)). A man stood up, and Allah's Messenger, peace and blessings be upon him and his progeny, asked: ((What is your name?)). The man replied: "Murra (meaning 'bitterness')." He, peace and blessings be upon him and his progeny, then said: ((Sit down)). He repeated: ((Who will milk this camel for us?)). A man stood up, and he, peace and blessings be upon him and his progeny, asked: ((What is your name?)). The man replied: "Harb (meaning 'war')." He, peace and blessings be upon him and his progeny, then said: ((Sit down)). The Prophet, peace and blessings be upon him and his progeny, repeated: ((Who will milk this camel for us?)). A man stood up, and the Prophet, peace and blessings be upon him and his progeny, asked: ((What is your name?)). The man replied: "Ya'īsh (meaning 'he lives')." He then said: ((Milk! Milk!)), and he milked.[87]

Concerning what was narrated from the Prophet regarding cupping and concerning clipping the moustache

It has reached us that Allah's Messenger, peace and blessings be upon him and his progeny, had cupping done by a man called Abu Ťayba. He, peace and blessings be upon him and his progeny, ordered that he be given a *šā* of dates as well as commanded that his people lower his dues he owed.[88] It has also reached us that he, peace and blessings be upon him and his progeny, used to say: ((If there is a cure that reaches a disease, cupping will reach it)).[89] And he, peace and blessings be upon him and his progeny, said: ((If there was something that would cure death, part of it would be cupping)).[90]

It is narrated that he, peace and blessings be upon him and his progeny, said: ((Clip your moustaches and leave your beards)).[91]

---

[86] Similarly narrated in ***Sharh at-Tajrīd, Musnad Imam Zayd, Mušannaf Ibn Abi Shayba, Sunan al-Bayhaqi, Ash-Shu'b al-Imān***. Not only does the report emphasise the prohibition of playing chess but also permits the destruction of the objects involved in such disobedience as well as permits the application of *ta'zīr* to the perpetrators. One view on this matter is that the imam of the Muslims has the choice whether to enact this punishment or not. Another view is that the imam would be obligated to apply such *ta'zīr* if he assumed that there would be no restraint without such punishment; otherwise, the threat of such punishment would be considered sufficient. [Ref. ***Ar-Rawḍat an-Naḍīr***]

[87] Similarly narrated in ***Al-Muwaṭṭa, Al-Mu'jam al-Kabīr***

[88] Similarly narrated in ***Al-Muwaṭṭa, Ŝahīh al-Bukhāri, Ŝahīh Muslim, Sunan at-Tirmidhi, Sunan ad-Dārimi, Musnad Ahmed, Sunan al-Bayhaqi, Musnad Abu Ya'la***

[89] Similarly narrated in ***Al-Muwaṭṭa, Al-Mu'jam as-Saghīr***

[90] Similarly narrated in ***Sahīfa 'Ali b. Musa, Musnad Ahmed, Ŝahīh al-Bukhāri, Ŝahīh Muslim, Sunan Ibn Mājah, Musnad Abu Ya'la, Sunan al-Bayhaqi, Ash-Shu'b al-Imān, Al-Mu'jam al-Kabīr, Al-Mu'jam al-Awsaṭ***

[91] Similarly narrated in ***Ŝahīh al-Bukhāri, Sunan Abu Dāwūd, Sunan at-Tirmidhi, Sunan an-Nisā'i, Musnad Ahmed, Al-Mu'jam al-Kabīr, Al-Mu'jam al-Awsaṭ, Al-Mu'jam as-Saghīr, Mušannaf Ibn Abi Shayba, Bihār al-Anwār***

Concerning what is encouraged of speech and actions related to travel

It has reached us that when Allah's Messenger, peace and blessings be upon him and his progeny, placed his foot in the stirrups of his she-camel—intending to travel, he would say:

> ((In the name of Allah! O Allah, You are the companion in travel, and the Successor regarding family and wealth. O Allah! Spread out the earth for us and make the journey easy for us. O Allah! I seek refuge in You from the hardship of travel and from returning to sorrow and a distressing sight regarding family and wealth!)).[92]

It has also reached us that Allah's Messenger, peace and blessings be upon him and his progeny, used to say:

> ((Verily, Allah is kind and loves kindness. He is pleased with it and helps you with it as long as it is not misplaced. When you ride beasts, stop them in their places of descent and quicken their pace when the land is barren. Travel by night, because the land is travelled faster at night than it is during the day. Beware of pitching tents on the road because it is the path of riding beasts and the resting places of snakes)).[93]

Concerning isolation (*al-wahda*)

It has reached us that Allah's Messenger, peace and blessings be upon him and his progeny, said: ((One is a devil, two are two devils, and three are a collective)).[94] It has also reached us that he, peace and blessings be upon him and his progeny, said: ((Satan concerns himself with one and two, but when there are three, he does not concern himself with them)).[95]

Concerning the virtue of those who are loyal to Muhammad's Progeny

Allah's Messenger, peace and blessings be upon him and his progeny, said:

> ((O 'Ali, the one who loves your offspring loves you, and the one who loves you loves me. The one who loves me loves Allah, and the one who loves Allah will enter Paradise. The one who hates them hates you, and the one who hates you hates me. The one who hates me hates Allah, and the one who hates Allah has a right upon Allah to place him in Hellfire)).[96]

Allah's Messenger, peace and blessings be upon him and his progeny, said: ((One does not love us, O Ahl al-Bayt, except that his feet will be firmly established until Allah saves him on the Day of Judgement)).

He, peace and blessings be upon him and his progeny, also said: ((My Ahl al-Bayt are like the ark of Noah. Whoever embarks upon them will be saved and whoever does not will be drowned)).[97]

He, peace and blessings be upon him and his progeny, said:

> ((My Ahl al-Bayt are a means of safety to the people of the earth. The stars are a means of safety to the people of the heavens. When my Ahl al Bayt depart from the earth, it is a promise to the people of the earth. When the star goes from the sky, it is a promise to the people of the heavens)).[98]

---

[92] Similarly narrated in ***Ŝahīh Muslim, Musnad Ahmed, Al-Muwatta, Sunan al-Bayhaqi, Ŝahīh Ibn Hibbān, Al-Mu'jam al-Kabīr, Sunan Abu Dāwūd, Mušannaf Ibn Abi Shayba, Ušūl al-Kāfi, Bihār al-Anwār***

[93] Similarly narrated in ***Al-Muwatta, Al-Mu'jam al-Kabīr, Ŝahīh Muslim, Musnad Ahmed, Al-Mu'jam al-Awsat, Mušannaf Ibn Abi Shayba, Ŝahīh Ibn Hibbān Sunan Ibn Mājah, Musnad Abu Ya'la, Sunan Abu Dāwūd, Sunan al-Bayhaqi, Ušūl al-Kāfi, Bihār al-Anwār***

[94] Similarly narrated in ***Al-Mustadrak, Ŝahīh Ibn al-Khuzayma, Mušannaf Ibn Abi Shayba, Kanz al-Ummāl***

[95] Similarly narrated in ***Al-Muwatta, Sunan al-Bayhaqi, Kanz al-Ummāl***

[96] Similarly narrated in ***Amāli Ahmed b. 'Isa, Al-Mustadrak, Hilayat al-Awliya, Al-Mu'jam al-Kabīr, Bihār al-Anwār***. It is also narrated that the Prophet, peace and blessings be upon him and his progeny, said similar to al-Hasan and al-Hussein, upon them be peace, in the following texts: ***Amāli Ahmed b. 'Isa, Sunan Ibn Mājah, Al-Mustadrak***

[97] Similarly narrated in ***Amāli Ahmed b. 'Isa, Amāli Abu Ťālib, Al-Mustadrak, Al-Mu'jam al-Kabīr, Musnad al-Bazzār, Majmu' az-Zawā'id, Bihār al-Anwār***

[98] Similarly narrated in ***Al-Mustadrak, Al-Mu'jam al-Kabīr, Majmu' az-Zawā'id, Bihār al-Anwār***

The best of this *Ummah* is the one who is loyal to Allah, His Messenger, and his Ahl al-Bayt—the Commander of Believers and his descendants—because Allah has commanded their alliance. The worst of this *Ummah* and the most oppressive is the one who hates Allah, His Messenger and his Ahl al-Bayt—the Commander of Believers and his descendants—because Allah has prohibited that in His Book as well as upon the tongue of His Prophet, Muhammad, peace and blessings be upon him and his progeny.

He has appointed them the caliphs of His earth, the imams of His creation, the shepherds of His wilderness, the safeguards of His revelation and the preservers of His Book. He entrusted them with it and made them the guides to it. He commanded that they be asked and given recourse in every knowledge of his duties to them, and He placed in them the knowledge of the Book, the final word, and the discernment of the ambiguous. They guide to the Most Gracious and call to righteousness and excellence. **{Light upon light. Allah guides to His light the one whom He wills}** **(Q. 24:35)**.

And the fear of Allah comes from His slaves who have been guided. Praise be to Allah, the Most High, the Exalted, and may the prayers be upon Muhammad, the Chosen One, as well as upon his chosen and noble Ahl al-Bayt and their loyal followers!

We simply ended by mentioning what we mentioned about some of the virtues of the Progeny of Muhammad, peace and blessings be upon him and his progeny, in order to conclude with their mention in the Book just as we began it with them. This is because Allah, similarly, began with them in revealing the truth and divine guidance, and by them, the Glorified will seal this world.

Here ends the **Book of Judgements** by the grace of Allah, the Possessor of might and honour! May Allah grant blessings and peace to Muhammad, the best of people, and his Ahl al-Bayt as long as eternity and as long as light differs from darkness! And peace be upon all the Messengers, and praise be to Allah, Lord of creation! Allah suffices us and is sufficient and He is the best of helpers! O our Lord, open between us and our people with truth, and You are the best of openers!

Biographies

A'isha bt. Abu Bakr	This wife of the Prophet was one of the most notorious during his life and afterwards. She, along with another wife, **Hafsa**, were the subjects of reproach in ***Surah at-Tahrīm* (Q. 66)**. Her hostility towards Imam **'Ali** came to a head when she, along with Ťalha and **az-Zubayr**, led an army against him in the Battle of the Camel. She died in the year 58 AH.
'Abdullah b 'Umar b. al-Khaṫṫāb	This son of the Companion **'Umar b. al-Khaṫṫāb** was among the early converts in Mecca along with his father. He witnessed the Battle of Khandaq and the subsequent battles during the Prophet's lifetime. However, despite narrating the virtues of **'Ali b. Abi Ťālib**, he was one of the few Companions who withheld the oath of allegiance from him and did not participate in any of his battles. He died in 73 AH.
'Abdullah b. al-Hasan b. al-Hasan	He was an early *sayyid* nicknamed 'al-Kāmil.' He was considered a religious authority of his time. He narrated on the authority of his father and **Muhammad b. 'Ali al-Bāqir** as well as his mother, Fāṫima bt. Al-Hussein. He died in prison in the year 145 AH.
'Abdullah b. Ḋumayra	He was the son of **Ḋumayra** and related traditions from his father. He also related traditions from **Abu Hurayra**. Traditionalists among the Generality considered him reliable, such as al-Ajali and Ibn Hibbān. At-Tirmidhi and Ibn Mājah also used his narrations as proof.
'Abdullah b. Ja'far b. Abi Ťālib	This cousin of the Prophet was the first Muslim to be born in Ethiopia during the first eEmigration. He was known for his generosity just like is father, Ja'far. He witnessed the conquest of the Levant. He died in Medina at the age of 80.
'Abdullah b. Mas'ūd	This Meccan Companion was one of the early converts. He is prided as being the first to openly recite the Qur'an in Mecca. He immigrated to both Ethiopia and later Medina. He was relied upon as an authority in Kufa and returned to Medina during the time of **'Uthmān b. Affān**. He died there in either 31 or 32 AH.
'Abdullah b. Sa'īd al-Maqburi	He was a hadith narrator who was weakened by many. Despite this, he was nevertheless relied upon by Imams Abu Ťālib and Murshid Billah. He is also utilised by two of the Sunnite compilers of the 'Sound Six' hadith collections, at-Tirmidhi and Ibn Māja.
'Abdullah b. Salām	This Companion was originally a Jewish rabbi who was said to have been a descendant of the prophet, Joseph. He was a noted scholar among the People of the Book. He embraced Islam when the Prophet emigrated to Medina. He died in 73 AH.
'Abdullah b. Ubayy b. Salūl	This Companion was a leading figure in Medina at the arrival of the Prophet. Tradition holds him as converting to Islam out of pretext. His antagonism of the Prophet's orders and alliance with the opposing Jews of Medina has earned him the moniker of 'the chief of the hypocrites.' Despite this, the Prophet never instigated violence against him. He died in 9 AH.

'Abdul-Malik b. Marwān b. al-Hakam	This Umayyad became the caliph in 65 AH after his father. He was an oppressive tyrant who, like his predecessors, pursued power at all costs. It is also narrated of him that when the caliphate came to him, he closed the Qur'an he was reciting from and said in derision: "This is my last time with you." He died in the year 86 AH.
Abu Bakr b. Abi Uways	He was a hadith narrator relied upon by the imams of Ahl al-Bayt as well as the traditionalists of the Generality, such as al-Bukhāri, Muslim, Ibn Mājah, Abu Dāwūd and others. Yahya b. Mu'īn and adh-Dhahabi considered him reliable. He was brother of **Ismā'īl b. Abi Uways**. He died in 232 AH.
Abu Bakr b. Abi Quhāfa	This early Companion's name is 'Abdullah b. 'Uthmān. He was an Emigrant and gave his daughter **A'isha** to the Prophet for marriage. After the death of the Prophet, he assumed the position of the Caliphate among a series of chaotic events and in the absence of the Prophet's immediate family. He maintained this role until his death in 13 AH.
Abu Hurayra	There is disagreement concerning this Companion's actual name. Although he only spent two years in the presence of the Prophet, he has curiously narrated the most hadith out of any other Companion—numbering to over 5000 purported traditions. This discrepancy has caused some to question his reliability. He served as amīr of Bahrain during **'Umar b. al-Khaṫṫāb's** reign and amīr of Medina at some time during the Umayyad dynasty. He died in 59 AH.
Abu Khālid al-Wāsiti	He was a hadith narrator from Kufa but later moved to Wāsiṫ. He was a Companion of Imam **Zayd b. 'Ali** who transmitted the ***Musnad Imam Zayd*** on the authority of the imam. Although the hadith scholars of the Generality weakened him and considered his narrations unreliable, Zaydi imams and scholars narrated traditions from him and considered him wholly trustworthy.
Abu Musa al-Asha'ri	This Companion's name was 'Abdullah b. Qays. It is debated whether he was one of the immigrants to Ethiopia with Ja'far b. Abi Ťālib. He moved to Kufa and was made a governor by **'Uthmān**. He was retained by **'Ali b. Abi Ťālib** until he instigated the Kufans to refrain from supporting **'Ali** in one of his battles.
Abu Sahl b. Sa'īd al-Maqburi	He was a hadith narrator who was accused of being a Mu'tazilite. Traditionalist Abu Hātim described him as reliable but claimed that he only narrated from his brother, **'Abdullah**. However, this claim is baseless as he also transmitted from **al-Fadl b. Dalham**. Traditionalist Ibn 'Udayy said that there was no criticism of him by the earliest authorities. Also, one of the Sunnite traditionalists who authored one of the 'Sound Six' hadith collections, Ibn Mājah, related hadith from him.
Abu Sayāra al-Muta'i	This Companion's name was Umayr b. al-A'lam. The only thing related from him was the hadith regarding the purification dues on honey. He is counted among the narrators from Greater Syria. Among the Generality, Ibn Mājah narrated from him.
Abu Ťalha	His given name was Zayd b. Sahl al-Anšāri. He fought in the Battle of Badr as well as the subsequent battles. He died in Medina in 34 AH.
Abu Usayd	This Companion's name was Mālik b. Rabi'a. He was an Anšār who fought in the Battle of Badr. In fact, he was one of the last remaining Companions who fought at Badr to die. He died in Medina around the age of thirty. Some reports say at the age of sixty.

Abul-A'war as-Sulami	He is 'Amr b. Sufyān b. 'Abdu sh-Shams. It is debated whether he was a Companion of the Prophet or not. He was one of **Mu'awiya**'s followers and was given governorship of Jordan. He fought alongside **Mu'awiya** in the Battle of Ŝiffīn.
Ahmed b. 'Isa b. Zayd	He was an imam, scholar and jurist of the Prophet's Descendants. He was also a narrator of hadith. He performed the Hajj pilgrimage thirty times by walking. He was imprisoned by Hārūn ar-Rashīd but left the prison and died while in hiding in 247 AH.
al-Fađl b. Dalham	He was a Basran hadith narrator who was declared reliable by Waki' but weakened by the likes of Yahya b. Mu'īn. He was labelled a Mu'tazilite but was nonetheless utilised as a narrator in four of the 'Sound Six' hadith collections. Al-Hākim also related hadith from him in his ***Al-Mustadrak*** and declared the chain of narrators as authentic. Ahmed narrated from him in his ***Musnad*** and stated that there was no problem in him. Ibn Hajar declared him 'reliable' in his ***Majmu' az-Zawā`id***.
Al-Hamza b. 'Abdul-Muttalib	He was the uncle and milk brother of the Prophet. He embraced Islam while in Mecca and was a staunch defender of the faith. He was known as the Lion of Allah and the Lion of the Messenger. He fought in the Battles of Badr and Uhud and died in the latter battle in 3 AH at the age of 57.
al-Hasan al-Bašri	Born in Medina, this prominent personality was a student of the Companions and enjoyed the status of being a 'Follower (*tabi'i*).' Much has been attributed to and from him regarding various subjects. He was said to be a student of **'Ali b. Abi Ťālib** and 'Abdullah b. al-'Abbās. He died in 110 AH.
Al-Hasan b. 'Ali b. Abi Ťālib	He was the oldest grandson of the Prophet and was born in Medina to **'Ali b. Abi Ťālib** and **Fātima bt. Muhammad**. He was named by the Prophet, and he along with his mother, father and brother were designated the 'Ahl al-Bayt' of the Prophet in the Qur'anic verse **Q. 33:33**. He fought in the Battles of the Camel and Ŝiffīn alongside his father. He led the funeral prayer over his father and assumed the office of Caliphate immediately afterwards. His rule was characterised by rebellion and disloyalty on the part of his subjects. He was forced to a ceasefire with **Mu'awiya b. Abi Sufyān**. He eventually died of poison by his wife at the behest of **Mu'awiya**.
Al-Hasan b. al-Qāsim b. Ibrāhīm	This son of Imam **al-Qāsim b. Ibrāhīm Rassi** was recognised as a prominent sayyid and head of the scholars of the Prophet's Descendants. He lived in Medina and left for Yemen with his nephew, Imam al-Hādi. He died there and his tomb is located near that of Imam al-Hādi and his son, al-Murtaḍa Muhammad b. Yahya.
Al-Hussein b. 'Ali al-Fakhi	In 169 AH, this Hasani *sayyid* was given the oath of allegiance by prominent members of the Prophet's Descendants in Medina. When he and his companions were on their way to Mecca for the Hajj pilgrimage, they were met by Abbasid forces and slaughtered while in the state of pilgrim sanctity in a place called Fakh.
Al-Hussein b. 'Ali b. Abi Ťālib	He was the younger brother of **al-Hasan b. 'Ali** and was born a year later in Medina. He was the last and youngest of the Companions of the Cloak whom were designated 'Ahl al-Bayt' in the Qur'anic verse **Q. 33:33**. He fought in the Battles of the Camel and Ŝiffīn. He remained in Kufa during the lifetime of his father, **'Ali b. Abi Ťālib** until the latter's death and returned with his brother, **al-Hasan**, to

Medina. After the murder of his brother, al-Hussein refused to give his oath of allegiance to Yazīd, the son of **Mu'awiya**. Consequently, he and his immediate family and followers were mercilessly pursued which resulted in their slaughter by the forces of Yazīd. They were martyred in Karbala, Iraq on the tenth of Muharram in 61 AH.

Al-Hussein b. al-Qāsim b. Ibrāhīm	This son of Imam **al-Qāsim b. Ibrāhīm Rassi** was a scholar and jurist who narrated the edicts and judgements of his father. It is through him that Imam al-Hādi related his grandfather's opinions and judgements. He died in 279 AH.
'Ali b. Abi Ťālib	He was the Prophet's cousin and son-in-law who attained an unparalleled status during the latter's lifetime. He was born in the Ka'ba and was the first to embrace Islam after the Prophet's wife Khadīja as well as the first to perform the ritual prayer alongside the Prophet. He was respected for his matchless knowledge, bravery and austerity. He remained in Medina during the Caliphates of the first three caliphs and had not fought in any battles after the death of the Prophet except during his own Caliphate. He later settled in Kufa and died there at the age of 63 by the poison dagger of a Kharijite dissenter on the 21st of Ramadan in 40 AH.
'Ali b. al-Hussein b. 'Ali	This imam was nicknamed 'Zayn al-Abidīn' because of his constant worship and piety. He was one of the only survivors of the Battle of Karbala and retired from fighting until the end of his life. He served as a religious authority of his time as well as earned the title 'Master (*sayyid*) of the Ahl al-Bayt' during his lifetime. He died between 92 and 95 AH.
Al-Jārūd al-Abadi	It is also said that his name was Jārūd b. 'Amr b. al-Mu'ala al-Abadi. He came from Bahrain to visit **'Ali b. Abi Ťālib** in 10 AH. He was killed during the caliphate of **'Umar b. al-Khaṫṫāb** in Persia during a war campaign in 21 AH.
Al-Qāsim b. Ibrāhīm b. Ismā`īl	This illustrious imam was known as Imam Rassi due to the Rass Mountains being his base of operations. He was prolific and unparalleled in the fields of theology, jurisprudence, spirituality, eloquence and more. He died in 246 AH.
Al-Walīd b. Uqba b. Abi Mu'ayṫ	He was one of the later Companions who entered Islam at the Conquest of Mecca. He was declared **{disobedient}** in the Qur'an in contrast to **'Ali b. Abi Ťālib** who was declared a **{believer}** in **Q. 32:18.** He became one of the emirs during the reign of **'Uthmān b. Affān** but was known to drink intoxicants and engage in other objectionable practices. He died in 61 AH.
'Ammār b. Yāsir	This Companion was among the earliest converts who was subsequently tortured by the Meccan idolaters. We witnessed and participated in all of the battles during the lifetime of the Prophet. He also remained loyal to **'Ali** after the Prophet's death and fought in the battles headed by him. Numerous virtues have been related regarding 'Ammār highlighting his loyalty and virtue. He died in 37 AH.
'Amr b. al-'Ās b. Wā`il	This Companion embraced Islam after the Conquest of Mecca. He came into prominence after being made governor of Egypt by **'Umar**. His post was later dismissed by **'Uthmān** but reinstated by **Mu'awiya**. He was one of the leaders of the rebellion against **'Ali** and his schemes, tricks and machinations are well-known in history. He died in the year 70 AH.

An-Nu'mān b. Bashīr	This Companion became a staunch supporter of **Mu'awiya** and his son, Yazīd. He fought alongside the Umayyad in the Battle of Ŝiffīn and governed the Syrian city Homš on behalf of **Mu'awiya** and Yazīd. He was later killed in the same city after having switched sides to support the rebellion against the Umayyads led by **Ibn az-Zubayr**.
Aws b. as-Sāmit al-Anŝāri	This Companion witnessed Badr and subsequent battles. He divorced his wife **Khawla bt. Tha'laba** by saying "You are to me as my mother's back!" Subsequently, the ***Surah al-Mujādila*** **(Q. 58)** was revealed about this incident. He died during the time of **'Uthmān b. Affān**.
Az-Zubayr b. al-Awwām	His mother was the Prophet's paternal aunt. He embraced Islam after **Abu Bakr** and then emigrated as an Emigrant. He fought in all of the battles of the Muslims during the Prophet's lifetime. He later reneged his oath of allegiance to **'Ali b. Abi Ťālib** and was one of the leaders of opposition in the Battle of the Camel. He died fleeing the battle in 36 AH.
Barīra	She was a slave purchased and manumitted by **A'isha**. It is disputed, however, as to which tribe she was originally a client of. She was the servant of **A'isha** before the latter purchased her. She was married to Mughayth who loved her dearly. When given the choice by the Prophet, however, she chose to divorce Mughayth.
Bilāl b. Rabāh al-Habashi	He was an eminent early Companion who served as the muezzin of the fledgling Muslim *Ummah*. He was also the personal servant and confidant of the Prophet. He died in Damascus in the year 20 AH at the age of 64.
Daylam al-Himyari	He is also mistaken as Daylam b. Fayrūz or Daylam b. al-Huwsha'. He saw the Prophet, peace and blessings be upon him and his progeny. One of the only narrated traditions we have from him is concerning intoxicating drinks. He eventually settled in Egypt.
Dhu ash-Shimālayn	This Companion's given name was Umayr b. 'Abdu 'Amr al-Khazā'i. He was martyred in the Battle of Badr. He is sometimes confused with someone known as Dhul-Yadayn who lived beyond the time of the Prophet.
Ḋumayra b. Abi Ḋumayra	This Companion was a freed slave of the Prophet, peace and blessings be upon him and his progeny. The scholars of hadith differ regarding his name. He narrated traditions from the Commander of Believers, **'Ali b. Abi Ťālib**.
Fātima bt. Muhammad	According to the reports by the imams of the Ahl al-Bayt, she was born to the Prophet Muhammad after the call to Prophethood, although the Generality narrates that she was born prior. She was considered the most beloved to the Prophet and was said to have resembled her father the most in speech, looks and gait. She was among the migrants to Medina and married **'Ali b. Abi Ťālib** by the order of Allah while she was fifteen. She birthed **al-Hasan b. 'Ali** and **al-Hussein b. 'Ali** and constituted the central figure of the Ahl al-Bayt named by Allah in the Qur'anic verse **Q. 33:33**. After the death of her father, her opposition to the subsequent Caliphate of **Abu Bakr b. Abi Quhāfa** was well known. She passed away four to six months after the death of the Prophet at the age of twenty or twenty-eight.

Fāṭima bt. Abi Hubaysh	She was a Companion who was also among the early Emigrants to Medina. It is narrated that she married 'Abdullah b. Jahsh, and she gave birth to a son named Muhammad.
Fāṭima bt. Qays	An early Companion who was among the Emigrants to Medina. She was a widow whose first husband died in the Battle of Badr. She was later approached for marriage by **Usāma b. Zayd**. She also related a hadith regarding the lodging and financial maintenance of a woman who was divorced irrevocably. She died sometime after 50 AH.
Hafsa bt. 'Umar b. al- Khaṭṭāb	She was one of the wives of the Prophet who married him in 3 AH. He then divorced her and remarried her at the tearful behest of her father **'Umar**. It is also related that he remarried her after being commanded by revelation. She, along with **A'isha**, often conspired against other wives. ***Surah at-Tahrīm*** **(Q. 66)** was revealed about them both. She died in 45 AH.
Hakīm b. Jābir	He was considered one of the chief elders of the Kufans. He died at the end of the rule of al-Hajjāj in the year 82 AH. It is also said that he died in the year 95 AH.
Hussein b. 'Abdullah b. Ḍumayra	He related hadith from his grandfather through his father. Although he is considered reliable by the imams and scholars of Ahl al-Bayt, he is considered 'rejected' by some of the hadith scholars of the Generality, such as Ahmed b. Hanbal, Yahya b. Mu'īn and Ibn Hajar al-Haythami. He died around 160 AH.
Ibn al-Kawwa	His name was 'Abdullah b. Awfa. He was a specialist in identifying tribal lineage (*al-ansāb*). He fought alongside **'Ali b. Abi Ṭālib** in the Battle of Ṣiffīn, but later became one of the leaders of the Kharijites and was appointed as their prayer leader. He came out against **Mu'awiya b. Abi Sufyān** and died in 80 AH.
Ibn az-Zubayr	This Companion's given name was 'Abdullah, and he was the son of **az-Zubayr b. al-Awwām**. He is credited as being the first of the Emigrants to be born after the Emigration. He partnered with his aunt, **A'isha bt. Abi Bakr**, in the Battle of the Camel. He died in Mecca after an abortive attempt to wrest the caliphate from the Umayyads in 73 AH.
Ibn Mughaffal	He was 'Abdullah b. Mughaffal. He was among the Companions who took the oath of allegiance of Ridwān. He went to Basra and died there in the year 60 AH.
Ibn Umm Maktūm	His name was 'Amr, and it is also said that his name was 'Abdullah b. 'Amr. He was among the earliest Emigrants who reached Medina before the Prophet, peace and blessings be upon him and his progeny. The Prophet, peace and blessings be upon him and his progeny, made him the prayer leader in Medina. He was martyred in the Battle of al-Qadasiya.
Ibrāhīm b. 'Abdullah	Known as '*Nafs ar-Radiyya*' (Tr. 'The Satisfied Soul'), he along with his brother, Imam **Muhammad b. 'Abdullah** *Nafs az-Zakiyya*, fought against the Abbasid army. He was declared imam after the death of his brother and given the oath of allegiance. However, he was soon after martyred in 145 AH.
Ismā'īl b. Abi Uways	He was a hadith narrator who was relied upon by the imams of Ahl al-Bayt as well as the traditionalists of the Generality. He is utilised by al-Bukhāri, Muslim, at-

Tirmidhi, Abu Dāwūd and others in their collections. He was the brother of **Abu Bakr b. Abi Uways**. He died in 226 AH.

Ja'far b. Muhammad b. 'Ali — Nicknamed 'as-Ŝādiq' (tr. 'The Truthful'), he was the son of Imam **Muhammad b. 'Ali** al-Bāqir. Imam Ja'far was a prominent imam known and respected for his vast knowledge and character. His knowledge of jurisprudence, hadith, theology and spirituality are referred to by Shi'ites universally. He died in 148 AH.

Jābir b. 'Abdullah — He was the last of the Companions to die in Medina. He took part in most military expeditions along with the Prophet. He also fought alongside **'Ali b. Abi Ťālib** in all the civil wars. He remained loyal and faithful to **'Ali** and the Ahl al-Bayt until his death in 73 AH at the age of 94.

Kharāsh b. Umayya al-Khazā'i — This Companion confederated with the Banu Makhzūm. He was a Medinan who witnessed the battles of al-Hudaybiya, Khaybar and others afterwards. He shaved the Prophet's head on the day of Hudaybiya and cupped him. He died in 66 AH.

Khawla bt. Tha'laba — This female Companion was married to **Aws b. as-Sāmit al-Anŝāri** and divorced by a custom prevalent among the pre-Islamic Arabs. The verse and subsequent penalty for such was revealed after she complained to the Messenger, peace and blessings be upon him and his progeny.

Mā'iz b. Mālik al-Aslami — He was a Companion from Medina who committed adultery. He came to the Prophet repentant for it and demanded to be stoned. The Prophet turned from him four times and inquired of his mental state. When it was confirmed that it was sound, he finally had him stoned. He then said of him: ((He is clothed in the rivers of Paradise!))

Mālik b. Anas — One of the four 'founders' of the orthodox Sunni schools of jurisprudence. He was born in Medina and utilised as his methodology the statements and actions of those Medinians he considered authoritative. He spent his whole life in Medina and died 179 AH.

Mirdās b. Nahīk — His name was also said to be Mirdās b. 'Amr al-Fadaki. This Muslim kept his faith hidden from his people, but when he proclaimed his faith to an invading Muslim army, he was killed by **Usāma b. Zayd**. Some reports have another Companion as his killer; however, the soundest view is that it was **Usāma**.

Mu'awiya b. Abi Sufyān b. Harb — He was a Companion who embraced Islam after the Conquest of Mecca. He, along with his father, was among those prisoners of war pardoned by the Messenger. He was one the Prophet's scribes but held no prominent post during the latter's lifetime. He made war against Imam **'Ali b. Abi Ťālib** in the Battle of Ŝiffīn. He later became a caliph and instituted the Umayyad dynasty. He died in the year 60 AH.

Muhammad b. 'Abdullah — Known as '*Nafs az-Zakiyya*' (Tr. 'The Pure Soul'), this *sayyid* was a fountainhead of knowledge and bravery. After receiving the oath of allegiance as imam, he led an abortive attempt to dethrone the treacherous Abbasids who initially pledged allegiance to him only to later betray him. He was subsequently martyred in 145 AH.

Muhammad b. 'Ali b. al-Hussein	Nicknamed 'al-Bāqir' (tr. 'The Opener') because of his ability to break knowledge open for the benefit of others, this imam was an unparalleled scholar who is considered an authority. He was the brother of Imam **Zayd b. 'Ali** and supported his rebellion. He died in 114 AH.
Muhammad b. al-Qāsim b. Ibrāhīm	This son of Imam **al-Qāsim b. Ibrāhīm Rassi** was given the oath of allegiance in Yemen. He was recognised as the Sheikh of the Progeny of Allah's Messenger. He was known as a scrupulous scholar and ascetic. He died in 281 AH.
Muhammad b. Ibrāhīm b. Ismā'īl	This prominent Hasani imam was given the oath of allegiance by prominent members of the Prophet's Descendants as well as many scholars. He was the younger brother of Imam **al-Qāsim b. Ibrāhīm Rassi**. Imam Muhammad was martyred at the age of 26 on the orders of al-Mamūn al-'Abbāsi in 199 AH.
Muhammad b. Rāshid al-Khazā'i	He was a Shi'ite narrator considered reliable by the likes of Sunni traditionalists, Ahmed b. Hanbal, Yahya b. Mu'īn, Ibn al-Madini and others. He was also narrated from by Muhammad b. Manšūr al-Murādi and some imams of Ahl al-Bayt. He died in 166 AH.
Musa b. 'Abdullah b. al-Hasan	He was a Hasani poet who narrated traditions on the authority of his ancestors. He was captured by Abu Ja'far al-Manšūr al-'Abbasi and lashed one-thousand times. He was then sent to Mecca and lived there until the time Hārūn ar-Rashīd. Al-Hādi as well as Muhammad al-Manšūr narrated from him.
Nasr b. Mazāhim al-Kufi	He was a narrator who was considered reliable by Zaydi imams. He was one of the companions and partisans of Imam **Muhammad b. Ibrāhīm**. He authored a work dedicated to the Battle of Ŝiffīn in which Imam 'Ali fought against **Mu'awiya b. Abi Sufyān**. He died in 212 AH.
Negus	His name was Aš-hama, the King of Ethiopia. He was a just Christian monarch who sheltered a group among the nascent Muslim *Ummah* when they sought refuge from the Meccan idolaters. He later embraced Islam and died in Ethiopia before the Conquest of Mecca. He was prayed over by the Prophet *in absentia* in Medina.
Qudāma b. Maž'ūn	He was an early Companion who immigrated to Ethiopia. He participated in the Battle of Badr as well as the subsequent battles. He served as a governor of Bahrain during the government of **'Umar b. al-Khaťťāb**. He was witnessed drinking intoxicants by **Abu Hurayra**, **al-Jārūd al-Abadi** and Alqama al-Hasi. The prescribed punishment was applied to him by **'Umar**. He died in 36 AH.
Rāfi b. Khudayj al-Hārithi	This Companion accompanied the Prophet in most of the battles of the Muslims with the exception of Badr, for which he was too young to participate. He was injured by an arrow in the Battle of Uhud which affected him until the end of his life. He also fought on the side of **'Ali b. Abi Ťālib** in the Battle of Ŝiffīn. He died in the year 74 AH at the age of 86.
Rifā'i b. Rāfi' al-Quraḍi	This Anŝāri Companion was from the tribe of Khazraj. He fought alongside the Prophet in the Battle of al-'Aqaba as well as alongside **'Ali b. Abi Ťālib** in the battles of al-Jamal and Ŝiffīn. He died in the beginning of **Mu'awiya's** rule. His two sons, 'Abdullah and Mu'ādh narrated from him.
Sa'īd b.	He was a hadith narrator who was declared reliable by many; there are no criticisms

Abu Sa'īd al-Maqburi	of him except that he was very old and may have made mistakes in hadith about four years before his death.
Sa'īd b. al-A'š	This Umayyad was made governor of Kufa by the third caliph, **'Uthmān b. Affān**. He was also made governor of Medina by **Mu'awiya b. Abi Sufyān**. He died in 59 AH.
Ŝafiya bt. Hayy b. Akhtab	She was one of the Prophet's wives who was of Israelite background and a descendant of Aaron, the brother of Moses. The Prophet married her and made manumission her dowry. She died in the year 50 AH and is buried in the Baqi' cemetery in Medina.
Ŝafwān b. Umayya	He was a Companion who was initially regarded as one of the pagan Arab nobles who was later pardoned by the Prophet. He witnessed the Battle of Hunayn as a disbeliever but then later embraced Islam after the Conquest of Mecca. He was one of those whose heart needed to be reconciled by the purification dues. He died in 42 AH.
Sawda bt. Zama'at b. 'Amr	She was one of the wives of the Prophet. She married him right after the passing of **Khadija**. She was included amongst those who immigrated to Ethiopia as well as those who immigrated to Medina. Because of her advanced age, she used to give her days with the Prophet to **A'isha**. She died in the year 55 AH.
Shurayh b. al-Hārith al-Kindi	He was a Follower famous for his service as a magistrate. He served this position for sixty years. He first served under the administration of **'Umar b. al-Khaťťāb** and continued in this office during the reigns of **'Ali b. Abi Ťālib** and **Mu'awiya b. Abu Sufyān**. He was said to have lived until the age of 108 or 110 in the year 80 AH.
Ŝirma b. Anas	It is said that his name was Ŝirma b. Qays, Ŝirma b. Mālik, Abu Qays b. Ŝirma or Qays b. Ŝirma. This Companion embraced Islam while he was an old man and was known as an accomplished poet. He was the one about whom the verse in **(Q. 2:187)** was revealed.
Tāwūs	His name was Dhakwān b. Kaysān al-Yamāni. He was a famous Follower who was well known for his knowledge of hadith and jurisprudence. His narrations of hadith are considered reliable by traditionalists. He died in 104 AH.
Umāma bt. Abul-'Ās b. ar-Rābi'	She was the granddaughter of Allah's Messenger, being born to his daughter, **Zaynab**. It is reported that the Prophet, peace and blessings be upon him and his progeny, once promised to give a necklace to 'the one I love most.' Everyone expected him to give it to **A'isha bt. Abi Bakr** but instead, he gave it to Umāma. Her aunt **Fāťima bt. Muhammad** bequeathed that **'Ali b. Abi Ťālib** marry Umāma after her death. She died in 50 AH.
'Umar b. al-Khaťťāb	This Companion embraced Islam after the first Emigrants emigrated to Ethiopia. He was considered a close Companion of the Prophet and gave his daughter **Hafsa** in marriage to him. He was selected as the second caliph by **Abu Bakr b. Abi Quhāfa** and assumed the role when the latter died. 'Umar was killed by Abu Lulu, the Persian slave of al-Mughīra b. Shu'ba, in 23 AH.

Umm Salama	This wife of the Prophet was named Hind bt. Abi Umayya. She was one of the earliest migrants to Ethiopia. She married the Messenger after the Battle of Badr. She was considered one of the wisest wives and remained loyal to **'Ali b. Abi Ťālib** and the Ahl al-Bayt. She died after the martyrdom of Imam **al-Hussein b. 'Ali** in the year 62 AH.
'Uqba b. al-Hārith b. Āmr	This Companion was said to have embraced Islam after the Conquest of Mecca. There is confusion as to whether he was nicknamed Abu Sarū'a or if it was his brother. Regardless, one of the only narrations we have from him is the incident involving a woman who claimed she breastfed him and his wife.
Usāma b. Zayd b. Hāritha	This Companion was born in Mecca and raised as a Muslim. He immigrated with the Prophet to Medina. Before he was twenty years old, he was placed in charge of an army, among whom included **Abu Bakr b. Abi Quhāfa** and **'Umar b. al-Khaṭṭāb**. He settled in various places but returned to Medina before dying in 54 AH.
Yahya b. 'Abdullah b. al-Hasan	This Hasani *sayyid* witnessed the Fakh massacre in which **al-Hussein b. 'Ali al-Fakhi** was slaughtered along with his companions. Hārūn ar-Rashīd tirelessly pursued Imam Yahya and assured him safety if the latter came out of hiding. Hārūn violated this trust and had him imprisoned and poisoned in Baghdad.
Yahya b. Zayd b. 'Ali	Following in the footsteps of his illustrious father, **Zayd b. 'Ali**, Imam Yahya similarly waged a jihad against the oppressive authorities and was martyred at the age of 28 on the orders of the Umayyad caliph, al-Walīd b. Yazīd b. 'Abdul-Mālik in 97 AH.
Zayd al-Khayr at-Tā'i	When this Companion came to the Prophet in a delegation, his name was Zayd al-Khayl. However, the Prophet changed his name to Zayd al-Khayr. He was an accomplished poet and died before returning to his hometown to spread Islam.
Zayd b. 'Ali b. al-Hussein	He was a leading imam in all fields of Islamic science and sought to spread knowledge of the Prophet's Progeny. Born in Medina during the Umayyad dynasty, he led a failed rebellion against the empire and was martyred in Kufa during the time of caliph, Hishām b. 'Abdul-Mālik.
Zayd b. Thābit	He accompanied Allah's Messenger to Medina at the age of eleven. He witnessed the Battle of Uhud and subsequent battles. He used to write the revelation for the Prophet and was ordered by **Abu Bakr b. Abi Quhāfa** to collect the Qur'an. He was also ordered by **'Uthmān b. Affān** to pen the master copy of the Qur'an. He was said to be a supporter of **'Uthmān** and never fought any of the battles alongside **'Ali b. Abi Ťālib**. He died in Medina in 45 AH.
Zaynab bt. Jahsh	She was one of the Prophet's wives whom he married when she was 35. She was previously married to his adopted son, Zayd b. Hāritha. When they divorced, the Prophet married her, and **Q. 33:40** was revealed to counter the criticism of the hypocrites. She died in 20 AH.
Zaynab bt. Muhammad	She was the eldest daughter of the Prophet, peace and blessings be upon him and his progeny. She was born when he was thirty years old. She was given in marriage to her maternal cousin, Abul-'Ās b. ar-Rābi'. She died in 8 AH.

Dictionary of Jurisprudential Terms

'Awl	A re-apportioned **inheritance** in which the heirs' shares exceed the usual amount
Abled	Term used to describe one who has enough wealth to provide his own livelihood as well as that of dependants, such as wives, small children and parents
Apostasy	The intentional denial of any of the central doctrines of Islam by word or deed, such as the denial of Allah's existence or the rejection of any of the Prophets
Aqīqa	The lamb that one sacrifices on behalf of a male or female child on the seventh day afer birth, which is afterwards eaten and/or distributed as charity
Audible	Term used to describe a verbal utterance whose minimum is that the person next to him should be able to hear him, and whose maximum is limitless; the woman's audible recitation should be lesser than that
Bequest	The establishment of a person other than oneself in one's affairs, or some of them, after the former's death
Bier	A transferable platform upon which the deceased is carried to the grave
Bint labūn	A camel that has reached two lunar years of age
Bint makhāḍ	A camel that has reached one lunar year of age
Bloodwite	A compensatory amount paid by the **clan** of the free offender due to unintentional **manslaughter**
Booty	A term used to refer to that which the Muslim military forces obtain or acquire from the disbelievers during a war campaign from which the **fifth** is due
Call to prayer	An announcement with specific wording that indicates the entrance of an **obligatory ritual prayer** time
Capital	Any item of wealth considered necessary to engage in a commercial **transaction** whose primary objective is profit
Carcass	The remains of an animal that died without being slaughtered according to the specifications of Islamic law by a mature and morally responsible Muslim
Circumambulation	A ritual of the **Hajj pilgrimage** and **Umra** in which the pilgrim briskly jogs and walks seven circuits with the Ka'ba to the left while in the state of ritual purity
Circumcision	The removal of the skin of a man's glans; an incision made on the top of a female's vulva
Claim	A conveyance for which none knows the evidence of its veracity or falsity
Claimant	One who states a **claim** contrary to what is apparent or seeks to take something from another's possession by means of a claim

Clan	The paternal relatives of a person who are to pay the **bloodwite** in the case of unintentional **manslaughter**
Clientage	The right to the inheritance of the wealth left by a manumitted slave
Combined pilgrimage	The performance of both the **Hajj pilgrimage** and **'Umra pilgrimage** without separating them while maintaining the **state of pilgrim sanctity** between them and driving a she-camel to Mina
Confession	The informing by a morally-responsible person on behalf of him/herself or another regarding a right that is necessary
Congregational prayer	A **ritual prayer** which morally-responsible Muslims pray together with one serving as the prayer leader and the others serving as a follower
Consummative marriage	A bond after a valid **marriage** in which **intercourse** with the spouse is possible and established
Co-partnership	A type of **partnership** in which the partners pool all their wealth collectively and utilise a portion as well as share in the benefit and loss
Creditor	A person to whom another person owes **wealth**
Cuckold	A man who pimps his wife or who remains with her after having certainty that she committed adultery without having repented for such
Cupping	The intentional extraction of blood or pus from a wound or incision made in the body
Dawn prayer	The two-**unit**, **audible**, **obligatory ritual prayer** that is prayed from the time before sunrise
Day of doubt	The 30th of Sha'bān when it is not proven that the new moon was witnessed due to cloudiness or any other reason; however, if one is certain that the new moon was not witnessed, it would not be considered the day of doubt
Deputation	The establishment of a person other than oneself in one's affairs, or some of them, before the former's death
Dhimmi	A non-Muslim subject of the **domain of Islam** who is obligated to pay **jizya** in order to be protected and exempted from military service
Discouraged	A term used to describe that for which its negligence earns praise and reward, but its performance does not earn blame and punishment
Disobedient	Term used to designate a morally-responsible Muslim who intentionally commits a **major sin** in the open
Divorce pronouncement	A specific expression made or implied by a specific person in order to relinquish a **marriage** contract

Dust purification	Term used to describe a method of intentional ritual purification in which one wipes the face and arms with clean and pure dust
Encouraged	A term used to describe that for which its performance earns praise and reward, but its negligence does not earn blame and punishment
Entrusted item	A property or possession left with a trustee for the sake of safekeeping and not commercial use
Eunuch	A person whose reproductive organs have been amputated
Expiation	An action or item of wealth due upon a morally-responsible Muslim who infringes on the rights of another
Fast	To refrain from specific things during a specific period of time which is binding on a specific person
Fast-breaking dues	An **obligatory** alms due from the dawn of the 1st of Shawwāl in which a morally-responsible Muslim male renders it on his behalf and on behalf of all for whom he is **obligatory** to financially maintain
Fear prayer	The shortened **ritual prayer** prayed when the Muslims are encountering an enemy in war
Financial maintenance	On the most basic level, it entails the providing of food, condiments (*idām*), medicines, wages for a nursemaid, support for the blind, a servant, clothing and shelter to the extent of that which is considered normal for the poor of that country
Fornication	Term used to encompass illegal sexual relations in which a living morally-responsible person wilfully inserts his penis in the vagina or anus of another living morally-responsible person for whom there is no legal relationship, such as marriage or ownership
Fortune-teller	One who is assumed to have knowledge of the unseen
Foundling	A dependent human being who is found as an outcast without a **guardian**
Friday congregational prayer	The **congregational prayer** and sermons that take place on Friday noon, which is considered an individual obligation upon the morally-responsible, free, healthy, Muslim male given the existence of its preconditions
Game	Any type of wild animal, fish or fowl that is hunted, caught, captured and trapped for the purpose of food
Gift	Bestowing something of inherent value during one's lifetime which is not compensation or specified as religious charity
Guaranty	The assumption of responsibility for a debt or commodity owned by another

Guardian	A free, morally-responsible, non-marriageable, Muslim male who has the responsibility to financially maintain his female relative in the absence of any other who is closer to her
Hajj pilgrimage	Term used to describe the visitation to the Sanctified House in which the assumption of the **pilgrim garb** makes certain actions **prohibited** and the stoning of the *jamrāt* makes those actions **permissible**
Hand to hand	Term used to refer to a payment that is made on the spot and not delayed
Heretic	A morally-responsible person who professes belief in Islam but openly manifests beliefs contrary to the Oneness of Allah, such as Dualism
Hermaphrodite	A human being with both male and female genitalia
Hiqqa	A camel that has reached three lunar years of age
Incontinence	The inability to willingly stop the flow of urine
Indemnity	The amount of wealth due for a non-fatal injury, which includes certain preconditions and stipulations
Indentured labourer	One who is contractually bound to slavery for a fixed period of time in order to repay a debt or any other requirement
Indirect heir	An heir that is neither a parent nor offspring of the deceased
Inheritance	The determined shares left by the deceased to his/her dependents
Insanity	The complete removal of the intellect as a matter of perpetuity
Insolvency	The condition in which a person has more debt than possessions and wealth
Intoxicant	Any substance which colludes the intellect of the one who partakes in it—whether the amount is a lot or a little; the one who partakes in such without a valid reason is declared openly **disobedient**, and whoever declares it to be religiously **permissible** is declared a disbeliever
Irrevocable divorce	Any valid **divorce** contrary to the preconditions of a **revocable divorce**, in which the divorcee is not permitted to renew a **marriage** contract with his former spouse until after she has remarried and divorced another
Jadha'	A camel that has reached four lunar years of age
Jamrat	The stone pillars that pilgrims stone as a ritual for the **Hajj pilgrimage**
Jizya	An amount of wealth paid by the **dhimmi** in the domains of Islam
Late noon prayer	The four-**unit**, **silent**, **obligatory ritual prayer** that is prayed from the time the shadow of an object is twice the size of the object

Liability	Legal or financial responsibility for an infringement
Life grant	A type of **gift** granted to a recipient and his/her successors—if so stipulated—during the lifetime of the giver or that of the recipient
Loaned item	A commodity which is permitted for the borrower to freely use on the condition that it not be damaged or exhausted
Magic	The apparent manifestation of ability to alter creation by supernatural means
Magistrate	A legal official whose job is to issue judgements and edicts between people
Major ritual impurity	The state in which a Muslim is forbidden from certain acts of worship due to **intercourse**, the emission of semen, **menstruation** and **postpartum bleeding**
Major sin	An act of disobedience that destines punishment for its performer in the absence of repentance
Make up (prayer)	Praying the **ritual prayer** after the necessary time has elapsed
Makūk	An old form of measurement that consisted of a *ṣā'* and a half
Manslaughter	The taking of another's life either intentionally or unintentionally
Manumission	The freeing of a human being from contracted bondage and ownership
Marriage	A contract that occurs with a woman that permits **intercourse** with her outside of ownership
Martyr	Term that refers to a male, upright Muslim who was killed in the way of Allah even by poison; The term 'killed in the way of Allah' refers to one who was killed in the battlefield or due to defending oneself or his wealth as well as defending another or his wealth.
Menstruation	Term used to denote the exiting of blood from the uterus at a specified time
Misappropriation	The unlawful harming of one that deprives such one of that which is beneficial, that which repels harm and loss as well as one's right of entitlement
Muezzin	The caller to the ritual prayer whose preconditions for validity include being morally-responsible, male, upright and ritually pure from **major ritual impurity**
Munāsakha	The transfer or removal of wealth from the deceased to the deceased before it is distributed with the knowledge of the sequence
Muta'	When a man contracts a **marriage** with a woman until an appointed time, after which the **marriage** is annulled
Muzābana	The unlawful exchange of dried dates on palms for measured or unmeasured dates

Needy	Term used to refer to those who are more impoverished than the **poor** in that they do not own or cannot afford any of the five things the **poor** owns
Neighbour	A person in a **partnership** for which **pre-emption** is established due to residing in proximity to the seller in the same courtyard even if it is not directly adjacent
Night prayer	The four-**unit**, **audible**, **obligatory ritual prayer** that is prayed from the time the twilight disappears
Noon prayer	The four-**unit**, **silent**, **obligatory ritual prayer** that is prayed from the time the sun passes the zenith
Oath	A specific statement or indication that requires the one who said it to complete or avoid a matter with the threat of **expiation** if otherwise not met
Oath of abstention	When one intentionally swears that he will abstain from **intercourse** with his wife for four months or more
Obligatory	A term used to describe that for which its negligence earns blame and punishment, and its performance earns reward and praise
Partnership	The established relationship of two or more who share in profit and gain
Permissible	Term used to describe that for which its negligence does not earn praise and reward, nor does its performance earn blame and punishment
Pilgrim garb	The two unstitched sheets that are **obligatory** and worn on the body of a morally-responsible Muslim male during the **Hajj pilgrimage** and **'Umra pilgrimage**
Poor	Term used to refer to those who own or can only afford five things: a dwelling; a garment; an item of furniture, such as a pillow or drinking vessel; a servant or slave; and an item of warfare, such as a war horse or weapon
Postpartum bleeding	Term used to denote the blood that exits the uterus due to and after childbirth
Pre-emption	A general right of priority given to a partner or the like to make a purchase or exchange
Prepayment	An expedited contract of exchange with stipulated conditions
Pre-prayer call	An announcement signalling the commencement of the **ritual prayer** while standing utilising the wording of the **call to prayer**
Prescribed punishments	Term used to encompass the prescribed physical penalties applied by the imam of the Muslims to a morally-responsible person with the intention of fulfilling the rights of Allah and those of the offended party
Price-marking	The pricing of a commodity in which a customer pays without knowing the various details that were included in the price, such as transportation costs

Prohibited	A term used to describe that for which its negligence earns praise and reward, and its performance earns blame and punishment
Proprietor	The primary owner of the wealth with which the **speculator** engages in a **speculative partnership**
Purification dues	The taking of a determined amount of wealth from a specific person at a specific time and distributing it to a specified group
Purification wash	The intentional washing of the entire body with the purpose of entering the state of **ritual purity** required for certain actions
Qīrāṭ	A twenty-fourth of a Meccan dinar and a twentieth of an Iraqi dinar
Qunūt	Term used to denote an audible supplication made in connection to the ritual prayer
Ready money	The collective term used to refer to the dinar and dirham, or gold and silver money in general
Redistribution	A term that refers to the **inheritance** shares that are reallocated among the heirs after the **inheritance** shares were already distributed
Religious seclusion	The act of staying in the mosques with specific conditions
Resale for profit	A contract or agreement that stipulates that a third party be given a commodity to sell and that the profits be shared between the giver and seller for every portion of the price
Restricted (person)	Term used to denote one who is prevented from pursuing his/her needs due to illness, fear of aggression and the like
Retaliatory compensation	A legally **prescribed punishment** that requires the morally-responsible offender to be punished in the same manner as such person intentionally inflicted to another
Revocable divorce	Any divorce that takes place for which there is consummation but no compensation which is prior to the third pronouncement of divorce
Ritual ablution	The intentional performance of a series of actions in which the limbs are washed and/or wiped in a specific order and manner
Ritual impurities	Substances whose presence requires one to remove them in order for an act of worship to be considered valid
Ritual prayer	An act of worship that consists of remembrances and pillars for which the declaration of Allah's greatness makes certain actions during it **prohibited** and the final salutations makes those actions **permissible** again
Ritual purity	The state in which someone or something is free of **ritual impurities** so that one can perform certain acts of worship that require it

Road (partner in)	A person in a **partnership** for which **pre-emption** is established due to the joint ownership of transit passageways, blocked paths and private boundaries between properties
Ruqba	A type of **gift** granted by the giver to the recipient on the condition that whichever one of them should die first, it shall belong to the giver's heirs
Sacred Site	The whole of Muzdalifa which is between 'Arafat and Mina; its boundaries are al-Ma`zimayn, al-Hiyāḍ and the valley of Muhassir
Sacrificed meat	The meat of any sound animal that a non-pilgrim Muslim slaughtered by severing the larynx, oesophagus and two ventricles while reciting the Name of Allah
Security deposit	A contract over a specific property by which one who has it in his possession deserves to continue holding it in order to replenish what was allocated to him
Separate joint pilgrimage	The performance of both the **Hajj pilgrimage** and **'Umra pilgrimage** with a separation between them and removing the **state of pilgrim sanctity** between them
Sepulchre	An excavation in the middle of a grave as opposed to the side as in a **tomb**
Settlement	A derogation of a right, in which case, the person is discharged from its fulfilment; in the case of indemnity, it is a forgiveness of such.
Sharecropping	The renting out of land and its crops to a human labourer to work on for a share of the land or its crops
Shareholder	A joint owner in wealth or property
Shighār	When two men marry their daughters to one another provided that each exempts the **dowry** from the other
Silent	Term used to describe an inaudible verbal utterance whose minimum is that one can only hear oneself and whose maximum is that another's ears cannot hear it
Slander	The accusation of **fornication** against a free, morally-responsible and capable Muslim without valid evidence
Sleep	A state in which the body is fully relaxed, the senses are at ease and the speech of other people is concealed; it is distinct from drowsiness
Solitary pilgrimage	The performance of the **Hajj pilgrimage** singularly without the **'Umra pilgrimage** either separately or combined
Speculative partnership	An agreed upon arrangement between two or more persons in which one person gives the other gold or silver money to conduct a transaction on the former's behalf, and the profit is shared among them based on the mutual agreement of the percentage of such shares

Speculator	The one with whom the **proprietor** forges a **speculative partnership** to engage in a transaction with the latter's wealth of the proprietor based on a mutually agreed-upon profit that is divided between them
Spoils	Term used to refer to that which is obtained after the laying down of arms in a military campaign against disbelievers; all of such is distributed amongst the Muslim soldiers
Straitened	Term used to describe one who does not possess enough wealth for one's livelihood
Suckling	An expression dealing with the relationship of people due to a mother's milk given to an unrelated person during the latter's infancy
Sunnah divorce	A valid **divorce** that takes place with the following preconditions: there is only one **divorce pronouncement**, the woman is pure from **menstruation** and/or **postpartum bleeding**, and he had not had sexual **intercourse** with her prior to such **menstruation** and/or **postpartum bleeding**.
Sunset prayer	The three-**unit**, **audible**, **obligatory ritual prayer** that is prayed from the beginning of the night once an evening star is visible
Suretyship	The transfer of debt from one trust to another, and the former is thereby absolved
Ta'zīr	A punishment carried out against an offender, which has no prescribed limits set by Islamic law; it is generally less than that of the **prescribed punishments**
Talbiya	It is the recitation of the following phrase: *Labayk Allāhumma labayk. labayk lā sharīka laka labayk. Inna al-hamda wan- ni'mata laka wal-mulk. Lā sharīka lak.*
Tashrīq	The three days after the Eid of Sacrifice
Tomb	A rectangular pit which is dug in the side of the grave in the direction of the *qibla* wherein the deceased is
Transaction	An exchange of things of value between two parties in which there is a mutually agreed upon offer and acceptance
Tyrant	An oppressive Muslim ruler who openly violates Islamic law and deprives the rightful from their rights
umm walad	A slave woman with whom it is **permissible** for her master to have intercourse and who is manumitted upon delivering his child
'Umra pilgrimage	The observance of the following pilgrimage rites: the assumption of pilgrim garb, circumambulations, brisk walk between Ŝafa and Marwa and the shaving/cutting of the hair
Unit (prayer)	A portion of the **ritual prayer** that consists of a standing, bowing and two prostrations

Unlawful pronouncement	Specific verbal expressions made to one's lawful wife in which **intercourse** or lustful glancing is consequently forbidden unless otherwise removed by **expiation**
Usury	An unlawful increase gained as profit from a **transaction**; the sale of an item before taking possession of it
Vaginal bleeding	A condition that resembles **menstruation** in that blood exits the uterus; however, it falls outside of the usual limits of **menstruation**
Vow	That which a person obligates upon him/herself to do, say or avoid which is not one of the Islamic legal obligations
Waiting period	A name for a period during which a woman lies in expectation, so that her marriage will be **permissible** after its termination
Wash	The contact of a limb with **water** until the **water** drips while being accompanied by the act of rubbing
Wasq	A unit of measure that equals sixty *ṣā*'s
Water	A natural substance that falls from the sky and emanates from the earth which remains in its original created state without resembling anything else; it is considered ritually pure and purifies other than it
Watering source (partner in)	A person in a **partnership** for which **pre-emption** is established due to the joint ownership of land where there are wells, man-made rivulets and other artificial sources utilised for drinking **water** that separate the two pieces of land
Wealthy	A term used to describe one who owns more than the minimum amount that obligates the **purification dues**
Wipe (ablution)	The passing of the wet hand over a limb without any excess dripping **water**
Withdrawal	The intentional removal of a man's penis from a woman's vagina during ejaculation

Index

ʻ

'Abdullah b. 'Abbās, 514, 515, 530
Ibn al-'Abbās, 208, 210
'Abdullah b. 'Umar, 70, 283, 296, 449, 515
'Abdullah b. Ḍumayra, 53, 63, 84, 95, 224, 228, 450, 533, 619, 624
'Abdullah b. Ja'far, 232, 619
'Abdul-Malik b. Marwān, 341, 620
'Abdul-Muṭṭalib, 115, 116, 232, 304, 306, 349, 558, 621
'Ali b. Abi Ṭālib, 5, 20, 22, 26, 27, 28, 30, 39, 40, 41, 43, 44, 50, 51, 53, 63, 66, 68, 70, 72, 81, 82, 83, 84, 85, 86, 91, 92, 95, 102, 103, 106, 108, 110, 111, 113, 114, 115, 120, 124, 127, 137, 148, 159, 163, 174, 175, 177, 188, 203, 213, 214, 223, 224, 226, 227, 228, 231, 233, 234, 239, 251, 254, 257, 259, 261, 269, 271, 272, 273, 277, 278, 279, 286, 288, 291, 296, 300, 304, 305, 316, 318, 326, 335, 336, 342, 358, 375, 378, 398, 411, 414, 416, 421, 422, 423, 424, 425, 426, 429, 431, 443, 445, 446, 449, 451, 453, 465, 466, 468, 470, 472, 474, 476, 478, 484, 485, 489, 490, 491, 492, 493, 494, 495, 496, 502, 516, 530, 533, 534, 535, 536, 540, 544, 548, 551, 552, 553, 559, 561, 569, 572, 579, 584, 588, 590, 594, 596, 597, 598, 599, 601, 603, 605, 610, 611, 619, 620, 621, 622, 623, 624, 625, 626, 627, 628
'Ali b. al-Hussein, 8, 70, 193, 204, 327, 353, 578, 622, 626, 628
'Ammār b. Yāsir, 579, 610, 622
'Amr b. al-'Āṣ, 86, 622
'awl, 24, 493, 494
'Umar b. al-Khaṭṭāb, 70, 157, 283, 288, 336, 416, 421, 422, 449, 619, 620, 622, 626, 627, 628
'Umra, 9, 10, 20, 180, 184, 186, 187, 193, 194, 195, 197, 200, 202, 203, 205, 209, 211, 212, 216, 269, 410, 595, 631, 635, 637, 638
'Uthmān b. Affān, 183, 451, 619, 622, 623, 627, 628

A

Aaron, 3, 42, 43, 44, 158, 627
ablution, 3, 4, 5, 11, 29, 30, 31, 51, 52, 53, 54, 55, 56, 57, 58, 59, 60, 61, 62, 63, 65, 67, 68, 69, 72, 82, 86, 87, 88, 93, 106, 121, 170, 208, 215, 275, 284, 595, 636, 639
Abraham, 3, 4, 5, 44, 73, 74, 82, 117, 180, 185, 190, 216, 250, 557, 610
Abu Bakr b. Abi Uways, 53, 63, 84, 95, 224, 450, 625
Abu Dharr, 609
Abu Hanīfa, 7, 30, 32, 33, 78, 87, 161, 235, 243, 379
Abu Hurayra, 79, 89, 92, 119, 318, 449, 600, 619, 620, 626
Abu Musa al-Asha'ri, 86, 620
Abul-A'war as-Sulami, 86, 621
accusation, 403, 426, 427, 432, 433, 452
adultery, 246, 321, 418, 423, 625, 631
agriculture, 22, 407, 444, 445, 558, 614
Ahl al-Bayt, 3, 6, 7, 8, 9, 10, 11, 18, 19, 20, 21, 22, 23, 24, 26, 27, 29, 30, 31, 32, 44, 45, 68, 75, 85, 87, 95, 108, 116, 187, 193, 204, 210, 228, 281, 282, 286, 289, 344, 366, 456, 463, 464, 492, 494, 516, 537, 540, 541, 567, 568, 576, 578, 585, 587, 597, 616, 617, 620, 621, 622, 623, 624, 625, 626, 628
A'isha bt. Abi Bakr, 53, 96, 119, 200, 242, 256, 290, 291, 296, 425, 588, 609, 619, 620, 623, 624, 627
al-'Abbās, 138, 535, 558, 621
alcohol *See* intoxicants
al-Hamza, 113, 115, 116, 304, 306
al-Hasan al-Baṣri, 231, 621
al-Hasan b. 'Ali, 5, 6, 18, 85, 251, 289, 565, 596, 597, 600, 610, 621, 623
al-Hassan, 43
al-Hussein, 43
al-Hussein b. 'Ali, 6, 8, 18, 46, 113, 578, 594, 599, 600, 622, 623, 628
al-Qāsim b. Ibrāhīm
Rassi, 5, 6, 8, 9, 16, 21, 46, 52, 53, 67, 75, 77, 84, 88, 100, 193, 285, 286, 317, 342, 411, 573, 621, 622, 626
Amīn, 84, 86
amnesty, 448
amputation, 21, 22, 439, 440, 441, 442, 443, 444, 445, 446, 447, 632
anal intercourse, 262, 417, 438
analogy, 3, 16, 17, 65, 68, 92, 143, 146, 212, 281, 287, 294, 321, 323, 343, 344, 437, 493, 502, 505, 506, 508, 509, 510, 512, 523
anger, 28, 30, 12, 46, 274, 299, 305, 419, 449, 458, 556, 566, 567, 585, 586, 588, 606, 611, 612
Anṣār, 57, 71, 157, 238, 273, 524, 532, 538, 578, 590, 599, 620
apostate
apostasy, 14, 25, 27, 168, 251, 252, 271, 438, 458, 503, 510, 511, 551, 593
aqīqa, 26, 525, 526
Arafat, 8, 9, 11, 25, 96, 105, 108, 162, 180, 187, 188, 189, 190, 194, 195, 197, 200, 201, 203, 209, 210, 284, 351, 554, 637
arrogance, 30, 38, 275, 291, 420, 607, 608, 609
Āshūra, 8, 162
asset, 365, 378, 391, 415, 504, 507
astrology, 30, 611
audible, 79, 81, 83, 84, 105, 630, 631, 635, 636, 638

B

backbiting, 30, 54, 608
Badr, 89, 449, 580, 620, 621, 623, 624, 626, 628
Bahrain, 449, 464, 620, 622, 626
Banu Hāshim, 577, 594
barīd, 96, 164, 165
Barīra, 256, 278, 623
barley, 104, 131, 134, 135, 143, 150, 318, 331, 334, 342,

343, 345, 354, 397, 444, 448, 533
Basra, 11, 588, 624
battlefield, 112, 609, 634
beard, 51, 84, 121, 465, 536, 602, 615
Bedouin, 16, 87, 141, 326, 333, 334, 446, 464, 482, 520, 539, 556, 609
bequest, 26, 27, 110, 176, 228, 247, 500, 504, 540, 542, 543, 544, 545, 552
Bilāl, 7, 48, 49, 56, 63, 71, 111, 114, 120, 183, 188, 207, 210, 218, 234, 251, 264, 269, 277, 318, 623
bint labūn, 125, 126, 128, 144, 146, 464
bint makhāḍ, 125, 126, 128, 144, 146
Bismillah ar-Rahmān ar-Rahīm, 75, 83, 84, 185, 534
Black Stone, 185, 200
blood, 4, 19, 30, 52, 53, 59, 61, 64, 65, 66, 67, 68, 72, 92, 101, 112, 166, 178, 181, 193, 194, 197, 228, 255, 267, 269, 299, 304, 306, 321, 328, 394, 418, 419, 437, 454, 455, 458, 460, 462, 463, 471, 473, 520, 522, 523, 528, 560, 568, 574, 581, 585, 588, 589,590, 592, 606, 631, 634, 635, 639
bloodwite, 426, 462, 466, 467, 469, 473, 475, 478, 631
Book of Allah *See* Qur'an
booty, 7, 27, 28, 29, 136, 137, 140, 148, 319, 462, 489, 551, 569, 570, 571, 575, 576, 577, 578, 579, 583, 584, 585, 588, 589, 590, 592
borrowing, 356
bowing, 25, 26, 41, 54, 76, 77, 85, 87, 89, 90, 93, 94, 422, 539, 557, 566, 638
breastfeeding, 262, 280, 297, 305, 593, 628
brisk walk, 186, 187, 190, 194, 200, 201, 203, 207, 210, 215, 638
burial, 111, 114, 118, 119, 120, 122
business
transactions, 129, 142, 144, 252, 316, 317, 323, 326, 335, 368, 369, 372, 373, 375, 376, 382, 443, 581

C

call to prayer, 4, 5, 70, 71, 72, 80, 81, 94, 105, 108, 189, 635
camel, 92, 169, 180, 182, 187, 193, 194, 198, 199, 204, 205, 206, 208, 209, 212, 213, 214, 215, 216, 217, 218, 258, 323, 333, 334, 335, 338, 345, 347, 348, 349, 354, 378, 384, 385, 390, 407, 411, 417, 440, 444, 447, 478, 520, 521, 524, 525, 557, 576, 615, 616, 630, 631, 633
capital, 149, 280, 343, 344, 347, 369, 370, 371, 372, 374, 375, 391
captivity, 317, 328, 575, 579, 580, 589, 590
carcass, 60, 140, 199, 299, 306, 319, 424, 454, 455, 514, 516, 518, 520, 522, 523, 528, 531, 535, 536, 608
castration, 23, 260, 470, 524
cat, 530
certainty, 15, 17, 38, 41, 55, 69, 71, 72, 142, 237, 244, 321, 322, 329, 397, 419, 516, 548, 597, 631
charity, 18, 20, 26, 30, 41, 53, 124, 130, 136, 138, 140, 141, 143, 169, 183, 184, 189, 190, 193, 205, 209, 211, 212, 213, 214, 215, 216, 256, 274, 284, 291, 362, 363, 378, 400, 401, 402, 411, 412, 437, 446, 460, 461, 525, 526, 540, 542, 557, 577, 578, 581, 584, 598, 609, 630, 632
cheese, 60, 104, 150, 531
chess, 448, 615
Children of Israel, 156, 460, 612
Christian, 8, 22, 25, 118, 119, 148, 149, 156, 231, 245, 247, 249, 253, 254, 365, 400, 426, 451, 463, 471, 478, 503, 510, 511, 515, 531, 557, 626
church, 101
circuit, 89
circumambulation, 185, 187, 190, 192, 194, 195, 197, 200, 203, 207, 208, 210, 214, 215
claim, 10, 47, 349, 380, 404, 477, 630
clan, 23, 44, 375, 440, 461, 462, 465, 467, 468, 469, 472, 473, 475, 479, 482, 571, 630
clay pellets, 517, 598
clientage, 256, 412, 504, 505, 506, 507, 508, 509, 510, 511, 512, 513, 592
combined pilgrimage, 193, 211, 214, 216
Commander of Believers
Imam 'Ali, 22, 29, 30, 39, 40, 41, 42, 43, 48, 49, 50, 51, 76, 77, 81, 83, 86, 90, 91, 92, 95, 102, 106, 108, 110, 111, 113, 114, 115, 120, 124, 127, 137, 148, 161, 163, 174, 175, 177, 183, 188, 203, 213, 214, 224, 226, 227, 231, 233, 234, 251, 254, 257, 259, 260, 261, 269, 271, 272, 273, 277, 278, 279, 288, 296, 300, 304, 305, 306, 316, 317, 318, 320, 324, 335, 342, 358, 398, 411, 414, 416, 421, 422, 423, 424, 425, 426, 429, 431, 434, 443, 445, 446, 449, 450, 451, 452, 453, 465, 466, 470, 472, 474, 476, 478, 484, 485, 489, 490, 491, 492, 493, 494, 495, 496, 502, 503, 504, 516, 530, 533, 534, 535, 536, 540, 548, 551, 552, 553, 557, 558, 559, 561, 566, 569, 572, 578, 579, 584, 588, 590, 596, 603, 605, 609, 610, 611, 615, 617, 623
commodity, 237, 314, 315, 323, 324, 325, 326, 327, 329, 330, 331, 332, 333, 337, 338, 346, 347, 354, 364, 368, 369, 370, 372, 373, 374, 386, 388, 402, 440, 545, 572, 582, 632, 634, 635, 636
Companions, 19, 20, 44, 50, 106, 107, 111, 120, 129, 157, 264, 416, 421, 453, 462, 515, 530, 531, 566, 585, 602, 613, 619, 620, 621, 622, 624, 625
compensation, 141, 157, 158, 184, 197, 209, 216, 239, 240, 277, 278, 284, 291, 297, 301, 323, 329, 369, 394, 426, 427, 456, 460, 461, 468, 472, 589, 632, 636
compensatory ransom, 184, 214, 216
confession, 386, 387, 392, 400, 419, 420, 421, 422, 423, 424, 426, 427, 440, 442, 444, 445, 469, 473, 474, 475, 500, 501, 511, 512, 554
congregation, 30, 31, 70, 80, 82, 88, 91, 94, 98, 100, 102, 108, 109, 167, 424, 603
conjecture, 17, 151, 321, 322
consciousness, 40, 74, 83, 86, 94, 152, 221, 223, 245, 370, 371, 529, 541, 548
consensus, 3, 18, 19, 20, 21, 22, 29, 30, 32, 68, 70, 73, 80, 83, 85, 87, 90, 96, 108, 116, 122, 169, 182, 190, 193, 204, 206, 228, 283, 284, 287, 289, 304, 307, 340, 416, 453, 516, 529, 568
consummative marriage, 425, 426, 427, 428, 429, 430,

431, 437, 459
contract of indentureship, 504, 548, 549, 593
contractual guaranty, 358, 362, 364
corn, 104, 150, 318, 334, 345, 397, 448, 533
cow
cows, 126, 128, 145, 146, 169, 199, 205, 206, 208, 209, 210, 212, 214, 215, 216, 333, 334, 335, 345, 349, 354, 384, 417, 524, 525, 531
credit, 326, 327, 347, 350, 368, 370, 372, 378, 402
creditor, 314, 315, 353, 388, 390, 394, 401
cross-legged, 54, 93, 94
crucifixion, 438, 446, 447, 459
cuckold, 438, 458
cupping, 30, 52, 163, 205, 615

D

dates, 8, 17, 18, 22, 13, 104, 134, 135, 150, 151, 153, 157, 274, 318, 323, 331, 334, 335, 337, 342, 343, 345, 348, 350, 352, 353, 355, 356, 379, 384, 388, 389, 397, 444, 445, 448, 456, 529, 533, 534, 615, 634
dawn prayer, 14, 18, 25, 26, 73, 74, 85, 89, 94, 96, 107, 108, 122, 165, 174, 186, 187, 188, 414, 417, 451, 585, 596
Day of Judgement, 1, 45, 47, 51, 71, 159, 189, 192, 198, 326, 327, 328, 396, 431, 511, 528, 542, 571, 572, 586, 587, 594, 598, 599, 600, 601, 604, 606, 607, 614, 616
death penalty, 168, 169, 199, 253, 426, 427, 432, 437, 438, 446, 447, 454, 455, 456, 458, 459, 461, 467, 468, 469, 470, 471, 472, 473, 475, 476, 477, 510, 551, 593
debt, 86, 101, 137, 143, 151, 153, 172, 217, 228, 247, 301, 314, 315, 339, 343, 354, 368, 369, 370, 373, 375, 382, 386, 391, 392, 394, 401, 402, 407, 465, 504, 551, 552, 553, 632, 633, 638
debtor, 314, 315, 327, 382, 392
declaration of Allah's greatness, 5, 6, 9, 20, 25, 32, 53, 74, 75, 76, 80, 81, 85, 90, 93, 105, 108, 116, 117, 188, 636
defendant, 380, 477, 559
delayed payment, 336
deputy, 227, 228, 259, 372, 382
dhimmi, 6, 10, 12, 13, 14, 19, 20, 21, 22, 23, 25, 27, 28, 29, 118, 130, 149, 201, 230, 231, 241, 245, 247, 248, 249, 252, 253, 254, 261, 271, 360, 365, 394, 400, 422, 426, 428, 429, 430, 433, 434, 437, 438, 443, 470, 471, 478, 503, 515, 544, 553, 560, 579, 581,589, 591, 593, 633
Dhul Shimālayn, 89
Dhul-Hijja, 105, 162, 181, 186, 188, 201
Dhul-Qa'da, 5, 181, 201
dinar, 47, 125, 134, 135, 138, 143, 144, 147, 170, 226, 318, 326, 330, 331, 334, 335, 338, 339, 340, 341, 342, 343, 344, 346, 347, 353, 354, 356, 359, 361, 364, 368, 369, 372, 373, 374, 378, 382, 390, 391, 394, 401, 417, 463, 548, 549, 552, 636
dirham, 7, 47, 125, 131, 133, 134, 135, 136, 138, 142, 147, 148, 150, 153, 170, 223, 225, 226, 238, 240, 260, 261, 292, 293, 318, 329, 334, 338, 339, 340, 341, 342, 345, 346, 356, 372, 373, 392, 411, 417, 439, 440, 441, 463, 464, 477, 533, 559, 584, 586, 589, 590, 606, 636
disbelief, 7, 40, 48, 101, 247, 248, 251, 253, 261, 262, 275, 438, 460, 461, 503, 610
disbeliever, 15, 26, 28, 39, 43, 101, 118, 274, 275, 306, 310, 312, 434, 449, 471, 510, 532, 551, 561, 579, 592, 627, 633
discharge, 3, 52, 59, 60, 64, 67, 92, 169
disobedient, 21, 28, 39, 40, 41, 45, 48, 87, 88, 98, 100, 117, 118, 151, 166, 168, 180, 227, 241, 275, 283, 284, 316, 317, 320, 321, 327, 396, 422, 423, 431, 433, 434, 454, 459, 460, 552, 560, 561, 562, 565, 566, 568, 569, 573, 579, 583, 599, 601, 604, 612, 622, 633
dispensation, 61, 164, 165, 170, 208, 236, 503, 537, 614
dissimulation, 88, 534
divorce, 65, 173, 221, 229, 230, 232, 233, 234, 235, 236, 238, 239, 240, 242, 243, 244, 245, 251, 252, 253, 255, 256, 257, 258, 259, 266, 267, 268, 269, 270, 271, 272, 273, 274, 275, 276, 277, 278, 279, 280, 281, 282, 283, 284, 285, 286, 287, 288, 289, 290, 291, 292, 293, 294, 295, 296, 297, 298, 299, 300, 301, 302, 303, 308, 309, 310, 320, 322, 401, 402, 423, 451, 555, 592, 593, 623, 624, 625, 628, 633, 636, 638
dog, 23, 25, 27, 30, 55, 92, 184, 213, 424, 477, 514, 515, 516, 517, 561, 608, 614
domain of Islam, 252, 510, 551, 589, 590, 591, 592, 593, 631
domain of war, 251, 252, 254, 263, 510, 551, 581, 588, 589, 590, 591, 592, 593
donkey, 55, 92, 183, 319, 334, 403, 413, 420, 421, 424, 576, 608
dowry, 221, 225, 226, 229, 230, 231, 232, 234, 235, 236, 237, 238, 239, 240, 241, 243, 244, 245, 251, 253, 255, 256, 257, 258, 259, 260, 261, 267, 270, 285, 288, 290, 294, 295, 301, 302, 311, 319, 324, 366, 412, 413, 414, 415, 425, 426, 549,593, 627, 637
dream, 30, 57, 71, 165, 253, 279, 613
drum, 12, 238
dues collector, 6, 127, 128, 129, 132, 145, 146, 150, 153
dung, 92, 319, 531
dust purification, 14, 57, 58, 60, 61, 62, 63, 64, 106, 118, 121, 196, 197, 275, 285
dye, 99, 211, 280, 536, 602

E

eclipse prayer, 103
Eid, 61, 104, 105, 106, 108, 149, 150, 151, 152, 162, 172, 176, 177, 188, 351, 524, 604, 638
Eid of the Fast-Breaking, 105
Eid of the Sacrifice, 105, 108
ejaculation, 57, 160, 205, 259
Emigrants, 57, 68, 482, 578, 586, 624, 627
eunuch, 260
ewe, 144, 145, 146, 184, 199, 205, 209, 210, 212, 213
executor, 110, 375, 544, 545
expedition, 28, 129, 326, 575, 580, 582, 585, 588
expiation, 156, 162, 163, 168, 169, 172, 173, 198, 199, 203, 204, 205, 206, 211, 212, 214, 216, 217, 218, 274, 275, 276, 293, 294, 396, 397, 398, 399, 400, 401, 402,

403, 460, 461, 462, 466, 469, 471, 473, 549, 572, 632, 635, 639

F

false hair, 536, 602
fast-breaking dues, 104, 149, 150, 151, 152
fasting, 156, 157, 158, 159, 160, 161, 162, 163, 164, 165, 166, 167, 168, 169, 170, 171, 172, 173, 174, 175, 176, 177, 178, 184, 209, 211, 212, 214, 217, 283, 471, 568, 586, 600
fat, 335, 337, 348, 349, 351, 354, 385, 524, 525, 531
Fātiha, 4, 20, 75, 76, 77, 78, 79, 83, 118, 326
Fāṭima bt. Muhammad, 18, 19, 43, 112, 166
Fātima bt. Abu Hubaysh, 67
festive gathering, 238, 532
fifth dues, 129, 130, 136, 137, 140, 577, 578, 581, 585, 589
final salutations, 31, 32, 53, 75, 80, 81, 82, 85, 86, 88, 89, 90, 91, 95, 99, 100, 102, 103, 104, 117, 181, 188, 636
financial ease, 550, 593
financial maintenance, 196, 243, 255, 263, 267, 268, 270, 280, 297, 298, 308, 309, 310, 311, 368, 372, 379, 385, 388, 406, 529, 624
fish, 25, 136, 329, 516, 530, 632
flogging, 260, 298, 400, 403, 416, 420, 421, 423, 424, 426, 427, 428, 429, 430, 431, 432, 433, 434, 436, 439, 449, 450, 451, 452, 453, 456
foetus, 23, 26, 65, 150, 252, 421, 467, 468, 469, 470, 523
foodstuffs, 150
forgiveness, 29, 27, 51, 65, 103, 104, 112, 113, 114, 116, 117, 157, 159, 160, 164, 175, 182, 184, 189, 192, 246, 396, 397, 432, 439, 461, 529, 542, 586, 595, 599, 600, 603, 605, 608, 637
fornication, 87, 88, 113, 114, 221, 223, 227, 230, 234, 237, 246, 318, 321, 386, 387, 399, 403, 416, 417, 418, 419, 420, 421, 422, 423, 424, 425, 426, 427, 428, 429, 430, 431, 432, 433, 434, 437, 440, 450, 451, 452, 453, 455, 459, 460, 567, 609, 637
fornicator, 72, 233, 234, 403, 416, 418, 422, 427, 429, 431, 432, 435, 436, 437, 442, 460
foundling, 414
Friday, 5, 30, 87, 89, 91, 94, 95, 105, 106, 108, 175, 177, 215, 276, 284, 603, 604, 632
funeral bier, 114, 115, 118, 120, 122, 175
funeral prayer, 116, 117, 120, 122, 597, 621
funeral procession, 115, 118

G

Gabriel, 13, 15, 27, 85, 135, 159, 417, 420, 463, 564, 599, 604, 610
gambling
games of chance, 615
game animal, 183, 198, 199, 211, 213, 214, 217, 514, 515, 516, 517, 530, 531, 598, 610
generosity, 30, 248, 354, 356, 363, 541, 594, 605, 606, 619
gift, 127, 136, 217, 231, 232, 239, 240, 241, 255, 256, 259, 285, 329, 353, 354, 362, 363, 365, 366, 378, 382, 389, 401, 410, 411, 412, 445, 461, 473, 513, 521, 529, 530, 542, 577, 583, 634, 637
glorification, 20, 65, 76, 77, 78, 80, 81, 89, 160, 175, 287, 522, 604
goat, 125, 128, 208, 209, 212, 213, 349, 385, 464, 524, 525, 526
gold, 17, 19, 26, 125, 131, 132, 134, 135, 136, 138, 142, 146, 147, 148, 153, 318, 339, 340, 345, 347, 368, 372, 379, 394, 401, 402, 417, 464, 525, 526, 534, 535, 537, 539, 583, 590, 636, 637
grandfather, 20, 21, 24, 25, 26, 28, 31, 32, 44, 48, 53, 63, 75, 76, 84, 95, 100, 111, 120, 164, 167, 207, 224, 225, 228, 230, 250, 254, 264, 269, 270, 277, 286, 289, 291, 297, 311, 317, 342, 411, 450, 453, 481, 482, 483, 484, 485, 486, 490, 491, 492, 494, 495, 505, 506, 524, 533, 566, 571, 600, 622, 624
grandmother, 254, 297, 481, 482, 483, 484, 492, 503, 512, 596
grapes, 132, 151, 337, 342, 348, 354, 448, 456, 532, 533, 534
grave *See* 'tomb'
greetings, 185, 200, 421, 556, 612, 614, 615
guarantee, 356, 382, 412, 413, 590, 600, 608
guardian, 34, 42, 46, 218, 223, 224, 225, 226, 228, 238, 239, 241, 242, 249, 260, 266, 267, 268, 288, 294, 295, 297, 302, 314, 375, 376, 387, 411, 421, 422, 472, 545, 549, 562, 593, 632

H

hadith, 3, 6, 15, 16, 19, 24, 34, 42, 44, 52, 53, 55, 76, 78, 79, 89, 106, 118, 119, 127, 163, 169, 198, 206, 223, 226, 228, 236, 238, 248, 251, 273, 286, 305, 308, 320, 322, 323, 343, 410, 412, 425, 430, 438, 453, 456, 463, 469, 513, 523, 536, 556, 564, 566, 567, 580, 597, 604, 610, 619, 620, 621, 623, 624, 625, 626, 627
Hafsa, 290, 291, 619, 624, 627
hair extensions, 536
Hajj, 96, 157, 169, 170, 180, 181, 182, 186, 187, 190, 193, 194, 195, 196, 197, 198, 200, 201, 202, 203, 204, 205, 206, 207, 209, 210, 211, 212, 215, 216, 218, 269, 540, 595, 621, 630, 631, 633, 635, 637
hand-to-hand, 318, 319, 334, 335, 336, 337, 338, 339, 340, 345, 347, 394, 402
heir, 110, 130, 176, 251, 257, 280, 297, 298, 311, 312, 332, 375, 387, 412, 413, 459, 480, 481, 490, 492, 493, 494, 495, 496, 497, 499, 500, 501, 502, 503, 504, 508, 510, 512, 542, 543, 544, 545, 548, 549, 550, 552, 553, 563, 591, 630, 633, 636, 637
Hell, 40, 41, 192, 274, 419, 458, 495, 535, 560, 585, 599, 604, 608, 613
henna, 133, 183, 269, 280, 602
heretic, 438, 458
hermaphrodite, 82, 498, 499, 506, 507
hiqqa, 125, 126, 144, 146
homosexuality, 431, 609
honey, 136, 137, 170, 236, 275, 288, 448, 533, 534, 620
horse, 55, 56, 76, 129, 139, 142, 144, 158, 216, 258, 295,

330, 334, 345, 348, 354, 411, 476, 557, 574, 575, 576, 577, 582, 583, 590, 599, 614, 635
hunger, 168, 308, 320, 403, 514, 520, 522, 528, 531, 538, 609
hunting, 25, 183, 213, 214, 514, 515, 517, 610, 614
husband, 11, 12, 13, 14, 15, 20, 65, 66, 67, 68, 112, 218, 221, 225, 229, 230, 231, 232, 233, 234, 235, 236, 239, 240, 241, 242, 243, 244, 245, 249, 250, 251, 252, 253, 255, 256, 257, 258, 259, 260, 263, 266, 268, 269, 270, 271, 272, 273, 278, 279, 280, 281, 288,289, 290, 292, 293, 296, 297, 298, 299, 300, 301, 302, 306, 307, 308, 309, 310, 413, 425, 428, 451, 480, 481, 482, 485, 486, 488, 489, 490, 491, 493, 494, 499, 500, 560, 592, 624

I

Ibn al-Mughaffal, 92
Ibn Umm Maktūm, 72, 624
idolater, 13, 55, 118, 223, 234, 245, 246, 252, 275, 328, 426, 429, 455, 461, 462
illness
  sickness, 10, 47, 53, 74, 106, 158, 164, 165, 184, 197, 207, 283, 314, 389, 430, 561, 613
images, 30, 317, 614
imam, 4, 5, 22, 28, 29, 32, 33, 43, 45, 46, 47, 48, 50, 89, 94, 95, 96, 97, 99, 100, 102, 104, 105, 108, 109, 120, 127, 128, 129, 130, 136, 137, 138, 139, 141, 142, 143, 148, 151, 159, 168, 184, 187, 188, 199, 215, 223, 224, 225, 226, 251, 252, 259, 260, 276, 277, 315, 316, 327, 333, 363, 366, 378, 386, 394, 407, 414, 416, 419, 421, 422, 423, 424, 425, 427, 428, 429, 430, 432, 433, 434, 435, 436, 437, 438, 439, 440, 441, 442, 443, 444, 445, 446, 447, 448, 450, 454, 455, 456, 458, 461, 465, 467, 473, 478, 497, 510, 524, 542, 548, 560, 561, 562, 563, 564, 565, 566, 568, 570, 571, 572, 573, 574, 575, 576, 577, 578, 579, 580, 581, 582, 583, 584, 585, 587, 588, 589, 590, 592, 593, 597, 604, 609, 615, 620, 621, 622, 624, 625, 626, 628, 635
imamate, 28, 42, 43, 45, 47, 108, 541, 562, 563, 564, 566, 587
immovable property, 360, 545
impure occurrence, 109, 121
impurities, 19, 51, 55, 56, 59, 68, 69, 92, 99, 100, 101, 151, 233, 448, 453, 636
impurity, 3, 19, 50, 55, 56, 58, 59, 60, 61, 62, 63, 71, 92, 93, 100, 101, 109, 121, 177, 200, 282, 285, 306, 453, 454, 516, 522, 528, 531, 614, 634
indemnity, 237, 254, 255, 257, 258, 259, 426, 427, 428, 440, 453, 455, 458, 460, 461, 462, 463, 464, 465, 466, 467, 468, 469, 470, 471, 472, 473, 474, 475, 476, 477, 478, 479, 502, 503, 521, 548, 557, 560, 637
indentured labour, 256, 257, 429, 504, 513
indentured labourer, 153, 216, 241, 251, 256, 257, 258, 399, 411, 412, 428, 435, 468, 469, 504, 548, 549, 552, 592, 593
independent judgement, 99, 407, 430, 455, 466, 576
inheritance, 113, 181, 224, 228, 229, 230, 247, 248, 249, 250, 256, 257, 280, 289, 308, 310, 311, 320, 365, 386, 387, 391, 392, 410, 412, 478, 480, 481, 482, 483, 484, 485, 486, 487, 488, 489, 490, 491, 492, 493, 494, 495, 496, 497, 498, 499, 500, 501, 502, 503, 504, 505, 506, 507, 508, 509, 510, 511, 512, 513, 523, 543, 544, 591, 630, 631, 636
injury, 50, 57, 58, 64, 67, 99, 100, 102, 184, 386, 404, 460, 461, 463, 464, 465, 467, 468, 469, 470, 473, 475, 476, 477, 479, 556, 560, 580, 598, 633
insanity, 278, 279, 387, 398, 399, 425, 427, 428, 430, 441, 442, 455, 545
insolvency, 346, 379, 382, 388, 389, 390, 391, 407
intellect, 12, 17, 22, 39, 53, 54, 70, 71, 81, 89, 92, 97, 106, 131, 138, 139, 143, 153, 164, 236, 238, 240, 245, 246, 249, 260, 263, 264, 272, 275, 278, 279, 281, 283, 296, 304, 307, 314, 321, 322, 323, 345, 387, 417, 423, 424, 427, 428, 440, 441, 448, 450, 451, 453, 465, 467, 477, 494, 520, 532, 533, 534, 545, 549, 559, 562, 594, 633
intention, 9, 10, 14, 22, 23, 24, 11, 109, 161, 166, 168, 169, 170, 175, 182, 185, 188, 199, 202, 206, 210, 211, 217, 218, 231, 235, 244, 276, 279, 291, 292, 293, 297, 315, 362, 396, 398, 400, 419, 426, 427, 434, 446, 458, 459, 465, 466, 470, 472, 473, 476, 479, 525, 550, 559, 575, 598, 631, 634, 635, 636
intercourse, 20, 57, 59, 66, 67, 68, 156, 157, 159, 163, 164, 165, 169, 175, 176, 177, 183, 186, 190, 197, 198, 207, 215, 222, 229, 230, 231, 233, 234, 235, 236, 239, 240, 241, 243, 244, 245, 249, 250, 251, 253, 254, 255, 256, 257, 258, 259, 260, 261, 262, 263, 264, 266, 267, 268, 270, 273, 274, 276, 277, 278, 282, 283, 286, 288, 289, 290, 291, 298, 300, 302, 309, 310, 318, 319, 324, 329, 379, 389, 402, 414, 417, 418, 425, 426, 427, 428, 438, 439, 452, 469, 549, 554, 592, 593, 598, 602, 631, 634, 635, 638, 639
intoxicants, 22, 26, 55, 60, 87, 101, 199, 258, 319, 403, 443, 448, 449, 450, 451, 453, 454, 455, 456, 533, 534, 622, 626
intoxication, 14, 278, 279, 449, 453, 534
Iraq, 6, 21, 29, 30, 32, 130, 134, 181, 341, 464, 581, 622
irrevocable divorce, 232, 233, 270, 271, 310
Islam (embraced), 29, 231, 251, 252, 253, 254, 310, 433, 434, 446, 458, 461, 478, 503, 510, 532, 551, 553, 557, 591, 592, 593, 619, 621, 622, 623, 625, 626, 627, 628
Ismā'īl b. Abi Uways, 228, 620

J

Ja'far b. Muhammad, 286, 534, 600
Jābir b. 'Abdullah, 218, 226, 412, 625
judhu', 125, 126, 144, 146
jamrat, 10, 11, 187, 190, 191, 192, 193, 197, 200, 207, 208, 209, 215, 287
Jesus, 33, 44, 48, 452, 612
Jew, 101, 118, 119, 149, 231, 245, 247, 249, 253, 254, 342, 348, 365, 400, 420, 421, 426, 451, 463, 471, 503, 510, 511, 515, 531, 538, 609, 614, 619
jihad, 48, 52, 289, 541, 542, 558, 565, 568, 569, 573, 578, 603, 628
jizya, 28, 29, 148, 149, 252, 463, 511, 581, 582, 589, 593,

631
joint pilgrimage, 194, 213, 637

K

Ka'ba, 184, 185, 186, 190, 192, 195, 197, 211, 212, 217, 568, 604, 622, 630
Kharijites, 569, 624
Khawla bt. Tha'laba, 12, 274, 623, 625
Khaybar, 129, 340, 420, 625
khula' divorce, 302
kindness, 30, 40, 221, 228, 242, 263, 284, 285, 317, 326, 416, 461, 571, 581, 583, 605, 606, 616
kohl, 65, 163, 176, 183, 269, 270, 424
Kufa, 11, 26, 30, 32, 56, 85, 129, 300, 352, 424, 451, 464, 569, 619, 620, 621, 622, 627, 628

L

late noon prayer, 61, 67, 73, 74, 78, 88, 89, 99, 108, 122, 188, 417
leather socks, 68, 69, 101, 112, 184, 196, 204, 534, 536
liability, 333, 359, 360, 379, 382, 384, 413, 414, 427, 440, 471, 472, 474, 475, 476, 477, 479, 560
litigant, 556, 559, 560
livestock, 6, 11, 18, 23, 55, 104, 125, 128, 129, 142, 143, 146, 198, 199, 208, 211, 213, 214, 323, 327, 328, 329, 334, 347, 348, 384, 445, 467, 468, 521, 523, 526, 536, 614
lizard, 26, 213, 530
loan, 20, 140, 339, 343, 355, 356, 372, 373, 378, 412, 413, 427
lodging, 243, 268, 270, 308, 309, 312, 624
Lot, 262, 417, 418, 431, 597, 598
lunar year, 127, 129, 135, 136, 142, 143, 144, 146, 147, 250, 251, 298, 305, 306, 543, 630, 633

M

Mā'iz b. Mālik al-Aslami, 113, 416, 419, 424, 440, 625
Magian, 101, 231, 253, 254, 451, 471, 502, 510, 511, 512, 515, 516, 531
magistrate, 236, 298, 299, 351, 356, 414, 416, 442, 556, 557, 559, 627
Mahdi, 567, 568
major ritual impurity, 48, 53, 55, 56, 57, 58, 59, 60, 62, 63, 64, 65, 93, 111, 121, 165, 197, 214, 522, 596, 634
major sins, 30, 87, 88, 419, 609
makūk, 334, 337, 343, 345, 417
manufacture, 18, 99, 340, 352, 370, 385, 443, 535
manumission, 152, 153, 154, 168, 172, 173, 178, 231, 238, 239, 254, 255, 256, 257, 258, 259, 260, 272, 274, 275, 294, 301, 320, 324, 330, 375, 385, 387, 397, 398, 399, 400, 401, 402, 434, 436, 461, 469, 473, 478, 481, 500, 503, 504, 505, 506, 508, 509, 510, 511, 512, 513, 530, 542, 544, 548, 549, 550, 551, 552, 553, 554, 555, 623, 631, 638
maqām, 185, 216, 557
marriage, 65, 66, 73, 130, 143, 177, 183, 198, 220, 221, 222, 223, 224, 225, 226, 227, 228, 229, 230, 231, 232, 233, 234, 235, 236, 237, 238, 239, 240, 241, 242, 243, 244, 245, 246, 247, 248, 249, 250, 251, 252, 253, 254, 255, 256, 257, 258, 259, 260, 261, 262, 263, 266, 267, 268, 270, 271, 272, 273, 278, 279, 280, 281, 282, 283, 284, 288, 289, 291, 292, 294, 295, 296, 297, 299, 300, 301, 302, 304, 306, 307, 308, 309, 310, 311, 320, 324, 366, 368, 378, 379, 401, 402, 414, 416, 418, 420, 422, 423, 424, 425, 426, 427, 428, 429, 430, 431, 432, 437, 438, 451, 452, 459, 469, 502, 523, 532, 544, 545, 549, 550, 555, 567, 571, 592, 601, 614, 620, 623, 624, 625, 627, 628, 631, 632, 633, 634, 637, 639
martyr, 46, 112, 113, 542
Marwa, 186, 187, 190, 194, 195, 200, 201, 203, 215, 638
maternal aunt, 221, 222, 232, 304, 312
maternal uncle, 220, 232
measureable, 134, 336, 337
Mecca, 42, 96, 105, 118, 181, 182, 186, 187, 190, 193, 194, 195, 197, 200, 201, 202, 203, 205, 209, 210, 214, 216, 251, 300, 341, 462, 565, 568, 610, 611, 619, 621, 622, 624, 625, 626, 627, 628
Medina, 21, 102, 115, 157, 174, 181, 205, 218, 298, 340, 341, 420, 438, 446, 456, 477, 524, 558, 568, 570, 585, 597, 610, 611, 619, 620, 621, 622, 623, 624, 625, 626, 627, 628
menstrual cycle, 65, 66, 266, 301, *See* menstruation
menstruation, 64, 65, 66, 67, 68, 74, 121, 165, 166, 171, 200, 208, 214, 232, 233, 252, 255, 266, 267, 268, 269, 283, 285, 289, 295, 296, 301, 400, 421, 452, 522, 592, 634, 638, 639
midwifery, 437
migration, 252, 558, 609
milk, 47, 60, 125, 171, 215, 241, 244, 251, 275, 276, 304, 305, 306, 307, 323, 329, 335, 337, 338, 349, 402, 430, 446, 521, 530, 532, 535, 615, 621, 638
milk relatives, 241, 251, 254, 276, 304, 306, 402, 621
milk-mother, 222
Mina, 173, 180, 186, 187, 188, 189, 190, 191, 192, 193, 194, 195, 198, 200, 202, 203, 207, 209, 210, 215, 216, 284, 631, 637
misappropriation, 138, 143, 384, 385, 427, 470, 528, 582
mithqal, 125, 129, 134, 135, 136, 142, 146, 147, 148, 318, 339, 341, 401, 402, 417, 464
Moses, 42, 43, 44, 48, 152, 158, 420, 438, 605, 606, 627
mosque, 30, 31, 52, 67, 74, 101, 157, 159, 167, 407, 569, 577, 636
Mu'awiya b. Abi Sufyān, 86, 621, 624, 625, 626, 627
Mu'tazilite, 620, 621
mudd, 53, 157, 211, 318, 402, 403
muezzin, 70, 71, 72, 91, 92, 94, 95, 623
Muhammad
  Allah's Messenger, 1, 3, 4, 5, 6, 7, 9, 10, 11, 15, 16, 21, 22, 23, 25, 27, 29, 32, 33, 34, 36, 38, 39, 40, 42, 44, 46, 51, 70, 71, 75, 76, 77, 81, 82, 83, 85, 99, 110, 116, 117, 118, 122, 135, 137, 157, 159, 182, 185, 186, 191, 192, 193, 204, 236, 238, 246, 264, 274, 275, 282, 285, 287, 290, 343, 348, 388, 397, 420, 456,

461, 492, 529, 538, 540, 541, 557, 558, 565, 566, 567, 568, 581, 587, 589, 594, 597, 599, 600, 607, 609, 610, 611, 616, 617, 619, 621, 623, 624, 625, 626, 627, 628
Muhammad b. 'Ali, 27, 44, 70, 165, 193, 204, 286, 606, 619, 625, 626
munāsakha, 493
music, 238, 443, 470, 582
musk, 115, 116, 136, 176, 184
muta', 226, 227, 228, 229
mutilation, 111, 209, 524
mutual cursing, 298, 299, 433, 451, 452
Muzdalifa, 180, 189, 190, 191, 192, 201, 207, 284, 637

N

nakedness, 50, 51, 73, 94, 107, 191, 235, 236, 264, 267, 447, 535, 598
needy, 13, 17, 130, 136, 138, 139, 140, 141, 147, 149, 150, 157, 158, 171, 172, 173, 175, 184, 189, 190, 211, 212, 213, 214, 215, 216, 217, 273, 274, 396, 397, 398, 400, 402, 403, 538, 577, 578, 609, 612
Negus, 117, 626
new moon, 156, 174, 175, 351, 631
night prayer, 67, 71, 73, 74, 89, 94, 400, 417, 596
Noah, 45, 616
non-marriageable, 112, 217, 218, 241, 244, 254, 255, 633
noon prayer, 67, 73, 78, 88, 95, 99, 102, 107, 109, 417, 633

O

oath
vow, 177, 210, 229, 243, 246, 258, 276, 277, 278, 291, 292, 293, 294, 295, 297, 322, 326, 327, 333, 346, 355, 356, 364, 375, 379, 380, 386, 396, 397, 398, 399, 400, 401, 402, 403, 404, 413, 420, 473, 474, 475, 477, 549, 558, 559, 560, 563, 564, 565, 572, 596, 619, 621, 622, 623, 624, 625, 626
oath of abstention, 276, 277, 278, 294, 295
oath of allegiance, 28, 246, 291, 327, 563, 564, 565, 570, 571, 572, 596, 619, 621, 622, 623, 624, 625, 626
obligation, 14, 16, 28, 39, 41, 45, 49, 52, 62, 70, 73, 78, 85, 98, 103, 124, 128, 133, 137, 141, 142, 145, 150, 152, 153, 154, 156, 159, 162, 163, 169, 170, 171, 172, 176, 180, 192, 193, 196, 206, 207, 221, 243, 258, 260, 284, 298, 311, 363, 364, 382, 391, 404, 416, 417, 430, 441, 453, 455, 460, 478, 504, 541, 562, 566, 568, 569, 570, 577, 581, 582, 584, 585, 586, 590, 594, 607, 632
Oneness, 39
oppressor, 28, 87, 138, 177, 195, 291, 299, 364, 396, 400, 572, 573, 597, 606
ornaments, 136, 269, 270, 528, 602
orphan, 26, 28, 136, 137, 140, 538, 577, 578, 597, 609
ostrich, 183, 212, 213, 214, 347, 597
over-inflation, 320
ownership, 127, 128, 129, 130, 132, 133, 136, 137, 138, 141, 142, 143, 145, 146, 150, 151, 153, 196, 200, 209, 214, 216, 231, 237, 242, 254, 255, 257, 273, 278, 293, 300, 314, 315, 316, 318, 320, 321, 324, 325, 329, 330, 331, 332, 333, 336, 339, 340,343, 344, 346, 349, 350, 351, 352, 353, 354, 355, 358, 359, 360, 361, 362, 363, 364, 365, 368, 369, 370, 372, 375, 376, 379, 382, 384, 385, 386, 388, 389, 390, 391, 406, 407, 408, 410, 413, 414, 427, 441, 442, 444, 445, 463, 464, 465, 467, 470, 471, 473, 476, 477, 479, 500, 504, 514, 515, 517, 524, 525, 533, 545, 550, 551, 552, 553, 554, 555, 558, 583, 596, 614, 632, 634, 636, 637, 639

P

Paradise, 19, 40, 41, 42, 43, 44, 51, 104, 107, 425, 460, 533, 558, 559, 560, 572, 573, 587, 598, 600, 601, 602, 604, 605, 608, 611, 612, 616, 625
partnership, 246, 248, 249, 254, 255, 331, 332, 333, 339, 355, 358, 359, 360, 361, 362, 363, 364, 365, 366, 368, 369, 370, 371, 372, 373, 374, 375, 376, 386, 403, 406, 407, 436, 500, 529, 540, 542, 545, 550, 553, 554, 589, 631,635, 636, 637, 638, 639
paternal aunt, 220, 221, 232, 304, 488, 490
paternal relatives, 308, 365, 486, 487, 489, 499
paternal uncle, 14, 220, 224, 232, 254, 263, 311, 481, 490, 499, 501, 502, 512, 542
pebbles, 180, 187, 190, 191, 207, 208, 215, 287, 319, 598
penis, 82, 260, 463, 465, 470, 498, 506, 507, 632, 639
People of the Book, 15, 25, 114, 135, 158, 247, 254, 306, 421, 426, 503, 510, 531, 619
pig, 55, 536
pilgrim, 181, 182, 183, 184, 186, 187, 188, 193, 194, 195, 196, 197, 198, 199, 200, 201, 202, 203, 204, 205, 206, 207, 209, 211, 212, 213, 214, 216, 217, 218, 540, 558, 621, 630, 631, 633, 637, 638
pilgrim garb, 181, 182, 186, 187, 193, 194, 195, 196, 197, 198, 200, 201, 202, 633, 638
pilgrim sanctity, 183, 194, 195, 197, 198, 199, 200, 201, 202, 203, 204, 205, 209, 211, 217, 218, 283, 621, 631, 637
Pilgrimage, 86, 105, 173, 180, 188
plaintiff, 258, 380, 403, 404, 477, 559
plantation, 348, 352, 358, 360, 374, 389
plucking, 602
plunder, 583, 584, 585
poor, 104, 130, 138, 139, 141, 142, 147, 149, 150, 152, 169, 190, 215, 220, 312, 392, 400, 402, 545, 571, 577, 578, 589, 590, 632, 635
pork, 299
possession *See* ownership
postpartum bleeding, 66, 171, 234, 255, 634, 638
prayer leader, 82, 84, 88, 89, 90, 91, 94, 96, 97, 98, 100, 102, 103, 104, 108, 109, 120, 122, 624, 631
precaution, 57, 97, 99, 151, 161, 227, 233, 267, 301, 321, 350, 358, 364, 472, 496, 499, 517, 560, 564, 596
predatory animals, 26, 64, 184, 319, 528, 530, 536
pre-ejaculatory fluid, 205, 206
pre-emption, 358, 359, 360, 361, 362, 363, 364, 365, 366, 375, 635, 637, 639

pregnant, 65, 66, 121, 122, 171, 172, 234, 250, 251, 255, 268, 269, 280, 284, 290, 291, 295, 308, 319, 390, 421, 423, 474, 499, 509, 542, 592, 593
pre-Islamic era, 12, 115, 223, 228, 274, 281, 340, 406, 520, 533, 566, 577
prepayment, 336, 342, 343, 344, 345, 346, 347, 348, 349, 350, 351, 352, 353, 354, 355, 356
pre-prayer call, 70, 71, 72, 91, 95, 105
pre-pubescent, 12, 13, 15, 22, 65, 152, 225, 238, 240, 242, 252, 253, 255, 295, 297, 298, 328, 336, 375, 398, 399, 401, 425, 442, 451, 592
prescribed punishment, 227, 237, 244, 245, 246, 254, 257, 258, 260, 298, 302, 382, 386, 394, 400, 403, 404, 416, 420, 421, 422, 423, 424, 425, 426, 427, 428, 429, 430, 431, 432, 433, 434, 435, 436, 437, 438, 439, 440, 441, 442, 445, 446, 449, 450, 451, 452,453, 455, 458, 533, 534, 549, 554, 560, 572, 626, 636
principal, 317, 382
private parts, 50, 51, 56, 58, 67, 111, 112, 121, 122, 233, 234, 244, 275, 417, 431, 437, 539, 608
profit, 129, 137, 142, 143, 316, 319, 326, 330, 333, 342, 343, 344, 369, 370, 371, 372, 373, 374, 375, 376, 533, 630, 635, 636, 637, 638, 639
Prophet's Descendants, 5, 11, 18, 19, 20, 21, 130, 597, 621, 626
proposal, 235, 237, 267, 271, 593
proprietor, 137, 333, 372, 373, 374, 375, 376, 638
prostatic discharge, 57
prostration, 5, 21, 76, 77, 84, 87, 89, 90, 93, 94, 119, 537
prostration verse, 21, 89
prostrations of forgetfulness, 83, 85, 89, 90
protected place, 439, 440, 441, 442, 443, 444, 445, 455
puberty
  pubescent, 10, 12, 174, 201, 225, 240, 252, 263, 279, 304, 350, 394, 414, 561, 589, 591, 596
public treasury, 127, 129, 333, 414, 427, 428, 440, 446, 453, 474, 494, 503, 591, 592
purification, 48, 49, 50, 51, 52, 53, 56, 57, 58, 59, 60, 61, 62, 63, 64, 66, 67, 68, 70, 71, 74, 88, 93, 106, 111, 112, 118, 121, 160, 181, 184, 255, 266, 301, 317, 319, 365, 439, 595, 620, 627, 632, 639
purification dues, 4, 13, 14, 26, 28, 48, 49, 53, 70, 74, 106, 124, 125, 126, 127, 128, 129, 130, 131, 132, 133, 134, 135, 136, 137, 138, 139, 140, 141, 142, 143, 144, 145, 146, 147, 148, 151, 152, 153, 154, 157, 167, 317, 319, 340, 341, 365, 400, 417, 462, 585, 620, 627, 639
purification wash, 48, 52, 53, 56, 57, 58, 59, 60, 61, 63, 64, 65, 66, 67, 68, 93, 106, 111, 121, 165, 181, 183, 184, 197, 200, 266, 301
pus, 30, 92, 101, 196, 631

Q

qibla, 5, 28, 17, 50, 65, 75, 77, 88, 89, 93, 94, 101, 102, 107, 110, 119, 120, 121, 174, 186, 191, 192, 193, 247, 522, 525, 580, 638
quantitative disparity, 319, 335, 337, 391, 402
Qudāma, 449, 626
qunūt, 25, 26, 85, 86
Qur'an, 11, 12, 13, 14, 15, 16, 17, 18, 19, 20, 23, 34, 42, 48, 53, 65, 66, 67, 68, 70, 73, 74, 75, 76, 78, 79, 80, 81, 83, 84, 85, 86, 87, 97, 102, 104, 106, 107, 136, 152, 156, 157, 158, 160, 175, 182, 185, 189, 216, 221, 246, 248, 251, 326, 340, 396, 399, 417, 418, 419, 422, 436, 438, 439, 449, 460, 480, 482, 489, 494, 522, 538, 539, 556, 566, 574, 575, 586, 598, 599, 602, 604, 607, 619, 620, 622, 628
Quraysh, 57, 119, 304, 462, 520, 610, 611

R

Rafidites, 48, 68, 282, 285, 289
rain, 38, 61, 99, 103, 359
raisins, 134, 135, 150, 331, 334, 337, 533, 534
ram, 216, 217, 520, 524
Ramadan, 27, 30, 31, 33, 48, 49, 150, 151, 156, 157, 158, 159, 161, 163, 164, 165, 166, 167, 168, 169, 170, 171, 172, 174, 175, 176, 177, 203, 283, 597, 622
ransom, 184, 189, 467, 470, 580, 592, 593
rape, 429
raṭl, 293, 335, 336, 337, 340, 341, 342
recitation, 20, 21, 22, 25, 53, 65, 68, 73, 74, 75, 76, 78, 79, 80, 81, 83, 84, 87, 89, 90, 96, 102, 103, 175, 189, 194, 326, 522, 630, 638
reclamation, 137, 143, 335, 338, 346, 363, 378, 410, 411, 412, 414
redistribution, 408, 494, 495, 499, 502, 504, 506, 508, 509, 511, 512, 545
religious seclusion, 159, 167, 175, 176, 177, 600
remarriage, 231, 232, 233, 234, 235, 236, 251, 252, 253, 267, 268, 271, 278, 288, 299, 300, 308
repentance, 12, 104, 113, 157, 168, 169, 199, 212, 230, 253, 274, 283, 397, 431, 437, 438, 439, 448, 454, 458, 459, 503, 510, 551, 572, 578, 580, 595, 603, 605, 609, 634
residency, 96, 98, 99
resident, 61, 68, 78, 88, 96, 97, 98, 102, 103, 159, 164, 165, 172, 474
retaliation, 320, 386, 460, 461, 464, 465, 466, 468, 475, 476, 477, 478, 584
revocation, 278, 282, 283, 287, 288, 295, 297, 300, 308, 309, 310, 315, 329, 353
riding beast, 16, 23, 104, 105, 107, 181, 182, 184, 196, 206, 207, 209, 213, 329, 410, 413, 445, 471, 472, 477
ritual purity, 52, 53, 54, 55, 60, 68, 72, 74, 82, 87, 88, 89, 109, 118, 191, 200, 208, 214, 215, 282, 289, 290, 291, 301, 630, 636

S

šā, 3, 13, 53, 131, 132, 150, 171, 211, 215, 274, 397, 403, 417, 531, 615, 634, 639
Sa'īd b. al-A'š, 113, 627
Sacred Site, 189, 197, 637
sacrifice, 25, 26, 36, 75, 108, 169, 173, 184, 185, 187, 188, 190, 193, 194, 195, 198, 199, 200, 201, 202, 203, 204,

205, 206, 207, 208, 209, 210, 211, 212, 214, 215, 216, 217, 218, 284, 351, 517, 520, 521, 522, 523, 524, 525, 526, 536, 538, 541, 565
sacrificial animal, 173, 190, 193, 195, 196, 209, 210, 216, 218
Ŝafa, 186, 187, 190, 194, 195, 200, 201, 203, 215, 638
sales, 314, 316, 319, 323, 324, 325, 326, 327, 328, 329, 330, 331, 332, 334, 335, 343, 348, 358, 359, 362, 364, 365, 366, 375, 379, 401, 402, 446, 639
Salmān, 175, 177, 596
Sanctified House, 180, 192, 197, 201, 399, 557, 599, 604, 633
Sanctified Site, 184, 185, 192, 213, 214, 216
Satan, 50, 75, 84, 90, 102, 111, 160, 264, 281, 289, 320, 321, 322, 448, 449, 453, 530, 532, 567, 574, 586, 602, 607, 613, 616
Sawda bt. Zama'at, 242, 627
scents, 51, 95, 176, 183, 186, 190, 195, 198, 201, 214, 217
scribe, 314, 315, 356, 404, 572
security deposit, 332, 356, 378, 379, 380, 390, 391
seeking permission, 115, 596
seeking the best choice (*al-istikhāra*), 602, 603
semen, 52, 56, 57, 205, 233, 234, 236, 244, 245, 300, 329, 500, 634
separate joint pilgrimage, 194, 199, 204, 205, 209, 210, 212, 213, 216
sepulchre, 118, 119
sermon, 38, 95, 104, 105, 108, 215, 569, 588, 597
settlement, 192, 271, 394, 467, 469, 473, 475, 559, 580
sharecropping, 406
Shawwāl, 150, 174, 181, 201, 203, 632
sheep, 56, 92, 125, 126, 127, 128, 129, 135, 142, 145, 146, 148, 169, 209, 212, 215, 216, 306, 320, 326, 334, 335, 337, 345, 349, 354, 384, 390, 417, 463, 464, 520, 521, 525, 531, 532
ship, 94
Shortening, 96, 98
shroud, 112, 113, 121
shrouding, 111, 115, 118, 119, 120, 122, 445
shyness, 30, 611
sickness, 47, 58, 99, 165, 171, 175, 197, 207, 238, 263, 269, 312, 386, 542
Ŝiffīn, 557, 569, 578, 621, 623, 624, 625, 626
silk, 47, 99, 338, 342, 345, 352, 535, 538, 571
silver, 17, 19, 26, 125, 131, 132, 134, 135, 136, 138, 142, 147, 148, 153, 205, 318, 339, 340, 345, 347, 368, 372, 394, 417, 439, 525, 526, 534, 535, 583, 636, 637
slander, 86, 183, 246, 250, 403, 419, 426, 427, 428, 431, 432, 433, 434, 435, 436, 449, 450, 451, 452, 453, 609
slave, 4, 6, 10, 11, 12, 13, 14, 15, 16, 17, 19, 20, 21, 22, 23, 24, 25, 26, 27, 28, 29, 1, 9, 13, 14, 23, 38, 39, 40, 41, 43, 44, 45, 47, 48, 49, 52, 60, 63, 72, 78, 80, 87, 88, 93, 104, 105, 106, 110, 117, 120, 137, 138, 139, 142, 149, 150, 152, 153, 154, 156, 159, 162, 165, 168, 169, 170, 172, 173, 176, 177, 178, 183, 185, 186, 189, 190, 191, 192, 194, 197, 201, 216, 217, 218, 220, 221, 222, 223, 224, 226, 228, 229, 230, 231, 238, 239, 240, 241, 242, 243, 245, 246, 248, 250, 251, 252, 254, 255, 256, 257, 258, 259, 260, 261, 266, 270, 271, 272, 273, 274, 275, 278, 279, 281, 282, 283, 284, 285, 286, 288, 289, 293, 294, 295, 296, 297, 300, 301, 305, 306, 308, 309, 311, 316, 319, 320, 321, 322, 324, 325, 327, 328, 329, 330, 331, 332, 333, 334, 335, 345, 354, 365, 372, 375, 378, 379, 382, 384, 385, 386, 387, 389, 390, 396, 397, 398, 399, 401, 402, 403, 404, 410, 411, 412, 414, 418, 423, 425, 426, 427, 428, 429, 430, 431, 432, 433, 434, 435, 436, 437, 438, 439, 443, 444, 446, 447, 448, 451, 452, 453, 456, 461, 462, 465, 467, 468, 469, 470, 471, 473, 474, 475, 477, 478, 479, 481, 500, 503, 504, 505, 506, 508, 509, 510, 511, 512, 513, 515, 522, 523, 528, 529, 530, 538, 540, 541, 542, 544, 545, 548, 549, 550, 551, 552, 553, 554, 555, 557, 560, 562, 563, 565, 574, 577, 579, 582, 585, 586, 587, 589, 590, 591, 592, 593, 598, 599, 601, 604, 605, 609, 612, 613, 617, 623, 627, 631, 635, 638
slave girl, 254, 255, 256, 258, 272, 305, 306, 389, 410, 411, 414, 426, 429, 582
solitary pilgrimage, 187, 204, 213
speculative partnership, 372, 373, 374, 375, 376, 636
splint, 58
spoils, 220, 332, 575, 576, 578, 581, 582, 583, 584, 588, 589, 591
statue, 614
stepdaughter, 234
stillbirth, 560
stillborn, 23, 113, 114, 468, 469, 474
stipulation, 12, 16, 18, 17, 153, 175, 212, 232, 243, 255, 258, 302, 323, 332, 337, 338, 342, 343, 345, 348, 349, 351, 362, 369, 372, 373, 374, 376, 406, 548, 550, 551, 552, 554, 636
stoning, 191, 192, 193, 194, 200, 207, 208, 215, 287, 416, 417, 418, 420, 421, 423, 424, 426, 440, 560, 633
straitened, 149, 150, 173, 275, 309, 311, 312, 320, 392, 469, 475, 550, 553, 554, 592, 593
suckling, 230, 284, 304, 305, 306, 307, 543
Sunnah, 3, 8, 12, 26, 9, 15, 16, 17, 18, 22, 24, 30, 31, 32, 39, 41, 52, 58, 85, 104, 106, 114, 151, 169, 191, 192, 228, 245, 467, 484, 494, 501, 524, 528, 529, 530, 566, 567, 573, 576, 594, 638
sunset prayer, 61, 67, 73, 77, 78, 91, 94, 107, 417
supererogatory, 54, 61, 74, 82, 89, 93, 96, 107, 108, 159, 176, 203, 284
supplication, 25, 50, 51, 74, 75, 76, 79, 80, 81, 85, 86, 117, 118, 174, 186, 191, 208, 442, 531, 542, 567, 599, 603, 607, 636
synagogue, 101

T

ta'zīr, 429, 434, 438, 439, 441, 442, 444, 445, 447, 597, 615, 638
talbiya, 182, 184, 186, 187, 188, 189, 190, 194, 195, 197, 198, 202, 211
Tarwiya, 9, 186, 187, 188, 194, 195, 209, 351
Tashrīq, 108, 162, 170, 188, 193, 195, 638
tattoo, 602

taxes, 129, 141, 589
testicles, 260, 463, 465, 470
testimony of faith, 25, 77, 89, 91, 97, 103, 104, 463
theft, 84, 142, 143, 199, 246, 260, 333, 384, 386, 403, 439, 440, 441, 442, 443, 444, 445, 446, 447, 450, 455, 459, 460, 525
tithe, 129, 130, 131, 132, 133, 136, 137, 141, 148, 149, 153, 154, 417
tomb, 111, 113, 118, 119, 621, 637
travel, 30, 68, 74, 96, 97, 98, 99, 108, 112, 164, 181, 196, 206, 241, 269, 278, 372, 462, 476, 565, 583, 616
traveller, 61, 63, 64, 88, 96, 98, 102, 103, 106, 130, 139, 140, 141, 158, 159, 164, 171, 172, 196, 275, 283, 327, 572, 578
treasure, 585
turban, 68, 87, 100, 115, 184, 204, 397

U

Uhud, 113, 610, 621, 626, 628
Umm Salama, 18, 59, 83, 165, 232, 242, 250, 261, 262, 537, 609, 628
umm walad, 14, 15, 16, 20, 21, 23, 27, 29, 26, 152, 154, 216, 256, 258, 270, 271, 293, 298, 301, 308, 324, 325, 329, 389, 400, 428, 435, 436, 468, 469, 549, 553, 592, 593, 638
Ummah, 3, 8, 9, 14, 38, 41, 46, 48, 49, 81, 91, 95, 107, 113, 118, 124, 157, 238, 248, 284, 285, 290, 321, 340, 343, 344, 417, 419, 453, 455, 456, 461, 478, 562, 563, 564, 566, 571, 607, 610, 617, 623, 626
uncertainty, 16, 12, 17, 32, 257, 258, 287, 317, 320, 321, 322, 328, 329, 330, 340, 342, 348, 372, 404, 406, 447
uncircumcised, 26, 114, 523
unconscious, 5, 10, 74, 93, 94, 197, 400
unintentional manslaughter, 178, 398, 399, 401, 466, 469, 472, 630, 631
unlawful pronouncements, 169, 170, 172, 173, 178, 212, 273, 274, 275, 276, 293, 294, 397, 398, 399, 401, 549
urine, 19, 55, 56, 60, 61, 92, 100, 101, 446, 498, 506, 507, 536, 633
Usāma b. Zayd, 462, 624, 625, 628
usury, 91, 124, 199, 314, 316, 317, 318, 326, 327, 328, 334, 336, 339, 343, 347, 353, 354, 567, 609, 639

V

vaginal bleeding, 64, 66, 67, 166, 269, 301, 302
verbal remembrance, 51, 80, 95, 188, 189, 208
vinegar, 26, 60, 170, 275, 349, 397, 531, 532, 533
virgin, 225, 226, 237, 241, 428, 452
voluntary prayers, 95, 99, 107, 109, 114

W

waiting period, 65, 66, 173, 229, 230, 231, 232, 233, 234, 235, 236, 237, 244, 249, 251, 252, 253, 254, 255, 266, 267, 268, 269, 270, 271, 273, 275, 277, 278, 280, 281, 282, 283, 284, 285, 286, 288, 289, 290, 291, 292, 294, 295, 296, 297, 299, 300, 301, 308, 310, 451, 592, 593
war, 13, 22, 27, 28, 29, 11, 43, 86, 96, 98, 124, 139, 252, 317, 328, 419, 437, 438, 446, 447, 448, 459, 461, 462, 463, 536, 537, 551, 568, 569, 570, 571, 573, 574, 575, 576, 577, 578, 579, 580, 581, 583, 585, 589, 590, 591, 592, 593, 615, 621, 622, 625, 630,632, 635
wasq, 131, 132, 417
water, 25, 26, 27, 14, 44, 50, 51, 53, 54, 55, 56, 57, 58, 59, 60, 61, 62, 63, 64, 67, 68, 69, 93, 94, 104, 106, 112, 113, 121, 131, 133, 136, 141, 148, 150, 154, 160, 165, 168, 170, 171, 192, 193, 196, 197, 263, 267, 275, 285, 327, 338, 397, 406, 407,459, 516, 517, 535, 542, 558, 572, 586, 604, 613, 639
wealth, 26, 28, 34, 47, 54, 64, 110, 124, 127, 128, 129, 130, 131, 132, 133, 134, 136, 137, 138, 139, 140, 141, 142, 143, 144, 145, 146, 148, 149, 151, 152, 153, 154, 181, 192, 193, 216, 217, 248, 249, 251, 252, 254, 257, 268, 275, 280, 302, 308, 314, 316, 317, 321, 333, 342, 353, 363, 368, 369, 370, 372, 373, 374, 375, 376, 378, 379, 382, 387, 388, 389, 390, 391, 396, 400, 401, 410, 411, 413, 417, 418, 427, 432, 448, 459, 463, 464, 465, 471, 472, 475, 478, 482, 483, 484, 485, 487, 488, 490, 491, 494, 495, 496, 499, 500, 501, 503, 504, 505, 506, 507, 508, 509, 510, 511, 512, 513, 528, 529, 538, 539, 540, 541, 542, 543, 544, 545, 548, 553, 558, 559, 560, 561, 562, 565, 566, 571, 577, 578, 581, 582, 583, 584, 586, 589, 590, 591, 600, 603, 604, 606, 609, 616, 630, 631, 632, 633, 634, 636, 637, 638
weaning, 305, 306, 543
weighable, 131, 336, 337, 345, 346, 354
wheat, 104, 131, 134, 135, 150, 153, 211, 318, 331, 334, 336, 337, 342, 343, 345, 347, 348, 353, 354, 355, 398, 444, 448, 456, 533, 534
widow, 232
wife, 54, 55, 57, 59, 65, 66, 67, 68, 82, 112, 156, 157, 159, 160, 163, 164, 165, 167, 169, 172, 173, 175, 177, 183, 186, 190, 192, 197, 198, 205, 206, 207, 215, 220, 221, 222, 223, 228, 229, 230, 231, 232, 233, 234, 235, 236, 239, 240, 241, 242, 243, 244, 245, 247, 249, 250, 251, 252, 253, 254, 257, 258, 259, 261, 262, 263, 264, 266, 267, 268, 270, 271, 272, 273, 274, 275, 276, 277, 278, 279, 280, 281, 282, 283, 284, 285, 286, 287, 288, 289, 290, 291, 292, 293, 294, 295, 296, 297, 298, 299, 300, 302, 304, 305, 308, 309, 310, 311, 320, 329, 387, 402, 412, 413, 418, 423, 424, 425, 428, 430, 433, 451, 452, 469, 470, 480, 481, 482, 486, 488, 491, 492, 493, 496, 498, 499, 500, 503, 509, 530, 537, 550, 560, 583, 596, 619, 621, 622, 623, 624, 627, 628, 630, 631, 635, 639
wine *See* intoxicants
witness, 34, 158, 174, 223, 224, 226, 227, 228, 229, 238, 243, 244, 266, 267, 269, 288, 294, 295, 298, 302, 314, 315, 316, 323, 356, 364, 386, 403, 404, 413, 416, 422, 423, 424, 426, 427, 428, 429, 430, 431, 432, 433, 434, 435, 436, 437, 440, 441, 442, 444, 449, 450, 452, 455, 521, 549, 554, 560, 561, 593
witr, 26, 31, 85, 86, 107, 605
womb, 65, 114, 118, 122, 125, 171, 234, 248, 250, 252, 268, 269, 275, 280, 295, 301, 306, 308, 329, 390, 421,

474, 513, 523, 550, 553, 592, 593, 599

Y

yearling, 126, 128, 144, 208, 209
yellowness, 67, 74
Yemen, 5, 6, 7, 8, 9, 10, 11, 29, 115, 130, 181, 203, 456, 464, 556, 621, 626
yoghurt, 104

Z

Zamzam, 185, 186, 192, 193
Zayd b. 'Ali
Imam Zayd, 8, 9, 10, 23, 24, 25, 26, 27, 28, 29, 30, 31, 32, 38, 46, 50, 53, 56, 72, 82, 111, 159, 166, 188, 204, 210, 223, 230, 254, 270, 277, 286, 317, 366, 453, 464, 524, 533, 568, 595, 597, 598, 599, 601, 610, 620, 626, 628
Zaynab bt. Jahsh, 232, 628
zenith, 99, 122, 187, 191, 192, 193, 201, 207, 208, 603, 635

www.ingramcontent.com/pod-product-compliance
Lightning Source LLC
Chambersburg PA
CBHW050804220426
43209CB00089BA/1709
* 9 7 8 1 7 3 9 5 2 2 8 7 2 *